# OPERATIONS RESEARCH

## An Introduction

SIXTH
EDITION

# OPERATIONS RESEARCH

## An Introduction

HAMDY A. TAHA

University of Arkansas, Fayetteville

PRENTICE HALL

Upper Saddle River, New Jersey 07458

Library of Congress Cataloging-in-Publication Data

Taha, Hamdy A.
   Operations research : an introduction / Hamdy A. Taha. — 6th ed.
     p.  cm.
   Includes bibliographical references and index.
   ISBN 0-13-272915-6
   1. Operations research.  2. Programming (Mathematics)  I. Title.
T57.6.T3  1997                        96-37160
003 -dc21                            CIP

Publisher: TOM ROBBINS
Acquisitions editor: ALICE DWORKIN
Production editor: RHODORA V. PENARANDA
Editor-in-chief: MARCIA HORTON
Managing Editor: BAYANI MENDOZA DELEON
Director of production and manufacturing: DAVID W. RICCARDI
Copy editor: ANDREA HAMMER
Cover designer: BRUCE KENSELAAR
Manufacturing buyer: DONNA SULLIVAN
Editorial assistant: NANCY GARCIA

©1997, 1992 by Prentice-Hall, Inc.
Simon & Schuster/ A Viacom Company
Upper Saddle River, NJ 07458

Preliminary edition © 1968 by Hamdy A. Taha. First and second editions © 1971 and 1976 by Hamdy A. Taha. Third and fourth editions © 1982 and 1987 by Macmillan Publishing Company.

The author and publisher of this book have used their best efforts in preparing this book. These efforts include the development, research, and testing of the theories and programs to determine their effectiveness. The author and publisher make no warranty of any kind, expressed or implied, with regard to these programs or the documentation contained in this book. The author and publisher shall not be liable in any event for incidental or consequential damages in connection with, or arising out of, the furnishing, performance, or use of these programs.

Printed in the United States of America

10 9 8 7 6 5 4 3 2

ISBN 0-13-272915-6

Prentice-Hall International (UK) Limited, *London*
Prentice-Hall of Australia Pty, Limited, *Sydney*
Prentice-Hall Canada Inc., *Toronto*
Prentice-Hall Hispanoamericana, S.A., *Mexico*
Prentice-Hall of India Private Limited, *New Delhi*
Prentice-Hall of Japan, Inc., *Tokyo*
Simon & Schuster Asia Pte. Ltd., *Singapore*
Editora Prentice-Hall do Brasil, Ltda., *Rio de Janeiro*

*To Karen*

Los ríos no llevan agua,
el sol las fuentes secó. . .
¡Yo sé donde hay una fuente
que no ha de secar el sol!
La fuente que no se agota
es mi propio corazón. . .

—*V. Ruiz Aguilera (1862)*

# Contents

# Preface

Since the first publication of *Operations Research: An Introduction* in 1971, I have made innumerable changes in both the style and content of the book. In planning for the sixth edition, I came to realize that these individual changes may have inadvertently impaired the continuity of the presentation. I also felt a definite need for adding new problems and updating old ones. I am confident that the sixth edition addresses both concerns properly.

The first 18 chapters have been totally rewritten. The remaining three chapters have been revised and updated. New material has been added, and old material has been condensed or deleted. The presentation rectifies a deficiency in the fifth edition in which the level of mathematics, particularly in linear programming, was thought to be erratic. The sixth edition introduces each topic at a level that suits the background of the beginning student and gradually increases the level of sophistication to meet the expectations of the more advanced student.

I have used numerical examples as the main vehicle for the presentation of the underlying ideas of different operations research techniques. Every solved example is followed by a set of problems designed to provide balanced coverage of model formulation, computation, and theory. The chapters close with comprehensive problems taken mostly from published case analyses. The sixth edition includes more than 1000 problems, a 60% increase over the fifth edition.

The book is organized in three parts: deterministic, probabilistic, and nonlinear models. The deterministic models include linear programming, networks, goal programming, integer programming, deterministic dynamic programming, and deterministic inventory models. The organization of the linear programming topic allows the beginning student to gain an immediate appreciation of the practical use of the technique, including the powerful concepts of dual prices and sensitivity analysis. The networks chapter has been streamlined to include more applications and more generalized algorithms, including Floyd's shortest route algorithm and the relationships between networks flow, linear programming, and the transportation and transshipment models. I have also included a condensed version of PERT-CPM in the networks chapter. The advanced topics of linear programming have been combined into one chapter. Goal programming is covered in a new chapter, and integer programming now places emphasis on new applications and the more promising branch-and-bound technique. New applications have been included in the deterministic dynamic programming chapter, and the deterministic inventory models have been grouped in a separate chapter.

Probabilistic models start with a review of basic probability and statistics, followed by a presentation of forecasting models. The material on decision analysis now includes the analytic hierarchy approach (AHP) and the role of utility functions in decision analysis. The method of solving games by linear programming has been simplified and strengthened. Probabilistic dynamic programming is now presented in a totally new chapter. It is followed by an updated chapter on probabilistic inventory models. The new presentation of queuing models allows the student to study both the applications and the theory, or to concentrate solely on the applications aspect of the topic. The basic principles of discrete simulation are covered in a new chapter, with the introduction to the simulation language SIMNET II now moved to Appendix B. The material on Markov chains has been updated to fit the new format of the book.

Although the topics of nonlinear programming remain the same as in the fifth edition, the material has been updated and strengthened.

The software accompanying the book include TORA and the student version of SIMNET II. TORA includes various algorithms designed to match the format of the book, and may be used as a tutorial tool or for problem solving. SIMNET II has all the capabilities of the commercial version; the only difference is the limited size of the problem.

The book includes five appendixes: Appendix A reviews of matrix algebra. An introduction to the simulation language SIMNET II is given in Appendix B. Appendix C deals with the installation and use of TORA and SIMNET II software. Appendix D includes tables for the normal, $t$, and chi-square distributions. Answers to odd-numbered problems are given in Appendix E.

## ACKNOWLEDGMENTS

Many of my colleagues have been supportive of my work with their encouragement and criticism. I am deeply indebted to all of them and welcome this opportunity to benefit further from their contributions. In particular, I wish to express my appreciation to Professors Guy Curry (Texas A&M University), Don E. Deal (University of Houston), Richard Francis (University of Florida), Yasser Hosni (Florida Central University), Allen C. Schuermann (Oklahoma State University),  and Evangelos Triantaphyllou (Louisiana State University).

I am pleased to acknowledge the smooth transition under the auspices of my new publisher, Prentice Hall. I am especially grateful to my editors, Bayani M. de Leon, Alice Dworkin, Marcia Horton, and Rhodora Peñaranda for their support throughout the production of the sixth edition.

*Hamdy A. Taha*

# OPERATIONS RESEARCH

## An Introduction

# Chapter 1

# Overview of Operations Research

## 1.1 MATHEMATICAL OPERATIONS RESEARCH MODELS

Imagine that you have a 5-week business commitment between Fayetteville (FYV) and Denver (DEN). You fly out of Fayetteville on Monday and return on Wednesday. A regular round-trip ticket costs $400, but a 20% discount is granted if the dates of the ticket span a weekend. A one-way ticket in either direction costs 75% of the regular price. How should you buy the tickets for the 5-week period?

We can look at the situation as a decision-making problem whose solution requires identifying three main components.

1. What are the decision **alternatives?**
2. Under what **restrictions** is the decision made?
3. What is an appropriate **objective criterion** for evaluating the alternatives?

The following alternatives are available for purchasing the tickets:

1. Buy five regular FYV-DEN-FYV.
2. Buy one FYV-DEN, four DEN-FYV-DEN that span weekends, and one DEN-FYV.
3. Buy one FYV-DEN-FYV to cover Monday of the first week and Wednesday of the last week and four DEN-FYV-DEN that span weekends to cover the remaining legs.

The restriction on these options is that you should be able to leave on Monday and return on Wednesday of the same week.

An obvious objective criterion for evaluating the proposed alternative is the price of the tickets. The alternative that yields the smallest cost is the best. Specifically, we have

Alternative 1 cost = 5 × 400 = $2000

Alternative 2 cost = .75 × 400 + 4 × 400 + .75 × 400 = $2200

Alternative 3 cost = 5 × (.8 × 400) = **$1600**

Thus, you should choose alternative 3.

The preceding example provides the principal components of an operations research (OR) model—namely, alternatives, restrictions, and an objective criterion. Generally, the alternatives of the decision problem may take the form of unknown variables. These variables are then used to construct the restrictions and the objective criterion in appropriate mathematical functions. The end result is a **mathematical model** relating the variables, constraints, and objective function. The solution of the model then yields the values of the decision variables that **optimize (maximize** or **minimize)** the value of the objective function while satisfying all the constraints. The resulting solution is referred to as the **optimum feasible solution.**

A typical OR mathematical model is usually organized as follows:

Maximize or minimize (Objective function)

Subject to (Constraints)

**Example 1.1-1.**

Suppose that you are asked to shape a piece of wire of length $L$ inches into a rectangular shape to maximize the enclosed area. What would be the optimum length and width of the rectangle?

The variables of the problem are the length $l$ and the width $w$ of the rectangle. The resulting area is thus $A = lw$ inches$^2$. Thus, we maximize $A$ under the restriction that the length of the perimeter of the rectangle, $2(l + w)$, be equal to the available length, $L$. The mathematical model is written as

$$\text{Maximize } A = lw$$

subject to

$$l + w = \frac{L}{2}$$

We can solve this model by using the constraint $l + w = \frac{L}{2}$ to substitute out one of the variables in the objective function, which gives

$$A = \left(\frac{L}{2} - w\right)w = \frac{Lw}{2} - w^2$$

From calculus, we know in this case that the maximum of the area $A$ occurs at the point where the slope of $A$ with respect to $w$ is zero, that is,

$$\frac{dA}{dw} = \frac{L}{2} - 2w = 0$$

The solution of the equation above is $w = \frac{L}{4}$. The sufficiency condition (second derivative) shows that $w = \frac{L}{4}$ is a maximum point. Hence, $l = \frac{L}{4}$, and the optimum solution indicates that, among all rectangular shapes, the square yields the largest enclosed area.

---

Though mathematical models are the cornerstone of most OR studies, there is more to the solution of the decision-making problem than the construction and solution of the mathematical model. Specifically, decision problems usually include important intangible factors that may not be readily quantifiable. Foremost among these factors is the presence of the human element in most decision environments. Indeed, decision situations have been reported where the effect of human behavior has so influenced the decision problem that the solution obtained from the mathematical model is deemed impractical. An illustration of these cases is a version of the widely circulated *elevator problem*. In response to tenants' complaints about the slow elevator service in a large office building, the situation was analyzed using a waiting-line model. However, the proposed solution to speed up the elevator service did not alleviate the problem. Further study of the situation revealed that the tenant's complaints were more a case of boredom, and the problem was solved by installing full-length mirrors at the elevator entrance. The complaints disappeared as the elevator users were kept occupied watching themselves and others while waiting for the elevator service.

The mathematical aspect of OR should be viewed in the wider context of the decision-making process. This point was recognized by the British scientists who pioneered the first OR activities during World War II. Although their work was concerned primarily with the optimum allocation of the limited war matériel, the OR team included scientists from sociology, psychology, and behavioral sciences in recognition of the importance of their contribution to the decision-making process.

## 1.2 OPERATIONS RESEARCH TECHNIQUES

In OR mathematical models, the decision variables may be integer or continuous, and the objective and constraint functions may be linear or nonlinear. The optimization problems posed by these models give rise to a variety of solution methods, each designed to account for the special mathematical properties of the model. The most prominent and successful of these techniques is **linear programming,** where all the objective and constraint functions are linear, and all the variables are continuous. Other techniques that deal with other types of mathematical models are **dynamic programming, integer programming, nonlinear programming, goal programming,** and **network programming,** to mention only a few.

Practically all operations research techniques result in computational algorithms that are iterative in nature. This means that the problem is solved in **iterations,** with each new iteration bringing the solution closer to the optimum. The iterative nature of the algorithms typically give rise to voluminous and tedious computations. It is thus imperative that these algorithms be executed by the computer.

The use of the computer as an essential tool for solving OR models gives rise to a prominent computational difficulty: that of machine roundoff error. Such error becomes more pronounced as the number of iterations increases. The problem is even more difficult when the variables of the model are restricted to integer values. Because the computer does all the computations in floating-point (noninteger) arithmetic, exact representation of (some) integer values is not possible, and proper tolerances must be implemented to account for these inherent approximations.

Some mathematical models may be so complex that it is impossible to solve them by any of the available optimization algorithms. In such cases, it may be necessary to abandon the search for the *optimal* solution and simply seek a *good* solution using **heuristics.** A heuristic normally applies *rules of thumb* to produce a good solution to the problem. The advantage of a heuristic over an exact optimization algorithm is that it is usually much faster to execute.

## 1.3 SIMULATION MODELING

Despite the impressive advances in mathematical modeling, many real situations still are well beyond the capabilities of representing systems mathematically. For one thing, the "rigidity" of mathematical representation may make it impossible to describe the decision problem by a mathematical model adequately. Alternatively, even when it is plausible to formulate a proper mathematical model, the resulting optimization problem may prove too complex for available solution algorithms.

An alternative approach to modeling complex system is **simulation.** Simulation modeling is the next best thing to observing a real system. It differs from mathematical modeling in that the relationship between the input and output need not be stated explicitly. Instead, it breaks down the real system into (small) modules and then imitates the actual behavior of the system by using logical relationships to link the modules together. Starting with the input module, the simulation computations move among the appropriate modules until the output result is realized.

Simulation computations, though usually simple, are voluminous. It is thus unthinkable to execute a simulation model without the use of the computer.

Simulation models are much more flexible in representing systems than their mathematical counterparts. The main reason for this flexibility is that simulation views the system at elemental level, whereas mathematical models tend to represent the system from a more global standpoint.

The flexibility of simulation is not without drawbacks. The development of a simulation model is usually costly in both time and resources. Moreover, the execution of some simulation models, even on the fastest computers, may be slow.

## 1.4  ART OF MODELING

An OR study must be rooted in *teamwork,* where both the OR analysts and the client work side by side. The OR analysts with their expertise in modeling will need the experience and cooperation of the client for whom the study is being carried out.

As a decision-making tool, OR must be viewed as both a science and an art. It is a science by virtue of the embodying mathematical techniques it presents, and it is an art because the success of all the phases that precede and succeed the solution of the mathematical model depends largely on the creativity and experience of the operations research team. Willemain (1994) advises that "effective [OR] practice requires more than analytical competence: It also requires, among other attributes, technical judgement (e.g., when and how to use a given technique) and skills in communication and organizational survival."

It is difficult to prescribe specific courses of actions (similar to those dictated by the precise theory of mathematical models) for these intangible factors. As such, we can offer only general guidelines for the implementation of OR in practice.

The principal phases for implementing OR in practice include

**1.** Definition of the problem

**2.** Construction of the model

**3.** Solution of the model

**4.** Validation of the model

**5.** Implementation of the solution

Of all five phases, only phase 3 dealing with *model solution* is the best defined and the easiest to implement in an OR study because it deals with mostly precise mathematical theory. The implementation of the remaining phases is more an art than it is a theory. Consequently, we cannot prescribe procedures for executing these phases.

**Problem definition** involves defining the scope of the problem under investigation. This is a function that should be carried out by the entire OR team. The end result of the investigation is to identify three principal elements of the decision problem—namely: (1) the description of the decision alternatives, (2) the determination of the objective of the study, and (3) the specification of the limitations under which the modeled system operates.

**Model construction** entails translating the problem definition into mathematical relationships. If the resulting model fits into one of the standard mathematical models, such as linear programming, a solution is usually attainable by using available algorithms. Alternatively, if the mathematical relationships are too complex to allow the determination of an analytic solution, the OR team may opt to simplify the model and use a heuristic approach, or the team may consider the use of simulation, if appropriate. In some cases, a combination of mathematical, simulation, and heuristic models may be appropriate for solving the decision problem.

**Model solution,** by far, is the simplest of all OR phases because it entails the use of well-defined optimization algorithms. An important aspect of the model solution phase is *sensitivity analysis*. It deals with obtaining additional information about the behavior of the "optimum" solution when the model undergoes some parameter variations. Sensitivity analysis is particularly needed when the parameters of the model cannot be estimated accurately. In these cases, it is important to study the behavior of the optimum solution in the neighborhood of the initial estimates of the model's parameters.

**Model validity** checks whether or not the proposed model does what it is supposed to do—that is, does the model provide a reasonable prediction of the behavior of the system under study? Initially, the OR team should be convinced that the output of the model does not contain "surprises." In other words, does the solution make sense? Are the results intuitively acceptable? On the formal side, a common method for checking the validity of a model is to compare its output with historical output data. The model is valid if, under similar input conditions, it reproduces past performance. Generally, however, there is no assurance that future performance will continue to duplicate past behavior. Also, because the model is usually based on careful examination of past data, the proposed comparison should be favorable. If the proposed model is representing a new (nonexisting) system, no historical data would be available to make the comparison. In such cases, we may resort to the use of simulation as an independent tool for verifying the output of the mathematical model.

**Implementation** of the solution of a validated model involves the translation of the model's results into operating instructions issued in understandable form to the individuals who will administer the recommended system. The burden of this task lies primarily with the OR team.

## 1.5 ABOUT THIS BOOK

Morse (1967) states that "the teaching of models is not equivalent to the teaching of modeling." The author has taken note of this important statement during the preparation of the sixth edition. A conscious effort has been made to bring about the art of modeling in OR. The realistic models presented throughout the book, the numerous application (word) problems, and the comprehensive cases given at the end of chapters provide insight into the analysis of practical situations.

The author believes that a first course in OR should give the student a good foundation in the mathematics of OR as well as an appreciation of its potential applications. This plan will provide OR users with the kind of confidence that normally would be missing if the principal training is concentrated solely on the philosophical and artistic aspects of OR. Once a fundamental knowledge of the mathematical foundation has been ensured, the students can increase their capabilities in the artistic side of OR modeling by studying case studies that are available in several journals and publications. The author particularly recommends *Interfaces* (published by the Institute of Management Science) as a rich source of interesting OR applications.

## SELECTED REFERENCES

EVANS, J., *Creative Thinking in the Decision and Management Sciences,* South-Western Publishing, Cincinnati, Ohio, 1991.

GASS, S., "Model World: Danger, Beware the User as a Modeler," *Interfaces,* Vol. 20, No. 3, pp. 60–64, 1990.

MORRIS, W., "On the Art of Modeling," *Management Science,* Vol. 13, pp. B707–B717, 1967.

WILLEMAIN, T. R., "Insights on Modeling from a Dozen Experts," *Operations Research,* Vol. 42, No. 2, pp. 213–222, 1994.

# PART

# I

# DETERMINISTIC MODELS

# Introduction To Linear Programming

## 2.1 INTRODUCTION

Linear programming (LP) is a mathematical modeling technique designed to *optimize* the usage of *limited* resources. Successful applications of LP exist in the areas of military, industry, agriculture, transportation, economics, health systems, and even behavioral and social sciences. The usefulness of the technique is enhanced by the availability of highly efficient computer codes. Indeed, LP, because of its high computational efficiency, is the basis for the development of solution algorithms of other (more complex) types of OR models, including integer, nonlinear, and stochastic programming.

The computations in LP, as in most OR models, are typically voluminous and tedious, and, hence, require the use of the computer. The user-friendly TORA software that accompanies this book is designed to alleviate this computational burden.

## 2.2 CONSTRUCTION OF THE LP MODEL

This section illustrates the basic elements of an LP model by using a simple two-variable example. The results provide concrete ideas for the solution and interpretation of the general LP problem.

---

**Example 2.2–1   (THE REDDY MIKKS COMPANY).**

Reddy Mikks produces both interior and exterior paints from two raw materials, $M1$ and $M2$. The following table provides the basic data of the problem:

| | Tons of raw material per ton of | | Maximum daily availability (tons) |
| --- | --- | --- | --- |
| | Exterior paint | Interior paint | |
| Raw material, $M1$ | 6 | 4 | 24 |
| Raw material, $M2$ | 1 | 2 | 6 |
| Profit per ton ($1000) | 5 | 4 | |

A market survey restricts the maximum daily demand of interior paint to 2 tons. Additionally, the daily demand for interior paint cannot exceed that of exterior paint by more than 1 ton. Reddy Mikks wants to determine the optimum (best) product mix of interior and exterior paints that maximizes the total daily profit.

The LP model, as in any OR model, includes three basic elements.

1. Decision **variables** that we seek to determine
2. **Objective** (goal) that we aim to optimize
3. **Constraints** that we need to satisfy

The proper definition of the decision variables is an essential first step toward the development of the model. Once the variables are defined, the task of constructing the objective function and the constraints should not be too difficult.

For the Reddy Mikks problem, we need to determine the amounts to be produced of exterior and interior paint. The variables of the model are thus defined as

$x_1$ = Tons produced daily of exterior paint

$x_2$ = Tons produced daily of interior paint

Using these definitions, the next task is to construct the objective function. A logical objective for the company is to increase as much as possible (i.e., maximize) the total daily profit from both exterior and interior paints. Letting $z$ represent the total daily profit (in thousands of dollars), we get

$$z = 5x_1 + 4x_2$$

The objective of the company is

$$\text{Maximize } z = 5x_1 + 4x_2$$

The last element of the model deals with the constraints that restrict raw materials usage and demand. The raw materials restrictions are expressed verbally as

$$\left(\begin{array}{c}\text{Usage of a raw material}\\ \text{by both paints}\end{array}\right) \le \left(\begin{array}{c}\text{Maximum raw material}\\ \text{availability}\end{array}\right)$$

From the data of the problem that

$$\text{Usage of raw material } M1 = 6x_1 + 4x_2 \text{ tons}$$

$$\text{Usage of raw material } M2 = 1x_1 + 2x_2 \text{ tons}$$

Because the daily availabilities of raw materials $M1$ and $M2$ are limited to 24 and 6 tons, respectively, the associated restrictions are given as

$$6x_1 + 4x_2 \leq 24 \quad \text{(Raw material } M1\text{)}$$

$$x_1 + 2x_2 \leq 6 \quad \text{(Raw material } M2\text{)}$$

There are two types of demand restrictions: (1) Maximum daily demand of interior paint is limited to 2 tons, and (2) excess of daily production of interior paint over that of exterior paint is at most 1 ton. The first restriction is straightforward and is expressed as $x_2 \leq 2$. The second restriction can be translated to state that the difference between the daily production of interior and exterior paints, $x_2 - x_1$, does not exceed 1 ton—that is, $x_2 - x_1 \leq 1$.

An implicit (or "understood-to-be") restriction on the model is that the variables $x_1$ and $x_2$ must not be negative. We thus add the **nonnegativity restrictions,** $x_1 \geq 0, x_2 \geq 0$, to account for this requirement. (We will see later in Chapter 3 that the nonnegativity restrictions are essential for the development of the solution algorithm of the LP model.)

The complete Reddy Mikks model is written as

$$\text{Maximize } z = 5x_1 + 4x_2$$

subject to

$$6x_1 + 4x_2 \leq 24$$
$$x_1 + 2x_2 \leq 6$$
$$-x_1 + x_2 \leq 1$$
$$x_2 \leq 2$$
$$x_1, \, x_2 \geq 0$$

Any solution that satisfies all the constraints of the model is a **feasible solution**. For example, the solution $x_1 = 3$ tons and $x_2 = 1$ ton is feasible because it does not violate any of the constraints, including the nonnegativity restrictions. To verify this result, we substitute $(x_1 = 3, x_2 = 1)$ in the left-hand side of each constraint to make sure that the inequalities are satisfied. For example, in the first constraint, $6x_1 + 4x_2 = 6 \times 3 + 4 \times 1 = 22$, which is less than the right-hand side of the constraint ($=24$). The value of the objective function associated with the solution $(x_1 = 3, x_2 = 1)$ is $z = 5 \times 3 + 4 \times 1 = 19$ (thousand dollars).

From the standpoint of the entire model, what we really are interested in is the **optimum feasible solution** that yields the maximum total profit. With some reflection, you should conclude that the model has a large (in fact, infinite) number of feasible solutions. As such, it is impossible to use direct substitutions to determine the optimum. Instead, we need efficient procedures that will locate the optimum solution systematically. The graphical method in Section 2.3 and its algebraic generalization in Chapter 3 provide such procedures.

---

In the preceding example, the objective and constraints functions are all linear. Intrinsic in the linearity assumptions are the following two properties:

**1. Proportionality** requires the contribution of each decision variable in both the objective function and the constraints to be *directly proportional* to the value of the variable. For example, if Reddy Mikks grants quantity discounts when the sales exceed certain limits, then the revenues will no longer be proportional to the amount of sales.

**2. Additivity** stipulates that the total contribution of all the variables in the objective function and in the constraints be the direct sum of individual contribution of each variable. For example, two *competing* products, where an increase in sales level of one product adversely affects that of the other, do not satisfy the additivity property.

### Problem set 2.2a

**1.** For the Reddy Mikks model, construct each of the following constraints and express them with a constant right-hand side:
   **(a)** The daily demand for interior paint exceeds that of exterior paint by *at least* 1 ton.
   **(b)** The daily usage of raw material, $M2$, is *at most* 6 tons and *at least* 3 tons.
   **(c)** The demand for interior paint cannot be less than the demand for exterior paint.
   **(d)** The minimum quantity that should be produced of both the interior and the exterior paint is 3 tons.
   **(e)** The proportion of interior paint to the total production of both interior and exterior paints must not exceed .5.
**2.** Determine the *optimum feasible solution* among the following solutions of the Reddy Mikks model:
   **(a)** $x_1 = 1, x_2 = 4$.
   **(b)** $x_1 = 2, x_2 = 2$.
   **(c)** $x_1 = 3, x_2 = 1.5$.
   **(d)** $x_1 = 2, x_2 = 1$.
   **(e)** $x_1 = 2, x_2 = -1$.
**3.** For the feasible solution $x_1 = 2, x_2 = 2$ of the Reddy Mikks model, determine
   **(a)** The unused amount of raw material, $M1$.
   **(b)** The unused amount of raw material, $M2$.
**4.** Suppose that Reddy Mikks sells its exterior paint to a single wholesaler at quantity discount. The end effect is that the profit per ton will be $5000 if the contractor buys no more than 2 tons daily and $4500 otherwise. Can this situation be modeled as an LP model?

## 2.3 GRAPHICAL LP SOLUTION

This section shows how a two-variable LP model is solved graphically. Although two-variable models rarely occur in practice (where a typical LP model may include thousands of variables and constraints), the ideas gleaned from the graphical procedure lay the foundation for the development of the general solution technique (called the simplex method) presented in Chapter 3.

The graphical procedure includes two basic steps:

**1.** The determination of the solution space that defines the feasible solutions that satisfy all the constraints of the model.

**2.** The determination of the optimum solution from among all the points in the feasible solution space.

The procedure is described for both a maximization and a minimization objective function.

### 2.3.1 Solution of a Maximization Model

**Example 2.3–1.**

We use the Reddy Mikks model to illustrate the two steps of the graphical procedure.
*Step 1. Determination of the Feasible Solution Space:*
First, as shown in Figure 2–1, let the horizontal axis $x_1$ and the vertical axis $x_2$ represent the exterior paint and interior paint variables, respectively. Next, consider the nonnegativity restrictions $x_1 \geq 0$ and $x_2 \geq 0$. These two constraints restrict the solution space area to the first quadrant (which lies above the $x_1$-axis and to the right of the $x_2$-axis).

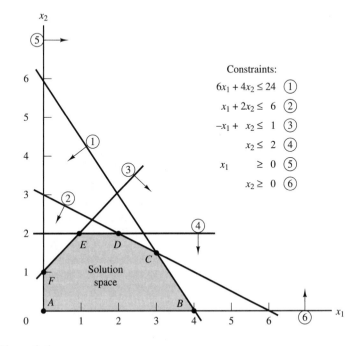

Constraints:

$$6x_1 + 4x_2 \leq 24 \quad \text{①}$$
$$x_1 + 2x_2 \leq 6 \quad \text{②}$$
$$-x_1 + x_2 \leq 1 \quad \text{③}$$
$$x_2 \leq 2 \quad \text{④}$$
$$x_1 \geq 0 \quad \text{⑤}$$
$$x_2 \geq 0 \quad \text{⑥}$$

**Figure 2–1**

The easiest way of accounting for the remaining four constraints is to replace the inequalities with equations and then plot the resulting straight lines. For example, the inequality $6x_1 + 4x_2 \leq 24$ is replaced with the straight line $6x_1 + 4x_2 = 24$. To plot this line, we need two distinct points, which can be secured by first setting $x_1 = 0$ to obtain $x_2 = \frac{24}{4} = 6$, and then setting $x_2 = 0$ to obtain $x_1 = \frac{24}{6} = 4$. Thus, the line passes through the two points $(0, 6)$ and $(4, 0)$ as shown by line (1) in Figure 2–1.

Next, we consider the effect of the inequality. All the inequality does is to divide the $(x_1, x_2)$-plane into two (half) spaces that occur on both sides of the plotted line; one side satisfies the inequality, and the other one does not. A procedure for determining the feasible side is to use the origin $(0, 0)$ as a reference point. For example, for the first constraint, $(0, 0)$ satisfies $6x_1 + 4x_2 \leq 24$ (that is, $6 \times 0 + 4 \times 0 = 0$, which is less than 24). This means that the feasible side of the constraint $6x_1 + 4x_2 \leq 24$ includes the origin. This result is shown by the directional arrow associated with constraint (1) in Figure 2–1.

In general, if the origin does not satisfy the inequality, then the directional arrow must point in the opposite side of $(0, 0)$. Also, if the line happens to pass through the origin, then we can choose another reference point to effect the desired result.

*Step 2. Determination of the Optimum Solution:*

Figure 2–1 provides the feasible solution space that is satisfied by all the constraints of the model. This space is delineated by the line segments joining the corner points A, B, C, D, E, and F. Any point within or on the boundary of the space *ABCDEF* is a feasible point, in the sense that it satisfies all the constraints. Because the feasible space

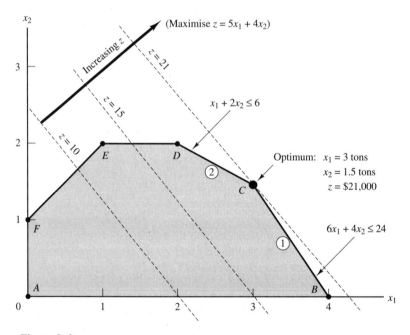

**Figure 2–2**

*ABCDEF* consists of an *infinite* number of points, we need a systematic procedure that identifies the optimum solution.

The determination of the optimum solution requires identifying the direction in which the profit function $z = 5x_1 + 4x_2$ increases (recall that we are *maximizing* z). We can do so by assigning z the (arbitrary) increasing values of 10 and 15, which would be equivalent to plotting the lines $5x_1 + 4x_2 = 10$ and $5x_1 + 4x_2 = 15$. Figure 2–2 super-imposes these two lines on the solution space of the model. The profit z thus can be increased in the direction shown in the figure until we reach the point in the solution space beyond which any further increase will put us outside the boundaries of *ABCDEF*. Such a point is the optimum.

In terms of Figure 2–2, the optimum solution is given by point C. The values of $x_1$ and $x_2$ are thus determined by solving the equations associated with lines (1) and (2); that is,

$$6x_1 + 4x_2 = 24$$

$$x_1 + 2x_2 = 6$$

The solution yields $x_1 = 3$ and $x_2 = 1.5$ with $z = 5 \times 3 + 4 \times 1.5 = 21$. This means that the optimum daily product mix of 3 tons of exterior paint and 1.5 tons of interior paint will yield a daily profit of $21,000.

It is not accidental that the optimum solution is associated with a **corner point** of the solution space where two lines intersect. Indeed, if we change the slope of the profit function z (by changing its coefficients), we will discover that the optimum solution is identified always by one of these *corner* points. This observation is the key idea for the development of the general *simplex algorithm,* which we will present in Chapter 3.

---

### Problem set 2.3a

1. Consider the following constraints:
   (a) $-3x_1 + x_2 \le 7$.  (b) $x_1 - 2x_2 \ge 5$.  (c) $2x_1 - 3x_2 \le 8$.
   (d) $x_1 - x_2 \le 0$.  (e) $-x_1 + x_2 \ge 0$.
   Determine the feasible space for each individual constraint, given that $x_1$, $x_2 \ge 0$.

2. Identify the direction of increase in z in each of the following cases:
   (a) Maximize $z = x_1 - x_2$.  (b) Maximize $z = -5x_1 - 6x_2$.
   (c) Maximize $z = -x_1 + 2x_2$.  (d) Maximize $z = -3x_1 + x_2$.

3. Determine the solution space and the optimum solution of the Reddy Mikks model for each of the following independent changes:
   (a) The maximum daily demand for exterior paint is 2.5 tons.
   (b) The daily demand for interior paint is at least 2 tons.
   (c) The daily demand for interior paint is exactly 1 ton higher than that for exterior paint.
   (d) The daily availability of raw material, $M1$, is at least 24 tons.
   (e) The daily availability of raw material, $M1$, is at least 24 tons, and the daily demand for interior paint exceeds that of exterior paint by at least 1 ton.

4. For the (original) Reddy Mikks model, identify the *corner* point(s) that define the optimum solution for each of the following objective functions:
   **(a)** $z = 3x_1 + x_2$.
   **(b)** $z = x_1 + 3x_2$.
   **(c)** $z = 6x_1 + 4x_2$.
   How does the solution in (c) differ from those in (a) and (b)?

5. Jack is an aspiring freshman at Ulern University. He realizes that "all work and no play make Jack a dull boy." As a result, Jack wants to apportion his available time of about 10 hours a day between work and play. He estimates that play is twice as much fun as work. He also wants to study at least as much as he plays. However, Jack realizes that if he is going to get all his homework assignments done, he cannot play more than 4 hours a day. How should Jack allocate his time to maximize his pleasure from both work and play?

### 2.3.2 Solution of a Minimization Model

---

**Example 2.3–2   (DIET PROBLEM).**

Ozark Farms uses at least 800 lb of special feed daily. The special feed is a mixture of corn and soybean meal with the following compositions:

| | lb per lb of feedstuff | | |
|---|---|---|---|
| Feedstuff | Protein | Fiber | Cost ($/lb) |
| Corn | .09 | .02 | .30 |
| Soybean meal | .60 | .06 | .90 |

The dietary requirements of the special feed stipulate at least 30% protein and at most 5% fiber. Ozark Farms wishes to determine the daily minimum-cost feed mix.

Because the feed mix consists of corn and soybean meal, the decision variables of the model are defined as

$x_1$ = lb of corn in the daily mix

$x_2$ = lb of soybean meal in the daily mix

The objective function seeks to minimize the total daily cost (in dollars) of the feed mix and is thus expressed as

$$\text{minimize } z = .3x_1 + .9x_2$$

The constraints of the model must reflect the daily amount needed and the dietary requirements. Because Ozark Farms needs 800 lb of feed a day, the associated constraint can be expressed as

$$x_1 + x_2 \geq 800$$

The protein dietary requirement constraint is developed next. The amount of protein included in $x_1$ lb of corn and $x_2$ lb of soybean meal is $(.09x_1 + .6x_2)$ lb. This quantity should equal at least 30% of the total feed mix $(x_1 + x_2)$ lb, thus yielding

$$.09x_1 + .6x_2 \geq .3(x_1 + x_2)$$

In a similar fashion, the fiber constraint is constructed as

$$.02x_1 + .06x_2 \leq .05(x_1 + x_2)$$

The preceding constraints are simplified by grouping all the coefficients of the $x_1$ and $x_2$ on the left-hand side of each inequality. The complete model thus becomes

$$\text{minimize } z = .3x_1 + .9x_2$$

subject to

$$x_1 + x_2 \geq 800$$
$$.21x_1 - .30x_2 \leq 0$$
$$.03x_1 - .01x_2 \geq 0$$
$$x_1, x_2 \geq 0$$

Figure 2–3 provides the graphical solution of the model. Unlike those of the Reddy Mikks model (Example 2.3–1), two of the constraints pass through the origin.

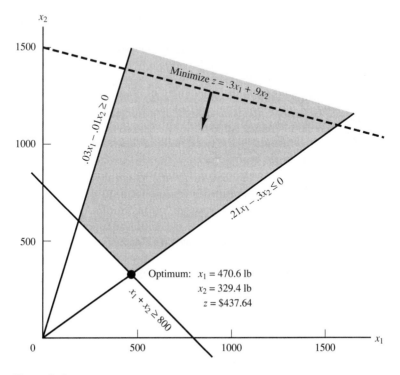

**Figure 2–3**

To plot each of the associated straight lines, we need one additional point, which can be obtained by assigning one of the variables a value and then solving for the other variable. For example, $x_1 = 200$ will yield $.21 \times 200 - .3x_2 = 0$, or $x_2 = 140$. This means that the straight line $.21x_1 - .3x_2 = 0$ passes through $(0, 0)$ and $(200, 140)$. Note also that the direction of feasibility for the two constraints that pass through the origin can be determined by using a reference point other than $(0, 0)$; for example, either $(100, 0)$ or $(0, 100)$ can be used as a reference point for the second and third constraints.

Because the present model seeks the minimization of the objective function, we need to reduce the value of $z$ as much as possible in the direction shown by the arrow in Figure 2–3. The optimum solution is the intersection of the two lines $x_1 + x_2 = 800$ and $.21x_1 - .3x_2 = 0$, which yields $x_1 = 470.59$ lb and $x_2 = 329.41$ lb. The associated minimum cost of the feed mix is $z = .3 \times 470.59 + .9 \times 329.42 = \$437.65$ per day.

---

**Problem set 2.3b**

**1.** Identify the direction of decrease in $z$ in each of the following cases:
   **(a)** Minimize $z = 4x_1 - 2x_2$.    **(b)** Minimize $z = -3x_1 + x_2$.
   **(c)** Minimize $z = -x_1 - 2x_2$.

**2.** For the diet model, suppose that the daily availability of corn is limited to 450 lb. Identify the new solution space, and determine the new optimum solution.

**3.** For the diet model, what type of optimum solution would the model yield if the feed mix should not exceed 800 lb a day? Does the solution make sense?

**4.** John must work at least 20 hours a week to supplement his income while attending school. He has the opportunity to work in two retail stores: in store 1, John can work between 5 and 12 hours a week, and in store 2 he is allowed to work between 6 and 10 hours. Both stores pay the same hourly wage. John thus wants to base his decision about how many hours to work in each store on a different criterion: work stress factor. Based on interviews with present employees, John estimates that, on a scale of 1 to 10, the stress factors are 8 and 6 at stores 1 and 2, respectively. Because stress mounts by the hour, he presumes that the total stress at the end of the week is proportional to the number of hours he works in the store. How many hours should John work in each store?

### 2.3.3 Slack, Surplus, and Unrestricted Variables

In the Reddy Mikks and diet models, we have used both $\leq$ and $\geq$ constraints. We have also solved both examples under the assumption that all the variables are nonnegative. This section defines two special variables, the **slack** and the **surplus,** that evolve in connection with the $\leq$ and $\geq$ constraints. It also introduces the concept of the **unrestricted variable** whose value can be positive, zero, or negative.

   ***Slack Variable.***    For constraints of the type ( $\leq$ ), the right-hand side normally represents the limit on the availability of a resource, and the left-hand side represents the usage of this limited resource by the different activities (variables) of the model. A *slack* thus represents the amount by which the available amount of the resource exceeds its usage by the activities. For example, mathematically, the constraint $6x_1 + 4x_2 \leq 24$ associated with the usage of raw material, $M1$, in the Reddy Mikks model is equivalent to $6x_1 + 4x_2 + s_1 = 24$, provided that $s_1 \geq 0$. The slack variable $s_1$ ( $= 24 - 6x_1 - 4x_2$) thus represents the unused amount of raw material, $M1$.

**Surplus Variable.**    Constraints of the type ( $\geq$ ) normally set minimum specification requirements. In this case, a *surplus* represents the excess of the left-hand side over the minimum requirement. For example, in the diet model, the constraint representing the minimum feed requirements, $x_1 + x_2 \geq 800$, is mathematically equivalent to $x_1 + x_2 - S_1 = 800$, provided that $S_1 \geq 0$. A positive value of $S_1$ signifies that a surplus amount of feed (over the minimum requirement of 800 lb) will be produced.

**Unrestricted Variable.**    In both the Reddy Mikks and the diet models, the nature of the variables requires them to assume nonnegative values. There are situations, where a variable can assume any real value. The following example illustrates a possible application.

---

**Example 2.3–3.**

McBurger fast-food restaurant sells quarter-pounder and cheeseburger. A quarter-pounder uses a quarter of a pound of meat, and a cheeseburger uses only .2 lb. The restaurant starts the day with 200 lb of meat but may order more at an additional cost of 25 cents per pound to cover the delivery cost. Any surplus meat at the end of the day is donated to HotSoup Charity. McBurger's profits are 20 cents from a quarter-pounder and 15 cents for a cheeseburger. All in all, McBurger does not expect to sell more than 900 sandwiches in any one day. How many of each sandwich should McBurger make?

Let us look at the constraints first. Letting $x_1$ and $x_2$ represent the daily number of quarter-pounders and cheeseburgers made, the use of meat will depend on whether McBurger stays within the initial limit of 200 lb or order additional meat. In the first case, the constraint is $.25x_1 + .2x_2 \leq 200$, and in the second case it becomes $.25x_1 + .2x_2 \geq 200$. The specific selection between the two constraints depends on which one yields a better optimum. In effect, we do not know whether the constraint should operate with a slack (first case) or with a surplus (second case). A logical way to account for the situation is to replace the two constraints with

$$.25x_1 + .2x_2 + x_3 = 200, x_3 \text{ unrestricted}$$

The fact that $x_3$ is unrestricted allows the variable to play the roles of both a slack and a surplus, as desired.

Next we consider the objective function. McBurger seeks to maximize the total profit, less any additional cost that may be incurred as a result of ordering special delivery of additional pounds of meat. The additional cost is incurred only if $x_3$ plays the role of a surplus, that is, if $x_3 < 0$.

Mathematically, dealing with an unrestricted variable is cumbersome. For this reason, we use a standard substitution that converts the unrestricted variable into two nonnegative variables—that is, let

$$x_3 = x_3^+ - x_3^-, \text{ where } x_3^+, x_3^- \geq 0$$

If $x_3^+ > 0$ and $x_3^- = 0$, $x_3^+$ plays the role of a slack. Otherwise, if $x_3^- > 0$ and $x_3^+ = 0$, then $x_3^-$ plays the role of surplus. (Chapter 3 shows that it is impossible that the optimal LP solution will yield positive values for $x_3^+$ and $x_3^-$ simultaneously.) Thus, the constraint can be expressed as

$$.25x_1 + .2x_2 + x_3^+ - x_3^- = 200$$

and the objective function is expressed directly as

$$\text{maximize } z = .20x_1 + .15x_2 - .25x_3^-$$

### Problem set 2.3c

**1.** In the Reddy Mikks model, consider the feasible solution $x_1 = 3$ tons and $x_2 = 1$ ton. Determine the value of the associated slacks for raw materials, $M1$ and $M2$.

**2.** In the diet model, determine the surplus amount of feed consisting of 500 lb of corn and 600 lb of soybean meal.

**3.** Two products are manufactured in a machining center. The productions times per unit of products 1 and 2 are 10 and 12 minutes, respectively. The total regular machine time is 2500 minutes per day. In any one day, the manufacturer can sell between 150 and 200 units of product 1, but no more than 45 units of product 2. Overtime may be used to meet the demand at an additional cost of $.50 per minute.

    **(a)** Assuming that the unit profits for products 1 and 2 are $6.00 and $7.50, respectively, formulate a model and determine the optimum production level for each product as well as any overtime needed in the center.

    **(b)** If the cost per overtime minute is increased to $1.50, should the company use overtime?

## 2.4 GRAPHICAL SENSITIVITY ANALYSIS

An LP model is a snapshot of a real situation in which the model parameters (objective and constraint coefficients) assume static values. It appears natural that we study the effect of making changes in the model parameters on a given optimum LP solution. This type of investigation is called **sensitivity analysis**.

This section investigates sensitivity analysis based on the graphical LP solution. Two cases are considered: (1) changes in the objective coefficients and (2) changes in the right-hand side of the constraints. Although the presentation is elementary and limited in scope, it does provide a fundamental insight into the significance of sensitivity analysis. In Chapter 4, the sensitivity analysis problem is presented in detail.

### 2.4.1 Changes in the Objective Function Coefficients

The general objective function in a two-variable LP problem can be written as

$$\text{maximize or minimize } z = c_1 x_1 + c_2 x_2$$

Changes in the coefficients $c_1$ and $c_2$ will change the slope of $z$. From the graphical LP solution in Section 2.3, a change in the slope of $z$ may lead to changing the optimum solution to a different *corner point* of the solution space. However, there is a range of variation for both $c_1$ and $c_2$ that will keep the current optimum unchanged. This is the information we seek to find by means of sensitivity analysis. More specifically, we are interested in determining the *range of optimality* for the ratio $\frac{c_1}{c_2}$ (or $\frac{c_2}{c_1}$) that will keep the optimum solution of a given model unchanged. The following example illustrates how the desired result can be reached by using graphical analysis.

---

**Example 2.4–1.**

We apply the sensitivity analysis procedure to the Reddy Mikks model (Example 2.2–1). In Figure 2–4, the optimum solution at $C$ provides the maximum value of $z = 5x_1 + 4x_2$. If we change the objective function to $z = c_1 x_1 + c_2 x_2$, then the solution at $C$ will remain optimum so long as the slope of $z$ lies between the slopes of the two lines intersecting at $C$—namely, $6x_1 + 4x_2 = 24$ (raw material, $M1$) and $x_1 + 2x_2 = 6$ (raw material, $M2$). We can express this relationship algebraically as

$$\frac{4}{6} \le \frac{c_2}{c_1} \le \frac{2}{1}, \quad c_1 \ne 0$$

or

$$\frac{1}{2} \le \frac{c_1}{c_2} \le \frac{6}{4}, \quad c_2 \ne 0$$

In the first condition, $c_1 \ne 0$ signifies that the objective function line cannot be horizontal. Similarly, in the second condition, $c_2 \ne 0$ means that $z$ cannot be vertical. As can be seen from Figure 2–4, the optimality range in this model (defined by the two lines intersecting at $C$) does not permit the objective function $z = c_1 x_1 + c_2 x_2$ to be a horizontal or vertical line. As a result, either of the given two conditions is applicable in this example. (For the cases where both $c_1$ and $c_2$ can assume zero values, the range for $\frac{c_1}{c_2}$ or $\frac{c_2}{c_1}$ must be partitioned into two sets in which the denominators are not allowed to be zero. See Problem 2.4a–1 for illustrations.)

What the conditions for $\frac{c_1}{c_2}$ and $\frac{c_2}{c_1}$ say is that values of $c_1$ and $c_2$ that satisfy the given inequalities will automatically keep the optimum solution unchanged at $C$. Note, that if $z = c_1 x_1 + c_2 x_2$ happens to coincide with $x_1 + 2x_2 = 6$, then alternative optima can occur anywhere on the line segment $CD$. Similarly, if it coincides with $6x_1 + 4x_2 = 24$, then all the points on the line segment $BC$ provide alternative optima.

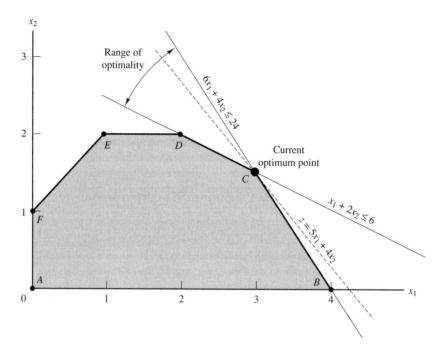

**Figure 2–4**

This observation, nevertheless, does not change the fact that $C$ remains optimum in both cases.

We can use the given conditions to determine the optimal range for one of the coefficients, assuming that the other coefficient remains the same as originally given in $z = 5x_1 + 4x_2$. Thus, if $c_2$ remains equal to 4, the associated optimal range for $c_1$ is determined from the condition $\frac{1}{2} \leq \frac{c_1}{c_2} \leq \frac{6}{4}$ by substituting $c_2 = 4$, which yields $4 \times \frac{1}{2} \leq c_1 \leq 4 \times \frac{6}{4}$, or $2 \leq c_1 \leq 6$. Similarly, if we specify $c_1 = 5$, then the condition $\frac{4}{6} \leq \frac{c_2}{c_1} \leq 2$ will yield $\frac{10}{3} \leq c_2 \leq 10$.

**Problem set 2.4a**

**1.** Determine graphically the range of optimality, $\frac{c_1}{c_2}$, for the following problems. Observe the special cases where $c_1$ or $c_2$ may assume a zero value.

**(a)** Maximize $z = 2x_1 + 3x_2$

subject to

$$3x_1 + 2x_2 \leq 5$$

$$-x_1 + x_2 \leq 0$$

$$x_1, x_2 \leq 0$$

**(b)** Maximize $z = 4x_1 + 3x_2$
subject to

$$3x_1 + 5x_2 \le 5$$

$$x_1 - x_2 \le 0$$

$$x_1, \ x_2 \le 0$$

**(c)** Maximize $z = x_1 + x_2$
subject to

$$-x_1 + x_2 \le 0$$

$$3x_1 - x_2 \le 3$$

$$x_1, \ x_2 \ge 0$$

2. In the diet problem of Example 2.3–2,
   **(a)** Determine the optimality range for the ratio of the cost per pound of corn to the cost per pound of soybean meal.
   **(b)** If the cost per pound of corn is increased by 20% and that of soybean meal is decreased by 5%, would the current solution remain optimal?
   **(c)** If the cost per pound of corn remains fixed at 30 cents and the cost per pound of soybean meal is increased to $1.10, would the current solution remain optimum?

3. B&K grocery store sells two types of soft drinks: the brand name A1 Cola and the cheaper store brand B&K Cola. The margin of profit on the A1 Cola is about 5 cents per can, whereas the B&K Cola grosses 7 cents per can. On the average, the store sells no more than 500 cans of both colas a day. Although A1 is a better recognized name, customers tend to buy more of the B&K brand because it is considerably cheaper. It is estimated that the B&K brand outsells the A1 brand by a ratio of at least 2:1. However, B&K sells at least 100 cans of A1 a day.
   **(a)** How many cans of each brand should the store carry daily to maximize profit?
   **(b)** Determine the ratio of the profits per can of A1 and B&K that will keep the optimum solution in (a) unchanged.

4. Baba Furniture Company employs four carpenters for 10 days to assemble tables and chairs. It takes 2 hours to assemble a table and 30 minutes to assemble a chair. Customers usually buy between four and six chairs with each table. The profits are $135 per table and $50 per chair. The company operates one 8-hour shift a day.
   **(a)** Determine the 10-day optimal production mix graphically.
   **(b)** Determine the range of the ratio of unit profits that will keep the optimum in (a) unchanged.

**(c)** If the present profits per table and chair are each reduced by 10%, use the answer in (b) to show how this change affects the optimum solution obtained in (a).

**(d)** If the present profits per table and chair are changed to $120 and $25, use sensitivity result in (b) to determine whether or not the solution in (a) will change.

5. The Bank of Elkins is allocating a maximum of $200,000 for personal and car loans during the next month. The bank charges 14% for personal loans and 12% for car loans. Both types of loans are repaid at the end of a 1-year period. Experience shows that about 3% of personal loans and 2% of car loans are never repaid. The bank usually allocates at least twice as much to car loans as to personal loans.

**(a)** Determine the optimal allocation of funds to the two types of loans and the net rate of return the bank will get from all the loans.

**(b)** Determine the optimality range for the ratio of car to personal interest rates that will keep the solution in (a) unchanged.

**(c)** Suppose that the percentage of unrepaid personal and car loans are changed to 4% and 3%, respectively, how would this change affect the optimum solution in (a)?

6. Electra produces two types of electric motors, each on a separate assembly line. The respective daily capacities of the two lines are 600 and 750 motors. Type 1 motor uses 10 units of a certain electronic component, and type 2 motor uses only 8 units. The supplier of the component can provide 8000 pieces a day. The profits per motor for types 1 and 2 are $60 and $40, respectively.

**(a)** Determine the optimum daily production mix.

**(b)** Determine the optimality range of the ratio of unit profits that will keep the solution in (a) unchanged.

7. Popeye Canning is contracted to receive 60,000 lb of ripe tomatoes at 7 cents per pound from which it produces both canned tomato juice and tomato paste. The canned products are packaged in 24-can cases. A can of juice requires 1 lb of fresh tomatoes, and a can of paste requires $\frac{1}{3}$ lb only. The company's share of the market is limited to 2000 cases of juice and 6000 cases of paste. The wholesale prices per case of juice and paste are $18 and $9, respectively.

**(a)** Develop an optimum production program for Popeye.

**(b)** Determine the ratio of the price per case of juice to the price per case of paste that will allow Popeye to produce more cases of juice than of paste.

8. Dean's Furniture Company assembles from precut lumber two types of kitchen cabinets: regular and deluxe. The regular cabinets are painted white, and the deluxe ones are varnished. Both the painting and the varnishing occur in one department. The daily capacity of the assembly department

can produce a maximum of 200 regular cabinets and 150 deluxe ones. Varnishing a deluxe unit takes twice as much time as painting a regular one. If the painting/varnishing department is dedicated to the deluxe units only, it can complete 180 units daily. The company estimates that the profits per unit for the regular and deluxe cabinets are $100 and $140, respectively.

**(a)** Formulate the problem as a linear program and find the optimal production schedule per day.

**(b)** Suppose that because of competition, the profits per unit of the regular and deluxe units must be reduced to $80 and $110, respectively. Use sensitivity analysis to determine whether or not the optimum solution in (a) remains unchanged.

## 2.4.2 Unit Worth of a Resource

In most LP models, constraints usually represent the usage of limited resources. For such constraints, the right-hand side provides the limit on the availability of the resource. In this section, we study the sensitivity of the optimum solution to changes in the availability of the resources. The analysis provides a single measure, called the **unit worth of the resource,** that quantifies the rate of change in the optimum value in the objective function as a result of making changes in the availability of a resource. The procedure is illustrated by the following example.

---

**Example 2.4–2.**

In the Reddy Mikks model, the first two constraints represent the limitations on the usages of raw materials, $M1$ and $M2$, respectively. Determine the worth per unit for each resource.

We start with the constraint for raw material, $M1$. Figure 2–5 shows that the current optimum occurs at point $C$, which is the intersection of the lines associated with raw materials, $M1$ and $M2$. When the availability of $M1$ changes (increases or decreases around the current level of 24 tons), the optimum solution point $C$ will "slide" along the line segment $DG$. Any change in $M1$ outside the range of this segment will make the intersection point $C$ infeasible (remember that $C$ is the intersection of the lines associated with $M1$ and $M2$). For this reason, we say that the end points $D = (2, 2)$ and $G = (6, 0)$ delineate the *feasibility range* for $M1$. The amount of $M1$ associated with $D = (2, 2)$ is computed as $6x_1 + 4x_2 = 6 \times 2 + 4 \times 2 = 20$ tons. Similarly, the amount of $M1$ associated with $G = (6, 0)$ is $6 \times 6 + 4 \times 0 = 36$ tons. Thus, the range of feasibility for $M1$ is $20 \leq M1 \leq 36$. Equivalently, if we define $M1 = 24 + D_1$, where $D_1$ is the change in the raw material above or below the current level of 24 tons, then we have $20 \leq 24 + D_1 \leq 36$, or, $-4 \leq D_1 \leq 12$. This means that the current level of $M1$ can be decreased by as much as 4 tons or increased by as much as 12 tons while guaranteeing that the optimum solution point will be given by the intersection $C$ of the lines associated with $M1$ and $M2$.

We now turn our attention to computing the worth per unit of raw material, $M1$. As the amount of $M1$ changes within the range $20 \leq M1 \leq 36$, the value of $z$ associated

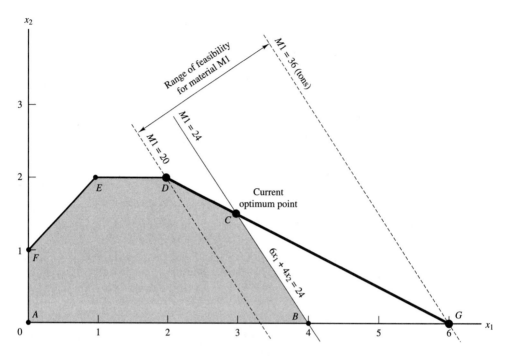

**Figure 2–5**

with the optimum point $C$ changes at a constant rate because $DG$ is a linear segment. Thus, letting $y_1$ represent the worth per unit of raw material, $M1$, we have

$$y_1 = \frac{\text{change in } z \text{ from } D \text{ to } G}{\text{change in } M1 \text{ from } D \text{ to } G}$$

Given $D = (2, 2)$ and $G = (6, 0)$, then

$$z \text{ at } D = 5 \times 2 + 4 \times 2 = 18 \text{ (thousand dollars)}$$

$$z \text{ at } G = 5 \times 6 + 4 \times 0 = 30 \text{ (thousand dollars)}$$

It then follows that

$$y_1 = \frac{30 - 18}{36 - 20} = \frac{3}{4} \text{ (thousand dollars per ton of } M1)$$

The result shows that a 1-ton change in $M1$ in the range $20 \le M1 \le 36$ will change the optimum value of $z$ by \$750.

Next, we consider raw material, $M2$. Figure 2–6 shows that the range of feasibility for $M2$ is delineated by the end points $B$ and $H$, where $B = (4, 0)$ and $H = (\frac{8}{3}, 2)$. Point $H$ is defined by the intersection of lines $ED$ and $BC$. Thus,

$$M2 \text{ at } B = x_1 + 2x_2 = 4 + 2 \times 0 = 4 \text{ tons}$$

$$M2 \text{ at } H = \frac{8}{3} + 2 \times 2 = \frac{20}{3} \text{ tons}$$

$z$ at $B = 5x_1 + 4x_2 = 5 \times 4 + 4 \times 0 = 20$ (thousand dollars)

$z$ at $H = 5 \times \frac{8}{3} + 4 \times 2 = \frac{64}{3}$ (thousand dollars)

It then follows that for $4 \le M2 \le \frac{20}{3}$, the worth per unit of $M2$, $y_2$, is computed as

$$y_2 = \frac{\dfrac{64}{3} - 20}{\dfrac{20}{3} - 4} = \frac{1}{2} \text{ (thousand dollar per ton of } M2)$$

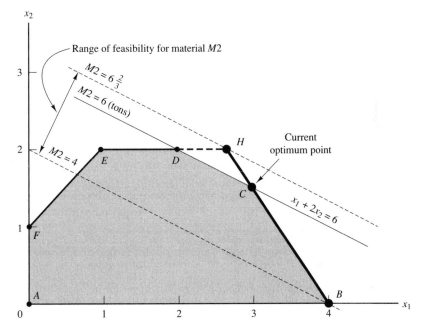

**Figure 2–6**

## Problem set 2.4b

1. Wild West produces two types of cowboy hats. Type 1 hat requires twice as much labor time as does each of the type 2. If all produced hats are of type 2 only, the company can produce a total of 400 hats a day. The market daily limits are 150 and 200 hats for types 1 and 2, respectively. The profit per type 1 hat is $8 and that of type 2 hat is $5.
   (a) Use the graphical solution to determine the number of hats that should be produced of each type.
   (b) Determine the worth of increasing the production capacity of the company by one type 2 hat and the range for which this result is applicable.

**(c)** If the demand limit on type 1 hat is decreased to 120, determine the corresponding effect on the optimal profit using the unit worth of the resource.

**(d)** What is the worth per unit increase in the market share of type 2 hat? By how much can the market share be increased while yielding the computed worth per unit?

**2.** A company produces two products, $A$ and $B$. The sales volume for $A$ is at least 80% of the total sales of both $A$ and $B$. However, the company cannot sell more than 100 unit of $A$ per day. Both products use one raw material whose maximum daily availability is limited to 240 lb a day. The usage rates of the raw material are 2 lb per unit of $A$ and 4 lb per unit of $B$. The unit prices for $A$ and $B$ are $20 and $50, respectively.

**(a)** Determine the optimal product mix for the company.

**(b)** Determine the worth per unit change in the availability of the raw material and its range of applicability.

**(c)** Use graphical sensitivity analysis to determine the effect of changing the maximum demand for product $A$ by $\pm 10$ units.

**3.** A company that operates 10 hours a day manufactures each of two products on three sequential processes. The following table summarizes the data of the problem:

| Product | Minutes per unit | | | Unit profit |
|---------|-----------|-----------|-----------|-------------|
|         | Process 1 | Process 2 | Process 3 |             |
| 1       | 10        | 6         | 8         | $2          |
| 2       | 5         | 20        | 10        | $3          |

**(a)** Determine the optimal mix of the two products.

**(b)** Suppose that the three processes are being considered for expansion, and you are required to prioritize them. Devise a logical way for achieving this goal.

**4.** Show & Sell can advertise its products on local radio or television (TV). The advertisement budget is limited to $10,000 a month. Each minute of radio advertisement costs $15 and each minute of TV commercials costs $300. Show & Sell likes to use radio advertisement at least twice as much as TVs. In the meantime, it is not practical to use more than 400 minutes of radio advertisement a month. Past experience shows that TV advertisement is estimated to be 25 times more effective than that of radio.

**(a)** Determine the optimum allocation of the budget to radio and TV advertisements.

**(b)** Determine the worth per unit of increasing the monthly limit on radio advertisement.

**(c)** If the monthly budget is increased to $15,000, use the unit worth definition to determine the resulting optimum measure of advertisement effectiveness.

5. Wyoming Electric Coop owns a steam-turbine power-generating plant. Because Wyoming is rich in coal deposits, the plant generates its steam from coal. This, however, creates the problem of meeting emission standards. Environmental Protection Agency regulations limit sulphur dioxide discharge to 2000 parts per million and smoke discharge from the plant stacks to 20 lb per hour. The Coop receives two grades of pulverized coals, C1 and C2, for use in the steam plant. The two grades are usually mixed together before burning. For simplicity, it can be assumed that the sulphur pollutant of the mixture (in parts per million) is a weighted average of the proportion of each grade used in the mixture. The following data are based on 1-ton consumption per hour of each of the two coal grades.

| Coal grade | Sulphur discharge in parts per million | Smoke discharge in lb per hour | Steam generated in lb per hour |
|---|---|---|---|
| C1 | 1800 | 2.1 | 12,000 |
| C2 | 2100 | .9 | 9000 |

**(a)** Determine the optimal ratio for mixing the two coal grades.
**(b)** Determine the effect of relaxing the smoke discharge limit by 1 lb on the amount of generated steam per hour.

6. The Continuing Education Division at the Ozark Community College offers a total of 30 courses each semester. The courses offered are usually of two types: practical, such as woodworking, word processing, and car maintenance; and humanistic, such as history, music, and fine arts. To satisfy the demands of the community, at least 10 courses of each type must be offered each semester. The division estimates that the revenues of offering practical and humanistic courses are approximately $1500 and $1000 per course, respectively.
**(a)** How should the college allocate its 30 courses?
**(b)** Determine the revenue from increasing the minimum requirement of the practical courses by one course.
**(c)** Determine the revenue from increasing the minimum requirement of the humanistic courses by one course.

7. The Burroughs Garment Company manufactures men shirts and women blouses for Walmark Discount Stores. Walmark will accept all the production supplied by Burroughs. The production process includes cutting, sewing, and packaging. Burroughs employs 25 workers in the cutting department, 35 in the sewing department, and 5 in the packaging department. The factory works one 8-hour shift, only 5 days a week. The following table gives the time requirements and profits per unit for the two garments:

| Garment | Minutes per unit | | | Unit profit($) |
|---------|---------|--------|-----------|------------|
|         | Cutting | Sewing | Packaging | |
| Shirts  | 20 | 70 | 12 | 2.50 |
| Blouses | 60 | 60 | 4  | 3.20 |

(a) Determine the optimal weekly production schedule for Burroughs.

(b) If Walmark minimum daily requirements are 2000 shirts and 3000 blouses, can these quantities be supplied by Burroughs's present 5-day work week? If not, can you suggest a way for Burroughs to meet these requirements? What will be the optimal production schedule in this case?

(c) Determine the worth per hour of cutting, sewing, and packaging.

(d) Suppose that overtime can be used in both the cutting and sewing departments, what should be the maximum hourly rate Burroughs should pay for overtime?

8. ChemLabs produces two domestic cleaning solutions, A and B, by processing two raw materials, I and II. The processing of 1 unit of raw material I costs $8 and produces .5 unit of solution A and .5 unit of solution B. Moreover, the processing of 1 unit of raw material II costs $5 and produces .6 unit of solution A and .4 unit of solution B. The daily demand for solution A lies between 10 and 15 units, and that for solution B lies between 12 and 20 units.

(a) Find the optimal mix of A and B that ChemLab should produce.

(b) Determine the worth per unit change in the demand limits for products A and B.

9. An assembly line consisting of three consecutive stations produces two radio models: HiFi-1 and HiFi-2. The following table provides the assembly times for the three workstations.

| Workstation | Minutes per unit | |
|-------------|--------|--------|
|             | HiFi-1 | HiFi-2 |
| 1 | 6 | 4 |
| 2 | 5 | 5 |
| 3 | 4 | 6 |

The daily maintenance for stations 1, 2, and 3 consumes 10%, 14%, and 12%, respectively, of the maximum 480 minutes available for each station each day.

(a) The company wishes to determine the optimal product mix that will minimize the idle (or unused) times in the three workstations.

(b) Determine the worth of decreasing the daily maintenance time for each station by 1 percentage point.

## 2.5 Computer Solution of LP Problems

The graphical procedure in Section 2.3 is used primarily to reveal some of the fundamental properties of the LP solution. In practice, where typical linear programming models may involve hundreds or even thousands of variables and constraints, the only feasible way to solve such models is by using an appropriate computer code.

In this section, the LP module of the software TORA is used to present the solution results of the linear programming problem. Although TORA can handle limited-size problems only, the type and quality of the output results is on par with those obtained from popular commercial codes.

---

**Example 2.5–1.**

Figure 2–7 presents the TORA solution of the Reddy Mikks model. We will use the interpretations given in the graphical method to explain the TORA output.

The output is divided into two main parts: (1) OPTIMUM SOLUTION SUMMARY and (2) SENSITIVITY ANALYSIS. In the OPTIMUM SOLUTION SUMMARY, we get the optimum values of the variables and the optimum objective value—namely, the amount of exterior paint, $x_1$, is 3 tons; amount of interior paint, $x_2$, is 1.5 tons; and the associated profit is \$21,000. It also provides information about the slack ($-$) and surplus ($+$) variables associated with the constraint. In the Reddy Mikks model, there are no ( $\geq$ ) constraints; hence, all the associated variables are slacks. The output shows that the slacks of the first two constraints are zero, which means that raw materials, $M1$ and $M2$, are consumed completely. The slack of the third constraint equals 2.5 tons, which means that the constraint is oversatisfied (because interior production is less than exterior production). The last slack associated with the fourth constraint shows that the production of interior paint is half a ton lower than the maximum limit specified by the maximum market demand.

The top two sections of SENSITIVITY ANALYSIS deal with making *single* changes in the coefficients of the objective function and the right-hand sides of the constraints. For example, the current optimum solution will remain unchanged so long as the profit per ton of exterior paint lies between \$2000 and \$6000. Also, the feasibility of the current solution is not affected so long as the daily availability of raw material, $M1$, stays between 20 and 36 tons. These are the same results obtained graphically in Example 2.4–2.

Changes in the coefficients of the objective function within the specified limits will not change the value of $x_1$ or $x_2$, but will affect the value of the objective function $z$ (see Section 2.4.1). However, changes in the right-hand side within the specified limits will alter the values of both the variables and the objective function (as explained in Section 2.4.2). Efficient methods for computing the new solution are given in Section 4.7.

We still have two additional columns to explain: the *reduced cost* of a variable and the *dual price* of a constraint. Let us start with the definition of reduced costs.

An LP variable is regarded as an economic activity that consumes (input) resources for the purpose of producing (output) profit. In this context, we have the following definition:

$$\begin{pmatrix} \text{Reduced cost per} \\ \text{unit of activity } j \end{pmatrix} = \begin{pmatrix} \text{Cost of consumed} \\ \text{resources per} \\ \text{unit of activity } j \end{pmatrix} - \begin{pmatrix} \text{Profit per unit} \\ \text{of activity } j \end{pmatrix}$$

```
                         *** OPTIMUM SOLUTION SUMMARY ***
```
---

Title: Reddy Mikks Model
Final iteration No: 3
Objective value (max) =    21.0000

---

| Variable | Value | Obj Coeff | Obj Val Contrib |
|---|---|---|---|
| x1 EXT | 3.0000 | 5.0000 | 15.0000 |
| x2 INT | 1.5000 | 4.0000 | 6.0000 |

---

| Constraint | RHS | Slack(−)/Surplus(+) |
|---|---|---|
| 1 (<) | 24.0000 | 0.0000− |
| 2 (<) | 6.0000 | 0.0000− |
| 3 (<) | 1.0000 | 2.5000− |
| 4 (<) | 2.0000 | 0.5000− |

```
                         *** SENSITIVITY ANALYSIS ***
```
Objective coefficients -- Single Changes:

---

| Variable | Current Coeff | Min Coeff | Max Coeff | Reduced Cost |
|---|---|---|---|---|
| x1 EXT | 5.0000 | 2.0000 | 6.0000 | 0.0000 |
| x2 INT | 4.0000 | 3.3333 | 10.0000 | 0.0000 |

Right-hand Side -- Single Changes:

---

| Constraint | Current RHS | Min RHS | Max RHS | Dual Price |
|---|---|---|---|---|
| 1 (<) | 24.0000 | 20.0000 | 36.0000 | 0.7500 |
| 2 (<) | 6.0000 | 4.0000 | 6.6667 | 0.5000 |
| 3 (<) | 1.0000 | −1.5000 | infinity | 0.0000 |
| 4 (<) | 2.0000 | 1.5000 | infinity | 0.0000 |

Objective Coefficients -- Simultaneous Changes d:

---

| Nonbasic Var | Optimality Condition |
|---|---|
| sx3 | 0.7500 +   0.2500 d1 +  −0.1250 d2 >= 0 |
| sx4 | 0.5000 +  −0.5000 d1 +   0.7500 d2 >= 0 |

Right-hand Side Ranging -- Simultaneous Changes D:

---

| Basic Var | Value/Feasibility Condition |
|---|---|
| x1 EXT | 3.0000 +   0.2500 D1 +  −0.5000 D2 >= 0 |
| x2 INT | 1.5000 +  −0.1250 D1 +   0.7500 D2 >= 0 |
| sx5 | 2.5000 +   0.3750 D1 +  −1.2500 D2 +   1.0000 D3 >= 0 |
| sx6 | 0.5000 +   0.1250 D1 +  −0.7500 D2 +   1.0000 D4 >= 0 |

**Figure 2–7**

If the activity's reduced cost per unit is positive, then the cost of its consumed resources per unit is higher than its profit per unit, and the activity should not be undertaken. This means that the value of its associated variable in the optimum solution should be zero. Alternatively, an activity that is economically attractive will have a zero reduced cost in the optimum solution, signifying an equilibrium point has been reached at which the output (unit profit) equals the input (unit cost of the resources). In Figure 2–7, both $x_1$ and $x_2$ have zero reduced cost because both are positive in the optimum solution.

Next, we consider the definition of **dual prices.** The dual price actually represents the unit worth of a resource, exactly as explained in Section 2.4.2—that is, it gives the contribution to the objective function resulting from a unit increase or decrease in the availability of a resource. The name dual price arose from the mathematical definition of the dual problem in linear programming (see Chapter 4). Other less common names for the dual price include **shadow prices** and **simplex multipliers.** Although the name *unit worth of a resource* used in Section 2.4.2 provides a more apt description of what the output result means, we will use the name *dual price* because it is standard in the output of all commercial LP codes.

In Figure 2–7, the dual prices for raw materials, $M1$ and $M2$ are .75 and .5, or \$750 and \$500 per ton, respectively. These are the same results obtained graphically in Example 2.4–2 and are valid for the respective ranges $20 \leq M1 \leq 36$ and $4 \leq M2 \leq 6\frac{2}{3}$ only. For example, if the availability of $M1$ is increased from its current level of 24 tons to 28 tons, then the optimum value of the objective function will increase by \$750 $\times$ $(28 - 24) = \$3000$.

The dual prices for the third and fourth constraints of the Reddy Mikks model are zero for the ranges $-1.5$ to $\infty$ and 1.5 to $\infty$, respectively. This result shows that increases in the resources representing the market limits for the production of interior and exterior paints have no effect on the optimum solution.

The remaining portion of the SENSITIVITY ANALYSIS output represents the effect on the optimum that results from making *simultaneous* changes in all the objective function coefficients or in the right-hand side of all the constraints. The changes in the objective coefficients assume that the objective function of the Reddy Mikks model is given as $z = (5 + d_1)x_1 + (4 + d_2)x_2$. The resulting conditions (associated with slacks $sx_3$ and $sx_4$) given by

$$.75 + .25d_1 - .125d_2 \geq 0$$

$$.50 - .50d_1 + .750d_2 \geq 0$$

are actually the same as the condition

$$\frac{1}{2} \leq \frac{c_1}{c_2} \leq \frac{6}{4}$$

which we derived in Section 2.4.1 from the graphical solution. Specifically, if we set $c_1 = 5 + d_1$ and $c_2 = 4 + d_2$, we will obtain the same conditions (verify!). Notice in this case that if the given conditions are satisfied for given values of $d_1$ and $d_2$, then only the optimum value of the objective function will change, but the values of the variables will remain unchanged. If the changes are such that the given conditions are not satisfied, a new optimum must be recomputed using the procedure given in Section 4.7.

Next, we consider making simultaneous changes in the right-hand sides of the constraints. For the Reddy Mikks model, the respective right-hand sides of the constraints are assumed to be $24 + D_1, 6 + D_2, 1 + D_3$, and $2 + D_4$. The given four conditions actually provide the new solution values in terms of $D_1, D_2, D_3$, and $D_4$. These solution values must be nonnegative to satisfy feasibility. For example, suppose that $D_1 = 5$, $D_2 = -1, D_3 = 1$, and $D4 = 2$, then

$$x_1 = 3 + .25 \times 5 - .5 \times -1 = 4.75$$

$$x_2 = 1.5 - .125 \times 5 + .75 \times -1 = .125$$

$$sx_5 = 2.5 + .375 \times 5 - 1.25 \times -1 + 1 \times 1 = 6.625$$

$$sx_6 = .5 + .125 \times 5 - .75 \times -1 + 1 \times 2 = 3.875$$

All the values are nonnegative; hence the specified changes will yield the new feasible solution $x_1 = 4.75$ tons, $x_2 = .125$ ton, and $z = 5 \times 4.75 + 4 \times .125 = 24.25$, or \$24,250. The resulting value of z exceeds the current value by $\Delta z = \$24,250 - \$21,000 = \$3,250$. This amount can also be computed as

$$\Delta z = D_1 y_1 + D_2 y_2 + D_3 y_3 + D_4 y_4$$

where $y_1, y_2, y_3$, and $y_4$ are the dual prices of the respective resources. Thus, we get

$$\Delta z = 5 \times \$750 + (-1) \times \$500 + 1 \times 0 + 2 \times 0 = \$3,250$$

This type of computation is valid if only the changes $D_i, i = 1, 2, 3, 4$, leads to a feasible solution. If the changes result in a negative value of any of the variables, then a new solution must be recomputed as discussed in Section 4.7.

---

### Problem set 2.5a

**1.** Figure 2–8 provides the TORA output for the diet model of Example 2.3–2.
    **(a)** Interpret the dual price of the first constraint.
    **(b)** If the minimum daily feed requirement is increased to 900, determine the new solution using the output information in Figure 2–8.
    **(c)** If the costs per pound of corn and soybean meal are changed to \$.40 and \$1.05, respectively, would the current solution remain optimum?
    **(d)** From the graphical solution, derive the optimality conditions given in Figure 2–8 for simultaneous changes in the objective function coefficients.

**2.** The LP model of Problem 2.4a–7 is given as

$$\text{Maximize} = 18x_1 + 9x_2$$

subject to

$$24x_1 + 8x_2 \leq 60,000$$

$$x_1 \leq 2000, x_2 \leq 6000$$

$$x_1, x_2 \geq 0$$

where $x_1$ and $x_2$ are the number of cases of juice and paste the company should produce. The solution of the model is given in Figure 2–9.

```
                        *** OPTIMUM SOLUTION SUMMARY ***
─────────────────────────────────────────────────────────────────────────
Title: Diet problem
Final iteration No: 3
Objective value (min) =  437.6471
─────────────────────────────────────────────────────────────────────────
Variable            Value        Obj Coeff     Obj Val Contrib

x1 Corn            470.5882       0.3000          141.1765
x2 Soy             329.4118       0.9000          296.4706
─────────────────────────────────────────────────────────────────────────
Constraint           RHS          Slack(−)/Surplus(+)

1 (>)              800.0000            0.0000+
2 (<)                0.0000            0.0000−
3 (>)                0.0000            0.0000+
```

```
                     *** SENSITIVITY ANALYSIS ***
Objective coefficients -- Single Changes:
─────────────────────────────────────────────────────────────────────────
Variable    Current Coeff    Min Coeff     Max Coeff    Reduced Cost

x1 Corn         0.3000         −0.6300        0.9000        0.0000
x2 Soy          0.9000          0.3000      infinity        0.0000
```

Right-hand Side -- Single Changes:

```
─────────────────────────────────────────────────────────────────────────
Constraint    Current RHS       Min RHS      Max RHS     Dual Price

1 (>)          800.0000          0.0000      infinity       0.5471
2 (<)            0.0000       −138.0000     168.0000        1.1765
3 (>)            0.0000       −infinity      10.8235        0.0000
```

Objective Coefficients -- Simultaneous Changes d:

```
─────────────────────────────────────────────────────────────────────────
Nonbasic Var   Optimality Condition

Sx3        −0.5471 +    −0.5882 d1 +    −0.4118 d2 <= 0
sx4        −1.1765 +     1.9608 d1 +    −1.9608 d2 <= 0
```

Right-hand Side Ranging -- Simultaneous Changes D:

```
─────────────────────────────────────────────────────────────────────────
Basic Var    Value/Feasibility Condition

x1 Corn    470.5882 +    0.5882 D1 +     1.9608 D2 >= 0
x2 Soy     329.4118 +    0.4118 D1 +    −1.9608 D2 >= 0
sx5         10.8235 +    0.0135 D1 +     0.0784 D2 +  −1.0000 D3 >= 0
```

**Figure 2–8**

*** OPTIMUM SOLUTION SUMMARY ***

Title: Problem 2.5a-2
Final iteration No: 4
Objective value (max) =63000.0000

| Variable | Value | Obj Coeff | Obj Val Contrib |
|---|---|---|---|
| x1 Juice | 500.0000 | 18.0000 | 9000.0000 |
| x2 Paste | 6000.0000 | 9.0000 | 54000.0000 |

| Constraint | RHS | Slack(−)/Surplus(+) |
|---|---|---|
| 1 (<) | 60000.0000 | 0.0000− |
| 2 (<) | 2000.0000 | 1500.0000− |
| 3 (<) | 6000.0000 | 0.0000− |

*** SENSITIVITY ANALYSIS ***

Objective coefficients -- Single Changes:

| Variable | Current Coeff | Min Coeff | Max Coeff | Reduced Cost |
|---|---|---|---|---|
| x1 Juice | 18.0000 | 0.0000 | 27.0000 | 0.0000 |
| x2 Paste | 9.0000 | 6.0000 | infinity | 0.0000 |

Right-hand Side -- Single Changes:

| Constraint | Current RHS | Min RHS | Max RHS | Dual Price |
|---|---|---|---|---|
| 1 (<) | 60000.0000 | 48000.0000 | 96000.0000 | 0.7500 |
| 2 (<) | 2000.0000 | 500.0000 | infinity | 0.0000 |
| 3 (<) | 6000.0000 | 1500.0000 | 7500.0000 | 3.0000 |

Objective Coefficients -- Simultaneous Changes d:

| Nonbasic Var | Optimality Condition |
|---|---|
| sx3 | $0.7500 + 0.0417 d_1 >= 0$ |
| sx5 | $3.0000 + 1.0000 d_2 + -0.3333 d_1 >= 0$ |

Right-hand Side Ranging -- Simultaneous Changes D:

| Basic Var | Value/Feasibility Condition |
|---|---|
| x2 Paste | $6000.0000 + 1.0000 D_3 >= 0$ |
| x1 Juice | $500.0000 + 0.0417 D_1 + -0.3333 D_3 >= 0$ |
| sx4 | $1500.0000 + -0.0417 D_1 + 1.0000 D_2 + 0.3333 D_3 >= 0$ |

**Figure 2–9**

(a) Determine the worth per unit of an additional pound of tomato.
(b) Is it worthwhile for the company to raise its market share for juice? For paste?
(c) If the company reduces the contracted amount of tomato to 50,000 lb, determine the new optimum solution.
(d) If the profit per case of juice is reduced to $15 and the profit per case of paste is increased to $10, will the current optimum solution change?
(e) If the amount of purchased tomato is increased to 80,000 lb and the market share of paste in increased to 7000, determine the new optimum solution.
(f) If the amount of purchased tomato is decreased to 30,000 lb and the market share of paste is increased to 8000 cases, would it be possible to determine the new solution from the data in Figure 2–9?

## 2.6 ANALYSIS OF SELECTED LP MODELS

This section presents realistic LP models in which the definition of the variables and the construction of the objective function and the constraints are not as straightforward as in the case of the two-variable model. Additionally, the TORA computer output of each model, similar to that presented in Section 2.5, will allow insightful interpretations of the solutions.

**Example 2.6–1 (BANK LOAN POLICY).**
The Thriftem Bank, a full-service facility, is in the process of formulating a loan policy involving a maximum of $12 million. The following table provides the pertinent data about the different types of loans the bank deals with:

| Type of loan | Interest rate | Probability of bad debt |
|---|---|---|
| Personal | .140 | .10 |
| Car | .130 | .07 |
| Home | .120 | .03 |
| Farm | .125 | .05 |
| Commercial | .100 | .02 |

Bad debts are unrecoverable and hence produce no interest revenue.
   Competition with other financial institutions in the area requires the bank to allocate at least 40% of the funds to farm and commerical loans. To assist the housing industry in the region, home loans must equal at least 50% of the personal, car, and home loans. The bank also has a stated policy specifiying that the overall ratio for bad debts on all loans may not exceed .04.
*Mathematical Model*
The variables of the model can be defined as follows:

$x_1$ = personal loans (in millions of dollars)
$x_2$ = car loans
$x_3$ = home loans
$x_4$ = farm loans
$x_5$ = commercial loans

The objective of the Thriftem Bank is to maximize its net return comprised of the difference between the revenue from interest and lost funds from bad debts. Because bad debts are not recoverable, both as principal and interest, the objective function is given as

$$\text{Maximize } z = .14(.9x_1) + .13(.93x_2) + .12(.97x_3) + .125(.95x_4)$$
$$+ .1(.98x_5) - .1x_1 - .07x_2 - .03x_3 - .05x_4 - .02x_5$$

This function simplifies to

$$\text{Maximize } z = .026x_1 + .0509x_2 + .0864x_3 + .06875x_4 + .078x_5$$

The problem has five constraints:

**1.** *Total funds*

$$x_1 + x_2 + x_3 + x_4 + x_5 \leq 12$$

**2.** *Farm and commercial loans*

$$x_4 + x_5 \geq .4 \times 12$$

or

$$x_4 + x_5 \geq 4.8$$

**3.** *Home loans*

$$x_3 \geq .5(x_1 + x_2 + x_3)$$

**4.** *Limit on bad debts*

$$\frac{.1x_1 + .07x_2 + .03x_3 + .05x_4 + .02x_5}{x_1 + x_2 + x_3 + x_4 + x_5} \leq .04$$

or

$$.06x_1 + .03x_2 - .01x_3 + .01x_4 - .02x_5 \leq 0$$

**5.** *Nonnegativity*

$$x_1 \geq 0, x_2 \geq 0, x_3 \geq 0, x_4 \geq 0, x_5 \geq 0$$

A subtle assumption in the preceding formulation is that all loans are issued at approximately the same time. This assumption allows us to ignore differences in the time values of the funds allocated to the different loans.

The output of the Bank Policy model is shown in Figure 2–10. It recommends home and commercial loans only. Of the remaining types, personal loans are the least attractive, not only because they have the smallest objective coefficient (= .026) but

*** OPTIMUM SOLUTION SUMMARY ***

Title: Bank Model
Final iteration No: 5
Objective value (max) =    0.9965

| Variable | Value | Obj Coeff | Obj Val Contrib |
|----------|-------|-----------|-----------------|
| x1 pers'nl | 0.0000 | 0.0260 | 0.0000 |
| x2 car     | 0.0000 | 0.0509 | 0.0000 |
| x3 home    | 7.2000 | 0.0864 | 0.6221 |
| x4 farm    | 0.0000 | 0.0688 | 0.0000 |
| x5 com'l   | 4.8000 | 0.0780 | 0.3744 |

| Constraint | RHS | Slack(−)/Surplus(+) |
|------------|-----|---------------------|
| 1 (<) | 12.0000 | 0.0000− |
| 2 (>) | 4.8000  | 0.0000+ |
| 3 (<) | 0.0000  | 3.6000− |
| 4 (<) | 0.0000  | 0.1680− |

*** SENSITIVITY ANALYSIS ***

Objective coefficients -- Single Changes:

| Variable | Current Coeff | Min Coeff | Max Coeff | Reduced Cost |
|----------|---------------|-----------|-----------|--------------|
| x1 pers'nl | 0.0260 | −infinity | 0.0864   | 0.0604 |
| x2 car     | 0.0509 | −infinity | 0.0864   | 0.0355 |
| x3 home    | 0.0864 | 0.0780    | infinity | 0.0000 |
| x4 farm    | 0.0688 | −infinity | 0.0780   | 0.0092 |
| x5 com'l   | 0.0780 | 0.0688    | 0.0864   | 0.0000 |

Right-hand Side -- Single Changes:

| Constraint | Current RHS | Min RHS | Max RHS | Dual Price |
|------------|-------------|---------|---------|------------|
| 1 (<) | 12.0000 | 4.8000  | infinity | 0.0864  |
| 2 (>) | 4.8000  | 0.0000  | 12.0000  | −0.0084 |
| 3 (<) | 0.0000  | −3.6000 | infinity | 0.0000  |
| 4 (<) | 0.0000  | −0.1680 | infinity | 0.0000  |

Objective Coefficients -- Simultaneous Changes d:

| Nonbasic Var | Optimality Condition |
|--------------|----------------------|
| x1 pers'nl | 0.0604 + | 1.0000 d3 − d1 >= 0 |
| x2 car     | 0.0355 + | 1.0000 d3 − d2 >= 0 |
| x4 farm    | 0.0092 + | 1.0000 d5 − d4 >= 0 |
| Sx6        | 0.0084 + | 1.0000 d3 +    −1.0000 d5 >= 0 |
| sx7        | 0.0864 + | 1.0000 d3 >= 0 |

Right-hand Side Ranging -- Simultaneous Changes D:

| Basic Var | Value/Feasibility Condition |
|-----------|-----------------------------|
| x3 home | 7.2000 + | 1.0000 D1 +    −1.0000 D2 >= 0 |
| x5 com'l | 4.8000 + | 1.0000 D2 >= 0 |
| sx9     | 3.6000 + | 0.5000 D1 +    −0.5000 D2 +    1.0000 D3 >= 0 |
| sx10    | 0.1680 + | 0.0100 D1 +     0.0100 D2 +    1.0000 D4 >= 0 |

**Figure 2–10**

also because their reduced cost is the highest among all the variables (= .0604). The re-duced cost means that the "profitability" of the personal loan variable must be in-creased by .0604 for the variable to be just profitable. Looking at the dual prices, the first constraint shows that an increase of 1 (million) dollars in allocated funds will in-crease the net return from all loans by .0864 (million) dollars. This is equivalent to an annual return of 8.64% on investment. Because the associated range is (4.8, ∞), this re-turn is guaranteed for any increase in allocated funds above the present $12 (million). A return of 8.64% appears to be low, especially since the lowest interest rate that the bank charges is 10%. The difference is attributed to bad debts, which are not recover-able both as principal and interest. Indeed, the highest objective coefficient in the model is .0864 (home loans). Interestingly, this coefficient happens to equal the dual price of constraint 1 (allocated funds). The conclusion from this observation is that any new additional funds will be allocated by the optimum solution to home loans.

Constraint 2 sets the minimum limit on the sum of farm and commercial loans. The negative dual price (= −.0084) shows that an increase in that limit will have an ad-verse effect on the net return. In other words, there is no economic advantage in setting a minimum limit on the amount of farm and commercial loans. This observation is con-sistent with the interpretation of the first constraint which stipulates that any new addi-tional funds will be allocated to home loans rather than to farm and commercial loans. As a matter of fact, if we were to remove the minimum limit requirement on farm and commercial loans, all the funds would be allocated to home loans (verify this conclusion by "yanking" constraint 2 using TORA's MODIFY option).

---

### Example 2.6–2   (LAND USE AND DEVELOPMENT).

The Birdeyes Real Estate Co. owns 800 acres of undeveloped land on a scenic lake in the heart of the Ozark Mountains. In the past, little or no regulation was applied to new developments around the lake. The lake shores are now dotted with vacation homes. Because of the lack of sewage service, septic tanks, mostly improperly installed, are in extensive use. Over the years, seepage from the septic tanks has resulted in a severe water pollution problem.

To curb further degradation in the quality of water, county officials approved stringent ordinances applicable to all future developments.

1. Only single-, double-, and triple-family homes can be constructed, with the sin-gle-family homes accounting for at least 50% of the total.

2. To limit the number of septic tanks, minimum lot sizes of 2, 3, and 4 acres are required for single-, double-, and triple-family homes, respectively.

3. Recreation areas of 1 acre each must be established at the rate of one area per 200 families.

4. To preserve the ecology of the lake, underground water may not be pumped for house or garden use.

The president of Birdeyes Real Estate is studying the possibility of developing the company's 800 acres. The new development will include single-, double-, and triple-family homes. It is estimated that 15% of the acreage will be consumed in the opening of streets and easements for utilities. Birdeyes estimates the returns from the different housing units as

| Housing unit | Single | Double | Triple |
|---|---|---|---|
| Net return per unit ($) | 10,000 | 12,000 | 15,000 |

The cost of connecting water service to the area is proportionate to the number of units constructed. However, the county stipulates that a minimum of $100,000 must be collected for the project to be economically feasible. Additionally, the expansion of the water system beyond its present capacity is limited to 200,000 gallons per day during peak periods. The following data summarize the cost of connecting water service as well as the water consumption assuming an average size family:

| Housing unit | Single | Double | Triple | Recreation |
|---|---|---|---|---|
| Water service cost per unit ($) | 1000 | 1200 | 1400 | 800 |
| Water consumption per unit (gal/day) | 400 | 600 | 840 | 450 |

*Mathematical Model*
The company must decide on the number of units to be constructed of each housing type together with the number of recreation areas satisfying county ordinances. Define

$x_1$ = number of units of single-family homes
$x_2$ = number of units of double-family homes
$x_3$ = number of units of triple-family homes
$x_4$ = number of recreation areas

The objective of the company is to maximize total return; that is

$$\text{Maximize } z = 10{,}000x_1 + 12{,}000x_2 + 15{,}000x_3$$

The constraints of the problem include

1. Limit on land use
2. Limit on the requirements for single-family homes relative to other styles
3. Limit on the requirements for recreation areas
4. Capital requirement for connecting water service
5. Limit on peak-period daily water consumption

These constraints are expressed mathematically as follows:

1. *Land use*

$$2x_1 + 3x_2 + 4x_3 + 1x_4 \leq 680 \,(= .85 \times 800)$$

2. *Single-family homes*

$$\frac{x_1}{x_1 + x_2 + x_3} \geq .5$$

or

$$.5x_1 - .5x_2 - .5x_3 \geq 0$$

3. *Recreation areas*

$$x_4 \geq \frac{x_1 + 2x_2 + 3x_3}{200}$$

or

$$200x_4 - x_1 - 2x_2 - 3x_3 \geq 0$$

4. *Capital*

$$1000x_1 + 1200x_2 + 1400x_3 + 800x_4 \geq 100,000$$

5. *Water consumption*

$$400x_1 + 600x_2 + 840x_3 + 450x_4 \leq 200,000$$

6. *Nonnegativity*

$$x_1 \geq 0, x_2 \geq 0, x_3 \geq 0, x_4 \geq 0$$

It is a good practice in model formulation to pay attention to the impact of computational roundoff error. In the preceding model, the coefficients in constraints 4 and 5 (capital and water consumption) are relatively larger than most of the coefficients in the remaining constraints. This inconsistency could lead to undesirable machine roundoff error resulting from the mixed manipulation of relatively large and relatively small coefficients. In our present example, we can rectify this potential problem by scaling down all the coefficients of in constraints 4 and 5 by the constant 1000. This reduces the constraints to

$$x_1 + 1.2x_2 + 1.4x_3 + 8x_4 \geq 100$$

$$.4x_1 + .6x_2 + .84x_3 + .45x_4 \leq 200$$

It is equally damaging computationally to deal with very small constraint coefficients. In such situations it may be advisable to scale up all the small coefficients to produce some consistency in the formulation of the model. Most software (TORA included) will attempt to achieve this consistency before solving the problem. However, it is a good modeling practice to implement this step during the formulation of the model.

Figure 2–11 provides the optimal solution of the model. We notice that linear programming does not provide integer solutions in general. The present solution yields SINGLE = 339.152 and RECR'N = 1.696 with DOUBLE = TRIPLE = 0. We can round this solution to SINGLE = 339 and RECR'N = 2 (which, incidentally, happens to be the optimum integer solution).

The optimum solution does not recommend the construction of double and triple homes, despite the fact that their returns per unit ($12,000 and $15,000) are higher in absolute sense than that for a single home. This result shows that the marginal returns as expressed in the objective function are not sufficient to judge the profitability of an activity. We must consider additionally the cost of the resources used by the activity. Indeed, this is what the *reduced cost* accomplishes. The present reduced costs of $3012.45 and $5024.94 for DOUBLE and TRIPLE provide the excess of the per unit cost of

\*\*\* OPTIMUM SOLUTION SUMMARY \*\*\*

Title: Land Development
Final iteration No: 6
Objective value (max) =3391521.2500

| Variable | Value | Obj Coeff | Obj Val Contrib |
|---|---|---|---|
| x1 SINGLE | 339.1521 | 10000.0000 | 3391521.2500 |
| x2 DOUBLE | 0.0000 | 12000.0000 | 0.0000 |
| x3 TRIPLE | 0.0000 | 15000.0000 | 0.0000 |
| x4 RECR'N | 1.6958 | 0.0000 | 0.0000 |

| Constraint | RHS | Slack(−)/Surplus(+) |
|---|---|---|
| 1 (<) | 680.0000 | 0.0000− |
| 2 (>) | 0.0000 | 169.5760+ |
| 3 (>) | 0.0000 | 0.0000+ |
| 4 (>) | 100.0000 | 240.5087+ |
| 5 (<) | 200.0000 | 63.5761− |

\*\*\* SENSITIVITY ANALYSIS \*\*\*

Objective coefficients -- Single Changes:

| Variable | Current Coeff | Min Coeff | Max Coeff | Reduced Cost |
|---|---|---|---|---|
| x1 SINGLE | 10000.0000 | 7993.3557 | infinity | 0.0000 |
| x2 DOUBLE | 12000.0000 | −infinity | 15012.4688 | 3012.4688 |
| x3 TRIPLE | 15000.0000 | −infinity | 20024.9351 | 5024.9351 |
| x4 RECR'N | 0.0000 | −2000000.1250 | 5000.0000 | 0.0000 |

Right-hand Side -- Single Changes:

| Constraint | Current RHS | Min RHS | Max RHS | Dual Price |
|---|---|---|---|---|
| 1 (<) | 680.0000 | 199.7012 | 996.8926 | 4987.5308 |
| 2 (>) | 0.0000 | −infinity | 169.5760 | 0.0000 |
| 3 (>) | 0.0000 | −340.0000 | 50988.0195 | −24.9377 |
| 4 (>) | 100.0000 | −infinity | 340.5087 | 0.0000 |
| 5 (<) | 200.0000 | 136.4239 | infinity | 0.0000 |

Objective Coefficients -- Simultaneous Changes d:

Nonbasic Var   Optimality Condition

| | | | |
|---|---|---|---|
| x2 DOUBLE | 3012.4688 + | 1.5012 d1 + | −0.0025 d4 − d2 >= 0 |
| x3 TRIPLE | 5024.9351 + | 2.0025 d1 + | −0.0050 d4 − d3 >= 0 |
| Sx6 | 24.9377 + | 0.0025 d1 + | −0.0050 d4 >= 0 |
| sx8 | 4987.5308 + | 0.4988 d1 + | 0.0025 d4 >= 0 |

Right-hand Side Ranging -- Simultaneous Changes D:

Basic Var    Value/Feasibility Condition

| | | | | |
|---|---|---|---|---|
| sx7 | 240.5087 + | 0.5007 D1 + | 0.0015 D3 + | −1.0000 D4 >= 0 |
| x1 SINGLE | 339.1521 + | 0.4988 D1 + | −0.0025 D3 >= 0 | |
| x4 RECR'N | 1.6958 + | 0.0025 D1 + | 0.0050 D3 >= 0 | |
| sx5 | 169.5760 + | 0.2494 D1 + | −1.0000 D2 + | −0.0012 D3 >= 0 |
| sx12 | 63.5761 + | −0.2006 D1 + | −0.0012 D3 + | 1.0000 D5 >= 0 |

**Figure 2–11**

resources over the marginal return. Thus, for either activity to be *just* profitable, we must either reduce the per unit cost of the resources or increase the marginal return by an amount equal to its reduced cost.

Constraints 2, 4, and 5 have positive slack/surplus values, which indicates that their resources are "abundant." As a result, their *dual prices* (worth per unit) are zero. Constraint 1 representing available land has a dual value of $4987.53, indicating that a 1-acre increase in available land is worth $4987.53 in net revenue. This information could be valuable in deciding on the purchase price of new land.

Constraint 4 has a dual price of $-$24.937, and because it is negative, any increase in its "resource" will affect the total revenue adversely. But why is it so? We can answer this question only if we know what the units of the "resource" of that constraint are. Let us look at the constraint once again:

$$200 \text{ RECR'N} - \text{SINGLE} - 2 \text{ DOUBLE} - 3 \text{ TRIPLE} \geq 0$$

The constraint specifies the minimum number of recreation areas (RECR'N) in relationship to the number of homes. As the constraint now stands, the units of its left-hand side are convoluted. However, if we divide the entire constraint by 200, we get

$$\text{RECR'N} - (.005 \text{ SINGLE} + .01 \text{ DOUBLE} + .015 \text{ TRIPLE}) \geq 0$$

The variable RECR'N represents the number of recreation areas. Since each recreation area occupies 1 acre, the units of RECR'N and those of the expression in parentheses must also be in acres. Thus an increase of 1 unit in the right-hand side (i.e., an increase from 0 to 1) can be interpreted as a 1-acre increase in RECR'N. With the new presentation of the constraint, we can say that the dual price represents the worth per acre increase in the recreation area. However, with the new constraint, the dual price must be $200 \times -24.937 = -\$4987.53$. (Actually, if you modify the constraint as shown and rerun the model, the TORA output will yield the new dual value directly— try it!)

The new dual price now tells us that an acre increase in recreation area will reduce the revenue by $4987.53. Interestingly, it exactly equals the dual price of the land use resource (constraint 2) but with opposite sign. The result makes economic sense, because an acre allocated to the recreation area is an acre taken away from constructing homes. It is thus no coincidence that the dual prices match.

---

### Example 2.6–3   (BUS SCHEDULING PROBLEM).

Progress City is studying the feasibility of introducing a mass transit bus system that will alleviate the smog problem by reducing in-city driving. The initial study seeks the determination of the minimum number of buses that can handle the transportation needs. After gathering necessary information, the city engineer noticed that the minimum number of buses needed fluctuates with the time of the day. Studying the data further, it became evident that the required number of buses can be approximated by constant values over successive intevals of 4 hours each. Figure 2–12 summarizes the engineer's findings. To carry out the required daily maintenance, each bus could operate only 8 successive hours a day.

*Mathematical representation*

It is required to determine the *number of buses to operate during different shifts* (variables) that will *meet the minimum demand* (constraints) while *minimizing the total number of daily buses in operation* (objective)

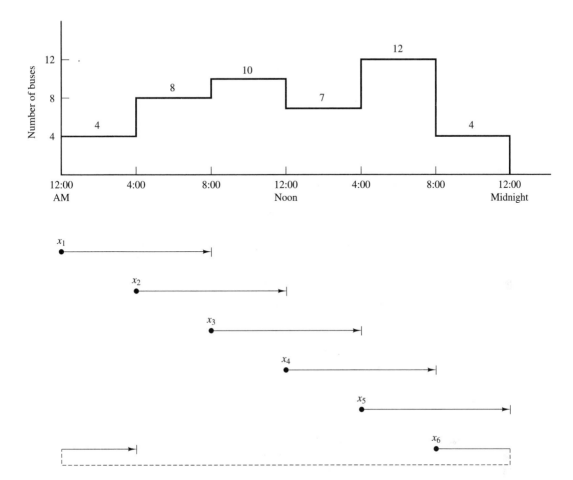

**Figure 2–12**

You may already have noticed that the definition of the variables is ambiguous. We know that each bus will run 8-hour shifts, but we do not know when a shift should start. If we follow a normal three-shift schedule (8:01 A.M.–4:00 P.M., 4:01 P.M.–12:00 midnight, and 12:01 A.M.–8:00 A.M.) and assume that $x_1$, $x_2$, and $x_3$ are the number of buses starting in the first, second, and third shifts, we can see from Figure 2–12 that $x_1 \geq 10$, $x_2 \geq 12$, and $x_3 \geq 8$, with the corresponding minimum number equal to $x_1 + x_2 + x_3 = 10 + 12 + 8 = 30$ buses daily.

This solution is acceptable only if the shifts *must* coincide with the normal three-shift schedule. It may be advantageous, however, to allow the optimization process to choose the "best" starting time for a shift. A reasonable way to accomplish this is to allow a shift to start every 4 hours. The bottom of Figure 2–12 illustrates this concept where (overlapping) shifts may start at 12:01 A.M., 4:01 A.M., 8:01 A.M., 12:01 P.M., 4:01 P.M., and 8:01 P.M., with each shift continuing for 8 consecutive hours. We are now ready to define the variables:

$x_1$ = number of buses starting at 12:01 A.M.

$x_2$ = number of buses starting at 4:01 A.M.

$x_3$ = number of buses starting at 8:01 A.M.

$x_4$ = number of buses starting at 12:01 P.M.

$x_5$ = number of buses starting at 4:01 P.M.

$x_6$ = number of buses starting at 8:01 P.M.

The mathematical model is written as

$$\text{Minimize } z = x_1 + x_2 + x_3 + x_4 + x_5 + x_6$$

subject to

$$
\begin{array}{llll}
x_1 & + x_6 \geq 4 & (\text{12:01 A.M.–4:00 A.M.}) \\
x_1 + x_2 & \geq 8 & (\text{4:01 A.M.–8:00 A.M.}) \\
x_2 + x_3 & \geq 10 & (\text{8:01 A.M.–12:00 noon}) \\
x_3 + x_4 & \geq 7 & (\text{12:01 P.M.–4:00 P.M.}) \\
x_4 + x_5 & \geq 12 & (\text{4:01 P.M.–8:00 P.M.}) \\
x_5 + x_6 & \geq 4 & (\text{8:01 P.M.–12:00 P.M.}) \\
x_j \geq 0 & j = 1\,2\ldots 6 &
\end{array}
$$

The output in Figure 2–13 shows that a total of 26 buses is needed to satisfy the demand. The optimum schedule calls for $x_1 = 4$ buses to start at 12:01 A.M., $x_2 = 10$ at 4:01 A.M., $x_4 = 8$ at 12:01 P.M., and $x_5 = 4$ at 4:01 P.M. The reduced costs are all zero, which indicates that the problem has alternative optimum solutions. The dual prices yield interesting information. A dual price of 1 indicates that a unit increase in the minimum number of buses required for the corresponding period is coupled with an equal increase in the total number of buses in operation. If the dual price is zero, an increase in the minimum requirements will not increase the total number of buses in operation. These changes, however, are limited by the ranges specified in Figure 2–13. For example, the minimum requirement for period 2 (constraint 2) can be increased from 8 to 14 without requiring a net increase in the total number of buses in operation. Similarly, each unit increase in the minimum requirement of period 3 beyond 10 will increase the total number of operations by an equal amount. This type of information is significant in analyzing the optimum solution.

A sensitivity analysis of the objective coefficients may not be meaningful in the present example because the nature of the model requires these coefficients to equal 1 always. If the objective function is restructured to reflect other measures (e.g., minimization of the operating cost of the buses), the situation will be different and a sensitivity analysis of these coefficients would be meaningful.

---

**Example 2.6–4 (TRIM-LOSS OR STOCK-SLITTING PROBLEM).**
The Pacific Paper Company produces paper rolls with a standard width of 20 feet each. Special customer orders with different widths are produced by slitting the standard rolls. Typical orders (which may vary from day to day) are summarized in the following table:

*** OPTIMUM SOLUTION SUMMARY ***

Title: Bus Model
Final iteration No: 5
Objective value (min) = 26.0000, ALTERNATIVE solution detected at x3

| Variable | Value | Obj Coeff | Obj Val Contrib |
|---|---|---|---|
| x1 12:01AM | 4.0000 | 1.0000 | 4.0000 |
| x2 4:00AM | 10.0000 | 1.0000 | 10.0000 |
| x3 8:00AM | 0.0000 | 1.0000 | 0.0000 |
| x4 12:01PM | 8.0000 | 1.0000 | 8.0000 |
| x5 4:01PM | 4.0000 | 1.0000 | 4.0000 |
| x6 8:01PM | 0.0000 | 1.0000 | 0.0000 |

| Constraint | RHS | Slack(−)/Surplus(+) |
|---|---|---|
| 1 (>) | 4.0000 | 0.0000+ |
| 2 (>) | 8.0000 | 6.0000+ |
| 3 (>) | 10.0000 | 0.0000+ |
| 4 (>) | 7.0000 | 1.0000+ |
| 5 (>) | 12.0000 | 0.0000+ |
| 6 (>) | 4.0000 | 0.0000+ |

*** SENSITIVITY ANALYSIS ***
==> DEGENERATE or ALTERNATE optimum. Ranges may not be unique
Objective coefficients -- Single Changes:

| Variable | Current Coeff | Min Coeff | Max Coeff | Reduced Cost |
|---|---|---|---|---|
| x1 12:01AM | 1.0000 | 0.0000 | 1.0000 | 0.0000 |
| x2 4:00AM | 1.0000 | 0.0000 | 1.0000 | 0.0000 |
| x3 8:00AM | 1.0000 | 1.0000 | infinity | 0.0000 |
| x4 12:01PM | 1.0000 | 1.0000 | 1.0000 | 0.0000 |
| x5 4:01PM | 1.0000 | 1.0000 | 1.0000 | 0.0000 |
| x6 8:01PM | 1.0000 | 1.0000 | infinity | 0.0000 |

Right-hand Side -- Single Changes:

| Constraint | Current RHS | Min RHS | Max RHS | Dual Price |
|---|---|---|---|---|
| 1 (>) | 4.0000 | 0.0000 | infinity | 1.0000 |
| 2 (>) | 8.0000 | −infinity | 14.0000 | 0.0000 |
| 3 (>) | 10.0000 | 4.0000 | infinity | 1.0000 |
| 4 (>) | 7.0000 | −infinity | 8.0000 | 0.0000 |
| 5 (>) | 12.0000 | 11.0000 | infinity | 1.0000 |
| 6 (>) | 4.0000 | 0.0000 | 5.0000 | 0.0000 |

Right-hand Side Ranging -- Simultaneous Changes D:

| Basic Var | Value/Feasibility Condition |
|---|---|
| x1 12:01AM | 4.0000 +    1.0000 D1 >= 0 |
| sx8 | 6.0000 +    1.0000 D1 +   −1.0000 D2 +    1.0000 D3 >= 0 |
| x2 4:00AM | 10.0000 +    1.0000 D3 >= 0 |
| sx10 | 1.0000 +   −1.0000 D4 +    1.0000 D5 +   −1.0000 D6 >= 0 |
| x4 12:01PM | 8.0000 +    1.0000 D5 +   −1.0000 D6 >= 0 |
| x5 4:01PM | 4.0000 +    1.0000 D6 >= 0 |

**Figure 2–13**

| Order | Desired width (ft) | Desired number of rolls |
|-------|--------------------|--------------------------|
| 1 | 5 | 150 |
| 2 | 7 | 200 |
| 3 | 9 | 300 |

In practice, an order is filled by setting the slitting knives to the desired widths. Usually, there are a number of ways in which a standard roll can be slit to fill a given order. Figure 2–14 shows three possible knife settings for the 20-foot roll. Although there are other feasible settings, we limit the discussion for the moment to considering settings *A, B,* and *C* in Figure 2–14. We can combine the given settings in a number of ways to fill orders for widths 5, 7, and 9 feet. The following are examples of feasible combinations:

**1.** Slit 300 (standard) rolls using setting *A* and 75 rolls using *B*.
**2.** Slit 200 rolls using setting *A* and 100 rolls using setting *C*.

Which combination is better? We can answer this question by considering the "waste" that each combination will produce. In Figure 2–14 the shaded portion represents surplus rolls not wide enough to fill the required orders. These surplus rolls are referred to as *trim loss*. We can evaluate the "goodness" of each combination by computing its trim loss. However, since the surplus rolls may have different widths, we should base the evaluation on the *area* of trim loss rather than the number of suplus rolls. Assuming that the standard roll has a length *L* feet, we can compute the trim-loss area as follows (see Figure 2–14):

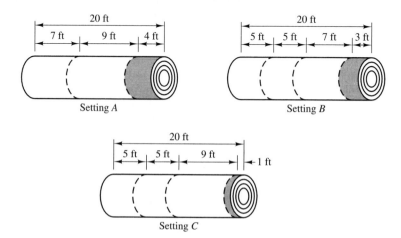

**Figure 2–14**

Combination 1:    $300(4 \times L) + 75(3 \times L) = 1425L$ ft$^2$

Combination 2:    $200(4 \times L) + 100(1 \times L) = 900L$ ft$^2$

These areas account only for the shaded portions in Figure 2–14. Any surplus production of the 5-, 7- and 9-foot rolls must be considered also in the computation of the trim-loss area. In combination 1, setting $A$ produces a surplus of $300 - 200 = 100$ extra 7-foot rolls and setting $B$ produces 75 extra 7-foot rolls. Thus the additional "waste" area is 175 $(7 \times L) = 1225L$ ft$^2$. Combination 2 does not produce surplus rolls of the 7- and 9-foot rolls but setting $C$ does produce $200 - 150 = 50$ extra 5-foot rolls, with an added waste area of 50 $(5 \times L) = 250L$ ft$^2$. As a result we have

$$\left( \begin{matrix} \text{Total trim loss area} \\ \text{for combination 1} \end{matrix} \right) = 1425L + 1225L = 2650L \text{ ft}^2$$

$$\left( \begin{matrix} \text{Total trim loss area} \\ \text{for combination 2} \end{matrix} \right) = 900L + 250L = 1150L \text{ ft}^2$$

Combination 2 is better because it yields a smaller trim-loss area.

To obtain the optimum solution to the problem, it is necessary to determine all possible knife settings and then generate *all* the feasible combinations. Although the determination of all the settings may not be too difficult, generating all feasible combinations may not be easy. The need for a systematic approach is thus evident. This is what the LP model will accomplish.

*Mathematical Representation*

We seek to determine the *knife setting combinations* (variables) that will *fill the required orders* (constraints) with the *least trim-loss area* (objective).

The definition of the variables as given must be translated in a way that the mill operator can use. Specifically, the variables are defined as *the number of standard rolls to be slit according to a given knife setting*. This definition requires identifying all possible knife settings as summarized in the following table. Settings 1, 2, and 3 are given in Figure 2–14. You should convince yourself of the validity of the remaining settings and that no "promising" settings have been forgotten. Remember that a promising setting cannot yield a trim-loss roll of width 5 feet or larger.

| Required width (ft) | Knife settings | | | | | | Minimum number of rolls |
|---|---|---|---|---|---|---|---|
| | 1 | 2 | 3 | 4 | 5 | 6 | |
| 5 | 0 | 2 | 2 | 4 | 1 | 0 | 150 |
| 7 | 1 | 1 | 0 | 0 | 2 | 0 | 200 |
| 9 | 1 | 0 | 1 | 0 | 0 | 2 | 300 |
| Trim loss per foot of length | 4 | 3 | 1 | 0 | 1 | 2 | |

To express the model mathematically, we define the variables as

$x_j$ = number of standard rolls to be slit according to setting $j, j = 1, 2, \ldots, 6$

*** OPTIMUM SOLUTION SUMMARY ***
------------------------------------------------------------------------
Title: Trim Loss Model
Final iteration No: 5
Objective value (min) = 262.5000
==> ALTERNATIVE solution detected at x4
------------------------------------------------------------------------

| Variable | Value | Obj Coeff | Obj Val Contrib |
|----------|-------|-----------|-----------------|
| x1 stng_1 | 0.0000 | 1.0000 | 0.0000 |
| x2 stng_2 | 0.0000 | 1.0000 | 0.0000 |
| x3 stng_3 | 25.0000 | 1.0000 | 25.0000 |
| x4 stng_4 | 0.0000 | 1.0000 | 0.0000 |
| x5 stng_5 | 100.0000 | 1.0000 | 100.0000 |
| x6 stng_6 | 137.5000 | 1.0000 | 137.5000 |

| Constraint | RHS | Slack(−)/Surplus(+) |
|------------|-----|---------------------|
| 1 (>) | 150.0000 | 0.0000+ |
| 2 (>) | 200.0000 | 0.0000+ |
| 3 (>) | 300.0000 | 0.0000+ |

*** SENSITIVITY ANALYSIS ***
Objective coefficients -- Single Changes:
==> DEGENERATE or ALTERNATE optimum. Ranges may not be unique
------------------------------------------------------------------------

| Variable | Current Coeff | Min Coeff | Max Coeff | Reduced Cost |
|----------|---------------|-----------|-----------|--------------|
| x1 stng_1 | 1.0000 | 0.8750 | infinity | −0.1250 |
| x2 stng_2 | 1.0000 | 0.8750 | infinity | −0.1250 |
| x3 stng_3 | 1.0000 | 0.5000 | 1.0000 | 0.0000 |
| x4 stng_4 | 1.0000 | 1.0000 | infinity | 0.0000 |
| x5 stng_5 | 1.0000 | 0.2500 | 1.2500 | 0.0000 |
| x6 stng_6 | 1.0000 | 1.0000 | 1.2000 | 0.0000 |

Right-hand Side -- Single Changes:
==> DEGENERATE or ALTERNATE optimum. Ranges may not be unique
------------------------------------------------------------------------

| Constraint | Current RHS | Min RHS | Max RHS | Dual Price |
|------------|-------------|---------|---------|------------|
| 1 (>) | 150.0000 | 100.0000 | 700.0000 | 0.2500 |
| 2 (>) | 200.0000 | 0.0000 | 300.0000 | 0.3750 |
| 3 (>) | 300.0000 | 25.0000 | infinity | 0.5000 |

**Figure 2–15**

The constraints of the model deal directly with satisfying the demand for rolls. If all the settings exhibited in the table are used, we get

$$\text{Number of 5-ft rolls produced} = 2x_2 + 2x_3 + 4x_4 + x_5$$

$$\text{Number of 7-ft rolls produced} = x_1 + x_2 + 2x_5$$

$$\text{Number of 9-ft rolls produced} = x_1 + x_3 + 2x_6$$

These amounts must equal at least 150, 200, and 300 rolls, respectively.

To construct the objective function, we observe that the total trim loss area is the difference between the total area of the standard rolls used and the total area representing all the orders. Thus

Total area of standard rolls $= 20L(x_1 + x_2 + x_3 + x_4 + x_5 + x_6)$

Total area of orders $= L(150 \times 5 + 200 \times 7 + 300 \times 9) = 4750L$

Given that the length $L$ of the standard roll is a constant, the objective function reduces to

$$\text{Minimize } z = x_1 + x_2 + x_3 + x_4 + x_5 + x_6$$

The general model may thus be written as

$$\text{Minimize } z = x_1 + x_2 + x_3 + x_4 + x_5 + x_6$$

subject to

$$
\begin{array}{llll}
2x_2 + 2x_3 + 4x_4 + x_5 & \geq 150 & \text{(5-ft rolls)} \\
x_1 + x_2 \phantom{+ 2x_3} + 2x_5 & \geq 200 & \text{(7-ft rolls)} \\
x_1 \phantom{+ x_2} + x_3 \phantom{+ 2x_5} + 2x_6 \geq 300 & & \text{(9-ft rolls)} \\
x_j \geq 0, \quad j = 1, 2, \ldots, 6
\end{array}
$$

The optimum solution of the model in Figure 2–15 indicates that the problem has alternative optima, which means that for the same number of standard rolls different settings may be used to satisfy the order. The given solution calls for cutting 25 standard rolls according to setting 3, 100 according to setting 5, and 137.5 according to setting 6. The solution is not implementable because $x_6$ is noninteger. We can either use an integer algorithm to solve the problem (see Chapter 9), or round the LP solution so that $x_6$ will assume the conservative value of 138 instead.

In view of the integer requirement for the variables, the solution is interpreted in a slightly different manner. For example, the dual price of .25 corresponding to constraint 1 signifies that an increase of 1 roll in the demand for the 5-foot rolls will require cutting an additional one-fourth of a standard 20-foot roll. This recommendation is impractical. We can recommend instead cutting an additional 20-foot roll for every four additional 5-foot rolls. This recommendation is valid so long as we are within the range $[100, 700]$ specified by the right-hand–side ranging. A similar analysis applies to the remaining dual prices.

### Problem set 2.6a

1. Consider the Thriftem Bank model of Example 2.6–1 and its solution in Figure 2–10.

   (a) Consider the output that pertains to making single changes in the right-hand side of the constraint. Explain why the minimum value allowed for the right-hand side of the first constraint equals $4.8 million. By the same token, explain why the maximum value of the right-hand side of the second constraint equals 12.

   (b) Suppose that the bank allocates all $12 million to farm and commercial loans. Compute the resulting net return for the bank in two different ways.

(c) Suppose that the funds available for making loans are increased to $20 million and that the minimum limit on farm and commercial loans is increased to $9 million. Would the new optimum solution continue to include home and commercial loans only? If so, find the new optimum solution.

2. Consider the Land Use model of Example 2.6–2. Suppose that Birdeyes can purchase an additional 100 virgin acres of land for $450,000. Use the results of the model in Figure 2–11 to provide the company with a decision regarding this purchase.

3. Consider the Bus Scheduling model of Example 2.6–3.
   (a) Use the output results in Figure 2–13 to determine the optimum total number of buses assuming that the minimum number of buses for the successive 6 periods are given as (i) (4, 12, 10, 7, 12, 4) and (ii) (4, 8, 7, 7, 12, 4).
   (b) Suppose that the minimum requirements are changed to (6,9,12,7,15,6). Use sensitivity analysis to determine whether the current solution remains feasible. If it is feasible, determine the new values of the variables.

4. Consider the trim-loss model of Example 2.6–4 and its solution in Figure 2–15.
   (a) If we slit 200 rolls using setting 1 and 100 rolls using setting 3, compute the associated trim-loss area.
   (b) Suppose that the only available standard roll is 15 feet wide. Generate all possible knife settings for producing 5-, 7-, and 9-foot rolls, and compute the associated trim loss per foot length.
   (c) In the original model, if the demand for 7-foot rolls is decreased by 80, what is the total number of standard 20-foot rolls that will be needed to fill the demand for of all three types of rolls?
   (d) In the original model, if the demand for 9-foot rolls is changed to 400, how many additional standard 20-foot rolls will be needed to satisfy the new demand?

5. Shale Oil, located on the island of Aruba, has a capacity of 600,000 barrels of crude oil per day. The final products from the refinery include two types of unleaded gasoline: regular and premium. The refining process encompasses three stages: (1) a distillation tower that produces a feedstock, (2) a cracker unit that produces gasoline stock by using a portion of the feedstock produced from the distillation tower, and (3) a blender unit that blends the gasoline stock form the cracker unit and the feedstock from the distillation tower. Both the regular and the premium gasoline can be produced from either the feedstock or the gasoline stock during the blending process, although at different production costs. The company estimates that the net profit per barrel of regular gasoline is $7.70 and $5.20, depending on whether it is blended from feedstock or from gasoline stock. The corresponding profit values for the premium grade are $12.30 and $10.40.

According to design specifications, it takes five barrels of crude oil to produce one barrel of feedstock. The cracker units cannot use more than 40,000 barrels of feedstock a day. All remaining feedstock is used directly in the blender unit to produce the end-product gasoline. The demand limits for regular and premium gasoline are 80,000 and 50,000 barrels per day.

**(a)** Develop a model for determining the optimum production schedule for the refinery.

**(b)** Suppose that the capacity of the distillation tower can be increased to 650,000 barrels of crude oil per day at an initial cost of $3,500,000 and a daily maintenance cost of $15,000. Would you recommend the expansion? State any assumptions that may be needed to reach a decision.

**6.** Hawaii Sugar Company produces brown sugar, processed (white) sugar, powdered sugar, and molasses from sugar cane syrup. The company purchases 4000 tons of syrup weekly and is contracted to deliver at least 25 tons weekly of each type of sugar. The production process starts by manufacturing brown sugar and molasses from the syrup. A ton of syrup produces .3 ton of brown sugar and .1 tons of molasses. Next, white sugar is produced by processing brown sugar. It takes 1 ton of brown sugar to produce .8 ton of white sugar. Finally, powdered sugar is produced from white sugar through a special grinding process that has a 95% conversion efficiency (1 ton of white sugar produces .95 ton of powdered sugar). The profits per ton for brown sugar, white sugar, powdered sugar, and molasses are $150, $200, $230, and $35, respectively.

**(a)** Formulate the problem as a linear program, and determine the weekly production schedule.

**(b)** Investigate the economic feasibility of expanding the processing capacity of the company to more than 4000 tons of syrup weekly.

**7.** Fox Enterprises is considering six projects for possible construction over the next 4 years. The expected (present value) returns, and cash outlays for the projects are given below. Fox is authorized to undertake any of the projects partially or completely. A partial undertaking of a project will prorate both return and cash outlays proportionately.

| | Cash outlay (1000$) | | | | |
| Project | Year 1 | Year 2 | Year 3 | Year 4 | Return ($1000) |
|---|---|---|---|---|---|
| 1 | 10.5 | 14.4 | 2.2 | 2.4 | 32.40 |
| 2 | 8.3 | 12.6 | 9.5 | 3.1 | 35.80 |
| 3 | 10.2 | 14.2 | 5.6 | 4.2 | 17.75 |
| 4 | 7.2 | 10.5 | 7.5 | 5.0 | 14.80 |
| 5 | 12.3 | 10.1 | 8.3 | 6.3 | 18.20 |
| 6 | 9.2 | 7.8 | 6.9 | 5.1 | 12.35 |
| Available funds ($1000) | 60.0 | 70.0 | 35.0 | 20.0 | |

**(a)** Formulate the problem as a linear program, and determine the optimal project mix that maximizes total returns.

**(b)** Suppose that no part of project 2 can be undertaken unless at least a portion of project 6 is undertaken. Modify the formulation of the model and find the new optimal solution.

**(c)** Is it worthwhile to borrow money in year 4?

**(d)** In the original model, suppose that any funds left at the end of 1 year are used in the immediately succeeding year. Find the new optimal solution, and determine how much each year "borrows" from the preceding year.

**(e)** Suppose that the yearly funds available for the first 3 years can be exceeded, if necessary, by borrowing from other financial activities within the company. Reformulate the model, and find the optimum solution. Would the new solution require borrowing in any year? If so, what is the rate of return on borrowed money?

**8.** Acme Manufacturing Company has received a contract to deliver home windows over the next 6 months. The successive demands for the six periods are 100, 250, 190, 140, 220, and 110, respectively. Production cost per window varies from month to month depending on labor, material, and utility costs. Acme estimates the production cost per window over the next 6 months to be $50, $45, $55, $48, $52, and $50, respectively. To take advantage of the fluctuations in manufacturing cost, Acme may elect to produce more than is needed to satisfy the demand of a given month and stock the excess units for delivery in later months. This, however, will incur storage costs at the rate of $8 per window per month assessed on end-of-month inventory.

**(a)** Develop a linear program to determine an optimum production schedule for Acme.

**(b)** Solve the problem assuming that Acme has an initial inventory of 25 windows at the beginning of the first month.

**(c)** The dual prices in periods 1, 2, 4, and 5 exactly equal the unit manufacturing costs for the same periods, whereas that of period 3 differs. Explain why.

**(d)** If the storage cost per window per month is increased to $9, will the optimum solution in (a) remain unchanged?

**9.** Investor Doe has four potential opportunities to invest a total of $100,000. The following table gives the cash flow for the four investments.

| Project | Cash flow ($1000) at the start of | | | | |
|---|---|---|---|---|---|
| | Year 1 | Year 2 | Year 3 | Year 4 | Year 5 |
| 1 | −1.00 | 0.50 | 0.30 | 1.80 | 1.20 |
| 2 | −1.00 | 0.60 | 0.20 | 1.50 | 1.30 |
| 3 | 0.00 | −1.00 | 0.80 | 1.90 | 0.80 |
| 4 | −1.00 | 0.40 | 0.60 | 1.80 | 0.95 |

The information in the table can be interpreted as follows: For project 1, $1.00 invested at the start of year 1 will yield $.50 at the start of year 2, $.30 at the start of year 3, $1.80 at the start of year 4, and $1.20 at the start of year 5. The remaining entries can be interpreted similarly. A 0.00 entry signifies no in or out cash flow. Doe also has the additional option of investing in a bank account that earns 6.5% annually. Funds accumulated from one year can be reinvested in the succeeding years.

**(a)** Formulate the problem as a linear program to determine the optimal allocation of funds to investment opportunities.

**(b)** Use the dual prices to determine the overall return on investment.

**(c)** If you wish to spend $1000 on pleasure at the end of year 1, how would this affect the accumulated amount at the start of year 5?

**(d)** If your pleasure spending is $1000 at the end of each of the first 4 years, determine the accumulated funds at the start of year 5.

**10.** Toolco has contracted with AutoMate to supply their automotive discount stores with wrenches and chisels. AutoMate's weekly demand consists of 1500 wrenches and 1200 chisels. Toolco's present one-shift capacity is not large enough to produce the requested units and must use overtime and possibly subcontracting with other tool shops. The result is an increase in the production cost per unit, as shown in the following table. The market restricts wrenches to chisels to a ratio of at least 2:1.

| Tool | Production type | Weekly production range (units) | Unit cost ($) |
|------|-----------------|----------------------------------|---------------|
| Wrenches | Regular | 0–550 | 2.00 |
| | Overtime | 551–800 | 2.80 |
| | Subcontracting | 801–∞ | 3.00 |
| Chisel | Regular | 0–620 | 2.10 |
| | Overtime | 621–900 | 3.20 |
| | Subcontracting | 901–∞ | 4.20 |

**(a)** Formulate the problem as a linear program, and determine the optimum production schedule for each tool.

**(b)** Relate the fact that the production cost function has increasing unit costs to the validity of the model.

**(c)** Relate the dual prices of the model to the unit production costs given in the table.

**(d)** What is the effect of increasing the production capacities of regular and overtime by one unit on the total production cost per week?

**11.** Four products are processed sequentially on two machines. The following table gives the pertinent data of the problem.

| | | Manufacturing time per unit (hr) | | | | |
|---|---|---|---|---|---|---|
| Machine | Cost per hr($) | Product 1 | Product 2 | Product 3 | Product 4 | Capacity (hr) |
| 1 | 10 | 2 | 3 | 4 | 2 | 500 |
| 2 | 5 | 3 | 2 | 1 | 2 | 380 |
| Unit selling price($) | | 65 | 70 | 55 | 45 | |

(a) Formulate the problem as an LP model, and find the optimum solution.

(b) Suppose that any additional capacity of machines 1 and 2 can only be acquired by using overtime. What is the maximum cost per hour the company should be willing to incur for either machine?

(c) By how much should the machining cost per unit of product 3 be reduced for it to be just profitable?

(d) In the original model, suppose that the selling prices for products 1, 3, and 4 are changed to $80, $65, and $60, respectively. Determine the limits on the selling price of product 2 that will leave the current values of the variables unchanged.

(e) In the original model, if the capacity of machine 1 is increased to 550 hours, determine the range on the capacity of machine 2 that will keep the current solution feasible.

12. A manufacturer produces three models, I, II, and III, of a certain product using raw materials $A$ and $B$. The following table gives the data for the problem.

| | Requirements per unit | | | |
|---|---|---|---|---|
| Raw material | I | II | III | availability |
| $A$ | 2 | 3 | 5 | 4000 |
| $B$ | 4 | 2 | 7 | 6000 |
| Minimum demand | 200 | 200 | 150 | |
| Profit per unit($) | 30 | 20 | 50 | |

The labor time per unit of model I is twice that of II and three times that of III. The entire labor force of the factory can produce the equivalent of 1500 units of model I. The market requirements specify the ratios $3 : 2 : 5$ for the production of the three respective models.

(a) Formulate the problem as a linear program, and find the optimum solution.

(b) Suppose that the manufacturer can purchase additional units of raw material $A$ at $12 per unit. Would it be advisable to do so?

(c) Would you recommend that the manufacturer purchase additional units of raw material $B$ at $5 per unit?

**(d)** Do you think it is advantageous for the manufacturer to increase the ratio of the units produced of model I to those of model II above the current ratio of 3:2?

**13.** HiRise Construction can bid on two 1-year projects. The quarterly cash flow (in millions of dollars) is given in the following table for the two projects.

| Project | Cash flow (in millions of $) at | | | | |
|---------|--------|--------|--------|---------|----------|
|         | 1/1/99 | 4/1/99 | 7/1/99 | 10/1/99 | 12/31/99 |
| I       | −1.0   | −3.1   | −1.5   | 1.8     | 5.0      |
| II      | −3.0   | −2.5   | 1.5    | 1.8     | 2.8      |

HiRise has cash funds of $1 million at the beginning of each quarter and may borrow an equal amount at 10% nominal annual interest rate. This means that if the amount borrowed in quarter $i$ is $B_i$, then $0 \le B_i \le 1$, for $i = 1, 2, 3, 4$. Any borrowed money must be returned at the end of the quarter. Surplus cash can earn quarterly interest at an 8% nominal annual rate. All money accumulated at the end of one quarter is invested in the succeeding quarter.

**(a)** Assume that HiRise is allowed partial or full participation in the two projects. Determine the level of participation that will maximize the net cash accumulated on 12/31/99.

**(b)** Is it possible in any quarter to borrow money and simultaneously end up with surplus funds? Explain.

**(c)** Give an economic interpretation of the resulting dual prices of the model.

**(d)** Show how the dual price associated with the upper bound on the borrowed money at the beginning of the third quarter can be derived from the dual prices associated with the balance equations representing the in-out cash flow at the five designated dates of the year.

**14.** In anticipation of the immense college expenses of their child, a couple has started an annual investment program on the child's 8th birthday that will last until the 18th birthday. The couple estimates that they will be able to invest the following amounts at the beginning of each year:

| Year       | 1    | 2    | 3    | 4    | 5    | 6    | 7    | 8    | 9    | 10   |
|------------|------|------|------|------|------|------|------|------|------|------|
| Amount($)  | 2000 | 2000 | 2500 | 2500 | 3000 | 3500 | 3500 | 4000 | 4000 | 5000 |

To avoid unpleasant surprises, the couple opts to invest the money safely in the following options: (1) Insured savings with 7.5% annual yield;

(2) six-year government bonds that yield 7.9% and have a current market price equal to 98% of face value; and (3) nine-year municipal bonds yielding 8.5%, with a current market price of 1.02 of its face value.

**(a)** How should the couple invest the money?

**(b)** Determine the rate of return associated with each year.

15. A business executive has the option to invest money in two plans: Plan A guarantees that each dollar invested will earn $.70 a year hence, and plan B guarantees that each dollar invested will earn $2 after 2 years. In plan A, investments can be made annually, and in plan B, investments are allowed for periods that are multiples of two years only.

**(a)** How should the executive invest $100,000 to maximize the earnings at the end of 3 years?

**(b)** Is it worthwhile for the executive to invest more money in the plans?

16. Consider the problem of assigning three types of aircraft to four routes according to the following data:

| Aircraft type | Capacity (passengers) | Number of aircraft | Number of daily trips on route | | | |
|---|---|---|---|---|---|---|
| | | | 1 | 2 | 3 | 4 |
| 1 | 50 | 5 | 3 | 2 | 2 | 1 |
| 2 | 30 | 8 | 4 | 3 | 3 | 2 |
| 3 | 20 | 10 | 5 | 5 | 4 | 2 |
| Daily number of customers | | | 1000 | 2000 | 900 | 1200 |

The associated costs, including the penalties for losing customers because of space unavailability, are

| Aircraft Type | Operating cost ($) per trip on route | | | |
|---|---|---|---|---|
| | 1 | 2 | 3 | 4 |
| 1 | 1000 | 1100 | 1200 | 1500 |
| 2 | 800 | 900 | 1000 | 1000 |
| 3 | 600 | 800 | 800 | 900 |
| Penalty ($) per lost customer | 40 | 50 | 45 | 70 |

**(a)** Determine the optimum allocation of aircraft to routes and determine the associated number of trips.

**(b)** Is it advantageous to increase the number of any of the three types of aircraft?

**(c)** Interpret the dual prices associated with the constraints representing the limits on the number of customers served on each route.

**17.** Two alloys, *A* and *B*, are made from four metals, I, II, III, and IV, according to the following specifications:

| Alloy | Specifications | Selling price ($) |
|-------|----------------|-------------------|
| A | At most 80% of I | 200 |
| | At most 30% of II | |
| | At least 50% of IV | |
| B | Between 40 and 60% of II | 300 |
| | At least 30% of III | |
| | At most 70% of IV | |

The four metals, in turn, are extracted from three ores according to the following data:

| Ore | Maximum quantity (tons) | I | II | III | IV | Others | Price/ton ($) |
|-----|-------------------------|---|----|----|----|--------|---------------|
| | | | | Constituents (%) | | | |
| 1 | 1000 | 20 | 10 | 30 | 30 | 10 | 30 |
| 2 | 2000 | 10 | 20 | 30 | 30 | 10 | 40 |
| 3 | 3000 | 5 | 5 | 70 | 20 | 0 | 50 |

**(a)** How much of each type of alloy should be produced? (*Hint:* Let $x_{ij}$ be tons of ore *i* allocated to alloy *k*, and define $w_k$ as tons of alloy *k* produced.)

**(b)** How much of each ore should be allocated to the production of each alloy?

**(c)** Which of the specification constraints contribute adversely to the optimum solution?

**(d)** What is the maximum price the company should be willing to pay per ton of ore 1? Ore 2? Ore 3?

**18.** A gambler plays a game that requires dividing bet money among four choices. The game has three outcomes. The following table gives the corresponding gain or loss per dollar for the different options of the game.

| Outcome | 1 | 2 | 3 | 4 |
|---------|----|----|----|----|
| | Return per dollar deposited in given choice | | | |
| 1 | −3 | 4 | −7 | 15 |
| 2 | 5 | −3 | 9 | 4 |
| 3 | 3 | −9 | 10 | −8 |

The gambler has a total of $500, which may be played only once. The exact outcome of the game is not known a priori. Because of this uncertainty, the gambler's strategy is maximize the *minimum* return produced by the three outcomes.

**(a)** How should the gambler allocate the $500 among the four choices? (*Hint:* The gambler's net return may be positive, zero, or negative.)

**(b)** Would you advise the gambler to bet additional funds?

## 2.7 SUMMARY

The graphical LP technique is used to draw general conclusions about the properties of the LP solution. It reveals that the optimum LP solution is associated with a corner point of the solution space. This key result is the basis for the development of the simplex method presented in Chapter 3 for solving the general linear programming problem. The graphical method also provides an insightful economic interpretation of the LP model.

## SELECTED REFERENCES

BAZARAA, M., J. JARVIS, and M. SHERALI, *Linear Programming and Network Flows,* 2nd ed., Wiley, New York, 1990.

SCHRAGE, L., *LINDO: An Optimization Modeling System, Text and Software,* 4th ed., Boyd and Fraser, Danvers, Mass., 1991.

WILLIAM, H., *Model Building in Mathematical Programming,* 3rd ed., Wiley, New York, 1990.

## COMPREHENSIVE PROBLEMS

■ **2–1.*** The Hi-C Company manufactures and cans three orange extracts: juice concentrate, regular juice, and jam. The products, which are intended for commercial use, are manufactured in 5-gallon cans. Jam uses Grade I oranges, and the remaining two products use Grade II. The following table lists the usages of orange as well as next year's demand:

| Product | Orange grade | Pounds of oranges per 5-gal can | Maximum Demand (cans) |
|---------|--------------|-------------------------------|----------------------|
| Jam | I | 5 | 10,000 |
| Concentrate | II | 30 | 12,000 |
| Juice | II | 15 | 40,000 |

*Motivated by "Red Brand Canners," *Stanford Business Cases 1965,* Graduate School of Business, Stanford University.

A market survey shows that the demand for regular juice is at least twice as high as that for the concentrate.

In the past, Hi-C bought Grade I and Grade II oranges seperately at the respective prices of 25 cents and 20 cents per pound. This year, an unexpected frost forced the growers to harvest and sell the crop early without being sorted to Grade I and Grade II. It is estimated that 30% of the 3,000,000-lb crop falls into Grade I and that only 60% into Grade II. For this reason, the crop is being offered at the uniform discount price of 19 cents per pound. Hi-C estimates that it will cost the company about 2.15 cents per pound to sort the oranges into Grade I and Grade II. The below-standard oranges (10% of the crop) will be discarded.

For the purpose of cost allocation, the Accounting Department uses the following argument to estimate the cost per pound of Grade I and Grade II oranges. Since 10% of the purchased crop will fall below Grade II standard, the effective average cost per pound can be computed as $\frac{(19 + 2.15)}{.9} = 23.5$ cents. Since the ratio of Grade I to Grade II in the purchased lot is 1 to 2, the corresponding average cost per pound based on the old prices is $\frac{(20 \times 2 + 25 \times 1)}{3} = 21.67$ cents. Thus, the increase in the average price ($= 23.5$ cents $- 21.67$ cents $= 1.83$ cents) should be reallocated to the two grades by using the 1:2 ratio, yielding a Grade I cost per pound of $25 + 1.83(\frac{1}{3}) = 25.61$ cents and a Grade II cost of $20 + 1.83(\frac{2}{3}) = 21.22$ cents. By using this information, the Accounting Department complies the following profitablity sheet for the three products.

|  | Product (5-gal can) | | |
|---|---|---|---|
|  | Jam | Concentrate | Juice |
| Sales price | $15.50 | $30.25 | $20.75 |
| Variable costs | 9.85 | 21.05 | 13.28 |
| Allocated fixed overhead | 1.05 | 2.15 | 1.96 |
| Total cost | $10.90 | $23.20 | $15.24 |
| Net profit | 4.60 | 7.05 | 5.51 |

Establish a production plan for the Hi-C Company.

■ **2–2.*** A steel company operates a foundry and two mills. The foundry casts three types of steel rolls that are machined in its machine shop before being shipped to the mills. Machined rolls are used by the mills for manufacturing various products.

At the beginning of each quarter, the mills prepare their monthly needs of rolls and submit them to the foundry. The foundry manager then draws a production plan that is essentially constrained by the machining capacity of the shop. Shortages are covered by direct purchase at a premium price from outside sources. A comparison between the cost per roll when acquired from the foundry and its outside purchase price is given in the table that follows. However, management points out that such shortage is not frequent and can be estimated to occur about 5% of the time.

*Based on S. Jain, K. Stott, and E. Vasold, "Orderbook Balancing Using a Combination of Linear Programming and Heuristic Techniques," *Interfaces,* Vol. 9, no. 1, November 1978, pp. 55–67.

| Roll type | Weight (lb) | Internal cost ($ per roll) | External purchase price ($ per roll) |
|-----------|-------------|----------------------------|--------------------------------------|
| 1         | 800         | 90                         | 108                                  |
| 2         | 1200        | 130                        | 145                                  |
| 3         | 1650        | 180                        | 194                                  |

Processing times on the four different machines in the machine shop are

| Machine type | Processing time per roll | | | Number of machines | Availabe hr per machine per month |
|--------------|--------|--------|--------|--------------------|-----------------------------------|
|              | Roll 1 | Roll 2 | Roll 3 |                    |                                   |
| 1            | 1      | 5      | 7      | 10                 | 320                               |
| 2            | 0      | 4      | 6      | 8                  | 310                               |
| 3            | 6      | 3      | 0      | 9                  | 300                               |
| 4            | 3      | 6      | 9      | 5                  | 310                               |

The demand for rolls by the two mills over the next 3 months is

| Month | Demand in tens of rolls | | | | | |
|-------|--------|--------|--------|--------|--------|--------|
|       | Mill 1 | | | Mill 2 | | |
|       | Roll 1 | Roll 2 | Roll 3 | Roll 1 | Roll 2 | Roll 3 |
| 1     | 50     | 20     | 40     | 20     | 10     | 0      |
| 2     | 0      | 30     | 50     | 30     | 20     | 20     |
| 3     | 10     | 0      | 30     | 0      | 40     | 20     |

Devise a production schedule for the machine shop.

■ **2–3.** ArkTec assembles PC computers for private clients. The orders for the next four quarters are 400, 700, 500, and 200, respectively. ArkTec has the option to produce more than is demanded for the quarter, in which case a holding cost of $100 per computer per quarter is incurred. Increasing production from one quarter to the next requires hiring additional employees, which increases the production cost per computer in that quarter by $60. Also, decreasing production from one quarter to the next would require laying off employees, which results in increasing the production cost per computer in that quarter by $50. How should ArkTec schedule the assembly of the computers to satisfy the demand for the four quarters?

■ **2–4.** The Beaver Furniture Company manufactures and assembles chairs, tables, and bookshelves. The plant produces semifinished products that are assembled in the company's assembling facility.

The (unassembled) monthly production capacity of the plant includes 3000 chairs, 1000 tables, and 580 bookshelves. The assembling facility employs 150 workers in two 8-hour shifts a day, 5 days a week. The average assembly times per chair, table, and bookshelf are 20, 40, and 15 minutes, respectively.

The size of the labor force in the assembly facility fluctuates because of the annual leaves taken by the employees. Pending requests for leaves include 20 workers for May, 25 for June, and 45 for July.

The sales forecast for the three products for the months of May, June, and July are estimated by the marketing department as

| Product | Sales forecast units | | | End-of-April inventory |
|---|---|---|---|---|
| | May | June | July | |
| Chair | 2800 | 2300 | 3350 | 30 |
| Table | 500 | 800 | 1400 | 100 |
| Bookshelf | 320 | 300 | 600 | 50 |

The production cost and selling price for the three products are

| Product | Unit cost ($) | Unit price ($) |
|---|---|---|
| Chair | 150 | 250 |
| Table | 400 | 750 |
| Bookshelf | 60 | 120 |

If a unit is not sold in the month in which it is produced, it is held over for possible sale in a later month. The storage cost is about 2% of the unit production cost. Should Beaver approve the proposed annual leaves?

# Chapter 3

# The Simplex Method

## 3.1 INTRODUCTION

The graphical method in Chapter 2 shows that the optimum LP solution is always associated with a *corner point* (also known mathematically as **extreme point**) of the solution space. This result is the key idea for the development of the general algebraic *simplex method* for solving any LP model.

The transition from the geometric extreme (or corner) point solution to the simplex method lies in identifying the extreme points algebraically. To achieve this goal, we first convert the model into the **standard LP form** by using slack or surplus variables to convert the inequality constraints into equations.

Our interest in the standard LP form lies in the **basic solutions** of the simultaneous linear equations. These (algebraic) basic solution completely define all the (geometric) extreme points of the solution space (see Section 7.2 for the proof). The simplex algorithm is designed to locate the optimum from among these basic solutions in an efficient manner.

## 3.2 STANDARD LP FORM AND ITS BASIC SOLUTIONS

This section first shows how the standard LP form is obtained. It then shows how the basic solutions are determined.

### 3.2.1 Standard LP Form

The use of basic solutions to solve the general LP model requires putting the problem in a standard form whose properties are

**1.** All the constraints (with the exception of the nonnegativity restrictions on the variables) are equations with nonnegative right-hand side.

**2.** All the variables are nonnegative.

**3.** The objective function may be of the maximization or the minimization type.

**1. Conversion of inequalities into equations.**    An inequality of the type $\leq$ ($\geq$) can be converted to an equation by augmenting its left-hand side with a *slack (surplus)* variable (see Section 2.3.3 for definitions of slacks and surplus).

***Example of $\leq$ constraint.***

$$x_1 + 2x_2 \leq 3$$

is equivalent to

$$x_1 + 2x_2 + s_1 = 3$$

where the slack $s_1 \geq 0$.

***Example of $\geq$ constraint.***

$$3x_1 + x_2 \geq 5$$

is equivalent to

$$3x_1 + x_2 - S_1 = 5$$

where the surplus $S_1 \geq 0$.

The right-hand side of an equation can always be made nonnegative by multiplying the equation by $-1$, if necessary. We also note that a ($\leq$) inequality can be converted to a ($\geq$) by multiplying both sides of the inequality by $-1$. For example, $2 < 4$ becomes $-2 > -4$ when we multiply both sides by $-1$.

**2. Conversion of unrestricted variable into nonnegative variables.**
An *unrestricted* variable $x_j$ can be expressed in terms of two *nonnegative* variables by using the substitution

$$x_j = x_j^+ - x_j^-, \quad x_j^+, x_j^- \geq 0$$

For example, for $x_j = -5$, we let $x_j^+ = 0$ and $x_j^- = 5$. If $x_j = +5$, then we take $x_j^+ = 5$ and $x_j^- = 0$. In both cases, $x_j^+$ and $x_j^-$ are nonnegative, as desired.

The substitution is effected in all the constraints and in the objective function. After solving the problem in terms of $x_j^+$ and $x_j^-$, the value of the original variable is then determined through back substitution.

**3. Conversion of maximization to minimization.**    The maximization of a function $f(x_1, x_2, \ldots, x_n)$ is equivalent to the minimization of $-f(x_1, x_2, \ldots, x_n)$, in the sense that both problems yield the same optimal values of $x_1, x_2, \ldots,$ and $x_n$.

**Example 3.2–1.**

Express the following LP model in standard form.

$$\text{Maximize } z = 2x_1 + 3x_2 + 5x_3$$

subject to

$$x_1 + x_2 - x_3 \geq -5$$
$$-6x_1 + 7x_2 - 9x_3 \leq 4$$
$$x_1 + x_2 + 4x_3 = 10$$
$$x_1, x_2 \geq 0$$

$$x_3 \text{ unrestricted}$$

The conversion is effected in the following manner:

**1.** Subtract the surplus $S_1$ from the left-hand side of the first constraint and then multiply both sides by $-1$ to obtain a nonnegative right-hand side. (Alternatively, we can multiply both sides of the $\geq$ inequality by $-1$ to convert it to $\leq$ with nonnegative right-hand side, and then augment a slack $s_1$ to the left-hand side.)

**2.** Add the slack $s_2$ to the left-hand side of the second constraint.

**3.** Because the third constraint is already in equation form, no slack or surplus is needed in this case.

**4.** Substitute unrestricted $x_3 = x_3^+ - x_3^-$ in the objective and all the constraints, where $x_3^+$ and $x_3^- \geq 0$.

The given operations yield the following standard LP.

$$\text{Maximize } z = 2x_1 + 3x_2 + 5x_3^+ - 5x_3^-$$

subject to

$$-x_1 - x_2 + x_3^+ - x_3^- + s_1 \qquad = 5$$
$$-6x_1 + 7x_2 - 9x_3^+ + 9x_3^- \qquad + s_2 = 4$$
$$x_1 + x_2 + 4x_3^+ - 4x_3^- \qquad = 10$$
$$x_1, \quad x_2, \quad x_3^+, \quad x_3^-, \quad x_4, \quad x_5 \geq 0$$

## Problem set 3.2a

**1.** Write the standard form of Example 3.2–1 assuming the first constraint is of the type $=$, the second constraint is of the type $\geq$, and the third constraint is of the type $\leq$. Additionally, $x_1$ is unrestricted and $x_3 \geq 0$.

**2.** Two different products, P1 and P2, can be manufactured by either of two different machines, M1 and M2. The unit processing time of either product on either machine is the same. The daily capacity of machine, M1, is 200 units (of either P1 or P2, or a mixture of both) and the daily capacity of machine, M2, is 250 units. The shop supervisor wants to balance the production schedule of the two machines such that the total number of units produced on one machine is within 5 units of the number produced on the other. The profit per unit of $P1$ is \$10 and that of $P2$ is \$15. Set up the problem in the standard LP form.

3. Show how the following objective function can be presented in the standard LP form:

$$\text{Minimize } z = \max\{|x_1 - x_2 + 3x_3|, |-x_1 + 3x_2 - x_3|\}$$

$$x_1, x_2, x_3 \geq 0$$

4. Show that the $m$ equations:

$$\sum_{j=1}^{n} a_{ij}x_j = b_i, \quad i = 1, 2, \ldots, m$$

are equivalent to the following $m + 1$ inequalities:

$$\sum_{j=1}^{n} a_{ij}x_j \leq b_i, \quad i = 1, 2, \ldots, m$$

$$\sum_{j=1}^{n} \left(\sum_{i=1}^{m} a_{ij}\right) x_j \geq \sum_{i=1}^{m} b_i$$

## 3.2.2 Determination of Basic Solutions

The standard LP form includes $m$ simultaneous linear equations in $n$ unknowns or variables ($m < n$). We divide the $n$ variables into two sets: (1) $n - m$ variables, to which we assign zero values; and (2) the remaining m variables, whose values are determined by solving the resulting $m$ equations. If the $m$ equations yield a *unique* solution, then the associated $m$ variables are called **basic variables** and the remaining $n - m$ zero variables are referred to as **nonbasic variables**. In this case, the resulting unique solution comprises a **basic solution**. If all the variables assume nonnegative values, then the basic solution is *feasible*. Otherwise, it is *infeasible*.

Based on the given definitions, the maximum number of *possible* basic solutions for $m$ equations in $n$ unknowns is

$$\binom{n}{m} = \frac{n!}{m! \, (n - m)!}$$

---

**Example 3.2–2.** Consider the following set of two equations in five unknowns ($m = 2, n = 5$).

$$x_1 + \phantom{2}x_2 + 4x_3 + 2x_4 + 3x_5 = 8$$

$$4x_1 + 2x_2 + 2x_3 + \phantom{2}x_4 + 6x_5 = 4$$

Identify a feasible basic solution, an infeasible basic solution, and variable combinations that do not produce basic solutions.

The maximum number of possible basic solutions is $\frac{5!}{3!2!} = 10$. We show subsequently that some of these combinations may not produce a basic solution at all.

By definition, a basic solution can include only two ($= m$) variables, which means that the associated number of *zero* nonbasic variables must be three ($= n - m$).

*Case 1. Basic feasible solution*

          Zero (nonbasic) variables: $(x_2, x_4, x_5)$

| | |
|---|---|
| Equations: | $x_1 + 4x_3 = 8$ |
| | $4x_1 + 2x_3 = 4$ |
| Solution: | *Unique* with $x_1 = 0$, $x_3 = 2$. |
| Status: | *Feasible* basic solution because the basic variables $x_1$ and $x_3$ are $\geq 0$. |

*Case 2. Basic infeasible solution*

          Zero (nonbasic) variables: $(x_3, x_4, x_5)$

| | |
|---|---|
| Equations: | $x_1 + x_2 = 8$ |
| | $4x_1 + 2x_2 = 4$ |
| Solution: | *Unique* with $x_1 = -6$, $x_2 = 14$ |
| Status: | *Infeasible* basic solution because $x_1 < 0$. |

*Case 3. Infinity of solutions*

          Zero (nonbasic) variables: $(x_1, x_2, x_5)$

| | |
|---|---|
| Equations: | $4x_3 + 2x_4 = 8$ |
| | $2x_3 + x_4 = 4$ |
| Solution: | No unique solution because the equations are *dependent* (if you divide the first equation by 2, you will obtain the second equation). |
| Status: | Infinity of solutions. |

*Case 4. Nonexisting solution*

          Zero (nonbasic) variables: $(x_1, x_3, x_4)$

| | |
|---|---|
| Equations: | $x_2 + 3x_5 = 8$ |
| | $2x_2 + 6x_5 = 4$ |
| Solution: | No solution exists because the equations are *inconsistent*. |
| Status: | Nonexisting solution. |

---

## Problem Set 3.2b

1. In Example 3.2–2, we examined four combinations of variables. Test the combinations $(x_1, x_4)$, $(x_1, x_5)$, and $(x_2, x_3)$ and identify the status of their solutions.

2. Consider the following LP:

$$\text{Maximize } z = 2x_1 + 3x_2$$

subject to

$$x_1 + 3x_2 \leq 6$$
$$3x_1 + 2x_2 \leq 6$$
$$x_1, x_2 \geq 0$$

(a) Express the problem in standard form.

(b) Determine all the basic solutions of the problem, and classify them as feasible and infeasible.

(c) Use direct substitution in the objective function to determine the best *basic feasible* solution.

(d) Verify graphically that the solution obtained in (c) is the optimum LP solution—hence, conclude that the optimum solution can be determined algebraically by considering the basic feasible solutions only.

(e) Show how the *infeasible* basic solution are represented on the graphical solution space.

3. Determine the optimum solution for each of the following LPs by enumerating all the basic solutions.

(a) Maximize $z = 2x_1 - 4x_2 + 5x_3 - 6x_4$

subject to

$$x_1 + 4x_2 - 2x_3 + 8x_4 \leq 2$$

$$-x_1 + 2x_2 + 3x_3 + 4x_4 \leq 1$$

$$x_1, x_2, x_3, x_4, \geq 0$$

(b) Minimize $z = x_1 + 2x_2 - 3x_3 - 2x_4$

subject to

$$x_1 + 2x_2 - 3x_3 + x_4 = 4$$

$$x_1 + 2x_2 + x_3 + 2x_4 = 4$$

$$x_1, x_2, x_3, x_4, \geq 0$$

4. Show that all the basic solutions of the following LP are infeasible.

$$\text{Maximize } z = x_1 + x_2$$

subject to

$$x_1 + 2x_2 \leq 6$$

$$2x_1 + x_2 \geq 16$$

$$x_1, x_2 \geq 0$$

### 3.2.3 Unrestricted Variables and Basic Solutions

In Section 2.3.3 we defined the unrestricted variables. We then showed in Section 3.2.1 that, in the standard form, an unrestricted variable $x_j$ must be substituted out in terms of two nonnegative variables as

$$x_j = x_j^+ - x_j^-, \quad x_j^+, x_j^- \geq 0$$

Based on the definition of basic solutions in Section 3.2.2, it is impossible for $x_j^+$ and $x_j^-$ to be basic variables simultaneously because they are dependent. Dependence follows from the fact that constraint coefficients of $x_j^+$ are the negatives of those of $x_j^-$. This means that in any basic solution at least one of the variables $x_j^+$ and $x_j^-$ must be nonbasic at zero level (see Problem 3.2c–1).

### Problem set 3.2c

1. Consider the following LP:

$$\text{Maximize } z = 2x_1 + 3x_2 + 5x_3$$

subject to

$$-6x_1 + 7x_2 - 9x_3 \geq 4$$

$$x_1 + x_2 + 4x_3 = 10$$

$$x_1, x_3 \geq 0$$

$$x_2 \text{ unrestricted}$$

The conversion to the standard form involves using the substitution $x_2 = x_2^+ - x_2^-$. Show that none of the basic solutions of the problem can include both $x_2^+$ and $x_2^-$ simultaneously.

2. Consider the following LP:

$$\text{Maximize } z = x_1 + 3x_2$$

subject to

$$x_1 + x_2 \leq 2$$

$$-x_1 + x_2 \leq 4$$

$$x_1 \text{ unrestricted}$$

$$x_2 \geq 0$$

   **(a)** Determine all the basic feasible solutions of the problem.
   **(b)** Use direct substitution in the objective function to determine the best basic solution.
   **(c)** Solve the problem graphically, and verify that the solution obtained in (c) is the optimum.

3. JoShop manufactures three products whose unit profits are $2, $5, and $3, respectively. The company has budgeted 80 hours of labor time and 65 hours of machine time for the production of three products. The labor requirements per unit of products 1, 2, and 3 are 2, 1, and 2 hours, respectively. The corresponding machine time requirements per unit are 1, 1, and .5 hour. JoShop regards the budgeted labor and machine hours as goals that may be exceeded, if necessary,

but at the additional cost of $15 per labor hour and $10 per machine hour. The respective unit profits for the three products are $2, $5, and $3.

(a) Formulate the problem as an LP, and determine all its basic feasible solution.

(b) Use the results in (a) to determine the optimum solution.

4. In an LP in which there are several unrestricted variables, a transformation of the type $x_j = x_j^+ - x_j^-, x_j^+, x_j^- \geq 0$ will double the corresponding number of nonnegative variables. We can, instead, replace $k$ unrestricted variables with exactly $k + 1$ nonnegative variables by using the substitution $x_j = x_j' - w, x_j', w \geq 0$. Use TORA to show that the two methods produce the same solution for the following LP:

$$\text{Maximize } z = -2x_1 + 3x_2 - 2x_3$$

subject to

$$4x_1 - x_2 - 5x_3 = 10$$

$$2x_1 + 3x_2 + 2x_3 = 12$$

$$x_1 \geq 0, \quad x_2, \quad x_3 \text{ unrestricted}$$

## 3.3 THE SIMPLEX ALGORITHM

Based on the development in Section 3.2, we can determine the LP optimum by exhaustively enumerating all the basic (feasible) solutions of the standard form. This procedure, however, is computationally inefficient. The simplex algorithm is designed to locate the optimum by concentrating on a selected number of the basic feasible solutions of the problem.

The simplex method always starts at a basic feasible solution and then attempts to find another basic feasible solution that will improve the objective value. This is possible only if an *increase* in a current zero (nonbasic) variable can lead to an improvement in the objective value. However, for a current zero variable to become positive, one of the current basic variables must be removed (become nonbasic at zero level) to guarantee that the new solution will include exactly $m$ basic variables (recall that we are interested in only *basic* solutions with exactly $m$ basic variables). In the terminology of the simplex method, the selected zero variable is the **entering variable,** and the removed basic variable is the **leaving variable.**

---

**Example 3.3–1.**

We use the Reddy Mikks model (Example 2.2–1) to explain the details of the simplex method. The main elements of the problem are summarized here for convenience. Let

$$x_1 = \text{Daily production of exterior paint in tons}$$
$$x_2 = \text{Daily production of interior paint in tons}$$

Exterior and interior paints are produced from two types of raw materials, M1 and M2. The first two constraints represent the limits on the raw material availability. Constraints

3 and 4 are concerned with limits on demand. The respective profit per ton for the exterior and the interior paints are $5000 and $4000. The objective of the problem is to maximize the total profit. For convenience, the unit profits are scaled down by 1000.

The problem is expressed in standard form as

$$\text{Maximize } z = 5x_1 + 4x_2 + 0s_1 + 0s_2 + 0s_3 + 0s_4$$

subject to

$$
\begin{aligned}
6x_1 + 4x_2 + s_1 \quad\quad\quad\quad\quad &= 24 \quad \text{(Raw material } M1) \\
x_1 + 2x_2 \quad + s_2 \quad\quad\quad\quad &= 6 \quad \text{(Raw material } M2) \\
-x_1 + x_2 \quad\quad\quad + s_3 \quad\quad &= 1 \quad \text{(Demand limit)} \\
x_2 \quad\quad\quad\quad + s_4 &= 2 \quad \text{(Demand limit)} \\
x_1, \ x_2, \ s_1, \ s_2, \ s_3, \ s_4 &\geq 0
\end{aligned}
$$

The variables $s_1, s_2, s_3, s_4$ are the slacks associated with the four ($\leq$) constraints. The standard form can be summarized in a compact tableau form as

| Basic | $z$ | $x_1$ | $x_2$ | $s_1$ | $s_2$ | $s_3$ | $s_4$ | Solution | |
|-------|-----|-------|-------|-------|-------|-------|-------|----------|---|
| $z$   | 1   | $-5$  | $-4$  | 0     | 0     | 0     | 0     | 0        | $z$-row |
| $s_1$ | 0   | 6     | 4     | 1     | 0     | 0     | 0     | 24       | $s_1$-row |
| $s_2$ | 0   | 1     | 2     | 0     | 1     | 0     | 0     | 6        | $s_2$-row |
| $s_3$ | 0   | $-1$  | 1     | 0     | 0     | 1     | 0     | 1        | $s_3$-row |
| $s_4$ | 0   | 0     | 1     | 0     | 0     | 0     | 1     | 2        | $s_4$-row |

Each of the bottom four rows represents a constraint equation whose right-hand side is given in the "solution" column. The z-row is obtained from

$$z - 5x_1 - 4x_2 = 0$$

The slack variables $s_1$, $s_2$, $s_3$, and $s_4$ provide an obvious starting *basic feasible* solution because once we assign zero values to the nonbasic variables $x_1$ and $x_2$, the "solution" column (right-hand side) automatically provides the values of the slacks—that is, $s_1 = 24, s_2 = 6, s_3 = 1$, and $s_4 = 2$. This result follows because of the special structure of the columns associated with the slacks. The associated value of $z$ is zero.

Is the starting solution optimal (in the sense that the variables $x_1$ and $x_2$ should remain at zero level)? The answer is no, because in the objective function $z = 5x_1 + 4x_2$ the profit will increase by $5 (thousand) per ton increase in $x_1$ and by $4 (thousand) per ton increase in $x_2$. Although either variable will increase the profit, we choose to increase $x_1$ because it offers a higher rate of increase in $z$ ($5 versus $4). In this case, $x_1$ is the *entering variable*. Applying the same reasoning to the starting tableau where the objective function is expressed as $z - 5x_1 - 4x_2 = 0$, the entering variable is spotted as the nonbasic variable having the *most negative* coefficient in the z-row.

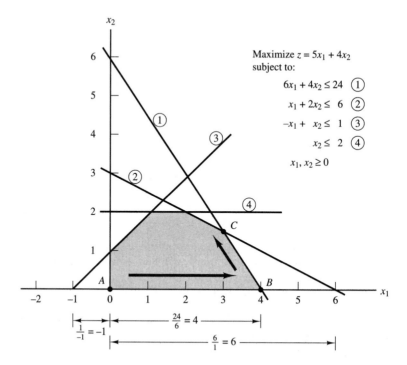

**Figure 3–1**

The entering variable $x_1$ must now be increased above zero level. Figure 3–1 shows that, starting at the origin $A$ ($x_1 = 0$, $x_2 = 0$), the largest value we can assign to $x_1$ without falling outside the feasible space is defined by point $B$ ($x_1 = 4, x_2 = 0$). This means that the solution will move from the extreme point $A$ to the improved extreme point $B$.

Because the simplex algorithm is algebraic, we need to show how extreme point $B$ can be determined from the tableau without the benefit of the graphical representation. From Figure 3–1, we can determine $B$ by considering the intercepts of the constraints with the $x_1$-axis. Algebraically, these intercepts are the **ratios** of the right-hand side of the equations (i.e., the coefficients of the "solution" column) to the corresponding constraint coefficients under $x_1$, as the following table shows.

| Basic | $x_1$ | Solution | Ratio (or Intercept) |
|-------|-------|----------|----------------------|
| $s_1$ | 6 | 24 | $\frac{24}{6} = 4$ (Minimum) |
| $s_2$ | 1 | 6 | $\frac{6}{1} = 6$ |
| $s_3$ | $-1$ | 1 | $-\frac{1}{1} = -1$ (Ignore) |
| $s_4$ | 0 | 2 | $\frac{2}{0} = \infty$ (Ignore) |

We are interested only in the *nonnegative* ratios (or intercepts) because they represent the direction of increase in $x_1$. Given that the coefficients of the "solution" column are, by design, always nonnegative, the resulting ratios will be *nonnegative* only if the denominator element is strictly positive. This is the reason we discard the ratios of equations 3 and 4, whose denominators are negative or zero.

The minimum nonnegative ratio provides the value of the entering variable $x_1$ in the new solution—namely, $x_1 = 4$ (compare with point $B$ in Figure 3–1). The corresponding increase in the value of the objective $z$ is ($5 \times 4$ tons) = \$20.

Next, we determine the *leaving variable* from among the current basic variables $s_1$, $s_2$, $s_3$, and $s_4$ that should be forced to zero level when $x_1$ enters. (Recall that a basic solution in this example must include exactly $m = 4$ basic variables.) Because $s_1$ is associated with the smallest (nonnegative) ratio, its value will be zero at the new point $B$. Thus, $s_1$ is the *leaving variable,* which automatically makes $x_1$ basic at level 4. Replacing the leaving variable $s_1$ with the entering variable $x_1$ produces the new basic solution ($x_1$, $s_2$, $s_3$, $s_4$).

The computation of the new basic solution is based on the **Gauss-Jordan row operations.** The following tableau, which is a replica of the starting tableau, identifies the **pivot column** as the one associated with the entering variable and the **pivot row** as the row associated with the leaving variable. The intersection of the pivot column and the pivot row define the **pivot element.**

| Basic | $z$ | $x_1$ | $x_2$ | $s_1$ | $s_2$ | $s_3$ | $s_4$ | Solution | |
|-------|-----|-------|-------|-------|-------|-------|-------|----------|---|
| $z$   | 1   | $-5$  | $-4$  | 0     | 0     | 0     | 0     | 0        | |
| $s_1$ | 0   | 6     | 4     | 1     | 0     | 0     | 0     | 24       | ← Pivot row |
| $s_2$ | 0   | 1     | 2     | 0     | 1     | 0     | 0     | 6        | |
| $s_3$ | 0   | $-1$  | 1     | 0     | 0     | 1     | 0     | 1        | |
| $s_4$ | 0   | 0     | 1     | 0     | 0     | 0     | 1     | 2        | |

Pivot
column

The Gauss-Jordan computations needed to produce the new basic solution include two types.

**1.** Pivot row

New pivot row = Current pivot row ÷ Pivot element

**2.** *All other rows, including z*

New Row = (Current row) − (Its pivot column coefficient) × (New pivot row)

Type 1 computation divides the pivot row ($s_1$-row) by the pivot element (= 6). The following tableau shows the new pivot row with the entering (nonbasic) variable $x_1$ replacing the leaving variable $s_1$. The solution column directly gives the new value of $x_1$ (= 4).

| Basic | $z$ | $x_1$ | $x_2$ | $s_1$ | $s_2$ | $s_3$ | $s_4$ | Solution |
|-------|-----|-------|-------|-------|-------|-------|-------|----------|
| $z$ | | | | | | | | |
| $x_1$ | 0 | 1 | $\frac{4}{6}$ | $\frac{1}{6}$ | 0 | 0 | 0 | $\frac{24}{6}=4$ ← New pivot row |
| $s_2$ | | | | | | | | |
| $s_3$ | | | | | | | | |
| $s_4$ | | | | | | | | |

Type 2 computations are applied to the remaining rows as follows:

**1.** $z$-row

$$
\begin{array}{rccccccc}
\text{Current } z\text{-row: } (1 & -5 & -4 & 0 & 0 & 0 & 0 & |\quad 0) \\
-(-5) \times \text{New pivot row: } (0 & 5 & \tfrac{10}{3} & \tfrac{5}{6} & 0 & 0 & 0 & |\quad 20) \\
= \text{ New } z\text{-row: } (1 & 0 & -\tfrac{2}{3} & \tfrac{5}{6} & 0 & 0 & 0 & |\quad 20)
\end{array}
$$

**2.** $s_2$-row

$$
\begin{array}{rccccccc}
\text{current } s_2\text{-row: } (0 & 1 & 2 & 0 & 1 & 0 & 0 & |\quad 6) \\
-(1) \times \text{new pivot row: } (0 & -1 & -\tfrac{2}{3} & -\tfrac{1}{6} & 0 & 0 & 0 & |\quad -4) \\
= \text{ new } s_2\text{-row: } (0 & 0 & \tfrac{4}{3} & -\tfrac{1}{6} & 1 & 0 & 0 & |\quad 2)
\end{array}
$$

**3.** $s_3$-row

$$
\begin{array}{rccccccc}
\text{current } s_3\text{-row: } (0 & -1 & 1 & 0 & 0 & 1 & 0 & |\quad 1) \\
-(-1) \times \text{new pivot row: } (0 & 1 & \tfrac{2}{3} & \tfrac{1}{6} & 0 & 0 & 0 & |\quad 4) \\
= \text{ new } s_3\text{-row: } (0 & 0 & \tfrac{5}{3} & \tfrac{1}{6} & 0 & 1 & 0 & |\quad 5)
\end{array}
$$

**4.** $s_4$-row   The new $s_4$-row remains the same as the current one because its coefficient in the *pivot column* is zero.

The new tableau corresponding to the new basic solution $(x_1, s_2, s_3, s_4)$ thus becomes

| Basic | $z$ | $x_1$ | $x_2$ | $s_1$ | $s_2$ | $s_3$ | $s_4$ | Solution |
|-------|-----|-------|-------|-------|-------|-------|-------|----------|
| $z$ | 1 | 0 | $-\frac{2}{3}$ | $\frac{5}{6}$ | 0 | 0 | 0 | 20 |
| $x_1$ | 0 | 1 | $\frac{2}{3}$ | $\frac{1}{6}$ | 0 | 0 | 0 | 4 |
| $s_2$ | 0 | 0 | $\frac{4}{3}$ | $-\frac{1}{6}$ | 1 | 0 | 0 | 2 |
| $s_3$ | 0 | 0 | $\frac{5}{3}$ | $\frac{1}{6}$ | 0 | 1 | 0 | 5 |
| $s_4$ | 0 | 0 | 1 | 0 | 0 | 0 | 1 | 2 |

Observe that the new tableau has the same properties as the starting tableau. When we set the nonbasic variables $x_2$ and $s_1$ to zero, the solution column automatically yields the new basic solution ($x_1 = 4$, $s_2 = 2$, $s_3 = 5$, $s_4 = 2$) together with the corresponding new value of $z$ ( $= 20$). This "conditioning" of the tableau is the result of the application of the Gauss-Jordan row operations.

An examination of the last tableau shows that it is not optimal because the nonbasic variable $x_2$ has a negative coefficient in the $z$-row. This reasoning, which is the same as the one we used with the starting tableau, becomes clear when we express the $z$-row as

$$z = \frac{2}{3}x_2 - \frac{5}{6}s_1 + 20$$

An increase in $x_2$ (above its current zero value) is advantageous because it will increase the value of $z$. Thus, $x_2$ is the entering variable.

Next, we determine the leaving variable by computing the ratios of the constraints with the *nonnegative* direction of the entering variable $x_2$.

| Basic | $x_2$ | Solution | Ratio |
|-------|-------|----------|-------|
| $x_1$ | $\frac{2}{3}$ | 4 | $4 \div \frac{2}{3} = 6$ |
| $s_2$ | $\frac{4}{3}$ | 2 | $2 \div \frac{4}{3} = \frac{3}{2}$ |
| $s_3$ | $\frac{5}{3}$ | 5 | $5 \div \frac{5}{3} = 3$ |
| $s_4$ | 1 | 2 | $2 \div 1 = 2$ |

The computations show that $s_2$ is the leaving variable and that $x_2$ will enter the new basic solution at the value $\frac{3}{2}$, the smallest (nonnegative) ratio. The corresponding increase in $z$ is $\left(\frac{2}{3} \times \frac{3}{2}\right) = 1$, yielding new $z = 20 + 1 = 21$.

The pivot row is now given by the $s_2$-row and the pivot column is associated with $x_2$. The pivot element thus equals $\frac{4}{3}$.

Next, we apply the Gauss-Jordan row operations as follows:

1. New pivot $s_2$-row = current $s_2$-row $\div \frac{4}{3}$.

2. New $z$-row = Current $z$-row $- \left(-\frac{2}{3}\right) \times$ New pivot row

3. New $x_1$-row = Current $x_1$-row $- \left(\frac{2}{3}\right) \times$ New pivot row

4. New $s_3$-row = Current $s_3$-row $- \left(\frac{5}{3}\right) \times$ New pivot row

5. New $s_4$-row = Current $s_4$-row $- (1) \times$ New pivot row

These computations produce the following tableau:

| Basic | $z$ | $x_1$ | $x_2$ | $s_1$ | $s_2$ | $s_3$ | $s_4$ | Solution |
|-------|-----|-------|-------|-------|-------|-------|-------|----------|
| $z$ | 1 | 0 | 0 | $\frac{3}{4}$ | $\frac{1}{2}$ | 0 | 0 | 21 |
| $x_1$ | 0 | 1 | 0 | $\frac{1}{4}$ | $-\frac{1}{2}$ | 0 | 0 | 3 |
| $x_2$ | 0 | 0 | 1 | $-\frac{1}{8}$ | $\frac{3}{4}$ | 0 | 0 | $\frac{3}{2}$ |
| $s_3$ | 0 | 0 | 0 | $\frac{3}{8}$ | $-\frac{5}{4}$ | 1 | 0 | $\frac{5}{2}$ |
| $s_4$ | 0 | 0 | 0 | $\frac{1}{8}$ | $-\frac{3}{4}$ | 0 | 1 | $\frac{1}{2}$ |

Since *none* of the $z$-row coefficients associated with the nonbasic variables $s_1$ and $s_2$ is negative, the last tableau is optimal.

The optimum solution can be read from the simplex tableau in the following manner. The optimal values of the variables in the "basic" column are given in the right-hand–side "solution" column and can be interpreted as

| Decision variable | Optimum value | Recommendation |
|-------------------|---------------|----------------|
| $x_1$ | 3 | Produce 3 tons of exterior paint daily |
| $x_2$ | $\frac{3}{2}$ | Produce 1.5 tons of interior paint daily |
| $z$ | 21 | Daily profit is $21,000 |

The simplex tableau offers a wealth of additional information that includes

**1.** The status of the resources
**2.** The worth per unit (dual prices) of the resources
**3.** All the data required to carry out sensitivity analysis on the optimal solution

We will show here how the status of the resources can be determined. The determination of the dual prices and the use of the tableau data to carry out sensitivity analysis are covered in Chapter 4.

The status of a resource is designated as scarce or abundant depending, respectively, on whether or not the activities (variables) of the model use the available amount of the resource completely. This information is secured from the optimum tableau by checking the value of the slack variable associated with the constraint representing the resource. If the slack value is zero, the resource is used completely and is classified as scarce. Otherwise, a positive slack indicates that the resource is abundant.

In the Reddy Mikks model, the four constraints are classified in the following manner:

| Resource | Slack value | Status |
|----------|-------------|--------|
| Raw material, $M1$ | $s_1 = 0$ | Scarce |
| Raw material, $M2$ | $s_2 = 0$ | Scarce |
| Demand limit 1 | $s_3 = \frac{5}{2}$ | Abundant |
| Demand limit 2 | $s_4 = \frac{1}{2}$ | Abundant |

The status of the resources indicates that an increase in the availability of raw materials, $M1$ and $M2$, is warranted because the two resources are scarce. The amount of increase can be determined by using appropriate sensitivity analysis procedures. This point was discussed in Sections 2.4 and 2.5, and will be examined more fully in Chapter 4.

Example 3.3–1 deals with maximization. In minimization, the selection of the leaving variables is the same as in the maximization case. For the entering variable, given that max $z = -\min(-z)$ as shown in Section 3.2.1, the minimization case selects the entering variable as the nonbasic variable with the most *positive* objective coefficient, and minimum $z$ is attained when all the $z$-row coefficients are nonpositive.

The rules for selecting the entering and leaving variables are referred to as the **optimality** and **feasibility conditions**. For convenience, we summarize these conditions and the steps of the simple method subsequently.

*Optimality condition.* The entering variable in a maximization (minimization) problem is the *nonbasic* variable having the most negative (positive) coefficient in the $z$-row. Ties are broken arbitrarily. The optimum is reached at the iteration where all the $z$-row coefficients of the nonbasic variables are nonnegative (nonpositive).

*Feasibility condition.* For both the maximization and the minimization problems, the leaving variable is the *basic* variable associated with the smallest nonnegative ratio. Ties are broken arbitrarily.

The steps of the simplex method are

**Step 0.** Determine a starting basic feasible solution.

**Step 1.** Select an *entering variable* using the optimality condition. Stop if there is no entering variable.

**Step 2.** Select a *leaving variable* using the feasibility condition.

**Step 3.** Determine the new basic solution by using the appropriate Gauss-Jordan computations. Go to step 1.

The simplex method computations are *iterative*, in the sense that fixed conditions and computations are applied to the current tableau to produce the next tableau. We thus refer to the successive tableaus as **iterations**.

A trace of the successive basic solutions of Example 3.3–1 on the graphical space in Figure 3–1 shows that the iterations start at extreme point $A$, move to extreme point $B$, and terminate at the optimum extreme point $C$. These iterations correspond to

**adjacent** extreme points where the path of the simplex method coincides with the **edges** of the solution space. The algorithm can never cut across the solution space by going from $A$ to $C$ directly. (See the **interior point algorithm,** Section 7.8, for an alternative solution method.)

### Problem set 3.3a

1. This problem is designed to reinforce your understanding of the simplex feasibility condition. In the first tableau in Example 3.3–1, we used the minimum (nonnegative) ratio test to determine the leaving variable. Such a condition guarantees that none of the new values of the basic variables will become negative. To demonstrate this point, apply TORA to the Reddy Mikks model and employ the "user-guided" option to force $s_2$, instead of $s_1$, to leave the basic solution. Now, look at the resulting simplex tableau, and you will note that $s_1$ assumes a negative value ($= -2$), meaning that the new solution is infeasible.

2. Consider the following set of constraints:

$$x_1 + 2x_2 + 2x_3 + 4x_4 \le 40$$
$$2x_1 - x_2 + x_3 + 2x_4 \le 8$$
$$4x_1 - 2x_2 + x_3 - x_4 \le 10$$
$$x_1, x_2, x_3, x_4 \ge 0$$

For each of the following objective functions, solve the problem using TORA's user-guided option:
(a) Maximize $z = 2x_1 + x_2 - 3x_3 + 5x_4$.
(b) Maximize $z = 8x_1 + 6x_2 + 3x_3 - 2x_4$.
(c) Maximize $z = 3x_1 - x_2 + 3x_3 + 4x_4$.
(d) Minimize $z = 5x_1 - 4x_2 + 6x_3 - 8x_4$.
(e) Minimize $z = -4x_1 + 6x_2 - 2x_3 + 4x_4$.

3. The following tableau represents a specific simplex iteration. All variables are nonnegative.

| Basic | $x_1$ | $x_2$ | $x_3$ | $x_4$ | $x_5$ | $x_6$ | $x_7$ | $x_8$ | |
|-------|-------|-------|-------|-------|-------|-------|-------|-------|-----|
| $z$   | 0     | $-5$  | 0     | 4     | $-1$  | $-10$ | 0     | 0     | 620 |
| $x_8$ | 0     | 3     | 0     | $-2$  | $-3$  | $-1$  | 5     | 1     | 12  |
| $x_3$ | 0     | 1     | 1     | 3     | 1     | 0     | 3     | 0     | 6   |
| $x_1$ | 1     | $-1$  | 0     | 0     | 6     | $-4$  | 0     | 0     | 0   |

(a) Determine the leaving variable if the entering variable is (i) $x_2$, (ii) $x_4$, (iii) $x_5$, (iv) $x_6$, (v) $x_7$.

**(b)** For each case in (a), and without using the Gauss-Jordan operations, determine the value of the entering variable and the corresponding increase or decrease in the value of the objective $z$.

**4.** Consider the following system of equations:

$$x_1 + 2x_2 - 3x_3 + 5x_4 + x_5 \qquad\qquad\quad = 4$$
$$5x_1 - 2x_2 \qquad\quad + 6x_4 \qquad + x_6 \qquad\qquad = 8$$
$$2x_1 + 3x_2 - 2x_3 + 3x_4 \qquad\qquad + x_7 \quad = 3$$
$$-x_1 \qquad\quad + x_3 + 2x_4 \qquad\qquad\qquad + x_8 = 0$$
$$x_1, x_2, \ldots, x_8 \geq 0$$

Let $x_5, x_6, \ldots$, and $x_8$ be a given initial basic feasible solution. If $x_1$ becomes basic, which of the given basic variables must become nonbasic at zero level for all the variables to remain nonnegative, and what would be the value of $x_1$ in the new solution? Repeat this procedure for $x_2, x_3$, and $x_4$.

**5. (a)** Solve the following LP *by inspection,* and justify the answer in terms of the basic solutions of the simplex method.

$$\text{Maximize } z = x_1$$

subject to

$$5x_1 + x_2 \qquad\qquad = 4$$
$$6x_1 \qquad + x_3 \qquad = 8$$
$$3x_1 \qquad\qquad + x_4 = 3$$
$$x_1, x_2, x_3, x_4, \geq 0$$

**(b)** Repeat (a) assuming that the objective function calls for minimizing $z = x_1$.

**6.** Solve the following problem *by inspection,* and justify the method of solution in terms of the basic solutions of the simplex method.

$$\text{Maximize } z = 5x_1 - 6x_2 + 3x_3 - 5x_4 + 12x_5$$

subject to

$$x_1 + 3x_2 + 5x_3 + 6x_4 + 3x_5 \leq 90$$
$$x_1, x_2, x_3, x_4, x_5 \geq 0$$

(*Hint:* A basic solution consists of one variable only.)

**7.** Consider the two-dimensional solution space in Figure 3–2

**(a)** Determine the optimum extreme point graphically assuming that the objective function is given as

$$\text{Maximize } z = 3x_1 + 6x_2$$

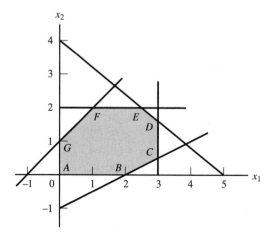

**Figure 3–2**

(b) If the simplex iterations start at point $A$, identify the path of the algorithm.

(c) Determine the entering variable, the corresponding ratios of the feasibility condition, and the change in the value of $z$, assuming that the starting iteration occurs at point $A$ and that the objective function is given as

$$\text{Maximize } z = 4x_1 + x_2$$

(d) Repeat (c), assuming that the objective function is

$$\text{Maximize } z = x_1 + 4x_2$$

**8.** Consider the three-dimensional LP solution space in Figure 3–3, whose feasible extreme points are $A, B, \ldots,$ and $J$.

(a) Which of the following pairs of extreme points are adjacent: $(A, B), (B, D), (E, H),$ and $(A, I)$?

(b) Suppose that the simplex iterations start at $A$ and that the optimum occurs at $H$. Indicate whether any of the following paths are *not* legitimate for the simplex algorithm, and state the reason.

(i) $A \rightarrow B \rightarrow G \rightarrow H$.

(ii) $A \rightarrow E \rightarrow I \rightarrow H$.

(iii) $A \rightarrow C \rightarrow E \rightarrow B \rightarrow A \rightarrow D \rightarrow H$.

**9.** For the solution space in Figure 3–3, all the constraints are of the type $\leq$ and all the variables $x_1, x_2,$ and $x_3$ are nonnegative. Suppose that $s_1, s_2, s_3,$ and $s_4$ ($\geq 0$) are the slacks associated with constraints represented by the planes $CEIJF, BEIHG, DFJHG,$ and $IJH$, respectively. Identify the basic and nonbasic variables associated with each feasible extreme point of the solution space.

**10.** Consider the solution space in Figure 3–3, where the simplex algorithm starts at point $A$. Determine the entering variable in the *first* iteration

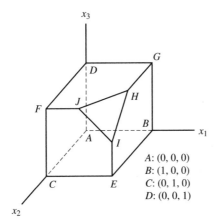

A: (0, 0, 0)
B: (1, 0, 0)
C: (0, 1, 0)
D: (0, 0, 1)

**Figure 3–3**

together with its value and the improvement in $z$ for each of the following objective functions:

(a) Maximize $z = x_1 - 2x_2 + 3x_3$.

(b) Maximize $z = 5x_1 + 2x_2 + 4x_3$.

(c) Maximize $z = -2x_1 + 7x_2 + 2x_3$.

(d) Maximize $z = x_1 + x_2 + x_3$.

**11.** Consider the following LP:

$$\text{Maximize } z = 16x_1 + 15x_2$$

subject to

$$40x_1 + 31x_2 \leq 124$$

$$-x_1 + x_2 \leq 1$$

$$x_1 \leq 3$$

$$x_1, x_2 \geq 0$$

Use TORA where appropriate to answer the following:

(a) Solve the problem by the simplex method, where the entering variable is the nonbasic variable with the *most* negative $z$-row coefficient.

(b) Resolve the problem by the simplex algorithm, always selecting the entering variable as the nonbasic variable with the *least* negative $z$-row coefficient.

(c) Compare the number of iterations in (a) and (b). Does the selection of the entering variable as the nonbasic variable with the *most* negative $z$-row coefficient lead to a smaller number of iterations? Explain the reason.

(d) Suppose that the sense of optimization is changed to minimization by multiplying $z$ by $-1$. How would this change affect the simplex iterations?

**12.** The Gutchi Company manufactures purses, shaving bags, and backpacks. The construction of the three products include leather and synthetic material, but leather seems to be the main limiting raw material. The production process requires two types of skilled labor: sewing and finishing. The following table gives the availability of the resources, their usage by the three products, and the profits per unit.

| | Resource requirements per unit | | | |
|---|---|---|---|---|
| Resource | Purse | Bag | Backpack | Daily availability |
| Leather (ft$^2$) | 2 | 1 | 3 | 42 ft$^2$ |
| Sewing (hr) | 2 | 1 | 2 | 40 hr |
| Finishing (hr) | 1 | .5 | 1 | 45 hr |
| Selling price ($) | 24 | 22 | 45 | |

Formulate the problem as a linear program, find the optimum solution using TORA, and determine the status of the resources.

## 3.4 ARTIFICIAL STARTING SOLUTION

In Example 3.3–1, starting the simplex iterations at a basic feasible solution guarantees that all the succeeding iterations will be feasible. For the LPs in which all the constraints are of the ( $\leq$ ) type (with nonnegative right-hand sides), the slacks offer a convenient starting basic feasible solution. A natural question then arises: How can we find a starting basic solution for models that involve (=) and ( $\geq$ ) constraints?

The most common procedure for starting LPs that do not have convenient slacks is to use **artificial variables**. These are variables that assume the role of slacks at the first iteration, only to be disposed of at a later iteration. Two closely related methods are proposed for effecting this result: the $M$-method and the two-phase method.

### 3.4.1 The M-Method

The $M$-method starts with the LP in the standard form. For any equation $i$ that does not have a slack, we augment an artificial variable $R_i$. Such a variable then becomes part of the starting basic solution. However, because artificials are extraneous to the LP model, we assign them a **penalty** in the objective function to force them to zero level at a later iteration of the simplex algorithm.

Given $M$ is a sufficiently large positive value, the variable $R_i$ is penalized in the objective function using $-MR_i$ in the case of maximization and $+MR_i$ in the case of minimization. Because of this penalty, the nature of the optimization process will logically attempt to drive $R_i$ to zero level during the course of the simplex iterations. The following example provides the details of the method.

**Example 3.4–1.**

$$\text{Minimize } z = 4x_1 + x_2$$

subject to

$$3x_1 + x_2 = 3$$
$$4x_1 + 3x_2 \geq 6$$
$$x_1 + 2x_2 \leq 4$$
$$x_1, x_2 \geq 0$$

The standard form is obtained by subtracting a surplus $x_3$ in the second constraint and adding a slack $x_4$ in the third constraint. We thus get

$$\text{Minimize } z = 4x_1 + x_2$$

subject to

$$3x_1 + x_2 \qquad\qquad = 3$$
$$4x_1 + 3x_2 - x_3 \qquad = 6$$
$$x_1 + 2x_2 \qquad + x_4 = 4$$
$$x_1, x_2, x_3, x_4 \geq 0$$

The first and second equations do not have variables that play the role of slacks. We thus use the artificial variables $R_1$ and $R_2$ in these two equations and penalize them in the objective function with $MR_1 + MR_2$. The resulting LP is given as

$$\text{Minimize } z = 4x_1 + x_2 + MR_1 + MR_2$$

subject to

$$3x_1 + x_2 \qquad + R_1 \qquad\qquad = 3$$
$$4x_1 + 3x_2 - x_3 \qquad + R_2 \qquad = 6$$
$$x_1 + 2x_2 \qquad\qquad\qquad + x_4 = 4$$
$$x_1, x_2, x_3, x_4, R_1, R_2, \geq 0$$

In the modified model, we can now use $R_1, R_2$, and $x_4$ as the starting basic feasible solution, as the following tableau demonstrates (for convenience, we have eliminated the $z$-column because it does not change in all the iterations).

| Basic | $x_1$ | $x_2$ | $x_3$ | $R_1$ | $R_2$ | $x_4$ | Solution |
|-------|-------|-------|-------|-------|-------|-------|----------|
| $z$ | $-4$ | $-1$ | 0 | $-M$ | $-M$ | 0 | 0 |
| $R_1$ | 3 | 1 | 0 | 1 | 0 | 0 | 3 |
| $R_2$ | 4 | 3 | $-1$ | 0 | 1 | 0 | 6 |
| $x_4$ | 1 | 2 | 0 | 0 | 0 | 1 | 4 |

Before proceeding with the simplex method computations, we need to make the $z$-row consistent with the rest of the tableau. Specifically, the value of $z$ associated with the starting basic solution $R_1 = 3$, $R_2 = 6$, and $x_4 = 4$ must be $3M + 6M + 0 = 9M$ rather than 0 as shown in the right-hand side of the $z$-row. This inconsistency stems from the fact that $R_1$ and $R_2$ have nonzero coefficients $(-M, -M)$ in the $z$-row (compare with the all-slack starting solution in Example 3.3–1, where the $z$-row coefficients of the slacks are zero). We can eliminate this inconsistency by substituting out $R_1$ and $R_2$ in the $z$-row using the appropriate constraint equations. In particular, notice the highlighted "1" elements in the $R_1$-row and the $R_2$-row. Multiplying *each* of the $R_1$-row and the $R_2$-row by $M$ and adding the *sum* to the $z$-row will in effect substitute out $R_1$ and $R_2$ in the objective row. We can summarize this step as

$$\text{New } z\text{-row} = \text{Old } z\text{-row} + M \times R_1\text{-row} + M \times R_2\text{-row}$$

This operation is applied to our example as

| | | | | | | | | |
|---|---|---|---|---|---|---|---|---|
| Old $z$-row: | $(-4$ | | $-1$ | $0$ | $-M$ | $-M$ | $0 \mid$ | $0)$ |
| $+ M \times R_1$-row: | $(3M$ | | $M$ | $0$ | $M$ | $0$ | $0 \mid$ | $3M)$ |
| $+ M \times R_2$-row: | $(4M$ | | $3M$ | $-M$ | $0$ | $M$ | $0 \mid$ | $6M)$ |
| = New $z$-row: | $(-4 + 7M$ | $-1 + 4M$ | $-M$ | $0$ | $0$ | $0 \mid$ | $9M)$ |

The modified tableau will thus become

| Basic | $x_1$ | $x_2$ | $x_3$ | $R_1$ | $R_2$ | $x_4$ | Solution |
|-------|-------|-------|-------|-------|-------|-------|----------|
| $z$ | $-4 + 7M$ | $-1 + 4M$ | $-M$ | $0$ | $0$ | $0$ | $9M$ |
| $R_1$ | $3$ | $1$ | $0$ | $1$ | $0$ | $0$ | $3$ |
| $R_2$ | $4$ | $3$ | $-1$ | $0$ | $1$ | $0$ | $6$ |
| $x_4$ | $1$ | $2$ | $0$ | $0$ | $0$ | $1$ | $4$ |

Notice that the new $z = 9M$, which is consistent now with the values of the starting basic feasible solution $R_1 = 3, R_2 = 6$, and $x_4 = 4$.

The last tableau is now ready for the application of the simplex method using the optimality and the feasibility conditions. Because we are minimizing the objective function, $x_1$, which has the most *positive* coefficient in the $z$-row ($= -4 + 7M$) is the entering variable. The ratios of the feasibility condition yield $R_1$ as the leaving variable.

Once the entering and the leaving variables have been determined, the new tableau can be computed by using the familiar Gauss-Jordan operations. Remember that in carrying out the row operations on the objective function, the expressions in $M$ must be dealt with algebraically. Thus, the new pivot row is multiplied by $-(-4 + 7M)$ and added to the current $z$-row to obtain the new objective row. The next tableau is thus given as

| Basic | $x_1$ | $x_2$ | $x_3$ | $R_1$ | $R_2$ | $x_4$ | Solution |
|-------|-------|-------|-------|-------|-------|-------|----------|
| $z$ | 0 | $\dfrac{1 + 5M}{3}$ | $-M$ | $\dfrac{4 - 7M}{3}$ | 0 | 0 | $4 + 2M$ |
| $x_1$ | 1 | $\dfrac{1}{3}$ | 0 | $\dfrac{1}{3}$ | 0 | 0 | 1 |
| $R_2$ | 0 | $\dfrac{5}{3}$ | $-1$ | $-\dfrac{4}{3}$ | 1 | 0 | 2 |
| $x_4$ | 0 | $\dfrac{5}{3}$ | 0 | $-\dfrac{1}{3}$ | 0 | 1 | 3 |

Note how the first simplex iteration forces the artificial variable $R_1$ out of the basic solution, which is consistent with the concept of penalizing these variables in the objective function.

The last tableau shows that $x_2$ and $R_2$ are the entering and leaving variables, respectively. The simplex computations must thus be continued for two more iterations to satisfy the optimality condition. The resulting optimum solution is $x_1 = \frac{2}{5}$, $x_2 = \frac{9}{5}$, $x_3 = 1$, and $z = \frac{17}{5}$ (see Problem 3.4a–1).

There are two observations regarding the use of the $M$-method.

**1.** The use of the penalty $M$ may not force the artificial variable to zero level in the final simplex iteration. If the LP problem does not have a feasible solution space (i.e., the constraints are not consistent), then the final simplex iteration will include at least one artificial variable at a positive level. This is an indication that the problem has no feasible solution.

**2.** Theoretically, the application of the $M$-technique requires $M \rightarrow \infty$. However, from the standpoint of using the computer $M$ must be finite and *sufficiently large*. How large is "sufficiently large" is an open question. Specifically, $M$ should be large enough to act as a penalty, but it should not be too large to impair the accuracy of the simplex computations. In particular, our main concern is about machine roundoff error that could result from manipulating a mixture of large and small numbers. The following example demonstrates our point.

**Example 3.4–2.**

Consider the following problem:

$$\text{Maximize } z = 0.2x_1 + 0.5x_2$$

subject to

$$3x_1 + 2x_2 \geq 6$$

$$x_1 + 2x_2 \leq 4$$

$$x_1, x_2 \geq 0$$

We will run two experiments that demonstrate the possible adverse impact of $M$ on the computations.

*Experiment 1*

Using TORA's user-guided option, apply the simplex method with $M = 10$, and then repeat it using $M = 999,999$. The first $M$ yields the correct solution $x_1 = 1$ and $x_2 = 1.5$, whereas the second gives the incorrect solution $x_1 = 4$ and $x_2 = 0$.

*Experiment 2*

Multiply the objective function by 1000 to get $z = 200x_1 + 500x_2$ and solve the problem using $M = 10$ and $M = 999,999$ and observe that the second value is the one that yields the correct solution in this case.

The conclusion from the two experiments is that the correct choice of the value of $M$ is data dependent. The unqualified theoretical requirement that requires $M$ to be selected "very large" can lead to serious roundoff error. Perhaps this is the reason the $M$-method is never implemented in commercial LP codes. Instead, the *two-phase method,* which we present in the next section, is used.

## Problem set 3.4a

1. Complete the simplex iteration of Example 3.4–1 and obtain the optimum solution.

2. In Example 3.4–1, identify the starting tableau for each of the following (independent) cases, and develop the associated $z$-row after substituting out all the artificial variables:
   **(a)** The third constraint is $x_1 + 2x_2 \geq 4$.
   **(b)** The second constraint is $4x_1 + 3x_2 \leq 6$.
   **(c)** The second constraint is $4x_1 + 3x_2 = 6$.
   **(d)** The objective function is to maximize $z = 4x_1 + x_2$.

3. Consider the following set of constraints:

$$-2x_1 + 3x_2 = 3 \qquad (1)$$
$$4x_1 + 5x_2 \geq 10 \qquad (2)$$
$$x_1 + 2x_2 \leq 5 \qquad (3)$$
$$6x_1 + 7x_2 \leq 3 \qquad (4)$$
$$4x_1 + 8x_2 \geq 5 \qquad (5)$$
$$x_1, x_2 \geq 0$$

For each of the following problems, develop the $z$-row after substituting out the artificial variables:
   **(a)** Maximize $z = 5x_1 + 6x_2$ subject to (1), (3), and (4).
   **(b)** Maximize $z = 2x_1 - 7x_2$ subject to (1), (2), (4), and (5).
   **(c)** Minimize $z = 3x_1 + 6x_2$ subject to (3), (4), and (5).
   **(d)** Minimize $z = 4x_1 + 6x_2$ subject to (1), (2), and (5).
   **(e)** Minimize $z = 3x_1 + 2x_2$ subject to (1) and (5).

4. Consider the following set of constraints:

$$x_1 + x_2 + x_3 = 7$$
$$2x_1 - 5x_2 + x_3 \geq 10$$
$$x_1, x_2, x_3 \geq 0$$

Solve the problem for each of the following objective functions:
(a) Maximize $z = 2x_1 + 3x_2 - 5x_3$.
(b) Minimize $z = 2x_1 + 3x_2 - 5x_3$.
(c) Maximize $z = x_1 + 2x_2 + x_3$.
(d) Minimize $z = 4x_1 - 8x_2 + 3x_3$.

5. Consider the problem

$$\text{Maximize } z = 2x_1 + 4x_2 + 4x_3 - 3x_4$$

subject to

$$x_1 + x_2 + x_3 = 4$$
$$x_1 + 4x_2 + x_4 = 8$$
$$x_1, x_2, x_3, x_4, \geq 0$$

Solve the problem using $x_3$ and $x_4$ for the starting basic feasible solution. Do not use any artificial variables.

6. Solve the following problem using $x_3$ and $x_4$ as starting basic feasible variables. Do not use any artificial variables.

$$\text{Minimize } z = 3x_1 + 2x_2 + 3x_3$$

subject to

$$x_1 + 4x_2 + x_3 \geq 7$$
$$2x_1 + x_2 + x_4 \geq 10$$
$$x_1, x_2, x_3, x_4, \geq 0$$

7. Consider the problem

$$\text{Maximize } z = x_1 + 5x_2 + 3x_3$$

subject to

$$x_1 + 2x_2 + x_3 = 3$$
$$2x_1 - x_2 = 4$$
$$x_1, x_2, x_3 \geq 0$$

The variable $x_3$ plays the role of a slack—hence, we do not need an artificial variable in the first constraint. However, in the second constraint, an artificial variable is needed. Use this starting solution (i.e., $x_3$ in the first constraint and $R_2$ in the second constraint) to solve this problem.

8. Show how the $M$-method will conclude that the following problem has no feasible solution.

$$\text{Maximize } z = 2x_1 + 5x_2$$

subject to

$$3x_1 + 2x_2 \geq 6$$

$$2x_1 + x_2 \leq 2$$

$$x_1, x_2 \geq 0$$

## 3.4.2 The Two-Phase Method

Example 3.4–2 demonstrates the adverse impact of the roundoff error on the accuracy of the $M$-method. The two-phase method is designed to alleviate the problem by eliminating the constant $M$ altogether. As the name suggests, the method solves the LP in two phases: Phase I attempts to find a starting basic feasible solution. If such a solution can be found, Phase II uses it to solve the original problem.

**Phase I.** Put the problem in the standard LP form, and add the necessary artificial variables to the constraints exactly as in the $M$-method to secure a starting basic solution. Next, find a basic solution of the resulting equations that *minimizes* the sum of the artificial variables. If the minimum value of the sum is positive, the LP problem has no feasible solution, which ends the solution process (recall that a positive artificial variable signifies that the corresponding original constraint is not satisfied). Otherwise, we move to Phase II.

**Phase II.** Use the feasible solution obtained in Phase I as a starting basic feasible solution for the *original* problem.

---

**Example 3.4–3.** We use the same problem in Example 3.4–1.
   *Phase I*

$$\text{Minimize } r = R_1 + R_2$$

subject to

$$3x_1 + x_2 \qquad + R_1 \qquad\qquad = 3$$

$$4x_1 + 3x_2 - x_3 \qquad + R_2 \qquad = 6$$

$$x_1 + 2x_2 \qquad\qquad\qquad + x_4 = 4$$

$$x_1, x_2, x_3, x_4, R_1, R_2 \geq 0$$

The associated tableau is given as

| Basic | $x_1$ | $x_2$ | $x_3$ | $R_1$ | $R_2$ | $x_4$ | Solution |
|-------|-------|-------|-------|-------|-------|-------|----------|
| $r$ | 0 | 0 | 0 | $-1$ | $-1$ | 0 | 0 |
| $R_1$ | 3 | 1 | 0 | 1 | 0 | 0 | 3 |
| $R_2$ | 4 | 3 | $-1$ | 0 | 1 | 0 | 6 |
| $x_4$ | 1 | 2 | 0 | 0 | 0 | 1 | 4 |

As in the *M*-method, $R_1$ and $R_2$ are substituted out in the *r*-row by using the following computations:

$$
\begin{array}{llrrrrrr}
\text{Old } r\text{-row:} & (0 & 0 & 0 & -1 & -1 & 0 & |\ \ 0) \\
+\ 1 \times R_1\text{-row:} & (3 & 1 & 0 & 1 & 0 & 0 & |\ \ 3) \\
+\ 1 \times R_2\text{-row:} & (4 & 3 & -1 & 0 & 1 & 0 & |\ \ 6) \\
=\ \text{New } r\text{-row:} & (7 & 4 & -1 & 0 & 0 & 0 & |\ \ 9)
\end{array}
$$

The new *r*-row

$$r + 7x_1 + 4x_2 - x_3 + 0R_1 + 0R_2 + 0x_4 = 9$$

is used now to solve Phase I of the problem, which yields the following optimum tableau (verify!):

| Basic | $x_1$ | $x_2$ | $x_3$ | $R_1$ | $R_2$ | $x_4$ | Solution |
|-------|-------|-------|-------|-------|-------|-------|----------|
| $r$ | 0 | 0 | 0 | $-1$ | $-1$ | 0 | 0 |
| $x_1$ | 1 | 0 | $\frac{1}{5}$ | $\frac{3}{5}$ | $-\frac{1}{5}$ | 0 | $\frac{3}{5}$ |
| $x_2$ | 0 | 1 | $-\frac{3}{5}$ | $-\frac{4}{5}$ | $\frac{3}{5}$ | 0 | $\frac{6}{5}$ |
| $x_4$ | 0 | 0 | 1 | 1 | $-1$ | 1 | 1 |

Because minimum $r = 0$, Phase I produces the basic feasible solution $x_1 = \frac{3}{5}$, $x_2 = \frac{6}{5}$, and $x_4 = 1$. At this point, the artificial variables have completed their mission, and we can eliminate their columns altogether from the tableau and move to Phase II.
*Phase II*
After deleting the artificial columns, the *original* problem is written as

$$\text{Minimize } z = 4x_1 + x_2$$

subject to

$$x_1 + \frac{1}{5}x_3 = \frac{3}{5}$$

$$x_2 - \frac{3}{5}x_3 = \frac{6}{5}$$

$$x_3 + x_4 = 1$$

$$x_1, x_2, x_3, x_4 \geq 0$$

Essentially, Phase I is a procedure that transforms the original constraint equations in a manner that provides a starting basic feasible solution for the problem. The tableau associated with Phase II problem is thus given as

| Basic | $x_1$ | $x_2$ | $x_3$ | $x_4$ | Solution |
|-------|-------|-------|-------|-------|----------|
| $z$ | $-4$ | $-1$ | $0$ | $0$ | $0$ |
| $x_1$ | $1$ | $0$ | $\frac{1}{5}$ | $0$ | $\frac{3}{5}$ |
| $x_2$ | $0$ | $1$ | $-\frac{3}{5}$ | $0$ | $\frac{6}{5}$ |
| $x_4$ | $0$ | $0$ | $1$ | $1$ | $1$ |

Again, because the basic variables $x_1$ and $x_2$ have nonzero coefficients in the $z$-row, they must be substituted out. The computation for modifying the $z$-row are

$$
\begin{array}{lrrrrrr}
\text{Old } z\text{-row:} & (-4 & -1 & 0 & 0 & | & 0) \\
+\, 4 \times x_1\text{-row:} & (4 & 0 & \frac{4}{5} & 0 & | & \frac{12}{5}) \\
+\, 1 \times x_2\text{-row:} & (0 & 1 & -\frac{3}{5} & 0 & | & \frac{6}{5}) \\
=\text{ New } z\text{-row:} & (0 & 0 & \frac{1}{5} & 0 & | & \frac{18}{5})
\end{array}
$$

The initial tableau of Phase II is thus given as

| Basic | $x_1$ | $x_2$ | $x_3$ | $x_4$ | Solution |
|-------|-------|-------|-------|-------|----------|
| $z$ | $0$ | $0$ | $\frac{1}{5}$ | $0$ | $\frac{18}{5}$ |
| $x_1$ | $1$ | $0$ | $\frac{1}{5}$ | $0$ | $\frac{3}{5}$ |
| $x_2$ | $0$ | $1$ | $-\frac{3}{5}$ | $0$ | $\frac{6}{5}$ |
| $x_4$ | $0$ | $0$ | $1$ | $1$ | $1$ |

Because we are minimizing, $x_3$ must enter the solution. Application of the simplex method computations will produce the optimum in one iteration (verify!).

The removal of the artificial variables at the end of Phase I is effected only when they are all *nonbasic* (as Example 3.4–2 illustrates). It is possible, however, that artificial variables may remain *basic* but at *zero* level at the end of Phase I. In this case, such variables, by necessity, form part of the Phase II starting basic solution. As such, the computations in Phase II must be modified to ensure that an artificial variable never becomes positive during Phase II iterations.

The rule for guaranteeing that a *zero* basic artificial variable never becomes positive during Phase II is simple. If in the pivot column, the constraint coefficient corresponding to the zero basic artificial variable is positive, it will define the *pivot element* automatically (because it corresponds to the minimum ratio of zero), and the artificial variable will become nonbasic in the next iteration. If the pivot element is zero, the next iteration will leave the artificial variable unchanged at zero level. That leaves us with the case of a negative pivot element. In this case, the minimum ratio will not be associated with the basic (zero) artificial variable. If the resulting minimum ratio happens to be positive, then the artificial variable will assume a positive value in the next iteration (do you see why?). To prevent this from happening, we *force* the artificial variable to leave the solution anyway. Because the artificial variable is at zero level, its removal from the basic solution should not affect the feasibility of the remaining basic variables. (You will find it helpful to summarize the three cases by using the tableau format.)

To summarize, the rule for Phase II calls for forcing the artificial variable to leave the basic solution any time its constraint coefficient in the pivot column is positive or negative. As a matter of fact, this rule can be applied at the end of Phase I to remove zero artificial variables from the basic solution before we ever start with Phase II (see Problem 3.4b–5).

### Problem set 3.4b

1. **(a)** In Phase I, why is the sum of the artificial variables always minimized?
   **(b)** If the LP is of the maximization type, do we maximize the sum of the artificial variables in Phase I?

2. For each case in Problem 3.4a–3, write the corresponding Phase I objective function.

3. Solve Problem 3.4a–4 by the two-phase method.

4. Write Phase I for the following problem, and then solve with TORA to show that the problem has no feasible solution.

$$\text{Maximize } z = 2x_1 + 5x_2$$

subject to

$$3x_1 + 2x_2 \geq 6$$
$$2x_1 + x_2 \leq 2$$
$$x_1, x_2 \geq 0$$

5. Consider the following problem:

$$\text{Maximize } z = 3x_1 + 2x_2 + 3x_3$$

subject to

$$2x_1 + x_2 + x_3 \leq 2$$
$$3x_1 + 4x_2 + 2x_3 \geq 8$$
$$x_1, x_2, x_3 \geq 0$$

**(a)** Use TORA to show that Phase I will terminate with a zero artificial basic variable.

**(b)** Use hand computations to carry out Phase II with the zero-artificial variable as part of the starting basic solution. Make sure that the artificial variables never assume positive values.

**(c)** Show that the zero-artificial variable can be driven out of the optimum basic solution of Phase I (before we start Phase II) by selecting an entering variable with a *nonzero* pivot element in the artificial variable row. Then carry out Phase II using the new basic solution.

**6.** Consider the following problem:

$$\text{Maximize } z = 3x_1 + 2x_2 + 3x_3$$

subject to

$$2x_1 + x_2 + x_3 = 2$$

$$x_1 + 3x_2 + x_3 = 6$$

$$3x_1 + 4x_2 + 2x_3 = 8$$

$$x_1, x_2, x_3 \geq 0$$

**(a)** Use TORA to show that Phase I terminates with two zero-artificial variables in the basic solution.

**(b)** Show that when the procedure of Problem 5(c) is applied at the end of Phase I, only one of the two zero-artificial variables can be made nonbasic.

**(c)** Show that the original constraint associated with the zero-artificial variable that cannot be made nonbasic in (b) must be redundant—hence, its row as well as the artificial variable itself can be dropped altogether at the start of Phase II.

**7.** Consider the following LP:

$$\text{Maximize } z = 3x_1 + 2x_2 + 3x_3$$

subject to

$$2x_1 + x_2 + x_3 \leq 2$$

$$3x_1 + 4x_2 + 2x_3 \geq 8$$

$$x_1, x_2, x_3 \geq 0$$

The optimal simplex tableau at the end of Phase I is given as

| Basic | $x_1$ | $x_2$ | $x_3$ | $x_4$ | $x_5$ | $R$ | Solution |
|-------|-------|-------|-------|-------|-------|-----|----------|
| $z$   | $-5$  | 0     | $-2$  | $-1$  | $-4$  | 0   | 0        |
| $x_2$ | 2     | 1     | 1     | 0     | 1     | 0   | 2        |
| $R$   | $-5$  | 0     | $-2$  | $-1$  | $-4$  | 1   | 0        |

Show that the nonbasic variables $x_1, x_3, x_4,$ and $x_5$ can never assume positive values at the end of Phase II. Hence, their columns can dropped before we start Phase II. In essence, the removal of these variables reduces the constraint equations of the problem to $x_2 = 2$. This means that it will not be necessary to carry out Phase II at all because the solution space is reduced to one point only.

The general conclusion from this problem is that any nonbasic variables that have *strictly negative* $z$-row coefficients at the end of Phase I must be dropped from the tableau as they can never assume positive values at the end of Phase II. Incidentally, negative $z$-row coefficients for nonartificial variables can only occur if an artificial variable is basic (at zero level) at the end of Phase I.

**8.** Consider the LP model

$$\text{Minimize } z = 2x_1 - 4x_2 + 3x_3$$

subject to

$$5x_1 - 6x_2 + 2x_3 \geq 5$$

$$-x_1 + 3x_2 + 5x_3 \geq 8$$

$$2x_1 + 5x_2 - 4x_3 \geq 4$$

$$x_1, x_2, x_3 \geq 0$$

Show how the inequalities can be modified to a set of equations that requires the use of single artificial variable only (instead of two).

## 3.5 SPECIAL CASES IN SIMPLEX METHOD APPLICATION

This section considers four special cases that arise in the application of the simplex method.

**1.** Degeneracy
**2.** Alternative optima
**3.** Unbounded solutions
**4.** Nonexisting (or infeasible) solutions

Our interest in studying these special cases is twofold: (1) to present a *theoretical* explanation for the reason these situations arise and (2) to provide a *practical* interpretation of what these special results could mean in a real-life problem.

### 3.5.1 Degeneracy

In the application of the feasibility condition of the simplex method a tie for the minimum ration may be broken arbitrarily for the purpose of determining the leaving variable. When this happens, one or more of the *basic* variables will be zero in the next iteration. In this case, the new solution is **degenerate**.

There is nothing alarming about dealing with a degenerate solution, with the exception of a small theoretical inconvenience, which we shall discuss shortly. From the practical standpoint, the condition reveals that the model has at least one *redundant* constraint. To be able to provide more insight into the practical and theoretical impacts of degeneracy, we consider a numeric example. The graphical illustration should enhance the understanding of ideas underlying this special situation.

**Example 3.5-1 (DEGENERATE OPTIMAL SOLUTION).**

$$\text{Maximize } z = 3x_1 + 9x_2$$

subject to

$$x_1 + 4x_2 \le 8$$

$$x_1 + 2x_2 \le 4$$

$$x_1, x_2 \ge 0$$

Let $x_3$ and $x_4$ be slack variables. The simplex iterations are given in the following tableux.

| Iteration | Basic | $x_1$ | $x_2$ | $x_3$ | $x_4$ | Solution |
|---|---|---|---|---|---|---|
| 0 | $z$ | $-3$ | $-9$ | 0 | 0 | 0 |
| $x_2$ enters | $x_3$ | 1 | 4 | 1 | 0 | 8 |
| $x_3$ leaves | $x_4$ | 1 | 2 | 0 | 1 | 4 |
| 1 | $z$ | $-\frac{3}{4}$ | 0 | $\frac{9}{4}$ | 0 | 18 |
| $x_1$ enters | $x_2$ | $\frac{1}{4}$ | 1 | $\frac{1}{4}$ | 0 | 2 |
| $x_4$ leaves | $x_4$ | $\frac{1}{2}$ | 0 | $-\frac{1}{2}$ | 1 | 0 |
| 2 | $z$ | 0 | 0 | $\frac{3}{2}$ | $\frac{3}{2}$ | 18 |
| (optimum) | $x_2$ | 0 | 1 | $\frac{1}{2}$ | $-\frac{1}{2}$ | 2 |
| | $x_1$ | 1 | 0 | $-1$ | 2 | 0 |

In the starting iteration, $x_3$ and $x_4$ tie for the leaving variable. This is the reason the basic variable $x_4$ has a zero value in iteration 1, thus resulting in a degenerate basic solution. The optimum is reached after an additional iteration is carried out.

What is the practical implication of degeneracy? Look at Figure 3-4, which provides the graphical solution to the model. Three lines pass through the optimum $x_1 = 0$, $x_2 = 2$. Because this is a two-dimensional problem, the point is *overdetermined* and one of the constraints is redundant. In practice, the mere knowledge that some resources are superfluous can prove valuable during the implementation of the solution. The in-

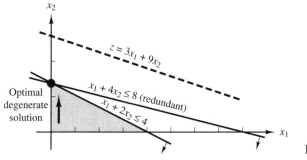

**Figure 3–4**

formation may also lead to discovering irregularities in the construction of the model. Unfortunately, there are no reliable techniques for identifying redundant constraints directly from the tableau.

From the theoretical standpoint, degeneracy has two implications. The first deals with the phenomenon of **cycling** or **circling**. If you look at iterations 1 and 2 in the tableaux, you will find that the objective value has not improved ($z = 18$). It is thus conceivable that the simplex procedure would repeat the *same sequence* of iterations, never improving the objective value and never terminating the computations. Although there are methods for eliminating cycling, these methods could lead to a drastic slowdown in computations. For this reason, most LP codes do not include provisions for cycling, relying on the fact that the percentage of such problems is too small to warrant a routine implementation of the cycling procedures.

The second theoretical point arises in the examination of iterations 1 and 2. Both iterations, although differing in classifying the variables as basic and nonbasic, yield identical values of all the variables and objective value, namely,

$$x_1 = 0, \quad x_2 = 2, \quad x_3 = 0, \quad x_4 = 0, \quad z = 18$$

Is it possible then to stop the computations at iteration 1 (when degeneracy first appears), even though it is not optimum? The answer is no, because the solution may be *temporarily* degenerate (see Problem 3.5a–2).

---

### Problem set 3.5a

1. Consider the graphical solution space in Figure 3–5. Suppose that the simplex iterations start at $A$ and that the optimum solution occurs at $D$ and that the objective function is defined such that at $A$, $x_1$ enters the solution first.
   **(a)** Identify (on the graph) the extreme points that define the simplex method path to the optimum point.
   **(b)** Determine the maximum possible number of simplex iterations needed to reach the optimum solution.

2. Show (both graphically and by the simplex method) that the following LP is *temporarily* degenerate.

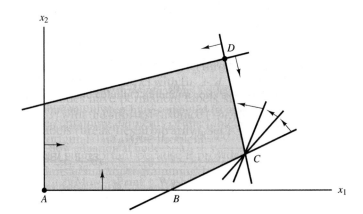

**Figure 3–5**

$$\text{Maximize } z = 3x_1 + 2x_2$$

subject to

$$4x_1 + 3x_2 \leq 12$$

$$4x_1 + x_2 \leq 8$$

$$4x_1 - x_2 \leq 8$$

$$x_1, x_2 \geq 0$$

3. Use TORA's interactive option to "thumb" through the successive simplex iteration of the following LP (developed by E. M. Beale). The starting all-slack basic feasible solution will reappear identically in iteration 7. The example illustrates the occurrence of *cycling* in the simplex iterations and the possibility of the simplex algorithm never converging to the optimum solution.

$$\text{Maximize } z = \frac{3}{4}x_1 - 20x_2 + \frac{1}{2}x_3 - 6x_4$$

subject to

$$\frac{1}{4}x_1 - 8x_2 - x_3 + 9x_4 \leq 0$$

$$\frac{1}{2}x_1 - 12x_2 - \frac{1}{2}x_3 + 3x_4 \leq 0$$

$$x_3 \leq 1$$

$$x_1, x_2, x_3, x_4 \geq 0$$

It is interesting that if all the coefficients in this LP are converted to integer values (by using proper multiples), then the simplex algorithm will reach the optimum in a finite number of iterations (try it!).

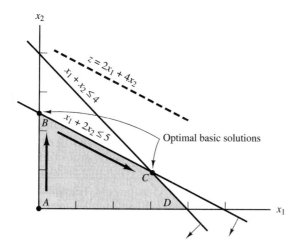

**Figure 3–6**

*(Warning:* Do not use TORA's automated option; otherwise, as expected, the iterations will cycle indefinitely.)

### 3.5.2 Alternative Optima

When the objective function is parallel to a *binding* constraint (i.e., a constraint that is satisfied as an equation by the optimal solution), the objective function will assume the *same optimal value* at more than one solution point. For this reason they are called **alternative optima.** The next example shows that there is an *infinity* of such solutions. The example also demonstrates the practical significance of encountering alternative optima.

---

**Example 3.5-2 (INFINITY OF SOLUTIONS).**

$$\text{Maximize } z = 2x_1 + 4x_2$$

subject to

$$x_1 + 2x_2 \le 5$$

$$x_1 + x_2 \le 4$$

$$x_1, x_2 \ge 0$$

Figure 3-6 demonstrates how alternative optima can arise in the LP model when the objective function is parallel to a binding constraint. Any point on the *line segment BC* represents an alternative optimum with the same objective value $z = 10$.

The iterations of the model are given by the following tableaux.

| Iteration | Basic | $x_1$ | $x_2$ | $x_3$ | $x_4$ | Solution |
|-----------|-------|-------|-------|-------|-------|----------|
| 0 | $z$ | $-2$ | $-4$ | 0 | 0 | 0 |
| $x_2$ enters | $x_3$ | 1 | 2 | 1 | 0 | 5 |
| $x_3$ leaves | $x_4$ | 1 | 1 | 0 | 1 | 4 |
| 1 (optimum) | $z$ | 0 | 0 | 2 | 0 | 10 |
| $x_1$ enters | $x_2$ | $\frac{1}{2}$ | 1 | $\frac{1}{2}$ | 0 | $\frac{5}{2}$ |
| $x_4$ leaves | $x_4$ | $\frac{1}{2}$ | 0 | $-\frac{1}{2}$ | 1 | $\frac{3}{2}$ |
| 2 | $z$ | 0 | 0 | 2 | 0 | 10 |
| (alternative | $x_2$ | 0 | 1 | 1 | $-1$ | 1 |
| optimum) | $x_1$ | 1 | 0 | $-1$ | 2 | 3 |

Iteration 1 gives the optimum $x_1 = 0, x_2 = \frac{5}{2}$, and $z = 10$, which coincides with point $B$ in Figure 3-6. How do we know from this tableau that the alternative optima exist? Look at the coefficients of the *non*basic variables in the $z$-equation of iteration 1. The coefficient of nonbasic $x_1$ is zero, indicating that $x_1$ can enter the basic solution without changing the value of $z$, but causing a change in the values of the variables. Iteration 2 does just that—letting $x_1$ enter the basic solution, which will force $x_4$ to leave. This results in the new solution point at $C(x_1 = 3, x_2 = 1, z = 10)$.

The simplex method determines only the two corner points $B$ and $C$. Mathematically, we can determine all the points $(\hat{x}_1, \hat{x}_2)$ on the line segment $BC$ as a nonnegative weighted average of the points $B$ and $C$. Thus, given $0 \le \alpha \le 1$ and

$$B: \ x_1 = 0, \quad x_2 = \frac{5}{2}$$

$$C: \ x_1 = 3, \quad x_2 = 1$$

then all the points on the line segment $BC$ are given by

$$\hat{x}_1 = \alpha(0) + (1 + \alpha)(3) = 3 - 3\alpha$$

$$\hat{x}_2 = \alpha\left(\frac{5}{2}\right) + (1 - \alpha)(1) = 1 + \frac{3}{2}\alpha$$

When $\alpha = 0$, $(\hat{x}_1, \hat{x}_2) = (3, 1)$, which is point $C$. When $\alpha = 1$, $(\hat{x}_1, \hat{x}_2) = (0, \frac{5}{2})$, which is point $B$. For values of $\alpha$ between 0 and 1, $(\hat{x}_1, \hat{x}_2)$ lies between $B$ and $C$.

In practice, alternative optima are useful because they allow us to choose from many solutions without experiencing any deterioration in the objective value. In the example, for instance, the solution at $B$ shows that activity 2 only is at a positive level, whereas at $C$ both activities are positive. If the example represents a product-mix situation, it may be advantageous from the standpoint of sales competition to produce two products rather than one. In this case, the solution at $C$ is recommended.

**Problem set 3.5b**

1. For the following LP, find three alternative optimal basic solutions, and then write a general expression for all the nonbasic alternative optima constituting these three basic solutions.

$$\text{Maximize } z = x_1 + 2x_2 + 3x_3$$

subject to

$$x_1 + 2x_2 + 3x_3 \le 10$$
$$x_1 + x_2 \qquad \le 5$$
$$x_1 \qquad\qquad \le 1$$
$$x_1, x_2, x_3 \ge 0$$

2. Show that all the alternative optima of the following LP are all nonbasic. Give a two-dimensional graphical demonstration of the type of solution space and objective function that will produce this result.

$$\text{Maximize } z = 2x_1 - x_2 + 3x_3$$

subject to

$$x_1 - x_2 + 5x_3 \le 10$$
$$2x_1 - x_2 + 3x_3 \le 40$$
$$x_1, x_2, x_3 \ge 0$$

3. For the following LP, show that the optimal solution is degenerate and that there exist alternative solutions that are all nonbasic.

$$\text{Maximize } z = 3x_1 + x_2$$

subject to

$$x_1 + 2x_2 \qquad \le 5$$
$$x_1 + x_2 - x_3 \le 2$$
$$7x_1 + 3x_2 - 5x_3 \le 20$$
$$x_1, x_2, x_3 \ge 0$$

### 3.5.3 Unbounded Solution

In some LP models, the values of the variables may be increased indefinitely without violating any of the constraints, meaning that the solution space is **unbounded** in at least one direction. As a result, the objective value may increase (maximization case) or decrease (minimization case) indefinitely. In this case, both the solution space and the optimum objective value are unbounded.

Unboundedness in a model can point to one thing only: The model is poorly constructed. The most likely irregularities in such models are that one or more nonredundant constraints are not accounted for, and the parameters (constants) of some constraints are not estimated correctly.

The following examples show how unboundedness, both in the solution space and the objective value, can be recognized in the simplex tableau.

---

**Example 3.5-3 (UNBOUNDED OBJECTIVE VALUE).**

$$\text{Maximize } z = 2x_1 + x_2$$

subject to

$$x_1 - x_2 \le 10$$

$$2x_1 \quad\quad \le 40$$

$$x_1, x_2 \ge 0$$

## Starting Iteration.

| Basic | $x_1$ | $x_2$ | $x_3$ | $x_4$ | Solution |
|-------|-------|-------|-------|-------|----------|
| $z$   | $-2$  | $-1$  | 0     | 0     | 0        |
| $x_3$ | 1     | $-1$  | 1     | 0     | 10       |
| $x_4$ | 2     | 0     | 0     | 1     | 40       |

In the starting tableau, both $x_1$ and $x_2$ are candidates for entering the solution. Because $x_1$ has the most negative coefficient, it is normally selected as the entering variable. However, *all* the *constraint* coefficients under $x_2$ are *negative* or *zero*, meaning that $x_2$ can be increased indefinitely without violating any of the constraints. Because each unit increase in $x_2$ will increase $z$ by 1, an infinite increase in $x_2$ will also result in an infinite increase in $z$. Thus, the problem has no bounded solution. This result can be seen in Figure 3-7. The solution space is unbounded in the direction of $x_2$, and the value of $z$ can be increased indefinitely.

---

The rule for recognizing unboundedness is as follows. If at any iteration the constraint coefficients of any *nonbasic* variable are nonpositive, then the *solution space* is unbounded in that direction. If, in addition, the objective coefficient of that variable is negative in the case of maximization or positive in the case of minimization, then the *objective value* also is unbounded.

### Problem set 3.5c

1. In Example 3.5–3, show that if, according to the optimality condition, we start with $x_1$ as the entering variable, then the simplex algorithm will lead eventually to an unbounded solution.

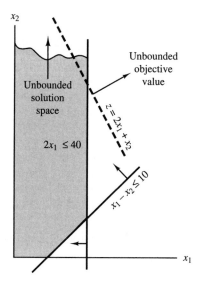

**Figure 3–7**

2. Consider the LP:

$$\text{Maximize } z = 20x_1 + 10x_2 + x_3$$

subject to

$$3x_1 - 3x_2 + 5x_3 \le 50$$
$$x_1 \quad + \quad x_3 \le 10$$
$$x_1 - \quad x_2 + 4x_3 \le 20$$
$$x_1, x_2, x_3 \ge 0$$

(a) By inspecting the constraints, determine the direction ($x_1$, $x_2$, or $x_3$) in which the solution space is unbounded.

(b) Without further computations, what can you conclude regarding the optimum objective value?

3. In some ill-constructed LP models, the solution space may be unbounded even though the problem may have a bounded objective value. Such an occurrence can point only to irregularities in the construction of the model. In large problems, it may be difficult to detect the existence of unboundedness by inspection. Devise a procedure for determining whether or not a solution space is unbounded, and apply it to the following model:

$$\text{Maximize } z = 40x_1 + 20x_2 + 2x_3$$

subject to

$$3x_1 - 3x_2 + 5x_3 \leq 50$$

$$x_1 \qquad + x_3 \leq 10$$

$$x_1 - x_2 + 4x_3 \leq 2$$

$$x_1, x_2, x_3 \geq 0$$

### 3.5.4 Infeasible Solution

If the constraints are not satisfied simultaneously, the model has no feasible solution. This situation can never occur if *all* the constraints are of the type $\leq$ (assuming non-negative right-hand-side constants), because the slacks provide a *feasible* solution. For other types of constraints, we use artificial variables. Although the artificials are penalized to force them to zero at the optimum, this can occur only if the model has a feasible space. Otherwise, at least one artificial variable will be *positive* in the optimum iteration.

From the practical standpoint, an infeasible space points to the possibility that the model is not formulated correctly.

---

**Example 3.5-4 (INFEASIBLE SOLUTION SPACE).**

$$\text{Maximize } z = 3x_1 + 2x_2$$

subject to

$$2x_1 + x_2 \leq 2$$

$$3x_1 + 4x_2 \geq 12$$

$$x_1, x_2 \geq 0$$

The following tableaux provides the simplex iterations of the model.

| Iteration | Basic | $x_1$ | $x_2$ | $x_4$ | $x_3$ | $R$ | Solution |
|-----------|-------|-------|-------|-------|-------|-----|----------|
| 0 | $z$ | $-3 - 3M$ | $-2 - 4M$ | $M$ | $0$ | $0$ | $-12M$ |
| $x_2$ enters | $x_3$ | $2$ | $1$ | $0$ | $1$ | $0$ | $2$ |
| $x_3$ leaves | $R$ | $3$ | $4$ | $-1$ | $0$ | $1$ | $12$ |
| 1 | $z$ | $1 + 5M$ | $0$ | $M$ | $2 + 4M$ | $0$ | $4 - 4M$ |
| (pseudo- | $x_2$ | $2$ | $1$ | $0$ | $1$ | $0$ | $2$ |
| optimum) | $R$ | $-5$ | $0$ | $-1$ | $-4$ | $1$ | $4$ |

Optimum iteration 1 shows that the artificial variable $R$ is *positive* ($= 4$) which indicates that the problem is infeasible. Figure 3-8 demonstrates the infeasible solution space. The simplex method, by allowing the artificial variable to be positive, in essence has reversed the direction of the inequality from $3x_1 + 4x_2 \geq 12$ to $3x_1 + 4x_2 \leq 12$. (Can you explain how?) The result is what we may call a **pseudo-optimal solution.**

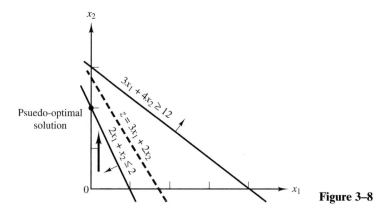

**Figure 3–8**

## Problem set 3.5d

**1.** Toolco produces three types of tools, $T1$, $T2$, and $T3$. The tools use two raw materials, $M1$ and $M2$, according to the data in the following table:

| Raw material | Number of units of raw materials per tool | | |
|---|---|---|---|
| | $T1$ | $T2$ | $T3$ |
| $M1$ | 3 | 5 | 6 |
| $M2$ | 5 | 3 | 4 |

The daily availability of raw materials is 1000 units and 1200 units, respectively. The manager in charge of production was informed by the marketing department that according to their research, the daily demand for all three tools must be at least 500 units. Would the manufacturing department be able to satisfy the demand? If not, what is the most Toolco can provide of the three tools?

**2.** Consider the LP model

$$\text{Maximize } z = 3x_1 + 2x_2 + 3x_3$$

$$2x_1 + x_2 + x_3 \le 2$$

$$3x_1 + 4x_2 + 2x_3 \ge 8$$

$$x_1, x_2, x_3 \ge 0$$

Show by the $M$-technique that the optimal solution includes an artificial basic variable. However, because its value is zero, the problem has a *feasible* optimal solution.

## 3.6 SUMMARY

The simplex method is based on the fundamental theory that the optimum solution of a linear program is associated with an extreme point and that extreme points are completely defined by the basic solutions of the standard form of the LP model. The use of artificial methods to find a starting solution for the model are designed to automate the simplex method for the computer. The chapter discusses the theoretical and practical implications of the special cases of degeneracy, alternative optimal, unboundedness, and infeasibility.

## SELECTED REFERENCES

BAZARAA, M., J. JARVIS, and H. SHERALI, *Linear Programming and Network Flows,* 2nd ed., Wiley, New York, 1990.

DANTZIG, G., *Linear Programming and Extensions,* Princeton University Press, Princeton, N.J., 1963.

NERING, E., and A. TUCKER, *Linear Programming and Related Problems,* Academic Press, Boston, 1992.

TAHA, H., "Linear Programming," Chapter II–1 in *Handbook of Operations Research,* J. Moder and S. Elmaghraby (eds.), Van Nostrand Reinhold, New York, 1978.

## COMPREHENSIVE PROBLEMS

■ **3–1** A small canning company produces five types of canned goods that are extracted from three types of fresh fruit. The manufacturing process uses two production departments that were originally designed with surplus capacities to accommodate possible future expansion. In fact, the company operates currently on a one-shift basis and can easily expand to two or three shifts to meet increase in demand. The real restriction for the time being appears to be the limited availability of fresh fruit. Because of the limited refrigeration capacity on the company's premises, fresh fruit must be brought in daily.

A young operations researcher has just joined the company. After analyzing the production situation, the analyst decided to formulate a master LP model for the plant. The model involves five decision variables (for the five products) and three constraints (for the raw materials). With three constraints and five variables, LP theory says that the optimum solution cannot include more than three products. "Aha," the analyst says, "the company is not operating optimally!"

The analyst schedules a meeting with the plant manager to discuss the details of the LP model. The manager, who seems to follow the modeling concept well, agrees with the analyst that the model is a close representation of reality.

The analyst then goes on to explain that, according to LP theory, the optimal product should not exceed three because the model has only three constraints. As such, it may be worthwhile to consider discontinuing the two nonprofitable products.

The manager listens attentively, then tells the analyst that the company is committed to producing all five products because of the competitive nature of the market and that, in no way, can the company discontinue any of the products. The operations research snaps back by saying that the only way for remedying the situation is to add at least two more constraints, in which case the optimal LP model will most likely include all five products.

At this point, the manager gets confused because the idea of having to add more restrictions to be able to produce more products does not suggest optimality. "That is what the LP theory says" is the answer the manager gets from the analyst.

What is your opinion of this "paradox"?

■ **3-2**[1] An LTL trucking company, specializing in less-than-truck-Load shipments, operates a number of terminals that are strategically located across the U.S. When the loads arrive at a terminal, they are sorted either for delivery to local customers or for transfer to other terminals. The terminal docks are staffed by *bid* and *casual* workers. *Bid* workers are union employees who are guaranteed a 40-hour work-week. A bid employee assigned to one of the standard three shifts of the day is expected to work the same shift for five consecutive days, but may start on any day of the week. *Casual* employees are hired temporarily for any number of hours to account for peak loads that may exceed the work capacity of available bid workers. Union contract restricts casual employees to less than 40 hours per week.

Loads arrive at the terminal at all hours of the day and, for all practical purposes, their level varies continuously with the time of the day. A study of historical data shows that the load level takes on a repetitive weekly pattern that peaks during the weekend (Friday through Sunday). The company's policy specifies that a load must be processed within 16 hours of its arrival at the terminal.

Develop a model to determine the weekly assignment of bid workers and the hiring of casual employees.

[1]Based on a study conducted by the author for a national LTL trucking company.

# Chapter 4

# Duality and Sensitivity Analysis

## 4.1 INTRODUCTION

The optimal solution of a linear programming problem represents a snapshot of the conditions that prevail at the time the model is formulated. In the real world, decision environments rarely remain static, and it is essential to equip LP with the capability to determine changes in the optimal solution that result from making changes in the parameters of the model. This is what *sensitivity analysis* does. It provides efficient computational techniques that allow us to study the dynamic behavior of the optimal solution.

We have already dealt with the topic of sensitivity analysis at an elementary level in Section 2.4. In this chapter, we present an algebraic treatment of the topic based on the use of *duality theory*.

Sensitivity analysis deals with making *discrete* changes in the parameters of the model. A generalization of this situation is the case in which the parameters change according to predetermined *continuous* functions. The technique, called *parametric programming,* will be presented in Section 7.7.

## 4.2. DEFINITION OF THE DUAL PROBLEM

The LP model we develop for a situation is referred to as the **primal** problem. The **dual** problem is a closely related mathematical definition that can be derived directly from the primal problem. This section provides the mathematical details of the dual model.

In most LP treatments, the dual is defined for various forms of the primal depending on the sense of optimization (maximization or minimization), the types of the constraints ($\leq$, $\geq$, and $=$), and the sign of the variables (nonnegative or unrestricted). This type of treatment may be confusing (see Problem 4.2a–7). In this book, we present a *single* definition that automatically subsumes *all* the forms of the primal. The definition assumes that the primal problem is expressed in the *standard form* (Section 3.2), which is defined as

$$\text{Maximize or minimize } z = \sum_{j=1}^{n} c_j x_j$$

subject to

$$\sum_{j=1}^{n} a_{ij} x_j = b_i, \quad i = 1, 2, \ldots, m$$

$$x_j \geq 0, \quad j = 1, 2, \ldots, n$$

The variables $x_j, j = 1, 2, \ldots, n$, include the surplus and slacks, if any. The standard form has three properties.

**1.** All the constraints are equations (with nonnegative right-hand side).
**2.** All the variables are nonnegative.
**3.** The sense of optimization may be maximization of minimization.

Remember that the standard form is always used to produce the starting tableau of the simplex method and that the solution of the dual problem can be obtained directly from the optimal primal simplex tableau, as will be shown in Section 4.3. Thus, by defining the dual from the standard primal, we automatically obtain a dual solution that is consistent with the simplex method computations.

The variables and constraints of the dual problem can be constructed symmetrically from the primal problem as follows:

**1.** A dual variable is defined for each of the $m$ primal constraint equations.
**2.** A dual constraint is defined for each primal of the $n$ primal variables.
**3.** The left-hand–side coefficients of the dual constraint equal the constraint (column) coefficients of the associated primal variable. Its right-hand side equals the objective coefficient of the same primal variable.
**4.** The objective coefficients of the dual equal the right-hand side of the primal constraint equations.

Table 4–1 summarizes this information pictorially with $y_1, y_2, \ldots,$ and $y_m$ representing the dual variables.

The rules for determining the sense of optimization, the type of the constraint, and the sign of the variables in the dual problem are summarized in Table 4–2. The following examples demonstrate the implementation of these rules.

**TABLE 4–1**

|  | Primal variables | | | | | | |
|---|---|---|---|---|---|---|---|
|  | $x_1$ | $x_2$ | $\ldots$ | $x_j$ | $\ldots$ | $x_n$ | |
| Dual variables | $c_1$ | $c_2$ | $\ldots$ | $c_j$ | $\ldots$ | $c_n$ | |
| $y_1$ | $a_{11}$ | $a_{12}$ | $\ldots$ | $a_{1j}$ | $\ldots$ | $a_{1n}$ | $b_1$ |
| $y_2$ | $a_{21}$ | $a_{22}$ | $\ldots$ | $a_{2j}$ | $\ldots$ | $a_{2n}$ | $b_2$ |
| . | . | . | | . | | . | . |
| . | . | . | $\ldots$ | . | $\ldots$ | . | . |
| . | . | . | | . | | . | . |
| $y_m$ | $a_{m1}$ | $a_{m2}$ | $\ldots$ | $a_{mj}$ | $\ldots$ | $a_{mn}$ | $b_m$ |
| | | | | $j$th Dual constraint | | | Dual objective |

**TABLE 4–2**

| Standard primal problem objective | Dual problem | | |
|---|---|---|---|
| | Objective | Constraints type | Variables sign |
| Maximization | Minimization | $\geq$ | Unrestricted |
| Minimization | Maximization | $\leq$ | Unrestricted |

**Example 4.2–1.**

| Primal | Standard primal | Dual variables |
|---|---|---|
| Maximize $z = 5x_1 + 12x_2 + 4x_3$ subject to $$x_1 + 2x_2 + x_3 \leq 10$$ $$2x_1 - x_2 + 3x_3 = 8$$ $$x_1, x_2, x_3 \geq 0$$ | Maximize $z = 5x_1 + 12x_2 + 4x_3 + 0x_4$ subject to $$x_1 + 2x_2 + x_3 + x_4 = 10$$ $$2x_1 - x_2 + 3x_3 + 0x_4 = 8$$ $$x_1, x_2, x_3, x_4 \geq 0$$ | $y_1$ $y_2$ |

*Dual Problem*

$$\text{Minimize } w = 10y_1 + 8y_2$$

subject to

$$y_1 + 2y_2 \geq 5$$

$$2y_1 - y_2 \geq 12$$

$$y_1 + 3y_2 \geq 4$$

$$\left.\begin{array}{r} y_1 + 0y_2 \geq 0 \\ y_1, y_2 \text{ unrestricted} \end{array}\right\} \Rightarrow (y_1 \geq 0, y_2 \text{ unrestricted})$$

**Example 4.2–2.**

| Primal | Standard primal | Dual variables |
|---|---|---|
| Minimize $z = 15x_1 + 12x_2$ subject to $\quad x_1 + 2x_2 \geq 3$ $\quad 2x_1 - 4x_2 \leq 5$ $\quad x_1, x_2 \geq 0$ | Minimize $z = 15x_1 + 12x_2 + 0x_3 + 0x_4$ subject to $\quad x_1 + 2x_2 - x_3 + \quad = 3$ $\quad 2x_1 - 4x_2 \quad + x_4 = 5$ $\quad x_1, x_2, x_3, x_4 \geq 0$ | $y_1$ $y_2$ |

*Dual Problem*

$$\text{Maximize } w = 3y_1 + 5y_2$$

subject to

$$y_1 + 2y_2 \leq 15$$

$$2y_1 - 4y_2 \leq 12$$

$$-y_1 \qquad \leq 0 \quad (\text{or } y_1 \geq 0)$$

$$y_2 \leq 0$$

$$y_1, y_2 \text{ unrestricted (redundant)}$$

**Example 4.2–3.**

| Primal | Standard primal | Dual variables |
|---|---|---|
| Maximize $z = 5x_1 + 6x_2$ subject to | Substitute $x_1 = x_1^+ - x_1^-$, to get Maximize $z = 5x_1^+ - 5x_1^- + 6x_2$ subject to | |
| $\quad x_1 + 2x_2 = 5$ | $\quad x_1^+ - x_1^- + 2x_2 \quad = 5$ | $y_1$ |
| $\quad -x_1 + 5x_2 \geq 3$ | $\quad -x_1^+ + x_1^- + 5x_2 - x_3 \quad = 3$ | $y_2$ |
| $\quad 4x_1 + 7x_2 \leq 8$ | $\quad 4x_1^+ - 4x_1^- + 7x_2 \quad + x_4 = 8$ | $y_3$ |
| $\quad x_1 \text{ unrestricted}$ | $\quad x_1^+, x_1^-, x_2 \geq 0$ | |
| $\quad x_2 \geq 0$ | | |

*Dual Problem*

$$\text{Minimize } z = 5y_1 + 3y_2 + 8y_3$$

subject to

$$\left.\begin{array}{r} y_1 - y_2 + 4y_3 \geq 5 \\ -y_1 + y_2 - 4y_3 \geq -5 \end{array}\right\} \Rightarrow (y_1 - y_2 + 4y_3 = 5)$$

$$2y_1 + 5y_2 + 7y_3 \geq 6$$

$$- y_2 \qquad\qquad \geq 0 \quad\Rightarrow (y_2 \leq 0)$$

$$y_3 \geq 0$$

$y_1$ unrestricted

$y_2, y_3$, unrestricted    (redundant)

The first and second constraints are replaced by an equation. The rule in this case is that an unrestricted primal variable always corresponds to an equality dual constraint, and conversely, a primal equation produces an unrestricted dual variable.

## Problem set 4.2a

1. In Example 4.2–1, derive the associated dual problem if the sense of optimization in the primal problem is changed to minimization.
2. Consider Example 4.2–1. The application of the simplex method to the primal requires the use of an artificial variable in the second constraint of the standard primal to secure a starting basic solution. Show that the presence of an artificial primal variable does not affect the definition of the dual because it leads to a redundant dual constraint.
3. In Example 4.2–2, derive the associated dual problem given that the primal problem is augmented with the third constraint $3x_1 + x_2 = 4$.
4. In Example 4.2–3, show that even if the sense of optimization in the primal is changed to minimization, an unrestricted primal variable always corresponds to an equality dual constraint.
5. Write the dual for each of the following primal problems:
   (a) Maximize $z = -5x_1 + 2x_2$
      subject to

$$-x_1 + x_2 \leq -2$$

$$2x_1 + 3x_2 \leq 5$$

$$x_1, x_2 \geq 0$$

   (b) Minimize $z = 6x_1 + 3x_2$
      subject to

$$6x_1 - 3x_2 + x_3 \geq 2$$

$$3x_1 + 4x_2 + x_3 \geq 5$$

$$x_1, x_2, x_3 \geq 0$$

**(c)** Maximize $z = 5x_1 + 6x_2$
subject to

$$x_1 + 2x_2 = 5$$

$$-x_1 + 5x_2 \geq 3$$

$$x_1 \text{ unrestricted}$$

$$x_2 \leq 0$$

(Notice that $x_2$ is nonpositive.)

**(d)** Minimize $z = 3x_1 + 4x_2 + 6x_3$
subject to

$$x_1 + x_2 \geq 10$$

$$x_1 \geq 0$$

$$x_2 \leq 0$$

$$x_3 \geq 0$$

**(e)** Maximize $z = x_1 + x_2$
subject to

$$2x_1 + x_2 = 5$$

$$3x_1 - x_2 = 6$$

$$x_1, x_2 \text{ unrestricted}$$

**6.** True or False?

**(a)** The dual of the dual problem yields the original primal.

**(b)** If the primal constraint is originally in equation form, the corresponding dual variable is necessarily unrestricted.

**(c)** If the primal constraint is of the type $\leq$, the corresponding dual variable will be nonnegative (nonpositive) depending on whether the primal objective is maximization (minimization).

**(d)** If the primal constraint is of the type $\geq$, the corresponding dual variable will be nonnegative (nonpositive) depending on whether the primal objective is minimization (maximization).

**(e)** An unrestricted primal variable will result in an equality dual constraint.

**7.** The following explicit rules are often listed in most operations research and linear programming books for constructing the dual problem. Show that these rules are a subsumed by the general definition given in Table 4–2.

| Maximization Problem | | Minimization Problem |
|:---:|:---:|:---:|
| Constraints | | Variables |
| $\geq$ | $\Leftrightarrow$ | $\leq 0$ |
| $\leq$ | $\Leftrightarrow$ | $\geq 0$ |
| $=$ | $\Leftrightarrow$ | Unrestricted |
| Variables | | Constraints |
| $\geq 0$ | $\Leftrightarrow$ | $\geq$ |
| $\leq 0$ | $\Leftrightarrow$ | $\leq$ |
| Unrestricted | $\Leftrightarrow$ | $=$ |

## 4.3 RELATIONSHIP BETWEEN THE OPTIMAL PRIMAL AND DUAL SOLUTIONS

The primal and dual problems are so closely related that the optimal solution of one problem can be secured directly (without further computations) from the optimal simplex tableau of the other problem. This result is based on the following property:

**Property I.**   *At any simplex iteration of the primal or the dual,*

$$\begin{pmatrix} \text{Objective coefficient} \\ \text{of variable } j \text{ in} \\ \text{one problem} \end{pmatrix} = \begin{pmatrix} \text{Left-hand side } minus \\ \text{right-hand side} \\ \text{of constraint } j \text{ in} \\ \text{the other problem} \end{pmatrix}$$

The property is symmetrical with respect to both the primal and the dual problems.

Property I can be used to determine the optimal solution of one problem (directly) from the optimal simplex tableau of the other. This result could be advantageous computationally if the computations associated with the solved problem is considerably less than those associated with the other problem. For example, if a model has 100 variables and 500 constraints, it is advantageous computationally to solve the dual because it has only 100 constraints.

---

**Example 4.3–1.**

Consider the primal and dual problems of Example 4.2–1, which are repeated here for convenience.

| Primal | Dual |
|---|---|
| Maximize $z = 5x_1 + 12x_2 + 4x_3$ <br> subject to <br> $x_1 + 2x_2 + x_3 \leq 10$ <br> $2x_1 - x_2 + 3x_3 = 8$ <br> $x_1, x_2, x_3 \geq 0$ | Minimize $w = 10y_1 + 8y_2$ <br> subject to <br> $y_1 + 2y_2 \geq 5$ <br> $2y_1 - y_2 \geq 12$ <br> $y_1 + 3y_2 \geq 4$ <br> $y_1 \geq 0, y_2$ unrestricted |

The following tableaux provide the simplex iterations for the primal problem.

| Iteration | Basic | $x_1$ | $x_2$ | $x_3$ | $x_4$ | $R$ | Solution |
|---|---|---|---|---|---|---|---|
| 0 | $z$ | $-5 - 2M$ | $-12 + M$ | $-4 - 3M$ | 0 | 0 | $-8M$ |
| | $x_4$ | 1 | 2 | 1 | 1 | 0 | 10 |
| | $R$ | 2 | $-1$ | 3 | 0 | 1 | 8 |
| 1 | $z$ | $-\dfrac{7}{3}$ | $-\dfrac{40}{3}$ | 0 | 0 | $\dfrac{4}{3} + M$ | $\dfrac{32}{3}$ |
| | $x_4$ | $\dfrac{1}{3}$ | $\dfrac{7}{3}$ | 0 | 1 | $-\dfrac{1}{3}$ | $\dfrac{22}{3}$ |
| | $x_3$ | $\dfrac{2}{3}$ | $-\dfrac{1}{3}$ | 1 | 0 | $\dfrac{1}{3}$ | $\dfrac{8}{3}$ |
| 2 | | $-\dfrac{3}{7}$ | 0 | 0 | $\dfrac{40}{7}$ | $-\dfrac{4}{7} + M$ | $\dfrac{368}{7}$ |
| | $x_2$ | $\dfrac{1}{7}$ | 1 | 0 | $\dfrac{3}{7}$ | $-\dfrac{1}{7}$ | $\dfrac{22}{7}$ |
| | $x_3$ | $\dfrac{5}{7}$ | 0 | 1 | $\dfrac{1}{7}$ | $\dfrac{2}{7}$ | $\dfrac{26}{7}$ |
| 3 | $z$ | 0 | 0 | $\dfrac{3}{5}$ | $\dfrac{29}{5}$ | $-\dfrac{2}{5} + M$ | $\dfrac{274}{5}$ |
| | $x_2$ | 0 | 1 | $-\dfrac{1}{5}$ | $\dfrac{2}{5}$ | $-\dfrac{1}{5}$ | $\dfrac{12}{5}$ |
| | $x_1$ | 1 | 0 | $\dfrac{7}{5}$ | $\dfrac{1}{5}$ | $\dfrac{2}{5}$ | $\dfrac{26}{5}$ |

Applying Property I to the starting solution variables $x_4$ and $R$ in optimal iteration 3, we obtain the following information:

| | Starting primal variables | $x_4$ | $R$ |
|---|---|---|---|
| | $z$-Equation coefficient (iteration 3) | $\dfrac{29}{5}$ | $-\dfrac{2}{5} + M$ |
| | Associated dual constraint | $y_1 \geq 0$ | $y_2 \geq -M$ |
| | Equation resulting from Property I | $y_1 - 0 = \dfrac{29}{5}$ | $y_2 - (-M) = -\dfrac{2}{5} + M$ |

The solution of the given equations yields $y_1 = \frac{29}{5}$ and $y_2 = -\frac{2}{5}$. If you solve the dual problem independently, you will obtain the same solution. Also, because of the symmetry of Property I with respect to the primal and the dual problem, a similar application to the starting variables in the optimal dual tableau will automatically yield the optimal primal solution $x_1 = \frac{26}{5}, x_2 = \frac{12}{5}$, and $x_3 = 0$ (use TORA to solve the dual and verify that the given assertion is true).

The application of Property I to the starting variables always results in easy-to-solve equations because each equation involves exacty one variable. Nothing, however, should prevent us from using any two of the other (primal) variables (that is, $x_1, x_2$, and $x_3$) to generate the desired equations. For example, at the optimal tableau, Property I equations associated with $x_1$ and $x_3$ are, respectively,

$$y_1 + 2y_2 - 5 = 0$$

$$y_1 + 3y_2 - 4 = \frac{3}{5}$$

The solution of these two equations still yields the same optimal dual values $y_1 = \frac{29}{5}$ and $y_2 = -\frac{2}{5}$. However, the equations are not as simple as those associated with $x_4$ and $R$ (convince yourself that any two of the variables $x_1, x_2, x_3, x_4$, and $R$ will produce the dual variables).

---

We present next a relationship between the primal and the dual, which, together with Property I, can be used to provide interesting economic interpretations of the linear programming problem.

***Property II.***   *For any pair of feasible primal and dual solutions,*

$$\begin{pmatrix} \text{Objective value in the} \\ maximization \text{ problem} \end{pmatrix} \le \begin{pmatrix} \text{Objective value in the} \\ minimization \text{ problem} \end{pmatrix}$$

*At the optimum, the relationship holds as a strict equation.*

---

**Example 4.3–2.**

In Example 4.2–1, the primal and dual problems can be shown (by inspection of the constraints) to have the feasible solutions $(x_1 = 0, x_2 = 0, x_3 = \frac{8}{3})$ and $(y_1 = 6, y_2 = 0)$. The associated values of the objective functions are then given as $z = 10\frac{2}{3}$ and $w = 60$. Conversely, the optimum solution for the two problems $(x_1 = \frac{26}{5}, x_2 = \frac{12}{5}, x_3 = 0)$ and $(y_1 = \frac{29}{5}, y_2 = -\frac{2}{5})$ yield $z = w = 54.8$. Both calculations demonstrate the property.

---

Property II reveals that for all feasible solutions of the primal and the dual, the objective value in the minimization problem always provides an upper bound on the objective value of the maximization problem. Given that the successive iterations of the maximization problem will result in increasing the value of the objective function, and those of the minimization problem will result in decreasing the value of the objective function. Eventually, in the course of the successive iterations, an equilibrium point will be reached where the maximization and the minimization objective values must be equal.

**Problem set 4.3a**

1. In Example 4.3–1, use the dual constraints associated with $x_2$ and $x_3$ to determine the optimal dual values, $y_1$ and $y_2$.

2. Consider the following LP:

$$\text{Maximize } z = 5x_1 + 2x_2 + 3x_3$$

subject to

$$x_1 + 5x_2 + 2x_3 = 30$$
$$x_1 - 5x_2 - 6x_3 \leq 40$$
$$x_1, x_2, x_3 \geq 0$$

The *optimal* solution yields the following objective equation:

$$z + 0x_1 - 23x_2 + 7x_3 + (5 + M)x_4 + 0x_5 = 150$$

where artificial $x_4$ and slack $x_5$ are the starting basic variables. Write the associated dual problem and determine its optimal solution from the optimal $z$-equation.

3. Consider the following LP:

$$\text{Maximize } z = x_1 + 5x_2 + 3x_3$$

subject to

$$x_1 + 2x_2 + x_3 = 3$$
$$2x_1 - x_2 \quad\quad = 4$$
$$x_1, x_2, x_3 \geq 0$$

**(a)** Write the associated dual problem.

**(b)** Given the information that the optimal basic variables are $x_1$ and $x_3$, determine the associated optimal dual solution.

4. Consider the following LP:

$$\text{Maximize } z = 2x_1 + 4x_2 + 4x_3 - 3x_4$$

subject to

$$x_1 + x_2 + x_3 \quad\quad = 4$$
$$x_1 + 4x_2 \quad\quad + x_4 = 8$$
$$x_1, x_2, x_3, x_4 \geq 0$$

Use the dual problem to verify that the basic solution $(x_1, x_2)$ is not optimal.

5. In Problem 4, the objective equation in the optimal tableau is

$$z + 2x_1 + 0x_2 + 0x_3 + 3x_4 = 16$$

Determine the associated optimal dual solution.

6. Determine a feasible solution to the following set of inequalities by using the dual problem:

$$2x_1 + 3x_2 \leq 12$$

$$-3x_1 + 2x_2 \leq -4$$

$$3x_1 - 5x_2 \leq 2$$

$$x_1 \text{ unrestricted}$$

$$x_2 \geq 0$$

(*Hint:* Augment the trivial objective function maximize $z = 0x_1 + 0x_2 + 0x_3$ to the inequalities, then solve the dual.)

7. Find the optimal value of the objective function for the following problem by only inspecting its dual. (Do not solve the dual by the simplex method.)

$$\text{Minimize } z = 10x_1 + 4x_2 + 5x_3$$

subject to

$$5x_1 - 7x_2 + 3x_3 \geq 50$$

$$x_1, \ x_2, \ x_3 \geq 0$$

8. Estimate a range for the optimal objective value for each of the following LPs:
   (a) Minimize $z = 5x_1 + 2x_2$
       subject to

$$x_1 - x_2 \geq 3$$

$$2x_1 + 3x_2 \geq 5$$

$$x_1, x_2 \geq 0$$

   (b) Maximize $z = x_1 + 5x_2 + 3x_3$
       subject to

$$x_1 + 2x_2 + x_3 = 3$$

$$2x_1 - x_2 \qquad = 4$$

$$x_1, x_2, x_3 \geq 0$$

   (c) Maximize $z = 2x_1 + x_2$
       subject to

$$x_1 - x_2 \le 10$$

$$2x_1 \qquad \le 40$$

$$x_1, \; x_2 \ge 0$$

(d) Maximize $z = 3x_1 + 2x_2$
    subject to

$$2x_1 + \; x_2 \le 3$$

$$3x_1 + 4x_2 \ge 12$$

$$x_1, \; x_2 \ge 0$$

9. In Problem 8(a), let $y_1$ and $y_2$ be the dual variables. Determine whether the
   following pairs of primal-dual solutions are optimal:
   (a) $(x_1 = 3, \; x_2 = 1; \; y_1 = 4, \; y_2 = 1)$
   (b) $(x_1 = 4, \; x_2 = 1; \; y_1 = 1, \; y_2 = 0)$
   (c) $(x_1 = 3, \; x_2 = 0; \; y_1 = 5, \; y_2 = 0)$

## 4.4 ECONOMIC INTERPRETATION OF DUALITY

The linear programming problem can be viewed as a resource allocation model in
which the objective is to maximize revenue or profit subject to the availability of limited resources. Looking at the problem from this standpoint, the associated dual
problem offers interesting economic interpretations of the LP resource allocation
model.

To formalize the discussion, we consider the following representation of the
general primal and dual problems in which the primal takes the role of a resource allocation model:

| Primal | Dual |
|---|---|
| Maximize $z = \sum_{j=1}^{n} c_j x_j$ <br> subject to <br><br> $\sum_{j=1}^{n} a_{ij} x_j \le b_i, \; i = 1, 2, \ldots, m$ <br><br> $x_j \ge 0, j = , 2, \ldots, n$ | Minimize $w = \sum_{i=1}^{m} b_i y_i$ <br> subject to <br><br> $\sum_{i=1}^{m} a_{ij} y_i \ge c_j, j = 1, 2, \ldots, n$ <br><br> $y_i \ge 0, i = 1, 2, \ldots, m$ |

From the standpoint of the resource allocation model, the primal problem has
$n$ economic activities and $m$ resources. The coefficient $c_j$ in the primal represents the
profit per unit of activity $j$. Resource $i$, whose maximum availability is $b_i$, is consumed at the rate of $a_{ij}$ units per unit of activity $j$.

### 4.4.1 Economic Interpretation of Dual Variables

Property II in Section 4.3 states that for any two primal and dual solutions, the values of the objective functions, when finite, must satisfy the following inequality:

$$z = \sum_{j=1}^{n} c_j x_j \leq \sum_{i=1}^{m} b_i y_i = w$$

The strict equality holds when both the primal and dual solutions are optimal.

Let us consider the optimal condition $z = w$ first. Given that the primal problem represents a resource allocation model, we can think of $z$ as representing profit dollars. Because $b_i$ represents the number of units available of resource $i$, it follows that the equation $z = w$ can be expressed dimensionally as

$$\$ = \sum_i (\text{units of resource } i) \, (\$ \text{ per unit of resource } i)$$

This means that the dual variables, $y_i$, must represent the *worth per unit* of resource $i$. (This same interpretation was obtained graphically in Section 2.4.2 without the use of duality.) In the literature, the variables $y_i$ are referred by the "technical" name **dual prices**. Other (equally nonsuggestive) names include **shadow prices** and **simplex multipliers**.

Using the same logic, the inequality $z < w$ associated with any two feasible primal and dual solutions is interpreted as

$$(\text{Profit}) < (\text{Worth of resources})$$

This relationship says that so long as the total return from all the activities is less than the worth of the resources, the corresponding primal and dual solutions cannot be optimal. Optimality (maximum return) is reached only when the resources have been exploited completely, which can happen only when the input (worth of the resources) equals the output (profit dollars). In economic terms, the system is said to remain *unstable* (nonoptimal) when the input (worth of the resources) exceeds the output (return). Stability occurs only when the two quantities are equal.

---

**Example 4.4–1.**

The Reddy Mikks model (Example 2.2–1) and its dual are given subsequently.

| Reddy Mikks primal | Reddy Mikks dual |
|---|---|
| Maximize  $z = 5x_1 + 4x_2$<br>subject to<br>$6x_1 + 4x_2 \leq 24$  (resource 1, M1)<br>$x_1 + 2x_2 \leq 6$  (resource 2, M2)<br>$-x_1 + x_2 \leq 1$  (resource 3)<br>$x_2 \leq 2$  (resource 4)<br>$x_1, x_2 \geq 0$ | Minimize  $w = 24y_1 + 6y_2 + y_3 + 2y_4$<br>subject to<br>$6y_1 + y_2 - y_3 \geq 5$<br>$4y_1 + 2y_2 + y_3 + y_4 \geq 4$<br>$y_1, y_2, y_3, y_4 \geq 0$ |
| Optimal solution:<br>$x_1 = 3, x_2 = 1.5, z = 21$ | Optimal solution:<br>$y_1 = .75, y_2 = .5, y_3 = y_4 = 0, w = 21$ |

Briefly, the Reddy Mikks model deals with the production of two types of paint (interior and exterior) using two raw materials $M1$ and $M2$ (resources 1 and 2) and subject to market conditions represented by the third and fourth constraints. The problem seeks to determine the tons of interior and exterior paints that should be produced to maximize profit (expressed in thousands of dollars).

The optimal dual solution shows that the worth per unit of raw material, $M1$ (resource 1), is $y_1 = .75$ (or \$750 per ton), whereas that of raw material, $M2$ (resource 2) is $y_2 = .5$ (or \$500 per ton). In Section 2.4.2, we showed graphically that these same results hold true for the ranges (20, 36) and (4, 6.67) for resources 1 and 2, respectively (these ranges will be derived algebraically also in Section 4.7.1). Thus, raw material, $M1$, can be increased from its present level of 24 tons to a maximum of 36 tons with a corresponding increase in profit of $12 \times \$750 = \$9000$. Similarly, the limit on raw material, $M2$, can be increased from 6 tons to a maximum of 6.67 tons, with a corresponding increase in profit of $.67 \times \$500 = \$335$. Similar interpretations can be given if the raw material levels are decreased below the current levels within the indicated ranges of applicability. The discussion does not imply that the given resources cannot be changed to levels outside the given ranges. It simply says that the worth per unit for each of resources 1 and 2 are guaranteed only within the specified ranges.

For resources 3 and 4, representing the market requirements, the dual prices (optimal dual values) are both zero, which indicates that their associated resources are abundant. Hence, their worth per unit is zero.

### Problem set 4.4a

1. In Example 4.4–1, compute the change in the optimal profit in each of the following two cases:
   (a) The constraint for raw material, $M1$ (resource 1), is $6x_1 + 4x_2 \le 22$.
   (b) The constraint for raw material, $M2$ (resource 2), is $x_1 + 2x_2 \le 4.5$.
   (c) The market condition represented by resource 4 is $x_2 \le 10$
2. NWAC Electronics manufactures four types of simple cables for a defense contractor. Each cable must go through four sequential operations: splicing, soldering, sleeving, and inspection. The following table gives the pertinent data of the situation.

| Cable | Minutes per unit | | | | Unit profit ($) |
|---|---|---|---|---|---|
| | Splicing | Soldering | Sleeving | Inspection | |
| SC320 | 10.5 | 20.4 | 3.2 | 5.0 | 9.40 |
| SC325 | 9.3 | 24.6 | 2.5 | 5.0 | 10.80 |
| SC340 | 11.6 | 17.7 | 3.6 | 5.0 | 8.75 |
| SC370 | 8.2 | 26.5 | 5.5 | 5.0 | 7.80 |
| Daily capacity (minutes) | 4800.0 | 9600.0 | 4700.0 | 4500.0 | |

The contractor guarantees that the minimum production level for each of the four cables is 100 units.

(a) Formulate the problem as a linear programming model, and use TORA to determine the optimum production schedule.

(b) Based on the dual prices generated by TORA, do you recommend making increases in the daily capacities of any of the four operations? Explain.

(c) Does the stipulation of minimum production requirements for the four cables represent an advantage or a disadvantage for NAWC Electronics? Provide an explanation based on the dual prices provided by TORA.

(d) Is it feasible to increase the capacity of soldering by 10% of its present limit while maintaining the present unit contribution to profit as specified by the dual price?

3. BagCo produces leather jackets and handbags. A jacket requires 8 m² of leather, and a handbag uses only 2 m². The labor requirements for the two products are 12 and 5 hours, respectively. The current weekly supplies of leather and labor are limited to 1200 m² and 1850 hours. The company sells the jackets and handbags at $350 and $120, respectively. The objective is to determine the production schedule that maximizes the net revenue. BagCo is considering an expansion of production. What is the maximum purchase price the company should pay for additional leather? For additional labor?

## 4.4.2 Economic Interpretation of Dual Constraints

The dual constraints can be interpreted by using the result of Property I in Section 4.3. Namely, at any primal iteration,

$$\text{(Objective coefficient of } x_j) = \sum_{i=1}^{m} a_{ij} y_i - c_j$$

We use dimensional analysis to interpret this equation. The profit per unit, $c_j$, of activity $j$ is in dollars per unit. Hence, for consistency, the quantity $\sum_{i=1}^{m} a_{ij} y_i$ must also be in dollars per unit. Next, because $c_j$ represents profit, the quantity $\sum_{i=1}^{m} a_{ij} y_i$, which appears in the equation with an opposite sign, must stand for cost. At the same time, given $a_{ij}$ is the amount of resource $i$ used by activity $j$, the dual variables $y_i$ must represent the **imputed cost** per unit of resource $i$, and we can think of the quantity $\sum_{i=1}^{m} a_{ij} y_i$ as the imputed cost of all the resources needed to produce 1 unit of activity $j$.

The maximization optimality condition of the simplex method says that an increase in the level of an unused (nonbasic) activity $j$ can improve profit only if its objective coefficient $(\sum_{i=1}^{m} a_{ij} y_i - c_j)$ is negative. In terms of the preceding interpretation, this condition states that

$$\begin{pmatrix} \text{Imputed cost of} \\ \text{used resources} \\ \text{per unit of activity } j \end{pmatrix} < \begin{pmatrix} \text{Profit per unit} \\ \text{of activity } j \end{pmatrix}$$

The maximization optimality condition thus says that it is economically advantageous to increase an activity to a positive level if its unit profit exceeds its unit imputed cost.

To familiarize you with the standard notation used in the literature, we introduce the definition

$$z_j = \sum_{i=1}^{m} a_{ij} y_i$$

to represent the imputed cost of used resources per unit of activity $j$. The notation $(z_j - c_j)$ is the objective coefficient of $x_j$ in the simplex tableau and is often referred to as the **reduced cost** of activity $j$. Indeed, some books use $z_j - c_j$ to compute the objective equation coefficient directly (in place of using the Gauss-Jordan row operations). The use of $z_j - c_j$ in the simplex computations is actually part of the *revised simplex method*, which will be discussed in Chapter 7.

---

**Example 4.4–2.**

TOYCO assembles three types of toys: trains, trucks, and cars using three operations. The daily limits on the available times for the three operations are 430, 460, and 420 minutes, respectively, and the profits per toy train, truck, and car are $3, $2, and $5, respectively. The assembly times per train at the three operations are 1, 3, and 1 minutes, respectively. The corresponding times per truck and per car are $(2,0,4)$ and $(1,2,0)$ minutes (a zero time indicates that the operation is not used).

Letting $x_1$, $x_2$, and $x_3$ represent the daily number of units assembled of trains, trucks and cars, the associated LP model and its dual are given as:

| TOYCO primal | TOYCO dual |
|---|---|
| Maximize  $z = 3x_1 + 2x_2 + 5x_3$<br>subject to<br>$x_1 + 2x_2 + \phantom{2}x_3 \leq 430$ (Operation 1)<br>$3x_1 + \phantom{2x_2} + 2x_3 \leq 460$ (Operation 2)<br>$x_1 + 4x_2 \phantom{+ 2x_3} \leq 420$ (Operation 3)<br>$x_1, x_2, x_3 \geq 0$ | Minimize  $z = 430y_1 + 460y_2 + 420y_3$<br>subject to<br>$y_1 + 3y_2 + \phantom{4}y_3 \geq 3$<br>$2y_1 + \phantom{3y_2 +} 4y_3 \geq 2$<br>$y_1 + 2y_2 \phantom{+ 4y_3} \geq 5$<br>$y_1, y_2, y_3 \geq 0$ |
| Optimal solution:<br>$x_1 = 0, x_2 = 100, x_3 = 230, z = \$1350$ | Optimal solution:<br>$y_1 = 1, y_2 = 2, y_3 = 0$ |

The optimal primal solution calls for producing toy trucks ($x_2 = 100$) and toy cars ($x_3 = 230$), but no toy trains ($x_1 = 0$). This means that, according to the present economy of scale, toy trains are not profitable. Nevertheless, competition dictates that TOYCO produce toy trains also. How can this be achieved? Looking at the problem from the standpoint of the interpretation of $z_1 - c_1$ for $x_1$, toy trains will become attractive economically only if $z_1 < c_1$. TOYCO thus can either increase the profit per unit $c_1$ by raising the unit selling price, or it can decrease the imputed cost of the used resources $z_1 (= y_1 + 3y_2 + y_3)$. An increase in unit profit may not be possible because TOYCO wishes to remain competitive in the market. A decrease in $z_1$ is more plausible because it entails making improvements in the assembly operations, mainly by reducing their unit usage of available operations times. Letting $r_1, r_2,$ and $r_3$ represent the proportions by which the unit times of the three operations are reduced, the problem requires determining $r_1, r_2,$ and $r_3$ such that the new imputed cost of the three operations falls below the units profit $c_1$—that is,

$$1(1 - r_1)y_1 + 3(1 - r_2)y_2 + 1(1 - r_3)y_3 < 3$$

For the given values of $y_1 = 1, y_2 = 2,$ and $y_3 = 0$, this inequality reduces to (verify!)

$$r_1 + 6r_2 > 4$$

Thus, any feasible values of $r_1$ and $r_2$ between 0 and 1 that satisfy $r_1 + 6r_2 > 4$ should render toy trains profitable. For example, $r_1 = .25$ and $r_2 = .2$ will produce $z_1 - c_1 = .25 + 6(.2) - 4 = -2.55$. Notice, however, that a unit reduction in the use of operation 2 is 6 times as effective as an equal reduction in the use of operation 1.

---

### Problem set 4.4b

1. In Example 4.4–2, suppose that for toy trains the per unit usage of operation 2 can be reduced from 3 minutes to at most 1.25 minutes. By how much must the per unit usage of operation 1 be reduced to make toy trains just profitable?

2. In Example 4.4–2, suppose that TOYCO is studying the possibility of introducing a fourth toy: fire trucks. The assembly does not make use of operation 1. Its unit assembly times on operations 2 and 3 are 1 and 3 minutes, respectively. The profit per unit is $4. Would you advise TOYCO to introduce the new product?

3. JoShop uses lathes and drill presses to produce four types of machine parts, $PP1, PP2, PP3,$ and $PP4$. The table below summarizes the pertinent data of the situation.

| Machine | Machining time in minutes per unit of | | | | Capacity (minutes) |
|---|---|---|---|---|---|
| | $PP1$ | $PP2$ | $PP3$ | $PP4$ | |
| Lathes | 2 | 5 | 3 | 4 | 5300 |
| Drill presses | 3 | 4 | 6 | 4 | 5300 |
| Unit profit ($) | 3 | 6 | 5 | 4 | |

For the parts that are not produced by the present optimum solution, determine the rate of deterioration in the optimum profit per unit increase of each of these products.

**4.** Consider the optimal solution of JoShop in Problem 3. The company estimates that for each of the parts with zero production in the optimum solution, an across-the-board 20% reduction in machining time can be realized through process improvements. Would these improvements make these parts profitable? If not, what is the minimum percentage reduction needed to realize profitability?

## 4.5 DUAL SIMPLEX METHOD

In this section, we introduce a different simplex algorithm that is motivated by the relationship between the primal and dual problems. The algorithm is designed to solve a class of LP models efficiently. The new method is essential for carrying out sensitivity analysis (see Section 4.7)

In the *dual simplex algorithm,* the LP problem starts (better than) optimum and infeasible. Successive iterations are designed to move toward feasibility without violating optimality. At the iteration when feasibility is restored, the algorithm ends. The dual simplex method contrasts with the regular (primal) simplex method of Chapter 3 in that the iterations start feasible and nonoptimal and continue to be feasible until optimality is achieved.

In the dual simplex method, the starting tableau must have an optimum objective row with at least one infeasible ($< 0$) basic variable. To maintain optimality and, simultaneously, move toward feasibility at each new iteration, the following two conditions are employed:

***Dual feasibility condition.***     The leaving variable, $x_r$, is the basic variable having the most negative value, with ties broken arbitrarily. If all the basic variables are nonnegative, the algorithm ends.

***Dual optimality condition.***     The entering variable is determined from among the nonbasic variables as the one corresponding to

$$\min_{\text{Nonbasic } x_j} \left\{ \left| \frac{z_j - c_j}{\alpha_{rj}} \right|, \alpha_{rj} < 0 \right\}$$

where $\alpha_{rj}$ is the constraint coefficient of the tableau associated with the row of the leaving variable $x_r$ and the column of the entering variable $x_j$. Ties are broken arbitrarily.

With some reflection, you will notice that the *dual optimality condition* is based on the same general idea used in the development of the *primal feasibility condition* in Chapter 3.

---

**Example 4.5–1.**

$$\text{Minimize } z = 3x_1 + 2x_2$$

subject to

$$3x_1 + x_2 \geq 3$$

$$4x_1 + 3x_2 \geq 6$$

$$x_1 + x_2 \leq 3$$

$$x_1, x_2 \geq 0$$

The starting tableau for the problem is given as

| Basic | $x_1$ | $x_2$ | $x_3$ | $x_4$ | $x_5$ | Solution |
|-------|-------|-------|-------|-------|-------|----------|
| $z$   | $-3$  | $-2$  | 0     | 0     | 0     | 0        |
| $x_3$ | $-3$  | $-1$  | 1     | 0     | 0     | $-3$     |
| $x_4$ | $-4$  | $-3$  | 0     | 1     | 0     | $-6$     |
| $x_5$ | 1     | 1     | 0     | 0     | 1     | 3        |

The variables $x_3$ and $x_4$ are surplus, whereas $x_5$ is a slack. We multiplied each of the equations associated with the surplus basic variables $x_3$ and $x_4$ by $-1$ so that the right-hand side will show directly which basic variables are infeasible ($x_3 = -3$, $x_4 = -6$, $x_5 = 3$). This will always be the procedure we use in the dual simplex algorithm. Also, $z_j - c_j \leq 0$ for all $j = 1, 2, \ldots, 5$, which indicates that the starting basic solution is optimal. (It is actually better than optimal because the starting solution is infeasible.) Thus, the preceding tableau satisfies the conditions required for the starting tableau of the dual simplex method—namely, optimum and infeasible.

The dual feasibility condition indicates that $x_4$ ($= -6$) is the leaving variable. Next, we apply the dual optimality condition to determine the entering variable using the following summary table.

| Variable | $x_1$ | $x_2$ | $x_3$ | $x_4$ | $x_5$ |
|----------|-------|-------|-------|-------|-------|
| z-row ($z_j - c_j$) | $-3$ | $-2$ | 0 | 0 | 0 |
| $x_4$-row, $\alpha_{4j}$ | $-4$ | $-3$ | 0 | 1 | 0 |
| Ratio $\left\| \dfrac{z_j - c_j}{\alpha_{4j}} \right\|$ | $\dfrac{3}{4}$ | $\dfrac{2}{3}$ | — | — | — |

The ratios show that $x_2$ is the entering variable. Notice that a variable $x_j$ is a candidate for entering the basic solution only if its $\alpha_{4j}$ is strictly negative. Thus, the basic variables $x_3$, $x_4$, and $x_5$ should not be considered.

The next tableau is obtained by using the familiar row operations, which gives.

**6.** Solve the following LP in three different ways (use TORA for convenience). Give your opinion about which method appears to be the most efficient computationally.

$$\text{Minimize } z = 6x_1 + 7x_2 + 3x_3 + 5x_4$$

subject to

$$5x_1 + 6x_2 - 3x_3 + 4x_4 \geq 12$$
$$x_2 - 5x_3 - 6x_4 \geq 10$$
$$2x_1 + 5x_2 + x_3 + x_4 \geq 8$$
$$x_1, x_2, x_3, x_4 \geq 0$$

**7.** *Generalized simplex algorithm.* The (primal) simplex algorithm we studied in Chapter 3 starts feasible but nonoptimal. The dual simplex starts (better than) optimal but infeasible. What if an LP model starts both nonoptimal and infeasible? We have seen that the primal simplex accounts for the infeasibility of the starting solution by using artificial variables. Similarly, the dual simplex accounts for the nonoptimality by using artificial constraints. Although these procedures are designed to enhance *automatic* computations, such details may cause one to lose sight of what the simplex algorithm truly entails—namely, that the optimum solution of an LP is associated with an extreme point (or basic) solution. Based on this observation, you should be able to "tailor" your own simplex algorithm for LP models that start both nonoptimal and infeasible. To illustrate the procedure, consider the LP model of Problem 5(a). The model can be put in the following tableau form in which the starting basic solution $(x_3, x_4, x_5)$ is both nonoptimal (because of $x_3$) and infeasible (because $x_4 = -8$). (Notice that the first equation has been multiplied by $-1$ to reveal the infeasibility directly in the "solution" column.)

| Basic | $x_1$ | $x_2$ | $x_3$ | $x_4$ | $x_5$ | $x_6$ | Solution |
|-------|-------|-------|-------|-------|-------|-------|----------|
| $z$   | 0     | 0     | $-2$  | 0     | 0     | 0     | 0        |
| $x_4$ | 1     | $-2$  | 2     | 1     | 0     | 0     | $-8$     |
| $x_5$ | $-1$  | 1     | 1     | 0     | 1     | 0     | 4        |
| $x_6$ | 2     | $-1$  | 4     | 0     | 0     | 1     | 10       |

Solve the problem without the use of any artificial variables or constraints as follows: Remove infeasibility first by applying a version of the dual simplex feasibility condition that selects $x_4$ as the leaving variable. To determine the entering variable, all we need is a nonbasic variable whose constraint coefficient in the $x_4$-row is strictly negative. The selection can be done without regard to maintaining optimality because it is nonexistent at this point any way (compare with the dual optimality condition). This procedure is repeated as necessary until the feasibility is satisfied. The next step will be to pay attention to optimality by applying the proper optimality condition of the primal simplex method.

The essence of this exercise is that the simplex method is not rigid. The literature abounds with variations of the simplex method (e.g., the primal-dual method, the symmetrical method, the crisscross method, and the multiplex method) that give the impression that each procedure is different, when, in effect, they all seek an extreme point solution, with a slant toward automation and computational efficiency.

**8.** The LP model of Problem 5(c) has no feasible solution. Show how this condition is detected by the *generalized simplex procedure* given in Problem 7.

**9.** The LP model of Problem 5(d) has no bounded solution. Show how this condition is detected by the *generalized simplex procedure* given in Problem 7.

## 4.6 PRIMAL-DUAL COMPUTATIONS

In carrying out sensitivity analysis, we are interested in one principal result: Will the changes in the model's coefficients change (the optimality or feasibility of) the current solution. If so, how can we determine the new optimum (if one exists)? We can always answer these questions by solving the problem anew; however, for typical practical problems with thousands of variables and constraints, this may be inefficient. To acquire the desired results efficiently, we need to understand how the simplex computations are affected when changes are made in the original coefficients of the model. In particular, how are the optimality (objective-row coefficients) and feasibility (right-hand side of the tableau) of the simplex tableau affected when such changes are made?

A compact way for tracking the simplex computations is by using matrices. For those of us with no prior experience in matrices, we need only three elementary matrix operations: (row vector) $\times$ (matrix), (matrix) $\times$ (column vector), and (scalar) $\times$ (matrix). These operations are introduced here for convenience. First we start with some definitions (see Appendix A for a more complete review of matrices):

**1.** A *matrix,* **A,** of size $(m \times n)$ is a rectangular array of elements with $m$ rows and $n$ columns.

**2.** A *row vector,* **V,** of size $n$ is a $(1 \times n)$ matrix.

**3.** A *column vector,* **P,** of size $m$ is an $(m \times 1)$ matrix.

We have shown in Section 4.3 how the dual values can be computed by solving a set of simultaneous linear equations. A more compact, yet equivalent, way for calculating the dual vector (or dual prices) is

$$\mathbf{Y} = \mathbf{C}_B \mathbf{B}^{-1}$$

where $\mathbf{C}_B$ is an $m$-row vector comprised of the *original* objective function coefficients $c_j$ associated with the basic vector $\mathbf{X}_B$ (see Section 7.4 for a validation of this formula). Thus, $z_j - c_j$ can be computed as

$$z_j - c_j = \sum_{i=1}^{m} a_{ij} y_i - c_j$$

$$= \mathbf{Y}\mathbf{P}_j - c_j$$

The second equation shows that $z_j - c_j$ is the difference between the left- and the right-hand sides of the dual constraints (also as shown in Section 4.4.2).

All the elements of the current tableau are computed from the current inverse $\mathbf{B}^{-1}$ and the *original* data of the problem. As will be shown in the next section, this point is crucial in carrying out the sensitivity analysis computations.

---

**Example 4.6–1.**

The LP of example 4.3–1 will be used to demonstrate the primal-dual computations. The primal and dual problems are restated here in matrix form.

| Primal | Dual |
|---|---|
| Maximize $z = (5, 12, 4)\begin{bmatrix} x_1 \\ x_2 \\ x_3 \end{bmatrix}$ <br> subject to <br><br> $\begin{bmatrix} 1 & 2 & 1 \\ 2 & -1 & 3 \end{bmatrix}\begin{bmatrix} x_1 \\ x_2 \\ x_3 \end{bmatrix} = \begin{bmatrix} 10 \\ 8 \end{bmatrix}$ <br><br> $x_1, x_2, x_3 \geq 0$ | Minimize $w = (y_1, y_2)\begin{bmatrix} 10 \\ 8 \end{bmatrix}$ <br> subject to <br><br> $(y_1, y_2)\begin{bmatrix} 1 & 2 & 1 \\ 2 & -1 & 3 \end{bmatrix} \geq (5, 12, 4)$ <br><br> $y_1 \geq 0$, $y_2$ unrestricted |

The given primal-dual computations apply to any of the simplex iterations. We demonstrate this point by using iteration 1 of the primal solution given in Example 4.3–1. We have

$$\mathbf{X}_B = \begin{bmatrix} x_4 \\ x_3 \end{bmatrix}, \quad \mathbf{C}_B = (0, 4)$$

(Note that the order of the elements of $\mathbf{C}_B$ must follow the same order specified by the basic vector $\mathbf{X}_B$; namely, $c_4$ then $c_3$.) We also obtain the inverse as

$$\mathbf{B}^{-1} = \begin{bmatrix} 1 & -\dfrac{1}{3} \\ 0 & \dfrac{1}{3} \end{bmatrix}$$

Thus, the associated dual vector is computed as

$$(y_1, y_2) = \mathbf{Y} = \mathbf{C}_B \mathbf{B}^{-1} = (0, 4)\begin{bmatrix} 1 & -\frac{1}{3} \\ 0 & \frac{1}{3} \end{bmatrix} = (0, \tfrac{4}{3})$$

The associated $z$-equation coefficients is computed as

$$z_1 - c_1 = \mathbf{Y}\mathbf{P}_1 - c_1 = (0, \tfrac{4}{3})\begin{bmatrix} 1 \\ 2 \end{bmatrix} - 5 = -\tfrac{7}{3}$$

In a similar manner, we compute $z_2 - c_2 = -\frac{40}{3}$, $z_3 - c_3 = 0$, $z_4 - c_4 = 0$, and $z_5 - c_5 = \frac{4}{3} + M$ (verify!).

We next show how the elements of the constraint equations are computed by using the inverse $\mathbf{B}^{-1}$ and the *original* constraint columns $\mathbf{P}_j$ and $\mathbf{b}$. The right-hand–side column of iteration 1 is computed as

$$\mathbf{X}_B = \mathbf{B}^{-1}\mathbf{b} = \begin{bmatrix} 1 & -\frac{1}{3} \\ 0 & \frac{1}{3} \end{bmatrix}\begin{bmatrix} 10 \\ 8 \end{bmatrix} = \begin{bmatrix} \frac{22}{3} \\ \frac{8}{3} \end{bmatrix}$$

Similarly, the left-hand–side columns of the constraints are illustrated by computing the column associated with $x_1$ as

$$\mathbf{B}^{-1}\mathbf{P}_1 = \begin{bmatrix} 1 & -\frac{1}{3} \\ 0 & \frac{1}{3} \end{bmatrix}\begin{bmatrix} 1 \\ 2 \end{bmatrix} = \begin{bmatrix} \frac{1}{3} \\ \frac{2}{3} \end{bmatrix}.$$

The remaining columns under $x_2, x_3, x_4, x_5$, and $R$ can be computed in a similar manner (verify!).

---

The main conclusion from Example 4.6–1 is that the entire simplex tableau at any iteration can be generated from the associated inverse $\mathbf{B}^{-1}$ and the *original* data of the model. Thus, in terms of carrying out sensitivity analysis on an optimum LP solution whose inverse basis is $\mathbf{B}^{-1}$, we can study the effect of any changes in the objective coefficients and the right-hand side of the constraints simply by re-computing all $z_j - c_j$ ($z$-equation) and $\mathbf{B}^{-1}\mathbf{b}$ (right-hand side of the tableau). If the results of the calculations show that the current basic vector $\mathbf{X}_B$ remains feasible and optimal, then there is nothing more to be done. Otherwise, additional computations are needed to recover optimality or feasibility. The next section details these computations.

### Problem set 4.6a

**1.** In the solution of Example 4.3–1, identify the inverse basis and verify all the elements of
   **(a)** Iteration 2.
   **(b)** Iteration 3.

**2.** Consider the following LP model:

$$\text{Maximize } z = 3x_1 + 2x_2 + 5x_3$$

subject to

$$x_1 + 2x_2 + x_3 + x_4 \qquad\qquad = 30$$
$$3x_1 \qquad + 2x_3 \qquad + x_5 \qquad = 60$$
$$x_1 + 4x_2 \qquad\qquad\qquad + x_6 = 20$$
$$x_1, x_2, x_3, x_4, x_5 \geq 0$$

Check the optimality and feasibility of the following basic solutions:

**(a)**
$$\mathbf{X}_B = \begin{bmatrix} x_4 \\ x_3 \\ x_6 \end{bmatrix}, \quad \mathbf{B}^{-1} = \begin{bmatrix} 1 & -\dfrac{1}{2} & 0 \\[2mm] 0 & \dfrac{1}{2} & 0 \\[2mm] 0 & 0 & 1 \end{bmatrix}$$

**(b)**
$$\mathbf{X}_B = \begin{bmatrix} x_2 \\ x_3 \\ x_1 \end{bmatrix}, \quad \mathbf{B}^{-1} = \begin{bmatrix} \dfrac{1}{4} & -\dfrac{1}{8} & \dfrac{1}{8} \\[2mm] \dfrac{3}{2} & -\dfrac{1}{4} & -\dfrac{3}{4} \\[2mm] -1 & \dfrac{1}{2} & \dfrac{1}{2} \end{bmatrix}$$

**(c)**
$$\mathbf{X}_B = \begin{bmatrix} x_2 \\ x_3 \\ x_6 \end{bmatrix}, \quad \mathbf{B}^{-1} = \begin{bmatrix} \dfrac{1}{2} & -\dfrac{1}{4} & 0 \\[2mm] 0 & \dfrac{1}{2} & 0 \\[2mm] -2 & 1 & 1 \end{bmatrix}$$

**3.** Consider the following LP model:

$$\text{Maximize } z = 4x_1 + 14x_2$$

subject to

$$2x_1 + 7x_2 + x_3 \qquad = 21$$
$$7x_1 + 2x_2 \qquad + x_4 = 21$$
$$x_1, x_2, x_3, x_4 \geq 0$$

Check the optimality and feasibility of each of the following basic solutions.

(a)    $\mathbf{X}_B = \begin{bmatrix} x_2 \\ x_4 \end{bmatrix}$,    $\mathbf{B}^{-1} = \begin{bmatrix} \dfrac{1}{7} & 0 \\ -\dfrac{2}{7} & 1 \end{bmatrix}$

(b)    $\mathbf{X}_B = \begin{bmatrix} x_2 \\ x_3 \end{bmatrix}$,    $\mathbf{B}^{-1} = \begin{bmatrix} 0 & \dfrac{1}{2} \\ 1 & -\dfrac{7}{2} \end{bmatrix}$

(c)    $\mathbf{X}_B = \begin{bmatrix} x_2 \\ x_1 \end{bmatrix}$,    $\mathbf{B}^{-1} = \begin{bmatrix} \dfrac{7}{45} & -\dfrac{2}{45} \\ -\dfrac{2}{45} & \dfrac{7}{45} \end{bmatrix}$

(d)    $\mathbf{X}_B = \begin{bmatrix} x_1 \\ x_4 \end{bmatrix}$,    $\mathbf{B}^{-1} = \begin{bmatrix} \dfrac{1}{2} & 0 \\ -\dfrac{7}{2} & 1 \end{bmatrix}$

4. Consider the following LP model:

$$\text{Minimize } z = 2x_1 + x_2$$

subject to

$$
\begin{aligned}
3x_1 + x_2 - x_3 \qquad\qquad &= 3 \\
4x_1 + 3x_2 \qquad - x_4 \qquad &= 6 \\
x_1 + 2x_2 \qquad\qquad + x_5 &= 3 \\
x_1, x_2, x_3, x_4, x_5 &\geq 0
\end{aligned}
$$

Compute the entire simplex tableau associated with the following basic solution and check its optimality and feasibility.

$$\mathbf{X}_B = \begin{bmatrix} x_1 \\ x_2 \\ x_5 \end{bmatrix}, \quad \mathbf{B}^{-1} = \begin{bmatrix} \dfrac{3}{5} & -\dfrac{1}{5} & 0 \\ -\dfrac{4}{5} & \dfrac{3}{5} & 0 \\ 1 & -1 & 1 \end{bmatrix}$$

5. Consider the following LP model:

$$\text{Maximize } z = 5x_1 + 12x_2 + 4x_3$$

subject to

$$x_1 + 2x_2 + x_3 + x_4 = 10$$
$$2x_1 - x_2 + 3x_3 = 2$$
$$x_1, x_2, x_3, x_4 \geq 0$$

(a) Identify the best solution from among the following basic feasible solutions:

(i)
$$\mathbf{X}_B = \begin{bmatrix} x_4 \\ x_3 \end{bmatrix}, \quad \mathbf{B}^{-1} = \begin{bmatrix} 1 & -\dfrac{1}{3} \\ 0 & \dfrac{1}{3} \end{bmatrix}$$

(ii)
$$\mathbf{X}_B = \begin{bmatrix} x_2 \\ x_1 \end{bmatrix}, \quad \mathbf{B}^{-1} = \begin{bmatrix} \dfrac{2}{5} & -\dfrac{1}{5} \\ \dfrac{1}{5} & \dfrac{2}{5} \end{bmatrix}$$

(iii)
$$\mathbf{X}_B = \begin{bmatrix} x_2 \\ x_3 \end{bmatrix}, \quad \mathbf{B}^{-1} = \begin{bmatrix} \dfrac{3}{7} & -\dfrac{1}{7} \\ \dfrac{1}{7} & \dfrac{2}{7} \end{bmatrix}$$

(b) Is the solution obtained in (a) optimum for the LP model?

6. The following is the optimal tableau for a maximization LP model with three ( $\leq$ ) constraints and all nonnegative variables. The variables $x_4$, $x_5$, and $x_6$ are the slacks associated with the three constraints. Determine the associated optimal objective value in two different ways by using the primal and dual objective functions.

| Basic | $x_1$ | $x_2$ | $x_3$ | $x_4$ | $x_5$ | Solution |
|-------|-------|-------|-------|-------|-------|----------|
| $z$ | 0 | 0 | 0 | 3 | 2 | ? |
| $x_3$ | 0 | 0 | 1 | 1 | $-1$ | 2 |
| $x_2$ | 0 | 1 | 0 | 1 | 0 | 6 |
| $x_1$ | 1 | 0 | 0 | $-1$ | 1 | 2 |

7. Consider the following LP model:

$$\text{Maximize } z = 5x_1 + 2x_2 + 3x_3$$

subject to

$$x_1 + 5x_2 + 2x_3 \leq b_1$$
$$x_1 - 5x_2 - 6x_3 \leq b_2$$
$$x_1, x_2, x_3 \geq 0$$

Specific constant values of $b_1$ and $b_2$ produce the following optimal tableau:

| Basic | $x_1$ | $x_2$ | $x_3$ | $x_4$ | $x_5$ | Solution |
|-------|-------|-------|-------|-------|-------|----------|
| $z$   | 0     | $a$   | 7     | $d$   | $e$   | 150      |
| $x_1$ | 1     | $b$   | 2     | 1     | 0     | 30       |
| $x_5$ | 0     | $c$   | $-8$  | $-1$  | 1     | 10       |

The constants $a$, $b$, $c$, $d$, and $e$ can be determined from the data of the original problem and the optimal feasible condition of the tableau. Determine
(a) The right-hand–side limits, $b_1$ and $b_2$, of constraints 1 and 2.
(b) The optimal dual solution.
(c) The elements $a$, $b$, and $c$ associated with the variable $x_2$.

## 4.7 POSTOPTIMAL OR SENSITIVITY ANALYSIS

Sensitivity analysis was treated at an elementary level in Sections 2.4. This section uses duality and the primal-dual computations to provide an in-depth treatment of the topic.

Sensitivity analysis is carried out after the (current) optimum solution of an LP model is obtained. The goal is to determine whether changes in the model's coefficients will leave the current solution unchanged, and if not, how a new optimum (assuming one exists) can be obtained efficiently.

In general, changes in the model can result in one of four cases.

1. The current (basic) solution remains unchanged.
2. The current solution becomes infeasible.
3. The current solution becomes nonoptimal.
4. The current solution becomes both nonoptimal and infeasible.

In case 2, we use the dual simplex method to recover feasibility, and in case 3, we use the (primal) simplex method to obtain the new optimum. In case 4, we use both the primal and the dual methods to obtain the new solution. The first three cases are investigated subsequently. The fourth case, being a combination of cases 2 and 3, is treated in Comprehensive Problem 4–3.

The TOYCO model of Example 4.4–2 will be used to explain the different procedures. Recall that the TOYCO model deals with the assembly of three types of toys: trains, trucks, and cars. Each assembly requires three successive operations. We wish to determine the number of units of each toy that will maximize profit. The model and its dual are repeated here for convenience.

| TOYCO primal | TOYCO dual |
|---|---|
| Maximize $z = 3x_1 + 2x_2 + 5x_3$ subject to | Minimize $z = 430y_1 + 460y_2 + 420y_3$ subject to |
| $x_1 + 2x_2 + x_3 \leq 430$ (Operation 1) $3x_1 + \phantom{2x_2} + 2x_3 \leq 460$ (Operation 2) $x_1 + 4x_2 \phantom{+ 2x_3} \leq 420$ (Operation 3) $x_1, x_2, x_3 \geq 0$ | $y_1 + 3y_2 + \phantom{4}y_3 \geq 3$ $2y_1 + \phantom{3y_2} + 4y_3 \geq 2$ $y_1 + 2y_2 \phantom{+ 4y_3} \geq 5$ $y_1, y_2, y_3 \geq 0$ |
| Optimal solution: $x_1 = 0, x_2 = 100, x_3 = 230, z = \$1350$ | Optimal solution: $y_1 = 1, y_2 = 2, y_3 = 0$ |

The associated optimum tableau for the primal is given as

| Basic | $x_1$ | $x_2$ | $x_3$ | $x_4$ | $x_5$ | $x_6$ | Solution |
|---|---|---|---|---|---|---|---|
| $z$ | 4 | 0 | 0 | 1 | 2 | 0 | 1350 |
| $x_2$ | $-\dfrac{1}{4}$ | 1 | 0 | $\dfrac{1}{2}$ | $-\dfrac{1}{4}$ | 0 | 100 |
| $x_3$ | $\dfrac{3}{2}$ | 0 | 1 | 0 | $\dfrac{1}{2}$ | 0 | 230 |
| $x_6$ | 2 | 0 | 0 | $-2$ | 1 | 1 | 20 |

## 4.7.1 Changes Affecting Feasibility

The feasibility of the current optimum solution may be affected only if (1) the right-hand side of the constraints, **b**, is changed, or (2) a new constraint is added to the model. In both cases, infeasibility occurs when at least one of elements of $\mathbf{B}^{-1}\mathbf{b}$ becomes negative—that is, one or more of the current basic variables become negative.

   ***Discrete changes in the right-hand side vector b.***    This section considers the case where specific discrete changes are made in one or more of the elements of the vector **b**. The following example illustrates the procedure.

---

**Example 4.7–1.**

   Suppose that TOYCO wants to expand its assembly lines by increasing the daily capacity of each line by 40% to 602, 644, and 588 minutes, respectively. With these increases, the only change that will take place in the optimum tableau is the right-hand side of the constraints (and the optimum objective value). Thus, using the formula $\mathbf{X}_B = \mathbf{B}^{-1}\mathbf{b}$, we get

$$\begin{bmatrix} x_2 \\ x_3 \\ x_6 \end{bmatrix} = \begin{bmatrix} \dfrac{1}{2} & -\dfrac{1}{4} & 0 \\ 0 & \dfrac{1}{2} & 0 \\ -2 & 1 & 1 \end{bmatrix} \begin{bmatrix} 602 \\ 644 \\ 588 \end{bmatrix} = \begin{bmatrix} 140 \\ 322 \\ 28 \end{bmatrix}$$

   Thus, the current basic variables, $x_2, x_3$, and $x_6$, remain feasible at the new values 140, 322, and 28. The associated optimum profit is $1890.

Although the new solution is appealing from the standpoint of increased profit, TOYCO recognizes that its implementation will take time. Another proposal was thus made to shift the slack capacity of operation 3 ($x_6 = 20$ minutes) to the capacity of operation 1, which changes the capacity mix of the three operations to 450, 460, and 400 minutes, respectively. The resulting solution is

$$
\begin{bmatrix} x_2 \\ x_3 \\ x_6 \end{bmatrix} = \begin{bmatrix} \frac{1}{2} & -\frac{1}{4} & 0 \\ 0 & \frac{1}{2} & 0 \\ -2 & 1 & 1 \end{bmatrix} \begin{bmatrix} 450 \\ 460 \\ 400 \end{bmatrix} = \begin{bmatrix} 110 \\ 230 \\ -40 \end{bmatrix}
$$

The resulting solution is infeasible because $x_6 = -20$. We apply the dual simplex method to recover feasibility. First, we modify the right-hand side of the tableau as shown by the shaded column. Notice that the associated value of $z = 3 \times 0 + 2 \times 110 + 5 \times 230 = \$1370$.

| Basic | $x_1$ | $x_2$ | $x_3$ | $x_4$ | $x_5$ | $x_6$ | Solution |
|-------|-------|-------|-------|-------|-------|-------|----------|
| $z$ | 4 | 0 | 0 | 1 | 2 | 0 | 1370 |
| $x_2$ | $-\frac{1}{4}$ | 1 | 0 | $\frac{1}{2}$ | $-\frac{1}{4}$ | 0 | 110 |
| $x_3$ | $\frac{3}{2}$ | 0 | 1 | 0 | $\frac{1}{2}$ | 0 | 230 |
| $x_6$ | 2 | 0 | 0 | $-2$ | 1 | 1 | $-40$ |

From the dual simplex, $x_6$ leaves and $x_4$ enters, which yields the following optimal feasible tableau (in general, the dual simplex may take more than one iteration to recover feasibility).

| Basic | $x_1$ | $x_2$ | $x_3$ | $x_4$ | $x_5$ | $x_6$ | Solution |
|-------|-------|-------|-------|-------|-------|-------|----------|
| $z$ | 5 | 0 | 0 | 0 | $\frac{5}{2}$ | $\frac{1}{2}$ | 1350 |
| $x_2$ | $\frac{1}{4}$ | 1 | 0 | 0 | 0 | $\frac{1}{4}$ | 100 |
| $x_3$ | $\frac{3}{2}$ | 0 | 1 | 0 | $\frac{1}{2}$ | 0 | 230 |
| $x_4$ | $-1$ | 0 | 0 | 1 | $-\frac{1}{2}$ | $-\frac{1}{2}$ | 20 |

The optimum solution remains essentially unchanged. This in turn means that the proposed shift in capacity allocation is not advantageous in this case.

---

### Problem set 4.7a

**1.** In the TOYCO model listed at the start of Section 4.7, would it be more advantageous to assign the 20-minute excess capacity of operation 3 to operation 2 instead of operation 1?

2. Suppose that TOYCO wants to change the capacities of the three operations according to the following cases:

$$(\textbf{a}) \begin{bmatrix} 460 \\ 500 \\ 400 \end{bmatrix} \quad (\textbf{b}) \begin{bmatrix} 500 \\ 400 \\ 600 \end{bmatrix} \quad (\textbf{c}) \begin{bmatrix} 300 \\ 800 \\ 200 \end{bmatrix} \quad (\textbf{d}) \begin{bmatrix} 450 \\ 700 \\ 350 \end{bmatrix}$$

Use sensitivity analysis to determine the optimum solution.

3. Consider the Reddy Mikks model of Example 2.2.–1. Its optimal tableau is given in Example 3.3–1. If the daily availabilities of raw materials, $M1$ and $M2$, are increased to 28 and 8 tons, respectively, use sensitivity analysis to determine the new optimal solution.

4. The Ozark Farm has 20,000 broilers that are fed for 8 weeks before being marketed. The weekly feed per broiler varies according to the following schedule:

| Week | 1 | 2 | 3 | 4 | 5 | 6 | 7 | 8 |
|------|------|------|------|------|------|------|------|------|
| lb/broiler | .26 | .48 | .75 | 1.00 | 1.30 | 1.60 | 1.90 | 2.10 |

To reach a desired weight gain in 8 weeks, the feed must meet specific nutritional needs by mixing feedstuffs. Although a typical list of feedstuffs is large, for simplicity we will limit the model to three ingredients only: limestone, corn, and soybean meal. The nutritional needs will also be limited to three types: calcium, protein, and fiber. The following table summarizes the nutritive content of the selected ingredients together with the cost data.

| Ingredient | Content (lb) per lb of | | | $ per lb |
|------------|---------|---------|-------|----------|
| | Calcium | Protein | Fiber | |
| Limestone | .380 | .00 | .00 | .12 |
| Corn | .001 | .09 | .02 | .45 |
| Soybean meal | .002 | .50 | .08 | 1.60 |

The feed mix must contain
(**a**) At least .8% but not more than 1.2% calcium
(**b**) At least 22% protein
(**c**) At most 5% crude fiber
Develop an optimal schedule for the 8-week feed period.

*Feasible range of the elements of b.*    Another way of looking at the effect of changing the availability of the resources (i.e., the right-hand–side vector **b**) is to determine the range for which the current solution remains feasible. The following example illustrates the procedure.

---

**Example 4.7–2.**

In the TOYCO model, suppose that we are interested in determining the feasibility range of the capacity of operation 1. We can do so by replacing the vector **b** with

$$\mathbf{b_1} = \begin{bmatrix} 430 + D_1 \\ 460 \\ 420 \end{bmatrix}$$

The amount $D_1$ represents the change in the capacity of operation 1 above and below the present level of 430 minutes. The current basic solution remains basic if $\mathbf{X_B} = \mathbf{B}^{-1}\mathbf{b_1} \geq \mathbf{0}$—that is,

$$\begin{bmatrix} x_2 \\ x_3 \\ x_6 \end{bmatrix} = \begin{bmatrix} \frac{1}{2} & -\frac{1}{4} & 0 \\ 0 & \frac{1}{2} & 0 \\ -2 & 1 & 1 \end{bmatrix} \begin{bmatrix} 430 + D_1 \\ 460 \\ 420 \end{bmatrix} = \begin{bmatrix} 100 + \frac{D_1}{2} \\ 230 \\ 20 - 2D_1 \end{bmatrix} \geq \begin{bmatrix} 0 \\ 0 \\ 0 \end{bmatrix}$$

The first condition ($x_2 \geq 0$) yields $D_1 \geq -200$, the second condition ($x_3 \geq 0$) is independent of $D_1$, and the third condition ($x_6 \geq 0$) yields $D_1 \leq 10$. Thus the current basic solution remains feasible for $-200 \leq D_1 \leq 10$. This is equivalent to varying the availability minutes of operation 1 in the range

$$430 - 200 \leq \text{(Operation 1 capacity)} \leq 430 + 10$$

or

$$230 \leq \text{(Operation 1 capacity)} \leq 440$$

The change in the optimal objective value associated with $D_1$ is $D_1 y_1$, where $y_1$ is the worth per unit (dual price) in dollars per minute of operation 1.

To illustrate the use of the determined range, suppose that the capacity of operation 1 is changed from the current level of 430 minutes to 400 minutes. The current basic solution remains feasible because the new capacity falls within the feasible range. To compute the new values of the variables we use $D_1 = 400 - 430 = -30$ to obtain

$$\begin{bmatrix} x_2 \\ x_3 \\ x_6 \end{bmatrix} = \begin{bmatrix} 100 + \frac{1}{2}(-30) \\ 230 \\ 20 - 2(-30) \end{bmatrix} = \begin{bmatrix} 85 \\ 230 \\ 80 \end{bmatrix}$$

To compute the associated change in the optimal value of the objective function, we first compute the dual prices as

$$(y_1, y_2, y_{3,}) = \mathbf{C}_B \mathbf{B}^{-1} = (2, 5, 0) \begin{bmatrix} \frac{1}{2} & -\frac{1}{4} & 0 \\ 0 & \frac{1}{2} & 0 \\ -2 & 1 & 1 \end{bmatrix} = (1, 2, 0)$$

Thus, the worth per minute of operation 1 is $y_1 = \$1$ per minute and the change in the optimal profit is $D_1 y_1 = -30 \times 1 = -\$30$. Remember that the given worth per unit, $y_1 = 1$, remains valid only within the specified range for $D_1$. Any change outside this range causes infeasibility—hence, the need for using the dual simplex method to determine the new solution, if one exists.

---

Similar procedures can be used to determine the feasible ranges for $D_2$ and $D_3$, the changes associated with operations 2 and 3 (see Problem 4.7b–1). The determination of $D_1, D_2$, and $D_3$ in the prescribed manner and their relationship to the optimal dual values $y_1, y_2$, and $y_3$ are valid only when each resource is considered individually. Should we decide to change the three resources *simultaneously*, a different set of conditions must be derived replacing the present vector $\mathbf{b}$ with the new vector $\mathbf{b}^*$ whose respective elements are $430 + D_1, 460 + D_2$, and $420 + D_3$ (see Problem 4.7b–2).

### Problem set 4.7b

1. In the TOYCO model, suppose that $D_2$ and $D_3$ represent the changes in the availability of operations 2 and 3.
   (a) Determine the range of variation for $D_2$ and $D_3$ that will maintain the feasibility of the current solution assuming that the changes are applied to one operation at a time.
   (b) Determine the worth per minute change in the capacities of operations 2 and 3.
   (c) If the availability of operation 2 is changed from the current 460 minutes to 500 minutes, determine the new solution and the corresponding change in the optimal profit.
   (d) If the availability of operation 3 is changed from 420 minutes to 450 minutes, find the new solution and its associated change in the optimal profit.
   (e) If the availability of operation 3 is changed from 420 minutes to 380 minutes, find the new optimal solution and the associated change in the optimal profit.

2. In the TOYCO model, suppose that the changes $D_1, D_2$, and $D_3$ are made *simultaneously* in the three operations.
   (a) Determine the conditions that will maintain the feasibility of the current optimum solution.
   (b) If the availabilities of operations 1, 2, and 3 are changed to 438, 500, and 410 minutes, respectively, use the conditions determined in (a) to show

that the current basic solution remains feasible, and determine the change in the optimal profit by using the optimal dual prices.

   **(c)** If the availabilities of the three operations are changed to 460, 440, and 380 minutes, respectively, use the conditions obtained in (a) to show that the current basic solution becomes infeasible, and then use the dual simplex method to determine the new solution.

**3.** Consider the TOYCO model.

   **(a)** Suppose that any additional time for operation 1 beyond its current capacity of 430 minutes per day must be done on an overtime basis at $50 an hour. The hourly cost includes both labor and the operation of the machine. Is it economically advantageous to use overtime with operation 1?

   **(b)** Suppose that the operator of operation 2 has agreed to work 2 hours of overtime daily at $45 an hour. Additionally, the cost of the operation itself is $10 an hour. What is the net effect of this activity on the daily profit?

   **(c)** Is it worthwhile to use overtime with operation 3?

   **(d)** Suppose that the daily availability of operation 1 is increased to 440 minutes. Any overtime used beyond the current maximum capacity will cost $40 an hour. Determine the new optimum solution, including the associated net profit.

   **(e)** Suppose that the availability of operation 2 is decreased by 15 minutes a day and that the hourly cost of the operation during regular time is $30. Is it advantageous to decrease the availability of operation 2?

**4.** The Gutchi Company manufactures purses, shaving bags, and backpacks. The construction of the three products requires leather and synthetic material, with leather being the limiting raw material. The production process uses two types of skilled labor: sewing and finishing. The following table gives the availability of the resources, their usage by the three products, and the profits per unit.

|                    | Resource requirements per unit | | |                     |
| ------------------ | ------ | ---- | -------- | ------------------- |
| Resource           | Purse  | Bag  | Backpack | Daily availability  |
| Leather (ft²)      | 2      | 1    | 3        | 42                  |
| Sewing (hr)        | 2      | 1    | 2        | 40                  |
| Finishing (hr)     | 1      | .5   | 1        | 45                  |
| Selling price ($)  | 24     | 22   | 45       |                     |

Formulate the problem as a linear program and find the optimum solution using TORA. Next, indicate whether the following changes in the resources will keep the current solution feasible. For the cases where feasibility is maintained, determine the new optimum solution (values of the variables and the objective function).

(a) Available leather is increased to 45 ft$^2$.
(b) Available leather is decreased by 1 ft$^2$.
(c) Available sewing hours are changed to 38 hours.
(d) Available sewing hours are changes to 46 hours.
(e) Available finishing hours are decreased to 15 hours.
(f) Available finishing hours are increased to 50 hours.
(g) Would you recommend hiring an additional sewing worker at $15 an hour?

5. HiDec produces two models of electronic gadgets that use resistors, capacitors, and chips. The following table summarizes the data of the situation:

| Resource | Unit resource requirements | | Maximum availability (units) |
|---|---|---|---|
| | Model 1 (units) | Model 2 (units) | |
| Resistor | 2 | 3 | 1200 |
| Capacitor | 2 | 1 | 1000 |
| Chips | 0 | 4 | 800 |
| Unit profit ($) | 3 | 4 | |

Let $x_1$ and $x_2$ be the amounts produced of Models 1 and 2, respectively. Following are the LP model and its associated optimal simplex tableau.

$$\text{Maximize } z = 3x_1 + 4x_2$$

subject to

$$2x_1 + 3x_2 \le 1200 \qquad \text{(Resistors)}$$
$$2x_1 + x_2 \le 1000 \qquad \text{(Capacitors)}$$
$$4x_2 \le 800 \qquad \text{(Chips)}$$
$$x_1, x_2 \ge 0$$

| Basic | $x_1$ | $x_2$ | $s_1$ | $s_2$ | $s_3$ | Solution |
|---|---|---|---|---|---|---|
| $z$ | 0 | 0 | $\frac{5}{4}$ | $\frac{1}{4}$ | 0 | 1750 |
| $x_1$ | 1 | 0 | $-\frac{1}{4}$ | $\frac{3}{4}$ | 0 | 450 |
| $s_3$ | 0 | 0 | $-2$ | 2 | 1 | 400 |
| $x_2$ | 0 | 1 | $\frac{1}{2}$ | $-\frac{1}{2}$ | 0 | 100 |

(a) Determine the status of each resource.

**(b)** In terms of the optimal profit, determine the worth of one resistor. One capacitor. One chip.

**(c)** Determine the range of applicability of the dual prices for each resource.

**(d)** If the available number of resistors is increased to 1300 units, find the new optimum solution.

**(e)** If the available number of chips is reduced to 350 units, will you be able to determine the new optimum solution directly from the given information? Explain.

**(f)** If the availability of capacitors is limited by the range of applicability computed in (c), determine the corresponding range of the optimal profit and the corresponding ranges for the number of units to be produced of Models 1 and 2.

**(g)** A new contractor is offering to sell HiDec additional resistors at 40 cents each but only if HiDec would purchase at least 500 units. Should HiDec accept the offer?

**6.** Gapco has a daily budget of 320 hours of labor and 350 units of raw material to manufacture two products. If necessary, the company can employ up to 10 hours daily of overtime labor hours at the additional cost of $2 an hour. It takes 1 labor hour and 3 units of raw material to produce one unit of product 1, and 2 labor hours and 1 unit of raw material to produce 1 unit of product 2. The profit per unit of product 1 is $10 and that of product is $12. Let $x_1$ and $x_2$ define the daily number of units produced of Products 1 and 2, and $x_3$ the daily hours of overtime used. The LP model and its associated optimal simplex tableau are then given as

$$\text{Maximize } z = 10x_1 + 12x_2 - 2x_3$$

subject to

$$x_1 + 2x_2 - x_3 \leq 320 \qquad \text{(Labor hours)}$$
$$3x_1 + x_2 \quad\;\; \leq 350 \qquad \text{(Raw material)}$$
$$x_3 \leq 10 \qquad \text{(Overtime)}$$
$$x_1, x_2, x_3 \leq 0$$

| Basic | $x_1$ | $x_2$ | $x_3$ | $s_1$ | $s_2$ | $s_3$ | Solution |
|-------|-------|-------|-------|-------|-------|-------|----------|
| $z$ | 0 | 0 | 0 | $\frac{26}{5}$ | $\frac{8}{5}$ | $\frac{16}{5}$ | 2256 |
| $x_2$ | 0 | 1 | 0 | $\frac{3}{5}$ | $-\frac{1}{5}$ | $\frac{3}{5}$ | 128 |
| $x_1$ | 1 | 0 | 0 | $-\frac{1}{5}$ | $\frac{2}{5}$ | $-\frac{1}{5}$ | 74 |
| $x_3$ | 0 | 0 | 1 | 0 | 0 | 1 | 10 |

**(a)** Determine the optimal solution of the problem.

**(b)** Determine the dual prices and the applicability ranges of their associated resources.

**(c)** Examine the dual prices for labor hours (constraint 1) and overtime hours (constraint 3). Shouldn't these two values be the same? Explain.

**(d)** Gapco currently pays an additional $2 per overtime hour. What is the most the company should be willing to pay?

**(e)** If Gapco can acquire additional 100 units of raw material daily at $1.50 a unit, would you advise the company to do so? What if the cost of raw material is $2 a unit?

**(f)** Suppose that Gapco is experiencing shortage in raw material and that it cannot acquire more that 200 units a day, determine the associated optimal solution.

**(g)** Suppose that Gapco can use no more than 8 hours of overtime daily, find the new optimum solution.

7. *The 100% feasibility rule.* A simplified rule can be used to test whether or not the *simultaneous* changes $D_1, D_2, \ldots,$ and $D_m$ in the right-hand–side vector **b** can maintain the feasibility of the current solution. Suppose that the right-hand–side $b_i$ of constraint $i$ is changed to $b_i + D_i$ *one at a time,* and that $p_i \le D_i \le q_i$ is the corresponding feasibility range obtained by using the procedure in Example 4.7–2. By definition, we have $p_i \le 0$ $(q_i \ge 0)$ because it represents the maximum allowable decrease (increase) in $b_i$. Next, define $r_i$ equal $\frac{D_i}{p_i}$ or $\frac{D_i}{q_i}$, depending on whether $D_i$ is negative or positive, respectively. By definition, we have $0 \le r_i \le 1$. The 100% rule thus says, given the changes $D_1, D_2, \ldots,$ and $D_m$, then a *sufficient* (but not necessary) condition for the current solution to remain feasible is that $r_1 + r_2 + \ldots + r_m \le 1$. If the condition is not satisfied, then the current solution may or may not remain feasible. Also, the rule is not applicable if $D_i$ falls outside the range $(p_i, q_i)$.

In reality, the 100% rule is too weak to be consistently useful. Even in the cases where feasibility can be confirmed, we still have to obtain the new solution by using the regular simplex feasibility conditions (as we did in Problem 2).

To demonstrate the weakness of the rule, apply it to parts (b) and (c) of Problem 2. The rule fails to confirm the feasibility of the solution in (b) and does not apply in (c) (because the changes in $D_i$ are outside the admissible ranges). Problem 8 further demonstrates this point.

8. Consider the problem

$$\text{Maximize } z = x_1 + x_2$$

subject to

$$2x_1 + x_2 \le 6$$

$$x_1 + 2x_2 \le 6$$

$$x_1, \ x_2 \ge 0$$

**(a)** Show that the optimal basic solution includes both $x_1$ and $x_2$ and that the feasibility ranges for the two constraints, considered one at a time, are $-3 \leq D_1 \leq 6$ and $-3 \leq D_2 \leq 6$.

**(b)** Suppose that the two resources are increased simultaneously by $\Delta > 0$ each. First, show that the basic solution remains feasible for all $\Delta > 0$. Next, show that the 100% rule will confirm feasibility only if the increase is in the range $0 < \Delta < 3$ units. Otherwise, the rule fails for $3 \leq \Delta \leq 6$ and does not apply for $\Delta > 6$.

**9.** Show that the 100% feasibility rule in Problem 7 is based on the condition $\mathbf{B}^{-1}\mathbf{b} \geq \mathbf{0}$.

***Addition of new constraints.***    The addition of a new constraint to an existing model can lead to one of two cases.

**1.** The new constraint is *redundant,* meaning that it is satisfied by the current optimum solution.

**2.** The new constraint is *violated,* in which case the dual simplex method must be used to (attempt to) recover feasibility.

Notice that the addition of a nonredundant constraint can only worsen the current optimum value of the objective function.

---

**Example 4.7–3.**

Suppose that TOYCO is changing the design of its toys, and that the change will require the addition of a fourth operation in the assembly lines. The daily capacity of the new operation is 500 minutes and the times per unit for the three products on this operation are 3, 1, and 1 minutes, respectively. The resulting constraint is thus constructed as $3x_1 + x_2 + x_3 \leq 500$. This constraint is redundant because it is satisfied by the current optimum solution $x_1 = 0$, $x_2 = 100$, and $x_3 = 230$. This means that the current optimum solution remains unchanged.

---

**Example 4.7–4.**

Suppose, instead, that TOYCO unit times on the fourth operation are actually 3, 3, and 1 minutes, respectively. All the remaining data of the model remain unchanged. In this case, the fourth constraint $3x_1 + 3x_2 + x_3 \leq 500$ will not be satisfied by the current optimum solution. We thus must augment the new constraint to the current optimum tableau as follows:

| Basic | $x_1$ | $x_2$ | $x_3$ | $x_4$ | $x_5$ | $x_6$ | $x_7$ | Solution |
|-------|-------|-------|-------|-------|-------|-------|-------|----------|
| $z$ | 4 | 0 | 0 | 1 | 2 | 0 | 0 | 1350 |
| $x_2$ | $-\frac{1}{4}$ | 1 | 0 | $\frac{1}{2}$ | $-\frac{1}{4}$ | 0 | 0 | 100 |
| $x_3$ | $\frac{3}{2}$ | 0 | 1 | 0 | $\frac{1}{2}$ | 0 | 0 | 230 |
| $x_6$ | 2 | 0 | 0 | $-2$ | 1 | 1 | 0 | 20 |
| $x_7$ | 3 | 3 | 1 | 0 | 0 | 0 | 1 | 500 |

Because the variables $x_2$ and $x_3$ are basic, we must substitute out their constraint coefficients in the $x_7$-row, which can be achieved by performing the following operation:

$$\text{New } x_7\text{-row} = \text{Old } x_7\text{-row} - [3 \times x_2\text{-row}) - 1 \times (x_3\text{-row})]$$

The new tableau is thus given as

| Basic | $x_1$ | $x_2$ | $x_3$ | $x_4$ | $x_5$ | $x_6$ | $x_7$ | Solution |
|-------|-------|-------|-------|-------|-------|-------|-------|----------|
| $z$ | 4 | 0 | 0 | 1 | 2 | 0 | 0 | 1350 |
| $x_2$ | $-\frac{1}{4}$ | 1 | 0 | $\frac{1}{2}$ | $-\frac{1}{4}$ | 0 | 0 | 100 |
| $x_3$ | $\frac{3}{2}$ | 0 | 1 | 0 | $\frac{1}{2}$ | 0 | 0 | 230 |
| $x_6$ | 2 | 0 | 0 | $-2$ | 1 | 1 | 0 | 20 |
| $x_7$ | $\frac{9}{4}$ | 0 | 0 | $-\frac{3}{2}$ | $\frac{1}{4}$ | 0 | 1 | $-30$ |

The application of the dual simplex method will produce the new optimum solution $x_1 = 0, x_2 = 90, x_3 = 230$, and $z = \$1330$ (verify!).

## Problem set 4.7c

1. In the TOYCO model, suppose the fourth operation has the following specifications: The maximum production rate based on 480 minutes a day is either 120 units of product 1, 480 units of product 2, or 240 units of product 3. Determine the optimal solution assuming that the daily capacity is limited to (a) 570 minutes (b) 548 minutes.

2. *Secondary constraints.* Instead of solving a problem using all of its constraints, we can start by identifying the so-called *secondary constraints.* These are the constraints that we suspect are the least restrictive in terms of the optimum solution. The model is solved using the remaining (primary) constraints. We may then augment the secondary constraints one at a time. A secondary constraint is discarded once it is found that it satisfies the available optimum. The process is continued until all the secondary constraints are accounted for.

    Apply the proposed procedure to the following LP:

    $$\text{Maximize } z = 5x_1 + 6x_2 + 3x_3$$

    subject to

    $$5x_1 + 5x_2 + 3x_3 \leq 50$$
    $$x_1 + x_2 - x_3 \leq 20$$

$$7x_1 + 6x_2 - 9x_3 \leq 30$$

$$5x_1 + 5x_2 + 5x_3 \leq 35$$

$$12x_1 + 6x_2 \quad\quad \leq 90$$

$$x_2 - 9x_3 \leq 20$$

$$x_1,\ x_2,\ x_3 \geq 0$$

### 4.7.2  Changes Affecting Optimality

The current solution will cease to be optimal only if the coefficients of the objective function, $z_j - c_j$, violate the optimality condition. Given the dual prices vector $\mathbf{Y} = \mathbf{C}_B \mathbf{B}^{-1}$ as defined in Section 4.6, the definition

$$z_j - c_j = \mathbf{Y}\mathbf{P}_j - c_j$$

tells us that the optimality of the solution can be affected only when we change the objective coefficients $c_j$ (and, hence, $\mathbf{C}_B$) or the unit resource usage vector $\mathbf{P}_j$. We will subsequently investigate each of these cases.

**Changes in the objective coefficients $c_j$.**    The effect of making changes in $c_j$ on optimality entails recomputing $z_j - c_j$ for the *nonbasic* variables only. The reason we do not need to recompute $z_j - c_j$ for the *basic* variables is that they will always equal zero regardless of the changes made in $c_j$ (see Section 7.4 for the proof).

The computational procedure is summarized as:

**1.** Compute the dual prices vector $\mathbf{Y} = \mathbf{C}_B \mathbf{B}^{-1}$ using the new vector $\mathbf{C}_B$ if it has been changed.

**2.** Compute $z_j - c_j = \mathbf{Y}\mathbf{P}_j - c_j$ for all the current *nonbasic* $x_j$. Two cases will result.

1. If the optimality condition is satisfied, the current solution will remain the same but at a new optimum value of the objective function. (If $\mathbf{C}_B$ is unchanged, the optimum objective value will remain the same, however).
2. If the optimality condition is not satisfied, we apply the (primal) simplex method to recover optimality.

---

**Example 4.7–5.**

In the TOYCO model, suppose that the company has a new pricing policy to meet or match the competition. The unit profits under the new policy are $4, $3, and $4 for train, truck, and car toys, respectively. This means that the new objective function is given as

$$\text{Maximize } z = 4x_1 + 3x_2 + 4x_3$$

Because the current basic solution $\mathbf{X}_B$ consists of $x_2, x_3$, and $x_6$, we have $\mathbf{C}_B = (3, 4, 0)$, and the dual prices vector is computed as

$$
\mathbf{Y} = \mathbf{C}_B \mathbf{B}^{-1} = (3, 4, 0) \begin{bmatrix} \dfrac{1}{2} & -\dfrac{1}{4} & 0 \\[2mm] 0 & \dfrac{1}{2} & 0 \\[2mm] -2 & 1 & 1 \end{bmatrix} = \left( \dfrac{3}{2}, \dfrac{5}{4}, 0 \right)
$$

The values of $z_j - c_j$ for the nonbasic variables $x_1, x_4$, and $x_5$ are computed from the formula $z_j - c_j = \mathbf{YP}_j - c_j$ as

$$
z_1 - c_1 = y_1 + 3y_2 + y_3 - 4 = \frac{3}{2} + 3\left(\frac{5}{4}\right) + 0 - 4 = \frac{5}{4}
$$

$$
z_4 - c_4 = y_1 - 0 = \frac{3}{2}
$$

$$
z_5 - c_5 = y_2 - 0 = \frac{5}{4}
$$

Note that $c_1 = 4$ in accordance with the new objective function.

The computation show that the current solution, $x_1 = 0$ train, $x_2 = 100$ trucks, and $x_3 = 230$ cars, is still optimal. The corresponding new profit is computed as $4 \times 0 + 3 \times 100 + 4 \times 230 = \$1220$.

Suppose now that the TOYCO objective function is changed to

$$
\text{Maximize } z = 6x_1 + 3x_2 + 4x_3
$$

This is the same as the preceding one except that the coefficient of $x_1$ has been changed from 4 to 6. As a result, only $z_1 - c_1$ needs to be recomputed, which gives

$$
z_1 - c_1 = y_1 + 3y_2 + y_3 - 6 = \frac{3}{2} + 3\left(\frac{5}{4}\right) + 0 - 6 = -\frac{3}{4}
$$

It follows that $x_1$ must enter the solution. The corresponding simplex tableau is then given as

| Basic | $x_1$ | $x_2$ | $x_3$ | $x_4$ | $x_5$ | $x_6$ | Solution |
|-------|-------|-------|-------|-------|-------|-------|----------|
| $z$ | $-\dfrac{3}{4}$ | 0 | 0 | $\dfrac{3}{2}$ | $\dfrac{5}{4}$ | 0 | 1350 |
| $x_2$ | $-\dfrac{1}{4}$ | 1 | 0 | $\dfrac{1}{2}$ | $-\dfrac{1}{4}$ | 0 | 100 |
| $x_3$ | $\dfrac{3}{2}$ | 0 | 1 | 0 | $\dfrac{1}{2}$ | 0 | 230 |
| $x_6$ | 2 | 0 | 0 | $-2$ | 1 | 1 | 20 |

The elements shown in the shaded cells are the new $z_j - c_j$ for the nonbasic variables $x_1, x_4$, and $x_5$. All the remaining elements of the tableau are the same as in the original optimal tableau. The new optimum solution is then determined by letting $x_1$ enter and $x_6$ leave, which yields $x_1 = 10, x_2 = 102.5, x_3 = 215$, and $z = \$1227.50$ (verify!).

Another way of investigating the effect of changes in the objective function coefficients is to compute the range of variation for each individual coefficient that will keep the current solution optimal. This is achieved by replacing the current $c_j$ with $c_j + d_j$, where $d_j$ represents the (positive or negative) amount of change.

The limits on $d_j$ may then be determined by computing the new $z_j - c_j$ and then implementing the proper optimality condition depending on whether the model is of the maximization or minimization type (see Problems 4.7d–3 and 4.7d–7).

### Problem set 4.7d

1. Invfestigate the optimality of the TOYCO solution for each of the following objective functions. If the solution changes, determine the new optimum. (The optimum tableau of TOYCO is given at the start of Section 4.7.)
   (a) $z = 2x_1 + x_2 + 4x_3$
   (b) $z = 3x_1 + 6x_2 + x_3$
   (c) $z = 8x_1 + 3x_2 + 9x_3$
2. Investigate the optimality of the Reddy Mikks solution (Example 4.4–1) for each of the following objective functions. If the solution changes, determine the new optimum. (The optimal tableau of the model is given in Example 3.3–1.)
   (a) $z = 3x_1 + 2x_2$
   (b) $z = 8x_1 + 10x_2$
   (c) $z = 2x_1 + 10x_2$
3. In the TOYCO model, suppose that the objective coefficients are changed, one at a time, as follows:
   (a) The unit profit of a toy train is $3 + d_1$ dollars.
   (b) The unit profit of a toy truck is $2 + d_2$ dollars.
   (c) The unit profit of a toy car $5 + d_3$ dollars.
   The changes $d_1, d_2$, and $d_3$ can be positive or negative. Use the proper conditions on $z_j - c_j$ to determine the admissible ranges that will keep the current solution optimal.
4. In the TOYCO model, use the solution in Problem 3 to indicate whether or not the current solution will remain optimal in each of the following (independent) cases. If the solution changes, determine the new one.
   (a) The unit profit of a toy train is increased from $3 to $5. To $8.
   (b) The units profit of a toy train is decreased from $3 to $2.
   (c) The unit profit of a toy truck is increased from $2 to $6.
   (d) The unit profit of a toy car is decreased from $5 to $2.
5. In the Reddy Mikks model, suppose that the following individual changes are implemented in the objective coefficients, one at a time:
   (a) The profit per ton of exterior paint is $5 + d_1$ thousand dollars.
   (b) The profit per ton of interior paint is $4 + d_2$ thousand dollars.

Assuming that $d_1$ and $d_2$ can be positive or negative, use the proper condition on $z_j - c_j$ to determine the admissible ranges that will keep the current solution optimal.

6. In the Reddy Mikks model, use the solution in Problem 5 to indicate whether or not the current solution will remain optimal in each of the following (independent) cases. If the solution changes, determine the new one.
   (a) The profit per ton of exterior paint is increased from $5000 to $7000. Decreased from $5000 to $4000.
   (b) The profit per ton of interior paint is increased from $4000 to $6000. Decreased from $4000 to $3000.

7. In Problem 3, suppose that the proposed changes $d_1, d_2$, and $d_3$ are instituted *simultaneously* in the TOYCO model.
   (a) Determine the conditions that will keep the current solution optimal.
   (b) Use the conditions obtained in (a) to determine the new solution (if a change occurs) in each of the following cases:
       (i) $z = 2x_1 + x_2 + 4x_3$
       (ii) $z = 3x_1 + 6x_2 + x_3$
       (iii) $z = 8x_1 + 3x_2 + 9x_3$

8. In Problem 5, suppose that the proposed changes $d_1$ and $d_2$ are instituted *simultaneously* in the Reddy Mikks model.
   (a) Determine the conditions that will keep the current solution optimal.
   (b) Use the conditions obtained in (a) to determine whether or not the current solution remains optimal in each of the following cases:
       (i) $z = 3x_1 + 2x_2$
       (ii) $z = 3x_1 + 9x_2$
       (iii) $z = 5x_1 + 5x_2$

9. In the Gutchi model of Problem 4.7b–4, determine the associated optimum solution for each of the following objective functions:
   (a) $z = 40x_1 + 22x_2 + 45x_3$
   (b) $z = 70x_1 + 22x_2 + 45x_3$
   (c) $z = 24x_1 + 10x_2 + 45x_3$
   (d) $z = 24x_1 + 20x_2 + 45x_3$
   (e) $z = 24x_1 + 22x_2 + 50x_3$
   (f) $z = 24x_1 + 22x_2 + 40x_3$

10. Consider the HiDec model in Problem 4.7b–5.
    (a) Find the unit profit range for Models 1 that will maintain the optimality of the current solution.
    (b) Find the unit profit range for model 2 that will keep the current solution optimal.
    (c) If the unit profit of model 1 is increased to $6, determine the new solution.
    (d) If the unit profit of model 2 is changed to $1, determine the new optimum solution.

(e) Determine the condition that will keep the current solution optimum if the unit profits of Models 1 and 2 are changed simultaneously.

(f) Suppose that the objective function is changed to

$$z = 5x_1 + 2x_2$$

Determine the associated optimum solution.

11. Consider the Gapco model in Problem 4.7b–6.

   (a) What is the least profit per unit Gapco can make from product 1 without changing the current production schedule?

   (b) If the profit per unit of product 2 is increased to $25, determine the associated optimum solution.

12. *The 100% optimality rule.* A rule similar to the *100% feasibility rule* outlined in Problem 4.7b–7 can also be developed for testing the effect of simultaneously changing all $c_j$ to $c_j + d_j, j = 1, 2, \ldots, n$, on the optimality of the current solution. Suppose that $u_j \leq d_j \leq v_j$ is the optimality range obtained as a result of changing each $c_j$ to $c_j + d_j$ one at a time using the procedure given in Problem 3. In this case, $u_j \leq 0$ ($v_j \geq 0$) because it represents the maximum allowable decrease (increase) in $c_j$ that will keep the current solution optimal. For the cases where $u_j \leq d_j \leq v_j$, define $r_j = \frac{d_j}{v_j}$ or $\frac{d_j}{u_j}$, depending on whether $d_j$ is positive or negative, respectively. By definition, $0 \leq r_j \leq 1$. The 100% rule says that a sufficient (but not necessary) condition for the current solution to remain optimal is that $r_1 + r_2 + \ldots + r_n \leq 1$. If the condition is not satisfied, the current solution may or may not remain optimal. The rule does not apply if $d_j$ falls outside the specified ranges.

   Apply the 100% optimality rule to the cases in Problem 1 to check if the given optimum solution remains unchanged. By comparing the results of the 100% rule with those of the optimality conditions used in Problem 1, demonstrate that the 100% rule is too weak to be consistently reliable as a decision-making tool.

13. Show that the 100% optimality rule (Problem 12) is derived from the conditions $z_j - c_j \geq 0$ for maximization problems and $z_j - c_j \leq 0$ for minimization problems.

***Addition of a new activity.***    The addition of a new activity in an LP model is equivalent to adding a new variable. Intuitively, the addition of a new activity is desirable only if it is profitable—that is, if it improves the optimal value of the objective function. This condition can be checked by computing $z_j - c_j = \mathbf{YP}_j - c_j$ for the new activity, where $\mathbf{Y}$ are the current optimal dual values and $\mathbf{P}_j$ and $c_j$ represent the resource usages and profit per unit of the new activity. If the computed $z_j - c_j$ satisfies the optimality condition, then the new activity is not desirable. Otherwise, the new activity is profitable and must be brought into the basic solution.

**Example 4.7–6.**

TOYCO recognizes that toy trains are not currently in production because they are not profitable. The company wants to replace toy trains with a new product, a toy fire engine, to be assembled on the existing facilities. TOYCO estimates the profit per toy fire engine to be \$4 and the assembly times per unit to be 1 minute on each of operations 1 and 2, and 2 minutes on operation 3.

Let $x_7$ represent the new fire engine product. Because the current basic vector $\mathbf{C}_B$ has not changed, the current dual values $\mathbf{Y} = (y_1, y_2, y_3) = (1, 2, 0)$ are applicable. We thus get

$$z_7 - c_7 = 1y_1 + 1y_2 + 2y_3 - 4 = 1 \times 1 + 1 \times 2 + 2 \times 0 - 4 = -1$$

The result shows that it is profitable to include $x_7$ in the optimal basic solution. To obtain the new optimum, we first compute

$$\mathbf{B}^{-1}\mathbf{P}_7 = \begin{bmatrix} \frac{1}{2} & -\frac{1}{4} & 0 \\ 0 & \frac{1}{2} & 0 \\ -2 & 1 & 1 \end{bmatrix} \begin{bmatrix} 1 \\ 1 \\ 2 \end{bmatrix} = \begin{bmatrix} \frac{1}{4} \\ \frac{1}{2} \\ 1 \end{bmatrix}$$

Thus, the current simplex tableau must be modified as follows

| Basic | $x_1$ | $x_2$ | $x_3$ | $x_7$ | $x_4$ | $x_5$ | $x_6$ | Solution |
|-------|-------|-------|-------|-------|-------|-------|-------|----------|
| $z$ | 4 | 0 | 0 | $-1$ | 1 | 2 | 0 | 1350 |
| $x_2$ | $-\frac{1}{4}$ | 1 | 0 | $\frac{1}{4}$ | $\frac{1}{2}$ | $-\frac{1}{4}$ | 0 | 100 |
| $x_3$ | $\frac{3}{2}$ | 0 | 1 | $\frac{1}{2}$ | 0 | $\frac{1}{2}$ | 0 | 230 |
| $x_6$ | 2 | 0 | 0 | 1 | $-2$ | 1 | 1 | 20 |

The new optimum is determined by letting $x_7$ enter the basic solution, in which case $x_6$ must leave.

The case of adding a new activity, as demonstrated earlier, also subsumes the case where changes are made in the resource usage vector $\mathbf{P}_j$ of an *existing* activity. For this reason, this case will not be considered separately.

### Problem set 4.7e

**1.** In the original TOYCO model (Example 4.4–2), toy trains are not part of the optimal product mix. The company recognizes that market competition will not allow raising the unit price of the toy. Instead, the company wants to concentrate on improving the assembly operation itself. This entails reducing the assembly time per unit in each of the three operations by a specified percentage, $p\%$. Determine the value of $p$ that will make toy trains just profitable. (The optimum tableau of the TOYCO model is given at the start of Section 4.7.)

2. In the TOYCO model, suppose that the company can reduce the unit times on operations 1, 2, and 3 for toy trains from the current levels of 1, 3, and 1 minutes to .5, 1, and .5 minutes, respectively. The profit per unit remains unchanged at $3. Determine the new optimum solution.

3. In the TOYCO model, suppose that a new toy (fire engine) require 3, 2, 4 minutes, respectively, on operations 1, 2, and 3. Determine the optimal solution when the profit per unit is given by
   (a) $5.
   (b) $10.

4. In the Reddy Mikks model, the company is considering the production of a cheaper brand of exterior paint whose input requirements per ton include .75 ton of each of raw materials, $M1$ and $M2$. Market conditions still dictate that the excess of interior paint over the production of *both* types of exterior paint be limited to 1 ton daily. The profit per ton of the new exterior paint is $3500. Determine the new optimal solution. (The model is explained in Example 4.4–1, and its optimum tableau is given in Example 3.3.–1.)

## 4.8 SUMMARY

This chapter has presented the dual problem and its economic interpretation. The chapter concludes with the topic of sensitivity analysis in which the different coefficients of the LP model are changed. The objective of sensitivity analysis is to determine the new optimal feasible solution, if one exists, in the most efficient manner.

## SELECTED REFERENCES

BRADLEY, S., A. HAX, and T. MAGNANTI, *Applied Mathematical Programming,* Addison-Wesley, Reading, Mass., 1977

BAZARAA, M., J. JARVIS, and H. SHERALI, *Linear Programming and Network Flows,* 2nd ed., Wiley, New York, 1990.

NERING, E., and A. TUCKER, *Linear Programming and Related Problems,* Academic Press, Boston, 1992.

## COMPREHENSIVE PROBLEMS

■ **4–1**[1] MANCO produces three products $P1$, $P2$, and $P3$. The production process uses raw materials, $R1$ and $R2$, which are processed on facilities, $F1$ and $F2$. The following table provides the pertinent data of the problem.

| Resource | Units | Usage per unit | | | Maximum daily capacity |
|----------|-------|----|----|----|----------|
|          |       | $P1$ | $P2$ | $P3$ |          |
| $F1$ | Minutes | 1 | 2 | 1 | 430 |
| $F2$ | Minutes | 3 | 0 | 2 | 460 |
| $R1$ | lb | 1 | 4 | 0 | 420 |
| $R2$ | lb | 1 | 1 | 1 | 300 |

The minimum daily demand for $P2$ is 70 units and the maximum demand for $P3$ is 240 units. The unit profit contributions of $P1$, $P2$, and $P3$ are $300, $200, and $500, respectively.

MANCO management is discussing means to improve the financial situation of the company. The following are the most prominent proposals:

1. The per unit profit of P3 can be increased by 20%, but this will reduce the market demand to 210 units instead of the present 240 units.
2. Raw material, $R2$, appears to be a critical factor in limiting current production. Additional units can be secured from a different supplier whose price per pound is $3 higher than the present supplier.
3. The capacities of $F1$ and $F2$ can be increased by up to 40 minutes a day, each for an additional cost of $35 per day.
4. The chief buyer of product $P2$ is requesting that its daily supply be increased from the present 70 units to 100 units.
5. The per unit processing time of $P1$ on $F2$ can be reduced from 3 to 2 minutes at an additional cost of $4 per day.

Discuss the feasibility of the these proposals, remembering that (some of) the proposals are not mutually exclusive.

■ **4–2** The Reddy Mikks Company is preparing a future expansion plan. A study of the market indicates that the company can increase its sales by about 25%. The following proposals are being studied for the development of an action plan. (Refer to Example 3.3–1 for the details of the model and its solution.)

[1]Based on D. Sheran, "Post-Optimal Analysis in Linear Programming—The Right Example," *IIE Transactions,* Vol. 16, No. 1, March 1984, pp. 99–102.

*Proposal 1.* Because a 25% increase roughly equals a $5250 increase in profit and the worth per additional ton of $M1$ and $M2$ are $750 and $500, respectively, the desired increase in production can be achieved by making a combined increase of $5250 ÷ ($750 + $500)/2 = 8.4 tons in each of $M1$ and $M2$.

*Proposal 2.* Increase the amounts of raw materials, $M1$ and $M2$ by 6 tons and 1 ton, respectively. These increments equal 25% of the current levels of $M1$ and $M2$ (= 24 and 6 tons, respectively). Because these two resources are *scarce* at the current optimum solution, a 25% increase in their availability produces an equivalent increase in the levels of production of interior and exterior paints, as desired.

What is your opinion of these proposals? Would you suggest a different approach for solving the problem?

■ **4–3** *Sensitivity analysis for cases affecting both optimality and feasibility.* Suppose that you are given the following simultaneous changes in the Reddy Mikks model:

1. The profit per ton of exterior and interior paints are $1000 and $4000, respectively.
2. The maximum daily availabilities of raw materials, $M1$ and $M2$, are 28 and 8 tons, respectively.
   
   (a) Show that the proposed changes will render the current basic solution both nonoptimal and infeasible.
   
   (b) Use the *generalized simplex algorithm* in Problem 4.5a–7 to determine the new optimal feasible solution.

# Chapter 5

# Transportation Model and Its Variants

## 5.1 DEFINITION OF THE TRANSPORTATION MODEL

The transportation model is a special class of the linear programming problem. It deals with the situation in which a commodity is shipped from **sources** (e.g., factories) to **destinations** (e.g., warehouses). The objective is to determine the amounts shipped from each source to each destination that minimize the total shipping cost while satisfying both the supply limits and the demand requirements. The model assumes that the shipping cost on a given route is directly proportional to the number of units shipped on that route. In general, the transportation model can be extended to areas other than the direct transportation of a commodity, including, among others, inventory control, employment scheduling, and personnel assignment.

The general problem is represented by the network in Figure 5–1. There are $m$ sources and $n$ destinations, each represented by a **node**. The **arcs** linking the sources and destinations represent the routes between the sources and the destinations. Arc

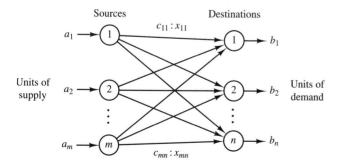

**Figure 5–1**

$(i, j)$ joining source $i$ to destination $j$ carries two pieces of information: (1) the transportation cost per unit, $c_{ij}$, and (2) the amount shipped, $x_{ij}$. The amount of supply at source $i$ is $a_i$ and the amount of demand at destination $j$ is $b_j$. The objective of the model is to determine the unknowns $x_{ij}$ that will minimize the total transportation cost while satisfying all the supply and demand restrictions.

**Example 5.1–1.**

MG Auto has three plants in Los Angeles, Detroit, and New Orleans, and two major distribution centers in Denver and Miami. The capacities of the three plants during the next quarter are 1000, 1500, and 1200 cars. The quarterly demand at the two distribution centers are 2300 and 1400 cars. The mileage chart between the plants and the distribution centers are given in Table 5–1.

**TABLE 5–1**

|             | Denver | Miami |
|-------------|--------|-------|
| Los Angeles | 1000   | 2690  |
| Detroit     | 1250   | 1350  |
| New Orleans | 1275   | 850   |

The trucking company in charge of transporting the cars charges 8 cents per mile per car. The transportation cost per car on the different routes, rounded to the closest dollar, are calculated as given in Table 5–2.

**TABLE 5–2**

|                     | Denver (1) | Miami (2) |
|---------------------|------------|-----------|
| Los Angeles (1)     | $80        | $215      |
| Detroit (2)         | $100       | $108      |
| New Orleans (3)     | $102       | $68       |

The LP model of the problem in Table 5–2 is given as

$$\text{Minimize } z = 80x_{11} + 215x_{12} + 100x_{21} + 108x_{22} + 102x_{31} + 68x_{32}$$

subject to

$$x_{11} + x_{12} \qquad\qquad\qquad = 1000 \quad \text{(Los Angeles)}$$

$$x_{21} + x_{22} \qquad\qquad\qquad = 1500 \quad \text{(Detroit)}$$

$$+ x_{31} + x_{32} = 1200 \quad \text{(New Orleans)}$$

$$x_{11} \qquad + x_{21} \qquad + x_{31} \qquad = 2300 \quad \text{(Denver)}$$

$$x_{12} \qquad + x_{22} \qquad + x_{32} = 1400 \quad \text{(Miami)}$$

$$x_{ij} \geq 0, \quad i = 1, 2, 3, \quad j = 1, 2$$

These constraints are all equations because the total supply from the three sources (= 1000 + 1500 + 1200 = 3700 cars) equals the total demand at the two destinations (= 2300 + 1400 = 3700 cars).

The LP model can be solved by the simplex method. However, the special structure of the constraints allows us to solve the problem more conveniently using the **transportation tableau** shown in Table 5–3.

**TABLE 5–3**

|  | Denver | Miami | Supply |
|---|---|---|---|
| Los Angeles | 80 $x_{11}$ | 215 $x_{12}$ | **1000** |
| Detroit | 100 $x_{21}$ | 108 $x_{22}$ | **1500** |
| New Orleans | 102 $x_{31}$ | 68 $x_{32}$ | **1200** |
| Demand | **2300** | **1400** |  |

The optimal solution (obtained by TORA) is summarized in Figure 5–2. It calls for shipping 1000 cars from Los Angeles to Denver, 1300 from Detroit to Denver, 200 from Detroit to Miami, and 1200 from New Orleans to Miami. The associated minimum transportation cost is $313,200.

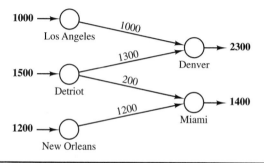

**Figure 5–2**

When the total supply does not equal the total demand, the transportation model is said to be **unbalanced**. We will show subsequently how an unbalanced model can always be balanced by adding a **dummy** source or destination. The reason we are interested in balancing the transportation model is that it allows the development of a solution algorithm that is based directly on the use of the transportation tableau.

**Example 5.1–2.**

In the MG model, suppose that the Detroit plant capacity is 1300 cars (instead of 1500). This means that the total supply (= 3500 cars) is less than the total demand (= 3700 cars), a situation that dictates that part of the demand at Denver and Miami may not be filled.

Because the demand exceeds the supply, a dummy source (plant) with a capacity of 200 cars (= 3700 − 3500) is added to balance the transportation model. In this case, the unit transportation cost from the dummy plant to the two destinations is zero because the plant does not exist. The unit transportation cost from the dummy source to the destinations may assume positive values as well. For example, to ensure that Miami will receive all its demand, we assign a high unit transportation cost (penalty) to the entry from the dummy source to Miami.

Table 5–4 gives the balanced model together with its optimum solution. The solution shows that the dummy plant ships 200 cars to Miami, which means that Miami will be 200 cars short of satisfying its demand of 1400 cars.

**TABLE 5–4**

|              | Denver | Miami | Supply |
|--------------|--------|-------|--------|
| Los Angeles  | 80     | 215   |        |
|              | **1000** |     | **1000** |
| Detroit      | 100    | 108   |        |
|              | **1300** |     | **1300** |
| New Orleans  | 102    | 68    |        |
|              |        | **1200** | **1200** |
| Dummy Plant  | 0      | 0     |        |
|              |        | **200** | **200** |
| Demand       | **2300** | **1400** |    |

We can also demonstrate the case in which the supply exceeds the demand by assuming that the demand at Denver is 1900 cars only. In this case, we need to add a dummy distribution center to "receive" the surplus supply. Again, the unit transportation costs to the dummy distribution center are zero, unless we wish to impose other conditions. For example, we can require a factory to "ship out" completely by assigning a high unit transportation cost from the designated factory to the dummy destination.

Table 5–5 gives the new model and its optimal solution (obtained by TORA). The solution shows that the Detroit plant will have a surplus of 400 cars.

**TABLE 5–5**

|  | Denver | Miami | Dummy |  |
|---|---|---|---|---|
| Los Angeles | 80 | 215 | 0 |  |
|  | **1000** |  |  | **1000** |
| Detroit | 100 | 108 | 0 |  |
|  | **900** | **200** | **400** | **1500** |
| New Orleans | 102 | 68 | 0 |  |
|  |  | **1200** |  | **1200** |
| Demand | **1900** | **1400** | **400** |  |

**Problem set 5.1a**

1. True or False?
   (a) To balance a transportation model, it may be necessary to add both a dummy source and a dummy destination.
   (b) The amounts shipped to a dummy destination represent surplus at the shipping source.
   (c) The amounts shipped from a dummy source represent shortages at the receiving destinations.
2. In each of the following cases, determine whether a dummy source or a dummy destination must be added to balance the model.
   (a) Supply: $a_1 = 10, a_2 = 5, a_3 = 4, a_4 = 6$

   Demand: $b_1 = 10, b_2 = 5, b_3 = 7, b_4 = 9$

   (b) Supply: $a_1 = 30, a_2 = 44$

   Demand: $b_1 = 25, b_2 = 30, b_3 = 10$
3. In Table 5–4 of Example 5.1–2, where a dummy plant is added, what does it mean in terms of the solution if the dummy plant "ships" 150 cars to Denver and 50 cars to Miami?

**4.** In Table 5–5 of Example 5.1–2, where a dummy destination is added, suppose that the Detroit plant must ship out *all* its production, how can this restriction be implemented in the model?

**5.** In Example 5.1–2, suppose that for the case where the demand exceeds the supply (Table 5–4), penalty costs are levied at the rate of $200 and $300 for each undelivered car at Denver and Miami, respectively. Additionally, no deliveries are made from the Los Angeles plant to the Miami distribution center. Set up the model, and determine the optimal shipping schedule for the problem using TORA.

**6.** Three electric power plants with capacities of 25, 40, and 30 million kWh supply electricity to three cities. The maximum demands at the three cities are estimated at 30, 35, and 25 million kWh. The price per million kWh at the three cities is given in Table 5–6.

**TABLE 5–6**

|  |  | City | |  |
|---|---|---|---|---|
|  |  | 1 | 2 | 3 |
|  | 1 | $600 | $700 | $400 |
| Plant | 2 | $320 | $300 | $350 |
|  | 3 | $500 | $480 | $450 |

During the month of August, there is a 20% increase in demand at each of the three cities, which can be met by purchasing electricity from another network at a premium rate of $1000 per million kWh. The network is not linked to city 3, however. The utility company wishes to determine the most economical plan for the distribution and purchase of additional energy.

**(a)** Formulate the problem as a transportation model.

**(b)** Solve the problem with TORA, and determine an optimal distribution plan for the utility company.

**(c)** Determine the cost of the additional power purchased by each of the three cities.

**7.** Solve Problem 6, assuming that there is a 10% power transmission loss through the network.

**8.** The National Parks Service is receiving four bids for logging at three pine forests in Arkansas. The three locations include 10,000, 20,000, and 30,000 acres. A single bidder can bid for at most 50% of the total acreage available. The bids per acre at the three locations are given in Table 5–7.

**TABLE 5-7**

|  |  | Location | | |
|---|---|---|---|---|
|  |  | 1 | 2 | 3 |
| Bidder | 1 | $520 | $210 | $570 |
|  | 2 | — | $510 | $495 |
|  | 3 | $650 | — | $240 |
|  | 4 | $180 | $430 | $710 |

**(a)** In the present situation, we need to *maximize* the total bidding revenue for the Parks Service. Show how the problem can be formulated as a transportation model.

**(b)** Use TORA to determine the acreage that should be assigned to each of the four bidders.

9. Three refineries with daily capacities of 6, 5, and 8 million gallons, respectively, supply three distribution areas with daily demands of 4, 8, and 7 million gallons, respectively. Gasoline is transported to the three distribution areas through a network of pipelines. The transportation cost is 10 cents per 1000 gallons per pipeline mile. Table 5–8 gives the mileage between the refineries and the distribution areas. Refinery 1 is not connected to distribution area 3.

**TABLE 5–8**

|  |  | Distribution area | | |
|---|---|---|---|---|
|  |  | 1 | 2 | 3 |
| Plant | 1 | 120 | 180 | — |
|  | 2 | 300 | 100 | 80 |
|  | 3 | 200 | 250 | 120 |

**(a)** Construct the associated transportation model.

**(b)** Use TORA to determine the optimum shipping schedule in the network.

10. In Problem 9, suppose that the capacity of refinery 3 is 6 million gallons only and that distribution area 1 must receive all its demand. Additionally, any shortages at areas 2 and 3 will incur a penalty of 5 cents per gallon.

(a) Formulate the problem as a transportation model.

(b) Solve the resulting model with TORA, and determine the optimum shipping schedule.

11. In Problem 9, suppose that the daily demand at area 3 drops to 4 million gallons. Surplus production at refineries 1 and 2 is diverted to other distribution areas by truck. The transportation cost per 100 gallons is $1.50 from refinery 1 and $2.20 from refinery 2. Refinery 3 can divert its surplus production to other chemical processes within the plant.

(a) Formulate the problem as a transportation model.

(b) Solve the model by TORA, and determine the optimum shipping schedule.

12. Three orange orchards supply crates of oranges to four retailers. The daily demand amounts at the four retailers are 150, 150, 400, and 100 crates, respectively. Supply at the three orchards is dictated by available regular labor and are estimated at 150, 200, and 250 crates daily. However, both orchards 1 and 2 have indicated that they could supply more crates, if necessary, by using overtime labor. Orchard 3 does not offer this option. The transportation costs per crate from the orchards to the retailers are given in Table 5–9.

**TABLE 5–9**

|          |   | Retailer |     |     |     |
|----------|---|----------|-----|-----|-----|
|          |   | 1        | 2   | 3   | 4   |
|          | 1 | $1       | $2  | $3  | $2  |
| Orchard  | 2 | $2       | $4  | $1  | $2  |
|          | 3 | $1       | $3  | $5  | $3  |

(a) Formulate the problem as a transportation model.

(b) Solve the problem by TORA.

(c) How many crates should orchards 1 and 2 supply using overtime labor?

13. Cars are shipped from three distribution centers to five dealers. The shipping cost is based on the mileage between the sources and the destinations, and is independent of whether the truck makes the trip with partial or full loads. Table 5–10 summarizes the mileage between the distribution centers and the dealers together with the monthly supply and demand figures given in *number* of cars. A full truck load includes 18 cars. The transportation cost per truck mile is $25.

**TABLE 5–10**

| | | | Dealer | | | |
|---|---|---|---|---|---|---|
| | 1 | 2 | 3 | 4 | 5 | Supply |
| 1 | 100 | 150 | 200 | 140 | 35 | **400** |
| Center 2 | 50 | 70 | 60 | 65 | 80 | **200** |
| 3 | 40 | 90 | 100 | 150 | 130 | **150** |
| Demand | **100** | **200** | **150** | **160** | **140** | |

**(a)** Formulate the associated transportation model.

**(b)** Determine the optimal shipping schedule using TORA.

**14.** MG Auto, of Example 5.1–1, produces four car models: $M1$, $M2$, $M3$, and $M4$. The Detroit plant produces models M1, M2, and $M4$. Models $M1$ and $M2$ are also produced in New Orleans. The Los Angeles plant manufactures models $M3$ and $M4$. The capacities of the various plants and the demands at the distribution centers are given in Table 5–11.

**TABLE 5–11**

| | Model | | | | |
|---|---|---|---|---|---|
| | $M1$ | $M2$ | $M3$ | $M4$ | Totals |
| Plant | | | | | |
| Los Angeles | — | — | 700 | 300 | 1000 |
| Detroit | 500 | 600 | — | 400 | 1500 |
| New Orleans | 800 | 400 | — | — | 1200 |
| Distribution center | | | | | |
| Denver | 700 | 500 | 500 | 600 | 2300 |
| Miami | 600 | 500 | 200 | 100 | 1400 |

The mileage chart is the same as given in Example 5.1–1, and the transportation rate remains equal to 8 cents per car mile for all models. Additionally, it is possible to substitute a percentage of the demand for some models from the supply of others according to the specifications in Table 5–12.

**TABLE 5–12**

| Distribution center | Percentage of demand | Interchangeable models |
|---|---|---|
| Denver | 10 | $M1, M2$ |
|  | 20 | $M3, M4$ |
| Miami | 10 | $M1, M2$ |
|  | 5 | $M2, M4$ |

**(a)** Formulate the corresponding transportation model.

**(b)** Determine the optimum shipping schedule using TORA.

(Hint: Add four new destinations corresponding to the new combinations $[M1, M2], [M3, M4], [M1, M2]$, and $[M2, M4]$. The demands at the new destinations are determined from the given percentages.)

## 5.2 NONTRADITIONAL TRANSPORTATION MODELS

The application of the transportation model is not limited to *transporting* commodities between geographical sources and destinations. This section presents two applications in the areas of production-inventory control and equipment maintenance.

---

**Example 5.2–1 (PRODUCTION-INVENTORY CONTROL).**

Boralis manufactures backpacks for serious hikers. The demand for its product occurs during March to June of each year. Boralis estimates the demand for the 4 months to be 100, 200, 180, and 300 units, respectively. The company uses part-time labor to manufacture the backpacks and, as such, its production capacity varies monthly. It is estimated that Boralis can produce 50, 180, 280, and 270 units for March to June, respectively. Because the production capacity and demand for the different months do not match, a current month's demand may be satisfied in one of three ways.

1. Current month's production
2. Surplus production in an earlier month
3. Surplus production in a later month

In the first case, the production cost per backpack is $40.00 The second case incurs an additional holding cost of $.50 per backpack per month. In the third case, an additional penalty cost of $2.00 per backpack is incurred for each month delay. Boralis wishes to determine the optimal production schedule for the 4 months.

The situation can be modeled as a transportation model by recognizing the following parallels between the elements of the production-inventory problem and the transportation model:

| | Transportation | Production-inventory |
|---|---|---|
| 1. | Source $i$ | 1. Production period $i$ |
| 2. | Destination $j$ | 2. Demand period $j$ |
| 3. | Supply amount at source $i$ | 3. Production capacity of period $i$ |
| 4. | Demand at destination $j$ | 4. Demand for period $j$ |
| 5. | Unit transportation cost from source $i$ to destination $j$ | 5. Unit cost (production + inventory + penalty) in period $i$ for period $j$ |

The resulting transportation model is given in Table 5–13.

**TABLE 5–13**

| | 1 | 2 | 3 | 4 | Capacity |
|---|---|---|---|---|---|
| 1 | $40.00 | $40.50 | $41.00 | $41.50 | **50** |
| 2 | $42.00 | $40.00 | $40.50 | $41.00 | **180** |
| 3 | $44.00 | $42.00 | $40.00 | $40.50 | **280** |
| 4 | $46.00 | $44.00 | $42.00 | $40.00 | **270** |
| Demand | **100** | **200** | **180** | **300** | |

The unit "transportation" cost from period $i$ to period $j$ is computed as

$$c_{ij} = \begin{cases} \text{Production cost in } i, & i = j \\ \text{Production cost in } i + \text{holding cost from } i \text{ to } j, & i < j \\ \text{Production cost in } i + \text{penaty cost from } i \text{ to } j, & i > j \end{cases}$$

For example,

$$c_{11} = \$40.00$$
$$c_{24} = \$40.00 + (\$.50 + \$.50) = \$41.00$$
$$c_{41} = \$40.00 + (\$2.00 + \$2.00 + \$2.00) = \$46.00$$

The optimal solution is summarized in Figure 5–3. The dashed lines indicate back-ordering, the dotted lines indicate production for a future period, and the solid lines show production in a period for itself.

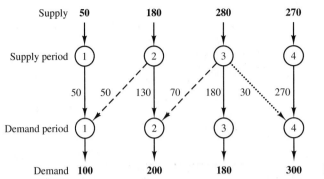

**Figure 5–3**

---

**Example 5.2–2   (EQUIPMENT MAINTENANCE).**

Arkansas Pacific operates a medium-sized saw mill. The mill prepares different types of wood that range from soft pine to hard oak according to a weekly schedule. Depending on the type of wood being milled, the demand for sharp blades varies from day to day according to the following 1-week (7-day) data:

| Day | Mon. | Tues. | Wed. | Thur. | Fri. | Sat. | Sun. |
|-----|------|-------|------|-------|------|------|------|
| Demand (blades) | 24 | 12 | 14 | 20 | 18 | 14 | 22 |

The mill can satisfy the daily demand in the following manner:

1. Buy new blades at the cost of $12 a blade.
2. Use an overnight sharpening service at the cost of $6 a blade, or a slow 2-day service at the cost of $3 a blade.

The situation can be represented as a transportation model with eight sources and seven destinations. The destinations represent the 7 days of the week. The sources of the model are defined as follows: Source 1 corresponds to buying new blades, which, in the extreme case, could provide sufficient supply to cover the demand for all 7 days. Sources 2 to 8 correspond to the 7 days of the week. The amount of supply for each of these sources equals the number of used blades at the end of the associated day. For example, source 2 (i.e., Monday) will have a supply of used blades equal to the demand for Monday. The unit transportation cost for the model could be $12, $6, or $3, depending on whether the blade is supplied from new blades, overnight sharpening, or 2-day sharpening. Notice that the overnight service means that used blades sent at the *end* of day $i$ will be in use at the *start* of day $i + 1$ or day $i + 2$. The 2-day service means that used blades sent at the *end* of day $i$ will be in use at the *start* of day $i + 3$ or any day thereafter. The "disposal" column is a dummy destination that receives the blades left unsharpened at the end of a day. The complete model is given in Table 5–14.

**TABLE 5–14**

| | 1 Mon. | 2 Tues. | 3 Wed. | 4 Thur. | 5 Fri. | 6 Sat. | 7 Sun. | 8 Disposal | |
|---|---|---|---|---|---|---|---|---|---|
| 1 New | $12 **24** | $12 **2** | $12 | $12 | $12 | $12 | $12 | $0 **98** | 124 |
| 2 Mon. | M | $6 **10** | $6 **8** | $3 **6** | $3 | $3 | $3 | $0 | 24 |
| 3 Tues. | M | M | $6 **6** | $6 | $3 **6** | $3 | $3 | $0 | 12 |
| 4 Wed. | M | M | M | $6 **14** | $6 | $3 | $3 | $0 | 14 |
| 5 Thur. | M | M | M | M | $6 **12** | $6 **8** | $3 | $0 | 20 |
| 6 Fri. | M | M | M | M | M | $6 **14** | $6 **4** | $0 | 18 |
| 7 Sat. | M | M | M | M | M | M | $6 **14** | $0 | 14 |
| 8 Sun. | M | M | M | M | M | M | M | $0 **22** | 22 |
| | 24 | 12 | 14 | 20 | 18 | 14 | 22 | 124 | |

The optimum solution (obtained by TORA) is summarized as follows:

| | | Sharpening service | | |
|---|---|---|---|---|
| Period | New blades | Overnight | 2-Day | Disposal |
| Mon. | 24 (Mon.) | 10 (Tues.) + 8 (Wed.) | 6 (Thur.) | 0 |
| Tues. | 2 (Tues.) | 6 (Wed.) | 6 (Fri.) | 0 |
| Wed. | 0 | 14 (Thur.) | 0 | 0 |
| Thur. | 0 | 12 (Fri.) | 8 (Sun.) | 0 |

*(continued)*

| Fri. | 0 | 14 (Sat.) | 0 | 4 |
| Sat. | 0 | 14 (Sun.) | 0 | 0 |
| Sun. | 0 | 0 | 0 | 22 |

Observe the interpretation of the solution. At the start of Monday, Arkansas Pacific buys 24 new blades. At the end of the same day, the company will have 24 used blades, 18 of which are sent to overnight service and 6 to 2-day service. Of the 18 overnight blades, 10 will be used on Tuesday, and 8 on Wednesday. The six 2-day blades will be used on Thursday. The rest of the tableau is interpreted similarly. The disposal column shows the number of used blades that will be left unsharpened at the end of a given day.

### Problem set 5.2a

1. In Example 5.2–1, suppose that the holding cost per unit is period dependent and is given by 40, 30, and 70 cents for periods 1, 2, and 3, respectively. The penalty and production costs remain as given in the example. Determine the optimum solution using TORA, and interpret the results.

2. In Example 5.2–2, suppose that the sharpening service offers 3-day service for $1 a blade on Monday and Tuesday (days 1 and 2), reformulate the problem, and interpret the solution obtained by TORA.

3. In example 5.2–2, if a sharpened blade is not used on the same day it is delivered, a holding cost of 50 cents per blade per day is incurred. Reformulate the model, and interpret the TORA solution.

4. JoShop wants to assign four different categories of machines to five types of tasks. The number of machines available in the four categories are 25, 30, 20, and 30. The number of jobs in the five tasks are 20, 20, 30, 10, and 25. Machine category 4 cannot be assigned to task type 4. Table 5–15 provides the unit cost (in dollars) of assigning a machine category to a task type. The objective of the problem is to determine the optimum number of machines in each category to be assigned to task type. Solve the problem by TORA, and interpret the solution.

**TABLE 5–15**

|  |  | \multicolumn{5}{c}{Task type} |
|  |  | 1 | 2 | 3 | 4 | 5 |
|---|---|---|---|---|---|---|
|  | 1 | 10 | 2 | 3 | 15 | 9 |
| Machine | 2 | 5 | 10 | 15 | 2 | 4 |
| category | 3 | 15 | 5 | 14 | 7 | 15 |
|  | 4 | 20 | 15 | 13 | — | 8 |

**5.** The demand for a perishable item over the next 4 months is 400, 300, 420, and 380 tons, respectively. The supply capacities for the same months are 500, 600, 200, and 300 tons. The purchase price per ton varies from month to month and is estimated at $100, $140, $120, and $150, respectively. Because the item is perishable, a current month's supply must be consumed within 3 months (including the current month). The storage cost per ton per month is $3. The nature of the item does not allow back-ordering. Solve the problem as a transportation model by TORA, and determine the optimum delivery schedule for the item over the next 4 months.

**6.** The demand for a special small engine over the next five quarters is 200, 150, 300, 250, and 400 units. The manufacturer supplying the engine has different production capacities estimated at 180, 230, 430, 300, and 300 for the same five periods. Back-ordering is not allowed, but the manufacturer may use overtime production to fill the demand, if necessary. The overtime capacity for each period equals half the capacity of the regular production. The production costs per unit for the five periods are $100, $96, $116, $102, and $106, respectively. The overtime production cost per engine is 50% higher than the regular production cost. If an engine is produced now for use in later periods, an additional storage cost of $4 per engine per period is incurred. Formulate the problem as a transportation model. Use TORA to determine the optimum number of engines to be produced during regular time and overtime of each period.

**7.** Periodic preventive maintenance is carried out on aircraft engines, where an important component must be replaced. The number of aircraft scheduled for such maintenance over the next 6 months is estimated at 200, 180, 300, 198, 230, and 290, respectively. All maintenance work is done during the first 2 days of the month, where a used component may be replaced with a new or an overhauled component. The overhauling of used components may be done in a local repair facility, where they will be ready for use at the beginning of next month, or they may be sent to a central repair shop where a delay of 3 months (including the month in which maintenance ocurrs) is expected. The repair cost in the local shop is $120 per component. At the central facility, the cost is only $35 per component. An overhauled component used in a later month will incur an additional storage cost of $1.50 per unit per month. New components may be purchased at $200 each in month 1, with a 5% price increase every 2 months. Formulate the problem as a transportation model, and solve by TORA to determine the optimal schedule for satisfying the demand for the component over the next 6 months.

## 5.3 THE TRANSPORTATION ALGORITHM

This section details the transportation algorithm. The algorithm follows the exact steps of the simplex method (Chapter 3). However, instead of using the regular simplex tableau, we take advantage of the special structure of the transportation model to present the algorithm in a more convenient form.

To facilitate the presentation of the details of the algorithm, we use the following numeric example.

---

**Example 5.3–1 (SUNRAY TRANSPORT).**

The SunRay Transport Company ships truckloads of grain from three silos to four mills. The supply (in truckloads) and the demand (also in truckloads) together with the unit transportation costs per truckload on the different routes are summarized in the transportation model in Table 5–16. The unit transportation costs, $c_{ij}$, (shown in the northeast corner of each box) are in hundreds of dollars.

**TABLE 5–16**

| | Mill 1 | Mill 2 | Mill 3 | Mill 4 | Supply |
|---|---|---|---|---|---|
| Silo 1 | 10 $x_{11}$ | 2 $x_{12}$ | 20 $x_{13}$ | 11 $x_{14}$ | **15** |
| Silo 2 | 12 $x_{21}$ | 7 $x_{22}$ | 9 $x_{23}$ | 20 $x_{24}$ | **25** |
| Silo 3 | 4 $x_{31}$ | 14 $x_{32}$ | 16 $x_{33}$ | 18 $x_{34}$ | **10** |
| Demand | 5 | 15 | 15 | 15 | |

The purpose of the model is to determine the minimum cost shipping schedule between the silos and the mills. This is equivalent to determining the quantity $x_{ij}$ shipped from silo $i$ to mill $j$ ($i = 1, 2, 3; j = 1, 2, 3, 4$).

---

The steps of the transportation algorithm are exact parallels of the simplex algorithm—namely, the following:

**Step 1.** Determine a *starting* basic feasible solution, and go to step 2.

**Step 2.** Use the optimality condition of the simplex method to determine the *entering variable* from among all the nonbasic variables. If the optimality condition is satisfied, stop. Otherwise, go to step 3.

**Step 3.** Use the feasibility condition of the simplex method to determine the *leaving variable* from among all the current basic variables, and find the new basic solution. Return to step 2.

Each of these steps is detailed subsequently.

### 5.3.1 Determination of the Starting Solution

A general transportation model with $m$ sources and $n$ destinations has $m + n$ constraint equations, one for each source and each destination. However, because the transportation model is always balanced (sum of the supply = sum of the demand), one of these equations must be redundant. Thus, the model has $m + n - 1$ independent constraint equations, which means that the starting basic solution consists of $m + n - 1$ basic variables. As an illustration, the starting solution in Example 5.3–1 includes $3 + 4 - 1 = 6$ basic variables.

The special structure of the transportation problem allows securing a nonartificial starting basic solution using one of three methods:

1. Northwest-corner method
2. Least-cost method
3. Vogel approximation method

The difference among the three methods is the "quality" of the starting basic solution they produce, in the sense that a better starting solution yields a smaller objective value. In general, the Vogel method yields the best starting basic solution, and the northwest-corner method yields the worst. The trade-off is that the northwest-corner method involves the least computations.

**The Northwest-corner method.**   The method starts at the northwest-corner cell (route) of the tableau (variable $x_{11}$).

**Step 1.**  Allocate as much as possible to the selected cell, and adjust the associated amounts of supply and demand by subtracting the allocated amount.

**Step 2.**  Cross out the row or column with zero supply or demand to indicate that no further assignments can be made in that row or column. If both the row and column net to zero simultaneously, cross out one only, and leave a zero supply (demand) in the uncrossed-out row (column).

**Step 3.**  If *exactly one* row or column is left uncrossed out, stop. Otherwise, move to the cell to the right if a column has just been crossed or the one below if a row has been crossed out. Go to step 1.

---

**Example 5.3–2.**

The application of the procedure to the model of Example 5.3–1 gives the starting basic solution in Table 5–17. The arrows show the order in which the allocated (circled) amounts are generated.

The starting basic solution is given as

$$x_{11} = 5, \ x_{12} = 10$$

$$x_{22} = 5, \ x_{23} = 15, \ x_{24} = 5$$

$$x_{34} = 10$$

**TABLE 5–17**

|   | 1 | 2 | 3 | 4 | Supply |
|---|---|---|---|---|--------|
| **1** | 10 ⑤→ | 2 ⑩ | 20 | 11 | 15 |
| **2** | 12 | 7 ⑤→ | 9 ⑮→ | 20 ⑤ | 25 |
| **3** | 4 | 14 | 16 | 18 ⑩ | 10 |
| Demand | 5 | 15 | 15 | 15 | |

The associated cost of the schedule is

$$z = 5 \times 10 + 10 \times 2 + 5 \times 7 + 15 \times 9 + 5 \times 20 + 10 \times 18 = \$520$$

**Least-cost method.**     The least-cost method finds a better starting solution by concentrating on the cheapest routes. Instead of starting with the northwest cell (as in the northwest-corner method), we start by assigning as much as possible to the cell with the smallest unit cost (ties are broken arbitrarily). We then cross out the satisfied row or column, and adjust the amounts of supply and demand accordingly. If both a row and a column are satisfied simultaneously, only one is crossed out, the same as in the northwest corner method. Next, we always look for the uncrossed-out cell with the smallest unit cost and repeat the process until we are left at the end with exactly one uncrossed-out row or column.

**Example 5.3–3.**   The least-cost method is applied to Example 5.3–1 in the following manner:

**1.** Cell $(1, 2)$ has the least unit cost in the tableau ( = \$2). The most that can be shipped through $(1,2,)$ is $x_{12} = 15$ truckloads, which happens to satisfy both row 1 and column 2 simultaneously. We arbitrarily cross out column 2 and adjust the supply in row 1 to 0.

**2.** The cell with the smallest uncrossed-out unit cost is $(3, 1)$. We assign $x_{31} = 5$, and cross out column 1, because it is satisfied and adjust the demand of row 3 to $10 - 5 = 5$ truckloads.

**3.** Continuing in the same manner, we successively assign 15 truckloads to cell $(2, 3), 0$ truckloads to cell $(1,4), 5$ truckloads to cell $(3,4)$, and 10 truckloads to cell $(2,4)$ (verify!).

The resulting starting solution is summarized in Table 5–18. The arrows show the order in which the allocations are made. The starting solution (consisting of 6 basic variables) is

$$x_{12} = 15, \; x_{14} = \; 0$$
$$x_{23} = 15, \; x_{24} = 10$$
$$x_{31} = \; 5, \; x_{34} = \; 5$$

**TABLE 5–18**

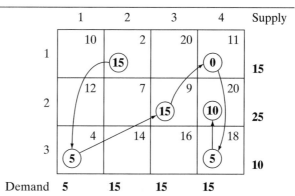

|        | 1  | 2  | 3  | 4  | Supply |
|--------|----|----|----|----|--------|
| 1      | 10 | 2 ⑮ | 20 | 11 ⓪ | **15** |
| 2      | 12 | 7  | 9 ⑮ | 20 ⑩ | **25** |
| 3      | 4 ⑤ | 14 | 16 | 18 ⑤ | **10** |
| Demand | 5  | 15 | 15 | 15 |        |

The associated objective value is

$$z = 15 \times 2 + 0 \times 11 + 15 \times 9 + 10 \times 20 + 5 \times 4 + 5 \times 18 = \$475$$

The quality of the least-cost starting solution is better than that of the northwest-corner method (Example 5.3–2) because it yields a smaller value of $z$ (\$475 versus \$520 in the northwest-corner method).

---

**Vogel approximation method (VAM).**    VAM is an improved version of the least-cost method that generally produces better starting solutions.

**Step 1.** For each row (each column) with *strictly positive* supply (demand), determine a penalty measure by subtracting the *smallest* unit cost element in the row (column) from the *next smallest* unit cost element in the same row (column).

**Step 2.** Identify the row or column with the largest penalty. Break ties arbitrarily. Allocate as much as possible to the variable with the least unit cost in the selected row or column. Adjust the supply and demand, and cross out the satisfied row *or* column. If a row and a column are satisfied simultaneously, only one of the two is crossed out, and the remaining row (column) is assigned zero supply (demand).

**Step 3. (a)** If exactly one row or column with zero supply or demand remains uncrossed out, stop.

**(b)** If one row (column) with *positive* supply (demand) remains uncrossed out, determine the basic variables in the row (column) by the least-cost method. Stop.

**(c)** If all the uncrossed out rows and columns have (remaining) zero supply and demand, determine the *zero* basic variables by the least-cost method. Stop.

**(d)** Otherwise, go to step 1.

**Example 5.3–4.**

VAM is applied to Example 5.3–1. Table 5–19 computes the first set of penalties.

**TABLE 5–19**

| | 1 | 2 | 3 | 4 | | Row penalty |
|---|---|---|---|---|---|---|
| 1 | 10 | 2 | 20 | 11 | 15 | 10 – 2 = 8 |
| 2 | 12 | 7 | 9 | 20 | 25 | 9 – 7 = 2 |
| 3 | 4 (5) | 14 | 16 | 18 | 10 | 14 – 4 = 10 |
| | 5 | 15 | 15 | 15 | | |
| Column penalty | 10 – 4 = 6 | 7 – 2 = 5 | 16 – 9 = 7 | 18 – 11 = 7 | | |

Because row 3 has the largest penalty (= 10) and cell (3, 1) has the smallest unit cost in that row, the amount 5 is assigned to $x_{31}$. Column 1 is now satisfied and hence is crossed out, and a new set of penalties is recomputed as Table 5–20 shows.

**TABLE 5–20**

| | 1 | 2 | 3 | 4 | | Row penalty |
|---|---|---|---|---|---|---|
| 1 | 10 | 2 (15) | 20 | 11 | 15 | 9 |
| 2 | 12 | 7 | 9 | 20 | 25 | 2 |
| 3 | 4 (5) | 14 | 16 | 18 | 10 | 2 |
| | 5 | 15 | 15 | 15 | | |
| Column penalty | — | 5 | 7 | 7 | | |

The new penalties now show row 1 has the highest penalty (= 9). Hence, we assign the maximum amount possible to cell (1, 2), which yields $x_{12} = 15$ and simultaneously satisfies both row 1 and column 2. We arbitrarily cross out column 2 and adjust the supply in row 1 to zero.

Continuing in the same manner, row 2 will produce the next highest penalty $(= 11)$, and we assign $x_{22} = 15$, which crosses out column 3 and leaves 10 units in row 2. Only column 4 is left, and it has a positive supply of 15 units. Applying the least-cost method to that column, we successively assign $x_{14} = 0$, $x_{34} = 5$, and $x_{24} = 10$ (verify!). The associated objective value for this solution is

$$z = 15 \times 2 + 0 \times 11 + 15 \times 9 + 10 \times 20 + 5 \times 4 + 5 \times 18 = \$475$$

This solution happens to have the same objective value as in the least-cost method. Usually, however, VAM is expected to produce better starting solutions for the transportation model.

### Problem set 5.3a

**1.** Compare the starting solutions obtained by the northwest-corner, least-cost, and Vogel methods for each of the following models:

| (a) | | | | | (b) | | | | | (c) | | | |
|---|---|---|---|---|---|---|---|---|---|---|---|---|---|
| 0 | 2 | 1 | **6** | | 1 | 2 | 6 | **7** | | 5 | 1 | 8 | **12** |
| 2 | 1 | 5 | **7** | | 0 | 4 | 2 | **12** | | 2 | 4 | 0 | **14** |
| 2 | 4 | 3 | **7** | | 3 | 1 | 5 | **11** | | 3 | 6 | 7 | **4** |
| **5** | **5** | **10** | | | **10** | **10** | **10** | | | **9** | **10** | **11** | |

### 5.3.2 Iterative Computations of the Algorithm

After determining the starting solution (using any of the three methods in Section 5.3.1), we use the following algorithm to determine the optimum solution:

**Step 1.** Use the simplex *optimality condition* to determine the *entering variable* as the current nonbasic variable that can improve the solution. If the optimality condition is satisfied, stop. Otherwise, go to step 2.

**Step 2.** Determine the *leaving variable* using the simplex *feasibility condition*. Change the basis, and return to step 1.

The change of basis computations do not involve the familiar row operations used in the simplex method. Instead, the special structure of the transportation model allows simpler computations.

**Example 5.3–5.**

Solve the transportation model of Example 5.3–1, starting with the northwest-corner solution.

Table 5–21 gives the northwest-corner starting solution as determined in Example 5.3–2 (Table 5–17).

**TABLE 5–21**

|     | 1 | 2 | 3 | 4 | Supply |
|-----|---|---|---|---|--------|
| 1   | 10<br>5 | 2<br>10 | 20 | 11 | 15 |
| 2   | 12<br>5 | 7<br>15 | 9<br>5 | 20 | 25 |
| 3   | 4 | 14 | 16 | 18<br>10 | 10 |
| Demand | 5 | 15 | 15 | 15 | |

The determination of the entering variable from among the current nonbasic variables (those that are not part of the starting basic solution) is done by computing the nonbasic coefficients in the $z$-row, using the **method of multipliers** (which, as we show in Section 5.4, is rooted in LP duality theory).

In the method of multipliers, we associate the multipliers $u_i$ and $v_j$ with row $i$ and column $j$ of the transportation tableau. For each current *basic* variable $x_{ij}$, these multipliers are shown in Section 5.4 to satisfy the following equations:

$$u_i + v_j = c_{ij}, \text{ for each } basic \ x_{ij}$$

In Example 5.3–1, we have 7 variables and 6 equations corresponding to the six basic variables. To solve these equations, the method of multipliers calls for arbitrarily setting $u_1 \equiv 0$, and then solving for the remaining variables as shown subsequently.

| Basic variable | $(u, v)$ Equation | Solution |
|----------------|-------------------|----------|
| $x_{11}$ | $u_1 + v_1 = 10$ | $u_1 \equiv 0 \rightarrow v_1 = 10$ |
| $x_{12}$ | $u_1 + v_2 = 2$ | $u_1 \equiv 0 \rightarrow v_2 = 2$ |
| $x_{22}$ | $u_2 + v_2 = 7$ | $v_2 = 2 \rightarrow u_2 = 5$ |
| $x_{23}$ | $u_2 + v_3 = 9$ | $u_2 = 5 \rightarrow v_3 = 4$ |
| $x_{24}$ | $u_2 + v_4 = 20$ | $u_2 = 5 \rightarrow v_4 = 15$ |
| $x_{34}$ | $u_3 + v_4 = 18$ | $v_4 = 15 \rightarrow u_3 = 3$ |

To summarize, we have

$$u_1 = 0, \ u_2 = 5, \ u_3 = 3$$
$$v_1 = 10, \ v_2 = 2, \ v_3 = 4, \ v_4 = 15$$

Next, we use the computed values of $u_i$ and $v_j$ to evaluate the nonbasic variables by computing

$$u_i + v_j - c_{ij}, \quad \text{for each } \textit{nonbasic } x_{ij}$$

The results of these evaluations are shown in the following table.

| Nonbasic variable | $u_i + v_j - c_{ij}$ |
|:---:|:---:|
| $x_{13}$ | $u_1 + v_3 - c_{13} = 0 + \ 4 - 20 = \ -16$ |
| $x_{14}$ | $u_1 + v_4 - c_{14} = 0 + 15 - 11 = \quad 4$ |
| $x_{21}$ | $u_2 + v_1 - c_{21} = 5 + 10 - 12 = \quad 3$ |
| $x_{31}$ | $u_3 + v_1 - c_{31} = 3 + 10 - \ 4 = \quad 9$ |
| $x_{32}$ | $u_3 + v_2 - c_{32} = 3 + \ 2 - 14 = \ -9$ |
| $x_{33}$ | $u_3 + v_3 - c_{33} = 3 + \ 4 - 16 = \ -9$ |

The preceding information, together with the fact that $u_i + v_j - c_{ij} = 0$ for each basic $x_{ij}$, is actually equivalent to computing the $z$-row of the simplex tableau as the foling summary shows.

| Basic | $x_{11}$ | $x_{12}$ | $x_{13}$ | $x_{14}$ | $x_{21}$ | $x_{22}$ | $x_{23}$ | $x_{24}$ | $x_{31}$ | $x_{32}$ | $x_{33}$ | $x_{34}$ |
|:---:|:---:|:---:|:---:|:---:|:---:|:---:|:---:|:---:|:---:|:---:|:---:|:---:|
| $z$ | 0 | 0 | $-16$ | 4 | 3 | 0 | 0 | 0 | 9 | $-9$ | $-9$ | 0 |

Because the transportation model seeks to *minimize* cost, the entering variable is the one having the *most positive* coefficient in the $z$-row. Thus, $x_{31}$ is the entering variable.

The preceding computations are usually done directly on the transportation tableau as shown in Table 5–22, meaning that it is not necessary really to write the $(u, v)$-equations explicitly. Instead, we start by setting $u_1 \equiv 0$. Then we can compute the $v$-values of all the columns that have *basic* variables in row 1. Next, we compute $u_2$ based on the $(u, v)$-equation of basic $x_{22}$. Now, given $u_2$, we can compute $v_3$ and $v_4$, which finally leads us to determining $u_3$. Once all the $u$'s and $v$'s are determined, we can evaluate the nonbasic variables by computing $u_i + v_j - c_{ij}$ for each nonbasic $x_{ij}$. These evaluations are shown in Table 5–22 in the boxed southeast corner of each cell.

**TABLE 5–22**

| | $v_1 = 10$ | $v_2 = 2$ | $v_3 = 4$ | $v_4 = 15$ | |
|---|---|---|---|---|---|
| $u_1 = 0$ | 10<br>5 | 2<br>10 | 20<br>$-16$ | 11<br>4 | 15 |
| $u_2 = 5$ | 12<br>3  5 | 7<br>15 | 9<br>5 | 20 | 25 |
| $u_3 = 3$ | 4<br>9 | 14<br>$-9$ | 16<br>$-9$  10 | 18 | 10 |
| Demand | 5 | 15 | 15 | 15 | |

Having determined $x_{31}$ as the entering variable, we need to determine the leaving variable. Remember that if $x_{31}$ enters the solution to become basic, we need to make one of the current basic variables nonbasic (at zero level) so that we always remain with the correct number of basic variables ($= 3 + 4 - 1 = 6$, in this example).

The leaving variable is determined in the following manner. The selection of $x_{31}$ as the entering variable means that we want to ship through this route because it reduces the total shipping cost. What is the most that we can ship through the new route? We observe in the Table 5–22 that if we ship an amount $\theta$ through route $(3, 1)$ (i.e., $x_{31} = \theta$), then the maximum value of $\theta$ is determined based on two conditions.

1. The supply limits and the demand requirements remain satisfied.
2. No negative shipments are allowed through any of the routes.

These two conditions determine the maximum value of $\theta$ and the leaving variable in the following manner. First, construct a *closed loop* that starts and ends at the entering variable cell, $(3, 1)$. The loop consists of *connected* horizontal and vertical segments only (no diagonals are allowed). Each corner of the resulting loop, with the exception of that in the entering variable cell, must coincide with a current basic variable. Table 5–23 shows the loop for $x_{31}$. Exactly one loop exists for a given entering variable.

**TABLE 5–23**

| | $v_1 = 10$ | $v_2 = 2$ | $v_3 = 4$ | $v_4 = 15$ | Supply |
|---|---|---|---|---|---|
| $u_1 = 0$ | 10<br>⊖ $5 - \theta$ | 2<br>⊕ $10 + \theta$ | 20<br>$-16$ | 11<br>4 | 15 |
| $u_2 = 5$ | 12<br>3 | 7<br>⊖ $5 - \theta$  15 | 9<br>⊕ $5 + \theta$ | 20 | 25 |
| $u_3 = 3$ | 4<br>⊕ $\theta$  9 | 14<br>$-9$ | 16<br>$-9$ | 18<br>⊖ $10 - \theta$ | 10 |
| Demand | 5 | 15 | 15 | 15 | |

Next, we assign the amount $\theta$ to the entering variable cell $(3, 1)$. For the supply and demand limits to remain satisfied, we must alternate between subtracting and adding the amount $\theta$ at the successive *corners* of the loop as shown in Table 5–23 (it is immaterial if the loop is traced in a clockwise or counterclockwise direction). The new values of the variables then remain nonnegative if

$$x_{11} = 5 - \theta \geq 0$$

$$x_{22} = 5 - \theta \geq 0$$

$$x_{34} = 10 - \theta \geq 0$$

The corresponding maximum value of $\theta$ is 5, which occurs when both $x_{11}$ and $x_{22}$ reach zero level. Because only one current basic variable must leave the basic solution, we can chose either $x_{11}$ or $x_{22}$ as the leaving variable. We arbitrarily chose $x_{11}$ to leave the solution.

The selection of $x_{31}$ ( $= 5$) as the entering variable and $x_{11}$ as the leaving variable requires adjusting the values of basic variables at the corners of the closed loop as Table 5–24 shows. Because each unit shipped through route $(3, 1)$ reduces the shipping cost by \$9 ( $= u_3 + v_1 - c_{31}$), the total cost associated with the new schedule is \$9 $\times$ 5 = \$45 less than in the previous schedule. Thus, the new cost is \$520 $-$ \$45 = \$475.

Given the new basic solution, we repeat the computation of the multipliers $u$ and $v$ as Table 5–24 shows. The entering variable is $x_{14}$. The closed loop shows that $x_{14} = 10$ and that the leaving variable is $x_{24}$.

**TABLE 5–24**

The new solution, shown in Table 5–25, costs \$4 $\times$ 10 = \$40 less than the preceding one, thus yielding the new cost \$475 $-$ \$40 = \$435. The new evaluations $u_i + v_j - c_{ij}$ for all nonbasic $x_{ij}$ are now negative. Thus, the solution in Table 5–25 is optimal.

**TABLE 5–25**

|  | $v_1 = -3$ | $v_2 = 2$ | $v_3 = 4$ | $v_4 = 11$ | Supply |
|---|---|---|---|---|---|
| $u_1 = 0$ | 10 <br> −13 **5** | 2 | 20 <br> −16 **10** | 11 | 15 |
| $u_2 = 5$ | 12 <br> −10 **10** | 7 <br> **15** | 9 | 20 <br> −4 **25** | 25 |
| $u_3 = 7$ | 4 <br> **5** | 14 <br> −5 | 16 <br> −5 **5** | 18 | 10 |
| Demand | 5 | 15 | 15 | 15 | |

The following table summarizes the optimum solution.

| From silo | To mill | Number of truckloads |
|---|---|---|
| 1 | 2 | 5 |
| 1 | 4 | 10 |
| 2 | 2 | 10 |
| 2 | 3 | 15 |
| 3 | 1 | 5 |
| 3 | 4 | 5 |

Optimal cost = $435

---

## Problem set 5.3b

1. In the transportation models in Table 5–26, use the northwest-corner method to find the starting solution, then determine the optimum solution.

**TABLE 5–26**

| (a) | | | | (b) | | | | (c) | | | |
|---|---|---|---|---|---|---|---|---|---|---|---|
| $0 | $2 | $1 | 6 | $0 | $4 | $2 | 8 | — | $3 | $5 | 4 |
| $2 | $1 | $5 | 9 | $2 | $3 | $4 | 5 | $7 | $4 | $9 | 7 |
| $2 | $4 | $3 | 5 | $1 | $2 | $0 | 6 | $1 | $8 | $6 | 19 |
| 5 | 5 | 10 | | 7 | 6 | 6 | | 5 | 6 | 19 | |

**2.** In the transportation problem in Table 5–27, the total demand exceeds the total supply. Suppose that the penalty costs per unit of unsatisfied demand are $5, $3, and $2 for destinations 1, 2, and 3, respectively. Determine the optimum solution.

**TABLE 5–27**

| $5 | $1 | $7 | **10** |
|----|----|----|--------|
| $6 | $4 | $6 | **80** |
| $3 | $2 | $5 | **15** |
| **75** | **20** | **50** | |

**3.** In Problem 2, suppose that there are no penalty costs, but that the demand at destination 3 must be satisfied completely. Find the optimal solution.

**4.** In the unbalanced transportation problem in Table 5–28, if a unit from a source is not shipped out (to any of the destinations), a storage cost is incurred at the rate of $5, $4, and $3 per unit for sources 1, 2, and 3, respectively. If additionally all the supply at source 2 must be shipped out completely to make room for a new product, determine the optimum shipping schedule.

**TABLE 5–28**

| $1 | $2 | $1 | **20** |
|----|----|----|--------|
| $3 | $4 | $5 | **40** |
| $2 | $3 | $3 | **30** |
| **30** | **20** | **20** | |

**5.** In a $3 \times 3$ transportation problem, let $x_{ij}$ be the amount shipped from source $i$ to destination $j$ and $c_{ij}$ be the corresponding transportation cost per unit. The amounts of supply at sources 1, 2, and 3 are 15, 30, and 85 units, respectively, and the demands at destinations 1, 2, and 3 are 20, 30, and 80 units, respectively. Assume that the starting northwest-corner solution is optimal and that the associated values of the multipliers are given as $u_1 = -2$, $u_2 = 3, u_3 = 5, v_1 = 2, v_2 = 5$, and $v_3 = 10$.
   **(a)** Find the associated optimal cost.
   **(b)** Determine the smallest value of $c_{ij}$ associated with each nonbasic variable that will maintain the optimality of the northwest-corner solution.

**6.** The transportation problem in Table 5–29 gives the indicated *degenerate* basic solution. Suppose that the multipliers associated with this solution are

$u_1 = 1, u_2 = -1, v_1 = 2, v_2 = 2$, and $v_3 = 5$ and that the unit cost for all (basic and nonbasic) *zero* $x_{ij}$ variables is given by

$$c_{ij} = i + j\theta, \ -\infty < \theta < \infty$$

**TABLE 5–29**

| | | | |
|---|---|---|---|
| 10 | | | 10 |
| | 20 | 20 | 40 |
| 10 | 20 | 20 | |

**(a)** If the given solution is optimal, determine the associated optimal value of the objective function.

**(b)** Determine the value of $\theta$ that will guarantee the optimality of the given solution. (*Hint:* Locate the zero basic variable.)

**7.** Consider the problem

$$\text{Minimize } z = \sum_{i=1}^{m} \sum_{j=1}^{n} c_{ij}x_{ij}$$

subject to

$$\sum_{j=1}^{n} x_{ij} \geq a_i, \ i = 1, 2, \cdots, m$$

$$\sum_{i=1}^{m} x_{ij} \geq b_j, \ j = 1, 2, \cdots, n$$

$$x_{ij} \geq 0, \ \text{all } i \text{ and } j$$

It may appear logical to assume that the optimum solution will require the first (second) set of inequalities to be replaced by equations if $\Sigma\, a_i \geq \Sigma\, b_j (\Sigma\, a_i \leq \Sigma\, b_j)$. The counterexample in Table 5–30 (Charnes, Glover, and Klingman, 1970) shows that this assumption is not correct.

**TABLE 5–30**

| | | | |
|---|---|---|---|
| $1 | $1 | $2 | 5 |
| $6 | $5 | $1 | 6 |
| 2 | 7 | 1 | |

Show that the application of the suggested procedure yields the solution $x_{11} = 2, x_{12} = 3, x_{22} = 4$, and $x_{23} = 2$, with $z = \$27$, which is worse than the feasible solution $x_{11} = 2, x_{12} = 7$, and $x_{23} = 6$, with $z = \$15$.

### 5.3.3 Simplex Method Explanation of the Method of Multipliers

The relationship between the method of multipliers and the simplex method can be explained by means of duality theory (Section 4.4.2). From the special structure of the LP representing the transportation model (see Example 5.1–1 for an illustration), the associated dual problem can be written as

$$\text{Maximize } z = \sum_{i=1}^{m} a_i u_i + \sum_{j=1}^{n} b_j v_j$$

subject to

$$u_i + v_j \le c_{ij}, \quad \text{all } i \text{ and } j$$

$$u_i \text{ and } v_j \text{ unrestricted}$$

where,

$a_i = $ Supply amount at source $i$

$b_j = $ Demand amount at destination $j$

$c_{ij} = $ Unit transportation cost from source $i$ to destination $j$

$u_i = $ Dual variable of the constraint associated with source $i$

$v_j = $ Dual variable of the constraint associated with destination $j$

From the primal-dual relationships (Section 4.3), the objective function coefficients of the variable $x_{ij}$ must equal the difference between the left- and the right-hand sides of the corresponding dual constraint—that is, $u_i + v_j - c_{ij}$. However, we know that this quantity must equal zero for each *basic variable,* which then produces the result

$$u_i + v_j = c_{ij}, \text{ for each } \textit{basic} \text{ variable } x_{ij}.$$

There are $m + n - 1$ such equations whose solution (after assuming an arbitrary value $u_1 \equiv 0$) yields the multipliers $u_i$ and $v_j$. Once these multipliers are computed, the entering variable is determined from all the *nonbasic* variables as the one having the largest positive $u_i + v_j - c_{ij}$.

The assignment of an arbitrary value to one of the dual variables (i.e., $u_1 = 0$) contradicts the presentation in Section 4.6 because it indicates that the dual values associated with a given basic solution are not unique. Problem 5.3c–2 shows why there is actually no contradiction in assuming an arbitrary dual value.

#### Problem set 5.3c

**1.** Write the dual problem for the LP of the transportation problem in Example 5.3–5 (Table 5–21). Compute the associated optimum *dual* objective value using the optimal dual values given in Table 5–25, and show that it yields the same value as the optimal cost given in the example.

**2.** In the transportation model, one of the dual variables assumes an arbitrary value. This means that for the same basic solution, the values of the associated dual variables are not unique. The result appears to contradict the theory of linear programming, where the dual values are determined as the product of the vector of the objective coefficients for the basic variables and the associated inverse basic matrix (see Section 4.6). Show that for the transportation model, although the inverse basis is unique, the vector of *basic* objective coefficients need not be so. Specifically, show that if $c_{ij}$ is changed to $c_{ij} + k$ for all $i$ and $j$, where $k$ is a constant, then the optimal values of $x_{ij}$ will remain the same. Hence, the use of an arbitrary value for a dual variable is implicitly equivalent to assuming that a specific constant $k$ is added to all $c_{ij}$.

## 5.4 THE ASSIGNMENT MODEL

"The best person for the job" is an apt description of what the assignment model seeks to accomplish. The situation can be illustrated by the assignment of workers to jobs, where any worker may undertake any job, albeit with varying degrees of skill. A job that happens to match a worker's skill costs less than that in which the operator is not as skillful. The objective of the model is to determine the optimum (least-cost) assignment of workers to jobs.

The general assignment model with $n$ workers and $n$ jobs is represented in Table 5–31.

**TABLE 5–31**

|        |       | \multicolumn{4}{c}{Jobs} |          |          |        |          |       |
|--------|-------|----------|----------|-----|----------|-------|
|        |       | 1        | 2        | ... | $n$      |       |
| Worker | 1     | $c_{11}$ | $c_{12}$ | ... | $c_{1n}$ | **1** |
|        | 2     | $c_{21}$ | $c_{22}$ | ... | $c_{2n}$ | **1** |
|        | .     | .        | .        |     | .        | .     |
|        | .     | .        | .        |     | .        | .     |
|        | .     | .        | .        |     | .        | .     |
|        | $n$   | $c_{n1}$ | $c_{n2}$ | ... | $c_{nn}$ | **1** |
|        |       | **1**    | **1**    | ... | **1**    |       |

The element $c_{ij}$ represents the cost of assigning worker $i$ to job $j$ ($i, j = 1, 2, \ldots,$ $n$). There is no loss in generality in assuming that the number of workers always equals the number of jobs because we can always add fictitious workers or fictitious jobs to effect this result.

The assignment model is actually a special case of the transportation model in which the workers represent the sources, and the jobs represent the destinations. The supply amount at each source and the demand amount at each destination exactly equals 1. The cost of "transporting" worker $i$ to job $j$ is $c_{ij}$. In effect, the assignment model can be solved directly as a regular transportation model. Nevertheless, the fact that all the supply and demand amounts equal 1 has led to the development of a simple solution algorithm called the **Hungarian method**. Although the new method appears to be totally unrelated to the transportation model, the algorithm is actually rooted in the simplex method, just as the transportation model is.

### 5.4.1 The Hungarian Method

We will use two examples to present the mechanics of the new algorithm. The next section provides a simplex-based explanation of the procedure.

---

**Example 5.4–1.**

Joe Klyne's three children, John, Karen, and Terri, want to earn some money to take care of personal expenses during a school trip to the local zoo. Mr. Klyne has chosen three chores for his children: mowing the lawn, painting the garage, and washing the family cars. To avoid anticipated siblings competitions, he asked them to submit (secret) bids for what they feel was a fair pay for each of the three chores. The understanding then was that all three children will abide by their father's decision as to who gets which chore. Table 5–32 summarizes the bids received.

**TABLE 5–32**

|        | Mow  | Paint | Wash |
|--------|------|-------|------|
| John   | $15  | $10   | $9   |
| Karen  | $9   | $15   | $10  |
| Terri  | $10  | $12   | $8   |

Based on this information, how should Mr. Klyne assign the chores?

The assignment problem will be solved by the Hungarian method.

**Step 1.** For the original cost matrix, identify each row's minimum, and subtract it from all the entries of the row.

**Step 2.** For the matrix resulting from step 1, identify each column's minimum, and subtract it from all the entries of the column.

**Step 3.** Identify the optimal assignment as the one associated with the zero elements of the matrix obtained in step 2.

Let $p_i$ and $q_j$ be row $i$ and column $j$ minimum costs as defined in steps 1 and 2, respectively. The row minimums of step 1 are computed from the original cost matrix as shown in Table 5–33.

**TABLE 5–33**

|        | Mow | Paint | Wash | Row minimum |
|--------|-----|-------|------|-------------|
| John   | 15  | 10    | **9**  | $p_1 = 9$ |
| Karen  | **9** | 15  | 10   | $p_2 = 9$ |
| Terri  | 10  | 12    | **8**  | $p_3 = 8$ |

Next, we subtract the row minimum from each respective row to obtain the reduced matrix in Table 5–34.

**TABLE 5–34**

|        | Mow | Paint | Wash |
|--------|-----|-------|------|
| John   | 6   | **1** | **0** |
| Karen  | **0** | 6   | 1    |
| Terri  | 2   | 4     | **0** |

Column minimum $q_1 = 0$     $q_2 = 1$     $q_3 = 0$

The application of step 2 yields the column minimums in Table 5–34. Subtracting these values from the respective columns, we get the reduced matrix in Table 5–35.

**TABLE 5–35**

|        | Mow | Paint | Wash |
|--------|-----|-------|------|
| John   | 6   | <u>**0**</u> | 0 |
| Karen  | <u>**0**</u> | 5 | 1 |
| Terri  | 2   | 3     | <u>**0**</u> |

The cells with underscored zero entries provide the optimum solution. This means that John gets to paint the garage, Karen gets to mow the lawn, and Terri gets to wash the family cars. The total cost to Mr. Klyne is $9 + 10 + 8 = \$27$. This amount also will always equal $(P_1 + p_2 + p_3) + (q_1 + q_2 + q_3) = (9 + 9 + 8) + (0 + 1 + 0) = \$27$. (A justification of this result is given in the next section.)

---

The given steps of the Hungarian method work well for the preceding example because the zero entries in the final matrix happen to produce a *feasible* assignment (in the sense that each child is assigned exactly one chore). In some cases, the zeros created by steps 1 and 2 may not yield a feasible solution directly. In this case, further steps are needed to find the optimal (feasible) assignment. The following example demonstrates this situation.

---

**Example 5.4–2.**

Suppose that the situation discussed in Example 5.4–1 is extended to four children and four chores. Table 5–36 summarizes the cost elements of the problem.

**TABLE 5–36**

|  |  | Chore | | | |
|---|---|---|---|---|---|
|  |  | 1 | 2 | 3 | 4 |
|  | 1 | \$1 | \$4 | \$6 | \$3 |
| Child | 2 | \$9 | \$7 | \$10 | \$9 |
|  | 3 | \$4 | \$5 | \$11 | \$7 |
|  | 4 | \$8 | \$7 | \$8 | \$5 |

The application of steps 1 and 2 to the matrix in Table 5–36 (using $p_1 = 1, p_2 = 7$, $p_3 = 4, p_4 = 5, q_1 = 0, q_2 = 0, q_3 = 3$, and $q_4 = 0$) yields the following reduced matrix in Table 5–37 (verify!):

**TABLE 5–37**

|  |  | Chore | | | |
|---|---|---|---|---|---|
|  |  | 1 | 2 | 3 | 4 |
|  | 1 | **0** | 3 | 2 | 2 |
| Child | 2 | 2 | **0** | **0** | 2 |
|  | 3 | **0** | 1 | 4 | 3 |
|  | 4 | 3 | 2 | **0** | **0** |

The locations of the zero entries do not allow assigning one chore to each child. For example, if we assign child 1 to chore 1, then column 1 will be eliminated, and child

3 will not have a zero entry in the remaining three columns. This obstacle can be accounted for by adding the following step to the procedure outlined in Example 5.4–1:

**Step 2a.** If no feasible assignment (with all zero entries) can be secured from steps 1 and 2,

(i) Draw the *minimum* number of horizontal and vertical lines in the last reduced matrix that will cover *all* the zero entries.

(ii) Select the *smallest uncovered* element, and subtract it from every uncovered element; then add it to every element at the intersection of two lines.

(iii) If no feasible assignment can be found among the resulting zero entries, repeat step 2a. Otherwise, go to step 3 to determine the optimal assignment.

The application of step 2a to the last matrix produces the three covering lines shown in Table 5–38.

**TABLE 5–38**

|  |  | \multicolumn{4}{c}{Chore} | | | |
|--|--|--|--|--|--|
|  |  | 1 | 2 | 3 | 4 |
|  | 1 | 0 | 3 | 2 | 2 |
|  | 2 | 2 | 0 | 0 | 2 |
| Child | 3 | 0 | 1 | 4 | 3 |
|  | 4 | 3 | 2 | 0 | 0 |

The smallest uncovered element (shown underscored) equals 1. This element is subtracted from all the uncovered elements and added to the intersection elements to produce the matrix in Table 5–39.

**TABLE 5–39**

|  |  | \multicolumn{4}{c}{Chore} | | | |
|--|--|--|--|--|--|
|  |  | 1 | 2 | 3 | 4 |
|  | 1 | **0** | 2 | 1 | 1 |
|  | 2 | 3 | 0 | **0** | 2 |
| Child | 3 | 0 | **0** | 3 | 2 |
|  | 4 | 4 | 2 | 0 | **0** |

The optimum solution (shown by the underscored zeros) calls for assigning child 1 to chore 1, child 2 to chore 3, child 3 to chore 2, and child 4 to chore 4. The associated optimal cost is $1 + 10 + 5 + 5 = \$21$. The same cost is also determined by summing the $p_i$'s, the $q_j$'s, and the element that was subtracted after the covering lines were constructed—that is $(1 + 7 + 4 + 5) + (0 + 0 + 3 + 0) + (1) = \$21$.

**Problem set 5.4a**

1. Solve the assignment models in Table 5–40.

**TABLE 5–40**

| (a) | | | | | (b) | | | | |
|---|---|---|---|---|---|---|---|---|---|
| $3 | $8 | $2 | $10 | $3 | $3 | $9 | $2 | $3 | $7 |
| $8 | $7 | $2 | $9 | $7 | $6 | $1 | $5 | $6 | $6 |
| $6 | $4 | $2 | $7 | $5 | $9 | $4 | $7 | $10 | $3 |
| $8 | $4 | $2 | $3 | $5 | $2 | $5 | $4 | $2 | $1 |
| $9 | $10 | $6 | $9 | $10 | $9 | $6 | $2 | $4 | $5 |

2. JoShop needs to assign four jobs it received to 4 workers. The varying skills of the workers give rise to varying costs for performing the jobs. Table 5–41 summarizes the cost data of the assignments. The data indicate that worker 1 cannot work on job 3, and worker 3 cannot work on job 4. Determine the optimal assignment.

**TABLE 5–41**

| | | Job | | | |
|---|---|---|---|---|---|
| | | 1 | 2 | 3 | 4 |
| | 1 | $50 | $50 | — | $20 |
| Worker | 2 | $70 | $40 | $20 | $30 |
| | 3 | $90 | $30 | $50 | — |
| | 4 | $70 | $20 | $60 | $70 |

3. In the JoShop model of Problem 2, suppose that an additional (fifth) worker becomes available for performing the four jobs at the respective costs of $60, $45, $30, and $80. Is it economical to replace one of the current four workers with the new one?

4. In the model of Problem 2, suppose that JoShop has just received a fifth job and that the respective costs of performing it by the four current workers are $20, $10, $20, and $80. Should the new job take priority over any of the four jobs JoShop already has?

5. A business executive must make the four round trips listed in Table 5–42 between the head office in Dallas and a branch office in Atlanta.

**TABLE 5–42**

| Departure date<br>from Dallas | Return date to<br>Dallas |
| --- | --- |
| Monday, June 3 | Friday, June 7 |
| Monday, June 10 | Wednesday, June 12 |
| Monday, June 17 | Friday, June 21 |
| Tuesday, June 25 | Friday, June 28 |

The price of a round-trip ticket from Dallas is $400. A discount of 25% is granted if the dates of arrival and departure of a ticket span a weekend (Saturday and Sunday). If the stay in Atlanta lasts more than 21 days, the discount is increased to 30%. A one-way ticket between Dallas and Atlanta (either direction) costs $250. How should the executive purchase the tickets?

6. Figure 5–4 gives a schematic layout of a machine shop with its existing work centers designated by squares 1, 2, 3, and 4. Four new work centers are to be added to the shop at the locations designated by circles $a, b, c,$ and $d$. The objective is to assign the new centers to the proposed locations in a manner that will minimize the total materials handling traffic between the existing

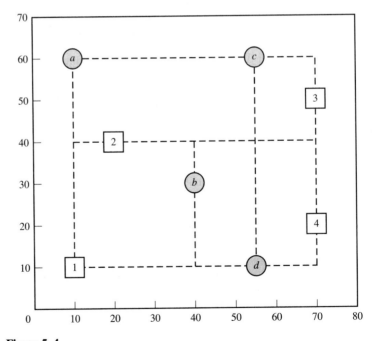

**Figure 5–4**

centers and the proposed ones. Table 5–43 summarizes the frequency of trips between the new centers and the old ones. Materials handling equipment travels along the rectangular aisles intersecting at the locations of the centers. For example, the one-way travel distance (in meters) between center 1 and center b is $30 + 20 = 50$ m.

**TABLE 5–43**

|  |  | New center | | | |
|---|---|---|---|---|---|
|  |  | a | b | c | d |
|  | 1 | 10 | 2 | 4 | 3 |
| Existing center | 2 | 7 | 1 | 9 | 5 |
|  | 3 | 0 | 8 | 6 | 2 |
|  | 4 | 11 | 4 | 0 | 7 |

## 5.4.2 Simplex Explanation of the Hungarian Method

The assignment problem in which $n$ workers are assigned to $n$ jobs can be represented as an LP model in the following manner: Let $c_{ij}$ be the cost of assigning worker $i$ to job $j$, and define

$$x_{ij} = \begin{cases} 1, & \text{if worker } i \text{ is assigned to job } j \\ 0, & \text{otherwise} \end{cases}$$

Then the LP model is given as

$$\text{Minimize } z = \sum_{i=1}^{n} \sum_{j=1}^{n} c_{ij} x_{ij}$$

subject to

$$\sum_{j=1}^{n} x_{ij} = 1, \ i = 1, 2, \cdots, n$$

$$\sum_{i=1}^{n} x_{ij} = 1, \ j = 1, 2, \cdots, n$$

$$x_{ij} = 0 \text{ or } 1$$

The optimal solution of the preceding LP model remains unchanged if a constant is added to or subtracted from any row or column of the cost matrix $(c_{ij})$. To prove this point, let $p_i$ and $q_j$ be constants subtracted from row $i$ and column $j$. Thus, the cost element $c_{ij}$ is changed to

$$c'_{ij} = c_{ij} - p_i - q_j$$

Next, we show that using the objective coefficients $c'_{ij}$ yields the same optimum values of $x_{ij}$ as when $c_{ij}$ is used.

$$\sum_i \sum_j (c_{ij} - p_i - q_j)x_{ij} = \sum_i \sum_j c_{ij}x_{ij} - \sum_i p_i\left(\sum_j x_{ij}\right) - \sum_j q_j\left(\sum_i x_{ij}\right)$$

$$= \sum_i \sum_j c_{ij}x_{ij} - \sum_i p_i(1) - \sum_j q_j(1)$$

$$= \sum_i \sum_j c_{ij}x_{ij} - \text{constant}$$

Because the new objective function differs from the original one by a constant, the optimum values of $x_{ij}$ must be the same in both cases. The development thus shows that steps 1 and 2 of the Hungarian method, which call for subtracting $p_i$ from row $i$ and then subtracting $q_j$ from column $j$, produce an equivalent assignment model. In this regard, if a feasible solution can be found among the created zero entries of the cost matrix created by steps 1 and 2, then it must be optimum because the cost in the modified matrix cannot be less than zero.

If the created zero entries cannot yield a feasible solution (as Example 5.4–2 demonstrates), then step 2a (dealing with the covering of the zero entries) must be applied. The validity of this procedure is again rooted in the simplex method of linear programming and can be explained based on duality theory (Chapter 4) and the complementary slackness theorem (Chapter 7). We will not present the details of the proof here because it is somewhat involved.

The reason $(p_1 + p_2 + \ldots p_n) + (q_1 + q_2 + \ldots + q_n)$ gives the optimal objective value is that it represents the dual objective function of the assignment model. This result can be seen through comparison with the dual objective function of the transportation model given in Section 5.3.3. (See Bazaraa et al [1990], pp. 499–508 for the details.)

## 5.5 THE TRANSSHIPMENT MODEL

The transshipment model recognizes that in real life it may be cheaper to ship through intermediate or *transient* nodes before reaching the final destination. This concept is more general than the one advanced by the regular transportation model, where direct shipments only are allowed between a source and a destination.

This section shows how a transshipment model can be converted to (and solved as) a regular transportation model using the idea of a **buffer**.

**Example 5.5–1.**

Two automobile plants, $P1$ and $P2$, are linked to three dealers, $D1$, $D2$, and $D3$, by way of two transit centers, $T1$ and $T2$ according to the network shown in Figure 5–5. The supply amounts at plants $P1$ and $P2$ are 1000 and 1200 cars, and the demand amounts at dealers

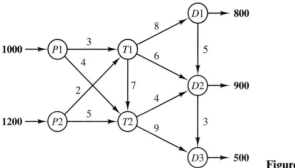

**Figure 5–5**

$D1, D2$, and $D3$, are 800, 900, and 300 cars. The shipping cost per car (in hundreds of dol-lars) between pairs of nodes are shown on the connecting links (or arcs) of the network.

Transshipment occurs in the network in Figure 5–5 because the entire supply amount of 2200 ( $= 1000 + 1200$) cars at nodes $P1$ and $P2$ could conceivably pass through any node of the network before ultimately reaching their destinations at nodes $D1, D2$, and $D3$. In this regard, the nodes of the network with both input and output arcs (i.e., $T1, T2, D1$, and $D2$) act as both sources and destinations, and are referred to as **transshipment nodes**. The remaining nodes are either **pure supply nodes** (i.e., $P1$ and $P2$) or **pure demand nodes** (i.e., $D3$). The transshipment model can be converted into a regular transportation model with six sources ($P1, P2, T1, T2, D1$, and $D2$) and five des-tinations ($T1, T2$, and $D1, D2$, and $D3$). The amounts of supply and demand at the dif-ferent nodes are computed as

Supply at a *pure supply node* = Original supply

Supply at a *transshipment node* = Original supply + buffer

Demand at a *pure demand node* = Original demand

Demand at a *transshipment node* = Original demand + Buffer

The buffer amount should be sufficiently large to allow all the *original* supply (or demand) units to pass through any of the *transshipment* nodes. Let $B$ be the desired buffer amount, then

$$B = \text{Total supply (or demand)}$$

$$= 1000 + 1200 \text{ (or } 800 + 900 + 500)$$

$$= 2200 \text{ cars}$$

Using the preceding information and the unit shipping costs given on the net-work, the equivalent regular transportation model is constructed as in Table 5–44.

The solution of the resulting transportation model (determined by TORA) is shown in Figure 5–6. Note the effect of transshipment: Dealer $D2$ receives 1400 cars, keeps 900 cars to satisfy its demand, and sends the remaining 500 cars to dealer $D3$.

**TABLE 5–44**

|      | T1 | T2 | D1 | D2 | D3 |           |
|------|----|----|----|----|----|-----------|
| P1   | 3  | 4  | M  | M  | M  | **1000**  |
| P2   | 2  | 5  | M  | M  | M  | **1200**  |
| T1   | 0  | 7  | 8  | 6  | M  | **B**     |
| T2   | M  | 0  | M  | 4  | 9  | **B**     |
| D1   | M  | M  | 0  | 5  | M  | **B**     |
| D2   | M  | M  | M  | 0  | 3  | **B**     |
|      | **B** | **B** | **800 + B** | **900 + B** | **500** | |

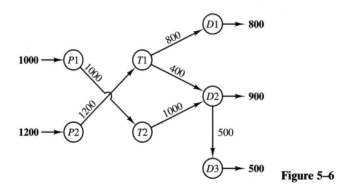

**Figure 5–6**

## Problem set 5.5a

**1.** The network in Figure 5–7 gives the shipping routes from nodes 1 and to nodes 5 and 6 by way of nodes 3 and 4. The unit shipping costs are shown on the respective arcs.

   **(a)** Develop the corresponding transshipment model.

   **(b)** Solve the problem by TORA, and show how the shipments are routed from the sources to the destinations.

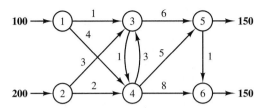

**Figure 5–7**

2. In Problem 1, suppose that source node 1 can be linked to source node 2 with a unit shipping cost of $1. The unit shipping cost from node 1 to node 3 is increased to $5. Formulate the problem as a transshipment model, and find the optimum shipping schedule.

3. The network in Figure 5–8 shows the routes for shipping cars from three plants (nodes 1, 2, and 3) to three dealers (nodes 6 to 8) by way of two distribution centers (nodes 4 and 5). The shipping costs per car (in $100) are shown on the arcs.

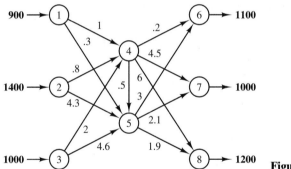

**Figure 5–8**

   **(a)** Solve the problem as a transshipment model, and find the optimum solution by TORA.
   **(b)** Suppose that distribution center 4 can sell 240 cars directly to customers. Find the new optimum solution.

4. Consider the transportation problem in which two factories supply three stores with a certain commodity. The number of supply units available at sources 1 and 2 are 200 and 300; those demanded at stores 1, 2, and 3 are 100, 200, and 50, respectively. Units may be transshipped among the factories and the stores before ultimately reaching their destination. It is desired to find the optimal shipping schedule (use TORA) based on the unit costs in Table 5–45.

**TABLE 5–45**

|  |  | Factory | | Store | | |
|---|---|---|---|---|---|---|
|  |  | 1 | 2 | 1 | 2 | 3 |
| Factory | 1 | $0 | $6 | $7 | $8 | $9 |
|  | 2 | $6 | $0 | $5 | $4 | $3 |
| Store | 1 | $7 | $2 | $0 | $5 | $1 |
|  | 2 | $1 | $5 | $1 | $0 | $4 |
|  | 3 | $8 | $9 | $7 | $6 | $0 |

5. Consider the oil pipeline network shown in Figure 5–9. The different nodes represent the pumping and the receiving stations. The distances in miles between the different stations are shown on the network. The transportation cost per gallon between two nodes is directly proportional to the length of the pipeline. Develop the associated transshipment model, and find the optimum solution using TORA.

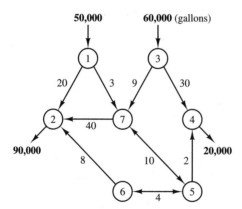

**Figure 5–9**

6. *Shortest-route problem.* Find the shortest route between nodes 1 and 7 of the network in Figure 5–10 by formulating the problem as a transshipment model. The distance between the different nodes are shown on the network. (*Hint:* Assume that node 1 has a net supply of 1 unit, and node 7 has a net demand also of 1 unit.)

7. In the transshipment model of Example 5.5–1, define $x_{ij}$ as the amount shipped from node $i$ to node $j$. The problem can be formulated as a linear program in which each node produces a constraint equation. Develop the

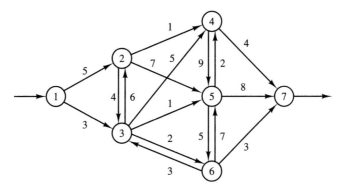

**Figure 5–10**

linear program, and show that the resulting formulation has the characteristic that the constraint coefficients, $a_{ij}$, of the variable $x_{ij}$ are defined as

$$a_{ij} = \begin{cases} 1, & \text{For constraint } i \\ -1, & \text{For constraint } j \\ 0, & \text{Otherwise} \end{cases}$$

8. An employment agency must provide the following laborers over the next
   5 months:

| Month | 1 | 2 | 3 | 4 | 5 |
|---|---|---|---|---|---|
| No. of laborers | 100 | 120 | 80 | 170 | 50 |

Because the cost of labor depends on the length of employment, it
may be more economical to keep more laborers than needed during some
months of the 5-month planning horizon. The following table estimates the
labor cost as a function of the length of employment:

| Months of employment | 1 | 2 | 3 | 4 | 5 |
|---|---|---|---|---|---|
| Cost per laborer ($) | 100 | 130 | 180 | 220 | 250 |

Formulate the problem as a linear program. Then, using proper algebraic manipulations of the constraint equations, show that the model can be

converted to a transshipment model, and find the optimum solution to the scheduling problem. (*Hint:* Use the transshipment characteristic in Problem 5.5a–7 to convert the constraints of the scheduling problem into those of the transshipment model.)

## 5.6 SUMMARY

The transportation model is a special LP whose structure allows the development of an efficient computational technique. The technique is based on duality theory. Related models include the assignment and the transshipment models. The transportation model also applies to nontransportation areas, such as production scheduling and inventory control.

The transportation model is but one class of the generalized network models covered in Chapter 6. Some recent surveys report that as much as 70% of the real-world mathematical programming problems can be treated as network-related models.

## SELECTED REFERENCES

BAZARAA, M., J. JARVIS, and H. SHERALI, *Linear Programming and Network Flows,* 2nd ed., Wiley, New York, 1990.

CHANRNES, A., F. GLOVER, and D. KLINGMAN, "A Note on a Distribution Problem," *Operations Research,* Vol. 18, pp. 1213–1216, 1970.

DANTZIG, G., *Linear Programming and Extensions,* Princeton University Press, Princeton, N.J., 1963.

MURTY, K., *Network Programming,* Prentice Hall, Upper Saddle River, N.J., 1992.

## COMPREHENSIVE PROBLEMS

■  5–1[1]  ABC Cola operates a plant in the northern section of the island nation of Tawanda. The plant produces soft drinks in three types of packages that include returnable glass bottles, aluminum cans, and nonreturnable plastic bottles. Returnable bottles are shipped to the distribution warehouses and must be returned empty for reuse in the plant.

Because of the continued growth in demand, ABC wants to build another plant either in the midsection or in the south of the island. The demand for the soft drinks (expressed in cases) over the next 5 years is given in Table 5–46.

[1]Based on T. Cheng and C. Chiu, "A Case Study of Production Expansion Planning in a Soft-Drink Manufacturing Company," *Omega,* Vol. 16, No. 6, pp. 521–532, 1988.

**TABLE 5–46**

|          | Year |      |      |      |      |
|----------|------|------|------|------|------|
| Package  | 1    | 2    | 3    | 4    | 5    |
| Returnables    | 2400 | 2450 | 2600 | 2800 | 3100 |
| Cans           | 1750 | 2000 | 2300 | 2650 | 3050 |
| Nonreturnables | 490  | 550  | 600  | 650  | 720  |

The planned production capacities for the existing plant extrapolated over the same 5-year horizon are given in Table 5–47.

**TABLE 5–47**

|          | Year |      |      |      |      |
|----------|------|------|------|------|------|
| Package  | 1    | 2    | 3    | 4    | 5    |
| Returnables    | 1800 | 1400 | 1900 | 2050 | 2150 |
| Cans           | 1250 | 1350 | 1400 | 1500 | 1800 |
| Nonreturnables | 350  | 380  | 400  | 400  | 450  |

The company owns six distribution warehouses: $N1$ and $N2$ are located in the north, $C1$ and $C2$ are located in the central section, and $S1$ and $S2$ are located in the south. The share of sales by each warehouse within its zone is given in Table 5–48.

**TABLE 5–48**

| Warehouse | Share Percentage |
|-----------|------------------|
| $N1$      | 85               |
| $N2$      | 15               |
| $C1$      | 60               |
| $C2$      | 40               |
| $S1$      | 80               |
| $S2$      | 20               |

Approximately 60% of the sales occur in the north, 15% in the central section, and 25% in the south.

The company wants to construct the new plant either in the central section or in the south. The transportation cost per case of returnable bottles is given in Table 5–49. It is estimated that the transportation costs per case of cans and per case of nonreturnables are 60% and 70%, respectively, that of the returnable bottles.

**TABLE 5–49**

| | Transportation cost per case ($) | | |
| Warehouse | Existing plant | Central plant | South plant |
| --- | --- | --- | --- |
| $N1$ | 0.80 | 1.30 | 1.90 |
| $N2$ | 1.20 | 1.90 | 2.90 |
| $C1$ | 1.50 | 1.05 | 1.20 |
| $C2$ | 1.60 | 0.80 | 1.60 |
| $S1$ | 1.90 | 1.50 | 0.90 |
| $S2$ | 2.10 | 1.70 | 0.80 |

Should the new plant be located in the central or the southern section of the country?

■ 5-2[2]  The construction of Brisbane International Airport requires the pipeline movement of about 1,355,000 $m^3$ of sand dredged from five clusters at a nearby bay to nine sites at the airport location. The sand is used to help stabilize the swampy grounds at the proposed construction area. Some of the sites to which the sand is moved are dedicated to building roads both within and on the perimeter of the airport. Excess sand from a site will then be moved by trucks to other outlying areas around the airport where a perimeter road will be built. The distances (in 100 m) between the source clusters and the sites are summarized in Table 5–50, which also shows the supply and demand quantities in 100 $m^3$ at the different locations.

(a) The project management has estimated a [volume ($m^3$) × distance (100 m)] sand movement of 2,495,000 units at the cost of $.65 per unit. Is the estimate given by the project management for sand movement on target?

[2]Based on C. Perry and M. Ilief "Earth Moving on Construction Projects," *Interfaces*, Vol. 13, No. 1, 1983, pp. 79–84.

**TABLE 5–50**

|   | 1 | 2 | 3 | 4 | 5 | 6 | 7 | 8 | 9 | Supply |
|---|---|---|---|---|---|---|---|---|---|--------|
| 1 | 22 | 26 | 12 | 10 | 18 | 18 | 11 | 8.5 | 20 | **960** |
| 2 | 20 | 28 | 14 | 12 | 20 | 20 | 13 | 10 | 22 | **201** |
| 3 | 16 | 20 | 26 | 20 | 1.5 | 28 | 6 | 22 | 18 | **71** |
| 4 | 20 | 22 | 26 | 22 | 6 | $\infty$ | 2 | 21 | 18 | **24** |
| 5 | 22 | 26 | 10 | 4 | 16 | $\infty$ | 24 | 14 | 21 | **99** |
| Demand | **62** | **217** | **444** | **315** | **50** | **7** | **20** | **90** | **150** | |

(b) The project management came to realize that sand movement to certain sites cannot be carried out until some of the roads are built. In particular, the perimeter road (destination 9) must be built before movement to certain sites can be effected. In Table 5–51, the blocked routes that require the completion of the perimeter road are marked with x. How should the sand movement be made to accommodate these restrictions?

**TABLE 5–51**

|   | 1 | 2 | 3 | 4 | 5 | 6 | 7 | 8 | 9 |
|---|---|---|---|---|---|---|---|---|---|
| 1 | x | x |   |   | x |   |   |   |   |
| 2 | x | x |   |   | x |   |   |   |   |
| 3 |   |   | x |   |   | x |   |   |   |
| 4 |   |   | x |   |   |   |   | x |   |
| 5 | x | x |   |   | x |   | x |   |   |

■ 5–3 Ten years ago, a wholesale dealer started a business distributing pharmaceuticals from a central warehouse (*CW*). Orders were delivered to customers by vans. The warehouse has since been expanded in response to growing demand. Additionally, two new warehouses (*W*1 and *W*2) have been constructed. The central warehouse, traditionally well stocked, occasionally supplied the new warehouses with some short items. The occasional supply of short items has grown into a large-scale operation in which the two new warehouses receive for redistribution about one-third of their stock directly from the central warehouse. Table 5–52 gives the number of orders shipped out by each of the three warehouses to customer locations, *C*1 to *C*6. A customer location is a town with several pharmacies.

**TABLE 5–52**

| Route | | No. of Orders |
|---|---|---|
| From | To | |
| CW | W1 | 2000 |
| CW | W2 | 1500 |
| CW | C1 | 4800 |
| CW | C2 | 3000 |
| CW | C3 | 1200 |
| W1 | C1 | 1000 |
| W1 | C3 | 1100 |
| W1 | C4 | 1500 |
| W1 | C5 | 1800 |
| W2 | C2 | 1900 |
| W2 | C5 | 600 |
| W2 | C6 | 2200 |

The dealer's delivery schedule has evolved over the years to its present status. In essence, the schedule was devised in a rather decentralized fashion with each warehouse determining its delivery zone based on "self-fulfilling" criteria. Indeed, in some instances, warehouse managers competed for new customers mainly to increase their "sphere of influence." For instance, the managers of the central warehouse boasts that their delivery zone includes not only regular customers but the other two warehouses as well. It is not unusual then that several warehouses deliver supplies to different pharmacies within the same town (customer location).

The distances in miles traveled by the vans between the different locations are given in Table 5–53. A vanload usually hauls 100 orders.

**TABLE 5–53**

|   | CW | W1 | W2 | C1 | C2 | C3 | C4 | C5 | C6 |
|---|---|---|---|---|---|---|---|---|---|
| CW | 0 | 5 | 45 | 50 | 30 | 30 | 60 | 75 | 80 |
| W1 | 5 | 0 | 80 | 38 | 70 | 30 | 8 | 10 | 60 |
| W2 | 45 | 80 | 0 | 85 | 35 | 60 | 55 | 7 | 90 |

**TABLE 5–53** *(continued)*

| | | | | | | | | | |
|------|----|----|----|----|----|----|----|----|----|
| $C1$ | 50 | 38 | 85 | 0  | 20 | 40 | 25 | 30 | 70 |
| $C2$ | 30 | 70 | 35 | 20 | 0  | 40 | 90 | 15 | 10 |
| $C3$ | 30 | 30 | 60 | 40 | 40 | 0  | 10 | 6  | 90 |
| $C4$ | 60 | 8  | 55 | 25 | 90 | 10 | 0  | 80 | 40 |
| $C5$ | 75 | 10 | 7  | 30 | 15 | 6  | 80 | 0  | 15 |
| $C6$ | 80 | 60 | 90 | 70 | 10 | 90 | 40 | 15 | 0  |

Evaluate the present distribution policy of the dealer.

■ 5–4   KeeWee Airlines flies eight two-way flights between Waco and Macon according to the schedule in Table 5–54. A crew can return to its home base (Waco or Macon) on the same day provided there is at least a 90-minute layover in the other city. Otherwise, the crew can return the next day. It is desired to pair the crews with the flights originating from the two cities to minimize the total layover time by all the crews.

**TABLE 5–54**

| Flight | From Waco | To Macon | Flight | From Macon | To Waco |
|--------|-----------|----------|--------|------------|---------|
| $W1$   | 6:00      | 8:30     | $M1$   | 7:30       | 9:30    |
| $W2$   | 8:15      | 10:45    | $M2$   | 9:15       | 11:15   |
| $W3$   | 13:30     | 16:00    | $M3$   | 16:30      | 18:30   |
| $W4$   | 15:00     | 17:30    | $M4$   | 20:00      | 22:00   |

Chapter **6**

# Network Models

## 6.1 SCOPE OF NETWORK APPLICATIONS

There is a multitude of operations research situations that can be conveniently modeled and solved as networks (nodes connected by branches). As illustrations, consider the following situations:

**1.** The design of an offshore natural-gas pipeline network connecting wellheads in the Gulf of Mexico to an inshore delivery point. The objective of the model is to minimize the cost of constructing the pipeline.

**2.** The determination of the shortest route between two cities in an existing network of roads.

**3.** The determination of the maximum capacity (in tons per year) of a coal slurry pipeline network joining the coal mines in Wyoming with the power plants in Houston. (Slurry pipelines transport coal by pumping water through specially designed pipes.)

**4.** The determination of the minimum-cost flow schedule from oil fields to refineries through a pipeline network.

**5.** The determination of the time schedule (start and completion dates) for the activities of a construction project.

The solution of these situations, and others like it, is accomplished through a variety of network optimization algorithms. This chapter will present five of these algorithms.

**1.** Minimal spanning tree (situation 1)
**2.** Shortest route algorithm (situation 2)

**3.** Maximum flow algorithm (situation 3)

**4.** Minimum-cost capacitated network algorithm (situation 4)

**5.** Critical path (CPM) algorithm (situation 5)

The situations for which these algorithms apply can also be formulated and solved as explicit linear programs. However, the proposed network-based algorithms are more efficient than the simplex method.

## 6.2 NETWORK DEFINITIONS

A network consists of a set of **nodes** linked by **arcs** (or **branches**). The notation for describing a network is $(N, A)$, where $N$ is the set of nodes, and $A$ is the set of arcs. As an illustration, the network in Figure 6–1 is described as

$N = \{1, 2, 3, 4, 5\}$

$A = \{(1,3), (1,2), (2,3), (2,4), (2,5), (3,4), (3,5), (4,5)\}$

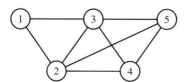

**Figure 6–1**

Associated with each network is some type of flow (e.g., oil products flow in a pipeline and automobile traffic flows in a road network). In general, the flow in a network is limited by the capacity of its arcs, which may be finite or infinite.

An arc is said to be **directed** or **oriented** if it allows positive flow in one direction and zero flow in the opposite direction. A **directed network** has all directed branches.

A **path** is a sequence of distinct branches that join two nodes regardless of the direction of flow in each branch. A path forms a **loop** or a **cycle** if it connects a node to itself. For example, in Figure 6–1, the branches $(2, 3), (3, 4)$, and $(4, 2)$ form a loop. A **directed loop** (or a **circuit**) is a loop in which all the branches are oriented in the same direction.

A **connected network** is such that every two distinct nodes are linked by at least one path. The network in Figure 6–1 demonstrates this type of network. A **tree** is a connected network that may involve only a subset of all the nodes of the network with no loops allowed, whereas a **spanning tree** is a tree that links all the nodes of the network. Figure 6–2 provides examples of a tree and a spanning tree.

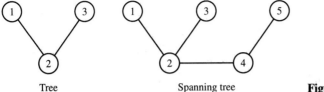

Tree                          Spanning tree                    **Figure 6–2**

**Problem set 6.2a**

1. For each network in Figure 6–3 determine (a) a path, (b) a loop, (c) a directed loop or a circuit, (d) a tree, and (e) a spanning tree.

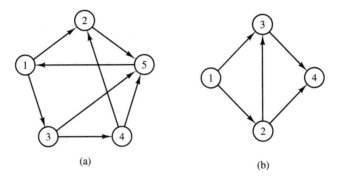

(a)                                            (b)

**Figure 6–3**

2. Determine the sets $N$ and $A$ for the networks in Figure 6–3.

3. Draw the network defined by

   $N = \{1, 2, 3, 4, 5, 6\}$

   $A = \{(1, 2), (1, 5), (2, 3), (2, 4), (3, 5), (3, 4), (4, 2), (4, 6), (5, 2), (5, 6)\}$

4. Consider eight equal squares arranged in three rows, with two squares in the first row, four in the second, and two in the third. The squares of each row are arranged symmetrically about the vertical axis. It is desired to fill the squares with distinct numbers in the range $1, 2, \ldots$, and 8 so that no two *adjacent* vertical, horizontal, or diagonal squares hold consecutive numbers. Express the problem as a network, and devise a systematic solution procedure based on the network representation.

5. Three inmates escorted by 3 guards must be transported by boat from San Francisco to the Alcatraz penitentiary island to serve their sentences. The boat cannot transfer more than two persons in either direction. The inmates are certain to overpower the guards if they outnumber them at any time. Develop a network model that designs the boat trips in a manner that ensures a smooth transfer of the inmates.

## 6.3 MINIMAL SPANNING TREE ALGORITHM

The minimal spanning tree algorithm deals with linking the nodes of a network, directly or indirectly, using the shortest length of connecting branches. A typical application occurs in the creation of a network of paved roads that link several rural towns, where the road between two towns may pass through one or more other towns. The most economical design of the road system calls for minimizing the total miles of paved roads, a result that is achieved by implementing the minimal spanning tree algorithm.

The steps of the procedure are given as follows. Let $N = \{1, 2, \ldots, n\}$ be the set of nodes of the network and define

$C_k$ = Set of nodes that have been permanently connected at iteration k of the algorithm

$\overline{C}_k$ = Set of nodes as yet to be connected permanently

**Step 0.** Set $C_0 = \varnothing$ and $\overline{C}_0 = N$.

**Step 1.** Start with *any* node, $i$, in the unconnected set $\overline{C}_0$ and set $C_1 = \{i\}$, which automatically renders $\overline{C}_1 = N - \{i\}$.
Set $k = 2$.

**General step k.** Select a node, $j^*$, in the unconnected set $\overline{C}_{k-1}$ that yields the shortest branch to a node in the connected set $C_{k-1}$. Link $j^*$ permanently to $C_{k-1}$ and remove it from $\overline{C}_{k-1}$, that is,

$$C_k = C_{k-1} + \{j^*\}, \overline{C}_k = \overline{C}_{k-1} - \{j^*\}$$

If the set of unconnected nodes, $\overline{C}_k$, is empty, stop. Otherwise, set $k = k + 1$ and repeat the step.

---

**Example 6.3–1.**

The Midwest TV Cable Company is in the process of providing cable service to five new housing development areas. Figure 6–4 depicts the potential TV linkages among the

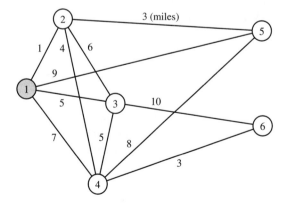

Figure 6–4

five areas. The cable miles are shown on each branch. It is desired to determine the most economical cable network.

The algorithm starts at node 1 (any other node will do as well), which gives

$$C_1 = \{1\}, \quad \overline{C}_1 = \{2, 3, 4, 5, 6\}$$

The iterations of the algorithm are summarized in Figure 6–5. The thin arcs provide all the candidate links between $C$ and $\overline{C}$. The thick branches represent the permanent links among the nodes of the connected set $C$, and the dashed branch represents the new (permanent) link added at each iteration.

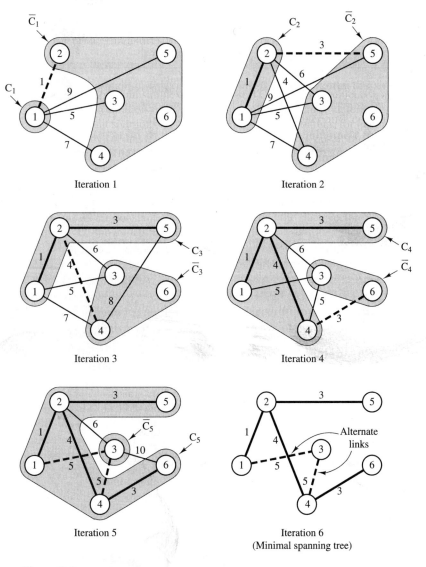

**Figure 6–5**

For example, in iteration 1, branch $(1, 2)$ is the shortest link ($= 1$ mile) among all the candidate branches from node 1 to nodes $2, 3, 4, 5,$ and 6 of the unconnected set $\overline{C}_1$. Hence, link $(1, 2)$ is made permanent and $j^* = 2$, which yields

$$C_2 = \{1, 2\}, \quad \overline{C}_2 = \{3, 4, 5, 6\}$$

The solution is given by the minimal spanning tree shown in iteration 6 of Figure 6–5. The resulting minimum cable miles needed to provide the desired cable service are $1 + 3 + 4 + 3 + 5 = 16$ miles.

---

### Problem set 6.3a

1. Solve Example 6.3–1 starting at node 5 (instead of node 1), and show that the algorithm produces the same solution.

2. Determine the minimal spanning tree of the network of Example 6.3–1 under each of the following separate conditions:
   (a) Nodes 5 and 6 are linked by a 2-mile cable.
   (b) Nodes 2 and 5 cannot be linked.
   (c) Nodes 2 and 6 are linked by a 4-mile cable.
   (d) The cable between nodes 1 and 2 is 8 miles long.
   (e) Nodes 3 and 5 are linked by a 2-mile cable.
   (f) Node 2 cannot be linked directly to nodes 3 and 5.

3. In intermodal transportation, loaded truck trailers are shipped between railroad terminals by placing the trailer on special flatbed carts. Figure 6–6 shows the location of the main railroad terminals in the United States and the existing railroad tracks. The objective is to decide which tracks should be "revitalized" to handle the intermodal traffic. In particular, the Los Angeles (LA) terminal must be linked directly to Chicago (CH) to accommodate the anticipated heavy traffic between the two locations. Other than that, all the remaining terminals can be linked, directly or indirectly, such that the total length (in miles) of the selected

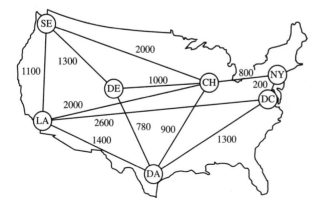

**Figure 6–6**

tracks is minimized. Determine the segments of the railroad tracks that must be included in the revitalization program.

4. Figure 6–7 gives the mileage of the feasible links connecting nine offshore natural gas wellheads with an inshore delivery point. Because the location of wellhead 1 is the closest to shore, it is equipped with sufficient pumping and storage capacity to pump the output of the remaining eight wells to the delivery point. Determine the minimum pipeline network that links the wellheads to the delivery point.

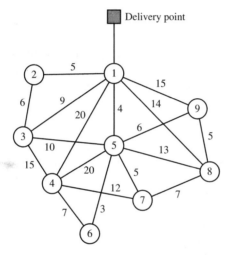

**Figure 6–7**

5. In Figure 6–7 of Problem 4, suppose that the wellheads can be divided into two groups depending on gas pressure: a high-pressure group that includes wells 2, 3, 4, and 6, and a low-pressure group that includes wells 5, 7, 8, and 9. Because of the pressure difference, it is not possible to link the wellheads of the two groups. At the same time, both groups must be connected to the delivery point through wellhead 1. Determine the minimum pipeline network for this situation.

6. Electro produces 15 electronic parts on 10 machines. The company wants to group the machines into cells designed to minimize the "dissimilarities" among the parts processed in each cell. A measure of "dissimilarity," $d_{ij}$, among the parts processed on machines $i$ and $j$ can be expressed as

$$d_{ij} = 1 - \frac{n_{ij}}{n_{ij} + m_{ij}}$$

where $n_{ij}$ is the number of parts shared between machines $i$ and $j$, and $m_{ij}$ is the number of parts that are used by either machine $i$ or $j$ only.

The following table assigns the parts to machines:

| Machine | Assigned parts |
| --- | --- |
| 1 | 1, 6 |
| 2 | 2, 3, 7, 8, 9, 12, 13, 15 |
| 3 | 3, 5, 10, 14 |
| 4 | 2, 7, 8, 11, 12, 13 |
| 5 | 3, 5, 10, 11, 14 |
| 6 | 1, 4, 5, 9, 10 |
| 7 | 2, 5, 7, 8, 9, 10 |
| 8 | 3, 4, 15 |
| 9 | 4, 10 |
| 10 | 3, 8, 10, 14, 15 |

**(a)** Express the problem as a network model.
**(b)** Show that the determination of the cells can be based on the minimal spanning tree solution.
**(c)** For the data given in the preceding table, construct the two- and three-cell solutions.

## 6.4 SHORTEST ROUTE PROBLEM

The shortest-route problem determines the shortest route between a source and destination in a transportation network. The same model can be used to model other situations as well, as illustrated by the folowing examples.

### 6.4.1 Examples of the Shortest-Route Applications

**Example 6.4–1 (EQUIPMENT REPLACEMENT).**
RentCar is developing a replacement plan for its car fleet for a 5-year (1996 to 2000) planning horizon. At the start of each year, a decision is made as to whether a car should be kept in operation or replaced. A car must be in service at least 1 year but must be replaced after 3 years. The following table provides the replacement cost as a function of the year a car is acquired and the number of years in operation.

| Year acquired | Replacement cost ($) for given years in operation | | |
|:---:|:---:|:---:|:---:|
| | 1 | 2 | 3 |
| 1996 | 4000 | 5400 | 9800 |
| 1997 | 4300 | 6200 | 8700 |
| 1998 | 4800 | 7100 | — |
| 1999 | 4900 | — | — |

The problem can be formulated as a network in which nodes 1 to 5 represent years 1996 to 2000. Arcs from node 1 (year 1996) can reach only nodes 2, 3, and 4 because a car must be in operation between 1 and 3 years. The arcs from the other nodes can be interpreted similarly. The length of each arc equals the replacement cost. The solution of the problem is equivalent to finding the shortest route between nodes 1 and 5.

Figure 6–8 shows the resulting network. Using TORA, the shortest route (shown by the thick path) is 1→3→5, with a total cost of $12,500. This solution means that the car acquired in 1996 (node 1) must be replaced after 2 years in 1998 (node 3). The replacement car will then be kept in operation until the end of the year 2000. The total cost of this replacement policy is $12,500 (= $5400 + $7100).

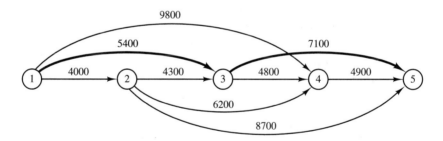

**Figure 6–8**

---

**Example 6.4–2 (MOST RELIABLE ROUTE).**
I. Q. Smart drives daily to work. Having just completed a course in network analysis, Smart is able to determine the shortest route to work. Unfortunately, the selected route is heavily patrolled by police, and with all the fines paid for speeding, the shortest route is not the best choice. Smart has thus decided to choose a route that maximizes the probability of *not* being stopped by police.

The network in Figure 6–9 shows the possible routes between home and work, and the associated probabilities of not being stopped on each segment. The probability of not being stopped on the way to work is thus the product of the probabilities associated with the successive segments of the selected route. For example, the probability of not receiving a fine on the route $1 \to 3 \to 5 \to 7$ is $.9 \times .3 \times .25 = .0675$. Smart's objective is to select the route that *maximizes* the probability of not being fined.

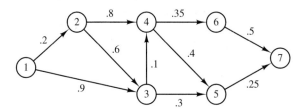

**Figure 6–9**

The problem can be formulated as a shortest-route model by using a logarithmic transformation that will convert the product probability into the sum of the logarithms of probabilities—that is, if $p_{1k} = p_1 \times p_2 \times \ldots \times p_k$ is the probability of not being stopped, then

$$\log p_{1k} = \log p_1 + \log p_2 + \ldots + \log p_k$$

Mathematically, the maximization of $p_{1k}$ is equivalent to the maximization of $\log p_{1k}$. Because $\log p_{1k} \leq 0$, the maximization of $\log p_{1k}$ is, in turn, equivalent to the minimization of $-\log p_{1k}$. Using this transformation, the individual probabilities $p_j$ in Figure 6–9 are replaced with $-\log p_j$, for all $j$ in the network, thus yielding the shortest-route network in Figure 6–10.

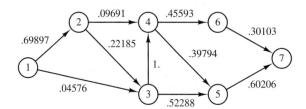

**Figure 6–10**

Using TORA, the shortest route in Figure 6–10 is defined by the nodes 1, 3, 5, and 7 with a corresponding "length" of 1.1707 ($= -\log p_{17}$). Thus, the maximum probability of not being stopped is $p_{17} = .0675$.

---

**Example 6.4–3 (THREE-JUG PUZZLE).**

An 8-gallon jug is filled with fluid. Given two empty 5- and 3-gallon jugs, we want to divide the 8 gallons of fluid into two equal parts by using the three jugs only. No other measuring devices are allowed. What is the smallest number of pourings needed to achieve this result?

You probably can guess the solution of this puzzle. Nevertheless, the solution process can be systematized by representing the problem as a shortest-route problem.

A node is defined to represent the amount of fluid in the 8-, 5-, and 3-gallon jugs, respectively. This means that the network starts with node $(8, 0, 0)$ and terminates with the desired solution node $(4, 4, 0)$. A new node is generated from the current node by pouring fluid from one jug to another.

Figure 6–11 shows different routes that lead from the start node $(8, 0, 0)$ to the sink node $(4, 4, 0)$. The arc between two successive nodes represents a single pouring, and hence can be assumed to have a unit length. The problem thus reduces to determining the shortest route between the source node $(8, 0, 0)$ and the sink node $(4, 4, 0)$.

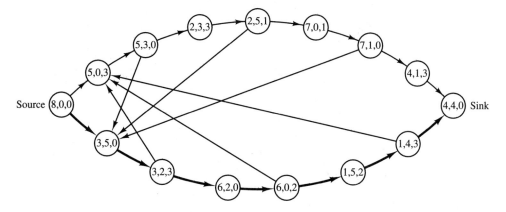

**Figure 6–11**

The optimal solution, given by the bottom path in Figure 6–11, requires 7 pourings.

## Problem set 6.4a

**1.** Reconstruct the equipment replacement model of Example 6.4–1, assuming that a car must be kept in service at least 2 years, with a maximum service life of 4 years. The planning horizon is from 1996 to 2002.

| | Replacement cost ($) for given years in operation | | |
| --- | --- | --- | --- |
| Year acquired | 2 | 3 | 4 |
| 1996 | 3800 | 4100 | 6800 |
| 1997 | 4000 | 4800 | 7000 |
| 1998 | 4200 | 5100 | 7200 |
| 1999 | 4800 | 5700 | — |
| 2000 | 5300 | — | — |

**2.** Figure 6–12 provides the communication network between two stations, 1 and 7. The probability that a link in the network will operate without failure is shown on each arc. Messages are sent from stations 1 to station 7, and the objective is to determine the route that will maximize the probability of a successful transmission. Formulate the situation as a shortest-route model, and solve with TORA.

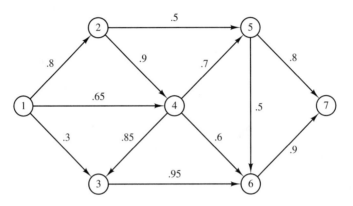

**Figure 6–12**

**3.** An old-fashioned electric toaster has two spring-loaded base-hinged doors. The two doors open outward in opposite directions away from the heating element. A slice of bread is toasted one side at a time by pushing open one of the doors with one hand and placing the slice with the other hand. After one side is toasted, the slice is turned over to get the other side toasted. It is desired to determine the sequence of operations (placing, toasting, turning, and removing) needed to toast three slices of bread in the shortest possible time. Formulate the problem as a shortest-route model using the following elemental times for the different operations:

| Operation | Time (seconds) |
|---|---|
| Place one slice in either side | 3 |
| Toast one side | 30 |
| Turn slice already in toaster | 1 |
| Remove slice from either side | 3 |

**4.** *Production planning.* DirectCo sells an item whose demand over the next 4 months is 100, 140, 210, and 180 units, respectively. The company can stock just enough supply to meet each month's demand, or it can overstock to meet the demand for two or more successive months. In the latter case, a holding cost of $1.20 is charged per overstocked unit per month. DirectCo estimates the unit purchase prices for the next 4 months to be $15, $12, $10, and $14, respectively. A setup cost of $200 is incurred each time a purchase order is placed. The company wants to develop a purchasing plan that will minimize the total costs of ordering, purchasing, and holding the item in stock. Formulate the problem as a shortest-route model, and use TORA to find the optimum solution.

**5.** *Knapsack Problem.* A hiker has a 5-ft³ backpack and needs to decide on the most valuable items to take on the hiking trip. There are three items from which to choose. Their volumes are 2, 3, and 4 ft³, and the hiker estimates their associated values on a scale from 0 to 100 as 30, 50, and 70, respectively. Express the problem as longest route network, and find the optimal solution. (*Hint:* A node in the network may be defined as [*i*, *v*], where *i* is the item number, and *v* is the volume remaining immediately before *i* is chosen.)

### 6.4.2 Shortest-Route Algorithms

This section presents two algorithms for solving both cyclic (i.e., containing loops) and acyclic networks.

**1.** Dijkstra's algorithm
**2.** Floyd's algorithm

Dijkstra's algorithm is designed to determine the shortest routes between the source node and every other node in the network. Floyd's algorithm is more general because it allows the determination of the shortest route between *any* two nodes in the network.

**Dijkstra's algorithm.**   The computations of the algorithm advance from a node $i$ to an immediately succeeding node $j$ using a special labeling procedure. Let $u_i$ be the shortest distance from source node 1 to node $i$, and define $d_{ij}$ ($\geq 0$) as the length of arc $(i, j)$. Then the label for node $j$ is defined as

$$[u_j, i] = [u_i + d_{ij}, i], d_{ij} \geq 0$$

Node labels in Dijkstra's algorithm are of two types: *temporary* and *permanent.* A temporary label can be replaced with another label if a shorter route to the same node can be found. At the point when it becomes evident that no better route can be found, the status of the temporary label is changed to permanent.

The steps of the algorithm are summarized as follows.

**Step 0.**   Label the source node (node 1) with the permanent label [0, —]. Set $i = 1$.

**Step *i.***

    **(a)** Compute the *temporary* labels $[u_i + d_{ij}, i]$ for each node $j$ that can be reached from node $i$, *provided $j$ is not permanently labeled*. If node $j$ is already labeled with $[u_j, k]$ through another node $k$ and if $u_i + d_{ij} < u_j$, replace $[u_j, k]$ with $[u_i + d_{ij}, i]$.

    **(b)** If *all* the nodes have permanent labels, stop. Otherwise, select the label $[u_r, s]$ with the shortest distance ($=u_r$) from among all the *temporary* labels (break ties arbitrarily). Set $i = r$ and repeat step *i*.

---

**Example 6.4–4.**

The network in Figure 6–13 gives the permissible routes and their lengths in miles between city 1 (node 1) and four other cities (nodes 2 to 5). We want to determine the shortest routes from city 1 to each of the remaining four cities.

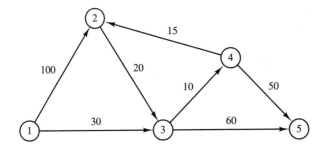

**Figure 6–13**

**Iteration 0.** Assign the *permanent* label $[0, —]$ to node 1.

**Iteration 1.** Nodes 2 and 3 can be reached from (the last permanently labeled) node 1. Thus, the list of labeled nodes (temporary and permanent) becomes

| Node | Label | Status |
|:---:|:---|:---:|
| **1** | **$[0, —]$** | **Permanent** |
| 2 | $[0 + 100, 1] = [100, 1]$ | Temporary |
| 3 | $[0 + 30, 1] = [30, 1]$ | ← Temporary |

For the two temporary labels $[100, 1]$ and $[30, 1]$, node 3 yields the smaller distance ($u_3 = 30$). Thus, the status of node 3 is changed to permanent.

**Iteration 2.** Nodes 4 and 5 can be reached from node 3, and the list of labeled nodes becomes

| Node | Label | Status |
|------|-------|--------|
| **1** | **[0, —]** | **Permanent** |
| 2 | [100, 1] | Temporary |
| **3** | **[30, 1]** | **Permanent** |
| 4 | [30 + 10, 3] = [40, 3] | ← Temporary |
| 5 | [30 + 60, 3] = [90, 3] | Temporary |

The status of the temporary label [40, 3] at mode 4 is changed to permanent ($u_4 = 40$).

**Iteration 3.**  Nodes 2 and 5 can be reached from node 4. Thus, the list of labeled nodes is updated as

| Node | Label | Status |
|------|-------|--------|
| **1** | **[0, —]** | **Permanent** |
| 2 | [40 + 15, 4] = [55, 4] | ← Temporary |
| **3** | **[30, 1]** | **Permanent** |
| **4** | **[40, 3]** | **Permanent** |
| 5 | [90, 3] or | |
| | [40 + 50, 4] = [90, 4] | Temporary |

Node 2's temporary label [100, 1] in iteration 2 is changed to [55, 4] in iteration 3 to indicate that a shorter route has been found through node 4. Also, in iteration 3, node 5 has two alternative labels with the same distance $u_5 = 90$.

The list for iteration 3 shows that node 2 must be permanently labeled.

**Iteration 4.**  Only node 3 can be reached from node 2. However, because node 3 is permanently labeled, it cannot be relabeled. The new list of labels thus remains the same as in iteration 3 except that the label at node 2 is permanent. This leaves node 5 as the only temporary label. Because node 5 does not lead to other nodes, its status is converted to permanent, and the process ends.

The computations of the algorithm can be carried out more easily on the network as Figure 6–14 demonstrates.

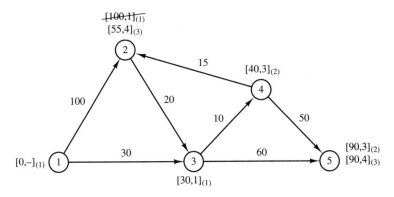

**Figure 6–14**

The shortest route between nodes 1 and any other node in the network is determined by starting at the desired destination node and backtracking through the nodes using the information given by the permanent labels. For example, the following sequence determines the shortest route from node 1 to node 2:

$$(2) \rightarrow [55, 4] \rightarrow (4) \rightarrow [40, 3] \rightarrow (3) \rightarrow [30, 1] \rightarrow (1)$$

Thus, the desired route is $1 \rightarrow 3 \rightarrow 4 \rightarrow 2$ with a total length of 55 miles.

---

## Problem set 6.4b

**1.** The network in Figure 6–15 gives the distances in miles between pairs of cities 1, 2, . . . , and 8. Find the shortest route between the following cities:
   **(a)** Cities 1 and 8
   **(b)** Cities 1 and 6
   **(c)** Cities 4 and 8
   **(d)** Cities 2 and 6

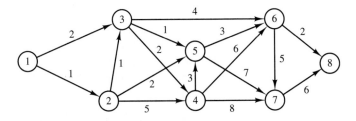

**Figure 6–15**

**2.** Determine the shortest route between node 1 and every other node in the network of Figure 6–16.

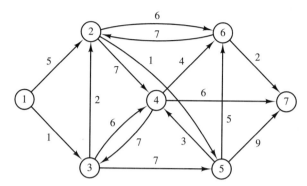

**Figure 6–16**

**3.** Determine the optimal solution of Problem 6.4a–1.
**4.** Determine the optimal solution of Problem 6.4a–2.
**5.** Determine the optimal solution of Problem 6.4a–4.

**Floyd's algorithm.**    Floyd's algorithm is more general than Dijkstra's because it determines the shortest route between *any* two nodes in the network. The algorithm represents an *n*-node network as a square matrix with *n* rows and *n* columns. Entry $(i, j)$ of the matrix gives the distance $d_{ij}$ from node $i$ to node $j$, which is finite if $i$ is linked directly to $j$, and infinite otherwise.

The idea of Floyd's algorithm is straightforward. Given three nodes $i$, $j$, and $k$ in Figure 6–17 with the connecting distances shown on the three arcs, it is shorter to reach $k$ from $i$ passing through $j$ if

$$d_{ij} + d_{jk} < d_{ik}$$

In this case, it is optimal to replace the direct route from $i \rightarrow k$ with the indirect route $i \rightarrow j \rightarrow k$. This **triple operation** exchange is applied systematically to the network using the following steps:

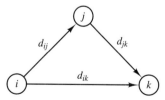

**Figure 6–17**

**Step 0.**  Define the starting distance matrix $D_0$ and node sequence matrix $S_0$ as given subsequently. The diagonal elements are marked with (—) to indicates that they are blocked. Set $k = 1$.

|         | 1 | 2 | ... | j | ... | n |
|---------|---|---|-----|---|-----|---|
| 1 | — | $d_{12}$ | ... | $d_{1j}$ | ... | $d_{1n}$ |
| 2 | $d_{21}$ | — | ... | $d_{2j}$ | ... | $d_{2n}$ |
| . | . | . | . | . | . | . |
| $D_0 = i$ | $d_{i1}$ | $d_{i2}$ | ... | $d_{ij}$ | ... | $d_{in}$ |
| . | . | . | . | . | . | . |
| n | $d_{n1}$ | $d_{n2}$ | ... | $d_{nj}$ | ... | — |

|         | 1 | 2 | ... | j | ... | n |
|---------|---|---|-----|---|-----|---|
| 1 | — | 2 | ... | j |  | n |
| 2 | 1 | — | ... | j |  | n |
| . | . | . | . | . | . | . |
| $S_0 = i$ | 1 | 2 |  | j |  | n |
| . | . | . | . | . | . | . |
| n | 1 | 2 |  | j |  | — |

**General step $k$.** Define row $k$ and column $k$ as *pivot row* and *pivot column*. Apply the *triple operation* to each element $d_{ij}$ in $D_{k-1}$, for all $i$ and $j$. If the condition

$$d_{ik} + d_{kj} < d_{ij}, (i \neq k, j \neq k, \text{and } i \neq j)$$

is satisfied, make the following changes:

**(a)** Create $D_k$ by replacing $d_{ij}$ in $D_{k-1}$ with $d_{ik} + d_{kj}$.

**(b)** Create $S_k$ by replacing $s_{ij}$ in $S_{k-1}$ with $k$. Set $k = k + 1$, and repeat step $k$.

Step $k$ of the algorithm can be explained more readily by representing $D_{k-1}$ as shown in Figure 6–18. Here, row $k$ and column $k$ define the current pivot row and column. Row $i$ represents any of the rows $1, 2, \ldots$, and $k - 1$, and row $p$ represents any of the rows $k + 1, k + 2, \ldots$, and $n$. Similarly, column $j$ represents any of the columns $1, 2, \ldots$, and $k - 1$, and column $q$ represents any of the columns $k + 1, k + 2, \ldots$, and $n$. The *triple operation* can be applied as follows. If the sum of the elements on the pivot row and the pivot column (shown by squares) is smaller than the associated intersection element (shown by a circle), then it is optimal to replace the intersection distance by the sum of the pivot distances.

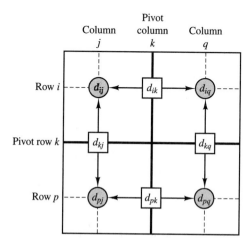

Figure 6–18

After $n$ steps, we can determine the shortest route between nodes $i$ and $j$ from the matrices $D_n$ and $S_n$ using the following rules:

**1.** From $D_n$, $d_{ij}$ gives the shortest distance between nodes $i$ and $j$.

**2.** From $S_n$, determine the intermediate node $k = s_{ij}$, which yields the route $i \rightarrow k \rightarrow j$. If $s_{ik} = k$ and $s_{kj} = j$, stop; all the intermediate nodes of the route have been found. Otherwise, repeat the procedure between nodes $i$ and $k$, and nodes $k$ and $j$.

---

**Example 6.4–5.**

For the network in Figure 6–19, find the shortest routes between every two nodes. The distances (in miles) are given on the arcs. Arc $(3, 5)$ is directional so that no traffic is allowed from node 5 to node 3. All the other arcs allow traffic in both directions.

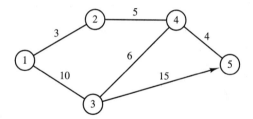

Figure 6–19

**Iteration 0.** The matrices $D_0$ and $S_0$ give the initial representation of the network. $D_0$ is symmetric except that $d_{53} = \infty$ because no traffic is allowed from node 5 to node 3.

$$D_0$$

|   | 1 | 2 | 3 | 4 | 5 |
|---|---|---|---|---|---|
| 1 | — | 3 | 10 | ∞ | ∞ |
| 2 | 3 | — | ∞ | 5 | ∞ |
| 3 | 10 | ∞ | — | 6 | 15 |
| 4 | ∞ | 5 | 6 | — | 4 |
| 5 | ∞ | ∞ | ∞ | 4 | — |

$$S_0$$

|   | 1 | 2 | 3 | 4 | 5 |
|---|---|---|---|---|---|
| 1 | — | 2 | 3 | 4 | 5 |
| 2 | 1 | — | 3 | 4 | 5 |
| 3 | 1 | 2 | — | 4 | 5 |
| 4 | 1 | 2 | 3 | — | 5 |
| 5 | 1 | 2 | 3 | 4 | — |

**Iteration 1.** The pivot row and the pivot column are given by the (shaded) first row and first column ($k = 1$), as shown in the $D_0$-matrix. The double-boxed elements, $d_{23}$ and $d_{32}$, are the only ones that can be improved by the *triple operation*. Thus, to obtain $D_1$ and $S_1$ from $D_0$ and $S_0$,

**1.** Replace $d_{23}$ with $d_{21} + d_{13} = 3 + 10 = 13$ and set $s_{23} = 1$.
**2.** Replace $d_{32}$ with $d_{31} + d_{12} = 10 + 3 = 13$ and set $s_{32} = 1$.

These changes are shown in boldface in matrices $D_1$ and $S_1$.

$$D_1$$

|   | 1 | 2 | 3 | 4 | 5 |
|---|---|---|---|---|---|
| 1 | — | 3 | 10 | ∞ | ∞ |
| 2 | 3 | — | **13** | 5 | ∞ |
| 3 | 10 | **13** | — | 6 | 15 |
| 4 | ∞ | 5 | 6 | — | 4 |
| 5 | ∞ | ∞ | ∞ | 4 | — |

$$S_1$$

|   | 1 | 2 | 3 | 4 | 5 |
|---|---|---|---|---|---|
| 1 | — | 2 | 3 | 4 | 5 |
| 2 | 1 | — | **1** | 4 | 5 |
| 3 | 1 | **1** | — | 4 | 5 |
| 4 | 1 | 2 | 3 | — | 5 |
| 5 | 1 | 2 | 3 | 4 | — |

**Iteration 2.** Set $k = 2$, as shown by the shaded row and column in $D_1$. The *triple operation* is applied to the double-boxed elements in $D_1$ and $S_1$. The changes are shown in boldface in $D_2$ and $S_2$.

$D_2$

|   | 1 | 2 | 3 | 4 | 5 |
|---|---|---|---|---|---|
| 1 | — | 3 | 10 | 8 | ∞ |
| 2 | 3 | — | 13 | 5 | ∞ |
| 3 | 10 | 13 | — | 6 | 15 |
| 4 | 8 | 5 | 6 | — | 4 |
| 5 | ∞ | ∞ | ∞ | 4 | — |

$S_2$

|   | 1 | 2 | 3 | 4 | 5 |
|---|---|---|---|---|---|
| 1 | — | 2 | 3 | 2 | 5 |
| 2 | 1 | — | 1 | 4 | 5 |
| 3 | 1 | 1 | — | 4 | 5 |
| 4 | 2 | 2 | 3 | — | 5 |
| 5 | 1 | 2 | 3 | 4 | — |

**Iteration 3.** Set $k = 3$, as shown by the shaded row and column in $D_2$. The new matrices are given by $D_3$ and $S_3$.

$D_3$

|   | 1 | 2 | 3 | 4 | 5 |
|---|---|---|---|---|---|
| 1 | — | 3 | 10 | 8 | 25 |
| 2 | 3 | — | 13 | 5 | 28 |
| 3 | 10 | 13 | — | 6 | 15 |
| 4 | 8 | 5 | 6 | — | 4 |
| 5 | ∞ | ∞ | ∞ | 4 | — |

$S_3$

|   | 1 | 2 | 3 | 4 | 5 |
|---|---|---|---|---|---|
| 1 | — | 2 | 3 | 2 | 3 |
| 2 | 1 | — | 1 | 4 | 3 |
| 3 | 1 | 1 | — | 4 | 5 |
| 4 | 2 | 2 | 3 | — | 5 |
| 5 | 1 | 2 | 3 | 4 | — |

**Iteration 4.** Set k = 4, as shown by the shaded row and column in $D_3$. The new matrices are given by $D_4$ and $S_4$.

$D_4$

|   | 1 | 2 | 3 | 4 | 5 |
|---|---|---|---|---|---|
| 1 | — | 3 | 10 | 8 | 12 |
| 2 | 3 | — | 11 | 5 | 9 |
| 3 | 10 | 11 | — | 6 | 10 |
| 4 | 8 | 5 | 6 | — | 4 |
| 5 | 12 | 9 | 10 | 4 | — |

$S_4$

|   | 1 | 2 | 3 | 4 | 5 |
|---|---|---|---|---|---|
| 1 | — | 2 | 3 | 2 | 4 |
| 2 | 1 | — | 4 | 4 | 4 |
| 3 | 1 | 4 | — | 4 | 4 |
| 4 | 2 | 2 | 3 | — | 5 |
| 5 | 4 | 4 | 4 | 4 | — |

**Iteration 5.** Set $k = 5$, as shown by the shaded row and column in $D_4$. No further improvements are possible in this iteration.

The final matrices $D_4$ and $S_4$ contain all the information needed to determine the shortest route between any two nodes in the network. For example, the shortest distance from node 1 to node 5 is $d_{15} = 12$.

To determine the associated route, recall that a segment $(i, j)$ represents a direct link only if $s_{ij} = j$. Otherwise, $i$ and $j$ are linked through at least one other intermediate node. Because $s_{15} = 4$ and $s_{45} = 5$, the route is initially given as $1 \rightarrow 4 \rightarrow 5$. Now, since $s_{14} \neq 4$, the segment $(1, 4)$ is not a *direct* link, and we need to determine its intermediate node(s). Given $s_{14} = 2$ and $s_{24} = 4$, the route $1 \rightarrow 4$ is replaced with $1 \rightarrow 2 \rightarrow 4$. Because $s_{12} = 2$ and $s_{24} = 4$, no further intermediate nodes exist.

The combined result now gives the optimal route as $1 \rightarrow 2 \rightarrow 4 \rightarrow 5$. The associated length of the route is 12 miles.

## Problem Set 6.4c

1. In Example 6.4–5, determine the shortest routes between each of the following pairs of nodes:
   **(a)** From node 5 to node 1.
   **(b)** From node 3 to node 5.
   **(c)** From node 5 to node 3.
   **(d)** From node 5 to node 2.

2. Apply Floyd's algorithm to the network in Figure 6–20. Arcs $(7, 6)$ and $(6, 4)$ are unidirectional, and all the distances are in miles. Determine the shortest route between the following pairs of nodes:
   **(a)** From node 1 to node 7.
   **(b)** From node 7 to node 1.
   **(c)** From node 6 to node 7.

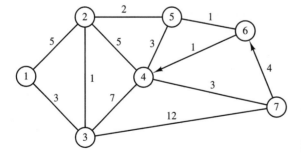

**Figure 6–20**

3. The Tell-All mobile-phone company services six geographical areas. The satellite distances (in miles) among the six areas are given in Figure 6–21. Tell-All needs to determine the most efficient message routes that should be established between each two areas in the network.

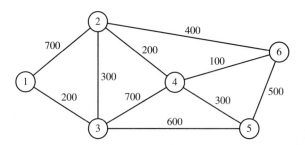

**Figure 6–21**

## 6.5 MAXIMAL FLOW MODEL

Consider a network of pipelines that transports crude oil from oil wells to refineries. Intermediate booster and pumping stations are installed at appropriate design distances to move the crude in the network. Each pipe segment has a finite maximum rate of crude flow (or capacity). A pipe segment may be unidirectional or bidirectional, depending on its design. A unidirectional segment has a finite capacity in one direction and a zero capacity in the opposite direction. Figure 6–22 demonstrates a typical pipeline network. How can we determine the maximum capacity of the network between the wells and the refineries?

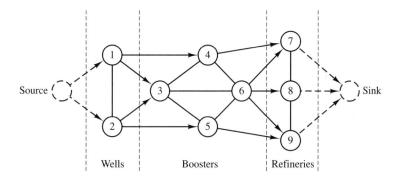

**Figure 6 – 22**

The solution of the proposed problem requires converting the network into one with a single source and a single sink. This requirement can be accomplished by using unidirectional infinite capacity arcs as shown in Figure 6–22.

Given arc $(i, j)$ with $i < j$, we use the notation $(\overline{C}_{ij}, \overline{C}_{ji})$ to represent the flow capacities in the two directions $i \rightarrow j$ and $j \rightarrow i$, respectively. To eliminate ambiguity, we place $\overline{C}_{ij}$ on the arc next to node $i$ with $\overline{C}_{ji}$ placed next to node $j$, as shown in Figure 6–23.

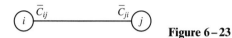

**Figure 6–23**

## 6.5.1  Enumeration of Cuts

A **cut** defines a set of arcs whose deletion from the network causes a complete disruption of flow between the source and sink nodes. The **cut capacity** equals the sum of the capacities of the associated arcs. Among *all* possible cuts in the network, the cut with the *smallest capacity* gives the maximum flow in the network.

---

**Example 6.5–1.**

Consider the network in Figure 6–24. The bidirectional capacities are shown on the respective arcs using the convention in Figure 6–23. For example, for arc (3, 4), the flow limit is 10 units from 3 to 4 and 5 units from 4 to 3.

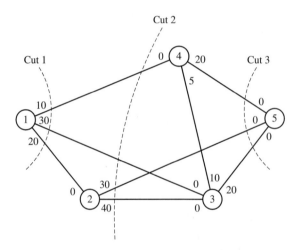

**Figure 6–24**

Figure 6–24 illustrates three cuts whose capacities are computed in the following table.

| Cut | Associated arcs | Capacity |
|-----|-----------------|----------|
| 1 | (1, 2), (1, 3), (1, 4) | 10 + 30 + 20 = 60 |
| 2 | (1, 3), (1, 4), (2, 3), (2, 5) | 30 + 10 + 40 + 30 = 110 |
| 3 | (2, 5), (3, 5), (4, 5) | 30 + 20 + 20 = 70 |

All we can get from the three cuts is that the maximum flow in the network does not exceed 60 units. We cannot tell what the maximal flow is until *all* the cuts in the network are enumerated. Unfortunately, the enumeration of all the cuts is not a simple task. Hence, the enumeration procedure cannot be used to determine the maximal flow in the network.

### Problem set 6.5a

1. For the network in Figure 6–24, determine two additional cuts, and find their capacities.

### 6.5.2 Maximal Flow Algorithm

The idea of the maximal flow algorithm is to find a **breakthrough path** with net *positive* flow that links the source and sink nodes. We will use this idea to develop the maximal flow algorithm.

Consider arc $(i, j)$ with (initial) capacities $(\overline{C}_{ij}, \overline{C}_{ji})$. As the computations of the algorithm progress, portions of these capacities will be committed to the flow in the arc. The **residuals** (or remaining capacities) of the arc are then changed accordingly. We use the notation $(c_{ij}, c_{ji})$ to represent these residuals. The network with the updated residuals is referred to as the **residue network**.

For a node $j$ that receives flow from node $i$, we define a label $[a_j, i]$, where $a_j$ is the flow from node $i$ to node $j$. The steps of the algorithm are thus summarized as follows.

**Step 1.** For all arcs $(i, j)$, set the residual capacity equal to the initial capacity—that is $(c_{ij}, c_{ji}) = (\overline{C}_{ij}, \overline{C}_{ji})$. Let $a_1 = \infty$ and label source node 1 with $[\infty, -]$. Set $i = 1$, and go to step 2.

**Step 2.** Determine $S_i$ as the set unlabeled nodes $j$ that can be reached directly from node $i$ by arcs with *positive* residuals (that is, $c_{ij} > 0$ for all $j \in S_i$). If $S_i \neq \varnothing$, go to step 3. Otherwise, go to step 4.

**Step 3.** Determine $k \in S_i$ such that

$$c_{ik} = \max_{j \in S_i} \{c_{ij}\}$$

Set $a_k = c_{ik}$ and label node $k$ with $[a_k, i]$. If the sink node has been labeled (i.e., $k = n$), and a *breakthrough path* is found, go to step 5. Otherwise, set $i = k$, and go to step 2.

**Step 4 (backtracking).** If $i = 1$, no further breakthroughs are possible; go to step 6. Otherwise, let $r$ be the node that has been labeled *immediately* before the current node $i$ and remove $i$ from the set of nodes that are adjacent to $r$. Set $i = r$, and go to step 2.

**Step 5 (determination of residue network).** Let $N_p = \{1, k_1, k_2, \ldots, n\}$ define the nodes of the $p$th breakthrough path from source 1 to sink $n$. Then the maximum flow along the path is computed as

$$f_p = \min\{a_1, a_{k1}, a_{k2}, \ldots a_n\}$$

The residual capacity of each arc along the breakthrough path is *decreased* by $f_p$ in the direction of the flow and *increased* by $f_p$ in the reverse direction—that is, for nodes $i$ and $j$ on the path, the residual flow is changed from the current $(c_{ij}, c_{ji})$ to

(a) $(c_{ij} - f_p, c_{ji} + f_p)$ if the flow is from $i$ to $j$

**(b)** $(c_{ij} + f_p, c_{ji} - f_p)$ if the flow is from $j$ to $i$

Reinstate any nodes that were removed in step 4. Set $i = 1$, and return to step 2 to attempt a new breakthrough path.

**Step 6    (solution).**

**(a)** Given that $m$ breakthrough paths have been determined, compute the maximal flow in the network as

$$F = f_1 + f_2 + \ldots + f_m$$

**(b)** Given that the *initial* and *final* residuals of arc $(i, j)$ are given by $(\overline{C}_{ij}, \overline{C}_{ji})$ and $(c_{ij}, c_{ji})$, respectively, the optimal flow is computed as follows: Let $(\alpha, \beta) = (\overline{C}_{ij} - c_{ij}, \overline{C}_{ji} - c_{ji})$. If $\alpha > 0$, the optimal flow from $i$ to $j$ is $\alpha$. Otherwise, if $\beta > 0$, the optimal flow from $j$ to $i$ is $\beta$. (It is impossible to have both $\alpha$ and $\beta$ positive.)

The backtracking process of step 4 is invoked when the algorithm becomes inadvertently "dead-ended" at an intermediate node before a breakthrough is realized. The flow adjustment in step 5 can be explained via the simple flow network in Figure 6–25. Network (a) gives the first breakthrough path $N_1 = \{1, 2, 3, 4\}$ with its maximum flow $f_1 = 5$. Thus, the residuals of each of arcs $(1, 2), (2, 3)$, and $(3, 4)$ are changed from $(5, 0)$ to $(0, 5)$, per step 5. Network (b) now gives the second breakthrough path $N_2 = \{1, 2, 3, 4\}$ with $f_2 = 5$. After making the necessary flow adjustments, we get network (c), where no further breakthroughs are possible. What happened in the transition from (b) to (c) is nothing but a cancellation of a previously committed flow in the direction $2 \to 3$. The algorithm is able to "remember" that a flow from 2 to 3 has been committed previously only because we have increased the capacity in the reverse direction from 0 to 5 (per step 5).

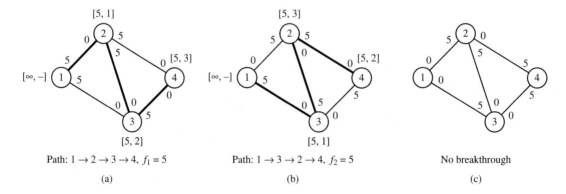

Path: $1 \to 2 \to 3 \to 4$, $f_1 = 5$   Path: $1 \to 3 \to 2 \to 4$, $f_2 = 5$   No breakthrough

          (a)                              (b)                          (c)

**Figure 6–25**

**Example 6.5–2.**

Determine the maximal flow in the network of Example 6.5–1 (Figure 6–24). Figure 6–26 provides a graphic summary of the algorithm. You will find it helpful to compare the description of the iterations with the graphic summary.

*Iteration 1.*

Set the initial residuals $(c_{ij}, c_{ji})$ equal to the initial capacities $(\overline{C}_{ij}, \overline{C}_{ji})$.

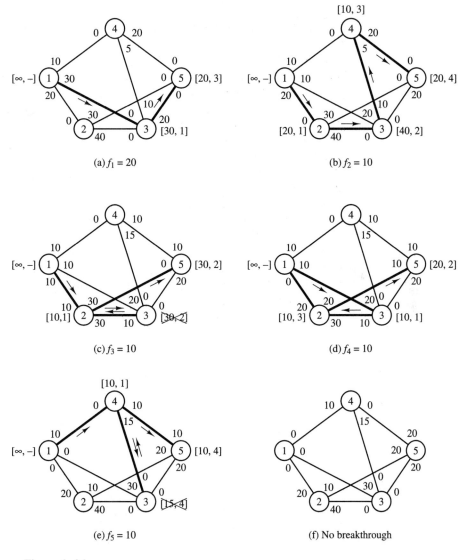

**Figure 6–26**

**Step 1.**  Set $a_1 = \infty$, and label node 1 with $[a_1, -]$. Set $i = 1$.

**Step 2.**  $S_1 = \{2, 3, 4\}(\neq \varnothing)$.

**Step 3.**  $k = 3$ because $c_{13} = \max\{c_{12}, \ c_{13}, \ c_{14}\} = \max\{20, \ 30, \ 10\} = 30$. Set $a_3 = c_{13} = 30$, and label node 3 with $[30, 1]$. Set $i = 3$, and repeat step 2.

**Step 2.**  $S_3 = \{4, 5\}$.

**Step 3.**  $k = 5$ and $a_5 = c_{35} = \max\{10, 20\} = 20$. Label node 5 with $[20, 3]$. Break-through is achieved. Go to step 5.

**Step 5.**  Breakthrough path is determined from the labels starting at node 5 and ending at node 1—that is, $(5) \to [20, 3] \to (3) \to [30, 1] \to (1)$. Thus, $N_1 = \{1, 3, 5\}$ and $f_1 = \min\{a_1, a_3, a_5\} = \{\infty, \ 30, \ 20\} = 20$. The residual capacities along path $N_1$ are

$$(c_{13}, \ c_{31}) = (30 - 20, \ 0 + 20) = (10, \ 20)$$

$$(c_{35}, \ c_{53}) = (20 - 20, \ 0 + 20) = (0, \ 20)$$

*Iteration 2.*

**Step 1.**  Set $a_1 = \infty$, and label node 1 with $[a_1, -]$. Set $i = 1$.

**Step 2.**  $S_1 = \{2, 3, 4\}$.

**Step 3.**  $k = 2$ and $a_2 = c_{12} = \max\{20, 10, 10\} = 20$. Set $i = 2$, and repeat step 2.

**Step 2.**  $S_2 = \{3, 5\}$.

**Step 3.**  $k = 3$ and $a_3 = c_{23} = 40$. Label node 3 with $[40, 2]$. Set $i = 3$, and repeat step 2.

**Step 2.**  $S_3 = \{4\}$ (note that $c_{35} = 0$—hence, node 5 cannot be included in $S_3$).

**Step 3.**  $k = 4$ and $a_4 = c_{34} = 10$. Label node 4 with $[10, 3]$. Set $i = 4$, and repeat step 2.

**Step 2.**  $S_4 = \{5\}$ (note that nodes 1 and 3 are already labeled—hence, they cannot be included in $S_4$).

**Step 3.**  $k = 5$ and $a_5 = c_{45} = 20$. Label node 5 with $[20, 4]$. Breakthrough has been achieved. Go to step 5.

**Step 5.**  $N_2 = \{1, 2, 3, 4, 5\}$ and $f_2 = \min\{\infty, 20, 40, 10, 20\} = 10$. The residuals along the path of $N_2$ are

$$(c_{12}, \ c_{21}) = (20 - 10, \ 0 + 10) = (10, \ 10)$$

$$(c_{23}, \ c_{32}) = (40 - 10, \ 0 + 10) = (30, \ 10)$$

$$(c_{34}, \ c_{43}) = (10 - 10, \ 5 + 10) = (0, \ 15)$$

$$(c_{45}, \ c_{54}) = (20 - 10, \ 0 + 10) = (10, \ 10)$$

*Iteration 3.*

**Step 1.**  Set $a_1 = \infty$ and label node 1 with $[a_1, -]$. Set $i = 1$.

**Step 2.**  $S_1 = \{2, 3, 4\}$.

**Step 3.**  $k = 2$ and $a_2 = c_{12} = \max\{10, 10, 10\} = 10$ (ties are broken arbitrarily). Label node 2 with $[10, 1]$. Set $i = 2$, and repeat step 2.

**Step 2.**  $S_2 = \{3, 5\}$.

**Step 3.**  $k = 3$ and $a_3 = c_{23} = 30$ (break ties arbitrarily). Label node 3 with $[30, 2]$. Set $i = 3$, and repeat step 2.

**Step 2.**  $S_3 = \varnothing$ (because $c_{34} = c_{35} = 0$). Go to step 4 to backtrack.

**Step 4.**  The label $[30, \mathbf{2}]$ at node 3 gives the immediately preceding node $r = 2$. Remove node 3 from further consideration *in this iteration* by crossing it out. Set $i = r = 2$, and repeat step 2.

**Step 2.** $S_2 = \{5\}$ (note that node 3 has been removed in the backtracking step).

**Step 3.** $k = 5$ and $a_5 = c_{25} = 30$. Label node 5 with $[30, 2]$. Breakthrough has been achieved; go to step 5.

**Step 5.** $N_3 = \{1, 2, 5\}$ and $f_3 = \min \{\infty, 10, 30\} = 10$. The residuals along the path of $N_3$ are

$$(c_{12}, c_{21}) = (10 - 10, \ 10 + 10) = (0, \ 20)$$

$$(c_{25}, c_{52}) = (30 - 10, \ 0 + 10) = (20, \ 10)$$

*Iteration 4.*

This iteration yields $N_4 = \{1, 3, 2, 5\}$ with $f_4 = 10$ (verify!).

*Iteration 5.*

This iteration yields $N_5 = \{1, 4, 5\}$ with $f_5 = 10$ (verify!).

*Iteration 6.*

No further breakthroughs are possible because all the arcs out of node 1 have zero residuals. We turn to step 6 to determine the solution.

**Step 6.** Maximal flow in the network is $F = f_1 + f_2 + \ldots + f_5 = 20 + 10 + 10 + 10 + 10 = 60$ units. The flow in the different arcs is computed by subtracting the last residuals in iterations 6 [i.e., $(c_{ij}, c_{ji})_6$] from the initial capacities $(\overline{C}_{ij}, \overline{C}_{ji})$ as the following table shows.

| Arc | $(\overline{C}_{ij}, \overline{C}_{ji}) - (c_{ij}, c_{ji})_6$ | Flow amount | Direction |
|---|---|---|---|
| $(1, 2)$ | $(20, 0) - (0, 20) = (20, -20)$ | 20 | $1 \rightarrow 2$ |
| $(1, 3)$ | $(30, 0) - (0, 30) = (30, -30)$ | 30 | $1 \rightarrow 3$ |
| $(1, 4)$ | $(10, 0) - (0, 10) = (10, -10)$ | 10 | $1 \rightarrow 4$ |
| $(2, 3)$ | $(40, 0) - (40, 0) = (0, 0)$ | 0 | — |
| $(2, 5)$ | $(30, 0) - (10, 20) = (20, -20)$ | 20 | $2 \rightarrow 5$ |
| $(3, 4)$ | $(10, 5) - (0, 15) = (10, -10)$ | 10 | $3 \rightarrow 4$ |
| $(3, 5)$ | $(20, 0) - (0, 20) = (20, -20)$ | 20 | $3 \rightarrow 5$ |
| $(4, 5)$ | $(20, 0) - (0, 20) = (20, -20)$ | 20 | $4 \rightarrow 5$ |

### Problem set 6.5b

1. In Example 6.5–2,
   **(a)** Determine the surplus capacities for all the arcs.
   **(b)** Determine the amount of flow through nodes 2, 3, and 4.
   **(c)** Can the network flow be increased by increasing the capacities in the directions $3 \rightarrow 5$ and $4 \rightarrow 5$?

2. Apply TORA to the network in Example 6.5–2, and verify the labels and flows for the iterations summarized in Figure 6–26.

**3.** Determine the maximal flow and the optimum flow in each arc for the network in Figure 6–27.

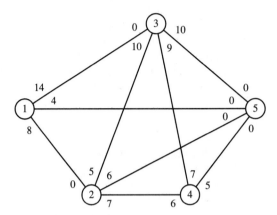

**Figure 6–27**

**4.** Three refineries send a gasoline product to two distribution terminals through a pipeline network. Any demand that cannot be satisfied through the network is acquired from other sources. The pipeline network is served by three pumping stations as shown in Figure 6–28. The product flows in the network in the direction shown by the arrows. The capacity of each pipe segment (shown directly on the arcs) are in million bbl per day. Determine the following:
   **(a)** The daily production at each refinery that matches the maximum capacity of the network.
   **(b)** The daily demand at each terminal that matches the maximum capacity of the network.
   **(c)** The daily capacity of each pump that matches the maximum capacity of the network.

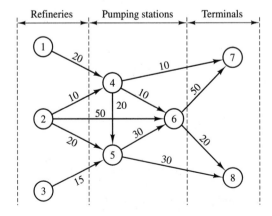

**Figure 6–28**

5. Suppose that the maximum daily capacity of pump 6 in the network of Figure 6–28 (Problem 4) is limited to 50 million bbl. Remodel the network to include this restriction. Then determine the maximum capacity of the network.

6. Chicken feed is transported by trucks from three silos to four chicken farms. Some of the silos cannot ship directly to some of the farms. The capacities of the other routes are limited by the number of trucks available and the number of trips made daily. The following table shows the daily amounts of supply at the silos and demand at the farms (in thousands of pounds). The cell entries of the table specify the daily capacities of the associated routes.

|  |  | Farm | | | |  |
| --- | --- | --- | --- | --- | --- | --- |
|  |  | 1 | 2 | 3 | 4 |  |
|  | 1 | 30 | 5 | 0 | 40 | **20** |
| Silo | 2 | 0 | 0 | 5 | 90 | **20** |
|  | 3 | 100 | 40 | 30 | 40 | **200** |
|  |  | **200** | **10** | **60** | **20** |  |

   **(a)** Determine the schedule that satisfies the most demand.
   **(b)** Will the proposed schedule satisfy all the demand at the farms?

7. In Problem 6, suppose that transshipping is allowed between silos 1 and 2 and silos 2 and 3. Suppose also that transshipping is allowed between farms 1 and 2, 2 and 3, and 3 and 4. The maximum two-way daily capacity on the proposed transshipping routes is 50 (thousand) lb. What is the effect of transshipping on the unsatisfied demands at the farms?

8. A parent has five (teenage) children and five household chores to assign to them. Past experience has taught the parent that forcing chores on a child is counterproductive. With this in mind, the children are asked to list their preferences among the five chores, as the following table shows:

| Child | Preferred chore |
| --- | --- |
| Rif | 3, 4, or 5 |
| Mai | 1 |
| Ben | 1 or 2 |
| Kim | 1, 2, or 5 |
| Ken | 2 |

The parent's modest goal now is to finish as many chores as possible while abiding by the children's preferences. Determine the maximum number of chores that can be completed and the assignment of chores to children.

9. Four factories are engaged in the production of four types of toys. The following table lists the toys that can be produced by each factory.

| Factory | Toys production mix |
|---------|---------------------|
| 1       | 1, 2, 3             |
| 2       | 2, 3                |
| 3       | 1, 4                |
| 4       | 3, 4                |

All toys require the same per unit labor and material. The daily capacities of the four factories are 250, 180, 300, and 100 toys, respectively. The daily demands for the four toys are 200, 150, 350, and 100 units, respectively. Determine the factories production schedules that will most satisfy the demands for the four toys.

10. The academic council at the U of A is seeking representation from among six students who are affiliated with four honor societies. The academic council representation includes three areas: mathematics, art, and engineering. At most two students in each area can be on the council. The following table shows the membership of the six students in the four honor societies:

| Society | Affiliated students |
|---------|---------------------|
| 1       | 1, 2, 3             |
| 2       | 1, 3, 5             |
| 3       | 3, 4, 5             |
| 4       | 1, 2, 4, 6          |

The students who are skilled in the areas of mathematics, art, and engineering are shown in the following table:

| Area        | Skilled students |
|-------------|------------------|
| Mathematics | 1, 2, 4          |
| Art         | 3, 4             |
| Engineering | 4, 5, 6          |

A student who is skilled in more than one area must be assigned exclusively to one area only. Can all four honor societies be represented on the council?

**11.** *Maximal/minimal flow in networks with lower bounds.* The maximal flow algorithm given in this section assumes that all the arcs have zero lower bounds. In some models, the lower bounds may be strictly positive, and we may be interested in finding the maximal or minimal flow in the network (see Comprehensive Problem 6–3). The presence of the lower bound poses difficulty because the network may not have a feasible flow at all. The objective of this exercise is to show that any maximal and minimal flow model with positive lower bounds can be solved using two steps.

**Step 1.** Find an initial feasible solution for the network with positive lower bounds.

**Step 2.** Using the feasible solution in step 1, find the maximal or minimal flow in the original network.

**(a)** Show that an arc $(i, j)$ with flow limited by $l_{ij} \leq x_{ij} \leq u_{ij}$ can be represented equivalently by a *sink* with demand $l_{ij}$ at node $i$ and a *source* with demand $l_{ij}$ at node $j$ with flow limited by $0 \leq x_{ij}' \leq u_{ij} - l_{ij}$.

**(b)** Show that finding a feasible solution for the original network is equivalent to finding the maximal flow $x_{ij}'$ in the network after (1) modifying the bounds on $x_{ij}$ to $0 \leq x_{ij}' \leq u_{ij} - l_{ij}$, (2) "lumping" all the resulting sources into one supersource with outgoing arc capacities $l_{ij}$, (3) "lumping" all the resulting sinks into one supersink with incoming arc capacities $l_{ij}$, and (4) connecting the terminal node $t$ to the source node $s$ in the original network by a return infinite capacity arc. A feasible solution exists if the maximal flow in the new network equals the sum of the lower bounds in the original network. Apply the procedure to the following network and find a feasible flow solution:

| Arc $(i, j)$ | $(l_{ij}, u_{ij})$ |
|:---:|:---:|
| $(1, 2)$ | $(5, 20)$ |
| $(1, 3)$ | $(0, 15)$ |
| $(2, 3)$ | $(4, 10)$ |
| $(2, 4)$ | $(3, 15)$ |
| $(3, 4)$ | $(0, 20)$ |

**(c)** Use the feasible solution for the network in (b) together with the maximal flow algorithm to determine the *minimal* flow in the original network. (*Hint:* First compute the residue network given the initial feasible solution. Next, determine the maximum flow *from the end* *node to the start node.* This is equivalent to finding the maximum flow that should be canceled from the start node to the end node. Now, combining the feasible and maximal flow solutions yields the minimal flow in the original network.)

**(d)** Use the feasible solution for the network in (b) together with the *maximal* flow model to determine the maximal flow in the original network. (*Hint:* As in part [c], start with the residue network. Next apply the breakthrough algorithm to the resulting residue network exactly as in the regular maximal flow model.)

## 6.6 MINIMUM-COST CAPACITATED FLOW PROBLEM

The minimum-cost capacitated flow problem generalizes the maximal flow model of Section 6.5 in four aspects.

1. All arcs are directional (one way).
2. A (nonnegative) unit flow cost is associated with each arc.
3. Arcs may have positive lower capacity limits.
4. Any node in the network may act as a source or as a sink.

The new model determines the flows in the different arcs that minimize the total cost while satisfying the flow restrictions on the arcs and the supply and demand amounts at the nodes. We first present the capacitated network flow model and its equivalent linear programming formulation. The linear programming formulation is then used as the basis for the development of a special capacitated simplex algorithm for solving the network flow model.

### 6.6.1 Network Representation

Consider a capacitated network $G = (N, A)$, where $N$ is the set of nodes, and $A$ is the set of arcs and define

$x_{ij}$ = amount of flow from node $i$ to node $j$

$u_{ij}$ ($l_{ij}$) = upper (lower) capacity of arc $(i, j)$

$c_{ij}$ = unit flow cost from node $i$ to node $j$

$f_i$ = net flow at node $i$

Figure 6–29 depicts these definitions on arc $(i, j)$. The label $[f_i]$ assumes a positive (negative) value when a net supply (demand) is associated with node $i$.

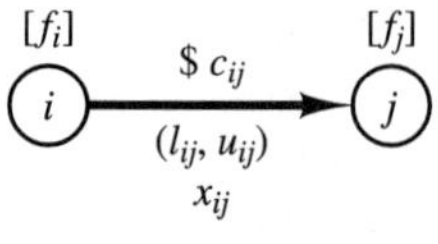

**Figure 6–29**

**Example 6.6–1.**

GrainCo supplies corn from three silos to three poultry farms. The supply amounts at the three silos are 100, 200, and 50 thousand bushels and the demand at the three farms are 150, 80, and 120 thousand bushels. GrainCo mostly uses railroads to transport the corn to the farms, with the exception of three routes where trucks are used.

Figure 6–30 summarizes the available route between the silos and the farms. The silos are represented by nodes 1, 2, and 3 whose supply amounts are [100], [200], and [50], respectively. The farms are represented by nodes 4, 5, and 6 whose demand amounts are [−150], [−80], and [−120], respectively. The routes allow transhipping between the silos. Arcs (1, 4), (3, 4), and (4, 6) are truck routes. These routes have minimum and maximum capacities. For example, the capacity of route (1, 4) is between 50 and 80 thousand bushels. All other routes use trainloads, whose maximum capacity is practically unlimited. The transportation costs per bushel are indicated on the respective arcs.

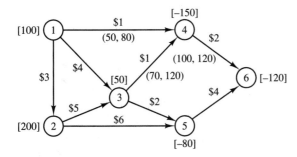

**Figure 6–30**

## Problem set 6.6a

1. A product is manufactured to satisfy demand over a 4-period planning horizon according to the following data:

| Period | Units of demand | Unit production cost ($) | Unit holding cost ($) |
|--------|-----------------|--------------------------|-----------------------|
| 1 | 100 | 24 | 1 |
| 2 | 110 | 26 | 2 |
| 3 | 95 | 21 | 1 |
| 4 | 125 | 24 | 2 |

Given that no back-ordering is allowed, represent the problem as a network model.

2. In Problem 1, suppose that back-ordering is allowed at a penalty of $1.50 per unit per period. Formulate the problem as a network model.

3. In Problem 1, suppose that the production capacities of periods 1 to 4 are 110, 95, 125, and 100 units, respectively, in which case the given demand cannot be satisfied without back-ordering. Assuming that the penalty cost for back-ordering is $1.5 per unit per period, formulate the problem as a network model.

4. Daw Chemical owns two plants that manufacture a basic chemical compound for two customers at the rate of 660 and 800 tons per month. The monthly production capacity of plant 1 is between 400 and 800 tons and that of plant 2 is between 450 and 900 tons. The production cost per ton in plants 1 and 2 are $25 and $28, respectively. Raw material for the plants is provided by two suppliers, who are contracted to ship at least 500 and 750 tons per month for plants 1 and 2 at the costs of $200 and $210 per ton, respectively. Daw Chemical also assumes the transportation cost of both the raw material and the final compound. The costs per ton of transporting the raw material from supplier 1 to plants 1 and 2 are $10 and $12. Similar costs from supplier 2 are $9 and $13, respectively. The transportation cost per ton from plant 1 to clients 1 and 2 are $3 and $4, and from plant 2 are $5 and $2, respectively. Assuming that 1 ton of raw material produces 1 ton of the final compound, formulate the problem as a network model.

5. Two nonintegrated public schools are required to change the racial balance of their enrollments by accepting minority students. Minority enrollment must be between 30% and 40% in both schools. Nonminority students live in two communities, and minority students live in three other communities. Traveled distances, in miles, from the five communities to the two schools are summarized in the following table:

| | | Roundtrip miles from school to | | | | |
| | | Minority areas | | | Nonminority areas | |
| School | Maximum enrollment | 1 | 2 | 3 | 1 | 2 |
|---|---|---|---|---|---|---|
| 1 | 1500 | 20 | 12 | 10 | 4 | 5 |
| 2 | 2000 | 15 | 18 | 8 | 6 | 5 |
| Student population | | 500 | 450 | 300 | 1000 | 1000 |

Formulate the problem as a network model to determine the number of minority and nonminority students enrolled in each school.

## 6.6.2 Linear Programming Formulation

The formulation of the capacitated network model as a linear program provides the foundation for the development of the capacitated simplex algorithm, which we will present in the next section. Using the notation introduced in Section 6.6.1, the linear program for the capacitated network is given as

$$\text{Minimize } z = \sum_{(i,j) \in A} \sum c_{ij} x_{ij}$$

subject to

$$\sum_{\substack{k \\ (j,k) \in A}} x_{jk} - \sum_{\substack{i \\ (i,j) \in A}} x_{ij} = f_j, \ j \in N$$

$$l_{ij} \leq x_{ij} \leq u_{ij}$$

The equation for node $j$ measures the net flow $f_j$ in node $j$ as

(Outgoing flow from node $j$) $-$ (Incoming flow into node $j$) $= f_j$

Node $j$ acts as a source if $f_j > 0$ and as a sink if $f_j < 0$.

We can always remove the lower bound $l_{ij}$ from the constraints by using the substitution

$$x_{ij} = x_{ij}' + l_{ij}$$

The new flow variable, $x_{ij}'$, has an upper limit of $u_{ij} - l_{ij}$. Additionally, the net flow at node $i$ becomes $[f_i] - l_{ij}$, and that at node $j$ is $[f_j] + l_{ij}$. Figure 6–31 shows the transformation of activity $(i, j)$ after the lower bound is substituted out.

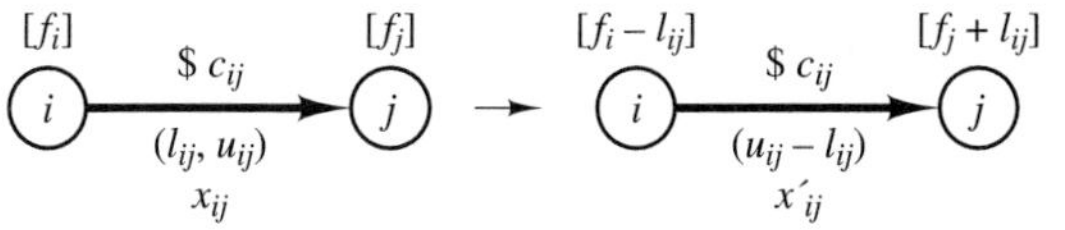

**Figure 6–31**

---

**Example 6.6–2.**

Write the linear program for the network in Figure 6–30, before and after the lower bounds are substituted out.

The main constraints of the linear program relate the input-output flow at each node, which yields the following LP:

|           | $x_{12}$ | $x_{13}$ | $x_{14}$ | $x_{23}$ | $x_{25}$ | $x_{34}$ | $x_{35}$ | $x_{46}$ | $x_{56}$ |         |
|-----------|------|------|------|------|------|------|------|------|------|---------|
| Minimize  | 3    | 4    | 1    | 5    | 6    | 1    | 2    | 2    | 4    |         |
| Node 1    | 1    | 1    | 1    |      |      |      |      |      |      | = 100   |
| Node 2    | −1   |      |      | 1    | 1    |      |      |      |      | = 200   |
|           |      |      |      |      |      |      |      |      |      | *Continued* |

| | $x_{12}$ | $x_{13}$ | $x_{14}$ | $x_{23}$ | $x_{25}$ | $x_{34}$ | $x_{35}$ | $x_{46}$ | $x_{56}$ | | |
|---|---|---|---|---|---|---|---|---|---|---|---|
| Node 3 | | $-1$ | | $-1$ | | $1$ | $1$ | | | $=$ | $50$ |
| Node 4 | | | $-1$ | | | $-1$ | | $1$ | | $=$ | $-150$ |
| Node 5 | | | | | $-1$ | | $-1$ | | $1$ | $=$ | $-80$ |
| Node 6 | | | | | | | | $-1$ | $-1$ | $=$ | $-120$ |
| Lower bounds | $0$ | $0$ | $50$ | $0$ | $0$ | $70$ | $0$ | $100$ | $0$ | | |
| Upper bounds | $\infty$ | $\infty$ | $80$ | $\infty$ | $\infty$ | $120$ | $\infty$ | $120$ | $\infty$ | | |

Note the arrangement of the constraints coefficients, where, the column associated with variable $x_{ij}$ has exactly one $+1$ in row $i$ and one $-1$ in row $j$. The rest of the coefficients are all 0. This structure is typical of network flow models.

The variables with lower bounds are substituted as

$$x_{14} = x_{14}' + 50$$
$$x_{34} = x_{34}' + 70$$
$$x_{46} = x_{46}' + 100$$

The resulting linear program is

| | $x_{12}$ | $x_{13}$ | $x_{14}'$ | $x_{23}$ | $x_{25}$ | $x_{34}'$ | $x_{35}$ | $x_{46}'$ | $x_{56}$ | | |
|---|---|---|---|---|---|---|---|---|---|---|---|
| Minimize | $3$ | $4$ | $1$ | $5$ | $6$ | $1$ | $2$ | $2$ | $4$ | | |
| Node 1 | $1$ | $1$ | $1$ | | | | | | | $=$ | $50$ |
| Node 2 | $-1$ | | | $1$ | $1$ | | | | | $=$ | $200$ |
| Node 3 | | $-1$ | | $-1$ | | $1$ | $1$ | | | $=$ | $-20$ |
| Node 4 | | | $-1$ | | | $-1$ | | $1$ | | $=$ | $-130$ |
| Node 5 | | | | | $-1$ | | $-1$ | | $1$ | $=$ | $-80$ |
| Node 6 | | | | | | | | $-1$ | $-1$ | $=$ | $-20$ |
| Upper bounds | $\infty$ | $\infty$ | $30$ | $\infty$ | $\infty$ | $50$ | $\infty$ | $20$ | $\infty$ | | |

The corresponding network after substituting out the lower bounds is shown in Figure 6–32. Note that the lower-bound substitution can be effected directly from Figure 6–30 using the substitution in Figure 6–31, and without the need to express the problem as a linear program first.

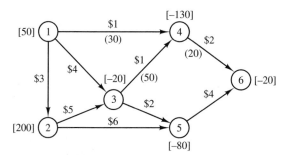

**Figure 6–32**

The next example provides an illustration of a network model that initially does not satisfy the "node flow" requirement (i.e., node output flow less node input flow equals node net flow), but that can be converted to this form readily through special manipulation of the constraints of the linear program.

---

**Example 6.6–3 (EMPLOYMENT SCHEDULING).**

The Tempo Employment Agency has a contract to provide workers over the next 4 months (January to April) according to the following schedule:

| Month | Jan. | Feb. | March | April |
|---|---|---|---|---|
| No. of workers | 100 | 120 | 80 | 170 |

Because of the erratic demand, it may be economical to retain more workers than needed in a given month. The cost of recruiting and maintaining the workers is a function of their employment period as the following table shows:

| Employment period (months) | 1 | 2 | 3 | 4 |
|---|---|---|---|---|
| Cost per worker ($) | 100 | 130 | 180 | 220 |

Let

$x_{ij}$ = number of workers hired at the *start* of month $i$ and terminated at the *start* of month $j$

For example, $x_{12}$ gives the number of workers hired in January for 1 month only.

To formulate the problem as a linear program for the 4-month period, we add the month of May (month 5), so that $x_{45}$ defines hiring in April for April. Naturally, May has no demand.

The constraints recognize that the demand for period $k$ can be satisfied by all $x_{ij}$ such that $i \leq k < j$. Letting $S_i \geq 0$ be the surplus number of workers in month $i$, the linear program is given as

|  | $x_{12}$ | $x_{13}$ | $x_{14}$ | $x_{15}$ | $x_{23}$ | $x_{24}$ | $x_{25}$ | $x_{34}$ | $x_{35}$ | $x_{45}$ | $s_1$ | $s_2$ | $s_3$ | $s_4$ |  |
|---|---|---|---|---|---|---|---|---|---|---|---|---|---|---|---|
|  | 100 | 130 | 180 | 220 | 100 | 130 | 180 | 100 | 130 | 100 |  |  |  |  | Minimize |
| Jan. | 1 | 1 | 1 | 1 |  |  |  |  |  |  | −1 |  |  |  | 100 |
| Feb. |  | 1 | 1 | 1 | 1 | 1 | 1 |  |  |  |  | −1 |  |  | 120 |
| March |  |  | 1 | 1 |  | 1 | 1 | 1 | 1 |  |  |  | −1 |  | 80 |
| April |  |  |  | 1 |  |  | 1 |  | 1 | 1 |  |  |  | −1 | 170 |

The preceding LP does not have the $(-1, +1)$ special structure of the network flow model (see Example 6.6–2). Nevertheless, the given linear program has special characteristics that allow converting it into an equivalent network flow model by using the following arithmetic manipulations:

1. In an n-equation linear program, create a new equation, $n + 1$, by multiplying equation $n$ by $-1$.
2. Leave equation 1 unchanged.
3. For $i = 2, 3, \ldots, n$, replace each equation $i$ with (equation $i$) − (equation $i - 1$).

The application of these manipulations to the employment scheduling example yields the following linear program whose structure fits the network flow model:

|  | $x_{12}$ | $x_{13}$ | $x_{14}$ | $x_{15}$ | $x_{23}$ | $x_{24}$ | $x_{25}$ | $x_{34}$ | $x_{35}$ | $x_{45}$ | $s_1$ | $s_2$ | $s_3$ | $s_4$ |  |
|---|---|---|---|---|---|---|---|---|---|---|---|---|---|---|---|
|  | 100 | 130 | 180 | 220 | 100 | 130 | 180 | 100 | 130 | 100 |  |  |  |  | Min |
| Jan. | 1 | 1 | 1 | 1 |  |  |  |  |  |  | −1 |  |  |  | 100 |
| Feb. | −1 |  |  |  | 1 | 1 | 1 |  |  |  | 1 | −1 |  |  | 20 |
| March |  | −1 |  |  | −1 |  |  | 1 | 1 |  |  | 1 | −1 |  | −40 |
| April |  |  | −1 |  |  | −1 |  | −1 |  | 1 |  |  | 1 | −1 | 90 |
| May |  |  |  | −1 |  |  | −1 |  | −1 | −1 |  |  |  | 1 | −170 |

Using the preceding formulation, the employment scheduling model can be represented equivalently by the minimum cost flow network shown in Figure 6–33. Actually, because the arcs have no upper bounds, the problem can be solved also as a transshipment model (see Section 5.5).

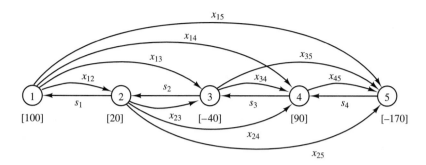

**Figure 6–33**

## Problem Set 6.6b

1. Write the linear program associated with the minimum cost flow network in Figure 6–34, before and after the lower bounds are substituted out.

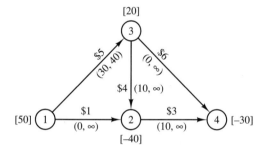

**Figure 6–34**

2. Use inspection to find a feasible solution to the minimum-cost network model of the employment scheduling problem in Example 6.6–3 (Figure 6–33). Interpret the solution by showing the pattern of hiring and firing that satisfies the demand for each month, and compute the associated total cost.

3. Reformulate the employment scheduling model of Example 6.6–3, assuming that a worker must be hired for at least 2 months. Write the linear program, and convert it to a minimum cost flow network.

4. Develop the linear program and the associated minimum-cost flow network for the employment scheduling model of Example 6.6–3 using the following 5-month demand data. The per worker costs of hiring and firing for periods of 1 to 5 months are $50, $70, $85, $100, and $130, respectively.

**(a)**

| Month | 1 | 2 | 3 | 4 | 5 |
|---|---|---|---|---|---|
| No. of workers | 200 | 220 | 300 | 50 | 240 |

**(b)**

| Month | 1 | 2 | 3 | 4 | 5 |
|---|---|---|---|---|---|
| No. of workers | 200 | 220 | 300 | 50 | 240 |

5. *Conversion of a capacitated network into an uncapacitated network.* Show that an arc $(i \rightarrow j)$ with capacitated flow $x_{ij} \leq u_{ij}$ can be replaced with two *uncapacitated* arcs $(i \rightarrow k)$ and $(j \rightarrow k)$ with a net (output) flow of $[-u_{ij}]$ at node $k$ and an additional (input) flow of $[+u_{ij}]$ at node $j$. The result is that the *capacitated* network can be converted to an *uncapacitated* transportation cost model (Section 5.1). Apply the resulting transformation to the network in Figure 6–35.

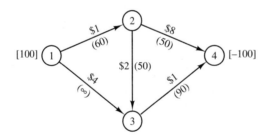

**Figure 6–35**

### 6.6.3  Capacitated Network Simplex Algorithm

The algorithm is based on the exact steps of the regular simplex method. However, it is designed to exploit the special network structure of the minimum-cost flow model.

Given $f_i$ is the net flow at node $i$ as defined in the linear program of Section 6.6.2, the capacitated simplex algorithm stipulates that the network must satisfy

$$\sum_{i=1}^{n} f_i = 0$$

The condition says that the total supply in the network equals the total demand. We can always satisfy this requirement by adding a balancing dummy source or destination, which we connect to all other nodes in the network by zero unit cost and infinite capacity arcs. However, the balancing of the network does not guarantee a feasible solution as this may be precluded by the restricting capacities of the arcs.

We will now present the steps of the capacitated algorithm. Familiarity with the simplex method and duality theory (Chapters 3 and 4) are essential. Also, knowledge of the upper-bounded simplex method (Section 7.5.2) should be helpful.

> **Step 0.** Determine a starting basic feasible solution (set of arcs) for the network. Go to step 1.
>
> **Step 1.** Determine an entering arc (variable) using the simplex method optimality condition. If the solution is optimal, stop; otherwise, go to step 2.
>
> **Step 2.** Determine the leaving arc (variable) using the simplex method feasibility condition. Change the basis, then go to step 1.

An $n$-node network with zero net flow (i.e., $f_1 + f_2 + \ldots + f_n = 0$) consists of $n - 1$ *independent* constraint equations. Thus, an associated basic solution must include $n - 1$ arcs. It can be proved that a basic solution always corresponds to a *spanning tree* of the network (see Section 6.3).

The entering arc (step 1) is determined by computing the objective coefficients $z_{ij} - c_{ij}$ for all the current nonbasic arcs $(i, j)$. If all $z_{ij} - c_{ij} \leq 0$, the current basis is optimum. Otherwise, we select the nonbasic arc with the most positive $z_{ij} - c_{ij}$ to enter the basis.

The computation of $z_{ij} - c_{ij}$ is based on duality, exactly as we did with the transportation model (see Section 5.3.3). Using the linear program defined in Section 6.6.2, let $w_i$ be the dual variable associated with the constraint of node $i$, then the dual problem (excluding the upper bounds) is given as

$$\text{Maximize } z = \sum_{i=1}^{n} f_i w_i$$

subject to

$$w_i - w_j \leq c_{ij}, \quad (i, j) \in A$$

$$w_i \text{ unrestricted in sign}, i = 1, 2, \ldots n$$

From the theory of linear programming, we have

$$w_i - w_j = c_{ij}, \text{ for basic arc } (i, j)$$

Because the original linear program (Section 6.6.2) has one redundant constraint by definition, we can assign an arbitrary value to one of the dual variables (compare with the transportation algorithm, Section 5.3). For convenience, we will set $w_1 = 0$. We then solve the (basic) equations $w_i - w_j = c_{ij}$ to determine the remaining dual values. Next, we compute $z_{ij} - c_{ij}$ for the nonbasic variables as

$$z_{ij} - c_{ij} = w_i - w_j - c_{ij}$$

The only remaining detail is to show how the leaving variable can be determined. This information is explained in the following numeric example.

---

**Example 6.6–4.**

A network of pipelines connects two water desalination plants to two cities. The daily supply amounts at the two plants are 40 and 60 million gallons and the daily demand amounts at cities 1 and 2 are 30 and 60 million gallons. Both plants 1 and 2 have direct links to each of cities 1 and 2. Desalinated water from plants 1 and 2 may also be transported to city 2 through a special pumping station. Additionally, plant 1 is linked to plant 2, and city 1 is linked to city 2. The model is already balanced because the supply at nodes 1 and 2 equals the demand at nodes 4 and 5. Figure 6–36 gives the associated network.

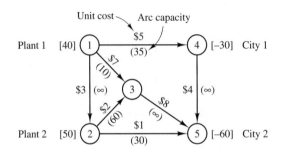

**Figure 6–36**

*Iteration 0*

**Step 0.** *Determination of a Starting Basic Feasible Solution:* The starting *feasible* spanning tree in Figure 6–37 (shown with solid arcs) is obtained by inspection. Normally, we use an artificial variable technique to find such a solution (for details, see Bazaraa et al., 1990, pp. 440–446).

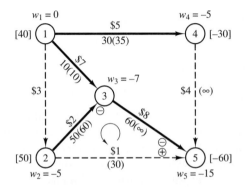

$z_{12} - c_{12} = 0 - (-5) - 3 = 2$
$z_{25} - c_{25} = -5 - (-15) - 1 = \mathbf{9}$
$z_{45} - c_{45} = -5 - (-15) - 4 = 6$

Arc (2, 5) reaches upper bound at 30.

Substitute $x_{25} = 30 - x_{52}$.

Reduce $x_{23}$ and $x_{35}$ each by 30.

**Figure 6–37**

In Figure 6–37, the basic feasible solution consists of (solid) arcs (1, 3), (1,4), (2, 3), and (3, 5) with the feasible flows of 30, 10, 50, and 60 units, respectively. This leaves (dashed) arcs (1, 2), (2, 5), and (4, 5) to represent the nonbasic variables. The notation $x(c)$ indicates that a flow of $x$ units is assigned to an arc with capacity is $c$. The default values for $x$ and $c$ are 0 and ∞, respectively.

*Iteration 1*

**Step 1.**    *Determination of the Entering Arc:* We obtain the dual values by solving the current basic equations

$$w_1 = 0$$

$$w_i - w_j = c_{ij}, \text{ for basic } (i, \ j)$$

we thus get,

Arc $(1, \ 3): w_1 - w_3 = 7$, hence $w_3 = -7$

Arc $(1, \ 4): w_1 - w_4 = 5$, hence $w_4 = -5$

Arc $(2, \ 3): w_2 - w_3 = 2$, hence $w_2 = -5$

Arc $(3, \ 5): w_3 - w_5 = 8$, hence $w_5 = -15$

Now, we compute $z_{ij} - c_{ij}$ for the nonbasic variables as

Arc $(1, \ 2): w_1 - w_2 - c_{12} = 0 - (-5) - 3 = 2$

Arc $(2, \ 5): w_2 - w_5 - c_{25} = (-5) - (-15) - 1 = \mathbf{9}$

Arc $(4, \ 5): w_4 - w_5 - c_{45} = (-5) - (-15) - 4 = 6$

Thus, arc $(2, 5)$ enters the basic solution.

**Step 2.**    *Determination of the leaving Arc:* From Figure 6–37, arc $(2, 5)$ forms a loop with basic arcs $(2, 3)$ and $(3, 5)$. *From the definition of the spanning tree, no other loop can be formed.* Because the flow in the new arc $(2, 5)$ must be increased, we adjust the flow in the arcs of the loops by an equal amount to maintain the feasibility of the new solution. To achieve this, we identify the positive $(+)$ flow in the loop by the direction of flow of the entering arc (i.e., from 2 to 5). We then assign $(+)$ or $(-)$ to the remaining arcs of the loop, depending on whether the flow of each arc is *with* or *against* the direction of flow of the entering arc. These sign conventions are shown in Figure 6–37.

To determine the maximum level of flow in the entering arc $(2, 5)$, we must guarantee that

**1.** The new flow in the current basic arcs of the loop cannot be negative.

**2.** The new flow in the entering arc cannot exceed its capacity.

The application of rule 1 shows that the flows in arcs $(2, 3)$ and $(3, 5)$ cannot be decreased by more than min{50, 60} = 50 units. Rule 2 stipulates that the flow in arc $(2, 5)$ can be increased to at most the arc capacity (= 30 units). Thus, the maximum flow change in the loop is min {30, 50} = 30 units. The flows in the loop are thus 30 units in arc $(2, 5)$, $50 - 30 = 20$ units in arc $(2, 3)$, and $60 - 30 = 30$ units in arc $(3, 5)$.

Because none of the current basic arcs leaves the basis at zero level, the new arc $(2, 5)$ must remain nonbasic at upper bound. However, to avoid dealing with nonbasic arcs that are not at zero flow level, we implement the substitution

$$x_{25} = 30 - x_{52}, \; 0 \le x_{52} \le 30$$

This substitution is effected in the flow equations associated with nodes 2 and 5 as follows. Consider

Current flow equation at node 2: $50 + x_{12} = x_{23} + x_{25}$

Current flow equation at node 5: $x_{25} + x_{35} + x_{45} = 60$

Then, the substitution $x_{25} = 30 - x_{52}$ gives

New flow equation at node 2: $20 + x_{12} + x_{52} = x_{23}$

New flow equation at node 5: $x_{35} + x_{45} = x_{52} + 30$

The results of these changes are shown in Figure 6–38. The direction of flow in arc $(2, 5)$ is now reversed to $5 \to 2$ with $x_{52} = 0$, as desired. The substitution also requires changing the unit cost of arc $(5, 2)$ to $-\$1$. We will indicate this direction reversal on the network by tagging the arc with an asterisk.

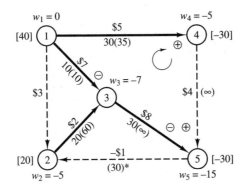

$z_{12} - c_{12} = 0 - (-5) - 3 = 2$
$z_{52} - c_{52} = -15 - (-5) - (-1) = -9$
$z_{45} - c_{45} = -5 - (-15) - 4 = \mathbf{6}$

Arc $(4, 5)$ enters at level 5.

Arc $(1, 4)$ leaves at upper bound.

Substitute $x_{14} = 35 - x_{41}$.

Reduce $x_{13}$ and $x_{35}$ each by 5.

**Figure 6–38**

*Iteration 2.*
Figure 6–38 summarizes the new values of $z_{ij} - c_{ij}$ (verify!) and shows that arc $(4, 5)$ enters the basic solution. It also defines the loop associated with the new entering arc and assigns the signs to its arcs.

The flow in arc $(4, 5)$ can be increased by the smallest of

1. Maximum allowable *increase* in entering arc $(4, 5) = \infty$
2. Maximum allowable *increase* in arc $(1, 4) = 35 - 30 = 5$ units
3. Maximum allowable *decrease* in arc $(1, 3) = 10$ units
4. Maximum allowable *decrease* in arc $(3, 5) = 30$ units

Thus, the flow in arc $(4, 5)$ can be increased to 5 units, which will make $(4, 5)$ basic and will force basic arc $(1, 4)$ to be nonbasic at its upper bound $(= 35)$.

Using the substitution $x_{14} = 35 - x_{41}$, the network is changed as shown in Figure 6–39, with arcs $(1, 3), (2, 3), (3, 5),$ and $(4, 5)$ forming the basic (spanning tree) solution. The reversal of flow in arc $(1, 4)$ changes its unit cost to $-\$5$. Also, convince yourself that the substitution in the flow equations of nodes 1 and 4 will net 5 *input* units at each node.

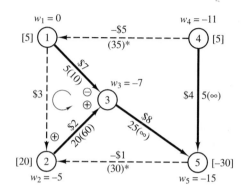

$$z_{12} - c_{12} = 0 - (-5) - 3 = 2$$
$$z_{41} - c_{41} = -11 - 0 - (-5) = -6$$
$$z_{52} - c_{52} = -15 - (-5) - (-1) = -9$$

Arc $(1, 2)$ enters at level 5.

Arc $(1, 3)$ leaves at level 0.

Increase $x_{23}$ by 5.

**Figure 6–39**

*Iteration 3.*

The computations of the new $z_{ij} - c_{ij}$ for the nonbasic arcs $(1, 2), (4, 1)$ and $(5, 2)$ are summarized in Figure 6–39, which shows that arc $(1, 2)$ enters at level 5, and arc $(1, 3)$ becomes nonbasic at level 0. The new solution is depicted in Figure 6–40.

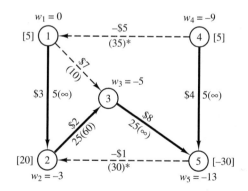

$$z_{13} - c_{13} = 0 - (-5) - 7 = -2$$
$$z_{41} - c_{41} = -9 - 0 - (-5) = -4$$
$$z_{52} - c_{52} = -13 - (-3) - (-1) = -9$$

Optimum solution:
$$x_{13} = 5, x_{13} = 0$$
$$x_{14} = 35 - 0 = 35$$
$$x_{23} = 25$$
$$x_{25} = 30 - 0 = 30$$
$$x_{35} = 25, x_{45} = 5$$
Total cost = \$495

**Figure 6–40**

*Iteration 4.*

The new $z_{ij} - c_{ij}$ in Figure 6–40 shows that the solution is optimum. The values of the original variables are obtained by back substitution as the shown in Figure 6–40.

## Problem set 6.6c

1. Solve Problem 6.6a–1 by the capacitated simplex algorithm, and also show that it can be solved by the transshipment model.
2. Solve Problem 6.6a–2 by the capacitated simplex algorithm, and also show that it can be solved by the transshipment model.
3. Solve Problem 6.6a–3 by the capacitated simplex algorithm.
4. Solve Problem 6.6a–4 by the capacitated simplex algorithm.
5. Solve Problem 6.6a–5 by the capacitated simplex algorithm.
6. Solve the employment scheduling problem of Example 6.6–3 by the capacitated simplex algorithm.
7. Wyoming Electric uses existing slurry pipes to transport coal (carried by pumped water) from three mining areas (1, 2, and 3) to three power plants (4, 5, and 6). Each pipe can transport at most 10 tons per hour. The transportation costs per ton and the capacity of the pipes per hour are given in the following table.

|   | 4 | 5 | 6 | |
|---|---|---|---|---|
| 1 | $5 | $8 | $4 | 8 |
| 2 | $6 | $9 | $12 | 10 |
| 3 | $3 | $1 | $5 | 18 |
|   | 16 | 6 | 14 | |

Determine the optimum shipping schedule.

8. The network in Figure 6–41 gives the distances among seven cities. Use the capacitated simplex algorithm to find the shortest distance between nodes 1 and 7. (*Hint:* Assume that nodes 1 and 7 have net flows of [+1] and [−1], respectively. All the other nodes have zero net flow.)

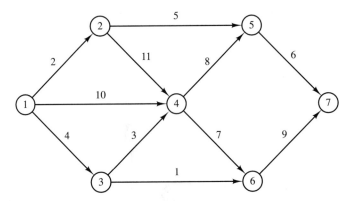

**Figure 6–41**

**9.** Show how the capacitated minimum-cost flow model can be specialized to represent the maximum flow model of Section 6.5. Apply the transformation to the network in Example 6.5–2. For convenience, assume that the flow capacity from 4 to 3 is zero. All the remaining data are unchanged.

## 6.7 CPM AND PERT

CPM (Critical Path Method) and PERT (Program Evaluation and Review Technique) are network-based methods designed to assist in the planning, scheduling, and control of projects. A project is defined as a collection of interrelated activities with each activity consuming time and resources. The objective of CPM and PERT is to provides analytic means for scheduling the activities. Figure 6–42 summarizes the steps of the techniques. First, we define the activities of the project, their precedence relationships, and their time requirements. Next, the project is translated into a network that shows the precedence relationships among the activities. The third step involves carrying out specific network computations that facilitate the development of the time schedule for the project.

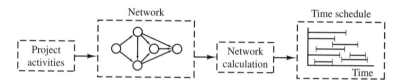

**Figure 6–42**

The two techniques, CPM and PERT, which were developed independently, differ in that CPM assumes deterministic activity durations. PERT, conversely, assumes probabilistic durations. This presentation concentrates on CPM only.

### 6.7.1 Network Representation

Each activity of the project is represented by a directional arc (more commonly known as *arrow*) pointing in the direction of progress in the project. The nodes of the network (also referred to as *events*) establish the precedence relationships among the different activities of the project.

Three rules are available for constructing the network.

**Rule 1.** *Each activity is represented by one and only one arrow in the network.*
**Rule 2.** *Each activity must be identified by two distinct end nodes.*

Figure 6–43 shows how a dummy activity can be used to represent two concurrent activities, A and B. By definition, a dummy activity, which is normally depicted by a dashed arrow, consumes no time or resources. Inserting a dummy activity in one of the four ways shown in Figure 6–43, we maintain the concurrence of *A* and *B*, and provide unique end nodes for the two concurrent activities (to satisfy rule 2).

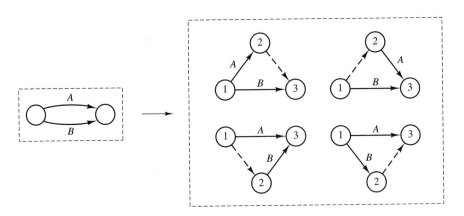

**Figure 6–43**

**Rule 3.** *To maintain the correct precedence relationships, the following questions must be answered as each activity is added to the network:*
  **(a)** *What activities must immediately precede the current activity?*
  **(b)** *What activities must follow the current activity?*
  **(c)** *What activities must occur concurrently with the current activity?*

The answers to these questions may require the use of dummy activities to ensure proper precedence among the activities. For example, suppose that the following precedence must be satisfied:

  **1.** Activity $C$ can start immediately after $A$ and $B$ are completed.
  **2.** Activity $E$ can start immediately after only $B$ is completed.

Part (a) of Figure 6–44 shows the incorrect representation of the precedence relationship because it requires both $A$ and $B$ to be completed before $E$ can start. In part (b) of the same figure, the use of a dummy activity rectifies the situation.

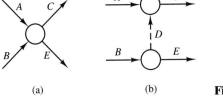

(a)                              (b)                    **Figure 6–44**

**Example 6.7–1.**
  A publisher has a contract with an author to publish a textbook. The (simplified) activities associated with the production of the textbook are given subsequently. Develop the associated network for the project.

| | Activity | Predecessor (s) | Duration (weeks) |
|---|---|---|---|
| A: | Manuscript proofreading by editor | — | 3 |
| B: | Sample pages prepared by typesetter | — | 2 |
| C: | Book cover design | — | 4 |
| D: | Preparation of artwork for book figures | — | 3 |
| E: | Author's approval of edited manuscript and sample pages | A, B | 2 |
| F: | Book typesetting | E | 4 |
| G: | Author checks typeset pages | F | 2 |
| H: | Author checks artwork | D | 1 |
| I: | Production of printing plates | G, H | 2 |
| J: | Book production and binding | C, I | 4 |

Figure 6–45 provides the network describing the precedence relationships among the different activities. The dummy activity $(2, 3)$ is used to produce unique end nodes for concurrent activities A and B. The numbering of the nodes is done in a manner that indicates the direction of progress in the project.

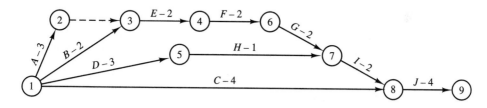

**Figure 6–45**

### Problem Set 6.7a

**1.** Construct the project network comprised of activities $A$ to $L$ with the following precedence relationships:

(a) $A$, $B$, and $C$, the first activities of the project, can be executed concurrently.

(b) $A$ and $B$ precede $D$.

(c) $B$ precedes $E$, $F$, and $H$.

(d) $F$ and $C$ precede $G$.

**(e)** *E* and *H* precede *I* and *J.*
**(f)** *C, D, F,* and *J* precede *K.*
**(g)** *K* precedes *L.*
**(h)** *I, G,* and *L* are the terminal activities of the project.

2. Construct the project network comprised of activities *A* to *P* that satisfies the following precedence relationships:

**(a)** *A, B,* and *C,* the first activities of the project, can be executed concurrently.
**(b)** *D, E,* and *F* follow *A.*
**(c)** *I* and *G* follow both *B* and *D.*
**(d)** *H* follows both *C* and *G.*
**(e)** *K* and *L* follow *I.*
**(f)** *J* succeeds both *E* and *H.*
**(g)** *M* and *N* succeed *F,* but cannot start until both *E* and *H* are completed.
**(h)** *O* succeeds *M* and *I.*
**(i)** *P* succeeds *J, L,* and *O.*
**(j)** *K, N,* and *P* are the terminal activities of the project.

3. The footings of a building can be completed in four connective sections. The activities for each section include (1) digging, (2) placing steel, and (3) pouring concrete. The digging of one section cannot start until that of the preceding section has been completed. The same restriction applies to pouring concrete. Develop the project network.

4. In Problem 3, suppose that 10% of the plumbing work can be started simultaneously with the digging of the first section but before any concrete is poured. After each section of the footings is completed, an additional 5% of the plumbing can be started provided that the preceding 5% portion is complete. Construct the project network.

5. An opinion survey involves designing and printing questionnaires, hiring and training personnel, selecting participants, mailing questionnaires, and analyzing the data. Construct the project network, stating all assumptions.

6. The activities in the following table describe the construction of a new house. Construct the associated project network.

| | Activity | Predecessor(s) | Duration (days) |
|---|---|---|---|
| *A:* | Clear site | — | 1 |
| *B:* | Bring utilities to site | — | 2 |
| *C:* | Excavate | *A* | 1 |
| *D:* | Pour foundation | *C* | 2 |
| *E:* | Outside plumbing | *B, C* | 6 *Continued* |

|     | Activity                          | Predecessor(s) | Duration (days) |
|-----|-----------------------------------|----------------|-----------------|
| *F:* | Frame house                      | *D*            | 10              |
| *G:* | Do electric wiring               | *F*            | 3               |
| *H:* | Lay floor                        | *G*            | 1               |
| *I:* | Lay roof                         | *F*            | 1               |
| *J:* | Inside plumbing                  | *E, H*         | 5               |
| *K:* | Shingling                        | *I*            | 2               |
| *L:* | Outside sheathing insulation     | *F, J*         | 1               |
| *M:* | Install windows and outside doors | *F*           | 2               |
| *N:* | Do brick work                    | *L, M*         | 4               |
| *O:* | Insulate walls and ceiling       | *G, J*         | 2               |
| *P:* | Cover walls and ceiling          | *O*            | 2               |
| *Q:* | Insulate roof                    | *I, P*         | 1               |
| *R:* | Finish interior                  | *P*            | 7               |
| *S:* | Finish exterior                  | *I, N*         | 7               |
| *T:* | Landscape                        | *S*            | 3               |

**7.** A company is in the process of preparing a budget for launching a new product. The following table provides the associated activities and their durations. Construct the project network.

|     | Activity                      | Predecessor(s) | Duration (days) |
|-----|-------------------------------|----------------|-----------------|
| *A:* | Forecast sales volume         | —              | 10              |
| *B:* | Study competitive market      | —              | 7               |
| *C:* | Design item and facilities    | *A*            | 5               |
| *D:* | Prepare production schedule   | *C*            | 3               |
| *E:* | Estimate cost of production   | *D*            | 2               |
| *F:* | Set sales price               | *B, E*         | 1               |
| *G:* | Prepare budget                | *E, F*         | 14              |

**8.** The activities involved in a candlelight choir service are listed in the following table. Construct the project network.

|        | Activity                      | Predecessor(s) | Duration (days) |
|--------|-------------------------------|----------------|-----------------|
| A:     | Select music                  | —              | 21              |
| B:     | Learn music                   | A              | 14              |
| C:     | Make copies and buy books     | A              | 14              |
| D:     | Tryouts                       | B, C           | 3               |
| E:     | Rehearsals                    | D              | 70              |
| F:     | Rent candelabra               | D              | 14              |
| G:     | Decorate candelabra           | F              | 1               |
| H:     | Set up decorations            | D              | 1               |
| I:     | Order choir robe stoles       | D              | 7               |
| J:     | Check out public address system | D            | 7               |
| K:     | Select music tracks           | J              | 14              |
| L:     | Set up public address system  | K              | 1               |
| M:     | Final rehearsal               | E, G, L        | 1               |
| N:     | Choir party                   | H, L, M        | 1               |
| O:     | Final program                 | I, N           | 1               |

**9.** The widening of a road section requires relocating ("reconductoring") 1700 feet of 13.8-kV overhead primary line. The following table summarizes the activities of the project. Construct the associated project network.

|        | Activity                              | Predecessor(s) | Duration (days) |
|--------|---------------------------------------|----------------|-----------------|
| A:     | Job review                            | —              | 1               |
| B:     | Advise customers of temporary outage  | A              | $\frac{1}{2}$   |
| C:     | Requisition stores                    | A              | 1               |

*Continued*

| | Activity | Predecessor(s) | Duration (days) |
|---|---|---|---|
| D: | Scout job | A | $\frac{1}{2}$ |
| E: | Secure poles and material | C, D | 3 |
| F: | Distribute poles | E | $3\frac{1}{2}$ |
| G: | Pole location coordination | D | $\frac{1}{2}$ |
| H: | Restake | G | $\frac{1}{2}$ |
| I: | Dig holes | H | 3 |
| J: | Frame and set poles | F, I | 4 |
| K: | Cover old conductors | F, I | 1 |
| L: | Pull new conductors | J, K | 2 |
| M: | Install remaining material | L | 2 |
| N: | Sag conductor | L | 2 |
| O: | Trim trees | D | 2 |
| P: | Deenergize and switch lines | B, M, N, O | $\frac{1}{9}$ |
| Q: | Energize and switch new line | P | $\frac{1}{2}$ |
| R: | Clean up | Q | 1 |
| S: | Return material to stores | I | 2 |

**10.** The following table gives the activities for buying a new car. Construct the project network.

| | Activity | Predecessor(s) | Duration (days) |
|---|---|---|---|
| A: | Conduct feasibility study | — | 3 |
| B: | Find potential buyer for present car | A | 14 |
| C: | List possible models | A | 1 |
| D: | Research all possible models | C | 3 |
| E: | Conduct interview with mechanic | C | 1 |
| F: | Collect dealer propaganda | C | 2 |

*Continued*

|  | Activity | Predecessor(s) | Duration (days) |
|---|---|---|---|
| *G:* | Compile pertinent data | *D, E, F* | 1 |
| *H:* | Choose top three models | *G* | 1 |
| *I:* | Test-drive all three choices | *H* | 3 |
| *J:* | Gather wearranty and financing data | *H* | 2 |
| *K:* | Choose one car | *I, J* | 2 |
| *L:* | Choose dealer | *K* | 2 |
| *M:* | Search for desired color and options | *L* | 4 |
| *N:* | Test-drive chosen model once again | *L* | 1 |
| *O:* | Purchase new car | *B, M, N* | 3 |

### 6.7.2 Critical Path Computations

The ultimate result in CPM is the construction of the time schedule for the project (see Figure 6–42). To achieve this objective conveniently, we carry out special computations that produce the following information:

**1.** Total duration needed to complete the project
**2.** Categorization of the activities of the project as *critical* and *noncritical*

An activity is said to be **critical** when there is no "leeway" in determining its start and finish times. As such, to complete the project without delay, each critical activity must be started and completed on time. A **noncritical** activity allows some scheduling slack, so that the start time of the activity may be advanced or delayed within limits without affecting the completion date of the entire project.

To carry out the necessary computations, we define an **event** as a point in time at which activities are terminated and others are started. In terms of the network, an event corresponds to a node. Next, we introduce the following definitions:

$\square_j$ = Earliest occurrence time of event $j$
$\Delta_j$ = Latest occurrence time of event $j$
$D_{ij}$ = Duration of activity $(i, j)$

The definitions of the *earliest* and *latest* occurrences of event $j$ are specified relative to the start and completion dates of the entire project.

The critical path calculations involve two passes: The **forward pass** determines the earliest occurrence times of the events, and the **backward pass** calculates their latest occurrence times.

**Forward pass (earliest occurrence times, □).**    In this pass, the computations start at node 1 and advance recursively to end node $n$.

> **Initial Step.**  Set $\square_1 \equiv 0$ to indicate that the project starts at time 0.
>
> **General Step $j$.**  Given that nodes $p, q, \ldots$, and $v$ are linked *directly* to node $j$ by incoming activities $(p, j), (q, j), \ldots$, and $(v, j)$ and that the earliest occurrence times of events (nodes) $p, q, \ldots$, and $v$ have already been computed, then the earliest occurrence time of event $j$ is computed as
>
> $$\square_j = \max \{\square_p + D_{pj}, \square_q + D_{qj}, \ldots \square_v + D_{vj}\}$$
>
> The forward pass is complete when $\square_n$ at node $n$ is computed. By definition $\square_j$ represents the longest path (duration) to node $j$

**Backward pass (latest occurrence times, △).**    Following the completion of the forward pass, the backward pass computations start at node $n$ and regress recursively to node 1.

> **Initial Step.**  Set $\triangle_n \equiv \square_n$ to indicate that the earliest and latest occurrence of the last event of the project are the same.
>
> **General Step $j$.**  Given that nodes $p, q, \ldots$, and $v$ are linked *directly* to node $j$ by *outgoing* activities $(j, p), (j, q), \ldots$, and $(j, v)$ and that the latest occurrence times of events (nodes) $p, q, \ldots$, and $v$ have already been computed, then the latest occurrence time of event $j$ is computed as
>
> $$\triangle_j = \min \{\triangle_p - D_{jp}, \triangle_q - D_{jq}, \ldots \triangle_v - D_{jv}\}$$

The backward pass is complete when $\triangle_1$ at node 1 is computed.

Based on the preceding calculations, an activity $(i, j)$ will be *critical* if it satisfies three conditions.

**1.** $\triangle_i = \square_i$
**2.** $\triangle_j = \square_j$
**3.** $\triangle_j - \triangle_i = \square_j - \square_i = D_{ij}$

The three conditions state that the earliest and latest occurrence times of the end events $i$ and $j$ are equal and that the duration $D_{ij}$ occupies their time span exactly. An activity that does not satisfy all three conditions is thus *noncritical*.

The critical activities of a network must constitute an uninterrupted path that spans the entire network from start to finish.

**Example 6.7–2.**

Determine the critical path for the project network in Figure 6–46. All the durations are in days.

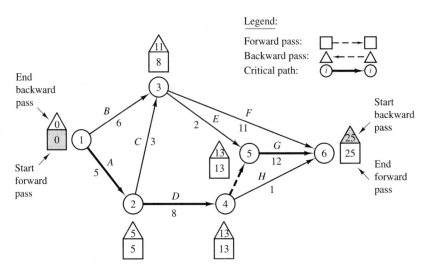

**Figure 6–46**

*Forward Pass.*

**Node 1.** Set $\square_1 = 0$.

**Node 2.** $\square_2 = \square_1 + D_{12} = 0 + 5 = 5$

**Node 3.** $\square_3 = \max \{\square_1 + D_{13}, \square_2 + D_{23}\} = \max \{0 + 6, 5 + 3\} = 8$

**Node 4.** $\square_4 = \square_2 + D_{24} = 5 + 8 = 13$

**Node 5.** $\square_5 = \max \{\square_3 + D_{35}, \square_4 + D_{45}\} = \max \{8 + 2, 13 + 0\} = 13$

**Node 6.** $\square_6 = \max \{\square_3 + D_{36}, \square_4 + D_{46}, \square_5 + D_{56}\}$

$\quad\quad\quad = \max \{8 + 11, 13 + 1, 13 + 12\} = 25$

The computations show that the project can be completed in 25 days.

*Backward Pass.*

**Node 6.** Set $\triangle_6 = \square_6 = 25$.

**Node 5.** $\triangle_5 = \triangle_6 - D_{56} = 25 - 12 = 13$

**Node 4.** $\triangle_4 = \min \{\triangle_6 - D_{46}, \triangle_5 - D_{45}\} = \min \{25 - 1, 13 - 0\} = 13$

**Node 3.** $\triangle_3 = \min\{\triangle_6 - D_{36}, \triangle_5 - D_{35}\} = \min\{25 - 11, 13 - 2\} = 11$

**Node 2.** $\triangle_2 = \min \{\triangle_4 - D_{24}, \triangle_3 - D_{23}\} = \min \{13 - 8, 11 - 3\} = 5$

**Node 1.** $\triangle_1 = \min\{\triangle_3 - D_{13}, \triangle_2 - D_{12}\} = \min \{11 - 6, 5 - 5\} = 0$

Correct computations will always result in $\triangle_1 = 0$.

The forward and backward pass computations are summarized in Figure 6–46. The rules for determining the critical activities show that the critical path is defined by

$1 \rightarrow 2 \rightarrow 4 \rightarrow 5 \rightarrow 6$, which spans the network from start (node 1) to finish (node 6). The sum of the durations of the critical activities $[(1, 2), (2, 4), (4, 5), \text{ and } (5, 6)]$ equals the duration of the project ($= 25$ days). Observe that activity $(4, 6)$ satisfies the first two conditions for a critical activity (namely, $\triangle_4 = \square_4 = 13$ and $\triangle_5 = \square_5 = 25$) but does not satisfy the third condition (namely, $\square_6 - \square_4 \neq D_{46}$). Hence, the activity is not critical.

### Problem set 6.7b

**1.** Determine the critical path for the project network in Figure 6–47.

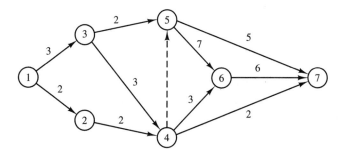

**Figure 6–47**

**2.** Determine the critical path for the project networks in Figure 6–48.

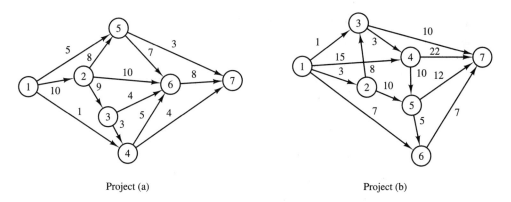

Project (a)                    Project (b)

**Figure 6–48**

**3.** Determine the critical path for the project in Problem 6.7a–6.

**4.** Determine the critical path for the project in Problem 6.7a–8.

**5.** Determine the critical path for the project in Problem 6.7a–9.

**6.** Determine the critical path for the project in Problem 6.7a–10.

### 6.7.3  Construction of the Time Schedule

This section shows how the information obtained from the calculations in Section 6.7.2 can be used to develop the time schedule. We recognize that for an activity $(i, j)$, $\Box_i$ represents the *earliest start time,* and $\triangle_j$ represents the *latest completion time.* This means that $(\Box_i, \triangle_j)$ delineates the (maximum) span during which the activity $(i, j)$ may be scheduled.

**Construction of Preliminary Schedule.**   The method for constructing a preliminary schedule is illustrated by an example.

---

**Example 6.7–3.**

Determine the time schedule for the project of Example 6.7–2 (Figure 6–46).

We can get a preliminary time schedule for the different activities of the project by delineating their respective time spans. Figure 6–49 provides this result. Two observations are in order.

**1.** The critical activities (shown by solid lines) are scheduled one right after the other to ensure that the project is completed within its specified 25-day duration.

**2.** The noncritical activities (shown by dashed lines) encompass spans that are larger than their respective durations, thus allowing slack (or "leeway") in scheduling them within their allotted spans.

How should we schedule the noncritical activities within their respective spans? Normally, it is preferable to start each noncritical activity as early as possible. In this manner, slack periods will remain opportunely available at the end of the allotted

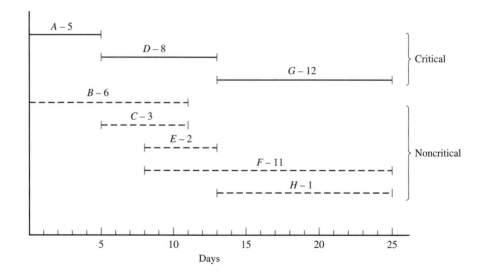

**Figure 6–49**

span, where they can be used to absorb possible unexpected delays in the execution of the activity. It may be necessary, however, to delay the start of a noncritical activity past its earliest time. For example, in Figure 6–49, suppose that each of the noncritical activities $E$ and $F$ requires the use of a bulldozer, and that only one is available. Scheduling both $E$ and $F$ as early as possible requires two bulldozers between times 8 and 10. We can remove the overlap by starting $E$ at time 8 and pushing the start time of $F$ to somewhere between times 10 and 14.

If all the noncritical activities can be scheduled as early as possible, the resulting schedule automatically is feasible. Otherwise, some precedence relationships may be destroyed if noncritical activities are delayed past their earliest time. Take, for example, activities $C$ and $E$ in Figure 6–49. In the project network (Figure 6–46), C must be completed before $E$. However, the spans of $C$ and $E$ in Figure 6–49 allow scheduling C between times 6 and 9, and E between times 8 and 10. This schedule does not guarantee that C will precede $E$. The example demonstrates the need for some "red flag" that automatically pinpoints the possible occurrence of such conflict in the schedule. We will show subsequently how the use of activity *slacks* or *floats* can be used to provide such information.

---

**Determination of the floats.**    Floats are the slack times available within the allotted span of the noncritical activity. The two most common floats are the **total float** and the **free float**.

Figure 6–50 gives a convenient summary for computing the total float ($TF_{ij}$) and the free float ($FF_{ij}$) for an activity $(i, j)$. The total float is the excess of the time span defined from the *earliest* occurrence of event $i$ to the *latest* occurrence of event $j$ over the duration of $(i, j)$—that is,

$$TF_{ij} = \triangle_j - \square_i - D_{ij}$$

The free float is the excess of the time span defined from the *earliest* occurrence of event $i$ to the *earliest* occurrence of event $j$ over the duration of $(i, j)$—that is,

$$FF_{ij} = \square_j - \square_i - D_{ij}$$

By definition, $FF_{ij} \leq TF_{ij}$.

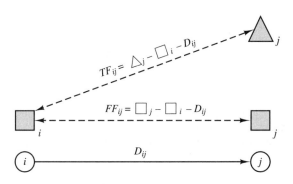

**Figure 6–50**

**Red-Flagging Rule.**   *For a noncritical activity $(i, j)$*

**(a)** *If $FF_{ij} = TF_{ij}$, then the activity can be scheduled anywhere within its $(\Box_i, \triangle_j)$ span without causing schedule conflict.*

**(b)** *If $FF_{ij} < TF_{ij}$, then the start of the activity can be delayed by no more than $FF_{ij}$ relative to its earliest start time $(\Box_i)$ without causing schedule conflict. Any delay larger than $FF_{ij}$ (but not more than $TF_{ij}$) must be accompanied by an equal delay relative to $\Box_j$ in the start time of all the activities leaving node $j$.*

The implication of the rule is that a noncritical activity $(i, j)$ will be red-flagged if its $FF_{ij} < TF_{ij}$. This red flag is important only if we decide to delay the start of the activity past its earliest start time, $\Box_i$, in which case we must pay attention to the start times of the activities leaving node $j$ to avoid schedule conflicts.

**Example 6.7–4.**

Compute the floats for the noncritical activities of the network in Example 6.7–2, and discuss their use in finalizing a schedule for the project.

The following table summarizes the computations of the total and free floats. It is more convenient to do the calculations directly on the network using the procedure in Figure 6–50.

| Noncritical activity | Duration | Total float ($TF$) | Free float ($FF$) |
|---|---|---|---|
| $B$ (1, 3) | 6 | $11 - 0 - 6 = 5$ | $8 - 0 - 6 = 2$ |
| $C$ (2, 3) | 3 | $11 - 5 - 3 = 3$ | $8 - 5 - 3 = 0$ |
| $E$ (3, 5) | 2 | $13 - 8 - 2 = 3$ | $13 - 8 - 2 = 3$ |
| $F$ (3, 6) | 11 | $25 - 8 - 11 = 6$ | $25 - 8 - 11 = 6$ |
| $H$ (4, 6) | 1 | $25 - 13 - 1 = 11$ | $25 - 13 - 1 = 11$ |

The computations red-flag activities $B$ and $C$ only because their $FF < TF$. The remaining activities ($E$, $F$, and $H$) have $FF = TF$, and hence may be scheduled anywhere between their earliest start and latest completion times.

To investigate the significance of the red-flagged activities, consider activity $B$. Because its $TF = 5$ days, this activity can start as early as time 0 or as late as time 5 (see Figure 6–49). However, because its $FF = 2$ days, starting $B$ anywhere between time 0 and time 2 will have no effect on the succeeding activities $E$ and $F$. If, however, activity $B$ must start at time $2 + \triangle(< 5)$, then the start times of activities $E$ and $F$ must be pushed forward past their earliest start time ($= 8$) by at least $\triangle$. In this manner, the precedence relationship between $B$ and its successors $E$ and $F$ is preserved.

Turning to red-flagged activity $C$, we note that its $FF = 0$. This means that *any* delay in starting $C$ past its earliest start time ($= 5$) must be coupled with at least an equal delay in the start of its successor activities $E$ and $F$.

**Problem set 6.7c**

1. Given an activity $(i, j)$ with duration $D_{ij}$ and its earliest start time $\square_i$ and its latest completion time $\triangle_j$, determine the earliest completion and the latest start times of $(i, j)$.

2. What are the total and free floats of a critical activity?

3. For each of the following activities, determine the maximum delay in the starting time relative to its earliest start time that will allow all the immediately succeeding activities to be scheduled anywhere between their earliest and latest completion times.
   (a) $TF = 10, FF = 10, D = 4$.
   (b) $TF = 10, FF = 5, D = 4$.
   (c) $TF = 10, FF = 0, D = 4$.

4. In Example 6.7–4, use the floats to answer the following:
   (a) Suppose that activity $B$ is started at time 1, and activity $C$ is started at time 5, determine the earliest start times for $E$ and $F$.
   (b) Suppose that activity $B$ is started at time 3, and activity $C$ is started at time 7, determine the earliest start times for $E$ and $F$.
   (c) Can activity $B$ start as late as time 6?

5. In the project of Example 6.7–2 (Figure 6–46), assume that the durations of activities $B$ and $F$ are changed from 6 and 11 days to 20 and 25 days, respectively.
   (a) Determine the critical path.
   (b) Determine the total and free floats for the network, and identify the red-flagged activities.
   (c) Suppose that activity $A$ is started at time 5, determine the earliest possible start times for activities $C, D, E,$ and $H$.
   (d) Suppose that activities $F, G,$ and $H$ require the same equipment. Determine the minimum number of units needed of this equipment.

6. Compute the floats and identify the red-flagged activities for the projects (a) and (b) in Figure 6–48, then develop the time schedules under the following conditions:

   *Project (a)*

   (i) Activity $(1, 5)$ cannot start any earlier than time 14.

   (ii) Activities $(5, 6)$ and $(5, 7)$ use the same equipment, of which only one unit is available.

   (iii) All other activities start as early as possible.

   *Project (b)*

   (i) Activity $(1, 3)$ must be scheduled at its earliest start time while accounting for the requirement that $(1, 2), (1, 3),$ and $(1, 6)$ use a special equipment, of which 1 unit only is available.

   (ii) All other activities start as early as possible.

## 6.8 SUMMARY

Network modeling provides a convenient way for solving complex problems. This chapter has presented a variety of network applications. Although these applications can be solved as linear programs, the special network algorithms are superior from the computational standpoint.

The capacitated network simplex method subsumes most of the specialized algorithms presented in the chapter. Nevertheless, these specialized algorithms are generally more efficient computationally.

## SELECTED REFERENCES

Ahuja, R., T. Magnati, and J. Orlin, *Network Flows: Theory, Algorithms, And Applications,* Prentice Hall, Upper Saddle River, N.J., 1993.

Bazaraa, M., J. Jarvis, and H. Sherali, *Linear Programming And Network Flow,* 2nd ed., Wiley, New York, 1990.

Evans, J.R., and E. Minieka, *Optimization Algorithms For Networks And Graphs,* 2nd ed., Marcel Dekker, New York, 1992.

Murty, K., *Network Programming,* Prentice Hall, Upper Saddle River, N.J., 1992.

## COMPREHENSIVE PROBLEMS

■ **6–1**  An outdoors person who lives in San Francisco (SF) wishes to spend a 15-day vacation visiting four national parks: Yosemite (YO), Yellowstone (YE), Grand Teton (GT), and Mount Rushmore (MR). The tour, which starts and ends in San Francisco, visits the parks in the following order: SF→YO→YE→GT→MR→SF, and includes a 2-day stay at each park. Travel from one park location to another is either by air or car. Each leg of the trip takes 1/2 day if traveled by air. Travel by car takes 1/2 day from SF to YO, 3 days from YO to YE, one day from YE to GT, 2 days from GT to MR, and 3 days from MR back to SF. The tradeoff is that car travel generally costs less but takes longer. Considering the fact that the individual must return to work in 15 days, the objective is to make the tour as inexpensively as possible within the 15-day limit. The following table provides the one-way cost of traveling by car and air. Determine the mode of travel on each leg of the tour.

| From | Air travel cost ($) to | | | | | Car travel cost ($) to | | | | |
|------|-----|-----|-----|-----|-----|-----|-----|-----|-----|-----|
|      | SF  | YO  | YE  | GT  | MR  | SF  | YO  | YE  | GT  | MR  |
| SF   | —   | 150 | 350 | 380 | 450 | —   | 130 | 175 | 200 | 230 |
| YO   | 150 | —   | 400 | 290 | 340 | 130 | —   | 200 | 145 | 180 |
| YE   | 350 | 400 | —   | 150 | 320 | 175 | 200 | —   | 70  | 150 |

*Continued*

| | Air travel cost ($) to | | | | | | Car travel cost ($) to | | | | |
|---|---|---|---|---|---|---|---|---|---|---|---|
| From | SF | YO | YE | GT | MR | | SF | YO | YE | GT | MR |
| GT | 380 | 290 | 150 | — | 300 | | 200 | 145 | 70 | — | 100 |
| MR | 450 | 340 | 320 | 300 | — | | 230 | 180 | 150 | 100 | — |

■ **6-2**[1]  A benefactor has donated valuable books to the Springdale Public Library. The books come in four heights: 12, 10, 8, and 6 inches. The head librarian estimates that 12 feet of shelving will be needed for the 12-inch books, 18 feet for the 10-inch ones, 9 feet for the 8-inch books, and 10 feet for the 6-inch ones. The construction cost of a shelf includes both a fixed cost and a variable cost per foot length as the following table shows.

| Shelf height (in) | Fixed cost ($) | Variable cost ($/ft length) |
|---|---|---|
| 12 | 25 | 5.50 |
| 10 | 25 | 4.50 |
| 8 | 22 | 3.50 |
| 6 | 22 | 2.50 |

Given that smaller books can be stored on larger shelves, how should the shelves be designed?

■ **6-3**   A shipping company wants to deliver five cargo shipments from ports $A$, $B$, and $C$ to ports $D$ and $E$. The delivery dates for the five shipments are

| Shipment | Shipping route | Delivery date |
|---|---|---|
| 1 | $A$ to $D$ | 10 |
| 2 | $A$ to $E$ | 15 |
| 3 | $B$ to $D$ | 4 |
| 4 | $B$ to $E$ | 5 |
| 5 | $C$ to $E$ | 18 |

The following table gives trip times (in days) between ports (the return trip times is assumed to take less time).

[1]Based on A. Ravindran, "On Compact Storage in Libraries," *Opsearch*, Vol. 8, No. 3, pp. 245–252, 1971.

The company wants to determine the minimum number of ships needed to carry out the given shipping schedule.

|   | A | B | C | D | E |
|---|---|---|---|---|---|
| A |   |   |   | 3 | 4 |
| B |   |   |   | 3 | 2 |
| C |   |   |   | 3 | 5 |
| D | 2 | 2 | 2 |   |   |
| E | 3 | 1 | 4 |   |   |

■ **6–4**[2] Several individuals have set up separate brokerage firms that traded in highly speculative stocks. The brokers operated under a loose financial system that allowed extensive interbrokerage transactions, including buying, selling, borrowing, and lending. For the group of brokers as a whole, the main source of income was the commission they received from sales to outside clients.

Eventually, the risky trading in speculative stocks became unmanageable, and all the brokers declared bankruptcy. At the time the bankruptcy was declared, the financial situation was that all brokers owed money to outside clients and the interbroker financial entanglements were so complex that almost every broker owed money to every other broker in the group.

The brokers whose assets could pay for their debts were declared solvent. The remaining brokers were referred to a legal body whose purpose was to resolve the debt situation in the best interest of outside clients. Because the assets and receivables of the nonsolvent brokers were less than their payables, all debts were prorated. The final effect was a complete liquidation of all the assets of the nonsolvent brokers.

In resolving the financial entanglements within the group of nonsolvent brokers, it was decided that the transactions would be executed only to satisfy certain legal requirements because, in effect, none of the brokers would be keeping any of the funds owed by others. As such, the legal body requested that the number of interbroker transactions be reduced to an absolute minimum. This means that if $A$ owed $B$ an amount $X$, and $B$ owed $A$ an amount $Y$, the two "loop" transactions were reduced to one whose amount is $|X - Y|$. This amount would go from $A$ to $B$ if $X > Y$ and from $B$ to $A$ if $Y > X$. If $X = Y$, the transactions were completely eliminated. The idea was to be extended to all loop transactions involving any number of brokers.

How would you handle this situation? Specifically, you are required to answer two questions.

1. How should the debts be prorated?
2. How should the number of interbroker transactions be reduced to a minimum?

[2]Based on H. Taha, "Operations Research Analysis of a Stock Market Problem," *Computers and Operations Research,* Vol. 18, No. 7, pp. 597–602, 1991.

# Chapter 7

# Advanced Linear Programming

## 7.1 INTRODUCTION

This chapter presents a rigorous treatment of the foundations of linear programming (LP). The presentation includes proofs of the validity of the simplex algorithm and duality theory. It also introduces efficient computational algorithms including the revised simplex method, upper and lower bounding, decomposition, and parametric programming. The chapter then presents the totally different Karmarkar interior point algorithm. The new algorithm is claimed to be more efficient than the simplex method in handing extremely large LPs.

The presentation in this chapter is based on the use of the compact matrix notation. If you have not already acquired a working knowledge of linear matrix algebra, you may want to consult Appendix A for a brief exposition of the topic.

## 7.2 VECTORS AND BASES

This section shows how the basic solutions are determined from the matrix form of the *standard LP*.

### 7.2.1 STANDARD LP IN MATRIX FORM

The standard LP form defined in Section 3.2.2 requires all the variables to be nonnegative and all the constraints to be equations with nonnegative right-hand side. Using matrix notation, the standard form is expressed as

$$\text{Maximize or minimize } z = \mathbf{CX}$$

subject to

$$(\mathbf{A}, \mathbf{I})\mathbf{X} = \mathbf{b}$$

$$\mathbf{X} \geq \mathbf{0}$$

where

$$\mathbf{I} = m\text{-identity matrix}$$

$$\mathbf{X} = (x_1, x_2, \ldots, x_n)^T, \quad \mathbf{C} = (c_1, c_2, \ldots, c_n)$$

$$\mathbf{A} = \begin{bmatrix} a_{11} & a_{12} & \cdots & a_{1,\,n-m} \\ a_{21} & a_{22} & \cdots & a_{2,\,n-m} \\ \vdots & \vdots & \vdots & \vdots \\ a_{m1} & a_{m2} & \cdots & a_{m,\,n-m} \end{bmatrix}, \quad \mathbf{b} = \begin{bmatrix} b_1 \\ b_2 \\ \vdots \\ b_m \end{bmatrix}$$

The $(m \times m)$ identity matrix, $\mathbf{I}$, can always be made to occupy the right-most position on the left-hand side of the equations through proper arrangement of the variables and by using artificial variables, if necessary.

---

**Example 7.2–1.**

The matrix notation is demonstrated by the following LP model.

$$\text{Maximize } z = 2x_1 + 3x_2$$

subject to

$$x_1 + x_2 \geq 5$$
$$x_1 + 2x_2 = 7$$
$$5x_1 - 2x_2 \leq 9$$
$$x_1, x_2 \geq 0$$

The associated standard LP in matrix form is expressed as

$$\text{Maximize } z = (2, 3, 0. - M, - M, 0) \begin{bmatrix} x_1 \\ x_2 \\ x_3 \\ x_4 \\ x_5 \\ x_6 \end{bmatrix}$$

subject to

$$\begin{bmatrix} 1 & 1 & -1 & 1 & 0 & 0 \\ 1 & 2 & 0 & 0 & 1 & 0 \\ 5 & -2 & 0 & 0 & 0 & 1 \end{bmatrix} \begin{bmatrix} x_1 \\ x_2 \\ x_3 \\ x_4 \\ x_5 \\ x_6 \end{bmatrix} = \begin{bmatrix} 5 \\ 7 \\ 9 \end{bmatrix}$$

$$x_j \geq 0, \quad j = 1, 2, \ldots, 6$$

It includes $n = 6$ variables and $m = 3$ constraint equations. The variables $x_3$ and $x_6$ are surplus and slack, respectively, and $x_4$ and $x_5$ are artificial.

The associated matrices are defined as

$$\mathbf{X} = (x_1, x_2, \ldots, x_6)^T$$

$$\mathbf{C} = (2, 3, 0, -M, -M, 0)$$

$$\mathbf{b} = (5, 7, 9)^T$$

$$\mathbf{A} = \begin{bmatrix} 1 & 1 & -1 \\ 1 & 2 & 0 \\ 5 & -2 & 0 \end{bmatrix}, \quad \mathbf{I} = \begin{bmatrix} 1 & 0 & 0 \\ 0 & 1 & 0 \\ 0 & 0 & 1 \end{bmatrix}$$

## Problem set 7.2a

1. In Example 7.2–1, suppose that the first and second constraints are changed to ($\leq$) and that the third constraint is changed to ($\geq$). Write the standard form in matrix form, and define the associated $\mathbf{X}, \mathbf{C}, \mathbf{A}, \mathbf{I}$, and $\mathbf{b}$.

2. Express each of the following linear programs in standard matrix form and identify the elements $\mathbf{A}, \mathbf{C}, \mathbf{b}$, and $\mathbf{X}$.

   (a) Maximize $z = 3x_1 + 2x_2 + 5x_3$
       subject to

$$7x_1 + 3x_2 - x_3 \leq 15$$
$$2x_1 - 2x_2 + 3x_3 \leq 20$$
$$x_1 + x_2 + x_3 \leq 5$$
$$x_1, x_2, x_3 \geq 0$$

   (b) Minimize $z = 2x_1 + 5x_2$
       subject to

$$3x_1 + 2x_2 \leq 5$$
$$4x_1 - x_2 \geq 2$$
$$x_1, x_2 \geq 0$$

   (c) Maximize $z = 6x_1 + 2x_2 + 3x_3$
       subject to

$$5x_1 + 2x_2 + 4x_3 = 20$$
$$3x_1 - x_2 + 2x_3 \leq 15$$
$$x_1, x_2, x_3 \geq 0$$

## 7.2.2 Vector Representation of a Basis

In the standard LP, the system of linear equations $(\mathbf{A}, \mathbf{I})\mathbf{X} = \mathbf{b}$ with $m$ equations and $n$ unknowns can be expressed in vector form as

$$\sum_{j=1}^{n} \mathbf{P}_j x_j = \mathbf{b}$$

where $\mathbf{P}_j$ represents the $j$th column vector of $(\mathbf{A}, \mathbf{I})$. A subset of $m$ vectors is said to form a **basis, B,** if, and only if, the selected $m$ vectors are **linearly independent.** Independence among the $m$ vectors of $\mathbf{B}$ is established if, and only if, the determinant of $\mathbf{B}$, $\det(\mathbf{B})$, is nonzero. In this case, $\mathbf{B}$ is said to be **nonsingular.**

---

**Example 7.2–2.**

The following system, expressed in vector form, has two linear equations and three unknowns ($m = 2$ and $n = 3$). Determine all its bases.

$$\begin{bmatrix} 1 \\ 2 \end{bmatrix} x_1 + \begin{bmatrix} 3 \\ -2 \end{bmatrix} x_2 + \begin{bmatrix} -1 \\ -2 \end{bmatrix} x_3 = \begin{bmatrix} 4 \\ 2 \end{bmatrix}$$

Each of $\mathbf{P}_1, \mathbf{P}_2, \mathbf{P}_3, \mathbf{P}_4$, and $\mathbf{b}$ is a two-dimensional vector, which can be represented generically as $(a_1, a_2)^T$. Figure 7–1 plots these vectors on the $(a_1, a_2)$-plane. For example, for $\mathbf{b} = (4, 2)^T, a_1 = 4$ and $a_2 = 2$.

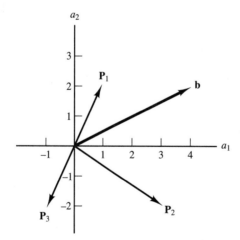

**Figure 7–1**

Because we are dealing with two equations ($m = 2$), a basis must include exactly two vectors, selected from among $\mathbf{P}_1, \mathbf{P}_2$, and $\mathbf{P}_3$. An examination of Figure 7–1 shows that the combinations $(\mathbf{P}_1, \mathbf{P}_2)$ and $(\mathbf{P}_2, \mathbf{P}_3)$ form bases because their associated vectors are independent. Conversely, the combination $(\mathbf{P}_1, \mathbf{P}_3)$ does not constitute a basis because $\mathbf{P}_1$ and $\mathbf{P}_3$ are dependent.

Algebraically, a combination forms a basis if its determinant does not equal zero. The following computations show that $(\mathbf{P}_1, \mathbf{P}_2)$ and $(\mathbf{P}_2, \mathbf{P}_3)$ are bases, and $(\mathbf{P}_1, \mathbf{P}_3)$ is not.

$$\det(\mathbf{P}_1, \mathbf{P}_2) = \det\begin{bmatrix} 1 & 3 \\ 2 & -2 \end{bmatrix} = (1 \times -2) - (2 \times 3) = -8 \neq 0$$

$$\det(\mathbf{P}_2, \mathbf{P}_3) = \det\begin{bmatrix} 3 & -1 \\ -2 & -2 \end{bmatrix} = (3 \times -2) - (-2 \times -1) = -8 \neq 0$$

$$\det(\mathbf{P}_1, \mathbf{P}_3) = \det\begin{bmatrix} 1 & -1 \\ 2 & -2 \end{bmatrix} = (1 \times -2) - (2 \times -1) = 0$$

### Problem set 7.2b

1. Show graphically (using vectors) and algebraically whether each of the following matrices forms a basis.

$$\mathbf{B}_1 = \begin{bmatrix} 1 & 2 \\ 2 & 3 \end{bmatrix}, \qquad \mathbf{B}_2 = \begin{bmatrix} 1 & 2 \\ 2 & 1 \end{bmatrix}$$

$$\mathbf{B}_3 = \begin{bmatrix} 2 & -4 \\ -1 & 2 \end{bmatrix}, \qquad \mathbf{B}_4 = \begin{bmatrix} 1 & 5 \\ 2 & 10 \end{bmatrix}$$

2. Consider the following system of equations:

$$\begin{bmatrix} 1 \\ 2 \\ 3 \end{bmatrix} x_1 + \begin{bmatrix} 0 \\ 2 \\ 1 \end{bmatrix} x_2 + \begin{bmatrix} 1 \\ 4 \\ 2 \end{bmatrix} x_3 + \begin{bmatrix} 2 \\ 0 \\ 0 \end{bmatrix} x_4 = \begin{bmatrix} 3 \\ 4 \\ 2 \end{bmatrix}$$

Determine if any of the following combinations forms a basis.
(a) $(\mathbf{P}_1, \mathbf{P}_2, \mathbf{P}_3)$
(b) $(\mathbf{P}_1, \mathbf{P}_2, \mathbf{P}_4)$
(a) $(\mathbf{P}_2, \mathbf{P}_3, \mathbf{P}_4)$

### 7.2.3 Basic Solutions

For the system $(\mathbf{A}, \mathbf{I})\mathbf{X} = \mathbf{b}$ of $m$ equations and $n$ unknowns ($m < n$), let $\mathbf{X}_B$ be a subset of $m$ elements of the $n$-vector $\mathbf{X}$, and define the ($m \times m$) matrix, $\mathbf{B}$, to comprise the vectors of $(\mathbf{A}, \mathbf{I})$ associated with $\mathbf{X}_B$. Assigning zero values to the remaining $n - m$ elements of $\mathbf{X}$, the system $(\mathbf{A}, \mathbf{I})\mathbf{X} = \mathbf{b}$ reduces to

$$\mathbf{B}\mathbf{X}_B = \mathbf{b}$$

If $\mathbf{B}$ is a *basis*, then we get the *unique* solution

$$\mathbf{X}_B = \mathbf{B}^{-1}\mathbf{b}$$

where $\mathbf{B}^{-1}$ is the inverse of $\mathbf{B}$. Under this condition, $\mathbf{X}_B$ is a **basic solution** of $(\mathbf{A}, \mathbf{I})\mathbf{X} = \mathbf{b}$. If $\mathbf{B}^{-1}\mathbf{b} \geq 0$, then $\mathbf{X}_B$ is feasible.

The conclusion from the preceding discussion is that in a system of $m$ linear equations and $n$ variables, the maximum number of basic solutions is given as

$$\left(\frac{n}{m}\right) = \frac{n!}{m!(n-m)!}$$

**Example 7.2–3.**

Determine all the basic solution of the system of equation in Example 7.2–2 and indicate whether or not they are feasible.

The following table summarizes the results. The inverse of **B** is determined by using one of the methods in Section A.2.7.

| **B** | **BX**$_B$ **= b** | Solution | Status |
|---|---|---|---|
| $(\mathbf{P}_1, \mathbf{P}_2)$ | $\begin{bmatrix} 1 & 3 \\ 2 & -2 \end{bmatrix} \begin{bmatrix} x_1 \\ x_2 \end{bmatrix} = \begin{bmatrix} 4 \\ 2 \end{bmatrix}$ | $\begin{bmatrix} x_1 \\ x_2 \end{bmatrix} = \begin{bmatrix} \frac{1}{4} & \frac{3}{8} \\ \frac{1}{4} & -\frac{1}{8} \end{bmatrix} \begin{bmatrix} 4 \\ 2 \end{bmatrix} = \begin{bmatrix} \frac{7}{4} \\ \frac{3}{4} \end{bmatrix}$ | Feasible |
| $(\mathbf{P}_1, \mathbf{P}_3)$ | (Not a basis) | — | — |
| $(\mathbf{P}_2, \mathbf{P}_3)$ | $\begin{bmatrix} 3 & -1 \\ -2 & -2 \end{bmatrix} \begin{bmatrix} x_2 \\ x_3 \end{bmatrix} = \begin{bmatrix} 4 \\ 2 \end{bmatrix}$ | $\begin{bmatrix} x_2 \\ x_3 \end{bmatrix} = \begin{bmatrix} \frac{1}{4} & -\frac{1}{8} \\ -\frac{1}{4} & -\frac{3}{8} \end{bmatrix} \begin{bmatrix} 4 \\ 2 \end{bmatrix} = \begin{bmatrix} \frac{3}{4} \\ -\frac{7}{4} \end{bmatrix}$ | Infeasible |

### Problem set 7.3a

1. In the following sets of equations, (a) and (b) have unique (basic) solutions, (c) has infinity of solutions, and (d) has no solution. Show how these results can be verified using graphical vector representation. From this exercise, state the general conditions that lead to unique solution, infinity of solutions, and no solution.

   **(a)**  $x_1 + 3x_2 = 2$          **(b)**  $2x_1 + 3x_2 = 1$

   $3x_1 + x_2 = 3$                    $2x_1 - x_2 = 2$

   **(c)**  $2x_1 + 6x_2 = 4$          **(d)**  $2x_1 - 4x_2 = 2$

   $x_1 + 3x_2 = 2$                    $-x_1 + 2x_2 = 1$

2. Identify graphically (using vectors) if each of the following sets of equations has a unique solution, infinity of solutions, or no solution. For the cases of unique solutions, indicate from the vector representation (and without solving the equations algebraically) whether the values of the $x_1$ and $x_2$ are positive, zero, or negative.

   **(a)** $\begin{bmatrix} 5 & 4 \\ 1 & -3 \end{bmatrix} \begin{bmatrix} x_1 \\ x_2 \end{bmatrix} = \begin{bmatrix} 1 \\ 1 \end{bmatrix}$          **(b)** $\begin{bmatrix} 2 & -2 \\ 1 & 3 \end{bmatrix} \begin{bmatrix} x_1 \\ x_2 \end{bmatrix} = \begin{bmatrix} 1 \\ 3 \end{bmatrix}$

**(c)** $\begin{bmatrix} 2 & 4 \\ 1 & 3 \end{bmatrix}\begin{bmatrix} x_1 \\ x_2 \end{bmatrix} = \begin{bmatrix} -2 \\ -1 \end{bmatrix}$      **(d)** $\begin{bmatrix} 2 & 4 \\ 1 & 2 \end{bmatrix}\begin{bmatrix} x_1 \\ x_2 \end{bmatrix} = \begin{bmatrix} 6 \\ 3 \end{bmatrix}$

**(e)** $\begin{bmatrix} -2 & 4 \\ 1 & -2 \end{bmatrix}\begin{bmatrix} x_1 \\ x_2 \end{bmatrix} = \begin{bmatrix} 2 \\ 1 \end{bmatrix}$      **(f)** $\begin{bmatrix} 1 & -2 \\ 0 & 0 \end{bmatrix}\begin{bmatrix} x_1 \\ x_2 \end{bmatrix} = \begin{bmatrix} 1 \\ 1 \end{bmatrix}$

**3.** True or False?

**(a)** The system $\mathbf{BX} = \mathbf{b}$ has a unique solution if $\mathbf{B}$ is nonsingular.

**(b)** The system $\mathbf{BX} = \mathbf{b}$ has no solution if $\mathbf{B}$ is singular and $\mathbf{b}$ is independent relative to the vectors of $\mathbf{B}$.

**(c)** The system $\mathbf{BX} = \mathbf{b}$ has infinity of solutions if $\mathbf{B}$ is singular, and $\mathbf{b}$ is dependent relative to the vectors of $\mathbf{B}$.

## 7.3 VALIDITY PROOFS OF THE SIMPLEX METHOD[1]

In Section 2.3, we demonstrated that the (finite) optimal solution of a two-variable LP is associated with an *extreme point* of the solution space. In Chapter 3, we made the transition from the graphical solution to the algebraic simplex algorithm by stating that the extreme points are totally defined by the basic solutions of the equations representing the solution space. This section proves this result. Because convex sets play a key role in the proofs, we first define these sets mathematically.

### 7.3.1 Definition of Convex Sets

A set $C$ in the $n$-dimensional space is said to be convex if the line segment joining any two *distinct* points in the set lies entirely in $C$. Mathematically, this means that if $\mathbf{X}'$ and $\mathbf{X}''$ are two distinct points in $C$, then their **convex combination,** defined as

$$\mathbf{X} = \lambda\mathbf{X}' + (1 - \lambda)\mathbf{X}'', \quad 0 \leq \lambda \leq 1$$

must also be in $C$. Figure 7–2 illustrates the definition where sets (a) and (b) are convex, and set (c) is nonconvex.

The *extreme points* of a convex set are those points in the set that cannot be expressed as a convex combination of any two *distinct* points in the same set. In

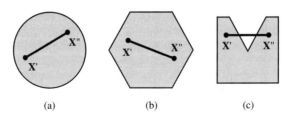

| (a) | (b) | (c) |

**Figure 7–2**

[1]This section may be skipped without loss of continuity.

Figure 7–2, the convex set (a) has an infinite number of extreme points (namely, the tangent points of the circle), and the set (b), which is typical of LP solution spaces, has only a finite number (= 6).

### Problem set 7.3b

1. Show that the set $Q = \{x_1, x_2 \mid x_1 + x_2 \leq 1, x_1 \geq 0, x_2 \geq 0\}$ is convex. Is the nonnegativity condition essential for the proof?

2. Show that the set $Q = \{x_1, x_2 \mid x_1 \geq 1 \text{ or } x_2 \geq 2\}$ is not convex.

3. Determine graphically the extreme points of the convex set $Q = \{x_1, x_2 \mid x_1 + x_2 \leq 2, x_1 \geq 0, x_2 \geq 0\}$, and then show that the entire feasible solution space can be determined as a convex combination of its extreme points. Hence, conclude that any (bounded) solution space is totally defined once its extreme points are known.

4. In the solution space in Figure 7–3 (drawn to scale), express the interior point (3, 1) as a convex combination of the extreme points A, B, C, and D, where each extreme point carries a strictly positive weight.

### 7.3.2 Optimality of the Simplex algorithm

The proof of optimality involves three interrelated theorems. Theorem 7.3–1 proves that the LP solution space forms a convex set (with a finite number of extreme points). Theorem 7.3–2 proves that the optimal LP solution in the simplex method is always associated with a feasible extreme point of the solution space. Finally, Theorem 7.3–3 provides the link between the (geometric) extreme points and the (algebraic) basic solutions by proving that all the extreme points of the solution space are identified by the basic solutions of the (standard) LP equations. The conclusion is that the optimal solution of the (standard) LP problem is associated with a basic (feasible) solution of the constraint equations.

For the purpose of the presentation, we define

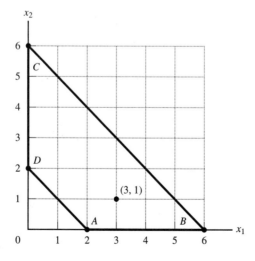

**Figure 7–3**

$$Q = \{\mathbf{X} \,|\, (\mathbf{A}, \mathbf{I})\mathbf{X} = \mathbf{b}, \mathbf{X} \geq \mathbf{0}\}$$

as the set of all feasible solutions of the linear program. It is assumed that the linear program has $m$ equations and $n$ unknowns.

**Theorem 7.3–1.**    *The set Q of all feasible solutions is convex.*

*Proof.* Define $\mathbf{X}^*$ as the convex combination of two distinct points, $\mathbf{X}'$ and $\mathbf{X}''$, in $Q$— that is,

$$\mathbf{X}^* = \lambda\mathbf{X}' + (1 - \lambda)\mathbf{X}'', \quad 0 \leq \lambda \leq 1$$

Then, $Q$ is convex if, and only if, $\mathbf{X}^*$ also lies in $Q$. To show that this is true, we note that $\mathbf{X}^* \geq \mathbf{0}$ by definition and that

$$\begin{aligned}
(\mathbf{A}, \mathbf{I})\mathbf{X}^* &= (\mathbf{A}, \mathbf{I})[\lambda\mathbf{X}' + (1 - \lambda)\mathbf{X}''] \\
&= \lambda(\mathbf{A}, \mathbf{I})\mathbf{X}' + (1 - \lambda)(\mathbf{A}, \mathbf{I})\mathbf{X}'' \\
&= \lambda\mathbf{b} + (1\lambda)\mathbf{b} \\
&= \mathbf{b}
\end{aligned}$$

**Theorem 7.3–2.**    *The optimum solution to the linear programming problem*

$$\textit{Maximize } z = \mathbf{CX}, \textit{ subject to } (\mathbf{A}, \mathbf{I})\,\mathbf{X} = \mathbf{b}, \ \mathbf{X} \geq \mathbf{0}$$

*when finite, must occur at an extreme of its feasible space Q.*

*Proof.* We can always assume that the set $Q$ is bounded by augmenting, when necessary, the redundant constraint $x_j \leq M$ (where $M$ is sufficiently large) for all $x_j$ that are unbounded. In this case, any feasible point in $Q$ can be expressed as a convex combination of the extreme points, $\mathbf{X}^{(k)}, k = 1, 2, \ldots, K$, of the solution space. Define $\mathbf{X}^*$ as the extreme point with the maximum objective value among all the extreme points of $Q$—that is,

$$z^* = \mathbf{CX}^* = \max_i \{\mathbf{CX}^{(i)}\}$$

We show that any nonextreme point, $\mathbf{X}'$, in the solution space $Q$ cannot yield a better objective value than $z^*$.

Because $\mathbf{X}'$ is not an extreme point, we can express it as a convex combination of the extreme points of $Q$—that is,

$$\mathbf{X}' = \sum_{k=1}^{K} \lambda_k\mathbf{X}^{(k)}, \quad \lambda_k \geq 0, \quad \sum_{k=1}^{K} \lambda_k = 1$$

Thus,

$$z' = \mathbf{CX}' = \mathbf{C}\left(\sum_{k=1}^{K} \lambda_k\mathbf{X}^{(k)}\right) = \sum_{k=1}^{K} \lambda_k(\mathbf{CX}^{(k)}) \leq \mathbf{CX}^* = z^*$$

which completes the proof.

Theorem 7.3.2 proves that the optimum LP solution is determined by concentrating solely on the extreme points of the solution space. The essence of the theorem is that the infinite feasible points in the solution space are now replaced with a finite number of candidates for the optimum—namely, the extreme points.

**Theorem 7.3–3.**    *A necessary and sufficient for a point* $X$ *to be an extreme point of the solution space* Q *is that* $X$ *be a basic (feasible) solution satisfying* $(A, I)X = b$ *and* $X \geq 0$.

*Proof.* The proof is based on contradiction (see Bazaraa et al [1990], pp. 89–91, for details).

**Problem set 7.3c**

1. Consider the following equations in vector form:

$$\begin{bmatrix} 2 \\ 1 \end{bmatrix} x_1 + \begin{bmatrix} 1 \\ 2 \end{bmatrix} x_2 + \begin{bmatrix} 1 \\ 1 \end{bmatrix} x_3 + \begin{bmatrix} 2 \\ -1 \end{bmatrix} x_4 + \begin{bmatrix} 4 \\ 2 \end{bmatrix} x_5 = \begin{bmatrix} 2 \\ 2 \end{bmatrix}$$

   The column vectors represent $P_1$ to $P_5$, and $b$, respectively.
   **(a)** Plot the vectors of the problem.
   **(b)** How many *distinct* extreme points are associated with the bases $(P_1, P_3)$, $(P_2, P_3)$, $(P_3, P_4)$, and $(P_3, P_5)$? Explain the significance of the result.
   **(c)** Suppose that all the variables are nonnegative. Can the vector combination $(P_1, P_4)$ form a *feasible* basis?

2. Consider the following systems of linear equations in which all $x_j \geq 0$.
   **(a)**
   $$2x_1 + 3x_2 + x_3 \qquad = 6$$
   $$x_1 + 2x_2 + \qquad + x_4 = 4$$
   **(b)**
   $$3x_1 + 6x_2 + 5x_3 + x_4 \qquad = 12$$
   $$2x_1 + 2x_2 + x_3 \qquad + 2x_5 = 8$$

   For each case, determine all the feasible extreme points by evaluating its basic feasible solutions. What is the relationship between the number of extreme points and the number of basic solutions?

3. Consider an LP in which the variable $x_k$ is unrestricted in sign. Prove that by substituting $x_k = x_k^+ - x_k^-$, where $x_k^+$ and $x_k^-$ are nonnegative, it is impossible in any simplex iteration for both $x_k^+$ and $x_k^-$ to assume positive values simultaneously.

4. Prove that the optimum solution of the LP

   Minimize $z = CX$,   subject to $(A, I)X = b$, $X \geq 0$

   when finite, occurs at an extreme point of the solution space.

**5.** In Problem 4, prove that if the optimum solution occurs at more than one extreme point, then the value of the objective function will remain the same at all the convex combinations of these extreme points.

## 7.4 GENERALIZED SIMPLEX TABLEAU IN MATRIX FORM

In Section 7.3, we proved that the optimum LP solution, when finite, is associated with an extreme point of the solution space. We also proved that all the extreme points are totally defined algebraically by the basic solutions of the system $(\mathbf{A}, \mathbf{I})\mathbf{X} = \mathbf{b}, \mathbf{X} \geq \mathbf{0}$. Thus, the optimum LP solution can be determined by concentrating solely on the basic solutions of the problem.

In the simplex method, we start with a feasible basis, **B,** and then move to a new feasible basis, $\mathbf{B}_{\text{next}}$, that produces a better (or, at least, no worse) value of the objective function, until we eventually reach the optimum solution. Thus, the basis **B** is the principal element that drives the computations in the simplex method. This point is demonstrated by developing a general simplex tableau in matrix form.

In the standard LP problem

$$\text{Maximize } z = \mathbf{CX}, \text{ subject to } (\mathbf{A}, \mathbf{I})\mathbf{X} = \mathbf{b}, \mathbf{X} \geq \mathbf{0}$$

we partition the vector **X** into $\mathbf{X}_{\text{I}}$ and $\mathbf{X}_{\text{II}}$ such that $\mathbf{X}_{\text{II}}$ corresponds to the starting basis $\mathbf{B} = \mathbf{I}$—that is, $\mathbf{X}_{\text{II}}$ is the *starting* basic feasible solution of the problem. The vector **C** is also partitioned to $\mathbf{C}_{\text{I}}$ and $\mathbf{C}_{\text{II}}$ corresponding to $\mathbf{X}_{\text{I}}$ and $\mathbf{X}_{\text{II}}$, respectively. The standard LP problem is thus written as

$$\begin{bmatrix} 1 & -\mathbf{C}_{\text{I}} & -\mathbf{C}_{\text{II}} \\ 0 & \mathbf{A} & \mathbf{I} \end{bmatrix} \begin{bmatrix} z \\ \mathbf{X}_{\text{I}} \\ \mathbf{X}_{\text{II}} \end{bmatrix} = \begin{bmatrix} 0 \\ \mathbf{b} \end{bmatrix}$$

At any simplex iteration, let $\mathbf{X}_B$ be the basic vector and define $\mathbf{C}_B$ as its associated objective function coefficients. Because all the nonbasic variables are zero, the standard LP reduces to $\mathbf{B}\mathbf{X}_B = \mathbf{b}$ and $z = \mathbf{C}_B\mathbf{X}_B$, and the current solution is

$$\begin{bmatrix} z \\ \mathbf{X}_B \end{bmatrix} = \begin{bmatrix} 1 & -\mathbf{C}_B \\ 0 & \mathbf{B} \end{bmatrix}^{-1} \begin{bmatrix} 0 \\ \mathbf{b} \end{bmatrix} = \begin{bmatrix} 1 & \mathbf{C}_B\mathbf{B}^{-1} \\ 0 & \mathbf{B}^{-1} \end{bmatrix} \begin{bmatrix} 0 \\ \mathbf{b} \end{bmatrix} = \begin{bmatrix} \mathbf{C}_B\mathbf{B}^{-1}b \\ \mathbf{B}^{-1}\mathbf{b} \end{bmatrix}$$

The method for inverting the partitioned matrix is in Section A.2.7.

The general simplex tableau is derived by premultiplying the original standard LP equations as follows:

$$\begin{bmatrix} 1 & \mathbf{C}_B\mathbf{B}^{-1} \\ 0 & \mathbf{B}^{-1} \end{bmatrix} \begin{bmatrix} 1 & -\mathbf{C}_{\text{I}} & -\mathbf{C}_{\text{II}} \\ 0 & \mathbf{A} & \mathbf{I} \end{bmatrix} \begin{bmatrix} z \\ \mathbf{X}_{\text{I}} \\ \mathbf{X}_{\text{II}} \end{bmatrix} = \begin{bmatrix} 1 & \mathbf{C}_B\mathbf{B}^{-1} \\ 0 & \mathbf{B}^{-1} \end{bmatrix} \begin{bmatrix} 0 \\ \mathbf{b} \end{bmatrix}$$

Carrying out the matrix manipulations, we obtain the general simplex tableau as

| Basic | $X_I$ | $X_{II}$ | Solution |
|-------|-------|----------|----------|
| $z$ | $C_B B^{-1} A - C_I$ | $C_B B^{-1} - C_{II}$ | $C_B B^{-1} b$ |
| $X_B$ | $B^{-1} A$ | $B^{-1}$ | $B^{-1} b$ |

The entire tableau is readily computed once the current basis $\mathbf{B}$ (and hence its inverse $\mathbf{B^{-1}}$) is known because the remaining elements of the tableau, $\mathbf{C}_B$, $\mathbf{C}_I$, $\mathbf{C}_{II}$, $\mathbf{A}$, and $\mathbf{b}$, are all obtained from the original data of the problem.

The preceding tableau is important because it provides the foundation for all the computational algorithms in linear programming. In particular, the development of the algorithms of the revised simplex, bounded variables, and decomposition is based on this tableau (see Section 7.5).

In the simplex method, the solution moves from one basis $\mathbf{B}$ to the next basis $\mathbf{B}_{next}$ by replacing a current *basic* vector in $\mathbf{B}$ (the *leaving vector*) with a *nonbasic* vector (the *entering vector*). The determination of the entering and leaving vectors is based on the following optimality and the feasibility conditions.

***Simplex optimality condition.*** From the general matrix tableau, the $z$-equation coefficient associated with the variable $x_j$ is

$$z_j - c_j = \mathbf{C}_B \mathbf{B}^{-1} \mathbf{P}_j - c_j$$

where $\mathbf{P}_j$ is the $j$th vector of $(\mathbf{A}, \mathbf{I})$ and $c_j$ is the $j$th element of $\mathbf{C}$. Noting that $(z_j - c_j)$ is always zero for all *basic* $x_j$ (see Problem 7.4a–8) and defining $NB$ as the set of indices for the nonbasic variables, we can write the objective equation as

$$z + \sum_{j \epsilon NB} (z_j - c_j)x_j = \mathbf{C}_B \mathbf{B}^{-1} \mathbf{b}$$

From the $z$-equation, an increase in the value of a nonbasic $x_j$ above zero will increase (decrease) the value of $z$ above its current level $\mathbf{C}_B \mathbf{B}^{-1} \mathbf{b}$ only if its current $z_j - c_j$ is strictly negative (positive). Otherwise, $x_j$ will not improve the current solution and must remain nonbasic at zero level. (See Problem 7.4a–9 for a related interpretation of $z_j - c_j$.)

***Simplex feasibility condition.*** The determination of the leaving vector is based on examining the constraint equation associated with the ith *basic* variable. Consider

$$(\mathbf{X}_B)_i + \sum_{j \epsilon NB} (\mathbf{B}^{-1} \mathbf{P}_j)_i x_j = (\mathbf{B}^{-1} \mathbf{b})_i$$

The notation $(\mathbf{V})_i$ is used to represent the ith element of the column vector $\mathbf{V}$.

Given $\mathbf{P}_k$ is the entering vector (as specified by the optimality condition), the entering variable, $x_k$, will increase above zero level. Because all the remaining nonbasic variables are zero, the constraint equation associated with basic $(\mathbf{X}_B)_i$ can be written as

$$(\mathbf{X}_B)_i = (\mathbf{B}^{-1}\mathbf{b})_i - (\mathbf{B}^{-1}\mathbf{P}_k)_i x_k$$

The equation shows that if $(\mathbf{B}^{-1}\mathbf{P}_k)_i > 0$, an increase in $x_k$ will not cause $(\mathbf{X}_B)_i$ to become negative if

$$(\mathbf{B}^{-1}\mathbf{b})_i - (\mathbf{B}^{-1}\mathbf{P}_k)_i x_k \geq 0, \text{ for all } i$$

Thus, the maximum value of the entering variable $x_k$ is computed as

$$x_k = \min_i \left\{ \frac{(\mathbf{B}^{-1}\mathbf{b})_i}{(\mathbf{B}^{-1}\mathbf{P}_k)_i} \, \middle| \, (\mathbf{B}^{-1}\mathbf{P}_k)_i > 0 \right\}$$

The basic variable responsible for producing the minimum ratio becomes the leaving variable.

---

**Example 7.4–1.**

Consider the following LP:

$$\text{Maximize } z = x_1 + 4x_2 + 7x_3 + 5x_4$$

subject to

$$2x_1 + x_2 + 2x_3 + 4x_4 = 10$$
$$3x_1 - x_2 - 2x_3 + 6x_4 = 5$$
$$x_1, x_2, x_3, x_4 \geq 0$$

Suppose that we are given the information that $\mathbf{B} = (\mathbf{P}_1, \mathbf{P}_2)$ forms a feasible basis.

**(a)** Show that $\mathbf{B}$ is not optimal.

**(b)** Determine the entering and leaving vectors and $\mathbf{B}_{\text{next}}$.

Given $\mathbf{B} = (\mathbf{P}_1, \mathbf{P}_2)$, then we have $\mathbf{X}_B = (x_1, x_2)^T$ and $\mathbf{C}_B = (1, 4)$. The inverse $\mathbf{B}^{-1}$ is computed as

$$\mathbf{B}^{-1} = \begin{bmatrix} 2 & 1 \\ 3 & -1 \end{bmatrix}^{-1} = \begin{bmatrix} \frac{1}{5} & \frac{1}{5} \\ \frac{3}{5} & -\frac{2}{5} \end{bmatrix}$$

Thus, the current basic solution is

$$\mathbf{X}_B = \begin{bmatrix} x_1 \\ x_2 \end{bmatrix} = \mathbf{B}^{-1}\mathbf{b} = \begin{bmatrix} \frac{1}{5} & \frac{1}{5} \\ \frac{3}{5} & -\frac{2}{5} \end{bmatrix} \begin{bmatrix} 10 \\ 5 \end{bmatrix} = \begin{bmatrix} 3 \\ 4 \end{bmatrix}$$

which yields $z = \mathbf{C}_B\mathbf{X}_B = 1 \times 3 + 4 \times 4 = 19$.

We check the optimality of the basis $\mathbf{B} = (\mathbf{P}_1, \mathbf{P}_2)$ by computing $z_j - c_j$ for the current nonbasic variables, $x_3$ and $x_4$—that is,

$$(z_3 - c_3, z_4 - c_4) = \mathbf{C}_B \mathbf{B}^{-1}[\mathbf{P}_3, \mathbf{P}_4] - (c_3, c_4)$$

$$= (1, 4) \begin{bmatrix} \dfrac{1}{5} & \dfrac{1}{5} \\ \dfrac{3}{5} & -\dfrac{2}{5} \end{bmatrix} \begin{bmatrix} 2 & 4 \\ -2 & 6 \end{bmatrix} - (7, 5) = (1, -3)$$

Because the LP is of the maximization type, $z_4 - c_4 = -3$ shows that $\mathbf{X}_B = (x_1, x_2)^T$ is not optimal and that the value of $z$ can be improved by allowing $x_4$ to enter the basic solution.

Given the entering variable $x_4$, either $x_1$ or $x_2$ must leave $\mathbf{X}_B$ (or, equivalently, either $\mathbf{P}_1$ or $\mathbf{P}_2$ must leave the basis $\mathbf{B}$). To determine the leaving variable, we compute

$$\begin{bmatrix} x_1 \\ x_2 \end{bmatrix} = \mathbf{B}^{-1}\mathbf{b} = \begin{bmatrix} 3 \\ 4 \end{bmatrix}, \quad \text{and } \mathbf{B}^{-1}\mathbf{P}_4 = \begin{bmatrix} 2 \\ 0 \end{bmatrix}$$

Because $\mathbf{B}^{-1}\mathbf{P}_4$ has only one *strictly positive* element ($=2$), the value of the entering variable $x_4$ is computed as

$$x_4 = \min_{i=1,2} \left\{ \frac{3}{2}, - \right\} = \frac{3}{2}$$

Thus, $\mathbf{P}_1$ leaves the basis $\mathbf{B}$ and is replaced by $\mathbf{P}_4$ to give

$$\mathbf{B}_{\text{next}} = (\mathbf{P}_4, \mathbf{P}_2) = \begin{bmatrix} 4 & 1 \\ 6 & -1 \end{bmatrix}$$

The corresponding new value of $z$ is $19 - (z_4 - c_4)x_4 = 19 - (-3) \times (\frac{3}{2}) = 23.5$.

## Problem set 7.4a

1. Consider the following LP:

$$\text{Maximize } z = 5x_1 + 12x_2 + 4x_3$$

subject to

$$x_1 + 2x_2 + x_3 + x_4 = 10$$
$$2x_1 - 2x_2 - x_3 \quad\;\; = 2$$
$$x_1, x_2, x_3, x_4 \geq 0$$

Check if each of the following vector sets forms a basis: $(\mathbf{P}_1, \mathbf{P}_2)$, $(\mathbf{P}_2, \mathbf{P}_3)$, $(\mathbf{P}_3, \mathbf{P}_4)$.

2. Complete the computations in Example 7.4–1 until optimality is achieved, and find the optimal solution.

3. In Example 7.4–1, can we start the simplex computations with $\mathbf{B} = (\mathbf{P}_2, \mathbf{P}_3)$? Explain.

4. Consider the following LP:

$$\text{Maximize } z = 4x_1 + 14x_2 - 2x_3$$

subject to

$$2x_1 + 7x_2 + x_3 \qquad\quad = 21$$

$$7x_1 + 2x_2 \qquad + x_4 = 21$$

$$x_1, x_2, x_3, x_4 \geq 0$$

Use matrix operations to check the feasibility and optimality of each of the following sets of basic variables:

   **(a)** $(x_2, x_4)$     **(b)** $(x_2, x_3)$     **(c)** $(x_2, x_1)$     **(d)** $(x_1, x_4)$

5. Consider the following LP:

$$\text{Minimize } z = 2x_1 + x_2$$

subject to

$$3x_1 + x_2 - x_3 \qquad\qquad = 3$$

$$4x_1 + 3x_2 \qquad - x_4 \qquad = 6$$

$$x_1 + 2x_2 \qquad\qquad + x_5 = 3$$

$$x_1, x_2, x_3, x_4, x_5 \geq 0$$

Compute the entire simplex tableau associated with $\mathbf{X}_B = (x_1, x_2, x_5)^T$ and determine if it is feasible and optimal.

6. The following is the optimal tableau of an LP.

| Basic | $x_1$ | $x_2$ | $x_3$ | $x_4$ | $x_5$ | Solution |
|-------|-------|-------|-------|-------|-------|----------|
| $z$   | 0     | 0     | 0     | 3     | 2     | ?        |
| $x_3$ | 0     | 0     | 1     | 1     | $-1$  | 2        |
| $x_2$ | 0     | 1     | 0     | 1     | 0     | 6        |
| $x_1$ | 1     | 0     | 0     | $-1$  | 1     | 2        |

The variables $x_3$, $x_4$, and $x_5$ are slacks in the original problem. Use matrix manipulation to reconstruct the original LP, and then compute the optimum value of the objective function in two different ways.

7. Consider the following LP:

$$\text{Maximize } z = c_1x_1 + c_2x_2 + c_3x_3 + c_4x_4$$

subject to

$$\mathbf{P}_1x_1 + \mathbf{P}_2x_2 + \mathbf{P}_3x_3 + \mathbf{P}_4x_4 = \mathbf{b}$$

$$x_1, x_2, x_3, x_4 \geq 0$$

The vectors $\mathbf{P}_1, \mathbf{P}_2, \mathbf{P}_3$, and $\mathbf{P}_4$ are shown in Figure 7–4. Assume that the current basis is $\mathbf{B} = (\mathbf{P}_1, \mathbf{P}_2)$.

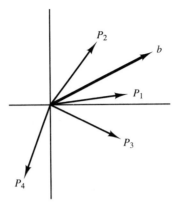

**Figure 7–4**

(a) If $\mathbf{P}_3$ enters the basis, which current basic vector must leave in order for the resulting basic solution to be feasible.

(b) Can $\mathbf{P}_4$ be part of a feasible basis?

8. Prove that, in any simplex iteration, $z_j - c_j = 0$, for all the associated *basic* variables.

9. Prove that if $z_j - c_j > 0$ ($< 0$) for all the nonbasic variables $x_j$ of a maximization (minimization) LP, then the optimum is unique. Otherwise, if $z_j - c_j = 0$ for a nonbasic $x_j$, then the problem has an alternative optimum.

10. In an all-slack starting basic solution, show using the matrix form of the tableau that the mechanical procedure used in Section 3.3 in which the objective equation is set as

$$z - \sum_{j=1}^{n} c_j x_j = 0$$

automatically computes the proper $z_j - c_j$ for all the variables in the starting tableau.

11. Using the matrix form of the simplex tableau, show that in an all-artificial starting basic solution, the procedure employed in Section 3.4.1 to substitute out the artificial variables in the objective function (using the constraint equations) actually computes the proper $z_j - c_j$ for all the variables in the starting tableau.

12. Consider an LP in which the variable $x_k$ is unrestricted in sign. Prove that by substituting $x_k = x_k^+ - x_k^-$, where $x_k^+$ and $x_k^-$ are nonnegative, it is impossible that $x_k^+$ and $x_k^-$ replace one another in an alternative optimum solution.

13. Given the LP in standard form with $m$ equations and $n$ unknowns, determine the number of *adjacent* extreme points that can be reached from a nondegenerate extreme point of the solution space. Why is nondegeneracy an issue in this case?

14. In applying the feasibility condition of the simplex method, suppose that $x_r = 0$ is a basic variable and that $x_j$ is the entering variable. Why is it necessary for $x_r$ to have

$(\mathbf{B}^{-1}\mathbf{P}_j)_r > 0$ to leave the solution? What is the problem if $(\mathbf{B}^{-1}\mathbf{P}_j)_r \leq 0$? (*Hint:* The answer is explained using the fact that basic $x_r$ must remain nonnegative.)

**15.** In the implementation of the feasibility condition of the simplex method, what are the conditions for encountering a degenerate solution for the first time? For continuing to obtain a degenerate solution in the next iteration? For removing degeneracy in the next iteration? Explain the answer mathematically.

**16.** What are the relationships between extreme points and basic solutions under degeneracy and nondegeneracy. What is the maximum number of iterations that can be performed at a given extreme point assuming no cycling?

**17.** Consider the LP, maximize $z = \mathbf{CX}$ subject to $\mathbf{AX} \leq \mathbf{b}$, $\mathbf{X} \geq \mathbf{0}$, where $\mathbf{b} \geq \mathbf{0}$. Suppose that the entering vector $\mathbf{P}_j$ is such that at least one element of $\mathbf{B}^{-1}\mathbf{P}_j$ is positive.
  **(a)** If $\mathbf{P}_j$ is replaced with $\beta\mathbf{P}_j$, where $\beta$ is a positive scalar, and provided $x_j$ remains the entering variable, find the relationship between the values of $x_j$ corresponding to $\mathbf{P}_j$ and $\beta\mathbf{P}_j$.
  **(b)** Answer part (a) if, additionally, $\mathbf{b}$ is replaced with $\alpha\mathbf{b}$, where $\alpha$ is a positive scalar.

**18.** Consider the LP, maximize $z = \mathbf{CX}$ subject to $\mathbf{AX} \leq \mathbf{b}$, $\mathbf{X} \geq \mathbf{0}$, where $\mathbf{b} \geq \mathbf{0}$. After obtaining the optimum solution, it is suggested that a nonbasic variable $x_j$ can be made basic (profitable) by reducing the resources requirements per unit of $x_j$ to $1/\beta$ of their original values, where $\beta$ is a scalar greater than 1. Because the requirements per unit are reduced, it is expected that the profit per unit of $x_j$ will also be reduced to $1/\beta$ of its original value. Will these changes make $x_j$ a profitable variable? What should be recommended for $x_j$ to be profitable?

**19.** Consider the LP, maximize $z = \mathbf{CX}$ subject to $(\mathbf{A}, \mathbf{I})\mathbf{X} = \mathbf{b}$, $\mathbf{X} \geq \mathbf{0}$. Define $x_B$ as the current basic vector, with $\mathbf{B}$ as its associated basis and $\mathbf{C}_B$ as its vector of objective coefficients. Show that if $\mathbf{C}_B$ is replaced with the new coefficients $\mathbf{D}_B$, the values of $z_j - c_j$ for the basic vector $\mathbf{X}_B$ will remain equal to zero. What is the significance of this result?

## 7.5 EFFICIENT COMPUTATIONAL ALGORITHMS

This section presents variations of the simplex method that include the **revised simplex algorithm,** the **bounded variables algorithm,** and the **decomposition algorithm.** These algorithms are primarily designed to enhance the computational efficiency of simplex method.

### 7.5.1 Revised Simplex Method

The revised simplex algorithm is based *exactly on the same steps* used in the tableau simplex method of Chapter 3. The only difference is that in chapter 3, the next iteration is computed by row operations. In the revised method, the crux of the computations is rooted in the basis $\mathbf{B}$ and its inverse $\mathbf{B}^{-1}$.

The sample iteration in Example 7.4–1 is typical of the computations in the revised method. The only additional detail deals with the determination of $\mathbf{B}^{-1}$ at each iteration. Instead of inverting $\mathbf{B}$ directly using one of the methods in Section A.7.4, the revised method uses the convenient **product form** method. We first show how the product form method works and then present the details of the revised simplex algorithm.

**Product form of the inverse.**　　In the simplex method, the successive bases, $\mathbf{B}$ and $\mathbf{B}_{next}$, differ only in one column vector, resulting from interchanging the entering and the leaving vectors. This situation is ideal for the application of the product form of inversion.

Given $\mathbf{B}^{-1}$, we can compute $\mathbf{B}^{-1}_{next}$ using the formula

$$\mathbf{B}^{-1}_{next} = \mathbf{E}\mathbf{B}^{-1}$$

To compute the matrix $\mathbf{E}$, let $\mathbf{P}_j$ and $\mathbf{P}_r$ be the entering and the leaving vectors in the current simplex iteration. Then $\mathbf{E}$ is defined as an $m$-identity matrix whose $r$th column is replaced by

$$\xi = \frac{1}{(\mathbf{B}^{-1}\mathbf{P}_j)_r} \begin{bmatrix} -(\mathbf{B}^{-1}\mathbf{P}_j)_1 \\ -(\mathbf{B}^{-1}\mathbf{P}_j)_2 \\ \vdots \\ +1 \\ \vdots \\ -(\mathbf{B}^{-1}\mathbf{P}_j)_m \end{bmatrix} \leftarrow r\text{th place}$$

provided that $(\mathbf{B}^{-1}\mathbf{P}_j)_r \neq 0$. If $(\mathbf{B}^{-1}\mathbf{P}_j)_r = 0$, then $\mathbf{B}^{-1}_{next}$ does not exist.

The validity of the formula $\mathbf{B}^{-1}_{next}$ is proved as follows. Define $\mathbf{F}$ as an $m$-identify matrix whose $r$th column is replaced by $\mathbf{B}^{-1}\mathbf{P}_j$—that is,

$$\mathbf{F} = (\mathbf{e}_1, \mathbf{e}_{r-1}, \mathbf{B}^{-1}\mathbf{P}_j, \mathbf{e}_{r+1}, \dots, \mathbf{e}_m)$$

Because $\mathbf{B}_{next}$ differs from $\mathbf{B}$ only in that its $r$th column is replaced with $\mathbf{P}_j$, then

$$\mathbf{B}_{next} = \mathbf{B}\mathbf{F}$$

Thus,

$$\mathbf{B}^{-1}_{next} = (\mathbf{B}\mathbf{F})^{-1} = \mathbf{F}^{-1}\mathbf{B}^{-1}$$

The formula follows by setting $\mathbf{E} = \mathbf{F}^{-1}$.

---

**Example 7.5–1.**

We are given the information

$$\mathbf{B} = \begin{bmatrix} 2 & 1 & 0 \\ 0 & 2 & 0 \\ 4 & 0 & 1 \end{bmatrix}, \quad \mathbf{B}^{-1} = \begin{bmatrix} \frac{1}{2} & -\frac{1}{4} & 0 \\ 0 & \frac{1}{2} & 0 \\ -2 & 1 & 1 \end{bmatrix}$$

Suppose that a new matrix $\mathbf{B}_{next}$ is obtained from $\mathbf{B}$ by replacing its third column vector $\mathbf{P}_3 = (0, 0, 1)^T$ with $\mathbf{V}_3 = (2, 1, 5)^T$. Determine $\mathbf{B}_{next}^{-1}$.

Because we are replacing the *third* column of $\mathbf{B}$, it follows that $r = 3$. From

$$\mathbf{B}^{-1}\mathbf{V}_3 = \begin{bmatrix} \frac{1}{2} & -\frac{1}{4} & 0 \\ 0 & \frac{1}{2} & 0 \\ -2 & 1 & 1 \end{bmatrix} \begin{bmatrix} 2 \\ 1 \\ 5 \end{bmatrix} = \begin{bmatrix} \frac{3}{4} \\ \frac{1}{2} \\ 2 \end{bmatrix} \leftarrow r = 3$$

we get

$$\xi = \frac{1}{2} \begin{bmatrix} -\frac{3}{4} \\ -\frac{1}{2} \\ +1 \end{bmatrix} = \begin{bmatrix} -\frac{3}{8} \\ -\frac{1}{4} \\ \frac{1}{2} \end{bmatrix}$$

Thus,

$$\mathbf{B}_{next}^{-1} = \begin{bmatrix} 1 & 0 & -\frac{3}{8} \\ 0 & 1 & -\frac{1}{4} \\ 0 & 0 & \frac{1}{2} \end{bmatrix} \begin{bmatrix} \frac{1}{2} & -\frac{1}{4} & 0 \\ 0 & \frac{1}{2} & 0 \\ -2 & 1 & 1 \end{bmatrix} = \begin{bmatrix} \frac{5}{4} & -\frac{5}{8} & -\frac{3}{8} \\ \frac{1}{2} & \frac{1}{4} & -\frac{1}{4} \\ -1 & \frac{1}{2} & \frac{1}{2} \end{bmatrix}$$

---

### Problem set 7.5a

**1.** In Example 7.5–1, suppose that, in addition to the given change in $\mathbf{P}_3$, the second vector $\mathbf{P}_2$ is changed to $\mathbf{V}_2 = (1, 1, 1)^T$. Find the corresponding inverse.

**2.** Consider the matrix $\mathbf{B}$ in Example 7.5–1. Suppose that the third vector $\mathbf{P}_3$ is replaced with the $\mathbf{V}_3 = \mathbf{P}_1 + 2\mathbf{P}_2$. This means that the resulting matrix is singular. Show how the product form of the inverse discovers the singularity of the matrix.

**3.** Use the product form of the inverse to verify whether each of the following equations has a unique solution, no solution, or infinity of solutions.

(a)  $x_1 + 2x_2 = 3$

$\quad\ \ x_1 + 4x_2 = 2$

(b)  $x_1 + 2x_2 = 5$

$\quad -x_1 - 2x_2 = -5$

$$
\begin{aligned}
\textbf{(c)} \quad x_1 + \phantom{x_2} + 1x_3 &= 5 \\
4x_1 + x_2 + 3x_3 &= 8 \\
x_1 + 3x_2 - 2x_3 &= 3
\end{aligned}
$$

**Revised simplex computations.**   The product form of the inverse is used in the revised simplex method in the following manner. Because the starting basis is always an identity matrix $\mathbf{I}$ (whose inverse is itself), $\mathbf{B}_i^{-1}$ associated with iteration $i$ can be determined as

$$
\mathbf{B}_i^{-1} = \mathbf{E}_i \mathbf{E}_{i-1} \dots \mathbf{E}_1 \mathbf{I}
$$

In this regard, it is never necessary to invert any raw data basis directly.

The steps of the revised simplex algorithm are essentially those of the tableau simplex method. The easiest way to verify this point is to summarize the revised method computations using the familiar simplex tableau format—that is,

| Basic | $x_1$ | $x_2$ | $\cdots$ | $x_j$ | $\cdots$ | $x_n$ | Solution |
|-------|-------|-------|----------|-------|----------|-------|----------|
| $z$ | $z_1 - c_1$ | $z_2 - c_2$ | $\cdots$ | $z_j - c_j$ | $\cdots$ | $z_n - c_n$ | $\mathbf{C}_B \mathbf{B}^{-1}$ |
| $\mathbf{X}_B$ | | | | $\mathbf{B}^{-1} \mathbf{P}_j$ | | | $\mathbf{B}^{-1} \mathbf{b}$ |

where

$$
z_j - C_j = \mathbf{C}_B \mathbf{B}^{-1} \mathbf{P}_j - c_j
$$

**Example 7.5–2.**

The Reddy Mikks model (Section 2.1) is resolved by the revised simplex algorithm. The same model was solved by the tableau method in Section 3.3. A comparison between the computations will show that the two methods are one and the same.

The standard form of the Reddy Mikks model can be expressed in matrix form as

$$
\text{Maximize } z = (5, 4, 0, 0, 0, 0)(x_1, x_2, x_3, x_4, x_5, x_6)^T
$$

subject to

$$
\begin{bmatrix}
6 & 4 & 1 & 0 & 0 & 0 \\
1 & 2 & 0 & 1 & 0 & 0 \\
-1 & 1 & 0 & 0 & 1 & 0 \\
0 & 1 & 0 & 0 & 0 & 1
\end{bmatrix}
\begin{bmatrix}
x_1 \\ x_2 \\ x_3 \\ x_4 \\ x_5 \\ x_6
\end{bmatrix}
=
\begin{bmatrix}
24 \\ 6 \\ 1 \\ 2
\end{bmatrix}
$$

$$
x_1, x_2, \dots, x_6 \geq 0
$$

we use the notation $(c_1, c_2, \dots, c_6)$ to represent the objective function coefficients and $(\mathbf{P}_1, \mathbf{P}_2, \dots, \mathbf{P}_6)$ to represent the columns of $(\mathbf{A}, \mathbf{I})$ of the constraint equations. The right-hand side of the constraints is represented by the vector $\mathbf{b}$.

In the following computations, we will give the algebraic formula for each step and its final numeric answer without detailing the arithmetic operations. You will find it instructive to fill in the gaps in each step.

**Iteration 0**

$$\mathbf{X}_{B_0} = (x_3, x_4, x_5, x_6)^T, \mathbf{C}_{B_0} = (0, 0, 0, 0)$$

$$\mathbf{B}_0 = (\mathbf{P}_3, \mathbf{P}_4, \mathbf{P}_5, \mathbf{P}_6) = \mathbf{I}, \mathbf{B}_0^{-1} = \mathbf{I}$$

Thus,

$$\mathbf{X}_{B_0} = \mathbf{B}_0^{-1}\mathbf{b} = (24, 6, 1, 2)^T, z = \mathbf{C}_{B_0}\mathbf{X}_{B_0} = 0$$

*Optimality Computations*

$$\mathbf{C}_{B_0}\mathbf{B}_0^{-1} = (0, 0, 0, 0)$$

$$\{z_j - c_j\}_{j=1,2} = \mathbf{C}_{B_0}\mathbf{B}_0^{-1}(\mathbf{P}_1, \mathbf{P}_2) - (c_1, c_2) = (-\mathbf{5}, -\mathbf{4})$$

Thus, $\mathbf{P}_1$ is the entering vector.
*Feasibility computations*

$$\mathbf{X}_{B_0} = (x_3, x_4, x_5, x_6)^T = (24, 6, 1, 2)^T$$

$$\mathbf{B}_0^{-1}\mathbf{P}_1 = (6, 1, -1, 0)^T$$

Hence,

$$x_1 = \min\left\{\frac{24}{6}, \frac{6}{1}, -, -\right\} = \min\{\mathbf{4}, 6, -, -\} = 4$$

and $\mathbf{P}_3$ becomes the leaving vector.

The results above can be summarized in the familiar simplex tableau format. The presentation should help convince you that the two method are the same.

| Basic | $x_1$ | $x_2$ | $x_3$ | $x_3$ | $x_4$ | $x_5$ | $x_6$ | Solution |
|-------|-------|-------|-------|-------|-------|-------|-------|----------|
| $z$ | $-5$ | $-4$ | 0 | 0 | 0 | 0 | 0 | 0 |
| $x_3$ | 6 | | | | | | | 24 |
| $x_4$ | 1 | | | | | | | 6 |
| $x_5$ | $-1$ | | | | | | | 1 |
| $x_6$ | 0 | | | | | | | 2 |

**Iteration 1**

$$\mathbf{X}_{B_1} = (x_1, x_4, x_5, x_6)^T, \mathbf{C}_{B_1} = (5, 0, 0, 0)$$

$$\mathbf{B}_1 = (\mathbf{P}_1, \mathbf{P}_4, \mathbf{P}_5, \mathbf{P}_6)$$

To compute $\mathbf{B}_1^{-1}$, we note that $\mathbf{B}_0^{-1}\mathbf{P}_1 = (6, 1, -1, 0)^T$. Because the *first* column of $\mathbf{B}_0$ is being replaced, $r = 1$ in the formation of $\xi$, and we get

$$\mathbf{B}_1^{-1} = \mathbf{E}\mathbf{B}_0^{-1} = \mathbf{EI} = \mathbf{E} = \begin{bmatrix} \dfrac{1}{6} & 0 & 0 & 0 \\[2mm] -\dfrac{1}{6} & 1 & 0 & 0 \\[2mm] \dfrac{1}{6} & 0 & 1 & 0 \\[2mm] 0 & 0 & 0 & 1 \end{bmatrix}$$

Thus,

$$\mathbf{X}_{B_1} = \mathbf{B}_1^{-1}\mathbf{b} = (4, 2, 5, 2)^T, \quad z = \mathbf{C}_{B_1}\mathbf{X}_{B_1} = 20$$

*Optimality Computations*

$$\mathbf{C}_{B_1}\mathbf{B}_1^{-1} = \left(\frac{5}{6}, 0, 0, 0\right)$$

$$\{z_j - c_j\}_{j=2, 3} = \mathbf{C}_{B_1}\mathbf{B}_1^{-1}(\mathbf{P}_2, \mathbf{P}_3) - (c_2, c_3) = \left(-\frac{2}{3}, \frac{5}{6}\right)$$

Thus, $\mathbf{P}_2$ is the entering vector.
*Feasibility computations*

$$\mathbf{X}_{B_1} = (x_1, x_4, x_5, x_6)^T = (4, 2, 5, 2)^T$$

$$\mathbf{B}_1^{-1}\mathbf{P}_2 = \left(\frac{2}{3}, \frac{4}{3}, \frac{5}{3}, 1\right)^T$$

Hence,

$$x_2 = \min\left\{6, \frac{3}{2}, 3, 2\right\} = \frac{3}{2}$$

and $\mathbf{P}_4$ becomes the leaving vector. (You will find it helpful to summarize the results above in the simplex tableau format as we did in iteration 0.)
**Iteration 2**

$$\mathbf{X}_{B_2} = (x_1, x_2, x_5, x_6)^T, \quad \mathbf{C}_{B_2} = (5, 4, 0, 0)$$

$$\mathbf{B}_2 = (\mathbf{P}_1, \mathbf{P}_2, \mathbf{P}_5, \mathbf{P}_6)$$

To compute $\mathbf{B}_2^{-1}$, we have $\mathbf{B}_1^{-1}\mathbf{P}_2 = (\frac{2}{3}, \frac{4}{3}, \frac{5}{3}, 1)^T$ and $r = 2$. We thus get

$$\mathbf{B}_2^{-1} = \mathbf{E}\mathbf{B}_1^{-1} = \begin{bmatrix} 1 & -\dfrac{2}{4} & 0 & 0 \\[2mm] 0 & \dfrac{3}{4} & 0 & 0 \\[2mm] 0 & -\dfrac{5}{4} & 1 & 0 \\[2mm] 0 & -\dfrac{3}{4} & 0 & 1 \end{bmatrix} \begin{bmatrix} \dfrac{1}{6} & 0 & 0 & 0 \\[2mm] -\dfrac{1}{6} & 1 & 0 & 0 \\[2mm] \dfrac{1}{6} & 0 & 1 & 0 \\[2mm] 0 & 0 & 0 & 1 \end{bmatrix} = \begin{bmatrix} \dfrac{1}{4} & -\dfrac{1}{2} & 0 & 0 \\[2mm] -\dfrac{1}{8} & \dfrac{3}{4} & 0 & 0 \\[2mm] \dfrac{3}{8} & -\dfrac{5}{4} & 1 & 0 \\[2mm] \dfrac{1}{8} & -\dfrac{3}{4} & 0 & 1 \end{bmatrix}$$

Thus,

$$\mathbf{X}_{B_2} = \mathbf{B}_2^{-1}\mathbf{b} = \left(3, \frac{3}{2}, \frac{5}{2}, \frac{1}{2}\right)^T, \quad z = \mathbf{C}_{B_2}\mathbf{X}_{B_2} = 21$$

*Optimality computations*

$$\mathbf{C}_{B_2}\mathbf{B}_2^{-1} = \left(\frac{3}{4}, \frac{1}{2}, 0, 0\right)$$

$$\{z_j - c_j\}_{j=3,4} = \mathbf{C}_{B_2}\mathbf{B}_2^{-1}(\mathbf{P}_3, \mathbf{P}_4) - (c_3, c_4) = \left(\frac{3}{4}, \frac{1}{2}\right)$$

Thus, $\mathbf{X}_{B_2}$ is optimal, and the computations end.

*Summary of optimal solution*

$$x_1 = 3, x_2 = 1.5, z = 21$$

The computations in the revised method has two advantages.

**1.** The number of arithmetic operations in the revised method may be smaller than in the tableau method, depending on the size ($m \times n$) of the problem and the sparsity (fraction of nonzero coefficients) of its $\mathbf{C}$, $\mathbf{A}$ and $\mathbf{b}$.

**2.** Because the computations in the revised method are based on $\mathbf{B}^{-1}$ and the *original data,* machine roundoff error is controlled by controlling the accuracy of $\mathbf{B}^{-1}$. This is in contrast with the tableau simplex method, where there is a propagation of roundoff error.

### Problem set 7.5b

**1.** In Example 7.5–2, summarize the data of iterations 1 and 2 in the tableau format of Section 3.3.

**2.** Solve the following LPs by the revised simplex method:
    **(a)** Maximize $z = 6x_1 + 2x_2 + 3x_3$
        subject to

$$2x_1 - x_2 + 2x_3 \leq 2$$
$$x_1 \qquad\quad 4x_3 \leq 4$$
$$x_1, x_2, x_3 \geq 0$$

**(b)** Maximize $z = 2x_1 + x_2 + 2x_3$
        subject to

$$4x_1 + 3x_2 + 8x_3 \leq 12$$
$$4x_1 + x_2 + 12x_3 \leq 8$$
$$4x_1 - x_2 + 3x_3 \leq 8$$
$$x_1, x_2, x_3 \geq 0$$

**(c)** Minimize $z = 2x_1 + x_2$
        subject to

$$3x_1 + x_2 = 3$$
$$4x_1 + 3x_2 \geq 6$$
$$x_1 + 2x_2 \leq 3$$
$$x_1, x_2 \geq 0$$

**(d)** Minimize $z = 5x_1 - 4x_2 + 6x_3 + 8x_4$
subject to

$$x_1 + 7x_2 + 3x_3 + 7x_4 \leq 46$$
$$3x_1 - x_2 + x_3 + 2x_4 \leq 20$$
$$2x_1 + 3x_2 - x_3 + x_4 \geq 18$$
$$x_1, x_2, x_3, x_4 \geq 0$$

3. Solve the following LP by the revised simplex method using the starting basic feasible vector $\mathbf{X}_{B_0} = (x_2, x_4, x_5)$.

$$\text{Minimize } z = 7x_2 + 11x_3 - 10x_4 + 26x_6$$

subject to

$$x_2 - x_3 + x_5 + x_6 = 6$$
$$x_2 - x_3 + x_4 + 3x_6 = 8$$
$$x_1 + x_2 - 3x_3 + x_4 + x_5 = 12$$
$$x_1, x_2, x_3, x_4, x_5, x_6 \geq 0$$

(*Hint:* Use the product form of the inverse to determine $\mathbf{B}_0^{-1}$, and then proceed with the revised method computations.)

4. Solve the following using the two-phase revised simplex method:
   **(a)** Problem 2-c.
   **(b)** Problem 2-d.
   **(c)** Problem 3 (discard the given starting $\mathbf{X}_{B_0}$).

5. *Revised dual simplex method.* The steps of the revised dual simplex method (using matrix manipulations) can be summarized as follows:

   **Step 0.** Let $\mathbf{B}_0 = \mathbf{I}$ be the starting basis and that at least one of the elements of $\mathbf{X}_{B_0}$ is negative (infeasible).
   **Step 1.** Compute $\mathbf{X}_B = \mathbf{B}^{-1}\mathbf{b}$, the current values of the basic variables. Select the leaving variable $x_r$ as the one having the most negative value. If all the elements of $\mathbf{X}_B$ are nonnegative, stop; the current solution is feasible.
   **Step 2.**
   **(a)** Compute $z_j - c_j = \mathbf{C}_B\mathbf{B}^{-1}\mathbf{P}_j - c_j$ for all the nonbasic variables $x_j$.
   **(b)** For all the nonbasic variables $x_j$, compute the constraint coefficients $(\mathbf{B}^{-1}\mathbf{P}_j)_r$ associated with the row of the leaving variable $x_r$.
   **(c)** The entering variable is associated with

   $$\theta = \min_j \left\{ \left| \frac{z_j - c_j}{(\mathbf{B}^{-1}\mathbf{P}_j)_r} \right|, (\mathbf{B}^{-1}\mathbf{P}_j)_r < 0 \right\}$$

   If all $(\mathbf{B}^{-1}\mathbf{P}_j)_r \geq 0$, no feasible solution exists.

**Step 3**. Obtain the new basis by interchanging the entering and leaving vectors ($\mathbf{P}_j$ and $\mathbf{P}_r$) using the formula $\mathbf{B}_{\text{next}}^{-1} = \mathbf{E}\mathbf{B}^{-1}$. Set $\mathbf{B}^{-1} = \mathbf{B}_{\text{next}}^{-1}$, and go to step 1.

Apply the method to the following problem:

$$\text{Minimize } z = 2x_1 + x_2$$

subject to

$$3x_1 + x_2 \geq 3$$
$$4x_1 + 3x_2 \geq 6$$
$$x_1 + 2x_2 \leq 3$$
$$x_1, x_2 \geq 0$$

### 7.5.2  Bounded Variables Algorithm

In LP models, variables may have explicit positive upper and lower bounds. For example, in production facilities, lower and upper bounds can represent the minimum and maximum demands for certain products. Bounded variables also arise prominently in the course of solving integer programming problems by the branch-and-bound algorithm (see Section 9.3.1).

The bounded algorithm is efficient computationally because it accounts for the bounds *implicitly*. We consider the lower bounds first because it is simpler. Given $\mathbf{X} \geq \mathbf{L}$, we can use the substitution

$$\mathbf{X} = \mathbf{L} + \mathbf{X}', \quad \mathbf{X}' \geq \mathbf{0}$$

throughout and solve the problem in terms of $\mathbf{X}'$ (whose lower bound now equals zero). The original $\mathbf{X}$ is determined by back substitution, which is legitimate because it guarantees that $\mathbf{X} = \mathbf{X}' + \mathbf{L}$ will remain nonnegative for all $\mathbf{X}' \geq \mathbf{0}$.

Next, consider the upper bounding constraints, $\mathbf{X} \leq \mathbf{U}$. The idea of direct substitution (i.e., $\mathbf{X} = \mathbf{U} - \mathbf{X}''$, $\mathbf{X}'' \geq \mathbf{0}$) is not correct because back substitution, $\mathbf{X} = \mathbf{U} - \mathbf{X}''$, does not ensure that $\mathbf{X}$ will remain nonnegative. A different procedure is thus needed.

Define the upper bounded LP model as

$$\text{Maximize } z = \{\mathbf{C}\mathbf{X} \,|\, (\mathbf{A}, \mathbf{I})\mathbf{X} = \mathbf{b}, \ \mathbf{0} \leq \mathbf{X} \leq \mathbf{U}\}$$

The bounded algorithm uses only the constraints $(\mathbf{A}, \mathbf{I})\mathbf{X} = \mathbf{b}$, $\mathbf{X} \geq \mathbf{0}$ explicitly, while accounting for $\mathbf{X} \leq \mathbf{U}$ implicitly through modification of the simplex feasibility condition.

Let $\mathbf{X}_B = \mathbf{B}^{-1}\mathbf{b}$ be a current basic feasible solution of $(\mathbf{A}, \mathbf{I})\mathbf{X} = \mathbf{b}$, $\mathbf{X} \geq \mathbf{0}$ and suppose that, according to the (regular) optimality condition, $\mathbf{P}_j$ is the entering vector. Then, *given that all the nonbasic variables are zero*, the constraint equation of the $i$th basic variable can be written as

$$(\mathbf{X}_B)_i = (\mathbf{B}^{-1}\mathbf{b})_i - (\mathbf{B}^{-1}\mathbf{P}_j)_i x_j$$

When the entering variable $x_j$ increases above zero level, $(\mathbf{X}_B)_i$ will *increase or decrease* depending on whether $(\mathbf{B}^{-1}\mathbf{P}_j)_i$ is negative or positive, respectively. Thus, in determining the value of the entering variable $x_j$, three conditions must be satisfied.

1. The basic variable $(\mathbf{X}_B)_i$ remains nonnegative—that is, $(\mathbf{X}_B)_i \geq 0$.
2. The basic variable $(\mathbf{X}_B)_i$ does not exceed its upper bound—that is, $(\mathbf{X}_B)_i \leq (\mathbf{U}_B)_i$, where $\mathbf{U}_B$ comprises the ordered elements of $\mathbf{U}$ corresponding to $\mathbf{X}_B$.
3. The entering variable $x_j$ cannot assume a value larger than its upper bound—that is, $x_j \leq u_j$, where $u_j$ is the $j$th element of $\mathbf{U}$.

The first condition $(\mathbf{X}_B)_i \geq 0$ requires that

$$(\mathbf{B}^{-1}\mathbf{b})_i - (\mathbf{B}^{-1}\mathbf{P}_j)_i x_j \geq 0$$

and is not violated if

$$x_j \leq \theta_1 \equiv \min_i \left\{ \frac{(\mathbf{B}^{-1}\mathbf{b})_i}{(\mathbf{B}^{-1}\mathbf{P}_j)_i} \mid (\mathbf{B}^{-1}\mathbf{P}_j)_i > 0 \right\}$$

This condition is the same as the feasibility condition of the regular simplex method.

Next, the condition $(\mathbf{X}_B)_i \leq (\mathbf{U}_B)_i$ specifies that

$$(\mathbf{B}^{-1}\mathbf{b})_i - (\mathbf{B}^{-1}\mathbf{P}_j)_i x_j \leq (\mathbf{U}_B)_i$$

which is not violated if

$$x_j \leq \theta_2 \equiv \min_i \left\{ \frac{(\mathbf{B}^{-1}\mathbf{b})_i - (\mathbf{U}_B)_i}{(\mathbf{B}^{-1}\mathbf{P}_j)_i} \mid (\mathbf{B}^{-1}\mathbf{P}_j)_i < 0 \right\}$$

Finally, the third condition is satisfied simply if $x_j \leq u_j$.

Combining the three restrictions together, $x_j$ enters the solution at the level that satisfies all three conditions—that is,

$$x_j = \min\{\theta_1, \theta_2, u_j\}$$

The change of basis for the next iteration depends on whether $x_j$ enters the solution at level $\theta_1$, $\theta_2$, or $u_j$. Assuming that $(\mathbf{X}_B)_r$ is the leaving variable, then we have the following rules:

1. $x_j = \theta_1$. $(\mathbf{X}_B)_r$ leaves the basic solution (becomes nonbasic) at level zero. The new iteration is generated in the normal simplex manner by using $x_j$ and $(\mathbf{X}_B)_r$ as the entering and the leaving variables, respectively.
2. $x_j = \theta_2$. $(\mathbf{X}_B)_r$ becomes nonbasic *at its upper bound*. The new iteration is generated as in the case of $x_j = \theta_1$, with one modification that accounts for the fact that $(\mathbf{X}_B)_r$ will be nonbasic at *upper bound*. Because the values of $\theta_1$ and $\theta_2$ are developed under the assumption that *all nonbasic variables are at zero level* (convince yourself that this is the case!), we must convert the new nonba-

sic $(\mathbf{X}_B)_r$ at upper bound to a nonbasic variable at zero level. This is achieved by using the substitution $(\mathbf{X}_B)_r = (\mathbf{U}_B)_r - (\mathbf{X}_B)'_r$, where $(\mathbf{X}_B)'_r \geq 0$. It is immaterial whether the substitution is made before or after the new basis is computed.

3. $x_j = u_j$. The basic vector $\mathbf{X}_B$ remains unchanged because $x_j = u_j$ stops short of forcing any of the current basic variables to reach its lower ($=0$) or upper bound. This means that $x_j$ will remain nonbasic *but at upper bound*. Following the argument just presented, the new iteration is generated by using the substitution $x_j = u_j - x'_j$.

A tie among $\theta_1$, $\theta_2$, and $u_j$ may be broken arbitrarily. However, it is preferable to implement the rule for $x_j = u_j$ because it entails less computations.

The substitution $x_j = u_j - x'_j$ will change the original $c_j$, $\mathbf{P}_j$, and $\mathbf{b}$ to $c'_j = -c_j$, $\mathbf{P}'_j = -\mathbf{P}_j$, and $\mathbf{b}$ to $\mathbf{b}' = \mathbf{b} - u_j\mathbf{P}_j$. This means that if the revised simplex method is used, all the computations (e.g., $\mathbf{B}^{-1}$, $\mathbf{X}_B$, and $z_j - c_j$), should be based on the updated values of $\mathbf{C}$, $\mathbf{A}$, and $\mathbf{b}$ at each iteration (see Problem 7.5c–5 for further details).

---

**Example 7.5–3.**

Solve the following LP model by the upper-bounding algorithm.

$$\text{Maximize } z = 3x_1 + 5y + 2x_3$$

subject to

$$x_1 + y + 2x_3 \leq 14$$

$$2x_1 + 4y + 3x_3 \leq 43$$

$$0 \leq x_1 \leq 4, \quad 7 \leq y \leq 10, \quad 0 \leq x_3 \leq 3$$

The lower bound on $y$ is accounted for by using the substitution $y = x_2 + 7$, where $0 \leq x_2 \leq 10 - 7 = 3$.

We will not use the revised simplex method to carry out the computations, to avoid being "sidetracked" by its computational details. Instead, we will use the compact tableau form. Problems 7.5c–5, 7.5c–6, and 7.5c–7 address the revised version of the algorithm.

**Iteration 0**

| Basic | $x_1$ | $x_2$ | $x_3$ | $x_4$ | $x_5$ | Solution |
|-------|------|------|------|------|------|----------|
| $z$   | $-3$ | $-5$ | $-2$ | $0$  | $0$  | $35$     |
| $x_4$ | $1$  | $1$  | $2$  | $1$  | $0$  | $7$      |
| $x_5$ | $2$  | $4$  | $3$  | $0$  | $1$  | $15$     |

We have $\mathbf{B} = \mathbf{B}^{-1} = \mathbf{I}$ and $\mathbf{X}_B = (x_4, x_5)^T = \mathbf{B}^{-1}\mathbf{b} = (7, 15)^T$. Given $x_2$ is the entering variable ($z_2 - c_2 = -5$), we then get

$$\mathbf{B}^{-1}\mathbf{P}_2 = (1, 4)^T$$

which yields

$$\theta_1 = \min\left\{\frac{7}{1}, \frac{15}{4}\right\} = 3.75, \text{ corresponding to } x_5$$

$$\theta_2 = \infty \, (\text{because } \mathbf{B}^{-1}\mathbf{P}_2 > \mathbf{0})$$

Given $x_2 \le 3$, it follows that

$$x_2 = \min\{3.75, \infty, 3\} = 3 = u_2$$

Thus, $\mathbf{X}_B$ remains unchanged, and $x_2$ becomes nonbasic at its upper bound. We use the substitution $x_2 = 3 - x_2'$ to obtain the new tableau as

| Basic | $x_1$ | $x_2'$ | $x_3$ | $x_4$ | $x_5$ | Solution |
|-------|-------|--------|-------|-------|-------|----------|
| $z$   | $-3$  | $5$    | $-2$  | $0$   | $0$   | $50$     |
| $x_4$ | $1$   | $-1$   | $2$   | $1$   | $0$   | $4$      |
| $x_5$ | $2$   | $-4$   | $3$   | $0$   | $1$   | $3$      |

The substitution in effect changes the original right-hand side vector from $\mathbf{b} = (7, 15)^T$ to $\mathbf{b}' = (4, 3)^T$. This change should be considered in future computations.

**Iteration 1**

The entering variable is $x_1$. The basic vector $\mathbf{X}_B$ and $\mathbf{B}^{-1}$ $(=\mathbf{I})$ are the same as in iteration 0. Thus,

$$\mathbf{B}^{-1}\mathbf{P}_1 = (1, 2)^T$$

We then get

$$\theta_1 = \min\left\{\frac{4}{1}, \frac{3}{2}\right\} = 1.5, \text{ corresponding to basic } x_5$$

$$\theta_2 = \infty \, (\text{because } \mathbf{B}^{-1}\mathbf{P}_2 > \mathbf{0})$$

Given $x_1 \le 4$, it follows that

$$x_1 = \min\{1.5, \infty, 4\} = 1.5 = \theta_1$$

Thus, the entering variable $x_1$ becomes basic, and the leaving variable $x_5$ becomes non-basic at zero level, which yields

| Basic | $x_1$ | $x_2'$ | $x_3$         | $x_4$ | $x_5$          | Solution        |
|-------|-------|--------|---------------|-------|----------------|-----------------|
| $z$   | $0$   | $-1$   | $\frac{5}{2}$ | $0$   | $\frac{3}{2}$  | $\frac{109}{2}$ |
| $x_4$ | $0$   | $1$    | $\frac{1}{2}$ | $1$   | $-\frac{1}{2}$ | $\frac{5}{2}$   |
| $x_1$ | $1$   | $-2$   | $\frac{3}{2}$ | $0$   | $\frac{1}{2}$  | $\frac{3}{2}$   |

**Iteration 2**

The new inverse is

$$\mathbf{B}^{-1} = \begin{bmatrix} 1 & -\dfrac{1}{2} \\ 0 & \dfrac{1}{2} \end{bmatrix}$$

New $\mathbf{X}_B = (x_4, x_1)^T = \mathbf{B}^{-1}\mathbf{b}' = (\frac{5}{2}, \frac{3}{2})^T$, where $\mathbf{b}' = (4, 3)^T$ as computed at the end of iteration 0. We select $x_2'$ as the entering variable, and, observing that $\mathbf{P}_2' = -\mathbf{P}_2$, we get

$$\mathbf{B}^{-1}\mathbf{P}_2' = (1, -2)^T$$

Thus,

$$\theta_1 = \min\left\{ \frac{\frac{5}{2}}{1}, - \right\} = 2.5, \text{ corresponding to basic } x_4$$

$$\theta_2 = \min\left\{ -, \frac{\frac{3}{2} - 4}{-2} \right\} = 1.25, \text{ corresponding to basic } x_1$$

Given $x_2' \le 3$, it thus follows that

$$x_2' = \min\{2.5, \mathbf{1.25}, 3\} = 1.25 = \theta_2$$

Thus, the entering variable $x_2'$ becomes basic and the leaving variable $x_1$ becomes nonbasic at upper bound, which yields

| Basic | $x_1$ | $x_2'$ | $x_3$ | $x_4$ | $x_5$ | Solution |
|---|---|---|---|---|---|---|
| $z$ | $-\dfrac{1}{2}$ | 0 | $\dfrac{7}{4}$ | 0 | $\dfrac{5}{4}$ | $\dfrac{215}{4}$ |
| $x_4$ | $\dfrac{1}{2}$ | 0 | $\dfrac{5}{4}$ | 1 | $-\dfrac{1}{4}$ | $\dfrac{13}{4}$ |
| $x_2'$ | $-\dfrac{1}{2}$ | 1 | $-\dfrac{3}{4}$ | 0 | $-\dfrac{1}{4}$ | $-\dfrac{3}{4}$ |

Next, because $x_1$ becomes nonbasic at its upper bound, we use the substitution $x_1 = 4 - x_1'$ to obtain

| Basic | $x_1'$ | $x_2'$ | $x_3$ | $x_4$ | $x_5$ | Solution |
|---|---|---|---|---|---|---|
| $z$ | $\dfrac{1}{2}$ | 0 | $\dfrac{7}{4}$ | 0 | $\dfrac{5}{4}$ | $\dfrac{223}{4}$ |
| $x_4$ | $-\dfrac{1}{2}$ | 0 | $\dfrac{5}{4}$ | 1 | $-\dfrac{1}{4}$ | $\dfrac{5}{4}$ |
| $x_2'$ | $\dfrac{1}{2}$ | 1 | $-\dfrac{3}{4}$ | 0 | $-\dfrac{1}{4}$ | $\dfrac{5}{4}$ |

which is now optimal and feasible.

The optimal values of $x_1$, $x_2$, and $x_3$ are obtained by back substitution as $x_1 = u_1 - x_1' = 4 - 0 = 4$, $x_2 = u_2 - x_2' = 3 - \frac{5}{4} = \frac{7}{4}$, and $x_3 = 0$. Finally, we get $y = l_2 + x_2 = 7 + \frac{7}{4} = \frac{35}{4}$. The associated optimal value of $z$ is $\frac{223}{4}$.

---

## Problem set 7.5c

**1.** Consider the following linear program:

$$\text{Maximize } z = 2x_1 + x_2$$

subject to

$$x_1 + x_2 \le 3$$
$$0 \le x_1 \le 2, \ \ 0 \le x_2 \le 2$$

**(a)** Solve the problem graphically, and trace the sequence of extreme points leading to the optimal solution.

**(b)** Solve the problem by the upper bounding algorithm and show that the method, produces the same sequence of extreme points as in the graphical optimal solution (use TORA to generate the iterations).

**(c)** How does the upper-bounding algorithm recognize the extreme points?

**2.** Solve the following problem by the bounded algorithm:

$$\text{Maximize } z = 6x_1 + 2x_2 + 8x_3 + 4x_4 + 2x_5 + 10x_6$$

subject to

$$8x_1 + x_2 + 8x_3 + 2x_4 + 2x_5 + 4x_6 \le 13$$
$$0 \le x_j \le 1, \ \ j = 1, 2, \dots, 6$$

**3.** Solve the following problems by the bounded algorithm:

**(a)** Minimize $z = 6x_1 - 2x_2 - 3x_3$
    subject to

$$2x_1 + 4x_2 + 2x_3 \le 8$$
$$x_1 - 2x_2 + 3x_3 \le 7$$
$$0 \le x_1 \le 2, \ \ 0 \le x_2 \le 2, \ \ 0 \le x_3 \le 1$$

**(b)** Minimize $z = 3x_1 + 5x_2 + 2x_3$
    subject to

$$x_1 + 2x_2 + 2x_3 \le 10$$
$$2x_1 + 4x_2 + 3x_3 \le 15$$
$$0 \le x_1 \le 4, \ \ 0 \le x_2 \le 3, \ \ 0 \le x_3 \le 3$$

start first with the entering variable. Given $\mathbf{C}_B$ and $\mathbf{B}^{-1}$ of the current basis of the master problem, then for nonbasic $\beta_{jk}$ we have

$$z_{jk} - c_{jk} = \mathbf{C}_B \mathbf{B}^{-1} \mathbf{P}_{jk} - c_{jk}$$

where,

$$c_{jk} = \mathbf{C}_j \hat{\mathbf{Y}}_{jk} \quad \text{and} \quad \mathbf{P}_{jk} = \begin{bmatrix} \mathbf{A}_j \hat{\mathbf{Y}}_{jk} \\ 0 \\ \vdots \\ 1 \\ \vdots \\ 0 \end{bmatrix}$$

Now, to decide which, if any, of the variable $\beta_{jk}$ should enter the solution, we must determine

$$z_{j*k*} - c_{j*k*} = \min_{\text{all } j \text{ and } k} \{z_{jk} - c_{jk}\}$$

If $z_{j*k*} - c_{j*k*} > 0$, then, according to the maximization optimality condition, $\beta_{j*k*}$ must enter the solution; otherwise, the optimum has been reached.

We still have not shown how $z_{j*k*} - c_{j*k*}$ is computed numerically. The secret lies in the following identity

$$\min_{\text{all } j \text{ and } k} \{z_{jk} - c_{jk}\} = \min_j \left\{ \min_k \{z_{jk} - c_{jk}\} \right\}$$

The reason we are able to establish this identity is that each convex set $\mathbf{D}_j \mathbf{X}_j = \mathbf{b}_j$, $\mathbf{X}_j \geq 0$ has its independent set of extreme points. In effect, what the identity says is that we can determine $z_{j*k*} - c_{j*k*}$ in two steps.

**1.** For each convex set $\mathbf{D}_j \mathbf{X}_j = \mathbf{b}_j$, $\mathbf{X}_j \geq 0$, determine the extreme point $\hat{\mathbf{Y}}_{jk*}$ that yields the smallest $z_{jk} - c_{jk}$—that is, $z_{jk*} - c_{jk*} = \min_k \{z_{jk} - c_{jk}\}$.
**2.** Next, determine $z_{j*k*} - c_{j*k*} = \min_j \{z_{jk*} - c_{jk*}\}$

From LP theory, we know that the optimum solution, when finite, must be associated with an extreme point of the solution space. Because each of the sets $\mathbf{D}_j \mathbf{X}_j = \mathbf{b}_j$, $\mathbf{X}_j \geq \mathbf{0}$ is bounded by definition, step 1 is thus mathematically equivalent to solving n linear programs of the form

$$\text{Minimize } w_j = \{z_j - c_j \mid \mathbf{D}_j \mathbf{X}_j = \mathbf{b}_j, \mathbf{X}_j \geq \mathbf{0}\}$$

Actually, the objective function $w_j$ is a linear function in $\mathbf{X}_j$ (see Problem 7.5d–8).

The determination of the entering variable $\beta_{j*k*}$ in the master problem reduces to solving $n$ (smaller) linear programs to determine the "entering" extreme point $\hat{\mathbf{Y}}_{j*k*}$. This approach precludes the need to determine all the extreme points of all $n$ convex sets. Once the desired extreme point is located, all the elements of the column vector $\mathbf{P}_{j*k*}$ are at hand. Given that information, we can then determine the leaving variable, and subsequently compute the next $\mathbf{B}^{-1}$ using the normal revised simplex method computations.

---

**Example 7.5–4.**

Solve the following LP by the decomposition algorithm:

$$\text{Maximize } z = 3x_1 + 5x_2 + x_4 + x_5$$

subject to

$$x_1 + x_2 \quad + x_4 + x_5 \qquad\qquad + x_8 = 40$$

$$5x_1 + x_2 + x_3 \qquad\qquad\qquad\qquad = 12$$

$$x_4 + x_5 - x_6 \qquad\qquad = 5$$

$$x_4 + 5x_5 \quad + x_7 \qquad = 50$$

$$x_1, x_2, x_3, x_4, x_5, x_6, x_7, x_8 \geq 0$$

The variables $x_3, x_7$, and $x_8$ are slacks and $x_6$ is a surplus.
The problem can be summarized as

| $x_1$ | $x_2$ | $x_3$ | $x_4$ | $x_5$ | $x_6$ | $x_7$ | $x_8$ | |
|-------|-------|-------|-------|-------|-------|-------|-------|-----|
| 3 | 5 | 0 | 1 | 1 | 0 | 0 | 0 | |
| 1 | 1 | 0 | 1 | 1 | 0 | 0 | 1 | 40 |
| 5 | 1 | 1 | | | | | | 12 |
| | | | 1 | 1 | −1 | 0 | | 5 |
| | | | 1 | 5 | 0 | 1 | | 50 |

The representation shows that the problem has the following two subproblems:
*Subproblem 1 (j = 1)*

$$\mathbf{X}_1 = (x_1, x_2, x_3)^T, \quad \mathbf{C}_1 = (3, 5, 0), \quad \mathbf{A}_1 = (1, 1, 0),$$

$$\mathbf{D}_1 = (5, 1, 1), \quad b_1 = 12$$

*Subproblem 2 (j = 2)*

$$\mathbf{X}_2 = (x_4, x_5, x_6, x_7)^T, \quad \mathbf{C}_2 = (1, 1, 0, 0), \quad \mathbf{A}_2 = (1, 1, 0, 0),$$

$$\mathbf{D}_2 = \begin{bmatrix} 1 & 1 & -1 & 0 \\ 1 & 5 & 0 & 1 \end{bmatrix}, \quad \mathbf{b}_2 = \begin{bmatrix} 5 \\ 50 \end{bmatrix}$$

The slack variable $x_8$ does not constitute a subproblem in the sense given previously. The variable thus must be kept as part of the master problem.

Using $x_9$ and $x_{10}$ as artificial variables, the starting tableau of the master problem can be written symbolically as

| $\beta_{11}$ | $\beta_{12}$ | $\cdots$ | $\beta_{1K1}$ | $\beta_{21}$ | $\beta_{22}$ | $\cdots$ | $\beta_{2K2}$ | $x_8$ | $x_9$ | $x_{10}$ | |
|---|---|---|---|---|---|---|---|---|---|---|---|
| $C_1\hat{Y}_{11}$ | $C_1\hat{Y}_{12}$ | $\cdots$ | $C_1\hat{Y}_{1K1}$ | $C_2\hat{Y}_{21}$ | $C_2\hat{Y}_{22}$ | $\cdots$ | $C_2\hat{Y}_{2K2}$ | 0 | $-M$ | $-M$ | |
| $A_1\hat{Y}_{11}$ | $A_1\hat{Y}_{12}$ | $\cdots$ | $A_1\hat{Y}_{1K1}$ | $A_2\hat{Y}_{21}$ | $A_2\hat{Y}_{22}$ | $\cdots$ | $A_2\hat{Y}_{1K1}$ | 1 | 0 | 0 | 40 |
| 1 | 1 | $\cdots$ | 1 | 0 | 0 | $\cdots$ | 0 | 0 | 1 | 0 | 1 |
| 0 | 0 | $\cdots$ | 0 | 1 | 1 | $\cdots$ | 1 | 0 | 0 | 1 | 1 |
| | Subproblem 1 | | | | Subproblem 2 | | | Starting basic solution | | | |

**Iteration 0**

$$\mathbf{X}_B = (x_8, x_9, x_{10})^T = (40, 1, 1)^T$$

$$\mathbf{C}_B = (0, -M, -M), \quad \mathbf{B} = \mathbf{B}^{-1} = \mathbf{I}$$

**Iteration 1**

*Subproblem 1 ($j = 1$).* We have

$$z_1 - c_1 = \mathbf{C}_B\mathbf{B}^{-1} \begin{bmatrix} \mathbf{A}_1\mathbf{X}_1 \\ 1 \\ 0 \end{bmatrix} - \mathbf{C}_1\mathbf{X}_1$$

$$= (0, -M, -M) \begin{bmatrix} (1, 1, 0)\begin{bmatrix} x_1 \\ x_2 \\ x_3 \end{bmatrix} \\ 1 \\ 0 \end{bmatrix} - (3, 5, 0)\begin{bmatrix} x_1 \\ x_2 \\ x_3 \end{bmatrix}$$

$$= -3x_1 - 5x_2 - M$$

Next, $\mathbf{D}_1\mathbf{X}_1 = \mathbf{b}_1$ reduces to $5x_1 + x_2 + x_3 = 12$. Thus, the corresponding LP is

$$\text{Minimize } w_1 = -3x_1 - 5x_2 - M$$

subject to

$$5x_1 + x_2 + x_3 = 12$$

$$x_1, x_2, x_3 \geq 0$$

The solution of this problem (by the simplex method) yields

$$\hat{\mathbf{Y}}_{11} = (0, 12, 0)^T, z_1^* - c_1^* = w_1^* = -60 - M$$

*Subproblem 2 (j = 2).* The associated linear program is given as

$$\text{Minimize } z_2 - c_2 = \mathbf{C}_B\mathbf{B}^{-1} \begin{bmatrix} \mathbf{A}_2\mathbf{X}_2 \\ 0 \\ 1 \end{bmatrix} - \mathbf{C}_2\mathbf{X}_2$$

$$= (0, -M, -M) \begin{bmatrix} (1, 1, 0, 0) \begin{bmatrix} x_4 \\ x_5 \\ x_6 \\ x_7 \end{bmatrix} \\ 0 \\ 1 \end{bmatrix} - (1, 1, 0, 0) \begin{bmatrix} x_4 \\ x_5 \\ x_6 \\ x_7 \end{bmatrix}$$

$$= -x_4 - x_5 - M$$

subject to

$$\begin{bmatrix} 1 & 1 & -1 & 0 \\ 1 & 5 & 0 & 1 \end{bmatrix} \begin{bmatrix} x_4 \\ x_5 \\ x_6 \\ x_7 \end{bmatrix} = \begin{bmatrix} 5 \\ 50 \end{bmatrix}$$

$$x_4, x_5, x_6, x_7 \geq 0$$

The optimal solution of the problem yields

$$\hat{\mathbf{Y}}_{21} = (50, 0, 45, 0)^T, z_2^* - c_2^* = -50 - M$$

Because the master problem is of the maximization type and $z_1^* - c_1^* < z_2^* - c_2^*$ and $z_1^* - c_1^* < 0$, it follows that $\beta_{11}$ associated with extreme point $\hat{\mathbf{Y}}_{11}$ must enter the solution.

To determine the leaving variable, consider

$$\mathbf{P}_{11} = \begin{bmatrix} \mathbf{A}_1\hat{\mathbf{Y}}_{11} \\ 1 \\ 0 \end{bmatrix} = \begin{bmatrix} (1, 1, 0) \begin{bmatrix} 0 \\ 12 \\ 0 \end{bmatrix} \\ 1 \\ 0 \end{bmatrix} = \begin{bmatrix} 12 \\ 1 \\ 0 \end{bmatrix}$$

Thus, $\mathbf{B}^{-1}\mathbf{P}_{11} = (12, 1, 0)^T$. Given $\mathbf{X}_B = (x_8, x_9, x_{10})^T = (40, 1, 1)^T$, it follows that $x_9$ (an artificial variable) leaves the basic solution (permanently).

We can now determine $\mathbf{B}_{\text{next}}^{-1}$ using the product form of the inverse (Section 7.5.1) by removing the vector associated with $x_9$ from the basis and introducing the vector $\mathbf{P}_{11}$, which gives (verify!)

$$\mathbf{B}^{-1} = \begin{bmatrix} 1 & -12 & 0 \\ 0 & 1 & 0 \\ 0 & 0 & 1 \end{bmatrix}$$

and the new basic solution is

$$\mathbf{X}_B = (x_8, \beta_{11}, x_{10})^T = \mathbf{B}^{-1}(40, 1, 1)^T = (28, 1, 1)^T$$

$$\mathbf{C}_B = (0, \mathbf{C}_1 \hat{\mathbf{Y}}_{11}, -M) = (0, 60, -M)$$

### Iteration 2

*Subproblem 1 ( j = 1).* You should verify that the associated linear program remains the same as for $j = 1$ in Iteration 1 (this is merely a coincidence and does not represent a general rule). The optimum solution yields $z_1^* - c_1^* = w_1 = 0$, which means that none of the remaining extreme points in Subproblem 1 can improve the solution to the master problem. (The optimum solution of Subproblem 1 is the same extreme point $\hat{\mathbf{Y}}_{11}$ whose variable $\beta_{11}$ is already basic. This is the reason $z_1^* - c_1^* = 0$.)

*Subproblem 2 ( j = 2).* Again, you should verify that the associated linear program is (coincidentally) the same as for $j = 2$ in Iteration 1. The optimum solution yields

$$\hat{\mathbf{Y}}_{22} = (50, 0, 45, 0)^T, \; z_2^* - c_2^* = -50 - M$$

Note that $\hat{\mathbf{Y}}_{22}$ is actually the same extreme point as $\hat{\mathbf{Y}}_{21}$. However, we use the subscript 2 for notational convenience to represent iteration 2.

From the results of the two subproblems, $z_2^* - c_2^* < 0$ indicates that $\beta_{22}$ associated with $\hat{\mathbf{Y}}_{22}$ enters the basic solution.

To determine the leaving variable, consider

$$\mathbf{P}_{22} = \begin{bmatrix} \mathbf{A}_2 \hat{\mathbf{Y}}_{22} \\ 0 \\ 1 \end{bmatrix} = \begin{bmatrix} (1, 1, 0, 0) \begin{bmatrix} 50 \\ 0 \\ 45 \\ 0 \end{bmatrix} \\ 0 \\ 1 \end{bmatrix} = \begin{bmatrix} 50 \\ 0 \\ 1 \end{bmatrix}$$

Thus, $\mathbf{B}^{-1}\mathbf{P}_{22} = (50, 0, 1)^T$. Because $\mathbf{X}_B = (x_8, \beta_{11}, x_{10})^T = (28, 1, 1)^T$, $x_8$ leaves. The new $\mathbf{B}^{-1}$ becomes (verify!)

$$\mathbf{B}^{-1} = \begin{bmatrix} \dfrac{1}{50} & -\dfrac{12}{50} & 0 \\ 0 & 1 & 0 \\ -\dfrac{1}{50} & \dfrac{12}{50} & 1 \end{bmatrix}$$

The new basic solution is

$$\mathbf{X}_B = (\beta_{22}, \beta_{11}, x_{10})^T = \mathbf{B}^{-1}(40, 1, 1)^T = \left( \dfrac{14}{25}, 1, \dfrac{11}{25} \right)^T$$

$$\mathbf{C}_B = (\mathbf{C}_2\hat{\mathbf{Y}}_{22}, \mathbf{C}_1\hat{\mathbf{Y}}_{11}, -M) = (50, 60, -M)$$

**Iteration 3**

*Subproblem 1 (j = 1).* You should verify that the associated objective function is

$$\text{Minimize } w_1 = \left(\frac{M}{50} - 2\right)x_1 + \left(\frac{M}{50} - 4\right)x_2 - \frac{12M}{50} + 48$$

The corresponding optimum solution yields $z_1^* - c_1^* = 0$, which shows that Subproblem 1 yields no improved extreme point.

*Subproblem 2 (j = 2).* The objective function can be shown to equal (verify!)

$$\text{Minimize } w_2 = \left(\frac{M}{50}\right)(x_3 + x_4) - M$$

The associated optimum solution is

$$\hat{\mathbf{Y}}_{23} = (5, 0, 0, 45)^T, z_2^* - c_2^* = -\frac{9M}{10}$$

*Nonbasic Variable $x_8$.* From the definition of the master problem, $z_j - c_j$ of $x_8$ must be computed and compared separately. Thus,

$$z_8 - c_8 = \mathbf{C}_B\mathbf{B}^{-1}\mathbf{P}_8 - c_8$$

$$= \left(1 + \frac{M}{50}, 48 - \frac{12M}{50}, -M\right)(1, 0, 0)^T - 0$$

$$= 1 + \frac{M}{50}$$

Thus, $x_8$ cannot improve the solution.

From the preceding information, $\beta_{23}$ associated with $\hat{\mathbf{Y}}_{23}$ enters the basic solution. To determine the leaving variable, consider

$$\mathbf{P}_{23} = \begin{bmatrix} \mathbf{A}_2\,\hat{\mathbf{Y}}_{23} \\ 0 \\ 1 \end{bmatrix} = \begin{bmatrix} (1, 1, 0, 0) \begin{bmatrix} 5 \\ 0 \\ 0 \\ 45 \end{bmatrix} \\ 0 \\ 1 \end{bmatrix} = \begin{bmatrix} 5 \\ 0 \\ 1 \end{bmatrix}$$

Thus, $\mathbf{B}^{-1}\mathbf{P}_{23} = (\frac{1}{10}, 0, \frac{9}{10})^T$. Given $\mathbf{X}_B = (\beta_{22}, \beta_{11}, x_{10})^T = (\frac{14}{25}, 1, \frac{11}{25})^T$, the artificial variable $x_{10}$ leaves the basic solution (permanently).

The new $\mathbf{B}^{-1}$ is (verify!)

$$\mathbf{B}^{-1} = \begin{bmatrix} \dfrac{1}{45} & -\dfrac{12}{45} & -\dfrac{5}{45} \\ 0 & 1 & 0 \\ -\dfrac{1}{45} & \dfrac{12}{45} & \dfrac{50}{45} \end{bmatrix}$$

and the new basic solution is given as

$$\mathbf{X}_B = (\beta_{22}, \beta_{11}, \beta_{23})^T = \mathbf{B}^{-1}(40, 1, 1)^T = \left(\frac{23}{45}, 1, \frac{22}{45}\right)^T$$

$$\mathbf{C}_B = (\mathbf{C}_2\hat{\mathbf{Y}}_{22,}\ \mathbf{C}_1\hat{\mathbf{Y}}_{11},\ \mathbf{C}_2\hat{\mathbf{Y}}_{23}) = (50, 60, 5)$$

**Iteration 4**

*Subproblem 1 (j = 1).* $w_1 = -2x_1 - 4x_2 + 48$. It yields $z_1^* - c_1^* = w_1^* = 0$.
*Subproblem 2 (j = 2).* $w_2 = 0x_4 + 0x_5 + 48 = 48$.
*Nonbasic Variable* $x_8$. $z_8 - c_8 = 1$. The preceding information shows that Interation 3 is optimal.

We can compute the optimum solution of the original problem by back substitution:

$$\mathbf{X}_1^* = (x_1, x_2, x_3)^T = \beta_{11}\hat{\mathbf{Y}}_{11} = 1(0, 12, 0)^T = (0, 12, 0)^T$$

$$\mathbf{X}_2^* = (x_4, x_5, x_6, x_7)^T = \beta_{22}\hat{\mathbf{Y}}_{22} + \beta_{23}\hat{\mathbf{Y}}_{23}$$

$$= \left(\frac{23}{45}\right)(50, 0, 45, 0)^T + \left(\frac{22}{45}\right)(5, 0, 0, 45)^T$$

$$= (28, 0, 23, 22)^T$$

All the remaining variables are zero. The optimum value of the objective function can be obtained by direct substitution.

---

## Problem set 7.5d

1. In each of the following cases, determine the feasible extreme points graphically and express the feasible solution space as a function of these extreme points. If the solution space is unbounded, add a proper artificial constraint.
   **(a)**

$$x_1 + 2x_2 \le 6$$
$$2x_1 + x_2 \le 8$$
$$-x_1 + x_2 \le 1$$
$$x_2 \le 2$$
$$x_1, x_2 \ge 0$$

   **(b)**

$$2x_1 + x_2 \le 2$$
$$3x_1 + 4x_2 \ge 12$$
$$x_1, x_2 \ge 0$$

   **(c)**

$$x_1 - x_2 \le 10$$
$$2x_1 \le 40$$
$$x_1, x_2 \ge 0$$

2. In Example 7.5–4, the feasible extreme points of subspaces $\mathbf{D}_1\mathbf{X}_1 = \mathbf{b}_1$, $\mathbf{X}_1 \geq \mathbf{0}$ and $\mathbf{D}_2\mathbf{X}_2 = \mathbf{b}_2$, $\mathbf{X}_2 \geq \mathbf{0}$ can be determined graphically. Use this information to express the associated master problem explicitly. Then show that the application of the revised simplex method to the master problem produces the same entering variable $\beta_{jk}$ as that generated by solving Subproblems 1 and 2. Hence, convince yourself that the determination of the entering variable $\beta_{jk}$ is exactly equivalent to solving the two minimization subproblems.

3. Consider the following linear program:

$$\text{Maximize } z = x_1 + 3x_2 + 5x_3 + 5x_3 + 2x_4$$

subject to

$$
\begin{aligned}
5x_1 + x_2 &\leq 9 \\
x_1 + 4x_2 &\leq 8 \\
5x_1 + 3x_2 + 4x_3 &\geq 10 \\
x_3 - 5x_4 &\leq 4 \\
x_3 + x_4 &\leq 10 \\
x_1, x_2, x_3, x_4 &\geq 0
\end{aligned}
$$

Construct the master problem explicitly by using the extreme points of the subspaces, and then solve the resulting problem directly by the revised simplex method.

4. Solve Problem 3 using the decomposition algorithm and compare the two procedures.

5. Apply the decomposition algorithm to the following problem:

$$\text{Maximize } z = 6x_1 + 7x_2 + 3x_3 + 5x_4 + x_5 + x_6$$

subject to

$$
\begin{aligned}
x_1 + x_2 + x_3 + x_4 + x_5 + x_6 &\leq 50 \\
x_1 + x_2 &\leq 10 \\
x_2 &\leq 8 \\
5x_3 + x_4 &\leq 12 \\
x_5 + x_6 &\geq 5 \\
x_5 + 5x_6 &\leq 50 \\
x_1, x_2, x_3, x_4, x_5, x_6 &\geq 0
\end{aligned}
$$

6. Indicate the necessary changes for applying the decomposition algorithm to minimization LPs. Then solve the following problem:

$$\text{Minimize } z = 5x_1 + 3x_2 + 8x_3 - 5x_4$$

subject to

$$x_1 + x_3 + x_3 + x_4 \geq 25$$
$$5x_1 + x_2 \leq 20$$
$$5x_1 - x_2 \geq 5$$
$$x_3 + x_4 = 20$$
$$x_1, x_2, x_3, x_4, \geq 0$$

7. Solve the following problem by the decomposition algorithm:

$$\text{Minimize } z = 10y_1 + 2y_2 + 4y_3 + 8y_4 + y_5$$

subject to

$$y_1 + 4y_2 - y_3 \qquad \geq 8$$
$$2y_1 + y_2 + y_3 \qquad \geq 2$$
$$3y_1 \qquad + y_4 + y_5 \geq 4$$
$$y_1 \qquad + 2y_4 - y_5 \geq 10$$
$$y_1, y_2, y_3, y_4, y_5 \geq 0$$

(*Hint:* Solve the dual problem first by decomposition.)

8. In the decomposition algorithm, suppose that the number of common constraints in the original problem is $r$. Show that the objective function for subproblem $j$ can be written as

$$\text{Minimize } w_j = z_j - c_j = (\mathbf{C}_B \mathbf{R} \mathbf{A}_j - \mathbf{C}_j) \mathbf{X}_j + \mathbf{C}_B \mathbf{V}_{r+j}$$

where $\mathbf{R}$ represents the first $r$ columns of $\mathbf{B}^{-1}$ and $\mathbf{V}_{r+j}$ is its $(r + j)$th column.

## 7.6 DUALITY

We have dealt with the dual problem at an elementary level in Chapter 4. This section presents a more rigorous treatment of duality and allows us to verify the special primal-dual relationships that formed the basis for sensitivity analysis in Chapter 4. The presentation also develops the foundation for the development of parametric programming.

### 7.6.1 Matrix Definition of the Dual Problem

Suppose that the standard form of the primal problem with $m$ constraints and $n$ variables is defined as

$$\text{Maximize } z = (\mathbf{C}_I, \mathbf{C}_{II})\mathbf{X}$$

subject to

$$(\mathbf{A}, \mathbf{I})\mathbf{X} = \mathbf{b}$$

$$\mathbf{X} \geq 0$$

The vector $\mathbf{X}$ can be partitioned to $(\mathbf{X}_I, \mathbf{X}_{II})$, where $\mathbf{X}_{II}$ is the starting basic vector with $m$ elements.

Letting $\mathbf{Y} = (y_1, y_2, \dots, y_m)$ represent the dual variables vector, the rules in Table 4–2 produce the following dual problem

$$\text{Minimize } w = \mathbf{Yb}$$

subject to

$$\mathbf{YA} \geq \mathbf{C}_I$$

$$\mathbf{Y} \geq \mathbf{C}_{II}$$

$$\mathbf{Y} \text{ unrestricted}$$

The constraints $\mathbf{Y} \geq \mathbf{C}_{II}$ may override unrestricted $\mathbf{Y}$.

#### Problem set 7.6a

1. Prove that the dual of the dual is the primal.
2. Suppose that the primal is given as min $z = \{\mathbf{CX} \mid \mathbf{AX} \geq \mathbf{b}, \mathbf{X} \geq 0\}$. Define the corresponding dual problem.

### 7.6.2 Optimal Dual Solution

This section establishes relationships between the primal and dual problems and shows how the optimal dual solution can be determined from the optimal primal solution. Let $\mathbf{B}$ be the current *optimal* primal basis, and define $\mathbf{C}_B$ as the objective function coefficients associated with the optimal vector $\mathbf{X}_B$.

**Theorem 7.6–1.**    Weak duality theory. *For any pair of* feasible *primal and dual solutions* $(\mathbf{X}, \mathbf{Y})$, *the value of the objective function in the* minimization *problem sets an upper bound on the value of the objective function in the* maximization *problem. For the* optimal *pair* $(\mathbf{X}^*, \mathbf{Y}^*)$, *the values of the objective functions are equal.*

*Proof.* The feasible pair $(\mathbf{X}, \mathbf{Y})$ satisfies all the restrictions of the two problems. Premultiplying both sides of the constraints of the maximization problem with (unrestricted) $\mathbf{Y}$, we get

$$\mathbf{Y}\,(\mathbf{A}, \mathbf{I})\,\mathbf{X} = \mathbf{Yb} = w$$

Also, for the minimization problem, postmultiplying both sides of each of the first two sets of constraints by $\mathbf{X}(\geq \mathbf{0})$, we get

$$\mathbf{Y}\,(\mathbf{A}, \mathbf{I})\,\mathbf{X} \geq (\mathbf{C}_{\mathrm{I}},\ \mathbf{C}_{\mathrm{II}})\mathbf{X}$$

or

$$\mathbf{Y}\,(\mathbf{A},\ \mathbf{I})\,\mathbf{X} \geq (\mathbf{C}_{\mathrm{I}},\ \mathbf{C}_{\mathrm{II}})\mathbf{X} = z$$

(The nonnegativity of the vector $\mathbf{X}$ is essential for maintaining the direction of the inequality.) Combining the two inequalities, it follows that $z \leq w$ for any *feasible* pair $(\mathbf{X}, \mathbf{Y})$.

Note that the theorem does not specify which problem is primal and which is dual. What is important is the sense of the optimization in each problem.

The implication of the theorem is that, given $z \leq w$ for any feasible solutions, the maximum of $z$ and the minimum of $w$ are achieved when the two objective values are equal. A consequence of this result is that the "goodness" of any feasible primal and dual solutions relative to the optimum may be checked by comparing the difference $(w - z)$ to $\frac{(z + w)}{2}$. The smaller the ratio $\frac{2(w - z)}{z + w}$, the closer the two solutions are to being optimal. The suggested *rule of thumb* should *not* be interpreted to imply that the optimal objective value is $\frac{(z + w)}{2}$.

What happens if one of the two problems has an unbounded objective value? The answer is that the other problem must be infeasible. For if it is not, then both problems have feasible solutions, and the relationship $z \leq w$ must hold—an impossible result because either $z = +\infty$ or $w = -\infty$ by assumption.

The next question is: If one problem is infeasible, is the other problem is unbounded? Maybe not! The following counterexample shows that both the primal and the dual can be infeasible:

**Primal.** Maximize $z = \{x_1 + x_2 \mid x_1 - x_2 \leq -1,\ -x_1 + x_2 \leq -1,\ x_1, x_2 \geq 0\}$

**Dual.** Minimize $w = \{-y_1 - y_2 \mid y_1 - y_2 \leq -1,\ -y_1 + y_2 \leq -1,\ y_1, y_2 \geq 0\}$

**Theorem 7.6–2.**  *Given the optimal primal basis* $\mathbf{B}$ *and its associated objective coefficient vector* $\mathbf{C}_B$, *the optimal solution of the dual problem is*

$$\mathbf{Y} = \mathbf{C}_B\mathbf{B}^{-1}$$

*Proof.* The proof rests on verifying two points: $\mathbf{Y} = \mathbf{C}_B\mathbf{B}^{-1}$ is a feasible dual solution and, $z = w$, per Theorem 7.6–1.

The feasibility of $\mathbf{Y} = \mathbf{C}_B\mathbf{B}^{-1}$ is guaranteed by the optimality of the primal, $z_j - c_j \geq 0$ for all $j$—that is,

$$\mathbf{C}_B\mathbf{B}^{-1}\mathbf{A} - \mathbf{C}_\mathrm{I} \geq \mathbf{0} \text{ and } \mathbf{C}_B\mathbf{B}^{-1} - \mathbf{C}_\mathrm{II} \geq \mathbf{0}$$

(See Section 7.4.) The desired result follows by substituting $\mathbf{Y}$ for $\mathbf{C}_B\mathbf{B}^{-1}$.

Next, we show that the associated $w = z$ by noting that

$$w = \mathbf{Yb} = \mathbf{C}_B\mathbf{B}^{-1}\mathbf{b}$$

Similarly, given the primal solution $\mathbf{X}_B = \mathbf{B}^{-1}\mathbf{b}$ (see Section 7.4), we get

$$z = \mathbf{C}_B\mathbf{X}_B = \mathbf{C}_B\mathbf{B}^{-1}\mathbf{b}$$

The dual variables $\mathbf{Y} = \mathbf{C}_B\mathbf{B}^{-1}$ are sometimes referred to as the *simplex multipliers*. They are also known as the *shadow prices*, a name that evolved from the economic interpretation of the dual variables (see Section 4.4.1).

---

**Example 7.6–1.**

The *optimal* basis for the following LP is $\mathbf{B} = (\mathbf{P}_1, \mathbf{P}_4)$. Write the dual and find its optimum solution using the optimal primal basis.

$$\text{Maximize } z = 3x_1 + 5x_2$$

subject to

$$x_1 + 2x_2 + x_3 \quad\quad = 5$$
$$-x_1 + 3x_2 \quad\quad + x_4 = 2$$
$$x_1, x_2, x_3, x_4 \geq 0$$

The dual problem is given as

$$\text{Minimize } w = 5y_1 + 2y_2$$

subject to

$$y_1 - y_2 \geq 3$$
$$2y_1 + 3y_2 \geq 5$$
$$y_1, y_2 \geq 0$$

We have $\mathbf{C}_B = (3, 0)$. The optimal basis and its inverse are given as

$$\mathbf{B} = \begin{bmatrix} 1 & 0 \\ -1 & 1 \end{bmatrix}, \text{ and } \mathbf{B}^{-1} = \begin{bmatrix} 1 & 0 \\ 1 & 1 \end{bmatrix}$$

The associated primal and dual values are

$$(x_1, x_4)^T = \mathbf{B}^{-1}\mathbf{b} = (5, 7)^T$$

$$(y_1, y_2) = \mathbf{C}_B\mathbf{B}^{-1} = (3, \ 0)$$

Both solutions are feasible and $z = w = 15$. Thus the two solutions are optimal.

---

Given $\mathbf{P}_j$ is the $j$th column of $(\mathbf{A}, \mathbf{I})$, we note from Theorem 7.6–2 that

$$z_j - c_j = \mathbf{C}_B\mathbf{B}^{-1}\mathbf{P}_j - c_j = \mathbf{YP}_j - c_j,$$

represents the difference between the left- and right-hand sides of the dual constraints. The maximization primal starts with $z_j - c_j < 0$ for at least one $j$, which means that the corresponding dual constraint of the form $\mathbf{YP}_j \geq c_j$ is not satisfied. When the primal optimal is reached we get $z_j - c_j \geq 0$, for all $j$, which means that the corresponding dual solution $\mathbf{Y} = \mathbf{C}_B\mathbf{B}^{-1}$ becomes feasible. We conclude that while the primal is seeking optimality, the dual is automatically seeking feasibility. This point is the basis for the development of the *dual simplex method* (Section 4.5) in which the iterations start better than optimal and infeasible and remain so until feasibility is acquired at the last iteration. This is in contrast with the (primal) simplex method (Chapter 3), which continues to be worse than optimal but feasible until optimality is achieved.

### Problem set 7.6b

1. Verify that the dual problem of the numeric example given at the end of Theorem 7.6–1 is correct. Then verify graphically that both the primal and dual problems have no feasible solution.

2. Consider the following LP:

$$\text{Maximize } z = 50x_1 + 30x_2 + 10x_3$$

   subject to

$$
\begin{aligned}
2x_1 + x_2 \quad\quad &= \ 1 \\
2x_2 \quad &= -5 \\
4x_1 \quad\quad + x_3 &= \ 6
\end{aligned}
$$

$$x_1, x_2, x_3 \geq 0$$

   **(a)** Write the dual.
   **(b)** Show by inspection that the primal is infeasible.
   **(c)** Show that the dual in (a) is unbounded.
   **(d)** From Problems 1 and 2, develop a general conclusion regarding the relationship between infeasibility and unboundedness in the primal and dual problems.

3. Consider the following LP:

$$\text{Maximize } z = 5x_1 + 12x_2 + 4x_3$$

subject to

$$2x_1 - x_2 + 3x_3 \quad\quad = 2$$

$$x_1 + 2x_2 + x_3 + x_4 = 5$$

$$x_1, x_2, x_3, x_4 \geq 0$$

**(a)** Write the dual.

**(b)** In each of the following cases, first verify that the given basis **B** is feasible for the primal. Next, using $\mathbf{Y} = \mathbf{C}_B \mathbf{B}^{-1}$, compute the associated dual values and verify whether or not the primal solution is optimal.

**(i)** $\mathbf{B} = (\mathbf{P}_4, \mathbf{P}_3)$    **(iii)** $\mathbf{B} = (\mathbf{P}_1, \mathbf{P}_2)$

**(ii)** $\mathbf{B} = (\mathbf{P}_2, \mathbf{P}_3)$    **(iv)** $\mathbf{B} = (\mathbf{P}_1, \mathbf{P}_4)$

**4.** Consider the following LP:

$$\text{Maximize } z = 2x_1 + 4x_2 + 4x_3 - 3x_4$$

subject to

$$x_1 + x_2 + x_3 \quad\quad = 4$$

$$x_1 + 4x_2 + \quad\; + x_4 = 8$$

$$x_1, x_2, x_3, x_4 \geq 0$$

**(a)** Write the dual problem.

**(b)** Verify that $\mathbf{B} = (\mathbf{P}_2, \mathbf{P}_3)$ is optimal by computing $z_j - c_j$ for all nonbasic $\mathbf{P}_j$.

**(c)** Find the associated optimal dual solution.

**5.** An LP model includes two variables $x_1$ and $x_2$ and three constraints of the type $\leq$. The associated slacks are $x_3$, $x_4$, and $x_5$. Suppose that the optimal basis is $\mathbf{B} = (\mathbf{P}_1, \mathbf{P}_2, \mathbf{P}_3)$, and its inverse is

$$\mathbf{B}^{-1} = \begin{bmatrix} 0 & -1 & 1 \\ 0 & 1 & 0 \\ 1 & 1 & -1 \end{bmatrix}$$

The optimal primal and dual solutions are given as

$$\mathbf{X}_B = (x_1,\ x_2,\ x_3)^T = (2,\ 6,\ 2)^T$$

$$\mathbf{Y} = (y_1,\ y_2,\ y_3) = (0,\ 3,\ 2)$$

Determine the optimal value of the objective function.

**6.** Prove the following relationship for the optimal primal and dual solutions:

$$\sum_{i=1}^{m} c_i (\mathbf{B}^{-1}\mathbf{P}_k)_i = \sum_{i=1}^{m} y_i a_{ik}$$

where $\mathbf{C}_B = (c_1, c_2, \ldots, c_m)$ and $\mathbf{P}_k = (a_{1k}, a_{2k}, \ldots, a_{mk})^T$, for $k = 1, 2, \ldots,$ $n$, and $(\mathbf{B}^{-1}\mathbf{P}_k)_i$ is the $i$th element of $\mathbf{B}^{-1}\mathbf{P}_k$.

**7.** Write the dual of

$$\text{Max } z = \{\mathbf{CX} \mid \mathbf{AX} = \mathbf{b}, \ \mathbf{X} \text{ unrestricted}\}$$

**8.** Show that the dual of

$$\text{Max } z = \{\mathbf{CX} \mid \mathbf{AX} \le \mathbf{b}, \ \mathbf{0} < \mathbf{L} \le \mathbf{X} \le \mathbf{U} < \infty\}$$

always possesses a feasible solution.

## 7.7 PARAMETRIC LINEAR PROGRAMMING

Parametric linear programming is an extension of the sensitivity analysis procedures we presented in Section 4.7. It investigates the changes in the optimum LP solution that result from *predetermined* continuous variations in the objective function coefficients and the right-hand side of the constraints.

Some LP presentations may give the impression that parametric linear programming applies to only linear parametric variations. Actually, the procedure can be applied to any quantifiable function, linear or nonlinear. The only difficulty with the nonlinear functions is that the computations may become cumbersome. We will concentrate primarily on the linear case. (See Problem 7.7a–5 for an illustration of the nonlinear case.)

Suppose that the LP is defined as

$$\text{Max } z = \left\{ \mathbf{CX} \mid \sum_{j=1}^{n} \mathbf{P}_j x_j = \mathbf{b}, \ \mathbf{X} \ge \mathbf{0} \right\}$$

Useful parametric analysis deals making parametric changes in the objective function and the right-hand side of the constraint. Typical parametric linear functions are

$$\mathbf{C}(t) = \mathbf{C} + t\,\mathbf{C}'$$

$$\mathbf{b}(t) = \mathbf{b} + t\,\mathbf{b}'$$

where $t$ is the parameter of variation and $\mathbf{C}'$ and $\mathbf{b}'$ are given vectors. For convenience, we will assume that $t \ge 0$.

The general idea of parametric analysis is to start with the optimal solution at $t = 0$. Then, using the optimality and feasibility conditions of the simplex method, we determine the range $0 \le t \le t_1$ for which the solution at $t = 0$ remains

According to these conditions, the basic solution $\mathbf{X}_{B_1}$ remains optimal for all $t \geq 1$. This means that $t_2 = \infty$ and the process ends. Observe that the optimality condition $-2 + 2t \geq 0$, automatically "remembers" that $\mathbf{X}_{B_1}$ is optimal for a range of $t$ that starts from the last critical value $t_1 = 1$. This will always be the case in parametric programming computations.

The optimal solution for the entire range of $t$ is summarized subsequently. The value of $z$ is computed by direct substitution.

| $t$ | $x_1$ | $x_2$ | $x_3$ | $z$ |
|---|---|---|---|---|
| $0 \leq t \leq 1$ | 0 | 5 | 30 | $160 + 140t$ |
| $t \geq 1$ | 0 | 0 | 30 | $150 + 150t$ |

## Problem set 7.7a

1. In example 7.7–1, suppose that $t$ is unrestricted in sign. Determine the range of $t$ for which $\mathbf{X}_{B_0}$ remains optimal.
2. Solve Example 7.7–1, assuming that the objective function is given as
   (a) Maximize $z = (3 + 3t)x_1 + 2x_2 + (5 - 6t)x_3$
   (b) Maximize $z = (3 - 2t)x_1 + (2 + t)x_2 + (5 + 2t)x_3$
   (c) Maximize $z = (3 + t)x_1 + (2 + 2t)x_2 + (5 - t)x_3$
3. Study the variation in the optimal solution of the following parameterized LP given $t \geq 0$.

$$\text{Minimize } z = (4 - t)\,x_1 + (1 - 3t)\,x_2 + (2 - 2t)\,x_3$$

subject to

$$3x_1 + x_2 + 2x_3 = 3$$
$$4x_1 + 3x_2 + 2x_3 \geq 6$$
$$x_1 + 2x_2 + 5x_3 \leq 4$$
$$x_1, x_2, x_3 \geq 0$$

4. The analysis in this section assumes that the optimal solution of the LP at $t = 0$ is obtained by the (primal) simplex method. In some problems, it may be more convenient to obtain the optimal solution by the dual simplex method (Section 4.5). Show how the parametric analysis can be carried out in this case, then analyze the LP of Example 4.5–1, assuming that the objective function is given as

$$\text{Minimize } z = (3 + t)\,x_1 + (2 + 4t)\,x_2$$

**5.** In Example 7.7–1, suppose that the objective function is nonlinear in $t$ ($t \geq 0$) and is defined as

$$\text{Maximize } z = (3 + 2t^2) x_1 + (2 - 2t^2) x_2 + (5 - t) x_3$$

Determine the first critical value $t_1$.

## 7.7.2 Parametric Changes in b

The parameterized right-hand side $\mathbf{b}(t)$ can only affect the feasibility of the problem. The critical values of $t$ are thus determined based on the following condition:

$$\mathbf{X}_{B_1} = \mathbf{B}_1^{-1}\mathbf{b}(t) \geq \mathbf{0}$$

---

**Example 7.7–2.**

$$\text{Maximize } z = 3x_1 + 2x_2 + 5x_3$$

subject to

$$x_1 + 2x_2 + x_3 \leq 40 - t$$
$$3x_1 \qquad + 2x_3 \leq 60 + 2t$$
$$x_1 + 4x_2 \qquad \leq 30 - 7t$$
$$x_1, \ x_2, \ x_3 \geq 0$$

Assume that $t \geq 0$.

At $t = t_0 = 0$, the problem is identical to that of Problem 7.7–1. We thus have

$$\mathbf{X}_{B_0} = (x_2, x_3, x_6)^T = (5, 30, 10)^T$$

$$\mathbf{B}_0^{-1} = \begin{bmatrix} \dfrac{1}{2} & -\dfrac{1}{4} & 0 \\[2mm] 0 & \dfrac{1}{2} & 0 \\[2mm] -2 & 1 & 1 \end{bmatrix}$$

To determine the first critical value $t_1$, we apply the condition $\mathbf{X}_{B_0} = \mathbf{B}_0^{-1}\mathbf{b}(t) \geq \mathbf{0}$ which yields

$$\begin{bmatrix} x_2 \\ x_3 \\ x_6 \end{bmatrix} = \begin{bmatrix} 5 - t \\ 30 + t \\ 10 - 3t \end{bmatrix} \geq \begin{bmatrix} 0 \\ 0 \\ 0 \end{bmatrix}$$

These inequalities are satisfied for $t \leq \frac{10}{3}$, meaning that $t_1 = \frac{10}{3}$ and that the basis $\mathbf{B}_0$ remains feasible for the range $0 \leq t \leq \frac{10}{3}$. However, the values of the basic variables $x_2$, $x_3$, and $x_6$ will change with $t$.

The value of the basic variable $x_6$ ($=10 - 3t$) will equal zero at $t = t_1 = \frac{10}{3}$, and will become negative for $t > \frac{10}{3}$. Thus, at $t = \frac{10}{3}$, we can determine the alternative basis $\mathbf{B}_1$ by applying the revised dual simplex method (see Problem 7.5b–5 for details). The leaving variable is $x_6$.

*Alternative Basis at $t = t_1 = \frac{10}{3}$*

Given $x_6$ is the leaving variable, we determine the entering variable as

$$\mathbf{X}_{B_0} = (x_2, \ x_3, \ x_6)^T, \ \mathbf{C}_{B_0} = (2, \ 5, \ 0)$$

Thus,

$$\{z_j - c_j\}_{j=1, 4, 5} = \{\mathbf{C}_{B_0} \mathbf{B}_0^{-1} \mathbf{P}_j - c_j\}_{j=1, 4, 5} = (4, \ 1, \ 2)$$

Next, we compute

$$\{(\mathbf{B}_0^{-1} \mathbf{P}_j)_{x_6}\}_{j=1, 4, 5} = \text{(row of } \mathbf{B}_0^{-1} \text{ associated with } x_6) \ (\mathbf{P}_1, \ \mathbf{P}_4, \ \mathbf{P}_5)$$

$$= \text{(third row of } \mathbf{B}_0^{-1}) \ (\mathbf{P}_1, \ \mathbf{P}_4, \ \mathbf{P}_5)$$

$$= (-2, \ 1, \ 1) \ (\mathbf{P}_1, \ \mathbf{P}_4, \ \mathbf{P}_5)$$

$$= (2, \ -2, \ 1)$$

The entering variable is thus associated with

$$\theta = \min\left\{ - , \ \left|\frac{1}{-2}\right|, \ - \right\} = \frac{1}{2}$$

which yields $\mathbf{P}_4$ as the entering vector.

The new basis $\mathbf{B}_1^{-1}$ is determined as

$$\mathbf{B}_1^{-1} = \mathbf{E}\mathbf{B}_0^{-1} = \begin{bmatrix} 1 & 1 & \frac{1}{4} \\ 0 & 1 & 0 \\ 0 & 0 & -\frac{1}{2} \end{bmatrix} \begin{bmatrix} \frac{1}{2} & -\frac{1}{4} & 0 \\ 0 & \frac{1}{2} & 0 \\ -2 & 1 & 1 \end{bmatrix} = \begin{bmatrix} 0 & 0 & \frac{1}{4} \\ 0 & \frac{1}{2} & 0 \\ 1 & -\frac{1}{2} & -\frac{1}{2} \end{bmatrix}$$

This gives $\mathbf{X}_{B_1} = (x_2, x_3, x_4)^T$.

The next critical value $t_2$ is determined from the condition $\mathbf{X}_{B_1} = \mathbf{B}^{-1}\mathbf{b}(t) \geq \mathbf{0}$, which yields

$$\begin{bmatrix} x_2 \\ x_3 \\ x_4 \end{bmatrix} = \begin{bmatrix} \dfrac{30 - 7t}{4} \\ 30 + t \\ \dfrac{-10 + 3t}{2} \end{bmatrix} \geq \begin{bmatrix} 0 \\ 0 \\ 0 \end{bmatrix}$$

These condition show that $\mathbf{B}_1$ remains feasible for $\frac{10}{3} \leq t \leq \frac{30}{7}$.

At $t = t_2 = \frac{30}{7}$ an alternative basis can be obtained by the revised dual simplex method. The leaving variable is $x_2$ because it corresponds the condition yielding the critical value $t_2$.

*Alternative Basis at* $t = t_2 = \frac{30}{7}$

Given $x_2$ is the leaving variable, we determine the entering variable as follows:

$$\mathbf{X}_{B_1} = (x_2, \, x_3, \, x_4)^T, \quad \mathbf{C}_{B_1} = (2, \, 5, \, 0)$$

Thus,

$$\{z_j - c_j\}_{j=1,5,6} = \{\mathbf{C}_{B_1} \mathbf{B}_1^{-1} \mathbf{P}_j - c_j\}_{j=1,5,6} = \left(5, \, \frac{5}{2}, \, \frac{1}{2}\right)$$

Next, we compute

$$\{(\mathbf{B}_1^{-1} \mathbf{P}_j)_{x_2}\}_{j=1,5,6} = (\text{Row of } \mathbf{B}_1^{-1} \text{ associated with } x_2) \, (\mathbf{P}_1, \, \mathbf{P}_5, \, \mathbf{P}_6)$$

$$= (\text{First row of } \mathbf{B}_1^{-1}) \, (\mathbf{P}_1, \, \mathbf{P}_5, \, \mathbf{P}_6)$$

$$= \left(0, \, 0, \, \frac{1}{4}\right) (\mathbf{P}_1, \, \mathbf{P}_5, \, \mathbf{P}_6)$$

$$= \left(\frac{1}{4}, \, 0, \, \frac{1}{4}\right)$$

Because these elements are all $\geq 0$, the problem has no feasible solution for $t > \frac{30}{7}$, and the parametric analysis ends at $t = t_2 = \frac{30}{7}$.

The optimal solution is summarized as

| $t$ | $x_1$ | $x_2$ | $x_3$ | $z$ |
|---|---|---|---|---|
| $0 \leq t \leq \frac{10}{3}$ | 0 | $5 - t$ | $30 + t$ | $160 + 3t$ |
| $\frac{10}{3} \leq t \leq \frac{30}{7}$ | 0 | $\frac{30 - 7t}{4}$ | $30 + t$ | $165 + \frac{3}{2}t$ |
| $t > \frac{30}{7}$ | | (No feasible solution exists) | | |

## Problem set 7.7b

1. In Example 7.7–2, find the first critical value $t_1$ and define the vectors of $\mathbf{B}_1$ in each of the following cases:
   (a) $\mathbf{b}(t) = (40 + 2t, \, 60 - 3t, \, 30 + 6t)^T$
   (b) $\mathbf{b}(t) = (40 - t, \, 60 + 2t, \, 30 - 5t)^T$

2. Study the variation in the optimal solution of the following parameterized LP given $t \geq 0$.

$$\text{Minimize } z = 4x_1 + x_2 + 2x_3$$

subject to

$$3x_1 + x_2 + 2x_3 = 3 + 3t$$

$$4x_1 + 3x_2 + 2x_3 \geq 6 + 2t$$

$$x_1 + 2x_2 + 5x_3 \leq 4 - t$$

$$x_1, x_2, x_3 \geq 0$$

3. The analysis in this section assumes that the optimal LP solution at $t = 0$ is obtained by the (primal) simplex method. In some problems, it may be more convenient to obtain the optimal solution by the dual simplex method (Section 4.5). Show how the parametric analysis can be carried out in this case, and then analyze the LP of Example 4.5–1, assuming that the right-hand side vector is

$$\mathbf{b}(t) = (3 + 2t, \ 6 - t, \ 3 - 4t)^T$$

Assume $t \geq 0$.

4. Solve Problem 2 assuming that the right-hand side is changed to

$$\mathbf{b}(t) = (3 + 3t^2, \ 6 + 2t^2, \ 4 - t^2)^T$$

Further assume that $t$ can be positive, zero, or negative.

## 7.8 KARMARKAR INTERIOR POINT ALGORITHM

The simplex method obtains the optimum solution by moving along edges of the solution space from one extreme point to the next. Although in practice the simplex method has served well in solving very large problems, theoretically the number of iterations needed to reach the optimum solution can grow exponentially. In fact, researchers have constructed LPs with $n$ variables in which all $2^n$ extreme points are encountered before the optimum is attained.[*]

In 1984, N. Karmarkar developed a polynomial-time algorithm that cuts across the interior of the solution space. The effectiveness of the algorithm appears to be in the solution of extremely large LPs.

We start by introducing the main idea of the Karmarkar method and then provide the computational details of the algorithm.

### 7.8.1 Basic Idea of the Interior-Point Algorithm

Consider the following (trivial) example:

---

[*]Try the following problem using TORA: maximize $z = x_1 + x_2$ subject to $x_1 \leq 1, 2x_1 + x_2 \leq 3, x_1, x_2 \geq 0$. The solution is attained after all $2^2 = 4$ feasible extreme points have been examined.

$$\text{Maximize } z = x_1$$

subject to

$$0 \le x_1 \le 2$$

Using $x_2$ as a slack variable, the problem can be rewritten as

$$\text{Maximize } z = x_1$$

subject to

$$x_1 + x_2 = 2$$

$$x_1, x_2 \ge 0$$

Figure 7–6 depicts the problem. The solution space is given by the line segment $AB$. The direction of increase in $z$ is in the positive direction of $x_1$.

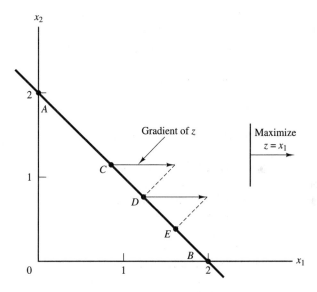

**Figure 7–6**

Let us start with any arbitrary *interior* (nonextreme) point $C$ in the feasible space (line $AB$). The **gradient** of the objective function (maximize $z = x_1$) at $C$ is the direction of fastest increase in $z$. If we locate an arbitrary point along the gradient and then project it perpendicularly on the feasible space (line $AB$), we obtain the new point $D$ with a better objective value $z$. Such improvement is obtained by moving in the direction of the projected gradient $CD$. If we repeat the procedure at $D$, we will determine a new point $E$ that is closer to the optimum at $B$. Conceivably, if we move (cautiously) in the direction of the **projected gradient,** we will "stumble" on the optimum point $B$. If we are minimizing $z$ (instead of maximizing), the procedure of the projected gradient will correctly move us *away* from point $B$ toward the minimum at point $A$ ($x_1 = 0$).

The given steps hardly define an algorithm in the normal sense, but the idea is intriguing! We need some modifications that will guarantee that (1) the steps generated along the projected gradient will not "overshoot" the optimum point at B, and (2) in the general $n$-dimensional case, the direction created by the projected gradient will not cause an "entrapment" of the algorithm at a nonoptimum point. This, basically, is what Karmarkar's interior-point algorithm accomplishes.

### 7.8.2 Interior-Point Algorithm

Several variants of Karmarkar's algorithm are in circulation. Our presentation follows the original algorithm. Karmarkar assumes that the LP is given as

$$\text{Minimize } z = \mathbf{CX}$$

subject to

$$\mathbf{AX} = 0$$

$$\mathbf{1X} = 1$$

$$\mathbf{X} \geq 0$$

All the constraints are homogeneous equations except for the constraint $\mathbf{1X} = \sum_{j=1}^{n} x_j = 1$, which defines an $n$-dimensional simplex. The validity of Karmarkar's algorithm rests on satisfying two conditions:

1. $\mathbf{X} = \left( \dfrac{1}{n}, \dfrac{1}{n}, ..., \dfrac{1}{n} \right)$ satisfies $\mathbf{AX} = \mathbf{0}$

2. $\min z = 0$

Karmarkar provides algebraic transformations for converting the general LP problem to this form. The following example illustrates how a general LP may be put in the homogeneous form $\mathbf{AX} = 0$ with $\mathbf{1X} = 1$. It also shows how the transformation results in $\mathbf{X} = (\frac{1}{n}, \frac{1}{n}, ..., \frac{1}{n})$ being a feasible solution of $\mathbf{AX} = 0$ (condition 1). The transformation needed to produce $\min z = 0$ (condition 2) will not be presented here because it is tedious.

---

**Example 7.8–1.**

Consider the problem.

$$\text{Maximize } z = y_1 + y_2$$

subject to

$$y_1 + 2y_2 \leq 2$$

$$y_1, y_2 \geq 0$$

The constraint $y_1 + 2y_2 \leq 2$ is converted into an equation by augmenting a slack variable $y_3 \geq 0$ to yield

$$y_1 + 2y_2 + y_3 = 2$$

Now define

$$y_1 + y_2 + y_3 \leq U$$

where $U$ is sufficiently large so as not to eliminate any feasible points in the original solution space. In our example, as can be determined from the equation $y_1 + 2y_2 + y_3 = 2$, $U = 5$ will be adequate. Augmenting a slack variable $y_4 \geq 0$, we obtain

$$y_1 + y_2 + y_3 + y_4 = 5$$

We can homogenize the constraint $y_1 + 2y_2 + y_3 = 2$ by multiplying the right-hand side by $\frac{(y_1 + y_2 + y_3 + y_4)}{5}$ because the latter fraction equals 1. This yields, after simplification,

$$3y_1 + 8y_2 + 3y_3 - 2y_4 = 0$$

To convert $y_1 + y_2 + y_3 + y_4 = 5$ to the simplex form, we define the new variable $x_i = \frac{y_i}{5}, i = 1, 2, 3, 4$, to obtain

$$\text{Maximize } z = 5x_1 + 5x_2$$

subject to

$$3x_1 + 8x_2 + 3x_3 - 2x_4 = 0$$

$$x_1 + x_2 + x_3 + x_4 = 1$$

$$x_j \geq 0, \quad j = 1, 2, 3, 4$$

Finally, we can ensure that the center $\mathbf{X} = (\frac{1}{n}, \frac{1}{n}, ..., \frac{1}{n})$ of the simplex is a feasible point for homogeneous equations by subtracting from the left-hand side of each equation an artificial variable whose coefficient equals the algebraic sum of all the constraint coefficients on the left-hand side—that is, $3 + 8 + 3 - 2 = 12$. The artificial variables are then added to the simplex equation and are penalized appropriately in the objective function. In our example, the artificial $x_5$ is augmented as follows:

$$\text{Maximize } z = 5x_1 + 5x_2 - Mx_5$$

subject to

$$3x_1 + 8x_2 + 3x_3 - 2x_4 - 12x_5 = 0$$

$$x_1 + x_2 + x_3 + x_4 + x_5 = 1$$

$$x_j \geq 0, \quad j = 1, 2, ..., 5$$

For this system of equations, the new simplex center $(\frac{1}{5}, \frac{1}{5}, ..., \frac{1}{5})$ is feasible for the homogeneous equation. The value $M$ in the objective nfunction is chosen sufficiently large to drive $x_5$ to zero (compare with the $M$-method, Section 3.4.1).

We now present the main steps of the algorithm. Figure 7–7 (a) provides a typical illustration of the solution space is three dimensions with the homogeneous set $\mathbf{AX} = \mathbf{0}$ consisting only of one equation. By definition, the solution space consisting of the line segment $AB$ lies entirely in the simplex $\mathbf{1X} = 1$ and passes through the feasible interior point $(\frac{1}{3}, \frac{1}{3}, \frac{1}{3})$. In a similar fashion, Figure 7–7 (b) provides an illustration of the solution space $ABC$ in four dimensions with the homogeneous set again consisting of one constraint only. In this case, the center of the simplex is given by $(\frac{1}{4}, \frac{1}{4}, \frac{1}{4}, \frac{1}{4})$.

Karmarkar's principal idea is to start from an interior point represented by the center of the simplex and then advance in the direction of the *projected gradient* to determine a new solution point. The new point must be strictly an interior point, meaning that all its coordinates must be positive. The validity the algorithm rests on this condition.

For the new solution point to be strictly interior, it must not lie on the boundaries of the simplex. (In terms of Figure 7–7, points $A$ and $B$ in three dimensions and lines $AB$, $BC$, and $AC$ in three dimensions must be excluded.) To guarantee this result, a sphere with its center coinciding with that of the simplex is inscribed tightly inside the simplex. In the $n$-dimensional case, the radius $r$ of this sphere equals $\frac{1}{\sqrt{n(n-1)}}$. Now a smaller sphere with radius $\alpha r$ $(0 < \alpha < 1)$ will be a subset of the sphere and any point in the intersection of the smaller sphere with the homogeneous system $\mathbf{AX} = \mathbf{0}$ will be an interior point, with all its coordinates being strictly positive. Thus, we can move as far as possible in this restricted space (intersection of $\mathbf{AX} = \mathbf{0}$ and the $\alpha r$-sphere) along the projected gradient to determine the new (necessarily improved) solution point.

The new solution point no longer will be at the center of the simplex. For the procedure to be iterative, we need to find a way to bring the *new* solution point to the center of a simplex. Karmarkar satisfies this requirement by proposing the following intriguing idea, called **projective transformation.** Let

$$y_i = \frac{\dfrac{x_i}{x_{ki}}}{\displaystyle\sum_{j=1}^{n} \dfrac{x_i}{x_{kj}}}, \quad i = 1, 2, ..., n$$

where $x_{ki}$ is the $i$th element of the current solution point $\mathbf{X}_k$. The transformation is valid, because all $x_{ki} > 0$ by design. You will also notice that $\sum_{i=1}^{n} y_i = 1$, or $\mathbf{1Y} = 1$, by definition. This transformation is equivalent to

$$\mathbf{Y} = \frac{\mathbf{D}_k^{-1}\mathbf{X}}{\mathbf{1D}_k^{-1}\mathbf{X}}$$

where $\mathbf{D}_k$ is a diagonal matrix whose $i$th diagonal elements equal $x_{ki}$. The transformation maps the $X$-space onto the $Y$-space uniquely because we can directly show that the last equation yields

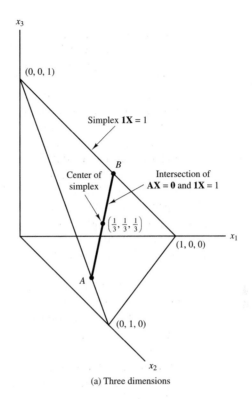

(a) Three dimensions

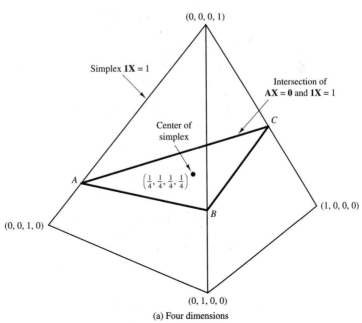

(a) Four dimensions

**Figure 7–7**

$$\mathbf{X} = \frac{\mathbf{D}_k\mathbf{Y}}{\mathbf{1D}_k\mathbf{Y}}$$

By definition, min $\mathbf{CX} = 0$. It follows that $\mathbf{1D}_k\mathbf{Y}$ must be positive, in which case our original linear program can be written as

$$\text{Minimize } z = \mathbf{CD}_k\mathbf{Y}$$

subject to

$$\mathbf{AD}_k\mathbf{Y} = \mathbf{0}$$

$$\mathbf{1Y} = 1$$

$$\mathbf{Y} \geq \mathbf{0}$$

The transformed problem has the same format as the original problem. We can thus start with the simplex center $\mathbf{Y} = (\frac{1}{n}, \frac{1}{n}, ..., \frac{1}{n})$ and repeat the iterative step. After each iteration, we can compute the values of the original $\mathbf{X}$ variables from the $\mathbf{Y}$ solution.

We show now how the new solution point can be determined for the transformed problem. Our problem at any iteration $k$ is given by

$$\text{Maximize } z = \mathbf{CD}_k\mathbf{Y}$$

subject to

$$\mathbf{AD}_k\mathbf{Y} = \mathbf{0}$$

$$\mathbf{Y} \text{ lies in the } \alpha r\text{-sphere}$$

Because the $\alpha r$-sphere is a subset of the space of the constraints $\mathbf{1X} = 1$ and $\mathbf{X} \geq \mathbf{0}$, these two constraints can be dispensed with. The optimum solution of the preceding problem can be shown to be

$$\mathbf{Y}_{\text{new}} = \mathbf{Y}_{\text{current}} + \alpha r \frac{\mathbf{c}_p}{\|\mathbf{c}_p\|}$$

where $\mathbf{Y}_{\text{current}} = (\frac{1}{n}, \frac{1}{n}, ..., \frac{1}{n})^t$ and $\mathbf{c}_p$ is the projected gradient, which can be shown to be computed as

$$\mathbf{c}_p = [\mathbf{I} - \mathbf{P}^T(\mathbf{PP}^T)^{-1}\mathbf{P}](\mathbf{CD}_k)^T$$

with $\mathbf{P} = \begin{pmatrix} \mathbf{AD}_k \\ \mathbf{1} \end{pmatrix}$

The specific selection of $\alpha$ is crucial in producing a potent algorithm. Normally, we would select $\alpha$ as large as possible to acquire large jumps in the solution. However, by choosing $\alpha$ too large, we may come too close to the prohibited boundaries of the simplex. There is no known general answer to this problem. Karmarkar suggests the use of $\alpha = \frac{(n-1)}{3n}$.

The steps of Karmarkar's algorithm are

**Step 0.** Start with the solution point $\mathbf{X}_0 = (\frac{1}{n}, \frac{1}{n}, ..., \frac{1}{n})$ and compute $r = \sqrt{\frac{1}{n(n-1)}}$ and $\alpha = \frac{(n-1)}{3n}$.

**General step k.**  Define

$$\mathbf{D}_k = \text{diag } \{x_{k1}, \ldots, x_{kn}\}$$

$$\mathbf{P} = \begin{pmatrix} \mathbf{A}\mathbf{D}_k \\ 1 \end{pmatrix}$$

and compute

$$\mathbf{Y}_{\text{new}} = \left( \frac{1}{n}, \ldots, \frac{1}{n} \right)^T + \alpha r \frac{\mathbf{c}_p}{\|\mathbf{c}_p\|}$$

$$\mathbf{X}_{k+1} = \frac{\mathbf{D}_k \mathbf{Y}_{\text{new}}}{1 \mathbf{D}_k \mathbf{Y}_{\text{new}}}$$

where $\mathbf{c}_p = [\mathbf{I} - \mathbf{P}^T(\mathbf{P}\mathbf{P}^T)^{-1}\mathbf{P}](\mathbf{c}\mathbf{D}_k)^T$

---

**Example 7.8–2.**

Consider the following linear program, which is already in the format specified by the Karmarkar algorithm.

$$\text{Minimize } z = x_1 - 2x_2$$

subject to

$$x_1 - 2x_2 + x_3 = 0$$

$$x_1 + x_2 + x_3 = 1$$

$$x_1, \ x_2, \ x_3 \geq 0$$

The example satisfies all the conditions of Karmarkar's algorithm—namely, $\mathbf{X} = \left( \frac{1}{3}, \frac{1}{3}, \frac{1}{3} \right)$ satisfies $x_1 - 2x_2 + x_3 = 0$ and the optimum value of $z$ [corresponding to the optimum solution $\left( \frac{2}{3}, \frac{1}{3}, 0 \right)$] is zero.

*Iteration 0*

$$\mathbf{X}_0 = \left( \frac{1}{3}, \frac{1}{3}, \frac{1}{3} \right), \quad r = \frac{1}{\sqrt{6}}, \quad \alpha = \frac{2}{9}, \quad z = \frac{-1}{3} = -.33333$$

*Iteration 1*

$$\mathbf{D}_0 = \begin{bmatrix} \frac{1}{3} & 0 & 0 \\ 0 & \frac{1}{3} & 0 \\ 0 & 0 & \frac{1}{3} \end{bmatrix}$$

$$\mathbf{c}\mathbf{D}_0 = \left( \frac{1}{3}, \ -\frac{2}{3}, \ 0 \right)$$

$$\mathbf{A}\mathbf{D}_0 = (1, \ -2, \ 1) \begin{bmatrix} \frac{1}{3} & 0 & 0 \\ 0 & \frac{1}{3} & 0 \\ 0 & 0 & \frac{1}{3} \end{bmatrix} = \left( \frac{1}{3}, \ -\frac{2}{3}, \ \frac{1}{3} \right)$$

$$\mathbf{P} = \begin{bmatrix} \dfrac{1}{3} & -\dfrac{2}{3} & \dfrac{1}{3} \\ 1 & 1 & 1 \end{bmatrix}$$

$$(\mathbf{P}\mathbf{P}^T)^{-1} = \begin{bmatrix} \dfrac{2}{3} & 0 \\ 0 & 3 \end{bmatrix}^{-1} = \begin{bmatrix} \dfrac{3}{2} & 0 \\ 0 & \dfrac{1}{3} \end{bmatrix}$$

$$\mathbf{c}_p = \left[ \begin{pmatrix} 1 & 0 & 0 \\ 0 & 1 & 0 \\ 0 & 0 & 1 \end{pmatrix} - \begin{pmatrix} \dfrac{1}{3} & 1 \\ -\dfrac{2}{3} & 1 \\ \dfrac{1}{3} & 1 \end{pmatrix} \begin{pmatrix} \dfrac{3}{2} & 0 \\ 0 & \dfrac{1}{3} \end{pmatrix} \begin{pmatrix} \dfrac{1}{3} & -\dfrac{2}{3} & \dfrac{1}{3} \\ 1 & 1 & 1 \end{pmatrix} \right] \begin{bmatrix} \dfrac{1}{3} \\ -\dfrac{2}{3} \\ 0 \end{bmatrix}$$

$$= \left( \dfrac{1}{6}, \ 0, \ -\dfrac{1}{6} \right)^T$$

$$\|\mathbf{c}_p\| = \sqrt{\left(\dfrac{1}{6}\right)^2 + 0 + \left(\dfrac{1}{6}\right)^2} = .2357$$

$$\dfrac{\alpha r}{\|\mathbf{c}_p\|} = \dfrac{\left(\dfrac{2}{9}\right)\left(\dfrac{1}{\sqrt{6}}\right)}{.2357} = .384901$$

$$\mathbf{Y}_{\text{new}} = \left( \dfrac{1}{3}, \dfrac{1}{3}, \dfrac{1}{3} \right)^T + .384901 \left( \dfrac{1}{6}, \ 0, \ \dfrac{-1}{6} \right)^T$$

$$= (.397483, .333333, .269183)^T$$

We now compute $\mathbf{X}_1$, the solution associated with $\mathbf{Y}_{\text{new}}$. Because $\mathbf{D}_0$ has equal diagonal elements $(= \frac{1}{3})$ and the fact that $\mathbf{1Y} = 1$, the formula $\mathbf{X}_1 = \mathbf{D}_0\mathbf{Y}_{\text{new}}/\mathbf{1D}_0\mathbf{Y}_{\text{new}}$ yields $\mathbf{X}_1 = \mathbf{Y}_{\text{new}} = (.397483, .333333, .269183)^T$. The corresponding value of $z = -.269183$, which is better than the preceding solution $\mathbf{X}_0$, whose $z = -.33333$.

If $\alpha$ is taken larger than the current value of $\frac{2}{9}$, the solution will move faster toward the optimum point $(\frac{2}{3}, \frac{1}{3}, 0)$. In fact, if we take $\alpha = 1$, the resulting $\mathbf{Y}_{\text{new}}$ will provide the optimum value directly. However, we *cannot* do this because $x_3 = 0$ will invalidate the assumption on which the projective transformation $\mathbf{Y}$ is based. This observation provides a glimpse at one of the uncertainties in the interior-point algorithm.

**Iteration 2**

$$\mathbf{D}_1 = \text{diag}\{.397485, .333333, .269182\}$$

$$\mathbf{cD}_1 = (.397485, -.666666, 0)$$

$$\mathbf{AD}_1 = (1, -2 = 1) \begin{bmatrix} .397485 & 0 & 0 \\ 0 & .333333 & 0 \\ 0 & 0 & .269182 \end{bmatrix}$$

$$= (.397485, -.666666, .269182)$$

$$\mathbf{P} = \begin{pmatrix} .397845 & -.666666 & .269182 \\ 1 & 1 & 1 \end{pmatrix}$$

$$\mathbf{c}_p = (.132402, .018152, -.150555)^T$$

$$\|\mathbf{c}_p\| = .201312$$

$$\frac{\alpha r}{\|\mathbf{c}_p\|} = \frac{\left(\frac{2}{9}\right)\left(\frac{1}{\sqrt{6}}\right)}{.201312} = .450653$$

$$\mathbf{Y}_{\text{new}} = \left(\frac{1}{3}, \frac{1}{3}, \frac{1}{3}\right)^T + .450653\,(.132402, .018152, -.150555)^T$$

$$= (.393001, .341514, .265486)^T$$

Now, to compute $\mathbf{X}_2$, we have

$$\mathbf{D}_1\mathbf{Y}_{\text{new}} = \begin{pmatrix} .156212 \\ .113838 \\ .071464 \end{pmatrix}, \quad \mathbf{1}\mathbf{D}_1\mathbf{Y}_{\text{new}} = .341514$$

$$\mathbf{X}_2 = \frac{\mathbf{D}_1\mathbf{Y}_{\text{new}}}{\mathbf{1}\mathbf{D}_1\mathbf{Y}_{\text{new}}} = \begin{pmatrix} .457411 \\ .333333 \\ .209256 \end{pmatrix}$$

$$z = .20934$$

Repeated application of the steps of the algorithm will move the solution closer to the optimum point $\left(\frac{2}{3}, \frac{1}{3}, 0\right)$. Karmarkar does provide an additional step for rounding the optimal solution to the optimum extreme point. The details of this step will not be presented here, however.

## Problem set 7.8a

**1.** Carry out one additional iteration in Example 7.8–2, and show that the solution is moving toward the optimum $z = 0$.

**2.** Carry out three iterations of Karmarkar's algorithm for the following problem:

$$\text{Maximize } z = -4x_1 + x_3 + x_4$$

subject to

$$-2x_1 + 2x_2 + x_3 - x_4 = 0$$
$$x_1 + x_2 + x_3 + x_4 = 1$$
$$x_1, \; x_2, \; x_3, \; x_4 \geq 0$$

**3.** Carry out three iterations of Karmarkar's algorithm for the following linear program:

$$\text{Maximize } z = 2x_1 + x_2$$

subject to

$$x_1 + x_2 \leq 4$$
$$x_1, \; x_2 \geq 0$$

## 7.9 SUMMARY

This chapter has presented the revised simplex method, the upper-bounding technique, and the decomposition algorithms. The thrust of these algorithms is to improve the efficiency and the accuracy of the results. Of the three methods, the revised simplex method and the upper-bounding techniques stand out as the two most promising techniques. The decomposition algorithm is not general enough to warrant inclusion in commercial codes. Besides, the current capacity and speed of today's computers preclude the need for implementing the decomposition principle.

Parametric programming is a useful tool. It converts the static LP solution into a general one that reflects the dynamic changes in the structure of the LP model.

Karmarkar's algorithm has not "caught on" as the "popular" method for solving LPs. Literature references to the use of the algorithm in practice are indeed scarce. Apparently, the use of the algorithm requires special computing hardware as well as the use of heuristics to condition the LP favorably for the application of the algorithm.

## REFERENCES

BAZRAA, M., J. JARVIS, AND H. SHERALI, *Linear Programming and Network Flows,* 2nd ed., Wiley, New York, 1990.

HOOKER, J., "Karmarkar's Linear Programming Algorithm," *Interfaces,* Vol. 16, No. 4, pp. 75–90, 1986.

NERING, E., and A. TUCKER, *Linear Programming and Related Problems,* Academic Press, Boston, 1992.

## COMPREHENSIVE PROBLEMS

■ **7-1** Suppose that you are given the points

$$A = (6, \; 4, \; 6, \; -2), \; B = (4, \; 12, \; -4, \; 8), \; C = (-4, \; 0, \; 8, \; 4)$$

Develop a systematic procedure that will allow determining whether or not each of the following points can expressed as a convex combination of *A*, B, and *C*:

(a)  (3, 5, 4, 2)

(b)  (5, 8, 4, 9).

■ **7–2.** Consider the following LP:

$$\text{Maximize } z = 3x_1 + 2x_2$$

subject to

$$x_1 + 2x_2 \le 6$$
$$2x_1 + x_2 \le 8$$
$$-x_1 + x_2 \le 1$$
$$x_1, x_2 \ge 0$$

Determine the optimum simplex tableau (use TORA for convenience), and then directly use the information in the optimum simplex tableau to determine the *second* best extreme-point solution (relative to the "absolute" optimum) for the problem. Verify the answer by solving the problem graphically. (*Hint:* Consult the extreme points that are *adjacent* to the optimum solution.)

■ **7–3.** *Interval programming.* Consider the following LP:

$$\text{Maximize } z = \{\mathbf{CX} \mid \mathbf{L} \le \mathbf{AX} \le \mathbf{U}, \ \mathbf{X} \ge \mathbf{0}\}$$

where **L** and **U** are constant column vectors. Define the slack vector $\mathbf{Y} \ge \mathbf{0}$ such that $\mathbf{AX} + \mathbf{Y} = \mathbf{U}$. Show that this LP is equivalent to

$$\text{Maximize } z = \{\mathbf{CX} \mid \mathbf{AX} + \mathbf{Y} = \mathbf{U}, \ \mathbf{0} \le \mathbf{Y} \le \mathbf{U} - \mathbf{L}, \ \mathbf{X} \ge \mathbf{0}\}$$

Use the proposed procedure to solve the following LP:

$$\text{Minimize } z = 5x_1 - 4x_2 + 6x_3$$

subject to

$$20 \le x_1 + 7x_2 + 3x_3 \le 46$$
$$10 \le 3x_1 - x_2 + x_3 \le 20$$
$$18 \le 2x_1 + 3x_2 - x_3 \le 35$$
$$x_1, x_2, x_3 \ge 0$$

■ **7–4.** Consider the following 0-1 integer LP:

$$\text{Minimize } z = \{\mathbf{CX} \mid \mathbf{AX} \le \mathbf{b}, \ \mathbf{X} \in (0, \ 1)\}$$

Suppose that $z_{\min}$ is a known upper bound on *z*. Define the constraint

$$\min_{\mu \ge 0} \ \max_{X = (0,\, 1)} \{\mu \, (\mathbf{b} - \mathbf{AX}) + (z_{\min} - \mathbf{CX})\} \ge 0$$

where $\mu \ge \mathbf{0}$. This constraint does not violate any of the restrictions of the original 0-1 problem. The min-max problem is one way of identifying the "tightest" such constraint through proper selection of $\mu (\ge \mathbf{0})$. Show that the proposed mixed 0-1 definition for determining $\mu$ actually reduces to solving an ordinary LP problem. (*Hint:* The integer restriction $\mathbf{X} = [0, 1]$ is equivalent to the continuous range $0 \leq \mathbf{X} \leq 1$. Use the dual problem to define the desired LP.)

■ **7-5.** The optimum solution of the LP in Problem 2 is given as $x_1 = \frac{10}{3}, x_2 = \frac{4}{3}$, and $z = \frac{38}{3}$ . Plot the change in optimum $z$ with $\theta$ given that $x_1 = \frac{10}{3} + \theta$, where $\theta$ is unrestricted in sign. Note that $x_1 = \frac{10}{3} + \theta$ tracks $x_1$ above and below its optimal value.

■ **7-6.** Suppose that the optimum linear program is represented as

$$\text{Maximize } z = c_0 - \sum_{j \in NB} (z_j - c_j)x_j$$

subject to

$$x_i = x_i^* - \sum_{j \in NB} \alpha_{ij} x_j, \, i = 1, 2, \ldots, m$$

$$\text{all } x_i \text{ and } x_j \geq 0$$

where $NB$ is the set of nonbasic variables. Suppose that for a current basic variable $x_i = x_i^*$ we impose the restriction $x_i \geq d_i$, where $d_i$ is the smallest integer greater than $x_i^*$. Estimate an upper bound on the optimum value of $z$ after the constraint is augmented to the problem. Repeat the same procedure assuming that the imposed restriction is $x_i \leq e_i$, where $e_i$ is the largest integer smaller than $x_i^*$.

■ **7-7.** Consider the following minimization LP:

$$\text{Minimize } z = (10t-4)x_1 + (4t-8)\, x_2$$

subject to

$$
\begin{aligned}
2x_1 + 2x_2 + x_3 \quad &= 8 \\
4x_1 + 2x_2 \quad\quad + x_4 &= 6 - 2t \\
x_1, \, x_2, \, x_3, \, x_4 &\geq 0
\end{aligned}
$$

where $-\infty \leq t \infty$ . The parametric analysis of the problem yields the following results:

$$-\infty \leq t \leq -5 : \text{Optimal basis is } \mathbf{B} = (\mathbf{P}_1, \, \mathbf{P}_4)$$

$$-5 \leq t \leq -1 : \text{Optimal basis is } \mathbf{B} = (\mathbf{P}_1, \, \mathbf{P}_2)$$

$$-1 \leq t \leq \quad 2 : \text{Optimal basis is } \mathbf{B} = (\mathbf{P}_2, \, \mathbf{P}_3)$$

Determine all the critical values of $t$ that may exist for $t \geq 2$.

# Chapter 8

# Goal Programming

## 8.1 SINGLE OBJECTIVE VERSUS MULTIPLE GOALS

The LP models presented in the preceding chapters are characterized by the optimization of a *single* objective function. There are situations where the system may have multiple (possibly conflicting) objectives. For example, aspiring politicians may promise to reduce the national debt and, simultaneously, offer income tax relief. In such situations, it may be impossible to find a single solution that optimizes the conflicting objectives. Instead, we may seek a *compromise* solution based on the relative importance of each objective.

This chapter presents the goal programming technique for solving multiobjective models. The principal idea is to convert the original multiple objectives into a single goal. The resulting model yields what is usually referred to as an **efficient solution** because it may not be optimum with respect to *all* the conflicting objectives of the problem.

## 8.2 A GOAL PROGRAMMING FORMULATION

The idea of goal programming is illustrated by an example.

---

**Example 8.2–1.**

Fairville is a small city with a population of about 20,000 residents. The city council is in the process of developing an equitable tax rate table. The annual taxation base for real estate property is $550 million. The annual taxation bases for food and drugs and for general sales are $35 million and $55 million, respectively. Annual local gasoline consumption is estimated at 7.5 million gallons. The city council wants to develop the tax rates based on four main goals.

**1.** Tax revenues must be at least \$16 million to meet the city's financial commitments.

**2.** Food and drug taxes cannot exceed 10% of all taxes collected.

**3.** General sales taxes cannot exceed 20% of all taxes collected.

**4.** Gasoline tax cannot exceed 2 cents per gallon.

Let the variables $x_p$, $x_f$, and $x_s$ represent the tax rates (expressed as proportions) for property, food and drug, and general sales and define the variable $x_g$ as the gasoline tax in cents per gallon. The goals of the city council are then expressed as

$$550x_p + 35x_f + 55x_s + .075x_g \geq 16 \qquad \text{(Tax revenue)}$$

$$35x_f \leq .1(550x_p + 35x_f + 55x_s + .075x_g) \qquad \text{(Food/drug tax)}$$

$$55x_s \leq .2(550x_p + 35x_f + 55x_s + .075x_g) \qquad \text{(General tax)}$$

$$x_g \leq 2 \qquad \text{(Gasoline tax)}$$

$$x_p, x_f, x_s, x_g \geq 0$$

These constraints are then simplified as

$$550x_p + 35x_f + 55x_s + .075x_g \geq 16$$

$$55x_p - 31.5x_f + 5.5x_s + .0075x_g \geq 0$$

$$110x_p + 7x_f - 44x_s + .015x_g \geq 0$$

$$x_g \leq 2$$

$$x_p, x_f, x_s, x_g \geq 0$$

Each of the inequalities of the model represents a goal that the city council aspires to satisfy. However, these goals may be in conflict and the best we can do is try to reach a compromise solution.

The manner in which goal programming reaches a compromise solution is achieved as follows. First, each inequality constraint is converted into a flexible goal in which the constraints may be violated, if necessary. In terms of the Fairville model, the flexible goals are expressed as follows:

$$550x_p + 35x_f + 55x_s + .075x_g + s_1^+ - s_1^- = 16$$

$$55x_p - 31.5x_f + 5.5x_s + .0075x_g + s_2^+ - s_2^- = 0$$

$$110x_p + 7x_f - 44x_s + .015x_g + s_3^+ - s_3^- = 0$$

$$x_g + s_4^+ - s_4^- = 2$$

$$x_p, x_f, x_s, x_g \geq 0$$

$$s_i^+, s_i^- \geq 0, \quad i = 1, 2, 3, 4$$

The nonnegative variables $s_i^+$ and $s_i^-$, $i = 1, 2, 3, 4$, are called **deviational variables** because they represent the deviations above and below the right-hand side of constraint $i$.

The deviational variables $s_i^+$ and $s_i^-$ are by definition dependent, and hence cannot be basic variables simultaneously. This means that in any simplex iteration, at most *one* of the two deviational variables can assume a positive value. If the original $i$th inequality is of the type $\leq$ and its $s_i^+ > 0$, then the $i$th goal will be satisfied; otherwise, if $s_i^- > 0$, goal $i$ will not be satisfied. In essence, the definition of $s_i^+$ and $s_i^-$ allows us to meet or violate the $i$th goal at will. This is the type of flexibility that goal programming seeks when it tries to reach a compromise solution. Naturally, a good compromise solution is the one that seeks the minimization of the amount by which each goal is violated.

In the Fairville model, given that the first three constraints are of the type $\geq$ and the fourth constraint is of the type $\leq$, the deviational variables $s_1^+, s_2^+, s_3^+,$ and $s_4^-$ represent the amounts by which the respective goals may be violated. Thus, the compromise solution should seek to satisfy the following four objectives as much as possible:

$$\text{Minimize } G_1 = s_1^+$$

$$\text{Minimize } G_2 = s_2^+$$

$$\text{Minimize } G_3 = s_3^+$$

$$\text{Minimize } G_4 = s_4^-$$

These functions are minimized subject to the constraint equations of the model.

---

How can we optimize a multiobjective model with possibly conflicting goals? Two methods have been developed for this purpose: (1) the weighting method and (2) the preemptive method. Both methods are based on converting the multiple objectives into a single function. The details of these methods are presented in the remainder of this chapter.

### Problem set 8.2a

1. Formulate the Fairville tax problem, assuming that the town council is specifying an additional goal, $G_5$, that requires gasoline tax to equal at least 1% of the total tax bill.

2. The NW Shopping Mall conducts special events to attract potential patrons to its premises. The two most popular events that seem to attract teenagers, the young/middle-aged group, and senior citizens are band concerts and art and craft shows. The costs per presentation of the band and art show are $1500 and $3000, respectively. The total (strict) annual budget allocated to the two events is $15,000. The mall manager estimates the attendance of the events as follows:

| | Number attending per presentation | | |
| --- | --- | --- | --- |
| Event | Teenagers | Young/middle age | Seniors |
| Band concert | 200 | 100 | 0 |
| Art Show | 0 | 400 | 250 |

The manager has set the minimum goals of 1000, 1200, and 800 for the attendance of teenagers, the young/middle-aged group, and seniors, respectively. Formulate the problem as a goal programming model.

3. Ozark University admission office is processing freshman applications for the upcoming academic year. The applications fall into three categories: in-state, out-of-state, and international. The male-female ratios for in-state and out-of-state applicants are 1 : 1 and 3 : 2, respectively. For the international students, the corresponding ratio is 8 : 1. The American College Test (ACT) score is an important factor in accepting new students. The statistics gathered by the university indicate that the average ACT score for in-state, out-of-state, and international students are 27, 26, and 23, respectively. The committee on admissions has established the following desirable goals for the new freshman class:

   (a) The incoming class is at least 1200 freshmen.
   (b) The average ACT score for all incoming students is at least 25.
   (c) International students constitute at least 10% of the incoming class.
   (d) The female-male ratio is at least 1 : 1.
   (e) Out-of-state students constitute at least 20% of the incoming class.

   Formulate the problem as a goal programming model.

4. Circle K farms consumes 3 tons of special feed daily. The feed, a mixture of limestone, corn, and soybean meal, must satisfy the following nutritional requirements:

   *Calcium.* At least 0.8% but not more than 1.2%.
   *Protein.* At least 22%.
   *Fiber.* At most 5%.

   The following table gives the nutritional content of the feed ingredient.

| Ingredient | lb per lb of ingredient | | |
| --- | --- | --- | --- |
| | Calcium | Protein | Fiber |
| Limestone | .380 | .00 | .00 |
| Corn | .001 | .09 | .02 |
| Soybean meal | .002 | .50 | .08 |

   Formulate the problem as a goal programming model, and state your opinion regarding the suitability of goal programming in this situation.

5. Mantel produces a toy carriage, whose final assembly must include four wheels and two seats. The factory producing the parts operates three shifts a day. The following table provides the amounts produced of each part in the three shifts.

|        | Units produced per run | |
|--------|--------|--------|
| Shift  | Wheels | Seats  |
| 1      | 500    | 300    |
| 2      | 600    | 280    |
| 3      | 640    | 360    |

Ideally, the number of produced wheels is exactly twice that of the number of seats (recall that each toy will include four wheels and two seats). However, because the production rates vary from shift to shift, exact balance in production may not be possible. Mantel is interested in determining the number of production runs in each shift that minimizes the imbalance in the production of the parts. The capacity limitations restricts the number of runs to between 4 and 5 for shift 1, 10 and 20 for shift 2, and 3 and 5 for shift 3. Formulate the problem as a goal programming model.

**6.** Camyo Manufacturing produces four parts that require the use of a lathe and a drill press. The two machines operate 10 hours a day. The following table provides the time in minutes required by each part:

| Part | Lathe | Drill press |
|------|-------|-------------|
| 1    | 5     | 3           |
| 2    | 6     | 2           |
| 3    | 4     | 6           |
| 4    | 7     | 4           |

It is desired to balance the use of the two machines by requiring the difference between their total operation times not to exceed 30 minutes. The market demand limits the number of units produced of each part to at least 10 units. Additionally, the number of units of part 1 may not exceed that of part 2. Formulate the problem as a goal programming model.

**7.** Two products are manufactured on two sequential machines. The following table gives the machining times in minutes per unit for the two products.

| Machine | Product 1 | Product 2 |
|---------|-----------|-----------|
| 1       | 5         | 3         |
| 2       | 6         | 2         |

The daily production quota for the two products are 80 and 60 units, respectively. Each machine runs 8 hours a day. Overtime, though not desirable, may be used if necessary to meet the production quota. Formulate the problem as a goal programming model.

8. Vista City hospital plans the short-stay assignment of surplus beds (those that are not already occupied) 4 days in advance. During the 4-day planning period about 30, 25, and 20 patients will require 1-, 2-, or 3-day stays, respectively. Surplus beds during the same period are estimated at 20, 20, 24, and 30. Use goal programming to resolve the problem of overadmission and underadmission in the hospital.

9. The Von Trapp family is in the process of moving to a new city where both parents have accepted new jobs. In trying to find an ideal location for their new home, the Von Trapps listed the following goals:
   **(a)** It should be as close as possible to Mrs. Von Trapp's place of work (within $\frac{1}{4}$ of a mile).
   **(b)** It should be as far as possible from the noise of the airport (at least 10 miles).
   **(c)** It should be reasonably close to a shopping mall (within 1 mile).

   In preparation for solving the problem, Mr. and Mrs. Von Trapp located the *x-y* coordinates (relative to a landmark in the city) of work, airport, and shopping mall as $(1, 1)$, $(20, 15)$, and $(4, 7)$, respectively (all distances are in miles). Formulate the problem as a goal programming model. (*Note:* The resulting constraints are not necessarily linear.)

10. *Regression analysis.* In a laboratory experiment, suppose that $y_i$ is the $i$th observed (independent) yield associated with the dependent observational measurements $x_{ij}, i = 1, 2, \ldots, m; j = 1, 2, \ldots, n$. It is desired to determine a linear regression fit into these data points. Let $b_j, j = 0, 1, \ldots, n$, be the regression coefficients. It is required to determine all $b_j$ such that the sum of the absolute deviations between the observed and the estimated yield is minimized. Formulate the problem as a goal programming model.

11. *Chebyshev problem.* An alternative goal for the regression model in Problem 10 is to minimize over $b_j$ the maximum of the absolute deviations. Formulate the problem as a goal programming model.

## 8.3 GOAL PROGRAMMING ALGORITHMS

This section presents two algorithms for solving the goal programming problem. Both methods are based on representing the multiple goals by a single objective function. In the **weighting method,** a single objective function is formed as the weighted sum of the functions representing the goals of the problem. The **preemptive method** starts by prioritizing the goals in order of importance. The model is then optimized using one goal at a time, and in such a manner that the optimum value of a higher-priority goal is not degraded by a lower priority goal.

The proposed two methods are distinct, in the sense that they will not generally produce the same solution. Neither method, however, can be claimed superior because each technique is designed to satisfy certain decision-making preferences.

### 8.3.1 The Weighting Method

Suppose that the goal programming model has $n$ goals and that the $i$th goal is given as

$$\text{Minimize } G_i, \ i = 1, 2, ..., n$$

The combined objective function used in the weighting method is then defined as

$$\text{Minimize } z = w_1 G_1 + w_2 G_2 + ... + w_n G_n$$

where $w_i, i = 1, 2, . . . , n$, are positive weights that reflect the decision maker's preferences regarding the relative importance of each goal. For example, $w_i = 1$, for all $i$, signifies that all the goals carry equal weights. The determination of the specific values of these weights is subjective. Indeed, the apparently sophisticated analytic procedures developed in the literature (see, e.g., Cohon, 1978) are still rooted in subjective assessments.

---

**Example 8.3–1.**

TopAd, a new advertising agency with 10 employees, has received a contract to promote a new product. The agency can advertise by radio and television. The following table provides data about the number of people reached by each type of advertisement, and the cost and labor requirements.

|  | Data/min advertisement | |
| --- | --- | --- |
|  | Radio | Television |
| Exposure (in millions of persons) | 4 | 8 |
| Cost (in thousands of dollars) | 8 | 24 |
| Assigned employees | 1 | 2 |

The contract prohibits TopAd from using more than 6 minutes of radio advertisement. Additionally, radio and television advertisements need to reach at least 45 million people. TopAd has set a budget goal of $100,000 for the project. How many minutes of radio and television minutes should TopAd use?

Let $x_1$ and $x_2$ be the minutes allocated to radio and television advertisements. The goal programming formulation for the problem is given as

$$\text{Minimize } G_1 = s_1^+ \text{ (Satisfy exposure goal)}$$

$$\text{Minimize } G_2 = s_2^- \text{ (Satisfy budget goal)}$$

subject to

$$4x_1 + 8x_2 + s_1^+ - s_1^- = 45 \quad \text{(Exposure goal)}$$

$$8x_1 + 24x_2 + s_2^+ - s_2^- = 100 \quad \text{(Budget goal)}$$

$$x_1 + 2x_2 \quad\quad\quad \le 10 \quad \text{(Personnel limit)}$$

$$x_1 \quad\quad\quad\quad\quad\quad \le 6 \quad \text{(Radio limit)}$$

$$x_1, x_2, s_1^+, s_1^-, s_2^+, s_2^- \ge 0$$

TopAd's management assumes that the exposure goal is twice as important as the budget goal. The combined objective function thus becomes

$$\text{Minimize } z = 2G_1 + G_2 = 2s_1^+ + s_2^-$$

The optimum solution is obtained by TORA as

$$z = 10$$

$$x_1 = 5 \text{ minutes}, x_2 = 2.5 \text{ minutes}, s_1^+ = 5 \text{ million persons}$$

All the remaining variables equal zero.

The fact that the optimum value of $z$ is not zero indicates that at least one of the goals is not met. Specifically, $s_1^+ = 5$ means that the exposure goal (of at least 45 million persons) is missed by 5 million individuals. Conversely, the budget goal (of not exceeding \$100,000) is not violated because $s_2^- = 0$.

Goal programming yields only an *efficient* solution to the problem, which is not necessarily optimum. For example, the solution $x_1 = 6$ and $x_2 = 2$ yields the same exposure ($4 \times 6 + 8 \times 2 = 40$ million persons), but costs less ($8 \times 6 + 24 \times 2 = \$96,000$. In essence, what goal programming does is to find a solution that *just satisfies* the goals of the model. Such "deficiency" in reaching the optimum solution raises questions regarding the viability of goal programming as an optimizing technique (see Example 8.3–3 for further discussion).

## Problem set 8.3a

1. Consider Problem 8.2a–1 dealing with the Fairville tax situation. Solve the problem, assuming that all five goals have the same weight. Are all the goals satisfied?

2. In Problem 8.2a–2, suppose that the goal of attracting young/middle-aged people is twice as important as either of the other two categories (teens and seniors). Find the associated solution, and check if all the goals have been met.

3. In the Ozark University admission situation described in Problem 8.2a–3, suppose that the limit on the size of the incoming freshmen class must be met, but the remaining requirements can be treated as flexible goals. Further, assume that the ACT score goal is twice as important as any of the remaining goals.

(a) Solve the problem, and specify whether or not all the goals are satisfied.

(b) If, in addition, the size of the incoming class can be treated as a flexible goal that is twice as important as the ACT goal, how would this change affect the solution?

4. In the Circle K model of Problem 8.2a–4, is it possible to satisfy all the nutritional requirements?

5. In Problem 8.2a–5, determine the solution, and specify whether or not the daily production of wheels and seats can be balanced.

6. In Problem 8.2a–6, suppose that the market demand goal is twice as important as that of balancing the two machines, and that no overtime is allowed. Solve the problem, and determine if the goals are met.

7. In Problem 8.2a–7, suppose that the production quota for the two products must be met, using overtime if necessary. Find a solution to the problem, and specify the amount of overtime, if any, needed to meet the production quota.

8. In the Vista City Hospital of Problem 8.2a–8, suppose that only the bed limits represent flexible goals and that all the goals have equal weights. Can all the goals be met?

9. The Malco Company has compiled the following table from the files of five of its employees to study the relationship between income and age, education (expressed in number of college years completed), and experience (expressed in number of years in the business).

| Age (yr) | Education (yr) | Experience (yr) | Annual income ($) |
|----------|----------------|------------------|-------------------|
| 30 | 4 | 5 | 40,000 |
| 39 | 5 | 10 | 48,000 |
| 44 | 2 | 14 | 38,000 |
| 48 | 0 | 18 | 36,000 |
| 37 | 3 | 9 | 41,000 |

Use the goal programming formulation in Problem 8.2a–10 to fit the data into the linear equation $y = b_0 + b_1 x_1 + b_2 x_2 + b_3 x_3$

10. Solve Problem 9 using the Chebyshev Method proposed in Problem 8.2a–11.

## 8.3.2 The Preemptive Method

In the preemptive method, the $n$ goals of the problem are ranked in order of importance as judged by the decision maker—that is,

$$\text{Minimize } G_1 = \rho_1 \quad \text{(Highest priority)}$$

$$\vdots$$

$$\text{Minimize } G_n = \rho_n \quad \text{(Lowest priority)}$$

The variable $\rho_i$ is the component of the deviational variables, $s_i^+$ or $s_i^-$, that describes goal $i$. For example, in the TopAd model (Example 8.3–1), $\rho_1 = s_1^+$ and $\rho_2 = s_2^-$.

The solution procedure solves one goal problem at a time, starting with the highest-priority goal $G_1$ and terminating with the lowest goal $G_n$. *The process is carried out such that the solution obtained from a lower-priority goal does not degrade any of the solutions already secured for the higher-priority goals.* This means that, for all $i \geq 1$, if $z(G_i)$ is the optimum objective value given goal $G_i$, then the optimization of lower goals $G_j$ $(j > i)$ cannot produce a solution that will worsen the value of $z(G_i)$.

The literature on goal programming presents a "special" simplex method that guarantees the nondegradation of higher priority solutions. The method uses the **column-dropping rule** that calls for eliminating a *nonbasic* variable $x_j$ with $z_j - c_j \neq 0$ from the optimal tableau of goal $G_k$ before the problem of goal $G_{k+1}$ is optimized. The rule recognizes that such nonbasic variables, if elevated above zero level in the optimization of succeeding goals, can degrade (but never improve) the quality of a higher priority goal. The procedure requires modifying the simplex tableau so it will carry the objective functions of all the goals of the model.

Unfortunately, the proposed simplex method modification makes goal programming more complicated than it really is. In this presentation, we show that the same results can be achieved in a more straightforward manner using the following steps:

**Step 0.** Identify the goals of the model and rank them in order of priority:
$G_1 = \rho_1 > G_2 = \rho_2 > \ldots > G_n = \rho_n$. Set $i = 1$.

**Step i.** Solve $LP_i$ that minimizes $G_i$, and let $\rho_i = \rho_i^*$ define the corresponding optimum value of the deviational variable $\rho_i$. If $i = n$, stop; $LP_n$ solves the $n$-goal program. Otherwise, augment the constraint $\rho_i = \rho_i^*$ to the constraints of the $G_i$-problem to ensure that the value of $\rho_i$ will not be degraded in future problems. Set $i = i + 1$, and repeat step $i$.

The successive addition of the special constraints $\rho_i = \rho_i^*$ may not be as "elegant" theoretically as the *column-dropping rule*. Nevertheless, it achieves the exact same result. More important, it is easier to understand.

Some may argue that the column-dropping rule offers computational advantages. Essentially, the column-dropping rule makes the problem smaller successively by removing variables, whereas our procedure makes the problem larger by adding new constraints. However, considering the nature of the additional constraints $(\rho_i = \rho_i^*)$, we should be able to modify the simplex algorithm so that the additional constraint can be implemented implicitly through direct substitution of the variable $\rho_i$. This substitution affects only the constraint in which $\rho_i$ appears and, in effect, reduces the number of variables as we move from one goal to the next. (We can also use the bounded simplex method of Section 7.5.2 by replacing $\rho_i = \rho_i^*$ with

$\rho_i \leq \rho_i^*$) In this regard, the column-dropping rule, aside from its possible theoretical appeal, does not appear to offer a particular computational advantage. For the sake of completeness, however, we will demonstrate how the column-dropping rule works in Example 8.3–3.

---

**Example 8.3–2.**

The problem of Example 8.3–1 is solved by the preemptive method. Assume that the exposure goal has a higher priority.

**Step 0.** $G_1 > G_2$

$$G_1: \text{Minimize } s_1^+ \quad \text{(Satisfy exposure goal)}$$

$$G_2: \text{Minimize } s_2^- \quad \text{(Satisfy budget goal)}$$

**Step 1.** Solve $LP_1$.

$$\text{Minimize } G_1 = s_1^+$$

subject to

$$
\begin{array}{llll}
4x_1 + 8x_2 + s_1^+ - s_1^- & = 45 & \text{(Exposure goal)} \\
8x_1 + 24x_2 \quad\quad\quad + s_2^+ - s_2^- & = 100 & \text{(Budget goal)} \\
x_1 + 2x_2 & \leq 10 & \text{(Personnel limit)} \\
x_1 & \leq 6 & \text{(Radio limit)}
\end{array}
$$

$$x_1, x_2, s_1^+, s_1^-, s_2^+, s_2^- \geq 0$$

The optimum solution (determined by TORA) is $x_1 = 5$ minutes, $x_2 = 2.5$ minutes, $s_1^+ = 5$ million people, with the remaining variables equal zero. The solution shows that the exposure goal, $G_1$, is violated by 5 million persons.

In $LP_1$, we have $\rho_1 = s_1^+$. Thus, the additional constraint we use with the $G_2$-problem is $s_1^+ = 5$.

**Step 2.** We need to solve $LP_2$, whose objective functions is

$$\text{Minimize } G_2 = s_2^-$$

subject to the same set of constraint as in step 1 plus the additional constraint $s_1^+ = 5$. We can solve the new problem by using TORA's MODIFY option to add the constraint $s_1^+ = 5$.

The optimization of $LP_2$ is not necessary because the optimum solution to problem $G_1$ already yields $s_2^- = 0$. Hence, the solution of $LP_1$ is automatically optimum for $LP_2$ (you can verify this answer by solving $LP_2$ with TORA). The solution $s_2^- = 0$ shows that $G_2$ is satisfied.

The additional constraint $s_1^+ = 5$ can also be accounted for by substituting out $s_1^+$ in the first constraint. The result is that the right-hand side of the exposure goal constraint will be changed from 45 to 40, thus reducing $LP_2$ to

$$\text{Minimize } G_2 = s_2^-$$

subject to

$$4x_1 + 8x_2 - s_1^- \qquad\qquad = 40 \quad \text{(Exposure goal)}$$

$$8x_1 + 24x_2 + \quad + s_2^+ - s_2^- = 100 \quad \text{(Budget goal)}$$

$$x_1 + 2x_2 \qquad\qquad\qquad \leq 10 \quad \text{(Personnel limit)}$$

$$x_1 \qquad\qquad\qquad\qquad \leq 6 \quad \text{(Radio limit)}$$

$$x_1, x_2, s_1^-, s_2^+, s_2^- \geq 0$$

The new formulation is one variable less than the one in LP1, which is the same idea conveyed by the column-dropping rule.

Next, we use an example to show that a better solution for the problem of Examples 8.3–1 and 8.3–2 can be obtained if the preemptive method is used to *optimize* objectives rather than to *satisfy* goals. The example also serves to demonstrate the *column-dropping rule* for solving goal programs.

**Example 8.3–3.**

The goals of Example 8.3–1 can be restated as

$$\text{Priority 1: Maximize exposure } (P_1)$$

$$\text{Priority 2: Minimize cost } (P_2)$$

Mathematically, the two objectives are given as

$$\text{Maximize } P_1 = 4x_1 + 8x_2 \quad \text{(exposure)}$$

$$\text{Minimize } P_2 = 8x_1 + 24x_2 \quad \text{(cost)}$$

The specific goal limits for exposure and cost (= 45 and 100) in Examples 8.3–1 and 8.3–2 are removed because we will allow the simplex method to determine these limits optimally.
The new problem can thus be stated as

$$\text{Maximize } P_1 = 4x_1 + 8x_2$$

$$\text{Minimize } P_2 = 8x_1 + 24x_2$$

subject to

$$x_1 + 2x_2 \leq 10$$

$$x_1 \qquad \leq 6$$

$$x_1, x_2 \geq 0$$

We first solve the problem using the procedure introduced in Example 8.3–2.

**Step 1.** Solve LP$_1$.

$$\text{Maximize } P_1 = 4x_1 + 8x_2$$

subject to

$$x_1 + 2x_2 \leq 10$$

$$x_1 \qquad \leq 6$$

$$x_1, x_2 \geq 0$$

The optimum solution (obtained by TORA) is $x_1 = 0$, $x_2 = 5$ with $P_1 = 40$, which shows that the most exposure we can get is 40 million persons.

**Step 2.** Add the constraint $4x_1 + 8x_2 \geq 40$ to ensure that goal $G_1$ is not degraded. Thus, we solve LP$_2$ as

$$\text{Minimize } P_2 = 8x_1 + 24x_2$$

subject to

$$x_1 + 2x_2 \leq 10$$

$$x_1 \qquad \leq 6$$

$$4x_1 + 8x_2 \geq 40 \qquad \text{(Additional constraint)}$$

$$x_1, x_2 \geq 0$$

The TORA optimum solution of LP$_2$ is $P_2 = \$96,000$, $x_1 = 6$ minutes, and $x_2 = 2$ minutes. It yields the same exposure ($P_1 = 40$ million people) but at a smaller cost. This solution, which results from optimizing the goals, is superior to the one in Example 8.3–2 that seeks only to satisfy the goals.

We solve the same problem by using the column-dropping rule. The rule calls for carrying the objective rows associated with all the goals in the simplex tableau, as we will show subsequently.

*LP$_1$ (Exposure Maximization):* The LP$_1$ simplex tableau carries both objective rows, $P_1$ and $P_2$. The optimality condition applies to the $P_1$-objective row only. The $P_2$-row plays a passive role in LP$_1$, but must be updated with the rest of the simplex tableau in preparation for the optimization of LP$_2$.

LP$_1$ is solved in two iterations as follows:

| Basic | $x_1$ | $x_2$ | $s_1$ | $s_2$ | Solution |
|-------|-------|-------|-------|-------|----------|
| $P_1$ | $-4$ | $-8$ | 0 | 0 | 0 |
| $P_2$ | $-8$ | $-24$ | 0 | 0 | 0 |
| $s_1$ | 1 | 2 | 1 | 0 | 10 |
| $s_2$ | 1 | 0 | 0 | 1 | 6 |
| $P_1$ | 0 | 0 | 4 | 0 | 40 |
| $P_2$ | 4 | 0 | 12 | 0 | 120 |
| $x_2$ | $\frac{1}{2}$ | 1 | $\frac{1}{2}$ | 0 | 5 |
| $s_2$ | 1 | 0 | 0 | 1 | 6 |

The last tableau yields the optimal solution $x_1 = 0$, $x_2 = 5$, and $P_1 = 40$.

The **column-dropping rule** calls for eliminating any *nonbasic* variable $x_j$ with $z_j - c_j \neq 0$ from the optimum tableau of $LP_1$ before $LP_2$ is optimized. The reason for doing this is that these variables, if left unchecked, could become positive in lower-priority optimization problems, thus degrading the quality of higher-priority solutions.

$LP_2$ *(Cost Minimization):* The column-dropping rule eliminates $s_1$ (with $z_j - c_j = 4$). We can see from the $P_2$-row that if $s_1$ is not eliminated, it will be the entering variable at the start of the $P_2$-iterations and will yield the optimum solution $x_1 = x_2 = 0$, which will degrade the optimum objective value of the $P_1$-problem from $P_1 = 40$ to $P_1 = 0$. (Try it!)

The $P_2$-problem is of the minimization type. Following the elimination of $s_1$, the variable $x_1$ with $z_j - c_j = 4$ ($> 0$) can improve the value of $P_2$. The following table shows the $LP_2$ iterations. The $P_1$-row has been deleted because it no longer serves a purpose in the optimization of $LP_2$.

| Iteration | Basic | $x_1$ | $x_2$ | $s_1$ | $s_2$ | Solution |
|---|---|---|---|---|---|---|
|   | $P_1$ |  |  |  |  | 40 |
|   | $P_2$ | 4 | 0 |  | 0 | 120 |
| 1 | $x_2$ | $\frac{1}{2}$ | 1 |  | 0 | 5 |
|   | $s_2$ | 1 | 0 |  | 1 | 6 |
|   | $P_1$ |  |  |  |  | 40 |
|   | $P_2$ | 0 | 0 |  | $-4$ | 96 |
| 2 | $x_2$ | 0 | 1 |  | $-\frac{1}{2}$ | 2 |
|   | $x_1$ | 1 | 0 |  | 1 | 6 |

The optimum solution ($x_1 = 6$, $x_2 = 2$) with a total exposure of $P_1 = 40$ and a total cost of $P_2 = 96$ is the same as obtained earlier.

---

### Problem set 8.3b

1. In Example 8.3–2, suppose that the budget goal is increased to $110,000. The exposure goal remains unchanged at 45 million persons. Show how the preemptive method will reach a solution.

2. Solve Problem 8.2a–1 (Fairville tax model) using the following priority ordering for the goals: $G_1 > G_2 > G_3 > G_4$.

3. Consider Problem 8.2a–2, which deals with the presentation of band concerts and art shows at the NW Mall. Suppose that the goals set for teens, the

young/middle-aged group, and seniors are referred to as $G_1$, $G_2$, and $G_3$, respectively. Solve the problem for each of the following priority orders:

**(a)** $G_1 > G_2 > G_3$

**(b)** $G_3 > G_2 > G_1$

   Show that the satisfaction of the goals (or lack of it) can be a function of the priority order.

**4.** Solve the Ozark University model (Problem 8.2a–3) using the preemptive method, assuming that the goals are prioritized in the same order given in the problem.

## 8.4 SUMMARY

Goal programming deals with decision problems involving conflicting objectives. The basic idea of the technique is to convert the multiobjective problem into one or more problems with one objective each. The quality of the final solution is influenced by the decision makers's ranking of the different objectives as well as by the "tightness" of the limits set for the goals. In this regard, goal programming seeks only an *efficient* solution that attempts to meet all the goals of the problem.

## REFERENCES

Cohon, T. L., *Multiobjective Programming and Planning,* Academic Press, New York, 1978.

Ignizio, J. P., and T. M. Cavalier, *Linear Programming,* Prentice-Hall, Upper Saddle River, N.J., 1994.

Steuer, R. E., *Multiple Criteria Optimization: Theory, Computations, and Application,* Wiley, New York, 1986.

## COMPREHENSIVE PROBLEMS

■ 8–1[1]   The Warehouzer Company manages three sites of forest land for timber production and reforestation with the respective areas of 100,000, 180,000, and 200,000 acres. The main timber products include three categories: sawlogs, plywood, and pulpwood. Several reforestation alternatives are available for each site, each with its cost, number of rotation years, return from rent, and production output. The following table summarizes this information.

---

[1]Based on Rustagi, K. P., *Forest Management Planning for Timber Production: A Goal Programming Approach,* Bulletin No. 89, Yale University, New Haven, 1976.

| Site | Alternative | Annual $/acre | | Rotation yr | Annual m³/acre | | |
|------|-------------|------|------|------|----------|---------|---------|
|      |             | Cost | Rent |      | Pulpwood | Plywood | Sawlogs |
| 1    | A1          | 1000 | 160  | 20   | 12       | 0       | 0       |
|      | A2          | 800  | 117  | 25   | 10       | 0       | 0       |
|      | A3          | 1500 | 140  | 40   | 5        | 6       | 0       |
|      | A4          | 1200 | 195  | 15   | 4        | 7       | 0       |
|      | A5          | 1300 | 182  | 40   | 3        | 0       | 7       |
|      | A6          | 1200 | 180  | 40   | 2        | 0       | 6       |
|      | A7          | 1500 | 135  | 50   | 3        | 0       | 5       |
| 2    | A1          | 1000 | 102  | 20   | 9        | 0       | 0       |
|      | A2          | 800  | 55   | 25   | 8        | 0       | 0       |
|      | A3          | 1500 | 95   | 40   | 2        | 5       | 0       |
|      | A4          | 1200 | 120  | 15   | 3        | 4       | 0       |
|      | A5          | 1300 | 100  | 40   | 2        | 0       | 5       |
|      | A6          | 1200 | 90   | 40   | 2        | 0       | 4       |
| 3    | A1          | 1000 | 60   | 20   | 7        | 0       | 0       |
|      | A2          | 800  | 48   | 25   | 6        | 4       | 0       |
|      | A3          | 1500 | 60   | 40   | 2        | 0       | 4       |
|      | A4          | 1200 | 65   | 15   | 2        | 0       | 3       |
|      | A5          | 1300 | 35   | 40   | 1        | 0       | 5       |

To guarantee sustained future production, each acre of reforestation in each alternative requires that as many acres as years in rotation be assigned to that alternative. The rent column represents the stumpage value per acre.

The goals of Warehouzer are:

1. Annual output of pulpwood, plywood, and sawlogs are 200,000, 150,000, and 350,000 cubic meters, respectively.
2. Annual reforestation budget is $2.5 million.
3. Annual return from land rent is $100 per acre.

How much land at each site should be assigned to each alternative?

■ 8–2    A charity organization runs a children's shelter. The organization relies on volunteer service from 8:00 A.M. until 2:00 P.M. Volunteers may begin work at the start of any hour between 8:00 A.M. and 11:00 A.M. A volunteer works a maximum of 6 hours and a minimum of 2 hours, and no volunteers work during lunch hour between 12:00 noon and 1:00 P.M. The charity has estimated its goal of needed volunteers throughout the day (from 8:00 A.M. to 2:00 P.M., and excluding the lunch hour between 12:00 noon and 1:00 P.M.) as 15, 16, 18, 20, and 16, respectively. The objective is to decide on the number of volunteers that should start at each hour such that the given goals are met as much as possible. Formulate and solve the problem as a goal-programming model.

# Chapter 9

# Integer Linear Programming

## 9.1 INTRODUCTION

Integer linear programs (ILPs) are linear programs in which some or all the variables are restricted to integer (or discrete) values. Despite decades of extensive research, computational experience with ILP has been less than satisfactory. To date, there does not exist an ILP computer code that can solve integer programming problems consistently.

This chapter starts with illustrative applications of integer programming, and then presents the ILP algorithms.

## 9.2 ILLUSTRATIVE APPLICATIONS

The ILP applications in this section start with simple formulations and then graduate to more complex ones. For convenience, we define a **pure** integer problem as the one in which all the variables are integer. If only some of the variables are integer, the problem is a **mixed** integer program.

---

**Example 9.2–1 (CAPITAL BUDGETING).**
Five projects are being evaluated over a 3-year planning horizon. The following table gives the expected returns for each project and the associated yearly expenditures.

| Project | Expenditures (million $)/yr | | | Returns (million $) |
| --- | --- | --- | --- | --- |
|  | 1 | 2 | 3 | |
| 1 | 5 | 1 | 8 | 20 |
| 2 | 4 | 7 | 10 | 40 |
| 3 | 3 | 9 | 2 | 20 |
| 4 | 7 | 4 | 1 | 15 |
| 5 | 8 | 6 | 10 | 30 |
| Available funds (million $) | 25 | 25 | 25 | |

Determine the projects to be executed over the 3-year horizon.

The problem reduces to a "yes-no" decision for each project. Define the binary variable $x_j$ as

$$x_j = \begin{cases} 1, & \text{Project } j \text{ is selected} \\ 0, & \text{Project } j \text{ is not selected} \end{cases}$$

The ILP model is thus given as

$$\text{Maximize } z = 20x_1 + 40x_2 + 20x_3 + 15x_4 + 30x_5$$

subject to

$$5x_1 + 4x_2 + 3x_3 + 7x_4 + 8x_5 \le 25$$
$$x_1 + 7x_2 + 9x_3 + 4x_4 + 6x_5 \le 25$$
$$8x_1 + 10x_2 + 2x_3 + x_4 + 10x_5 \le 25$$

$$x_1, x_2, x_3, x_4, x_5 = (0, 1)$$

The optimum integer solution (obtained by TORA) is $x_1 = x_2 = x_3 = x_4 = 1$, $x_5 = 0$, with $z = 95$ (million $). The solution shows that all but project 5 must be selected.

It is interesting to compare the continuous LP solution with the ILP solution. The LP optimum, obtained by replacing $x_j = (0, 1)$ with $0 \le x_j \le 1$ for all $j$, yields $x_1 = .5789$, $x_2 = x_3 = x_4 = 1$, $x_5 = .7368$, and $z = 108.68$ (million $). The solution is meaningless because two of the variables assume fractional values. We may be tempted to *round* the solution, which yields $x_1 = x_5 = 1$. The resulting solution is infeasible because the constraints are violated. More important, the concept of *rounding* does not apply here because $x_j$ represents the "yes-no" decision for which fractional values are meaningless.

**Problem set 9.2a[1]**

1. In the capital budgeting model of Example 9.2–1, suppose that project 5 must be selected if either project 1 or project 3 is selected. Modify the model to include the new restriction and find the optimum solution with TORA.

2. Five items are to be loaded in a vessel. The weight $w_i$ and volume $v_i$ together with the value $r_i$ for item $i$ are tabulated subsequently.

| Item $i$ | Unit weight, $w_i$ (tons) | Unit volume, $v_i$ (yd$^3$) | Unit worth, $r_i$ (100 $) |
|---|---|---|---|
| 1 | 5 | 1 | 4 |
| 2 | 8 | 8 | 7 |
| 3 | 3 | 6 | 6 |
| 4 | 2 | 5 | 5 |
| 5 | 7 | 4 | 4 |

The maximum allowable cargo weight and volume are 112 tons and 109 yd$^3$, respectively. Formulate the ILP model, and find the most valuable cargo using TORA.

3. Suppose that you have 7 full wine bottles, 7 half-full, and 7 empty. You would like to divide the 21 bottles among three individuals so that each will receive exactly 7. Additionally, each individual must receive the same quantity of wine. Express the problem as an ILP constraint equations, and find a solution using TORA. (*Hint:* Use a dummy objective function in which all the objective coefficients are zeros.)

4. An eccentric sheikh left a will for the distribution of his herd of camels among his three children: Tarek receives at least one-half of the herd, Sharif gets at least-one third, and Maisa gets at least one-ninth. The remainder goes to a charity organization. The will does not specify the size of the herd except to say that it is an odd number of camels and that the named charity receives exactly one camel. How many camels did the sheikh leave in the estate, and how many did each child get?

5. A farm couple is sending their three boys to the market to sell 90 apples with the objective of educating them about money and numbers. Jim, the oldest, carries 50 apples; Bill, the middle one, carries 30; and John, the

youngest, carries only 10. The parents have stipulated five rules: (a) The selling price is either $1 for 7 apples or $3 for 1 apple, or a combination of the two prices. (b) Each child may exercise one or both options of the selling price. (c) Each of the three children must return with exactly the same amount of money. (d) Each child must return with an even number of dollars (no cents). (e) The amount received by each child must be the largest possible under the stipulated conditions. Given that the three kids are able to sell all they have, how can they satisfy their parents conditions?

6. Once upon a time, there was a captain of a merchant ship who wanted to reward three crew members for their valiant effort in saving the ship's cargo during an unexpected storm in the high seas. The captain put aside a certain sum of money in the purser's office and instructed the first officer to distribute it equally among the three mariners after the ship had reached shore. One night, one of the sailors, unbeknownst to the others, went to the purser's office and decided to claim (an equitable) one-third of the money in advance. After dividing the money into three equal shares, an extra coin remained, which the mariner decided to keep (in addition to one-third of the money). The next night, the second mariner got the same idea and, repeating the same three-way division with what was left, ended up keeping an extra coin as well. The third night, the third mariner also took a third of what was left, plus an extra coin that could not be divided. When the ship reached shore, the first officer divided what was left of the money equally among the three mariners, also to be left with an extra coin. To simplify things, the first officer put the extra coin aside and gave the three mariners their allotted equal shares. How much money was in the safe to start with? Formulate the problem as an ILP, and find the solution using TORA. (*Hint:* The problem has a countably infinite number of integer solutions. For convenience, assume that we are interested in determining the smallest sum of money that satisfies the problem. Then, boosting the resulting solution by 1, augment it as a lower bound and obtain the next smallest solution. Continuing in this manner, a general solution pattern will evolve.)

7. You have the following three-letter words: AFT, FAR, TVA, ADV, JOE, FIN, OSF, and KEN. Suppose that we assign numeric values to the alphabet starting with $A = 1$ and ending with $Z = 26$. Each word is scored by adding numeric codes of its three letters. For example, AFT has a score of $1 + 6 + 20 = 27$. You are to select five of the given eight words that yield the maximum total score. Simultaneously, the selected five words must satisfy the following conditions:

$$\begin{pmatrix} \text{sum of letter 1} \\ \text{scores} \end{pmatrix} < \begin{pmatrix} \text{sum of letter 2} \\ \text{scores} \end{pmatrix} < \begin{pmatrix} \text{sum of letter 3} \\ \text{scores} \end{pmatrix}$$

Formulate the problem as an ILP, and find the optimum solution using TORA.

8. The Record-a-Song Company has contracted with a rising star to record eight songs. The durations of the different songs are 8, 3, 5, 5, 9, 6, 7, and 12 minutes, respectively. Record-a-Song plans on using a two-sided cassette tape for the recording. Each side has a capacity of 30 minutes. The company would like to distribute the songs on the two sides in a balanced manner. This means that the length of the songs on each side should be about the same, as much as possible. Formulate the problem as an ILP, and find the optimum solution.

9. In Problem 8, suppose that the nature of the melodies dictates that songs 3 and 4 cannot be recorded on the same side. Formulate the problem as an ILP. Would it be possible to use a 25-minute tape (each side) to record the eight songs? If not, use ILP to determine the minimum tape capacity needed to make the recording.

---

**Example 9.2–2 (FIXED-CHARGE PROBLEM).**

I have been approached by three telephone companies to subscribe to their long-distance service in the United States. MaBell will charge a flat $16 per month plus $.25 a minute. PaBell will charge $25 a month but will reduce the per minute cost to $.21. As for BabyBell, the flat monthly charge is $18, and the cost per minute is $.22. I usually make an average of 200 minutes of long-distance calls a month. Assuming that I do not pay the flat monthly fee unless I make calls and that I can apportion my calls among all three companies as I please, how should I use the three companies to minimize my monthly telephone bill?

This problem can be solved readily without ILP. Nevertheless, it is instructive to formulate it as an integer program.

Define

$x_1$ = MaBell long-distance minutes per month

$x_2$ = PaBell long-distance minutes per month

$x_3$ = BabyBell long-distance minutes per month

$y_1$ = 1 if $x_1 > 0$ and 0 if $x_1 = 0$

$y_2$ = 1 if $x_2 > 0$ and 0 if $x_2 = 0$

$y_3$ = 1 if $x_3 > 0$ and 0 if $x_3 = 0$

We can ensure that $y_j$ will equal 1 if $x_j$ is positive by using the constraint

$$x_j \leq My_j, \quad j = 1, 2, 3$$

where $M$ is a sufficiently large value that will not limit the value of $x_j$ artificially. Because I make about 200 minutes a month, then $x_j \leq 200$ for all $j$, and it is safe to take $M = 200$.

The complete model is

$$\text{Minimize } z = .25x_1 + .21x_2 + .22x_3 + 16y_1 + 25y_2 + 18y_3$$

subject to

$$x_1 + x_2 + x_3 = 200$$

$$x_1 \qquad\qquad \leq 200y_1$$

$$x_2 \qquad \leq 200y_2$$

$$x_3 \leq 200y_3$$

$$x_1, x_2, x_3 \geq 0$$

$$y_1, y_2, y_3 = (0, 1)$$

The formulation shows that the $j$th monthly flat fee will be part of the objective function $z$ only if $y_j = 1$, which can happen only if $x_j > 0$ (per the last three constraints of the model). If $x_j = 0$ at the optimum, then the minimization of $z$, together with the fact that the coefficient of $y_j$ is strictly positive, will force $y_j$ to equal zero, as desired.

The optimum solution yields $x_3 = 200$, $y_3 = 1$, and all the remaining variables equal to zero, which shows that BabyBell should be selected as my long-distance carrier. Observe that the information conveyed by $y_3 = 1$ is redundant because the same result is implied by $x_3 > 0$ (= 200). Actually, the main reason for using $y_1, y_2$, and $y_3$ is to account for the monthly flat fee. In effect, the three binary variables convert an ill-behaved (non-linear) model into an analytically manageable formulation. This conversion has resulted in introducing the integer (binary) variables in an otherwise continuous problem.

The concept of "flat fee" is typical of what is known in the literature as the **fixed charge problem**.

### Problem set 9.2b

1. Jobco is planning to produce at least 2000 widget on three machines. The minimum lot size on any machine is 500 widget. The following table gives the pertinent data of the situations.

| Machine | Setup cost | Production cost/unit | Capacity (units) |
|---|---|---|---|
| 1 | 300 | 2 | 600 |
| 2 | 100 | 10 | 800 |
| 3 | 200 | 5 | 1200 |

Formulate the problem as an ILP, and find the optimum solution using TORA.

2. Oilco is considering two potential drilling sites for reaching four targets (possible oil wells). The following table provides the preparation costs at each of the two sites and the cost of drilling from site $i$ to target $j$ ($i = 1, 2$, $j = 1, 2, 3, 4$).

| Site | Drilling cost (million $) to target | | | | Preparation cost (million $) |
|------|---|---|---|---|------|
|      | 1 | 2 | 3 | 4 |      |
| 1    | 2 | 1 | 8 | 5 | 5    |
| 2    | 4 | 6 | 3 | 1 | 6    |

Formulate the problem as an ILP, and find the optimum solution using TORA.

3. Three industrial sites are considered for locating manufacturing plants. The plants send their supplies to three customers. The supply at the plants and the demand at the customers, together with the unit transportation cost from the plants to the customers are given in the following table.

|   | 1 | 2 | 3 | Supply |
|---|---|---|---|--------|
| 1 | $10 | $15 | $12 | 1800 |
| 2 | $17 | $14 | $20 | 1400 |
| 3 | $15 | $10 | $11 | 1300 |
| Demand | 1200 | 1700 | 1600 | |

In addition to the transportation costs, fixed costs also are incurred at the rate of $10,000, $15,000, and $12,000 for plants 1, 2, and 3, respectively. Formulate the problem as an ILP and find the optimum solution using TORA.

**Example 9.2–3 (TRAVELING SALESMAN PROBLEM).**

The daily production schedule at the Rainbow Company includes batches of white (W), yellow (Y), red (R), and black (B) paints. Because Rainbow uses the same facilities for all four types of paint, proper cleaning between batches is necessary. The following table summarizes the clean-up time in minutes when the row-designated color is followed by the column-designated color. For example, when white is followed by yellow, the clean-up time is 10 minutes. Because a color cannot follow itself, the corresponding entries are assigned infinite setup time. Determine the optimal sequencing for the daily production of the four colors that will minimize the associated total clean-up time.

| Current paint | Clean-up min given next paint is | | | |
|---------------|--------|--------|--------|--------|
|               | White  | Yellow | Black  | Red    |
| White         | $\infty$ | 10   | 17     | 15     |
| Yellow        | 20     | $\infty$ | 19   | 18     |
| Black         | 50     | 44     | $\infty$ | 25   |
| Red           | 45     | 40     | 20     | $\infty$ |

Figure 9–1 summarizes the problem. Each paint is represented by a node, and the directional arcs represent the clean-up time needed to reach one node from the other. The situation thus reduces to determining the *shortest loop* that starts at one node (paint) and passes through each of the remaining three nodes exactly once before returning back to the starting node. Problems of this type are known generically as the **traveling salesman** problem because they paraphrase the situation in which a person desires to determine the *shortest tour* for visiting n cities, with each city visited exactly once.

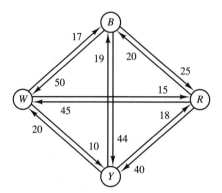

**Figure 9–1**

We can solve this problem by exhaustively enumerating the six $[(4 - 1)! = 3! = 6]$ possible loops of the network. The following table shows that $W \rightarrow Y \rightarrow R \rightarrow B \rightarrow W$ is the optimum loop.

| Production loop | Total clean-up time |
|---|---|
| $W \rightarrow Y \rightarrow B \rightarrow R \rightarrow W$ | $10 + 19 + 25 + 45 = 99$ |
| $\mathbf{W \rightarrow Y \rightarrow R \rightarrow B \rightarrow W}$ | $\mathbf{10 + 18 + 20 + 50 = 98}$ |
| $W \rightarrow B \rightarrow Y \rightarrow R \rightarrow W$ | $17 + 44 + 18 + 45 = 124$ |
| $W \rightarrow B \rightarrow R \rightarrow Y \rightarrow W$ | $17 + 25 + 40 + 20 = 102$ |
| $W \rightarrow R \rightarrow B \rightarrow Y \rightarrow W$ | $15 + 20 + 44 + 20 = 99$ |
| $W \rightarrow R \rightarrow Y \rightarrow B \rightarrow W$ | $15 + 40 + 19 + 50 = 124$ |

Exhaustive enumeration of the loops is practical only for small problems (e.g., an 11-node network has $10! = 3,628,800$ loops). Consequently, a more efficient formulation is needed.

Define

$x_{ij} = 1$ if node $j$ is reached from node $i$ and zero otherwise A necessary condition for a tour (loop) is that city $i$ connects to one city only and that city $j$ is reached from exactly one city. Letting $M$ be a sufficiently large positive value, we can formulate the Rainbow problem as

$$\text{Minimize } z = Mx_{WW} + 10x_{WY} + 17x_{WB} + 15x_{WR} + 20x_{YW} + Mx_{YY} + 19x_{YB} + 18x_{YR}$$

$$+ 50x_{BW} + 44x_{BY} + Mx_{BB} + 25x_{BR} + 45x_{RW} + 40x_{RY} + 20x_{RB} + Mx_{RR}$$

subject to

$$x_{WW} + x_{WY} + x_{WB} + x_{WR} = 1$$
$$x_{YW} + x_{YY} + x_{YB} + x_{YR} = 1$$
$$x_{BW} + x_{BY} + x_{BB} + x_{BR} = 1$$
$$x_{RW} + x_{RY} + x_{RB} + x_{RR} = 1$$
$$x_{WW} + x_{YW} + x_{BW} + x_{RW} = 1$$
$$x_{WY} + x_{YY} + x_{BY} + x_{RY} = 1$$
$$x_{WB} + x_{YB} + x_{BB} + x_{RB} = 1$$
$$x_{WR} + x_{YR} + x_{BR} + x_{RR} = 1$$
$$x_{ij} = (0, 1) \text{ for all } i \text{ and } j$$

Solution is a tour (loop)

Except for the requirement that the solution must be a tour, the formulation is an assignment model. There is no guarantee that the optimal solution of the assignment model alone will produce a tour. Most likely, it will consist of subtours that link subsets of the nodes together. For this reason, exact algorithms based on the assignment have been developed for solving the problem. These algorithms vary in their complexity and computational efficiency (see Taha, 1975, pp. 304–316 for details).

## Problem set 9.2c

**1.** A manager has a total of 10 employees working on six projects. There are overlaps among the assignments as the following table shows:

|     | Project |     |     |     |     |     |
|-----|---|---|---|---|---|---|
|     | 1 | 2 | 3 | 4 | 5 | 6 |
| 1   |   | X |   | X | X |   |
| 2   | X |   | X |   | X |   |
| 3   |   | X | X | X |   | X |
| 4   |   |   | X | X | X |   |
| 5   | X | X | X |   |   |   |
| 6   | X | X | X | X |   | X |
| 7   | X | X |   |   | X | X |
| 8   | X |   | X | X |   |   |
| 9   |   |   |   |   | X | X |
| 10  | X | X |   | X | X | X |

The manager must meet all 10 employees once a week to discuss their progress. Currently, the meeting with each employee lasts about 20 minutes—that is, a total of 3 hours and 20 minutes for all 10 employees. A suggestion is made to reduce the total time by holding group meetings, depending on the projects the employees share. The manager wants to schedule the projects in a way that will reduce the traffic (number of employees) in and out of the meeting room. How should the projects be scheduled?

2. A book salesperson who lives in Basin must call once a month on four customers located in Wald, Bon, Mena, and Kiln. The following table gives the distances in miles among the different cities.

|       | Basin | Wald | Bon | Mena | Kiln |
|-------|-------|------|-----|------|------|
| Basin | 0     | 120  | 220 | 150  | 210  |
| Wald  | 120   | 0    | 80  | 110  | 130  |
| Bon   | 220   | 110  | 0   | 160  | 185  |
| Mena  | 150   | 110  | 160 | 0    | 190  |
| Kiln  | 210   | 130  | 185 | 190  | 0    |

The objective is to minimize the total distance traveled by the salesperson. Formulate the problem as an ILP.

3. In Problem 2, suppose that Wald, Bon, Mena, and Kiln are designated as cities 1, 2, 3, and 4, and that hometown Basin is split into two cities that are designated as cities 0 and 5. Thus, a tour starts at city 0, passes (in some order) through 1, 2, 3, and 4, and terminates at 5. Define $v_i$ for city $i$ ($i = 0, 1, \ldots, 5$) such that $0 \leq v_i \leq 5$, and let $x_{ij} = 1$ if city $i$ is followed by city $j$ in the tour and zero otherwise. Show that the constraints

$$v_i - v_j + 5x_{ij} \leq 4, \ i = 0, 1, \ldots, 4, \ j = 1, 2, \ldots, 5$$

guarantee the elimination of all subtours in the solution of the problem.

---

**Example 9.2–4 (SET COVERING PROBLEM).**

To promote safety for students, the U of A Security Department is in the process of installing emergency telephones at selected locations on campus. The department wants to install the minimum number of telephones provided that each of the camps main streets is served by at least one telephone. Figure 9–2 maps the principal streets (A to K) on campus.

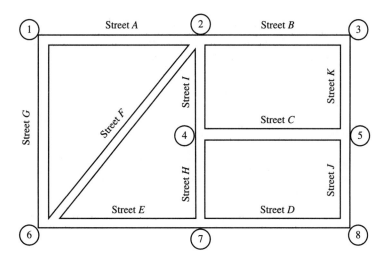

**Figure 9–2**

It is logical to place the telephones at the intersections of streets so that each telephone will serve at least two streets. Figure 9–2 shows that the layout of the streets requires a maximum of eight telephone locations.

Define

$$x_j = 1 \text{ if a telephone is installed in location } j \text{ and } 0$$

$$\text{otherwise, } j = 1, 2, ..., 8$$

The constraints of the problem require installing at least one telephone on each of the 11 streets (A to K). Thus, the model becomes

$$\text{Minimize } z = x_1 + x_2 + x_3 + x_4 + x_5 + x_6 + x_7 + x_8$$

subject to

$$
\begin{aligned}
x_1 + x_2 & & & \geq 1 \quad (\text{Street } A) \\
x_2 + x_3 & & & \geq 1 \quad (\text{Street } B) \\
x_4 + x_5 & & & \geq 1 \quad (\text{Street } C) \\
x_7 + x_8 & \geq 1 \quad (\text{Street } D) \\
x_6 + x_7 & & \geq 1 \quad (\text{Street } E) \\
x_2 \quad\quad + x_6 & & & \geq 1 \quad (\text{Street } F) \\
x_1 \quad\quad\quad + x_6 & & & \geq 1 \quad (\text{Street } G) \\
x_4 \quad\quad\quad + x_7 & & \geq 1 \quad (\text{Street } H)
\end{aligned}
$$

$$x_2 \quad + x_4 \qquad\qquad\qquad \geq 1 \ \text{(Street } I)$$

$$x_5 \qquad\qquad + x_8 \geq 1 \ \text{(Street } J)$$

$$x_3 \quad + x_5 \qquad\qquad \geq 1 \ \text{(Street } K)$$

$$x_j = (0, \ 1), \quad j = 1, \ 2, \ ..., 8$$

The optimum solution of the problem (obtained by TORA) requires installing four telephones at intersections 1, 2, 5, and 7.

The preceding model is typical of what is generically known as the **set covering problem**. In this model, all the variables are binary. For each constraint, all the left-hand-side coefficients are 0 or 1, and the right-hand side is of the form ($\geq 1$). The objective function always minimizes $c_1 x_1 + c_2 x_2 + ... + c_n x_n$, where $c_j > 0$ for all $j = 1, 2, ..., n$. In the present example, $c_j = 1$ for all $j$. However, if $c_j$ represents the installation cost in location $j$, then these coefficients may assume values other than 1.

**Problem set 9.2d**

1. ABC is an LTL trucking company that delivers loads on a daily basis to five customers. The following routes have been chosen to reach the customers:

*Route 1.*   1, 2, 3, 4
*Route 2.*   4, 3, 5
*Route 3.*   1, 2, 5
*Route 4.*   2, 3, 5
*Route 5.*   1, 4, 2
*Route 6.*   1, 3, 5

The segments of each route are dictated by the capacity of the truck delivering the loads. For example, on route 1, the truck has enough capacity to deliver the loads to only customers 1, 2, 3, and 4. The following table lists distances (in miles) among the truck terminal (ABC) and the customers.

| | ABC | 1 | 2 | 3 | 4 | 5 |
|---|---|---|---|---|---|---|
| ABC | 0 | 10 | 12 | 16 | 9 | 8 |
| 1 | 10 | 0 | 32 | 8 | 17 | 10 |
| 2 | 12 | 32 | 0 | 14 | 21 | 20 |
| 3 | 16 | 8 | 14 | 0 | 15 | 18 |
| 4 | 9 | 17 | 21 | 15 | 0 | 11 |
| 5 | 8 | 10 | 20 | 18 | 11 | 0 |

The objective is to make the daily deliveries to the five customers using the shortest possible driving distance. The solution may be such that the same customer is served by more than one route. In the implementation of the solution, only one of these routes is used. Formulate the problem as an ILP and solve using TORA.

2. The U of A is in the process of forming a committee to handle the students' grievances. The directives received from the administration is to include at least one female, one male, one student, one administrator, and one faculty member. Ten individuals (identified, for simplicity, by the letters *a* to *j*) have been nominated. The mix of these individuals in the different categories is given as follows:

| Category | Individuals |
|---|---|
| Females | *a, b, c, d, e* |
| Males | *f, g, h, i, j* |
| Students | *a, b, c, j* |
| Administrators | *e, f* |
| Faculty | *d, g, h, i* |

The U of A wants to form the smallest committee while guaranteeing a representation of each of the five categories. Formulate the problem as an ILP, and find the optimum solution using TORA.

3. Washington County includes six towns that need emergency ambulance service. The ambulance stations may be placed in any or all of the six towns. However, because of the proximity of some of the towns, a single station may serve more than one community. The stipulation is that the station must be within 15 minutes of driving time from the towns it serves. The table below gives the driving times in minutes among the six towns.

|   | 1 | 2 | 3 | 4 | 5 | 6 |
|---|---|---|---|---|---|---|
| 1 | 0 | 23 | 14 | 18 | 10 | 32 |
| 2 | 23 | 0 | 24 | 13 | 22 | 11 |
| 3 | 14 | 24 | 0 | 60 | 19 | 20 |
| 4 | 18 | 13 | 60 | 0 | 55 | 17 |
| 5 | 10 | 22 | 19 | 55 | 0 | 12 |
| 6 | 32 | 11 | 20 | 17 | 12 | 0 |

Formulate an ILP whose solution will produce the smallest number of stations and their locations. Find the solution using TORA.

**4.** The treasures of King Tut are on display in a museum in New Orleans. The layout of the museum is shown in Figure 9–3, with the different rooms joined by open doors. A guard standing at a door can watch two adjoining rooms. The museum wants to ensure guard presence in every room, using the minimum number possible. Formulate the problem as an ILP, and find the optimum solution with TORA.

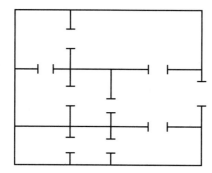

**Figure 9–3**

---

**Example 9.2–5 (EITHER-OR CONSTRAINTS).**

Jobco uses a single machine to process three jobs. Both the processing time and the due date (in days) for each job are given in the following table. The due dates are measured from the zero datum, the assumed start time of the first job.

| Job | Processing time (d) | Due date (d) | Late penalty ($/d) |
|-----|-----|-----|-----|
| 1 | 5 | 25 | 19 |
| 2 | 20 | 22 | 12 |
| 3 | 15 | 35 | 34 |

The objective of the problem is to determine the minimum late-penalty sequence for processing the three jobs.

Define

$x_j$ = Completion date in days for job $j$ (measured from the zero datum)

The problem has two types of constraints: (1) the noninterference constraints guaranteeing that no two jobs are processed concurrently and (2) the due date constraints. Consider the noninterference constraints first.

Two jobs $i$ and $j$ with processing time $p_i$ and $p_j$ will not be processed concurrently if

$$\text{Either } x_i \geq x_j + p_j \text{ or } x_j \geq x_i + p_i$$

depending on whether job $j$ precedes job $i$, or vice versa.

Because all mathematical programs deal with *simultaneous* constraints only, we transform the **either-or** constraints by introducing the following auxiliary binary variable:

$$y_{ij} = \begin{cases} 1, & \text{if } i \text{ precedes } j \\ 0, & \text{if } j \text{ precedes } i \end{cases}$$

For $M$ sufficiently large, the *either-or* constraint is converted to the following two *simultaneous* constraints

$$My_{ij} + (x_i - x_j) \geq p_j \text{ and } M(1 - y_{ij}) + (x_j - x_i) \geq p_i$$

The conversion guarantees that only one of the two constraints can be active at any one time. If $y_{ij} = 0$, the first constraint is active, and the second is redundant (because its left-hand side will include $M$, which is much larger than $p_i$). If $y_{ij} = 1$, the first constraint is redundant, and the second is active.

Next, the due date constraint is considered. Given $d_j$ is the due date for job $j$, let $s_j$ be an unrestricted variable. Then, the associated constraint is

$$x_j + p_j + s_j = d_j$$

If $s_j \geq 0$, the due date is met, and if $s_j < 0$, a late penalty is incurred. Using the standard substitution

$$s_j = s_j^+ - s_j^-, s_j^+ \text{ and } s_j^- \geq 0$$

The constraint becomes

$$x_j + s_j^+ - s_j^- = d_j - p_j$$

The late penalty cost is proportional to $s_j^-$.

The model for the given problem is

$$\text{Minimize } z = 19s_1^- + 12s_2^- + 34s_3^-$$

subject to

$$
\begin{array}{lclclclclcr}
x_1 & - & x_2 & & & + & My_{12} & & & & \geq 20 \\
-x_1 & + & x_2 & & & - & My_{12} & & & & \geq 5 - M \\
x_1 & & & - & x_3 & + & My_{13} & & & & \geq 15 \\
-x_1 & & & + & x_3 & - & My_{13} & & & & \geq 5 - M \\
& & x_2 & - & x_3 & & & + & My_{23} & & \geq 15 \\
& & -x_2 & + & x_3 & & & - & My_{23} & & \geq 20 - M \\
x_1 & & & & & & & + & s_1^+ - s_1^- & & = 25 - 5 \\
& & x_2 & & & & & & + s_2^+ - s_2^- & & = 22 - 20 \\
& & & & x_3 & & & & + s_3^+ - s_3^- & = & 35 - 15 \\
\end{array}
$$

$$x_1, \ x_2, \ x_3, \ s_1^+, \ s_1^-, \ s_2^+, \ s_2^-, \ s_3^+, \ s_3^- \ \geq 0$$

$$y_{12}, \ y_{13}, \ y_{23} = (0, \ 1)$$

The integer variables, $y_{12}, y_{13}$, and $y_{23}$, are introduced to convert the either-or constraints into simultaneous constraints. The resulting model is a *mixed* ILP.

To solve the model, we choose $M = 100$, a value that is larger than the sum of the processing times for all three activities.

The optimal solution (obtained by TORA) is $x_1 = 20$, $x_2 = 0$, and $x_3 = 25$. Thus, the optimal processing sequence is $2 \rightarrow 1 \rightarrow 3$. The solution calls for completing job 2 at time $0 + 5 = 5$, job 1 at time $= 20 + 5 = 25$, and job 3 at $25 + 15 = 40$ days. Job 3 is delayed by $40 - 35 = 5$ days past its due date at a cost of $5 \times \$34 = \$170$.

### Problem set 9.2e

1. A game board consists of nine equal squares. You are required to fill each square with a number between 1 and 9 such that the sum of the numbers in each row and each column equals 15. Determine the number in each square for the following cases:

   (a) No two adjacent numbers in any row or any column are equal.

   (b) The numbers in all the squares are distinct.

   Express the problem as ILP constraints, and solve with TORA.

2. A machine is used to produce two interchangeable products. The daily capacity of the machine can produce at most 20 units of product 1 and 10 units of product 2. Alternatively, the machine can be adjusted to produce at most 12 units of product 1 and 22 units of product 2 daily. Market analysis shows that the maximum daily demands for the two products combined is 35 units. Suppose that the unit profit for the two respective products are $10 and $12, which of the two machine settings should be selected. Formulate the problem as an ILP, and find the optimum using TORA. (*Note:* This two-dimensional problem can be solved by inspecting the graphical solution space. This is not the case for the *n*-dimensional problem.)

3. Gapco manufactures three products, whose daily labor and raw material requirements are given in the following table.

| Product | Required daily labor (hr/unit) | Required daily raw material (lb/unit) |
|---------|:---:|:---:|
| 1 | 3 | 4 |
| 2 | 4 | 3 |
| 3 | 5 | 6 |

The profits per unit of the three products are $25, $30, and $22, respectively. Gapco has two options for locating its plant. The two locations differ primarily in the availability of labor and raw material as shown in the following table:

| Location | Available daily labor (hr) | Available daily raw material (lb) |
|----------|----------------------------|------------------------------------|
| 1 | 100 | 100 |
| 2 | 90 | 120 |

Formulate the problem as a mixed ILP, and use TORA to determine the optimum location of the plant.

4. Consider the job-shop scheduling problem that produces two end products using a single machine. The precedence relationships among the eight operations are summarized in Figure 9–4. Let $p_j$ be the processing time for operations $j$ ($= 1, 2, \ldots, n$). The due dates measured from the zero datum, for products 1 and 2, are $d_1$ and $d_2$, respectively. An operation, once started, must be completed before another starts. Formulate the problem as a mixed ILP.

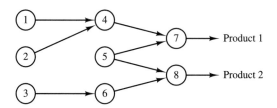

**Figure 9–4**

5. Jaco owns a plant in which three products are manufactured. The labor and raw material requirements for the three products are given in the following table.

| Product | Required daily labor (hr/unit) | Required daily raw material (lb/unit) |
|---------|-------------------------------|----------------------------------------|
| 1 | 3 | 4 |
| 2 | 4 | 3 |
| 3 | 5 | 6 |
| Daily availability | 100 | 100 |

The profit per unit for the three products are $25, $30, and $45, respectively. If product 3 is to be manufactured at all, then its production level must be at least 5 units daily. Formulate the problem as a mixed ILP, and find the optimal mix using TORA.

6. Show how the nonconvex shaded solution spaces in Figure 9–5 can be represented by a set of simultaneous constraints. Then use TORA to find the optimum solution that maximizes $z = 2x_1 + 3x_2$ subject to the solution space given in (a).

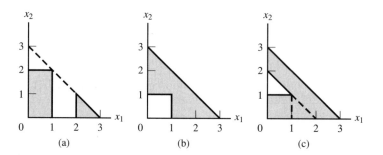

(a)                     (b)                     (c)

**Figure 9–5**

7. Suppose that it is required that *any* $k$ out of the following $m$ constraints must be active:

$$g_i(x_1, x_2, ..., x_n) \le b_i, \quad i = 1, 2, ..., m$$

Show how this condition my be represented.

8. In the following constraint, the right-hand side may assume one of values, $b_1, b_2, ...,$ and $b_m$.

$$g(x_1, x_2, ..., x_n) \le b_1, b_2, ..., \text{ or } b_m$$

Show how this condition is represented.

## 9.3 INTEGER PROGRAMMING ALGORITHMS

The ILP algorithms are based on exploiting the tremendous computational success of LP. The strategy of these algorithms involves three steps.

**Step 1.** Relax the solution space of the ILP by replacing any binary variable $y$ with the continuous range $0 \le y \le 1$, and deleting the integer restrictions on all the integer variables. The result of the relaxation is a regular LP.

**Step 2.** Solve the LP, and identify its continuous optimum.

**Step 3.** Starting from the continuous optimum point, add special constraints that iteratively modify the LP solution space in a manner that will eventually render an optimum extreme point that satisfies the integer requirements.

Two general methods have been developed for generating the special constraints referred to in step 3.

**1.** Branch-and-bound (B&B) method
**2.** Cutting plane method

Although neither method is consistently effective in solving ILPs, computational experience shows that the branch-and-bound method is far more successful than the cutting plane method.

### 9.3.1  Branch-and-Bound (B&B) Algorithm

The basics of the B&B algorithm will be explained by a numerical example.

---

**Example 9.3–1.**
Consider the following ILP:

$$\text{Maximize } z = 5x_1 + 4x_2$$

subject to

$$x_1 + x_2 \leq 5$$

$$10x_1 + 6x_2 \leq 45$$

$$x_1, x_2 \geq 0 \text{ and integer}$$

The ILP solution space is shown in Figure 9–6 by dots. The associated LP problem, LP0, is defined by dropping the integer restrictions and its optimum solution is given as $x_1 = 3.75, x_2 = 1.25$, and $z = 23.75$.

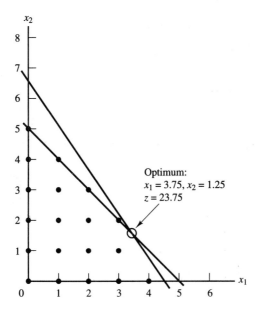

Optimum:
$x_1 = 3.75, x_2 = 1.25$
$z = 23.75$

**Figure 9–6**

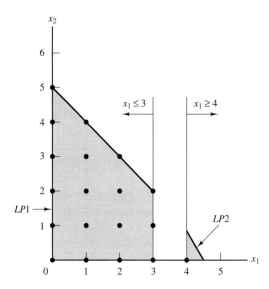

**Figure 9–7**

Because the optimum LP0 solution does not satisfy the integer requirements, the B&B algorithm modifies the solution space in a manner that eventually identifies the ILP optimum. First, we select one of the integer variables whose value at LP0 is not integer. Selecting $x_1$ ($= 3.75$) arbitrarily, the region $3 < x_1 < 4$ of the LP0 solution space contains no integer values of $x_1$, and, hence, can be eliminated as nonpromising. This is equivalent to replacing the original LP0 with two new LPs, LP1 and LP2, defined as

LP1 space $=$ LP0 space $+$ $(x_1 \leq 3)$
LP2 space $=$ LP0 space $+$ $(x_1 \geq 4)$

Figure 9–7 depicts the LP1 and LP2 spaces. The two spaces contain the same feasible integer points of the original ILP, which means that dealing with LP1 and LP2 is the same as dealing with the original LP0.

If we *intelligently* continue to remove the regions that do not include integer solutions by imposing the appropriate constraints (such as $3 < x_1 < 4$), we will eventually produce LPs whose optimum extreme points satisfy the integer restrictions. In effect, we will be solving the ILP by dealing with a succession of (continuous) LPs.

The new restrictions, $x_1 \leq 3$ and $x_1 \geq 4$, are mutually exclusive, so that LP1 and LP2 must be dealt with as separate LPs as Figure 9–8 shows. This dichotomization gives rise to the concept of **branching** in the B&B algorithm. In this case, $x_1$ is the **branching variable**.

The optimum ILP lies in either LP1 or LP2. Hence, both subproblems must be examined. We arbitrarily examine LP1 (associated with $x_1 \leq 3$) first.

$$\text{Maximize } z = 5x_1 + 4x_2$$

subject to

$$x_1 + x_2 \leq 5$$

$$10x_1 + 6x_2 \leq 45$$

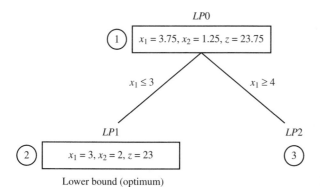

$$x_1 \leq 3$$
$$x_1, x_2 \geq 0$$

The solution of LP1 (which can be solved efficiently by the upper-bounded algorithm of Section 7.5.2) yields the optimum solution

$$x_1 = 3, x_2 = 2, \text{ and } z = 23$$

The LP1 solution satisfies the integer requirements for $x_1$ and $x_2$. Hence, LP1 is said to be **fathomed**. This means that LP1 need not be investigated any further because it does not include any *better* ILP solution.

We cannot at this point judge the "quality" of the integer solution from LP1, for LP2 may yield a better integer solution (with a higher value of $z$). All we can say is that $z = 23$ is a **lower bound** on the optimum (maximum) objective value of the original ILP. This means that any unexamined subproblem that cannot yield a better objective value must be discarded as nonpromising. If an unexamined subproblem can produce a better integer solution, then the lower bound must be updated subsequently.

Given the lower bound $z = 23$, we examine LP2 (the only remaining unexamined subproblem). Because optimum $z = 23.75$ at LP0 *and all the coefficients of the objective function happen to be integers*, it is impossible that LP2 (which is more restrictive than LP0) will produce a better integer solution. As a result, we discard LP2 and conclude that it is *fathomed*.

The B&B algorithm is now complete because both LP1 and LP2 have been examined and fathomed (the first for producing an integer solution and the second for showing that it cannot produce a better integer solution). We thus conclude that the optimum ILP solution is the one associated with the lower bound—namely, $x_1 = 3$, $x_2 = 2$, and $z = 23$.

Two questions remain unanswered regarding the procedure.

**1.** At LP0, could we have selected $x_2$ as the *branching variable* in place of $x_1$?

**2.** When selecting the next subproblem to be examined, could we have solved LP2 first instead of LP1?

The answer to both questions is "yes." However, the ensuing computations could differ dramatically. Figure 9–9, in which LP2 is examined first, illustrates this point. The optimum LP2 solution is $x_1 = 4, x_2 = .83$, and $z = 23.33$ (verify using TORA). Because

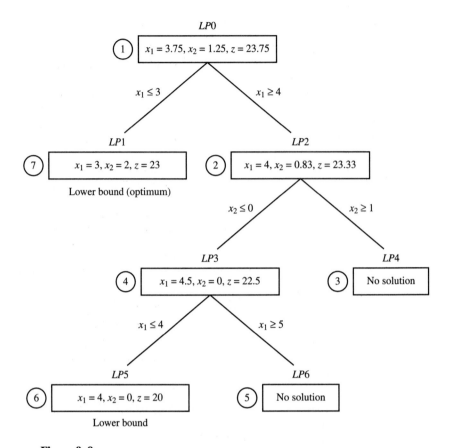

**Figure 9–9**

$x_2$ (= .83) is noninteger, LP2 is investigated further by creating subproblems LP3 and LP4 using the respective branches $x_2 \leq 0$ and $x_2 \geq 1$, respectively. This means that

$$\text{LP3 space} = \text{LP2 space} \quad + (x_2 \leq 0)$$
$$= \text{LP0 space} + (x_1 \geq 4) + (x_2 \leq 0)$$
$$\text{LP4 space} = \text{LP2 space} \quad + (x_2 \geq 1)$$
$$= \text{LP0 space} + (x_1 \geq 4) + (x_2 \geq 1)$$

We have three outstanding subproblems that must be examined: LP1, LP3, and LP4. Suppose that we arbitrarily examine LP4 first. LP4 has no solution, and hence it is fathomed. Next, let us examine LP3. The optimum solution is $x_1 = 4.5$, $x_2 = 0$, and $z = 22.5$. The noninteger value of $x_1$ (= 4.5) leads to the two branches $x_1 \leq 4$ and $x_1 \geq 5$, and the creation of subproblems LP5 and LP6 from LP3.

$$\text{LP5 space} = \text{LP0 space} + (x_1 \geq 4) + (x_2 \leq 0) + (x_1 \leq 4)$$
$$\text{LP6 space} = \text{LP0 space} + (x_1 \leq 4) + (x_2 \leq 0) + (x_1 \geq 5)$$

Now, subproblems LP1, LP5, and LP6 remain unexamined. LP6 is fathomed because it has no feasible solution. Next, LP5 has the integer solution ($x_1 = 4$, $x_2 = 0$, $z = 20$), and, hence, yields a lower bound ($z = 20$) on the optimum ILP solution. We are left with subproblem LP1, whose solution is also integer ($x_1 = 3$, $x_2 = 2$, $z = 23$). Thus, the lower bound is updated to $z = 23$. Because *all* the subproblems have been fathomed, the optimum solution is associated with the most up-to-date lower bound—namely, $x_1 = 3$, $x_2 = 2$, and $z = 23$.

The solution sequence in Figure 9–9 (LP0, LP2, LP4, LP3, LP6, LP5, LP1) is a worst-case scenario that, nevertheless, may occur in practice. The example points to a principal weaknesses of the B&B algorithm: How do we select the next subproblem to be examined, and how do we choose its branching variable?

In Figure 9–8, we happen to "stumble" on a good lower bound at the very first subproblem, LP1, thus allowing us to fathom LP2 without further computations and to terminate the B&B search. In essence, we completed the procedure by solving one subproblem only. In Figure 9–9, we had to examine seven subproblems before the B&B algorithm is terminated. Although there are heuristics for enhancing the ability of B&B to "guess" which branch can lead to an improved ILP solution (see Taha, 1975, pp. 154–171), there is no solid theory that will always yield consistent results.

---

We now summarize the B&B algorithm. Assuming a maximization problem, set an initial lower bound $z = -\infty$ on the optimum objective value of ILP. Set $i = 0$.

**Step 1.** (fathoming/bounding). Select LP$i$, the next subproblem to be examined. Solve LP$i$, and attempt to fathom it using one of three conditions.

    **(a)** The optimal $z$-value of LP$i$ cannot yield a better objective value than the current lower bound.

    **(b)** LP$i$ yields a better feasible integer solution than the current lower bound.

    **(c)** LP$i$ has no feasible solution.

    Two cases will arise.

    **(a)** If LP$i$ is fathomed, update the lower bound if a better ILP solution is found. If all subproblems have been fathomed, stop; the optimum ILP is associated with the current lower bound, if any. Otherwise, set $i = i + 1$, and repeat step 1.

    **(b)** If LP$i$ is not fathomed, go to step 2 to effect branching.

**Step 2.** (branching). Select one of the integer variables $x_j$, whose optimum value $x_j^*$ in the LP$i$ solution is not integer. Eliminate the region $[x_j^*] < x_j < [x_j^*] + 1$ (where $[v]$ defines the largest integer $\leq v$) by creating two LP subproblems that correspond to

$$x_j \leq [x_j^*] \text{ and } x_j \geq [x_j^*] + 1$$

Set $i = i + 1$, and go to step 1.

The given steps apply to maximization problems. For minimization, we replace the lower bound with an upper bound (whose initial value is $z = +\infty$ ).

The B&B algorithm can be extended directly to mixed problems (in which only some of the variables are integer). If a variable is continuous, we simply never select it as a branching variable. A feasible subproblem provides a new bound on the objective value if the values of the discrete variables are integer and the objective value is improved relative to the current bound.

### Problem set 9.3a

1. Solve the ILP of Example 9.3–1 by the B&B algorithm starting with $x_2$ as the branching variable. Solve the subproblems with TORA using the MODIFY option for the upper and lower bounds. Start the procedure by solving the subproblem associated with $x_2 \leq [x_2^*]$.

2. Develop the B&B tree for each of the following problems. For convenience, always select $x_1$ as the branching variable at node 0.

   **(a)** Maximize $z = 3x_1 + 2x_2$
   
   subject to
   
   $$2x_1 + 2x_2 \leq 9$$
   $$3x_1 + 3x_2 \geq 18$$
   $$x_1, x_2 \geq \text{and integer}$$

   **(b)** Maximize $z = 2x_1 + 3x_2$
   
   subject to
   
   $$5x_1 + 7x_2 \leq 35$$
   $$4x_1 + 9x_2 \leq 36$$
   $$x_1, x_2 \geq \text{and integer}$$

   **(c)** Maximize $z = x_1 + x_2$
   
   subject to
   
   $$2x_1 + 5x_2 \leq 16$$
   $$6x_1 + 5x_2 \leq 27$$
   $$x_1, x_2 \geq \text{and integer}$$

   **(d)** Minimize $z = 5x_1 + 4x_2$
   
   subject to
   
   $$3x_1 + 2x_2 \geq 5$$
   $$2x_1 + 3x_2 \geq 7$$
   $$x_1, x_2 \geq \text{and integer}$$

   **(e)** Maximize $z = 5x_1 + 7x_2$
   
   subject to
   
   $$2x_1 + x_2 \leq 13$$
   $$5x_1 + 9x_2 \leq 41$$
   $$x_1, x_2 \geq \text{and integer}$$

3. Repeat Problem 2, assuming that $x_1$ is continuous.

4. Show graphically that the following ILP has no feasible solution, and then verify the result using B&B.

$$\text{Maximize } z = 2x_1 + x_2$$

subject to

$$10x_1 + 10x_2 \le 9$$

$$10x_1 + 5x_2 \ge 1$$

$$x_1, x_2 \ge \text{ and integer}$$

5. Solve the following problems by B&B.

(a) Maximize $z = 18x_1 + 14x_2 + 8x_3 + 4x_4$
  subject to

$$15x_1 + 12x_2 + 7x_3 + 4x_4 + x_5 \le 37$$

$$x_1, x_2, x_3, x_4, x_5 = (0, 1)$$

(b) Maximize $z = x_1 + 2x_2 + 5x_3$
  subject to

$$\left| -x_1 + 10x_2 - 3x_3 \right| \ge 15$$

$$2x_1 + x_2 + x_3 \le 10$$

$$x_1, x_2, x_3 \ge 0$$

### 9.3.2 Zero-One Implicit Enumeration Algorithm

Any integer variable $x$ with a finite upper bound $u$ (i.e., $0 \le x \le u$) can be expressed in terms of 0–1 (binary) variables using the substitution

$$x = 2^0 y_0 + 2^1 y_1 + 2^2 y_2 + \ldots + 2^k y_k$$

where $k$ is the smallest integer satisfying $2^{k+1} - 1 \ge u$ and $y_0, y_1, \ldots,$ and $y_k$ are 0–1 variables. This result, together with what appeared at one time to be a simple algorithm for solving 0–1 ILP, has raised hope that the general ILP may be solved more efficiently as a 0–1 problem. Unfortunately, this line of investigation failed to produce a computational breakthrough.

The first special 0–1 algorithm, called the **additive algorithm,** was developed in 1965, some 7 years after the development of B&B. Initially, the algorithm appeared unrelated to the general B&B algorithm because it did not require solving LPs, and its principal computation involved only simple additions and subtractions. However, shortly after, the link between the two algorithms became apparent, in the sense that the additive algorithm is but a special case of the general B&B algorithm.

The design of the fathoming heuristic in the additive algorithm requires presenting the 0–1 problem in a convenient form that satisfies the following requirements:

**1.** The objective function is of the minimization type with all *nonnegative* coefficients.

**2.** All the constraints must be of the type ($\leq$), with negative right-hand sides, if necessary. These constraints are then converted to equations by using (continuous) slack variables to the left-hand side of the constraints.

Any $0-1$ integer problem can satisfy these conditions as the following example demonstrates.

---

**Example 9.3–2.**

Convert the following $0-1$ problem to satisfy the starting requirements of the additive algorithm.

$$\text{Maximize } z = 3x_1 - 5x_2$$

subject to

$$x_1 + x_2 = 5$$
$$4x_1 + 6x_2 \geq 4$$
$$x_1, x_2 = (0, 1)$$

We first convert the problem to minimization with all ($\leq$) constraints as follows:

**(a)** Multiply $z$ by $-1$ to get minimize $w = -3x_1 + 5x_2$.
**(b)** Convert the constraint equation into two constraints of the type ($\leq$) to obtain $x_1 + x_2 \leq 5$ and $-x_1 - x_2 \leq -5$.
**(c)** Multiply the second constraint by $-1$ to get $-4x_1 - 6x_2 \leq -4$.

Using the slacks $s_1, s_2$, and $s_3$ for the three constraints, the problem is written as

$$\text{Minimize } w = -3x_1 + 5x_2$$

subject to

$$x_1 + x_2 + s_1 = 5$$
$$-x_1 - x_2 + s_2 = -5$$
$$-4x_1 - 6x_2 + s_3 = -4$$
$$x_1, x_2 = (0, 1)$$
$$s_1, s_2, s_3 \geq 0$$

To ensure that the objective function coefficients are nonnegative, substitute $x_j = 1 - x_j'$ for any $x_j$ with negative coefficient in the objective function. Thus, we substitute $x_1 = 1 - x_1'$ and adjust the right-hand side of the constraints accordingly. The additive algorithm now deals with $x_1'$ and $x_2$.

---

As in the B&B, branching in the additive algorithm is also based on the use of a branching variable $x_j$. The main difference is that the two branches are associated with the strict equations $x_j = 0$ and $x_j = 1$ because $x_j$ is a binary variable. Bounding is treated in the same manner as in the B&B algorithm, in the sense that an improved integer solution provides an upper bound on the minimum value of the objective function.

The fathoming of the subproblems can occur in one of three ways.

**1.** The subproblem cannot lead to a feasible solution.
**2.** The subproblem cannot yield a better upper bound.
**3.** The subproblem yields a feasible integer solution.

These rules are the same as in B&B. The main difference is that we do not solve LPs. Instead, we use heuristics.

The following numeric example demonstrates the additive algorithm and its fathoming tests.

---

**Example 9.3–3 (ADDITIVE ALGORITHM).**
Solve the following $0-1$ problem.

$$\text{Maximize } w = 3y_1 + 2y_2 - 5y_3 - 2y_4 + 3y_5$$

subject to

$$y_1 + y_2 + y_3 + 2y_4 + y_5 \le 4$$
$$7y_1 \qquad + 3y_3 - 4y_4 + 3y_5 \le 8$$
$$11y_1 - 6x_2 \qquad + 3y_4 - 3y_5 \ge 3$$
$$y_1, y_2, y_3, y_4, y_5 = (0, 1)$$

The problem can be put in the initial form required by the additive algorithm (see Example 9.3–2) using the following operations:
**(a)** Multiply the objective function by $-1$.
**(b)** Multiply the third constraint by $-1$.
**(c)** Add the slacks $s_1, s_2,$ and $s_3$ to convert the three constraints into equations.
**(d)** Substitute $y_1 = 1 - x_1, y_2 = 1 - x_2, y_5 = 1 - x_5, y_3 = x_3,$ and $y_4 = x_4$ to produce all positive objective coefficients.

The conversion results in the following objective function (verify!):

$$\text{Minimize } z' = 3x_1 + 2x_2 + 5x_3 + 2x_4 + 3x_5 - 8$$

For convenience, we will ignore the constant $-8$ and replace $z' + 8$ with $z$, so that the resulting converted problem reads as (verify!)

$$\text{Minimize } z = 3x_1 + 2x_2 + 5x_3 + 2x_4 + 3x_5$$

subject to

$$-x_1 - x_2 + x_3 + 2x_4 - x_5 + s_1 = 1$$
$$-7x_1 \qquad + 3x_3 - 4x_4 - 3x_5 + s_2 = -2$$
$$11x_1 - 6x_2 \qquad - 3x_4 - 3x_5 + s_3 = -1$$
$$x_1, x_2, x_3, x_4, x_5 = (0, 1)$$

Because the converted problem seeks the minimization of an objective function with all positive coefficients, a logical starting solution should consist of all-zero binary variables. In this case, the slacks will act as basic variables, and their values are given by the right-hand sides of the equations. The solution is summarized in following tableau.

| Basic | $x_1$ | $x_2$ | $x_3$ | $x_4$ | $x_5$ | $s_1$ | $s_2$ | $s_3$ | Solution |
|-------|-------|-------|-------|-------|-------|-------|-------|-------|----------|
| $s_1$ | $-1$ | $-1$ | $1$ | $2$ | $-1$ | $1$ | $0$ | $0$ | $1$ |
| $s_2$ | $-7$ | $0$ | $3$ | $-4$ | $-3$ | $0$ | $1$ | $0$ | $-2$ |
| $s_3$ | $11$ | $-6$ | $0$ | $-3$ | $-3$ | $0$ | $0$ | $1$ | $-1$ |
| Objective coefficients | $3$ | $2$ | $5$ | $2$ | $3$ | | | | |

As you will see subsequently, the application of the fathoming tests at each subproblem will only require changing the right-most column of the tableau.

Given an initial all-zero binary solution, the associated slack solution is

$$(s_1, s_2, s_3) = (1, -2, -1), z = 0$$

If all the slacks were nonnegative, we would conclude that the all-zero binary solution is optimum. However, because some of the slacks are infeasible (negative), we need to elevate one or more binary variables to level 1 to achieve feasibility (or conclude that the problem has no feasible solution).

The elevation of (some of) the zero binary variables to level 1 occurs in the additive algorithm *one at a time*. The chosen variable is called the branching variable, and its selection is based on the use of special tests.

The branching variable must have the potential to reduce the infeasibility of the slacks. Looking at the preceding tableau, $x_3$ cannot be selected as a branching variable because its constraint coefficients in the second and third constraints are nonnegative. Thus, setting $x_3 = 1$ can only worsen the infeasibility of $s_2$ and $s_3$. Conversely, each of the remaining variables has at least one negative constraint coefficient in constraints 2 and 3—hence, a combination of these variables may produce feasible slacks. We can thus exclude $x_3$ and consider $x_1, x_2, x_4$, and $x_5$ as the only possible candidates for the branching variable.

The selection of the branching variable from among the candidates $x_1, x_2, x_4$, and $x_5$ is based on the use of *measure of slack infeasibility*. This measure, which is based on the assumption that a zero-variable $x_j$ will be elevated to level 1, is defined as

$$I_j = \sum_{\text{all } i} \min\{0, s_i - a_{ij}\}$$

where $s_i$ is the current value of slack $i$ and $a_{ij}$ is the constraint coefficient of the variable $x_j$ in constraint $i$.

Actually, $I_j$ is nothing but the sum of the *negative* slacks resulting from elevating $x_j$ to level 1. The seemingly complicated formula can be simplified to

$$I_j = \sum_{\text{all } i} (\text{negative } s_i \text{ value given } x_j = 1)$$

For example, when we set $x_1 = 1$, we get $s_1 = 1 - (-1) = 2, s_2 = -2 - (-7) = 5$, and $s_3 = -1 - 11 = -12$. Thus, $I_1 = -12$. Similarly, $I_2 = -2, I_4 = -1$, and $I_5 = 0$ (remember that $x_3$ was excluded as nonpromising). Because $I_5$ yields the smallest measure of infeasibility, $x_5$ is selected as the branching variable. Figure 9–10 shows the two branches associated with $x_5 = 1$ and $x_5 = 0$, and the creation of nodes 1 and 2. Node 1 yields the feasible slack values $(s_1, s_2, s_3) = (2, 1, 2)$ and $z = 3$. Thus, node 1 is fathomed and $\bar{z} = 3$ defines the current *upper bound* on the optimal objective value.

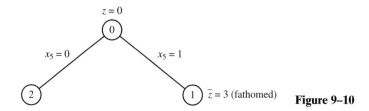

**Figure 9–10**

Having fathomed node 1, we move to node 2, for which $x_5 = 0$. Here, we have

$$(s_1, \ s_2, \ s_3) = (-1, \ 2, \ -1), \ z = 2$$

which is infeasible. The variables $x_1, x_2, x_3$, and $x_4$ are the candidates for the branching variable. (Note that although the solutions at node 0 and node 2 are identical, node 2 differs in that $x_5$ is no longer a branching candidate.) As with node 1, $x_3$ is not promising because it does not move $s_2$ and $s_3$ toward feasibility. The variables $x_1$ and $x_3$ also are not promising because their objective coefficient (3 and 5) will yield a worse objective value than the current upper bound ($\bar{z} = 3$). For the remaining variables, $x_2$ and $x_4$, we compute the measures of infeasibility as

$$I_2 = -2, I_4 = -1$$

Thus, $x_4$ is the branching variable at node 2.

Figure 9–11 shows the branches $x_4 = 1$ and $x_4 = 0$, leading to nodes 3 and 4. At node 3 (defined by fixing $x_5 = 0$ and $x_4 = 1$), we get

$$(s_1, s_1, s_3) = (-1, 2, 2), z = 2$$

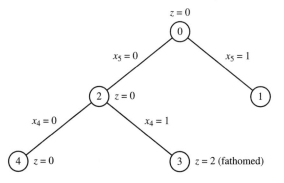

**Figure 9–11**

which is infeasible. The candidates for branching are $x_1$, $x_2$, and $x_3$. However, elevating any of these variable to level 1 will worsen the value of $z$ relative to the current upper bound $\bar{z} = 3$). Thus, all the candidate variables are excluded, and node 3 is fathomed.

Next, at the remaining node 4, defined by $x_5 = x_4 = 0$, we have

$$(s_1, s_2, s_3) = (1, -2, -1), z = 0$$

The variables $x_1$ and $x_3$ are excluded by the upper bound test. (Note that $x_3$ can also be excluded because it cannot reduce slack feasibility). The remaining variable, $x_2$, cannot be excluded by the upper bound or the slack feasibility tests. Hence, $x_2$ is the branching variable.

Figure 9–12 shows the addition of nodes 5 and 6 emanating from node 4. At node 5, we have

$$(s_1, s_2, s_3) = (2, -2, 5), z = 2$$

and $x_1$ and $x_3$ as the branching candidates. The variable $x_1$ is excluded by the upper-bound test, and $x_3$ is excluded by both the slack feasibility and upper-bound tests. This means that node 5 is fathomed. Node 6 is also fathomed because neither $x_1$ nor $x_3$ can produce a better feasible solution.

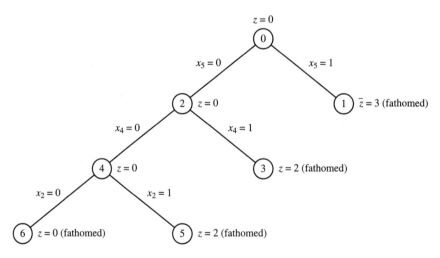

**Figure 9–12**

All the "dangling" nodes in Figure 9–12 have now been fathomed, and the B&B ends. The optimum solution is associated with node 1—that is, $x_5 = 1, z = 3$, and all the other variables are zero. In terms of the original variables, the solution is $y_1 = y_2 = 1$ and $y_3 = y_4 = y_5 = 0$ with $w = 5$.

Figure 9–12 shows that the smaller the number of branches leading to a *fathomed* node, the more efficient is the algorithm. For example, node 1 is defined by fixing one branch ($x_5 = 1$), and its fathoming automatically accounts for $2^{5-1} = 16$ binary solutions (all those that have $x_5 = 1$). Conversely, node 3 is defined by fixing two binary variables, and its fathoming implicitly accounts for $2^{5-2} = 8$ binary solutions only.

The tests proposed in Example 9.3–3 are mere heuristics, and their strength in excluding nonpromising variables depends on how "clever" we design them. Indeed, the complete additive algorithm includes more powerful tests than have been outlined in Example 9.3–3. These tests, however, are all in the spirit of the simple heuristics presented earlier.

**Problem set 9.3b**

**1.** Solve by the additive algorithm.

**(a)** Maximize $z = 3x_1 + x_2 + 3x_3$
subject to

$$-x_1 + 2x_2 + x_3 \leq 4$$
$$4x_2 - 3x_3 \leq 2$$
$$x_1 - 3x_2 + 2x_3 \leq 3$$
$$x_1, x_2, x_3 = (0, 1)$$

**(b)** Minimize $z = 2x_1 + 4x_2 + 6x_3$
subject to

$$8x_1 - 4x_2 - x_3 \geq 5$$
$$6x_1 - 3x_2 - 2x_3 \geq 2$$
$$-2x_1 + 9x_2 + 7x_3 \geq 4$$
$$x_1, x_2, x_3 = (0, 1)$$

**(c)** Minimize $z = -5x_1 + 7x_2 + 10x_3$
subject to

$$-x_1 - 3x_2 + 5x_3 \geq 0$$
$$2x_1 + 6x_2 - 3x_3 \geq 4$$
$$-x_2 + 2x_3 \geq 2$$
$$x_1, x_2, x_3 = (0, 1)$$

**2.** Show by the additive algorithm that the following problem has no feasible solution.

$$\text{Maximize } z = 2x_1 + x_2$$

subject to

$$10x_1 + 10x_2 \leq 9$$
$$10x_1 + 5x_2 \geq 1$$
$$x_1, x_2 = (0, 1)$$

3. Solve the capital budgeting problem of Example 9.2–1 using the additive algorithm.

4. Solve the following problem, assuming that only one of the given two constraints holds.

$$\text{Maximize } z = x_1 + 2x_2 - 3x_3$$

subject to

$$20x_1 + 15x_2 - x_3 \leq 10$$
$$12x_1 - 3x_2 + 4x_3 \leq 20$$
$$x_1, x_2, x_3 = (0, 1)$$

### 9.3.3 Cutting Plane Algorithm

As in the B&B algorithm, the cutting plane algorithm also starts at the continuous optimum LP solution. However, rather than using branching and bounding, it modifies the solution space by successively adding specially constructed constraints (called **cuts**). We first demonstrate the idea by a graphical example, and then show how the cuts are implemented algebraically.

---

**Example 9.3–4.**

Demonstrate graphically how the cutting plane algorithm may be used to solve the following ILP.

$$\text{Maximize } z = 7x_1 + 10x_2$$

subject to

$$-x_1 + 3x_2 \leq 6$$
$$7x_1 + x_2 \leq 35$$
$$x_1, x_2 \geq 0 \text{ and integer}$$

The cutting plane algorithm modifies the solution space by adding *cuts* that produce an optimum integer extreme point. Figure 9–13 gives an example of two such cuts. Initially, we start with the continuous LP optimum $(x_1, x_2) = (4\frac{1}{2}, 3\frac{1}{2})$ and $z = 66\frac{1}{2}$. Next, we add cut I, which produces the (continuous) LP optimum $(x_1, x_2) = (4\frac{4}{7}, 3)$ with $z = 62$. Then, we add cut II, which, together with cut I and the original constraints, produces the LP optimum $(x_1, x_2) = (4, 3)$ and $z = 58$. The last solution is all integer, as desired.

The added cuts do not eliminate any of the original feasible integer points, but must pass through at least one feasible or infeasible integer point. These are basic requirements of any cut.

In general, it may take any (finite) number of cuts to reach the desired all-integer extreme point. Indeed, the number of cuts needed to produce the desired integer solution appears to be independent of the size of the problem, in the sense that a problem with a small number of variables and constraints may require more cuts than a larger problem.

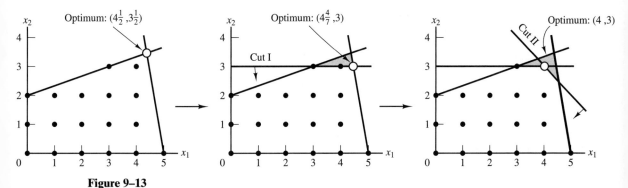

**Figure 9–13**

### Problem set 9.3c

1. In Example 9.3–4, show graphically whether or not each of the following constraints can form a legitimate cut:
   (a) $x_1 + 2x_2 \leq 10$
   (b) $2x_1 + x_2 \leq 10$
   (c) $3x_2 \leq 10$
   (d) $3x_1 + x_2 \leq 15$

2. In Example 9.3–4, show graphically how the following two (legitimate) cuts can lead to the optimum integer solution:

   *Cut I.*    $x_1 + 2x_2 \leq 10$
   *Cut II.*    $3x_1 + x_2 \leq 15$

**Algebraic development of cuts.** The cutting plane algorithm starts by solving the continuous LP problem. In the optimum LP tableau, we select one of the rows, called the **source row,** for which the basic variable is noninteger. The desired cut is constructed from the fractional components of the coefficients of the source row. For this reason, it is referred to as the **fractional cut.**

We now develop the fractional cut. Rather than using complex notations, the construction of the cut is explained by a numeric example.

---

**Example 9.3–5.**

Given the slacks $x_3$ and $x_4$ for constraints 1 and 2, the optimum LP tableau of Example 9.3–4 is

| Basic | $x_1$ | $x_2$ | $x_3$ | $x_4$ | Solution |
|-------|-------|-------|-------|-------|----------|
| $z$ | 0 | 0 | $\frac{63}{22}$ | $\frac{31}{22}$ | $66\frac{1}{2}$ |
| $x_2$ | 0 | 1 | $\frac{7}{22}$ | $\frac{1}{22}$ | $3\frac{1}{2}$ |
| $x_1$ | 1 | 0 | $-\frac{1}{22}$ | $\frac{3}{22}$ | $4\frac{1}{2}$ |

*Cut II.*   $3x_1 + x_2 \leq 15$

**Algebraic development of cuts.**   The cutting plane algorithm starts by solving the continuous LP problem. In the optimum LP tableau, we select one of the rows, called the **source row,** for which the basic variable is noninteger. The desired cut is constructed from the fractional components of the coefficients of the source row. For this reason, it is referred to as the **fractional cut.**

We now develop the fractional cut. Rather than using complex notations, the construction of the cut is explained by a numeric example.

---

**Example 9.3–5.**

Given the slacks $x_3$ and $x_4$ for constraints 1 and 2, the optimum LP tableau of Example 9.3–4 is

The optimum continuous solution is $x_1 = 4\frac{1}{2}, x_2 = 3\frac{1}{2}, x_3 = 0, x_4 = 0$, and $z = 66\frac{1}{2}$. The pure integer cut is developed under the assumption that all the variables are integer. Note also that because the original objective coefficients are integer, then the value of $z$ associated with an integer solution also must be integer.

The information in the optimum tableau can be written in equation form as

$$z\text{equation: } z + \frac{63}{22}x_3 + \frac{31}{22}x_4 = 66\frac{1}{2}$$

$$x_2\text{equation: } x_2 + \frac{7}{22}x_3 + \frac{1}{22}x_4 = 3\frac{1}{2}$$

$$x_1\text{equation: } x_1 - \frac{1}{22}x_3 + \frac{3}{22}x_4 = 4\frac{1}{2}$$

Because $z$, $x_1$, and $x_2$ must be integer in this example and all of them happen to have fractional values in the optimum tableau, any of the three equations can be used as a *source row* for generating the cut. Let us arbitrarily select the $z$-equation for this purpose:

$$z + \frac{63}{22}x_3 + \frac{31}{22}x_4 = 66\frac{1}{2} \quad (z\text{-source row})$$

To construct the fractional cut, each of the *noninteger* coefficients are factored into integer and fractional components, *provided that the fractional component is strictly positive.* For example,

$$\frac{5}{2} = \left(2 + \frac{1}{2}\right)$$

$$-\frac{7}{3} = \left(-3 + \frac{2}{3}\right)$$

The factoring of the $z$-source row yields

$$z + \left(2 + \frac{19}{22}\right)x_3 + \left(1 + \frac{19}{22}\right)x_4 = \left(66 + \frac{1}{2}\right)$$

Moving all the integer components to the left-hand side and all the fractional components to the right-hand side, we get

Because $x_3 = x_4 = 0$ in the LP optimum tableau, the cut is not satisfied (because it yields $\frac{1}{2} \le 0$). Thus, its addition to the optimum tableau moves the resulting optimal extreme point toward satisfying the integer restriction.

We can develop cuts also from the $x_1$-source row and the $x_2$-source row in the same manner. Consider the $x_1$-row first. We have

$$x_1 - \frac{1}{22} x_3 + \frac{3}{22} x_4 = 4\tfrac{1}{2} \quad (x_1 \text{source row})$$

The factoring operation yields

$$x_1 + \left(-1 + \frac{21}{22}\right) x_3 + \left(0 + \frac{3}{22}\right) x_4 = \left(4 + \frac{1}{2}\right)$$

The associated cut is

$$-\frac{21}{22} x_3 - \frac{3}{22} x_4 + \frac{1}{2} \le 0$$

Similarly,

$$x_2 + \frac{7}{22} x_3 + \frac{1}{22} x_4 = 3\tfrac{1}{2} \quad (x_2 \text{source row})$$

yields

$$x_2 + \left(0 + \frac{7}{22}\right) x_3 + \left(0 + \frac{1}{22}\right) x_4 = \left(3 + \frac{1}{2}\right)$$

Hence, the cut is given as

$$-\frac{7}{22} x_3 - \frac{1}{22} x_4 + \frac{1}{2} \le 0$$

Any of three cuts can be used in the first iteration of the cutting plane algorithm. In this regard, we really did not need to generate all three cuts before selecting one of them.

Arbitrarily selecting the cut generated from the $x_2$-row, we can write it as

$$-\frac{7}{22} x_3 - \frac{1}{22} x_4 + s_1 = -\frac{1}{2}, \ s_1 \ge 0 \quad \text{(Cut I)}$$

This constraint is added as a secondary constraint to the LP optimum tableau as follows:

| Basic | $x_1$ | $x_2$ | $x_3$ | $x_4$ | $s_1$ | Solution |
|-------|-------|-------|-------|-------|-------|----------|
| $z$ | 0 | 0 | $\frac{63}{22}$ | $\frac{31}{22}$ | 0 | $66\frac{1}{2}$ |
| $x_2$ | 0 | 1 | $\frac{7}{22}$ | $\frac{1}{22}$ | 0 | $3\frac{1}{2}$ |
| $x_1$ | 1 | 0 | $-\frac{1}{22}$ | $\frac{3}{22}$ | 0 | $4\frac{1}{2}$ |
| $s_1$ | 0 | 0 | $-\frac{7}{22}$ | $-\frac{1}{22}$ | 1 | $-\frac{1}{2}$ |

$$x_2 + \left(0 + \frac{7}{22}\right)x_3 + \left(0 + \frac{1}{22}\right)x_4 = \left(3 + \frac{1}{2}\right)$$

| Basic | $x_1$ | $x_2$ | $x_3$ | $x_4$ | $s_1$ | Solution |
|-------|-------|-------|-------|-------|-------|----------|
| $z$   | 0     | 0     | 0     | 1     | 9     | 62       |
| $x_2$ | 0     | 1     | 0     | 0     | 1     | 3        |
| $x_1$ | 1     | 0     | 0     | $\frac{1}{7}$ | $-\frac{1}{7}$ | $4\frac{4}{7}$ |
| $x_3$ | 0     | 0     | 1     | $\frac{1}{7}$ | $-\frac{22}{7}$ | $1\frac{4}{7}$ |

Hence, the cut is given as

$$-\frac{7}{22}x_3 - \frac{1}{22}x_4 + \frac{1}{2} \le 0$$

Any of three cuts can be used in the first iteration of the cutting plane algorithm. In this regard, we really did not need to generate all three cuts before selecting one of them.

Arbitrarily selecting the cut generated from the $x_2$-row, we can write it as

$$-\frac{7}{22}x_3 - \frac{1}{22}x_4 + s_1 = -\frac{1}{2}, \ s_1 \ge 0 \quad \text{(Cut I)}$$

| Basic | $x_1$ | $x_2$ | $x_3$ | $x_4$ | $s_1$ | $s_2$ | Solution |
|-------|-------|-------|-------|-------|-------|-------|----------|
| $z$   | 0     | 0     | 0     | 1     | 9     | 0     | 62       |
| $x_2$ | 0     | 1     | 0     | 0     | 1     | 0     | 3        |
| $x_1$ | 1     | 0     | 0     | $\frac{1}{7}$ | $-\frac{1}{7}$ | 0 | $4\frac{4}{7}$ |
| $x_3$ | 0     | 0     | 1     | $\frac{1}{7}$ | $-\frac{22}{7}$ | 0 | $1\frac{4}{7}$ |
| $s_2$ | 0     | 0     | 0     | $-\frac{1}{7}$ | $-\frac{6}{7}$ | 1 | $-\frac{4}{7}$ |

| Basic | $x_1$ | $x_2$ | $x_3$ | $x_4$ | $s_1$ | $s_2$ | Solution |
|-------|-------|-------|-------|-------|-------|-------|----------|
| $z$   | 0     | 0     | 0     | 0     | 3     | 7     | 58       |
| $x_2$ | 0     | 1     | 0     | 0     | 1     | 0     | 3        |
| $x_1$ | 1     | 0     | 0     | 0     | $-1$  | 1     | 4        |
| $x_3$ | 0     | 0     | 1     | 0     | $-4$  | 1     | 1        |
| $x_4$ | 0     | 0     | 0     | 1     | 6     | $-7$  | 4        |

The optimum solution ($x_1 = 4, x_2 = 3, z = 58$) is all integer. It is not accidental that all the coefficients of the last tableau are integers. This is a typical characteristic of the implementation of the fractional cut.

---

It is important to point out that the fractional cut assumes that *all* the variables, *including slack and surplus,* are integer. This means that the cut deals with only the pure integer problem.

The importance of this assumption is illustrated by an example. Consider the constraint

$$x_1 + \frac{1}{3}x_2 \leq \frac{13}{2}$$

$$x_1, x_2 \geq 0 \text{ and integer}$$

From the standpoint of solving the associated ILP, the constraint is treated as an equation by using the nonnegative slack $s_1$—that is,

$$x_1 + \frac{1}{3}x_2 + s_1 = \frac{13}{2}$$

The application of the fractional cut assumes that the constraint has a feasible integer solution in all $x_1, x_2$ and $s_1$. An examination of the equation reveals that it can have a feasible integer solution in $x_1$ and $x_2$ *only if $s_1$ is noninteger.* Thus, the application of the fractional cut will yield no feasible integer solution because *all* the variables, $x_1$, $x_2$, and $s_1$, cannot be integer simultaneously. Nevertheless, the constraint does have feasible integer solutions for the variables of concern, $x_1$ and $x_2$.

There are two ways to remedy this situation.

**1.** We multiply the entire constraint by a proper constant to remove all the fractions. For example, the given constraint above is multiplied by 6 to obtain

$$6x_1 + 2x_2 \leq 39$$

Any integer solution of $x_1$ and $x_2$ automatically yields integer slack. However, this type of conversion is appropriate for only simple constraints as the magnitudes of the integer coefficients may become extremely large in some cases.

**2.** Use a special cut, called the **mixed cut,** which allows only a subset of variables to assume integer values, with all the other variables (including slack and surplus) remaining continuous. The details of this cut will not be presented in this chapter (see Taha, 1975, pp. 198–202)

### Problem set 9.3d

**1.** Express cuts I and II of Example 9.3–5 in terms of $x_1$ and $x_2$ and show that they are the same ones used graphically in Figure 9–13.

**2.** Show that the fractional cut does not yield a feasible solution for the following problem unless all the fractions in the constraint are eliminated.

$$\text{Maximize } z = x_1 + 2x_2$$

subject to

$$x_1 + \frac{1}{2}x_2 \le \frac{13}{4}$$

$$x_1, x_2 \ge 0 \text{ and integer}$$

**3.** Solve the following problems by the fractional cut, and compare the true optimum integer solution with the solution obtained by rounding the continuous optimum.

(a)  Maximize $z = 4x_1 + 6x_2 + 2x_3$
     subject to

$$4x_1 - 4x_2 \qquad \le 5$$
$$-x_1 + 6x_2 \qquad \le 5$$
$$-x_1 + \phantom{6}x_2 + x_3 \le 5$$

$$x_1, x_2, x_3 \ge 0 \text{ and integer}$$

(b)  Maximize $z = 3x_1 + x_2 + 3x_3$
     subject to

$$-x_1 + 2x_2 + \phantom{2}x_3 \le 4$$
$$4x_2 - 3x_3 \le 2$$
$$x_1 - 3x_2 + 2x_3 \le 3$$

$$x_1, x_2, x_3 \ge 0 \text{ and integer}$$

## 9.4 SUMMARY

The most important factor affecting computations in integer programming is the number of integer variables. Because available algorithms do not solve the ILP problem consistently, it is advantageous computationally to reduce the number of integer variables in the ILP model as much as possible. The following suggestions may prove helpful:

1.  Approximate integer variables by continuous ones wherever possible.
2.  For the integer variables, restrict their feasible ranges as much as possible.
3.  Avoid the use of nonlinearity in the model.

The importance of the integer problem in practice is not yet matched by efficient solution algorithms. It is unlikely that a new theoretical breakthrough will be achieved in the area of integer programming. Instead, new technological advances in computers may offer the best hope for improving the efficiency of ILP algorithms.

## SELECTED REFERENCES

NEMHAUSER, G., and L. WOLSEY, *Integer and Combinatorial Optimization,* Wiley, New York, 1988.

PARKER, G., and R. RARDIN, *Discrete Optimization,* Academic Press, Orlando, FL, 1988.

SALKIN, H., and K. MATHUR, *Foundations of Integer Programming,* North-Holland, New York, 1989.

TAHA, H., *Integer Programming: Theory, Applications, and Computations,* Academic Press, Orlando, FL, 1975.

## COMPREHENSIVE PROBLEMS

■ **9–1**  A development company owns 90 acres of land in a growing metropolitan area, where it intends to construct office buildings and a shopping center. The developed property is rented for 7 years and then sold. The sale price for each building is estimated at 10 times its operating net income in the last year of rental. The company estimates that the project will include a 4.5-million-square-foot shopping center. The master plan calls for constructing three high-rise and four garden office buildings.

The company is faced with a scheduling problem. If a building is completed too early, it may stay vacant; if it is completed too late, potential tenants may be lost to other projects. The demand for office space over the next 7 years based on appropriate market studies is

| Year | Demand (thousands of ft$^2$) | |
|:---:|:---:|:---:|
| | High-rise space | Garden space |
| 1 | 200 | 100 |
| 2 | 220 | 110 |
| 3 | 242 | 121 |
| 4 | 266 | 133 |
| 5 | 293 | 146 |
| 6 | 322 | 161 |
| 7 | 354 | 177 |

The following table lists the proposed capacities of the seven buildings:

| Garden | Capacity ($ft^2$) | High-rise buildings | Capacity ($ft^2$) |
|--------|-------------------|---------------------|-------------------|
| 1      | 60,000            | 1                   | 350,000           |
| 2      | 60,000            | 2                   | 450,000           |
| 3      | 75,000            | 3                   | 350,000           |
| 4      | 75,000            | —                   | —                 |

The gross rental income is estimated at $25 per square foot. The operating expenses are $5.75 and $9.75 per square foot for the garden and high-rise buildings, respectively. The associated construction costs are $70 and $105 per square foot, respectively. Both the construction cost and the rental income are estimated to increase at roughly the inflation rate of 4%.

How should the company schedule the construction of the seven buildings?

■ **9–2**[2] In a National Collegiate Athletic Association women's gymnastic meet, competition includes four events: vault, uneven bars, balance beam, and floor exercises. Each team may enter the competition with six gymnasts per event. A gymnast is evaluated on a scale of 1 to 10. Past statistics for the U of A team produce the following scores:

**U of A Scores for Gymnast**

| | 1 | 2 | 3 | 4 | 5 | 6 |
|-------|---|---|----|---|----|----|
| Vault | 6 | 9 | 8  | 8 | 4  | 10 |
| Bars  | 7 | 9 | 7  | 8 | 9  | 5  |
| Beam  | 9 | 8 | 10 | 9 | 9  | 8  |
| Floor | 6 | 6 | 5  | 9 | 10 | 9  |

The total score for a team is determined by summarizing the top five individual scores for each event. An entrant may participate as a specialist in one event or an "all- rounder" in all four events but not both. A specialist is allowed to compete in at most three events, and at least four of the team participants must be all-rounders. Set up an ILP model that can be used to select the competing team, and find the optimum solution using TORA.

■ **9–3**[3] In 1990, approximately 180,000 telemarketing centers employing 2 million individuals were in operation in the United States. In the year 2000, it is estimated that more than 700,000 companies will be employing approximately 8 million people in tele-

[2]Based on P. Ellis and R. Corn, "Using Bivalent Integer Programming to Select Teams of Intercollegiate Women's Gymnastic Competition, "*Interfaces,* Vol. 14, No. 3, pp. 41-46, 1984.

[3]Based on T. Spencer, A. Brigandi, D. Dargon, and M. Sheehan, "AT&T's Telemarketing Site Selection System Offers Customer Support," *Interfaces,* Vol. 20, No. 1, pp. 83–96, 1990.

marketing their products. The questions of how many telemarketing centers to employ and where to locate them are of paramount importance.

The ABC company is in the process of deciding on the number of telemarketing centers to employ and their locations. A center may be located in one of several candidate areas selected by the company and may serve (partially or completely) one or more geographical areas. A geographical area is usually identified by one or more (telephone) area codes. ABC's telemarketing concentrates on eight area codes: 501, 918, 316, 417, 314, 816, 502, and 606. The following table provides the candidate locations, their served areas, and the cost of establishing the center.

| Center location | Served area codes | Cost ($) |
|---|---|---|
| Dallas, TX | 501, 918, 316, 417 | 500,000 |
| Atlanta, GA | 314, 816, 502, 606 | 800,000 |
| Louisville, KY | 918, 316, 417, 314, 816 | 400,000 |
| Denver, CO | 501, 502, 606 | 900,000 |
| Little Rock, AR | 417, 314, 816, 502 | 300,000 |
| Memphis, TN | 606, 501, 316, 417 | 450,000 |
| St. Louis, MO | 816, 502, 606, 314 | 550,000 |

Customers in all area codes can access any of the centers 24 hours a day.

The communication costs per hour between the centers and the area codes are given in the following table.

| To | From area code | | | | | | | |
|---|---|---|---|---|---|---|---|---|
| | 501 | 918 | 316 | 417 | 314 | 816 | 502 | 606 |
| Dallas, TX | $14 | $35 | $29 | $32 | $25 | $13 | $14 | $20 |
| Atlanta, GA | $18 | $18 | $22 | $18 | $26 | $23 | $12 | $15 |
| Louisville, KY | $22 | $25 | $12 | $19 | $30 | $17 | $26 | $25 |
| Denver, CO | $24 | $30 | $19 | $14 | $12 | $16 | $18 | $30 |
| Little Rock, AR | $19 | $20 | $23 | $16 | $23 | $11 | $28 | $12 |
| Memphis, TN | $23 | $21 | $17 | $21 | $20 | $23 | $20 | $10 |
| St. Louis, MO | $17 | $18 | $12 | $10 | $19 | $22 | $16 | $22 |

ABC wold like to select between three and four centers. Where should they be located?

# Chapter 10

# Deterministic Dynamic Programming

## 10.1 INTRODUCTION

Dynamic programming (DP) determines the optimum solution to an $n$-variable problem by decomposing it into $n$ *stages* with each stage comprising a single-variable subproblem. The computational advantage is that we will be optimizing single-variable, instead of $n$-variable, subproblems. The main contribution of DP is the **principle of optimality,** a framework for decomposing the problem into stages. Because the nature of the stage differs depending on the optimization problem, DP does not provide the computational details for optimizing each stage. Such details are improvised and designed by the problem solver.

## 10.2 RECURSIVE NATURE OF COMPUTATIONS IN DP

Computations in DP are done recursively, in the sense that the optimum solution of one subproblem is used as an input to the next subproblem. By the time we solve the last subproblem, we will have at hand the optimum solution for the entire problem. The manner in which the recursive computations are carried out depends on how we decompose the original problem. In particular, the subproblems are normally linked together by some common constraints. As we move from one subproblem to the next, we must account for the feasibility of these constraints.

---

**Example 10.2–1   (SHORTEST ROUTE PROBLEM).**

Suppose that you want to select the shortest highway route between two cities. The network in Figure 10–1 provides the possible routes between the starting city at node 1 and the destination city at node 7. The routes pass through intermediate cities designated by nodes 2 to 6.

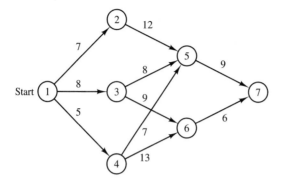

**Figure 10–1**

We can solve this problem by exhaustively enumerating all the routes between nodes 1 and 7 (there are five such routes). However, in a large network, exhaustive enumeration is not efficient computationally.

To solve the problem by DP, we first decompose it into *stages*. The vertical (dashed) lines in Figure 10–2 delineate the three stages of the problem. Next, we carry out the computations for each stage separately.

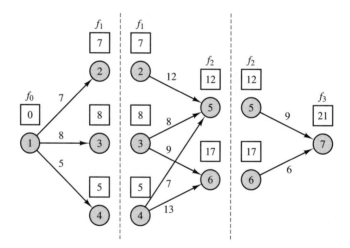

**Figure 10–2**

The general idea is to compute the shortest (cumulative) distances to all the terminal nodes of a stage and then use these distances as input data to the immediately succeeding stage. Considering the nodes associated with stage 1, we can see that nodes 2, 3, and 4 are each connected to the starting node 1 by a single arc (see Figure 10–2). Hence, for stage 1 we have

*Stage 1 Summary Results*

Shortest distance to node 2 = 7 miles (from node 1)

Shortest distance to node 3 = 8 miles (from node 1)

Shortest distance to node 4 = 5 miles (from node 1)

Next, we move to stage 2 to determine the shortest (cumulative) distances to nodes 5 and 6. Considering node 5 first, we see from Figure 10–2 that there are three possible routes to reach node 5—namely, (2, 5), (3, 5), and (4, 5). This information, together with the shortest distances to nodes 2, 3, and 4 determines the shortest (cumulative) distance to node 5 as

$$\begin{pmatrix} \text{Shortest distance} \\ \text{to node 5} \end{pmatrix} = \min_{i=2,3,4} \left\{ \begin{pmatrix} \text{Shortest distance} \\ \text{to node } i \end{pmatrix} + \begin{pmatrix} \text{Distance from} \\ \text{node } i \text{ to node 5} \end{pmatrix} \right\}$$

$$= \min \begin{Bmatrix} 7 + 12 = 19 \\ 8 + \ \ 8 = 16 \\ 5 + \ \ 7 = 12 \end{Bmatrix} = 12 \quad \text{(from node 4)}$$

Similarly, for node 6 we have

$$\begin{pmatrix} \text{Shortest distance} \\ \text{to node 6} \end{pmatrix} = \min_{i=3,4} \left\{ \begin{pmatrix} \text{Shortest distance} \\ \text{to node } i \end{pmatrix} + \begin{pmatrix} \text{Distance from} \\ \text{node } i \text{ to node 6} \end{pmatrix} \right\}$$

$$= \min \begin{Bmatrix} 8 + \ \ 9 = 17 \\ 5 + 13 = 18 \end{Bmatrix} = 17 \text{ (from node 3)}$$

*Stage 2 Summary Results*

Shortest distance to node 5 = 12 miles (from node 4)

Shortest distance to node 6 = 17 miles (from node 3)

The last step is to consider stage 3. The destination node 7 can be reached from either nodes 5 or 6. Using the summary results from stage 2 and the distances from nodes 5 and 6 to node 7, we get

$$\begin{pmatrix} \text{Shortest distance} \\ \text{to node 7} \end{pmatrix} = \min \begin{Bmatrix} 12 + 9 = 21 \\ 17 + 6 = 23 \end{Bmatrix} = 21 \text{ (from node 5)}$$

*Stage 3 Summary results*

Shortest distance to node 7 = 21 miles (from node 5)

The given computations show that the shortest distance between nodes 1 and 7 is 21 miles. The cities that define the optimum route are determined as follows. From stage 3 summary, node 7 is linked to node 5. Next, from stage 2 summary, node 4 is linked to node 5. Finally, from stage 1 summary, node 4 is linked to node 1. Thus, the optimum route is defined as 1–4–5–7.

We now show how the DP recursive computations can be expressed mathematically. Let $f_i(x_i)$ be the shortest distance to node $x_i$ at stage $i$, and define $d(x_{i-1}, x_i)$ as the distance from node $x_{i-1}$ to node $x_i$, then, $f_i$ is computed from $f_{i-1}$ using the following recursive equation:

$$f_i(x_i) = \min_{\substack{\text{all feasible} \\ (x_{i-1}, x_i)\ \text{routes}}} \{d(x_{i-1}, x_i) + f_{i-1}(x_{i-1})\}, i = 1, 2, 3$$

Starting at $i = 1$, the recursion defines $f_0(x_0) \equiv 0$. The equation shows that the shortest distances $f_i(x_i)$ at stage $i$ must be expressed in terms of the next node, $x_i$. In the terminology of DP, $x_i$ is referred to as the **state** of the system at stage $i$. In effect, the *state* of the system at stage $i$ is regarded as the information that links the stages together, such that optimal decisions for the remaining stages can be made without reexamining how the decisions for the previous stages were reached. The proper definition of the *state* allows us to consider each stage separately and guarantee that the solution is feasible for all the stages.

The definition of the *state* leads to the following unifying framework.

***Principle of Optimality.*** Future decisions for the remaining stages will constitute an optimal policy regardless of the policy adopted in previous stages.

The implementation of the principle is evident in the computations in Example 10.2–1. For example, in stage 3, we only use of the shortest distances to nodes 5 and 6, and do not concern ourselves with how these nodes are reached from node 1.

### Problem set 10.2a

1. Solve Example 10.2–1, assuming the following routes are used:

$$d(1, 2) = 5, d(1, 3) = 9, d(1, 4) = 8$$
$$d(2, 5) = 10, d(2, 6) = 17$$
$$d(3, 5) = 4, d(3, 6) = 10$$
$$d(4, 5) = 9, d(4, 6) = 9$$
$$d(5, 7) = 8$$
$$d(6, 7) = 9$$

2. I am an avid hiker. Last summer, my friend G. Don and I went on a 5-day hike-and-camp trip in the beautiful White Mountains in New Hampshire. We decided to limit our hiking to an area comprising three well-known peaks: Mounts Washington, Jefferson, and Adams. Mount Washington has a 6-mile base-to-peak trail. The corresponding base-to-peak trails for Mounts Jefferson and Adams are 4 and 5 miles, respectively. The trails joining the bases of the three mountains are 3 miles between Mounts Washington and Jefferson, 2 miles between Mounts Jefferson and Adams, and 5 miles between Mounts Adams and Washington. We started on the first day at the base of Mount Washington and returned to the same spot at the end of 5 days. Our goal was to hike as many miles as we could. We also decided to climb exactly one mountain each day and to camp at the base of the mountain we would be climbing the next day. Additionally, we

decided that the same mountain could not be visited in any two consecutive days. How did we schedule our hike?

## 10.3 FORWARD AND BACKWARD RECURSION

Example 10.2–1 uses **forward recursion** in which the computations proceed from stage 1 to stage 3. The same example can be solved by **backward recursion,** starting at stage 3 and ending at stage 1.

Both the forward and backward recursions yield the same solution. Although the forward procedure appears more logical, DP literature invariably uses backward recursion. The reason for this preference is that, in general, backward recursion may be more efficient computationally. We will demonstrate the use of backward recursion by applying it to Example 10.2–1. The demonstration will also provide the opportunity to present the DP computations in a compact tabular form.

---

**Example 10.3–1.**
The backward recursive equation for Example 10.2–1 is given as

$$f_i(x_i) = \min_{\substack{\text{all feasible} \\ \text{routes } (x_i, x_{i+1})}} \{d(x_i, x_{i+1}) + f_{i+1}(x_{i+1})\}, \quad i = 1, 2, 3$$

where $f_4(x_4) \equiv 0$ for $x_4 = 7$. The associated order of computations is $f_3 \rightarrow f_2 \rightarrow f_1$.
*Stage 3.* Because node 7 ($x_4 = 7$) is connected to nodes 5 and 6 ($x_3 = 5$ and 6) with exactly one route each, there are no alternatives to choose from, and stage 3 results can be summarized as

|       | $d(x_3, x_4)$ | Optimum solution | |
|-------|:---:|:---:|:---:|
| $x_3$ | $x_4 = 7$ | $f_3(x_3)$ | $x_4^*$ |
| 5     | 9 | 9 | 7 |
| 6     | 6 | 6 | 7 |

*Stage 2.* Route (2, 6) is not a feasible alternative because it does not exist. Given $f_3(x_3)$ from stage 3, we can then compare the feasible alternatives as shown in the following tableau:

|       | $d(x_2, x_3) + f_3(x_3)$ | | Optimum solution | |
|-------|:---:|:---:|:---:|:---:|
| $x_2$ | $x_3 = 5$ | $x_3 = 6$ | $f_2(x_2)$ | $x_3^*$ |
| 2     | 12 + 9 = 21 | — | 21 | 5 |
| 3     | 8 + 9 = 17 | 9 + 6 = 15 | 15 | 6 |
| 4     | 7 + 9 = 16 | 13 + 6 = 19 | 16 | 5 |

The optimum solution of stage 2 reads as follows: If you are in cities 2 or 4, the shortest route passes through city 5, and if you are in city 3, the shortest route passes through city 6.

*Stage 1.* From node 1, we have three alternative routes: $(1, 2)$, $(1, 3)$, and $(1, 4)$. Using $f_2(x_2)$ from stage 2, we can compute the following tableau.

| | $d(x_1, x_2) + f_2(x_2)$ | | | Optimum solution | |
| --- | --- | --- | --- | --- | --- |
| $x_1$ | $x_2 = 2$ | $x_2 = 3$ | $x_2 = 4$ | $f_1(x_1)$ | $x_2^*$ |
| 1 | $7 + 21 = 28$ | $8 + 15 = 23$ | $5 + 16 = 21$ | 21 | 4 |

The optimum solution at stage 1 shows that city 1 is linked to city 4. Next, the optimum solution at stage 2 shows that city 4 is linked to city 5. Finally, the optimum solution at stage 3 indicates that city 5 is linked to city 7. Thus, the complete route is given as 1–4–5–7, and the associate distance is 21 miles.

### Problem set 10.3a

1. For Problem 10.2a–1, develop the backward recursive equation, and use it to find the optimum solution.
2. For Problem 10.2a–2, develop the backward recursive equation, and use it to find the optimum solution.
3. For the network in Figure 10–3, it is desired to determine the shortest route between cities 1 to 7. Define the stages and the states, using backward recursion and then solve the problem.

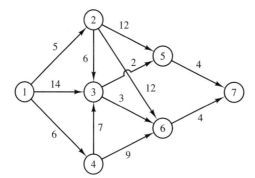

**Figure 10–3**

## 10.4 SELECTED DP APPLICATIONS

This section presents four applications, each of which is selected to provide a new idea in the implementation of dynamic programming. As you study each application, pay special attention to the three basic elements of a DP model:

1. Definition of the *stages*
2. Definition of the *alternatives* at each stage
3. Definition of the *states* for each stage

Of the three elements, the definition of the *state* is usually the subtlest. The applications presented subsequently show that the definition of the state varies depending on the situation being modeled. Nevertheless, as you investigate each application, you will find it helpful to consider the following questions:

1. What relationships bind the stages together?
2. What information is needed to make feasible decisions at the current stage without reexamining the decisions made at the previous stages?

My teaching experience indicates that the understanding of the concept of the *state* can be enhanced by questioning the validity of the way it is defined in the book. Try a different definition that may appear "more logical" to you, and use it in the recursive computations. You will eventually discover that the definitions presented here provide the correct way for solving the problem. Meanwhile, the proposed mental process should enhance your understanding of the concept of the state.

### 10.4.1 Cargo-Loading Model

The cargo-loading model deals with the problem of loading items on a vessel with limited volume or weight capacity. Each item produces a level of revenue. The objective is to load the vessel with the most valuable cargo.

Before presenting the DP model, we remark that the cargo-loading problem is also known as the **fly-away kit** problem, in which a jet pilot must determine the most valuable (emergency) items to take aboard the jet; and the **knapsack** problem, in which a soldier (or a hiker) must decide on the most valuable items to carry in a backpack. It appears that the three names were chosen to ensure equal representation of the navy, air force, and army!

The (backward) recursive equation is developed for the general problem of an $n$-item $W$-ton vessel. Let $m_i$ be the number of units of item $i$ in the cargo. The general problem is represented by the following integer LP:

$$\text{Maximize } z = r_1 m_1 + r_2 m_2 + \dots + r_n m_n$$

subject to

$$w_1 m_1 + w_2 m_2 + \dots + w_n m_n \leq W$$

$$m_1, m_2, \dots, m_n \geq 0 \text{ and integer}$$

The three elements of the model are

1. *Stage $i$* is represented by item $i$, $i = 1, 2, \dots, n$.

**2.** The *alternatives* at stage $i$ are represented by $m_i$, the number of units of item $i$ included in the cargo. The associated return is $r_i m_i$. Defining $[\frac{W}{w_i}]$ as the largest integer less than or equal to $\frac{W}{w_i}$, it follows that $m_i = 0, 1, \ldots, [\frac{W}{w_i}]$.

**3.** The *state* at stage $i$ is represented by $x_i$ the total weight assigned to stages (items) $i, i + 1, \ldots$, and $n$, combined. This definition reflects the fact that the weight constraint is the only restriction that links all $n$ stages together.

Define

$$f_i(x_i) = \text{maximum return for stages } i, i + 1, \text{ and } n, \text{ given state } x_i$$

The simplest way to determine recursive equation is a two-step procedure.

*Step 1.* Express $f_i(x_i)$ as a function of $f_i(x_{i+1})$ as follows:

$$f_i(x_i) = \max_{\substack{m_i=0, 1, \ldots, \frac{W}{w_i} \\ x_i=0, 1, \ldots, W}} \{r_i m_i + f_{i+1}(x_{i+1})\}, \quad i = 1, 2, \ldots, n$$

where $f_{n+1}(x_{n+1}) \equiv 0$.

*Step 2.* Express $x_{i+1}$ as a function $x_i$ to ensure that the left-hand side, $f_i(x_i)$, is a function of $x_i$ only. By definition, $x_i - x_{i+1}$ represents the weight consumed at stage $i$—that is, $x_i - x_{i+1} = w_i m_i$, or $x_{i+1} = x_i - w_i m_i$. Thus, the proper recursive equation is given as

$$f_i(x_i) = \max_{\substack{m_i=0, 1, \ldots, \frac{W}{w_i} \\ x_i=0, 1, \ldots, W}} \{r_i m_i + f_{i+1}(x_i - w_i m_i)\}, \quad i = 1, 2, \ldots, n$$

---

**Example 10.4–1.**

A 4-ton vessel is loaded with one or more of three items. The following table gives the unit weight, $w_i$, in tons and the unit revenue, $r_i$, in thousands of dollars for item $i$. How should the vessel be loaded to maximize the total return?

| Item $i$ | $w_i$ | $r_i$ |
|----------|-------|-------|
| 1 | 2 | 31 |
| 2 | 3 | 47 |
| 3 | 1 | 14 |

Because the unit weights $w_i$ and the maximum weight $W$ all assume integer values, the state $x_i$ can assume integer values only.

*Stage 3.* The exact weight to be allocated to stage 3 (item 3) is not known in advance, but must assume one of the values $0, 1, \ldots$, and 4 (because $W = 4$ tons). The states $x_3 = 0$ and $x_3 = 4$, respectively, represent the extreme cases of not shipping item 3 at all and of allocating the entire vessel to it. The remaining values of $x_3$ ($= 1, 2,$ and 3) imply a partial allocation of the vessel capacity to item 3. In effect, the given range of values for $x_3$ covers all the possible allocations of the vessel capacity to item 3.

Because $w_3 = 1$ ton per unit, the maximum number of units of item 3 that can be loaded is $[\frac{4}{1}] = 4$, which means that the possible values of $m_3$ are 0, 1, 2, 3, and 4. An alternative $m_3$ is feasible only if $w_3 m_3 \le x_3$. Thus, all the infeasible alternatives (those for which $w_3 m_3 > x_3$) are excluded. The following equation is the basis for comparing the alternatives of stage 3.

$$f_3(x_3) = \max_{m_3} \{14 m_3\}, \quad \max m_3 = \left[\frac{4}{1}\right] = 4$$

The following tableau compares the feasible alternatives for each value of $x_3$.

| | 14$m_3$ | | | | | Optimum solution | |
|---|---|---|---|---|---|---|---|
| $x_3$ | $m_3 = 0$ | $m_3 = 1$ | $m_3 = 2$ | $m_3 = 3$ | $m_3 = 4$ | $f_3(x_3)$ | $m_3^*$ |
| 0 | 0 | — | — | — | — | 0 | 0 |
| 1 | 0 | 14 | — | — | — | 14 | 1 |
| 2 | 0 | 14 | 28 | — | — | 28 | 2 |
| 3 | 0 | 14 | 28 | 42 | — | 42 | 3 |
| 4 | 0 | 14 | 28 | 42 | 56 | 56 | 4 |

*Stage 2*

$$f_2(x_2) = \max_{m_2} \{47\, m_2 + f_3(x_2 - 3 m_2)\}, \; \max\{m_2\} = \left[\frac{4}{3}\right] = 1$$

| | 47$m_2$ + $f_3(x_2 - 3m_2)$ | | Optimum solution | |
|---|---|---|---|---|
| $x_2$ | $m_2 = 0$ | $m_2 = 1$ | $f_2(x_2)$ | $m_2^*$ |
| 0 | 0 + 0 = 0 | — | 0 | 0 |
| 1 | 0 + 14 = 14 | — | 14 | 0 |
| 2 | 0 + 28 = 28 | — | 28 | 0 |
| 3 | 0 + 42 = 42 | 47 + 0 = 47 | 47 | 1 |
| 4 | 0 + 56 = 56 | 47 + 14 = 61 | 61 | 1 |

*Stage 1*

$$f_1(x_1) = \max_{m_1} \{31\, m_1 + f_2(x_1 - 2 m_1)\}, \; \max\{m_1\} = \left[\frac{4}{2}\right] = 2$$

| | | $31m_1 + f_2(x_1 - 2m_1)$ | | Optimum solution | |
| --- | --- | --- | --- | --- | --- |
| $x_1$ | $m_1 = 0$ | $m_1 = 1$ | $m_1 = 2$ | $f_1(x_1)$ | $m_1^*$ |
| 0 | 0 + 0 = 0 | — | — | 0 | 0 |
| 1 | 0 + 14 = 14 | — | — | 14 | 0 |
| 2 | 0 + 28 = 28 | 31 + 0 = 31 | — | 31 | 1 |
| 3 | 0 + 47 = 47 | 31 + 14 = 45 | — | 47 | 0 |
| 4 | 0 + 61 = 61 | 31 + 28 = 59 | 62 + 0 = 62 | 62 | 2 |

The optimum solution is now determined in the following manner: Given W = 4 tons, from stage 1, $x_1 = 4$ gives the optimum alternative $m_1^* = 2$, which means that 2 units of item 1 will be loaded on the vessel. This allocation leaves $x_2 = x_1 - 2m_2^*$ = 4 - 2 × 2 = 0. From stage 2, $x_2 = 0$ yields $m_2^* = 0$, which, in turn, gives $x_3 = x_2 - 3m_2 = 0 - 3 × 0 = 0$. Next, from stage 3, $x_3 = 0$ gives $m_3^* = 0$. Thus, the complete optimal solution is $m_1^* = 2$, $m_2^* = 0$, and $m_3 = 0$. The associated return is \$62,000.

In the table for stage 1, we actually need to obtain the optimum for $x_1 = 4$ only because this is the last stage to be considered. However, the computations for $x_1 = 0, 1, 2,$ and 3 are included to allow carrying out sensitivity analysis. For example, what would happen if the vessel capacity is 3 tons in place of 4 tons? The new optimum solution can be determined by starting with $x_1 = 3$ at stage 1 and continuing in the same manner as we did for $x_1 = 4$.

The cargo-loading example represents a typical *resource allocation* model in which a limited resource is apportioned among a finite number of (economic) activities. The objective is to maximize an associated return function. In such models, the definition of the state at each stage will be similar to the definition given for the cargo-loading model. Namely, the state at stage $i$ is the total resource amount allocated to stages $i, i + 1, \ldots ,$ and $n$.

### Problem set 10.4a

1. In Example 10.4–1, determine the optimum solution, assuming that the maximum weight capacity of the vessel is 3 tons.

2. Solve the cargo-loading problem of Example 10.4–1 for each of the following sets of data:
   (a) $w_1 = 4, r_1 = 70, w_2 = 1, r_2 = 20, w_3 = 2, r_3 = 40, W = 6$
   (b) $w_1 = 1, r_1 = 30, w_2 = 2, r_2 = 60, w_3 = 3, r_3 = 80, W = 4$

3. A wilderness hiker must pack three items: food, first-aid kits, and clothes. The backpack has a capacity of 3 ft$^3$. Each unit of food takes 1 ft$^3$. A first-

aid kit occupies $\frac{1}{4}$ ft$^3$ and each piece of cloth takes about $\frac{1}{2}$ ft$^3$. The hiker assigns the priority weights 3, 4, and 5 to food, first aid, and clothes, which means that clothes are the most valuable of the three items. From experience, the hiker must take at least 1 unit of each item and no more than two first-aid kits. How many of each item should the hiker take?

4. A student must select 10 elective courses from four different departments, with at least one course from each department. The 10 courses are allocated to the four departments in a manner that maximizes "knowledge." The student measures knowledge on a 100-point scale and comes up with the following chart:

|            | No. of courses |    |    |     |     |     |     |
|------------|------|----|----|-----|-----|-----|-----|
| Department | 1    | 2  | 3  | 4   | 5   | 6   | ≥7  |
| I          | 25   | 50 | 60 | 80  | 100 | 100 | 100 |
| II         | 20   | 70 | 90 | 100 | 100 | 100 | 100 |
| III        | 40   | 60 | 80 | 100 | 100 | 100 | 100 |
| IV         | 10   | 20 | 30 | 40  | 50  | 60  | 70  |

How should the student select the courses?

5. I have a small backyard garden that measures 10 × 20 feet. This spring I plan to plant three types of vegetables: tomatoes, green beans, and corn. The garden is organized in 20-foot rows. The corn and tomatoes rows are 2 feet wide, and the beans rows are 3 feet wide. I like tomatoes the most and beans the least, and on a scale of 1 to 10, I would assign 10 to tomatoes, 7 to corn, and 3 to beans. Regardless of my preferences, my wife insists that I plant at least one row of green beans and no more than two rows of tomatoes. How many rows of each vegetable should I plant?

6. Habitat for Humanity is a wonderful charity organization that builds homes for needy families using volunteer labor. An eligible family can chose from three home sizes: 1000, 1100, and 1200 ft$^2$. Each size house requires a certain number of labor volunteers. The Fayetteville chapter has received five applications for the upcoming 6 months. The committee in charge assigns a score to each application based on several factors. A higher score signifies more need. For the upcoming 6 months, the Fayetteville chapter can count on a maximum of 23 volunteers. The following data summarize the scores for the applications and the required number of volunteers. Which applications should the committee approve?

| Application | House size (ft²) | Score | Required no. of volunteers |
|---|---|---|---|
| 1 | 1200 | 78 | 7 |
| 2 | 1000 | 64 | 4 |
| 3 | 1100 | 68 | 6 |
| 4 | 1000 | 62 | 5 |
| 5 | 1200 | 85 | 8 |

**7.** Sheriff Bassam is up for reelection in Washington county. The funds available for the campaign are about $10,000. Although the reelection committee would like to launch the campaign in all five precincts of the county, the limited funds dictate otherwise. The following table lists the voting population and the amount of funds needed to launch an effective campaign in each precinct. The choice for each precinct is either to receive all allotted funds or none. How should the funds be allocated?

| Precinct | Population | Required funds ($) |
|---|---|---|
| 1 | 3100 | 3500 |
| 2 | 2600 | 2500 |
| 3 | 3500 | 4000 |
| 4 | 2800 | 3000 |
| 5 | 2400 | 2000 |

**8.** An electronic device consists of three components. The three components are in series so that the failure of one component causes the failure of the device. The reliability (probability of no failure) of the device can be improved by installing one or two standby units in each component. The following table charts the reliability, $r$, and the cost. The total capital

| No. of units in parallel | Component 1 | | Component 2 | | Component 3 | |
|---|---|---|---|---|---|---|
| | $r_1$ | $c_1$ ($) | $r_2$ | $c_2$ ($) | $r_3$ | $c_3$ ($) |
| 1 | .6 | 1000 | .7 | 3000 | .5 | 2000 |
| 2 | .8 | 2000 | .8 | 5000 | .7 | 4000 |
| 3 | .9 | 3000 | .9 | 6000 | .9 | 5000 |

available for the construction of the device is \$10,000. How should the device be constructed? (*Hint:* The objective is to maximize the reliability, $r_1 r_2 r_3$, of the device. This means that the decomposition of the objective function is multiplicative rather than additive.)

**9.** Solve the following model by DP:

$$\text{Maximize } z = y_1 y_2 \ldots y_n$$

subject to

$$y_1 + y_2 + \ldots + y_n = c$$
$$y_i \geq 0, i = 1, 2, \ldots, n$$

(*Hint:* This problem is similar to Problem 8, except that the variables $y_i$ are continuous.)

**10.** Solve the following problem by DP:

$$\text{Minimize } z = y_1^2 + y_2^2 + \ldots + y_n^2$$

subject to

$$y_1 y_2 \ldots y_n = c$$
$$y_i > 0, i = 1, 2, \ldots, n$$

**11.** Solve the following problem by DP:

$$\text{Maximize } z = (y_1 + 2)^2 + y_2 y_3 + (y_4 - 5)^2$$

subject to

$$y_1 + y_2 + y_3 + y_4 \leq 5$$
$$y_i \geq 0 \text{ and integer, } i = 1, 2, 3, 4$$

**12.** Solve the following problem by DP:

$$\text{Minimize } z = \max\{f(y_1), f(y_2), \ldots, f(y_n)\}$$

subject to

$$y_1 + y_2 + \ldots + y_n = c$$
$$y_i \geq 0, i = 1, 2, \ldots, n$$

Provide the solution for the special case of $n = 3$, $c = 10$, and $f(y_1) = y_1 + 5, f(y_2) = 5y_2 + 3,$ and $f(y_3) = y_3 - 2$.

## 10.4.2 Work Force Size Model

In some construction projects, hiring and firing are exercised to maintain a labor force that meets the needs of the project. Given that the activities of hiring and firing both incur additional costs, how should the labor force be maintained throughout the life of the project?

Let us assume that the project will be executed over the span of $n$ weeks and that the minimum labor force required in week $i$ is $b_i$ laborers. Under ideal conditions, we would like the size of the labor force in week $i$ to be exactly $b_i$. However, depending on the cost parameters, it may be more economical to allow the size of the labor force to vary above and below the minimum requirements. Given $x_i$ is the actual number of laborers employed in week $i$, two costs can be incurred in week $i$: (1) $C_1(x_i - b_i)$, the cost maintaining an excess labor force $x_i - b_i$; and (2) $C_2(x_i - x_{i-1})$, the cost of hiring an additional $x_i - x_{i-1}$ laborers.

The elements of the DP model are defined as follows:

1. *Stage* $i$ is represented by week $i$, $i = 1, 2, \ldots, n$.

2. The *alternatives* at stage $i$ is $x_i$, the number of laborers in week $i$.

3. The *state* at stage $i$ is represented by the number of laborers at stage (week) $i - 1, x_{i-1}$.

The DP recursive equation is given as

$$f_i(x_{i-1}) = \min_{x_i \geq b_i} \{C_1(x_i - b_i) + C_2(x_i - x_{i-1}) + f_{i+1}(x_i)\},$$

$$i = 1, 2, \ldots, n$$

where $f_{n+1}(x_n) \equiv 0$. The computations start at stage $n$ with $x_n = b_n$ and terminates at stage 1.

---

**Example 10.4–2.**

A construction contractor estimates that the size of the work force needed over the next 5 weeks to be 5, 7, 8, 4, and 6 workers, respectively. Excess labor kept on the force will cost \$300 per worker per week, and new hiring in any week will incur a fixed cost of \$400 plus \$200 per worker per week.

Expressing $C_1$ and $C_2$ in hundreds of dollars, we have

$$b_1 = 5, b_2 = 7, b_3 = 8, b_4 = 4, b_5 = 6$$

$$C_1(x_i - b_i) = 3(x_i - b_i), x_i > b_i, i = 1, 2, \ldots, 5$$

$$C_2(x_i - x_{i-1}) = 4 + 2(x_i - x_{i-1}), x_i > x_{i-1}, i = 1, 2, \ldots, 5$$

*Stage 5 ($b_5 = 6$)*

|  | $C_1(x_5 - 6) + C_2(x_5 - x_4)$ | Optimum solution | |
|---|---|---|---|
| $x_4$ | $x_6 = 6$ | $f_5(x_4)$ | $x_5^*$ |
| 4 | $3(0) + 4 + 2(2) = 8$ | 8 | 6 |
| 5 | $3(0) + 4 + 2(1) = 6$ | 6 | 6 |
| 6 | $3(0) + 0 \qquad\qquad = 0$ | 0 | 6 |

*Stage 4 ($b_4 = 4$)*

| | $C_1(x_4 - 4) + C_2(x_4 - x_3) + f_5(x_4)$ | | | Optimum solution | |
|---|---|---|---|---|---|
| $x_3$ | $x_4 = 4$ | $x_4 = 5$ | $x_4 = 6$ | $f_4(x_3)$ | $x_4^*$ |
| 8 | $3(0) + 0 + 8 = 8$ | $3(1) + 0 + 6 = 9$ | $3(2) + 0 + 0 = 6$ | 6 | 6 |

*Stage 3 ($b_3 = 8$)*

| | $C_1(x_3 - 8) + C_2(x_3 - x_2) + f_4(x_3)$ | Optimum solution | |
|---|---|---|---|
| $x_2$ | $x_3 = 8$ | $f_3(x_2)$ | $x_6^*$ |
| 7 | $3(0) + 4 + 2(1) + 6 = 12$ | 12 | 8 |
| 8 | $3(0) + 0 \qquad\qquad + 6 = 6$ | 6 | 8 |

*Stage 2 ($b_2 = 7$)*

| | $C_1(x_2 - 7) + C_2(x_3 - x_2) + f_3(x_2)$ | | Optimum solution | |
|---|---|---|---|---|
| $x_1$ | $x_2 = 7$ | $x_2 = 8$ | $f_2(x_1)$ | $x_2^*$ |
| 5 | $3(0) + 4 + 2(2) + 12 = 20$ | $3(1) + 4 + 2(3) + 6 = 19$ | 19 | 8 |
| 6 | $3(0) + 4 + 2(1) + 12 = 18$ | $3(1) + 4 + 2(2) + 6 = 17$ | 17 | 8 |
| 7 | $3(0) + 0 \qquad\quad + 12 = 12$ | $3(1) + 4 + 2(1) + 6 = 15$ | 12 | 7 |
| 8 | $3(0) + 0 \qquad\quad + 12 = 12$ | $3(1) + 0 \qquad\quad + 6 = 9$ | 9 | 8 |

*Stage 1 ($b_1 = 5$)*

| | $C_1(x_1 - 5) + C_2(x_1 - x_0) + f_2(x_1)$ | | | | Optimum solution | |
|---|---|---|---|---|---|---|
| $x_0$ | $x_1 = 5$ | $x_1 = 6$ | $x_1 = 7$ | $x_1 = 8$ | $f_1(x_0)$ | $x_1^*$ |
| 0 | $3(0) + 4 + 2(5)$ $+ 19 = 33$ | $3(1) + 4 + 2(6)$ $+ 17 = 36$ | $3(2) + 4 + 2(7)$ $+ 12 = 36$ | $3(2) + 4 + 2(8)$ $+ 9 = 35$ | 33 | 5 |

The optimum solution is determined as

$$x_0 = 0 \to x_1^* = 5 \to x_2^* = 8 \to x_3^* = 8 \to x_4^* = 6 \to x_5 = 6$$

The solution can be translated to the following plan:

| Week $i$ | Minimum labor force $(b_i)$ | Actual labor force $(x_i)$ | Decision |
|----------|-----------------------------|---------------------------|----------|
| 1 | 5 | 5 | Hire 5 workers |
| 2 | 7 | 8 | Hire 3 workers |
| 3 | 8 | 8 | No change |
| 4 | 4 | 6 | Fire 2 workers |
| 5 | 6 | 6 | No change |

### Problem set 10.4b

1. Solve Example 10.4–2 for each of the following minimum labor requirements:
   (a) $b_1 = 6, b_2 = 5, b_3 = 3, b_4 = 6, b_5 = 8$
   (b) $b_1 = 8, b_2 = 4, b_3 = 7, b_4 = 8, b_5 = 2$

2. In Example 10.4–2, suppose that a severance pay of $100 is incurred for each fired worker, determine the optimum solution.

3. Luxor Travel arranges 1-week tours to southern Egypt. The agency is contracted to provide tourist groups with seven, four, seven, and eight rental cars over the next 4 weeks, respectively. Luxor Travel subcontracts with a local car dealer to supply its rental needs. The dealer charges a rental fee of $220 per car per week, plus a flat fee of $500 for any rental transaction. Luxor, however, may elect not to return the rental cars at the end of the week, in which case the agency will be responsible only for the weekly rental ($220). What is the best way for Luxor Travel to handle the rental situation?

4. GECO is contracted for the next 4 years to supply aircraft engines at the rate of four engines a year. Available production capacity and production costs vary from year to year. GECO can produce five engines in year 1, six in year 2, three in year 3, and five in year 4. The corresponding production costs per engine over the next 4 years are $300,000, $330,000, $350,000, and $420,000, respectively. GECO can elect to produce more than it needs in a certain year, in which case the engines must be properly stored until they are shipped to customers. The storage cost per engine also varies from year to year, and is estimated to be $20,000 for year 1, $30,000 for year 2, $40,000 for year 3, and $50,000 for year 4. Currently, at the start of year 1, GECO has one engine ready for shipping. Develop an optimal production plan for GECO.

5. Toyco produces five electronic games ($E1, E2, \ldots$, and $E5$) and five mechanical toys ($M1, M2, \ldots$, and $M5$). Market research shows that the order of preference for the electronic games is $E1 \rightarrow E2 \rightarrow \ldots \rightarrow E5$, in the sense

that a customer would buy a higher preference if available. In a similar manner, the order of preference for the toys is $M1 \rightarrow M2 \rightarrow \ldots \rightarrow M5$. The weekly demands for the five electronic games are 100, 180, 90, 250, and 190 units, respectively. As for the mechanical toys, the weekly demands are 300, 190, 240, 280, and 260, respectively. The unit production costs for $E1, E2, \ldots$, and $E5$ are $10, $12, $8, $9, and $6, respectively. Also, the unit production costs for $M1, M2, \ldots$, and $M5$ are $4, $5, $3, $2, and $3, respectively. Toyco incurs a setup cost of $500 for the production of any of the games or the toys. Determine the optimum production schedule for Toyco.

## 10.4.3 Equipment Replacement Model

The longer a machine stays in service, the higher will be its maintenance cost, and the lower will be its productivity. When a machine reaches a certain age, it may be more economical to replace it. The problem thus reduces to determining the most economical age of a machine.

Suppose that we are studying the machine replacement problem over a span of $n$ years. At the *start* of each year, we decide whether to keep the machine in service for 1 more year or to replace it with a new one. Let $r(t)$ and $c(t)$ represent the yearly revenue and operating cost of a $t$-year-old machine. Further, assume that $s(t)$ is the salvage value of the machine that has been in service for $t$ years. The cost of acquiring a new machine in any year is $I$.

The elements of the DP model are

**1.** *Stage i* is represented by year $i$, $i = 1, 2, \ldots, n$.

**2.** The *alternatives* at stage (year) $i$ call for either *keeping* or *replacing* the machine at the *start* of year $i$.

**3.** The *state* at stage $i$ is the age of the machine at the start of year $i$.

Define

$$f_i(t) = \text{maximum net income for years } i, i + 1, \ldots, \text{and } n$$

$$\text{given that the machine is } t \text{ years old at the } start \text{ of year } i$$

The recursive equation is derived as

$$f_i(t) = \max \begin{cases} r(t) - c(t) + f_{i+1}(t + 1), & \text{if KEEP} \\ r(0) + s(t) - I - c(0) + f_{i+1}(1), & \text{if REPLACE} \end{cases}$$

where $f_{n+1}(.) \equiv 0$.

---

**Example 10.4–3.**

A company needs to determine the optimal replacement policy for a current 3-year-old machine over the next 4 years ($n = 4$)—that is, until the *start* of year 5. The following table gives the data of the problem. The company requires that a 6-year-old machine be replaced. The cost of a new machine is $100,000.

| Age, t (yr) | Revenue, r(t) ($) | Operating cost, c(t) ($) | Salvage value, s(t) ($) |
|:---:|:---:|:---:|:---:|
| 0 | 20,000 | 200 | – |
| 1 | 19,000 | 600 | 80,000 |
| 2 | 18,500 | 1200 | 60,000 |
| 3 | 17,200 | 1500 | 50,000 |
| 4 | 15,500 | 1700 | 30,000 |
| 5 | 14,000 | 1800 | 10,000 |
| 6 | 12,200 | 2200 | 5,000 |

The determination of the feasible values for the age of the machine at each stage is somewhat tricky. Figure 10–4 summarizes the network representing the problem. At the *start* of year 1, we have a 3-year-old machine. We can either replace (R) it or keep (K) it for another year. At the start of year 2, if replacement occurs, the new machine will be 1 year old; otherwise, the old machine will be 4 years old. The same logic applies at the start of years 2 to 4. If a 1-year-old machine is replaced at the start of years 2 and 3, its replace-

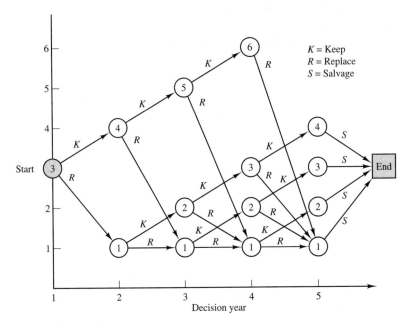

**Figure 10–4**

ment will be 1 year old at the start of the following year. Also, at the start of year 4, a 6-year-old machine must be replaced, and at the end of year 4, we salvage ($S$) the machines.

The network shows that at the start of year 2, the possible ages of the machine are 1 and 4 years. For the start of year 3, the possible ages are 1, 2, and 5 years, and for the start of year 4, the possible ages are 1, 2, 3, and 6 years.

The solution of the network in Figure 10–4 is equivalent to finding the longest route from the start of year 1 to the end of year 4. We will use the tabular form to solve the problem.

*Stage 4*

| | $K$ | $R$ | Optimum solution | |
|---|---|---|---|---|
| $t$ | $r(t) + s(t+1) - c(t)$ | $r(0) + s(t) + s(1) - c(0) - I$ | $f_4(t)$ | Decision |
| 1 | $19.0 + 60 - \;.6 = 78.4$ | $20 + 80 + 80 - .2 - 100 = 79.8$ | 79.8 | $R$ |
| 2 | $18.5 + 50 - 1.2 = 67.3$ | $20 + 60 + 80 - .2 - 100 = 59.8$ | 67.3 | $K$ |
| 3 | $17.2 + 30 - 1.5 = 45.7$ | $20 + 50 + 80 - .2 - 100 = 49.8$ | 49.8 | $R$ |
| 6 | (Must replace) | $20 + \;\;5 + 80 - .2 - 100 = \;\;4.8$ | 4.8 | $R$ |

*Stage 3*

| | $K$ | $R$ | Optimum solution | |
|---|---|---|---|---|
| $t$ | $r(t) - c(t) + f_4(t+1)$ | $r(0) + s(t) - c(0) - I + f_4(1)$ | $f_3(t)$ | Decision |
| 1 | $19.0 - \;.6 + 67.3 = 85.7$ | $20 + 80 - .2 - 100 + 79.8 = 79.6$ | 85.7 | $K$ |
| 2 | $18.5 - 1.2 + 49.8 = 67.1$ | $20 + 60 - .2 - 100 + 79.8 = 59.6$ | 67.1 | $K$ |
| 5 | $14.0 - 1.8 + \;\;4.8 = 17.0$ | $20 + 10 - .2 - 100 + 79.8 = 19.6$ | 19.6 | $R$ |

*Stage 2*

| | $K$ | $R$ | Optimum solution | |
|---|---|---|---|---|
| $t$ | $r(t) - c(t) + f_3(t+1)$ | $r(0) + s(t) - c(0) - I + f_3(1)$ | $f_2(t)$ | Decision |
| 1 | $19.0 - \;.6 + 67.1 = 85.5$ | $20 + 80 - .2 - 100 + 85.7 = 85.5$ | 85.5 | $K$ or $R$ |
| 4 | $15.5 - 1.7 + 19.6 = 33.4$ | $20 + 30 - .2 - 100 + 85.7 = 35.5$ | 35.5 | $R$ |

*Stage 1*

|   |   K   |   R   | Optimum solution |   |
|---|---|---|---|---|
|   |   |   | $f_1(t)$ | Decision |
| $t$ | $r(t) - c(t) + f_2(t+1)$ | $r(0) + s(t) - c(0) - I + f_2(1)$ | | |
| 3 | $17.2 - 1.5 + 35.5 = 51.2$ | $20 + 50 - .2 - 100 + 85.5 = 55.3$ | 55.3 | R |

Figure 10–5 summarizes the order in which the optimal solution is obtained. At the start of year 1, the optimal decision given $t = 3$ is to replace the machine. Thus, the new machine will be 1 year old at the start of year 2, and $t = 1$ at the start of year 2 calls for either keeping or replacing the machine. If it is replaced, the new machine will be 1 year old at the start of year 3; otherwise, the kept machine will be 2 years old. The process is continued in this manner until year 4 is covered.

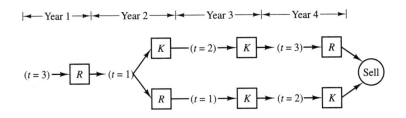

**Figure 10–5**

The alternative optimal policies starting in year 1 are $(R, K, K, R)$ and $(R, R, K, K)$. The total cost is \$55,300.

---

### Problem set 10.4c

1. Develop the network, and find the optimal solution for the model in Example 10.4–3 in each of the following cases:
   (a) The machine is 2 years old at the start of year 1.
   (b) The machine is 1 year old at the start of year 1.
   (c) The machine is bought new at the start of year 1.

2. My son, age 13, has a lawn-mowing business with 10 customers. For each customer, he cuts the grass 3 times a year, which earns him \$50 for each mowing. He has just paid \$200 for a new mower. The maintenance and operating cost of the mower is \$120 for the first year in service, which increases by 20% a year thereafter. A 1-year-old mower has a resale value of \$150, which decreases by 10% a year thereafter. My son, who plans to keep his business until he is 16, thinks that it is more economical to buy a new mower every 2 years. He bases his decision on the fact that the price of a new mower will only increase by 10% a year. Is his decision justified?

3. Circle Farms owns a 2-year-old tractor and wants to develop a replacement policy for its tractors over the next 5 years. A tractor must be kept in service for at least 2 years, but must be disposed of after 5 years. The current purchase price of a tractor is $40,000 and increases by 10% a year. The salvage value of a 2-year-old tractor is $30,000 and decreases by 10% a year. The current annual operating cost of the tractor is $1300 but is expected to increase by 10% a year.

   **(a)** Formulate the problem as a shortest-route problem.

   **(b)** Develop the associated recursive equation.

   **(c)** Determine the optimal replacement policy of the tractor over the next 5 years.

4. Consider the equipment replacement problem over a period of $n$ years. A new piece of equipment costs $c$ dollars, and its resale value after $t$ years in operation is $s(t) = 2(n - t)$ for $n > t$ and zero otherwise. The annual revenue is a function of the age $t$ and is given by $r(t) = n^2 - t^2$ for $n > t$ and zero otherwise.

   **(a)** Formulate the problem as a DP model.

   **(b)** Find the optimal replacement policy given $c = \$10{,}000, n = 5$, and the equipment is 2 years old.

5. Solve Problem 4, assuming that the equipment is 1 year old and that $n = 4$, $c = \$6000, r(t) = \frac{n}{(1+t)}$.

## 10.4.4 Investment Model

Suppose that you want to invest the amounts $P_1, P_2, \ldots, P_n$ at the start of each of the next $n$ years. You have two investment opportunities in two banks: First Bank pays an interest rate $r_1$ and Second Bank pays interest $r_2$, both compounded annually. To encourage deposits, both banks pay bonuses on new investments in the form of a percentage of the amount invested. The bonus percentages vary from year to year and are given in year $i$ by $q_{i1}$ for First Bank and $q_{i2}$ for Second Bank. They are due at the end of the year in which the investment is made and may be reinvested in either bank in the immediately succeeding year. This means that only bonuses and fresh new money may be invested in either bank. However, once an investment is deposited in either bank, it must remain there until the end of the $n$-year horizon. Devise the investment schedule over the next $n$ years.

The elements of the DP model are

**1.** *Stage i* is represented by year $i, i = 1, 2, \ldots, n$

**2.** The *alternatives* at stage $i$ are $I_i$ and $\bar{I}_i$ the amounts invested in First Bank and Second Bank, respectively.

**3.** The *state*, $x_i$, at stage $i$ is represented by the amount of capital available for investment at the start of year $i$.

We note that $\bar{I}_i = x_i - I_i$ by definition. Thus

$$x_i = P_i + q_{i-1,1}I_{i-1} + q_{i-1,2}(x_{i-1} - I_{i-1})$$

$$= P_i + (q_{i-1,1} - q_{i-1,2}) I_{i-1} + q_{i-1,2}x_{i-1}, i = 2, 3, \ldots, n$$

where $x_1 = P_1$. The reinvestment amount $x_i$ includes only new money plus any bonus from investments made in year $i - 1$.

Define

$$f_i(x_i) = \text{optimal value of the investments for years } i,$$
$$i + 1, \ldots, \text{and } n, \text{ given } x_i \text{ at the start of year } i$$

Next, define $s_i$ as the accumulated sum at the end of year $n$, given $I_i$ and $(x_i - I_i)$ are the investments made in year $i$ in First Bank and Second Bank, respectively. Letting $\alpha_i = (1 + r_i), i = 1, 2$, the problem can be stated as

$$\text{Maximize } z = s_1 + s_2 + \ldots s_n$$

where

$$s_i = I_i\alpha_1^{n+1-i} + (x_i - I_i)\alpha_2^{n+1-i}$$

$$= (\alpha_1^{n+1-i} - \alpha_2^{n+1-i})I_i + \alpha_2^{n+1-i}x_i, i = 1, 2, \ldots, n - 1$$

$$s_n = (\alpha_1 + q_{n1} - \alpha_2 - q_{n2}) I_n + (\alpha_2 + q_{n2})x_n$$

The terms $q_{n1}$ and $q_{n2}$ in $s_n$ are added because the bonuses for year $n$ are part of the final accumulated sum of money from the investment.

The backward DP recursive equation is thus given as

$$f_i(x_i) = \max_{0 \leq I_i \leq x_i} \{s_i + f_{i+1}(x_{i+1})\}, \quad i = 1, 2, \ldots, n - 1$$

where $x_{i+1}$ is defined in terms of $x_i$ as given previously, and $f_{n+1}(x_{n+1}) \equiv 0$.

---

**Example 10.4–4.**

Suppose that you want to invest $4000 now and $2000 at the start of years 2 to 4. The interest rate offered by First Bank is 8% compounded annually, and the bonus percentages over the next 4 years are 1.8, 1.7, 2.1, and 2.5, respectively. The annual interest rate offered by Second Bank is .2% lower than that of First Bank, but its bonus is higher by .5%. The objective is to maximize the accumulated capital at the end of 4 years.

Using the notation introduced previously, we have

$$P_1 = \$4,000, P_2 = P_3 = P_4 = \$2,000$$

$$\alpha_1 = (1 + .08) = 1.08$$

$$\alpha_2 = (1 + .078) = 1.078$$

$$q_{11} = .018, q_{21} = .017, q_{31} = .021, q_{41} = .025$$

$$q_{12} = .023, q_{22} = .022, q_{32} = .026, q_{42} = .030$$

*Stage 4*

$$f_4(x_4) = \max_{0 \leq I_4 \leq x_4} \{s_4\}$$

where

$$s_4 = (\alpha_1 + q_{41} - \alpha_2 - q_{42})I_4 + (\alpha_2 + q_{42})x_4 = -.003I_4 + 1.108x_4$$

The function $s_4$ is linear in $I_4$ in the range $0 \le I_4 \le x_4$, and its maximum occurs at $I_4 = 0$ because of the negative coefficient of $I_4$. Thus, the optimum solution for stage 5 can be summarized as

| | Optimum solution | |
|---|---|---|
| State | $f_4(x_4)$ | $I_4^*$ |
| $x_4$ | $1.108x_4$ | 0 |

*Stage 3*

$$f_3(x_3) = \max_{0 < I_3 < x_3} \{s_3 + f_4(x_4)\}$$

where

$$s_3 = (1.08^2 - 1.078^2)I_3 + 1.078^2x_3 = .00432I_3 + 1.1621x_3$$

$$x_4 = 2000 - .005I_3 + .026x_3$$

thus,

$$f_3(x_3) = \max_{0 \le I_3 \le x_3} \{.00432I_3 + 1.1621x_3 + 1.108(2000 - .005I_3 + .026x_3\}$$

$$= \max_{0 \le I_3 \le x_3} \{2216 - .00122I_3 + 1.1909x_3\}$$

| | Optimum solution | |
|---|---|---|
| State | $f_3(x_3)$ | $I_3^*$ |
| $x_3$ | $2216 + 1.1909x_3$ | 0 |

*Stage 2*

$$f_2(x_2) = \max_{0 \le I_2 \le x_2} \{s_2 + f_3(x_3)\}$$

where

$$s_2 = (1.08^3 - 1.078^3)I_2 + 1.078^3x_2 = .006985I_2 + 1.25273x_2$$

$$x_3 = 2000 - .005I_2 + .022x_2$$

thus,

$$f_2(x_2) = \max_{0 \le I_2 \le x_2} \{.006985I_2 + 1.2527x_2 + 2216$$

$$+ 1.1909(2000 - .005I_2 + .022x_2)\}$$

$$= \max_{0 \le I_2 \le x_2} \{4597.8 + .0010305I_2 + 1.27893x_2\}$$

| | Optimum solution | |
|---|---|---|
| State | $f_2(x_2)$ | $I_2^*$ |
| $x_2$ | $4597.8 + 1.27996x_2$ | $x_2$ |

*Stage 1*

$$f_1(x_1) = \max_{0 < I_1 < x_1} \{s_1 + f_2(x_2)\}$$

where

$$s_1 = (1.08^4 - 1.078^4) I_1 + 1.078^4 x_1 = .01005I_1 + 1.3504x_1$$
$$x_2 = 2000 - .005I_1 + .023x_1$$

Thus,

$$f_1(x_1) = \max_{0 \le I_1 \le x_1} \{.01005I_1 + 1.3504x_1 + 4597.8$$
$$+ 1.27996(2000 - .005I_1 + .023x_1)\}$$
$$= \max_{0 \le I_1 \le x_1} \{7157.7 + .00365I_1 + 1.37984x_1\}$$

| | Optimum solution | |
|---|---|---|
| State | $f_1(x_1)$ | $I_1^*$ |
| $x_1 = \$4000$ | $7157.7 + 1.38349x_2$ | $\$4000$ |

Working backward, we get

$$x_2 = 2000 - .005 \times 4000 + .023 \times 4000 = \$2072$$
$$x_3 = 2000 - .005 \times 2072 + .022 \times 2072 = \$2035.22$$
$$x_4 = 2000 - .005 \times 0 + .026 \times \$2035.22 = \$2052.92$$

The optimum solution is thus summarized as

| Optimum solution | Decision |
|---|---|
| $I_1^* = x_1$ | Invest $x_1 = \$4000$ in First Bank |
| $I_2^* = x_2$ | Invest $x_2 = \$2072$ in First Bank |
| $I_3^* = 0$ | Invest $x_3 = \$2035.22$ in Second Bank |
| $I_4^* = 0$ | Invest $x_4 = \$2052.92$ in Second Bank |

### Problem set 10.4d

1. Solve Example 10.4–4, assuming that $r_1 = .085$ and $r_2 = .08$. Additionally, assume that $P_1 = \$5000, P_2 = \$4000, P_3 = \$3000$, and $P_4 = \$2000$.

2. An investor with an initial capital of \$10,000 must decide at the end of each year how much to spend and how much to invest in a savings account. Each dollar invested returns $\alpha = \$1.09$ at the end of the year. The satisfaction derived from spending $\$y$ in any one year is quantified by the equivalence of owning $g(y) = \$\sqrt{y^!}$. Solve the problem by DP for a span of $n = 5$ years.

3. A farmer owns $k$ sheep. At the end of each year, a decision is made as to how many to sell or keep. The profit from selling a sheep in year $i$ is $p_i$. The sheep kept in year $i$ will double in number in year $i + 1$. The farmer plans to sell out completely at the end of $n$ years.
   **(a)** Derive the general recursive equation for the problem.
   **(b)** Solve the problem for $n = 3$ years, $k = 2$ sheep, $p_1 = \$100, p_2 = \$130$, and $p_3 = \$120$.

### 10.4.5 Inventory Models

DP has important applications in the area of inventory control. Chapters 11 and 16 present some of these applications. The models in Chapter 11 are deterministic, and those in Chapter 16 are probabilistic.

## 10.5 PROBLEM OF DIMENSIONALITY

In all the DP models we presented, the *state* at any stage is represented by a single variable. For example, in the cargo-loading model (Section 10.4.1), the problem specifies the weight of the item as the only restriction on the cargo. More realistically, the volume of the vessel may also be another viable restriction. In such a case, the *state* at any stage is said to be two-dimensional because it consists of two variables: weight and volume.

The increase in the number of state variables increases the computations at each stage. This is particularly evident for the DP models with tabular computations in which the number of rows in each tableau must correspond to all possible combinations of the state variables. This computational difficulty is so prominent in DP that it is referred to in the literature as the **curse of dimensionality**.

The following example is chosen to demonstrate the *curse of dimensionality*. It also serves to show how a linear program may be solved by DP.

---

**Example 10.5–1.**

Acme Manufacturing produces two products. The daily capacity of the manufacturing process is 430 minutes. Product 1 requires 2 minutes per unit, and product 2 requires 1 minute per unit. There is no limit on the amount produced of product 1, but the maximum daily demand for product 2 is 230 units. The unit profit of product 1 is \$2 and that of product 2 is \$5. Find the optimal solution by DP.

The problem is represented by the following linear program:

$$\text{Maximize } zx = 2x_1 + 5x_2$$

subject to

$$2x_1 + x_2 \leq 430$$

$$x_2 \leq 230$$

$$x_1, x_2 \geq 0$$

The elements of the DP model are

1. *Stage i* corresponds to product $i, i = 1, 2$.
2. *Alternative* $x_i$ is the amount of product $i, i = 1, 2$.
3. *State* $(v_2, w_2)$ represents the amounts of resources 1 and 2 (production time and demand limits) used in stage 2.
4. *State* $(v_1, w_1)$ represents the amounts of resources 1 and 2 (production time and demand limits) used in stages 1 and 2.

*Stage 2*

Define $f_2(v_2, w_2)$ as the maximum profit for stage 2 (product 2), given the state $(v_2, w_2)$. Then

$$f_2(v_2, w_2) = \max_{\substack{0 \leq x_2 \leq v_2 \\ 0 \leq x_2 \leq w_2}} \{5x_2\}$$

Thus, $\max\{5x_2\}$ occurs at $x_2 = \min\{v_2, w_2\}$, and the solution for stage 2 is

|  | Optimum solution | |
|---|---|---|
| State | $f_2(v_2, w_2)$ | $x_2$ |
| $(v_2, w_2)$ | $5 \min\{v_2, w_2\}$ | $\min\{v_2, w_2\}$ |

*Stage 1*

$$f_1(v_1, w_1) = \max_{0 \leq 2x_1 \leq v_1} \{2x_1 + f_2(v_1 - 2x_1, w_1)\}$$

$$= \max_{0 \leq 2x_1 \leq v_1} \{2x_1 + 5\min(v_1 - 2x_1, w_1)\}$$

The optimization of stage 1 requires the solution of a minimax problem, which, generally, is difficult. For the present problem, we set $v_1 = 430$ and $w_1 = 230$, which gives $0 \leq 2x_1 \leq 430$. Because $\min(430 - 2x_1, 230)$ is the lower envelope of two intersecting lines (verify!), it follows that

$$\min(430 - 2x_1, 230) = 2x_1 + \begin{cases} 230, & 0 \leq x_1 \leq 100 \\ 430 - 2x_1, & 100 \leq x_1 \leq 215 \end{cases}$$

and

$$f_1(430, 230) = \max_{x_1} \begin{cases} 2x_1 + 1150, & 0 \le x_1 \le 100 \\ -8x_1 + 2150, & 100 \le x_1 \le 215 \end{cases}$$

You can verify graphically that the optimum value of $f_1(430, 230)$ occurs at $x_1 = 100$. Thus, we get

| State | Optimum solution $f_1(v_1, w_1)$ | $x_1$ |
|-------|--------------------------------|-------|
| (430, 230) | 1350 | 100 |

To determine the optimum value of $x_2$, we note that

$$v_2 = v_1 - 2x_1 = 430 - 200 = 230$$
$$w_2 = w_1 - 0 \ \ = 230$$

Consequently,

$$x_2 = \min(v_2, w_2) = 230$$

The complete optimum solution is thus summarized as

$$x_1 = 100 \text{ units}, x_2 = 230 \text{ units}, z = \$1350.$$

## Problem set 10.5a

**1.** Solve th e following problems by DP.

   **(a)** Maximize $z = 4x_1 + 14x_2$

      subject to

$$2x_1 + 7x_2 \le 21$$
$$7x_1 + 2x_2 \le 21$$
$$x_1, x_2 \ge 0$$

   **(b)** Maximize $z = 8x_1 + 7x_2$

      subject to

$$2x_1 + \ x_2 \le \ 8$$
$$5x_1 + 2x_2 \le 15$$
$$x_1, x_2 \ge 0 \text{ and integer}$$

   **(c)** Maximize $z = 7x_1^2 + 6x_1 + 5x_2^2$

      subject to

$$x_1 + 2x_2 \le 10$$

$$x_1 - 3x_2 \leq 9$$
$$x_1, x_2 \geq 0$$

**2.** In the $n$-item cargo-loading problem of Example 10.4–1, suppose that the weight and volume limitations of the vessel are given by $W$ and $V$, respectively. Given $w_i$, $v_i$, and $r_i$ are the weight, value, and revenue per unit of item $i$, write the DP backward recursive equation for the problem.

## 10.6 SUMMARY

This chapter has presented several deterministic DP applications. The principle of optimality provides the framework for decomposing DP problems into stages. Although the principle of optimality is "vague" about the details of how each stage is optimized, its application has greatly facilitated the solution of many complex problems that otherwise were not solvable.

## SELECTED REFERENCES

BERTSEKAS, D., *Dynamic Programming: Deterministic and Stochastic Models,* Prentice Hall, Upper Saddle River, N.J., 1987.

DENARDO, E., *Dynamic Programming Theory and Applications,* Prentice Hall, Upper Saddle River, N.J., 1982

DREYFUS, S., and A. LAW, *The Art and Theory of Dynamic Programming,* Academic Press, New York, 1977.

SNIEDOVICH, M., *Dynamic Programming,* Marcel Dekker, New York, 1991.

## COMPREHENSIVE PROBLEM

■ **10–1** A company reviews the status of heavy equipment at the end of each year, and a decision is made either to keep the equipment an extra year or to replace it. However, equipment that has been in service for 3 years must be replaced. The company wishes to develop a replacement policy for its fleet over the next 10 years. The following table provides the pertinent data. The equipment is new at the start of year 1.

| Purchase yr | Purchase price ($) | Maintenance cost ($) for given age (yr) | | | Salvage value ($) for given age (yr) | | |
|---|---|---|---|---|---|---|---|
| | | 0 | 1 | 2 | 1 | 2 | 3 |
| 1 | 10,000 | 200 | 500 | 600 | 9,000 | 7,000 | 5,000 |
| 2 | 12,000 | 250 | 600 | 680 | 11,000 | 9,500 | 8,000 |
| 3 | 13,000 | 280 | 550 | 600 | 12,000 | 11,000 | 10,000 |
| 4 | 13,500 | 320 | 650 | 700 | 12,000 | 11,500 | 11,000 |
| 5 | 13,800 | 350 | 590 | 630 | 12,000 | 11,800 | 11,200 |
| 6 | 14,200 | 390 | 620 | 700 | 12,500 | 12,000 | 11,200 |
| 7 | 14,800 | 410 | 600 | 620 | 13,500 | 12,900 | 11,900 |
| 8 | 15,200 | 430 | 670 | 700 | 14,000 | 13,200 | 12,000 |
| 9 | 15,500 | 450 | 700 | 730 | 15,500 | 14,500 | 13,800 |
| 10 | 16,000 | 500 | 710 | 720 | 15,800 | 15,000 | 14,500 |

# Chapter 11

# Deterministic Inventory Models

## 11.1 INTRODUCTION

A business or an industry usually maintains a reasonable inventory of goods to ensure smooth operation. Traditionally, inventory is viewed as a necessary evil—too little of it causes costly interruptions, too much results in idle capital. The inventory problem determines the inventory level that balances the two extreme cases.

An important factor in the formulation and solution of an inventory model is that the demand (per unit time) of an item may be *deterministic* (known with certainty) or *probabilistic* (described by a probability distribution). This chapter is devoted to the presentation of deterministic models. The (usually more complex) probabilistic models are discussed in Chapter 16.

## 11.2 GENERAL INVENTORY MODEL

The nature of the inventory problem consists of repeatedly placing and receiving orders of given sizes at set intervals. From this standpoint, an **inventory policy** answers the following two questions:

1. *How much* to order?
2. *When* to order?

The answer to the first question determines the *economic order quantity* (EOQ) by minimizing the following cost model:

$$\begin{pmatrix} \text{Total} \\ \text{inventory} \\ \text{cost} \end{pmatrix} = \begin{pmatrix} \text{Purchasing} \\ \text{cost} \end{pmatrix} + \begin{pmatrix} \text{Setup} \\ \text{cost} \end{pmatrix} + \begin{pmatrix} \text{Holding} \\ \text{cost} \end{pmatrix} + \begin{pmatrix} \text{Shortage} \\ \text{cost} \end{pmatrix}$$

All these costs must be expressed in terms of the desired order quantity and the time between orders.

   **1.** *Purchasing cost* is based on the price per unit of the item. It may be constant, or it may be offered at a discount that depends on the size of the order.

   **2.** *Setup cost* represents the fixed charge incurred when an order is placed. This cost is independent of the size of the order.

   **3.** *Holding cost* represents the cost of maintaining the inventory in stock. It includes the interest on capital as well as the cost of storage, maintenance, and handling.

   **4.** *Shortage cost* is the penalty incurred when we run out of stock. It includes potential loss of income as well as the more subjective cost of loss in customer's goodwill.

   The answer to the second question (when to order?) depends on the type of inventory system with which we are dealing. If the system requires **periodic review** (e.g., every week or month), the time for receiving a new order coincides with the start of each period. Alternatively, if the system is based on **continuous review,** new orders are placed when the inventory level drops to a prespecified level, called the **reorder point.**

   The inventory models in this chapter encompass two types of deterministic models: static and dynamic. The static models have constant demand over time. In the dynamic models, the demand varies.

## 11.3 STATIC EOQ MODELS

This section presents three variations of the economic order quantity model with static demand.

### 11.3.1 Classic EOQ model

The simplest of the inventory models involves constant rate demand with instantaneous order replenishment and no shortage. Let

$$y \ = \ \text{Order quantity (number of units)}$$
$$D \ = \ \text{Demand rate (units per unit time)}$$
$$t_0 \ = \ \text{Ordering cycle length (time units)}$$

Using these definitions, the inventory level follows the pattern depicted in Figure 11–1. An order of size $y$ units is placed and received instantaneously when the inventory level is zero. The stock is then depleted uniformly at the constant demand rate $D$. The ordering cycle for this pattern is

$$t_0 = \frac{y}{D} \ \text{time units}$$

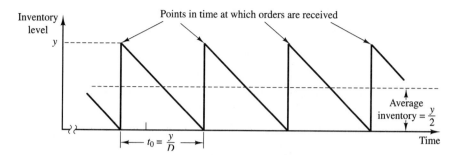

**Figure 11–1**

The resulting average inventory level is given as

$$\text{Average inventory level} = \frac{y}{2} \text{ units}$$

The cost model requires two cost parameters.

$K$ = Setup cost associated with the placement of an order (dollars per order)

$h$ = Holding cost (dollars per inventory unit per unit time)

The total cost *per unit time* (TCU) is thus computed as

$$\text{TCU}(y) = \text{Setup cost per unit time} + \text{Holding cost per unit time}$$

$$= \frac{\text{Setup cost} + \text{Holding cost per cycle } t_0}{t_0}$$

$$= \frac{K + h\left(\frac{y}{2}\right)t_0}{t_0}$$

$$= \frac{K}{\frac{y}{D}} + h\left(\frac{y}{2}\right)$$

The optimum value of the order quantity $y$ is determined by minimizing TCU($y$) with respect to $y$. Assuming $y$ is continuous, a necessary condition for finding the optimal value of $y$ is

$$\frac{d\,\text{TCU}\,(y)}{dy} = -\frac{KD}{y^2} + \frac{h}{2} = 0$$

The condition is also sufficient because TCU($y$) is convex. The solution of the equation yields the EOQ $y^*$ as

$$y^* = \sqrt{\frac{2KD}{h}}$$

The optimum inventory policy for the proposed model is summarized as

$$\text{Order } y^* = \sqrt{\frac{2\,KD}{h}} \text{ units every } t_0^* = \frac{y^*}{D} \text{ time units}$$

Actually, a new order need not be received at the instant it is ordered as the preceding discussion suggests. Instead, a positive **lead time, $L$,** may occur between the placement and the receipt of an order as Figure 11–2 demonstrates. In this case, the **reorder point** occurs when the inventory level drops to LD units.

Figure 11–2 assumes that the lead time $L$ is less than the cycle length $t_0^*$, which is not necessarily the case in general. To account for this situation, we define the *effective* lead time as

$$L_e = L - n t_0^*$$

where $n$ is the largest integer not exceeding $\frac{L}{t_0^*}$. This result is justified because after $n$ cycles of $t_0^*$ each, the inventory situation acts as if the interval between placing an order and receiving another is $L_e$. Thus, the reorder point occurs at $L_e D$ units, and the inventory policy can be restated as

Order the quantity $y^*$ whenever the inventory level drops to $L_e D$ units.

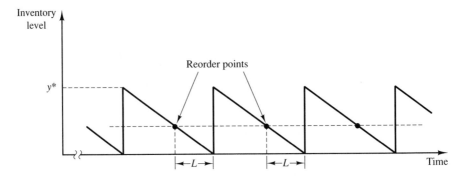

**Figure 11–2**

---

**Example 11.3–1.**

Neon lights on the U of A campus are replaced at the rate of 100 units per day. The physical plant orders the neon lights periodically. It costs $100 to initiate a purchase order. A neon light kept in storage is estimated to cost about $.02 per day. The lead time between placing and receiving an order is 12 days. Determine the optimal inventory policy for ordering the neon lights.

From the data of the problem, we have

$D$ = 100 units per day

$K$ = $100 per order

$h$ = $.02 per unit per day

$L$ = 12 days

Thus,

$$y^* = \sqrt{\frac{2KD}{h}} = \sqrt{\frac{2 \times \$100 \times 100}{.02}} = 1000 \text{ neon lights}$$

The associated cycle length is

$$t_0^* = \frac{y^*}{D} = \frac{1000}{100} = 10 \text{ days}$$

Because the lead time $L = 12$ days exceeds the cycle length $t_0^*$ ( $= 10$ days), we must compute $L_e$. The number of integer cycles included in $L$ is

$$n = (\text{Largest integer} \leq \tfrac{L}{t_0^*})$$
$$= (\text{Largest integer} \leq \tfrac{12}{10})$$
$$= 1$$

Thus,

$$L_e = L - nt_0^* = 12 - 1 \times 10 = 2 \text{ days}$$

The reorder point thus occurs when the inventory level drops to

$$L_e D = 2 \times 100 = 200 \text{ neon lights}$$

The inventory policy for ordering the neon lights is

Order 100 units whenever the inventory level drops to 200 units.

The daily inventory cost associated with the proposed inventory policy is

$$\text{TCU} (y) = \frac{K}{\frac{y}{D}} + h \left( \frac{y}{2} \right)$$

$$= \frac{\$100}{\frac{1000}{100}} + \$.02 \left( \frac{1000}{2} \right) = \$20 \text{ per day}$$

---

### Problem set 11.3a

1. In each of the following cases, no shortage is allowed, and the lead time between placing and receiving an order is 30 days. Determine the optimal inventory policy and the associated cost per day.
   (a) $K = \$100, h = \$.05, D = 30$ units per day
   (b) $K = \$50, \ \ h = \$.05, D = 30$ units per day
   (c) $K = \$100, h = \$.01, D = 40$ units per day
   (d) $K = \$100, h = \$.04, D = 20$ units per day

2. McBurger orders ground meat at the start of each week to cover the week's demand of 300 lb. The fixed cost per order is $20. It costs about $.03 per lb per day to refrigerate and store the meat.
   (a) Determine the inventory cost per week of the present ordering policy.

**(b)** Determine the optimal inventory policy that McBurger should use, assuming zero lead time between the placement and receipt of an order.

**(c)** Determine the difference in the cost per week between McBurger's current and optimal ordering policies.

**3.** A company stocks an item that is consumed at the rate of 50 units per day. It costs the company $20 each time an order is placed. An inventory unit held in stock for a week will cost $.35.

**(a)** Determine the optimum inventory policy, assuming a lead time of 1 week.

**(b)** Determine the optimum number of orders per year (based on 365 days per year).

**4.** Two inventory policies have been suggested by the purchasing department of a company:

> *Policy 1.* Order 150 units, given a reorder point of 50 units and a lead time of 10 days.
>
> *Policy 2.* Order 200 units, given a reorder point of 75 units and a lead time of 15 days.

The setup cost per order is $20, and the holding cost per unit inventory per day is $.02.

**(a)** Which of the two policies should the company adopt?

**(b)** If you were in charge of devising an inventory policy for the company, what would you recommend?

**5.** Walmark Store compresses and palletizes empty merchandise cartons for recycling. The store generates five pallets a day. The cost of storing a pallet in the store's back lot is $.10 per day. The company that moves the pallets to the recycling center charges a flat fee of $100 for the rental of its loading equipment plus a variable transportation cost of $3 per pallet. Graph the change in number of pallets with time, and devise an optimal policy for hauling the pallets to the recycling center.

**6.** A hotel uses an external laundry service to provide clean towels. The hotel generates 600 soiled towels a day. The laundry service picks up the soiled towels and replaces them with clean ones at regular intervals. There is a fixed charge of $81 for each pickup and delivery service, in addition to the variable cost of $.60 per towel. It costs the hotel $.02 a day to store a soiled towel and $.01 per day to store a clean one. How often should the hotel use the pickup and delivery service? (*Hint:* There are two types of inventory items in this situation. As the level of the soiled towels increases, that of clean towels decreases at an equal rate.)

**7.** Consider the inventory situation in which the stock is replenished uniformly (rather than instantaneously) at the rate $a$. Consumption occurs at the constant rate $D$. Because consumption also occurs during the replenishment period, it is necessary to have $a > D$. The setup cost is $K$ per order, and the holding cost is $h$

per unit per unit time. If $y$ is the order size and no shortage is allowed, show that

**(a)** The maximum inventory level is $y(1 - \frac{D}{a})$.

**(b)** The total cost per unit time given $y$ is

$$TCU(y) = \frac{KD}{y} + \frac{h}{2}\left(1 - \frac{D}{a}\right)y$$

**(c)** The economic order quantity is

$$y^* = \sqrt{\frac{2KD}{h\left(1 - \frac{D}{a}\right)}}, \quad D < a$$

**(d)** Show how the EOQ under instantaneous replenishment can be derived from the formula in (c).

**8.** A company can produce an item or buy it from a contractor. If it is produced, it will cost \$20 each time the machines are set up. The production rate is 100 units per day. If it is bought from a contractor, it will cost \$15 each time an order is placed. The cost of maintaining the item in stock, whether bought or produced, is \$.02 per unit per day. The company's usage of the item is estimated at 260,000 units annually. Assuming that no shortage is allowed, should the company buy or produce?

**9.** In Problem 7, suppose additionally that shortage is allowed and that the shortage cost per unit per unit time is $p$. If $w$ is the maximum shortage, show that the following results apply:

$$TCU(y, w) = \frac{KD}{y} + \frac{h\left\{y\left(1 - \frac{D}{a}\right) - w\right\}^2 + pw^2}{2\left(1 - \frac{D}{a}\right)y}$$

$$y^* = \sqrt{\frac{2KD(p + h)}{ph\left(1 - \frac{D}{a}\right)}}$$

$$w^* = \sqrt{\frac{2KDh\left(1 - \frac{D}{a}\right)}{p(p + h)}}$$

### 11.3.2 EOQ with Price Breaks

This model is the same as in Section 11.3.1, except that the inventory item may be purchased at a discount if the size of the order, $y$, exceeds a given limit, $q$—that is, the unit purchasing price, $c$, is given as

$$c = \begin{cases} c_1, & \text{if } y \le q \\ c_2, & \text{if } y > q \end{cases}$$

where $c_1 > c_2$. Hence,

$$\text{Purchasing cost per unit time} = \begin{cases} \dfrac{c_1 y}{t_0} = \dfrac{c_1 y}{\left(\dfrac{y}{D}\right)} = Dc_1, & y \le q \\[3mm] \dfrac{c_2 y}{t_0} = \dfrac{c_2 y}{\left(\dfrac{y}{D}\right)} = Dc_2, & y > q \end{cases}$$

Using the notation in Section 11.3.1, the total cost per unit time is

$$\text{TCU}(y) = \begin{cases} \text{TCU}_1(y) = Dc_1 + \dfrac{KD}{y} + \dfrac{h}{2} y, & y \le q \\[3mm] \text{TCU}_2(y) = Dc_2 + \dfrac{KD}{y} + \dfrac{h}{2} y, & y > q \end{cases}$$

The functions $\text{TCU}_1$ and $\text{TCU}_2$ are graphed in Figure 11–3. Because the two functions differ only by a constant amount, their minima must coincide at

$$y_m = \sqrt{\frac{2KD}{h}}$$

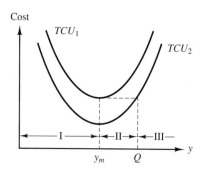

Figure 11–3

The cost function $\text{TCU}(y)$ starts on the left with $\text{TCU}_1(y)$ and drops to $\text{TCU}_2(y)$ at the price break point $q$. Figure 11–3 reveals that the determination of the optimum order quantity $y^*$ depends on where the price break point, $q$, lies with respect to zones I, II, and III delineated by $(0, y_m), (y_m, Q)$, and $(Q, \infty)$, respectively. The value of $Q\ (> y_m)$ is determined from the equation

$$\text{TCU}_2(Q) = \text{TCU}_1(y_m)$$

Figure 11–4 shows how the desired optimum quantity $y^*$ is determined—namely,

$$y^* = \begin{cases} y_m, & \text{if } q \text{ is in zones I or III} \\ q, & \text{if } q \text{ is in zone II} \end{cases}$$

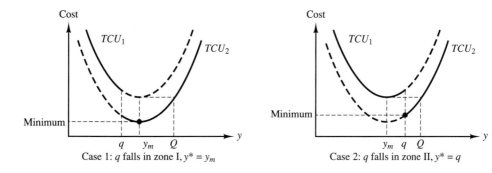

Case 1: $q$ falls in zone I, $y^* = y_m$

Case 2: $q$ falls in zone II, $y^* = q$

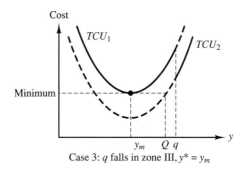

Case 3: $q$ falls in zone III, $y^* = y_m$

**Figure 11–4**

The steps for determining $y^*$ are

**Step 1.** Determine $y_m = \sqrt{\frac{2KD}{h}}$. If $q$ is in zone I, then $y^* = y_m$. Otherwise, go to step 2.

**Step 2.** Determine $Q$ from the equation $\text{TCU}_2(Q) = \text{TCU}_1(y_m)$ and define zones II and III. If $q$ is in zone II, $y^* = q$. Otherwise, $q$ is in zone III, and $y^* = y_m$.

---

**Example 11.3–2.**

LubeCar specializes in fast automobile oil change. The garage buys car oil in bulk at $3 per gallon. A price discount of $2.50 per gallon is available if LubeCar purchases more than 1000 gallons. The garage services approximately 150 cars per day, and each oil change requires 1.25 gallons. LubeCar stores bulk oil at the cost of $.02 per gallon per day. Also, the cost of placing an order for bulk oil is $20. There is a 2-day lead time for delivery. Determine the optimal inventory policy.

The consumption of oil per day is

$$D = 150 \text{ cars} \times 1.25 \text{ gallons per day} = 187.5 \text{ gallons per day}$$

We also have

$$h = \$.02 \text{ per gallon per day}$$
$$K = \$20 \text{ per order}$$
$$L = 2 \text{ days}$$

$$c_1 = \$3 \text{ per gallon}$$
$$c_2 = \$2.50 \text{ per gallon}$$
$$q = 1000 \text{ gallons}$$

*Step 1*    Compute

$$y_m = \sqrt{\frac{2KD}{h}} = \sqrt{\frac{2 \times 20 \times 187.5}{.02}} = 612.37 \text{ gallons}$$

Because $q = 1000$ is larger than $y_m = 612.37$, we move to step 2.

*Step 2*    Determine $Q$ from

$$\text{TCU}_2(Q) = \text{TCU}_1(y_m)$$

or

$$c_2D + \frac{KD}{Q} + \frac{hQ}{2} = c_1D + \frac{KD}{y_m} + \frac{hy_m}{2}$$

Substitution yields

$$2.5 \times 187.5 + \frac{20 \times 187.5}{Q} + \frac{.02Q}{2} = 3 \times 187.5 + \frac{20 \times 187.5}{612.37} + \frac{.02 \times 612.37}{2}$$

Simplification gives

$$.01Q^2 - 106Q + 3750 = 0$$

The equation that yields $Q = 10564.5$ ( $> y_m$). Thus,

$$\text{Zone II} = (612.37, 10564.5)$$
$$\text{Zone III} = (10564.5, \infty)$$

Because $q$ ( $= 1000$) falls in zone II, the optimal order quantity is $y^* = q = 1000$ gallons. Given a 2-day lead time, the reorder point is $2D = 2 \times 187.5 = 375$ gallons. Thus, the optimal inventory policy is
    Order 1000 gallons when the inventory level drops to 375 gallons.

---

### Problem set 11.3b

1. Consider the hotel laundry service situation in Problem 11.3a–6. The normal charge for washing a soiled towel is \$.60, but the laundry service will charge only \$.50 if the hotel supplies them in lots of at least 2500 towels. Should the hotel take advantage of the discount?

2. An item is consumed at the rate of 30 items per day. The holding cost per unit per day is \$.05, and the setup cost is \$100. Suppose that no shortage is allowed and that the purchasing cost per unit is \$10 for any quantity not exceeding 500 units and \$8 otherwise. Determine the optimal inventory policy, given a 21-day lead time.

3. An item sells for $25 a unit, but a 10% discount is offered for lots of 150 units or more. A company uses this item at the rate of 20 units per day. The setup cost for ordering a lot is $50, and the holding cost per unit per day is $.30. Should the company take advantage of the discount?

4. In Problem 3, determine the range on the price discount percentage that when offered for lots of size 150 units or more will not result in any financial advantage to the company.

5. In the inventory model discussed in this section, suppose that the holding cost per unit per unit time is $h_1$ for quantities below $q$ and $h_2$ otherwise, $h_1 > h_2$. Show how the economic lot size is determined.

### 11.3.3 Multi-Item EOQ with Storage Limitation

This model deals with $n$ ($> 1$) items, whose individual inventory fluctuations follow the same pattern in Figure 11–1 (no shortage allowed). The difference is that the items are competing for a limited storage space.

Define for item $i, i = 1, 2, \dots, n$,

$D_i$ = Demand rate

$K_i$ = Setup cost

$h_i$ = Unit holding cost per unit time

$y_i$ = Order quantity

$a_i$ = Storage area requirement per inventory unit

$A$ = Maximum available storage area for all $n$ items

Under the assumption of no shortage, the mathematical model representing the inventory situation is given as

$$\text{Minimize TCU}(y_1, y_{22}, \dots, y_n) = \sum_{i=1}^{n} \left( \frac{K_i D_i}{y_i} + \frac{h_i y_i}{2} \right)$$

subject to

$$\sum_{i=1}^{n} a_i y_i \leq A$$

$$y_i > 0, i = 1, 2, \dots, n$$

The steps for the solution of the model are

**Step 1.** Compute the *unconstrained* optimal values of the order quantities as

$$y_i^* = \sqrt{\frac{2K_i D_i}{h_i}}, i = 1, 2, \dots, n$$

**Step 2.** Check if the unconstrained optimal values $y_i^*$ satisfy the storage constraint. If it does, stop; $y_i^*, i = 1, 2, \ldots, n$ are optimal. Otherwise, go to step 3.

**Step 3.** The storage constraint must be satisfied in equation form. Use the Lagrange multipliers method to determine the constrained optimal values of the order quantities.

In step 3, the Lagrangean function is formulated as

$$L(\lambda, y_1\ y_2, \ldots, y_n) = \text{TCU}(y_1, y_2, \ldots, y_n) - \lambda\left(\sum_{i=1}^{n} a_i\, y_i - A\right)$$

$$= \sum_{i=1}^{n}\left(\frac{K_i D_i}{y_i} + \frac{h_i y_i}{2}\right) - \lambda\left(\sum_{i=1}^{n} a_i y_i - A\right)$$

where $\lambda(< 0)$ is the Lagrange multiplier.[1]

Because the Lagrangean function is convex, the optimal values of $y_i$ and $\lambda$ are determined from the following necessary conditions:

$$\frac{\partial L}{\partial y_i} = -\frac{K_i D_i}{y_i^2} + \frac{h_i}{2} - \lambda\, a_i = 0$$

$$\frac{\partial L}{\partial \lambda} = -\sum_{i=1}^{n} a_i y_i + A = 0$$

The second equation shows that the storage constraint must be satisfied in equation form at the optimum.

From the first equation,

$$y_i^* = \sqrt{\frac{2K_i D_i}{h_i - 2\lambda^* a_i}}$$

The formula shows that $y_i^*$ is dependent on the value of $\lambda^*$. For $\lambda^* = 0$, $y_i^*$ gives the unconstrained solution.

The value of $\lambda^*$ can be found in the following manner: Because by definition $\lambda < 0$ for the minimization case, we successively decrement $\lambda$ by a reasonably small amount and use it in the given formula to compute the associated $y_i^*$. The desired $\lambda^*$ yields $y_i^*$s that satisfy the storage constraint in equation form.

---

**Example 11.3–3.**

The following data describe three inventory items.

[1]See Section 20.2.1 for the details of the Lagrangean method. The application of the method is correct in this case because $\text{TCU}(y_1, y_2, \ldots, y_n)$ is convex, and the problem has a single linear constraint and hence a convex solution space. The procedure may not be correct under other conditions or when the problem has more than one constraint as explained in Section 20.2.2.

| Item | $K_i$ | $D_i$ | $h_i$ | $a_i$ |
|------|-------|-------|-------|-------|
| $i$ | ($) | (units per day) | ($) | (ft²) |
| 1 | 10 | 2 | .3 | 1 |
| 2 | 5 | 4 | .1 | 1 |
| 3 | 15 | 4 | .2 | 1 |

Total available storage area = 25 ft²

We arbitrarily select $\lambda$ in decrements of .1. The resulting computations are summarized in the table below.

| $\lambda$ | $y_1$ | $y_2$ | $y_3$ | $\sum_{i=1}^{3} a_i y_i - A$ |
|-----------|-------|-------|-------|------------------------------|
| 0 | 11.5 | 20.0 | 24.5 | +31.0 |
| −.1 | 8.9 | 11.5 | 17.3 | +12.7 |
| −.2 | 7.6 | 8.9 | 14.1 | +5.6 |
| −.3 | 6.7 | 7.6 | 12.2 | +1.5 |
| −.4 | 6.0 | 6.7 | 11.0 | −1.3 |

The last column of the table shows that the storage equation is satisfied somewhere in the range $-.3 > \lambda > -.4$. We can use a proper numerical analysis technique to search for the value of $\lambda$ in the specified range. Applying such a procedure, we get $\lambda^* \approx -.345$, which gives

$$y_1^* \approx 6.35 \text{ units}, \ y_2^* \approx 7.11 \text{ units}, \ y_3^* \approx 11.6 \text{ units}$$

In the preceding example, the computations always start from $\lambda = 0$, which may lead to inefficient computations. The situation may be improved through better selection of the initial value of $\lambda$. A procedure, suggested by Don Deal of the University of Houston, is outlined in Problem 11.3c–4.

### Problem set 11.3c

**1.** Solve the model of Example 11.3–3, assuming that we require the sum of the average inventories for all the items to be less than 25 units.

**2.** The following data describe four inventory items. The company wishes to determine the economic order quantity for each of the four items such that the total number of orders per year (365 days) is at most 150.

| Item $i$ | $K_i$ ($) | $D_i$ (units/d) | $h_i$ ($) |
|---|---|---|---|
| 1 | 100 | 10 | .1 |
| 2 | 50 | 20 | .2 |
| 3 | 90 | 5 | .2 |
| 4 | 20 | 10 | .1 |

**3.** Solve Problem 2, assuming that the only restriction is a limit of $10,000 on the amount of capital that can be invested in inventory. The purchase cost per unit of items 1, 2, 3, and 4 are $10, $5, $10, and $10, respectively.

**4.** Use the partial derivative equations of the inventory model in this section to show that the starting value of optimal $\lambda$ can be approximated by

$$\lambda^* \approx \frac{\bar{h}}{2\bar{a}} - \frac{n^2 \bar{a} \, \overline{KD}}{A^2}$$

where

$$\bar{h} = \frac{\sum\limits_{i=1}^{n} h_i}{n}, \bar{a} = \frac{\sum\limits_{i=1}^{n} a_i}{n}, \overline{KD} = \frac{\sum\limits_{i=1}^{n} K_i D_i}{n}$$

The exact value of $\lambda$ lies above or below $\lambda^*$. Apply the approximation to Example 11.3–3.

## 11.4 DYNAMIC EOQ MODELS

The models presented here differ from those in Section 11.3 in two aspects: (1) The inventory level is reviewed periodically over a finite number of equal periods; and (2) the demand per period, though deterministic, is dynamic, in the sense that it may vary from one period to the next.

A situation in which variable deterministic demand occurs is the **materials requirement planning** (MRP). The idea of the approach is described by an example. Suppose that the quarterly demand over the next year for two final models, $M1$ and $M2$, of a given product are 100 and 150 units, respectively. Deliveries of the quarterly

lots are made at the end of each quarter. The production lead time is 2 months for
$M1$ and 1 month for $M2$. Each unit of $M1$ and $M2$ uses 2 units of a subassembly $S$.
The lead time for the production of $S$ is 1 month.

Figure 11–5 depicts the production schedules for $M1$ and $M2$. The schedules
start with the quarterly demand for the two models (shown by solid arrows) occurring at the end of months 3, 6, 9, and 12. Given the lead times of 2 and 1 months for
$M1$ and $M2$, the dashed arrows then show the planned starts of each production lot.

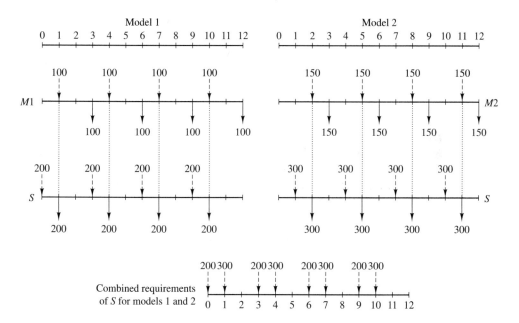

**Figure 11–5**

To start the production of the two models on time, the delivery of subassembly
$S$ must coincide with the occurrence of the dashed $M1$ and $M2$ arrows. This information is shown by the solid arrows in the $S$-chart, where the resulting $S$-demand is 2
units per unit of $M1$ or $M2$. Using a lead time of 1 month, the dashed arrows on the
$S$-chart give the production schedules for $S$. From these two schedules, the combined
demand for $S$ corresponding to $M1$ and $M2$ can then be determined as shown at the
bottom of Figure 11–5. The resulting *variable* (but known) demand for $S$ is typical of
the situation where dynamic EOQ occurs. In essence, given the indicated variable
demand for S, how much should be produced at the start of each month to reduce
the total production-inventory cost?

Two models are presented in this section. The first model assumes no setup (ordering) cost, and the second one does. This seemingly "small" detail makes a difference in the complexity of the model.

**Problem set 11.4a**

1. In Figure 11–5 determine the combined requirements for subassembly $S$ in each of the following cases:
   (a) Lead time for $M1$ is only one period.
   (b) Lead time for $M1$ is three periods.

### 11.4.1 No-Setup Model

This model involves a planning horizon with $n$ equal periods. Each period has a limited production capacity that can include several production levels (e.g., regular time and overtime represent two production levels). A current period may produce items for later periods, in which case an inventory holding cost must be charged.

The general assumptions of the model are

1. No setup cost is incurred in any period.
2. No shortage is allowed.
3. The unit production cost function in any period either is constant or has increasing marginal costs (i.e., convex).
4. The unit holding cost in any period is constant.

The assumption of no shortage signifies that the demand for a current period cannot be filled from the production of future periods. This assumption requires the cumulative production capacity for periods $1, 2, \ldots$, and $i$ to equal at least the cumulative demand for the same inclusive periods.

Figure 11–6 illustrates the unit production cost function with increasing margins. For example, regular time and overtime production correspond to two levels in which the unit production cost during overtime is higher than that during regular time.

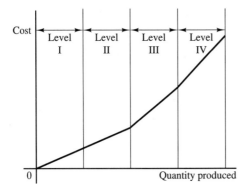

Figure 11–6

The $n$-period problem can be formulated as a transportation model (see Chapter 5) with $kn$ sources and $n$ destinations, where $k$ is the number of production levels per period (e.g., if each period uses regular time and overtime, then $k = 2$). The production capacity of each of the $kn$ production-level sources provides the supply amounts. The demand amounts are specified by each period's demand. The unit "transportation" cost from a source to a destination is the sum of the applicable production and holding costs per unit. The solution of the problem as a transportation model determines the minimum-cost production amounts in each production level.

The resulting transportation model can be solved without using the familiar transportation technique we presented in Chapter 5. The validity of the new solution algorithm follows from the special assumptions of no shortage and a convex production-cost function.

**Example 11.4–1.**

Metalco produces draft deflectors for use in home fireplaces during the months of December to March. The demand starts slow, peaks in the middle of the season, and tapers off toward the end. Because of the popularity of the product, Metalco may use overtime to satisfy the demand. The following table provides the production capacities and the demands for the four winter months.

| | Capacity | | |
|---|---|---|---|
| Month | Regular (units) | Overtime (units) | Demand (units) |
| 1 | 90 | 50 | 100 |
| 2 | 100 | 60 | 190 |
| 3 | 120 | 80 | 210 |
| 4 | 110 | 70 | 160 |

The unit production cost in any period is \$6 during regular time and \$9 during overtime. The holding cost per unit per month is \$.10.

To ensure that the model has a feasible solution when no shortage is allowed, it is required that the cumulative supply (production capacity) up to any month at least equals the associated cumulative demand, as the following table shows.

| Month | Cumulative supply | Cumulative demand |
|---|---|---|
| 1 | 90 + 50 = 140 | 100 |
| 2 | 140 + 100 + 60 = 300 | 100 + 190 = 290 |
| 3 | 300 + 120 + 80 = 500 | 290 + 210 = 500 |
| 4 | 500 + 110 + 70 = 680 | 500 + 160 = 660 |

Table 11–1 summarizes the model and its solution. The symbols $R_i$ and $O_i$ represent the regular time and overtime production levels in period $i$, $i = 1, 2, 3, 4$. Because the cumulative supply at period 4 exceeds the cumulative demand, a dummy surplus destination is added to balance the model as shown in Table 11–1. All the "transportation" routes from a previous to a current period are blocked because no shortage is allowed.

**TABLE 11–1**

| | 1 | 2 | 3 | 4 | Surplus | |
|---|---|---|---|---|---|---|
| $R_1$ | 6 — **90** | 6.1 | 6.2 | 6.3 | 0 | **90** |
| $O_1$ | 9 — **10** | 9.1 — **30** | 9.2 — **10** | 9.3 | 0 | **50 → 40 → 10** |
| $R_2$ | (blocked) | 6 — **100** | 6.1 | 6.2 | 0 | **100** |
| $O_2$ | (blocked) | 9 — **60** | 9.1 | 9.2 | 0 | **60** |
| $R_3$ | (blocked) | (blocked) | 6 — **120** | 6.1 | 0 | **120** |
| $O_3$ | (blocked) | (blocked) | 9 — **80** | 9.1 | 0 | **80** |
| $R_4$ | (blocked) | (blocked) | (blocked) | 6 — **110** | 0 | **110** |
| $O_4$ | (blocked) | (blocked) | (blocked) | 9 — **50** | 0 — **20** | **70 → 20** |
| | **100** ↓ **10** | **190** ↓ **90** ↓ **30** | **210** ↓ **90** ↓ **10** | **160** ↓ **50** | **20** | |

The unit "transportation" costs are computed as the sum of the applicable production and holding costs. For example, the unit cost from $R_1$ to period 1 equals the unit production cost $6 only. The unit cost from $O_1$ to period 4 equals the unit production cost plus the unit holding cost from periods 1 to 4—that is, $9 + (\$.1 + \$.1 + \$.1) = \$9.30$. Finally, the unit cost to the *surplus* destination is zero.

The optimal solution is obtained in one pass by starting from column 1 and moving, one column at a time, toward the *surplus* column. For each respective column, the demand is satisfied by using the cheapest routes in that column.[2]

Starting with column 1, the route $(R_1, 1)$ has the cheapest unit cost, and we assign the most we can to it—namely, min(90, 100) = 90 units, which leaves 10 unsatisfied units in column 1. Next, we move to the next-cheapest route $(O_1, 1)$ in column 1 and assign min(50, 10) = 10, which now satisfies the demand for period 1.

After satisfying the demand for period 1, we move to column 2. The assignments in this column occur in the following order: 100 units to $(R_2, 2)$, 60 units to $(O_2, 2)$, and 30 units to $(O_1, 2)$. The respective unit "transportation" costs associated with these assignments are $6, $9, and $9.10. We did not use the route $(R_1, 2)$, whose unit cost is $6.10, because all the supply of $R_1$ has been assigned to period 1.

Continuing in the same manner, we satisfy the demands of column 3 and then column 4. The optimum solution, shown in boldface in Table 11–1, is summarized as

**Period 1 regular time.**   Produce 90 units for period 1.

**Period 1 overtime.**   Produce 40 units: 10 for period 1, 30 for period 2, and 10 for period 3.

**Period 2 regular time.**   Produce 100 units for period 2.

**Period 2 overtime.**   Produce 60 units for period 2.

**Period 3 regular time.**   Produce 120 units for period 3.

**Period 3 overtime.**   Produce 80 units for period 3.

**Period 4 regular time.**   Produce 110 units for period 4.

**Period 4 overtime.**   Produce 50 units for period 4, and leave 20 units of idle capacity.

The associated total cost is $90 \times \$6 + 10 \times \$9 + 30 \times \$9.10 + 100 \times \$6 + 60 \times \$9 + 10 \times \$9.20 + 120 \times \$6 + 80 \times \$9 + 110 \times \$6 + 50 \times \$9 = \$4685$.

## Problem set 11.4b

**1.** Solve example 14.4–1, assuming that the unit production and holding costs are as given in the following table.

| Period $i$ | Regular time unit cost ($) | Overtime unit cost ($) | Unit holding cost ($) to period $i + 1$ |
|:---:|:---:|:---:|:---:|
| 1 | 5.00 | 7.50 | .10 |
| 2 | 3.00 | 4.50 | .15 |
| 3 | 4.00 | 6.00 | .12 |
| 4 | 1.00 | 1.50 | .20 |

[2]For a proof of the optimality of this procedure, see S. M. Johnson, "Sequential Production Planning over Time at Minimum Cost," *Management Science,* Vol. 3, pp. 435–437, 1957.

**2.** An item is manufactured to meet known demand for four periods according to the following data:

|  | Unit production cost (\$) for period | | | |
|---|---|---|---|---|
| Production range (units) | 1 | 2 | 3 | 4 |
| 1–3 | 1 | 2 | 2 | 3 |
| 4–11 | 1 | 4 | 5 | 4 |
| 12–15 | 2 | 4 | 7 | 5 |
| 16–25 | 5 | 6 | 10 | 7 |
| Unit holding cost to next period (\$) | .30 | .35 | .20 | .25 |
| Total demand (units) | 11 | 4 | 17 | 29 |

(a) Find the optimal solution, indicating the number of units to be produced in each period.

(b) Suppose that 10 additional units are needed in period 4. Where should they be produced?

**3.** The demand for a product over the next five periods may be filled from regular production, overtime production, or subcontracting. Subcontracting may be used only if all the overtime capacity has been used. The following table gives the supply, demand, and cost data of the situation.

| | Production capacity (units) | | | |
|---|---|---|---|---|
| Period | Regular time | Overtime | Subcontracting | Demand |
| 1 | 100 | 50 | 30 | 153 |
| 2 | 40 | 60 | 80 | 200 |
| 3 | 90 | 80 | 70 | 150 |
| 4 | 60 | 50 | 20 | 200 |
| 5 | 70 | 50 | 100 | 203 |

The unit production costs for the three levels in each period are \$4, \$6, and \$7, respectively. The unit holding cost per period is \$.50. Determine the optimal solution.

### 11.4.2 Setup Model

This situation assumes that no shortage is allowed and that a setup cost is incurred whenever a new production lot is started. Two solution methods will be presented: an exact dynamic programming algorithm and a heuristic.

Figure 11–7 summarizes the inventory situation schematically. The symbols shown in the figure are defined for period $i$, $i = 1, 2, \ldots, n$, as

$z_i$ = Amount ordered
$D_i$ = Demand for period $i$
$x_i$ = Inventory at the start of period $i$

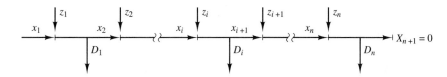

**Figure 11–7**

The cost elements of the situation are defined as

$K_i$ = Setup cost in period $i$
$h_i$ = Unit inventory holding cost from period $i$ to $i + 1$

The associated production cost function for period $i$ is

$$C_i(z_i) = \begin{cases} 0, & z_i = 0 \\ K_i + c_i(z_i), & z_i > 0 \end{cases}$$

where $c_i(z_i)$ is the marginal production cost function given $z_i$.

**Dynamic programming algorithm with general cost function.**    Because no shortage is allowed, the inventory model seeks to minimize the sum of production and holding costs for all $n$ periods. For simplicity, the holding cost for period $i$ is based on the end-of-period inventory

$$x_{i+1} = x_i + z_i - D_i$$

We can use either the forward or the backward recursive equation (see Chapter 10) to construct the dynamic programming model. We will use the forward recursive formulation because it is useful in solving the special case of nonincreasing marginal costs.

For the forward recursive equation, the *state* at *stage* (period) $i$ is defined as $x_{i+1}$, the end-of-period inventory level, where, as Figure 11–7 shows,

$$0 \leq x_{i+1} \leq D_{i+1} + \ldots + D_n$$

This inequality recognizes that, in the extreme case, the remaining inventory, $x_{i+1}$, can satisfy the demand for all the remaining periods.

Let $f_i(x_{i+1})$ be the minimum inventory cost for periods $1, 2, \ldots,$ and $i$ given the end-of-period inventory $x_{i+1}$. The forward recursive equation is thus given as

$$f_1(x_2) = \min_{0 \le z_1 \le D_1 + x_2} \{C_1(z_1) + h_1 x_2\}$$

$$f_i(x_{i+1}) = \min_{0 \le z_i \le D_i + x_{i+1}} \{C_i(z_i) + h_i x_{i+1} + f_{i-1}(x_{i+1} + D_i - z_i)\},$$

$$i = 2, 3, \ldots, n$$

**Example 11.4–2.**

Find the optimal solution for the three-period inventory situation given subsequently. The demand occurs in discrete units, and the starting inventory is $x_1 = 1$ unit. The unit production cost is \$10 for the first 3 units and \$20 for each additional unit.

| Period $i$ | Demand $D_i$ (units) | Setup cost $K_i$ (\$) | Holding cost $h_i$ (\$) |
|---|---|---|---|
| 1 | 3 | 3 | 1 |
| 2 | 2 | 7 | 3 |
| 3 | 4 | 6 | 2 |

The production cost function for period $i$ is $C_i(z_i) = K_i + c_i(z_i)$ for $z_i > 0$, where

$$c_i(z_i) = \begin{cases} 10z_i, & 0 \le z_i \le 3 \\ 30 + 20(z_i - 3), & z_i \ge 4 \end{cases}$$

*Stage 1*    $D_1 = 3, 0 \le x_2 \le 2 + 4 = 6$

| | | | $C_1(z_1) + h_1 x_2$ | | | | | | | Optimal solution | |
|---|---|---|---|---|---|---|---|---|---|---|---|
| | | $z_1 = 2$ | 3 | 4 | 5 | 6 | 7 | 8 | | | |
| $x_2$ | $h_1 x_2$ | $C_1(z_1) = 23$ | 33 | 53 | 73 | 93 | 113 | 133 | $f_1(x_2)$ | $z_1^*$ |
| 0 | 0 | 23 | | | | | | | 23 | 2 |
| 1 | 1 | | 34 | | | | | | 34 | 3 |
| 2 | 2 | | | 55 | | | | | 55 | 4 |
| 3 | 3 | | | | 76 | | | | 76 | 5 |
| 4 | 4 | | | | | 97 | | | 97 | 6 |
| 5 | 5 | | | | | | 118 | | 118 | 7 |
| 6 | 6 | | | | | | | 139 | 139 | 8 |

Because $x_1 = 1$, the smallest value of $z_1$ is $D_1 - x_1 = 3 - 1 = 2$.

*Stage 2*    $D_2 = 2, 0 \le x_3 \le 4$

| | | $C_2(z_2) + h_2 x_3 + f_1(x_3 + D_2 - z_2)$ | | | | | | | Optimal solution | |
|---|---|---|---|---|---|---|---|---|---|---|
| | | $z_2 = 0$ | 1 | 2 | 3 | 4 | 5 | 6 | | |
| $x_3$ | $h_2 x_3$ | $C_2(z_2) = 0$ | 17 | 27 | 37 | 57 | 77 | 97 | $f_2(x_3)$ | $z_2^*$ |
| 0 | 0 | 0 + 55 = 55 | 17 + 34 = 51 | 27 + 23 = 50 | | | | | 50 | 2 |
| 1 | 3 | 3 + 76 = 79 | 20 + 55 = 75 | 30 + 34 = 64 | 40 + 23 = 63 | | | | 63 | 3 |
| 2 | 6 | 6 + 97 = 103 | 23 + 76 = 99 | 33 + 55 = 88 | 43 + 34 = 77 | 63 + 23 = 86 | | | 77 | 3 |
| 3 | 9 | 9 + 118 = 127 | 26 + 97 = 123 | 36 + 76 = 112 | 46 + 55 = 101 | 66 + 34 = 100 | 86 + 23 = 109 | | 100 | 4 |
| 4 | 12 | 12 + 139 = 151 | 29 + 118 = 147 | 39 + 97 = 136 | 49 + 76 = 125 | 69 + 55 = 124 | 89 + 34 = 123 | 109 + 23 = 132 | 123 | 5 |

*Stage 3*    $D_3 = 4, x_4 = 0$

| | | $C_3(z_3) + h_3 x_4 + f_2(x_4 + D_3 - z_3)$ | | | | | Optimal solution | |
|---|---|---|---|---|---|---|---|---|
| | | $z_3 = 0$ | 1 | 2 | 3 | 4 | | |
| $x_4$ | $h_3 x_4$ | $C_3 z_3 = 0$ | 16 | 26 | 36 | 56 | $f_3(x_4)$ | $z_3^*$ |
| 0 | 0 | 0 + 123 = 123 | 16 + 100 = 116 | 26 + 77 = 103 | 36 + 63 = 99 | 56 + 50 = 106 | 99 | 3 |

The solution is given as $z_1^* = 2$, $z_2^* = 3$, and $z_3^* = 3$, which costs a total of $99.

## Problem set 11.4c

1. Consider Example 11.4–2.
   (a) Does it make sense to have $x_4 > 0$?
   (b) For each of the following two cases, determine the feasible ranges for $z_1, z_2, z_3, x_1, x_2$, and $x_3$. (You will find it helpful to represent each situation as in Figure 11–7.)
       (i) $x_1 = 4$ and all the remaining data are the same.
       (ii) $x_1 = 0, D_1 = 5, D_2 = 4$, and $D_3 = 5$.
2. Find the optimal solution for the following four-period inventory model.

| Period $i$ | Demand $D_i$ (units) | Setup cost $K_i$ ($) | Holding cost $h_i$ ($) |
|:---:|:---:|:---:|:---:|
| 1 | 5 | 5 | 1 |
| 2 | 2 | 7 | 1 |
| 3 | 3 | 9 | 1 |
| 4 | 3 | 7 | 1 |

The unit production cost is $1 for the first 6 units and $2 for additional units.

3. Suppose that the inventory-holding cost is based on the *average* inventory during the period. Develop the corresponding forward recursive equation.

4. Develop the backward recursive equation for the model, and then use it to solve Example 11.4–2.

5. Develop the backward recursive equation for the model, assuming that the inventory-holding cost is based on the *average* inventory in the period.

**Dynamic programming algorithm with constant or decreasing marginal costs.** The DP given previously can be used with any cost function. A special case occurs when both the unit production and unit holding costs are *nonincreasing* (concave) functions of the production quantity and the inventory level, respectively. This situation typically occurs when the unit cost function is constant or when a quantity discount is allowed.

Under the given conditions, it can be proved that[3]

1. Given a zero initial inventory ($x_1 = 0$), it is optimal to satisfy the demand in any period $i$ either from new production or from entering inventory, but never from both—that is, $z_i x_i = 0$. (For the cases with positive initial inventory, $x_1 > 0$, the amount can be written off from the demands of the successive periods until it is exhausted.)

2. The optimal production quantity, $z_i$, for period $i$ must either be zero or satisfy the exact demand for one or more contiguous succeeding periods.

These two properties, when used with the forward dynamic programming algorithm, result in simplified computations.

**Example 11.4–3.**
A four-period inventory models operates with the following data:

[3]See H. Wagner and T. Whitin, "Dynamic Version of the Economic Lot Size Model," *Management Science,* Vol. 5, pp. 89–96, 1958. The proof is developed under the restrictive assumption of constant and identical cost functions for all the periods. The assumption was later relaxed by A. Veinott Jr. of Stanford University, to include distinct concave cost functions.

| Period $i$ | Demand $D_i$ (units) | Setup cost $K_i$ ($) |
|---|---|---|
| 1 | 76 | 98 |
| 2 | 26 | 114 |
| 3 | 90 | 185 |
| 4 | 67 | 70 |

The initial inventory $x_1 = 15$ units. The unit production cost is $2, and the unit holding cost per period is $1 for all the periods. (The unit production and holding costs are taken the same for all the periods only for simplicity.)

The solution is determined by the forward algorithm except that the values of $x_{i+1}$ and $z_i$ assume "lump" sums as dictated by the cost function properties. Because $x_1 = 15$, the demand for the first period is decreased by an equivalent amount to $76 - 15 = 61$ units.

*Stage 1*    $D_1 = 61$

| | | | $C_1(z_1) + h_1 x_2$ | | | Optimal solution | |
|---|---|---|---|---|---|---|---|
| | | | $z_1 = 61$ | 87 | 177 | 244 | |
| $x_2$ | $h_1 x_2$ | $C_1(z_1) = 220$ | 272 | 452 | 586 | $f_1(x_2)$ | $z_1^*$ |
| 0 | 0 | 220 | — | — | — | 220 | 61 |
| 26 | 26 | — | 298 | — | — | 298 | 87 |
| 116 | 116 | — | — | 568 | — | 568 | 177 |
| 183 | 183 | — | — | — | 769 | 769 | 244 |
| Order in 1 for | | 1 | 1, 2 | 1, 2, 3 | 1, 2, 3, 4 | | |

*Stage 2*    $D_2 = 26$

| | | | $C_2(z_2) + h_2 x_3 + f_1(x_3 + D_2 - z_2)$ | | | Optimal solution | |
|---|---|---|---|---|---|---|---|
| | | | $z_1 = 0$ | 26 | 166 | 183 | |
| $x_3$ | $h_2 x_3$ | $C_2(z_2) = 0$ | 166 | 346 | 480 | $f_2(x_3)$ | $z_2^*$ |
| 0 | 0 | 0 + 298 = 298 | 166 + 220 = 386 | — | — | 298 | 0 |
| 90 | 90 | 90 + 568 = 586 | — | 436 + 220 = 656 | — | 656 | 116 |
| 157 | 157 | 157 + 769 = 926 | — | — | 637 + 220 = 857 | 857 | 183 |
| Order in 2 for | | — | 2 | 2, 3 | 2, 3, 4 | | |

*Stage 3*     $D_3 = 90$

| | | $C_3(z_3) + h_3x_4 + f_2(x_4 + D_3 - z_3)$ | | | Optimal solution | |
|---|---|---|---|---|---|---|
| | | $z_3 = 0$ | 90 | 157 | | |
| $x_4$ | $h_3x_4$ | $C_3(z_3) = 0$ | 365 | 499 | $f_3(x_4)$ | $z_3^*$ |
| 0 | 0 | $0 + 656 = 656$ | $365 + 298 = 663$ | — | 656 | 0 |
| 67 | 67 | $67 + 857 = 924$ | — | $566 + 298 = 864$ | 864 | 157 |
| Order in 3 for | | — | 3 | 3, 4 | | |

*Stage 4*     $D_4 = 67$

| | | $C_4(z_4) + h_4x_5 + f_3(x_3 + D_4 - z_4)$ | | Optimal solution | |
|---|---|---|---|---|---|
| | | $z_4 = 0$ | 67 | | |
| $x_5$ | $h_4x_5$ | $C_4(z_4) = 0$ | 204 | $f_4(x_5)$ | $z_4^*$ |
| 0 | 0 | $0 + 864 = 864$ | $204 + 656 = 860$ | 860 | 67 |
| Order in 4 for | | — | 4 | | |

The optimal policy is thus given by $z_1^* = 61 = z_2^* = 116 = z_3^* = 0$, and $z_4^* = 67$, at a total cost of \$860.

A special case of the nonincreasing (concave) cost functions occurs when the production cost for period i is defined by the linear function

$$C_i(z_i) = K_i + c_iz_i, z_i > 0, i = 1, 2,..., n$$

provided that $c_1 \geq c_2 \geq ... \geq c_n$. Under this condition the forward dynamic programming algorithm can be modified to produce further savings in computations.

The new algorithm defines stage $i$ for period $i$ where ordering is made in each of the preceding periods for periods up to and including current period $i$. This is expressed mathematically as

$$f_i = \min \begin{cases} C_1 + h_1(D_2 + ... + D_i) + ... + h_{i-1}D_i & \text{(Order in 1)} \\ C_2 + h_2(D_3 + ... + D_i) + ... + h_{i-1}D_i + f_1 & \text{(Order in 2)} \\ \vdots & \\ C_{i-1} + h_{i-1}D_i + f_{i-2} & \text{(Order in } i - 1) \\ C_i + f_{i-1} & \text{(Order in } i) \end{cases}$$

where

$f_i$ = Minimum total cost for periods 1 to $i, i = 1, 2,..., n$

$C_k$ = Total setup plus production cost for ordering in period $k$ the amount

$z_k$ = $D_k + ... + D_i$ for periods $k$ to $i, k \leq i$

The state of the system is suppressed because it corresponds directly to the number of preceding periods, $i$.

The computations of the algorithm can be reduced by making use of the following theorem:

**Planning Horizon Theorem.**    *If for period $i^*$ the minimum cost occurs such that the demand at $i^*$ is satisfied by ordering in a previous period $i^{**} < i^*$, then for all future periods $i > i^*$ it is sufficient to compute the optimal inventory policy by ordering in periods $i^{**}, i^{**} + 1, \ldots,$ and $i$ only. In particular, if the optimal policy calls for ordering in $i^*$ for the same period $i^*$ (i.e., $i^* = i^{**}$), then for any future period $i > i^*$ it is always optimal to order in $i^*$ regardless of future demands. In this case, $i^*$ marks the start of a planning horizon.*

---

**Example 11.4–4.**

Find the optimal inventory policy for the following six-period inventory situation: The unit production cost is $2 for all the periods.

The model computations shown in Table 11–2 are carried out on a row-by-row basis, starting with row 1. Each column represents a decision alternative defining period $k$ in which the demand for periods $k, k + 1, \ldots,$ and $i$ is filled. Each row represents the

| Period $i$ | $D_i$ (units) | $K_i$ ($) | $h_i$ ($) |
|:---:|:---:|:---:|:---:|
| 1 | 10 | 20 | 1 |
| 2 | 15 | 17 | 1 |
| 3 | 7 | 10 | 1 |
| 4 | 20 | 18 | 3 |
| 5 | 13 | 5 | 1 |
| 6 | 25 | 50 | 1 |

limiting period up to which the demand is filled. Thus, for each $i$, the optimum value of $f_i$ is obtained by considering all feasible decision alternatives $k$ ($\leq i$) and then selecting the alternative yielding the minimum cumulative cost. For example, given $i = 3$, we have three options: (a) order in period 1 for periods 1 to 3, (b) order in period 2 for periods 2 and 3, and (c) order in period 3 for period 3. The entries in Table 11–2 above the main diagonal are infeasible because back-ordering is not allowed.

To illustrate the use of the planning horizons, in row 3 ($i = 3$), $f_3$ occurs in column 2 ($k = 2$). This means that it is optimal at this point to order for period 3 (and period 2) in period 2. This is equivalent to having $i^{**} = 2$ and $i^* = 3$. According to the theorem, for all the succeeding rows ($i > 3$), the calculations may go back to period 2 only. Period 2 thus marks the start of a *sub*horizon. Moving to row 4, we see that $f_4$ occurs in column 4, which signifies that it is optimal to order for period 4 in period 4. Thus, $i^{**} = i^* = 4$, and

# TABLE 11-2

| | k = 1[a] | k = 2 | k = 3 | k = 4 | k = 5 | k = 6 |
|---|---|---|---|---|---|---|
| **i = 1** (1)[b] | 20 | | | | | |
| (2) | 10 × 2 = 20 | | | | | |
| (3) | 0 | | | | | |
| (4) | $\dfrac{0}{f_1 \to 40^*}$ | | | | | |
| **i = 2** (1) | 20 | 17 | | | | |
| (2) | (10 + 15) × 2 = 50 | 15 × 2 = 30 | | | | |
| (3) | 15 × 1 = 15 | 0 | | | | |
| (4) | $\dfrac{0}{f_2 \to 85^*}$ | $\dfrac{f_1 = 40}{87}$ | | | | |
| **i = 3** (1) | 20 | 17 | 10 | | | |
| (2) | (10 + 15 + 7) × 2 = 64 | (15 + 7) × 2 = 44 | 7 × 2 = 14 | | | |
| (3) | 22 × 1 + 7 × 1 = 29 | 7 × 1 = 7 | 0 | | | |
| (4) | $\dfrac{0}{113}$ | $\dfrac{f_1 = 40}{f_3 \to 108^*}$ | $\dfrac{f_2 = 85}{109}$ | | | |
| **i = 4** (1) | | 17 | 10 | 18 | | |
| (2) | | (15 + 7 + 20) × 2 = 84 | (7 + 20) × 2 = 54 | 20 × 2 = 40 | | |
| (3) | | 27 × 1 + 20 × 1 = 47 | 20 × 1 = 20 | 0 | | |
| (4) | | $\dfrac{f_1 = 40}{188}$ | $\dfrac{f_2 = 85}{169}$ | $\dfrac{f_3 = 108}{f_4 \to 166^*}$ | | |
| **i = 5** (1) | | | | 18 | 5 | |
| (2) | | | | (20 + 13) × 2 = 66 | 13 × 2 = 26 | |
| (3) | | | | 13 × 3 = 39 | 0 | |
| (4) | | | | $\dfrac{f_3 = 108}{231}$ | $\dfrac{f_4 = 166}{f_5 \to 197^*}$ | |
| **i = 6** (1) | | | | | 5 | 50 |
| (2) | | | | | (13 + 25) × 2 = 76 | 25 × 2 = 50 |
| (3) | | | | | 25 × 1 = 25 | 0 |
| (4) | | | | | $\dfrac{f_4 = 166}{f_6 \to 272^*}$ | $\dfrac{f_5 = 197}{297}$ |

[a] Place order in period k for periods up to and including i.

[b] (1) Setup cost, (2) purchasing cost, (3) holding costs, and (4) optimum total cost from preceeding periods.

$i = 4$ marks the start of a planning horizon. As such, the entries in columns 1 to 3 need not be computed in the succeeding rows (5 and 6). Continuing in this manner, we see in Table 11–2 that another planning horizon starts in period 5, with the result that in row 6, only the computation in columns 5 and 6 need to be carried out. The conclusion then is that periods 1, 4, and 5 mark the start of three planning horizons for the problem.

The advantage of the planning horizon theorem is that it eliminates the computations in the blank entries below the main diagonal of the table. The more blank entries we have, the more efficient the computations will be.

The optimal inventory policy is obtained by considering the last row in Table 11–2. Thus, $f_6$ indicates that it is optimal to order in period 5 the amount $z_5 = 38$ for periods 5 and 6. Next, from row 4 ( $= 5 - 1$ ), $f_4$ requires ordering $z_4 = 20$ for period 4 alone. Now, in row 3 ( $= 4 - 1$ ), $f_3$ calls for ordering in period 2 the amount $z_2 = 22$ for periods 2 and 3. Finally, the amount $z_1 = 10$ is ordered in period 1. The total cost for the entire problem is \$272.

## Problem set 11.4d

1. Solve Example 11.4–3, assuming that the initial inventory is 80 units.
2. Solve the following 10-period deterministic inventory model. Assume an initial inventory of 50 units.
3. Find the optimal inventory policy for the following five-period model. The unit production cost is \$20 for the first 30 items and \$10 for any

| Period $i$ | Demand $D_i$ (units) | Unit production cost (\$) | Unit holding cost (\$) | Setup cost (\$) |
|------------|----------------------|---------------------------|------------------------|-----------------|
| 1  | 150 | 6 | 1 | 100 |
| 2  | 100 | 6 | 1 | 100 |
| 3  | 20  | 4 | 2 | 100 |
| 4  | 40  | 4 | 1 | 200 |
| 5  | 70  | 6 | 2 | 200 |
| 6  | 90  | 8 | 3 | 200 |
| 7  | 130 | 4 | 1 | 300 |
| 8  | 180 | 4 | 4 | 300 |
| 9  | 140 | 2 | 2 | 300 |
| 10 | 50  | 6 | 1 | 300 |

additional units (quantity discount). The unit holding cost is \$1 per period.

**4.** In Example 11.4–4, determine the optimal inventory policy (directly from Table 11–2), assuming that the inventory problem includes only the first five periods.

| Period $i$ | Demand $D_i$ (units) | Setup cost $K_i$ ($) |
|:---:|:---:|:---:|
| 1 | 50 | 80 |
| 2 | 70 | 70 |
| 3 | 100 | 60 |
| 4 | 30 | 80 |
| 5 | 60 | 60 |

**5.** Solve Problem 2, assuming a constant unit production cost of $6 for all the periods. Identify the planning horizons and subhorizons for the problem.

**6.** Solve Problem 3, assuming a constant unit production cost of $25 for all the periods.

**Silver-Meal heuristic.** The heuristic model is valid only for the inventory situations in which the unit production costs are constant and identical for all the periods. For this reason, it seeks to balance only the setup and holding costs.

The heuristic identifies the successive future periods whose demand can be filled from current period's production. The objective is to minimize the associated setup and holding cost per period.

Suppose that we produce in period $i$ for periods $i, i + 1, \ldots,$ and $t, i \leq t$, and define TC($i, t$) as the associated setup and holding costs for the same periods. Mathematically, using the same notation of the DP models, then

$$
TC(i, t) = \begin{cases} K_i, & t = i \\ K_i + h_i D_{i+1} + (h_i + h_{i+1}) D_{i+2} + \ldots \\ \quad + (h_i + h_{i+1} + \ldots + h_{t-1}) D_t, & t > i \end{cases}
$$

Next, define TCU($i, t$) as the associated cost per period—that is,

$$
TCU(i, t) = \frac{TC(i, t)}{t - i + 1}
$$

Thus, given a current period $i$, the heuristic determines $t^*$ that minimizes TCU($i, t$).

The function TC($i, t$) can be computed recursively as follows:

$$
TC(i, i) = K_i
$$

$$TC\,(i, t) = TC\,(i, t - 1) + (h_i + h_{i+1} + \ldots + h_{t-1})D_t,$$
$$t = i + 1, i + 2, \ldots, n$$

The steps of the heuristic are

**Step 0.** Set $i = 1$.

**Step 1.** Determine the local minimum $t^*$ that satisfies

$$TCU(i, t^* - 1) \geq TCU\,(i, t^*)$$

and

$$TCU\,(i, t^* + 1) \geq TCU\,(i, t^*)$$

Then, the heuristic calls for ordering the amount $(D_i + D_{i+1} + \ldots + D_{t^*})$ in period $i$ for periods $i, i + 1, \ldots,$ and $t^*$.

**Step 2.** Set $i = t^* + 1$. If $i > n$, stop; the entire planning horizon has been covered. Otherwise, go to step 1.

### Example 11.4–5.

The heuristic is applied to Example 11.4–4, where the unit production cost is $2 for all the periods. The unit holding cost is $1 for all but period 4, where it equals $3.

*Iteration 1*    $(i = 1,\ K_1 = \$20)$

The function $TC(1, t)$ is computed recursively in $t$. For example, given $TC(1, 1) = \$20$,

| Period $t$ | $D_t$ | TC(1, $t$) | TCU(1, $t$) |
|:---:|:---:|:---:|:---:|
| 1 | 10 | $20 | $\frac{20}{1}$ = $20.00 |
| 2 | 15 | $20 + 1 \times 15 = \$35$ | $\frac{35}{2}$ = $17.50 |
| 3 | 7 | $35 + (1 + 1) \times 7 = \$49$ | $\frac{49}{3}$ = $16.33 |
| 4 | 20 | $49 + (1 + 1 + 1) \times 20 = \$109$ | $\frac{109}{4}$ = $27.25 |

$TC(1, 2) = TC(1, 1) + h_1 D_2 = 20 + 1 \times 15 = \$35$.

The local minimum occurs at $t^* = 3$, which calls for ordering $10 + 15 + 7 = 32$ units in period 1 for periods 1 to 3. Set $i = t^* + 1 = 3 + 1 = 4$.

*Iteration 2*    $(i = 4, K_4 = \$18)$.

| Period $t$ | $D_t$ | TC(4, $t$) | TCU(4, $t$) |
|:---:|:---:|:---:|:---:|
| 4 | 10 | $18 | $\frac{18}{1}$ = $18.00 |
| 5 | 13 | $18 + 3 \times 13 = \$57$ | $\frac{57}{2}$ = $28.50 |

The value $t^* = 1$ call for ordering 20 units in period 4 for period 4. Set $i = 4 + 1 = 5$.

*Iteration 3*   $(i = 5, K_5 = \$5)$

| Period $t$ | $D_t$ | TC(5, t) | TCU(5, t) |
|:---:|:---:|:---:|:---:|
| 5 | 13 | $5 | $\frac{5}{1} = \$5$ |
| 6 | 25 | $5 + 1 \times 25 = \$30$ | $\frac{30}{2} = \$15$ |

Because $t^* = 1$, we order 13 units in period 5 for period 5. Next, set $i = 5 + 1 = 6$. Because $i = 6$ is the last period of the planning horizon. We must order 25 unit in period 6 for period 6.

The following table compares the solutions obtained from the heuristic and the exact dynamic programming algorithm. We have deleted the unit production cost in the dynamic programming model because it is not included in the heuristic computations.

| Period | Heuristic | | Dynamic programming | |
|:---:|:---:|:---:|:---:|:---:|
| | Units produced | Cost ($) | Units produced | Cost ($) |
| 1 | 32 | 49 | 10 | 20 |
| 2 | 0 | 0 | 22 | 24 |
| 3 | 0 | 0 | 0 | 0 |
| 4 | 20 | 18 | 20 | 18 |
| 5 | 13 | 5 | 38 | 30 |
| 6 | 25 | 50 | 0 | 0 |
| Total | 90 | 122 | 90 | 92 |

The production schedule given by the heuristic costs about 32% more than that of the dynamic programming solution ($122 versus $92). The "inadequate" performance of the heuristic may be the result of the data used in the problem. Specifically, the extreme irregularities of the setup costs for periods 5 and 6 may be to blame for this poor performance. Nevertheless, the example shows that the heuristic does not have the capability to "look ahead" for better scheduling opportunities. For example, ordering in period 5 for periods 5 and 6 (instead of ordering for each period separately) can save $25, which will bring the total heuristic cost to $97.

**Problem set 11.4e**

**1.** The demand for fishing poles is at its minimum during the month of December and reaches its maximum during the month of April. Fishing Hole, Inc., estimates the December demand at 50 poles. It increases by 10 poles a month until it reaches 90 in April. Thereafter, the demand decreases by 5 poles a month. The setup cost for a production lot is $250 except during the peak demand months of February to April, where it increases to $300. The production cost per pole is approximately constant at $15 throughout the year, and the holding cost per pole per month is $1. How should Fishing Hole schedule its production facilities?

**2.** A small publisher reprints a novel to satisfy the demand over the next 12 months. The demand estimates for the successive months are 100, 120, 50, 70, 90, 105, 115, 95, 80, 85, 100, and 110. The setup cost for reprinting the book is $200.00 and the holding cost per book per month is $1.20. Determine the reprint schedule for the publisher.

## 11.5 SUMMARY

The inventory problem deals with *how much* and *when* to order an inventory item. These decisions are made by minimizing an appropriate cost function that encompasses the ordering, holding, and shortage costs. This chapter has presented various deterministic models. The degree of complexity of the model is primarily a function of the nature of the demand. In particular, static demand usually results in simpler models. Those in which the demand is dynamic may require the use of dynamic programming, and thus are more complex. Chapter 16 will consider the inventory problem under probabilistic demand conditions.

## SELECTED REFERENCES

SILVER, E., and R. PETERSON, *Decision Systems for Inventory Management and Production Control,* 2nd ed., Wiley, New York, 1985.

TERSINE, R., *Principles of Inventory and Materials Management,* 3rd ed., North Holland, New York, 1988.

WATERS, C., *Inventory Control and Management,* Wiley, New York, 1992.

## COMPREHENSIVE PROBLEMS

■ **11–1** The distribution center of the retailer Walmark Stores deals on a daily basis in buying many staple, nonfashionable inventory items. Steady demand for the various items comes from the numerous stores Walmark owns. In the past, decisions regarding *how much* and *when* to order were relegated to the buyers, whose main purpose was to acquire the items in sufficiently large quantities to guarantee the low purchase prices. This policy was carried out without conscious concern of the inventory status of the items. Indeed, decisions regarding how much to buy were based on the annual dollar usage of the item at the distribution center level. For example, if an item is purchased for $25 a unit and consumed at the rate of 10,000 units a year, then its annual dollar usage is estimated at $250,000. The main guideline the buyers used was that the higher the annual dollar usage of an item, the higher should be its stock level in the distribution center. This guideline translated into expressing the amount of inventory that must be kept on hand at the distribution center as the period between replenishment. For example, a buyer may purchase a prespecified amount of an item every three months.

To exercise better inventory control, Walmark decided to enlist the help of an operations research consultant. After studying the situation, the consultant concluded that the consumption rate of most items in the distribution center is, for all practical purposes, constant and that Walmark operates under the general policy of not allowing shortages. The study further indicated that the inventory-holding cost for all the items under consideration is a constant percentage of the unit purchase price. Furthermore, the fixed cost a buyer incurs with each purchase is the same regardless of the item involved. Armed with this information, the consultant was able to develop a single curve for any single item that relates the annual dollar usage to the average time between replenishment. This curve was then used to decide on which items currently are overstocked or understocked. How did the analyst do it?

■ **11–2** A company manufactures a final product that requires the use of a single component. The company purchases the component from an outside supplier. The demand rate for the final product is constant at about 20 units per week. Each unit of the final product uses 2 units of the purchased component. The following inventory data are available:

|                              | Component | Product |
| ---------------------------- | :-------: | :-----: |
| Setup cost per order ($)     |    80     |   100   |
| Unit holding cost per week ($) |    2    |    5    |
| Lead time (wk)               |     2     |    3    |

Unfilled demand of the final product is backlogged and costs about $8 per lost unit per week. Shortage in the purchased component is not expected to occur. Devise an ordering policy for the purchase of the component and the production of the final product.

■ **11–3** A company deals with a seasonal item, for which the monthly demand fluctuates appreciably. The demand data (in number of units) over the past 5 years are given subsequently.

| Mo | Yr | | | | |
|---|---|---|---|---|---|
| | 1 | 2 | 3 | 4 | 5 |
| Jan. | 10 | 11 | 10 | 12 | 11 |
| Feb. | 50 | 52 | 60 | 50 | 55 |
| March | 8 | 10 | 9 | 15 | 10 |
| April | 99 | 100 | 105 | 110 | 120 |
| May | 120 | 100 | 110 | 115 | 110 |
| June | 100 | 105 | 103 | 90 | 100 |
| July | 130 | 129 | 125 | 130 | 130 |
| Aug. | 70 | 80 | 75 | 75 | 78 |
| Sept. | 50 | 52 | 55 | 54 | 51 |
| Oct. | 120 | 130 | 140 | 160 | 180 |
| Nov. | 210 | 230 | 250 | 280 | 300 |
| Dec. | 40 | 46 | 42 | 41 | 43 |

Because of the fluctuations in demand, the inventory control manager has chosen a policy that orders the item quarterly on January 1, April 1, July 1, and October 1. The order size covers the demand for each quarter. The lead time between placing an order and receiving it is 3 months. Estimates for the current year's demand are taken equal to the demand for year 5, plus an additional 10% safety factor.

A new staff member believes that a better policy can be determined by using the economic order quantity based on the average monthly demand for the year. Fluctuations in demand can be "smoothed" out by placing orders to cover the demands for consecutive months, with the size of each order approximately equal to the economic lot size. Unlike the manager, the new staff member believes that the estimates for next year's demand should be based on the average of years 4 and 5.

The company bases its inventory computations on a holding cost of $.50 per unit inventory per month. A setup cost of $55 is incurred when a new order is placed.

Suggest an inventory policy for the company.

# PART

# II

# PROBABILISTIC MODELS

# Chapter 12

# Review of Basic Probability

## 12.1 INTRODUCTION

All the techniques presented in the preceding chapters assume that all the data are known with certainty. This assumption is not true for all situations. For example, the demand for electric power during the summer months can vary randomly from year to year, depending on weather conditions. In such cases, it is usually not appropriate to represent the demand by a single deterministic value. Instead, we can use observed or historical data to describe the demand by a probability distribution.

## 12.2 LAWS OF PROBABILITY

Probability is associated with performing an **experiment** whose **outcomes** occur randomly. The conjunction of all the outcomes of an experiment is referred to as the **sample space** and any subset of the sample space is known as an **event**. As an illustration, in the experiment of rolling a (six-faced) die, the outcome of a roll corresponds to a face of the die: 1 to 6; hence, the associated sample space is defined by the set $\{1, 2, 3, 4, 5, 6\}$. An example of an event is that a roll will turn up an even value (2, 4, or 6).

An experiment may deal with a continuous sample space as well. For example, the time between failures of an electronic component may assume any nonnegative value.

If, in an $n$-trial experiment, an event $E$ occurs $m$ times, then the probability, $P\{E\}$, of realizing the event $E$ is defined mathematically as

$$P\{E\} = \lim_{n \mapsto \infty} \frac{m}{n}$$

The definition implies that if the experiment is repeated *indefinitely* ($n \to \infty$), then the desired probability is represented by the long-run fraction $\frac{m}{n}$. You can verify this definition by flipping a coin, whose outcomes are head ($H$) or tail ($T$). The longer you repeat the experiment, the closer will be the estimate of $P\{H\}$ (or $P\{T\}$) to the theoretical value of .5.

By definition,

$$0 \le P\{E\} \le 1$$

with $P\{E\}$ equal to 0 if the event $E$ is impossible, and 1 if it is certain. For example, in a six-faced die experiment, rolling a 7 is impossible, whereas rolling an integer value from 1 to 6 is certain.

### Problem set 12.2a

1. In a survey conducted in the State of Arkansas high schools to study the correlation between senior year scores in mathematics and enrolling in engineering colleges, 400 out of 1000 surveyed seniors have studied mathematics. Out of those who studied mathematics, only 150 have enrolled in engineering.

    **(a)** Estimate the probability that a student who studied mathematics is enrolled in engineering. Is not enrolled in engineering.

    **(b)** Estimate the probability that a student neither studied mathematics nor enrolled in engineering.

2. Consider a random gathering of $n$ persons. Determine the smallest $n$ such that it is more likely that two persons or more have the same birthday. (*Hint:* Assume no leap years and that all days of the year are equally likely to be a person's birthday.)

### 12.2.1 Addition Law of Probability

Given two events, $E$ and $F$, $E + F$ represents the **union** of $E$ and $F$, and $EF$ represents their **intersection**. The events $E$ and $F$ are **mutually exclusive** if they do not intersect—that is, if the occurrence of one event precludes the occurrence of the other. Based on these definitions, the addition law of probability can be stated as

$$P\{E + F\} = \begin{cases} P\{E\} + P\{F\}, & E \text{ and } F \text{ mutually exclusive} \\ P\{E\} + P\{F\} - P\{EF\}, & \text{otherwise} \end{cases}$$

---

**Example 12.2–1.**

Consider the experiment of rolling a die. The sample space of the experiment is $\{1, 2, 3, 4, 5, 6\}$. For a fair die, we have

$$P\{1\} = P\{2\} = P\{3\} = P\{4\} = P\{5\} = P\{6\} = \frac{1}{6}$$

Define

$$E = \{1, 2, 3, \text{ or } 4\}$$
$$F = \{3, 4, \text{ or } 5\}$$

The outcomes 3 and 4 are common between $E$ and $F$—hence, $EF = \{3$ or $4\}$. Thus,

$$P\{E\} = P\{1\} + P\{2\} + P\{3\} + P\{4\} = \frac{1}{6} + \frac{1}{6} + \frac{1}{6} + \frac{1}{6} = \frac{2}{3}$$

$$P\{F\} = P\{3\} + P\{4\} + P\{5\} = \frac{1}{2}$$

$$P\{EF\} = P\{3\} + P\{4\} = \frac{1}{3}$$

It then follows that

$$P\{E + F\} = P\{E\} + P\{F\} - P\{EF\} = \frac{2}{3} + \frac{1}{2} - \frac{1}{3} = \frac{5}{6}$$

Intuitively, the result makes sense because $(E + F) = \{1, 2, 3, 4, 5\}$, whose probability of occurrence is $\frac{5}{6}$.

---

### Problem set 12.2b

**1.** In the die-rolling experiment, compute the probability of $E + F$ given that $E$ represents the even outcomes less than 6 and $F$ represents the odd outcomes greater than 1. Are $E$ and $F$ mutually exclusive?

**2.** Ann, Jim, John, and Liz are scheduled to compete in a racquetball tournament. Ann is twice as likely to beat Jim, and Jim is judged to be at the same level as John. Liz's past winning record against John is one out of three.
  **(a)** What is the probability that Jim will win the tournament?
  **(b)** What is the probability that a woman will win the tournament?

### 12.2.2 Conditional Law of Probability

Given the two events $E$ and $F$ with $P\{F\} > 0$, the conditional probability of $E$ given $F$, $P\{E|F\}$, is defined as

$$P\{E|F\} = \frac{P\{EF\}}{P\{F\}}, \quad P\{F\} > 0$$

If $E$ is a subset of (i.e., contained in) $F$, then $P\{EF\} = P\{E\}$.
  The two events, $E$ and $F$, are *independent* if and only if

$$P\{E|F\} = P\{E\}$$

In this case, the conditional probability law reduces to

$$P\{EF\} = P\{E\}P\{F\}$$

**Example 12.2–2.**

You are playing a game in which another person is rolling a die. You cannot see the die, but you are given information about the outcomes. Your job is to predict the outcome of each roll. Determine the probability that the outcome is a 6, given that you are told that the roll has turned up an even number.

Let $E = \{6\}$, and define $F = \{2, 4, \text{ or } 6\}$. Thus,

$$P\{E \mid F\} = \frac{P\{EF\}}{P\{F\}} = \frac{P\{E\}}{P\{F\}} = \frac{\left(\dfrac{1}{6}\right)}{\left(\dfrac{1}{2}\right)} = \frac{1}{3}$$

Note that $P\{EF\} = P\{E\}$ because $E$ is a subset of $F$.

### Problem set 12.2c

1. In Example 12.2–2, suppose that you are told that the outcome is less than 6, determine the probability of getting an even number.

2. Suppose that you roll two dice independently and record the number that turns up for each die.
   **(a)** What is the probability that both numbers are even?
   **(b)** What is the probability that the sum of the two numbers is 10?
   **(c)** What is the probability that the two numbers differ by at least 3?

3. You can toss a fair coin up to 7 times. You will win $100 if at least three tails appear before a head is encountered. What are your chances of winning the $100?

4. *Bayes theorem.* Given the two events $A$ and $B$, show that

$$P\{A \mid B\} = \frac{P\{B \mid A\} P\{A\}}{P\{B\}}$$

   where $P\{B\} > 0$.

5. The percentages of batteries supplied to a retailer by Factories $A$ and $B$ are 75% and 25%, respectively. The percentages of defectives produced by the two factories are known to be 1% and 2%, respectively. A customer has just bought a battery randomly from the retailer.
   **(a)** What is the probability that the battery is defective?
   **(b)** If the battery you bought is defective, what is the probability that it came from Factory $A$? (*Hint:* Use Bayes theorem in Problem 4.)

6. Statistics show that 70% of all men have some form of prostate cancer. The PSA test will show positive 90% of the time for inflicted men and 10% of the time for healthy men. What is the probability that a man who tested positive does have prostate cancer?

## 12.3 RANDOM VARIABLES AND PROBABILITY DISTRIBUTIONS

The outcomes of an experiment are either naturally numeric or can be represented on a numeric scale. For example, the outcomes of rolling a die are naturally numeric—namely, 1 to 6. Conversely, the testing of an item produces two outcomes: bad and good. In such a case, we can use the numeric code 0 to represent "bad" and 1 to represent "good." The numeric representation of the outcomes produces what is known as a **random variable**.

A random variable, $x$, may be **discrete** or **continuous**. For example, the random variable associated with the die-rolling experiment is discrete with $x = 1$ to 6, whereas the interarrival time at a service facility is continuous with $x \geq 0$.

Each continuous or discrete random variable $x$ has a **probability density function** (pdf), $f(x)$ or $p(x)$, that assigns probability measures to it. These functions must satisfy the conditions in the following table.

|  | Random variable, $x$ | |
| --- | --- | --- |
| Characteristic | Discrete | Continuous |
| Applicability range | $x = a,\ a + 1, \ldots, b$ | $a \leq x \leq b$ |
| Conditions for the pdf | $p(x) \geq 0$ | $f(x) \geq 0$ |
|  | $\sum_{x=a}^{b} p(x) = 1$ | $\int_{a}^{b} f(x)dx = 1$ |

A pdf, $p(x)$ or $f(x)$, must be nonnegative (otherwise, the probability of some event may be negative!). Also, the probability of the entire sample space must equal 1.

An important probability measure is the **cumulative density function** (CDF), defined as

$$P\{x \leq X\} = \begin{cases} P(X) = \sum_{x=a}^{x} p(x), & x \text{ discrete} \\[3mm] F(X) = \int_{a}^{X} f(x)\,dx, & x \text{ continuuous} \end{cases}$$

**Example 12.3–1.**

Consider the case of rolling a fair die. Let $x = \{1, 2, 3, 4, 5, 6\}$ be the random variable representing the face of the die that turns up. The pdf and CDF of $x$ are defined as

$$p(x) = \frac{1}{6}, \quad x = 1, 2, \ldots, 6$$

$$P(X) = \frac{X}{6}, \quad X = 1, 2, \ldots, 6$$

Figure 12–1 graphs the two functions. The pdf $p(x)$ is a *uniform* discrete function because all the values of the random variables occur with equal probabilities.

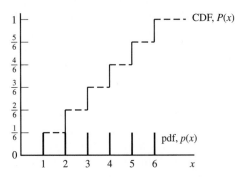

**Figure 12–1**

The continuous counterpart of uniform $p(x)$ is illustrated by the following experiment. A needle of length $l$ is pivoted in the center of a circle whose diameter also equals $l$. After marking an arbitrary reference point on the circumference, we spin the needle clockwise and measure the circumference distance $x$ from where the pointer stops to the marked point. Thus, the random variable $x$ is continuous in the range $0 \leq x \leq \pi l$. There is no reason to believe that the needle will tend to stop more often in a specific region of the circumference. Hence, all the values of $x$ in the specified range are equally likely to occur, and the distribution of $x$ must be uniform.

The pdf of $x$, $f(x)$, is defined as

$$f(x) = \frac{1}{\pi l}, \quad 0 \leq x \leq \pi l$$

The associated CDF, $F(X)$, is computed as

$$F(X) = P\{x \leq X\} = \int_0^X f(x)\, dx = \int_0^X \frac{1}{\pi l}\, dx = \frac{X}{\pi l}, \quad 0 \leq X \leq \pi l$$

Figure 12–2 graphs the two functions.

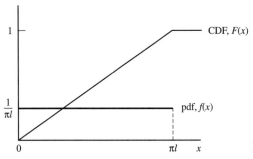

**Figure 12–2**

### Problem set 12.3a

1. The number of units, $x$, needed of an item may assume one of the discrete values from 1 to 5. The probability, $p(x)$, is directly proportional to the number of units needed. The constant of proportionality is $K$.
   (a) Determine the pdf and CDF of $x$, and graph the resulting functions.
   (b) Find the probability that $x$ will assume an even value.

2. Consider the following function:

$$f(x) = \frac{k}{x^2}, \qquad 10 \le x \le 20$$

   (a) Find the value of the constant $k$ that will make $f(x)$ a pdf.
   (b) Determine the CDF, and find the probability that $x$ is (i) larger than 12, and (ii) between 13 and 15.

3. The daily demand for unleaded gasoline is uniformly distributed between 750 and 1250 gallons. The gasoline tank, with a capacity of 1100 gallons, is refilled daily at midnight. What is the probability that the tank will be empty just before a refill?

## 12.4 EXPECTATION OF A RANDOM VARIABLE

Given $h(x)$ is a real function of a random variable $x$, we define the **expected value** of $h(x)$, $E\{h(x)\}$, as the (long-run) weighted average with respect to the pdf of $x$. Mathematically, given $p(x)$ and $f(x)$ are, respectively, the discrete and continuous pdfs of $x$, $E\{h(x)\}$ is computed as

$$E\{h(x)\} = \begin{cases} \sum_{x=a}^{b} h(x)p(x), & x \text{ discrete} \\ \int_{a}^{b} h(x)f(x)dx, & x \text{ continuous} \end{cases}$$

---

**Example 12.4–1.**

During the first week of each month, I (like most people) pay all my bills and answer a few letters. I usually buy 20 first-class mail stamps each month for this purpose. The number of stamps I will be using is random from 10 to 24, with equal probabilities. What is the average number of stamps left?

The pdf of the number of stamps used is

$$p(x) = \frac{1}{15}, \quad x = 10, 11, ..., 24.$$

The number of stamps left is given as

$$h(x) = \begin{cases} 20 - x, & x = 10, 11, ..., 19 \\ 0, & \text{otherwise} \end{cases}$$

Thus,

$$E\{h(x)\} = \left(\frac{1}{15}\right)[(20 - 10) + (20 - 11) + (20 - 12) + \ldots$$

$$+ (20 - 19)] + \left(\frac{5}{15}\right)(0) = 2\tfrac{2}{3} \text{ stamps}$$

The product $\left(\frac{5}{15}\right)(0)$ is needed to complete the expected value of $h(x)$. Specifically, the probability of being left with *zero* extra stamps is

$$P\{x \geq 20\} = P(20) + P(21) + P(22) + P(23) + P(24) = 5\left(\frac{1}{15}\right) = \frac{5}{15}$$

---

### Problem set 12.4a

1. In Example 12.4–1, compute the average number of extra stamps that will meet your maximum possible demand.
2. The results of Example 12.4–1 and of Problem 1 show *positive* averages for *both* the surplus and shortage of stamps. Are these results inconsistent? Explain.

### 12.4.1 Mean and Variance of a Random Variable

The **mean** of $x$, $E\{x\}$, is a numeric measure of the central tendency (or weighted sum) of the random variable. The **variance**, var$\{x\}$, is a measure of the dispersion of $x$ around the mean $E\{x\}$. A larger variance indicates a higher degree of uncertainty in the description of the random variable.

The formulas for the mean and variance can be derived from the general definition $E\{h(x)\}$ as follows: For $E\{x\}$, use $h(x) = x$, and for var$\{x\}$ use $h(x) = (x - E\{x\})^2$. Thus,

$$E\{x\} = \begin{cases} \sum_{x=a}^{b} xp(x), & x \text{ discrete} \\ \int_{a}^{b} xf(x)\, dx, & x \text{ continuous} \end{cases}$$

$$\text{var}\{x\} = \begin{cases} \sum_{x=a}^{b} (x - E\{x\})^2 p(x), & x \text{ discrete} \\ \int_{a}^{b} (x - E\{x\})^2 f(x)\, dx, & x \text{ continuous} \end{cases}$$

The basis for the development of the formulas can be seen more readily by examining the discrete case. Here, $E\{x\}$ is the *weighted sum* of the discrete values of $x$. Also, var$\{x\}$ is the *weighted sum* of the square of the deviation around $E\{x\}$. The continuous case can be interpreted similarly, with integration replacing summation.

**Example 12.4–2.**

We compute the mean and variance for each of the two experiments in Example 12.3–1.
*Case 1 (Die Rolling)*
    The pdf is $p(x) = \frac{1}{6}, x = 1, 2, \ldots, 6$.
Thus,

$$E\{x\} = 1\left(\frac{1}{6}\right) + 2\left(\frac{1}{6}\right) + 3\left(\frac{1}{6}\right) + 4\left(\frac{1}{6}\right) + 5\left(\frac{1}{6}\right) + 6\left(\frac{1}{6}\right) = 3.5$$

$$\mathrm{var}\{x\} = \left(\frac{1}{6}\right)[(1 - 3.5)^2 + (2 - 3.5)^2 + (3 - 3.5)^2 + (4 - 3.5)^2$$

$$+ (5 - 3.5)^2 + (6 - 3.5)^2] = 2.917$$

*Case 2 (Needle Spinning)*
    Suppose that the length of the needle is 1 inch.
Then,

$$f(x) = \frac{1}{3.14}, \quad 0 \le x \le 3.14$$

The mean and variance are computed as

$$E(x) = \int_0^{3.14} x \, \frac{1}{3.14} \, dx = 1.57$$

$$\mathrm{var}(x) = \int_0^{3.14} (x - 1.57)^2 \, \frac{1}{3.14} \, dx = .822$$

## Problem set 12.4b

1. Compute the mean and variance of the random variable defined in Problem 12.3a–1.

2. Compute the mean and variance of the random variable in Problem 12.3a–2.

3. Show that the mean and variance of a uniform random variable $x$, $a \le x \le b$, are

$$E\{x\} = \frac{b + a}{2}$$

$$\mathrm{var}\{x\} = \frac{(b - a)^2}{12}$$

4. Given the pdf $f(x), a \le x \le b$, prove that

$$\mathrm{var}\{x\} = E\{x^2\} - (E\{x\})^2$$

**5.** Given the pdf $f(x), a \leq x \leq b$, and $y = cx + d$, where $c$ and $d$ are constants. Prove that

$$E\{y\} = cE\{x\} + d$$
$$\text{var}\{y\} = c^2\text{var}\{x\}$$

## 12.4.2 Mean and Variance of Joint Random Variables

Consider the two continuous random variables $x_1$, $a_1 \leq x_1 \leq b_1$, and $x_2$, $a_2 \leq x_2 \leq b_2$. Define $f(x_1, x_2)$ as the **joint pdf** of $x_1$ and $x_2$ and $f_1(x_1)$ and $f_2(x_2)$ as the **marginal pdfs** of $x_1$ and $x_2$, respectively. Then

$$f(x_1, x_2) \geq 0, a_1 \leq x_1 \leq b_1, a_2 \leq x_2 \leq b_2$$

$$\int_{a_1}^{b_1} dx_1 \int_{a_2}^{b_2} dx_2 \, f(x_1, x_2) = 1$$

$$f_1(x_1) = \int_{a_2}^{b_2} f(x_1, x_2) \, dx_2$$

$$f_2(x_2) = \int_{a_1}^{b_1} f(x_1, x_2) \, dx_1$$

$$f(x_1, x_2) = f_1(x_1) f_2(x_2), \text{ if } x_1 \text{ and } x_2 \text{ are independent}$$

The same formulas apply to discrete pdfs by replacing integration with summation.

This section discusses functions involving more than one random variable. In particular, we consider two cases:

**(1)** $y = x_1 x_2$
**(2)** $y = c_1 x_1 + c_2 x_2$

where $x_1$ and $x_2$ are jointly distributed according to the pdf $f(x_1, x_2)$.

If $x_1$ and $x_2$ are independent, then

$$E\{x_1 x_2\} = E\{x_1\}E\{x_2\}$$

Conversely, and regardless of whether or not $x_1$ and $x_2$ are independent, we can prove that

$$E\{c_1 x_1 + c_2 x_2\} = c_1 E\{x_1\} + c_2 E\{x_2\}$$

Also,

$$\text{var}\{c_1 x_1 + c_2 x_2\} = c_1^2 \text{var}\{x\} + c_2^2 \text{var}\{x_2\} + 2c_1 c_2 \text{cov}\{x_1, x_2\}$$

where

$$\text{cov}\{x_1, x_2\} = E\{(x_1 - E\{x_1\})(x_2 - E\{x_2\})$$

$$= E(x_1x_2 - x_1E\{x_2\} - x_2E\{x_1\} + E\{x_1\}E\{x_2\})$$

$$= E\{x_1x_2\} - E\{x_1\}E\{x_2\}$$

If $x_1$ and $x_2$ are *independent,* then $E\{x_1 x_2\} = E\{x_1\}E\{x_2\}$ and $\text{cov}\{x_1, x_2\} = 0$. The converse is not true, in the sense that two *dependent* variables may have a zero covariance.

---

**Example 12.4–3.**

A lot includes four defective (D) items and six good (G) ones. You select one item randomly and test it. Then, without replacement, you test a second item. Let the random variables $x_1$ and $x_2$ represent the outcomes for the first and second items, respectively.

(a) Determine the joint pdf of $x_1$ and $x_2$.

(b) Determine the marginal distribution of $x_2$.

(c) Suppose that you get \$5 for each good item you select but must pay \$6 if it is defective. Determine the mean and variance of your revenue after two items have been selected.

Let $p(x_1, x_2)$ as the joint pdf of $x_1$ and $x_2$, and define $p_1(x_1)$ and $p_2(x_2)$ as the marginal pdfs of $x_1$ and $x_2$. First, we determine $p_1(x_1)$ as

$$p_1(G) = \frac{6}{10}, \ p_1(D) = \frac{4}{10}$$

Next, we know that $x_2$, the second outcome, depends on $x_1$. Hence, to determine $p_2(x_2)$, we first determine the joint pdf $p(x_1, x_2)$, from which we can determine the marginal distribution $p_2(x_2)$. Thus,

$$P\{x_2 = G | x_1 = G\} = \frac{5}{9}$$

$$P\{x_2 = G | x_1 = B\} = \frac{6}{9}$$

$$P\{x_2 = B | x_1 = G\} = \frac{4}{9}$$

$$P\{x_2 = B | x_1 = B\} = \frac{3}{9}$$

To determine $p(x_1, x_2)$, we use the formula $P\{AB\} = P\{A | B\}P\{B\}$ (see Section 12.2.2). Thus, we have

$$P\{x_2 = G, x_1 = G\} = \frac{5}{9} \times \frac{6}{10} = \frac{5}{15}$$

$$P\{x_2 = G, x_1 = B\} = \frac{6}{9} \times \frac{4}{10} = \frac{4}{15}$$

$$P\{x_2 = B, x_1 = G\} = \frac{4}{9} \times \frac{6}{10} = \frac{4}{15}$$

$$P\{x_2 = B, x_1 = B\} = \frac{3}{9} \times \frac{4}{10} = \frac{2}{15}$$

We thus summarize the joint pdf as

$$p(x_1, x_2) =$$

|  | $x_2 = G$ | $x_2 = B$ | $p_1(x_1)$ |
|---|---|---|---|
| $x_1 = G$ | $\frac{5}{15}$ | $\frac{4}{15}$ | $\frac{9}{15}$ |
| $x_1 = B$ | $\frac{4}{15}$ | $\frac{2}{15}$ | $\frac{6}{15}$ |
| $p_2(x_2)$ | $\frac{9}{15}$ | $\frac{6}{15}$ | |

The marginal distributions $p_1(x_1)$ and $p_2(x_2)$ can be determined by, respectively, summing the columns and the rows of the joint pdf. It is interesting that, contrary to intuition, $p_1(x_1) = p_2(x_2)$.

The expected revenue can be determined from the joint distribution by recognizing that $G$ produces \$5 and $B$ yields $-\$6$. Thus,

$$\text{Expected revenue} = (\$5 + \$5)\left(\frac{5}{15}\right) + (\$5 - \$6)\left(\frac{4}{15}\right)$$

$$+ (-\$6 + \$5)\left(\frac{4}{15}\right) + (-\$6 - \$6)\left(\frac{2}{15}\right) = \$1.20$$

The same result can be determined by recognizing that the expected revenue for both selections equals the sum of the expected revenue for each individual selection (even though the two variables are *not* independent)—that is,

Expected revenue=(Selection 1 expected revenue)+(Selection 2 expected revenue)

$$= \left[\$5\left(\frac{9}{15}\right) - \$6\left(\frac{6}{15}\right)\right] + \left[\$5\left(\frac{9}{15}\right) - \$6\left(\frac{6}{15}\right)\right]$$

$$= \$.60 + \$.60 = \$1.20$$

To compute the variance of the total revenue, we note that

$$\text{var\{revenue\}} = \text{var\{revenue 1\}} + \text{var\{revenue 2\}} + 2\,\text{cov\{revenue 1, revenue 2\}}$$

Because $p_1(x_1) = p_2(x_2)$, then var{revenue 1} = var{revenue 2}. To compute the variance, we use the formula (see Problem 12.4b–4),

$$\text{var}\{x\} = E\{x^2\} - (E\{x\})^2$$

Thus,

$$\text{var\{revenue 1\}} = \left[(5)^2\left(\frac{9}{15}\right) + (-6)^2\left(\frac{6}{15}\right)\right] - .6^2 = 29.04$$

Next, to compute the covariance, we use the formula

$$\text{cov}\{x_1, x_2\} = E\{x_1 x_2\} - E\{x_1\}E\{x_2\}$$

$E\{x_1 x_2\}$ can be computed from the joint pdf of $x_1$ and $x_2$. Thus, we have

$$\text{Covariance} = \left[ (5 \times 5)\left(\frac{5}{15}\right) + (5 \times -6)\left(\frac{4}{15}\right) + (-6 \times 5)\left(\frac{4}{15}\right) \right.$$

$$\left. + (-6 \times -6)\left(\frac{2}{15}\right) \right] - .6 \times .6 = -3.23$$

Thus,

$$\text{Variance} = 29.04 + 29.04 + 2(-3.23) = 51.62$$

### Problem set 12.4c

**1.** The joint pdf of $x_1$ and $x_2$, $p(x_1, x_2)$, is

|  | $x_2 = 3$ | $x_2 = 5$ | $x_2 = 7$ |
|---|---|---|---|
| $x_1 = 1$ | .2 | 0 | .2 |
| $x_1 = 2$ | 0 | .2 | 0 |
| $x_1 = 3$ | .2 | 0 | .2 |

$p(x_1, x_2) = $

(a) Find the marginal pdfs $p_1(x_1)$ and $p_2(x_2)$.
(b) Are $p_1(x_1)$ and $p_2(x_2)$ independent?
(c) Compute $E\{x_1 + x_2\}$.
(d) Compute $\text{cov}\{x_1, x_2\}$.
(e) Compute $\text{var}\{5x_1 - 6x_2\}$

## 12.5 FOUR COMMON PROBABILITY DISTRIBUTIONS

In Sections 12.3 and 12.4 we discussed the (discrete and continuous) uniform distribution. This section adds four more pdfs that are encountered often in operations research studies: the discrete binomial and Poisson, and the continuous exponential and the normal.

### 12.5.1 Binomial Distribution

Suppose that a manufacturer produces a certain product in lots of $n$ items each. The fraction of defective items in each lot is estimated from historical data to equal $p$. We are interested in determining the pdf of the number of defectives in a lot.

There are $C_x^n = \frac{x!(n-x)!}{n!}$ distinct combinations of having $x$ defectives in a lot of $n$ items, and the probability of getting each such combination is $p^x(1-p)^{n-x}$. It follows (from the addition law of probability) that the probability of $k$ defectives in a lot of $n$ items is

$$P\{x = k\} = C_k^n\, p^k(1-p)^{n-k}, \quad k = 1, 2, \ldots, n$$

This is the binomial distribution with parameters $n$ and $p$. Its mean and variance are given by

$$E\{x\} = np$$

$$\text{var}\{x\} = np(1-p)$$

---

**Example 12.5–1.**

An individual's daily chores require making 10 round-trips by car between two towns. Once through with all 10 trips, the individual can take the rest of the day off, a good enough motivation to drive above the speed limit. Experience shows that there is a 40% chance of getting a speeding ticket on any round-trip.

**(a)** What is the probability that the day will be finished without a speeding ticket?

**(b)** If each speeding ticket costs $80, what is the average daily fine?

The probability of getting a ticket on any one trip is $p = .4$. Thus, the probability of not getting a ticket in any one day is

$$P\{x = 0\} = C_0^{10}(.4)^0(.6)^{10} = .006$$

This means that there is less than 1% chance of finishing the day without a fine. In fact, the average fine per day can be computed as

$$\text{Average fine} = \$80E\{x\}$$

$$= \$80(np) = 80 \times 10 \times .4 = \$320$$

---

### Problem set 12.5a

1. A fair die is rolled 10 times. What is the probability that the rolled die will not show an even number?

2. Suppose that five fair coins are tossed independently. What is the probability that exactly one of the coins will be different from the remaining four?

3. A fortune teller claims to predict whether or not people will amass financial wealth in their lifetime by examining their handwriting. To verify this claim, 10 millionaires and 10 university professors were asked to provide samples of their handwriting. The samples are then paired, one millionaire and one professor, and presented to the fortune teller. We say that the claim is true if the fortune teller makes at least eight correct predictions. What is the probability that the claim is a "fluke?"

**4.** Prove the formulas given for the mean and variance of the binomial distribution.

### 12.5.2 Poisson Distribution

Customers arrive at a bank or a grocery store in a "totaly random" fashion, meaning that there is no way to predict when someone will arrive. The pdf for describing the number of such arrivals during a specified period follows the Poisson distribution.

Let $x$ be the number of events (e.g., arrivals) that take place during a specified time unit (e.g., a minute or an hour). The Poisson pdf is then given as

$$P\{x = k\} = \frac{\lambda^k e^{-\lambda}}{k!}, \quad k = 1, 2, \ldots$$

The mean and variance of the Poisson are

$$E\{x\} = \lambda$$

$$\text{var}\{x\} = \lambda$$

Intuitively, $E\{x\} = \lambda$ must represent the average number of events that occur per unit time. In essence, the parameter $\lambda$ is defined as the rate (number per unit time) at which the events occur.

The Poisson distribution figures out prominently in the study of queues (see Chapter 17).

---

**Example 12.5–2.**

Repair jobs arrive at a small-engine repair shop in a totally random fashion at the rate of 10 per day.

(a) What is the average number of jobs that are received daily at the shop?

(b) What is the probability that no jobs will arrive during any 1 hour, assuming that the shop is open 8 hours a day?

The average number of jobs received per day equals $\lambda = 10$ jobs per day. To compute the probability of no arrivals per *hour*, we need to compute the arrival rate per hour—namely, $\lambda_{\text{hour}} = \frac{10}{8} = 1.25$ jobs per hour. Thus

$$P\{\text{no arrivals per hour}\} = \frac{(\lambda_{\text{hour}})^0 e^{-\lambda_{\text{hour}}}}{0!}$$

$$= \frac{1.25^0 e^{-1.25}}{0!} = .2865$$

---

### Problem set 12.5b

**1.** Customers arrive at a service facility according to a Poisson distribution at the rate of four per minute. What is the probability that at least one customer will arrive in any given 30-second interval?

2. The Poisson distribution with parameter $\lambda$ approximates the binomial distribution with parameters $(n, p)$ when $n$ becomes sufficiently large, $p$ becomes sufficiently small, and $\lambda$ approximately equals $np$ (mathematically, we say that $n \to \infty$, $p \to 0$, and $np \to \lambda$). Demonstrate this result for the situation where a manufactured lot is known to contain 1% defective items. If a sample of 10 items is taken from the lot, compute the probability of the sample having at most one defective item, first by using the (exact) binomial distribution and then by using the (approximate) Poisson distribution. Show that the approximation will not be acceptable if the value of $p$ is increased to, say, 0.5.

3. Prove the formulas for the mean and variance of the Poisson distribution.

### 12.5.3 Negative Exponential Distribution

If the *number* of arrivals at a service facility during a specified period occurs according to a Poisson distribution, then, automatically, the distribution of the *intervals* between successive arrivals must follow the negative exponential (or, simply, the exponential) distribution. Specifically, if $\lambda$ is the rate at which the Poisson events occur, then the distribution of the time, $x$, between successive arrivals is given as

$$f(x) = \lambda e^{-\lambda x}, \quad x > 0$$

Figure 12–3 graphs $f(x)$.

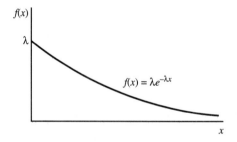

**Figure 12–3**

The mean and variance of the exponential distribution are

$$E\{x\} = \frac{1}{\lambda}$$

$$\text{var}\{x\} = \frac{1}{\lambda^2}$$

The mean $E\{x\}$ is consistent with the definition of $\lambda$. If $\lambda$ is the *rate* at which events occur, then $\frac{1}{\lambda}$ is the average interval between successive events.

---

**Example 12.5–3.**

Cars arrive at a gas station randomly every 2 minutes, on the average. Determine the probability that the interarrival time of cars does not exceed 1 minute.

The desired probability is of the form $P\{x \le A\}$, where $A = 1$ minute in the present example. The determination of this probability is the same as computing the CDF of $x$—namely,

$$P\{x \le A\} = \int_0^A \lambda e^{-\lambda x} dx$$

$$= -e^{-\lambda x} \Big|_0^A$$

$$= 1 - e^{-\lambda A}$$

Now, the rate of arrival for the example is computed as

$$\lambda = \frac{1}{2} \text{ arrival per minute}$$

Thus,

$$P\{x \le 1\} = 1 - e^{-(1/2)(1)} = .39$$

## Problem set 12.5c

**1.** Walmark Store gets its customers from within town and the surrounding rural areas. Town customers arrive at the rate of 5 per minute, and rural customers arrive at the rate of 7 per minute. Arrivals are totally random. Determine the probability that the interarrival time for all customers is less than 5 seconds.

**2.** Prove the formulas for the mean and variance of the exponential distribution.

### 12.5.4 Normal Distribution

The normal distribution describes many random phenomena that occur in every day life, including test scores, weights, heights, and many others. The pdf of the normal distribution is defined as

$$f(x) = \frac{1}{\sqrt{2\pi\sigma^2}} e^{-\frac{(x-\mu)^2}{2\sigma^2}} \qquad -\infty < x < \infty$$

where

$$E\{x\} = \mu$$

$$\text{var}\{x\} = \sigma^2$$

The notation $N(\mu, \sigma)$ is usually used to represent a normal distribution with mean $\mu$ and standard deviation $\sigma$.

Figure 12–4 graphs the normal $f(x)$. The pdf is symmetrical around the mean $\mu$.

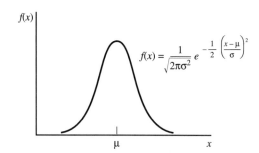

$$f(x) = \frac{1}{\sqrt{2\pi\sigma^2}}\, e^{-\frac{1}{2}\left(\frac{x-\mu}{\sigma}\right)^2}$$

**Figure 12–4**

The importance of the normal distribution stems also from the fact that the average of a sample taken from any distribution can always be approximated by the normal distribution. This remarkable result is based on the following theorem:

**Central Limit Theorem.**    *Let $x_1, x_2, \ldots,$ and $x_n$, be independent and identically distributed random variable each with mean $\mu$ and standard deviation $\sigma$ and define*

$$s_n = x_1 + x_2 + \ldots + x_n$$

*As $n$ becomes large ($n \to \infty$), the distribution of $s_n$ becomes asymptotically normal with mean $n\mu$ and variance $n\sigma^2$, regardless of the original distribution of $x_1, x_2, \ldots,$ and $x_n$.*

The central limit theorem particularly tells us that the distribution of the *average* of a sample of size $n$ drawn from any distribution is asymptotically normal with mean $\mu$ and variance $\frac{\sigma^2}{n}$.

The CDF of the normal random variable cannot be determined in a closed form. As a result, normal tables (see Table 1 in Appendix D) have been prepared for this purpose. These tables apply to the **standard normal,** for which the mean is zero and the variance is 1. Any normal random variable, $x$ (with mean $\mu$ and variance $\sigma^2$), can be converted to a standard normal, $z$, by using the transformation

$$z = \frac{x - \mu}{\sigma}$$

About 99.98% of the area under any normal distribution is enclosed in the range $\mu - 3\sigma \le x \le \mu + 3\sigma$. This range is known as the 3-sigma limits.

---

**Example 12.5–4.**

The inside diameter of a cylinder has the specifications $1 \pm .03$ in. The machining process output follows a normal distribution with mean 1 in and standard deviation .1 in. Determine the percentage of production that will meet the specifications.

Let $x$ represent the output of the process. The probability that a cylinder will meet specifications is

$$P\{1 - .03 \le x \le 1 + .03\} = P\{.97 \le x \le 1.03\}$$

Given $\mu = 1$ and $\sigma = .1$, the equivalent standard normal probability statement is

$$P\{.97 \le x \le 1.03\} = P\left\{ \frac{.97 - 1}{.1} \le z \le \frac{1.03 - 1}{.1} \right\}$$

$$= P\{-.3 \le z \le .3\}$$

$$= P\{z \le .3\} - P\{z \le -.3\}$$

$$= P\{z \le .3\} - [1 - P\{z \le .3\}]$$

$$= 2P\{z \le .3\} - 1$$

$$= 2 \times .6179 - 1$$

$$= .2358$$

The given probability statements can be justified by picturing the shaded area in Figure 12–5. Notice that $P\{z \le -.3\} = 1 - P\{z \le .3\}$ because of the symmetry of the pdf. The value .6179 $(= P\{z \le .3\}$ is obtained from the standard normal table (Table 1 in Appendix D).

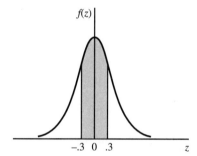

$f(z)$

−.3 0 .3    $z$    **Figure 12–5**

## Problem set 12.5d

1. The college of engineering at U of A requires a minimum ACT score of 26. The test score among high school seniors in a given schools district is normally distributed with mean 22 and standard deviation 2.
   (a) Determine the percentage of high school seniors who are potential engineering recruits.
   (b) If U of A does not accept any student with an ACT score less than 17, determine the percentage of students that will not be eligible for admission at U of A.

2. The weights of individuals who seek a helicopter ride in an amusement park has a mean of 180 lb and a standard deviation of 15 lb. The helicopter can carry five persons but has a maximum weight capacity of 1000 lb. What is the probability that helicopter will not take off with five persons aboard? (*Hint:* Apply the central limit theorem.)

3. The inside diameter of a cylinder is normally distributed with a mean of 1 in and a standard deviation of .01 in. A solid rod is assembled inside each

cylinder. The diameter of the rod is also normally distributed with a mean of .99 in and a standard deviation of .01 in. Determine the percentage of rod-cylinder pairs that will not fit in an assembly. (*Hint:* The difference between two normal random variables is also normal.)

## 12.6 EMPERICAL DISTRIBUTIONS

In the preceding sections, we have discussed the properties of the pdfs and CDFs of random variables and have given examples of four common distributions. How do we determine these distributions in practice?

The determination, actually estimation, of any pdf is rooted in the raw data we collect about the situation under study. For example, to estimate the pdf of the interarrival time of customers at a grocery store, we first record the clock time of the arriving customers. The desired interarrival data is the differences between successive arrival times.

This section shows how sampled data can be converted into pdfs based on the following steps:

**Step 1.** Summarize the raw data in the form of an appropriate frequency histogram, and determine the associated empirical pdf.

**Step 2.** Use the *goodness-of-fit test* to test if the resulting empirical pdf is sampled from a known theoretical pdf.

The details of the procedure are given subsequently.

**Frequency histogram.** A frequency histogram is constructed from raw data by dividing the range of the data (minimum value to maximum value) into nonoverlapping cells. Given the boundaries $(I_{i-1}, I_i)$ for cell $i$, the corresponding frequency is determined as the count (or tally) of all the raw data values, $x$, that satisfy $I_{i-1} < x \le I_i$.

---

**Example 12.6–1.**

The data in the following table represents the service time (in minutes) in a service facility for a sample of 60 customers.

| | | | | | | | | | |
|---|---|---|---|---|---|---|---|---|---|
| .7 | .4 | 3.4 | 4.8 | 2.0 | 1.0 | 5.5 | 6.2 | 1.2 | 4.4 |
| 1.5 | 2.4 | 3.4 | 6.4 | 3.7 | 4.8 | 2.5 | 5.5 | .3 | 8.7 |
| 2.7 | .4 | 2.2 | 2.4 | .5 | 1.7 | 9.3 | 8.0 | 4.7 | 5.9 |
| .7 | 1.6 | 5.2 | .6 | .9 | 3.9 | 3.3 | .2 | .2 | 4.9 |
| 9.6 | 1.9 | 9.1 | 1.3 | 10.6 | 3.0 | .3 | 2.9 | 2.9 | 4.8 |
| 8.7 | 2.4 | 7.2 | 1.5 | 7.9 | 11.7 | 6.3 | 3.8 | 6.9 | 5.3 |

The minimum and maximum values of the data are .2 and 11.7, respectively. We thus choose 12 cells each of width 1 minute in the range $(0, 12)$. The proper selection of the cell width is crucial in capturing the shape of the empirical distribution. Although there are no hard rules for determining the optimal cell width, a general rule of thumb is to use from 10 to 20 cells. In practice, it may be necessary to try different widths before encountering an acceptable histogram (the interactive capability of TORA should prove useful in this regard).

The following table summarizes the histogram information for the given raw data. The relative frequency column, $f_i$, is computed by dividing the entries of the observed frequency column, $o_i$, by the total number of observations $(n = 60)$. For example, $f_1 = \frac{11}{60} = .1833$. The cumulative frequency column, $F_i$, is generated by summing the values of $f_i$ successively. Thus, $F_1 = f_1 = .1833$ and $F_2 = F_1 + f_2 = .1833 + .1333 = .3166$.

| Cell interval | Observations tally | Observed frequency, $o_i$ | Relative frequency, $f_i$ | Cumulative relative frequency, $F_i$ |
|---|---|---|---|---|
| $(0, 1)$ | ⫾⫾⫾ ⫾⫾⫾ ⫾ | 11 | .1883 | .1883 |
| $(1, 2)$ | ⫾⫾⫾ ⫾⫾⫾ | 8 | .1333 | .3166 |
| $(2, 3)$ | ⫾⫾⫾ ⫾⫾⫾⫾ | 9 | .1500 | .4666 |
| $(3, 4)$ | ⫾⫾⫾ ⫾⫾ | 7 | .1167 | .5833 |
| $(4, 5)$ | ⫾⫾⫾ ⫾ | 6 | .1000 | .6833 |
| $(5, 6)$ | ⫾⫾⫾ | 5 | .0833 | .7666 |
| $(6, 7)$ | ⫾⫾⫾⫾ | 4 | .0667 | .8333 |
| $(7, 8)$ | ⫾⫾ | 2 | .0333 | .8666 |
| $(8, 9)$ | ⫾⫾⫾ | 3 | .0500 | .9166 |
| $(9, 10)$ | ⫾⫾⫾ | 3 | .0500 | .9666 |
| $(10, 11)$ | ⫾ | 1 | .0167 | .9833 |
| $(11, 12)$ | ⫾ | 1 | .0167 | 1.000 |
| Totals | | 60 | 1.0000 | |

The value of $f_i$ and $F_i$ provide the equivalences of the pdf and the CDF for the service time, $t$. Because the frequency histogram provides a discretized version of the continuous service time, we can convert the resulting CDF into a piecewise continuous function by joining the resulting points with linear segments. Figure 12–6 provides the empirical pdf and CDF for the example. The CDF, as given by the histogram, is defined at the cells' midpoints.

We can now estimate the mean, $\bar{t}$, and variance, $s_t^2$, of the empirical distribution as follows. Let $N$ be the number of cells in the histogram, and define $\bar{t}_i$ as the midpoint of cell $i$, then

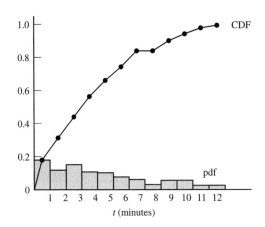

**Figure 12–6**

$$\bar{t} = \sum_{i=1}^{N} f_i \bar{t}_i$$

$$s_t^2 = \sum_{i=1}^{N} f_i(\bar{t}_i - \bar{t})^2$$

Applying these formulas to the present example, we get

$$\bar{t} = .1833 \times .5 + .133 \times 1.5 + \ldots + 11.5 \times .0167 = 3.934 \text{ minutes}$$

$$s_t^2 = .1833 \times (.5 - 3.934)^2 + .133 \times (1.5 - 3.934)^2 + \ldots$$
$$+ .0167 \times (11.5 - 3.934)^2 = 8.646 \text{ minutes}^2$$

**Goodness-of-fit test.** The goodness-of-fit test checks whether the sample used in determining the empirical distribution is drawn from a specific theoretical distribution. An initial evaluation of the data can be made by comparing the empirical CDF with the CDF of the assumed theoretical distribution. If the two CDFs do not deviate from one another excessively, then it is likely that the sample is drawn from the proposed theoretical distribution. This initial "hunch" can be strengthened further by applying the goodness-of-fit test. The following example provides the details of the proposed procedure.

**Example 12.6–2.**

Test the data in Example 12.6–1 for a hypothesized exponential distribution.

Our first task is to specify the function that define the theoretical distribution. Because, as computed in Example 12.6–1, $\bar{t} = 3.934$ minutes, then $\lambda = \frac{1}{3.934} = .2542$ service per munite for the hypothesized exponential distribution (see Section 12.5.3), and the associated pdf and CDF are given as

$$f(t) = .2542e^{-.2542t}, \quad t > 0$$

$$F(T) = \int_0^T f(t)dt = 1 - e^{-.2542T}, \quad T > 0$$

We can use the CDF, $F(T)$, to compute the theoretical CDF for $T = .5, 1.5, \ldots,$ and 11.5, and then compare them graphically with empirical value $F_i, i = 1, 2, \ldots, 12,$ as computed in Example 12.6–1. For example,

$$F(.5) = \; = 1 - e^{-(.2542 \times .5)} \approx .12$$

Figure 12–7 provides the resulting comparison. A cursory examination of the two graphs suggests that the exponential distribution may, indeed, provide a reasonable fit for the observed data.

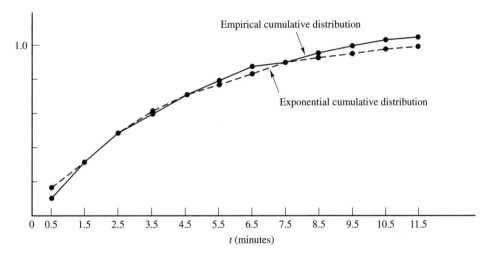

**Figure 12–7**

The next step is to implement a goodness-of-fit test. Two such tests exist: (1) the **Kolmogrov-Smirnov** test, and (2) the **chi-square** test. We will limit our discussion here to the chi-square test.

The chi-square test is based on a measurement of the deviation between the empirical and theoretical frequencies corresponding to the different cells of the developed histogram. Specifically, the theoretical frequency, $n_i$, corresponding to the observed frequency, $o_i$, of cell $i$, is computed as

$$n_i = n\int_{I_{i-1}}^{I_i} f(t)dt$$

$$= n(F(I_i) - F(I_{i-1}))$$

$$= 60(e^{-.2542I_{i-1}} - e^{-.2542I_i})$$

Given $o_i$ and $n_i$ for each cell $i$ of the histogram, a measure of the deviation between the empirical and observed frequencies is computed as

$$\chi^2 = \sum_{i=1}^{N} \frac{(o_i - n_i)^2}{n_i}$$

As $N \to \infty$, $\chi^2$ is asymptotically a chi-square pdf with $N - k - 1$ degrees of freedom, where $k$ is the number of parameters estimated from the raw (or histogrammed) data and used for defining the theoretical distribution.

The null hypothesis stating that the observed sample is drawn from the theoretical distribution $f(t)$ is accepted if

$$\chi^2 < \chi^2_{N-k-1, 1-\alpha}$$

where $\chi^2_{N-k-1, 1-\alpha}$ is the chi-square value for $N - k - 1$ degrees of freedom and $\alpha$ significance level.

The computations of the test are shown in the following table:

| Cell | Observed frequency, $o_i$ | Theoretical frequency, $n_i$ | $\frac{(o_i - n_i)^2}{n_i}$ |
|------|--------------------------|------------------------------|------------------------------|
| (0, 1) | 11 | 13.47 | .435 |
| (1, 2) | 8 | 10.44 | .570 |
| (2, 3) | 9 | 8.10 | .100 |
| (3, 4) | 7 | 6.28 | .083 |
| (4, 5) | 6 | 4.87 | |
| (5, 6) | 5 | 3.88 | |
| (6, 7) | 4 | 2.93 | |
| (7, 8) | 2 | 2.27 | |
| (8, 9) | 3 } 25 | 1.76 } 21.71 | .499 |
| (9, 10) | 3 | 1.37 | |
| (10, 11) | 1 | 1.06 | |
| (11, 12) | 1 | .82 | |
| (12, ∞) | 1 | 2.75 | |
| Totals | $n = 60$ | $n = 60$ | $\chi^2$-value 1.705 |

As a rule of thumb, the expected theoretical frequency in any cell must be at least 5. This requirement is usually resolved by combining successive cells until the rule is satisfied. In the preceding table, the rule requires forming a single (4, ∞)-cell. The resulting number of cells becomes $N = 5$. Because we are estimating one parameter from the observed data (namely, $\lambda$), the degrees of freedom for the chi-square must equal $5 - 1 - 1 = 3$. If we assume a significance level $\alpha = .05$, the chi-square table (Table 3 in Appendix D) yields the critical value $\chi^2_{3,.05} = 7.815$. Because the $\chi^2$-value ($= 1.705$) is less than the critical value, we accept the hypothesis that the sample is drawn from the hypothesized exponential pdf.

---

### Problem set 12.6a

**1.** The following data represent the interarrival time (in minutes) at a service facility:

| 4.3 | 3.4 | .9 | .7 | 5.8 | 3.4 | 2.7 | 7.8 |
|-----|-----|-----|-----|-----|-----|-----|-----|
| 4.4 | .8 | 4.4 | 1.9 | 3.4 | 3.1 | 5.1 | 1.4 |
| .1 | 4.1 | 4.9 | 4.8 | 15.9 | 6.7 | 2.1 | 2.3 |
| 2.5 | 3.3 | 3.8 | 6.1 | 2.8 | 5.9 | 2.1 | 2.8 |
| 3.4 | 3.1 | .4 | 2.7 | .9 | 2.9 | 4.5 | 3.8 |
| 6.1 | 3.4 | 1.1 | 4.2 | 2.9 | 4.6 | 7.2 | 5.1 |
| 2.6 | .9 | 4.9 | 2.4 | 4.1 | 5.1 | 11.5 | 2.6 |
| .1 | 10.3 | 4.3 | 5.1 | 4.3 | 1.1 | 4.1 | 6.7 |
| 2.2 | 2.9 | 5.2 | 8.2 | 1.1 | 3.3 | 2.1 | 7.3 |
| 3.5 | 3.1 | 7.9 | .9 | 5.1 | 6.2 | 5.8 | 1.4 |
| .5 | 4.5 | 6.4 | 1.2 | 2.1 | 10.7 | 3.2 | 2.3 |
| 3.3 | 3.3 | 7.1 | 6.9 | 3.1 | 1.6 | 2.1 | 1.9 |

**(a)** Develop three histograms for the data based on cell widths of .5, 1, and 1.5 minutes, respectively (use TORA for convenience).

**(b)** Compare graphically the cumulative distribution of the empirical CDF and that of a corresponding exponential distribution.

**(c)** Test the hypothesis that the given sample is drawn from an exponential distribution. Use a 95% confidence level.

**(d)** Which of the three histograms is "best" for the purpose of testing the null hypothesis?

**2.** The following data represent the period (in seconds) needed to transmit a message.

| | | | | |
|------|------|------|------|------|
| 25.8 | 67.3 | 35.2 | 36.4 | 58.7 |
| 47.9 | 94.8 | 61.3 | 59.3 | 93.4 |
| 17.8 | 34.7 | 56.4 | 22.1 | 48.1 |
| 48.2 | 35.8 | 65.3 | 30.1 | 72.5 |
| 5.8 | 70.9 | 88.9 | 76.4 | 17.3 |
| 77.4 | 66.1 | 23.9 | 23.8 | 36.8 |
| 5.6 | 36.4 | 93.5 | 36.4 | 76.7 |
| 89.3 | 39.2 | 78.7 | 51.9 | 63.6 |
| 89.5 | 58.6 | 12.8 | 28.6 | 82.7 |
| 38.7 | 71.3 | 21.1 | 35.9 | 29.2 |

Test the hypothesis that these data are drawn from a uniform distribution at a 95% confidence level, given the following additional information about the theoretical uniform distribution:

**(a)** The range of the distribution is between 0 and 100.

**(b)** The range of the distribution is estimated from the sample data.

**(c)** The maximum limit on the range of the distribution is 100, but the minimum limit must be estimated from the sample data.

**3.** An automatic device is used to count the volume of traffic at a busy intersection. The device records the time a car arrives at the intersection on a continuous time scale, starting from zero. The following table provides the (cumulative) arrival time (in minutes) for the first 60 cars. Construct a suitable histogram to test the hypothesis that the interarrival time is drawn from an exponential distribution. Use a 95% confidence level.

| Arrival | Arrival time (min) | Arrival | Arrival time (min) | Arrival | Arrival time (min) | Arrival | Arrival time (min) |
|---------|--------------------|---------|--------------------|---------|--------------------|---------|--------------------|
| 1 | 5.2 | 16 | 67.6 | 31 | 132.7 | 46 | 227.8 |
| 2 | 6.7 | 17 | 69.3 | 32 | 142.3 | 47 | 233.5 |
| 3 | 9.1 | 18 | 78.6 | 33 | 145.2 | 48 | 239.8 |
| 4 | 12.5 | 19 | 86.6 | 34 | 154.3 | 49 | 243.6 |
| 5 | 18.9 | 20 | 91.3 | 35 | 155.6 | 50 | 250.5 |
| 6 | 22.6 | 21 | 97.2 | 36 | 166.2 | 51 | 255.8 |
| 7 | 27.4 | 22 | 97.9 | 37 | 169.2 | 52 | 256.5 |
| 8 | 29.9 | 23 | 111.5 | 38 | 169.5 | 53 | 256.9 |

*Continued*

| Arrival | Arrival time (min) | Arrival | Arrival time (min) | Arrival | Arrival time (min) | Arrival | Arrival time (min) |
|---------|--------------------|---------|--------------------|---------|--------------------|---------|--------------------|
| 9 | 35.4 | 24 | 116.7 | 39 | 172.4 | 54 | 270.3 |
| 10 | 35.7 | 25 | 117.3 | 40 | 175.3 | 55 | 275.1 |
| 11 | 44.4 | 26 | 118.2 | 41 | 180.1 | 56 | 277.1 |
| 12 | 47.1 | 27 | 124.1 | 42 | 188.8 | 57 | 278.1 |
| 13 | 47.5 | 28 | 1127.4 | 43 | 201.2 | 58 | 283.6 |
| 14 | 49.7 | 29 | 127.6 | 44 | 218.4 | 59 | 299.8 |
| 15 | 67.1 | 30 | 127.8 | 45 | 219.9 | 60 | 300.0 |

## 12.7 SUMMARY

This chapter provides a quick review of basic probability theory. It also summarizes the characteristics of the most common discrete and continuous probability distributions. The chapter closes with a presentation of empirical distributions.

## SELECTED REFERENCES

FELLER, W., *An Introduction to Probability Theory and Its Applications,* 2nd ed., Vols. 1 and 2, Wiley, New York, 1967.

PAPOULIS, A., *Probability and Statistics,* Prentice Hall, Upper Saddle River, N.J., 1990

PARZEN, E., *Modern Probability Theory and Its Applications,* Wiley, New York, 1960.

ROSS, S., *Introduction to Probability Models,* 5th ed., Academic Press, New York, 1993.

# Chapter 13

# Forecasting Models

## 13.1 INTRODUCTION

In decision making, we deal with devising future plans. The data describing the decision situation must thus be representative of what occurs in the future. For example, in inventory control, we base our decisions on the nature of demand for the controlled item during a specified planning horizon. Also, in financial planning, we need to predict the pattern of cash flow over time.

This chapter presents three techniques for forecasting future changes in the level of a desired variable as a function of time:

1. Moving average
2. Exponential smoothing
3. Regression

The main symbols used in this chapter are

$y_t$ = Actual (or observed) value of the random variable in period $t$
$y_t^*$ = Estimated value of the random variable in period $t$
$\epsilon_t$ = Random component (or noise) in period $t$

## 13.2 MOVING AVERAGE TECHNIQUE

The underlying assumption for this technique is that the time series is stable, in the sense that its data are generated by the following constant process:

$$y_t = b + \epsilon_t$$

where $b$ is an unknown constant parameter estimated from the historical data. The random error $\epsilon_t$ is assumed to have a zero expected value and a constant variance. Additionally, the data for the different periods are not correlated.

The moving average technique assumes that the most recent $n$ observations are equally important in estimating the parameter $b$. Thus, at a current period $t$, if the data for the most recent $n$ periods are $y_{t-n+1}, y_{t-n+2}, \ldots$, and $y_t$, then the *estimated* value for period $t + 1$ is computed as

$$y^*_{t+1} = \frac{y_{t-n+1} + y_{t-n+2} + \ldots + y_t}{n}$$

There is no exact rule for selecting the moving average base, $n$. If the variations in the variable remain reasonably constant over time, a large $n$ is recommended. Otherwise, a small value of $n$ is advisable if the variable exhibits changing patterns. In practice, the value of $n$ ranges between 2 and 10.

**Example 13.2–1.**

The demand (in number of units) for an inventory item over the past 24 months is summarized in Table 13–1. Use the moving average technique to forecast next month's demand ($t = 25$).

**TABLE 13–1**

| Month, $t$ | Demand, $y_t$ | Month, $t$ | Demand, $y_t$ |
|:---:|:---:|:---:|:---:|
| 1 | 46 | 13 | 54 |
| 2 | 56 | 14 | 42 |
| 3 | 54 | 15 | 64 |
| 4 | 43 | 16 | 60 |
| 5 | 57 | 17 | 70 |
| 6 | 56 | 18 | 66 |
| 7 | 67 | 19 | 57 |
| 8 | 62 | 20 | 55 |
| 9 | 50 | 21 | 52 |
| 10 | 56 | 22 | 62 |
| 11 | 47 | 23 | 70 |
| 12 | 56 | 24 | 72 |

To check the applicability of the moving average technique, we analyze the nature of the given data. Figure 13–1 plots the demand time series, $y_t$. The plot shows that the data exhibit an upward trend with time. Generally speaking, this trend means that the moving average would not be a good predictor of future demand. In particular, the use of a large base, $n$, for the moving average is not advisable in this case because it will suppress the data trend. Conversely, if we use a small $n$, we will be in a better position to capture the nature of the trend in the data.

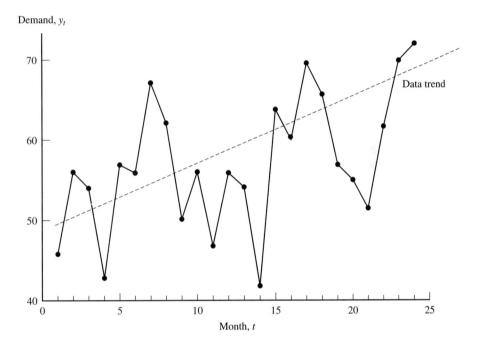

**Figure 13–1**

If we use $n = 3$, the estimated demand for next month ($t = 25$) will equal the average of the demands for months 22 to 24—that is,

$$y_{25}^* = \frac{62 + 70 + 72}{3} = 68 \text{ units}$$

The estimated demand of 68 units for $t = 25$ is also used as an estimate for $t = 26$—that is,

$$x_{26}^* = \frac{70 + 72 + 68}{3} = 70 \text{ units}$$

When the *actual* demand for $t = 25$ becomes known, we should use it to reestimate the demand for $t = 26$ as the average for periods 23, 24, and 25.

**Problem set 13.2a**

1. In Example 13.2–1, estimate the demand for $t = 25$ based on $n = 12$. What effect does larger $n$ have on suppressing the trend of the data?

2. The number of air conditioning units sold over the past 24 months is given in Table 13–2. Analyze the data from the standpoint of the applicability of the moving average technique.

**TABLE 13–2**

| Mo | Sales | Mo | Sales |
|----|-------|----|-------|
| 1  | 25    | 13 | 40    |
| 2  | 15    | 14 | 35    |
| 3  | 30    | 15 | 50    |
| 4  | 38    | 16 | 60    |
| 5  | 58    | 17 | 66    |
| 6  | 62    | 18 | 90    |
| 7  | 85    | 19 | 105   |
| 8  | 88    | 20 | 85    |
| 9  | 60    | 21 | 60    |
| 10 | 40    | 22 | 55    |
| 11 | 40    | 23 | 50    |
| 12 | 38    | 24 | 45    |

3. Table 13–3 gives the number of individuals who visit a tourist area by car and air over a 10-year period. Analyze the data from the standpoint of the applicability of the moving average technique.

**TABLE 13–3**

| Yr  | 1980 | 1981 | 1982 | 1983 | 1984 | 1985 | 1986 | 1987 | 1988 | 1989 |
|-----|------|------|------|------|------|------|------|------|------|------|
| Car | 1042 | 1182 | 1224 | 1338 | 1455 | 1613 | 1644 | 1699 | 1790 | 1885 |
| Air | 500  | 522  | 540  | 612  | 715  | 790  | 840  | 900  | 935  | 980  |

4. Table 13–4 gives the sales in millions of dollars for a department store. Analyze the data from the standpoint of the applicability of the moving average technique.

**TABLE 13–4**

| Yr | 1980 | 1981 | 1982 | 1983 | 1984 | 1985 | 1986 | 1987 | 1988 | 1989 |
|---|---|---|---|---|---|---|---|---|---|---|
| Sales | 21.0 | 23.2 | 23.2 | 24.0 | 24.9 | 25.6 | 26.6 | 27.4 | 28.5 | 29.6 |

**5.** The U of A offers off-campus courses at five different locations around the state. Table 13–5 summarizes the enrollment data over a 6-year period. The data for each year is categorized by semester: fall (1), spring (2), and summer (3). It is desired to use these data to estimate the enrollment for next year. Analyze the given data from the standpoint of the applicability of the moving average technique.

**TABLE 13–5**

|  |  | Course location | | | | |
|---|---|---|---|---|---|---|
| Semester | | 1 | 2 | 3 | 4 | 5 |
| 1989 | | | | | | |
| | 1 | 288 | 136 | 48 | 165 | 59 |
| | 2 | 247 | 150 | 49 | 168 | 46 |
| | 3 | 117 | 69 | 14 | 61 | 15 |
| 1990 | | | | | | |
| | 1 | 227 | 108 | 41 | 108 | 28 |
| | 2 | 239 | 106 | 46 | 128 | 43 |
| | 3 | 101 | 50 | 15 | 54 | 16 |
| 1991 | | | | | | |
| | 1 | 240 | 126 | 31 | 104 | 46 |
| | 2 | 261 | 134 | 19 | 83 | 38 |
| | 3 | 138 | 48 | 9 | 56 | 32 |
| 1992 | | | | | | |
| | 1 | 269 | 149 | 17 | 90 | 51 |
| | 2 | 301 | 113 | 25 | 54 | 28 |
| | 3 | 119 | 50 | 14 | 17 | 6 |

*Continued*

|          | Course location |     |     |     |     |
|----------|-----|-----|-----|-----|-----|
| Semester | 1   | 2   | 3   | 4   | 5   |
| 1993     |     |     |     |     |     |
| 1        | 226 | 102 | 22  | 16  | 30  |
| 2        | 241 | 110 | 16  | 0   | 24  |
| 3        | 125 | 46  | 7   | 0   | 12  |
| 1994     |     |     |     |     |     |
| 1        | 231 | 88  | 2   | 0   | 1   |
| 2        | 259 | 66  | 3   | 0   | 27  |
| 3        | 102 | 23  | 0   | 0   | 0   |

## 13.3 EXPONENTIAL SMOOTHING

The exponential smoothing technique assumes that the process is constant, the same assumption used in the development of the moving average method. However, it is designed to alleviate a drawback in the moving average method, where the same weight on all the data is used in computing the average. Specifically, exponential smoothing places a larger weight on the most recent observation.

Define $\alpha(0 < \alpha < 1)$ as the **smoothing constant,** and assume that the time series points for the past $t$ periods are $y_1, y_2, \ldots, y_t$. Then, $y_{t+1}^*$, the estimate for period $t + 1$ is computed as

$$y_{t+1}^* = \alpha y_t + \alpha(1 - \alpha)y_{t-1} + \alpha(1 - \alpha)^2 y_{t-2} + \ldots$$

Because the respective coefficients of $y_t, y_{t-1}, y_{t-2}, \ldots$ are progressively smaller, the new procedure puts more weight on the more recent data points.

The formula for computing $y_{t+1}^*$ can be simplified as follows:

$$y_{t+1}^* = \alpha y_t + (1 - \alpha)\{\alpha y_{t-1} + \alpha(1 - \alpha)y_{t-2} + \alpha(1 - \alpha)^2 y_{t-3} + \ldots\}$$

$$= \alpha y_t + (1 - \alpha)y_t^*$$

In this manner, $y_{t+1}^*$ can be computed recursively from $y_t^*$. The recursive equation is started by skipping the estimate $y_1^*$ at $t = 1$ and assuming that the estimate for $t = 2$ is taken equal to the actual data value for $t = 1$—that is, $y_2^* = y_1$. Actually, any reasonable procedure can be used to start the computations. For example, some suggest estimating $y_0^*$ as the average of a "reasonable" number of periods at the start of the time series.

The selection of the smoothing constant $\alpha$ is crucial in estimating future forecasts. A large value of $\alpha$ implies that recent observations carry heavier weights. In practice, the value of $\alpha$ lies between .01 and .30.

**Example 13.3–1.**

Apply the exponential smoothing technique to the data in Example 13.2–1. Choose $\alpha = .1$.

Table 13–6 summarizes the results. The computations are started by skipping $y_1^*$ and assuming that $y_2^* = y_1 = 46$ units.

**TABLE  13–6**

| $i$ | $y_i$ | $y_i^*$ | $i$ | $y_i$ | $y_i^*$ |
|---|---|---|---|---|---|
| 1 | 46 | — | 13 | 54 | .1(56) + .9(51.63) = 52.07 |
| 2 | 56 | 46 | 14 | 42 | .1(54) + .9(52.07) = 52.26 |
| 3 | 54 | .1(56) + .9(46) = 47 | 15 | 64 | .1(42) + .9(52.26) = 51.23 |
| 4 | 43 | .1(54) + .9(47) = 47.7 | 16 | 60 | .1(64) + .9(51.23) = 52.50 |
| 5 | 57 | .1(43) + .9(47.7) = 47.23 | 17 | 70 | .1(60) + .9(52.50) = 53.26 |
| 6 | 56 | .1(57) + .9(47.23) = 48.21 | 18 | 66 | .1(70) + .9(53.26) = 54.93 |
| 7 | 67 | .1(56) + .9(48.21) = 48.98 | 19 | 57 | .1(66) + .9(54.93) = 56.04 |
| 8 | 62 | .1(67) + .9(48.98) = 50.79 | 20 | 55 | .1(57) + .9(56.04) = 56.14 |
| 9 | 50 | .1(62) + .9(50.79) = 51.91 | 21 | 52 | .1(55) + .9(56.14) = 56.02 |
| 10 | 56 | .1(50) + .9(51.91) = 51.72 | 22 | 62 | .1(52) + .9(56.02) = 55.62 |
| 11 | 47 | .1(56) + .9(51.72) = 52.15 | 23 | 70 | .1(62) + .9(55.62) = 56.26 |
| 12 | 56 | .1(47) + .9(52.15) = 51.63 | 24 | 72 | .1(70) + .9(56.26) = 57.63 |

From the given computations, the estimate for $t = 25$ is computed as

$$y_{25}^* = \alpha y_{24} + (1 - \alpha)y_{24}^*$$

$$= .1(72) + .9(57.63) = 59.07 \text{units}$$

This estimate is considerably different from that given by the moving average ($= 68$ units). A larger value of $\alpha$ will produce a closer estimate for $t = 25$.

## Problem set 13.3a

**1.** Apply exponential smoothing to the data of Problem 13.2a–2. Use $\alpha = .2$.
**2.** Apply exponential smoothing to the data of Problem 13.2a–3. Use $\alpha = .2$.
**3.** Apply exponential smoothing to the data of Problem 13.2a–4. Use $\alpha = .2$.
**4.** Apply exponential smoothing to the data of Problem 13.2a–5. Use $\alpha = .2$.

## 13.4 REGRESSION

Regression analysis determines the relationship between a *dependent* variable (e.g., demand for an item) and an *independent* variable (e.g., time). The general regression formula between the dependent variable $x$ and the independent variable $y$ is given as

$$y = b_0 + b_1x + b_2x^2 + \ldots + b_nx^n + \epsilon$$

where $b_0, b_1, \ldots, b_n$ are unknown parameters. The random error $\epsilon$ has a zero mean and a constant standard deviation.

The simplest form of the regression model assumes that the dependent variable varies linearly with time—that is,

$$y^* = a + bx$$

The constants $a$ and $b$ are determined from the time series data based on the **least-square criterion** that seeks to minimize the sum of the square of the differences between the observed and the estimated values. Let $(y_i, x_i)$ represent the $i$th point of the raw data representing the time series, $i = 1, 2, \ldots, n$, and define

$$S = \sum_{i=1}^{n} (y_i - a - bx_i)^2$$

as the sum of the square of the deviations between the observed and estimated values. The values of $a$ and $b$ are determined by solving the following necessary conditions for the minimization of $S$—that is,

$$\frac{\partial S}{\partial a} = -2\sum_{i=1}^{n} (y_i - a - bx_i) = 0$$

$$\frac{\partial S}{\partial b} = -2\sum_{i=1}^{n} (y_i - a - bx_i)x_i = 0$$

After some algebraic manipulations, we obtain the following solution:

$$b = \frac{\sum_{i=1}^{n} y_i x_i - n\overline{y}\overline{x}}{\sum_{i=1}^{n} x_i^2 - n\overline{x}^2}$$

$$a = \overline{y} - b\overline{x}$$

where

$$\bar{x} = \frac{\sum\limits_{i=1}^{n} x_i}{n}$$

$$\bar{y} = \frac{\sum\limits_{i=1}^{n} y_i}{n}$$

The equations show that we need to compute $b$ first, from which the value of $a$ can be computed.

The estimates of $a$ and $b$ are valid for any probabilistic distribution of $y_i$. However, if $y_i$ is normally distributed with a constant standard deviation, a confidence interval can be established on the mean value of the estimator at $x = x^0$ (i.e., $y^0 = a + bx^0$) as

$$(a + bx^0) \pm t_{\alpha/2,\,n-2} \sqrt{\frac{\sum\limits_{i=1}^{n}(y_i - y_i^*)^2}{n - 2}} \sqrt{\frac{1}{n} + \frac{(x^0 - \bar{x})^2}{\sum\limits_{i=1}^{n} x_i^2 - n\bar{x}^2}}$$

The expression $(y_i - y_i^*)$ represents the deviation between the $i$th observed and estimated values of the dependent variable.

For future predicted values of the dependent variable, $y$, we are interested in determining its **prediction interval** (rather than the confidence interval on its mean value). As would be expected, the prediction interval of a future value is wider than the confidence interval on the mean value. Indeed, the formula for the prediction interval is the same as that of the confidence interval except that the term $\frac{1}{n}$ under the second square root is replaced with $\frac{(n + 1)}{n}$.

We can test how well the linear estimator $y^* = a + bx$ fits the raw data by computing the *correlation coefficient, r,* using the formula

$$r = \frac{\sum\limits_{i=1}^{n} y_i x_i = -n\bar{y}\,\bar{x}}{\sqrt{\left(\sum\limits_{i=1}^{n} x_i^2 - n\bar{x}^2\right)\left(\sum\limits_{i=1}^{n} y_i^2 - n\bar{y}^2\right)}}$$

where $-1 \leq r \leq 1$.

If $r = \pm 1$, then a perfect linear fit occurs between $x$ and $y$. In general, the closer the value of $|r|$ to 1, the better is the linear fit. If $r = 0$, then $y$ and $x$ may be independent. Actually, $r = 0$ is only a necessary but not sufficient condition for independence, as it is possible for two *dependent* variables to yield $r = 0$.

---

**Example 13.4–1.**

Apply the linear regression model to the data in Example 13.2–1, which are repeated in Table 13–7 for convenience.

**TABLE 13–7**

| Mo, $x_i$ | Demand, $y_i$ | Mo, $x_i$ | Demand, $y_i$ |
|-----------|---------------|-----------|---------------|
| 1         | 46            | 13        | 54            |
| 2         | 56            | 14        | 42            |
| 3         | 54            | 15        | 64            |
| 4         | 43            | 16        | 60            |
| 5         | 57            | 17        | 70            |
| 6         | 56            | 18        | 66            |
| 7         | 67            | 19        | 57            |
| 8         | 62            | 20        | 55            |
| 9         | 50            | 21        | 52            |
| 10        | 56            | 22        | 62            |
| 11        | 47            | 23        | 70            |
| 12        | 56            | 24        | 72            |

From the data in Table 13–7, we get

$$\sum_{i=1}^{24} y_i x_i = 17{,}842 , \sum_{i=1}^{24} x_i = 300, \sum_{i=1}^{24} x_i^2 = 4900$$

$$\sum_{i=1}^{24} y_i = 1374, \sum_{i=1}^{24} y_i^2 = 80{,}254$$

Hence,

$$\bar{x} = 12.5, \bar{y} = 57.25$$

$$b = \frac{17{,}842 - 24 \times 57.25 \times 12.5}{4900 - 24 \times 12.5^2} = .58$$

$$a = 57.25 - .58 + 12.5 = 50$$

The estimated demand is thus given as

$$y^* = 50 + .58x$$

For example, at $x = 25$, $y^* = 50 + .58(25) = 64.5$ units.
The correlation coefficient is computed as

$$r = \frac{17,842 - 24 \times 57.25 \times 12.5}{\sqrt{4900 - 24 \times 12.5^2)(80,254 - 24 \times 57.25^2)}} = .493$$

The relatively low value of $r$ shows that $y^* = 50 + .58x$ may not be a good linear fit for the raw data. Normally, a reasonable fit requires $.75 \le |r| \le 1$.

Suppose that we wish to compute the 95% confidence interval for the given linear estimator. First, we need to compute the sum of the squares of the deviations about the fitted line. Table 13–8 summarizes this information.

From the $t$-tables in Appendix D, we get

**TABLE  13–8**

| $x$ | $y$ | $y^*$ | $(y - y^*)^2$ |
|-----|-----|-------|---------------|
| 1 | 46 | 50.58 | 20.98 |
| 2 | 56 | 51.16 | 23.43 |
| 3 | 54 | 51.74 | 5.11 |
| 4 | 43 | 54.32 | 86.86 |
| 5 | 57 | 52.90 | 16.81 |
| 6 | 56 | 53.48 | 6.35 |
| 7 | 67 | 54.06 | 152.77 |
| 8 | 62 | 54.64 | 54.17 |
| 9 | 50 | 55.22 | 27.25 |
| 10 | 56 | 55.80 | 0.04 |
| 11 | 47 | 56.38 | 87.98 |
| 12 | 56 | 56.96 | 0.92 |
| 13 | 54 | 57.54 | 12.53 |
| 14 | 42 | 58.12 | 259.85 |
| 15 | 64 | 58.70 | 28.09 |
| 16 | 60 | 59.28 | 0.52 |
| 17 | 70 | 59.86 | 102.82 |
| 18 | 66 | 60.44 | 30.91 |

*Continued*

| $x$ | $y$ | $y^*$ | $(y - y^*)^2$ |
|-----|-----|-------|---------------|
| 19  | 57  | 61.02 | 16.16         |
| 20  | 55  | 61.60 | 43.56         |
| 21  | 52  | 62.18 | 103.63        |
| 22  | 62  | 62.76 | 0.58          |
| 23  | 70  | 63.34 | 44.53         |
| 24  | 72  | 63.92 | 65.29         |

$$\sum_{i=1}^{24} (y_i - y_i^*)^2 = 1088.70$$

$$t_{.025,\,22} = 2.074$$

Hence, the desired confidence interval is computed as

$$(50 + 58x^0) \pm 2.074 \sqrt{\frac{1088.7}{24 - 2}} \sqrt{\frac{1}{24} + \frac{(x^0 - 12.5)^2}{4900 - 24 \times 12.5^2}}$$

This can be simplified to

$$(50 + .58x^0) \pm 14.59 \sqrt{.042 + \frac{(x^0 - 12.5)^2}{1150}}$$

To illustrate the computation of the prediction interval, suppose that we are interested in establishing a prediction interval on the demand estimate for next month ($x^0 = 25$). In this case, the coefficient .042 must be replaced with 1.042, and the resulting prediction interval is computed as ($64.5 \pm 15.82$) or ($46.68, 80.32$). We thus say that there is a 95% chance that the demand at $x = 25$ will fall between 46.68 units and 80.32 units).

## Problem set 13.4a

1. Apply linear regression to the data of Problem 13.2a–2.
2. Apply linear regression to the data of Problem 13.2a–3.
3. Apply linear regression to the data of Problem 13.2a–4.
4. Apply linear regression to the data of Problem 13.2a–5.
5. In linear regression, prove that the sum of differences between the predicted and estimated values over all the data points always equals zero—that is,

$$\sum_{i=1}^{n} (y_i - y_i^*) = 0$$

## 13.5 SUMMARY

This chapter presents three forecasting techniques: the moving average, exponential smoothing, and regression. Each technique is suitable for specific characteristics of the time series representing the historical data. There are other forecasting techniques available in the literature. For example, the exponential smoothing method can be modified to account for both seasonal variations and for trends.

## SELECTED REFERENCES

BROWN, R.G., *Smoothing, Forecasting, and Prediction of Discrete Time Series,* Prentice Hall, Upper Saddle River, N.J., 1972.

MONTGOMERY, D., and E. PECK, *Introduction to Linear Regression Analysis,* Wiley, New York, 1991.

WILLIS, R. E., *A Guide to Forecasting for Planners and Managers,* Prentice Hall, Upper Saddle River, N.J., 1987.

## COMPREHENSIVE PROBLEM

■ **13–1**  A published argument advocates that the recent rise in the mean score of the Scholastic Aptitude Test (SAT) for high school students in the United States is attributed to demographic reasons rather than to improvement in teaching methods. Specifically, the argument states that the decrease in the number of children per family has created environments in which kids are interacting more frequently with adults (namely, their parents), which increases their intellectual skills. Conversely, children of large families are not as "privileged" intellectually because of the immature influence of their siblings.

What is your opinion regarding the development of a predictive regression equation for the SAT scores based on this argument?

# Chapter 14

# Decision Analysis and Games

## 14.1 DECISION ENVIRONMENTS

Decision analysis involves the use of a rational process for selecting the best of several alternatives. The "goodness" of a selected alternative depends on the quality of the data used in describing the decision situation. From this standpoint, a decision-making process can fall into one of three categories.

**1.** Decision-making under **certainty** in which the data are known deterministically.

**2.** Decision-making under **risk** in which the data can be described by probability distributions.

**3.** Decision-making under **uncertainty** in which the data cannot be assigned relative weights that represent their degree of relevance in the decision process.

In effect, under certainty, the data are well defined, and under uncertainty, the data are ambiguous. Decision-making under risk thus represents the "middle-of-the-road" case.

This chapter presents selected decision models of the three categories.

## 14.2 DECISION-MAKING UNDER CERTAINTY

Linear programming models (Chapters 2 to 8) provide an example of decision making under certainty. These models are suitable for only situations in which the decision alternatives can be interrelated by well-defined mathematical linear functions. This section presents a different approach for the situations in which ideas, feelings, and emotions are quantified to provide a numeric scale for prioritizing decision alternatives. The approach is known as the analytic hierarchy approach (AHP).

### 14.2.1 Analytic Hierarchy Approach

Before presenting the details of AHP, we use an example that demonstrates the manner in which the various decision alternatives are evaluated.

---

**Example 14.2–1.**

Martin Hans, a bright high school senior, has received full academic scholarships from three institutions: U of A, U of B, and U of C. To select a university, Martin lists two main criteria: location and academic reputation. Being the excellent student he is, he judges academic reputation to be five times as important as location, which gives a weight of approximately 83% to reputation and 17% to location. He then uses a systematic analysis (which will be detailed later) to rank the three universities from the standpoint of location and reputation. The analysis produces the following estimates:

> *Location.*   U of A (12.9%), U of B (27.7%), and U of C (59.4%)
> *Reputation.* U of A (54.5%), U of B (27.3%), and U of C (18.2%)

The structure of the decision problem is summarized in Figure 14–1. The problem involves a single hierarchy (level) with two criteria (location and reputation) and three decision alternatives (U of A, U of B, and U of C).

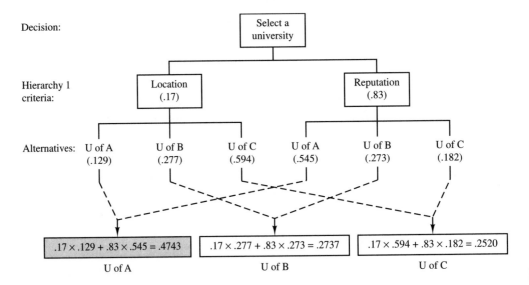

**Figure 14–1**

The ranking of the three universities is based on computing a *composite* weight for each university as:

U of A = .17 × .129 + .83 × .545 = **.4743**

U of B = .17 × .277 + .83 × .273 = .2737

U of C = .17 × .594 + .83 × .182 = .2520

On the basis of these calculations, U of A has the highest composite weight, and hence represents the most likely choice for Martin.

---

The general structure of AHP may include several hierarchies of criteria. Suppose in Example 14.2–1 that Martin's twin sister, Jane, was also accepted with full scholarships to the three universities. However, their parents stipulate that they both must attend the same university so they can share one car. Figure 14–2 summarizes the decision problem, which now involves two hierarchies of criteria. The values $p$ and $q$ (presumably equal) at the first hierarchy represent the relative weights given to Jane's and Martin's opinions about the selection process. The second hierarchy uses the weights $(p_1, p_2)$ and $(q_1, q_2)$ to reflect Martin's and Jane's individual opinions about the criteria of location and reputation of each university. The remainder of the decision structure can be interpreted similarly. Note that $p + q = 1$, $p_1 + p_2 = 1$, $q_1 + q_2 = 1$, $p_{11} + p_{12} + p_{13} = 1$, $p_{21} + p_{22} + p_{23} = 1$, $q_{11} + q_{12} + q_{13} = 1$, $q_{21} + q_{22} + q_{23} = 1$. The determination of the U of A composite weight, shown in Figure 14–2, demonstrates the manner in which the computations are carried out.

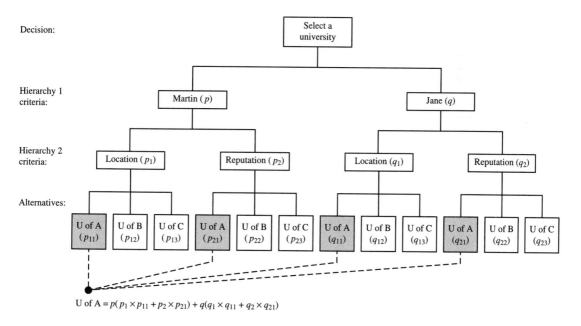

$$\text{U of A} = p(p_1 \times p_{11} + p_2 \times p_{21}) + q(q_1 \times q_{11} + q_2 \times q_{21})$$

**Figure 14–2**

**Problem set 14.2a**

1. Suppose that the following weights are specified for the situation of Martin and Jane:

$$p = .5, q = .5$$

$$p_1 = .17, p_2 = .83$$

$$p_{11} = .129, p_{12} = .277, p_{13} = .594$$

$$p_{21} = .545, p_{22} = .273, p_{23} = .182$$

$$q_1 = .3, q_2 = .7$$

$$q_{11} = .2, q_{12} = .3, q_{13} = .5$$

$$q_{21} = .5, q_{22} = .2, q_{23} = .3$$

Based on this information, rank the three universities.

**Determination of the weights.**    The crux of AHP is the determination of the relative weights used in Example 14.2–1 to rank the decision alternatives. Assuming that we are dealing with $n$ criteria at a given hierarchy, the procedure establishes an $n \times n$ *pairwise comparison matrix*, $\mathbf{A}$, that reflects the decision maker's judgment of the relative importance of the different criteria. The pairwise comparison is made such that the criterion in row $i$ ($i = 1, 2, ..., n$) is ranked relative to each of the criteria represented by the $n$ columns. Letting $a_{ij}$ define the element $(i, j)$ of $\mathbf{A}$, AHP proposes the use of a discrete scale from 1 to 9 in which $a_{ij} = 1$ signifies that $i$ and $j$ are *equally important*, $a_{ij} = 5$ reflects the opinion that $i$ is *strongly more important* than $j$, and $a_{ij} = 9$ indicates that $i$ is *extremely more important* than $j$. Other intermediate values between 1 and 9 are interpreted correspondingly. For consistency, $a_{ij} = k$ should automatically imply that $a_{ji} = \frac{1}{k}$. Also, all the diagonal elements $a_{ii}$ of $\mathbf{A}$ must equal 1 because they rank a criterion relative to itself.

---

**Example 14.2–2.**

We show how the comparison matrix $\mathbf{A}$ is determined for Martin's decision problem of Example 14.2–1. We start with the main hierarchy dealing with the criteria of reputation and location of a university. In Martin's judgment, the reputation of a university is *strongly more important* than its location, and hence he assigns the entry $(1, 2)$ of $\mathbf{A}$ the value 5—that is, $a_{12} = 5$. This assignment automatically implies that $a_{21} = \frac{1}{5}$. Letting $R$ and $L$ represent the criteria of reputation and location, the associated comparison matrix is given as

$$\mathbf{A} = \begin{array}{c} \\ R \\ L \end{array} \begin{array}{cc} R & L \\ \left[ \begin{array}{cc} 1 & 5 \\ \frac{1}{5} & 1 \end{array} \right] \end{array}$$

The relative weights of $R$ and $L$ can be determined from $\mathbf{A}$ by dividing the elements of each column by the sum of the elements of the same column. Thus, we divide the elements of columns 1 by $(1 + \frac{1}{5} = 1.2)$ and those of column 2 by $(5 + 1 = 6)$ to normalize **A**. The desired relative weights, $w_R$ and $w_L$, are then computed as the row average of the resulting normalized matrix. Thus,

$$
\begin{array}{cc}
 & R \quad L \qquad\qquad \text{Row Averages} \\
\mathbf{N} = \begin{array}{c} R \\ L \end{array} \begin{bmatrix} .83 & .83 \\ .17 & .17 \end{bmatrix} & \begin{array}{l} w_R = (.83 + .83) \div 2 = .83 \\ w_L = (.17 + .17) \div 2 = .17 \end{array}
\end{array}
$$

The computations yield $w_R = .83$ and $w_L = .17$, the weight used in Figure 14–1. The columns of **N** are identical, a characteristic that occurs only when the decision maker exhibits perfect *consistency* in specifying the entries of the comparison matrix **A**. This point is discussed further subsequently.

The relative weights of the alternatives U of A, U of B, and U of C are determined within each of the $R$ and $L$ criteria using the following two comparison matrices:

$$
\mathbf{A}_R = \begin{array}{c} \\ A \\ B \\ C \end{array} \begin{array}{c} A \quad B \quad C \\ \begin{bmatrix} 1 & 2 & 3 \\ \dfrac{1}{2} & 1 & \dfrac{3}{2} \\ \dfrac{1}{3} & \dfrac{2}{3} & 1 \end{bmatrix} \end{array}
$$

Column sums $= [1.83, 3.67, 5.5]$

$$
\mathbf{A}_L = \begin{array}{c} \\ A \\ B \\ C \end{array} \begin{array}{c} A \quad B \quad C \\ \begin{bmatrix} 1 & \dfrac{1}{2} & \dfrac{1}{5} \\ 2 & 1 & \dfrac{1}{2} \\ 5 & 2 & 1 \end{bmatrix} \end{array}
$$

Column sums $= [8, 3.5, 1.7]$

The elements of $\mathbf{A}_R$ and $\mathbf{A}_L$ are determined based on Martin's judgment regarding relative importance of the three universities.

Dividing all the entries by the sum of the elements in their respective columns, we obtain the following normalized matrices:

$$
\begin{array}{cc}
 & \quad A \quad\quad B \quad\quad C \qquad\qquad \text{Row Averages} \\
\mathbf{N}_R = \begin{array}{c} A \\ B \\ C \end{array} \begin{bmatrix} .545 & .545 & .545 \\ .273 & .273 & .273 \\ .182 & .182 & .182 \end{bmatrix} & \begin{array}{l} w_{RA} = (.545 + .545 + .545) \div 3 = .545 \\ w_{RB} = (.273 + .273 + .273) \div 3 = .273 \\ w_{RC} = (.182 + .182 + .182) \div 3 = .182 \end{array}
\end{array}
$$

$$
\begin{array}{cc}
 & \quad A \quad\quad B \quad\quad C \qquad\qquad \text{Row Averages} \\
\mathbf{N}_L = \begin{array}{c} A \\ B \\ C \end{array} \begin{bmatrix} .125 & .143 & .118 \\ .250 & .286 & .294 \\ .625 & .571 & .588 \end{bmatrix} & \begin{array}{l} w_{LA} = (.125 + .143 + .118) \div 3 = .129 \\ w_{LB} = (.250 + .286 + .294) \div 3 = .277 \\ w_{LC} = (.625 + .571 + .588) \div 3 = .594 \end{array}
\end{array}
$$

The values $(w_{RA}, w_{RB}, w_{RC}) = (.545, .273, .182)$ give the respective weights for U of A, U of B, and U of C from the standpoint of academic reputation. Similarly, $(w_{LA}, w_{LB}, w_{LC}) = (.129, .277, .594)$ provide the relative weights regarding location.

---

**Consistency of the comparison matrix.** In Example 14.2–2, we notice that all the columns of the normalized matrices $\mathbf{N}$ and $\mathbf{N}_R$ are identical, and those of $\mathbf{N}_L$ are not. Identical columns indicate that the resulting relative weights remain the same regardless of how the comparison is made. As such, the original comparison matrices $\mathbf{A}$ and $\mathbf{A}_R$ are said to be *consistent*. Matrix $\mathbf{A}_L$ thus is not consistent.

Consistency means that the decision is exhibiting coherent judgment in specifying the pairwise comparison of the criteria or alternatives. Mathematically, we say that a comparison matrix $\mathbf{A}$ is consistent if

$$a_{ij}a_{jk} = a_{ik}, \text{ for all } i, j, \text{ and } k$$

For example, in matrix $\mathbf{A}_R$ of Example 14.2–2, $a_{13} = 3$ and $a_{12}a_{23} = 2 \times \frac{3}{2} = 3$. This property requires all the columns (and rows) of $\mathbf{A}$ to be linearly dependent. In particular, the columns of any $2 \times 2$ comparison matrix are dependent, and hence a $2 \times 2$ matrix is always consistent.

It is unusual for all comparison matrices to be consistent. Indeed, given that human judgment is the basis for the construction of these matrices, some degree of inconsistency is expected and should be tolerated provided that it is not "unreasonable."

To determine whether or not a level of consistency is "reasonable," we need to develop a quantifiable measure for the comparison matrix $\mathbf{A}$. We have seen in Example 14.2–2 that a perfectly consistent $\mathbf{A}$ produces a normalized matrix $\mathbf{N}$ in which all the columns are identical—that is,

$$\mathbf{N} = \begin{bmatrix} w_1 & w_1 & \cdots & w_1 \\ w_2 & w_2 & \cdots & w_2 \\ \vdots & \vdots & \vdots & \vdots \\ w_n & w_n & \cdots & w_n \end{bmatrix}$$

It then follows that the corresponding comparison matrix $\mathbf{A}$ can be determined from $\mathbf{N}$ by dividing the elements of column $i$ by $w_i$ (which is the reverse process of determining $\mathbf{N}$ from $\mathbf{A}$). We thus have

$$\mathbf{A} = \begin{bmatrix} 1 & \dfrac{w_1}{w_2} & \cdots & \dfrac{w_1}{w_n} \\ \dfrac{w_2}{w_1} & 1 & \cdots & \dfrac{w_2}{w_n} \\ \vdots & \vdots & \vdots & \vdots \\ \dfrac{w_n}{w_1} & \dfrac{w_n}{w_2} & \cdots & 1 \end{bmatrix}$$

From the given definition of $\mathbf{A}$, we have

$$
\begin{bmatrix}
1 & \dfrac{w_1}{w_2} & \cdots & \dfrac{w_1}{w_n} \\[2mm]
\dfrac{w_2}{w_1} & 1 & \cdots & \dfrac{w_2}{w_n} \\[2mm]
\vdots & \vdots & \vdots & \vdots \\[2mm]
\dfrac{w_n}{w_1} & \dfrac{w_n}{w_2} & \cdots & 1
\end{bmatrix}
\begin{bmatrix} w_1 \\ w_2 \\ \vdots \\ w_n \end{bmatrix}
=
\begin{bmatrix} nw_1 \\ nw_2 \\ \vdots \\ nw_n \end{bmatrix}
= n
\begin{bmatrix} w_1 \\ w_2 \\ \vdots \\ w_n \end{bmatrix}
$$

More compactly, we say that $\mathbf{A}$ is consistent if, and only if,

$$\mathbf{A}\mathbf{w} = n\mathbf{w}$$

where $\mathbf{w}$ is a column vector of the relative weights $w_i, i = 1, 2, \ldots, n$.

For the case where $\mathbf{A}$ is not consistent, the relative weight, $w_i$, is approximated by the average of the $n$ elements of row $i$ in the normalized matrix $\mathbf{N}$ (see Example 14.2–2). Letting $\overline{\mathbf{w}}$ be the computed estimate, it can be shown that

$$\mathbf{A}\overline{\mathbf{w}} = n_{\max}\overline{\mathbf{w}}$$

where $n_{\max} \geq n$. In this case, the closer $n_{\max}$ is to $n$, the more consistent is the comparison matrix $\mathbf{A}$. As a result, AHP computes the *consistency ratio* as

$$CR = \frac{CI}{RI}$$

where

$$CI = \text{Consistency index of } \mathbf{A}$$

$$= \frac{n_{\max} - n}{n - 1}$$

$$RI = \text{Random consistency index of } \mathbf{A}$$

$$= \frac{1.98(n - 2)}{n}$$

The random consistency index, $RI$, was determined empirically as the average $CI$ of a large sample of randomly generated comparison matrices, $\mathbf{A}$.

The ratio $CR$ is used to test consistency as follows. If $CR \leq .1$, the level of inconsistency is acceptable. Otherwise, the inconsistency in $\mathbf{A}$ is high and the decision maker is advised to check the pairwise comparison elements $a_{ij}$ of $\mathbf{A}$ to produce a more consistent matrix.

The value of $n_{\max}$ is computed from $\mathbf{A}\overline{\mathbf{w}} = n_{\max}\overline{\mathbf{w}}$ by observing that the $i$th equation is

$$\sum_{j=1}^{n} a_{ij}\overline{w}_j = n_{\max}\overline{w}_i, \quad i = 1, 2, \ldots, n$$

Given $\sum_{i=1}^{n} \overline{w}_i = 1$, we get

$$\sum_{i=1}^{n}\left(\sum_{j=1}^{n} a_{ij}\,\overline{w}_j\right) = n_{\max}\sum_{i=1}^{n}\overline{w}_i = n_{\max}$$

This means that the value of $n_{\max}$ can be determined by first computing the column vector $\mathbf{A}\overline{\mathbf{w}}$ and then summing its elements.

---

**Example 14.2–3.**

In Example 14.2–2, the matrix $\mathbf{A}_L$ is inconsistent because the columns of its $\mathbf{N}_L$ are not identical. Test the consistency of $\mathbf{N}_L$.

We start by computing $n_{\max}$. From Example 14.2–2, we have

$$\overline{w}_1 = .129, \overline{w}_2 = .277, \overline{w}_3 = .594$$

Thus,

$$\mathbf{A}_L\overline{w} = \begin{bmatrix} 1 & \frac{1}{2} & \frac{1}{5} \\ 2 & 1 & \frac{1}{2} \\ 3 & 2 & 1 \end{bmatrix}\begin{bmatrix} .129 \\ .277 \\ .594 \end{bmatrix} = \begin{bmatrix} 0.3863 \\ 0.8320 \\ 1.7930 \end{bmatrix}$$

This yields

$$n_{\max} = .3863 + .8320 + 1.793 = 3.0113$$

Hence, for n = 3,

$$CI = \frac{n_{\max} - n}{n - 1} = \frac{3.0113 - 3}{3 - 1} = .00565$$

$$RI = \frac{1.98(n - 2)}{n} = \frac{1.98 \times 1}{3} = .66$$

$$CR = \frac{CI}{RI} = \frac{.00565}{.66} = .00856$$

Because $CR < .1$, the level of inconsistency in $\mathbf{A}_L$ is acceptable.

---

### Problem set 14.2b

**1.** The personnel department at C&H has narrowed the search for a prospective employee to three candidates: Steve ($S$), Jane ($J$), and Maisa ($M$). The final selection is based on three criteria: personal interview ($I$), experience ($E$), and references ($R$). The department uses matrix $\mathbf{A}$ (given subsequently) to establish the preferences among the three criteria. After interviewing the three candidates and compiling the data regarding their experiences and references, the matrices $\mathbf{A}_I, \mathbf{A}_E$, and $\mathbf{A}_R$ are constructed. Which of the three candidates should be hired? Assess the consistency of the data.

$$\mathbf{A} = \begin{array}{c} \\ I \\ E \\ R \end{array} \begin{array}{ccc} I & E & R \\ \left[\begin{array}{ccc} 1 & 2 & \dfrac{1}{4} \\ \dfrac{1}{2} & 1 & \dfrac{1}{5} \\ 4 & 5 & 1 \end{array}\right] \end{array} \qquad \mathbf{A}_I = \begin{array}{c} \\ S \\ J \\ M \end{array} \begin{array}{ccc} S & J & M \\ \left[\begin{array}{ccc} 1 & 3 & 4 \\ \dfrac{1}{3} & 1 & \dfrac{1}{5} \\ \dfrac{1}{4} & 5 & 1 \end{array}\right] \end{array}$$

$$\mathbf{A}_E = \begin{array}{c} \\ S \\ J \\ M \end{array} \begin{array}{ccc} S & J & M \\ \left[\begin{array}{ccc} 1 & \dfrac{1}{3} & 2 \\ 3 & 1 & \dfrac{1}{2} \\ \dfrac{1}{2} & 2 & 1 \end{array}\right] \end{array} \qquad \mathbf{A}_R = \begin{array}{c} \\ S \\ J \\ M \end{array} \begin{array}{ccc} S & J & M \\ \left[\begin{array}{ccc} 1 & \dfrac{1}{2} & 1 \\ 2 & 1 & \dfrac{1}{2} \\ 1 & 2 & 1 \end{array}\right] \end{array}$$

2. Kevin and June Park ($K$ and $J$) are in the process of buying a new house. Three houses, $A$, $B$, and $C$, are available. The Parks have agreed on two criteria for the selection of the house: yard work ($Y$) and proximity to work ($W$), and have developed the following comparison matrices. Rank the three houses in order of priority, and compute the consistency ratio for each matrix.

$$\mathbf{A} = \begin{array}{c} \\ K \\ J \end{array} \begin{array}{cc} K & J \\ \left[\begin{array}{cc} 1 & 2 \\ \dfrac{1}{2} & 1 \end{array}\right] \end{array}$$

$$\mathbf{A}_K = \begin{array}{c} \\ Y \\ W \end{array} \begin{array}{cc} Y & W \\ \left[\begin{array}{cc} 1 & \dfrac{1}{3} \\ 3 & 1 \end{array}\right] \end{array}$$

$$\mathbf{A}_J = \begin{array}{c} \\ Y \\ W \end{array} \begin{array}{cc} Y & W \\ \left[\begin{array}{cc} 1 & 4 \\ \dfrac{1}{4} & 1 \end{array}\right] \end{array}$$

$$\mathbf{A}_{KY} = \begin{array}{c} \\ A \\ B \\ C \end{array} \begin{array}{ccc} A & B & C \\ \left[\begin{array}{ccc} 1 & 2 & 3 \\ \dfrac{1}{2} & 1 & 2 \\ \dfrac{1}{3} & \dfrac{1}{2} & 1 \end{array}\right] \end{array}$$

$$
\mathbf{A}_{KW} = \begin{array}{c} \\ A \\ B \\ C \end{array} \overset{\begin{array}{ccc} A & B & C \end{array}}{\begin{bmatrix} 1 & 2 & \frac{1}{2} \\ \frac{1}{2} & 1 & \frac{1}{3} \\ 2 & 3 & 1 \end{bmatrix}}
$$

$$
\mathbf{A}_{JY} = \begin{array}{c} \\ A \\ B \\ C \end{array} \overset{\begin{array}{ccc} A & B & C \end{array}}{\begin{bmatrix} 1 & 4 & 2 \\ \frac{1}{4} & 1 & 3 \\ \frac{1}{2} & \frac{1}{3} & 1 \end{bmatrix}}
$$

$$
\mathbf{A}_{JW} = \begin{array}{c} \\ A \\ B \\ C \end{array} \overset{\begin{array}{ccc} A & B & C \end{array}}{\begin{bmatrix} 1 & \frac{1}{2} & 4 \\ 2 & 1 & 3 \\ \frac{1}{4} & \frac{1}{3} & 1 \end{bmatrix}}
$$

**3.** A new author sets three criteria for selecting a publisher for an OR textbook: royalty percentage ($R$), marketing ($M$), and advance payment ($A$). Two publishers, $H$ and $P$, have expressed interest in the book. Using the following comparison matrices, rank the two publishers and assess the consistency of the decision.

$$
\mathbf{A} = \begin{array}{c} \\ R \\ M \\ A \end{array} \overset{\begin{array}{ccc} R & M & A \end{array}}{\begin{bmatrix} 1 & 1 & \frac{1}{4} \\ 1 & 1 & \frac{1}{5} \\ 4 & 5 & 1 \end{bmatrix}} \qquad \mathbf{A}_R = \begin{array}{c} \\ H \\ P \end{array} \overset{\begin{array}{cc} H & P \end{array}}{\begin{bmatrix} 1 & 2 \\ \frac{1}{2} & 1 \end{bmatrix}}
$$

$$
\mathbf{A}_M = \begin{array}{c} \\ H \\ P \end{array} \overset{\begin{array}{cc} H & P \end{array}}{\begin{bmatrix} 1 & \frac{1}{2} \\ 2 & 1 \end{bmatrix}} \qquad \mathbf{A}_A = \begin{array}{c} \\ H \\ P \end{array} \overset{\begin{array}{cc} H & P \end{array}}{\begin{bmatrix} 1 & 1 \\ 1 & 1 \end{bmatrix}}
$$

**4.** A professor of political science wants to predict the outcome of a school board election. Three candidates, Ivy ($I$), Bahrn ($B$), and Smith ($S$) are running for one position. The professor places the voters into three categories:

left ($L$), center ($C$), and right ($R$). The candidates are judged based on three factors: educational experience ($E$), stand on issues ($S$), and personal character ($P$). The following are the comparison matrices for the first hierarchy of left, center, and right.

$$
\mathbf{A} = \begin{array}{c c} & \begin{array}{c c c} L & C & R \end{array} \\ \begin{array}{c} L \\ C \\ R \end{array} & \left[ \begin{array}{c c c} 1 & 2 & \frac{1}{2} \\ \frac{1}{2} & 1 & \frac{1}{5} \\ 2 & 5 & 1 \end{array} \right] \end{array}
\qquad
\mathbf{A}_L = \begin{array}{c c} & \begin{array}{c c c} E & S & P \end{array} \\ \begin{array}{c} E \\ S \\ P \end{array} & \left[ \begin{array}{c c c} 1 & 3 & \frac{1}{2} \\ \frac{1}{3} & 1 & \frac{1}{3} \\ 2 & 3 & 1 \end{array} \right] \end{array}
$$

$$
\mathbf{A}_c = \begin{array}{c c} & \begin{array}{c c c} E & S & P \end{array} \\ \begin{array}{c} E \\ S \\ P \end{array} & \left[ \begin{array}{c c c} 1 & 2 & 2 \\ \frac{1}{2} & 1 & 1 \\ \frac{1}{2} & 1 & 1 \end{array} \right] \end{array}
\qquad
\mathbf{A}_R = \begin{array}{c c} & \begin{array}{c c c} E & S & P \end{array} \\ \begin{array}{c} E \\ S \\ P \end{array} & \left[ \begin{array}{c c c} 1 & 1 & 9 \\ 1 & 1 & 8 \\ \frac{1}{9} & \frac{1}{8} & 1 \end{array} \right] \end{array}
$$

The professor was able to generate nine more comparison matrices to account for the three candidates at the second hierarchy representing experience, stand on issues, and personal character. The AHP process was then used to reduce these matrices to the following relative weights:

| Candidate | Left | | | Center | | | Right | | |
|---|---|---|---|---|---|---|---|---|---|
|  | $E$ | $S$ | $P$ | $E$ | $S$ | $P$ | $E$ | $S$ | $P$ |
| Ivy | .1 | .2 | .3 | .3 | .5 | .2 | .7 | .1 | .3 |
| Bahrn | .5 | .4 | .2 | .4 | .2 | .4 | .1 | .4 | .2 |
| Smith | .4 | .4 | .5 | .3 | .3 | .4 | .2 | .5 | .5 |

Using this information, determine the winning candidate and assess the consistency of the decision.

**5.** A school district is in dire need of reducing expenses to meet new budgetary restrictions at its elementary schools. Two options are available: Delete the physical education program ($E$), or delete the music program ($M$). The superintendent of the district has formed a committee with equal-vote representation from the School Board ($S$) and the Parent-Teacher Association ($P$) to study the situation and make a recommendation. The committee has decided to study the issue from the standpoint of budget restriction $(B)$ and students' needs $(N)$. The analysis produced the following comparison matrices:

$$\mathbf{A}_S = \begin{array}{c} \\ B \\ N \end{array}\begin{array}{cc} B & N \\ \left[\begin{array}{cc} 1 & 1 \\ 1 & 1 \end{array}\right] \end{array} \quad \mathbf{A}_P = \begin{array}{c} \\ B \\ N \end{array}\begin{array}{cc} B & N \\ \left[\begin{array}{cc} 1 & 2 \\ \frac{1}{2} & 1 \end{array}\right] \end{array}$$

$$\mathbf{A}_{SB} = \begin{array}{c} \\ E \\ M \end{array}\begin{array}{cc} E & M \\ \left[\begin{array}{cc} 1 & \frac{1}{2} \\ 2 & 1 \end{array}\right] \end{array} \quad \mathbf{A}_{SN} = \begin{array}{c} \\ E \\ M \end{array}\begin{array}{cc} E & M \\ \left[\begin{array}{cc} 1 & \frac{1}{3} \\ 3 & 1 \end{array}\right] \end{array}$$

$$\mathbf{A}_{PB} = \begin{array}{c} \\ E \\ M \end{array}\begin{array}{cc} E & M \\ \left[\begin{array}{cc} 1 & \frac{1}{3} \\ 3 & 1 \end{array}\right] \end{array} \quad \mathbf{A}_{PN} = \begin{array}{c} \\ E \\ M \end{array}\begin{array}{cc} E & M \\ \left[\begin{array}{cc} 1 & 2 \\ \frac{1}{2} & 1 \end{array}\right] \end{array}$$

Analyze the decision problem, and make a recommendation.

**6.** An individual is in the process of buying a car and has narrowed the choices to three models, $M1$, $M2$, and $M3$. The deciding factors include purchase price (PP), maintenance cost (MC), cost of city driving (CD), and cost of rural driving (RD). The following table provides the relevant data for a 3-year operation:

| Car Model | PP ($) | MC ($) | CD ($) | RD ($) |
|---|---|---|---|---|
| $M1$ | 6,000 | 1800 | 4500 | 1500 |
| $M2$ | 8,000 | 1200 | 2250 | 750 |
| $M3$ | 10,000 | 600 | 1125 | 600 |

Use the cost data to develop the comparison matrices. Assess the consistency of the matrices, and determine the choice model.

## 14.3 DECISION-MAKING UNDER RISK

Under the conditions of risk, the payoffs associated with each decision alternative are usually described by probability distributions. For this reason, decision making under risk is usually based on the *expected value criterion* in which decision alternatives are compared based on the maximization of expected profit or the minimization of expected cost. This approach has limitations, in the sense that it may not be applicable to certain situations. Ramifications to the expected value criterion have thus been introduced to account for these eventualities. This section presents the prominent techniques for making decisions under risk.

### 14.3.1 Expected Value Criterion

The expected value criterion seeks the maximization of expected (average) profit or the minimization of expected cost. The data of the problem assumes that the payoff (or cost) associated with each decision alternative is probabilistic.

**Decision tree analysis.**    The following example considers simple decision situations with a finite number of decision alternatives and explicit payoff matrices.

---

**Example 14.3–1.**

Suppose that you want to invest $10,000 in the stock market by buying shares in one of two companies: $A$ and $B$. Shares in Company A are risky but could yield a 50% return on investment during the next year. If the stock market conditions are not favorable (i.e., "bear" market), the stock may lose 20% of its value. Company B provides safe investments with 15% return in a "bull" market and only 5% in a "bear" market. All the publications you have consulted (and there is always a flood of them at the end of the year!) are predicting a 60% chance for a "bull" market and 40% for a "bear" market. Where should you invest your money?

The decision problem can be summarized as follows:

|                         | 1-year return on investment | |
| --- | --- | --- |
| Decision alternative | "Bull" market ($) | "Bear" market ($) |
| Company A stock | 5000 | $-2000$ |
| Company B stock | 1500 | 500 |
| Probability of occurrence | .6 | .4 |

The problem can also be represented as a **decision tree** as shown in Figure 14–3. Two types of nodes are used in the tree: a square ($\Box$) represents a *decision point* and a circle ($\bigcirc$) represents a *chance event*. Thus, two branches emanate from decision point 1 to represent the two alternatives of investing in stocks $A$ or $B$. Next, the two branches emanating from chance events 2 and 3 represent the "bull" and the "bear" markets with their respective probabilities and payoffs.

From Figure 14–3, the expected 1-year return for the two alternatives are

$$\text{For stock } A = \$5000 \times .6 + (-2000) \times .4 = \textbf{\$2,200}$$

$$\text{For stock } B = \$1500 \times .6 +\quad \$500 \times .4 = \$1,100$$

Based on these computations, your decision is to invest in stock $A$.

---

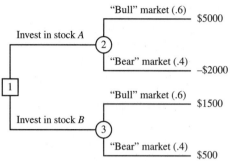

**Figure 14–3**

In the terminology of decision theory, the "bull" and the "bear" markets in the preceding example are referred to as **states of nature,** whose chances of occurrence are probabilistic (.6 versus .4). In general, a decision problem may include $n$ states of nature and $m$ alternatives. If $p_j (>0)$ is the probability of occurrence for state of nature $j$ and $a_{ij}$ is the payoff of alternative $i$ given state of nature $j$ ($i = 1, 2, ..., m; j = 1,$ $2, ..., n$), then the expected payoff for alternative $i$ is computed as

$$EV_i = a_{i1} p_1 + a_{i2} p_2 + \ ... \ + a_{in} p_n, \quad i = 1, 2, ..., n$$

where, by definition, $p_1 + p_2 + \ ... \ + p_n = 1$.

The best alternative is the one associated with $EV_i^* = \max_i \{EV_i\}$ or $EV_i^* = \min_i \{EV_i\}$ depending, respectively, on whether the payoff of the problem represents profit (income) or loss (expense).

### Problem set 14.3a

**1.** You have been invited to play the Fortune Wheel game on television. The wheel operates electronically with two buttons that produce hard ($H$) or soft ($S$) spin of the wheel. The wheel itself is divided into white ($W$) and red ($R$) half-circle regions. You have been told that the wheel is designed to stop with a probability of .3 in the white region and .7 in the red region. The payoff you get for the game is

|     | $W$       | $R$      |
| --- | --------- | -------- |
| $H$ | $800      | $200     |
| $S$ | – $2500   | $1000    |

Draw the associated decision tree, and specify a course of action.

2. Farmer McCoy can plant either corn or soybeans. The probabilities that the next harvest prices of these commodities will go up, stay the same, or go down are .25, .30, and .45, respectively. If the prices go up, the corn crop will net $30,000 and the soybeans will net $10,000. If the prices remain unchanged, McCoy will (barely) break even. But if the prices go down, the corn and soybeans crops will sustain losses of $35,000 and $5000, respectively.

   (a) Represent McCoy's problem as a decision tree.

   (b) Which crop should McCoy plant?

3. You have the chance to invest in three mutual funds: utility, aggressive growth, and global. The value of your investment will change depending on the market conditions. There is a 10% chance the market will go down, 50% chance it will remain moderate, and 40% chance it will perform well. The following table provides the percentage change in the investment value under the three conditions:

| Alternative | Percent return on investment | | |
| --- | --- | --- | --- |
| | Down market (%) | Moderate market (%) | Up market (%) |
| Utility | +5 | +7 | +8 |
| Aggressive growth | −10 | +5 | +30 |
| Global | +2 | +7 | +20 |

   (a) Represent the problem as a decision tree.

   (b) Which mutual fund should you select?

4. You have the chance to invest your money in either a 7.5% bond that sells at face value or an aggressive growth stock that pays only 1% dividend. If inflation is feared, the interest rate will go up to 8%, in which case the principal value of the bond will go down by 10%, and the stock value will go down by 20%. If recession is anticipated, the interest rate will go down to 6%. Under this condition, the principal value of the bond is expected to go up by 5%, and the stock value will increase by 20%. If the economy remains unchanged, the stock value will go up by 8% and the bond principal value remains the same. Economists estimate a 20% chance that inflation will rise and 15% that recession will set in. Assume that you are basing your investment decision on next year's economic conditions.

   (a) Represent the problem as a decision tree.

   (b) Would you invest in stocks or bonds?

5. AFC is about to launch its new Wings 'N Things fast food nationally. The research department is convinced that Wings 'N Things will be a great success and wants to introduce it immediately without advertisement in all AFC

outlets. The marketing department sees "things" differently and wants to unleash an intensive advertisement campaign. The advertisement campaign will cost $100,000 and if successful will produce $950,000 revenue. If the campaign is unsuccessful (there is a 30% chance it won't be), the revenue is estimated at only $200,000. If no advertisement is used, the revenue is estimated at $400,000 with probability .8 if the customers are receptive and $200,000 with probability .2 if they are not.

**(a)** Draw the associated decision tree.

**(b)** What course of action should AFC follow in launching the new product?

**6.** A fair coin is flipped three successive times. You receive $1.00 for each head ($H$) that turns up and an additional $.25 for each two successive heads that appear (remember that $HHH$ includes two sets of $HH$). However, you give back $1.10 for each tail ($T$) that shows up. You have the options to either play or not play the game.

**(a)** Draw the decision tree for the game.

**(b)** Would you favor playing this game?

**7.** You have the chance to play the following game in a gambling casino. A fair die is rolled twice, leading to four outcomes: (1) Both rolls show an even match, (2) both rolls show an odd match, (3) the outcomes are either even-odd or odd-even, and (4) all other outcomes. You are allowed to bet your money on exactly two outcomes with equal dollar amounts. For example, you can bet equal dollars on even-match (outcome 1) and odd-match (outcome 2). The payoff for each dollar you bet is $2.00 for the first outcome, $1.95 for the second and the third outcomes, and $1.50 for the fourth outcome.

**(a)** Draw the decision tree for the game.

**(b)** Which two choices would you make?

**(c)** Do you think you can ever come out ahead in this game?

**8.** Acme Manufacturing produces lots of widget with .8%, 1%, 1.2%, and 1.4% defectives according to the respective probabilities .4, .3, .25, and .05. Three customers, A, B, and C, are contracted to receive lots with no more than .8%, 1.2%, and 1.4% defectives, respectively. Acme will be penalized $1000 per percentage point if the percentage of defectives is higher than specified in the contract. Conversely, supplying higher-quality lots than required costs Acme $500 per percentage point. Assume that the lots are not inspected before shipment.

**(a)** Draw the associated decision tree.

**(b)** Which of the three customers should have the highest priority to receive their order?

**9.** TriStar plans to open a new plant in Arkansas. The company can open a full-sized plant now or a small-sized plant that can be expanded 2 years later if demand conditions are favorable (i.e., high demand). The time horizon for the decision problem is 10 years. TriStar estimates that the probability for high and low demands over the next 10 years is .75 and .25, respectively. The cost of the immediate construction of a large plant is $5 million, and a small plant costs $1 million. The expansion of the small plant 2 years from now costs $4.2 million. The income from the operation over the next 10 years is given in the following table:

|  | Estimated annual income (in $1000) | |
|---|---|---|
| Alternative | High demand | Low demand |
| Full-sized plant now | 1000 | 300 |
| Small-sized plant now | 250 | 200 |
| Expanded plant in 2 years | 900 | 200 |

   **(a)** Develop the associated decision tree, remembering that after 2 years TriStar has the options to expand or not expand the small plant.
   **(b)** Develop a construction strategy for TriStar over the next 10 years. (For simplicity, ignore the time value of money.)
**10.** Rework Problem 9, assuming that the annual interest rate is 10% and that the decisions are made considering the time value of money (*Note:* You need compound interest tables to solve this problem.)
**11.** Rework Problem 9, assuming that the demand can be high, medium, and low with probabilities .7, .2, and .1, respectively. Expansion of the small plant will occur only if the demand in the first 2 years is high. The following table gives the annual income.

|  | Estimated annual income (in $1,000) | | |
|---|---|---|---|
| Alternative | High demand | Medium demand | Low demand |
| Full-sized plant now | 1000 | 500 | 300 |
| Small-sized plant now | 400 | 280 | 150 |
| Expanded plant in 2 years | 900 | 600 | 200 |

   **More complex decision situations.**    To demonstrate the use of the expected value criterion further, we consider the situations in which the payoff of the decision problem is a mathematical function of the decision alternatives. In these cases, the use of decision tree representation, though possible, may not be as instructive as in the preceding examples.

**Example 14.3–2.**

Sunray Electric Coop uses a fleet of 20 trucks to service its electric network. The company wants to develop a periodic preventive maintenance for the fleet. The probability $p_t$ of a breakdown after $t$ months from the last preventive maintenance is estimated as

| $t$   | 1   | 2   | 3   | 4   | 5   | 6   | 7   | 8   | 9  | $\geq 10$ |
|-------|-----|-----|-----|-----|-----|-----|-----|-----|----|-----------|
| $p_t$ | .05 | .07 | .10 | .13 | .18 | .23 | .33 | .43 | .5 | .55       |

A random breakdown costs $200 per truck, and a scheduled maintenance costs only $50. Sunray wants to determine the optimal period (in months) between scheduled preventive maintenances.

Define $N$, the number of months between successive maintenances, as the maintenance cycle length that we desire to determine. Two types of costs occur during an $N$-period maintenance cycle: (1) the breakdown cost during the first $N - 1$ months, and (2) the maintenance cost at the end of the cycle. The second cost (preventive maintenance) is $50 times the fleet size of 20 trucks, or $1000 per maintenance cycle. The breakdown cost must be based on the average number of trucks that randomly break down during the first $N - 1$ periods of the cycle. Here, we have two states of nature in month $t$: breakdown with probability $p_t$ and no breakdown with probability $1 - p_t$. Thus, the expected number of breakdowns in period $t$ equals the fleet size times $p_t$, or $20p_t$. From this result, the expected total number of broken trucks during the first $N - 1$ months of the cycle is the sum of the expected number of broken trucks in the individual months—that is, $20p_1 + 20p_2 + \ldots$ $20p_{N-1} = 20(p_1 + p_2 + \ldots + p_{N-1})$. Letting $EC(N)$ be the total expected cost per maintenance cycle, we get

$$EC(N) = \$1000 + \$200 \times 20(p_1 + p_2 + \ldots + p_{n-1})$$

Sunray's decision problem reduces to determining the cycle length $N$ that will minimize, $ECPM(N)$, the total cost per month—that is,

$$ECPM(N) = \frac{EC(N)}{N}$$

$$= \frac{1000 + 4000 \sum_{t=1}^{N-1} p_t}{N}$$

The minimization of the function $ECPM(N)$ cannot be determined in closed form. Instead, we use the following tabular form to determine the answer:

| $N$ | $p_N$ | $\displaystyle\sum_{t=1}^{N-1} p_t$ | $ECPM(N)$ |
|---|---|---|---|
| 1 | .05 | .00 | $1000.00 |
| 2 | .07 | .05 | 600.00 |
| 3 | .10 | .12 | 493.33 |
| Optimal $N \rightarrow$ 4 | .13 | .22 | 470.00 |
| 5 | .18 | .35 | 480.00 |
| 6 | .23 | .53 | 520.00 |

The computations show that $ECPM(N)$ reaches its minimum at $N = 4$. Thus, preventive maintenance occurs every 4 months.

---

The decision problem of Example 14.3–2 can also be represented as a decision tree. You are asked to do so in Problem 14.3b–1.

### Problem set 14.3b

1. In Example 14.3–2, assume that the cost of preventive maintenance per truck is $75 and the cost per breakdown is $200. The probability of a breakdown in period 1 is .03, and it increases by .01 for periods 2 to 10. For periods 11 and up, the breakdown probability remains constant at .13.
   (a) Develop the associated decision tree.
   (b) Determine the optimal maintenance cycle length.
2. Daily demand for loaves of bread at a grocery store are specified by the following probability distribution:

| $n$ | 100 | 150 | 200 | 250 | 300 |
|---|---|---|---|---|---|
| $p_n$ | .20 | .25 | .30 | .15 | .10 |

The store pays 55 cents a loaf and sells it for $1.20 each. Any loaves that are not sold by the end of the day are disposed of at 25 cents each. Assume that the stock level is restricted to one of the demand levels specified for $p_n$.
   (a) Develop the associated decision tree.
   (b) How many loaves should be stocked daily?

3. In Problem 2, suppose that the store wishes to extend the decision problem to a 2-day horizon. The alternatives for the second day depend on the demand in the first day. If day 1's demand equals the amount stocked, the store will continue to order the same quantity for day 2. If the demand on day 1 exceeds the amount stocked, the store can order any of the higher-level stocks. Finally, if day 1's demand is less than the amount stocked, the store can only order any of the lower-level stocks. Develop the associated decision tree, and determine the optimal ordering strategy.

4. An automatic machine produces $\alpha$ (thousands of) units of a product per day. As $\alpha$ increases, the proportion of defectives, $p$, goes up according to the following probability density function

$$f(p) = \begin{cases} \alpha p^{\alpha-1}, & 0 \le p \le 1 \\ 0, & \text{otherwise} \end{cases}$$

Each defective item incurs a loss of \$50. A good item yields \$5 profit.

**(a)** Why is it not convenient to develop a decision tree for this problem?

**(b)** Determine the value of $\alpha$ that maximizes the expected profit.

5. The outer diameter, $d$, of a cylinder is processed on an automatic machine with upper and lower tolerance limits of $d + t_U$ and $d - t_L$. The production process can be described as a normal distribution with mean $\mu$ and standard deviation $\sigma$. An oversized cylinder is reworked at the cost of $c_1$ dollars. An undersized cylinder must be salvaged at the cost of $c_2$ dollars. Determine the optimal setting $d$ for the machine.

6. In production processes, maintenance action is applied periodically to cutting tools. If the rate of tool sharpening decreases, the percentage of defective items increases and vice versa. Let $S_U$ and $S_L$ be the upper and lower limits allowed in a given manufacturing process for a measurable dimension machined by the tool. Further, let $\mu(t)$ be the average of the process after $t$ time units have elapsed since the last sharpening, with $\mu(0)$ being the (ideal) initial setting of the tool. The cost of sharpening the tool is $c_1$ and the cost of a defective item is $c_2$. Production occurs in lots of size $Q$ at the rate of $r$ items per unit time and the actual output of the process is normal with mean $\mu(t)$ and a constant variance $\sigma$.

**(a)** Determine an expression for the expected cost of sharpening the tool and reworking the defectives as a function of the interval $T$ between successive sharpenings.

**(b)** Show that the optimal value of $T$ is independent of $Q$, and interpret the result.

**(c)** Determine a numerical value for $T$ using the data, $c_1 = \$10, c_2 = \$48.85$, $\alpha = 10$ items per hour, $\mu(t) = \mu(0) + t$, and $\sigma = 1$.

(*Hint:* Approximate the number of tool sharpenings during the production of lot $Q$ by $\frac{Q}{\alpha T}$. Also, use numerical integration to determine the optimal value of $T$.)

**7.** *Aspiration level criterion.* Acme Manufacturing uses an industrial chemical in one of its processes. The shelf life of the chemical is 1 month, following which any amount left is destroyed. The use of the chemical, in gallons, by Acme occurs randomly according to the following distribution:

$$f(x) = \begin{cases} \dfrac{200}{x^2}, & 100 \le x \le 200 \\[2mm] 0, & \text{otherwise} \end{cases}$$

The actual consumption of the chemical occurs uniformly during the month. Acme wants to determine the level of the chemical that satisfies two conflicting criteria (or aspiration levels):

**(1)** The average excess quantity for the month does not exceed 20 gallons.

**(2)** The average shortage quantity for the month does not exceed 40 gallons.

### 14.3.2 Variations of the Expected Value Criterion

This section addresses three issues relating to the expected value criterion. The first issue deals with the determination of *posterior probabilities* based on experimentation, the second issue deals with the *utility* versus the actual value of money, and the third issue modifies the expected value criterion so it can "accommodate" short-term decision problems.

**Posterior (Bayes) probabilities.**    The probabilities used in the expected value criterion are usually secured from historical data (see Section 12.6). In some cases, we may be able to modify these probabilities advantageously using current information. Such information is usually obtained through sampling or experimentation. The resulting probabilities are referred to as **posterior (or Bayes) probabilities,** as opposed to the **prior probabilities** determined from raw data. The following example shows how the expected value criterion presented in Section 14.3.1 can be modified to take advantage of new information provided by the posterior probabilities.

---

**Example 14.3–3.**

In Example 14.3–1, the (prior) probabilities of .6 and .4 of a "bull" and a "bear" market were determined from available financial publications. Instead of relying solely on these publications, suppose that you have decided to conduct a more "personal" investigation by consulting a friend who has done well in the stock market. The friend offers the general opinion of "for" or "against" investment. This opinion is further quantified in the following manner: If it is a "bull" market, there is a 90% chance the vote will be "for." If it is a "bear" market, the chance of a "for" vote is lowered to 50%. How do you make use of this additional information?

The statement made by the friend actually provides conditional probabilities of "for/against," given the states of nature "bull" and "bear" markets. To simplify the presentation, let us use the following symbols:

$v_1$ = "For" vote
$v_2$ = "Against" vote
$m_1$ = "Bull" market
$m_2$ = "Bear" market

The friend's statement may be written in the form of probability statements as

$$P\{v_1|m_1\} = .9, \, P\{v_1|m_2\} = .1$$
$$P\{v_2|m_1\} = .5, \, P\{v_2|m_2\} = .5$$

With this additional information, the decision problem can be summarized as follows:

**1.** If the friend's recommendation is "for," would you invest in stocks $A$ or $B$?
**2.** If the friend's recommendation is "against," would you invest in stocks $A$ or $B$?

Actually, the problem can be summarized in the form of a decision tree as shown in Figure 14–4. Node 1 is a chance event representing the "for" and "against" probabilities. Nodes 2 and 3 are decision points for choosing between stocks $A$ and $B$ given the friend's vote is "for" and "against," respectively. Finally, nodes 4 to 7 are chance events representing the "bull" and "bear" markets.

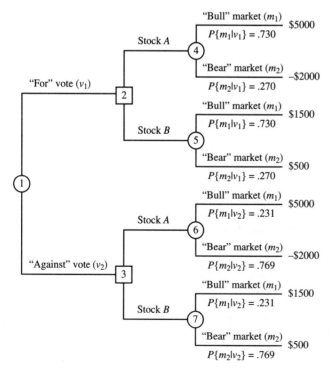

**Figure 14–4**

To evaluate the different alternatives in Figure 14–4, it is necessary to compute the *posterior* probabilities $P\{m_i \mid v_j\}$ shown on the $m_1$-and $m_2$-branches associated with chance nodes 4 to 7. These posterior probabilities are computed considering the additional information provided by the friend's "for/against" recommendation and are computed according to the following general steps:

**Step 1.** The conditional probabilities $P\{v_j \mid m\}$ of the problem can be summarized as

$$
P\{v_j \mid m_i\} = \quad
\begin{array}{c|c|c|}
 & v_1 & v_2 \\
\hline
m_1 & .9 & .1 \\
\hline
m_2 & .5 & .5 \\
\hline
\end{array}
$$

**Step 2.** Compute the joint probabilities as

$$P\{m_i, v_j\} = P\{v_j \mid m_i\}P\{m_i\}, \quad \text{for all } i \text{ and } j$$

Given the *prior* probabilities $P\{m_1\} = .6$ and $P\{m_2\} = .4$, the joint probabilities are determined by multiplying the first and the second rows of the table in step 1 by .6 and .4, respectively. We thus get

$$
P\{m_i, v_j\} = \quad
\begin{array}{c|c|c|}
 & v_1 & v_2 \\
\hline
m_1 & .54 & .06 \\
\hline
m_2 & .20 & .20 \\
\hline
\end{array}
$$

The sum of all the entries in the table equals 1.

**Step 3.** Compute the absolute probabilities as

$$P\{v_j\} = \sum_{\text{all } i} P\{m_i, v_j\}, \quad \text{for all } j$$

These probabilities are computed from the table in step 2 by summing the respective columns, which yields

$$
\begin{array}{c|c|}
P\{v_1\} & P\{v_2\} \\
\hline
.74 & .26 \\
\hline
\end{array}
$$

***Step 4.*** Determine the desired posterior probabilities as

$$P\{m_i \mid v_j\} = \frac{P\{m_i, v_j\}}{P\{v_j\}}$$

These probabilities are computed by dividing each column in the table of step 2 by the element of the corresponding column in the table of step 3, which (rounded to three digits) yields

$$P\{m_i \mid v_j\} = $$

|       | $v_1$ | $v_2$ |
|-------|-------|-------|
| $m_1$ | .730  | .231  |
| $m_2$ | .270  | .769  |

These are the probabilities shown in Figure 14–4. They are different from the original prior probabilities $P\{m_1\} = .6$ and $P\{m_2\} = .4$.

We are now ready to evaluate the alternatives based on the expected payoffs for nodes 4 to 7—that is,

*"For" Vote*

Stock $A$ at node 4 = 5000 × .730 + (−2000) × .270 = **$3110**

Stock $B$ at node 5 = 1500 × .730 + 500 × .270 = 1230

*Decision.* Invest in stock $A$.

*"Against" Vote*

Stock $A$ at node 6 = 5000 × .231 + (−2000) × .769 = −**$383**

Stock $B$ at node 7 = 1500 × .231 + 500 × .769 = **$731**

*Decision.* Invest in stock B.

Observe that the preceding decisions are equivalent to saying that the expected payoffs at decision nodes 2 and 3 are $3110 and $731, respectively (see Figure 14–4). Thus, given the probabilities $P\{v_1\} = .74$ and $P\{v_2\} = .26$ as computed in step 3, we can compute the expected payoff for the entire decision tree. (See Problem 14.3c–3.)

---

### Problem set 14.3c

1. Despite the fact that it is the rainy season of the year, JimmyBob has the desire to go fishing tomorrow, but only if it is not raining. Based on past weather data, there is a 70% chance it will rain during the rainy season. The

6:00 P.M. weather report forecasts an 85% chance of rain tomorrow. Should JimmyBob plan on fishing tomorrow?

2. Elektra receives 75% of its electronic components from vendor $A$ and the remaining 25% from vendor $B$. The percentage of defectives from vendors $A$ and $B$ are 1% and 2%, respectively. When a random sample of size 5 taken from a received lot is inspected, only one defective unit is found. Determine the probability that the lot is received from vendor $A$. Repeat the same for vendor $B$. (*Hint:* The probability of a defective item in a sample is binomial.)

3. In Example 14.3–3, suppose that you have the additional option of investing the original $10,000 in a safe certificate of deposit that yields 8% interest. Your friend's advice still applies to investing in only the stock market.
   (a) Draw the associated decision tree.
   (b) What is the optimal decision in this case? (*Hint:* Make use of $P\{v_1\}$ and $P\{v_2\}$ given in step 3 of Example 14.3–3 to determine the expected value of investing in the stock market.)

4. You are the author of what promises to be a successful novel. You have the option to either publish the novel yourself or through a publisher. The publisher is offering you $20,000 for signing the contract. If the novel is successful, it will sell 200,000 copies. If it isn't, it will sell only 10,000 copies. The publisher pays royalties at the rate of $1 per copy. A market survey by the publisher indicates that there is a 70% chance that the novel will be successful. If, conversely, you publish the novel yourself, you will incur an initial cost of $90,000 for printing and marketing, but each copy sold will net you $2.
   (a) Based on the given information, would you accept the publisher's offer or publish the book yourself?
   (b) Suppose that you contracted a literary agent to conduct a survey concerning the potential success of the novel. From past experience, the company advises you that when a novel is successful, the survey will predict the wrong outcome 20% of the time. When the novel is not successful, the survey will give the correct prediction 85% of the time. How would this information affect your decision?

5. Consider Farmer McCoy's decision situation in Problem 14.3a-2. The farmer has the additional option of using the land as a grazing range, in which case he is guaranteed a payoff of $7500. The farmer has also secured additional information from a broker regarding the degree of stability of future commodity prices. The broker's assessment of "favorable" and "unfavorable" is further quantified by the following conditional probabilities:

$$P\{a_j \mid s_i\} = \begin{array}{c|cc}
 & a_1 & a_2 \\
\hline
s_1 & .15 & .85 \\
s_2 & .50 & .50 \\
s_3 & .85 & .15 \\
\end{array}$$

where $a_1$ and $a_2$ represent the "favorable" and "unfavorable" assessment by the broker, and $s_1$ to $s_3$ represent the "down/same/up" change in future prices, respectively.

**(a)** Draw the associated decision tree.

**(b)** Specify the optimal decision for the problem.

**6.** In Problem 14.3a–5, suppose that the AFC management has decided to test-market its Wings 'N Things in selective locations. The outcome of the test is either "good" ($a_1$) or "bad" ($a_2$). The test yields the following conditional probabilities with and without the advertisement campaign:

$P\{a_j \mid v_i\}$—With campaign

| | $a_1$ | $a_2$ |
|---|---|---|
| $v_1$ | .95 | .05 |
| $v_2$ | .3 | .7 |

$P\{a_j \mid w_i\}$—No campaign

| | $a_1$ | $a_2$ |
|---|---|---|
| $w_1$ | .8 | .2 |
| $w_2$ | .4 | .6 |

The symbols $v_1$ and $v_2$ represent "success" and "no success," and $w_1$ and $w_2$ represent "receptive" and "not receptive."

**(a)** Develop the associated decision tree.

**(b)** Determine the best course of action for AFC.

**7.** Historical data at Acme Manufacturing estimates a 5% chance that a manufactured lot of widget will be unacceptable (bad). A bad lot has 15% defective items, and a good lot includes only 4% defective items. Letting $a = a_1(=a_2)$ indicate that the lot is good (bad), the associated prior probabilities are given as

$$P\{a = a_1\} = .95 \quad \text{and} \quad P\{a = a_2\} = .05$$

Instead of shipping lots based solely on prior probabilities, a test sample of two items is taken from each lot, which gives rise to three possible outcomes.

Both items are good ($s_1$).

One item is good ($s_2$).

Both items are defective ($s_3$).

**(a)** Determine the posterior probabilities $P\{a_i|s_j\}, i = 1, 2; j = 1, 2, 3$.

**(b)** Suppose that the manufacturer ships lots to two customers, $A$ and $B$. The contracts specify that the defectives for $A$ and $B$ should not exceed 5% and 8%, respectively. A penalty of $100 is incurred per percentage point above the maximum limit. Supplying better quality lots than the contract specifies costs the manufacturer $80 per percentage point. Develop the associated decision tree, and determine a priority strategy for shipping the lots.

**Utility functions.**    In the preceding presentation, the expected value criterion has been applied to only situations where the payoff is *actual* money. There are cases where the *utility* rather than the actual value should be used in the analysis. To illustrate this point, suppose that there is a 50–50 chance that a $20,000 investment will produce a profit of $40,000 or be lost completely. The associated expected profit is $40,000 \times .5 - 20,000 \times .5 = \$10,000$. Although there is a net expected profit, different individuals may vary in interpreting the result. An investor who is willing to accept risk may undertake the investment for a 50%-chance to make a $40,000 profit. Conversely, a conservative investor may not be willing to risk losing $20,000. From this standpoint, we say that different individuals exhibit different attitudes toward risk. This is translated to say that individuals exhibit different *utility* with respect to risk.

The determination of the utility is subjective. It depends on our attitude toward accepting risk. In this section, we present a systematic procedure for quantifying the attitude of the decision maker toward risk. The end result is a utility function that takes the place of actual money.

In the preceding investment illustration, the best payoff is $40,000, and the worst is −$20,000. We thus establish an arbitrary, but logical, utility scale, $U$, from 0 to 100, in which 0 equals the utility of −$20,000 and 100 the utility of $40,000—that is, $U(-\$20,000) = 0$ and $U(\$40,000) = 100$. Next, we determine the utility of points between −$20,000 and $40,000, with the objective of establishing the general shape of the utility function.

If the decision maker's attitude is indifferent toward risk, then the resulting utility function will be a straight line joining $(0, -\$20,000)$ and $(100, \$40,000)$. In this case, both the actual money and its utility should produce consistent decisions. For the more realistic cases, the utility function can take other forms that reflect the attitude of the decision maker toward risk. Figure 14–5 illustrates the cases of individuals $X$, $Y$, and $Z$. Individual $X$ is **risk averse** (or cautious) because of exhibiting higher sensitivity to loss than to profit. Individual $Z$ is the opposite, and hence is a **risk seeker**. This observation follows because for individual $X$, a $10,000 change above and below $0 shows that the profit change increases the utility by the amount *ab,* which is less than the decrease *bc* resulting from incurring an equal cash loss—that is, *ab* < *bc.* For the same ± $10,000 changes, individual *Z* exhibits opposite behavior because *de* > *ef.* Further, individual *Y* is **risk neutral** because the suggested changes yield equal changes in utility. In general, an individual may be both a risk-averse person and a risk seeker, in which case the associated utility curve will follow an elongated *S*-shape.

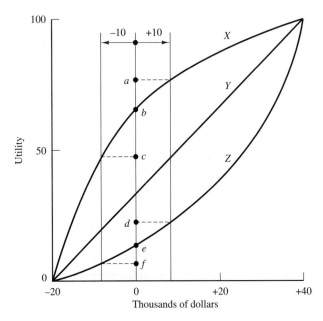

**Figure 14–5**

Utility curves similar to the ones demonstrated in Figure 14–5 are determined by "quantifying" the decision maker's attitude toward risk for different levels of cash money within the specified range. Thus, in our example, the desired range is (−$20,000 to $40,000), and the corresponding utility range is (0 to 100). What we would like to do is to specify the utility associated with intermediate cash values, such as −$10,000, $0, $10,000, $20,000, and $30,000. The procedure starts by establishing a **lottery** for a cash amount *x* whose expected utility is given as:

$$U(x) = pU(-20{,}000) + (1 - p)U(\$40{,}000), \quad 0 \le p \le 1$$

$$= 0p + 100\,(1 - p)$$

$$= 100 - 100p$$

To determine $U(x)$, we ask the decision maker to state a preference between a *guaranteed* cash amount *x* and the chance to play a lottery in which a loss of −$20,000 occurs with probability *p,* and a profit of $40,000 is realized with probabil-

criterion produces optimistic results because it is equivalent to applying the *best of the best* conditions. We can adjust the degree of optimism (or pessimism) through a proper selection of the value of $\alpha$ in the specified $(0, 1)$ range. In the absence of strong feeling regarding optimism and pessimism, $\alpha = .5$ may be an appropriate choice.

If $v(a_i, s_j)$ represents loss, then the criterion must be changed to

$$\min_{a_i} \left\{ \alpha \min_{s_j} v(a_i, s_j) + (1 - \alpha) \max_{s_j} v(a_i, s_j) \right\}$$

---

**Example 14.4–1.**

National Outdoors School (NOS) is preparing a summer campsite in the heart of Alaska to train individuals in wilderness survival. NOS estimates that attendance can fall into one of four categories: 200, 250, 300, and 350 persons. The cost of the campsite will be minimum if it is built to meet the demand exactly. Deviations above or below the ideal demand levels incurs additional costs resulting from building surplus (unused) capacity or lost income opportunities when some of the demand is not satisfied. Letting $a_1$ to $a_4$ represent the sizes of the campsites (200, 250, 300, and 350 persons) and $s_1$ to $s_4$ the level of attendance, the following table summarizes the cost matrix (in thousands of dollars) for the situation.

|       | $s_1$ | $s_2$ | $s_3$ | $s_4$ |
|-------|-------|-------|-------|-------|
| $a_1$ | 5     | 10    | 18    | 25    |
| $a_2$ | 8     | 7     | 12    | 23    |
| $a_3$ | 21    | 18    | 12    | 21    |
| $a_4$ | 30    | 22    | 19    | 15    |

The problem is analyzed using all four criteria.

*Laplace*   Given $P\{s_j\} = \frac{1}{4}, j = 1$ to 4, the expected values for the different actions are computed as

$$E\{a_1\} = \frac{1}{4}(5 + 10 + 18 + 25) = \$14,500$$

$$E\{a_2\} = \frac{1}{4}(8 + 7 + 12 + 23) = \$12,500 \leftarrow \text{Optimum}$$

$$E\{a_3\} = \frac{1}{4}(21 + 18 + 12 + 21) = \$18,000$$

$$E\{a_4\} = \frac{1}{4}(30 + 22 + 19 + 15) = \$21,500$$

*Minimax*   The minimax criterion produces the following matrix:

|       | $s_1$ | $s_2$ | $s_3$ | $s_4$ | Row max |
|-------|-------|-------|-------|-------|---------|
| $a_1$ | 5     | 10    | 18    | 25    | 25      |
| $a_2$ | 8     | 7     | 12    | 23    | 23      |
| $a_3$ | 21    | 18    | 12    | 21    | **21** ← Minimax |
| $a_4$ | 30    | 22    | 19    | 15    | 30      |

*Savage*    The regret matrix is determined by subtracting 5, 7, 12, and 15 from columns 1 to 4, respectively. Thus,

|       | $s_1$ | $s_2$ | $s_3$ | $s_4$ | Row max |
|-------|-------|-------|-------|-------|---------|
| $a_1$ | 0     | 3     | 6     | 10    | 10      |
| $a_2$ | 3     | 0     | 0     | 8     | **8** ← Minimax |
| $a_3$ | 16    | 11    | 0     | 6     | 16      |
| $a_4$ | 25    | 15    | 7     | 0     | 25      |

*Hurwicz*    The following table summarizes the computations.

| Alternative | Row min | Row max | $\alpha$(Row min) + (1 − $\alpha$)(Row max) |
|-------------|---------|---------|---------------------------------------------|
| $a_1$       | 5       | 25      | $25 - 20\alpha$ |
| $a_2$       | 7       | 23      | $23 - 16\alpha$ |
| $a_3$       | 12      | 21      | $21 - 9\alpha$  |
| $a_4$       | 15      | 30      | $30 - 15\alpha$ |

Using an appropriate $\alpha$, we can determine the optimum alternative. For example, at $\alpha = .5$, either $a_1$ or $a_2$ will yield the optimum, whereas at $\alpha = .25$, $a_3$ is the optimum.

## Problem set 14.4a

**1.** Hank is an intelligent student and usually makes good grades, provided that he has the chance to review the course material the night before the test.

For tomorrow's test, Hank is faced with a small problem. His fraternity brothers are having an all-night party in which he would like to participate. Hank has three options.

$a_1$ = Party all night
$a_2$ = Divide the night equally between studying and partying
$a_3$ = Study all night

The professor giving tomorrow's exam is unpredictable, in the sense that the test can be easy ($s_1$), moderate ($s_2$), or tough ($s_3$). Depending on the toughness of the test and the amount of review Hank does, the following test score combinations can be anticipated:

|       | $s_1$ | $s_2$ | $s_3$ |
|-------|-------|-------|-------|
| $a_1$ | 85    | 60    | 40    |
| $a_2$ | 92    | 85    | 81    |
| $a_3$ | 100   | 88    | 82    |

**(a)** Recommend a course of action for Hank (based on each of the four criteria of decisions under uncertainty).

**(b)** Suppose that Hank is more interested in the letter grade he will get. The dividing scores for the passing letter grades A to D are 90, 80, 70, and 60, respectively. Otherwise, for scores below 60, the grade is F. Would this attitude toward grades call for a change in Hank's course of action?

**2.** For the upcoming planting season, Farmer McCoy has four options.

$a_1$ = Plant corn
$a_2$ = Plant wheat
$a_3$ = Plant soybeans
$a_4$ = Use the land for grazing

The payoffs associated with the different actions are influenced by the amount of rainfall, which could be one of four states.

$s_1$ = Heavy rainfall
$s_2$ = Moderate rainfall
$s_3$ = Light rainfall
$s_4$ = Drought season

The payoff matrix (in thousands of dollars) is estimated as

|       | $s_1$ | $s_2$ | $s_3$ | $s_4$ |
|-------|-------|-------|-------|-------|
| $a_1$ | $-20$ | 60    | 30    | $-5$  |
| $a_2$ | 40    | 50    | 35    | 0     |
| $a_3$ | $-50$ | 100   | 45    | $-10$ |
| $a_4$ | 12    | 15    | 15    | 10    |

Develop a course of action for Farmer McCoy.

3. One of $N$ machines must be selected for manufacturing $Q$ units of a specific product. The minimum and maximum demands for the product are $Q^*$ and $Q^{**}$, respectively. The total production cost for $Q$ items on machine $i$ involves a fixed cost $K_i$ and variable cost per unit $c_i$, and is given as

$$TC_i = K_i + c_i Q$$

(a) Devise a solution for the problem under each of the four criteria of decisions under uncertainty.

(b) Solve the problem for the following set of data, assuming $1000 \le Q \le 4000$:

| Machine $i$ | $K_i$ ($) | $C_i$ ($) |
|-------------|-----------|-----------|
| 1           | 100       | 5         |
| 2           | 40        | 12        |
| 3           | 150       | 3         |
| 4           | 90        | 8         |

## 14.5 GAME THEORY

Game theory deals with decision situations in which two *intelligent* opponents have conflicting objectives. Typical examples include launching advertisement campaigns for competing products and planning war strategies for opposing armies. These situations are in contrast with the ones we have studied so far where *nature* is viewed as a nonmalevolent opponent.

In a game conflict, two opponents, known as **players,** will each have a (finite or infinite) number of alternatives or **strategies.** Associated with each pair of strategies is a **payoff** that one player pays to the other. Such games are known as **two-person zero-sum games** because the gain by one player equals the loss to the other. In this regard, it suffices to summarize the game in terms of the payoff to one player. Designating the two players as $A$ and $B$ with $m$ and $n$ strategies, respectively, the game is usually represented by the payoff matrix to player $A$ as

|        | $B_1$    | $B_2$    | $\cdots$ | $B_n$    |
|--------|----------|----------|----------|----------|
| $A_1$  | $a_{11}$ | $a_{12}$ | $\cdots$ | $a_{1n}$ |
| $A_2$  | $a_{21}$ | $a_{22}$ | $\cdots$ | $a_{2n}$ |
| $\cdot$ | $\cdot$ | $\cdot$  | $\cdot$  | $\cdot$  |
| $\cdot$ | $\cdot$ | $\cdot$  | $\cdot$  | $\cdot$  |
| $\cdot$ | $\cdot$ | $\cdot$  | $\cdot$  | $\cdot$  |
| $A_m$  | $a_{m1}$ | $a_{m1}$ | $\cdots$ | $a_{mn}$ |

The representation indicates that if $A$ uses strategy $i$ and $B$ uses strategy $j$, the payoff to $A$ is $a_{ij}$, which means that the payoff to $B$ is $-a_{ij}$.

### 14.5.1 Optimal Solution of Two-Person Zero-Sum Games

Because games are rooted in conflict of interest, the optimal solution selects one or more strategies for each player such that any change in the chosen strategies does not improve the payoff to either player. These solutions can be in the form of a single **pure** strategy or several strategies that are **mixed** according to predetermined probabilities. The following two examples demonstrate the two cases.

---

**Example 14.5–1.**

Two companies, $A$ and $B$, sell two brands of flu medicine. Company $A$ advertises in radio ($A_1$), television ($A_2$), and newspapers ($A_3$). Company $B$, in addition to using radio ($B_1$), television ($B_2$), and newspapers ($B_3$), also mails brochures ($B_4$). Depending on the cleverness and the intensity of the advertisement campaign, each company can capture a portion of the market from the other. The following matrix summarizes the percentage of the market captured or lost by company $A$.

|            | $B_1$ | $B_2$ | $B_3$ | $B_4$ | Row min |
|------------|-------|-------|-------|-------|---------|
| $A_1$      | 8     | $-2$  | 9     | $-3$  | $-3$    |
| $A_2$      | 6     | 5     | 6     | 8     | **5** Maximin |
| $A_3$      | $-2$  | 4     | $-9$  | 5     | $-9$    |
| Column max | 8     | **5** | 9     | 8     |         |
|            |       | Minimax |     |       |         |

The solution of the game is based on securing the *best of the worst* for each player. If Company $A$ selects strategy $A_1$, then regardless of what $B$ does, the worst that can happen is that $A$ would lose 3% of the market share to $B$. This is represented by the minimum value of the entries in row 1. Similarly, strategy $A_2$ worst outcome is for $A$ to capture 5% of the market from $B$, and the strategy $A_3$ worst outcome is for $A$ to lose 9% to $B$. These results are listed in the "row min" column. To achieve the *best* of the *worst*, Company $A$ chooses strategy $A_2$ because it corresponds to the maximin value, or the largest element in the "row min" column.

Next, consider Company $B$'s strategy. Because the given payoff matrix is for $A$, $B$'s *best of the worst* criterion requires determining the minimax value. The result is that strategy $B_2$ should be $B$'s choice.

The optimal solution of the game calls for selecting strategies $A_2$ and $B_2$—that is, both companies should use television advertisements. The payoff will be in favor of company $A$ because its market share will increase by 5%. In this case, we say that the **value of the game** is 5%, and that $A$ and $B$ are using a **saddle-point** solution.

The saddle-point solution guarantees that neither company is tempted to select a better strategy. If $B$ moves to another strategy ($B_1, B_3$, or $B_4$), Company $A$ can stay with strategy $A_2$, which ensures that $B$ will lose a worse share of the market (6% or 8%). By the same token, $A$ does not want to use a different strategy because if $A$ moves to strategy $A_3$, $B$ can move to $B_3$ and realize a 9% increase in market share. A similar conclusion is realized if $A$ moves to $A_1$.

The optimal saddle-point solution of a game need not be characterized by pure strategies. Instead, the solution may require mixing two or more strategies randomly, as the following example illustrates.

---

**Example 14.5–2.**

Two players, $A$ and $B$, play the coin-tossing game. Each player, unbeknownst to the other, chooses a head ($H$) or a tail ($T$). Both players would reveal their choices simultaneously. If they match ($HH$ or $TT$), player $A$ receives \$1 from $B$. Otherwise, $A$ pays $B$ \$1.

The following payoff matrix for player A gives the row-min and the column-max values corresponding to $A$'s and $B$'s strategies, respectively.

|       | $B_H$ | $B_T$ | Row min |
|-------|-------|-------|---------|
| $A_H$ | 1     | −1    | −1      |
| $A_T$ | −1    | 1     | −1      |
| Column max | 1 | 1  |         |

The maximin and the minimax values of the game are −\$1 and \$1, respectively. Because the two values are not equal, the game does not have a pure strategy solution. In particular, if $A_H$ is used by player $A$, player $B$ will select $B_T$ to receive \$1 from $A$. If this happens, $A$ can move to strategy $A_T$ to reverse the outcome of the game by receiving \$1 from $B$. The continuous temptation by either player to switch to another strategy shows that a pure strategy solution is not acceptable. Instead, both players must use proper random mixes of their respective strategies. In this case, the optimal value of the game will occur somewhere between the maximin and the minimax values of the game—that is,

maximin (lower) value ≤ value of the game ≤ minimax (upper) value

(See Problem 14.5a–5). Thus, in the coin-tossing example, the value of the game must lie between −$1 and +$1.

---

## Problem set 14.5a

1. Determine the saddle-point solution, the associated pure strategies, and the value of the game for each of the following games. The payoffs are for player $A$.

   **(a)**

   |       | $B_1$ | $B_2$ | $B_3$ | $B_4$ |
   |-------|-------|-------|-------|-------|
   | $A_1$ | 8     | 6     | 2     | 8     |
   | $A_2$ | 8     | 9     | 4     | 5     |
   | $A_3$ | 7     | 5     | 3     | 5     |

   **(b)**

   |       | $B_1$ | $B_2$ | $B_3$ | $B_4$ |
   |-------|-------|-------|-------|-------|
   | $A_1$ | 4     | −4    | −5    | 6     |
   | $A_2$ | −3    | −4    | −9    | −2    |
   | $A_3$ | 6     | 7     | −8    | −9    |
   | $A_4$ | 7     | 3     | −9    | 5     |

2. The following games give $A$'s payoff. Determine the values of $p$ and $q$ that will make the entry $(2, 2)$ of each game a saddle point:

   **(a)**

   |       | $B_1$ | $B_2$ | $B_3$ |
   |-------|-------|-------|-------|
   | $A_1$ | 1     | $q$   | 6     |
   | $A_2$ | $p$   | 5     | 10    |
   | $A_3$ | 6     | 2     | 3     |

**(b)**

|       | $B_1$ | $B_2$ | $B_3$ |
|-------|-------|-------|-------|
| $A_1$ | 1     | $q$   | 6     |
| $A_2$ | $p$   | 5     | 10    |
| $A_3$ | 6     | 2     | 3     |

**3.** Specify the range for the value of the game in each of the following case assuming that the payoff, c is for player A:

**(a)**

|       | $B_1$ | $B_2$ | $B_3$ | $B_4$ |
|-------|-------|-------|-------|-------|
| $A_1$ | 1     | 9     | 6     | 0     |
| $A_2$ | 2     | 3     | 8     | 4     |
| $A_3$ | $-5$  | $-2$  | 10    | $-3$  |
| $A_4$ | 7     | 4     | $-2$  | $-5$  |

**(b)**

|       | $B_1$ | $B_2$ | $B_3$ | $B_4$ |
|-------|-------|-------|-------|-------|
| $A_1$ | $-1$  | 9     | 6     | 8     |
| $A_2$ | $-2$  | 10    | 4     | 6     |
| $A_3$ | 5     | 3     | 0     | 7     |
| $A_4$ | 7     | $-2$  | 8     | 4     |

**(c)**

|       | $B_1$ | $B_2$ | $B_3$ |
|-------|-------|-------|-------|
| $A_1$ | 3     | 6     | 1     |
| $A_2$ | 5     | 2     | 3     |
| $A_3$ | 4     | 2     | $-5$  |

**(d)**

|         | $B_1$ | $B_2$ | $B_3$ | $B_4$ |
|---------|-------|-------|-------|-------|
| $A_1$   | 3     | 7     | 1     | 3     |
| $A_2$   | 4     | 8     | 0     | -6    |
| $A_3$   | 6     | -9    | -2    | 4     |

4. Two companies promote two competing products. Each product currently controls 50% of the market. Because of recent improvements in the two products, the two companies are now preparing to launch an advertisement campaign. If neither company advertises, equal market shares will continue. If either company launches a stronger campaign, the other is certain to lose a proportional percentage of its customers. A survey of the market shows that 50% of potential customers can be reached through television, 30% through newspapers, and 20% through radio.

   **(a)** Formulate the problem as a two-person zero-sum game, and select the appropriate advertisement media for each of the two companies.

   **(b)** Determine a range for the value of the game. Can each company operate with a single pure strategy?

5. Let $a_{ij}$ be the $(i,j)$th element of a payoff matrix with $m$ strategies for player $A$ and $n$ strategies for player $B$. The payoff is for player $A$. Prove that

$$\max_i \min_j a_{ij} \le \min_j \max_i a_{ij}$$

### 14.5.2 Solution of Mixed Strategy Games

Games with mixed strategies can be solved either graphically or by linear programming. The graphical solution is suitable for games in which at least one player has exactly two pure strategies. The method is interesting because it explains the idea of a saddle point graphically. Linear programming can be used to solve any two-person zero-sum game.

   **Graphical solution of games.**   We start with the case of $(2 \times n)$ games in which player $A$ has two strategies.

|                | $y_1$<br>$B_1$ | $y_2$<br>$B_2$ | $\cdots$ | $y_n$<br>$B_n$ |
|----------------|----------------|----------------|----------|----------------|
| $x_1: A_1$     | $a_{11}$       | $a_{12}$       | $\cdots$ | $a_{1n}$       |
| $1 - x_1: A_2$ | $a_{21}$       | $a_{22}$       | $\cdots$ | $a_{2n}$       |

The game assumes that player $A$ mixes strategies $A_1$ and $A_2$ with the respective probabilities $x_1$ and $1 - x_1, 0 \leq x_1 \leq 1$. Player $B$ mixes strategies $B_1$ to $B_n$ with the probabilities $y_1, y_2, \ldots,$ and $y_n$, where $y_j \geq 0$ for $j = 1, 2, \ldots, n$ and $y_1 + y_2 + \ldots + y_n = 1$. In this case, $A$'s expected payoff corresponding to $B$'s $j$th pure strategy is computed as

$$(a_{1j} - a_{2j})x_1 - a_{2j}, j = 1, 2, \ldots n$$

Player $A$ thus seeks to determine the value of $x_1$ that maximizes the minimum expected payoffs—that is,

$$\max_{x_1} \ \min_j \ \{(a_{1j} - a_{2j})x_1 - a_{2j}\}$$

---

**Example 14.5–3.**

Consider the following $2 \times 4$ game. The payoff is for player $A$.

|       | $B_1$ | $B_2$ | $B_3$ | $B_4$ |
|-------|-------|-------|-------|-------|
| $A_1$ | 2     | 2     | 3     | $-1$  |
| $A_2$ | 4     | 3     | 2     | 6     |

The game has no pure strategy solution, and hence the strategies must be mixed. $A$'s expected payoffs corresponding to $B$'s pure strategies are given as

| $B$'s pure strategy | $A$'s expected payoff |
|---------------------|-----------------------|
| 1                   | $-2x_1 + 4$           |
| 2                   | $-x_1 + 3$            |
| 3                   | $x_1 + 2$             |
| 4                   | $-7x_1 + 6$           |

Figure 14–6 plots the four straight lines associated with $B$'s pure strategies. To determine the *best of the worst,* the lower envelope of the four lines (shown by the heavy line segments) represents the minimum (worst) expected payoff for $A$ regardless of what $B$ does. The maximum (best) of the lower envelope corresponds to the maximin solution point at $x_1^* = .5$. This point is the intersection of lines 3 and 4. Player A's optimal solution thus calls for mixing $A_1$ and $A_2$ with probabilities .5, and .5, respectively. The corresponding value of the game, $v$, is determined by substituting $x_1 = .5$ in either of the functions for lines 3 and 4, which gives

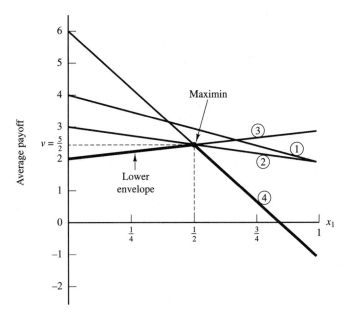

**Figure 14–6**

$$v = \begin{cases} \dfrac{1}{2} + 2 = \dfrac{5}{2}, & \text{from line 3} \\[2ex] -7\left(\dfrac{1}{2}\right) + 6 = \dfrac{5}{2}, & \text{from line 4} \end{cases}$$

Player $B$'s optimal mix is determined by the two strategies that define the lower envelope of the graph. This means that $B$ can mix strategies $B_3$ and $B_4$, in which case $y_1 = y_2 = 0$ and $y_4 = 1 - y_3$. As a result, $B$'s expected payoffs corresponding to $A$'s pure strategies are given as

| $A$'s pure strategy | $B$'s expected payoff |
|:---:|:---:|
| 1 | $4y_3 - 1$ |
| 2 | $-4y_3 + 6$ |

The *best of the worst* solution for $B$ is the minimum point on the *upper* envelope of the given two lines (you will find it instructive to plot the two lines and identify the upper envelope). This process is equivalent to solving the equation

$$4y_3 - 1 = -4y_3 + 6$$

The solution gives $y_3 = \frac{7}{8}$, which yields the value of the game as $v = 4 \times \left(\frac{7}{8}\right) - 1 = \frac{5}{2}$.

The solution of the game calls for player $A$ to mix $A_1$ and $A_2$ with equal probabilities and for player $B$ to mix $B_3$ and $B_4$ with probabilities $\frac{7}{8}$ and $\frac{1}{8}$. (Actually, the game has alternative solutions for $B$ because the maximin point in Figure 14–6 is determined by more than two lines. Any nonnegative combination of these alternative solutions is also a legitimate solution for the problem.)

---

For the games in which player $A$ has $m$ strategies and player $B$ has only two, the situation can be treated similarly. The main difference is that we will be plotting $B$'s expected payoff corresponding to $A$'s pure strategies. As a result, we will be seeking the minimax, rather than the maximin, point of the *upper envelope* of the plotted lines.

### Problem set 14.5b

1. Solve the coin-tossing game of Example 14.5–2 graphically.

2. Robin is a frequent traveler between two cities, where she has the option of traveling one of two routes: Route $A$ is a fast four-lane highway, and route $B$ is a long windy road. The highway patrol has a limited police force. If the full force is allocated to either route, Robin, with her passionate desire for driving superfast, is certain to receive a $100 speeding ticket. If the force is split 50–50 between the two routes, there is a 50% chance Robin will get a $100 ticket on route $A$ and a 30% chance that she will get the same fine on route $B$. Additionally, the longer route $B$ costs $15 more in gasoline than route $A$. Develop a strategy for both Robin and the police.

3. Solve the following games graphically. The payoff is for Player A.

   **(a)**

   |        | $B_1$ | $B_2$ | $B_3$ |
   |--------|-------|-------|-------|
   | $A_1$  | 1     | $-3$  | 7     |
   | $A_2$  | 2     | 4     | $-6$  |

   **(b)**

   |        | $B_1$ | $B_2$ |
   |--------|-------|-------|
   | $A_1$  | 5     | 8     |
   | $A_2$  | 6     | 5     |
   | $A_3$  | 5     | 7     |

4. Consider the following two-person, zero-sum game:

|       | $B_1$ | $B_2$ | $B_3$ |
|-------|-------|-------|-------|
| $A_1$ | 5.0   | 50.0  | 50.0  |
| $A_2$ | 1.0   | 1.0   | 0.1   |
| $A_3$ | 10.0  | 1.0   | 10.0  |

(a) Verify that the strategies $(\frac{1}{6}, 0, \frac{5}{6})$ for $A$ and $(\frac{49}{54}, \frac{5}{54}, 0)$ for $B$ are optimal, and determine the value of the game.

(b) Show that the optimal value of the game equals

$$\sum_{i=1}^{3} \sum_{j=1}^{3} a_{ij} x_i y_j$$

**Linear programming solution of games.**    Game theory bears a strong relationship to linear programming, in the sense that a two-person zero-sum game can be expressed as a linear program, and vice versa. In fact, G. Dantzig (1963, p. 24) states that when J. von Neumann, father of game theory, when first introduced to the simplex method in 1947, immediately recognized this relationship and further pointed out and stressed the concept of *duality* in linear programming. This section illustrates the solution of games by linear programming.

Player $A$'s optimal probabilities $x_i$, $i = 1, 2, \ldots, m$, can be determined by solving the following maximin problem,

$$\max_{x_i} \left\{ \min \left( \sum_{i=1}^{m} a_{i1} x_i, \sum_{i=1}^{m} a_{i2} x_i, \ldots, \sum_{i=1}^{m} a_{in} x_i \right) \right\}$$

$$x_1 + x_2 + \ldots + x_m = 1$$

$$x_i \geq 0, \quad i = 1, 2, \ldots, m$$

To transform the problem into a linear program, let

$$v = \min \left( \sum_{i=1}^{m} a_{i1} x_i, \sum_{i=1}^{m} a_{i2} x_i, \ldots, \sum_{i=1}^{m} a_{in} x_i \right)$$

The equation implies that

$$\sum_{i=1}^{m} a_{ij} x_i \geq v, \quad j = 1, 2, \ldots, n$$

Player $A$'s problem thus can be written as

Maximize $z = v$

subject to

$$\sum_{i=1}^{m} a_{ij} x_i \geq v, \quad j = 1, 2, \ldots, n$$

$$x_1 + x_2 + \ldots + x_m = 1$$

$$x_i \geq 0, \quad i = 1, 2, \ldots, m$$

$v$ unrestricted

Note that the value of the game, $v$, is unrestricted in sign.

Player $B$'s optimal strategies $y_1, y_2, \ldots,$ and $y_n$ are determined by solving the problem

$$\min_{y_j} \left\{ \max \left( \sum_{j=1}^{n} a_{1j} y_j, \sum_{j=1}^{n} a_{2j} y_j, \ldots, \sum_{j=1}^{n} a_{mj} y_j \right) \right\}$$

$$y_1 + y_2 + \ldots + y_n = 1$$

$$y_j \geq 0, \quad j = 1, 2, \ldots, n$$

Using a procedure similar to that followed with $A$'s problem, $B$'s problem reduces to

$$\text{Minimize } w = v$$

subject to

$$\sum_{j=1}^{n} a_{ij} y_j \leq v, \quad i = 1, 2, \ldots, m$$

$$y_1 + y_2 \ldots, y_m = 1$$

$$y_j \geq 0, \quad j = 1, 2, \ldots, n$$

$v$ unrestricted

The two problems optimize the same (unrestricted) variable $v$, the value of the game. The reason is that $B$'s problem is the dual of $A$'s problem (you are asked to prove this claim in Problem 14.5c–6 using the definition of duality in Chapter 4). This means that the optimal solution of one problem automatically yields the optimal solution to the other.

---

**Example 14.5–4.**

Solve the following game by linear programming.

|       | $B_1$ | $B_2$ | $B_3$ | Row min |
|-------|-------|-------|-------|---------|
| $A_1$ | 3     | −1    | −3    | −3      |
| $A_2$ | −2    | 4     | −1    | **−2**  |
| $A_3$ | −5    | −6    | 2     | −6      |
| Column max | 3 | 4 | **2** | |

The value of the game, $v$, lies between $-2$ and $2$.

*Player A's Linear Program*

$$\text{Maximize } z = v$$

subject to

$$3x_1 - 2x_2 - 5x_3 - v \geq 0$$

$$-x_1 + 4x_2 - 6x_3 - v \geq 0$$

$$-3x_1 - x_2 + 2x_3 - v \geq 0$$

$$x_1 + x_2 + x_3 = 1$$

$$x_1, x_2, x_3 \geq 0$$

$$v \text{ unrestricted}$$

The optimum solution, obtained by TORA, is $x_1 = .3945$, $x_2 = .3119$, $x_3 = .2936$, and $v = -.9083$.

The associated dual solution is $y_1 = -.3211$, $y_2 = -.0826$, $y_3 = -.5963$. The reason $y_1, y_2$, and $y_3$ are not positive, as they should be, is that $A$'s problem is a maximization with $\geq$ constraints, a condition that requires the associated dual variables to be negative (see Chapter 4). To see that this is the case, change all $\geq$ constraint in $A$'s problem to $\leq$ by multiplying both sides of each inequality by $-1$. The resulting dual values will be nonnegative, as desired (see Problem 14.5c–1). Indeed, in Problem 14.5c–6, the derivation of the dual directly from $A$'s problem will show that the dual problem representing $B$'s problem must have $y_i \leq 0$ but at the same time requires $-y_1 - y_2 - \ldots - y_n = 1$, which is the same as requiring $y_i \geq 0$ and $y_1 + y_2 + \ldots + y_n = 1$. Happily, all of this sign "confusion" can be avoided by changing $A$'s $\geq$ constraints into $\leq$.

*Player B's Linear Program*

$$\text{Minimize } z = v$$

subject to

$$3y_1 - y_2 - 3y_3 - v \leq 0$$

$$-2y_1 + 4y_2 - y_3 - v \leq 0$$

$$-5y_1 - 6y_2 + 2y_3 - v \leq 0$$

$$y_1 + y_2 + y_3 = 1$$

$$y_1, y_2, y_3 \geq 0$$

$$v \text{ unrestricted}$$

The solution by TORA yields $y_1 = .3211$, $y_2 = .0826$, $y_3 = .5963$, and $v = -.9083$. The associated dual solution is $x_1 = -.3945$, $y_2 = -.3119$, $x_3 = -.2936$. The dual values are negative because, as with $A$'s problem, the minimization problem has $\leq$ constraints. Conversion of the constraints to $\geq$ should rectify the situation.

**Problem set 14.5c**

1. Show in Example 14.5–4 that if the constraints of $A$'s problem are converted to $\leq$ and those of $B$'s problem are converted to $\geq$, then the dual values obtained from either problem will be nonnegative.

2. On a picnic outing, 2 two-person teams are playing hide-and-seek. There are four hiding locations (A, B, C, and D), and the two members of the hiding team can hide separately in any two of the four locations. The other team will then have the chance to search any two locations. The searching team gets a bonus point if they find both members of the hiding team. If they miss both, they lose a point. Otherwise, the game is a draw.
   **(a)** Set up the problem as a two-person zero-sum game.
   **(b)** Determine the optimal strategy and the value of the game.
   **(c)** Does the problem have alternative solutions?
   **(d)** Is this a fair game—that is, does it have a zero value?

3. UA and DU are setting up their strategies for the 1994 national championship college basketball game. Assessing the strengths of their respective "benches," each coach came up with four strategies for rotating their players during the game. The ability of each team in scoring 2-pointers, 3-pointers, and free throws is a key factor in determining the final score of the game. The following table summarizes the net points UA will score per possession as a function of the different strategies contemplated by each team:

|          | $DU_1$ | $DU_2$ | $DU_3$ | $DU_4$ |
|----------|--------|--------|--------|--------|
| $UA_1$   | 3      | -2     | 1      | 2      |
| $UA_2$   | 2      | 3      | -3     | 0      |
| $UA_3$   | -1     | 2      | -2     | 2      |
| $UA_4$   | -1     | -2     | 4      | 1      |

   **(a)** Solve the game by linear programming, and determine a strategy for the championship game.
   **(b)** Based on the given information, which of the two teams is projected to win the championship?
   **(c)** Suppose that the entire game will have a total of 60 possessions (30 for each team). Predict the expected number of points by which the championship will be won.

4. Colonel Blotto's army is fighting the enemy army for the control of two strategic locations. Blotto has two regiments, and the enemy has three. A location will fall to the army that attacks with more regiments. Otherwise, the result of the battle is a draw.

(a) Formulate the problem as a two-person zero-sum game, and solve by linear programming.

(b) Which army will win the battle?

5. In the two-player, two-finger Morra game, each player shows one or two fingers, and simultaneously guesses the number of fingers the opponent will show. The player making the correct guess wins an amount equal to the total number of fingers shown. Otherwise, the game is a draw. Set up the problem as a two-person zero-sum game, and solve by linear programming.

6. Show that the dual of $A$'s problem yields $B$'s problem and that the following two cases yield consistent results:

(a) $A$'s problem is as defined in Section 14.5.2.

(b) $A$'s problem is as in (a) except that the all $\geq$ constraints are first converted to $\leq$.

## 14.6 SUMMARY

This chapter has presented the decision criteria for problems with both perfect (deterministic) and imperfect (probabilistic or unknown) data. Further applications of the procedures with imperfect data will be presented in the succeeding chapters. In particular, the expected value criterion is used predominantly in the chapters on inventory, queueing, simulation, and Markovian decision processes. This does not mean that the others are not applicable. Rather, the expected value criterion is traditionally used because of its simplicity.

## SELECTED REFERENCES

CHEN, S., and HWANG, C., *Fuzzy Multiple Attribute Decision Making,* Springer-Verlag, Berlin, 1992.

DANTZIG, G. B., *Linear Programming and Extensions,* Princeton University Press, Princeton, N.J., 1963.

MEYERSON, R., *Game Theory: Analysis of Conflict,* Harvard University Press, Cambridge, Mass., 1991.

SAATY, T. L., *Fundamentals of Decision Making,* RWS Publications, Pittsburgh, 1994.

## COMPREHENSIVE PROBLEMS

■ 14–1[1]   A shop manager is considering three alternatives to an existing milling machine.

(a) Retrofit the existing mill with a power feed (PF).

[1]Based on S. Weber, "A Modified Analytic Hierarchy Process for Automated Manufacturing Decisions," *Interfaces,* Vol. 23, No. 4, pp. 75–84, 1993.

(b) Buy a new mill with a computer-aided design (CAD) feature.

(c) Replace the mill with a machining center (MC).

The three alternatives are evaluated based on two criteria: monetary and performance. The following table provides the pertinent data:

| Criterion | Units | PF | CAD | MC |
|---|---|---|---|---|
| Monetary | | | | |
| Initial cost ($) | | 12,000 | 25,000 | 120,000 |
| Maintenance cost ($) | | 2000 | 4000 | 15,00 |
| Training cost ($) | | 3000 | 8000 | 20,00 |
| Performance | | | | |
| Production rate | Units/d | 8 | 14 | 40 |
| Setup time | min | 30 | 20 | 3 |
| Scrap | lb/d | 440 | 165 | 44 |

The manager surmises that the monetary criterion is $1\frac{1}{2}$ times as important as the performance criterion. Additionally, the production rate is 2 times as important as the setup time, and 3 times as important as the scrap. The setup time is regarded as 4 times as important as the scrap. As for the monetary criteria, the manager estimates that the maintenance and training costs are of equal importance, and the initial cost is 2 times as important as either of these two costs.

Analyze the situation, and make an appropriate recommendation.

■ 14–2[2]   A company operates a catalog sales operation encompassing more than 200,000 items stocked in many regional warehouses. In the past, the company considered it essential to keep accurate records of the actual inventory in each warehouse. As a result, full inventory count was ordered every year—an intense and unwelcome activity that is done grudgingly by all warehouses. The company followed each count by an audit that sampled about 100 items per warehouse to check the quality of the logistical operation in each region. The result of the audit indicated that, on the average, only 64% of the items in each warehouse matched the actual inventory, which was unacceptable. To remedy the situation, the company ordered more frequent counts of the expensive and fast-moving items. A system analyst was assigned the task of setting up procedures for targeting these items.

Instead of responding directly to the company's request for identifying the target items, the system analyst decided to identify the cause of the problem. The analyst ended up changing the goal of the study from "How can we increase the *frequency* of inventory

[2]Based on I. Millet, "A Novena to Saint Anthony, or How to Find Inventory by Not Looking," *Interfaces,* Vol. 24, No. 2, pp. 69–75, 1994.

counts?" to "How can we increase the *accuracy* of inventory counts?" The study led to the following analysis: Given that the proportion of accurately counted items in a warehouse is $p$, the analyst assumed that it is reasonable to assume that there is a 95% chance that an item that was counted correctly in the first place will again be recounted correctly in a subsequent recount. For the proportion $1 - p$ that was not counted correctly in the first round, the chance of a correct recount is 80%. Using this information, the analyst used a decision tree to develop a break-even chart that compared the count accuracy in the first and second rounds. The end result was that the warehouses that had an accuracy level above the break-even threshold were not required to recount inventory. The surprising result of the proposed solution was a zealous effort on the part of each warehouse to get the count right the first time around, with a resounding across-the-board improvement in count accuracy in all the warehouses.

How did the analyst convince management of the viability of the proposed threshold for recounting?

■ 14–3[3]   In the airline industry, working hours are ruled by agreements with the unions. In particular, the maximum length of tour of duty may be limited to 16 hours for Boeing–747 flights and 14 hours for Boeing–707. If these limits are exceeded because of unexpected delays, the crew must be replaced by a fresh one. The airlines maintain reserve crews for such eventualities. The average annual cost of a reserve crew member is estimated at $30,000. Conversely, an overnight delay resulting from the unavailability of a reserve crew could cost as much as $50,000 for each delay. A crew member is on call 12 consecutive hours a day for 4 days of the week and may *not* be called on during the remaining 3 days of the week. The B–747 crew may also be served by two B–707 crews.

The following table summarizes the callout probabilities for reserve crews based on 3-year historical data.

| Trip category | Trip hr | Callout probability | |
| --- | --- | --- | --- |
| | | B-747 | B-707 |
| 1 | 14.0 | .014 | .072 |
| 2 | 13.0 | .0 | .019 |
| 3 | 12.5 | .0 | .006 |
| 4 | 12.0 | .016 | .006 |
| 5 | 11.5 | .003 | .003 |
| 6 | 11.0 | .002 | .003 |

As an illustration, the data indicate that for 14-hour trips, the probability of a callout is .014 for B-747 and .072 for B707.

[3]Based on A. Gaballa, "Planning Callout Reserves for Aircraft Delays," *Interfaces,* Vol. 9, No. 2, Part 2, pp. 78–86, 1979.

The following is a typical *peak* day schedule:

| Time of day | Aircraft | Trip category |
|-------------|----------|---------------|
| 8:00 | 707 | 3 |
| 9:00 | 707 | 6 |
| | 707 | 2 |
| 10:00 | 707 | 3 |
| 11:00 | 707 | 2 |
| | 707 | 4 |
| 15:00 | 747 | 6 |
| 16:00 | 747 | 4 |
| 19:00 | 747 | 1 |

The present policy for reserve crews calls for using two (seven-member) crews between 5:00 and 11:00, four between 11:00 and 17:00, and two between 17:00 and 23:00.

Evaluate the effectiveness of the present reserve crew policy. Specifically, is the present reserve crew size too large, too small, or just right?

# Chapter 15

# Probabilistic Dynamic Programming

## 15.1 INTRODUCTION[1]

Probabilistic dynamic programming (DP) differs from deterministic DP (Chapter 10) in that the states and the returns at each stage are probabilistic. Probabilistic DP arises particularly in the treatment of stochastic inventory models and in Markovian decision processes. These two topics are treated separately in Chapters 16 and 19, and hence will not be treated in this chapter. Instead, we will present some general examples that are designed to bring about the stochastic nature of DP.

## 15.2 A GAME OF CHANCE

A variation of the Russian roulette game calls for spinning a wheel marked along the perimeter with $n$ consecutive numbers: 1 to $n$. The probability that the wheel will stop at number $i$ after one spin is $p_i$. A player pays \$$x$ for the privilege of spinning the wheel up to $m$ spins. The resulting payoff to the player is double the number produced in the *last* spin. Assuming that the game (of up to $m$ spins each) is repeated a reasonably large number of times, devise an optimal strategy for the player.

We can construct the problem as a DP model using the following definitions:

**1.** *Stage $i$* is represented by spin $i$ of the wheel, $i = 1, 2, ..., m$.

**2.** The *alternatives* at each stage include either spinning the wheel once more or ending the game.

[1]This chapter is a continuation of the material in Chapter 10 on deterministic dynamic programming.

**3.** The *state j* of the system at stage *i* is represented by one of the numbers 1 to *n* that was obtained in the *last* spin.

Let

$$f_i(j) = \text{Maximum expected return given that the game is at stage}$$
$$\text{(spin) } i \text{ and that } i \text{ is the outcome of the } last \text{ spin}$$

We thus have

$$\begin{pmatrix} \text{Expected pay off at stage } i \\ \text{given last spin's outcome } j \end{pmatrix} = \begin{cases} 2j, & \text{if game ends} \\ \sum_{k=1}^{n} p_k f_{i+1}(k), & \text{if game continues} \end{cases}$$

The recursive equation may then be written as

$$f_{m+1}(j) = 2j$$

$$f_i(j) = \max \begin{cases} \text{End: } 2j, \\ \text{Spin: } \sum_{k=1}^{n} p_k f_{i+1}(k) & i = 2, 3, ..., m \end{cases}$$

$$f_1(0) = \sum_{k=1}^{n} p_k f_2(k)$$

The rationale for the recursive equation is that at the first spin ($i = 1$), the state of the system is $j = 0$ because the game has just started. Hence, $f_1(0) = p_1 f_2(1) + p_2 f_2(2) + \dots + p_n f_2(n)$. After the last spin ($i = m$), the only option open to us is to end the game regardless of the outcome $j$ of the $m$th spin. Thus, $f_{m+1}(j) = 2j$.

The recursive calculations start with $f_{m+1}$ and terminate with $f_1(0)$, thus producing $m + 1$ computational stages. Because $f_1(0)$ is the expected return from all $m$ spins, and given that the game costs \$x, it follows that

$$\text{Expected net return} = f_1(0) - x$$

---

**Example 15.2–1.**

Suppose that the perimeter of the Russian roulette wheel is marked with the numbers 1 to 5. The probability $p_i$ of stopping at the number $i$ is given by $p_1 = .3, p_2 = .25, p_3 = .2, p_4 = .15$, and $p_5 = .1$. The player pays \$5 for a maximum of four spins. Determine the optimal strategy for each of the four spins and find the associated expected net return.

*Stage 5*

$$f_5(j) = 2j$$

| Spin 4 outcome | Optimum solution | |
|:---:|:---:|:---:|
| $j$ | $f_5(j)$ | Decision |
| 1 | 2 | End |
| 2 | 4 | End |
| 3 | 6 | End |
| 4 | 8 | End |
| 5 | 10 | End |

*Stage 4*

$$f_4(j) = \max \{2j,\ p_1 f_5(1) + p_2 f_5(2) + p_3 f_5(3) + p_4 f_5(4) + p_5 f_5(5)\}$$

$$= \max \{2j,\ .3 \times 2 + .25 \times 4 + .2 \times 6 + .15 \times 8 + .1 \times 10\}$$

$$= \max \{2j,\ 5\}$$

| Spin 3 outcome | Expected return | | Optimum solution | |
|:---:|:---:|:---:|:---:|:---:|
| $j$ | End | Spin | $f_4(j)$ | Decision |
| 1 | 2 | 5 | 5 | Spin |
| 2 | 4 | 5 | 5 | Spin |
| 3 | 6 | 5 | 6 | End |
| 4 | 8 | 5 | 8 | End |
| 5 | 10 | 5 | 10 | End |

*Stage 3*

$$f_3(j) = \max \{2j,\ p_1 f_4(1) + p_2 f_4(2) + p_3 f_4(3) + p_4 f_4(4) + p_5 f_4(5)\}$$

$$= \max \{2j,\ .3 \times 5 + .25 \times 5 + .2 \times 6 + .15 \times 8 + .1 \times 10\}$$

$$= \max \{2j,\ 6.15\}$$

| Spin 2 outcome | Expected return | | Optimum solution | |
|:---:|:---:|:---:|:---:|:---:|
| $j$ | End | Spin | $f_3(j)$ | Decision |
| 1 | 2 | 6.15 | 6.15 | Spin |
| 2 | 4 | 6.15 | 6.15 | Spin |
| 3 | 6 | 6.15 | 6.15 | Spin |
| 4 | 8 | 6.15 | 8.00 | End |
| 5 | 10 | 6.15 | 10.00 | End |

*Stage 2*

$$f_2(j) = \max \{2j, \; p_1 f_3(1) + p_2 f_3(2) + p_3 f_3(3) + p_4 f_3(4) + p_5 f_3(5)\}$$

$$= \max \{2j, \; .3 \times 6.15 + .25 \times 6.15 + .2 \times 6.15 + .15 \times 8 + .1 \times 10\}$$

$$= \max \{2j, \; 6.8125\}$$

| Spin 1 outcome | Expected return | | Optimum solution | |
|:---:|:---:|:---:|:---:|:---:|
| $j$ | End | Spin | $f_3(j)$ | Decision |
| 1 | 2 | 6.81 | 6.81 | Spin |
| 2 | 4 | 6.81 | 6.81 | Spin |
| 3 | 6 | 6.81 | 6.81 | Spin |
| 4 | 8 | 6.81 | 8.00 | End |
| 5 | 10 | 6.81 | 10.00 | End |

*Stage 1*

$$f_1(0) = p_1 f_2(1) + p_2 f_2(2) + p_3 f_2(3) + p_4 f_2(4) + p_5 f_2(5)$$

$$= .3 \times 6.8125 + .25 \times 6.8125 + .2 \times 6.8125 + .15 \times 8 + .1 \times 10$$

$$= 7.31$$

The only option available at the start of the game is to spin.
From the preceding tableaux, the optimal solution is

| Spin No. | Optimal strategy |
|:---:|:---:|
| 1 | Game starts, spin |
| 2 | Continue if spin 1 produces 1, 2, or 3; else, end the game |
| 3 | Continue if spin 2 produces 1, 2, or 3; else, end the game |
| 4 | Continue if spin 3 produces 1 or 2; else, end the game |

The expected net return of the game is $7.31 − $5.00 = $2.31.

## Problem set 15.2a

**1.** In Example 15.2–1, suppose that the wheel is marked with the numbers 1 to 8 and that the wheel will stop at any of these numbers with equal probabilities. Assuming that each game includes a total of five spins, develop an optimal strategy for the game.

**2.** I would like to sell my used car to the highest bidder. Studying the market, I have concluded that I am likely to receive four types of offers with equal probabilities: very low at about $1050, low at about $1900, medium at about $2500, and high at about $3000. I decided to advertise the car for up to 3 consecutive days. At the end of each day, I would decide whether or not to accept the best offer made that day. What should be my optimal strategy regarding the acceptance of an offer?

## 15.3 INVESTMENT PROBLEM

An individual wishes to invest up to $$C$ thousand in the stock market over the next $n$ years. The investment plan calls for buying the stock at the start of the year and selling it at the end of the same year. Accumulated money may then be reinvested

(in whole or part) at the start of the following year. The degree of risk in the investment is represented by expressing the return probabilistically. A study of the market
shows that the return on investment is affected by $m$ (favorable or unfavorable)
market conditions and that condition $i$ yields a return $r_i$ with probability $p_i, i = 1, 2,$
..., $m$. How should the amount $C$ be invested to realize the highest accumulation at
the end of $n$ years?

Define

$x_i$ = Amount of funds available for investment at the start of year $i$ ($x_1 = C$)
$y_i$ = Amount actually invested at the start of year $i$ ($y_i \leq x_i$)

The elements of the DP model can be described as

1. *Stage $i$* is represented by year $i$.
2. The *alternatives* at stage $i$ are given by $y_i$.
3. The *state* at stage $i$ is given by $x_i$.

Let

$f_i(x_i)$ = Maximum expected funds for years $i, i + 1, ...,$ and $n$, given $x_i$
at the start of year $i$

For market condition $k$, we have

$$x_{i+1} = (1 + r_k)y_i + (x_i - y_i) = r_k y_i + x_i, k = 1, 2, ..., m$$

Given that market condition $k$ occurs with probability $p_k$, the DP recursive equation
is written as

$$f_i(x_i) = \max_{0 \leq y_i \leq x_i} \left\{ \sum_{k=1}^{m} p_k f_{i+1}(x_i + r_k y_i) \right\}, i = 1, 2, ..., n$$

where $f_{n+1}(x_{n+1}) = x_{n+1}$ because no investment occurs after year $n$. It follows that

$$f_n(x_n) = \max_{0 \leq y_n \leq x_n} \left\{ \sum_{k=1}^{m} p_k(x_n + r_k y_n) \right\}$$

$$= x_n \sum_{k=1}^{m} p_k(1 + r_k)$$

$$= x_n(1 + p_1 r_1 + p_2 r_2 + ... + p_m r_m)$$

The function in {.} is linear in $y_n$, and hence its maximum value occurs at $y_n = x_n$.

---

**Example 15.3–1.**

In the preceding investment model, suppose that you want to invest $10,000 over the
next 4 years. There is a 40% chance that you will double your money, a 20% chance that

you will break even, and a 40% chance that you will lose the entire initial investment. Devise an optimal investment strategy.

Using the notation of the model, we have

$$C = \$10,000, n = 4, m = 3$$

$$p_1 = .4, p_2 = .2, p_3 = .4$$

$$r_1 = 2, r_2 \, 0, r_3 = -1$$

*Stage 4*

$$f_4(x_4) = x_4(1 + .4 \times 2 + .2 \times 0 + .4 \times -1) = 1.4x_4$$

Thus, we get

|  | Optimum solution | |
|---|---|---|
| State | $f_4(x_4)$ | $y_4^*$ |
| $x_4$ | $1.4x_4$ | $x_4$ |

*Stage 3*

$$f_3(x_3) = \max_{0 \leq y_3 \leq x_3} \{p_1 f_4(x_3 + r_1 y_3) + p_2 f_4(x_3 + r_2 y_3) + p_3 f_4(x_3 + r_3 y_3)\}$$

$$= \max_{0 \leq y_3 \leq x_3} \{.4 \times 1.4(x_3 + 2y_3) + .2 \times 1.4(x_3 + 0y_3) + .4 \times 1.4[x_3 + (-1)y_3]\}$$

$$= \max_{0 \leq y_3 \leq x_3} \{1.4x_3 + .56y_3\}$$

$$= 1.96x_3$$

Thus, we get

|  | Optimum solution | |
|---|---|---|
| State | $f_3(x_3)$ | $y_3^*$ |
| $x_3$ | $1.96x_3$ | $x_3$ |

*Stage 2*

$$f_2(x_2) = \max_{0 \leq y_2 \leq x_2} \{p_1 f_3(x_2 + r_1 y_2) + p_2 f_3(x_2 + r_2 y_2) + p_3 f_3(x_2 + r_3 y_2)\}$$

$$= \max_{0 \leq y_2 \leq x_2} \{.4 \times 1.96(x_2 + 2y_2) + .2 \times 1.96(x_2 + 0y_2) + .4 \times 1.96[x_2 + (-1)y_2]\}$$

$$= \max_{0 \le y_2 \le x_2} \{1.96x_2 + .784y_2\}$$

$$= 2.744x_2$$

Thus, we get

|       | Optimum solution | |
| :---: | :---: | :---: |
| State | $f_2(x_2)$ | $y_2^*$ |
| $x_2$ | $2.744x_2$ | $x_2$ |

*Stage 1*

$$f_1(x_1) = \max_{0 \le y_1 \le x_1} \{p_1 f_2(x_1 + r_1 y_1) + p_2 f_2(x_1 + r_2 y_1) + p_3 f_2(x_1 + r_3 y_1)\}$$

$$= \max_{0 \le y_i \le x_i} \{.4 \times 2.744(x_1 + 2y_1) + .2 \times 2.744(x_1 + 0y_1) + .4 \times 2.744[x_1 + (-1)y_1]\}$$

$$= \max_{0 \le y_i \le x_i} \{2.744x_1 + 1.0976y_1\}$$

$$= 3.8416x_1$$

Thus, we get

|       | Optimum solution | |
| :---: | :---: | :---: |
| State | $f_1(x_1)$ | $y_1^*$ |
| $x_1$ | $3.8416x_1$ | $x_1$ |

The optimal investment policy can thus be summarized as follows: Because $y_i^* = x_i$ for $i = 1$ to 4, the optimal solution calls for investing all available funds at the start of each year. The accumulated funds at the end of 4 years are $3.8416x_1 = 3.8416(\$10,000) = \$38,416$.

---

### Problem set 15.3a

**1.** In Example 15.3–1, find the optimal investment strategy, assuming that the probabilities $p_k$ and return $r_k$ vary for the 4 years according to the following data:

| Yr | $r_1$ | $r_2$ | $r_3$ | $p_1$ | $p_2$ | $p_3$ |
|----|-------|-------|-------|-------|-------|-------|
| 1  | 2     | 1     | .5    | .1    | .4    | .5    |
| 2  | 1     | 0     | −1    | .4    | .4    | .2    |
| 3  | 4     | −1    | −1    | .2    | .4    | .4    |
| 4  | .8    | .4    | .2    | .6    | .2    | .2    |

2. A 10-m3 compartment is available for storing three items. The volumes needed to store 1 unit of items 1 to 3 are 2, 1, and 3 m3, respectively. The probabilistic demand for the items is described as follows:

| | Probability of demand | | |
|---|---|---|---|
| No. of units | Item 1 | Item 2 | Item 3 |
| 1 | .5 | .3 | .3 |
| 2 | .5 | .4 | .2 |
| 3 | .0 | .2 | .5 |
| 4 | .0 | .1 | .0 |

The shortage cost per unit for items 1 to 3 are $8, $10, and $15, respectively. How many units of each item should be held in the compartment?

3. HiTec has just started to produce supercomputers for a limited period of 3 years. The annual demand, D, for the new computer is described by the following distribution:

$$p(D = 1) = .5, \ p(D = 2) = .3, \ p(D = 3) = .2$$

The production capacity of the plant is three computers annually at the cost of $5 million each. The actual number of computers produced per year may not equal the demand exactly. An unsold computer at the end of a year incurs $1 million in storage and maintenance costs. A loss of $2 million occurs if the delivery of a computer is delayed by 1 year. HiTec would not accept new orders beyond year 4 but will continue production in year 5 to satisfy any unfilled demand at the end of year 4. Determine the optimal annual production schedule for HiTec.

4. The PackRat Outdoors Company owns three sports centers in downtown Little Rock. On Easter Day, bicycle riding is a desirable outdoors activity.

The company owns a total of eight rental bikes to be allocated to the three centers with the objective of maximizing revenues. The demand for the bikes and the hourly rental cost varies by location and are described by the following distributions:

|  | Probability of demand | | |
|---|---|---|---|
| No. of bikes | Center 1 | Center 2 | Center 3 |
| 0 | .1 | .02 | 0 |
| 1 | .2 | .03 | .15 |
| 2 | .3 | .10 | .25 |
| 3 | .2 | .25 | .30 |
| 4 | .1 | .30 | .15 |
| 5 | .1 | .15 | .10 |
| 6 | 0 | .05 | .025 |
| 7 | 0 | .05 | .025 |
| 8 | 0 | .05 | 0 |
| Rental cost/hr ($) | 6 | 7 | 5 |

How should PackRat allocate the eight bikes to the three centers?

## 15.4 MAXIMIZATION OF THE EVENT OF ACHIEVING A GOAL

In Section 15.3, we are interested in maximizing the optimal expected return. Another useful criterion for the problem is the maximization of the probability of achieving a certain level of return. We illustrate the model by using the investment situation in Section 15.3.

Using the notation in Section 15.3, the definitions of the *stage, i, alternative, $y_i$,* and *state, $x_i$,* remain the same. The two models differ in the definition of the objective criterion. Our goal in the current model is to maximize the probability of realizing a certain cumulative sum of money, $S$, at the end of $n$ years. From this standpoint, define

$f_i(x_i) = $ Probability of realizing the amount $S$ given $x_i$ is the amount of funds available at the start of year $i$ and that an optimal policy is implemented for years $i, i + 1, \ldots,$ and $n$

The DP recursive equation is thus given as

$$f_n(x_n) = \max_{0 \le y_n \le x_n} \left\{ \sum_{k=1}^{m} p_k P\{x_n + r_k y_n \ge S\} \right\}$$

$$f_i(x_i) = \max_{0 \le y_i \le x_i} \left\{ \sum_{k=1}^{m} p_k f_{i+1}(x_i + r_k y_i) \right\}, \quad i = 1, 2, ..., n - 1$$

The recursive formula is based on the conditional probability law

$$P\{A\} = \sum_{j=1}^{m} P\{A \mid B_j\} P\{B_j\}$$

In this case, $f_{i+1}(x_i + r_k y_i)$ plays the role of $P\{A \mid B_j\}$.

---

**Example 15.4–1.**

An individual wants to invest $2000. Available options allow doubling the amount invested with probability .3 or losing all of it with probability .7. Investments are sold at the end of the year, and reinvestment, in whole or part, starts again at the beginning of the following year. The process is repeated for three consecutive years. The objective is to maximize the probability of realizing $4000 at the end of the third year.

Using the notation of the model, we say that $r_1 = 1$ with probability .3, and $r_2 = -1$ with probability .7.

*Stage 3*

At stage 3, the state $x_3$ can be as small as $0 and as large as $8000. The minimum value is realized when the entire investment is lost, and the maximum value occurs when the investment is doubled at the end of each of the first 2 years. The recursive equation for stage 3 is thus written as

$$f_3(x_3) = \max_{y_3 = 0, 1, ..., x_3} \{.3P\{x_3 + y_3 \ge 4\} + .7P\{x_3 - y_3 \ge 4\}\}$$

where $x_3 = 0, 1, ..., 8$.

The tableau on page 582 details the computations for stage 3. All the shaded entries are infeasible because they do not satisfy the condition $y_3 \le x_3$. Also, in carrying out the computations, we notice that

$$P\{x_3 + y_3 \ge 4\} = 0, \text{ if } x_3 + y_3 < 4$$

$$P\{x_3 - y_3 \ge 4\} = 0, \text{ if } x_3 - y_3 < 4$$

Otherwise, these probabilities equal 1.

Although the tableau, on page 582 shows that alternative optima exist for $x_3 = 1$, 3, 4, 5, 6, 7, and 8, the optimum (last) column only provides the smallest optimum $y_3$. The assumption here is that the investor is not going to invest more than what is absolutely necessary to achieve the desired goal.

$$.3P(x_3 + y_3 \geq 4) + .7P(x_3 - y_3 \geq 4)$$

| $x_3$ | $y_3 = 0$ | 1 | 2 | 3 | 4 | 5 | 6 | 7 | 8 | Optimum $f_3$ | Optimum $y_3$ |
|---|---|---|---|---|---|---|---|---|---|---|---|
| 0 | $.3\times0+$ $.7\times0=0$ | | | | | | | | | 0 | 0 |
| 1 | $.3\times0+$ $.7\times0=0$ | $.3\times0+$ $.7\times0=0$ | | | | | | | | 0 | 0 |
| 2 | $.3\times0+$ $.7\times0=0$ | $.3\times0+$ $.7\times0=0$ | $.3\times1+$ $.7\times0=.3$ | | | | | | | .3 | 2 |
| 3 | $.3\times0+$ $.7\times0=0$ | $.3\times1+$ $.7\times0=.3$ | $.3\times1+$ $.7\times0=.3$ | $.3\times1+$ $.7\times0=.3$ | | | | | | .3 | 1 |
| 4 | $.3\times1+$ $.7\times1=1$ | $.3\times1+$ $.7\times0=.3$ | $.3\times1+$ $.7\times0=.3$ | $.3\times1+$ $.7\times0=.3$ | $.3\times1+$ $.7\times0=.3$ | | | | | 1 | 0 |
| 5 | $.3\times1+$ $.7\times1=1$ | $.3\times1+$ $.7\times1=1$ | $.3\times1+$ $.7\times0=.3$ | $.3\times1+$ $.7\times0=.3$ | $.3\times1+$ $.7\times0=.3$ | $.3\times1+$ $.7\times0=.3$ | | | | 1 | 0 |
| 6 | $.3\times1+$ $.7\times1=1$ | $.3\times1+$ $.7\times1=1$ | $.3\times1+$ $.7\times1=1$ | $.3\times1+$ $.7\times0=.3$ | $.3\times1+$ $.7\times0=.3$ | $.3\times1+$ $.7\times0=.3$ | $.3\times1+$ $.7\times0=.$ | | | 1 | 0 |
| 7 | $.3\times1+$ $.7\times1=1$ | $.3\times1+$ $.7\times1=1$ | $.3\times1+$ $.7\times1=1$ | $.3\times1+$ $.7\times1=1$ | $.3\times1+$ $.7\times0=.3$ | $.3\times1+$ $.7\times0=.3$ | $.3\times1+$ $.7\times0=.3$ | $.3\times1+$ $.7\times0=.3$ | | 1 | 0 |
| 8 | $.3\times1+$ $.7\times1=1$ | $.3\times1+$ $.7\times1=1$ | $.3\times1+$ $.7\times1=1$ | $.3\times1+$ $.7\times1=1$ | $.3\times1+$ $.7\times1=1$ | $.3\times1+$ $.7\times0=.3$ | $.3\times1+$ $.7\times0=.3$ | $.3\times1+$ $.7\times0=.3$ | $.3\times1+$ $.7\times0=.3$ | 1 | 0 |

*Stage 2*

$$f_2(x_2) = \max_{y_2=0,1,\ldots,x_2} \{.3f_3(x_2 + y_2) + .7f_3(x_2 - y_2)\}$$

| $x_2$ | $.3f_3(x_2 + y_2) + .7f_3(x_2 - y_2)$ | | | | | Optimum | |
|---|---|---|---|---|---|---|---|
| | $y_2 = 0$ | 1 | 2 | 3 | 4 | $f_2$ | $y_2$ |
| 0 | .3 × 0 + <br> .7 × 0 = 0 | | | | | 0 | 0 |
| 1 | .3 × 0 + <br> .7 × 0 = 0 | .3 × .3 + <br> .7 × 0 = .9 | | | | .09 | 1 |
| 2 | .3 × .3 + <br> .7 × .3 = .3 | .3 × .3 + <br> .7 × 0 = .09 | .3 × 1 + <br> .7 × 0 = .3 | | | .30 | 0 |
| 3 | .3 × .3 + <br> .7 × .3 = .3 | .3 × 1 + <br> .7 × .3 = .51 | .3 × 1 + <br> .7 × 0 = .3 | .3 × 1 + <br> .7 × 0 = .3 | | .51 | 1 |
| 4 | .3 × 1 + <br> .7 × 1 = 1 | .3 × 1 + <br> .7 × .3 = .51 | .3 × 1 + <br> .7 × .3 = .51 | .3 × 1 + <br> .7 × 0 = .3 | .3 × 1 + <br> .7 × 0 = .3 | 1 | 0 |

*Stage 1*

$$f_1(x_1) = \max_{y_1=0,1,2} \{.3f_2(x_1 + y_1) + .7f_2(x_1 - y_1)\}$$

| $x_1$ | $.3f_2(x_1 + y_1) + .7f_2(x_1 - y_1)$ | | | Optimum | |
|---|---|---|---|---|---|
| | $y_1 = 0$ | 1 | 2 | $f_1$ | $y_1$ |
| 2 | .3 × .3 + .7 × .3 <br> = .3 | .3 × .51 + .7 × .09 <br> = .216 | .3 × 1 + .7 × 0 <br> = .3 | .3 | 0 |

The optimum strategy is determined in the following manner: Given the initial investment $x_1 = \$2000$, stage 1 computations yields $y_1 = 0$, which means that no investment should be made in year 1. The decision not to invest in year 1 leaves the investor with $2000 at the start of year 2. From the stage 2 tableau, $x_2 = 2$ yields $y_2 = 0$, indicating once again that no investment should occur in year 2. Next, using $x_3 = 2$, stage 3 shows that $y_3 = 2$, which calls for investing the entire amount in year 3. The associated maximum probability for realizing the goal $S = 4$ is $f_1(2) = .3$.

## Problem set 15.4a

**1.** In Example 15.4–1, stage 1 indicates the alternative optima $y_1 = 0$ and $y_1 = 2$. Show that $y_1 = 2$ (i.e., invest all in year 1) will still lead to the same investment strategy for all 3 years—namely, the associated maximum probability remains equal to .3.

**2.** Solve Example 15.4–1 using the following data: The investor's goal is to maximize the probability of realizing at least $6000 at the end of year 3. The amount available to the investor is $1000 and the probability of doubling the money in any year is .6.

**3.** You and a friend can play the following game in the Tropicana Casino. You bet a certain amount of money, and each of you flips a fair coin independently. For each $1 you bet, Tropicana will pay back $3 (that gives a net gain of $2) if the outcome is *HH*. Otherwise, you lose the amount you bet. Assuming that you and your friend have a total of $1, determine the game strategy given that the objective is to maximize the probability of ending up with $4 after three games.

## SELECTED REFERENCES

BERTSEKAS, D., *Dynamic Programming: Deterministic and Stochastic Models*, Prentice Hall, Upper Saddle River, N.J., 1987.

COOPER, L., and M. COOPER, *Introduction to Dynamic Programming*, Pergamon Press, New York, 1981.

SMITH, D., *Dynamic Programming: A Practical Introduction*, Ellis Horwood, London, 1991.

## COMPREHENSIVE PROBLEM

■ **15–1** UPPS uses trucks to deliver orders to customers. The company wants to develop a replacement policy for its fleet over the next 5 years. The annual operating cost of a new truck is normally distributed with mean $300 and standard deviation $50. The mean and standard deviation of the operating cost increases by 10% a year thereafter. The current price of a new truck is $20,000, and it is expected to increase by 12% a year. Because of the extensive use of the truck, there is a chance that it might break down irreparably at any time. The trade-in value of a truck depends on whether it is broken or in working order. At the start of year 6, the truck is salvaged, and its salvage value again depends on its condition (broken or in working order). The following table provides the data of the situation as a function of the age of the truck:

| Truck age (yr) | 0 | 1 | 2 | 3 | 4 | 5 | 6 |
|---|---|---|---|---|---|---|---|
| Probability of breakdown | .01 | .05 | .10 | .16 | .25 | .40 | .60 |

If the truck is in working condition, its trade-in value after 1 year of operation is 70% of the purchase price and decreases by 15% a year thereafter. The trade-in value of the truck is halved if it is broken. The salvage value of the truck at the start of year 6 is $200 if it is in working condition and $50 if it is broken. Develop the optimal replacement policy for the truck.

# Chapter 16

# Probabilistic Inventory Models

## 16.1 INTRODUCTION[1]

Chapter 11 provides the foundation of inventory modeling under deterministic conditions. This chapter deals with probabilistic inventory models in which the demand is described by a probability distribution. The developed models are categorized broadly under *continuous* and *periodic* review situations. The periodic review models includes both single-period and multiperiod cases.

## 16.2 CONTINUOUS REVIEW MODELS

This section presents two models: (1) a "propabilitized" version of the deterministic EOQ (Section 11.3.1) that uses a buffer stock to account for probabilistic demand, and (2) a more exact probabilistic EOQ model that includes the probabilistic demand directly in the formulation.

### 16.2.1 "Probabilitized" EOQ Model

Some practitioners have sought to adapt the deterministic EOQ model (Section 11.3.1) to reflect the probabilistic nature of demand by using an approximation that superimposes a constant buffer stock on the inventory level throughout the entire planning horizon. The size of the buffer is determined such that the probability of running out of stock *during lead time* (the period between placing and receiving an order) does not exceed a prespecified value.

[1]This chapter is a continuation of the material in Chapter 11 on deterministic inventory models.

Let

$L$  = Lead time between placing and receiving an order

$x_L$ = Random variable representing demand during lead time

$\mu_L$ = Average demand during lead time

$\sigma_L$ = Standard deviation of demand during lead time

$B$  = Buffer stock size

$\alpha$  = Maximum allowable probability of running out of stock during lead time

The main assumption of the model is that the demand, $x_L$, during lead time $L$ is normally distributed with mean $\mu_L$ and standard deviation $\sigma_L$—that is, $N(\mu_L, \sigma_L)$.

Figure 16–1 depicts the relationship between the buffer stock, $B$, and the parameters of the deterministic EOQ model that include the lead time $L$, the average demand during lead time, $\mu_L$, and the EOQ, $y^*$. Note that $L$ must equal the *effective* lead time as defined in Section 11.3.1.

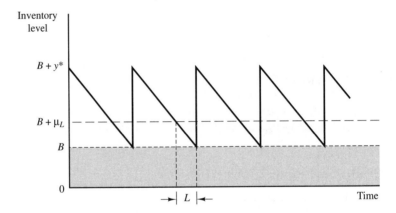

**Figure 16–1**

The probability statement used to determine $B$ can be written as

$$P\{x_L \geq B + \mu_L\} \leq \alpha$$

By definition (see Section 12.5.4),

$$z = \frac{x_L - \mu_L}{\sigma_L}$$

is a $N(0, 1)$ random variable. Thus, we have

$$P\left\{z \geq \frac{B}{\sigma_L}\right\} \leq \alpha$$

Figure 16–2 defines $K_\alpha$, which is determined from the standard normal tables (see Appendix D) such that

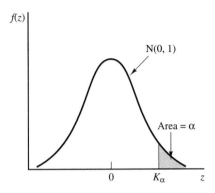

**Figure 16–2**

$$P\{z \geq K_\alpha\} = \alpha$$

Hence, the buffer size must satisfy

$$B \geq \sigma_L K_\alpha$$

The demand during the lead time, $L$, usually is described by a probability density function *per unit time* (e.g., per day or week), from which we can determine the distribution of the demand during $L$. Specifically, given that the demand per unit time is normal with mean $D$ and standard deviation $\sigma$, then, in general, the demand during $L$ is $N(\mu_L, \sigma_L)$, where

$$\mu_L = DL$$
$$\sigma_L = \sqrt{\sigma^2 L}$$

The formula for $\sigma_L$ requires $L$ to be (rounded to) an integer value.

---

**Example 16.2–1.**

In Example 11.3–1 dealing with determining the inventory policy of neon lights, it was determined that EOQ = 1000 units. If the *daily* demand is normal with mean $D = 100$ lights and standard deviation $\sigma = 10$ lights—that is, $N(100, 10)$—determine the buffer size so that the probability of running out of stock is below $\alpha = .05$.

From Example 11.3–1, the effective lead time is $L = 2$ days. Thus,

$$\mu_L = DL = 100 \times 2 = 200 \text{ units}$$
$$\sigma_L = \sqrt{\sigma^2 L} = \sqrt{10^2 \times 2} = 14.14 \text{ units}$$

From the normal tables (Appendix D), $K_{.05} = 1.64$. Hence, the buffer size is computed as

$$B \geq 14.14 \times 1.64 \approx 23 \text{ neon lights}$$

Given the EOQ $y^* = 1000$ lights, the optimal inventory policy with buffer $B$ calls for ordering 1000 units whenever the inventory level drops to 223 ($= B + \mu_L = 23 + 2 \times 100$) units.

---

**Problem set 16.2a**

1. In Example 16.2–1, determine the optimal inventory policy for each of the following cases:
   **(a)** Lead time = 15 days.
   **(b)** Lead time = 23 days.
   **(c)** Lead time = 8 days.
   **(d)** Lead time = 10 days.

2. A music store sells a best-selling compact disc. The daily demand for the disc is approximately normally distributed with mean 200 discs and a standard deviation of 20 discs. The cost of keeping the discs in the store is $.04 per disc per day. It costs the store $100 to place a new order. The supplier normally specifies a 7-day lead time for delivery. Assuming that the store wants to limit the probability of running out of discs during the lead time to no more than .02, determine the store's optimal inventory policy.

3. The daily demand for camera films at a gift shop in a resort area is normally distributed with a mean of 30 rolls and a standard deviation of 5 rolls. The cost of holding a roll in the shop is $.02. A fixed cost of $30 is incurred each time a new order of films is placed by the shop. The shop's inventory policy calls for ordering 150 rolls whenever the inventory level drops to 80 units while simultaneously maintaining a constant buffer of 20 rolls at all times.
   **(a)** For the stated inventory policy, determine the probability of running out of stock during the lead time.
   **(b)** Given the data of the situation, recommend an inventory policy for the shop, assuming that the probability of running out of films during the lead time does not exceed .10.

### 16.2.2 Probabilistic EOQ Model

There is no reason to believe that the "probabilitized" EOQ model in Section 16.2.1 will produce an optimal inventory policy. The fact that pertinent information regarding the probabilistic nature of demand is initially ignored, only to be "revived" in a totally independent manner at a later stage of the calculations, is sufficient to refute optimality. To remedy the situation, a more accurate model is presented in which the probabilistic nature of the demand is included directly in the formulation of the model.

Unlike the case in Section 16.2.1, the new model allows shortage of demand as Figure 16–3 demonstrates. The policy calls for ordering the quantity $y$ whenever the inventory drops to level $R$. As in the deterministic case, the reorder level $R$ is a function of the lead time between placing and receiving an order. The optimal values of $y$ and $R$ are determined by minimizing the expected cost per unit time that includes the sum of the setup, holding, and shortage costs.

The model has three assumptions.

1. Unfilled demand during lead time is backlogged.

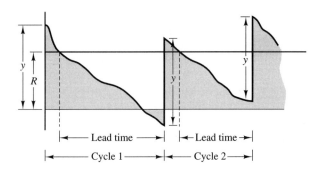

**Figure 16–3**

**2.** No more than one outstanding order is allowed.

**3.** The distribution of demand during lead time remains stationary (un-changed) with time.

To develop the total cost function per unit time, let

$f(x)$ = pdf of demand, $x$, during lead time
$D$   = Expected demand per unit time
$h$   = Holding cost per inventory unit per unit time
$p$   = Shortage cost per inventory unit
$K$   = Setup cost per order

Based on these definitions, the elements of the cost function are now determined.

   **1.** *Setup cost.* The approximate number of orders per unit time is $\frac{D}{y}$, so that the setup cost per unit time is $\frac{KD}{y}$.

   **2.** *Expected holding cost.* The average inventory is

$$I = \frac{(y + E\{R - x\}) + E\{R - x\}}{2} = \frac{y}{2} + R - E\{x\}$$

The expected holding cost per unit time thus equals $hI$.

   The formula is based on the average of the beginning and ending expected in-ventories of a cycle, $y + E\{R - x\}$ and $E\{R - x\}$, respectively. As an approximation, the expression ignores the case where $R - E\{x\}$ may be negative.

   **3.** *Expected shortage cost.* Shortage occurs when $x > R$. Thus, the expected shortage quantity per cycle is

$$S = \int_{R}^{\infty} (x - R)f(x)dx$$

Because $p$ is assumed to be proportional to the shortage quantity only, the expected shortage cost per cycle is $pS$, and, based on $D/y$ cycles per unit time, the shortage cost per unit time is $pDS/y$.

The resulting total cost function per unit time is

$$TCU(y, R) = \frac{DK}{y} + h\left(\frac{y}{2} + R - E\{x\}\right) + \frac{pD}{y}\int_R^\infty (x - R)f(x)dx$$

The solutions for optimal $y^*$ and $R^*$ are determined from

$$\frac{\partial TCU}{\partial y} = -\left(\frac{DK}{y^2}\right) + \frac{h}{2} - \frac{pDS}{y^2} = 0$$

$$\frac{\partial TCU}{\partial R} = h - \left(\frac{pD}{y}\right)\int_R^\infty f(x)dx = 0$$

We thus get

$$y^* = \sqrt{\frac{2D(K + pS)}{h}} \tag{1}$$

$$\int_{R^*}^\infty f(x)dx = \frac{hy^*}{pD} \tag{2}$$

Because $y^*$ and $R^*$ cannot be determined in closed forms from (1) and (2), a numeric algorithm, developed by Hadley and Whitin (1963, pp. 169–174), is used to find the solutions. The algorithm is proved to converge in a finite number of iterations, provided a feasible solution exists.

For $R = 0$, the last two equations, respectively, yield

$$\hat{y} = \sqrt{\frac{2D(K + pE\{x\})}{h}}$$

$$\tilde{y} = \frac{pD}{h}$$

If $\tilde{y} \geq \hat{y}$, unique optimal values of $y$ and $R$ exist. The solution procedure recognizes that the smallest value of $y^*$ is $\sqrt{2KD/h}$, which is achieved when $S = 0$.

The steps of the algorithm are

**Step 0.** Use the initial solution $y_1 = y^* = \sqrt{2KD/h}$, and let $R_0 = 0$. Set $i = 1$, and go to step $i$.

**Step i.** Use $y_i$ to determine $R_i$ from Equation (2). If $R_i \approx R_{i-1}$, stop; the optimal solution is $y^* = y_i$, and $R^* = R_i$. Otherwise, use $R_i$ in Equation (1) to compute $y_i$. Set $i = i + 1$, and repeat step $i$.

---

**Example 16.2–2.**

Electro uses resin in its manufacturing process at the rate of 1000 gallons per month. It cost Electro $100 to place an order for a new shipment. The holding cost per gallon per month is $2, and the shortage cost per gallon is $10. Historical data show that the demand during lead time is uniform over the range (0, 100) gallons. Determine the optimal ordering policy for Electro.

Using the symbols of the model, we have

$D$ = 1000 gallons per month
$K$ = \$100 per order
$h$ = \$2 per gallon per month
$p$ = \$10 per gallon
$f(x)$ = $1/100, 0 \le x \le 100$
$E\{x\}$ = 50 gallons

First, we need to check whether the problem has a feasible solution. Using the equations for $\hat{y}$ and $\tilde{y}$, we get

$$\hat{y} = \sqrt{\frac{2 \times 1000(100 + 10 \times 50)}{2}} = 774.6 \text{ gallons}$$

$$\tilde{y} = \frac{10 \times 1000}{2} = 5000 \text{ gallons}$$

Because $\tilde{y} \ge \hat{y}$, unique solutions exist for $y^*$ and $R^*$.

The expression for $S$ is computed as

$$S = \int_R^{100} (x - R)\frac{1}{100}dx = \frac{R^2}{200} - R + 50$$

Using $S$ in Equations (1) and (2), we obtain

$$y_i = \sqrt{\frac{2 \times 1000(100 + 10S)}{2}} = \sqrt{100{,}000 + 10{,}000S} \quad \text{gallons} \tag{3}$$

$$\int_{R_i}^{100} \frac{1}{100}dx = \frac{2y_i}{10 \times 1000}$$

The last equation yields

$$R_i = 100 - \frac{y_i}{50}, \tag{4}$$

We now use Equations (3) and (4) to determine the solution.

*Iteration 1*

$$y_1 = \sqrt{\frac{2KD}{h}} = \sqrt{\frac{2 \times 1000 \times 100}{2}} = 316.23 \text{ gallons}$$

$$R_1 = 100 - \frac{316.23}{50} = 93.68 \text{ gallons}$$

*Iteration 2*

$$S = \frac{R_1^2}{200} - R_1 + 50 = .19971 \text{ gallon}$$

$$y_2 = \sqrt{100,000 + 10,000 \times .19971} = 319.37 \text{ gallons}$$

Hence,

$$R_2 = 100 - \frac{319.39}{50} = 93.612$$

*Iteration 3*

$$S = \frac{R_2^2}{200} - R_2 + 50 = .20399 \text{ gallon}$$

$$y_3 = \sqrt{100,000 + 10,000 \times .20399} = 319.44 \text{ gallons}$$

Thus,

$$R_3 = 100 - \frac{319.44}{50} = 93.611 \text{ gallons}$$

Because $R_2$ and $R_3$ are approximately equal, the approximate optimal solution is given by

$$R^* \approx 93.61 \text{ gallons}, y^* \approx 319.4 \text{ gallons}$$

Thus, the optimal inventory policy calls for ordering approximately 320 gallons whenever the inventory level drops to 94 gallons.

---

### Problem set 16.2b

1. For the data given in Example 16.6–2, determine the following:
   (a) The approximate number of orders per month.
   (b) The expected monthly setup cost.
   (c) The expected holding cost per month.
   (d) The expected shortage cost per month.
   (e) The probability of running out of stock during lead time.
2. Solve Example 16.2–2, assuming that the demand during lead time is uniform between 0 and 50 gallons.
3. In Example 16.2–2, suppose that the demand during lead time is uniform between 40 and 60 gallons. Compare the solution with that obtained in Example 16.2–2, and interpret the results. (*Hint:* In both problems $E\{x\}$ is the same, but the variance in the present problem is smaller.)
4. Find the optimal solution for Example 16.2–2, assuming that the demand during lead time is normal with a mean of 100 gallons and a standard deviation of 2 gallons—that is, $N(100, 2)$. Assume that $D = 10,000$ gallons per month, $h = \$2$ per gallon per month, $p = \$4$ per gallon, and $K = \$20$.

## 16.3 SINGLE-PERIOD MODELS

Single-item inventory models occur when an item is ordered only once to satisfy the demand for the period. For example, seasonal fashion items become obsolete at the end of the season. This section presents two models representing the no-setup and the setup cases.

The symbols used in the development of the models include

$c$      = Purchasing (or production) cost per unit
$K$     = Setup cost per order
$h$      = Holding cost per unit during the period
$p$      = Penalty cost per shortage unit during the period
$D$     = Probabilistic demand during the period
$f(D)$ = pdf of demand during the period
$y$      = Order quantity
$x$      = Amount on hand before an order is placed

The model determines the optimal value of $y$ that minimizes the sum of the expected purchasing (or production), holding, and shortage costs. Given optimal $y$ ($= y^*$), the inventory policy calls for ordering $y^* - x$ if $x < y$; otherwise, no order is placed.

### 16.3.1 No-Setup Model

The assumptions of this model are

1. Demand occurs instantaneously at the start of the period immediately after the order is received.
2. No setup cost is incurred.

Figure 16–4 demonstrates the inventory position after the demand, $D$, is satisfied. If $D < y$, the quantity $y - D$ is held during the period. Otherwise, if $D > y$, a shortage amount $D - y$ will result.

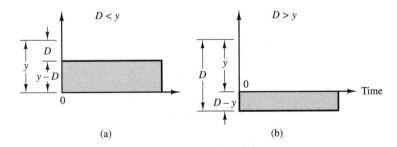

(a)    (b)

**Figure 16–4**

The expected cost for the period, $E\{C(y)\}$, is expressed as

$$E\{C(y)\} = c(y - x) + h\int_0^y (y - D)f(D)dD + p\int_y^\infty (D - y)f(D)dD$$

It can be shown that $E\{C(y)\}$ is convex in $y$ and, hence, has a unique minimum. Thus, taking the first derivative of $E\{C(y)\}$ with respect to $y$ and equating it to zero, we get

$$c + h\int_0^y f(D)dD - p\int_y^\infty f(D)dD = 0$$

or

$$c + hP\{D \le y\} + p(1 - P\{D \le y\}) = 0$$

or

$$P\{D \le y^*\} = \frac{p - c}{p + h}$$

The right-hand side of the last formula is referred to as the **critical ratio**. The value of $y^*$ is defined only if the critical ratio is nonnegative—that is, $p \ge c$. The case where $p < c$ is nonsensical because it implies that cost of purchasing the item is higher than the penalty for not providing it.

The preceding development assumes that the demand $D$ is continuous. If $D$ is discrete, then $f(D)$ is defined at only discrete points and the cost function is defined as

$$E\{C(y)\} = c(y - x) + h\sum_{D=0}^y (y - D)f(D) + p\sum_{D=y+1}^\infty (D - y)f(D)$$

The necessary conditions for optimality are

$$E\{C(y - 1)\} \ge E\{C(y)\} \quad \text{and} \quad E\{C(y + 1)\} \ge E\{C(y)\}$$

These conditions also are sufficient in this case because $E\{C(y)\}$ is a convex function. After some algebraic manipulations, the application of these conditions yields the following inequalities for determining $y^*$:

$$P\{D \le y^* - 1\} \le \frac{p - c}{p + h} \le P\{D \le y^*\}$$

---

**Example 16.3–1.**

The owner of a newsstand wants to determine the number of *USA Now* newspapers that must be stocked at the start of each day. It costs 30 cents to buy a copy, and the owner sells it for 75 cents. The sale of the newspaper typically occurs between 7:00 and 8:00 A.M. Newspapers left at the end of the day are recycled for an income of 5 cents a copy. How many copies should the owner stock every morning, assuming that the demand for the day can be described as

**(a)** A normal distribution with mean 300 copies and standard deviation 20 copies.

**(b)** A discrete pdf, $f(D)$, defined as

| $D$ | 200 | 220 | 300 | 320 | 340 |
|------|-----|-----|-----|-----|-----|
| $f(D)$ | .1 | .2 | .4 | .2 | .1 |

The holding and penalty costs are not defined directly in this situation. However, the data of the problem tell us that each unsold copy will cost the owner $30 - 5 = 25$ cents and that the penalty for running out of stock is 75 cents per copy. Thus, in terms of the parameters of the inventory problem, we can assume that $c = 30$ cents per copy, $h = 25$ cents per copy per day, and $p = 75$ cents per copy per day.

First, we determine the critical ratio as

$$\frac{p - c}{p + h} = \frac{75 - 30}{75 + 25} = .45$$

*Case (a)*

The demand $D$ is $N(300, 20)$. Define the $N(0, 1)$ standard normal random variable as

$$z = \frac{D - 300}{20}$$

Then,

$$\frac{y^* - 300}{20} = -.125$$

because, from the standard normal tables (Appendix D),

$$P\{z \le -.125\} \approx .45$$

Hence, the optimal order quantity is $y^* = 297.5$ (or approximately 280) copies.

*Case (b)*

The demand $D$ follows a discrete pdf, $f(D)$. First, we determine the CDF $P\{D \le y\}$ as

| $y$ | 200 | 220 | 300 | 320 | 340 |
|---|---|---|---|---|---|
| $P\{D \le y\}$ | .1 | .3 | .7 | .9 | 1.0 |

For the computed critical ratio of .45, we have

$$P\{D \le 220\} \le .45 \le P\{D \le 300\}$$

If follows that $y^* = 300$ copies.

## Problem set 16.3a

**1.** For the single-period model, show that for the discrete demand the optimal order quantity is determined from

$$P\{D \le y^* - 1\} \le \frac{p - c}{p + h} \le P\{D \le y^*\}$$

**2.** The demand for an item during a single period occurs instantaneously at the start of the period. The associated pdf is exponential with mean 10 units. Because of the difficulty in estimating the cost parameters, the order quantity is determined such that the probability of either surplus or shortage does not exceed .1. Is it possible to satisfy the two conditions simultaneously?

3. In a single-period inventory situation, the unit purchasing cost of a product is $10, and its unit holding cost is $1. If the order quantity is 4 units, find the permissible range of the unit penalty cost implied by the optimal conditions. Assume that the demand occurs instantaneously at the start of the period and that demand pdf is given as

| $D$ | 0 | 1 | 2 | 3 | 4 | 5 | 6 | 7 | 8 |
|---|---|---|---|---|---|---|---|---|---|
| $f(D)$ | .05 | .1 | .1 | .2 | .25 | .15 | .05 | .05 | .05 |

4. In his Engineering Economy class, Professor Porter Stone teaches his students to "play" the stock market. The stock market game lasts for 10 days and starts by assuming that the value of the selected stock will rise by 1% a day. In any one day there is also a chance that the market will decline as given by the following table:

| Day | 1 | 2 | 3 | 4 | 5 | 6 | 7 | 8 | 9 | 10 |
|---|---|---|---|---|---|---|---|---|---|---|
| Percent decline | 5. | 5. | .8 | .1 | 1.4 | .6 | 1.2 | .2 | .3 | .1 |
| $P\{\text{decline}\}$ | .06 | .02 | .05 | .07 | .10 | .13 | .15 | .20 | .12 | .10 |

The objective is to maximize the accumulated value of the stock. If you were a participant in Professor Stone's class, when should you start the game?

5. The U of A Bookstore offers a program of reproducing class notes for participating professors. Professor Yataha teaches a freshmen-level class, where an enrollment of between 200 and 250 students, uniformly distributed, is expected. It costs the bookstore $10 to produce each copy, which it then sells to the students for $25 a copy. The students purchase their books at the start of the semester. Any unsold copies of Professor Yataha's notes are shredded for recycling. In the meantime, once the bookstore runs out of copies, no additional copies are printed, and the students are responsible for securing the notes from other sources. If the bookstore wants to maximize its revenues, how many copies should it print?

6. QuickStop provides its customers with coffee and donuts at 6:00 A.M. each day. The convenience store buys the donuts for 7 cents a piece and sells them for 25 cents a piece until 8:00 A.M. After 8:00 A.M., the donuts sell for

5 cents a piece. The number of customers buying donuts each day is uniformly distributed between 30 and 50. Each customer usually orders 3 donuts with coffee. Approximately how many dozen donuts should Quick-Stop stock every morning to maximize revenues?

**7.** Colony Shop is stocking heavy coats for next winter. Colony pays $50 per coat and sells it at a 100% markup. At the end of the winter season, Colony conducts a sale and offers the coats at $55 each. The demand for coats during the winter season is more than 20 but less than or equal to 30, all with equal probabilities. Because the winter season is short, the unit holding cost is negligible. Also, Colony's manager does not believe that any penalty would result from coat shortages. Determine the optimal order quantity that will maximize the revenue for Colony Shop.

**8.** For the single-period model, suppose that the demand occurs uniformly during the period (rather than instantaneously at the start of the period), develop the associated cost model, and find the optimal order quantity.

**9.** Solve Example 16.3–1, assuming that the demand is continuous and that it occurs uniformly during the period and that the pdf of demand is uniform between 0 and 100. (*Hint:* You need to make use of the results of Problem 8.)

**10.** It is desired to maximize the expected profit in a single-period model. The demand occurs instantaneously at the *end* of the period. Let $c$, $r$, and $v$ be the unit purchasing cost, unit selling price, and unit salvage value for the item. Assuming that the demand $D$ is continuous and is described by the pdf $f(D)$, develop an expression for the total expected profit and determine the optimal order quantity.

## 16.3.2 Setup Model (s-S Policy)

The present model differs from the one in Section 16.3.1 in that a setup cost $K$ is incurred. Using the same notation, the total expected cost per period is

$$E\{\overline{C}(y)\} = K + E\{C(y)\}$$

$$= K + c(y - x) + h\int_0^y (y - D)f(D)dD + p\int_y^\infty (D - y)f(D)dD$$

As shown in Section 16.3.1, the optimum value $y^*$ must satisfy

$$P\{y \le y^*\} = \frac{p - c}{p + h}$$

Because $K$ is a constant, the minimum value of $E\{\overline{C}(y)\}$ must also occur at $y^*$ as Figure 16–5 shows. The values $s$ and $S$ shown in the figure will be defined shortly.

In Figure 16–5, $S = y^*$ and the value of $s$ ($< S$) is determined from the equation

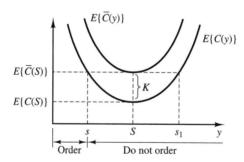

Figure 16–5

$$E\{C(s)\} = E\{\overline{C}(S)\} = K + E\{C(S)\}, \quad s < S$$

(The equation yields another value $s_1 > S$, which is ignored.)

Given that the amount on hand before an order is placed is $x$ units, how much should be ordered? This question is investigated under three conditions.

1. $x < s$.
2. $s \leq x \leq S$.
3. $x > S$.

*Case 1* $(x < s)$.   Because $x$ is already on hand, its equivalent cost is given by $E\{C(x)\}$. If any additional amount $y - x$ $(y > x)$ is ordered, the corresponding cost given $y$ is $E\{\overline{C}(y)\}$, which includes the setup cost $K$. From Figure 16–5, we have

$$\min_{y>x} E\{\overline{C}(y)\} = E(\overline{C}(S)) < E\{C(x)\}$$

Thus the optimal inventory policy in this case is to order $S - x$ units.

*Case 2* $(s \leq x \leq S)$.   From Figure 16–5, we have

$$E\{C(x)\} \leq \min_{y>x} E\{\overline{C}(y)\} = E(\overline{C}(S))$$

Thus, it is no more costly *not* to order in this case. Hence, $y^* = x$.

*Case 3* $(x > S)$.   From Figure 16–5, we have for $y > x$,

$$E\{C(x)\} < E\{\overline{C}(y)\}$$

This condition indicates that it is more economical not to order in this case—that is, $y^* = x$.

The optimal inventory policy, frequently referred to as the *s-S policy*, is summarized as

$$\text{If } x < s, \text{ order } S - x$$

If $x \geq s$, do not order

(The optimality of the $s$-$S$ policy is guaranteed because the associated cost function is convex. If the convexity property does not hold, the $s$-$S$ policy is not optimal.)

---

**Example 16.3–2.**

The daily demand for an item during a single period occurs instantaneously at the start of the period. The pdf of the demand is uniform between 0 and 10 units. The unit holding cost of the item during the period is $.50, and the unit penalty cost for running out of stock is $4.50. The unit purchase cost is $.50. A fixed cost of $25 is incurred each time an order is placed. Determine the optimal inventory policy for the item.

First we determine $y^*$. We have

$$\frac{p - c}{p + h} = \frac{4.5 - .5}{4.5 + .5} = .8$$

Thus, given

$$P\{D \leq y^*\} = \int_0^{y^*} \frac{1}{10}\, dD = \frac{y^*}{10}$$

then, $S = y^* = 8$.

The expected cost function is given as

$$E\{C(y)\} = .5(y - x) + .5\int_0^y \frac{1}{10}(y - D)dD + 4.5\int_y^{10} \frac{1}{10}(D - y)dD$$

$$= .5(y - x) + .05\left[yD - \frac{D^2}{2}\right]_0^y + .45\left[\frac{D^2}{2} - Dy\right]_y^{10}$$

$$= .25y^2 - 4y + 22.5 - .5x$$

The value of $s$ is determined by solving

$$E\{C(s)\} = K + E\{C(S)\}$$

This yields

$$.25s^2 - 4s + 22.5 - .5x = 25 + .25S^2 - 4S + 22.5 - .5x$$

Given $S = 8$, the preceding equation reduces to

$$s^2 - 16s - 36 = 0$$

The solution of this equation is $s = -2$ or $s = 18$. The value of $s = 18$ ($> S$) is disregarded. Because the remaining value is negative ($= -2$), $s$ has no feasible value. The optimal solution thus calls for not ordering at all (Figure 16–6). This conclusion usually happens when the cost function is "flat" or when the setup cost is high relative to the other costs of the model.

---

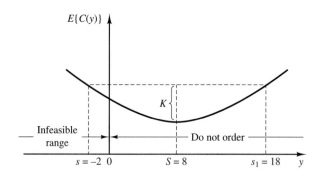

**Figure 16–6**

### Problem set 16.3b

1. Determine the optimal inventory policy for the situation in Example 16.3–2, assuming that the setup cost is $5.

2. In the single-period model in Section 16.3.1, suppose instead that the profit is to be maximized and that a setup cost $K$ is incurred. Given $r$ is the unit selling price and using the information in Section 16.3.1, develop an expression for the expected profit and determine the optimal order quantity. Solve the problem numerically for $r = \$3, c = \$2, p = \$4, h = \$1$, and $K = \$10$. The demand pdf is uniform between 0 and 10.

3. Work Problem 16.3a–6, assuming that there is a fixed cost of $10 associated with the delivery of donuts.

## 16.4 MULTIPERIOD MODEL

This section presents a multiperiod model under the assumption of no setup cost. Additionally, the model allows backlog of demand and assumes a zero-delivery lag. It further assumes that the demand $D$ in any period is described by a stationary pdf $f(D)$.

The multiperiod model considers the discounted value of money. If $\alpha\ (< 1)$ is the discount factor per period, then an amount $\$A$ after $n$ periods is equivalent to $\$\alpha^n A$ now.

Suppose that the inventory situation encompasses $n$ periods and that unfilled demand can be backlogged exactly one period. Define

$F_i(x_i)$ = Maximum expected profit for periods $i, i + 1, \ldots$, and $n$, given that $x_i$ is the amount on hand before an order is placed in period $i$

Using the notation in Section 16.3 and assuming that $r$ is the revenue per unit, the inventory situation can be formulated using the following dynamic programming model (see Chapter 15):

$$F_i(x_i) = \max_{y_i \geq x_i} \left\{ -c(y_i - x_i) + \int_0^{y_i} [rD - h(y_i - D)] f(D) dD \right.$$

$$+ \int_{y_i}^{\infty} [ry_i + \alpha r (D - y_i) - p(D - y_i)] f(D) dD$$

$$\left. + \alpha \int_0^{\infty} F_{i+1}(y_i - D) f(D) \, dD \right\}, \quad i = 1, 2, \ldots, n$$

where $f_{n+1}(y_n - D) \equiv 0$. The value of $x_i$ may be negative because unfilled demand is backlogged. The quantity $\alpha r(D - y_i)$ in the second integral is included because $(D - y_i)$ is the unfilled demand in period $i$ that must be filled in period $i + 1$.

The problem can be solved recursively. For the case where the number of periods is infinite, the recursive equation reduces to

$$F(x) = \max_{y \geq x} \left\{ -c (y - x) + \int_0^y [rD - h(y - D)] f(D) \, dD \right.$$

$$+ \int_y^{\infty} [ry + \alpha r(D - y) - p(D - y)] f(D) dD$$

$$\left. + \alpha \int_0^{\infty} F(y - D) f(D) dD \right\}$$

where $x$ and $y$ are the inventory levels for each period before and after and order is received, respectively.

The optimal value of $y$ can be determined from the following necessary condition, which also happened to be sufficient because the expected revenue function $F(x)$ is concave.

$$\frac{\partial(.)}{\partial y} = -c - h \int_0^y f(D) dD + \int_y^{\infty} [(1 - \alpha)r + p] f(D) dD$$

$$+ \alpha \int_0^{\infty} \frac{\partial F(y - D)}{\partial y} f(D) dD = 0$$

The value of

$$\frac{\partial F(y - D)}{\partial y}$$

is determined as follows. If there are $\beta(> 0)$ more units on hand at the start of the next period, the profit for the next period will increase by $c\beta$, for this much less has to be ordered. This means that

$$\frac{\partial F(y - D)}{\partial y} = c$$

The necessary condition thus becomes

$$-c - h\int_0^y f(D)dD + [(1 - \alpha)r + p]\left(1 - \int_0^y f(D)dD\right) + \alpha c\int_0^\infty f(D)dD = 0$$

The optimum inventory level $y*$ is thus determined from

$$\int_0^{y*} f(D)dD = \frac{p + (1 - \alpha)(r - c)}{p + h + (1 - \alpha)r}$$

The optimal inventory policy for each period given its entering inventory level $x$ is thus given as

If $x < y*$, order $y* - x$

If $x \geq y*$, do not order

### Problem set 16.4a

1. Consider a two-period probabilistic inventory model in which the demand is backlogged, and orders are received with zero-delivery lag. The demand pdf per period is uniform between 0 and 10, and the cost parameters are given as

Unit selling price = $2

Unit purchase price = $1

Unit holding cost = $.10

Unit penalty cost = $3

Discount factor = .8

Find the optimal inventory policy for the two periods, assuming that the initial inventory for period 1 is zero.

2. The pdf of the demand per period in an infinite-horizon inventory model is given as

$$f(D) = .08D, 0 \leq D \leq 5$$

The unit cost parameters are

Selling price = $10

Purchase price = $8

$$\text{Penalty cost} = \$1$$

$$\text{Discount factor} = .9$$

Determine the optimal inventory policy assuming zero delivery lag and that the unfilled demand is backlogged.

**3.** Consider the infinite horizon inventory situation with zero delivery lag and backlogged demand. Develop the optimal inventory policy based on the minimization of cost given that

$$\text{Holding cost for } z \text{ units} = hz^2$$

$$\text{Penalty cost for } z \text{ units} = px^2$$

Show that for the special case where $h = p$, the optimal solution is independent of pdf of demand.

## 16.5 SUMMARY

The inventory models presented in this chapter deal with probabilistic demand. The proposed solutions range from the use of a probabilistic version of the deterministic EOQ to more complex situations, where the model is solved by dynamic programming. The probabilistic nature of the demand has led to complex models that, perhaps, are not useful in practice. Nevertheless, there have been reported cases of successful probabilistic inventory implementations.

## SELECTED REFERENCES

HADLEY, G., and T. WHITIN, *Analysis of Inventory Systems,* Prentice Hall, Upper Saddle River, N.J., 1963.

SILVER, E. and R. PETERSON, *Decision Systems for Inventory Management and Production Planning,* 2nd ed., Wiley, New York, 1985.

TERSINE, R. *Principles of Inventory and Materials Management,* North Holland, New York, 1982

## COMPREHENSIVE PROBLEMS

■ 16–1[2] A telephone company operates *telephone centers* that provide residential services to customers in their respective domains. There are more than 60 telephone models to choose from. Currently, each phone center holds from 15 to 75 days of stock. The management considers such stock levels to be excessive because they are replenished on a daily basis from a central warehouse. At the same time, the management wants to ensure that sufficient stock is maintained at the telephone centers to ensure a service level of 95% for the customers. The team studying the problem started by col-

---

[2]Based on R. Cohen and F. Dunford, "Forecasting for Inventory Control: An Example of When "Simple" Means "Better," *Interfaces,* Vol. 16, No. 6, pp. 95–99, 1986.

lecting pertinent data. The objective of the team was to establish an optimal stock level for each telephone model. The following table shows the number of sets issued in a day of the green, desk-top, rotary-dial model (Green 500).
Similar tables were developed for all the models.

The desired cost parameters needed to determine the optimal stock level for each telephone model are difficult to estimate, and, thus, the application of tradi-

| Sets issued | 0 | 1 | 2 | 3 | 4 |
|---|---|---|---|---|---|
| Frequency | 189 | 89 | 20 | 4 | 1 |

tional inventory models is impossible. This is when the team has decided to use a more basic approach for determining appropriate stock levels for the different phone models. The development is based on the observation that both regression and time series analyses failed to detect appreciable trends in demand.

Suggest a method for determining adequate stock levels for the different models. State all the assumptions made to reach a decision.

■ 16-2[3] The inventory manager of a small retail stores places orders for items to take advantage of special offers or to combine orders received from one supplier. The result is that both the order quantity and the cycle length (interval between successive orders) are effectively random. Moreover, because the manager's policy is driven mostly by noninventory considerations, the order quantity and cycle length can be considered independent, in the sense that shorter cycle lengths do not necessarily mean smaller order quantities and vice versa.

The following table provides typical data for three items that were ordered simultaneously. The data show that both the order quantity and the cycle length are random. Moreover, a cursory look at the entries of the table reveals the lack of correlation between the order quantity and the cycle length.

A goodness-for-fit analysis of the complete set of data (see Chapter 12) reveals that the distribution of the demand rates (order quantity divided by cycle length) for the three items follow a Weibull distribution, $f(r)$, of the form

| Cycle length (mo) | Order quantity (units) | | |
|---|---|---|---|
| | Item 1 | Item 2 | Item 3 |
| 2.3 | 10 | 8 | 1 |
| 2.6 | 4 | 6 | 0 |
| .4 | 1 | 4 | 2 |

*continued*

[3]Based on A. Holt, "Multi-Item Inventory Control for Fluctuating Reorder Intervals," *Interfaces*, Vol. 16, No. 3, pp. 60–67, 1986.

| Cycle length (mo) | Order quantity (units) | | |
|:---:|:---:|:---:|:---:|
| | Item 1 | Item 2 | Item 3 |
| 2.0 | 8 | 6 | 2 |
| 1.2 | 7 | 0 | 2 |
| 1.4 | 0 | 10 | 1 |
| 1.7 | 1 | 2 | 0 |
| 1.3 | 0 | 5 | 2 |
| 1.1 | 9 | 4 | 3 |
| 1.8 | 4 | 6 | 2 |
| 1.6 | 2 | 0 | 0 |
| .5 | 5 | 3 | 1 |
| 2.1 | 10 | 7 | 2 |
| 2.3 | 4 | 12 | 4 |
| 2.4 | 8 | 9 | 3 |
| 2.1 | 10 | 8 | 5 |
| 2.2 | 9 | 13 | 2 |
| 1.8 | 12 | 8 | 4 |
| .7 | 6 | 4 | 2 |
| 2.1 | 5 | 4 | 0 |

$$f(r) = \frac{2r}{\alpha} e^{-r^2/\alpha}, \quad r \geq 0$$

where $r$ is the demand rate for the item. Similarly, the analysis shows that the distribution of the *reciprocal* of the cycle length, $s(x)$, is exponential of the form

$$s(x) = \beta e^{-\beta(x-a)}, \quad x \geq a$$

where $a$ is the minimum value assumed by $x$.

The determination of the optimal order quantity is based on the maximization of the expected profit per month which is defined as

$$\text{Expected profit} = \int \left[ \frac{1}{t} \int u(q, r, t) f(r) dr \right] g(t) dt$$

$$= \int \left[ x \int u\left(q, r, \frac{1}{x}\right) f(r) dr \right] s(x) dx$$

where $t$ and $g(t)$ are the cycle length and its density function. The profit function $u(q, r, t)$ is based on $p$, the net unit profit for the item, $h$, the holding cost per unit per month, and $K$, the fixed order cost.

(a) Use the data for the three items to determine the probability density function for each demand rate.

(b) Use the data for the cycle length to determine $s(x)$.

(c) Develop the mathematical expression for $u(q, r, t)$.

Determine the optimal order quantity for the three items given the following cost data: $p_1 = \$100$, $p_2 = \$150$, $p_3 = \$125$, $h_1 = \$2$, $h_2 = \$1.20$, $h_3 = \$1.65$, and $K = \$30$.

# Chapter 17

# Queueing Systems

## 17.1 WHY STUDY QUEUES?

Waiting for service is part of our daily life. We wait to eat at restaurants, we "queue up" at the check-out counters in grocery stores, and we "line up" for service in post offices. And the waiting phenomenon is not an experience limited to human beings only: Jobs wait to be processed on a machine, planes circle in a stack before given permission to land at an airport, and cars stop at traffic lights. Unfortunately, we cannot eliminate waiting without incurring inordinate expenses. In fact, all we can hope to achieve is to reduce the adverse impact of waiting to acceptable levels.

The study of queues determines the measures of performance of a queueing situation, including the average waiting time and the average queue length, among others. This information is then used to decide on an appropriate level of service for the facility, as the following example demonstrates.

---

**Example 17.1–1.**

Customers at McBurger fast-food restaurant complain of slow service. The restaurant currently employs three cashiers. The manager has commissioned a study with a consulting firm to investigate the complaint. The study reveals the following relationship between the number of cashiers and the waiting time for service:

| No. of cashiers | 1 | 2 | 3 | 4 | 5 | 6 | 7 |
|---|---|---|---|---|---|---|---|
| Average waiting time (min) | 16.2 | 10.3 | 6.9 | 4.8 | 2.9 | 1.9 | 1.3 |

An examination of these data shows a 7-minute average waiting time for the present 3-cashier situation. The manager wants it reduced to about 3 minutes.

From the given results, the average waiting time falls below 3 minutes when the number of cashiers is five or more. Indeed, the five-cashier situation results in an average waiting time of 2.9 minutes.

---

The results of queueing analysis may also be used in the context of a cost optimization model, where the sum of the costs of offering the service and waiting is minimized. Figure 17–1 depicts a typical cost model (in dollars per unit time) where the cost of service increases with the increase in the level of service. At the same time, the cost of waiting decreases with the increase in level of service. The main problem with implementing cost models is the difficulty of estimating the unit cost of waiting, particularly when human behavior impacts the operation of the model (see Section 17.9).

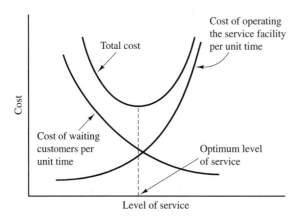

Figure 17–1

### Problem set 17.1a

1. Suppose that further analysis of the McBurger restaurant reveals the following additional results:

| No. of cashiers | 1 | 2 | 3 | 4 | 5 | 6 | 7 |
|---|---|---|---|---|---|---|---|
| Idleness (%) | 0 | 8 | 12 | 18 | 29 | 36 | 42 |

   **(a)** What is the efficiency of the operation (reflected by the percentage of time the employees are busy) when the number of cashiers is five?
   **(b)** The manager wants to keep the average waiting time around 3 minutes and, simultaneously, maintain the efficiency of the facility at approximately 90%. Can these goals be achieved? Explain.

2. Acme Metal Jobshop is in the process of purchasing a multipurpose drill press. Two models, $A$ and $B$, are available with hourly operating costs of $18 and $25, respectively. Model $A$ is slower than model $B$. Queueing analysis of similar machines shows that when $A$ is used, the average number of jobs in the queue is 4, which is 30% higher than the queue size in $B$. A delayed job represents a lost opportunity for profit, which is estimated by Acme at $10 waiting job per hour. Which model should Acme purchase?

## 17.2 ELEMENTS OF A QUEUEING MODEL

The principal actors in a queueing situation are the **customer** and the **server.** Customers are generated from a **source.** On arrival at the **facility,** they can start service immediately or wait in a **queue** if the facility is occupied. When a facility completes a service, it automatically "pulls" a waiting customer, if any, from the queue. If the queue is empty, the facility becomes idle until a new customer arrives.

From the standpoint of analyzing queues, the arrival of customers is represented by the **interarrival time** and the service is described by the **service time** per customer. Generally, the interarrival and service times can be probabilistic as in the operation of a post office or deterministic as in the arrival of applicants for job interviews.

**Queue size** plays a role in the analysis of queues, and it may have a finite size as in the buffer area between two successive machines, or it may be infinite as in mail order facilities.

The **queue discipline,** which represents the order in which customers are selected from a queue, is an important factor in the analysis of queueing models. The most common discipline is first come, first served (FCFS). Other disciplines include last come, first served (LCFS) and service in random order (SIRO). Customers may also be selected from the queue based on some order of **priority.** For example, rush jobs at a shop are processed ahead of regular jobs.

The queueing behavior of customers plays a role in waiting-line analysis. "Human" customers may **jockey** from one queue to another in hopes of reducing their waiting. They may also **balk** from joining a queue altogether because they anticipate a long delay, or they may **renege** from a queue because they have been waiting too long.

The design of the service facility may include a single server or several parallel servers (e.g., post office operation). The servers may also be arranged in series, (e.g., jobs are processed on successive machines).

The source from which customers are generated may be finite or infinite. A **finite source** limits the customers arriving for service (e.g., machines requesting the service of a repairperson). Alternatively, an **infinite source** is forever "abundant" (e.g., calls arriving at a telephone exchange).

Variations in the elements of a queueing situation give rise to a variety of queueing models. The remainder of this chapter provides examples of these models.

### Problem set 17.2a

**1.** In each of the following situations, identify the customer and the server:
   **(a)** Planes arriving at an airport.
   **(b)** Taxi stand.
   **(c)** Tools checked out from a crib in a machining shop.
   **(d)** Letters processed in a post office.
   **(e)** Registration for classes in a university.
   **(f)** Legal court cases.
   **(g)** Check-out operation in a supermarket.
   **(h)** Parking lot operation.

2. For each of the situations in Problem 1, identify the following: (a) nature of the calling source (finite or infinite), (b) nature of arriving customers (individually or in bulk), (c) type of the interarrival time (probabilistic or deterministic), (d) definition and type of service time, (f) queue capacity (finite or infinite), and (g) queue discipline.

3. Study the following system and identify all the associated queueing situations. For each situation, define the customers, the server(s), the queue discipline, the service time, the maximum queue length, and the calling source.

   Orders for jobs are received at a workshop for processing. On receipt, the supervisor decides whether it is a rush or a regular job. Some of these orders require the use of one of several identical machines. The remaining orders are processed in a two-stage production line, of which two are available. In each of the two groups, one facility is assigned to handle rush jobs.

   Jobs arriving at any facility are processed in order of arrival. Completed orders are shipped on arrival from a shipping zone having a limited capacity.

   Sharpened tools for the different machines are supplied from a central tool crib. When a machine breaks down, a repairperson is summoned from the service pool to make the repair. Machines working on rush orders always receive priorities both in acquiring new tools from the crib and receiving repair service.

4. True or False?
   **(a)** An impatient waiting customer may elect to *renege*.
   **(b)** If a long waiting time is anticipated, an arriving customer may elect to *balk*.
   **(c)** *Jockeying* from one queue to another is exercised in hopes of reducing waiting time.

5. In each of the situations in Problem 1, discuss the possibility of the customers exercising jockeying, balking, and reneging.

## 17.3  ROLE OF EXPONENTIAL DISTRIBUTION

In most queueing situations, the arrival of customers occurs in a totally random fashion. Randomness means that the occurrence of an event (e.g., arrival of a customer or completion of a service) is not influenced by the length of time that has elapsed since the occurrence of the last event.

Random interarrival and service times are described quantitatively for the purpose of queueing modeling by the **exponential distribution,** which is defined as

$$f(t) = \lambda e^{-\lambda t}, \quad t > 0$$

where $E\{t\} = \frac{1}{\lambda}$ (see Section 12.5.3 for more details). The fact that the exponential distribution is **completely random** is illustrated by the following example: If it is now 8:20 A.M. and the last arrival has occurred at 8:02 A.M., the probability that the next arrival will occur by 8:29 is a function of the interval from 8:20 to 8:29 only, and is totally independent of the length of time that has elapsed since the occurrence of the last event (8:02 to 8:20). This result is referred to as the **forgetfulness** or **lack of memory** of the exponential.

### 17.3.1 Forgetfulness Property

Given $t$ is exponentially distributed as defined by $f(t)$, if $S$ is the interval since the occurrence of the last event, then the forgetfulness property is described by a probability statement as:

$$P\{t > T + S \mid t > S\} = P\{t > T\}$$

To prove this result, we note that

$$P\{t > Y\} = 1 - P\{t < Y\} = e^{-\lambda Y}$$

Thus,

$$P\{t > T + S \mid t > S\} = \frac{P\{t > T + S, t > S\}}{P\{t > S\}} = \frac{P\{t > T + S\}}{P\{t > S\}}$$

$$= \frac{e^{-\lambda(T+S)}}{e^{-\lambda S}} = e^{-\lambda T}$$

$$= P\{t > T\}$$

---

**Example 17.3–1.**

A service machine always has a standby unit for immediate replacement on failure. The time to failure of the machine (or its standby unit) is exponential and occurs every 45 minutes, on the average. The machine operator claims that the machine "has the habit" of breaking down every night around 8:30 P.M. Analyze the operator's claim.

The average failure rate of the machine is $\lambda = \frac{60}{40} = 1.5$ failures per hour. Thus, the exponential distribution of the time to failure is

$$f(t) = 1.5e^{-1.15t}, \quad t > 0$$

Regarding the operator's claim, we know off hand that it cannot be correct because it conflicts with the fact that the time between breakdowns is exponential and, hence, totally random. The probability that a failure will occur by 8:30 P.M. cannot be used to support or refute the operator's claim because the value of such probability depends on the time of the day (relative to 8:30 P.M.) at which it is computed. For example, if it is 8:20 P.M. now, the probability that the operator's claim will be right tonight is

$$p\left\{t < \frac{10}{60}\right\} = 1 - e^{-1.5\left(\frac{10}{60}\right)} = 0.22$$

which is low. If it is 7:00 P.M. now, the probability that a failure will occur by 8:30 P.M. increases to approximately .9 (verify!). These two extreme values show that the operator's claim cannot be analyzed based on probability estimates and that we must rely on the characteristics of the exponential distribution (total randomness) in refuting the claim.

**Problem set 17.3a**

1. **(a)** Explain your understanding of the relationship between the arrival rate $\lambda$ and the average interarrival time. What are the units describing each variable?
   **(b)** In each of the following cases, determine the average arrival rate per hour, $\lambda$, and the average interarrival time in hours.
      **(i)** One arrival occurs every 10 minutes.
      **(ii)** Two arrivals occur every 6 minutes.
      **(iii)** Number of arrivals in a 30-minute period is 10.
      **(iv)** The average interval between successive arrivals is .5 hour.
   **(c)** In each of the following cases, determine the average service rate per hour, $\mu$, and the average service time in hours.
      **(i)** One service is completed every 12 minutes.
      **(ii)** Two departures occur every 15 minutes.
      **(iii)** Number of customers served in a 30-minute period is 5.
      **(iv)** The average service time is .3 hour.

2. In example 17.3–1, determine the following:
   **(a)** The average number of failures in 1 week, assuming the service is offered 24 hours a day, 7 days a week.
   **(b)** The probability of at least one failure in a 2-hour period.
   **(c)** The probability that the next failure will *not* occur within 3 hours.
   **(d)** If no failure has occurred 3 hours after the last failure, what is the probability that interfailure time is at least 4 hours?

3. The time between arrivals at the State Revenue Office is exponential with mean value .05 hour. The office opens at 8:00 A.M.
   **(a)** Write the exponential distribution that describes the interarrival time.
   **(b)** Find the probability that no customers will arrive at the office by 8:15 A.M.
   **(c)** It is now 8:35 A.M. The last customer entered the office at 8:26. What is the probability that the next customer will arrive before 8:38 A.M.? That the next customer will not arrive by 8:40 A.M.?
   **(d)** What is the average number of customers who will arrive between 8:10 and 8:45 A.M.?

4. Suppose that the time between breakdowns for a machine is exponential with mean 6 hours. If the machine has worked without failure during the last 3 hours, what is the probability that it will continue without failure during the next hour? That it will break down during the next .5 hour?

## 17.3.2 Derivation of the Exponential Distribution

The properties of the exponential distribution can be understood further by stating the main axioms on which the distribution is based.

**Theorem 17.3–1.**    *The exponential distribution is based on three axioms:*

*Axiom 1:  Given N(t), the number of events during the interval (0, t), the probability process describing N(t) has stationary independent increments, in the sense that the probability of an event occurring in the interval (T, T + S) depends only on the length of S.*

*Axiom 2:  The probability of an event occurring in a sufficiently small time interval h > 0 is positive but less than 1.*

*Axiom 3:  In a sufficiently small time interval h > 0, at most one event can occur—that is, P{N(h) > 1} = 0.*

*Proof.* Define $p_n(t)$ as the probability of $n$ events occurring during $t$. By axiom 1, the probability of no event occurring during $t + h$, $h > 0$ and sufficiently small, is

$$p_0(t + h) = p_0(t)p_0(h)$$

Based on the remaining two axioms, it can be shown that the solution of the preceding equation is

$$p_0(t) = e^{-\lambda t}, \quad t > 0$$

where $\lambda$ is a positive constant (see Parzen [1962, pp. 121–123] for details of the proof).

Define $f(t)$ as the probability density function of the interval $t$ between successive events, $t > 0$. We then have

$$P\{\text{interevent time} > T\} = P\{\text{no event during } T\}$$

This statement translates to

$$\int_T^\infty f(t)dt = p_0(T), \quad T > 0$$

Substituting and rearranging terms we get

$$\int_0^T f(t)dt = 1 - e^{-\lambda t}, \quad T > 0$$

Taking the derivative of both sides with respect to $T$, we get the exponential distribution

$$f(t) = \lambda e^{-\lambda t}, \quad t > 0$$

The mean value of the exponential is $\frac{1}{\lambda}$ time units, where $\lambda$ is the rate (number of events per unit time) at which the events are generated.

### Problem set 17.3b

**1.** True or False?
   **(a)** Under the exponential assumptions, two events can occur during a very small time interval.

**(b)** If the interevent time is exponential, then no matter how small an interval $h$ is, the probability that no event will occur during $h$ is always positive.

2. The time between arrivals at the game room in the student union is exponential with mean 10 minutes.
   **(a)** What is the arrival rate per hour?
   **(b)** What is the probability that no students will arrive at the game room during the next 15 minutes?
   **(c)** What is the probability that at least one student will visit the game room during the next 20 minutes?

3. The manager of a new fast-food restaurant wants to quantify the arrival process of customers by estimating the fraction of interarrival time intervals that will be (a) less than 2 minutes, (b) more than 3 minutes, and (c) between 2 and 3 minutes. Arrivals in similar restaurants occur at the rate of 35 customers per hour. The interarrival time is exponentially distributed.

4. Ann and Jim, two employees in a fast-food restaurant, play the following game while waiting for customers to arrive: Jim pays Ann 2 cents if the next customer does not arrive within 1 minute; otherwise, Ann pays Jim 2 cents. Determine Jim's average payoff in an 8-hour period. The interarrival time is exponential with mean 1.5 minute.

5. Suppose that in Problem 4 the rules of the game are such that Jim pays Ann 2 cents if the next customer arrives after 1.5 minutes, and Ann pays Jim an equal amount if the next arrival is within 1 minute. For arrivals within the range 1 to 1.5 minutes, the game is a draw. Determine Jim's expected payoff in an 8-hour period.

6. In Problem 4, suppose that Ann pays Jim 2 cents if the next arrival occurs within 1 minute and 3 cents if the interarrival time is between 1 and $1\frac{1}{2}$ minutes. Ann receives from Jim 5 cents if the interarrival time is between $1\frac{1}{2}$ and 2 minutes and 6 cents if it is larger than 2 minutes. Determine Ann's expected payoff in an 8-hour period.

7. A customer arriving at McBurger Fast-food Restaurant within 4 minutes of the immediately preceding customer will be served without any wait. If the interarrival time is between 4 and 5 minutes, the waiting time will be about 1 minute. If the interarrival time is longer than 5 minutes, the waiting time will be about 2 minutes. The interarrival time is exponential with mean 6 minutes.
   **(a)** Determine the probability that an arriving customer will not wait.
   **(b)** Determine the average waiting time per arriving customer.

8. The time between failures of a Kencore refrigerator is known to be exponential with mean value 9000 hours (about 1 year of operation) and the company issues a 1-year warranty on the refrigerator. What are the chances that a breakdown repair will be covered by the warranty?

9. The U of A runs two bus lines on campus: red and green. The red line serves north campus, and the green line serves south campus with a transfer station linking the two lines. Green buses arrive randomly (exponential interarrival time) at the transfer station every 10 minutes. Red buses also arrive randomly every 7 minutes.

   **(a)** What is the probability distribution of the waiting time for a student arriving on the red line to get on the green line?

   **(b)** What is the probability distribution of the waiting time for a student arriving on the green line to get on the red line?

10. Prove that the mean and standard deviation of the exponential distribution are equal.

## 17.4 PURE BIRTH AND DEATH MODELS (RELATIONSHIP BETWEEN THE EXPONENTIAL AND POISSON DISTRIBUTIONS)

This section presents two queueing situations: The first allows arrivals only (pure birth), and the second allows departures only (pure death). An example of the pure birth model is the creation of birth certificates for newly born babies. The pure death model may be demonstrated by the random withdrawal of inventory items from stock.

Both the pure birth and pure death models are developed based on the axioms of Theorem 17.3–1. A by-product of the development is to show the close relationship between the exponential and the Poisson distributions, in the sense that one distribution automatically defines the other.

### 17.4.1 Pure Birth Model

Given that arrivals occur at the rate $\lambda$ customers per unit time, then, for a sufficiently small time interval $h > 0$, Theorem 17.3–1 shows that

$$p_0(h) = e^{-\lambda h} = 1 - \lambda h + \frac{(\lambda h)^2}{2!} - \ldots = 1 - \lambda h + 0(h^2)$$

Axiom 3 states that during $h > 0$, at most one event (arrival) can occur. Thus, as $h \to 0$,

$$p_1(h) = 1 - p_0(h) \approx \lambda h$$

This result shows that the probability of an arrival occurring during $h$ is directly proportional to $h$, with the arrival rate $\lambda$ being the constant of proportionality.

To derive the Poisson distribution based on the axioms of Theorem 17.3–1, define $p_n(t)$ as the probability of $n$ arrivals during $t$. Thus, for $h > 0$ and sufficiently small,

$$p_n(t + h) \approx p_n(t)(1 - \lambda h) + p_{n-1}(t)\lambda h \quad n > 0$$

$$p_0(t + h) \approx p_0(t)(1 - \lambda h), \quad n = 0$$

In the first equation, $n$ arrivals will be realized during the $t + h$ if there are $n$ arrivals during $t$ and no arrivals during $h$, or $n - 1$ arrivals during $t$ and one arrival during $h$. All other combinations are not allowed by Axiom 3 of Theorem 17.3–1. The product law of probability is applicable to the right-hand side of the equation by the independence condition of Axiom 1. For the second equation, zero arrivals during $t + h$ can occur only if no arrivals occur during $h$.

Rearranging the terms and taking the limits as $h \to 0$, we get

$$p'_n(t) = \lim_{h \to 0} \frac{p_n(t + h) - p_n(t)}{h}$$

$$= -\lambda p_n(t) + \lambda p_{n-1}(t), \quad n > 0$$

$$p'_0(t) = \lim_{h \to 0} \frac{p_0(t + h) - p_0(t)}{h}$$

$$= -\lambda p_0(t)$$

where $p'_n(t)$ is the first derivative of $p_n(t)$ with respect to $t$.

The solution of the preceding difference-differential equations yields

$$p_n(t) = \frac{(\lambda t)^n e^{-\lambda t}}{n!}, \quad n = 0, 1, 2, \ldots$$

which is the **Poisson distribution** with mean $E\{n \mid t\} = \lambda t$ arrivals during $t$. The variance of the Poisson distribution also equals $\lambda t$.

The preceding result shows that if the time between arrivals is exponential with mean $\frac{1}{\lambda}$, then the number of arrivals during a specific period $t$ is Poisson with mean $\lambda t$. The converse is true also.

---

**Example 17.4–1.**

Babies are born in a sparsely populated state at the rate of one birth every 12 minutes. The time between births follows an exponential distribution. Find the following:

    **(a)** The average number of births per year.
    **(b)** The probability that no births will occur in any one day.
    **(c)** The probability of issuing 50 birth certificates by the end of the next 3 hours given that 40 certificates were issued during the last 2 hours.

The birth rate per day is computed as

$$\lambda = \frac{24 \times 60}{12} = 120 \text{ births/day}$$

The number of births per year in the state is

$$\lambda t = 120 \times 365 = 43{,}800 \text{ births/ year}$$

The probability of no births in any one day is computed from the Poisson distribution as

$$p_0(1) = \frac{(120 \times 1)^0 e^{-120 \times 11}}{0!} \approx 0$$

To compute the probability of issuing 50 certificates by the end of 3 hours given that 40 certificates were issued during the first 2 hours, we notice that because the distribution of the number of births is Poisson, the required probability reduces to having 10 (= 50 − 40) births in one (= 3 − 2) hour. Given $\lambda = \frac{60}{12} = 5$ births per hour, we get

$$p_{10}(1) = \frac{(5 \times 1)^{10} e^{-5 \times 1}}{10!} = .01813$$

Queueing formulas involve tedious computations, and it is advisable to use the TORA software to carry out these calculations. Figure 17–2 provides the TORA output for the pure birth model with $\lambda t = (5 \times 1) = 5$ births per day.

```
Problem title: Fig 17-2
Scenario 1 -- Pure Birth Model

Poisson with lambda*t = 5.00000

Values of p(n) for n=0 to 17, else p(n) < .00001

 0 0.00674   1 0.03369   2 0.08422   3 0.14037   4 0.17547
 5 0.17547   6 0.14622   7 0.10444   8 0.06528   9 0.03627
10 0.01813  11 0.00824  12 0.00343  13 0.00132  14 0.00047
15 0.00016  16 0.00005  17 0.00001

Cumulative values of p(n) for n=0 to 17

 0 0.00674   1 0.04043   2 0.12465   3 0.26503   4 0.44049
 5 0.61596   6 0.76218   7 0.86663   8 0.93191   9 0.96817
10 0.98630  11 0.99455  12 0.99798  13 0.99930  14 0.99977
15 0.99993  16 0.99998  17 0.99999
```

**Figure 17–2**

## Problem Set 17.4a

1. In example 17.4–1, suppose that the clerk who enters the information from birth certificates into the computer normally waits until at least 5 certificates have accumulated. Find the probability that the clerk will be entering a new batch every hour.

2. An art collector travels to art auctions once a month on the average. Each trip is guaranteed to produce exactly one purchase. The time between trips is exponentially distributed. Determine the following:
   **(a)** The probability that the collector will not purchase any art pieces in a 3-month period.

**(b)** The probability that the collector will not purchase more than eight art pieces per year.

**(c)** The probability that the time between successive trips will exceed 1 month.

3. In a bank operation, at most one arrival can occur during a very small interval $h$. The probability of an arrival occurring is directly proportional to $h$ with the proportionality constant equal to 2. Determine the following:

**(a)** The average number of arrivals during 5 time units.

**(b)** The probability that no arrival will occur during the next .5 time unit.

**(c)** The probability that at least one arrival will occur during the next .5 time unit.

**(d)** The probability that the time between two successive arrivals is at least 3 time units (*Hint:* See Axiom 3 of Theorem 17.3–1.)

4. The time between arrivals at L&J restaurant is exponential with mean 5 minutes. The restaurant opens for business at 11:00 A.M. Determine the following:

**(a)** The probability of having 10 customers in the restaurant at 11:12 A.M. given that there were 8 at 11:05 A.M.

**(b)** The probability that a new customer will arrive between 11:28 and 11:33 A.M. given that the last customer arrived at 11:25 A.M.

5. The Springdale Public Library receives books according to a Poisson distribution with mean 25 books per day. Each shelf in the stacks holds 100 books. Determine the following:

**(a)** The average number of shelves that will be stacked with new books each (30-day) month.

**(b)** The probability that more than 10 bookcases will be needed each month, given that a bookcase has 5 shelves.

6. The U of A runs two bus lines on campus: red and green. The red line serves north campus and the green line serves south campus with a transfer station linking the two lines. Green buses arrive randomly (according to a Poisson distribution) at the transfer station every 10 minutes. Red buses also arrive randomly every 7 minutes.

**(a)** What is the probability that two buses will stop at the station during a 5-minute interval?

**(b)** A student whose dormitory is located next to the station has a class in 10 minutes. Either bus will take the student to the classroom building. The ride takes 5 minutes, after which the student will walk for about 3 minutes to reach the classroom. What is the probability that the student will make it to class on time?

7. Prove that the mean and variance of the Poisson distribution during an interval $t$ equal $\lambda t$, where $\lambda$ is the arrival rate.

8. Derive the Poisson distribution from the difference-differential equations of the pure birth model. *Hint:* The solution of the general differential equation

$$y' + a(t)\, y = b(t)$$

is

$$y = e^{-\int a(t)dt} \left\{ \int b(t) e^{\int a(t)dt} dt + \text{constant} \right\}$$

### 17.4.2 Pure Death Model

In the pure death model, the system starts with $N$ customers at time 0 with no other arrivals allowed. Departures occur at the rate $\mu$ customers per unit time. To develop the difference-differential equations for the probability of $n$ customers *remaining* after $t$ time units, $p_n(t)$, we follow the arguments used with the pure birth model (Section 17.4–1). Thus,

$$p'_N(t) = -\mu p_N(t)$$
$$p'_n(t) = -\mu p_n(t) + \mu p_{n+1}(t), \quad 0 < n < N$$
$$p'_0(t) = \mu p_1(t)$$

The solution of these equations yields

$$p_n(t) = \frac{(\mu t)^{N-n} e^{-\mu t}}{(N-n)!}, \quad n = 1, 2, \ldots, N$$

$$p_0(t) = 1 - \sum_{n=1}^{N} p_n(t)$$

which is a **truncated Poisson** distribution.

---

**Example 17.4–2.**

The florist section in a grocery store stocks 18 dozen roses at the beginning of each week. On the average, the florist sells 3 dozens a day (one dozen at a time), but the actual demand follows a Poisson distribution. Whenever the stock level reaches 5 dozens, a new order of 18 new dozens is placed for delivery at the beginning of the following week. Because of the nature of the item, all roses left at the end of the week are discarded. Determine the following:

**(a)** The probability of placing an order *on or before* the end of each day of the week.

**(b)** The average number of dozen roses that will be discarded at the end of the week.

Because purchases occur at the rate of $\mu = 3$ dozens per day, the probability of placing an order by the end of day $t$ is given as

$$p_{n \le 5}(t) = p_0(t) + p_1(t) + \ldots + p_5(t)$$

$$= p_0(t) + \sum_{n=1}^{5} \frac{(3t)^{18-n}e^{-3t}}{(18-n)!}, \qquad t = 1, 2, \ldots, 7$$

Using TORA's multiple scenarios corresponding to $t = 1, 2, \ldots,$ and 7, we get

| $t$ (days) | 1 | 2 | 3 | 4 | 5 | 6 | 7 |
|---|---|---|---|---|---|---|---|
| $\mu t$ | 3 | 6 | 9 | 12 | 15 | 18 | 21 |
| $p_{n \le 5}(t)$ | .0000 | .0088 | .1242 | .4240 | .7324 | .9083 | .9755 |

The average number of dozen roses discarded at the end of the week ($t = 7$) is computed (using TORA) as

$$E\{n \mid t = 7\} = \sum_{n=0}^{18} n p_n(7) = .664 \text{ dozen}$$

### Problem set 17.4b

1. In Example 17.4–2,
   (a) Use TORA to verify the values for $p_{n \le 5}(t)$, for $t = 1, 2, \ldots,$ and 7.
   (b) Use TORA to compute $p_n(7)$, $n = 1, 2, \ldots, 18$, and then verify that these probabilities yield $E\{n \mid t = 7\} = .664$ dozen.

2. In Example 17.4–2, determine
   (a) The probability that the stock is depleted after 3 days.
   (b) The average number of dozen roses left at the end of the second day.
   (c) The probability that at least one dozen is purchased by the end of the fourth day, given that the last dozen was bought at the end of the third day.
   (d) The probability that the time remaining until the next purchase is at most half a day given that the last purchase occurred a day earlier.
   (e) The probability that no purchases will occur during the first day.

3. The Springdale High School band is performing a benefit jazz concert in its 400-seat auditorium. Local businesses buy the tickets in blocks of 10 and donate them to youth organizations. Tickets go on sale to business entities for 4 hours only the day before the concert. The process of placing orders for tickets is Poisson with a mean 10 calls per hour. Any (blocks of) tickets remaining after the box office is closed are sold at a discount as "rush tickets" 1 hour before the concert starts. Determine
   (a) The probability that it will be possible to buy rush tickets.
   (b) The average number of rush tickets available.

4. Each morning, the refrigerator in a small machine shop is stocked with two cases (24 cans per case) of soft drinks for use by the shop's 10 employees. The employees can quench their thirst at any time during the 8-hour work day (8:00 A.M. to 4:00 P.M.), and each employee is known to consume approxi-

mately 2 cans a day, but the process is totally random (Poisson distribution). What is the probability that an employee will not find a drink at noon (the start of the lunch period)? Just before the shop closes?

5. A freshman student receives a bank deposit of $100 a month from home to cover incidentals. Withdrawal checks of $20 each occur randomly during the month and are spaced according to an exponential distribution with a mean value of 1 week. Determine the probability that the student will run out of the incidental money before the end of the month (i.e., the end of the fourth week).

6. Inventory is withdrawn from a stock of 80 items according to a Poisson distribution at the rate of 5 items per day. Determine the following:
   (a) The probability that 10 items are withdrawn during the first 2 days.
   (b) The probability that no items are left at the end of 4 days.
   (c) The average number of items withdrawn over a 4-day period.

7. A machine shop has just stocked 10 spare parts for the repair of a machine. Stock replenishment of size 10 pieces occurs every 7 days. The time between breakdowns is exponential with mean 1 day. Determine the probability that the machine will remain broken for 2 days because of the unavailability of parts.

8. Demand for an item occurs according to a Poisson distribution with mean 3 per day. The maximum stock level is 25 items, which occurs on each Monday immediately after a new order is received. The order size depends on the number of units left at the end of the week on Saturday (the business is closed on Sundays). Determine the following:
   (a) The average weekly size of the order.
   (b) The probability of incurring shortage when the business opens on Friday morning.
   (c) The probability that the weekly order size exceeds 10 units.

9. Prove that the distribution of the time between departures corresponding to the truncated Poisson in the pure death model is an exponential distribution with mean $1/\mu$ time units.

10. Derive the truncated Poisson distribution from the difference-differential equations of the pure death model of using induction. (*Note:* See the hint in Problem 17.4a–8.)

## 17.5 GENERALIZED POISSON QUEUEING MODEL

This section develops a general queueing model that combines both arrivals and departures based on the Poisson assumptions—that is, the interarrival and the service times follow the exponential distribution. The model is the basis for the derivation of the specialized Poisson models in Section 17.6.

The development of the generalized model is based on the long-run or **steady-state** behavior of the queueing situation, which is achieved after the system has been in operation for a sufficiently long period. This type of analysis contrasts with the **transient** (or warm-up) behavior that prevails during the early operation of the system. One reason for not discussing the transient behavior in this chapter is that it is analytically complex. Another reason is that the study of most queueing situations occurs under steady-state conditions.

The generalized model assumes that both the arrival and departure rates are *state dependent,* meaning that they depend on the number of customers in the service facility. For example, at a highway toll booth, the attendant tends to speed up the collection of toll during rush hours. Also, in a shop with a specific number of machines, the rate of breakdown decreases as the number of broken machines increases because only working machines are capable of generating new breakdowns.

Define

$n$ = Number of customers in the system (in queue plus in service)
$\lambda_n$ = Arrival rate of customers given $n$ in the system
$\mu_n$ = Departure rate of customers given $n$ in the system
$p_n$ = Steady-state probability of $n$ customers in the system

The generalized model derives $p_n$ as a function of $\lambda_n$ and $\mu_n$. These probabilities are then used to determine the system's measures of performance, such as the average queue length, the average waiting time, and the average utilization of the facility.

The probabilities $p_n$ are determined by using the **transition-rate diagram** in Figure 17–3. The queueing system is in state $n$ when the number of customers in the system is $n$. From the axioms of the Poisson process given in Theorem 17.3–1, the probability of more than one event occurring during a small interval $h$ tends to zero as $h \to 0$. This means that for $n > 0$, state $n$ can change only to two possible states: $n - 1$ when a departure occurs at the rate $\mu_n$, and $n + 1$ when an arrival occurs at the rate $\lambda_n$. State 0 can only change to state 1 when an arrival occurs at the rate $\lambda_0$. Notice that $\mu_0$ is undefined because no departures can occur if the system is empty.

Under steady-state conditions, for $n > 0$, the *expected* rates of flow into and out of state $n$ must be equal. Based on the fact that state $n$ can be changed to states $n - 1$ and $n + 1$ only, we get

$$\begin{pmatrix} \text{Expected rate of} \\ \text{flow into state } n \end{pmatrix} = \lambda_{n-1}p_{n-1} + \mu_{n+1}p_{n+1}$$

Similarly,

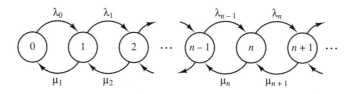

**Figure 17–3**

$$\left(\begin{array}{c}\text{Expected rate of}\\ \text{flow out of state } n\end{array}\right) = (\lambda_n + \mu_n)p_n$$

Thus, equating the two rates, we get the following **balance equation:**

$$\lambda_{n-1}p_{n-1} + \mu_{n+1}p_{n+1} = (\lambda_n + \mu_n)p_n, \qquad n = 1, 2, \ldots$$

From Figure 17–3, the balance equation associated with $n = 0$, is

$$\lambda_0 p_0 = \mu_1 p_1$$

The balance equations are solved recursively in terms of $p_0$ as follows: For $n = 0$, we have

$$p_1 = \left(\frac{\lambda_0}{\mu_1}\right) p_0$$

Next, for $n = 1$, we have

$$\lambda_0 p_0 + \mu_2 p_2 = (\lambda_1 + \mu_1)p_1$$

Substituting $p_1 = \left(\frac{\lambda_0}{\mu_0}\right)p_0$ and simplifying, we get (verify!)

$$p_2 = \left(\frac{\lambda_1 \lambda_0}{\mu_2 \mu_1}\right) p_0$$

In general, we can show by induction that

$$p_n = \left(\frac{\lambda_{n-1}\lambda_{n-2}\cdots\lambda_0}{\mu_n \mu_{n-1}\cdots\mu_1}\right) p_0, \, n = 1, 2, \, \ldots$$

The value of $p_0$ is determined from the equation $\Sigma_{n=0}^{\infty} p_n = 1$

---

**Example 17.5–1.**

B&K Groceries operates with three check-out counters. The sign by the check-out area advises the customers that an additional counter will be opened any time the number of customers in any lane exceeds three. This means that for fewer than four customers, only one counter will be in operation. For four to six customers, two counters will be open. For more than six customers, all three counters will be open. The customers arrive at the counters area according to a Poisson distribution, with a mean of 10 customers per hour. The average check-out time per customer is exponential with mean 12 minutes. Determine the steady-state probability $p_n$ of $n$ customers in the check-out area.

From the information of the problem, we have

$$\lambda_n = \lambda = 10 \text{ customers per hour}, \quad n = 0, 1, \, \ldots$$

$$\mu_n = \begin{cases} \frac{60}{12} = 5 \text{ customers per hour}, & n = 0, 1, 2, 3 \\ 2 \times 5 = 10 \text{ customers per hour}, & n = 4, 5, 6 \\ 3 \times 5 = 15 \text{ customers per hour}, & n = 7, 8, \, \ldots \end{cases}$$

Thus,

$$p_1 = \left(\frac{10}{5}\right) p_0 = 2p_0$$

$$p_2 = \left(\frac{10}{5}\right)^2 p_0 = 4p_0$$

$$p_3 = \left(\frac{10}{5}\right)^3 p_0 = 8p_0$$

$$p_4 = \left(\frac{10}{5}\right)^3 \left(\frac{10}{10}\right) p_0 = 8p_0$$

$$p_5 = \left(\frac{10}{5}\right)^3 \left(\frac{10}{10}\right)^2 p_0 = 8p_0$$

$$p_6 = \left(\frac{10}{5}\right)^3 \left(\frac{10}{10}\right)^3 p_0 = 8p_0$$

$$p_n = \left(\frac{10}{5}\right)^3 \left(\frac{10}{10}\right)^3 \left(\frac{10}{15}\right)^{n-6} p_0 = 8\left(\frac{2}{3}\right)^{n-6} p_0, \quad n = 7, 8, \ldots$$

The value of $p_0$ is determined from the equation

$$p_0 + p_0 \left[ 2 + 4 + 8 + 8 + 8 + 8 + 8\left(\frac{2}{3}\right) + 8\left(\frac{2}{3}\right)^2 + 8\left(\frac{2}{3}\right)^3 + \cdots \right] = 1$$

or, equivalently

$$p_0 \left\{ 31 + 8\left[ 1 + \left(\frac{2}{3}\right) + \left(\frac{2}{3}\right)^2 + \cdots \right] \right\} = 1$$

Using the geometric sum series

$$\sum_{i=0}^{\infty} x^i = \frac{1}{1 - x}, \; |x| < 1$$

we get

$$p_0 \left[ 31 + 8\left( \frac{1}{1 - \frac{2}{3}} \right) \right] = 1$$

Thus, $p_0 = \frac{1}{55}$.

Given $p_0$, we can now determine any of the probabilities of the problem. For example, the probability that only one counter will be open is computed as the probability that there are at most three customers in the system—that is,

$$p_0 + p_1 + p_2 + p_3 = (1 + 2 + 4 + 8)\left(\frac{1}{55}\right) \approx .273$$

The probability reasonably assumes that B&K will have at least one counter open even when no customers are present.

We can use $p_n$ to determine measures of performance for the B&K situation. For example, the mean number of idle servers is computed as

$$3p_0 + 2(p_1 + p_2 + p_3) + 1(p_4 + p_5 + p_6) + 0(p_7 + p_8 + \ldots) = 1 \text{ counter}$$

### Problem set 17.5a

1. In Example 17.5–1, determine the following:
   **(a)** The probability distribution of the number of open counters.
   **(b)** The average number of busy counters.
   **(c)** The average number of idle counters.

2. In the B&K model of Example 17.5–1, suppose that the interarrival time at the check-out area is exponential with mean 5 minutes and that the check-out time per customer is also exponential with mean 10 minutes. Suppose further that B&K will install a fourth counter and that all counters will open based on increments of two customers. Determine the following:
   **(a)** The steady-state probabilities $p_n$ for all $n$.
   **(b)** The probability that a fourth counter will be needed.
   **(c)** The average number of idle counters.

3. In the B&K model of Example 17.5–1, suppose that all three counters are always open and that the operation is set up such that the customer will go to the first empty counter. Determine the following:
   **(a)** The probability that all three counters will be in use.
   **(b)** The probability that an arriving customer will not wait.

4. First Bank of Springdale operates a one-lane drive-in ATM machine. Cars arrive according to a Poisson distribution at the rate of 12 cars per hour. The time per car needed to complete the ATM transaction is exponential with mean 6 minutes. The lane can accommodate a total of 10 cars. Once the lane is full, other arriving cars must seek service elsewhere. Determine the following:
   **(a)** The probability that an arriving car will not be able to use the ATM machine because the lane is full.
   **(b)** The probability that a car will not be able to use the ATM machine immediately on arrival.
   **(c)** The average number of cars in the lane.

5. Have you ever heard someone repeat the contradictory statement, "The place is so crowded no one goes there any more"? This statement can be interpreted as saying that the opportunity for reneging increases with the increase in the number of customers seeking service. A possible platform for modeling this situation is to say that the arrival rate at the system decreases as the number of customers in the system increases. More specifically, we consider the simplified case of M&M Pool Club where customers usually arrive in pairs to "shoot pool." The normal arrival rate is 6 pairs (of people) per hour. However, once the number of pairs in the pool hall exceeds 8, the arrival rate drops to 5 pairs per hour. The arrival process is assumed to follow the Poisson distribution. Each pair shoots pool for an exponential time with mean 30 minutes. The pool hall has a total of 5 tables and can accommodate no more than 12 pairs at any one time. Determine the following:
   **(a)** The probability that customers will begin reneging.

**(b)** The probability that all tables are in use.

**(c)** The average number of tables in use.

**(d)** The average number of pairs waiting for a pool table to be available.

6. A barbershop can serve one customer at a time. In addition, there are three seats for waiting customers. This means that the shop cannot have more than four customers at any one time. Customers arrive according to a Poisson distribution with mean four per hour. The time to get a haircut is exponential with mean 15 minutes. Determine the following:

**(a)** The steady-state probabilities.

**(b)** The expected number of customers in the shop.

**(c)** The probability that customers will go elsewhere because all the seats in the shop are occupied.

7. Consider a one-server queueing situation in which the arrival and service rates are given by

$$\lambda_n = 10 - n, n = 0, 1, 2, 3$$

$$\mu_n = \frac{n}{2} + 5, n = 1, 2, 3, 4$$

This situation is equivalent to reducing the arrival rate and increasing the service rate as the number in the system, $n$, increases.

**(a)** Set up the transition diagram and determine the balance equation for the system.

**(b)** Determine the steady-state probabilities.

8. Consider the single queue model where only one customer is allowed in the system. Customers who arrive and find the facility busy never return. Assume that arrivals occur according to a Poisson distribution with mean $\lambda$ per unit time and that the service time is exponential with mean $\frac{1}{\mu}$ time units.

**(a)** Set up the transition diagram and determine the balance equations.

**(b)** Determine the steady-state probabilities.

**(c)** Determine the average number in the system.

9. The induction proof for deriving the general solution of the generalized model is applied as follows. Consider

$$p_k = \prod_{i=0}^{k-1}\left(\frac{\lambda_i}{\mu_{i+1}}\right)p_0, k = n, n - 1, n - 2$$

We substitute for $p_{n-1}$ and $p_{n-2}$ in the general difference equation involving $p_n$, $p_{n-1}$, and $p_{n-2}$ to derive the desired expression for $p_n$. Verify this procedure.

## 17.6 SPECIALIZED POISSON QUEUES

Figure 17–4 depicts the specialized Poisson queueing situation with $c$ identical parallel servers. A waiting customer is selected from the queue to start service with the first free server. The arrival rate at the system is $\lambda$ customers per unit time. All parallel servers offer equal services, meaning that the service rate for any server is $\mu$ customers per unit time. The number of customers in the *system* is defined to include those *in service* and those waiting *in queue*.

A convenient notation for summarizing the characteristics of queueing situation in Figure 17–4 is given by the following format:

$$(a/b/c) : (d/e/f)$$

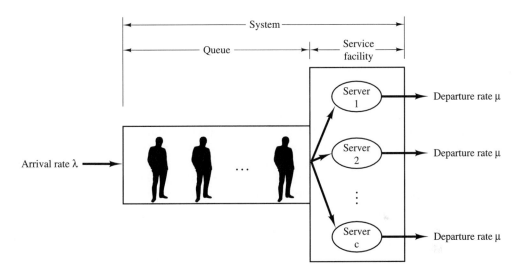

**Figure 17–4**

where

$a$ = Description of the arrivals distribution
$b$ = Description of the departures (service time) distribution
$c$ = Number of parallel servers ($= 1, 2, \ldots, \infty$)
$d$ = Queue discipline
$e$ = Maximum number (finite or infinite) allowed in the system (in queue plus in service)
$f$ = Size of the calling source (finite or infinite)

The standard notation for representing the arrivals and departures distributions (symbols *a* and *b*) are

$M$ = Markovian (or Poisson) arrivals or departures distribution (or equivalently exponential interarrival or service time distribution)

$D$ = Constant (deterministic) time

$E_k$ = Erlang or gamma distribution of time (or equivalently the sum of independent exponential distributions)

$GI$ = General (generic) distribution of interarrival time

$G$ = General (generic) distribution of service time

The queue discipline notation (symbol *d*) include

FCFS = First come, first served

LCFS = Last come, first served

SIRO = Service in random order

GD   = General discipline (i.e., any type of discipline)

To illustrate the use of the notation, the model $(M/D/10) : (GD/N/\infty)$ uses Poisson arrivals (or exponential interarrival time), constant service time, and 10 parallel servers. The queue discipline is GD, and there is a limit of $N$ customers on the entire system. The size of the source from which customers arrive is infinite.

As a historical note, the first three elements of the notation $(a/b/c)$, were devised by D. G. Kendall in 1953 and are known in the literature as the **Kendall notation.** Later in 1966, A. M. Lee added the symbols *d* and *e* to the notation. I added the last element, symbol *f*, in 1968.

Before presenting the details of the specialized Poisson queues, we show how the steady-state measures of performance of the generalized queueing situation can be derived from the steady-state probabilities $p_n$ given in Section 17.5

### 17.6.1 Steady-State Measures of Performance

The most commonly used measures of performance in a queueing situation are

$L_s$ = Expected number of customers in *system*

$L_q$ = Expected number of customers in *queue*

$W_s$ = Expected waiting time in *system*

$W_q$ = Expected waiting time in *queue*

$\bar{c}$ = Expected number of busy servers

Recall the *system* includes both the *queue* and the *service facility.*

We show now how these measures are derived (directly or indirectly) from the steady-state probability of *n* in the system, $p_n$. Specifically, we have

$$L_s = \sum_{n=1}^{\infty} np_n$$

$$L_q = \sum_{n=c+1}^{\infty} (n - c)p_n$$

The relationship between $L_s$ and $W_s$ (also $L_q$ and $W_q$) is known as **Little's formula,** and is given as

$$L_s = \lambda_{\text{eff}} W_s$$

$$L_q = \lambda_{\text{eff}} W_q$$

These relationships are valid under rather general conditions. The parameter $\lambda_{\text{eff}}$ is the *effective* arrival rate at the system. It equals the (nominal) arrival rate $\lambda$ when all arriving customers can join the system. Otherwise, if some customers cannot join because the system is full (e.g., a parking lot), then $\lambda_{\text{eff}} < \lambda$. We will show subsequently how $\lambda_{\text{eff}}$ is determined.

A direct relationship also exists between $W_s$ and $W_q$. By definition,

$$\begin{pmatrix} \text{Expected waiting} \\ \text{time in system} \end{pmatrix} = \begin{pmatrix} \text{Expected waiting} \\ \text{time in queue} \end{pmatrix} + \begin{pmatrix} \text{Expected service} \\ \text{time} \end{pmatrix}$$

This translates as

$$W_s = W_q + \frac{1}{\mu}$$

Next, we can relate $L_s$ and $L_q$ by multiplying both sides of the last formula by $\lambda_{\text{eff}}$, which together with Little's formula give

$$L_s = L_q + \frac{\lambda_{\text{eff}}}{\mu}$$

By definition, the difference between the average number in the system, $L_s$, and the average number in the queue, $L_q$, must equal the average number of *busy* servers, $\bar{c}$. We thus have,

$$\bar{c} = L_s - L_q = \frac{\lambda_{\text{eff}}}{\mu}$$

The percentage utilization of the servers is thus computed as $(\frac{\bar{c}}{c})100$.

---

**Example 17.6–1.**

Visitors parking at Ozark College is limited to only five spaces. Cars making use of this space arrive according to a Poisson distribution at the rate of six cars per hour. Parking time is exponentially distributed with a mean of 30 minutes. Visitors who cannot find an empty space immediately on arrival may temporarily wait inside the lot until a parked car leaves. That temporary space can hold only three cars. All other cars that cannot park or find a temporary waiting space must go elsewhere. Determine the following:

**(a)** The probability $p_n$ of $n$ cars being in the system.

**(b)** The effective rate at which cars arrive at the lot.

**(c)** The average number of cars in the lot.

**(d)** The average time a car waits for a parking space inside the lot.

**(e)** The average number of *occupied* parking spaces.

We note first that a parking space acts as a server so that the system has a total of $c = 5$ parallel servers. Also, the maximum capacity of the system is $5 + 3 = 8$ cars.

The probability $p_n$ can be determined as a special case of the generalized model in Section 17.5. Specifically, we have

$$\lambda_n = 6 \text{ cars/hour}, n = 0, 1, 2, \ldots, 8$$

$$\mu_n = \begin{cases} n\left(\dfrac{60}{30}\right) = 2n \text{ cars/hour}, & n = 1, 2, \ldots, 5 \\ 5\left(\dfrac{60}{30}\right) = 10 \text{ cars/hour}, & n = 6, 7, 8 \end{cases}$$

From Section 17.5, we thus get

$$p_n = \begin{cases} \dfrac{\left(\dfrac{6}{2}\right)^n}{n!} p_0, & n = 1, 2, \ldots, 5 \\ \dfrac{\left(\dfrac{6}{2}\right)^n}{5!5^{n-5}} p_0, & n = 6, 7, 8 \end{cases}$$

The value of $p_0$ is thus computed by substituting $p_n$, $n = 1, 2, \ldots, 8$, in the following equation

$$p_0 + p_1 + \ldots + p_8 = 1$$

or

$$p_0 + p_0\left(\frac{3}{1!} + \frac{3^2}{2!} + \frac{3^3}{3!} + \frac{3^4}{4!} + \frac{3^5}{5!} + \frac{3^6}{5!5^1} + \frac{3^7}{5!5^2} + \frac{3^8}{5!5^3}\right) = 1$$

This yields $p_0 = .04812$ (verify!). From $p_0$, we can now compute $p_1$ through $p_8$ as

| $n$ | 1 | 2 | 3 | 4 | 5 | 6 | 7 | 8 |
|---|---|---|---|---|---|---|---|---|
| $p_n$ | .14436 | .21654 | .21654 | .16240 | .09744 | .05847 | .03508 | .02105 |

The effective arrival rate $\lambda_{\text{eff}}$ can be computed by observing the schematic diagram in Figure 17–5, where customers arrive from the source at the rate $\lambda$ cars per hour. An arriving car may then be able to enter the parking lot or go elsewhere with rates $\lambda_{\text{eff}}$ or $\lambda_{\text{lost}}$, which means that $\lambda = \lambda_{\text{eff}} + \lambda_{\text{lost}}$. A car will not be able to enter the parking lot if there are 8 cars already there. This means that the proportion of cars that will *not* be able to enter the lot must equal $p_8$. Thus,

$$\lambda_{\text{lost}} = \lambda p_8 = 6 \times .02105 = .1263 \text{ cars per hour}$$

$$\lambda_{\text{eff}} = \lambda - \lambda_{\text{lost}} = 6 - .1263 = 5.8737 \text{ cars per hour}$$

The average number of cars in the lot (those waiting for or occupying a space) equals $L_s$, the average number in the system. We can compute $L_s$ from $p_n$ as

$$L_s = 0p_0 + 1p_1 + \ldots 8p_8 = 3.1286 \text{ cars}$$

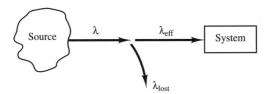

**Figure 17–5**

A car waiting in the temporary space is actually a car waiting in queue. Thus, its waiting time until a space is found is $W_q$. To determine $W_q$, we use the definition

$$W_q = W_s - \frac{1}{\mu}$$

Because

$$W_s = \frac{L_s}{\lambda_{\text{eff}}} = \frac{3.1286}{5.8737} = .53265 \text{ hour}$$

we compute $W_q$ as

$$W_q = .53265 - \frac{1}{2} = .03265 \text{ hour}$$

The average number of occupied parking spaces is the same as the average number of "busy servers," and hence is computed as

$$\bar{c} = L_s - L_q = \frac{\lambda_{\text{eff}}}{\mu} = \frac{5.8737}{2} = 2.9368 \text{ spaces}$$

---

### Problem set 17.6a

1. In Example 17.6–1, do the following:
   (a) Compute $L_q$ directly using the formula $\sum_{n=c+1}^{\infty}(n-c)p_n$.
   (b) Compute $W_s$ from $L_q$.
   (c) Compute the average number of cars that will not be able to enter the parking lot during an 8-hour period.
   (d) Show that the average number of empty spaces equals $\sum_{n=0}^{c-1}(c-n)p_n$.
2. Solve Example 17.6–1 using the following data: number of parking spaces $= 6$, number of temporary spaces $= 4$, $\lambda = 10$ cars per hour, and average parking time $= 45$ minutes.

### 17.6.2 Single-Server Models

This section presents two models for the single server case ($c = 1$). Customers are assumed to arrive at the constant rate $\lambda$ customers per unit time. The service rate is also constant and equal to $\mu$ customers per unit time. The first model sets no limit on the size of the system, and the second model assumes that the system size is finite. Both models assume an infinite-capacity source.

The results of the two models (and indeed of all the remaining models in Section 17.6) are derived as special cases of the results of the generalized model of Section 17.5.

The Kendall notation will be used to summarize the characteristics of each situation. Because the derivations of $p_n$ in Section 17.5 and of all the measures of performance in Section 17.6.1 are totally independent of a specific queue discipline, the symbol GD (general discipline) will be used with the notation.

**(M/M/1) : (GD/$\infty$/$\infty$).**    Using the notation of the generalized model, we have

$$\lambda_n = \lambda \text{ and } \mu_n = \mu, \text{ for all } n = 0, 1, 2, \ldots$$

Also, $\lambda_{\text{eff}} = \lambda$ and $\lambda_{\text{lost}} = 0$, because all arriving customers can join the system.

Define $\rho = \frac{\lambda}{\mu}$. The expression for $p_n$ in the generalized model then reduces to

$$p_n = \rho^n p_0, \quad n = 0, 1, 2, \ldots$$

To determine the value of $p_0$, we use the identity

$$p_0(1 + \rho + \rho^2 + \ldots) = 1$$

Assuming $\rho < 1$, the geometric series will have the finite sum $(\frac{1}{1-\rho})$, which yields $p_0 = 1 - \rho$.

The general formula for $p_n$ is thus given as

$$p_n = (1 - \rho)\rho^n, \quad n = 1, 2, \ldots \ (\rho < 1)$$

which is a geometric distribution.

The mathematical derivation of $p_n$ imposes the condition $\rho < 1$, which means that the arrival rate $\lambda$ must be strictly less than the service rate $\mu$ for the system to reach stability (steady-state conditions). If $\lambda \geq \mu$, the geometric series will not converge, and hence the steady-state probabilities $p_n$ will not exist. In this case, the queueing situation will always operate in a transient state in which the queue length increases indefinitely with time.

The measure of performance $L_s$ can be derived in the following manner:

$$L_s = \sum_{n=0}^{\infty} np_n = \sum_{n=0}^{\infty} n(1 - \rho)\rho^n$$

$$= (1 - \rho)\rho \frac{d}{d\rho} \sum_{n=0}^{\infty} \rho^n$$

$$= (1 - \rho)\rho \frac{d}{d\rho} \left(\frac{1}{1 - \rho}\right) = \frac{\rho}{1 - \rho}$$

Because $\lambda_{\text{eff}} = \lambda$ for the present situation, the remaining measures of performance are computed using the relationships in Section 17.6.1, thus yielding

$$W_s = \frac{L_s}{\lambda} = \frac{1}{\mu(1 - \rho)}$$

$$W_q = W_s - \frac{1}{\mu} = \frac{\rho}{\mu(1 - \rho)}$$

$$L_q = \lambda W_q = \frac{\rho^2}{1 - \rho}$$

$$\bar{c} = L_s - L_q = \rho$$

---

**Example 17.6–2.**

Automata car wash facility operates with only one bay. Cars arrive according to a Poisson distribution, with a mean of 4 cars per hour, and may wait in the facility's parking lot if the bay is busy. The time for washing and cleaning a car is exponential, with a mean of 10 minutes. Cars that cannot park in the lot can wait in the street bordering the wash facility. This means that for all practical purposes, there is no limit on the size of the system. The manager of the facility wants to determine the size of the parking lot.

For this situation, we have $\lambda = 4$ cars per hour, and $\mu = \frac{60}{10} = 6$ cars per hour. Because $\rho = \frac{\lambda}{\mu} < 1$, the system can operate under steady-state conditions.

The TORA output of the model, shown in Figure 17–6, is obtained by entering the data in the following order: $\lambda = 4$, $\mu = 6$, $c = 1$, system limit $= \infty$, and source limit $= \infty$.

The output shows that the average number of cars waiting in the queue, $L_q$, is 1.33 cars. We cannot use $L_q$ as the sole basis for the determination of the number of parking spaces because the design should, in some sense, reflect the maximum possible length of the queue. For example, it is more plausible that we design the parking lot such that an arriving car will find a parking space at least 90% of the time.

Suppose that $s$ is the unknown variable representing the number of parking spaces. Having $s$ parking spaces is equivalent to having $s + 1$ spaces in the *system* (queue plus wash bay). An arriving car will find a space 90% of the time if there are *at most* $s$ cars in the system. This condition is equivalent to the following probability statement:

$$p_0 + p_1 + \ldots + p_s \geq .9$$

From Figure 17–6, the *cumulative* values of $p_n$ are .86831 and .91221 for $n = 4$ and $n = 5$, respectively. This means that the condition is satisfied for $s \geq 5$ parking spaces.

The number of spaces $s$ can be determined also by using the mathematical definition of $p_n$—that is,

$$(1 - \rho)(1 + \rho + \rho^2 + \ldots + \rho^s) \geq .9$$

The sum of the truncated geometric series equals $\frac{1 - \rho^{s+1}}{1 - \rho}$. Thus the condition reduces to

$$(1 - \rho^{s+1}) \geq .9$$

Simplification of the inequality yields

$$\rho^{s+1} \leq .1$$

```
Problem title: Figure 17-6
Scenario 1 -- (M/M/1):(GD/*/*)
```

| Lambda = | 4.00000 | Lambda eff = | 4.00000 |
|----------|---------|--------------|---------|
| Mu =     | 6.00000 | Rho =        | 0.66667 |
| Ls =     | 2.00000 | Lq =         | 1.33333 |
| Ws =     | 0.50000 | Wq =         | 0.33333 |

```
Values of p(n) for n=0 to 25, else p(n) < .00001

 0 0.33333   1 0.22222   2 0.14815   3 0.09877   4 0.06584
 5 0.04390   6 0.02926   7 0.01951   8 0.01301   9 0.00867
10 0.00578  11 0.00385  12 0.00257  13 0.00171  14 0.00114
15 0.00076  16 0.00051  17 0.00034  18 0.00023  19 0.00015
20 0.00010  21 0.00007  22 0.00004  23 0.00003  24 0.00002
25 0.00001

Cumulative values of p(n) for n=0 to 25

 0 0.33333   1 0.55556   2 0.70370   3 0.80247   4 0.86831
 5 0.91221   6 0.94147   7 0.96098   8 0.97399   9 0.98266
10 0.98844  11 0.99229  12 0.99486  13 0.99657  14 0.99772
15 0.99848  16 0.99898  17 0.99932  18 0.99955  19 0.99970
20 0.99980  21 0.99987  22 0.99991  23 0.99994  24 0.99996
25 0.99997
```

**Figure 17–6**

Taking the logarithms on both sides, we get

$$s \geq \frac{\ln(.1)}{\ln\left(\frac{4}{6}\right)} - 1 = 4.679$$

Thus, $s \geq 5$ parking spaces.

## Problem set 17.6b

1. In Example 17.6–2, do the following.
   (a) Determine the percent utilization of the wash bay.
   (b) Determine the probability that an arriving car must wait in the parking lot prior to entering the wash bay.
   (c) If there are seven parking spaces, determine the probability that an arriving car will find an empty parking space.
   (d) How many parking spaces should be provided so that an arriving car may find a parking space 99% of the time?
2. John Macko is a student at OzarkU. He does odd jobs to supplement his income. Job requests come every 5 days on the average, but the time between requests is exponential. The time for completing a job is also exponential with mean 4 days.

**(a)** What is the probability that John will be out of jobs?

**(b)** If John gets about $50 a job, what is his average monthly income?

**(c)** If at the end of the semester, John decides to subcontract on the outstanding jobs at $40 each, how much, on the average, should he expect to pay?

3. Over the years, Detective Columbo, of the Fayetteville Police Department, has had a phenomenal success in solving every single crime case. It is only a matter of time before any case is solved. Columbo admits that the time per case is "totally random," but, on the average, each investigation will take about a week and half. Crimes in peaceful Fayetteville are not very common. They occur randomly at the rate of two crimes per month. Detective Columbo is asking for an assistant to share the heavy work load. Analyze Columbo's claim, particularly from the standpoint of the following points:

**(a)** The average number of cases awaiting investigation.

**(b)** The percentage of time the detective remains busy.

**(c)** The average time needed to solve a case.

4. Cars arrive at the Lincoln Tunnel toll gate according to a Poisson distribution, with a mean of 90 cars per hour. The time for passing the gate is exponential with mean 38 seconds. Drivers complain of the long waiting time, and authorities are willing to reduce the average passing time to 30 seconds by installing automatic toll collecting devices, provided two conditions are satisfied: (1) The average number of waiting cars in the present system exceeds 5 units, and (2) the percentage of the gate idle time with the new device installed does not exceed 10%. Can the new device be justified?

5. A fast-food restaurant has one drive-in window. Cars arrive according to a Poisson distribution at the rate of 2 cars every 5 minutes. The space in front of the window can accommodate at most 10 cars, including the one being served. Other cars can wait outside this space if necessary. The service time per customer is exponential, with a mean of 1.5 minutes. Determine the following:

**(a)** The probability that the facility is idle.

**(b)** The expected number of customers waiting to be served.

**(c)** The expected waiting time until a customer reaches the window to place an order.

**(d)** The probability that the waiting line will exceed the 10-space capacity.

6. Customers arrive at a one-window drive-in bank according to a Poisson distribution, with a mean of 10 per hour. The service time per customer is exponential, with a mean of 5 minutes. There are three spaces in front of the window, including the car being served. Other arriving cars line up outside this 3-car space.

**(a)** What is the probability that an arriving car can enter one of the 3-car spaces?

**(b)** What is the probability that an arriving car will wait outside the designated 3-car space?

**(c)** How long is an arriving customer expected to wait before starting service?

(d) How many car spaces should be provided in front of the window so that an arriving car can find a space there at least 20% of the time?

7. In the $(M/M/1) : (GD/\infty/\infty)$, give a plausible argument as to why $L_s$ does not equal $L_q + 1$, in general. Under what condition will the equality hold?

8. For the $(M/M/1) : (GD/\infty/\infty)$, derive the expression for $L_q$ using the basic definition $\sum_{n=2}^{\infty}(n - 1)p_n$.

9. For the $(M/M/1) : (GD/\infty/\infty)$ show that
   (a) The expected number in the queue given that the queue is not empty $= \frac{1}{(1-\rho)}$.
   (b) The expected waiting time in the queue for those who must wait $= \frac{1}{(\mu - \lambda)}$.

***Waiting Time Distribution for $(M/M/1) : (FCFS/\infty/\infty)^1$.***     The derivation of $p_n$ in the generalized model of Section 17.5 is *totally* independent of the queue discipline. This means that the average measures of performance, $W_s$, $W_q$, $L_s$, and $L_q$ apply to all queue disciplines.

Although the *average* waiting time is independent of the queue discipline, its probability density function does depend on the queue discipline used. We illustrate this point by deriving the waiting time distribution for the $(M/M/1)$ model based on the FCFS discipline.

Let $\tau$ be the amount of time a person *just arriving* must wait in the *system* (i.e., until the service is completed). Based on FCFS discipline, if there are $n$ customers in the system ahead of an arriving customer, then

$$\tau = t_1' + t_2 + \ldots + t_{n+1}$$

where $t_1'$ is the time needed for the customer actually in service to complete service and $t_2, t_3, \ldots, t_n$ are the service times for $n - 1$ customers in the queue. The time $t_{n+1}$ represents the service time for the arriving customer.

Define $w(\tau \mid n + 1)$ as the conditional density function of $\tau$ given $n$ customers in the system ahead of the arriving customer. Because the distribution of the service time is exponential, the forgetfulness property (Section 17.4) tells us that $t_1'$ is also exponential with the same distribution. Thus, $\tau$ is the sum of $n + 1$ identically distributed and independent exponential random variables. From probability theory, $w(\tau \mid n + 1)$ follows a gamma distribution with parameters $\mu$ and $n + 1$. We thus have

$$w(\tau) = \sum_{n=0}^{\infty} w(\tau \mid n + 1)p_n$$

$$= \sum_{n=0}^{\infty} \frac{\mu(\mu t)^n e^{-\mu t}}{n!}(1 - \rho)\rho^n$$

---

[1]This material may be skipped without loss of continuity.

$$= (1 - \rho)\mu e^{-\mu\tau} \sum_{n=0}^{\infty} \frac{(\lambda\tau)^n}{n!}$$

$$= \mu(1 - \rho)e^{-\mu(1-\rho)\tau}, \qquad \tau > 0$$

which is an exponential distribution with mean $W_s = \frac{1}{\mu(1-\rho)}$.

---

**Example 17.6–3.**

In the car wash facility model of Example 17.6–2, it is reasonable to assume that this service is performed based on FCFS discipline. Assess the reliability of using $W_s$ as an estimate of the waiting time in the system.

One way of answering this question is to estimate the proportion of customers whose waiting time exceeds $W_s$. Noting that $W_s = \frac{1}{\mu(1-\rho)}$, we get

$$P\{\tau > W_s\} = 1 - \int_0^{W_s} w(\tau)d\tau$$

$$= e^{-\mu(1-\rho)W_s} = e^{-1} \approx .368$$

Thus, under FCFS discipline, about 37% of the customers will wait longer than $W_s$. This appears excessive, particularly that the current $W_s$ for the car wash facility is high (= .5 hour). We note that the computed probability (= $e^{-1} \approx .368$) is independent of the rates $\lambda$ and $\mu$ for any $(M/M/1)$ (FCFS/$\infty$/$\infty$), which means that its value cannot be reduced. Thus, if we design the system based on the average $W_s$, then we should expect 36.8% of the customers to wait more than the average waiting time.

The situation can be improved in two ways: (1) We can increase the service rate $\mu$ to bring the value of $W_s$ down to an acceptable level, or (2) we can select the service rate such that the probability that the waiting time exceeds a prespecified value (say, 10 minutes) remains under a reasonably small percentage (say, 10%). The first method is equivalent to finding $\mu$ such that $W_s < \overline{T}$, and the second method would find $\mu$ by solving the inequality $P\{\tau > \overline{T}\} < \alpha$, where $\overline{T}$ and $\alpha$ are to be specified by the user.

---

## Problem set 17.6c

1. In Problem 17.6b–3, determine the probability that detective Columbo will take more than 1 week to solve a crime case.

2. In Example 17.6–3, compute the following:
   (a) The standard deviation of the waiting time $\tau$ in the system.
   (b) The probability that the waiting time in the system will vary by half a standard deviation around the mean value.

3. In Example 17.6–3, determine the service rate $\mu$ that satisfies the condition $W_s < 10$ minutes.

4. In Example 17.6–3, determine the service rate $\mu$ that will satisfy the condition $P\{\tau > 10 \text{ minutes}\} < .1$.

5. Consider Problem 17.6b–5. To attract more business, the owner of the restaurant will give free drinks to any customer who waits more than 5 minutes.

Given that a drink costs 50 cents, how much will it cost daily to offer free drinks? Assume that the restaurant is open for 12 hours a day.

**6.** Show that for the $(M/M/1) : (FCFS/\infty/\infty)$, the distribution of waiting time in the queue is

$$w_q(t) = \begin{cases} 1 - \rho, & t = 0 \\ \mu\rho(1 - \rho)e^{-(\mu-\lambda)t}, & t > 0 \end{cases}$$

Then find $W_q$ from $w_q(t)$.

**$(M/M/1)(GD/N/\infty)$.**    This model differs from $(M/M/1):(GD/\infty/\infty)$ in that there is a limit $N$ on the number in the system (maximum queue length $= N - 1$). Examples of this situation include manufacturing situations in which a machine may have a limited buffer area, and the one-lane, drive-in window in a fast-food restaurant.

Once the number of customers in the system reaches $N$, no more arrivals are allowed. Thus, we have

$$\lambda_n = \begin{cases} \lambda, & n = 0, 1, \ldots, N - 1 \\ 0, & n = N, N + 1, \ldots \end{cases}$$

$$\mu_n = \mu, \quad n = 0, 1, \ldots$$

Using $\rho = \frac{\lambda}{\mu}$, we get

$$p_n = \begin{cases} \rho^n p_0, & n \leq N \\ 0, & n > N \end{cases}$$

The value of $p_0$ is determined from the equation $\sum_{n=0}^{\infty} p_n = 1$, which yields

$$p_0(1 + \rho + \rho^2 + \ldots + \rho^N) = 1$$

or

$$p_0 = \begin{cases} \dfrac{1 - \rho}{1 - \rho^{N+1}}, & \rho \neq 1 \\ \dfrac{1}{N + 1}, & \rho = 1 \end{cases}$$

Thus,

$$p_n = \begin{cases} \dfrac{(1 - \rho)\rho^n}{1 - \rho^{N+1}}, & \rho \neq 1 \\ \dfrac{1}{N + 1}, & \rho = 1 \end{cases} \quad n = 0, 1, \ldots, N$$

The value of $\rho = \frac{\lambda}{\mu}$ need *not* be less than 1 in this model, because arrivals at the system are controlled by the system limit $N$. This means that $\lambda_{\text{eff}}$, rather than $\lambda$, is the rate that matters in this case. Because customers will be lost when there are $N$ in the system, then, as shown in Figure 17–5,

$$\lambda_{\text{lost}} = \lambda p_n$$

$$\lambda_{\text{eff}} = \lambda - \lambda_{\text{lost}} = \lambda(1 - p_N)$$

We should expect $\lambda_{\text{eff}}$ to be less $\mu$.

The expected number of customers in the system is computed as

$$L_s = \sum_{n=0}^{N} n p_n$$

$$= \frac{1 - \rho}{1 - \rho^{N+1}} \sum_{n=0}^{N} n \rho^n$$

$$= \frac{(1 - \rho)\rho}{1 - \rho^{N+1}} \frac{d}{d\rho} \left( \frac{1 - \rho^{N+1}}{1 - \rho} \right)$$

$$= \frac{\rho\{1 - (N + 1)\rho^N + N\rho^{N+1}\}}{(1 - \rho)(1 - \rho^{N+1})}, \qquad \rho \neq 1$$

When $\rho = 1$, $L_s = \frac{N}{2}$ (verify!). We can derive $W_s$, $W_q$, and $L_q$ from $L_s$ using $\lambda_{\text{eff}}$ as shown in Section 17.6.1.

The use of a hand calculator to compute the queueing formulas is at best cumbersome (the formulas will get more complex in later models!). I recommend the use of TORA to handle these computations.

---

**Example 17.6–4.**

Consider the car wash facility of Example 17.6–2. Suppose that the facility has a total of four parking spaces. If the parking lot is full, newly arriving cars balk to other facilities. The owner wishes to determine the impact of the limited parking space on losing customers to the competition.

In terms of the notation of the model, the limit on the system is $N = 4 + 1 = 5$. The input data for TORA are 4, 6, 1, 5, and $\infty$, respectively, and the output of the model is given in Figure 17–7.

```
Problem title: Figure 17-7
Scenario 1 -- (M/M/1):(GD/5/*)

Lambda =      4.00000          Lambda eff =        3.80752
Mu =          6.00000          Rho =         0.66667

Ls =          1.42256          Lq =          0.78797
Ws =          0.37362          Wq =          0.20695

Values of p(n) for n=0 to 5, else p(n) < .00001

 0 0.36541   1 0.24361   2 0.16241   3 0.10827   4 0.07218
 5 0.04812

Cumulative values of p(n) for n=0 to 5

 0 0.36541   1 0.60902   2 0.77143   3 0.87970   4 0.95188
 5 1.00000
```
                                                                        **Figure 17–7**

Because the limit on the system is $N = 5$, the proportion of lost customers is $p_5 = .04812$, which, based on a 24-hour day, is equivalent to losing $(\lambda p_5) \times 24 = 4 \times .04812 \times 24 = 4.62$ cars a day. A decision regarding increasing the size of the parking lot should be based on the value of lost business.

Looking at the problem from a different angle, the expected total time in the system, $W_s$, is .3736 hour, or approximately 22 minutes, down from 30 minutes in Example 17.6–3 when all arriving cars are allowed to join the facility. This reduction of about 25% is secured at the expense of losing about 4.8% of all potential customers because of the limited parking space.

---

**Problem set 17.6d**

1. In Example 17.6–4, determine the following:
   (a) The probability that an arriving car will go into the wash bay immediately on arrival.
   (b) The expected waiting time until a service starts.
   (c) The expected number of empty parking spaces.
   (d) The probability that all parking spaces are occupied.
   (e) The percent reduction in the average service time that will limit the average time in the system to about 15 minutes.

   (*Hint:* Use trial and error, with TORA, to answer part [e]).

2. Consider the car wash facility of Example 17.6–4. Determine the number of parking spaces such that the percentage of cars cannot find a space is limited to 1%.

3. Barber Joe gives a haircut according to an exponential distribution with mean 12 minutes. Because of his popularity, customers usually arrive (according to a Poisson distribution) at a rate much higher than Joe can handle: six customers per hour. Joe really will feel comfortable if the arrival rate is effectively reduced to about four customers per hour. To accomplish this goal, he came up with the idea of providing limited seating in the waiting area so that newly arriving customers would go elsewhere when they discover that all the seats are taken. How many seats should Joe provide to accomplish his goal?

4. The final assembly of electric generators at Electro is produced at the Poisson rate of 10 generators per hour. The generators are then conveyed on a belt to the inspection department for final testing. The belt can hold a maximum of 7 generators. An electronic sensor will automatically stop the conveyor once it is full, preventing the final assembly department from assembling more units until a space becomes available. The time to inspect the generators is exponential, with a mean of 15 minutes.
   (a) What is the probability that the final assembly department will stop production?
   (b) What is the average number of generators on the conveyor belt?
   (c) The production engineer claims that interruptions in the assembly department may be reduced by increasing the capacity of the belt. In fact,

the engineer claims that the capacity can be increased to the point where the assembly department can operate 95% of the time without interruption. Is this claim justifiable?

5. A cafeteria can seat a maximum of 50 persons. Customers arrive in a Poisson stream at the rate of 10 per hour and are served (one at a time) at the rate of 12 per hour.
   (a) What is the probability that an arriving customer will not eat in the cafeteria because it is full?
   (b) Suppose that three customers (with random arrival times) would like to be seated together. What is the probability that their wish can be fulfilled? (Assume that arrangements can be made to seat them together as long as three seats are available).

6. Patients arrive at a clinic according to a Poisson distribution at the rate of 20 patients per hour. The waiting room does not accommodate more than 14 patients. Examination time per patient is exponential, with a mean of 8 minutes.
   (a) What is the probability that an arriving patient will not wait?
   (b) What is the probability that an arriving patient will find a vacant seat in the room?
   (c) What is the expected waiting time until a patient leaves the clinic?

7. The probabilities $p_n$ of $n$ customers in the system for an $(M/M/1) : (GD/5/\infty)$ are given subsequently.

| $n$ | 0 | 1 | 2 | 3 | 4 | 5 |
|-----|-----|-----|-----|-----|-----|-----|
| $p_n$ | .399 | .249 | .156 | .097 | .061 | .038 |

The arrival rate $\lambda$ is five customers per hour. The service rate $\mu$ is eight customers per hour.
   (a) Compute the probability that an arriving customer will be able to enter the system.
   (b) Compute the rate at which the arriving customers will not be able to enter the system.
   (c) Compute the expected number in the system.
   (d) Compute the average waiting time in the queue.

8. Show that when $\rho = 1$ for the $(M/M/1) : (GD/N/\infty)$, the expected number in the system, $L_s$, equals $\frac{N}{2}$. (*Hint:* $1 + 2 + \cdots + i = \frac{i(i + 1)}{2}$.)

9. Show that $\lambda_{\text{eff}}$ for the $(M/M/1) : (GD/N/\infty)$ can be computed from the formula

$$\lambda_{\text{eff}} = \mu(L_s - L_q)$$

### 17.6.3 Multiple-Server Models

This section considers three queueing models with multiple parallel servers. The first two models are the multiserver versions of the models in Section 17.6.2. The third model treats the case in which the number of parallel servers is infinite.

**$(M/M/c) : (GD/\infty/\infty)$.**    In this model, there are $c$ parallel servers. The arrival rate is $\lambda$ and the service rate per server is $\mu$. Because there is no limit on the number in the system, $\lambda_{\text{eff}} = \lambda$.

The effect of using $c$ parallel servers is a proportionate increase in the service rate of the facility to $n\mu$ if $n \leq c$ and $c\mu$ if $n > c$. Thus, in terms of the generalized model (Section 17.5), $\lambda_n$ and $\mu_n$ are defined as

$$\lambda_n = \lambda, \qquad n \geq 0$$

$$\mu_n = \begin{cases} n\mu, & n \leq c \\ c\mu, & n > c \end{cases}$$

Thus,

$$p_n = \begin{cases} \dfrac{\lambda^n}{\mu(2\mu)(3\mu)\ldots(n\mu)} p_0 = \dfrac{\lambda^n}{n!\mu^n} p_0, & n \leq c \\[3ex] \dfrac{\lambda^n}{\mu(2\mu)\ldots(c-1)\mu(c\mu)^{n-c+1}} p_0 = \dfrac{\lambda^n}{c!c^{n-c}\mu^n} p_0, & n > c \end{cases}$$

Letting $\rho = \frac{\lambda}{\mu}$, and assuming $\frac{\rho}{c} < 1$, the value of $p_0$ is determined from $\sum_{n=0}^{\infty} p_n = 1$, which gives,

$$p_0 = \left\{ \sum_{n=0}^{c-1} \frac{\rho^n}{n!} + \frac{\rho^c}{c!} \sum_{n=c}^{\infty} \left( \frac{\rho}{c} \right)^{n-c} \right\}^{-1}$$

$$= \left\{ \sum_{n=0}^{c-1} \frac{\rho^n}{n!} + \frac{\rho^c}{c!} \left( \frac{1}{1 - \dfrac{\rho}{c}} \right) \right\}^{-1}, \qquad \frac{\rho}{c} < 1$$

The expression for $L_q$ can be determined as follows:

$$L_q = \sum_{n=c}^{\infty} (n - c)p_n$$

$$= \sum_{k=0}^{\infty} k p_{k+c}$$

$$= \sum_{k=0}^{\infty} k \frac{\rho^{k+c}}{c^k c!} p_0$$

$$= \frac{\rho^c \rho}{c! \, c} \sum_{k=0}^{\infty} k \left( \frac{\rho}{c} \right)^{k-1} p_0$$

$$= \frac{\rho^{c+1}}{(c-1)!(c-\rho)^2} P_0$$

Because $\lambda_{\text{eff}} = \lambda$, then $L_s = L_q + \rho$. The values of $W_s$ and $W_q$ can be determined by dividing $L_s$ and $L_q$ by $\lambda$.

---

**Example 17.6–5.**

A community is served by two cab companies. Each company owns two cabs, and the two companies are known to share the market almost equally. This is evident by the fact that calls arrive at each company's dispatching office at the rate of eight per hour. The average time per ride is 12 minutes. Calls arrive according to a Poisson distribution, and the ride time is exponential. The two companies recently were bought by an investor who is interested in consolidating them into a single dispatching office to provide faster service to customers. Analyze the new owner's proposal.

From the standpoint of queueing, the cabs are the servers, and the cab ride is the service. Each company can be represented by the model $(M/M/2) : (GD/\infty/\infty)$ with $\lambda = 8$ calls per hour and $\mu = \frac{60}{12} = 5$ rides *per cab* per hour. Consolidation will result in the model $(M/M/4) : (GD/\infty/\infty)$ with $\lambda = 2 \times 8 = 16$ calls per hour and $\mu = 5$ rides *per cab* per hour

A suitable measure for comparing the two models is the average time a customer waits for a ride—that is, $W_q$. Figure 17–8 provides the TORA output for the two scenarios. The results show that the waiting time for a ride is .356 hour ($\approx 21$ minutes) for the two-cab situation and .149( $\approx 9$ minutes) for the consolidated situation, a remarkable reduction of more than 50% and clear evidence that the consolidation of the two companies is warranted.

```
Problem title: Figure 17-8
Comparative measures: Nbr of scenarios = 2
```

| Nbr | c | Lambda | Mu | l'da_eff | Ls | Ws | Lq | Wq |
|-----|---|--------|-----|----------|-------|-------|-------|-------|
| 1 | 2 | 8.000 | 5.000 | 8.000 | 4.444 | 0.556 | 2.844 | 0.356 |
| 2 | 4 | 16.000 | 5.000 | 16.000 | 5.586 | 0.349 | 2.386 | 0.149 |

**Figure 17–8**

The conclusion from the preceding analysis is that **pooling of services** is always a more efficient mode of operation. This result is true even if the separate installations happen to be very busy.

---

**Problem set 17.6e**

**1.** In Example 17.6–5, determine the following:

   **(a)** The probability that all cabs in each of the two companies are "on call."

   **(b)** The probability that all cabs in the consolidated company will be "on call."

(c) The expected number of idle cabs in each of the two situations.

(d) The number of cabs that the consolidated company should have to limit the average waiting time for a ride to 5 minutes or less.

2. In the cab company example, suppose that the average time per ride is actually about 14 minutes, so that the utilization $(= \frac{\lambda}{\mu c})$ for the two- and four-cab operations increases to more than 93%. Is it still worthwhile to consolidate the two companies into one?

3. Determine the minimum number of parallel servers needed in each of the following (Poisson arrival/departure) situations to guarantee that the operation of the queueing situation will be stable (i.e., the queue length will not grow indefinitely):

(a) Customer arrive every 5 minutes and are served at the rate of 10 customers per hour.

(b) The average interarrival time is 2 minutes, and the average service time is 6 minutes.

(c) The arrival rate is 30 customers per hour, and the service rate per server is 40 customers per hour.

4. Customers arrive at Thrift Bank according to a Poisson distribution, with a mean of 45 customers per hour. Transactions per customer last about 5 minutes and is exponentially distributed. The bank wants to use a single-line multiple-teller operation, similar to the ones used in airports and post offices. The manager is conscious of the fact that customers may switch to other banks if they perceive that their wait in line is "excessive." For this reason, the manager wants to limit the average waiting time in the queue to no more than 30 seconds. How many tellers should the bank provide?

5. McBurger Fast-Food Restaurant has three cashiers. Customers arrive according to a Poisson distribution every 3 minutes and form one line to receive service by the first available cashier. It takes about 5 minutes, exponentially distributed, to fill an order. The waiting room inside the restaurant is limited. However, the food is good, and customers are willing to line up outside the restaurant, if necessary. Determine the size of the waiting room inside the restaurant (excluding those at the cashiers) such that an arriving customer does not wait outside the restaurant, with a probability of at least .999.

6. A small post office has two open windows. Customers arrive according to a Poisson distribution at the rate of 1 every 3 minutes. However, only 80% of them seek service at the windows. The service time per customer is exponential, with a mean of 5 minutes. All arriving customers form one line and access available windows on a FCFS basis.

(a) What is the probability that an arriving customer will wait in line?

(b) What is the probability that both windows are idle?

(c) What is the average length of the waiting line?

(d) Would it be possible to offer reasonable service with only one window? Explain.

**7.** U of A computer center is equipped with four identical mainframe computers. The number of users at any time is 25. Each user is capable of submitting a job through a terminal every 15 minutes, on the average, but the actual time between submissions is exponential. Arriving jobs will automatically go to the first available computer. The execution time per submission is exponential with mean 2 minutes. Compute the following:

**(a)** The probability that a job is not executed immediately on submission.

**(b)** The average time until the output of a job is returned to the user.

**(c)** The average number of jobs awaiting execution.

**(d)** The percentage of time the entire computer center is idle.

**(e)** The average number of idle computers.

**8.** Drake Airport services rural, suburban, and transit passengers. The arrival distribution for each of the three groups is Poisson with mean rates of 15, 10, and 7 passengers per hour, respectively. The time to check in a passenger is exponential with mean 6 minutes. Determine the number of counters that should be provided at Drake under each of the following conditions:

**(a)** The total average time to check a customer in is less than 15 minutes.

**(b)** The percentage of idleness of the counters does not exceed 10%.

**(c)** The probability that all counters are idle does not exceed .17.

**9.** In the United States, the use of single-line, multiple-server queues is common in post offices and in passenger check-in counters at airports. However, both grocery stores and banks (especially in smaller communities) tend to favor single-line, single-server implementations, despite the fact that single-line, multiple-server queues offer a more efficient operation. Comment on this observation.

**10.** In 1994, a leading U.S. long-distance telephone company announced through well-publicized television advertisements that collect-call callers would realize substantial savings if they would place their calls through a centralized 1–800 telephone number, instead of using the regional operator. The use of the 1–800 number is being promoted because it provides financial advantage to the company. Why is it so?

**11.** For the $(M/M/c) : (GD/\infty/\infty)$ model, Morse (1958, p. 103) gives the approximation for $L_q = \frac{\rho}{(c-\rho)}$, provided that $\frac{\rho}{c} \to 1$. Use this information to show that the ratio of the average waiting time in the $(M/M/c) : (GD/\infty/\infty)$ model to that in the $(M/M/1) : (GD/\infty/\infty)$ model approaches $\frac{1}{c}$ as $\frac{\rho}{c} \to 1$. Thus, for $c = 2$, the average waiting time can be reduced by 50%. The conclusion from this exercise is that it is always advisable to pool services.

**12.** In the derivation of $p_n$ for the $(M/M/c) : (GD/\infty/\infty)$ model, indicate which part of the derivation requires the condition $\frac{\rho}{c} < 1$. Explain in your own words the meaning of the condition. What will happen if the condition is not satisfied?

**13.** Prove that $L_s = L_q + \bar{c}$ starting with the definition $L_q = \sum_{n=c+1}^{\infty}(n-c)p_n$, where $\bar{c}$ is the average number of busy servers. Hence, show that $\bar{c} = \frac{\lambda_{\text{eff}}}{\mu}$.

**14.** Show that $p_n$ for the $(M/M/1) : (GD/\infty/\infty)$ model can be obtained from that of the $(M/M/c) : (GD/\infty/\infty)$ by setting $c = 1$.

**15.** Show that for the $(M/M/c) : (GD/\infty/\infty)$ that

$$L_q = \frac{c\rho}{(c - \rho)^2} p_c$$

**16.** For the $(M/M/c) : (GD/\infty/\infty)$ model, show that
  **(a)** The probability that a customer is waiting is $\{\frac{\rho}{(c - \rho)}\} p_c$
  **(b)** The average number in the queue given that it is not empty is $\frac{c}{(c - \rho)}$.
  **(c)** The expected waiting time in the queue for customers who must wait is $\frac{1}{\mu(c - \rho)}$.

**17.** Prove that the probability density function of waiting time in the queue for the $(M/M/c) : (GD/\infty/\infty)$ model is given as

$$w_q(T) = \begin{cases} 1 - \dfrac{\rho^c}{(c - 1)!(c - \rho)} p_0, & T = 0 \\ \dfrac{\mu\rho^c e^{-\mu(c-\rho) T}}{(c - 1)!} p_0, & T > 0 \end{cases}$$

(*Hint:* Convert the $c$-channel case into an *equivalent* single channel for which

$$P\{t > T\} = P\{\min_{1 \le i \le c} t_i > T\} = \{e^{-\mu T}\}^c = e^{-\mu c T}$$

where $t$ is the service time in the equivalent single channel.)

**18.** Prove that for $w_q(T)$ in Problem 17,

$$P\{T > y\} = P\{T > 0\} e^{-(c\mu - \lambda) y}$$

where $P\{T > 0\}$ is the probability that an arriving customer must wait.

**19.** Prove that the waiting time in the system for the $(M/M/c) : (FCFS/\infty/\infty)$ model has the following probability density function:

$$w(\tau) = \mu e^{-\mu\tau} + \frac{\rho^c \mu e^{-\mu\tau}}{(c - 1)!(c - \rho - 1)} \left\{ \frac{1}{c - \rho} - e^{-\mu(c-\rho-1)\tau} \right\} p_0, \quad \tau \ge 0$$

(*Hint:* $\tau$ is the convolution of the waiting time in queue, $T$ [see Problem 17], and the service time distribution.)

**$(M/M/c) : (GD/N/\infty), c \le N.$**    This model differs from that of the $(M/M/c) :$ $(GD/\infty/\infty)$ model in that a limit $N$ is set on the capacity of the system (i.e., the maximum queue size is $N - c$). The arrival and service rates are $\lambda$ and $\mu$. The effective arrival rate $\lambda_{\text{eff}}$ is less than $\lambda$ because of the limit, $N$, set on the capacity of the system.

In terms of the generalized model (Section 17.5), $\lambda_n$ and $\mu_n$ for the current model are defined as

$$\lambda = \begin{cases} \lambda, & 0 \le n \le N \\ 0, & n > N \end{cases}$$

$$\mu = \begin{cases} n\mu, & 0 \le n \le c \\ c\mu, & c \le n \le N \end{cases}$$

Substituting $\lambda_n$ and $\mu_n$ in the general expression in Section 17.5 and noting that $\rho = \frac{\lambda}{\mu}$, we get

$$p_n = \begin{cases} \dfrac{\rho^n}{n!} p_0, & 0 \le n < c \\[3mm] \dfrac{\rho^n}{c!c^{n-c}} p_0, & c \le n \le N \end{cases}$$

where

$$p_0 = \begin{cases} \left[ \displaystyle\sum_{n=0}^{c-1} \dfrac{\rho^n}{n!} + \dfrac{\rho^c \left( 1 - \left( \frac{\rho}{c} \right)^{N-c+1} \right)}{c! \left( 1 - \frac{\rho}{c} \right)} \right]^{-1}, & \dfrac{\rho}{c} \ne 1 \\[6mm] \left[ \displaystyle\sum_{n=0}^{c-1} \dfrac{\rho^n}{n!} + \dfrac{\rho^c}{c!} (N - c + 1) \right]^{-1}, & \dfrac{\rho}{c} = 1 \end{cases}$$

Next, we compute $L_q$ for the case where $\frac{\rho}{c} \ne 1$ as

$$L_q = \sum_{n=c}^{N} (n - c) p_n$$

$$= \sum_{j=0}^{N-c} j p_{j+c}$$

$$= \frac{\rho^c \rho}{c! c} \sum_{j=0}^{N-c} j \left( \frac{\rho}{c} \right)^{j-1} p_0$$

$$= \frac{\rho^{c+1}}{cc!} \frac{d}{d\left( \frac{\rho}{c} \right)} \sum_{j=0}^{N-c} \left( \frac{\rho}{c} \right)^j$$

$$= \frac{\rho^{c+1}}{(c-1)!(c-\rho)^2} \left\{ 1 - \left( \frac{\rho}{c} \right)^{N-c+1} - (N - c + 1) \left( 1 - \frac{\rho}{c} \right) \left( \frac{\rho}{c} \right)^{N-c} \right\} p_0$$

It can be shown that for $\frac{\rho}{c} = 1$, $L_q$ is given as

$$L_q = \frac{\rho^c (N - c)(N - c + 1)}{2c!} p_0, \qquad \frac{\rho}{c} = 1$$

To determine $W_q$, and hence $W_s$ and $L_s$, we need to obtain the value of $\lambda_{\text{eff}}$. Because no customer can enter the system once the limit $N$ is reached, we have

$$\lambda_{\text{lost}} = \lambda p_N$$

$$\lambda_{\text{eff}} = \lambda - \lambda_{\text{lost}} = (1 - P_N)\lambda$$

**Example 17.6–6.**

In the consolidated cab company problem of Example 17.6–5, suppose that new funds cannot be secured to purchase additional cabs. The owner was advised by a friend that one way to reduce the waiting time is for the dispatching office to inform new customers of potential excessive delay once the waiting list reaches six customers. This move is certain to get new customers to seek service elsewhere, but will reduce the waiting time for those already on the waiting list. Investigate the plausibility of the friend's advice.

Limiting the waiting list to 6 customers is equivalent to setting $N = 6 + 4 = 10$ customers. We are thus investigating the model $(M/M/4) : (GD/10/\infty)$, where $\lambda = 16$ customers per hour and $\mu = 5$ rides per hour. Figure 17–9 gives the TORA output of the model.

```
Problem title: Figure 17-9
Scenario 1 -- (M/M/4):(GD/10/*)
```

| Lambda = | 16.00000 | Lambda eff = | 15.42815 |
|----------|----------|--------------|----------|
| Mu =     | 5.00000  | Rho =        | 3.20000  |
| Ls =     | 4.23984  | Lq =         | 1.15421  |
| Ws =     | 0.27481  | Wq =         | 0.07481  |

```
Values of p(n) for n=0 to 10, else p(n) < .00001

  0 0.03121   1 0.09986   2 0.15977   3 0.17043   4 0.13634
  5 0.10907   6 0.08726   7 0.06981   8 0.05584   9 0.04468
 10 0.03574

Cumulative values of p(n) for n=0 to 10

  0 0.03121   1 0.13106   2 0.29084   3 0.46126   4 0.59760
  5 0.70667   6 0.79393   7 0.86374   8 0.91958   9 0.96426
 10 1.00000
```

**Figure 17–9**

The average waiting time, $W_q$, before setting a limit on the capacity of the system is .149 hour ($\approx$ 9 minutes) (see Figure 17–8), which is about twice the new average of .075 hour ($\approx$ 4.5 minutes). This remarkable reduction is achieved at the expense of losing about 3.6% of potential customers ($p_{10} = .03574$). However, this result does not reflect the possible loss of customer goodwill on the operation of the company.

### Problem set 17.6f

1. In Example 17.6–6, determine the following:
   (a) The expected number of idle cabs.
   (b) The probability that a calling customer will be the last to be put on the list.

    (c) The limit on the waiting list if it is desired to keep the waiting time in the queue to below 3 minutes.

2. Eat & Gas convenience store operates a two-pump gas station. The lane leading to the pumps can house at most five cars, including those being serviced. Arriving cars go elsewhere if the lane is full. The distribution of arriving cars is Poisson with mean 20 per hour. The time to fill up and pay for the purchase is exponential with mean 6 minutes. Determine the following:

    (a) The percentage of cars that will seek business elsewhere.

    (b) The percentage of time one of the pumps is in use.

    (c) The percent utilization of the two pumps.

    (d) The probability that an arriving car will find an empty space in the lane.

    (e) The capacity of the lane that will ensure that, on the average, no more than 10% of the arriving cars are turned away.

    (f) The capacity of the lane that will ensure, on the average, that the probability that both pumps are idle is .05 or less.

3. A small engine repair shop is run by three mechanics. Early in March of each year, people bring in their tillers and lawn mowers for service and maintenance. The shop is willing to accept all the tillers and mowers that the customers bring in. However, when a new customers sees the floor of the shop covered with waiting jobs, they go elsewhere to secure more prompt service. The floor shop can house a maximum of 15 mowers or tillers, including those being serviced. The customers arrive at the shop every 10 minutes on the average, and it takes a mechanic an average of 30 minutes to complete each job. Both the interarrival and the service times are exponential. Determine the following:

    (a) The average number of idle mechanics:

    (b) The amount of business lost to competition per 10-hour day because of the limited capacity of the shop.

    (c) The probability that the next arriving customer will be serviced by the shop.

    (d) The probability that at least one of the mechanics will be idle.

    (e) The average number of tillers or mowers awaiting service.

    (f) A measure of the overall productivity of the shop.

4. At U of A, newly enrolled freshmen students are notorious for wanting to drive their cars to class (even though most of them are required to live on campus and can conveniently make use of the university free transit system). During the first couple of weeks of the fall semester, traffic havoc prevails on campus as freshmen try desperately to find parking spaces. With an unusual dedication, the students wait patiently in the walkways of the parking lot for someone to leave so they can park their cars. Let us consider the following specific scenario. The parking lot has 30 parking spaces but can also accommodate 10 more cars in the walkways. These additional 10 cars cannot park in the walkways permanently and must await the availability of one of the 30

parking spaces. Freshman students arrive at the parking lot according to a Poisson distribution, with a mean of 20 cars per hour. The parking time per car averages about 60 minutes but actually follows an exponential distribution.

**(a)** What is the percentage of freshmen who are turned away because they cannot enter the lot?

**(b)** What is the probability that an arriving car will wait in the walkways?

**(c)** What is the probability that an arriving car will occupy the only remaining parking space on the lot?

**(d)** Determine the average number of occupied parking spaces.

**(e)** Determine the average number of spaces that are occupied in the walkways.

**(f)** Determine the number of freshmen who will not make it to class during an 8-hour period because the parking lot is totally full.

**5.** Verify the expression for $p_0$ for the $(M/M/c) : (GD/N/\infty)$ given that $\frac{\rho}{c} \neq 1$.

**6.** Prove the following equality for the $(M/M/c) : (GD/N/\infty)$

$$\lambda_{\text{eff}} = \mu \bar{c}$$

where $\bar{c}$ is the number of busy servers.

**7.** Verify the expression for $p_0$ and $L_q$ for the $(M/M/c) : (GD/N/\infty)$ when $\frac{\rho}{c} = 1$.

**8.** For the $(M/M/c) : (GD/N/\infty)$ model in which $N = c$, define $\lambda_n$ and $\mu_n$ in terms of the generalized model (Section 17.4), then show that the expression for $p_n$ is given as

$$p_n = \frac{\rho^n}{n!} p_0, \quad n = 1, 2, \ldots, c$$

where

$$p_0 = \left\{ 1 + \sum_{n=1}^{c} \frac{\rho^n}{n!} \right\}^{-1}$$

**$(M/M/\infty) : (GD/\infty/\infty)$—Self-Service Model.**    In this model, the number of servers is unlimited because the customer is also the server. A typical example is taking the written part of a driver's license test. Self-service gas stations and 24-hour ATM banks do not fall under this model's description because the servers in these cases are actually the gas pumps and the ATM machines.

The model assumes that the arrival rate, $\lambda$, is constant. The service rate, $\mu$, is also constant. In terms of the generalized model of Section 17.5, we have

$$\lambda_n = \lambda, \quad n = 0, 1, 2, \ldots$$

$$\mu_n = n\mu, \quad n = 0, 1, 2, \ldots$$

Thus,

$$P_n = \frac{\lambda^n}{n!\mu^n}P_0 = \frac{\rho^n}{n!}P_0, \quad n = 0, 1, 2, \ldots$$

Because $\Sigma_{n=0}^{\infty}P_n = 1$, it follows that

$$P_0 = \frac{1}{1 + \rho + \frac{\rho^2}{2!} + \cdots} = \frac{1}{e^\rho} = e^{-\rho}$$

As a result,

$$P_n = \frac{e^{-\rho}\rho^n}{n!}, \quad n = 0, 1, 2, \ldots$$

which is Poisson with mean $L_s = \rho$. As should be expected, $L_q = W_q = 0$ because it is a self-service model.

---

**Example 17.6–7.**

An investor invests $1000 a month in one type of stock market security. Because the investor must wait for good "buy" opportunity, the actual time at which the purchase is made is totally random. The investor usually keeps the securities for about 3 years on the average but will sell them at random times when "sell" opportunity presents itself. Although the investor is generally recognized as a shrewd stock market player, past experience indicates that about 25% of the securities decline at about 20% a year. The remaining 75% appreciate at the rate of about 12% a year. Estimate the investor's (long-run) average equity in the stock market.

This situation can be treated as an $(M/M/\infty) : (GD/\infty/\infty)$ because, for all practical purposes, the investor does not have to wait in line to buy or to sell securities. The average time between order placements is 1 month, which yields $\lambda = 12$ securities per year. The rate of selling securities is $\mu = \frac{1}{3}$ security per year.

Given the values of $\lambda$ and $\mu$, we obtain

$$L_s = \rho = \frac{\lambda}{\mu} = 36 \text{ securities}$$

The estimate of the (long-run) average *annual* net worth of the investor is

$$(.25L_s \times \$1000)(1 - .20) + (.75L_s \times \$1000)(1 + .12) = \$63,990$$

---

**Problem set 17.6g**

**1.** In Example 17.6–7, compute the following:
   **(a)** The probability that the investor will sell out completely.
   **(b)** The probability that the investor will own more than 10 securities.
   **(c)** The probability that the investor will own between 30 and 40 securities, inclusive.
   **(d)** The investor's net annual equity if only 10% of the securities depreciate by 30% a year, and the remaining 90% appreciate by 15% a year.

**2.** New drivers are required to pass written tests before they are given the road driving test. These tests are usually administered by the city police department. Records at the City of Springdale show that the average number of written tests is 100 per 8-hour day. The average time needed to complete the test is about 30 minutes. However, the actual arrival of test takers and the time each spends on the test are totally random. Determine the following:

   **(a)** The average number of seats the police department should provide in the test hall.

   **(b)** The probability that the number of test takers will exceed the average number of seats provided in the test hall.

   **(c)** The probability that no tests will be administered in any one day.

**3.** Show (by using TORA) that for small $\rho = .1$, the values of $W_s, L_s, W_s, W_q$ and $p_n$ for the $(M/M/c) : (GD/\infty/\infty)$ model can be estimated reliably using the less cumbersome formulas of the $(M/M/\infty) : (GD/\infty/\infty)$ model for $c$ as small as 10 servers.

**4.** Repeat Problem 3 for large $\rho = 9$ and show that the same conclusion holds except that the value of $c$ must be higher (at least 20). From the results of Problems 3 and 4, what general conclusion can be drawn regarding the use of the $(M/M/\infty) : (GD/\infty/\infty)$ to estimate the results of the $(M/M/\infty) : (GD/\infty/\infty)$ model.

### 17.6.4 Machine Servicing Model—(M/M/R) : (GD/K/K), R < K

The setting for this model is a shop that includes a total of K machines. Whenever a machine breaks down, it calls for the service of one of $R$ available repair persons. The rate of breakdown *per machine* is $\lambda$ breakdowns per unit time. A repair person will service broken machines at the rate of $\mu$ machine per unit time. All breakdowns and services are assumed to follow the Poisson distribution.

   This model differs from all the preceding ones in that the calling source is finite, in the sense that there is a limit on the number of calls that the source can generate. We can see this point by realizing that when all the machines in the shop are broken, no more calls for service will be generated. In essence, only machines in working order can break down and hence can generate calls for service.

   Given the rate of breakdown per machine, $\lambda$, the rate of breakdown for the *entire shop* is proportional to the number of machines that are in working order. In terms of the queueing model, having $n$ machines *in the system* signifies that $n$ machines are broken. Thus, the rate of breakdown for the entire shop is computed as

$$\lambda_n = (K - n)\lambda, \quad 0 \le n \le K$$

In terms of the generalized model of Section 17.5, we have

$$\lambda_n = \begin{cases} (K - n)\lambda, & 0 \le n \le K \\ 0, & n \ge K \end{cases}$$

$$\mu_n = \begin{cases} n\mu, & 0 \le n \le R \\ R\mu, & R \le n \le K \\ 0, & n > K \end{cases}$$

From the generalized model, we can then obtain (verify!)

$$p_n = \begin{cases} \binom{K}{n} \rho^n p_0, & 0 \le n \le R \\ \binom{K}{n} \dfrac{n!\rho^n}{R!R^{n-R}} p_0, & R \le n \le K \end{cases}$$

$$p_0 = \left\{ \sum_{n=0}^{R} \binom{K}{n}\rho^n + \sum_{n=R+1}^{K} \binom{K}{n} \frac{n!\rho^n}{R!R^{n-R}} \right\}^{-1}$$

It is difficult in this model to obtain a closed form for $L_s$ or $L_q$, and hence they must be computed using the following basic definitions:

$$L_s = \sum_{n=0}^{K} n\, p_n$$

The value of $\lambda_{\text{eff}}$ can be computed as

$$\lambda_{\text{eff}} = E\{\lambda(K - n)\} = \lambda(K - L_s)$$

Using the formulas in Section 17.6.1, we can compute the remaining measures of performance $W_s$, $W_q$, and $L_q$.

---

**Example 17.6–8.**

Toolco operates a machine shop with a total of 22 machines. Each machine is known to break down once every 2 hours, on the average. It takes an average of 12 minutes to complete a repair. Both the time between breakdowns and the repair time follow the exponential distribution. Toolco is interested in determining the number of repair persons needed to keep the shop running "smoothly."

The situation can be analyzed by investigating the productivity of the machines as a function of the number of repair persons. Such productivity measure can be defined as

$$\left( \begin{matrix} \text{Machines} \\ \text{productivity} \end{matrix} \right) = \frac{\text{Available machines} - \text{Broken machines}}{\text{Available machines}} \times 100$$

$$= \frac{22 - L_s}{22} \times 100$$

Figure 17–10 provides TORA comparative measures for $R = 1$ to $4$, given $\lambda = .5$ breakdowns per hour per machine and $\mu = 5$ repairs per hour. The associated productivities are computed in the following table:

| Repair person, $R$ | 1 | 2 | 3 | 4 |
|---|---|---|---|---|
| Machines productivity (100%) | 45.44 | 80.15 | 88.79 | 90.45 |
| Marginal increase (100%) | — | 34.71 | 8.64 | 1.66 |

```
Problem title: figure 17-10
Comparative measures: Nbr of scenarios = 4
```

| Nbr | c | Lambda | Mu | l'da_eff | Ls | Ws | Lq | Wq |
|---|---|---|---|---|---|---|---|---|
| 1 | 1 | 0.500 | 5.000 | 4.998 | 12.004 | 2.402 | 11.004 | 2.202 |
| 2 | 2 | 0.500 | 5.000 | 8.816 | 4.368 | 0.495 | 2.604 | 0.295 |
| 3 | 3 | 0.500 | 5.000 | 9.767 | 2.466 | 0.252 | 0.513 | 0.052 |
| 4 | 4 | 0.500 | 5.000 | 9.950 | 2.100 | 0.211 | 0.110 | 0.011 |

**Figure 17–10**

The results show that it is not acceptable to employ one repair person only because the associated productivity is low ($= 45.44\%$). By increasing the number of repair persons to two, the productivity jumps by 34.71% to 80.15%. When we employ three repair persons, the productivity increases only by about 8.64% to 88.79%, whereas four repair persons will increase the productivity by 1.66% only to 90.45%.

Judging from these results, the use of two repair persons is justifiable. The case of using three repair persons is not as strong because it raises the productivity by only 8.64%. Perhaps a monetary comparison between the cost of hiring a third repair person, and the income attributed to the 8.64% increase in productivity can be used to settle this point (see Section 17.10 for discussion of cost models). As for hiring a fourth repair person, the meager increase of 1.66% in productivity does not justify such an action.

## Problem set 17.6h

1. In Example 17.6–8, do the following:
   (a) Verify the values of $\lambda_{eff}$ given in Figure 17–10.
   (b) Compute the expected number of idle repair persons given $R = 4$.
   (c) Compute the probability that all repair persons are idle given $R = 3$.
   (d) Compute the probability that most repair persons are idle given $R = 3$ and $R = 4$.

2. In Example 17.6–8, define and compute the productivity of the repair persons for $R = 1$ to 4. Use this information in conjunction with the measure of machines productivity to decide on the number of repairpersons Toolco should hire.

3. In the computations in Figure 17–10, it may appear confusing that the average rate of machine breakdown in the shop, $\lambda_{eff}$, increases with the increase in $R$. Explain why the increase in $\lambda_{eff}$ should be expected.

4. An operator attends five automatic machines. After each machine completes a batch run, the operator must reset it before a new batch is started.

The time to complete a batch run is exponential with mean 45 minutes. The setup time is also exponential with mean 8 minutes.
  **(a)** Determine the average number of machines that are being set up.
  **(b)** Compute the probability that all machines are in working order.
  **(c)** Determine the average time a machine is down.

5. KleenAll is a service company that performs a variety of odd jobs, such as yard work, tree pruning, and house painting. The company's four employees leave the office with the first assignment of the day. After completing an assignment, the employee would call the office requesting instruction for the next job to be performed. The time to complete an assignment is exponential, with a mean of 45 minutes. The travel time between jobs is also exponential, with a mean of 20 minutes.
  **(a)** Determine the average number of employees who are traveling between jobs.
  **(b)** Compute the probability that no employee is on the road.

6. After a long wait, the Newborns were rewarded with quintuplets, two boys and three girls, thanks to the wonders of new medical advances. During the first 5 months, the babies' life consisted of two states: awake (and mostly crying) and asleep. According to the Newborns, the babies' "awake-asleep" activities never coincided. Instead, the whole affair appears to be totally random. In fact, Mrs. Newborn, a statistician by profession, believes that the length of time each baby cries is exponential, with a mean of 30 minutes. The amount of sleep each baby gets also happens to be exponential, with a mean of 2 hours. Determine the following:
  **(a)** The average number of babies who are awake at any one time.
  **(b)** The probability that all babies are asleep.
  **(c)** The probability that the Newborns will not be happy because more babies are awake (and crying) than are asleep.

7. Verify the expression for $p_n$ for the $(M/M/R) : (GD/K/K)$ model.

8. Show that the rate of breakdown in the shop can be computed from the formula

$$\lambda_{\text{eff}} = \mu \overline{R}$$

where $\overline{R}$ is the average number of busy repair persons.

9. Verify the following results for the special case of one repair person $(R = 1)$:

$$p_n = \frac{K! \rho^n}{(K - n)!} p_0$$

$$p_0 = \left\{ 1 + \sum_{n=1}^{R} \frac{K! \rho^n}{(K - n)!} \right\}^{-1}$$

$$L_s = K - \frac{(1 - p_0)}{\rho}$$

## 17.7 (M/G/1) : (GD/∞/∞)—POLLACZEK-KHINTCHINE (P-K) FORMULA

Queueing models in which the arrivals and departures do not follow the Poisson distribution are complex. In general, it is advisable in such cases to use simulation as an alternative tool for analyzing these situations (see Chapter 18).

    This section presents one of the few non-Poisson queues for which analytic results are available. It deals with the case in which the service time, $t$, is represented by any probability distribution with mean $E\{t\}$ and variance $\text{var}\{t\}$. The results of the model include the basic measures of performance $L_s$, $L_q$, $W_s$, and $W_q$. The model does not provide a closed form expression for $p_n$ because of analytic intractability.

    Let $\lambda$ be the arrival rate at the single-server facility. Given $E\{t\}$ and $\text{var}\{t\}$ of the service time distribution and that $\lambda E\{t\} < 1$, it can be shown using sophisticated probability/Markov chain analysis that

$$L_s = \lambda E\{t\} + \frac{\lambda^2(E^2\{t\} + \text{var}\{t\})}{2(1 - \lambda E\{t\})}, \quad \lambda E\{t\} < 1$$

Because $\lambda_{\text{eff}} = \lambda$, the remaining measures of performance ($L_q$, $W_s$, and $W_q$) can be derived from $L_s$, as explained in Section 17.6.1.

---

**Example 17.7–1.**

In the Automata car wash facility of Example 17.6–2, suppose that a new system is installed so that the service time for all cars is constant and equal to 10 minutes. How does the new system affect the operation of the facility?

    From Example 17.6–2, $\lambda_{\text{eff}} = \lambda = 4$ cars per hour. The service time is constant so that $E\{t\} = \frac{10}{60} = \frac{1}{6}$ hour and $\text{var}\{t\} = 0$. Thus,

$$L_s = 4\left(\frac{1}{6}\right) + \frac{4^2\left[\left(\frac{1}{6}\right)^2 + 0\right]}{2\left(1 - \frac{4}{6}\right)} = 1.333 \text{ cars}$$

$$L_q = 1.333 - \left(\frac{4}{6}\right) = .667 \text{ car}$$

$$W_s = \frac{1.333}{4} = .333 \text{ hour}$$

$$W_q = \frac{.667}{4} = .167 \text{ hour}$$

These results may also be obtained by using TORA.

    It is interesting that even though the arrival and departure rates are the same as in the Poisson case of Example 17.6–2 ($\lambda = 4$ cars per hour and $\mu = \frac{1}{E\{t\}} = 6$ cars per hour), the expected waiting time is lower in the current model because the service time is constant, as the following table shows.

|  | $(M/M/1):(GD/\infty/\infty)$ | $(M/D/1):(GD/\infty/\infty)$ |
|---|---|---|
| $W_s$ (hr) | .5 | .333 |
| $W_q$ (hr) | .333 | .167 |

The results make sense because a constant service time indicates *more certainty* in the operation of the facility.

---

### Problem set 17.7a

**1.** In Example 17.7–1, compute the percentage of time the facility is idle.

**2.** Solve Example 17.7–1 assuming that the service time distribution is given as follows:
   **(a)** Uniform between 8 and 20 minutes.
   **(b)** Normal with $\mu = 12$ minutes and $\sigma = 3$ minutes.
   **(c)** Discrete with values equal to 4, 8, and 15 minutes and probabilities .2, .6, and .2, respectively.

**3.** Layson Roofing Inc. installs shingle roofs on new and old residences in Arkansas. Prospective customers request the service randomly at the rate of nine jobs per 30-day month and are placed on a waiting list to be processed on a FCFS basis. Homes sizes vary, but it is fairly reasonable to assume that the roof areas are uniformly distributed between 150 and 300 squares. The work crew can usually complete 75 squares a day. Determine the following:
   **(a)** Layson's average backlog of roofing jobs.
   **(b)** The average time a customer waits until a roofing job is completed.
   **(c)** If the work crew is increased to the point where they can complete 150 squares a day, how would this affect the average time until a job is completed?

**4.** Optica, Ltd. makes prescription glasses according to orders received from customers. Each worker is specialized in certain types of glasses. The company has been experiencing unusual delays in the processing of bifocal and trifocal prescriptions. The workers in charge receives 30 orders per 8-hour day. The time to complete a prescription is normally distributed, with a mean of 12 minutes and a standard deviation of 3 minutes. After spending between 2 and 4 minutes, uniformly distributed, to inspect the glasses, the worker can start on a new prescription. Determine the following:
   **(a)** The percentage of time the worker is idle.
   **(b)** The average backlog of bifocal and trifocal prescriptions in Optica.
   **(c)** The average time until a prescription is filled.

**5.** A product arrives according to a Poisson distribution at the rate of one every 45 minutes. The product requires two tandem operations attended by one worker. The first operation uses a semiautomatic machine that completes its cycle in exactly 28 minutes. The second operation makes adjustments and minor changes, and its time depends on the condition of the product when it leaves operation 1. Specifically, the time of operation 2 is uniform between 3 and 6 minutes. Because each operation requires the complete attention of the worker, a new item cannot be loaded on the semiautomatic machine until the current item has cleared operation 2.

**(a)** Determine the number of items that are awaiting processing on the semiautomatic machine.

**(b)** What is the percentage of time the worker will be idle?

**(c)** How much time is needed, on the average, for an arriving item to clear operation 2?

**6.** $(M/D/1) : (\text{GD}/\infty/\infty)$. Show that for the case where the service time is constant $\{(\text{i.e., } \text{var}\{t\} = 0)\}$, the P-K formula reduces to

$$L_s = \rho + \frac{\rho^2}{2(1 - \rho)}$$

where $\mu = \frac{1}{E\{t\}}$ and $\rho = \frac{\lambda}{\mu} = \lambda E\{t\}$.

**7.** $(M/E_m/1) : (\text{GD}/\infty/\infty)$. Given that the service time is Erlang with parameters $m$ and $\mu$ (i.e., $E\{t\} = \frac{m}{\mu}$ and $\text{var}\{t\} = \frac{m}{\mu^2}$), show that the P-K formula reduces to

$$L_s = m\rho + \frac{m(1 + m)\rho^2}{2(1 - m\rho)}$$

**8.** Show that the P-K formula reduces to $L_s$ of the $(M/M/1) : (\text{GD}/\infty/\infty)$ when the service time is exponential with a mean of $\frac{1}{\mu}$ time units.

**9. (a)** In a service facility with $c$ parallel servers, suppose that customers arrive according to a Poisson distribution, with a mean rate of $\lambda$. Arriving customers are assigned to servers (busy or free) on a strict rotational basis. Determine the probability distribution of the interarrival time.

**(b)** Suppose in part (a) that arriving customers are assigned randomly to the $c$ servers with probabilities $\alpha_i$, $\alpha_i \geq 0$, $i = 1, 2, \ldots, c$, and $\alpha_1 + \alpha_2 + \ldots + \alpha_c = 1$. Determine the probability distribution of the interarrival time.

## 17.8 OTHER QUEUEING MODELS

The preceding sections have concentrated on the Poisson queueing models. Queueing literature is rich with other types of models. In particular, queues with priority for service, network queues, and non-Poisson queues form an important body of the queueing theory literature. These models can be found in most specialized books on queueing theory.

## 17.9 QUEUEING DECISION MODELS

The *service level* in a queuing facility is a function of the service rate, $\mu$, and the number of parallel servers, $c$. This section presents two decision models for determining "suitable" service levels for queueing systems: (1) a cost model, and (2) an aspiration-level model. Both models recognize that higher service levels reduce the waiting time in the system. The models make use of the measures of performance developed earlier for the different queueing situations to strike a balance between the conflicting factors of service level and waiting.

### 17.9.1 Cost Models

Cost models attempt to balance two conflicting costs:

**1.** Cost of offering the service
**2.** Cost of delay in offering the service (customer waiting time)

The two types of costs conflict because an increase in one automatically causes reduction in the other and vice versa (see Figure 17–1).

Letting $x = (\mu$ or $c)$ represent the *service level,* the cost model can be expressed as

$$ETC(x) = EOC(x) + EWC(x)$$

where

ETC = Expected total cost *per unit time*
EOC = Expected cost of operating the facility *per unit time*
EWC = Expected cost of waiting *per unit time*

The simplest forms for EOC and EWC are the following linear functions:

$$EOC(x) = C_1 x$$

$$EWC(x) = C_2 L_s$$

where

$C_1 = $ *marginal* cost per unit of $s$ per unit time
$C_2 = $ cost of waiting per unit time per (waiting) customer

The following two examples illustrate the use of the cost model. The first example assumes $x$ to equal the service rate, $\mu$, and the second assumes $x$ to equal the number of parallel servers, $c$.

**Example 17.9–1.**

KeenCo Publishing is in the process of purchasing a high-speed commercial copier. Four models whose specifications are summarized below have been proposed by vendors.

| Copier model | Operating cost ($/hr) | Speed (sheets/min) |
|:---:|:---:|:---:|
| 1 | 15 | 30 |
| 2 | 20 | 36 |
| 3 | 24 | 50 |
| 4 | 27 | 66 |

Jobs arrive at KeenCo according to a Poisson distribution with a mean of four jobs per 24-hour day. Job size is random but averages about 10,000 sheets per job. Contracts with the customers specify a penalty cost for late delivery at the rate of $80 per jobs per day. Which copier should KeenCo purchase?

Let the subscript $i$ represent copier model $i$ ($i = 1, 2, 3, 4$). The total expected cost *per day* associated with copier $i$ is thus expressed as:

$$\text{ETC}_i = \text{EOC}_i + \text{EWC}_i$$

$$= C_{1i} \times 24 + C_{2i}L_{si}$$

$$= 24C_{1i} + 80L_{si}, \quad i = 1, 2, 3, 4$$

The values of $C_{1i}$ are given by the data of the problem. We determine $L_{si}$ by recognizing that, for all practical purposes, each copier can be treated as an $(M/M/1)$ : $(GD/\infty/\infty)$ model. The arrival rate is $\lambda = 4$ jobs/day. The service rate $\mu_i$ associated with model $i$ is given as

| Model $i$ | Service rate $\mu_i$ (jobs/d) |
|:---:|:---:|
| 1 | 4.32 |
| 2 | 5.18 |
| 3 | 7.20 |
| 4 | 9.50 |

We illustrate the determination of the service rate by considering model 1.

$$\text{Average time per job} = \frac{10,000}{30} \times \frac{1}{60} = 5.56 \text{ hours}$$

Thus,

$$\mu_1 = \frac{24}{5.56} = 4.32 \text{ jobs/day}$$

The values of $L_{si}$, computed by TORA, are given in the following table:

| Model $i$ | $\lambda_i$ (Jobs/d) | $\mu_i$ (Jobs/d) | $L_{si}$ (Jobs) |
|-----------|---------------------|------------------|-----------------|
| 1         | 4                   | 4.32             | 12.50           |
| 2         | 4                   | 5.18             | 3.39            |
| 3         | 4                   | 7.20             | 1.25            |
| 4         | 4                   | 9.50             | 0.73            |

The costs for the four models are computed as follows:

| Model $i$ | $EOC_i$ ($) | $EWC_i$ ($) | $ETC_i$ ($) |
|-----------|-------------|-------------|-------------|
| 1         | 360.00      | 1000.00     | 1360.00     |
| 2         | 480.00      | 271.20      | 751.20      |
| **3**     | **576.00**  | **100.00**  | **676.00**  |
| 4         | 648.00      | 58.40       | 706.40      |

Thus, model 3 produces the lowest cost.

## Problem set 17.9a

1. In Example 17.9–1, do the following:
   (a) Verify the values of $\mu_2$, $\mu_3$, and $\mu_4$ given in the example.
   (b) Suppose that the penalty of $80 per job per day is levied only on jobs that are *not* "in progress" at the end of the day. Which copier yields the lowest total cost per day?

2. Metalco is in the process of hiring a repair person for a 10-machine shop. Two candidates are under consideration. The first candidate can carry out repairs at the rate of 5 machines per hour and earns $15 an hour. The second candidate, being more skillful, receives $20 an hour and can repair 8 machines per hour. Metalco estimates that each broken machine will incur $50 an hour because of lost production. Assuming that machine breakdowns occur according to a Poisson distribution with a mean of 3 per hour and that the repair time is exponential, which repair person should be hired?

3. B&K Groceries is opening a new store boasting "state-of-the-art" check-out scanners. Mr. Bih, one of the owners of B&K, has limited the choices to two scanners: scanner A can process 10 items a minute, and the better-quality scanner B can scan 15 items a minute. The daily (10 hours) cost of operating and maintaining the scanners are $25 and $35 for models A and B, respectively. Customers who finish shopping arrive at each cashier according to a Poisson

distribution at the rate of 10 customers per hour. Each customer's cart carries between 25 and 35 items, uniformly distributed. Mr. Bih estimates that the average cost per waiting customer per minute to be about 10 cents. Which scanner should B&K acquire? (*Hint:* The service time per customer is not exponential. It is uniformly distributed.)

4. H&I Industry produces a special machine according to customer specifications with regard to the numbers of pieces the machine can produce per hour. H&I charges $50 per unit increase in the production rate. A shop owner is considering buying one of these machines and wants to decide on the most economical speed (in pieces per hour) to be ordered. From past experience, the owner estimates that orders from customers arrive at the shop according to Poisson distribution at the rate of three orders per hour. Each order averages about 500 pieces. Contracts between the owner and the customers specify a penalty of $100 per late order per hour.

   (a) Assuming that the actual production time per order is exponential, develop a general cost model as a function of the production rate, $\mu$.
   (b) From the cost model in (a), determine an expression for the optimal production rate.
   (c) Using the data given in the problem, determine the optimal production rate the owner should request from H&I.

5. Jobs arrive at a machine shop according to a Poisson distribution at the rate of 80 jobs per week. An automatic machine represents the bottleneck in the shop. It is estimated that a unit increase in the production rate of the machine will cost $250 per week. Delayed jobs normally result in lost business, which is estimated to be $500 per job per week. Determine the associated optimum production rate for the machine based on the given information.

6. Pizza Unlimited sells two franchised restaurant models. Model $A$ has a capacity of 80 groups of customers, and model $B$ can seat 100 groups. The monthly cost of operating model $A$ is $12,000 and that of model B is $16,000. A prospective investor wants to set up a pizza restaurant and estimates that groups of customers, each occupying one table, arrive according to a Poisson distribution at a rate of 25 groups per hour. If all the tables are occupied, customers will go elsewhere. Model $A$ will serve 10 groups per hour, and model $B$ will serve 13 groups per hour. Because of the variation in group sizes and in the types of orders, the service time is exponential. The investor estimates that the average cost of lost business per customer per hour is $3. A delay in serving waiting customers is estimated to cost an average of $.50 per customer per hour.

   (a) Develop a cost model that considers the cost of lost customers (in addition to the cost of operating the restaurant and the cost of waiting).
   (b) Assuming that the restaurant will be open for business 10 hours a day, which model would you recommend for the investor?

7. Suppose in Problem 6 that the investor can choose any desired restaurant capacity based on a specific marginal cost for each additional capacity unit

requested. Derive the associated general cost model, and define all its components and terms.

**8.** Second Time Around sells popular used items on consignments from clients. Its operation can be viewed as an inventory problem in which the stock is replenished and depleted randomly according to Poisson distributions with rates $\lambda$ and $\mu$ items per day. Every time unit the item is out of stock, Second Time loses $\$C_1$ because of lost opportunities, and every time unit an item is held in stock, a holding cost $\$C_2$ is incurred.

   **(a)** Develop an expression for the expected total cost per unit time.

   **(b)** Determine the optimal value of $\rho = \frac{\lambda}{\mu}$. What condition must be imposed on the relative values of $C_1$ and $C_2$ in order for the obtained result to be consistent with the assumptions of the $(M/M/1) : (GD/\infty/\infty)$ model?

---

**Example 17.9–2.**

In a multiclerk tool crib facility, requests for tool exchange occur according to a Poisson distribution, with a mean of $17\frac{1}{2}$ requests per hour. Each clerk can handle an average of 10 requests per hour. The cost of hiring a new clerk in the facility is $\$12$ an hour. The cost of lost production per waiting machine per hour is approximately $\$50$ an hour. Determine the optimal number of clerks for the facility.

The situation corresponds to an $(M/M/c)$ model in which it is desired to determine the optimum value of $c$. Thus, we have $x = c$, and the corresponding cost model becomes,

$$\text{ETC}(c) = C_1 c + C_2 L_s(c)$$
$$= 12c + 50L_s(c)$$

Note that $L_s(c)$ is a function of the number of (parallel) clerks in the crib.

We use the $(M/M/1) : (GD/\infty/\infty)$ model with $\lambda = 17.5$ requests per hour and $\mu = 10$ requests per hour. In this regard, the model will reach steady state only if $c > \frac{\lambda}{\mu}$ —that is, for the present example, $c$ must at least equal 2. The following table provides the necessary calculation for determining optimal $c$. The values of $L_s(c)$ are determined by TORA

| $c$ | $L_s(c)$ (requests) | $\text{ETC}(c)$ ($\$$) |
|---|---|---|
| 2 | 7.467 | 397.35 |
| 3 | 2.217 | 142.35 |
| **4** | **1.842** | **140.10** |
| 5 | 1.769 | 148.45 |
| 6 | 1.754 | 159.70 |

Thus, optimal number of clerks is 4.

**Problem set 17.9b**

1. Resolve Example 17.9–2, assuming that $C_1 = \$20$ and $C_2 = \$45$.

2. Tasco Oil owns a pipeline booster unit that operates continuously. The time between breakdowns is exponential, with a mean of 20 hours. The repair time is exponential with mean 10 hours. In a particular station, two repair persons attend 10 boosters. The hourly wage for each repair person is $18. Pipeline schedule losses are estimated to be $30 per broken booster per hour. Tasco is studying the possibility of hiring an additional repair person.
   **(a)** Will there be any cost savings as a result of hiring a third repair person?
   **(b)** What is the schedule loss in dollars per breakdown when the number of repair persons on duty is two? Three?

3. A company leases a wide-area telecommications service (WATS) telephone line for $1500 a month. The office is open 200 working hours per month. At all other times, the WATS line service is used for other purposes and is not available for company business. Access to the WATS line during business hours is extended to 100 executives, each of whom may need the line at any time but average twice per 8-hour day with exponential time between calls. An executive will always wait for the WATS line if it is busy at an estimated inconvenience of 1 cent per minute of waiting. It is assumed that no additional needs for calls will arise while the executive waits for a given call. The normal cost of calls (not using the WATS line) averages about 50 cents per minute, and the duration of each call is exponential, with a mean of 6 minutes. The company is considering leasing (at the same price) a second WATS line to assist in handling the heavy traffic of calls.
   **(a)** Is the single WATS line saving the company money over a no-WATS system? How much is the company gaining or losing per month over the no-WATS system?
   **(b)** Should the company lease a second WATS line? How much would it gain or lose over the single WATS case by leasing an additional line?

4. A machine shop includes 20 machines and 3 repair persons. A working machine breaks down randomly according to a Poisson distribution. The repair time per machine is exponential, with a mean of 6 minutes. A queueing analysis of the situation shows that an average of 57.8 calls for repair per 8-hour day are generated for the entire shop and that a machine remains broken an average of 4.5 minutes before being attended by a repair person. Suppose that the rate of production per machine is 20 units per hour and that each produced unit generates $2 in revenue. Further, assume that a repair person is paid at the rate of $20 an hour. Compare the cost of hiring the repair persons against the cost of lost revenue when machines are broken.

5. The necessary condition for ETC($c$) (defined earlier) to assume a minimum value at $c = c^*$ are

$$\text{ETC}(c^* - 1) \geq \text{ETC}(c^*) \text{ and } \text{ETC}(c^* + 1) \geq \text{ETC}(c^*)$$

Show that these conditions reduce to

$$L_s(c^*) - L_s(c^* + 1) \leq \frac{C_1}{C_2} \leq L_s(c^* - 1) - L_s(c^*)$$

**6.** Apply the result of Problem 5 to Example 17.9–2 and show that it yields $c^* = 4$.

### 17.9.2 Aspiration Level Model

The viability of the cost model depends on how well we can estimate the cost parameters. Generally, these parameters are difficult to estimate, particularly the one associated with the waiting time of the customer. The aspiration level model seeks to alleviate this difficulty by working directly with the measures of performance of the queueing situation. The idea is to determine an acceptable range for the service level ($\mu$ or $c$) by specifying reasonable limits on *conflicting* measures of performance. Such limits are the *aspiration levels* the decision maker wishes to accomplish.

We illustrate the procedure by applying it to the multiple server model, where it is desired to determine an "acceptable" number of servers, $c^*$. We do so by considering the following two (conflicting) measures of performance:

**1.** The average waiting time in the system, $W_s$
**2.** The idleness percentage of the servers, $X$

The value of $W_s$ can be computed using TORA for the $(M/M/c)$ model. The idleness percentage can be computed as follows:

$$X = \frac{c - \bar{c}}{c} \times 100 = \frac{c - (L_s - L_q)}{c} \times 100 = \left(1 - \frac{\lambda_{\text{eff}}}{c\mu}\right) \times 100$$

(See Problem 17.6e–13 for the proof.)

The problem reduces to determining the number of servers $c^*$ such that

$$W_s \leq \alpha \quad \text{and} \quad X \leq \beta$$

where $\alpha$ and $\beta$ are the levels of aspiration specified by the decision maker. For example, we may stipulate that $\alpha = 3$ minutes and $\beta = 10\%$.

The solution of the problem may be determined by plotting $W_s$ and $X$ as a function of $c$ as shown in Figure 17–11. By locating $\alpha$ and $\beta$ on the graph, we can immediately determine an acceptable range for $c^*$. If the two conditions cannot be satisfied simultaneously, then one or both must be relaxed before a feasible range can be determined.

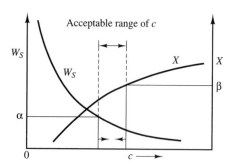

**Figure 17–11**

---

**Example 17.9–3.**

In Example 17.9–2, suppose that it is desired to determine the number of clerks such that the expected waiting time until a tool is received stays below 5 minutes. Simultaneously, it is also required that the percentage of idleness to be at most 20%.

Off hand, and before any calculations are made, an aspiration limit of 5 minutes on the waiting time until a tool is received (i.e., $W_s \leq 5$ minutes) is definitely unreachable because, according to the data of the problem, the average service time alone is 6 minutes. The following table summarizes $W_s$ and $\overline{X}$ as a function of $c$ and demonstrates this observation. Essentially, for $c \geq 5$, $W_s = 6$ minutes. This means that there will be no waiting time in the queue. The table also shows that any increase in the number of servers can only increase the idleness $\overline{X}$.

| $c$ | 2 | 3 | 4 | 5 | 6 | 7 | 8 |
|---|---|---|---|---|---|---|---|
| $W_s$ (min) | 25.6 | 7.6 | 6.3 | 6.0 | 6.0 | 6.0 | 6.0 |
| $\overline{X}$ (%) | | 12.5 | 41.7 | 56.3 | 65.0 | 70.8 | 75.0 | 78.0 |

There is really nothing that we can do in this situation because the problem cannot be solved by increasing the number of servers. Rather, we should either reduce the service time or recognize that the source of the problem is that tools are being requested at a an unreasonably high rate ($\lambda = 17.5$ requests per hour). This, most likely, is the area that should be addressed. For example, we may want to investigate the reason for such high demand for tool replacement. Could it be that the design of the tool itself is inadequate? Or could it be that the operators of the machines are purposely trying to disrupt production to express grievances?

---

## Problem set 17.9c

**1.** A shop uses 10 identical machines. Each machine breaks down once every 7 hours on the average. It takes 4 hours on the average to repair a broken machine. Both the breakdown and repair processes follow the Poisson distribution. Determine the following:

   **(a)** The number of repair persons needed such that the average number of broken machines is less than 4.

(b) The number of repair persons needed so that the expected delay time until a machine is repaired is less than 4 hours.

2. In the cost model in Section 17.9.1, it is generally difficult to estimate the cost parameter $C_2$ (cost of waiting). It may be helpful to compute the cost $C_2$ implied by the aspiration levels. In such a case, we assume that we are given $C_1$. Using the aspiration level model to determine $c^*$, we can then estimate the implied $C_2$ by using the following inequality:

$$L_s(c^*) - L_s(c^* + 1) \le \frac{C_1}{C_2} \le L_s(c^* - 1) - L_s(c^*)$$

(See Problem 17.9b–5 for the derivation.) Apply the procedure to the problem in Example 17.9–2, assuming $c^* = 3$ and $C_1 = \$12.00$.

## 17.10 SUMMARY

Queueing theory provides models for analyzing the operation of service facilities where arrivals and departures occur randomly. The Poisson and exponential distribution play important roles in queueing analysis because they represent totally random processes. Although queueing models can be analyzed with other distributions as well, the resulting models usually are not analytically tractable.

Queueing analysis does not solve problems per se. It provides the measures of performance that can be used within the framework of some decision models.

## SELECTED REFERENCES

Hall, R., *Queueing Methods for Service and Manufacturing,* Prentice Hall, Upper Saddle River, N.J., 1991.

Lipsky, L., *Queueing Theory, A Linear Algebraic Approach,* Macmillan, New York, 1992.

Morse, P., *Queues, Inventories, and Maintenance,* Wiley, New York, 1958.

Parzen, E., *Stochastic Processes,* Holden-Day, San Francisco, 1962.

Saaty, T., *Elements of Queueing Theory with Applications,* Dover, New York, 1983.

Tijms, H.C., *Stochastic Models—An Algorithmic Approach,* Wiley, New York, 1994.

## COMPREHENSIVE PROBLEMS

■ 17–1[2] The Bank of Elkins currently operates a traditional drive-in station and two "robo" lanes that connect to the inside of the bank through a pneumatic cartridge. The bank would like to expand the existing facilities so that an arriving car would complete its business in no more than 4 minutes, on the average. This time limit was based on psychological studies that show that customers base their impatience on the movement of the minute hand between two marks, which on most watches represents five minutes. To collect the necessary data, the team observed the operation of the existing

[2]Based on B. L. Foote, "A Queueing Case Study in Drive-In Banking," *Interfaces,* Vol. 6, No. 4., pp. 31–37, 1976.

tellers. After studying the system for a while, a member of the team noticed that there was a marked difference between the time a customer spends in the drive-in lane and the time the teller carries out the necessary bank transactions. In fact, the time a car spends in the system consisted of (1) realizing the car in front had moved, (2) move to the teller window, (3) give the teller instructions, (4) teller takes action, and (5) move out. During the first second and fifth components of this time period, the teller is forcibly idle. Indeed, the observation revealed that during each cycle, the teller was busy serving the customer only 40% of the time. Based on this information, the team discovered that there was room for reducing the operating cost of the present system.

What was the team's suggestion for improving the operations of the existing drive-in operation? Discuss all the implications of the suggestion.

■ 17–2 A state-run child abuse center operates from 9:00 A.M. to 9:00 P.M. daily. Calls reporting cases of child abuse arrive in a completely random fashion, as should be expected. The following table gives the number of calls recorded on an hourly basis over a period of 7 days:

| Starting hour | Total no. of calls for days | | | | | | |
|---|---|---|---|---|---|---|---|
| | 1 | 2 | 3 | 4 | 5 | 6 | 7 |
| 9:00 | 4 | 6 | 8 | 4 | 5 | 3 | 4 |
| 10:00 | 6 | 5 | 5 | 3 | 6 | 4 | 7 |
| 11:00 | 3 | 9 | 6 | 8 | 4 | 7 | 5 |
| 12:00 | 8 | 11 | 10 | 5 | 15 | 12 | 9 |
| 13:00 | 10 | 9 | 8 | 7 | 10 | 16 | 6 |
| 14:00 | 8 | 6 | 10 | 12 | 12 | 11 | 10 |
| 15:00 | 10 | 9 | 12 | 4 | 10 | 6 | 8 |
| 16:00 | 8 | 6 | 9 | 14 | 12 | 10 | 7 |
| 17:00 | 5 | 10 | 10 | 8 | 10 | 10 | 9 |
| 18:00 | 5 | 4 | 6 | 5 | 6 | 7 | 5 |
| 19:00 | 3 | 4 | 6 | 2 | 3 | 4 | 5 |
| 20:00 | 4 | 3 | 6 | 2 | 2 | 3 | 4 |
| 21:00 | 1 | 2 | 2 | 3 | 3 | 5 | 3 |

The table does not include lost calls resulting from the caller receiving a busy signal. For those calls that are actually received, each call lasts randomly for up to 12 minutes with an average of 7 minutes. Past calls show that the center has been experiencing a 15% annual rate of increase in telephone calls. The center would like to determine the number of telephone lines that must be installed to provide adequate service now and in the future. In particular, special attention is given to reducing the adverse effect of a caller receiving a busy signal.

■ 17-3 A manufacturing company employs three trucks to transport materials among six departments. Truck users have been demanding that a fourth truck be added to the fleet to alleviate the problem of excessive delays. The trucks do not have a home station from which they can be called. Instead, management considers it more efficient to keep the trucks in (semi-) continuous motion about the factory. A department requesting the use of a truck must await its arrival in the vicinity. If the truck is available, it will respond to the call. Otherwise, the department must await the appearance of another truck. The following table gives the frequency of the number of calls per hour:

| Calls/hr | Frequency |
|----------|-----------|
| 0 | 30 |
| 1 | 90 |
| 2 | 99 |
| 3 | 102 |
| 4 | 120 |
| 5 | 100 |
| 6 | 60 |
| 7 | 47 |
| 8 | 30 |
| 9 | 20 |
| 10 | 12 |
| 11 | 10 |
| 12 | 4 |

The service time for each department (in minutes) is approximately the same. The following table summarizes a typical service time histogram for one of the departments:

| Service time, $t$ | Frequency |
|---|---|
| $0 \leq t < 10$ | 61 |
| $10 \leq t < 20$ | 34 |
| $20 \leq t < 30$ | 15 |
| $30 \leq t < 40$ | 5 |
| $40 \leq t < 50$ | 8 |
| $50 \leq t < 60$ | 4 |
| $60 \leq t < 70$ | 4 |
| $70 \leq t < 80$ | 3 |
| $80 \leq t < 90$ | 2 |
| $90 \leq t < 100$ | 2 |

Recommend a course of action for the management.

■ 17–4 A young industrial engineer, Jon Micks, was recently hired by Metalco. The company owns a 30-machine shop and has hired 6 repair person to take care of repairs. The shop operates for one shift that starts at 8:00 A.M. and ends 4:00 P.M. Mr. Micks' first assignment is to study the effectiveness of the repair service in the shop. To that end, Jon collected the following data from the repair log for three randomly selected machines:

| Machine 5 | | Machine 18 | | Machine 23 | |
|---|---|---|---|---|---|
| Failure hour | Repair hour | Failure hour | Repair hour | Failure hour | Repair hour |
| 8:05 | 8:15 | 8:01 | 8:09 | 8:45 | 8:58 |
| 10:02 | 10:14 | 9:10 | 9:18 | 9:55 | 10:06 |
| 10:59 | 11:09 | 11:03 | 11:16 | 10:58 | 11:08 |
| 12:22 | 12:35 | 12:58 | 13:06 | 12:21 | 12:32 |
| 14:12 | 14:22 | 13:49 | 13:58 | 12:59 | 13:07 |
| 15:09 | 15:21 | 14:30 | 14:43 | 14:32 | 14:43 |
| 15:33 | 15:42 | 14:57 | 15:09 | 15:09 | 15:17 |
| 15:48 | 15:59 | 15:32 | 15:42 | 15:50 | 16:00 |

In addition to the preceding information, by checking the repair records for five randomly selected days, Jon was able to compile the following data representing the number of broken machines (including those being repaired) at the beginning of every hour of the work day:

| Date | | | | | | | | |
|------|------|------|-------|-------|-------|-------|-------|-------|
|      | 8:00 | 9:00 | 10:00 | 11:00 | 12:00 | 13:00 | 14:00 | 15:00 |
| 10/2  | 6 | 6 | 9 | 6 | 8 | 8 | 7 | 7 |
| 10/29 | 9 | 8 | 5 | 9 | 5 | 5 | 6 | 8 |
| 11/4  | 6 | 6 | 5 | 7 | 7 | 8 | 6 | 5 |
| 12/1  | 9 | 5 | 9 | 7 | 5 | 7 | 5 | 5 |
| 1/19  | 6 | 5 | 8 | 5 | 9 | 8 | 8 | 6 |

Total no. of broken machines at the hour of

Mr. Micks has a meeting with his supervisor, Becky Steele, regarding the data he has collected. He states that he is confident that the breakdown/repair process in the shop is totally random and that it is safe to assume that the situation can be described as a Poisson queue. Ms. Steele confirms that her long experience in the shop indicates that the situation is indeed totally random. Based on this observation, she examined Jon's data, and after making some computations, she announced to Jon that there was something wrong with the data. How did Ms. Steele reach that conclusion?

■ 17–5 The Yellow Cab Company owns four taxis. The taxi service operates for 10 hours daily. Calls arrive at the dispatching office according to a Poisson distribution with mean 20 calls per hour. The length of the ride is known to be exponential with mean 11.5 minutes. Because of the high demand on the cab service, Yellow limits the waiting list at the dispatching office to 16 customers. Once the limit is reached, future customers are advised to seek service elsewhere because of the expected long wait.

The Company manager, Kyle Yellowstone, is afraid that he may be losing too much business and thus would like to consider increasing the size of his fleet. Yellowstone estimates that the average income per ride is about $5. He also estimates that a new cab can be purchased for $18,000. A new cab is kept in service for 5 years and then sold for $3500. The annual cost of maintaining and operating a taxi is $20,000 a year. Can Mr. Yellowstone justify increasing the size of his fleet, and if so, by how many? For the analysis, assume a 10% annual interest rate.

# Chapter 18

# Simulation Modeling

## 18.1 WHAT IS SIMULATION?

Simulation is the next best thing to observing a real system in operation. It allows us to collect pertinent information about the behavior of the system by executing a computerized model. The collected data are then used to design the system. Simulation is not an optimization technique. Rather, it is a technique for estimating the measures of performance of the modeled system.

Simulation has been used in all aspects of science and technology as the following partial list demonstrates:

1. Basic science
   (a) Estimation of the area under a curve or, more generally, evaluation of multiple integrals
   (b) Estimation of the constant $\pi$ ($= 3.14159$)
   (c) Matrix inversion
   (d) Study of particle diffusion
2. Practical situations
   (a) Industrial problems, including the design of queueing systems, communication networks, inventory control, and chemical processes
   (b) Business and economic problems, including consumer behavior, price determination, economic forecasting, and total firm operation
   (c) Behavioral and social problems, including population dynamics, environmental health effects, epidemiological studies, and group behavior
   (d) Biomedical systems, including fluid balance, electrolyte distribution in the human body, blood cell proliferation, and brain activities
   (e) War strategies and tactics

Estimation of simulation output is based on *random sampling,* much the same way we do when observing a real situation. This means that the output of simulation is subject to random variations, and thus, as in any statistical experiment, must be examined using formal statistical inference tests. This important point is stressed throughout the chapter.

## 18.2 MONTE CARLO SIMULATION

Monte Carlo simulation refers to the use of random sampling to estimate the output of an experiment. It is regarded as the forerunner to present-day simulation.

This section uses an example to demonstrate the procedure. The objective of the example is to stress the statistical nature of the simulation experiment.

---

**Example 18.2–1.**

We will use Monte Carlo sampling to estimate the area of a circle whose equation is

$$(x - 1)^2 + (y - 2)^2 = 25$$

The radius of the circle is $r = 5$ cm, and its center is $(x, y) = (1, 2)$.

The procedure for estimating the area requires enclosing the circle "snugly" in a square whose side equals the diameter of the circle as shown in Figure 18–1. The corner points are determined from the geometry of the square.

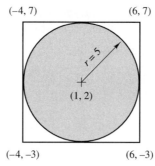

$(-4, 7)$                 $(6, 7)$

$r = 5$

$(1, 2)$

$(-4, -3)$           $(6, -3)$    **Figure 18–1**

The estimation of the area of the circle is based on the assumption that all the points in the square are equally likely to occur. Thus, if out of a random sample of $n$ points in the square, $m$ are found to fall within the circle, then

$$\left(\begin{array}{c}\text{Area of}\\\text{the circle}\end{array}\right) \approx \frac{m}{n}\left(\begin{array}{c}\text{Area of}\\\text{the square}\end{array}\right) = \frac{m}{n}(10 \times 10)$$

The idea is implemented by representing the coordinates $x$ and $y$ of a point in the square by the following uniform distributions:

$$f(x) = \frac{1}{10}, \quad -4 \leq x \leq 6$$

$$f(y) = \frac{1}{10}, \quad -3 \le y \le 7$$

Both functions equal zero outside the indicated ranges.

Let $R_1$ and $R_2$ be two distinct random numbers between 0 and 1. Then an equally likely random point $(x, y)$ in the square is determined as

$$x = -4 + [6 - (-4)]R_1 = -4 + 10\,R_1$$

$$y = -3 + [7 - (-3)]R_2 = -3 + 10\,R_2$$

Table 18–1 gives a small list of $(0, 1)$ random numbers. These numbers are generated by using special arithmetic operations as will be explained in Section 18.5.

**TABLE 18–1**

| | | | | | |
|---|---|---|---|---|---|
| .0589 | .3529 | .5869 | .3455 | .7900 | .6307 |
| .6733 | .3646 | .1281 | .4871 | .7698 | .2346 |
| .4799 | .7676 | .2867 | .8111 | .2871 | .4220 |
| .9486 | .8931 | .8216 | .8912 | .9534 | .6991 |
| .6139 | 3919 | .8261 | .4291 | .1394 | .9745 |
| .5933 | .7876 | .3866 | .2302 | .9025 | .3428 |
| .9341 | .5199 | .7125 | .5954 | .1605 | .6037 |
| .1782 | .6358 | .2108 | .5423 | .3567 | .2569 |
| .3473 | .7472 | .3575 | .4208 | .3070 | .0546 |
| .5644 | .8954 | .2926 | .6975 | .5513 | .0305 |

For each pair of distinct random numbers $(R_1, R_2)$, we can generate a (uniform) random point $(x, y)$ in the square by using the given formulas. A sample point $(x', y')$ falls within the circle if

$$(x' - 1)^2 + (y' - 2)^2 \le 25$$

For example, given $R_1 = .0589$ and $R_2 = .6733$, then

$$x' = -4 + 10R_1 = -4 + 10(.0589) = -3.411$$

$$y' = -3 + 10R_2 = -3 + 10(.6733) = 3.733$$

Because $(-3.411 - 1)^2 + (3.733 - 2)^2 = 22.46$ is less than 25, the point $(x', y')$ falls inside the circle.

We investigate now the effect of random sampling on the accuracy of estimating the area of the circle. Figure 18–2 summarizes the results for various sample sizes ranging from $n = 100$ to $n = 10,000$. The experiment is replicated 10 times for each $n$, with each replication using a different sequence of $(0, 1)$ random numbers. The figure graphs the estimates for replications 1 and 2 only, together with the mean and standard deviation for all 10 replications.

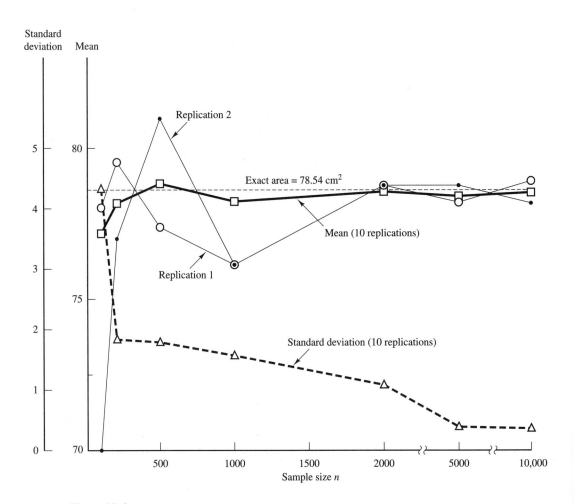

**Figure 18–2**

The following conclusions can be drawn from the results of the experiment:

**1.** The estimate of the area of the circle improves as the sample size increases, as demonstrated in Figure 18–2 by replications 1 and 2.

2. The average of all 10 replications for each sample size $n$ provides a better estimate of the area than any one replication. In Figure 18–2, the mean of the 10 replications approaches the exact area (= 78.54 cm²) more rapidly than the estimates provided by the individual replications.

3. The "accuracy" of the mean value of all 10 replications increases with the sample size, $n$, as evident by the decline in the value of the standard deviation.

Because of the random variation in the output of the experiment, it is essential to express the results as a confidence interval. Letting $\bar{A}$ and $s$ be the mean and variance of $N$ replications, the $100(1 - \alpha)\%$ confidence interval for the true area $A$ is

$$\bar{A} - \frac{s}{\sqrt{N}}\, t_{\alpha/2,\, N-1} \leq A \leq \bar{A} + \frac{s}{\sqrt{N}}\, t_{\alpha/2,\, N-1}$$

where $t_{\alpha/2,\, N-1}$ is the $\frac{100\alpha}{2}$ percentage point of the $t$-distribution with $N - 1$ degrees of freedom (see the $t$-table in Appendix D). (Note that $N$ equals the number of replications, which is distinct from $n$, the sample size.) In terms of the present experiment, we would be interested in establishing the confidence interval based on the largest sample size (i.e., $n = 10{,}000$). Given $N = 10$, $\bar{A} = 78.57$ cm², and $s = .47$ cm², the resulting 95% confidence interval is $78.23 \leq A \leq 78.9$.

The example poses two questions regarding the simulation experiment:

1. How large should the sample size, $n$, be?
2. How many replications, $N$, are needed?

The answers depend on the nature of the simulation experiment. As in any statistical experiment, higher values of $n$ and $N$ provide more reliable simulation results. The drawback is that higher values of $n$ and $N$ imply higher costs for conducting the simulation experiment.

---

### Problem set 18.2a

1. In Example 18.2–1, do the following:
   **(a)** Estimate the area of the circle using the first two columns of the $(0, 1)$ random numbers in Table 18–1. (For convenience, go down each column, selecting $R_1$ first and then $R_2$.)
   **(b)** Suppose that the equation of the circle is

   $$(x - 3)^2 + (y + 2)^2 = 16$$

   Define the corresponding distributions $f(x)$ and $f(y)$, and then show how a sample point $(x, y)$ can be determined using the $(0, 1)$ random pair $(R_1, R_2)$.

2. Use Monte Carlo sampling to estimate the area of the lake shown in Figure 18–3. Base the estimate on the first two columns of $(0, 1)$ random numbers in Table 18–1.

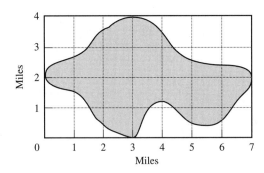

**Figure 18–3**

3. Consider the game in which two players, Jan and Jim, take turns in tossing a fair coin. If the outcome is heads, Jan gets $10 from Jim. Otherwise, Jim gets $10 from Jan.
   (a) How is the game simulated as a Monte Carlo experiment?
   (b) Run the experiment for 5 replications of 10 tosses each. Use the first five columns of the $(0, 1)$ random numbers in Table 18–1, with each column corresponding to one replication.
   (c) Establish a 95% confidence interval on Jan's winnings.
   (d) Compare the confidence interval in (c) with Jan's expected theoretical winnings.

4. Consider the following definite integral:

$$\int_0^1 x^2 dx$$

   (a) Develop the Monte Carlo experiment to estimate the integral.
   (b) Use the first four columns in Table 18–1 to evaluate the integral based on 4 replications of size 10 each. Compute a 95% confidence interval, and compare it with the exact value of the integral.

5. Simulate five wins or losses of the following game of craps: The player rolls two fair dice. If the outcome sum is 7 or 11, the player wins $10. Otherwise, the player records the resulting sum (called *point*) and keeps on rolling the dice until the outcome sum matches the recorded *point*, in which case the player wins $10. If a 7 is obtained, the player loses $10.

6. The lead time for receiving an order can be 1 or 2 days, with equal probabilities. The demand *per day* assumes the values 0, 1, and 2 with the respective probabilities of .2, .5, and .3. Use the random numbers in Table 18–1 (starting with column 1) to estimate the joint distribution of the demand and lead time. From the joint distribution, estimate the pdf of demand during lead time. (*Hint:* The demand during lead time assumes discrete values from 0 to 4.)

7. Consider the Buffon needle experiment. A horizontal plane is ruled with parallel lines spaced $D$ cm apart. A needle of length $d$ cm $(d < D)$ is

dropped randomly on the plane. The objective of the experiment is to determine the probability that either end of the needle touches or crosses one of the lines. Define

> $h$ = Perpendicular distance from the needle center to a (parallel) line
> $\theta$ = Inclination angle of the needle with a line

**(a)** Show that the needle will touch or cross a line only if

$$h \le \frac{d}{2}\sin\theta, \quad 0 \le h \le \frac{D}{2}, \ 0 \le \theta \le \pi$$

**(b)** Design the Monte Carlo experiment, and provide an estimate of the desired probability.

**(c)** Use the first four columns of Table 18–1 to obtain 4 replications of size 10 each of the desired probability. Determine a 95% confidence interval for the estimate.

**(d)** Prove that the theoretical probability is given by the formula

$$p = \frac{2d}{\pi D}$$

Use the result in (c) together with this formula to estimate $\pi$.

## 18.3 TYPES OF SIMULATION

The execution of present-day simulation is based generally on the sampling idea of the Monte Carlo method. It differs in that it is concerned with the study of the behavior of real systems as a function of time. Two distinct types of simulation models exist.

**1. Continuous models** deal with systems whose behavior changes *continuously* with time. A typical example of a continuous simulation is the study of world population dynamics. Continuous simulation models usually are represented in terms of difference-differential equations that describe the interactions among the different elements of the system.

**2. Discrete models** deal with systems whose behavior changes only at given instants. A typical example occurs in waiting lines where we are interested in estimating such measures as the average waiting time or the length of the waiting line. Such measures change only when a customer enters or leaves the system. At all other instants, nothing from the standpoint of collecting statistics occurs in the system.

The instants at which changes in the system occur identify the model's **events** (e.g., arrival and departure of customers). The fact that these events occur at discrete points gives rise to the name **discrete event simulation**.

Although both continuous and discrete simulations are important tools in practice, the discrete type is the one that is usually presented in conjunction with operations research topics. The reason is that discrete simulation is more closely allied with queueing models (see Chapter 17). Indeed, it is fair to state that practically all discrete simulation situations can be described in some form or another as queueing models.

This chapter concentrates on discussing the basics of discrete event simulation. We start with a description of events and how they can be generated in a simulation model. Next, we present the procedures for collecting simulation statistics and discuss the statistical aspect of the simulation experiment. The chapter also emphasizes the role of the computer and simulation languages in the execution of simulation models.

**Problem set 18.3a**

1. Categorize the following situations as either discrete or continuous (or a combination of both). In each case, specify the objective of developing the simulation model.

   **(a)** Orders for an item arrive randomly at a warehouse. An order that cannot be filled immediately from available stock must await the arrival of new shipments.

   **(b)** World population is affected by the availability of natural resources, food production, environmental conditions, educational level, health care, and capital investments.

   **(c)** Goods arrive on pallets at a receiving bay of an automated warehouse. The pallets are loaded on a lower conveyor belt and lifted through an up-elevator to an upper conveyor that moves the pallets to corridors. The corridors are served by cranes that pick up the pallets from the conveyor and place them in storage bins.

2. Explain why you would agree or disagree with the following statement: "Most discrete event simulation models can be viewed in some form or another as queueing systems consisting of *sources* from which customers are generated, *queues* where customers may wait, and *facilities* where customers are served."

## 18.4 ELEMENTS OF DISCRETE EVENT SIMULATION

This section shows how the concept of events is implemented and how the statistics of the simulated system are collected.

### 18.4.1 Generic Definition of Events

All discrete-event simulations describe, directly or indirectly, queueing (or waiting line) situations in which customers arrive, wait in a queue if necessary, and then receive service before they depart the system. In general, any discrete-event model is composed of a network of interrelated queues.

Given that a discrete-event model is in reality a composite of queues, we notice that for the purpose of collecting statistics (measures of performance) changes in the system (e.g., queue length and status of the service facility) can only occur when a customer arrives at the queue and when a customer leaves the facility after being served. This means that the two principal events in any discrete simulation model are an arrival and a departure. These are the only two instants at which we need to examine the system. At all other times, no changes affecting the statistics of the system occur.

---

**Example 18.4–1.**

Metalco Jobshop receives two types of jobs: regular and rush. All jobs are processed on two consecutive machines with ample buffer areas. Rush jobs always assume nonpreemptive priority over regular jobs. Identify the events of the situation.

This situation consists of two tandem queues corresponding to the two machines, respectively. At first thought, one may be inclined to identify the events of the situation as follows:

A11: A regular job arrives at machine 1.
A21: A rush job arrives at machine 1.
D11: A regular job departs machine 1.
D21: A rush job departs machine 1.
A12: A regular job arrives at machine 2.
A22: A rush job arrives at machine 2.
D12: A regular job departs machine 2.
D22: A rush job departs machine 2.

In reality, we only have exactly two events: an arrival of a (new) job at the shop and a departure of a (completed) job from a machine. First notice that events D11 and A12 coincide exactly and hence are not distinguishable. The same observation applies to D21 and A22. Next, in discrete simulation we can use one (arrival or departure) event for both types of jobs and simply "tag" the event with an **attribute** that identifies the job type as either regular or rush. (We can think of the attribute in this case as a *personal identification number,* and, indeed, it is.) Given this reasoning, the events of the model reduce to (1) an arrival A (at the shop) and (2) a departure D (from each machine). The actions associated with the departure event will depend on the machine at which they occur.

Having defined the basic events of a simulation model, we now show how the model is executed. Figure 18–4 gives a schematic representation of typical occurrences

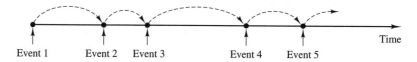

**Figure 18–4**

of events on the simulation time scale. After all the actions associated with a current event have been performed, the simulation advances by "jumping" to the next chronological event. In essence, the execution of the simulation occurs at the instants at which the events occur.

How does the simulation determine the occurrence time of the events? The arrival events are separated by the interarrival time (the interval between successive arrivals), and the departure events are specified by the service time in the facility. These times may be deterministic (e.g., a train arriving at a station every 5 minutes) or probabilistic (e.g., the random arrival of customers at a bank). If the time between events is deterministic, the determination of their occurrence times is straightforward. If it is probabilistic, we use a special procedure to sample the interevent time from the corresponding probability distribution. This point is discussed in the next section.

---

### Problem set 18.4a

1. Identify the discrete events needed to simulate the following situation: Two types of jobs arrive from two different sources. Both types are processed on a single machine, with priority given to the jobs arriving from the first source.

2. Jobs arrive at a constant rate at a carousel conveyor system. Three service stations are spaced equally around the carousel. If the server is idle when a job arrives at the station, the job is removed from the conveyor for processing. Otherwise, the job continues to rotate about the carousel until a server becomes available. A processed job is stored in an adjacent shipping area. Identify the discrete events needed to simulate this situation.

3. Cars arrive at a two-lane, drive-in bank, where each lane can house a maximum of four cars. If the two lanes are full, arriving cars seek service elsewhere. If at any time one lane is at least two cars longer than the other, the last car in the longer lane will jockey to the last position in the shorter lane. The bank operates the drive-in facility from 8:00 A.M. to 3:00 P.M. each work day. Define the discrete events for the situation.

4. The cafeteria at Elmdale Elementary provides a single-tray, fixed-menu lunch to all its pupils. Kids arrive at the dispensing window every 30 seconds. It takes 18 seconds to receive the lunch tray. Map the arrival-departure events on the time scale for the first five pupils.

### 18.4.2 Sampling from Probability Distributions

Randomness in simulation arises when the interval, $t$, between successive events is probabilistic. This section presents methods for generating successive random samples ($t = t_1, t_2, \ldots$) from a probability distribution $f(t)$. All the methods are rooted in the use of independent and identically distributed uniform $(0, 1)$ random numbers.

***Inverse Method.***    Suppose that it is desired to obtain a random sample $x$ from the (continuous or discrete) probability density function $f(x)$. The inverse method first determines a closed form expression of the cumulative density function $F(x) = P\{y \leq x\}$, where $0 \leq F(x) \leq 1$, for all defined values of $y$. Given $R$ is a random value obtained from a uniform $(0, 1)$ distribution, and assuming that $F^{-1}$ is the inverse of $F$, the steps of the method are as follows:

**Step 1.** Generate the $(0, 1)$ random number $R$.
**Step 2.** Compute the desired sample $x = F^{-1}(R)$.

Figure 18–5 illustrates the procedure for both a continuous and a discrete random distribution. The uniform $(0, 1)$ random value $R_1$ is projected from the vertical $F(x)$-scale to yield the desired sample value $x_1$ on the horizonal scale.

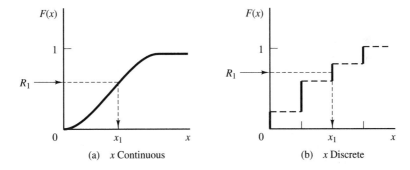

(a)   $x$ Continuous                                      (b)   $x$ Discrete

**Figure 18–5**

The validity of the proposed procedure rests on showing that the random variable $z = F(x)$ is uniformly distributed in the interval $0 \leq z \leq 1$, as the following theorem proves.

**Theorem 18.4–1.**    *Given the cumulative density function $F(x)$ of the random variable $x$, $-\infty \leq x \leq \infty$, the random variable $z = F(x)$, $0 \leq z \leq 1$, has the following probability density function:*

$$f(z) = 1, \quad 0 \leq z \leq 1$$

*which is a uniform $(0, 1)$ distribution.*

*Proof.*    The random variable is uniformly distributed if, and only if,

$$P\{z \leq Z\} = Z, \quad 0 \leq Z \leq 1$$

This result follows directly from the following equalities:

$$P\{z \leq Z\} = P\{F(x) \leq Z\} = P\{x \leq F^{-1}(Z)\} = F[F^{-1}(Z)] = Z$$

Additionally, $0 \leq Z \leq 1$ because $0 \leq P\{z \leq Z\} \leq 1$.

**Example 18.4–2 (EXPONENTIAL DISTRIBUTION).**

The time, $t$, between customers arrivals at a barbershop is represented by an exponential distribution with mean $E\{t\} = \frac{1}{\lambda}$ time units; that is,

$$f(t) = \lambda e^{-\lambda t}, \quad t > 0$$

Determine a random sample $t$ from $f(t)$.

The cumulative density function is determined as

$$F(t) = \int_0^t \lambda e^{-\lambda x} dx = 1 - e^{-\lambda t}, \, t > 0$$

Setting $R = F(t)$, we can solve for $t$, which yields

$$t = -\left(\frac{1}{\lambda}\right) \ln (1 - R)$$

Because $1 - R$ is the complement of $R$, we may replace $1 - R$ with $R$.

In terms of simulation, the result means that the occurrences of the events are spaced $t$ time units apart. For example, given $\lambda = 4$ customers per hour and $R = .9$, a sample of the period until the arrival of the next customer is computed as

$$t_1 = -\left(\frac{1}{4}\right) \ln (1 - .9) = .577 \text{ hour} = 34.5 \text{ minutes}$$

The values of $R$ used to obtain successive samples must be selected *randomly* from a uniform $(0, 1)$ distribution. We will show later in Section 18.5 how these $(0, 1)$ random values are generated during the execution of the simulation.

## Problem set 18.4b

1. In Example 18.4–2, suppose that the first customer arrives at time 0. Use the first three random numbers in column 1 of Table 18–1 to generate the arrival times of the next three customers and plot the resulting events on the time scale.

2. *Uniform distribution.* Suppose that the time needed to manufacture a part on a machine is uniformly distributed in the interval $[a, b]$, $a < b$—that is,

$$f(t) = \frac{1}{b - a}, \quad a \leq t \leq b$$

Determine an expression for the sample $t$ given the random number $R$.

3. Jobs are received randomly at a one-machine shop. The time between arrivals is exponential with mean 2 hours. The time needed to manufacture a job is uniform between 1.1 and 2 hours. Assume that the first job arrives at time 0. Determine the arrival and departure time for the first five jobs using the $(0, 1)$ random numbers in column 1 of Table 18–1.

4. The demand for an expensive spare part of a passenger jet is 0, 1, 2, or 3 units per day with probabilities .2, .3, .4, and .1, respectively. The airline

maintenance shop starts operation with a stock of 5 units, and will bring the stock level back to 5 units immediately after it drops below 2 units.

(a) Devise the procedure for determining demand samples.

(b) How many days will elapse until the first replenishment occurs? Use successive values of $R$ from the first column in Table 18–1.

5. In a simulation situation, TV units are inspected for possible defects. There is an 80% chance that a unit will pass inspection, in which it is sent to packaging. Otherwise, the unit is repaired. We can represent the situation symbolically in one of two ways.

> goto REPAIR/.2, PACKAGE/.8
> goto PACKAGE/.8, REPAIR/.2

These two representations appear equivalent. Yet, when a given sequence of $(0, 1)$ random numbers is applied to the two representations, different decisions (REPAIR or PACKAGE) may result. Explain why.

6. A player tosses a fair coin repeatedly until a head occurs. The associated payoff is $2^n$, where $n$ is the number of tosses until a head is realized.

(a) Devise the sampling procedure of the game.

(b) Use the random numbers in column 1 of Table 18–1 to determine the cumulative payoff after two heads are realized.

7. *Triangular distribution.* In simulation, the lack of data may make it impossible to determine the probability distribution associated with a simulation activity. In most of these situations, it may be easy to describe the desired variable by estimating its smallest, most likely, and largest values. These three values are sufficient to define a triangular distribution, which can then be used as "rough cut" estimation of the "true" distribution.

(a) Develop the formula for sampling from the following triangular distribution whose parameters are $a$, $b$, and $c$, where $a < b < c$:

$$f(x) = \begin{cases} \dfrac{2(x - a)}{(b - a)(c - a)}, & a \le x \le b \\[2ex] \dfrac{2(c - x)}{(c - b)(c - a)}, & b \le x \le c \end{cases}$$

(b) Generate three samples from a triangular distribution with parameters $(1, 3, 7)$ using the first three random numbers in column 1 of Table 18–1.

8. (a) Develop the sampling procedure for a probability distribution that consists of a rectangle flanked on the left and right sides by two symmetrical right triangles. The respective ranges for the triangle on left, the rectangle, and the triangle on right are $[a, b]$, $[b, c]$, and $[c, d]$, $a < b < c < d$. Each triangle has the same height as the rectangle.

(b) Determine five samples with $(a, b, c, d) = (1, 2, 4, 6)$ using the first five random numbers in column 1 of Table 18–1.

9. *Geometric distribution.* Show how a random sample can be obtained from the following geometric distribution:

$$f(x) = p(1 - p)^x, \quad x = 0, 1, 2, \ldots$$

where $x$ is the number of (Bernoulli) failures until a success occurs, and $p$ is the probability of a success, $0 < p < 1$. Generate five samples for $p = .6$.

10. *Weibull distribution.* Show how a random sample can be obtained from the Weibull distribution whose pdf is defined as

$$f(x) = \alpha \beta^{-\alpha} x^{\alpha-1} e^{-(\frac{x}{\beta})^\alpha}, \quad x > 0$$

where $\alpha > 0$ is the shape parameter, and $\beta > 0$ is the scale parameter.

The inverse method works well when the cumulative density function $F(x)$ is analytically tractable. Distributions, such as the gamma, normal, and Poisson, do not fall in this category. The methods listed in the remainder of this section show how these distributions are sampled.

***Convolution Method.*** The basic idea of the convolution method is to express the desired sample as the statistical sum of other easy-to-sample random variables. Typical among these distributions are the Erlang and the Poisson whose sample can be obtained from the exponential distribution samples.

---

**Example 18.4–3 (ERLANG DISTRIBUTION).**

The $m$-Erlang random variable is defined as the statistical sum (convolutions) of $m$ independent and identically distributed exponential random variables. Let $y$ represent the $m$-Erlang random variable, then

$$y = y_1 + y_2 + \ldots + y_m$$

where $y_i, i = 1, 2, \ldots, m,$ are independent and identically distributed exponential random variables whose probability density function is defined as

$$f(y_i) = \lambda e^{-\lambda y_i}, \ y_i > 0, \quad i = 1, 2, \ldots, m$$

From Example 18.4–2, the $i$th exponential distribution can be sampled as

$$y_i = -\left(\frac{1}{\lambda}\right) \ln (R_i), \quad i = 1, 2, \ldots, m$$

Thus, the $m$-Erlang sample is computed as

$$y = -\left(\frac{1}{\lambda}\right) \{\ln (R_1) + \ln(R_2) + \cdots + \ln(R_m)\}$$

$$= -\left(\frac{1}{\lambda}\right) \ln (R_1 R_2 \ldots R_m)$$

To illustrate the use of the formula, suppose that $m = 3$, and $\lambda = 4$ events per hour. The first 3 random numbers in column 1 of Table 18–1 yield $R_1 R_2 R_3 = (.0589)(.6733)(.4799) = .0190$, which yields $y = -(\frac{1}{4})\ln(.019) = .991$ hour.

---

### Example 18.4–4 (POISSON DISTRIBUTIONS).

If the distribution between the occurrence of successive events is exponential, then the distribution of the number of events per unit time must be Poisson and vice versa. We use this relationship to sample the Poisson distribution.

Assume that the Poisson distribution has a mean value of $\lambda$ events per unit time. Then the time between events is exponential with mean $\frac{1}{\lambda}$ time units. This means that a Poisson sample, $n$, will occur during $t$ time units if, and only if,

$$\text{Period till event } n \text{ occurs} \leq t \leq \text{ Period till event } n + 1 \text{ occurs}$$

This condition translates to

$$t_1 + t_2 + \ldots t_n \leq t \leq t_1 + t_2 + \ldots t_{n+1}, \quad n > 0$$

$$0 \leq t \leq t_1, \quad n = 0$$

where $t_i$ is a sample from the exponential distribution with mean $\frac{1}{\lambda}$. From the result in Example 18.4–3, we have

$$-\left(\frac{1}{\lambda}\right) \ln (R_1 R_2 \ldots R_n) \leq t < -\left(\frac{1}{\lambda}\right) \ln (R_1 R_2 \ldots R_{n+1}), \quad n > 0$$

$$0 \leq t < -\left(\frac{1}{\lambda}\right) \ln (R_1), \quad n = 0$$

which reduces to

$$R_1 R_2 \ldots R_n \geq e^{-\lambda t} > R_1 R_2 \ldots R_{n+1}, \quad n > 0$$

$$1 \geq e^{-\lambda t} > R_1, \quad n = 0$$

To illustrate the implementation of the sampling process, suppose that $\lambda = 4$ events per hour and that we wish to obtain a sample for a period $t = .5$ hour. This gives $e^{-\lambda t} = .1353$. Using the random numbers in column 1 of Table 18–1, we note that $R_1 = .0589$ is less than $e^{-\lambda t} = .1353$. Hence, the corresponding sample is $n = 0$.

---

### Example 18.4–5 (NORMAL DISTRIBUTION).

The Central Limit Theorem states that the sum (convolution) of $n$ independent and identically distributed random variables tends to be normally distributed as $n$ becomes sufficiently large. We use this result to generate sample from normal distribution with mean $\mu$ and standard deviation $\sigma$.

Define

$$x = R_1 + R_2 + \ldots + R_n$$

The random variable is asymptotically normal by the Central Limit Theorem. Given that the uniform $(0, 1)$ random number $R$ has a mean of $\frac{1}{2}$ and a variance of $\frac{1}{12}$, it follows that $x$ has a mean of $\frac{n}{2}$ and a variance of $\frac{n}{12}$. Thus, a random sample, $y$, from a normal distribution with mean $\mu$ and standard deviation $\sigma$, $N(\mu, \sigma)$, can be computed from $x$ as

$$y = \mu + \sigma \left( \frac{x - \dfrac{n}{2}}{\sqrt{\dfrac{n}{12}}} \right)$$

In practice, we take $n = 12$ for convenience, which reduces the formula to

$$y = \mu + \sigma (x - 6)$$

To illustrate the use of this method, suppose that we wish to generate a sample from a $N(10, 2)$ (mean $\mu = 10$ and standard deviation $\sigma = 2$). Taking the sum of the first 12 random numbers in columns 1 and 2 of Table 18–1, we get $x = 6.1094$. Thus, $y = 10 + 2(6.1094 - 6) = 10.2188$.

The disadvantage of this procedure is that it requires generating 12 $(0, 1)$-random numbers for each normal sample, which is computationally inefficient. A more efficient procedure calls for using the transformation

$$x = \sqrt{-2 \ln (R_1)} \, \cos (2\pi R_2)$$

Box and Muller (1958) prove that $x$ is a standard $N(0, 1)$. Thus, $y = \mu + \sigma x$ will produce a sample from $N(\mu, \sigma)$. The new procedure is more efficient because it requires two $(0, 1)$ random numbers only.

Actually, the Box-Muller method is even more efficient than stated because they prove that the preceding formula will produce another $N(0, 1)$ sample simply by replacing $\cos(2\pi R_2)$ with $\sin(2\pi R_2)$. This means that the two random numbers $R_1$ and $R_2$ may be used to generate *two* simultaneous $N(0, 1)$ samples.

To illustrate the implementation of the Box-Muller procedure to the normal distribution $N(10, 2)$, the first two random numbers in column 1 of Table 18–1 yield the following $N(0, 1)$ samples:

$$x_1 = \sqrt{-2 \ln (.0589)} \, \cos(2\pi \times .6733) \approx -1.103$$

$$x_2 = \sqrt{-2 \ln (.0589)} \, \sin(2\pi \times .6733) \approx -2.108$$

Thus, the corresponding $N(10, 2)$ samples are

$$y_1 = 10 + 2(-1.103) = 7.794$$

$$y_2 = 10 + 2(-2.108) = 5.7823$$

---

### Problem set 18.4c[1]

**1.** In Example 18.4–3, compute an Erlang sample, given $m = 4$ and $\lambda = 5$ events per hour.

[1]For all the problems of this set, use the random numbers in Table 18–1 starting with those of column 1.

2. In Example 18.4–4, generate three Poisson samples during a 2-hour period given that the mean of the Poisson is 5 events per hour.

3. In Example 18.5–5, generate two samples from $N(8, 1)$ by using both the convolution method and the Box-Muller method.

4. Jobs arrive at Metalco jobshop according to a Poisson distribution, with a mean of six jobs per day. The shop includes five machining centers to which the supervisor assigns received jobs on a strict rotational basis. Determine one sample of the interval between the arrival of jobs at the first machine center.

5. The ACT scores for the 1994 senior class at Springdale High is normal, with a mean of 27 points and a standard deviation of 3 points. Suppose that we draw a random sample of six seniors from that class. Use the Box-Muller method to determine the mean and standard deviation of the sample.

6. Psychology professor Yataha is conducting a learning experiment in which mice are trained to find their way around a restricted maze. The base of the maze is square. The mouse enters the maze at one of the four corners and must find its way through the maze to exit at the same point where it entered. The design of the maze is such that the mouse must pass by each of the remaining three corner points exactly once before it exits. The multipaths of the maze connect the four corners in a strict clockwise order. Professor Yataha estimates that the time the mouse takes to reach one corner point from another is uniformly distributed between 10 and 20 seconds, depending on the path it takes. Develop a sampling procedure for the time a mouse spends in the maze.

7. In Problem 6, suppose that once a mouse makes an exit from the maze, another mouse instantly enters. Develop a sampling procedure for the number of mice that exit the maze in 5 minutes.

8. *Negative Binomial.* Show how a random sample can be determined from the negative binomial whose distribution is given as

$$f(x) = \binom{y+x-1}{x} p^y (1 - p)^x, \quad x = 0, 1, 2, \ldots$$

where $x$ is the number of failures until the $y$th success occurs in a sequence of $n$ independent Bernoulli trials and $p$ is the probability of success, $0 < p < 1$. (*Hint:* The negative binomial is the convolution of independent geometric samples. See Problem 18.4b–9.)

*Acceptance-Rejection Method.*    The acceptance-rejection method is designed to handle complex pdfs for which the preceding methods cannot be applied. The general idea of the method is to replace the complex pdf $f(x)$ with a more analytically manageable "proxy" pdf $h(x)$. Samples from $h(x)$ can then be used to determine samples from the original pdf $f(x)$.

Define the **majorizing function** $g(x)$ such that it dominates $f(x)$ in its entire range—that is,

$$g(x) \geq f(x), \quad -\infty < x < \infty$$

Next, define the proxy pdf, $h(x)$, by normalizing $g(x)$ as

$$h(x) = \frac{g(x)}{\int_{-\infty}^{\infty} g(y)d(y)}, \quad -\infty < x < \infty$$

The steps of the acceptance-rejection method are thus given as

**Step 1.** Obtain a sample $x = x_1$ from $h(x)$ using the inverse or the convolution method.

**Step 2.** Obtain a $(0, 1)$ random number $R$.

**Step 3.** If $R \leq \frac{f(x_1)}{g(x_1)}$, accept $x_1$ as a proper sample of $f(x)$. Otherwise, discard $x_1$ and return to step 1.

The validity of the method is based on the following equality:

$$P\{x \leq a \,|\, x = x_1 \text{ is accepted, } -\infty < x_1 < \infty\} = \int_{-\infty}^{a} f(y)dy, \quad -\infty < a < \infty$$

This probability statement states that the sample $x = x_1$ that satisfies the condition of step 3 in reality is a sample from the original pdf $f(x)$, as desired.

The efficiency of the proposed method is enhanced by the decrease in the rejection probability of step 3. This probability depends on the specific choice of the majorizing function $g(x)$ and should decrease with the selection of a $g(x)$ that "majorizes" $f(x)$ more "snugly."

---

**Example 18.4–5 (BETA DISTRIBUTION).**

Apply the acceptance-rejection to the following beta distribution:

$$f(x) = 6x\,(1 - x), \quad 0 \leq x \leq 1$$

Figure 18–6 depicts $f(x)$ and a majorizing function $g(x)$.

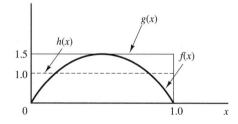

**Figure 18–6**

The height of the majorizing function $g(x)$ equals the maximum of $f(x)$, which occurs at $x = .5$. Thus, the height of the rectangle is $f(.5) = 1.5$. This means that

$$g(x) = 1.5, \quad 0 < x < 1$$

The proxy pdf $h(x)$, also shown in Figure 18–6, is computed as

$$h(x) = \frac{g(x)}{\text{Area under } g(x)} = \frac{1.5}{1 \times 1.5} = 1, \quad 0 < x < 1$$

The following steps demonstrate the procedure using the $(0, 1)$ random sequence in Table 18–1.

**Step 1.** Using $R = .0589$ gives the sample $x = .0589$ from $h(x)$.

**Step 2.** $R = .6733$.

**Step 3.** Because $\frac{f(.0589)}{g(.0589)} = \frac{.3326}{1.5} = .2217$ is less than $R = .6733$, we accept the sample $x_1 = .0589$.

To obtain a second sample, we continue as follows:

**Step 1.** Using $R = .4799$ (from column 1 of Table 18–1), we get $x = .4799$ from $h(x)$.

**Step 2.** $R = .9486$.

**Step 3.** Because $\frac{f(.4799)}{g(.4799)} = .9984$ is larger than $R = .9486$, we reject $x = .4799$ as a valid beta sample.

This means that the steps must be repeated again with "fresh" random numbers until the condition of step 3 is satisfied.

---

The efficiency of the acceptance-rejection method is enhanced by selecting a majorizing function $g(x)$ that "jackets" $f(x)$ as tightly as possible while yielding an analytically tractable proxy $h(x)$. For example, the method will be more efficient if the rectangular majorizing function $g(x)$ in Figure 18–5 is replaced with a step-pyramid function (see Problem 18.4d-2 for an illustration). The larger the number of steps, the more tightly will $g(x)$ majorize $f(x)$, and hence the higher is the probability of accepting a sample. However, a "tight" majorizing function generally entails additional computations which, if excessive, may offset the savings resulting from increasing the probability of acceptance.

### Problem set 18.4d

1. In Example 18.4–5, continue the steps of the procedure until a valid sample is obtained. Use the $(0, 1)$ random numbers in Table 18–1 in the same order in which they are used in the example.

2. Consider the beta pdf of example 18.4–5. Determine a two-step pyramid majorizing function $g(x)$ with two equal jumps each of height $\frac{1.5}{2} = .75$. Obtain one beta sample based on the new majorizing function using the same $(0, 1)$ random sequence in Table 18–1 that was employed in Example 18.4–5. The conclusion, in general, is that a tighter majorizing function will increase the probability of acceptance. Observe, however, that the magnitude of the computations associated with the new function is larger.

3. Determine the functions $g(x)$ and $h(x)$ for applying the acceptance-rejection method to the following function:

$$f(x) = \frac{\sin(x) + \cos(x)}{2}, \qquad 0 \le x \le \frac{\pi}{2}$$

Use the $(0, 1)$ random numbers from column 1 in Table 18–1 to generate two samples from $f(x)$. (*Hint:* For convenience, use a rectangular $g(x)$ over the defined range of $f(x)$.)

**4.** The interarrival time of customers at HairKare is described by the following distribution:

$$f_1(t) = \frac{k_1}{t}, \qquad 12 \le t \le 20$$

The time to receive a hair cut is represented by the following distribution:

$$f_2(t) = \frac{k_2}{t^2}, \qquad 18 \le t \le 22$$

The constant $k_1$ and $k_2$ are determined such that $f_1(t)$ and $f_2(t)$ are probability density functions. Use the acceptance-rejection method (and the random numbers in Table 18–1) to determine when the first customer will leave HairKare and when the next customer will arrive. Assume that the first customer arrives at $T = 0$.

## 18.5 GENERATION OF RANDOM NUMBERS

Uniform $(0, 1)$ random numbers play a key role in sampling from distributions. True $(0, 1)$ random numbers can only be generated by electronic devices. Because simulation models are executed on the computer, the use of electronic devices to generate random numbers is much too slow for that purpose. Additionally, electronic devices are activated by laws of chance, and hence it will be impossible to duplicate the same sequence of random numbers at will. This point is important because the debugging, verification, and validation of the simulation model often require duplicating the same sequence of random numbers.

The only plausible method for generating $(0, 1)$ random numbers for use in simulation is based on arithmetic operations. Such numbers are not truly random because they can be generated in advance. It is thus more appropriate to refer to them as **pseudorandom numbers**.

The most common arithmetic operation for generating $(0, 1)$ random numbers is the **multiplicative congruential method**. Given the parameters $u_0$, $b$, $c$, and $m$, a pseudorandom number $R_n$ can be generated from the formula:

$$u_n = (bu_{n-1} + c) \bmod (m), \qquad n = 1, 2, \ldots$$

$$R_n = \frac{u_n}{m}, \qquad n = 1, 2, \ldots$$

The initial value $u_0$ is usually referred to as the **seed** of the generator.

**Example 18.5–1.**

Generate three random numbers based on the multiplicative congruential method using the following initial values: $b = 9, c = 5, u_0 = 11$, and $m = 12$.

$$u_1 = (9 \times 11 + 5) \bmod 12 = 8, \ R_1 = \frac{8}{12} = .6667$$

$$u_2 = (9 \times 8 + 5) \bmod 12 = 5, \ R_2 = \frac{5}{12} = .4167$$

$$u_3 = (9 \times 5 + 5) \bmod 12 = 4, R_3 = \frac{4}{12} = .3333$$

The specific choices of $u_0, b, c$, and $m$ are crucial in determining the (statistical) quality of the generator as well as its cycle length (before the generated sequence repeats itself). "Casual" implementations of the congruential formula will not produce a good random number generator. Reliable generators, in addition to producing a sufficiently long cycle length, must also be tested statistically to ensure that the obtained sequence is generated from independent and identically distributed uniform $(0, 1)$ distributions. This point must be heeded when using "canned" software for random number generators.

Variations of the multiplicative congruential method that improve the quality of the generator are also available. A good discussion on the subject is available in Law and Kelton (1991).

### Problem set 18.5a

1. Show that the selection of $b, c, u_0$, and $m$ in Example 18.5–1 produces repetitive numbers quickly.

2. Find a random number generator for your computer, and use to generate 500 $(0, 1)$-random numbers. Histogram the resulting values and visually convince yourself that the obtained numbers reasonably follow the $(0, 1)$ uniform distribution. Actually, to test the sequence properly, you would need to apply the following tests: chi-square goodness of fit (see Section 12.6), runs test for independence, and correlation test (see Law and Kelton [1991] for details).

## 18.6 MECHANICS OF DISCRETE SIMULATION

As stated earlier, all discrete simulation models represent, in some form or another, queueing situations with two basic events: arrivals and departures. These events define the instants at which changes in the system's statistics can occur.

This section details how typical statistics are collected in a simulation model. The vehicle of explanation is a single queue model.

**Example 18.6–1.**

The interarrival time of customers at HairKare Barbershop is exponential with mean 12 minutes. The shop is operated by only one barber who gives two types of haircut: a crew cut that takes about 10 minutes and a regular cut that takes about 15 minutes. One out of every four customers, on the average, requires a crew cut, but the process is random. It is desired to compute the following:

1. The average utilization of the barber
2. The average number of waiting customers
3. The average time a customer waits in queue

The logic of the simulation model can be described in terms of its arrival and departure events as follows:

**ARRIVAL EVENT**

1. Generate and store chronologically the occurrence time of the next arrival event (= current simulation time + interarrival time).
2. If the *facility* (barber) is idle
    (a) Start service and declare the facility busy. Update the facility utilization statistics.
    (b) Generate and store chronologically the time of the departure event for the customer (= current simulation time + service time).
3. If the facility is busy, place the customer in the queue and update the queue statistics.

**DEPARTURE EVENT**

1. If the queue is empty, declare the facility idle. Update the facility utilization statistics.
2. If the queue is not empty
    (a) Select a customer (FCFS) from the queue, and place it in the facility. Update the queue and facility utilization statistics.
    (b) Generate and store chronologically the occurrence time of the departure event for the customer (= current simulation time + service time).

From the data of the problem, the interarrival time is exponential with mean 12 minutes, and the service time is discrete (10 minutes with probability .25 or 15 minutes with probability .75). Letting $p$ and $q$ represent random samples of interarrival and service times, then, as explained in Section 18.4.2, we get

$$p = -10 \ln (R) \text{ minutes}, \quad 0 \le R \le 1$$

$$q = \begin{cases} 10 \text{ minutes}, & 0 \le R \le .25 \\ 15 \text{ minutes}, & .25 < R \le 1 \end{cases}$$

For the purpose of this example, we use $R$ from Table 18–1, starting with column 1. We also use the symbol $T$ to represent the simulation clock time. We further assume that the first customer arrives at $T = 0$ and that the facility starts empty.

***Arrival Event at* T = 0 *(Customer 1).***    Customer 2 will arrive at $T = 0 + p_1$, where

$$p_1 = -10 \ln(.0589) = 28.3 \text{ minutes}$$

Because the facility is idle at $T = 0$, customer 1 starts service immediately. The corresponding service time is then computed by using $R = .6733$, which yields $q_1 = 15$ minutes. This means that customer 1 will leave the shop at $T = 0 + 15 = 15$. The occurrence times of the arrival event for customer 2, and the departure event for customer 1 ($T = 28.3$ and $T = 15$) produce the following *chronological* list of future events:

1. Departure at $T = 15$
2. Arrival at $T = 28.3$

Thus, the next most imminent event is a departure at $T = 15$.

***Departure Event at* T $= 15$ *(Customer 1).***    Because the queue is empty, the facility is declared idle. At the same time, we record that the facility has been busy between $T = 0$ and $T = 15$. The updated list of future events is

1. Arrival at $T = 28.3$

The next chronological event is an arrival occurring at $T = 28.3$.

***Arrival Event at* T $= 28.3$ *(Customer 2).***    Customer 3 will arrive after $p_2 = -10$ $\ln(.4799) = 7.34$ minutes—that is, at $T = 28.3 + 7.34 = 35.64$. Because the facility is idle, customer 2 starts service and the facility is declared busy. Given $R = .9486$, the corresponding service time is $q_2 = 15$ minutes. Thus, the departure event for customer 2 occurs at $T = 28.3 + 15 = 43.3$. The list of future events is updated as

1. Arrival at $T = 35.64$
2. Departure at $T = 43.3$

The next chronological event is an arrival occurring at $T = 35.64$.

***Arrival Event at* T $= 35.64$ *(Customer 3).***    Customer 4 will arrive at

$$T = 35.64 + [-10 \ln(.6139)] = 40.52$$

Because the facility is currently busy (until $T = 43.3$), customer 3 is placed in queue at $T = 35.64$. The updated list of future events is

1. Arrival at $T = 40.52$
2. Departure at $T = 43.3$

***Arrival event at* T $= 40.52$ *(Customer 4).***    Customer 5 will arrive at

$$T = 40.52 + [-10 \ln(.5933)] = 45.74$$

Because the facility continues to be busy (until $T = 43.3$), customer 4 is placed second in the queue at $T = 40.52$. The updated list of future events is

1. Departure at $T = 43.3$
2. Arrival at $T = 45.74$

***Departure Event at* T = 43.3 *(Customer 2).*** The first customer in the queue (customer 3) starts service. Given $R = .9341$, the associated departure time occurs at

$$T = 43.3 + 15 = 58.3$$

The facility continues to be busy, and the length of the queue is reduced by 1 at $T = 43.3$. The updated list of future events is

1. Arrival at $T = 45.74$
2. Departure at $T = 58.3$

***Arrival Event at* T = 45.74 *(Customer 5).*** Customer 6 arrives at

$$T = 45.74 + [-10 \ln(.1782)] = 62.99$$

Customer 5 is placed last in the queue at $T = 45.74$.

The preceding computations demonstrate all the possibilities of the simulation model logic. We will thus stop the computations at this point and show how the desired statistics of the model are calculated.

Let us assume that the simulation is run (executed) for 50 time units. Figure 18–7 summarizes the changes in the length of the queue and the utilization of the facility as a function of the simulation time.

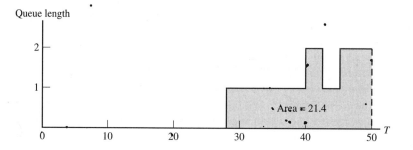

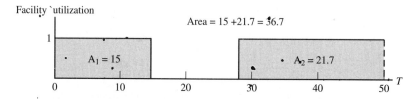

**Figure 18–7**

The queue length and the facility utilization are known as **time-based** variables because their variation is a function of time. As result, their average values are computed as

$$\left(\begin{array}{c}\text{Average value of a} \\ \text{time-based variable}\end{array}\right) = \frac{\text{Area under curve}}{\text{Simulated period}}$$

Implementing this formula for the data in Figure 18–7, we get

$$\text{Average queue length} = \frac{21.4}{50} = .428 \text{ customer}$$

$$\text{Average facility utilization} = \frac{36.7}{50} = .734 \text{ barber}$$

The average waiting time in the queue is an **observation-based** variable whose value is computed as

$$\begin{pmatrix} \text{Average value of an} \\ \text{observation-based variable} \end{pmatrix} = \frac{\text{Sum of observations}}{\text{Number of observations}}$$

Examination of Figure 18–7 reveals that the area under the queue-length curve actually equals the sum of the waiting time for the three customers who joined the queue. Specifically, the first waiting customer (customer 3) entered the queue at $T = 35.64$ and left at $T = 43.3$, the second waiting customer (customer 4) entered at $T = 40.52$ and continued to be in the queue at the end of the simulated period ($T = 50$), and the third customer (customer 5) entered at $T = 45.74$ and also continued to be in the queue at $T = 50$. Thus, the sum of the waiting time for the three customers is $(43.3 - 35.64) + (50 - 40.52) + (50 - 45.74) = 21.4$ minutes, which equals the area under the queue-length curve.

The average waiting time in the queue is thus computed as $\frac{21.4}{3} = 7.13$ minutes. This average applies only to those customers who have experienced positive waiting time. To obtain the average for all the customers ($= 5$) whether they experienced positive waiting time or not, we compute the average as $\frac{21.4}{5} = 4.28$ minutes.

The (tedious) computations in Example 18.6–1 point to the need for using the computer as an essential tool for executing simulation models. Indeed, several specialized simulation languages (e.g., SIMNET II, GPSS, and SIMAN) have been developed to automate these types of computations. Section 18.9 gives an overview of simulation languages.

### Problem set 18.6a

1. In Example 18.6–1, continue the simulation until customer 5 has been serviced. Use the random numbers in Table 18–1 in the same order in which they are used in the example. Compute the resulting average queue length, average facility utilization and average waiting time in the queue.

2. Suppose that the barbershop of Example 18.6–1 is operated by two barbers, and customers are served on a FCFS basis. Suppose further that the time to get a haircut is uniformly distributed between 15 and 30 minutes. The interarrival time of customers is exponential, with a mean of 10 minutes. Simulate the system manually for 75 time units. From the results of the simulation, determine the average time a customer waits in queue, the average number of customers waiting, and the average utilization of the barbers. Use the random numbers in Table 18–1.

**3.** Classify the following variables as either *observation-based* or *time-based*:
   **(a)** Time-to-failure of an electronic component.
   **(b)** Inventory level of an item.
   **(c)** Order quantity of an inventory item.
   **(d)** Number of defective items in a lot.
   **(e)** Time needed to grade test papers.
   **(f)** Number of cars in the parking lot of a car-rental agency.

**4.** The following table represents the variation in the number of waiting customers in a queue as a function of the simulation time.

| Simulation time, $T$ (hr) | No. of waiting customers |
|---|---|
| $0 \leq T \leq 3$ | 0 |
| $3 < T \leq 4$ | 1 |
| $4 < T \leq 6$ | 2 |
| $6 < T \leq 7$ | 1 |
| $7 < T \leq 10$ | 0 |
| $10 < T \leq 12$ | 2 |
| $12 < T \leq 18$ | 3 |
| $18 < T \leq 20$ | 2 |
| $20 < T \leq 25$ | 1 |

Compute the following measures of performance:
   **(a)** The average length of the queue.
   **(b)** The average waiting time in the queue for those who must wait.

**5.** Suppose that the barbershop of Example 18.6–1 is operated by three barbers. Assume further that the utilization of the servers (barbers) is summarized as given in the following table:

| Simulation time, $T$ (hr) | No. of busy servers |
|---|---|
| $0 < T \leq 10$ | 0 |
| $10 < T \leq 20$ | 1 |
| $20 < T \leq 30$ | 2 |

*continued*

| Simulation time, $T$ (hr) | No. of busy servers |
|:---:|:---:|
| $30 < T \leq 40$ | 0 |
| $40 < T \leq 60$ | 1 |
| $60 < T \leq 70$ | 2 |
| $70 < T \leq 80$ | 3 |
| $80 < T \leq 90$ | 1 |
| $90 < T \leq 100$ | 0 |

Determine the following measures of performance:
(a) The average utilization of the facility.
(b) The average busy time of the facility.
(c) The average idle time of the facility.

## 18.7 METHODS FOR GATHERING STATISTICAL OBSERVATIONS

Simulation is a statistical experiment. Its output must be interpreted using proper statistical inference tools (e.g., confidence intervals and hypothesis testing). To accomplish this task, the observations of the simulation experiment must satisfy three conditions:

1. Observations are drawn from stationary (identical) distributions.
2. Observations are sampled from a normal population.
3. Observations are independent.

It so happens that, in the strict sense, none of these conditions is satisfied by the simulation. Nevertheless, we can ensure that these conditions remain statistically viable by restricting the manner in which the simulation observations are gathered.

First, we consider the question of stationarity. We have seen in Example 18.2–1 that the accuracy of estimating the area of a circle by Monte Carlo increases with the sample size. Indeed, an examination of Figure 18–2 reveals that the estimate of the area changes erratically for small sample sizes because the simulation output is not stationary. The output stabilizes to (approximately) the exact area value as the sample sizes increases. Thus, the effect of nonstationarity can be suppressed by using a sufficiently large sample size.

Simulation output is a function of the length of the simulated period. The initial period of erratic behavior is usually referred to as the **transient** or **warm-up period**. When the output stabilizes, the system is said to be operating under **steady state**. The length of the transient period depends largely on the characteristics of the model, and there is no way to predict the start point of steady state in advance. In general, the longer is the simulation run, the better is the chance of reaching steady state.

We consider next the requirement that simulation observations must be drawn from a normal population. This requirement is realized by using the *central limit theorem* (see Section 12.5.4), which states that the distribution of the average of a sample is asymptotically normal regardless of the population from which the sample is drawn. The central limit theorem is thus the main vehicle for satisfying the normal distribution assumption.

The third condition deals with the independence of the observations. The nature of the simulation experiment does not guarantee independence among successive simulation observations. However, by using sample averages to represent simulation observations, we can also alleviate the problem of lack of independence. This is particularly true when we increase the time base used to compute the sample average.

The concepts of transient and steady states are valid only in what is called a **nonterminating simulation**—that is, the simulation that applies to systems whose operation continues indefinitely. In the case of a **terminating simulation** (e.g., bank operation where the bank typically opens for 8 hours a day), the transient behavior is part of the normal operation of the system and hence cannot be ignored. The only recourse here is to increase the number of observations as much as possible.

Having discussed the peculiarities of the simulation experiment and the means to circumvent them, we present the three most common methods for collecting observations in simulation.

**1.** Subinterval method
**2.** Replication method
**3.** Regenerative (or cycles) method

### 18.7.1 Subinterval Method

Figure 18–8 illustrates the idea of the subinterval method. Essentially, suppose that the simulation is executed for $T$ time units (i.e., run length $= T$) and that it is desired to collect $n$ observations. The subinterval method calls for truncating the initial tran-

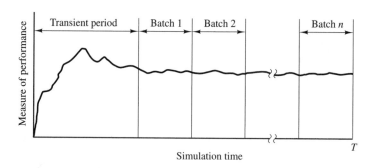

**Figure 18–8**

sient period first, and then subdividing the remainder of the simulation run into $n$ equal subintervals (or batches). The average of the desired measure of performance (e.g., queue length or waiting time in queue) within each subinterval is then used to represent a single observation. The truncation of the initial transient period implies that no statistical data are collected during that period.

The advantage of the subinterval method is that the effect of the transient (nonstationary) conditions is mitigated, particularly for those observations that are collected toward the end of the simulation run. The disadvantage of the method is that successive batches with common boundary conditions are correlated. The correlation problem can be alleviated by increasing the time for each batch.

**Example 18.7–1.**

Figure 18–9 shows the change in queue length in a single queue model as a function of the simulation time. The simulation run length is $T = 35$ hours, and the length of the transient period is estimated to equal 5 hours. It is desired to collect 5 observations— that is, $n = 5$. The corresponding time base for each batch thus equals $\frac{(35 - 5)}{5} = 6$ hours.

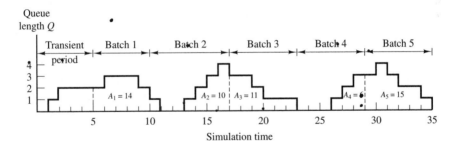

**Figure 18–9**

Let $\overline{Q}_i$ represent the average queue length in batch $i$. Because the queue length is a time-based variable, we have

$$\overline{Q}_i = \frac{A_i}{t}, \quad i = 1, 2, ..., 5$$

where $A_i$ is the area under the queue length curve, and $t$ is the time base per batch. In the present example, $t = 6$ hours.

The data in Figure 18–9 produce the following observations:

| Observation $i$ | 1 | 2 | 3 | 4 | 5 |
|---|---|---|---|---|---|
| $A_i$ | 14 | 10 | 11 | 6 | 15 |
| $\overline{Q}_i$ | 2.33 | 1.67 | 1.83 | 1.00 | 2.5 |
| Sample mean = 3.32 | | Sample variance = .35 | | | |

The sample mean and variance can be used to compute a confidence interval, if desired.

The computation of the sample variance in Example 18.7–1 is based on the following familiar formula:

$$ s^2 = \sqrt{\frac{\displaystyle\sum_{i=1}^{n} x_i - \bar{x}}{n - 1}} $$

This formula is only an approximation of the true variance because it ignores the effect of autocorrelation between the successive batches. The exact formula can be found in Law and Kelton (1991, pp. 282–286).

## 18.7.2 Replication Method

In the replication method, each observation is represented by an independent simulation run in which the transient period is truncated, as illustrated in Figure 18–10. The computation of the observation averages for each batch is the same as in the subinterval method. The only difference is that the standard variance formula is applicable because the batches are not correlated.

The advantage of the replication method is that each simulation run is driven by a distinct (0,1) random number stream, which yields observations that are truly statistically independent. The disadvantage is that each observation may be heavily biased by the initial effect of the transient conditions. Such a problem may be alleviated by making the run length sufficiently large.

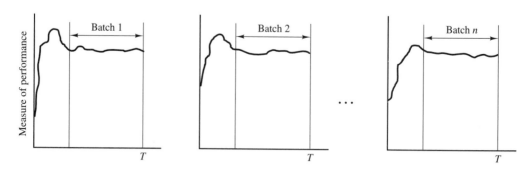

**Figure 18–10**

## 18.7.3 Regenerative (Cycle) Method

The regenerative method may be regarded as an extended case of the subinterval method. The motivation behind the new method is that it attempts to reduce the effect of autocorrelation that characterizes the subinterval method by requiring similar starting conditions for each batch. For example, if the variable we are dealing with is the queue length, each batch would start at an instant where the queue length is zero. Unlike the subinterval method, the nature of the regenerative method may result in unequal time bases for the different batches.

Although the regenerative method may reduce autocorrelation, it has the disadvantage of yielding a smaller number of batches for a given run length. This follows because we cannot predict when a new batch will start or how long a batch will last. Under steady-state conditions, however, we should expect the starting points for the successive batches to be more or less evenly spaced.

The computation of the average for batch $i$ in the regenerative method is generally defined as the ratio of two random variables $a_i$ and $b_i$—that is, $x_i = \frac{a_i}{b_i}$. The definitions of $a_i$ and $b_i$ depend on the variable being computed. Specifically, if the variable is *time based,* then $a_i$ would represent the area under the curve and $b_i$ would equal the associated time base. If the variable is *observation based,* then $a_i$ would be the total sum of the observations within batch $i$ and $b_i$ would be the associated number of observations.

Because $x_i$ is the ratio of two random variables, an unbiased estimate of the sample average can be shown to be

$$\bar{y} = \frac{\sum_{i=1}^{n} y_i}{n}$$

where

$$y_i = \frac{n\bar{a}}{\bar{b}} - \frac{(n-1)(n\bar{a} - a_i)}{n\bar{b} - b_i}, \quad i = 1, 2, ..., n$$

$$\bar{a} = \frac{\sum_{i=1}^{n} a_i}{n}$$

$$\bar{b} = \frac{\sum_{i=1}^{n} b_i}{n}$$

In this case, a confidence interval can be set on the true mean by using the mean and standard deviation of $y_i$.

---

**Example 18.7–2.**

Figure 18–11 represents the number of busy servers in a single facility with three parallel servers. The length of the simulation run is 35 time units, and the length of the transient period is 4 time units. It is desired to estimate the average utilization of the facility based on the regenerative method.

Busy
servers

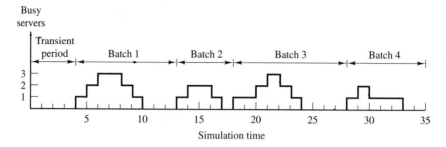

**Figure 18–11**

After truncating the transient period, Figure 18–11 yields four batches with the
common characteristic of starting with three idle servers. A summary of the computations is given in the following table:

| Batch $i$ | $a_i$ | $b_i$ | $y_i$ |
|:---------:|:-----:|:-----:|:-----:|
| 1 | 12 | 9 | 1.32 |
| 2 | 6 | 5 | 1.24 |
| 3 | 10 | 6 | 1.65 |
| 4 | 6 | 5 | 1.24 |
| | $\bar{a} = 8.5$ | $\bar{b} = 6.25$ | $\bar{y} = 1.363, s_y = .195$ |

The computation of $y_i$ is based on the following formula:

$$y_i = \frac{4 \times 8.5}{6.25} - \frac{(4-1)(4 \times 8.5 - a_i)}{4 \times 6.25 - b_i} = 5.44 - \frac{3(34 - a_i)}{25 - b_i}$$

**Problem set 18.7a**

1. In example 18.7–1, use the subinterval method to compute the average
   waiting time in the queue for those who must wait.

2. In a simulation model, the subinterval method is used to compute batches
   averages. The transient period is estimated to be 100, and each batch has a
   time base of 100 time units as well. Using the following data that provides
   the waiting times for customers as a function of the simulation time, estimate the 95% confidence interval for the mean waiting time.

| Time interval | Waiting times |
|:---:|:---:|
| 0–100 | 10, 20, 13, 14, 8, 15, 6, 8 |
| 100–200 | 12, 30, 10, 14, 16 |
| 200–300 | 15, 17, 20, 22 |
| 300–400 | 10, 20, 30, 15, 25, 31 |
| 400–500 | 15, 17, 20, 14, 13 |
| 500–600 | 25, 30, 15 |

3. In Example 18.7–2, suppose that the start points of the observations corre-spond to the points in time where all the servers have just become idle. Thus, in Figure 18–11, these points correspond to $t = 10, 17, 24$, and 33. Compute the 95% confidence interval for the utilization of the servers based on the new definition of the regenerative points.

4. In a single-server queueing situation, the system is simulated for 100 hours. The results of the simulation show that the server was busy during the fol-lowing time intervals: $(0, 10), (15, 20), (25, 30), (35, 60), (70, 80)$, and $(90, 95)$. Otherwise, the server was idle. The length of the transient period is esti-mated to be 10 hours.

   (a) Define the start points needed to implement the regenerative method.

   (b) Compute the 95% confidence interval for the average utilization of the server based on the use of the regenerative method.

   (c) Apply the subinterval method to the same problem using a sample size $n = 5$. Compute the corresponding 95% confidence interval, and com-pare it with the one obtained from the regenerative method.

## 18.8 SIMULATION LANGUAGES

The execution of simulation models entails two distinct types of computations: (1) File manipulations that deal with the chronological storage and processing of the model's events, and (2) arithmetic and bookkeeping computations associ-ated with the generation of random samples and the collection of model statis-tics. The first type of computation involves extensive logic development in list processing, and the second type entails tedious and time-consuming calculations. The nature of these computations makes the computer an essential tool for exe-cuting simulation models, and, in turn, prompts the development of special com-puter simulation languages for performing these computations conveniently and efficiently.

Available discrete simulation languages fall into two broad categories:

**1.** Event scheduling
**2.** Process oriented

In event scheduling languages, the user details the actions associated with the occurrence of each event, in much the same way they are given in Example 18.6–1. The main contribution of the language in this case is to automate the sampling process from distributions, the chronological storage and retrieval of events, and the collection of model statistics.

Process-oriented languages uses blocks or nodes that can be linked together to form a network that describes the movements of **transactions** or **entities** (i.e., customers) in the system. For example, the three most prominent blocks/nodes in any process simulation language are the *source* from which transactions are created, the *queue* where they can wait if necessary, and the *facility* where service is performed. Each of these blocks/nodes is defined with all the information needed to drive the simulation automatically. For example, once the interarrival time for the source is specified, the process-oriented language automatically "knows" when arrival events will occur. In effect, each block/node of the model has standing instructions that define exactly *how* and *when* transactions are moved in the simulation network.

Process-oriented languages are internally driven by the same actions used in event-scheduling languages. The difference is that these actions are automated to relieve the user of the tedious computational and logical details. In a way, we can regard process-oriented languages as being based on the input-output concept of the "black box" approach. This essentially means that process-oriented languages trade modeling flexibility for simplicity and ease of use.

Prominent event-scheduling languages include SIMSCRIPT, SLAM, and SIMAN. Over the years, these languages have evolved to include process-oriented capabilities. All three languages allow the user to write (a portion of) the model in higher-level language, such as FORTRAN or C. This capability is necessary to allow the user to model complex logic that otherwise cannot be achieved directly by the regular facilities of these languages. A major reason for this limitation is the restrictive and perhaps convoluted manner in which these languages move transactions (or entities) among the model's queues and facilities.

The oldest process-oriented language is GPSS. This language, which was first developed in the early 1960s, has evolved over the years to accommodate new modeling needs of complex systems. To use this language effectively, the user must master the "inner works" of some 80 different blocks. Despite long years of experience with GPSS, the language still possesses some modeling peculiarities that are difficult to justify. An example of these peculiarities is the need to approximate continuous distributions by piecewise linear ones. It is true that some recent versions of the language have provided direct capabilities for some of the continuous distributions (e.g., exponential and normal). However, with the present tremendous capability of the computer, it is difficult to understand why such an obstacle has persisted for so long.

A new process-oriented simulation language, called SIMNET II, is designed to allow modeling complex situations directly. SIMNET II uses three nodes: a *source* that creates transactions, a *queue* where transactions may wait, and a *facility* where service is performed. A fourth node, named *auxiliary*, viewed as an infinite-capacity facility, is designed to enhance the modeling capabilities of the language.

Figure 18–12 demonstrates the application of SIMNET II to a single server model. Each node is given an arbitrary name followed by the symbol *S, *Q, *F, or *A to represent a source, a queue, a facility, or an auxiliary, respectively. Transactions arrive from source ARIV, enter queue WAIT if necessary, and are served in facility SRVR before being TERMinated from the system. The interarrival time is EX(10), which is an exponential distribution, with a mean of 10 time units. Similarly, the service time is EX(15). Before the transaction exits the model, it computes its time in the system, SYS TIME, on a branch (*B) to TERM(inate). The simulation is executed for a RUN-LENGTH of 480 time units. Appendix B provides more details

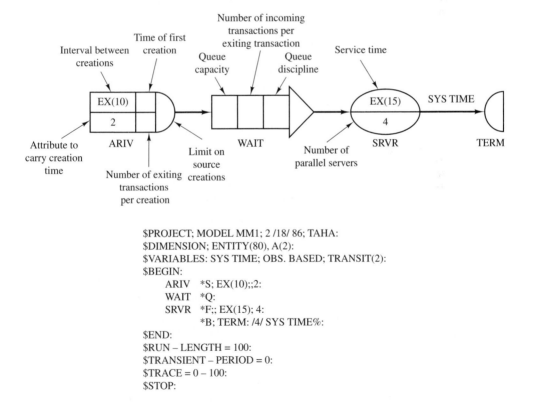

```
$PROJECT; MODEL MM1; 2 /18/ 86; TAHA:
$DIMENSION; ENTITY(80), A(2):
$VARIABLES: SYS TIME; OBS. BASED; TRANSIT(2):
$BEGIN:
     ARIV  *S; EX(10);;2:
     WAIT  *Q:
     SRVR  *F;; EX(15); 4:
           *B; TERM: /4/ SYS TIME%:
$END:
$RUN – LENGTH = 100:
$TRANSIENT – PERIOD = 0:
$TRACE = 0 – 100:
$STOP:
```

**Figure 18–12**

about SIMNET II. The student version of the language is given on the diskette accompanying this book.

### Problem set 18.9a[2]

1. Patrons arrive randomly at a three-clerk post office. The interarrival time is exponential with mean 5 minutes. The time a clerk spends with a patron is exponential with 10 minutes. All arriving patrons form one queue and wait for the first available free clerk. Run a simulation model of the system for 480 minutes to determine the following:

   **(a)** The average number of patrons waiting in the queue.

   **(b)** The average utilization of the clerks.

2. Television units arrive for inspection on a conveyor belt at the constant rate of 5 units per hour. The inspection time takes between 10 and 15 minutes, uniformly distributed. Past experience shows that 20% of inspected units must be adjusted and then sent back for reinspection. The adjustment time is also uniformly distributed between 6 and 8 minutes. Run a simulation model for 480 minutes to compute the following:

   **(a)** The average time a unit takes until it passes inspection.

   **(b)** The average number of times a unit must be reinspected before it exits the system.

3. A mouse is trapped in a maze and desperately "wants out." After spending between 1 and 3 minutes, uniformly distributed, of trying, there is a 30% chance that it will choose the right path. Otherwise, it will wander around aimlessly for between 2 and 3 minutes, uniformly distributed, and eventually end up where it started, only to try once again. The mouse can "try freedom" as many times as it pleases, but there is a limit to everything. With so much energy expended in trying and retrying, the mouse is sure to die if it does not make it within a period that is normally distributed, with a mean of 10 minutes and a standard deviation of 2 minutes. Write a simulation that will estimate the probability that the mouse will be free. For the purpose of estimating the probability, assume that 100 mice will be processed by the model.

4. In the final stage of automobile manufacturing, a car moving on a transporter is situated between two parallel workstations to allow work to be done on both the left and right sides of the car simultaneously. The operation times for the left and right sides are uniform between 15 and 20 minutes and 18 and 22 minutes, respectively. The transporter arrives at the stations area every 20 minutes. Simulate the process for 480 minutes to determine the utilization of the left and right stations.

5. Cars arrive at a one-bay car wash facility where the interarrival time is exponential, with a mean of 10 minutes. Arriving cars line up in a single lane that can accommodate at most five waiting cars. If the lane is full, newly ar-

---

[2]Work these problems by using SIMNET II [Appendix B], a simulation language of your choice, or by using BASIC, FORTRAN, or C.

riving cars will go elsewhere. It takes between 10 and 15 minutes, uniformly distributed, to wash a car. Simulate the system for 960 minutes, and compute the time a car spends in the facility.

## 18.9 SUMMARY

Simulation is a highly flexible tool that can be used effectively for analyzing complex systems. It also has the drawback that its output is subject to statistical error and hence must be interpreted by appropriate statistical tests. The special nature of the simulation experiment makes it difficult to gather observations that are both independent and representative of the steady-state conditions. However, by using special methods for collecting data, these difficulties may be alleviated.

All simulation languages use events to drive the simulation model. Discrete-event languages are more flexible but are also more difficult to use than the process-oriented languages.

## SELECTED REFERENCES

Box, G., and M. Muller, "A Note on the Generation of Random Normal Deviates," *Annals of Mathematical Statistics,* Vol. 29, pp. 610–611, 1958.

Law, A., and Kelton, W., *Simualtion Modeling & Analysis,* 2nd ed., McGraw-Hill, New York, 1991.

Ross, S., *A Course in Simulation,* Macmillan, New York, 1990.

Taha, H., *Simulation Modeling and SIMNET,* Prentice Hall, Upper Saddle River, N.J., 1988.

# Chapter 19

# Markovian Decision Process

## 19.1 SCOPE OF THE MARKOVIAN DECISION PROBLEM: THE GARDENER EXAMPLE[1]

This chapter presents an application of dynamic programming to the solution of a stochastic decision process that can be described by a finite number of states. The transition probabilities between the states are described by a Markov chain. The reward structure of the process is also described by a matrix whose individual elements represent the revenue (or cost) resulting from moving from one state to another. Both the transition and revenue matrices depend on the decision alternatives available to the decision maker. The objective of the problem is to determine the optimal policy that maximizes the expected revenue over a finite or infinite number of stages.

We use an example as a vehicle of explanation throughout the chapter. The example paraphrases several important applications in the areas of inventory, replacement, cash flow management, and regulation of water reservoir capacity.

Every year, at the beginning of the gardening season, a gardener applies chemical tests to check the soil's condition. Depending on the outcomes of the tests, the garden's productivity for the new season falls in one of three states: (1) good, (2) fair, and (3) poor.

Over the years, the gardener observed that current year's productivity depends only on last year's soil condition. The transition probabilities over a 1-year period from one productivity state to another can be represented in terms of the following Markov chain:

---

[1]A review of Markov chains is given in Section 19.6

$$
\begin{array}{c}
\text{State of} \\
\text{the system} \\
\text{next year} \\
\overbrace{\quad\quad\quad\quad\quad}
\end{array}
$$

$$
\begin{array}{cc}
\begin{array}{c} \\ \text{State of} \\ \text{the system} \\ \text{this year} \end{array}
&
\begin{array}{c}
\phantom{1} \quad 1 \quad\; 2 \quad\; 3 \\
\begin{array}{c} 1 \\ 2 \\ 3 \end{array}
\left[
\begin{array}{ccc}
.2 & .5 & .3 \\
0 & .5 & .5 \\
0 & 0 & 1
\end{array}
\right] = \mathbf{P}^1
\end{array}
\end{array}
$$

The transition probabilities in $\mathbf{P}^1$ indicate that the productivity for a current year can be no better than last year's. For example, if the soil condition for this year is fair (state 2), next year's productivity may remain fair with probability .5 or become poor (state 3), also with probability .5.

The gardener can alter the transition probabilities $\mathbf{P}^1$ by invoking other courses of action. Typically, fertilizer is applied to boost the soil condition, which yields the following transition matrix $\mathbf{P}^2$.

$$
\mathbf{P}^2 = \begin{array}{c} \\ 1 \\ 2 \\ 3 \end{array}
\begin{array}{c}
\phantom{1}\; 1 \quad\;\; 2 \quad\;\; 3 \\
\left[
\begin{array}{ccc}
.3 & .6 & .1 \\
.1 & .6 & .3 \\
.05 & .4 & .55
\end{array}
\right]
\end{array}
$$

To put the decision problem in perspective, the gardener associates a return function (or a reward structure) with the transition from one state to another. The return function expresses the gain or loss during a 1-year period, depending on the states between which the transition is made. Because the gardener has the option of using or not using fertilizer, gain and losses vary depending on the decision made. The matrices $\mathbf{R}^1$ and $\mathbf{R}^2$ summarize the return functions in hundreds-of dollars associated with the matrices $\mathbf{P}^1$ and $\mathbf{P}^2$, respectively.

$$
\mathbf{R}^1 = \| r_{ij}^1 \| = \begin{array}{c} \\ 1 \\ 2 \\ 3 \end{array}
\begin{array}{c}
\phantom{1}\; 1 \quad 2 \quad\;\; 3 \\
\left[
\begin{array}{ccc}
7 & 6 & 3 \\
0 & 5 & 1 \\
0 & 0 & -1
\end{array}
\right]
\end{array}
$$

$$
\mathbf{R}^2 = \| r_{ij}^2 \| = \begin{array}{c} \\ 1 \\ 2 \\ 3 \end{array}
\begin{array}{c}
\phantom{1}\; 1 \quad 2 \quad\;\; 3 \\
\left[
\begin{array}{ccc}
6 & 5 & -1 \\
7 & 4 & 0 \\
6 & 3 & -2
\end{array}
\right]
\end{array}
$$

The elements $r_{ij}^2$ of $\mathbf{R}^2$ consider the cost of applying the fertilizer. For example, if the system is in state 1 and remains in state 1 during next year, its gain will be $r_{11}^2 = 6$ compared with $r_{11}^1 = 7$ when no fertilizer is used.

What kind of a decision problem does the gardener have? First, we must know whether the gardening activity will continue for a limited number of years or indefinitely. These situations are referred to as **finite-stage** and **infinite-stage** decision problems. In both cases, the gardener would determine the *best* course of action (fertilize or do not fertilize) given the outcome of the chemical tests (state of the system). The optimization will be based on the maximization of expected revenue.

The gardener may also be interested in evaluating the expected revenue resulting from prespecified course of action for a given state of the system. For example, fertilizer may be applied whenever the soil condition is poor (state 3). The decision-making process in this case is said to be represented by a **stationary policy**.

Each stationary policy will be associated with a different transition and return matrices, which are constructed from the matrices $\mathbf{P}^1, \mathbf{P}^2, \mathbf{R}^1$ and $\mathbf{R}^2$. For example, for the stationary policy calling for applying fertilizer only when the soil condition is poor (state 3), the resulting transition and return matrices are given as

$$\mathbf{P} = \begin{bmatrix} .2 & .5 & .3 \\ 0 & .5 & .5 \\ .05 & .4 & .55 \end{bmatrix}, \quad \mathbf{R} = \begin{bmatrix} 7 & 6 & 3 \\ 0 & 5 & 1 \\ 6 & 3 & -2 \end{bmatrix}$$

These matrices differ from $\mathbf{P}^1$ and $\mathbf{R}^1$ in the third rows only, which are taken directly from $\mathbf{P}^2$ and $\mathbf{R}^2$. The reason is that $\mathbf{P}^2$ and $\mathbf{R}^2$ are the matrices that result when fertilizer is applied in *every* state.

### Problem set 19.1a

1. In the gardener model, identify the matrices $\mathbf{P}$ and $\mathbf{R}$ associated with the stationary policy that calls for using fertilizer whenever the soil condition is fair or poor.
2. Identify all the stationary policies for the gardener model.

## 19.2 FINITE-STAGE DYNAMIC PROGRAMMING MODEL

Suppose that the gardener plans to "retire" from gardening in $N$ years. We are interested in determining the optimal course of action for each year (to fertilize or not to fertilize). Optimality here calls for accumulating the highest expected revenue at the end of $N$ years.

Let $k = 1$ and 2 represent the two courses of action (alternatives) available to the gardener. The matrices $\mathbf{P}^k$ and $\mathbf{R}^k$ representing the transition probabilities and reward function for alternative $k$ were given in Section 19.1 and are summarized here for convenience.

$$\mathbf{P}^1 = \|p_{ij}^1\| = \begin{bmatrix} .2 & .5 & .3 \\ 0 & .5 & .5 \\ 0 & 0 & 1 \end{bmatrix}, \quad \mathbf{R}^1 = \|r_{ij}^1\| = \begin{bmatrix} 7 & 6 & 3 \\ 0 & 5 & 1 \\ 0 & 0 & -1 \end{bmatrix}$$

$$\mathbf{P}^2 = \|p_{ij}^2\| = \begin{bmatrix} .3 & .6 & .1 \\ .1 & .6 & .3 \\ .05 & .4 & .55 \end{bmatrix}, \quad \mathbf{R}^2 = \|r_{ij}^2\| = \begin{bmatrix} 6 & 5 & -1 \\ 7 & 4 & 0 \\ 6 & 3 & -2 \end{bmatrix}$$

The gardener's problem is expressed as a finite-stage dynamic programming (DP) model as follows. For the sake of generalization, suppose that the number of states for each stage (year) is $m$ ($= 3$ in the gardener's example) and define

$f_n(i)$ = Optimal *expected* revenue of stages $n, n + 1, ..., N$, given that the state of the system (soil condition) at the beginning of year $n$ is $i$

The *backward* recursive equation relating $f_n$ and $f_{n+1}$ can be written as

$$f_n(i) = \max_k \left\{ \sum_{j=1}^m p_{ij}^k [r_{ij}^k + f_{n+1}(j)] \right\}, \quad n = 1, 2, ..., N$$

where $f_{N+1}(j) \equiv 0$ for all $j$.

A justification for the equation is that the *cumulative* revenue, $r_{ij}^k + f_{n+1}(j)$, resulting from reaching state $j$ at stage $n + 1$ from state $i$ at stage $n$ occurs with probability $p_{ij}^k$. Letting

$$v_i^k = \sum_{j=1}^m p_{ij}^k r_{ij}^k$$

the DP recursive equation can be written as

$$f_N(i) = \max_k \{v_i^k\}$$

$$f_n(i) = \max_k \left\{ v_i^k + \sum_{j=1}^m p_{ij}^k f_{n+1}(j) \right\} \quad n = 1 \, 2 \, ... \, N - 1$$

To illustrate the computation of $v_i^k$, consider the case in which no fertilizer is used ($k = 1$).

$$v_1^1 = .2 \times 7 + .5 \times 6 + .3 \times 3 = 5.3$$
$$v_2^1 = 0 \times 0 + .5 \times 5 + .5 \times 1 = 3$$
$$v_3^1 = 0 \times 0 + 0 \times 0 + 1 \times -1 = -1$$

Thus, if the soil condition is good, a single transition yields 5.3 for that year; if it is fair, the yield is 3, and if it is poor, the yield is $-1$.

---

**Example 19.2-1.**

In this example, we solve the gardener's problem using the data summarized in the matrices $\mathbf{P}^1, \mathbf{P}^2, \mathbf{R}^1$, and $\mathbf{R}^2$, given a horizon of 3 years only ($N = 3$).

Because the values of $v_i^k$ will be used repeatedly in the computations, they are summarized here for convenience. Recall that $k = 1$ represents "do not fertilize" and $k = 2$ represents "fertilize."

| $i$ | $v_i^1$ | $v_i^2$ |
|-----|---------|---------|
| 1   | 5.3     | 4.7     |
| 2   | 3       | 3.1     |
| 3   | $-1$    | .4      |

*Stage 3*

|   |   | $v_i^k$ |   | Optimal Solution |   |
|---|---------|---------|---------|---------|-----|
| $i$ | $k = 1$ | $k = 2$ | $f_3(i)$ | $k^{\boldsymbol{\cdot}}$ |
| 1 | 5.3 | 4.7 | 5.3 | 1 |
| 2 | 3 | 3.1 | 3.1 | 2 |
| 3 | $-1$ | .4 | .4 | 2 |

*Stage 2*

|   | $v_i^k + p_{i1}^k f_3(1) + p_{i2}^k f_3(2) + p_{i3}^k f_3(3)$ | | Optimal Solution | |
|---|---|---|---|---|
| $i$ | $k = 1$ | $k = 2$ | $f_2(i)$ | $k^{\boldsymbol{\cdot}}$ |
| 1 | $5.3 + .2 \times 5.3 + .5 \times 3.1$ $+ .3 \times .4 = 8.03$ | $4.7 + .3 \times 5.3 + .6 \times 3.1$ $+ .1 \times .4 = 8.19$ | 8.19 | 2 |
| 2 | $3 + 0 \times 5.3 + .5 \times 3.1$ $+ .5 \times .4 = 4.75$ | $3.1 + .1 \times 5.3 + .6 \times 3.1$ $+ .3 \times .4 = 5.61$ | 5.61 | 2 |
| 3 | $-1 + 0 \times 5.3 + 0 \times 3.1$ $+ 1 \times .4 = -.6$ | $.4 + .05 \times 5.3 + .4 \times 3.1$ $+ .55 \times .4 \approx 2.31$ | 2.13 | 2 |

*Stage 1*

|   | $v_i^k + p_{i1}^k f_2(1) + p_{i2}^k f_2(2) + p_{i3}^k f_2(3)$ | | Optimal Solution | |
|---|---|---|---|---|
| $i$ | $k = 1$ | $k = 2$ | $f_1(i)$ | $k^{\boldsymbol{\cdot}}$ |
| 1 | $5.3 + .2 \times 8.19 + .5 \times 5.61$ $+ .3 \times 2.13 \approx 10.38$ | $4.7 + .3 \times 8.19 + .6 \times 5.61$ $+ .1 \times 2.13 \approx 10.74$ | 10.74 | 2 |
| 2 | $3 + 0 \times 8.19 + .5 \times 5.61$ $+ .5 \times 2.13 = 6.87$ | $3.1 + .1 \times 8.19 + .6 \times 5.61$ $+ .3 \times 2.13 \approx 7.92$ | 7.92 | 2 |
| 3 | $-1 + 0 \times 8.19 + 0 \times 5.61$ $+ 1 \times 2.13 = 1.13$ | $.4 + .05 \times 8.19 + .4 \times 5.61$ $+ .55 \times 2.13 \approx 4.23$ | 4.23 | 2 |

The optimal solution shows that for years 1 and 2, the gardener should apply fertilizer ($k* = 2$) regardless of the state of the system (soil condition as revealed by the chemical tests). In year 3, fertilizer should be applied only if the system is in state 2 or 3 (fair or poor soil condition). The total expected revenues for the three years are $f_1(1) = 10.74$ if the state of the system in year 1 is good, $f_1(2) = 7.92$ if it is fair, and $f_1(3) = 4.23$ if it is poor.

---

The finite-horizon problem can be generalized in two ways. First, the transition probabilities and their return functions need not be the same every year. Second, a discounting factor may be applied to the expected revenue of the successive stages so that the values of $f_1(i)$ would represent the *present value* of the expected revenues of all the stages.

The first generalization requires the return values $r_{ij}^k$ and transition probabilities $p_{ij}^k$ to be functions of the stage, $n$. In this case, the DP recursive equation becomes

$$f_N(i) = \max_k \{v_i^{k,N}\}$$

$$f_n(i) = \max_k \left\{ v_k^{k,n} + \sum_{j=1}^m p_{ij}^{k,n} f_{n+1}(j) \right\}, \quad n = 1, 2, \dots, N-1$$

where

$$v_i^{k,n} = \sum_{j=1}^m p_{ij}^{k,n} r_{ij}^{k,n}$$

The second generalization is accomplished as follows. Let $\alpha(< 1)$ be the discount factor per year such that D dollars a year from now are equivalent to $\alpha$ D dollars now. The new recursive equation becomes

$$f_N(i) = \max_k \{v_i^k\}$$

$$f_n(i) = \max_k \left\{ v_i^k + \alpha \sum_{j=1}^m p_{ij}^k f_{n+1}(j) \right\}, \quad n = 1, 2, \dots, N-1$$

### Problem set 19.2a

1. A company reviews the state of one of its important products annually and decides whether it is successful (state 1) or unsuccessful (state 2). The company must decide whether or not to advertise the product to further promote the sales. The following matrices, $P_1$ and $P_2$, provide the transition probabilities with and without advertisement during any year. The associated returns are given by the matrices $R_1$ and $R_2$. Find the optimal decisions over the next 3 years.

$$P^1 = \begin{bmatrix} .9 & .1 \\ .6 & .4 \end{bmatrix}, \quad R^1 = \begin{bmatrix} 2 & -1 \\ 1 & -3 \end{bmatrix}$$

$$P^2 = \begin{bmatrix} .7 & .3 \\ .2 & .8 \end{bmatrix}, \quad R^2 = \begin{bmatrix} 4 & 1 \\ 2 & -1 \end{bmatrix}$$

2. A company can advertise through radio, TV, or newspaper. The weekly costs of advertisement on the three media are estimated at $200, $900, and $300, respectively. The company can classify its sales volume during each week as (1) fair, (2) good, or (3) excellent. A summary of the transition probabilities associated with each advertisement medium follows.

Radio

|   | 1 | 2 | 3 |
|---|---|---|---|
| 1 | .4 | .5 | .1 |
| 2 | .1 | .7 | .2 |
| 3 | .1 | .2 | .7 |

TV

|   | 1 | 2 | 3 |
|---|---|---|---|
| 1 | .7 | .2 | .1 |
| 2 | .3 | .6 | .1 |
| 3 | .1 | .7 | .2 |

Newspaper

|   | 1 | 2 | 3 |
|---|---|---|---|
| 1 | .2 | .5 | .3 |
| 2 | 0 | .7 | .3 |
| 3 | 0 | .2 | .8 |

The corresponding weekly returns (in thousands of dollars) are

Radio

$$\begin{bmatrix} 400 & 520 & 600 \\ 300 & 400 & 700 \\ 200 & 250 & 500 \end{bmatrix}$$

TV

$$\begin{bmatrix} 1000 & 1300 & 1600 \\ 800 & 1000 & 1700 \\ 600 & 700 & 1100 \end{bmatrix}$$

Newspaper

$$\begin{bmatrix} 400 & 530 & 710 \\ 350 & 450 & 800 \\ 250 & 400 & 650 \end{bmatrix}$$

Find the optimal advertisement policy over the next 3 weeks.

3. A company is introducing a new product into the market. If the sales are high, there is a .5 probability that they will remain so next month. If they are not, the probability that they will become high next month is only .2. If the company advertises and the sales are high, the probability that they will remain high next month will increase to .8. Conversely, an advertising campaign while the sales are low will raise the probability to only .4.

If no advertisement is used and the sales are high, the returns are expected to be 10 if the sales remain high next month and 4 if they do not. The corresponding returns if the product starts with high sales are 7 and −2. Using advertisement will result in returns of 7 if the product starts with high sales and continues to be so and 6 if it does not. If the sales start low, the returns are 3 and −5, depending on whether of not they remain high.

Determine the company's optimal policy over the next 3 months.

4. *Inventory Problem.* An appliance store can place orders for refrigerators at the beginning of each month for immediate delivery. A fixed cost of $100 is incurred every time an order is placed. The storage cost per refrigerator per month is $5. The penalty for running out of stock is estimated at $150 per refrigerator per month. The monthly demand is given by the following pdf:

| Demand $x$ | 0 | 1 | 2 |
|---|---|---|---|
| $p(x)$ | .2 | .5 | .3 |

The store's policy is that the maximum stock level should not exceed two refrigerators in any single month. Determine the following:

(a) The transition probabilities for the different decision alternatives of the problem.

(b) The expected inventory cost per month as a function of the state of the system and the decision alternative.

(c) The optimal ordering policy over the next 3 months.

5. Repeat Problem 4 assuming that the pdf of demand over the next quarter changes according to the following table:

| Demand $x$ | Month | | |
|:---:|:---:|:---:|:---:|
| | 1 | 2 | 3 |
| 0 | .1 | .3 | .2 |
| 1 | .4 | .5 | .4 |
| 2 | .5 | .2 | .4 |

6. The market value of a used car is estimated at $2000. The owner can get more than this amount but is willing to entertain offers from he first three prospective buyers who respond to the advertisement (which means that a decision must be made not later than the time the third offer is received). The offers are expected to be $2000, $2200, $2400 and $2600, with equal probabilities. Naturally, once an offer is accepted, all later offers are discarded. The objective is to set an acceptance limit that can be used to evaluate each offer. These limits may be $2000, $2200, $2400, or $2600. Develop an optimal plan for the owner.

## 19.3 INFINITE-STAGE MODEL

The steady-state behavior of a Markovian process is independent of the initial state of the system. We are interested in evaluating policies for which the associated Markov chains allow the existence of a steady-state solution. (Section 19.6 provides the conditions under which a Markov chain can yield steady-state probabilities.)

There are two methods for solving the infinite-stage problem. The first method calls for evaluating *all* possible stationary policies of the decision problem. This is equivalent to an *exhaustive enumeration* process and can be used only if the number of stationary policies is reasonably small.

The second method, called policy iteration, is generally more efficient because it determines the optimum policy iteratively.

### 19.3.1 Exhaustive Enumeration Method

Suppose that the decision problem has total of $S$ stationary policies, and assume that $\mathbf{P}^s$ and $\mathbf{R}^s$ are the (one-step) transition and revenue matrices associated with the policy, $s = 1, 2, \ldots, S$. The steps of the enumeration method are as follows.

**Step 1.** Compute $v_i^s$, the expected one-step (one-period) revenue of policy $s$ given state $i, i = 1, 2, \ldots, m$.

**Step 2.** Compute $\pi_i^s$, the long-run stationary probabilities of the transition matrix $\mathbf{P}^s$ associated with policy $s$. These probabilities, when they exist, are computed from the equations

$$\pi^s \mathbf{P}^s = \pi^s$$

$$\pi_1^s + \pi_2^s + \cdots + \pi_m^s = 1$$

where $\pi^s = (\pi_1^s, \pi_2^s, \ldots, \pi_m^s)$.

**Step 3.** Determine $E^s$, the expected revenue of policy $s$ per transition step (period), by using the formula

$$E^s = \sum_{i=1}^{m} \pi_i^s v_i^s$$

**Step 4.** The optimal policy $s*$ is determine such that

$$E^{s*} = \max_s \{E^s\}$$

We illustrate the method by solving the gardener problem for an infinite-period planning horizon.

---

**Example 19.3-1.**

The gardener problem has a total of eight stationary policies, as the following table shows:

| Stationary policy, $s$ | Action |
|---|---|
| 1 | Do not fertilize at all. |
| 2 | Fertilize regardless of the state. |
| 3 | Fertilize whenever in state 1. |
| 4 | Fertilize whenever in state 2. |
| 5 | Fertilize whenever in state 3. |
| 6 | Fertilize whenever in state 1 or 2. |
| 7 | Fertilize whenever in state 1 or 3. |
| 8 | Fertilize whenever in state 2 or 3. |

The matrices $\mathbf{P}^s$ and $\mathbf{R}^s$ for policies 3 through 8 are derived from those of policies 1 and 2. We thus have

$$\mathbf{P}^1 = \begin{bmatrix} .2 & .5 & .3 \\ 0 & .5 & .5 \\ 0 & 0 & 1 \end{bmatrix}, \quad \mathbf{R}^1 = \begin{bmatrix} 7 & 6 & 3 \\ 0 & 5 & 1 \\ 0 & 0 & -1 \end{bmatrix}$$

$$\mathbf{P}^2 = \begin{bmatrix} .3 & .6 & .1 \\ .1 & .6 & .3 \\ .05 & .4 & .55 \end{bmatrix}, \quad \mathbf{R}^2 = \begin{bmatrix} 6 & 5 & -1 \\ 7 & 4 & 0 \\ 6 & 3 & -2 \end{bmatrix}$$

$$\mathbf{P}^3 = \begin{bmatrix} .3 & .6 & .1 \\ 0 & .5 & .5 \\ 0 & 0 & 1 \end{bmatrix}, \quad \mathbf{R}^3 = \begin{bmatrix} 6 & 5 & -1 \\ 0 & 5 & 1 \\ 0 & 0 & -1 \end{bmatrix}$$

$$\mathbf{P}^4 = \begin{bmatrix} .2 & .5 & 3 \\ .1 & .6 & .3 \\ 0 & 0 & 1 \end{bmatrix}, \quad \mathbf{R}^4 = \begin{bmatrix} 7 & 6 & 3 \\ 7 & 4 & 0 \\ 0 & 0 & -1 \end{bmatrix}$$

$$\mathbf{P}^5 = \begin{bmatrix} .2 & .5 & .3 \\ 0 & .5 & .5 \\ .05 & .4 & .55 \end{bmatrix}, \quad \mathbf{R}^5 = \begin{bmatrix} 7 & 6 & 3 \\ 0 & 5 & 1 \\ 6 & 3 & -2 \end{bmatrix}$$

$$\mathbf{P}^6 = \begin{bmatrix} .3 & .6 & .1 \\ .1 & .6 & .3 \\ 0 & 0 & 1 \end{bmatrix}, \quad \mathbf{R}^6 = \begin{bmatrix} 6 & 5 & -1 \\ 7 & 4 & 0 \\ 0 & 0 & -1 \end{bmatrix}$$

$$\mathbf{P}^7 = \begin{bmatrix} .3 & .6 & .1 \\ 0 & .5 & .5 \\ .05 & .4 & .55 \end{bmatrix}, \quad \mathbf{R}^7 = \begin{bmatrix} 6 & 5 & -1 \\ 0 & 5 & 1 \\ 6 & 3 & -2 \end{bmatrix}$$

$$\mathbf{P}^8 = \begin{bmatrix} .2 & .5 & .3 \\ .1 & .6 & .3 \\ .05 & .4 & .55 \end{bmatrix}, \quad \mathbf{R}^8 = \begin{bmatrix} 7 & 6 & 3 \\ 7 & 4 & 0 \\ 6 & 3 & -2 \end{bmatrix}$$

The values of $v_i^k$ can thus be computed as given in the following table.

|     | $v_i^s$ | | |
| --- | --- | --- | --- |
| $s$ | $i = 1$ | $i = 2$ | $i = 3$ |
| 1 | 5.3 | 3 | −1 |
| 2 | 4.7 | 3.1 | .4 |
| 3 | 4.7 | 3 | −1 |

*continued*

|       |         | $v_i^s$ |         |
|-------|---------|---------|---------|
| $s$   | $i = 1$ | $i = 2$ | $i = 3$ |
| 4     | 5.3     | 3.1     | −1      |
| 5     | 5.3     | 3       | .4      |
| 6     | 4.7     | 3.1     | −1      |
| 7     | 4.7     | 3       | .4      |
| 8     | 5.3     | 3.1     | .4      |

The computations of the stationary probabilities are achieved by using the equations

$$\boldsymbol{\pi}^s \mathbf{P}^s = \boldsymbol{\pi}^s$$

$$\pi_1 + \pi_2 + \cdots + \pi_m = 1$$

As an illustration, consider $s = 2$. The associated equations are

$$.3\pi_1 + .1\pi_2 + .05\pi_3 = \pi_1$$

$$.6\pi_1 + .6\pi_2 + .4\pi_3 = \pi_2$$

$$.1\pi_1 + .3\pi_2 + .55\pi_3 = \pi_3$$

$$\pi_1 + \pi_2 + \pi_3 = 1$$

(Notice that one of the first three equations is redundant.) The solution yields

$$\pi_1^2 = \frac{6}{59}, \quad \pi_2^2 = \frac{31}{5}, \quad \pi_3^2 = \frac{22}{59}$$

In this case, the expected yearly revenue is

$$E^2 = \sum_{i=1}^{3} \pi_i^2 v_i^2$$

$$= \frac{1}{59} (6 \times 4.7 + 31 \times .31 + 22 \times .4) = 2.256$$

The following table summarizes $\pi^k$ and $E^k$ for all the stationary policies. (Although this will not affect the computations in any way, note that each of policies 1, 3, 4, and 6 has an absorbing state: state 3. This is the reason $\pi_1 = \pi_2 = 0$ and $\pi_3 = 1$ for all these policies.)

| $s$ | $\pi_1^s$      | $\pi_2^s$       | $\pi_3^s$      | $E^s$  |
|-----|----------------|-----------------|----------------|--------|
| 1   | 0              | 0               | 1              | −1.    |
| 2   | $\frac{6}{59}$ | $\frac{31}{59}$ | $\frac{22}{59}$| 2.256  |

continued

| $s$ | $\pi_1^s$ | $\pi_2^s$ | $\pi_3^s$ | $E^s$ |
|---|---|---|---|---|
| 3 | 0 | 0 | 1 | .4 |
| 4 | 0 | 0 | 1 | $-1.$ |
| 5 | $\frac{5}{154}$ | $\frac{69}{154}$ | $\frac{80}{154}$ | 1.724 |
| 6 | 0 | 0 | 1 | $-1.$ |
| 7 | $\frac{5}{137}$ | $\frac{62}{137}$ | $\frac{70}{137}$ | 1.734 |
| 8 | $\frac{12}{135}$ | $\frac{69}{135}$ | $\frac{54}{135}$ | 2.216 |

Policy 2 yields the largest expected yearly revenue. The optimum long-range policy calls for applying fertilizer regardless of the state of the system.

## Problem set 19.3a

1. Solve problem 19.2a-1 for an infinite number of periods using the exhaustive emuneration method.

2. Solve problem 19.2a-2 for an infinite planning horizon using the exhaustive enumeration method.

3. Solve problem 19.2a-3 by the exhaustive enumeration method assuming an infinite horizon.

### 19.3.2 Policy Iteration Method Without Discounting

To appreciate the difficulty associated with the exhaustive enumeration method, let us assume that the gardener had four courses of action (alternatives) instead of two: do not fertilize, fertilize once during the season, fertilize twice, and fertilize three times. In this case, the gardener would have a total of $4^3 = 256$ stationary policies. By increasing the number of alternatives from 2 to 4, the number of stationary policies "soars" exponentially from 8 to 256. Not only is it difficult to enumerate all the policies explicitly, but the amount of computations may also be prohibitively large.

The policy iteration method is based on the following development. For any specific policy, we showed in Section 19.2 that the expected total return at stage $n$ is expressed by the recursive equation

$$f_n(i) = v_i + \sum_{j=1}^{m} p_{ij} f_{n+1}(j), \quad i = 1, 2, \dots, m$$

This recursive equation is the basis for the policy iteration method. However, the present form must be modified slightly to allow us to study the asymptotic behavior of the process. We define $\eta$ as the number of stages *remaining* for consideration. This is in contrast with $n$ in the equation, which defines the $n$th stage. The recursive equation is thus written as

$$f_\eta(i) = v_i + \sum_{j=1}^{m} P_{ij} f_{\eta-1}(j), \quad i = 1, 2, ..., m$$

Note that $f_\eta$ is the cumulative expected revenue given that $\eta$ is the number of stages remaining for consideration. With the new definition, the asymptotic behavior of the process can be studied by letting $\eta \to \infty$.

Given that

$$\pi = (\pi_1, \pi_2, ... \pi_m)$$

is the steady-state probability vector of the transition matrix $P = \|p_{ij}\|$ and

$$E = \pi_1 v_1 + \pi_2 v_2 + \cdots + \pi_m v_m$$

is the expected revenue per stage is computed in Section 19.3.1, it can be shown that for very large $\eta$,

$$f_\eta(i) = \eta E + f(i)$$

where $f(i)$ is a constant term representing the asymptotic intercept of $f_\eta(i)$ given the state $i$.

Because $f_\eta(i)$ is the cumulative optimum return for $\eta$ remaining stages given the state $i$ and $E$ is the expected revenue *per stage*, we can see intuitively why $f_\eta(i)$ equals $\eta E$ plus a correction factor $f(i)$ that accounts for the specific state $l$. This result assumes that $\eta$ is very large.

Now, using this information, the recursive equation is written as

$$\eta E + f(i) = v_i + \sum_{j=1}^{m} p_{ij} \{(\eta - 1)E + f(j)\}, \quad i = 1, 2, ..., m$$

Simplifying this equation, we get

$$E = v_i + \sum_{j=1}^{m} p_{ij} f(j) - f(i), \quad i = 1, 2, ..., m$$

which results in $m$ equations and $m + 1$ unknowns, unknowns being $f(1), f(2), ..., f(m)$, and $E$.

As in section 19.3.1, our objective is to determine the optimum policy that yields the maximum value of $E$. Because there are $m$ equations in $m + 1$ unknowns, the optimum value of $E$ cannot be determined in one step. Instead, an iterative approach is utilized which, starting with an arbitrary policy, will determine a new policy that yields a better value of $E$. The iterative process ends when two successive policies are identical.

The iterative process consists of two steps.

1. *Value determination step.* Choose arbitrary policy $s$. Using its associated matrices $\mathbf{P}^s$ and $\mathbf{R}^s$ and arbitrarily assuming $f^s(m) = 0$, solve the equations

$$E^s = v_i^s + \sum_{j=1}^{m} p_{ij}^s f^s(j) - f^s(i), \quad i = 1, 2, ..., m$$

in the unknowns $E^s, f^s(1), ...,$ and $f^s(m - 1)$. Go to the policy improvement step.

2. *Policy improvement step.* For each state $i$, determine the alternative $k$ that yields

$$\max_{k} \left\{ v_i^k + \sum_{j=1}^{m} p_{ij}^k f^s(j) \right\}, \quad i = 1, 2, ..., m$$

[The values of $f^s(j), j = 1, 2, . . . , m$, are those determined in the value determination step.] The resulting optimum decisions for states $1, 2, . . . , m$ constitute the new policy $t$. If $s$ and $t$ are identical, $t$ is optimum. Otherwise, set $s = t$ and return to the value determination step.

The optimization problem of the policy improvement step needs clarification. Our objective in this step is to obtain $\max \{E\}$. As given,

$$E = v_i + \sum_{j=1}^{m} p_{ij} f(j) - f(i)$$

Because $f(i)$ does not depend on the alternatives $k$, the maximization of $E$ over the alternatives $k$ is equivalent to the maximization problem given in the policy improvement step.

---

**Example 19.3-2.**

We solve the gardener example by the policy iteration method.

Let us start with the arbitrary policy that calls for not applying fertilizer. The associated matrices are

$$\mathbf{P} = \begin{bmatrix} .2 & .5 & .3 \\ 0 & .5 & .5 \\ 0 & 0 & 1 \end{bmatrix}, \quad \mathbf{R} = \begin{bmatrix} 7 & 6 & 3 \\ 0 & 5 & 1 \\ 0 & 0 & -1 \end{bmatrix}$$

The equations of the value iteration step are

$$E + f(1) - .2f(1) - .5f(2) - .3f(3) = 5.3$$
$$E + f(2) \qquad\quad - .5f(2) - .5f(3) = 3$$
$$E + f(3) \qquad\qquad\qquad\quad - f(3) = -1$$

If we arbitrarily let $f(3) = 0$, the equations yield the solution

$$E = -1, f(1) \approx 12.88, f(2) = 8, f(3) = 0$$

Next, we apply the policy improvement step. The associated calculations are shown in the following tableau.

| | | | Optimal solution | |
|---|---|---|---|---|
| | $v_i^k + p_{i1}^k f(1) + p_{i2}^k f(2) + p_{i3}^k f(3)$ | | | |
| $i$ | $k = 1$ | $k = 2$ | $f(i)$ | $k^*$ |
| 1 | $5.3 + .2 \times 12.88 + .5 \times 8$ $+ .3 \times 0 = 11.875$ | $4.7 + .3 \times 12.88 + .6 \times 8$ $+ .1 \times 0 = 13.36$ | 13.36 | 2 |
| 2 | $3 + 0 \times 12.88 + .5 \times 8$ $+ .5 \times 0 = 7$ | $3.1 + .1 \times 12.88 + .6 \times 8$ $+ .3 \times 0 = 9.19$ | 9.19 | 2 |
| 3 | $-1 + 0 \times 12.88 + 0 \times 8$ $+ 1 \times 0 = -1$ | $.4 + .05 \times 12.88 + .4 \times 8$ $+ .55 \times 0 = 4.24$ | 4.24 | 2 |

The new policy calls for applying fertilizer regardless of the state. Because the new policy differs from the preceding one, the value determination step is entered again. The matrices associated with the new policy are

$$\mathbf{P} = \begin{bmatrix} .3 & .6 & .1. \\ .1 & .6 & .3 \\ .05 & .4 & .55 \end{bmatrix}, \quad \mathbf{R} = \begin{bmatrix} 6 & 5 & -1 \\ 7 & 4 & 0 \\ 6 & 3 & -2 \end{bmatrix}$$

These matrices yield the following equations:

$$E + f(1) - .3f(1) - .6f(2) - .1f(3) = 4.7$$
$$E + f(2) - .1f(1) - .6f(2) - .3f(3) = 3.1$$
$$E + f(3) - .05f(1) - .4f(2) - .55f(3) = .4$$

Again, letting $f(3) = 0$, we get the solution

$$E = 2.26, \ f(1) = 6.75, \ f(2) = 3.79, \ f(3) = 0$$

The computations of the policy improvement step are given in the following tableau.

| | | | Optimal solution | |
|---|---|---|---|---|
| | $v_i^k + p_{i1}^k f(1) + p_{i2}^k f(2) + p_{i3}^k f(3)$ | | | |
| $i$ | $k = 1$ | $k = 2$ | $f(i)$ | $k^*$ |
| 1 | $5.3 + .2 \times 6.75 + .5 \times 3.79$ $+ .3 \times 0 = 8.54$ | $4.7 + .3 \times 6.75 + .6 \times 3.79$ $+ .1 \times 0 = 8.99$ | 8.99 | 2 |
| 2 | $3 + 0 \times 6.75 + .5 \times 3.79$ $+ .5 \times 0 = 4.89$ | $3.1 + .1 \times 6.75 + .6 \times 3.79$ $+ .3 \times 0 = 6.05$ | 6.05 | 2 |
| 3 | $-1 + 0 \times 6.75 + 0 \times 3.79$ $+ 1 \times 0 = -1$ | $.4 + .05 \times 6.75 + .4 \times 3.79$ $+ .55 \times 0 = 2.25$ | 2.25 | 2 |

The new policy, which calls for applying fertilizer regardless of the state, is identical with the preceding one. Thus the last policy is optimal and the iterative process ends. This is the same conclusion obtained by the exhaustive enumeration method (Section 19.3.1). Note, however, that the policy iteration method converges quickly to the optimum policy, a typical characteristic of the new method.

---

## Problem set 19.3b

1. Assume in Problem 19.2a-1 that the planning horizon is infinite. Solve the problem by the policy iteration method.
2. Solve problem 19.2a-2 by the policy iteration method, assuming an infinite planning horizon. Compare the results with those of Problem 18-8.
3. Solve Problem 19.2a-3 by the policy iteration method assuming an infinite planning horizon, and compare the results with those of Problem 18-9.

## 19.3.3 Policy Iteration Method with Discounting

The policy iteration algorithm can be extended to include discounting. Given that a $\alpha\ (< 1)$ is the discount factor, the finite-stage recursive equation can be written as (see Section 19.2)

$$f_\eta(i) = \max_k \left\{ v_i^k + \alpha \sum_{j=1}^m p_{ij}^k f_{\eta-1}(j) \right\}$$

(Note that $\eta$ represents the number of stages *to go*.) It can be proved that as $\eta \to \infty$ (infinite stage model), $f_\eta(i) = f(i)$, where $f(i)$ is the expected present-worth (discounted) revenue given that the system is in state $i$ and operating over an infinite horizon. Thus the long-run behavior of $f_\eta(i)$ as $\eta \to \infty$ is independent of the value of $\eta$. This is in contrast with the case of no discounting where $f_\eta(i) = \eta E + f(i)$. This result should be expected since in discounting the effect of future revenues will asymptotically diminish to zero. Indeed, the present worth $f(i)$ should approach a constant value as $\eta \to \infty$.

Given this information, the steps of the policy iterations are modified as follows.

1. *Value determination step*. For and arbitrary policy $s$ with its matrices $\mathbf{P}^s$ and $\mathbf{R}^s$, solve the $m$ equations

$$f^s(i) = v_i^s + \alpha \sum_{j=1}^m p_{ij}^s f^s(j), \quad i = 1, 2, ..., m$$

in the $m$ unknowns $f^s(1), f^s(2), ..., f^s(m)$.

**2.** *Policy improvement step.* For each state $i$, determine the alternative $k$ that yields

$$\max_k \left\{ v_i^k + \alpha \sum_{j=1}^m p_{ij}^k f^s(j) \right\}, \quad i = 1, 2, \ldots, m$$

where $f^s(j)$ are those obtained from the value determination step. If the resulting policy $t$ is the same as $s$, stop; $t$ is optimum. Otherwise, set $s = t$ and return to the value determination step.

---

**Example 19.3-3.**

We will solve Example 19.3-2 using the discounting factor $\alpha = .6$.

Starting with the arbitrary policy, $s = \{1, 1, 1\}$. The associated matrices **P** and **R** (**P**$^1$ and **R**$^1$ in Example 19.3-1) yield the equations

$$f(1) - .6[.2f(1) + .5f(2) + .3f(3)] = \quad 5.3$$

$$f(2) - .6[\qquad\quad .5f(2) + .df(3)] = \quad 3$$

$$f(3) - .6[\qquad\qquad\qquad\qquad f(3)] = -1$$

The solution of these equations yields

$$f_1 \approx 6.6, \ f_2 \approx 3.21, \ f_3 = -2.5$$

A summary of the policy improvement iteration is given in the following tableau:

| | $v_i^k +\ .6\,[\,p_{i1}^k f(1) +\ p_{i2}^k f(2) +\ p_{i3}^k f(3)\,]$ | | Optimal Solution | |
|---|---|---|---|---|
| $i$ | $k = 1$ | $k = 2$ | $f(i)$ | $k^{*}$ |
| 1 | $5.3 + .6[.2 \times 6.6 + .5 \times 3.21$ $+ .3 \times -2.5] = 6.61$ | $4.7 + .6[.3 \times 6.6 + .6 \times 3.21$ $+ .1 \times -2.5] = 6.89$ | 6.89 | 2 |
| 2 | $3 + .6[0 \times 6.6 + .5 \times 3.21$ $+ .5 \times -2.5] = 3.21$ | $3.1 + .6[.1 \times 6.6 + .6 \times 3.21$ $+ .3 \times -2.5] = 4.2$ | 4.2 | 2 |
| 3 | $-1 + .6[0 \times 6.6 + 0 \times 3.21$ $+ 1 \times -2.5] = -2.5$ | $.4 + .6[.05 \times 6.6 + .4 \times 3.21$ $+ .55 \times -2.5] = .54$ | .54 | 2 |

The value determination step using **P**$^2$ and **R**$^2$ (Example 19.3–1) yields the following equations:

$$f(1) - .6[3f(1)\ + .6f(2) + .1f(3)] \quad = 4.7$$

$$f(2) - .6[.1f(1)\ + .6f(2) + .3f(3)] \quad = 3.1$$

$$f(3) - .6[.05f(1) + .4f(2) + .55f(3)] = \quad .4$$

The solution of these equations yields

$$f(1) = 8.88, \ f(2) = 6.62, \ f(3) = 3.37$$

The policy improvement step yields the following tableau:

| | $v_i^k + .6[p_{i1}^k f(1) + p_{i2}^k f(2) + p_{i3}^k f(3)]$ | | Optimal Solution | |
|---|---|---|---|---|
| $i$ | $k = 1$ | $k = 2$ | $f(i)$ | $k^*$ |
| 1 | 5.3 + .6[.2 × 8.88 + .5 × 6.62 + .3 × 3.37] = 8.95 | 4.7 + .6[.3 × 8.88 + .6 × 6.62 + .1 × 3.37] = 8.88 | 8.95 | 1 |
| 2 | 3 + .6[0 × 8.88 + .5 × 6.62 + .5 × 3.37] = 5.99 | 3.1 + .6[.1 × 8.88 + .6 × 6.62 + .3 × 3.37] = 6.62 | 6.62 | 2 |
| 3 | −1 + .6[0 × 8.88 + 0 × 6.62 + 1 × 3.37] = 1.02 | .4 + .6[.05 × 8.88 + .4 × 6.62 + .55 × 3.37] = 3.37 | 3.37 | 2 |

Because the new policy $\{1, 2, 2\}$ differs from the preceding one, the value determination step is entered again using $\mathbf{P}^8$ and $\mathbf{R}^8$ (Example 19.3-1). This results in the following equations:

$$f(1) - .6[.2f(1) + .5f(2) + .3f(3)] = 5.3$$

$$f(2) - .6[.1f(1) + .6f(2) + .3f(3)] = 3.1$$

$$f(3) - .6[.05f(1) + .4f(2) + .55f(3)] = .4$$

The solution of these equations yields

$$f(1) = 8.98, \quad f(2) = 6.63, \quad f(3) = 3.38$$

The policy improvement step yields the following tableau:

| | $v_i^k + .6[p_{i1}^k f(1) + p_{i2}^k f(2) + p_{i3}^k f(3)]$ | | Optimal Solution | |
|---|---|---|---|---|
| $i$ | $k = 1$ | $k = 2$ | $f(i)$ | $k^*$ |
| 1 | 5.3 + .6[.2 × 8.98 + .5 × 6.63 + .3 × 3.38] = 8.98 | 4.7 + .6[.3 × 8.98 + .6 × 6.63 + .1 × 3.38] = 8.91 | 8.98 | 1 |
| 2 | 3 + .6[0 × 8.98 + .5 × 6.63 + .5 × 3.38] = 6.00 | 3.1 + .6[.1 × 8.98 + .6 × 6.63 + .3 × 3.38] = 6.63 | 6.63 | 2 |
| 3 | −1 + .6[0 × 8.98 + 0 × 6.63 + 1 × 3.38] = 1.03 | .4 + .6[.05 × 8.98 + .4 × 6.63 + .55 × 3.38] = 3.37 | 3.37 | 2 |

Because the new policy $\{1, 2, 2\}$ is identical with the preceding one, it is optimal. Note that discounting has resulted in a different optimal policy that calls for not applying fertilizer if the state of the system is good (state 3).

**Problem set 19.3c**

**1.** Repeat the problems listed, assuming the discount factor $\alpha = .9$.

    **(a)** Problem 19.3b-1.

    **(b)** Problem 19.3b-2.

    **(c)** Problem 19.3b-3.

## 19.4 LINEAR PROGRAMMING SOLUTION

The infinite-stage Markovian decision problems, both with discounting and without, can be formulated and solved as linear programs. We consider the no-discounting case first.

    In Section 19.3.1 we showed that the infinite-stage Markovian problem with no discounting ultimately reduces to determining the optimal policy $s^*$, which corresponds to

$$\max_{s \in S}\left\{ \sum_{j=1}^{m} \pi_i^s \, v_i^s \, \Big| \, \pi^s \mathbf{P}^s = \pi^s, \quad \pi_1^s + \pi_2^s + \ldots + \pi_m^s = 1, \quad \pi_i^s \geq 0 \; i = 1, 2, \ldots, m \right\}$$

where $S$ is the collection of all possible policies of the problem. The constraints of the problem ensure that $\pi_i^s$, $i = 1, 2, \ldots, m$, represent the steady-state probabilities of the Markov chain $\mathbf{P}^s$.

    We solved this problem in Section 19.3.1 by exhaustively enumerating all the elements $s$. Specifically, each policy $s$ is specified by a fixed set of actions (as exemplified by the gardener problem in Example 19.3-1).

    The problem is the basis for the development of the LP formulation of the Markovian decision problem. However, we need to modify the unknowns of the problem such that the optimal solution *automatically* determines the optimal action (alternative) $k$ when the system is in state $i$. The collection of all the optimal actions will then define $s^*$, the optimal policy.

    This objective is achieved as follows. Let

$q_i^k = $ Conditional probability of choosing alternative $k$ given that the system is in state $i$

The problem may thus be expressed as

$$\text{Maximize } E = \sum_{i=1}^{m} \pi_i \left( \sum_{k=1}^{k} q_i^k v_i^k \right)$$

subject to

$$\pi_j = \sum_{i=1}^{m} \pi_i \, p_{ij}, \quad j = 1, 2, \ldots, m$$

$$\pi_1 + \pi_2 + \cdots + \pi_m = 1$$

$$q_i^1 + q_i^2 + \cdots + q_i^K = 1, \quad i = 1, 2, \dots, m$$

$$\pi_i \geq 0, \ q_i^k \geq 0, \text{ all } i \text{ and } k$$

Note that $p_{ij}$ is a function of the policy selected and hence of the specific alternatives $k$ of the policy.

We shall see shortly that the problem can be converted into a linear program by making proper substitutions involving $q_i^k$. Observe, however, that the formulation is equivalent to the original one in Section 19.3.1 only if $q_i^k = 1$ for exactly *one* $k$ for each $i$, as this will reduce the sum $\sum_{k=1}^{K} q_i^k v_i^k$ to $v_i^{k*}$, where $k*$ is the optimal alternative chosen. Fortunately, the linear program we develop here does account for this condition automatically.

Define

$$w_{ik} = \pi_i q_i^k, \quad \text{for all } i \text{ and } k$$

By definition $w_{ik}$ represents the *joint* probability of state $i$ making decision $k$. From probability theory

$$\pi_i = \sum_{k=1}^{K} w_{ik}$$

Hence,

$$q_i^k = \frac{w_{ik}}{\sum_{k=1}^{K} w_{ik}}$$

We thus see that the restriction $\sum_{i=1}^{m} \pi_i = 1$ can be written as

$$\sum_{i=1}^{m} \sum_{k=1}^{K} w_{ik} = 1$$

Also, the restriction $\sum_{k=1}^{K} q_i^k = 1$ is automatically implied by the way we defined $q_i^k$ in terms of $w_{ik}$. (Verify!) Thus the problem can be written as

$$\text{Maximize } E = \sum_{i=1}^{m} \sum_{k=1}^{K} v_i^k w_{ik}$$

subject to

$$\sum_{k=1}^{K} w_{jk} - \sum_{i=1}^{m} \sum_{k=1}^{K} p_{ij}^k w_{ik} = 0, \quad j = 1, 2, \dots, m$$

$$\sum_{i=1}^{m} \sum_{k=1}^{K} w_{ik} = 1$$

$$w_{ik} \geq 0, \ i = 1, 2, \dots, m; \ k = 1, 2, \dots, K$$

The resulting model is a linear program in $w_{ik}$. Its optimal solution automatically guarantees that $q_i^k = 1$ for one $k$ for each $i$. First, note that the linear program has $m$ independent equations (one of the equations associated with $\pi = \pi \mathbf{P}$ is redundant). Hence, the problem must have $m$ basic variables. It can be shown that $w_{ik}$ must be strictly positive for at least one $k$ for each $i$. From these two results, we conclude that

$$q_i^k = \frac{w_{ik}}{\sum_{k=1}^{K} w_{ik}}$$

can assume a binary value (0 or 1) only. (As a matter of fact, the preceding result also shows that $\pi_i = \sum_{k=1}^{K} w_{ik} = w_{ik*}$, where $k*$ is the alternative corresponding to $w_{ik} > 0$.)

---

**Example 19.4-1.**

The following is an LP formulation of the gardener problem without discounting:

$$\text{Maximize } E = 5.3w_{11} + 4.7w_{12} + 3w_{21} + 3.1w_{22} - w_{31} + .4w_{32}$$

subject to

$$w_{11} + w_{12} - (.2w_{11} + .3w_{12} \qquad\qquad + .1w_{22} \qquad\qquad + .05w_{32}) = 0$$

$$w_{21} + w_{22} - (.5w_{11} + .6w_{12} + .52w_{21} + .6w_{22} \qquad\qquad + .4w_{32}) = 0$$

$$w_{31} + w_{32} - (.3w_{11} + .1w_{12} + .5w_{21} + .3w_{22} + w_{31} + .55w_{32}) = 0$$

$$w_{11} + W_{12} + w_{21} + w_{22} + w_{31} + w_{32} = 1$$

$$w_{ik} \geq 0, \quad \text{for all } i \text{ and } k$$

The optimal solution is $w_{11} = w_{12} = w_{31} = 0$ and $w_{12} = \frac{6}{59}, w_{22} = \frac{31}{59}$, and $w_{32} = \frac{22}{59}$. This result means that $q_1^2 = q_2^2 = q_3^2 = 1$. Thus, the optimal policy selects alternative 2 ($k = 2$) for $i = 1, 2$, and 3. The optimal value of $E$ is $4.7(\frac{6}{59}) + 3.1(\frac{31}{59}) + .4(\frac{22}{59}) = 2.256$. It is interesting that the positive values of $w_{ik}$ exactly equal the values of $\pi_i$ associated with the optimal policy in the exhaustive enumeration procedure of Example 19.3-1. This observation demonstrates the direct relationship between the two methods.

---

We next consider the Markovian decision problem with discounting. In Section 19.3.2 the problem is expressed by the recursive equation

$$f(i) = \max_k \left\{ v_i^k + \alpha \sum_{j=1}^{m} p_{ij}^k f(j) \right\}, \quad i = 1, 2, ..., m$$

These equations are equivalent to

$$f(i) \geq \alpha \sum_{j=1}^{m} p_{ij}^k f(j) + v_i^k, \quad \text{for all } i \text{ and } k$$

provided that $f(i)$ achieves its minimum value for each $i$. Now consider the objective function

$$\text{Minimize} \sum_{i=1}^{m} b_i \, f(i)$$

where $b_i$ ($> 0$ for all $i$) is an arbitrary constant. It can be shown that the optimization of this function subject to the inequalities given will result in the minimum value of $f(i)$. Thus, the problem can be written as

$$\text{Minimize} \sum_{i=1}^{m} b_i \, f(i)$$

subject to

$$f(i) - \alpha \sum_{i=1}^{m} p_{ij}^k \, f(j) \geq v_i^k, \quad \text{for all } i \text{ and } k$$

$$f(i) \text{ unrestricted} \quad i = 1, 2, \dots, m$$

Now the dual of the problem is

$$\text{Maximize} \sum_{i=1}^{m} \sum_{k=1}^{K} v_i^k \, w_{ik}$$

subject to

$$\sum_{k=1}^{K} w_{jk} - \alpha \sum_{i=1}^{m} \sum_{k=1}^{K} p_{ij}^k \, w_{ik} = b_j, \quad j = 1, 2, \dots, m$$

$$w_{ik} \geq 0, \quad \text{for } i = 1, 2, \dots, m; \ k = 1, 2, \dots, K$$

---

**Example 19.4-2.**

Consider the gardener example with discounting factor $\alpha = .6$. If we let $b_1 = b_2 = b_3 = 1$, the dual LP problem may be written as

$$\text{Maximize } 5.3w_{11} + 4.7w_{12} + 3w_{21} + 3.1w_{22} - w_{31} + .4w_{32}$$

subject to

$$w_{11} + w_{12} - .6[.2w_{11} + .3w_{12} \qquad\qquad + .1w_{22} \qquad\quad + .05w_{32}] = 1$$

$$w_{21} + w_{22} - .6[.5w_{11} + .6w_{12} + .5w_{21} + .6w_{22} \qquad\quad + .4w_{32}] = 1$$

$$w_{31} + w_{32} - .6[.3w_{11} + .1w_{12} + .5w_{21} + .3w_{22} + w_{31} + .55w_{32}] = 1$$

$$w_{ik} \geq 0, \quad \text{for all } i \text{ and } k$$

The optimal solution is $w_{12} = w_{21} = w_{31} = 0$ and $w_{11} = 1.5678$, $w_{22} = 3.3528$, and $w_{32} = 2.8145$. The solution shows that that optimal policy is $(1, 2, 2)$.

---

**Problem set 19.4a**

**1.** Formulate the following problems as linear programs.
   **(a)** Problem 19.3b-1.
   **(b)** Problem 19.3b-2.
   **(c)** Problem 19.3b-3.
**2.** Formulate the problems in Problem 19.3c-1 as linear programs.

## 19.5 SUMMARY

This chapter provides models for the solution of the Markovian decision problem, including the finite-stage models solved by DP. The infinite-stage model, it is shown that exhaustive enumeration is not practical for large problems. The DP based policy iteration algorithm is more efficient computationally. Discounting is shown to result in a possible change of the optimal policy in comparison with the case where no discounting is used. This conclusion applies to both the finite- and infinite-stage models.

The LP formulation is interesting but it is not as efficient computationally as the policy iteration algorithm, particularly for large values of $m$ and $k$.

Markovian decision problem has applications in inventory, maintenance, replacement, and water resources.

## 19.6 APPENDIX: REVIEW OF MARKOV CHAINS

Consider the discrete points in time $\{t_k\}$ for $k = 1, 2, \ldots$, and let $\xi_{t_k}$ be the random variable that characterizes the state of the system at $t_k$. The family of random variables $\{\xi_{t_k}\}$ forms a **stochastic process**. The states at time $t_k$ actually represent the (exhaustive and mutually exclusive) outcomes of the system at that time. The number of states may thus be finite or infinite. For example, the Poisson distribution

$$P_n(t) = \frac{e^{-\lambda t}(\lambda t)^n}{n!}, \qquad n = 0, 1, 2, \ldots$$

represents a stochastic process with an infinite number of states. The random variable $n$ represents the number of occurrences between 0 and $t$ (assuming that the system starts at time 0). The states of the system at any time $t$ are thus given by $n = 0$, $1, 2, \ldots$ .

Another example is the coin-tossing game with $k$ trials. Each trial may be viewed as a point in time. The resulting sequence of trials forms a stochastic process. The state of the system at any trial is either a head or a tail.

This section presents a summary of a class of stochastic systems that includes **Markov processes** and **Markov chains**. A Markov chain is a special case of Markov processes. It is used to study the short- and long-run behavior of certain stochastic systems.

### 19.6.1 Markov Processes

The occurrence of a future state in a Markov process depends on the immediately preceding state and only on it. If $t_0 < t_1 < \ldots t_n$ $(n = 0, 1, 2, \ldots)$ represents points in time, the family of random variables $\{\xi_{tn}\}$ is a Markov process if it possesses the following **Markovian property**:

$$P\{\xi_{t_n} = x_n | \xi_{t_{n-1}} = x_{n-1}, \ldots, \xi_{t_0} = x_0\} = P\{\xi_{t_n} = x_n | \xi_{t_{n-1}} = x_{n-1}\}$$

for all possible values of $\xi_{t0}, \xi_{t1}, \ldots, \xi_{tn}$.

The probability $p_{x_{n-1},x_n} = P\{\xi_{t_n} = x_n | \xi_{t_{n-1}} = x_{n-1}\}$ is called the **transition probability**. It represents the *conditional* probability of the system being in $x_n$ at $t_n$, given it was in $x_{n-1}$ at $t_{n-1}$. This probability is also referred to as the **one-step transition** because it describes the system between $t_{n-1}$ and $t_n$. An $m$-step transition probability is thus defined by

$$p_{x_n, x_{n+m}} = P\{\xi_{t_{n+m}} = x_{n+m} | \xi_{t_n} = x_n\}$$

### 19.6.2 Markov Chains

Let $E_1, E_2, \ldots, E_j$ $(j = 0, 1, 2, \ldots)$ represent the exhaustive and mutually exclusive outcomes (states) of a system at any time. Initially, at time $t_0$, the system may be in any of these states. Let $a_j^{(0)}$ $(j = 0, 1, 2, \ldots)$ be the absolute probability that the system is in state $E_j$ at $t_0$. Assume further that the system is Markovian.

Define

$$p_{ij} = P\{\xi_{t_n} = j | \xi_{t_{n-1}} = i\}$$

as the one-step transition probability of going from state $i$ at $t_{n-1}$ to state $j$ at $t_n$ and assume that these probabilities are stationary over time. The transition probabilities from state $E_i$ to state $E_j$ can be more conveniently arranged in a matrix form as follows:

$$\mathbf{P} = \begin{bmatrix} p_{00} & p_{01} & p_{02} & p_{03} & \cdots \\ p_{10} & p_{11} & p_{12} & p_{13} & \cdots \\ p_{20} & p_{21} & p_{22} & p_{23} & \cdots \\ p_{30} & p_{31} & p_{32} & p_{33} & \cdots \\ \vdots & \vdots & \vdots & \vdots & \end{bmatrix}$$

The matrix $\mathbf{P}$ is called a **homogeneous transition** or stochastic matrix because all the transition probabilities $p_{ij}$ are fixed and independent of time. The probabilities $p_{ij}$ must satisfy the conditions

$$\sum_j p_{ij} = 1, \quad \text{for all } i$$

$$p_{ij} \geq 0, \quad \text{for all } i \text{ and } j$$

The **Markov chain** is now defined. *A transition matrix $\mathbf{P}$ together with the initial probabilities $\{a_j^{(0)}\}$ associated with the states $E_j$ completely define a Markov chain.* One usually thinks of a Markov chain as describing the transitional behavior of a system over equal intervals. Situations exist where the length of the interval depends on the characteristics of the system and hence may not be equal. This case is referred to as **imbedded Markov chains**.

***Absolute and Transition Probabilities.***   Given $\{a_j^{(0)}\}$ and **P** of a Markov chain, the absolute probabilities of the system after a specified number of transitions are determined as follows. Let $\{a_j^{(n)}\}$ be the absolute probabilities of the system after $n$ transitions, that is, at $t_n$. The general expression of $\{a_j^{(n)}\}$ in terms of $\{a_j^{(0)}\}$ and **P** can be found as follows:

$$a_j^{(1)} = a_1^{(0)} p_{1j} + a_2^{(0)} p_{2j} + a_3^{(0)} p_{3j} + \cdots = \sum_i a_i^{(0)} p_{ij}$$

Also,

$$a_j^{(2)} = \sum_i a_i^{(1)} p_{ij} = \sum_i \left( \sum_k a_k^{(0)} p_{ki} \right) p_{ij} = \sum_k a_k^{(0)} \left( \sum_i p_{ki} p_{ij} \right) = \sum_k a_k^{(0)} p_{kj}^{(2)}$$

where $p_{kj}^{(2)} = \Sigma_i p_{ik} p_{ij}$ is the **two-step** or **second-order transition probability**—that is, the probability of going from state $k$ to state $j$ in exactly two transitions.

It can be shown by induction that

$$a_j^{(n)} = \sum_i a_i^{(0)} \left( \sum_k p_{ik}^{(n-1)} p_{kj} \right) = \sum_i a_i^{(0)} p_{ij}^{(n)}$$

where $p_{ij}^{(n)}$ is the $n$-step or $n$-order transition probability given by the recursive formula

$$p_{ij}^{(n)} = \sum_k p_{ik}^{(n-1)} p_{kj}$$

In general, for all i and j,

$$p_{ij}^{(n)} = \sum_k p_{ik}^{(n-m)} p_{kj}^{(m)}, \quad 0 < m < n$$

These equations are known as **Chapman–Kolomogorov** equations.

The elements of a higher transition matrix $\left\| p_{ij}^{(n)} \right\|$ can be obtained directly by matrix multiplication. Thus,

$$\left\| p_{ij}^{(2)} \right\| = \left\| p_{ij} \right\| \left\| p_{ij} \right\| = \mathbf{P}^2$$

$$\left\| p_{ij}^{(3)} \right\| = \left\| p_{ij}^2 \right\| \left\| p_{ij} \right\| = \mathbf{P}^3$$

and, in general,

$$\left\| p_{ij}^{(n)} \right\| = \mathbf{P}^{n-1} \mathbf{P} = \mathbf{P}^n$$

Hence, if the absolute probabilities are defined in vector form as

$$\mathbf{a}^{(n)} = \{ a_1^{(n)}, a_2^{(n)}, a_3^{(n)}, \ldots \}$$

then

$$\mathbf{a}^{(n)} = \mathbf{a}^{(0)} \mathbf{P}^n$$

**Example 19.6-1.**

     Consider the following Markov chain with two states,

$$\mathbf{P} = \begin{bmatrix} .2 & .8 \\ .6 & .4 \end{bmatrix}$$

with $\mathbf{a}^{(0)} = (.7 \ .3)$. Determine $\mathbf{a}^{(1)}, \mathbf{a}^{(4)},$ and $\mathbf{a}^{(8)}$.

$$\mathbf{P}^2 = \begin{bmatrix} .2 & .8 \\ .6 & .4 \end{bmatrix}\begin{bmatrix} .2 & .8 \\ .6 & .4 \end{bmatrix} = \begin{bmatrix} .52 & .48 \\ .36 & .64 \end{bmatrix}$$

$$\mathbf{P}^4 = \mathbf{P}^2\mathbf{P}^2 = \begin{bmatrix} .52 & .48 \\ .36 & .64 \end{bmatrix}\begin{bmatrix} .52 & .48 \\ .36 & .64 \end{bmatrix} \approx \begin{bmatrix} .443 & .557 \\ .417 & .583 \end{bmatrix}$$

$$\mathbf{P}^8 = \mathbf{P}^4\mathbf{P}^4 = \begin{bmatrix} .443 & .557 \\ .417 & .583 \end{bmatrix}\begin{bmatrix} .443 & .557 \\ .417 & .583 \end{bmatrix} \approx \begin{bmatrix} .4281 & .5719 \\ .4274 & .5726 \end{bmatrix}$$

Thus,

$$\mathbf{a}^{(1)} = (.7 \ .3)\begin{bmatrix} .2 & .8 \\ .6 & .4 \end{bmatrix} = (.32 \ .68)$$

$$\mathbf{a}^{(4)} = (.7 \ .3)\begin{bmatrix} .443 & .557 \\ .417 & .583 \end{bmatrix} = (.435 \ .565)$$

$$\mathbf{a}^{(8)} = (.7 \ .3)\begin{bmatrix} .4281 & .5719 \\ .4274 & .5726 \end{bmatrix} = (.4279 \ .5721)$$

     The rows of $\mathbf{P}^8$ tend to be identical. Also, $\mathbf{a}^{(8)}$ tends to be identical with the rows of $\mathbf{P}^{(8)}$. This is the result of the long-run properties of Markov chains, which implies that the long-run absolute probabilities are independent of $\mathbf{a}^{(0)}$. In this case the resulting probabilities are known as the **steady-state probabilities**.

     ***Classification of States in Markov Chains.***    In Markov chains, we may be interested in the behavior of the system over a short period of time. In this case the absolute probabilities are computed as shown in the preceding section. A more important study involves the long-run behavior of the system as the number of transitions tends to infinity. In such a case we need a systematic procedure that will predict the long-run behavior of the system. This section defines the states in Markov chains. These definitions will be useful in studying the long-run behavior of the system.

     ***Irreducible Markov Chain.***    A Markov chain is said to be **irreducible** if every state $E_j$ can be reached from every other state $E_j$ after a finite number of transitions that—is, for $i \neq j$,

$$P_{ij}^{(n)} > 0, \quad \text{for } 1 \leq n < \infty$$

In this case all the states of the chain **communicate**.

*Closed Set and Absorbing States.*    In a Markov chain, a set $C$ of states is said to be closed if the system, once in one of the states of $C$, will remain in $C$ indefinitely. A special example of a closed set is a single state $E_j$ with transition probability $p_{jj} = 1$. In this case, $E_j$ is called an **absorbing state**. All the states of an irreducible chain must from a closed set and no subset can be closed. The closed set $C$ must also satisfy all the conditions of a Markov chain and hence may be studied independently.

---

**Example 19.6-2.**

Consider the following Markov chain:

$$P = \begin{array}{c} \\ 0 \\ 1 \\ 2 \\ 3 \end{array} \begin{array}{cccc} 0 & 1 & 2 & 3 \end{array} \\ \left[ \begin{array}{cccc} \frac{1}{2} & \frac{1}{4} & \frac{1}{4} & 0 \\ 0 & 0 & 1 & 0 \\ \frac{1}{3} & 0 & \frac{1}{3} & \frac{1}{3} \\ 0 & 0 & 0 & 1 \end{array} \right]$$

This chain is illustrated graphically in Figure 19-1. The figure shows that the four states do *not* constitute an irreducible chain, because state 0, 1, and 2 cannot be reached from state 3. State 3, by itself, forms a closed set and hence it is absorbing. One can also say that state 3 forms an irreducible chain.

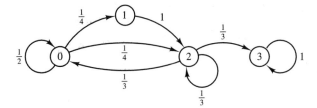

**Figure 19–1**

---

*First Return Times.*    An important definition in Markov chains theory is the **first return time**. Given that the system is initially in state $E_j$, it may return to $E_j$ *for the first time* at the $n$th step, $n \geq 1$. The number of steps before the system returns to $E_j$ is called the first return time.

Let $f_{jj}^{(n)}$ denote the probability that the first return to $E_j$ occurs at the $n$th step. Then given the transition matrix

$$P = \|p_{ij}\|$$

an expression for $f_{jj}^{(n)}$ can be determined as follows:

$$p_{jj} = f_{jj}^{(1)}$$

$$p_{jj}^{(2)} = f_{jj}^{(2)} + f_{jj}^{(1)}p_{jj}$$

or

$$f_{jj}^{(2)} = p_{jj}^{(2)} - f_{jj}^{(1)}p_{jj}$$

By induction

$$p_{jj}^{(n)} = f_{jj}^{(n)} + \sum_{m=1}^{n-1} f_{jj}^{(m)} p_{jj}^{(n-m)}$$

which yields the required expression as

$$f_{jj}^{(n)} = p_{jj}^{(n)} - \sum_{m=1}^{n-1} f_{jj}^{(m)} p_{jj}^{(n-m)}$$

The probability of *at least* one return to state $E_j$ is then given by

$$f_{jj} = \sum_{n=1}^{\infty} f_{jj}^{(n)}$$

Thus, the system is certain to return to $j$ if $f_{jj} = 1$. In this case, if $\mu_{jj}$ defines the mean return (recurrence) time,

$$\mu_{jj} = \sum_{n=1}^{\infty} n f_{jj}^{(n)}$$

If $f_{jj} < 1$, it is not certain that the system will return to $Ej$ and, consequently, $\mu_{jj} = \infty$.

The states of a Markov chain can be classified based on the definition of the first return times as follows:

1. A state is **transient** if $f_{jj} < 1$; that is $\mu_{jj} = \infty$.
2. A state is **recurrent** (persistent) if $f_{jj} = 1$.
3. A recurrent state is **null** if $\mu_{jj} = \infty$ and **nonnull** if $\mu_{jj} < \infty$ (finite).
4. A state is **periodic** with period $t$ if a return is possible only in $t$, $2t$, $3t$, ... steps. This means that $p_{jj}^{(n)}$ whenever $n$ is not divisible by $t$.
5. A recurrent state is **ergodic** if it is nonnull and aperiodic (not periodic).

*Ergodic Markov Chains.*    If all its states of a Markov chain are ergodic, then the chain is *irreducible*. In this case, the absolute probabilities

$$\mathbf{a}^{(n)} = \mathbf{a}^{(0)}\mathbf{P}^n$$

always converges uniquely to a limiting distribution as $n \to \infty$, where the limiting distribution is independent of the initial probabilities $\mathbf{a}^{(0)}$.

The following theorem is now in order:

**Theorem 19.6-1.**   *All the states in an irreducible infinite Markov chain may belong to one, and only one, of the following three classes: transient state, recurrent null state, of recurrent nonnull state. In every case all the states communicate and they have the same period. For the special case where the chain has a finite number of states, the chain cannot consist of transient states only nor can it contain any null states.*

***Limiting Distribution of Irreducible Chains.***   Example 19.6-1 shows that as the number of transitions increases, the absolute probability becomes independent of the initial distribution. This was referred to as the long-run property of Markov chains. In this section determination of the limiting (long-run) distribution of an irreducible chain is presented. The discussion will be restricted to the aperiodic type, because this is the only type needed in this text. In addition, the analysis of the periodic case is rather involved.

The existence of a limiting distribution in an irreducible aperiodic chain depends on the class of its states. Thus, considering the three classes given in Theorem 19.6-1, the following theorem can be stated:

**Theorem 19.6-2.**   *In an irreducible aperiodic Markov chain,*
  **(a)** *If the states are all transient or all null, then $p_{ij}^{(n)} \to 0$ as $n \to \infty$ for all i and j and no limiting distribution exists.*
  **(b)** *If all the states are ergodic, then*

$$\lim_{n \to \infty} a_j^{(n)} = \beta_j, \quad j = 0, 1, 2, \dots$$

*where $\beta_j$ is the limiting (steady-state) distribution. The probabilities $\beta_j$ exist uniquely and are independent of $a_j^{(0)}$. In this case, $\beta_j$ can be determined from the set of equations*[†]

$$\beta_j = \sum_i \beta_i p_{ij}$$

$$1 = \sum_j \beta_j$$

*The mean recurrence time for state j is then given by*

$$\mu_{jj} = \frac{1}{\beta_j}$$

---

**Example 19.6-3.**

Consider Example 19.6-1. To determine its steady-state probability distribution, one has

[†]One of the equations $\beta_j = \sum_i \beta_i p_{ij}$ is redundant.

$$\beta_1 = .2\beta_1 + .6\beta_2$$

$$\beta_2 = .8\beta_1 + .4\beta_2$$

$$1 = \beta_1 + \beta_2$$

The solution yields $\beta_1 = 0.4286$ and $\beta_2 = 0.5714$. These results are very close to the values of $\mathbf{a}^{(8)}$ (and the rows of $\mathbf{P}^8$) in example 19.6-1. Next we have

$$\mu_{11} = \frac{1}{\beta_1} = 2.3$$

$$\mu_{22} = \frac{1}{\beta_2} = 1.75$$

so that the mean recurrent time for the first and second states are 2.3 and 1.75 steps, respectively.

---

**Example 19.6-4.**

Consider the following Markov chain with three states:

$$
\mathbf{P} = \begin{array}{c} \\ 0 \\ 1 \\ 2 \end{array}
\begin{array}{ccc} 0 & 1 & 2 \end{array}
\left[ \begin{array}{ccc}
\frac{1}{2} & \frac{1}{4} & \frac{1}{4} \\
\frac{1}{2} & \frac{1}{4} & \frac{1}{4} \\
0 & \frac{1}{2} & \frac{1}{2}
\end{array} \right]
$$

This is called a **doubly stochastic matrix,** since

$$\sum_{i=1}^{s} p_{ij} = \sum_{j=1}^{s} p_{ij} = 1$$

where $s$ is the number of states. In such cases, the steady-state probabilities are $\beta_j = \frac{1}{s}$ for all $j$. Thus, for the matrix given,

$$\beta_0 = \beta_1 = \beta_2 = \frac{1}{3}$$

---

**Problem set 19.6a**

**1.** Classify the following Markov chains and find their stationary distributions.

$$
\textbf{(a)} \quad \left[ \begin{array}{ccc}
\frac{1}{4} & \frac{1}{4} & \frac{1}{2} \\
\frac{1}{4} & \frac{3}{4} & 0 \\
\frac{1}{2} & 0 & \frac{1}{2}
\end{array} \right]
$$

**(b)** $\begin{bmatrix} q & p & 0 & 0 & 0 \\ q & 0 & p & 0 & 0 \\ q & 0 & 0 & p & 0 \\ q & 0 & 0 & 0 & p \\ l & 0 & 0 & 0 & 0 \end{bmatrix}$,     $p + q = 1$

**2.** Find the mean recurrence time for each state of the following Markov chain:

$$\begin{bmatrix} \dfrac{1}{3} & \dfrac{1}{3} & \dfrac{1}{3} \\[2mm] \dfrac{1}{2} & \dfrac{1}{4} & \dfrac{1}{4} \\[2mm] \dfrac{1}{5} & \dfrac{3}{5} & \dfrac{1}{5} \end{bmatrix}$$

## SELECTED REFERENCES

DERMAN, C., *Finite State Markovian Decision Processes,* Academic Press, New York, 1970.

HOWARD, R., *Dynamic Programming and Markov Processes,* MIT Press, Cambridge, Mass., 1960.

# NONLINEAR MODELS

# Chapter 20

# Classical Optimization Theory

## 20.1 INTRODUCTION

Classical optimization theory uses differential calculus to determine points of maxima and minima (extrema) for unconstrained and constrained functions. The methods may not be suitable for efficient numerical computations. However, the underlying theory provides the basis for devising most nonlinear programming algorithms. (see Chapter 21).

This chapter develops necessary and sufficient conditions for determining unconstrained extrema, the *Jacobian* and *Lagrangean* methods for problems with equality constraints, and the *Kuhn-Tucker* conditions for problems with inequality constraints.

## 20.2 UNCONSTRAINED PROBLEMS

An extreme point of a function $f(\mathbf{X})$ defines either a maximum or a minimum of the function. Mathematically, a point $\mathbf{X}_0 = (x_1, \ldots, x_j, \ldots, x_n)$ is a maximum if

$$f(\mathbf{X}_0 + \mathbf{h}) \leq f(\mathbf{X}_0)$$

for all $\mathbf{h} = (h_1, \ldots, h_j, \ldots, h_n)$ such that $|h_j|$ is sufficiently small for all $j$. In other words, $\mathbf{X}_0$ is a maximum if the value of $f$ at every point in the neighborhood of $\mathbf{X}_0$ does not exceed $f(\mathbf{X}_0)$. In a similar manner, $\mathbf{X}_0$ is a minimum if for $\mathbf{h}$ as defined

$$f(\mathbf{X}_0 + \mathbf{h}) \geq f(\mathbf{X}_0)$$

Figure 20–1 illustrates the maxima and minima of a single-variable function $f(x)$ over the interval $[a, b]$. The points $x_1, x_2, x_3, x_4$, and $x_6$ are all extrema of $f(x)$. These include $x_1, x_3$, and $x_6$ as maxima and $x_2$ and $x_4$ as minima. Because

$$f(x_6) = \max\{f(x_1), f(x_3), f(x_6)\}$$

$f(x_6)$ is called **global** or **absolute** maximum, and $f(x_1)$ and $f(x_3)$ are **local** or **relative** maxima. Similarly, $f(x_4)$ is a local minimum and $f(x_2)$ is a global minimum.

Although $x_1$ (in Figure 20–1) is a maximum point, it differs from remaining local maxima in that the value of $f$ corresponding to at least one point in the neighborhood of $x_1$ is equal to $f(x_1)$. In this respect, $x_1$ is called a **weak maximum** compared with $x_3$, for example, where $f(x_3)$ defines a **strong maximum**. A weak maximum thus implies (an infinite number of) alternative maxima. Similar results may be developed for the weak minimum at $x_4$. In general, $\mathbf{X}_0$ is a weak maximum if $f(\mathbf{X}_0 + \mathbf{h}) \le f(\mathbf{X}_0)$ and a strong maximum if $f(\mathbf{X}_0 + \mathbf{h}) < f(\mathbf{X}_0)$, where $\mathbf{h}$ is as defined earlier.

In Figure 20–1, the first derivative (slope) of $f$ vanishes at all extrema. However, this property is also satisfied at **inflection** and **saddle** points, such as $x_5$. If a point with zero slope (gradient) is not an extremum (maximum or minimum), then it must automatically be an inflection or a saddle point.

### 20.2.1 Necessary and Sufficient Conditions

This section develops the necessary and sufficient conditions for an $n$-variable function $f(\mathbf{X})$ to have extrema. It is assumed that the first and second partial derivatives of $f(\mathbf{X})$ are continuous at every $\mathbf{X}$.

**Theorem 20.2-1.**   *A necessary condition for $\mathbf{X}_0$ to be an extreme point of $f(\mathbf{X})$* is *that*

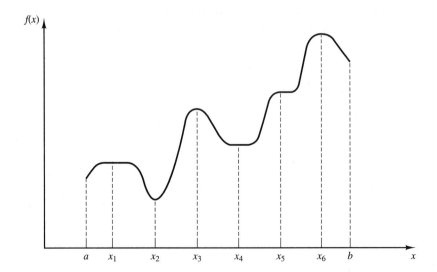

**Figure 20–1**

$$\nabla f(\mathbf{X}_0) = \mathbf{0}$$

*Proof.*    By Taylor's theorem, for $0 < \theta < 1$,

$$f(\mathbf{X}_0 + \mathbf{h}) - f(\mathbf{X}_0) = \nabla f(\mathbf{X}_0)\mathbf{h} + \left(\frac{1}{2}\right)\mathbf{h}^T\mathbf{H}\mathbf{h}\bigg|_{\mathbf{X}_0 + \theta\mathbf{h}}$$

where $\mathbf{h}$ is as defined earlier.

For sufficiently small $|h_j|$, the remainder term $(\frac{1}{2})\mathbf{h}^T\mathbf{H}\mathbf{h}$ is of the order $h_j^2$ hence

$$f(\mathbf{X}_0 + \mathbf{h}) - f(\mathbf{X}_0) = \nabla f(\mathbf{X}_0)\mathbf{h} + 0(h_j^2) \approx \nabla f(\mathbf{X}_0)\mathbf{h}$$

It is shown by contradiction that $\nabla f(\mathbf{X}_0)$ must vanish at a minimum point $\mathbf{X}_0$. Suppose it does not; then for a specific $j$,

$$\frac{\partial f(\mathbf{X}_0)}{\partial x_j} < 0 \quad \text{or} \quad \frac{\partial f(\mathbf{X}_0)}{\partial x_j} > 0$$

must hold. By selecting $h_j$ with appropriate sign, it is always possible to have

$$h_j \frac{\partial f(\mathbf{X}_0)}{\partial x_j} < 0$$

By setting all other $h_j$ equal to zero, Taylor's expansion yields

$$f(\mathbf{X}_0) + \mathbf{h}) < f(\mathbf{X}_0)$$

This result contradicts the assumption that $\mathbf{X}_0$ is a minimum point. Consequently, $\nabla f(\mathbf{X}_0)$ must vanish. A similar proof can be established for the maximization case.

Because the necessary condition is also satisfied for inflection and saddle points, it is more appropriate to refer to the points obtained from the solution of

$$\nabla f(\mathbf{X}_0) = \mathbf{0}$$

as **stationary** points. The next theorem establishes the sufficiency conditions for $\mathbf{X}_0$ to be an extreme point.

**Theorem 20.2-2.**    *A sufficient condition for a stationary point $\mathbf{X}_0$ to be an extremum is for the Hessian matrix $\mathbf{H}$ evaluated at $\mathbf{X}_0$ to be*

**(i)**  *Positive definite when $\mathbf{X}_0$ is a minimum point.*

**(ii)**  *Negative definite when $\mathbf{X}_0$ is a maximum point.*

*Proof.*  By Taylor's theorem, for $0 < \theta < 1$,

$$f(\mathbf{X}_0 + \mathbf{h}) - f(\mathbf{X}_0) = \nabla f(\mathbf{X}_0)\mathbf{h} + \left(\frac{1}{2}\right)\mathbf{h}^T\mathbf{H}\mathbf{h}\bigg|_{\mathbf{X}_0 + \theta\mathbf{h}}$$

Because $\mathbf{X}_0$ is a stationary point, by Theorem 20.2-1, $\nabla f(\mathbf{X}_0) = \mathbf{0}$. Thus,

$$f(\mathbf{X}_0 + \mathbf{h}) - f(\mathbf{X}_0) = \left(\frac{1}{2}\right)\mathbf{h}^T\mathbf{H}\mathbf{h}\bigg|_{\mathbf{X}_0 + \theta\mathbf{h}}$$

If $\mathbf{X}_0$ is a minimum point, then

$$f(\mathbf{X}_0 + \mathbf{h}) > f(\mathbf{X}_0)$$

for all nonnull $h$. Thus, for $\mathbf{X}_0$ to be a minimum point, it must be true that

$$\left(\frac{1}{2}\right)\mathbf{h}^T\mathbf{H}\mathbf{h}\bigg|_{\mathbf{X}_0 + \theta\mathbf{h}} > 0$$

The continuity of the second partial derivative guarantees that the expression $(\frac{1}{2})\mathbf{h}^T\mathbf{H}\mathbf{h}$ has the same sign at both $\mathbf{X}_0$ and $\mathbf{X}_0 + \theta\mathbf{h}$. Because $\mathbf{h}^T\mathbf{H}\mathbf{h}|_{\mathbf{X}_0}$ defines a quadratic form (see Section A.3), this expression (and hence $\mathbf{h}^T\mathbf{H}\mathbf{h}|_{\mathbf{X}_0 + \theta\mathbf{h}}$) is positive if and only if $\mathbf{H}|_{\mathbf{X}_0}$ is positive-definite. This means that a sufficient condition for the stationary point $\mathbf{X}_0$ to be a minimum is that the Hessian matrix evaluated at the same point is positive-definite. A similar proof for the maximization case shows that the corresponding Hessian matrix must be negative-definite.

---

**Example 20.2-1.**

Consider the function

$$f(x_1, x_2, x_3) = x_1 + 2x_3 + x_2 x_3 - x_1^2 - x_2^2 - x_3^2$$

The necessary condition

$$\nabla f(\mathbf{X}_0) = \mathbf{0}$$

gives

$$\frac{\partial f}{\partial x_1} = 1 - 2x_1 = 0$$

$$\frac{\partial f}{\partial x_2} = x_3 - 2x_2 = 0$$

$$\frac{\partial f}{\partial x_3} = 2 + x_2 - 2x_3 = 0$$

The solution of these simultaneous equations is given by

$$\mathbf{X}_0 = \left(\frac{1}{2}, \frac{2}{3}, \frac{4}{3}\right)$$

To establish sufficiency, consider

$$\mathbf{H}\bigg|_{\mathbf{X}_0} = \begin{bmatrix} \dfrac{\partial^2 f}{\partial x_1^2} & \dfrac{\partial^2 f}{\partial x_1\,\partial x_2} & \dfrac{\partial^2 f}{\partial x_1\,\partial x_3} \\[2mm] \dfrac{\partial^2 f}{\partial x_2\,\partial x_1} & \dfrac{\partial^2 f}{\partial x_2^2} & \dfrac{\partial^2 f}{\partial x_2\,\partial x_3} \\[2mm] \dfrac{\partial^2 f}{\partial x_3\,\partial x_1} & \dfrac{\partial^2 f}{\partial x_3\,\partial x_3} & \dfrac{\partial^2 f}{\partial x_3^2} \end{bmatrix}_{\mathbf{X}_0} = \begin{bmatrix} -2 & 0 & 0 \\ 0 & -2 & 1 \\ 0 & 1 & -2 \end{bmatrix}$$

The principal minor determinants of $\mathbf{H}\big|_{\mathbf{X}_0}$ have the values $-2, 4$, and $-6$, respectively. Thus, as shown in Section A.3, $\mathbf{H}\big|_{\mathbf{X}_0}$ is negative-definite and $\mathbf{X}_0 = (\frac{1}{2}, \frac{2}{3}, \frac{4}{3})$ represents a maximum point.

In general, if $\mathbf{H}\big|_{\mathbf{X}_0}$ is indefinite, $\mathbf{X}_0$ must be a saddle point. For the case where it is nonconclusive, $\mathbf{X}_0$ may or may not be an extremum and the development of a sufficiency condition becomes rather involved because higher-order terms in Taylor's expansion must be considered. (See Theorem 20.2-3 for an illustration of this pint to single-variable functions.) In some cases such complex procedures may not be necessary since the diagonalization of $\mathbf{H}$ may lead to more conclusive information. The following example illustrates this point.

**Example 20.2-2.**

Consider the function

$$f(x_1, x_2) = 8x_1x_2 + 3x_2^2$$

Thus,

$$\nabla f(x_1, x_2) = (8x_2, 8x_1 + 6x_2) = (0, 0)$$

This gives the stationary point $\mathbf{X}_0 = (0, 0)$. The Hessian matrix at $\mathbf{X}_0$ is

$$\mathbf{H} = \begin{bmatrix} 0 & 8 \\ 8 & 6 \end{bmatrix}$$

which is nonconclusive. By using one of the diagonalization methods, the transformed Hessian matrix becomes

$$\mathbf{H}_t = \begin{bmatrix} -\dfrac{64}{6} & 0 \\ 0 & 6 \end{bmatrix}$$

The principal minor determinants test shows that $\mathbf{H}_t$ (and hence $\mathbf{H}$) is indefinite. Thus $\mathbf{X}_0$ is a saddle point.

The sufficiency condition established by Theorem 20.2-2 applies to single-variable functions. Given $y_0$ is a stationary point, then

**(i)** $f''(y_0) < 0$ is a sufficient condition for $y_0$ to be maximum.

**(ii)** $f''(y_0) > 0$ is a sufficient condition for $y_0$ to be minimum.

If in the single-variable case $f''(y_0)$ vanishes, higher-order derivatives must be investigated as the following theorem requires.

**Theorem 20.2-3.**    *If at a stationary point $y_0$ of $f(y)$, the first $(n-1)$ derivatives vanish and $f^{(n)}(y) \neq 0$, then at $y = y_0, f(y)$ has*

(i) *An inflection point if n is odd.*

(ii) *An extreme point if n is even. This extreme point will be a maximum if* $f^{(n)}_{(y_0)} < 0$ *and a minimum if* $f^{(n)}_{(y_0)} > 0$.

---

**Example 20.2-3.**

Consider the two functions

$$f(y) = y^4 \quad \text{and} \quad g(y) = y^3$$

For $f(y) = y^4$

$$f'(y) = 4y^3 = 0$$

which yields the stationary point $y_0 = 0$. Now

$$f'(0) = f''(0) = f^{(3)}(0) = 0$$

But $f^{(4)}(0) = 24 > 0$; hence, $y_0 = 0$ is a minimum point (see Figure 20-2).
For $g(y) = y^3$,

$$g'(y) = 3y^2 = 0$$

This yields $y_0 = 0$ as a stationary point. Because $g^{(n)}(0)$ is not zero at $n = 3$, $y_0 = 0$ is an inflection point.

---

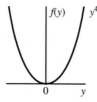

**Figure 20–2**

## Problem set 20.2a

1. Examine the following functions for extreme points.
   (a) $f(x) = x^3 + x$
   (b) $f(x) = x^4 + x^2$
   (c) $f(x) = 4x^4 - x^2 + 5$
   (d) $f(x) = (3x - 2)^2 (2x - 3)^2$
   (e) $f(x) = 6x^5 - 4x^3 + 10$

2. Examine the following functions for extreme points.
   (a) $f(\mathbf{X}) = x_1^3 + x_2^3 - 3x_1 x_2$
   (b) $f(\mathbf{X}) = 2x_1^2 + x_2^2 + x_3^2 + 6(x_1 + x_2 + x_3) + 2x_1 x_2 x_3$

3. Verify that the function

$$f(x_1, x_2, x_3) = 2x_1x_2x_3 - 4x_1x_3 - 2x_2x_3 + x_1^2 + x_2^2 + x_3^2 - 2x_1 - 4x_2 + 4x_3$$

has the stationary points $(0, 3, 1), (0, 1, -1), (1, 2, 0), (2, 1, 1),$ and $(2, 3, -1).$ Use the sufficiency condition to find the extreme points.

4. Solve the following simultaneous equations by converting the system to a nonlinear objective function with no constraints.

$$x_2 - x_1^2 = 0$$
$$x_2 - x_1 = 2$$

(*Hint:* min $f^2(x_1, x_2)$ occurs at $f(x_1, x_2) = 0$.)

5. Prove Theorem 20.2-3.

### 20.2.2 The Newton-Raphson Method

The necessary condition $\nabla f(\mathbf{X}) = \mathbf{0}$ generally may be difficult to solve numerically. The Newton-Raphson method is an iterative procedure for solving simultaneous nonlinear equations. Although the method is presented here in this context, it is actually part of the **gradient methods** for optimizing unconstrained functions numerically (see Section 21.1.2)

Consider the simultaneous equations

$$f_i(\mathbf{X}) = 0, \quad i = 1, 2, ..., m$$

Let $\mathbf{X}^k$ be a given point. Then by Taylor's expansion

$$f_i(\mathbf{X}) \approx f_i(\mathbf{X}^k) + \nabla f_i(\mathbf{X}^k)(\mathbf{X} - \mathbf{X}^k), \quad i = 1, 2, ..., m$$

Thus the original equations may be approximated by

$$f_i(\mathbf{X}^k) + \nabla f_i(\mathbf{X}^k)(\mathbf{X} - \mathbf{X}^k) = 0, \quad i = 1, 2, ..., m$$

These equations may be written in matrix notation as

$$\mathbf{A}_k + \mathbf{B}_k(\mathbf{X} - \mathbf{X}^k) = \mathbf{0}$$

Under the assumption that all $f_i(\mathbf{X})$ are independent, $\mathbf{B}_k$ is nonsingular. Thus

$$\mathbf{X} = \mathbf{X}^k - \mathbf{B}_k^{-1}\mathbf{A}_k$$

The idea of the method is to start from an initial point $\mathbf{X}^0$. By using the foregoing equation, a new pint $\mathbf{X}^{k+1}$ can always be determined from $\mathbf{X}^k$. The procedure is terminated with $\mathbf{X}^m$ as the solution when $\mathbf{X}^m \approx \mathbf{X}^{m-1}$.

A geometric interpretation of the method is illustrated by a single-variable function in Figure 20-3. The relationship between $x^k$ and $x^{k+1}$ for a single-variable function $f(x)$ reduces to

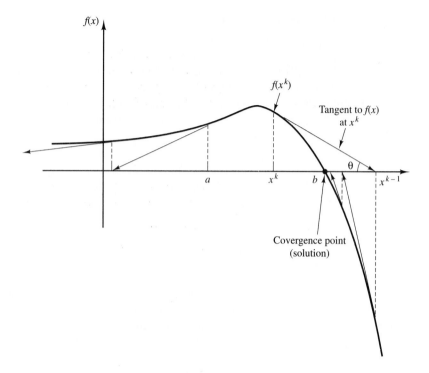

**Figure 20–3**

$$x^{k+1} = x^k - \frac{f(x^k)}{f'(x^k)}$$

or

$$f'(x^k) = \frac{f(x^k)}{x^k - x^{k+1}}$$

Figure 20-3 shows that $x^{k+1}$ is determined from the slope of $f(x)$ at $x^k$, where $\tan\theta = f'(x^k)$.

One difficulty with the method is that convergence is not always guaranteed unless the function $f$ is well behaved. In Figure 20-3, if the initial point is $a$, the method will diverge. There is no easy way for locating a "good" initial point.

### Problem set 20.2b

**1.** Apply the Newton-Raphson method to Problems 20.2a-1(c) and 20.2a-2(b).

## 20.3 CONSTRAINED PROBLEMS

This section deals with the optimization of constrained continuous functions. Section 20.3.1 introduces the case with equality constraints and Section 20.3.2 introduces the other case with inequality constraints. The presentation in Section 20.3.1 is covered for the most part in Beightler et al. (1979, pp. 45-55).

### 20.3.1 Equality Constraints

This section presents two methods: The **Jacobian** and the **Lagrangean**. The **Lagrangean** procedure can be developed logically from the Jacobian method. This relationship provides an interesting economic interpretation of the Lagrangean method.

*Constrained Derivatives (Jacobian) Method.* Consider the problem

$$\text{Minimize } z = f(\mathbf{X})$$

subject to

$$\mathbf{g}(\mathbf{X}) = \mathbf{0}$$

where

$$\mathbf{X} = (x_1, x_2, ..., x_n)$$
$$\mathbf{g} = (g_1, g_2, ..., g_m)^T$$

The functions $f(\mathbf{X})$ and $g_i(\mathbf{X})$, $i = 1, 2, ..., m$, are assumed to be twice continuously differentiable.

The idea of using constrained derivatives is to find a closed-form expression for the first partial derivatives of $f(\mathbf{X})$ at all points that satisfy the constraints $\mathbf{g}(\mathbf{X}) = \mathbf{0}$. The corresponding stationary points are identified as the points at which these partial derivatives vanish. The sufficiency conditions introduced in Section 20.2 can then be used to check the identity of stationary points.

To clarify this concept, consider $f(x_1, x_2)$ illustrated in Figure 20–4. This function is to be minimized subject to the constraint

$$g_1(x_1, x_2) = x_2 - b = 0$$

where $b$ is a constant. From Figure 20–4, the curve designated by the three points $A$, $B$, and $C$ represents the values of $f(x_1, x_2)$ for which the given constraint is always satisfied. The constrained derivatives method defines the gradient of $f(x_1, x_2)$ at any point on the curve $ABC$. Point $B$ at which the constrained derivative vanishes is a stationary point for the constrained problem.

The method is now developed mathematically. By Taylor's theorem, for the points $\mathbf{X} + \Delta\mathbf{X}$ in the feasible neighborhood of $\mathbf{X}$, we have

$$f(\mathbf{X} + \Delta\mathbf{X}) - f(\mathbf{X}) = \nabla f(\mathbf{X})\Delta\mathbf{X} + O(\Delta x_j^2)$$

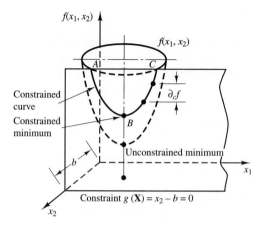

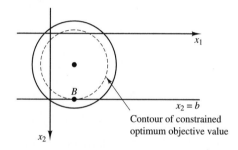

**Figure 20–4**

and

$$g(X + \Delta X) - g(X) = \nabla g(X)\Delta X + O(\Delta x_j^2)$$

As $\Delta x_j \to 0$, the equations reduce to

$$\partial f(X) = \nabla f(X)\partial X$$

and

$$\partial g(X) = \nabla g(X)\partial X$$

Because $g(X) = 0$, $\partial g(X) = 0$ for feasibility, and it follows that

$$\partial f(X) - \nabla f(X)\partial X = 0$$

$$\nabla g(X)\partial X = 0$$

This reduces to $(m + 1)$ equations in $(n + 1)$ unknowns, the unknowns being given by $\partial f(X)$ and $\partial(X)$. The unknown $\partial f(X)$ is determined as soon as $\partial(X)$ is known. This means that we have $m$ equations in $n$ unknowns.

If $m > n$, at least $(m - n)$ equations are redundant. After eliminating this redundancy, the system effectively has $m \leq n$. For the case where $m = n$, the solution is $\partial(\mathbf{X}) = \mathbf{0}$. This shows that $\mathbf{X}$ has no feasible neighborhood and that the solution space consists of one point only. Such case is trivial. The remaining case, where $m < n$, will be considered in detail.

Let

$$\mathbf{X} = (\mathbf{Y}, \mathbf{Z})$$

where

$$\mathbf{Y} = (y_1, y_2, ..., y_m) \text{ and } \mathbf{Z} = (z_1, z_2, ..., z_{n-m})$$

are called the *dependent* and *independent* variables, respectively. Rewriting the gradient vectors of $f$ and $\mathbf{g}$ in terms of $\mathbf{Y}$ and $\mathbf{Z}$, we get

$$\nabla f(\mathbf{Y}, \mathbf{Z}) = (\nabla_{\mathbf{Y}} f, \nabla_{\mathbf{Z}} f)$$

$$\nabla g(\mathbf{Y}, \mathbf{Z}) = (\nabla_{\mathbf{Y}} g, \nabla_{\mathbf{Z}} g)$$

Define

$$\mathbf{J} = \nabla_{\mathbf{Y}} \mathbf{g} = \begin{bmatrix} \nabla_{\mathbf{Y}} g_1 \\ \vdots \\ \nabla_{\mathbf{Y}} g_m \end{bmatrix}$$

$$\mathbf{C} = \nabla_{\mathbf{Z}} \mathbf{g} = \begin{bmatrix} \nabla_{\mathbf{Z}} g_1 \\ \vdots \\ \nabla_{\mathbf{Z}} g_m \end{bmatrix}$$

$\mathbf{J}_{m \times m}$ is called the **Jacobian matrix** and $\mathbf{C}_{m \times n - m}$ the **control matrix**. The Jacobian $\mathbf{J}$ is assumed nonsingular. This is always possible, since the given $m$ equations are independent by definition. The components of the vector $\mathbf{Y}$ can thus be selected from those of $\mathbf{X}$ such that $\mathbf{J}$ is nonsingular.

The original set of equations in $\partial f(\mathbf{X})$ and $\partial \mathbf{X}$ can be written as

$$\partial f(\mathbf{Y}, \mathbf{Z}) = \nabla_{\mathbf{Y}} f \, \partial \mathbf{Y} + \nabla_{\mathbf{Z}} f \, \partial \mathbf{Z}$$

and

$$\mathbf{J} \partial \mathbf{Y} = -\mathbf{C} \partial \mathbf{Z}$$

Because $\mathbf{J}$ is nonsingular, its inverse $\mathbf{J}^{-1}$ exists. Hence,

$$\partial \mathbf{Y} = -\mathbf{J}^{-1} \mathbf{C} \partial \mathbf{Z}$$

Substituting for $\partial \mathbf{Y}$ in the equation for $\partial f(\mathbf{Y}, \mathbf{Z})$ gives $\partial f$ as a function of $\partial \mathbf{Z}$—that is,

$$\partial f(\mathbf{Y}, \mathbf{Z}) = (\nabla_{\mathbf{Z}} f - \nabla_{\mathbf{Y}} f \mathbf{J}^{-1} \mathbf{C}) \partial \mathbf{Z}$$

From this equation, the constrained derivative with respect to the independent vector $\mathbf{Z}$ is given by

$$\nabla_c f = \frac{\partial_c f(\mathbf{Y}, \mathbf{Z})}{\partial_c \mathbf{Z}} = \nabla_z f - \nabla_\mathbf{Y} f \mathbf{J}^{-1} \mathbf{C}$$

where $\nabla_c f$ represents the **constrained gradient** vector of $f$ with respect to $\mathbf{Z}$. Thus, $\nabla_c f(\mathbf{Y}, \mathbf{Z})$ must be null at the stationary points.

The sufficiency conditions are similar to those developed in Section 20.2. The Hessian matrix will correspond to the independent vector $\mathbf{Z}$. In the meantime, the elements of the Hessina matrix must be the *constrained* second derivatives. To show how this is obtained, let

$$\nabla_c f = \nabla_z f - \mathbf{WC}$$

It thus follows the *i*th row of the (constrained) Hessian matrix is $\frac{\partial \nabla_c f}{\partial z_i}$. Notice that $\mathbf{W}$ is a function of $\mathbf{Y}$ and $\mathbf{Y}$ is a function of $\mathbf{Z}$. Thus, the partial derivative of $\nabla_c f$ with respect to $z_i$ is based on the following chain rule:

$$\frac{\partial w_j}{\partial z_i} = \frac{\partial w_j}{\partial y_j} \frac{\partial y_j}{\partial z_i}$$

---

**Example 20.3-1.**

Consider the following problem:

$$f(\mathbf{X}) = x_1^2 + 3x_2^2 + 5x_1 x_3^2$$

$$g_1(\mathbf{X}) = x_1 x_3 + 2x_2 + x_2^2 - 11 = 0$$

$$g_2(\mathbf{X}) = x_1^2 + 2x_1 x_2 + x_3^2 - 14 = 0$$

Given the feasible point $\mathbf{X}^0 = (1, 2, 3)$, it is required to study the variation in $f(=\partial_c f)$ in the feasible neighborhood of $\mathbf{X}^0$.

Let

$$\mathbf{Y} = (x_1, x_3) \quad \text{and} \quad \mathbf{Z} = x_2$$

Thus,

$$\nabla_\mathbf{Y} f = \left( \frac{\partial f}{\partial x_1}, \frac{\partial f}{\partial x_3} \right) = (2x_1 + 5x_3^2, 10x_1 x_3)$$

$$\nabla_\mathbf{Z} f = \frac{\partial f}{\partial x_2} = 6x_2$$

$$\mathbf{J} = \begin{bmatrix} \dfrac{\partial g_1}{\partial x_1} & \dfrac{\partial g_1}{\partial x_3} \\ \dfrac{\partial g_2}{\partial x_1} & \dfrac{\partial g_2}{\partial x_3} \end{bmatrix} = \begin{bmatrix} x_3 & x_1 \\ 2x_1 + 2x_2 & 2x_3 \end{bmatrix}$$

$$\mathbf{C} = \begin{bmatrix} \dfrac{\partial g_1}{\partial x_2} \\ \dfrac{\partial g_2}{\partial x_2} \end{bmatrix} = \begin{bmatrix} 2x_2 + 2 \\ 2x_1 \end{bmatrix}$$

An estimate of $\partial_c f$ in the feasible neighborhood of the feasible point $\mathbf{X}^0 = (1, 2, 3)$ resulting from a small change $\partial x_2 = .01$ is obtained as follows:

$$\mathbf{J}^{-1}\mathbf{C} = \begin{bmatrix} 3 & 1 \\ 6 & 6 \end{bmatrix}^{-1} \begin{bmatrix} 6 \\ 2 \end{bmatrix} = \begin{bmatrix} \dfrac{6}{12} & -\dfrac{1}{12} \\ -\dfrac{6}{12} & \dfrac{3}{12} \end{bmatrix} \begin{bmatrix} 6 \\ 2 \end{bmatrix} \approx \begin{bmatrix} 2.83 \\ -2.50 \end{bmatrix}$$

Hence, the incremental value of constrained $f$ is given as

$$\partial_c f = (\nabla_{\mathbf{Z}} f - \nabla_{\mathbf{Y}} f \mathbf{J}^{-1}\mathbf{C}) \, \partial \mathbf{Z} = \left( 6(2) - (47, 30) \begin{bmatrix} 2.83 \\ -2.5 \end{bmatrix} \right) \partial x_2$$

$$\approx -46 \partial x_2 = -.46$$

By specifying the value of $\partial x_2$ for the *independent* variable $x_2$, feasible values of $\partial x_1$ and $\partial x_2$ are automatically determined for the dependent variables $x_1$ and $x_3$ from the formula

$$\partial \mathbf{Y} = -\mathbf{J}^{-1}\mathbf{C} \, \partial \mathbf{Z}$$

This gives for $\partial x_2 = .01$,

$$\begin{bmatrix} \partial x_1 \\ \partial x_3 \end{bmatrix} = -\mathbf{J}^{-1}\mathbf{C} \, \partial x_2 = \begin{bmatrix} -.0283 \\ .0250 \end{bmatrix}$$

To check the value of $\partial_c f$ obtained, we can compute the value of $f$ at $\mathbf{X}^0$ and $\mathbf{X}^0 + \partial \mathbf{X}$. Thus

$$\mathbf{X}^0 + \partial \mathbf{X} = (1 - .0283, 2 + .01, 3 + .025) = (.9717, 2.01, 3.025)$$

This yields

$$f(\mathbf{X}^0) = 58 \quad \text{and} \quad f(\mathbf{X}^0 + \partial \mathbf{X}) = 57.523$$

or

$$\partial_c f = f(\mathbf{X}^0 + \partial \mathbf{X}) - f(\mathbf{X}^0) = -.477$$

This indicates a decrease in the value of $f$ as obtained by the formula for $\partial_c f$. The difference between the two answers ($-.477$ and $-.46$) is the result of the linear approximation at $\mathbf{X}^0$. The formula is good only for very small variation around $\mathbf{X}^0$.

### Problem set 20.3a

**1.** Consider Example 20.3-1.
   **(a)** Compute $\partial_c f$ by the two methods presented in the example, using $\partial x_2 = .001$ instead of $\partial x_2 = .01$. Does the effect of linear approximation become more negligible with the decrease in the value of $\partial x_2$?
   **(b)** Specify a relationship among $\partial x_1$, $\partial x_2$, and $\partial x_3$ at the feasible point $\mathbf{X}^0 = (1, 2, 3)$ that will keep the point $(x_1^0 + \partial x_1, x_2^0 + \partial x_2, x_3^0 + \partial x_3)$ feasible.

**(c)** If $\mathbf{Y} = (x_2, x_3)$ and $\mathbf{Z} = x_1$, what is the value of $\partial x_1$ that will produce the same value of $\partial_c f$ given in the example?

**(d)** Verify that the result in part (c) will yield $\partial_c f = -.46$.

---

**Example 20.3-2.**

This example illustrates the use of constrained derivatives. Consider the problem

$$\text{Minimize } f(\mathbf{X}) = x_1^2 + x_2^2 + x_3^2$$

subject to

$$g_1(\mathbf{X}) = x_1 + x_2 + 3x_3 - 2 = 0$$
$$g_2(\mathbf{X}) = 5x_1 + 2x_2 + x_3 - 5 = 0$$

We determine the constrained extreme points as follows. Let

$$\mathbf{Y} = (x_1, x_2) \quad \text{and} \quad \mathbf{Z} = x_3$$

Thus,

$$\nabla_{\mathbf{Y}} f = \left( \frac{\partial f}{\partial x_1}, \frac{\partial f}{\partial x_2} \right) = (2x_1, 2x_2), \quad \nabla_{\mathbf{Z}} f = \frac{\partial f}{\partial x_3} = 2x_3$$

$$\mathbf{J} = \begin{bmatrix} 1 & 1 \\ 5 & 2 \end{bmatrix}, \quad \mathbf{J}^{-1} = \begin{bmatrix} -\dfrac{2}{3} & \dfrac{1}{3} \\ \dfrac{5}{3} & -\dfrac{1}{3} \end{bmatrix}, \quad \mathbf{C} = \begin{bmatrix} 3 \\ 1 \end{bmatrix}$$

Hence,

$$\nabla_c f = \frac{\partial_c f}{\partial_c x_3} = 2x_3 - (2x_1, 2x_2) \begin{bmatrix} -\dfrac{2}{3} & \dfrac{1}{3} \\ \dfrac{5}{3} & -\dfrac{1}{3} \end{bmatrix} \begin{bmatrix} 3 \\ 1 \end{bmatrix}$$

$$= \frac{10}{3} x_1 - \frac{28}{3} x_2 + 2x_3$$

At a stationary point, $\nabla_c f = 0$ which together with $g_1(\mathbf{X}) = 0$ and $g_2(\mathbf{X}) = 0$ give the required stationary point(s). Specifically, the equations

$$\begin{bmatrix} 10 & -28 & 6 \\ 1 & 1 & 3 \\ 5 & 2 & 1 \end{bmatrix} \begin{bmatrix} x_1 \\ x_2 \\ x_3 \end{bmatrix} = \begin{bmatrix} 0 \\ 2 \\ 5 \end{bmatrix}$$

give the solution

$$\mathbf{X}^0 \approx (.81, .35, .28)$$

The identity of this stationary point is now checked by considering the sufficiency condition. Given $x_3$ is the independent variable, it follows from $\nabla_c f$ that

$$\frac{\partial_c^2 f}{\partial_c x_3^2} = \frac{10}{3} \left( \frac{dx_1}{dx_3} \right) - \frac{28}{3} \left( \frac{dx_2}{dx_3} \right) + 2 = \left( \frac{10}{3}, -\frac{28}{3} \right) \begin{bmatrix} \dfrac{dx_1}{dx_3} \\ \dfrac{dx_2}{dx_3} \end{bmatrix} + 2$$

From the Jacobian method,

$$
\begin{bmatrix} dx_1 \\ dx_3 \\ dx_2 \\ dx_3 \end{bmatrix} = -\mathbf{J}^{-1}\mathbf{C} = \begin{bmatrix} \dfrac{5}{3} \\ 3 \\ -\dfrac{14}{3} \end{bmatrix}
$$

Substitution gives $\dfrac{\partial_c^2 f}{\partial_c x_3^2} = \dfrac{460}{9} > 0$. Hence, $\mathbf{X}^0$ is the minimum point.

---

The use of the Jacobian method as presented may be hindered, in general, by the difficulty of determining $\mathbf{J}^{-1}$ for a large number of constraints. This difficulty can be overcome by applying Cramer's rule to solve for $\partial f$ in terms of $\partial \mathbf{Z}$. Thus, if $z_j$ represents the $j$th element of $\mathbf{Z}$ and $y_i$ represents the $i$th element of $\mathbf{Y}$, it can be shown that

$$
\frac{\partial_c f}{\partial_c z_j} = \frac{\dfrac{\partial(f, g_1, \ldots, g_m)}{\partial(z_j, y_1, \ldots, y_m)}}{\dfrac{\partial(g_1, \ldots, g_m)}{\partial(y_1, \ldots, y_m)}}
$$

where

$$
\frac{\partial(f, g_1, \ldots, g_m)}{\partial(z_j, y_1, \ldots, y_m)} \equiv \begin{vmatrix} \dfrac{\partial f}{\partial z_j} & \dfrac{\partial f}{\partial y_1} & \cdots & \dfrac{\partial f}{\partial y_m} \\ \dfrac{\partial g_1}{\partial z_j} & \dfrac{\partial g_1}{\partial y_1} & \cdots & \dfrac{\partial g_1}{\partial y_m} \\ \vdots & \vdots & & \vdots \\ \dfrac{\partial g_m}{\partial z_j} & \dfrac{\partial g_m}{\partial y_1} & \cdots & \dfrac{\partial g_m}{\partial y_m} \end{vmatrix}
$$

and

$$
\frac{\partial(g_1, \ldots, g_m)}{\partial(y_1, \ldots, y_m)} \equiv \begin{vmatrix} \dfrac{\partial g_1}{\partial y_1} & \cdots & \dfrac{\partial g_1}{\partial y_m} \\ \vdots & & \vdots \\ \dfrac{\partial g_m}{\partial y_1} & \cdots & \dfrac{\partial g_m}{\partial y_m} \end{vmatrix} = |\mathbf{J}|
$$

Thus, the necessary conditions become

$$
\frac{\partial_c f}{\partial_c z_j} = 0, \quad j = 1, 2, \ldots, n - m
$$

Similarly, in the matrix expression

$$
\frac{\partial \mathbf{Y}}{\partial \mathbf{Z}} = -\mathbf{J}^{-1}\mathbf{C}
$$

the $(i, j)$th element is given by

$$\frac{\partial y_i}{\partial z_j} = -\frac{\dfrac{\partial(g_1, \ldots, g_m)}{\partial(y_1, \ldots, y_{i-1}, z_j, y_{i+1}, \ldots, y_m)}}{\dfrac{\partial(g_1, \ldots, g_m)}{\partial(y_1, \ldots, y_m)}}$$

which represents the rate of variation of the dependent variable $y_i$ with respect to the independent variable $z_j$.

To obtain the sufficiency condition the $i$th element of $\mathbf{W} \equiv \nabla_{\mathbf{Y}} f \mathbf{J}^{-1}$ is given by

$$w_i = \frac{\dfrac{\partial(g_1, \ldots, g_{i-1}, f, g_{i+1}, \ldots, g_m)}{\partial(y_1, \ldots, y_m)}}{\dfrac{\partial(g_1, \ldots, g_m)}{\partial(y_1, \ldots, y_m)}}$$

To illustrate the application of the method, we determine the necessary condition for example 20.3-2.

$$\frac{\partial_c f}{\partial_c x_3} = \frac{\begin{vmatrix} 2x_3 & 2x_1 & 2x_2 \\ 3 & 1 & 1 \\ 1 & 5 & 2 \end{vmatrix}}{\begin{vmatrix} 1 & 1 \\ 5 & 2 \end{vmatrix}} = \frac{10}{3}x_1 - \frac{28}{3}x_2 + 2x_3$$

*Sensitivity Analysis in the Jacobian Method.*    The Jacobian method can be used to study the sensitivity of the optimal value of $f$ because of small changes in the right-hand sides of the constraints. Specifically, what effect will changing $g_i(\mathbf{X}) = 0$ to $g_i(\mathbf{X}) = \partial g_i$ have on the value of $f$? This type of investigation is called **sensitivity analysis** and, in some sense, is similar to that carried out in linear programming (see Chapter 4). However, sensitivity analysis in nonlinear programming is valid only in the small neighborhood of the extreme point. The development will be helpful in studying the Lagrangean method.

It is shown that

$$\partial f(\mathbf{Y}, \mathbf{Z}) = \nabla_{\mathbf{Y}} f \, \partial \mathbf{Y} + \nabla_{\mathbf{Z}} f \, \partial \mathbf{Z}$$

$$\partial \mathbf{g} = \mathbf{J} \, \partial \mathbf{Y} + \mathbf{C} \, \partial \mathbf{Z}$$

Suppose that $\partial \mathbf{g} \neq \mathbf{0}$; then

$$\partial \mathbf{Y} = \mathbf{J}^{-1} \partial \mathbf{g} - \mathbf{J}^{-1} \mathbf{C} \, \partial \mathbf{Z}$$

Substituting in the equation for $\partial f(\mathbf{Y}, \mathbf{Z})$ gives

$$\partial f(\mathbf{Y}, \mathbf{Z}) = \nabla_{\mathbf{Y}_0} f \mathbf{J}^{-1} \, \partial \mathbf{g} + \nabla_c f \, \partial \mathbf{Z}$$

where

$$\nabla_c f = \nabla_{\mathbf{Z}} f - \nabla_{\mathbf{Y}_0} f \mathbf{J}^{-1} \mathbf{C}$$

as defined previously. The expression for $\partial f(\mathbf{Y}, \mathbf{Z})$ can be used to study variation in $f$ in the feasible neighborhood of a feasible point $\mathbf{X}^0$ resulting from small changes $\partial \mathbf{g}$ and $\partial \mathbf{Z}$.

Now, at the extreme (indeed, any stationary) point $\mathbf{X}_0 = (\mathbf{Y}_0, \mathbf{Z}_0)$, the constrained gradient $\nabla_c f$ must vanish. Thus

$$\partial f(\mathbf{Y}_0, \mathbf{Z}_0) = \nabla_{\mathbf{Y}_0} f \mathbf{J}^{-1} \ \partial \mathbf{g}(\mathbf{Y}_0, \mathbf{Z}_0)$$

or

$$\frac{\partial f}{\partial \mathbf{g}} = \nabla_{\mathbf{Y}_0} f \mathbf{J}^{-1}$$

evaluated at $\mathbf{X}_0$. The effect of the small change $\partial \mathbf{g}$ on the *optimum* value of $f$ can be studied by evaluating the rate of change of $f$ with respect to $\mathbf{g}$. These rates are usually referred to as **sensitivity coefficients**.

---

**Example 20.3-3.**

Consider the same problem of Example 20.3-2. The optimum point is given by $\mathbf{X}_0 = (x_1^0, x_2^0, x_3^0) = (.81, .35, .28)$. Since $\mathbf{Y}_0 = (x_1^0, x_2^0)$, then

$$\nabla_{\mathbf{Y}_0} f = \left( \frac{\partial f}{\partial x_1}, \frac{\partial f}{\partial x_2} \right) = (2x_1^0, 2x_2^0) = (1.62, .70)$$

Consequently,

$$\left( \frac{\partial f}{\partial g_1}, \frac{\partial f}{\partial g_2} \right) = \nabla_{\mathbf{Y}_0} f \mathbf{J}^{-1} = (1.62, .7) \begin{bmatrix} -\dfrac{2}{3} & \dfrac{1}{3} \\ \dfrac{5}{3} & -\dfrac{1}{3} \end{bmatrix} = (.0876, .3067)$$

This implies that for $\partial g_1 = 1$, $f$ will increase *approximately* by .0867. Similarly, for $\partial g_1 = 1$, $f$ will increase *approximately* by .3067.

---

*Application of the Jacobian Method to an LP Problem.*    Consider the linear programming problem

$$\text{Maximize } z = 2x_1 + 3x_2$$

subject to

$$x_1 + x_2 + x_3 \qquad = 5$$

$$x_1 - x_2 \qquad + x_4 = 3$$

$$x_1, x_2\, x_3, x_4 \geq 0$$

For the nonnegativity constraints $x_j \geq 0$, let $w_j^2$ be the corresponding (nonnegative) slack variable. Thus $x_j - w_j^2 = 0$, or $x_j = w_j^2$. With this substitution, the nonnegativity conditions become implicit and the original problem becomes

$$\text{Maximize } z = 2w_1^2 + 3w_2^2$$

subject to

$$w_1^2 + w_2^2 + w_3^2 = 5$$
$$w_1^2 - w_2^2 + w_4^2 = 3$$

To apply the Jacobian method, let

$$\mathbf{Y} = (w_1, w_2) \quad \text{and} \quad \mathbf{Z} = (w_3, w_4)$$

(In the terminology of linear programming, $\mathbf{Y}$ and $\mathbf{Z}$ correspond to the basic and nonbasic variables, respectively.) Thus

$$\mathbf{J} = \begin{bmatrix} 2w_1 & 2w_2 \\ 2w_1 & -2w_2 \end{bmatrix}, \quad \mathbf{J}^{-1} = \begin{bmatrix} \dfrac{1}{4w_1} & \dfrac{1}{4w_1} \\ \dfrac{1}{4w_2} & \dfrac{-1}{4w_2} \end{bmatrix}, \quad w_1 \text{ and } w_2 \neq 0$$

$$\mathbf{C} = \begin{bmatrix} 2w_3 & 0 \\ 0 & 2w_4 \end{bmatrix}, \quad \nabla_{\mathbf{Y}} f = (4w_1, 6w_2), \quad \nabla_{\mathbf{Z}} f = (0, 0)$$

so that

$$\nabla_c f = (0, 0) - (4w_1, 6w_2) \begin{bmatrix} \dfrac{1}{4w_1} & \dfrac{1}{4w_1} \\ \dfrac{1}{4w_2} & \dfrac{-1}{4w_2} \end{bmatrix} \begin{bmatrix} 2w_3 & 0 \\ 0 & 2w_4 \end{bmatrix} = (-5w_3, w_4)$$

The solution of the equations comprised of $\nabla_c f = \mathbf{0}$ and the constraints of the problem yield the stationary point $(w_1 = 2, w_2 = 1, w_3 = 0, w_4 = 0)$. The Hessian is given by

$$\mathbf{H}_c = \begin{bmatrix} \dfrac{\partial_c^2 f}{\partial_c w_3^2} & \dfrac{\partial_c^2 f}{\partial_c w_3 \, \partial_c w_4} \\ \dfrac{\partial_c^2 f}{\partial_c w_3 \, \partial_c w_4} & \dfrac{\partial_c^2 f}{\partial_c w_4^2} \end{bmatrix} = \begin{bmatrix} -5 & 0 \\ 0 & 1 \end{bmatrix}$$

Because $\mathbf{H}_c$ is indefinite, the stationary point does not yield a maximum.

Actually, the result is not surprising, because the (nonbasic) variables $w_3$ and $w_4$ (and hence $x_3$ and $x_4$) equal zero, as contemplated by the theory of linear programming. Thus, depending on the specific choice of $\mathbf{Y}$ and $\mathbf{Z}$, the Jacobian method solution determines the corresponding extreme point of the solution space. This may or may not be the optimal solution. The Jacobian method has the power to identify the optimum point through the use of the sufficiency conditions.

The preceding discussion suggests that one has to keep on altering the specific choices of $\mathbf{Y}$ and $\mathbf{Z}$ until the sufficiency condition is satisfied. Thus, let $\mathbf{Y} = (w_2, w_4)$, $\mathbf{Z} = (w_1, w_3)$. Then the corresponding constrained gradient vector becomes

$$\nabla_c f = (4w_1, 0) - (6w_2, 0) \begin{bmatrix} \dfrac{1}{2w_2} & 0 \\ \dfrac{1}{2w_4} & \dfrac{1}{2w_4} \end{bmatrix} \begin{bmatrix} 2w_1 & 2w_3 \\ 2w_1 & 0 \end{bmatrix} = (-2w_1, 6w_3)$$

The corresponding stationary point is given by $w_1 = 0, w_2 = \sqrt{5}, w_3 = 0, w_4 = \sqrt{8}$. Because

$$\mathbf{H}_c = \begin{bmatrix} -2 & 0 \\ 0 & -6 \end{bmatrix}$$

is negative-definite, the solution is a maximum point.

The result is verified graphically in Figure 20-5. The first solution ($x_1 = 4$, $x_2 = 1$) is not optimal, whereas the second ($x_1 = 0, x_2 = 5$) is. You can verify that the remaining two extreme points of the solution space are not optimal. In fact, the extreme point ($x_1 = 0, x_2 = 0$) can be shown by the sufficiency condition to yield a minimum point.

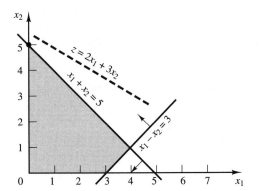

Figure 20–5

The sensitivity coefficients $\nabla_{\mathbf{Y}_0} f \mathbf{J}^{-1}$ when applied to linear programming yield its dual values. To illustrate this point for the given numerical example, let $u_1$ and $u_2$ be the corresponding dual variables. At the optimum point ($w_1 = 0, w_2 = \sqrt{5}$, $w_3 = 0, w_4 = \sqrt{8}$), these dual variables are given by

$$(u_1, u_2) = \nabla_{\mathbf{Y}_0} \mathbf{J}^{-1} = (6w_2, 0) \begin{bmatrix} \dfrac{1}{2w_2} & 0 \\ \dfrac{1}{2w_2} & \dfrac{1}{2w_4} \end{bmatrix} = (3, 0)$$

The corresponding dual objective value is $5u_1 + 3u_2 = 15$, which is the same as the optimal primal objective value. The given solution also satisfies the dual constraints and hence is optimal and feasible. This shows that the sensitivity coefficients are the same as the dual variables. In fact, both have the same interpretation.

It is now possible to draw some general conclusions from the application of the Jacobian method to the linear programming problem. From the numerical example, the necessary conditions require the independent variables to equal zero. Also, the sufficiency conditions indicate that the Hessian matrix is a diagonal matrix. Thus, all its diagonal elements must be positive for a minimum and negative for a maximum.

The observations suggest that the necessary condition is equivalent to specifying that only basic (feasible) solutions are needed to locate the optimum solution. In this case the independent variables are equivalent to the nonbasic variables in the linear programming problem. Also, the sufficiency condition suggests that there is a strong relationship between the diagonal elements of the Hessian matrix and the optimality indicator $z_j - c_j$ (see Section 7.4) in the simplex method.[1]

### Problem set 20.3b

1. Suppose that Example 20.3-2 is solved in the following manner. First, solve the constraints expressing $x_1$ and $x_2$ in terms of $x_3$; then use the resulting equations to express the objective function in terms of $x_3$ only. By taking the derivative of the new objective function with respect to $x_3$, we can determine the points of maxima and minima.

   (a) Would the derivative of the new objective function (expressed in terms of x3) be different from that obtained by the Jacobian method?

   (b) What is the prime difference between the procedure outlined and the Jacobian method?

2. Apply the Jacobian method to Example 20.3-1 by selecting $\mathbf{Y} = (x_2, x_3)$ and $\mathbf{Z} = (x_1)$.

3. Solve by the Jacobian method:

$$\text{Minimize } f(\mathbf{X}) = \sum_{i=1}^{n} x_i^2$$

   subject to

---

[1] For a formal proof of the validity of these results for the general linear programming problem, see H. Taha and G. Curry, "Classical Derivation of the Necessary and Sufficient Conditions for Optimal Linear Programs," *Operations Research,* Vol. 19, 1971, pp. 1045–1049. The paper shows that the key ideas of the simplex method can be derived by the Jacobian method.

$$\prod_{i=1}^{n} x_i = C$$

where $C$ is a positive constant. Suppose that the right-hand side of the constraint is changed to $C + \delta$, where $\delta$ is a small positive quantity. Find the corresponding change in the optimal value of $f$.

4. Solve by the Jacobian method

$$\text{Minimize } f(\mathbf{X}) = 5x_1^2 + x_2^2 + 2x_1x_2$$

subject to

$$g(\mathbf{X}) = x_1x_2 - 10 = 0$$

(a) Find the change in the optimal value of $f(\mathbf{X})$ if the constraint is replaced by $x_1x_2 - 9.99 = 0$

(b) Find the change in value of $f(\mathbf{X})$ in the neighborhood of the feasible point $(2, 5)$ given that $x_1x_2 = 9.99$ and $\partial x_1 = .01$.

5. Consider the problem:

$$\text{Maximize } f(\mathbf{X}) = x_1^2 + 2x_2^2 + 10x_3^2 + 5x_1x_2$$

subject to

$$g_1(\mathbf{X}) = x_1 + x_2^2 + 3x_2x_3 - 5 = 0$$
$$g_2(\mathbf{X}) = x_1^2 + 5x_1x_2 + x_3^2 - 7 = 0$$

Apply the Jacobian method to find $\partial f(\mathbf{X})$ in the feasible neighborhood of the feasible point $(1, 1, 1)$. Assume that this feasible neighborhood is specified by $\partial g_1 = -.01$, $\partial g_2 = .02$, and $\partial x_1 = .01$.

6. Consider the problem

$$\text{Minimize } f(\mathbf{X}) = x_1^2 + x_2^2 + x_3^2 + x_4^2$$

subject to

$$g_1(\mathbf{X}) = x_1 + 2x_2 + 3x_3 + 5x_4 - 10 = 0$$
$$g_2(\mathbf{X}) = x_1 + 2x_2 + 5x_3 + 6x_4 - 15 = 0$$

Show that by selecting $x_3$ and $x_4$ as the independent variables, the Jacobian method fails to give the solution. Then solve the problem using $x_1$ and $x_3$ as the independent variables and apply the sufficiency condition to examine the resulting stationary point. Find the sensitivity coefficients of the problem.

7. Consider the linear programming problem.

$$\text{Maximize } f(\mathbf{X}) = \sum_{j=1}^{n} c_j x_j$$

subject to

$$g_i(\mathbf{X}) = \sum_{j=1}^{n} a_{ij}x_j - b_i = 0 \quad i = 1, 2, \ldots, m$$

$$x_j \geq 0, \quad j = 1, 2, \ldots, n$$

Neglecting the nonnegativity constraint, show that the constrained derivatives $\nabla_c f(\mathbf{X})$ for this problem yield the same expression for $\{z_j - c_j\}$ defined by the optimality condition of the linear programming problem (Section 7.5.1)—that is,

$$\{z_j - c_j\} = \{\mathbf{C}_B \mathbf{B}^{-1} \mathbf{P}_j - c_j\}, \quad \text{for all } j$$

Can the constrained-derivative method be applied directly to the linear programming problem? Why or why not?

***Lagrangean Method.***    The sensitivity coefficients of the Jacobian method,

$$\frac{\partial f}{\partial \mathbf{g}} = \nabla_{\mathbf{Y}_0} \mathbf{J}^{-1}$$

can be used to solve the constrained problem with equality constraints. Let

$$\lambda = \nabla_{\mathbf{Y}_0} \mathbf{J}^{-1} = \frac{\partial f}{\partial \mathbf{g}}$$

Thus,

$$\partial f - \boldsymbol{\lambda}\, \partial \mathbf{g} = 0$$

This equation satisfies the necessary conditions for stationary points because the expression for $\frac{\partial f}{\partial \mathbf{g}}$ is computed such that $\nabla_c f = \mathbf{0}$. A more convenient form for presenting these equations, is to take their partial derivatives with respect to all $x_j$. This yields

$$\frac{\partial}{\partial x_j}(f - \boldsymbol{\lambda}\mathbf{g}) = 0, \quad j = 1, 2, \ldots, n$$

The resulting equations together with the constraint equations $\mathbf{g} = \mathbf{0}$ yield the feasible values of $\mathbf{X}$ and $\boldsymbol{\lambda}$ that satisfy the *necessary* conditions for stationary points.

     The procedure described defines the *Lagrangean method* for identifying the stationary points of optimization problems with *equality* constraints. The procedure can be developed formally as follows. Let

$$L(\mathbf{X}, \boldsymbol{\lambda}) = f(\mathbf{X}) - \boldsymbol{\lambda}\mathbf{g}(\mathbf{X})$$

The function $L$ is called the **Lagrangean function** and the parameters $\boldsymbol{\lambda}$ the **Lagrange multipliers**. By definition, these multipliers have the same interpretation as the sensitivity coefficients of the Jacobian method.

     The equations

$$\frac{\partial L}{\partial \boldsymbol{\lambda}} = 0 \quad \text{and} \quad \frac{\partial L}{\partial \mathbf{X}} = \mathbf{0}$$

give the necessary conditions for determining, stationary points of $f(\mathbf{X})$ subject to $\mathbf{g}(\mathbf{X}) = \mathbf{0}$. The sufficiency conditions for the Lagrangean method will be stated without proof. Define

$$\mathbf{H}^B = \left[ \begin{array}{c|c} \mathbf{0} & \mathbf{P} \\ \hline \mathbf{P}^T & \mathbf{Q} \end{array} \right]_{(m+n) \times (m+n)}$$

where

$$\mathbf{P} = \begin{bmatrix} \nabla g_1(\mathbf{X}) \\ \vdots \\ \nabla g_m(\mathbf{X}) \end{bmatrix}_{m \times n} \quad \text{and} \quad \mathbf{Q} = \left\| \frac{\partial^2 L(\mathbf{X}, \boldsymbol{\lambda})}{\partial x_i \, \partial x_j} \right\|_{n \times n}, \quad \text{for all } i \text{ and } j$$

The matrix $\mathbf{H}^B$ is called the **bordered Hessian matrix**.

Given the stationary point $(\mathbf{X}_0, \boldsymbol{\lambda}_0)$ for the Lagrangean function $L(\mathbf{X}, \boldsymbol{\lambda})$ and the bordered Hessian matrix $\mathbf{H}^B$ evaluated at $(\mathbf{X}_0, \boldsymbol{\lambda}_0)$, then $\mathbf{X}_0$ is

1. A maximum point if, starting with the principal major determinant of order $(2m + 1)$, the *last* $(n - m)$ principal minor determinants of $\mathbf{H}^B$ form an alternating sign pattern starting with $(-1)^{m+1}$.
2. A minimum point if, starting with the principal minor determinant of order $(2m + 1)$, the *last* $(n - m)$ principal minor determinants of $\mathbf{H}^B$ have the sign of $(-1)^m$.

These conditions are sufficient for identifying an extreme point. In other words, a stationary point may be an extreme point without satisfying these conditions.

Other conditions exist that are both necessary and sufficient for identifying extreme points. The disadvantage is that this procedure may be computationally intractable. Define the matrix

$$\Delta = \begin{bmatrix} \mathbf{0} & \mathbf{P} \\ \mathbf{P}^T & \mathbf{Q} - \mu \mathbf{I} \end{bmatrix}$$

evaluated at the stationary point $(\mathbf{X}_0, \boldsymbol{\lambda}_0)$, where $\mu$ is an unknown parameter. Consider the determinant $|\Delta|$; then each of the real $(n - m)$ roots $u_i$ of the polynomial

$$|\Delta| = 0$$

must be

1. Negative if $\mathbf{X}_0$ is a maximum point.
2. Positive if $\mathbf{X}_0$ is a minimum point.

**Example 20.3-4.**

Consider the same problem of Example 20.3-2. The Lagrangean function is

$$L(\mathbf{X}, \boldsymbol{\lambda}) = x_1^2 + x_2^2 + x_3^2 - \lambda_1(x_1 + x_2 + 3x_3 - 2) - \lambda_2(5x_1 + 2x_2 + x_3 - 5)$$

This yields the following necessary conditions:

$$\frac{\partial L}{\partial x_1} = 2x_1 - \lambda_1 - 5\lambda_2 = 0$$

$$\frac{\partial L}{\partial x_2} = 2x_2 - \lambda_1 - 2\lambda_2 = 0$$

$$\frac{\partial L}{\partial x_3} = 2x_3 - 3\lambda_1 - \lambda_2 = 0$$

$$\frac{\partial L}{\partial \lambda_1} = -(x_1 + x_2 + 3x_3 - 2) = 0$$

$$\frac{\partial L}{\partial \lambda_2} = -(5x_1 + 2x_2 + x_3 - 5) = 0$$

The solution to these simultaneous equations yields

$$\mathbf{X_0} = (x_1, x_2, x_3) = (.81, .35, .28)$$

$$\boldsymbol{\lambda} = (\lambda_1, \lambda_2) = (.0867, .3067)$$

This solution combines the results of Examples 20.3-2 and 20.3-3. The values of the Lagrange multipliers $\boldsymbol{\lambda}$ are the same as the sensitivity coefficients obtained in Example 20.3-3. This shows that these coefficients are independent of the choice of the dependent vector $\mathbf{Y}$ in the Jacobian method.

To show that the given point is a minimum, consider

$$\mathbf{H}^B = \begin{bmatrix} 0 & 0 & 1 & 1 & 3 \\ 0 & 0 & 5 & 2 & 1 \\ 1 & 5 & 2 & 0 & 0 \\ 1 & 2 & 0 & 2 & 0 \\ 3 & 1 & 0 & 0 & 2 \end{bmatrix}$$

Because $n = 3$ and $m = 2$, it follows that $n - m = 1$. Thus we need to check the determinant of $\mathbf{H}^B$ only, which must have the sign of $(-1)^2$ at a minimum. Because det $\mathbf{H}^B = 460 > 0$, $\mathbf{X}^0$ is a minimum point.

A method that is sometimes convenient for solving equations resulting from the necessary conditions is to select successive numerical values of $\boldsymbol{\lambda}$ and then solve the equations in $\mathbf{X}$. This is repeated until for some $\boldsymbol{\lambda}$, the resulting $\mathbf{X}$ satisfies all the active constraints in equation form. This method was illustrated in Chapter 11 as an application to the single-constraint inventory problem (see example 11.3-3). This procedure is tedious computationally. One may resort to an appropriate numerical technique, such as the Newton-Raphson method (Section 20.2.2) to solve the resulting equations.

---

**Example 20.3-5.**

Consider the problem

$$\text{Minimize } z = x_1^2 + x_2^2 + x_3^2$$

subject to

$$4x_1 + x_2^2 + 2x_3 - 14 = 0$$

The Lagrangean function is

$$L(\mathbf{X}, \lambda) = x_1^2 + x_2^2 + x_3^2 - \lambda(4x_1 + x_2^2 + 2x_3 - 14)$$

This yields the following necessary conditions:

$$\frac{\partial L}{\partial x_1} = 2x_1 - 4\lambda = 0$$

$$\frac{\partial L}{\partial x_2} = 2x_2 - 2\lambda x_2 = 0$$

$$\frac{\partial L}{\partial x_3} = 2x_3 - 2\lambda = 0$$

$$\frac{\partial L}{\delta \lambda} = -(4x_1 + x_2^2 + 2x_3 - 14) = 0$$

whose solutions are

$$(\mathbf{X}_0, \lambda_0)_1 = (2, 2, 1, 1)$$

$$(\mathbf{X}_0, \lambda_0)_2 = (2, -2, 1, 1)$$

$$(\mathbf{X}_0, \lambda_0)_3 = (2.8, 0, 1.4, 1.4)$$

Applying the sufficiency conditions yields

$$\mathbf{H}^B = \begin{pmatrix} 0 & 4 & 2x_2 & 2 \\ 4 & 2 & 0 & 0 \\ 2x_2 & 0 & 2 - 2\lambda & 0 \\ 2 & 0 & 0 & 2 \end{pmatrix}$$

Because $m = 1$ and $n = 3$, for a stationary point to be a minimum, the sign of the last $(3 - 1) = 2$ principal minor determinants must be that of $(-1)^m = -1$. Thus, for $(\mathbf{X}_0, \lambda_0)_1 = (2, 2, 1, 1)$,

$$\begin{vmatrix} 0 & 4 & 4 \\ 4 & 2 & 0 \\ 4 & 0 & 0 \end{vmatrix} = -32 < 0 \quad \text{and} \quad \begin{vmatrix} 0 & 4 & 4 & 2 \\ 4 & 2 & 0 & 0 \\ 4 & 0 & 0 & 0 \\ 2 & 0 & 0 & 2 \end{vmatrix} = -64 < 0$$

For $(\mathbf{X}_0, \lambda_0)_2 = (2, -2, 1, 1)$,

$$\begin{vmatrix} 0 & 4 & -4 \\ 4 & 2 & 0 \\ -4 & 0 & 0 \end{vmatrix} = -32 < 0 \quad \text{and} \quad \begin{vmatrix} 0 & 4 & -4 & 2 \\ 4 & 2 & 0 & 0 \\ -4 & 0 & 0 & 0 \\ 2 & 0 & 0 & 2 \end{vmatrix} = -64 < 0$$

Finally, for $(\mathbf{X}_0, \boldsymbol{\lambda}_0)_3 = (2.8, 0, 1.4, 1.4)$,

$$\begin{vmatrix} 0 & 4 & 0 \\ 4 & 2 & 0 \\ 0 & 0 & -.8 \end{vmatrix} = 12.8 > 0 \quad \text{and} \quad \begin{vmatrix} 0 & 4 & 0 & 2 \\ 4 & 2 & 0 & 0 \\ 0 & 0 & -.8 & 0 \\ 2 & 0 & 0 & 2 \end{vmatrix} = 32 > 0$$

This shows that $(\mathbf{X}_0)_1$ and $(\mathbf{X}_0)_2$ are minimum points. The fact that $(\mathbf{X}_0)_3$ does not satisfy the sufficiency conditions of either a maximum or a minimum does not mean that it is not an extreme point. This follows because the given conditions are sufficient only.

To illustrate the use of the other sufficiency condition that employs the roots of polynomial, consider

$$\Delta = \begin{bmatrix} 0 & 4 & 2x_2 & 2 \\ 4 & 2 - \mu & 0 & 0 \\ 2x_2 & 0 & 2 - 2\lambda - \mu & 0 \\ 2 & 0 & 0 & 2 - \mu \end{bmatrix}$$

Now, for $(\mathbf{X}_0, \boldsymbol{\lambda}_0)_1 = (2, 2, 1, 1)$

$$|\Delta| = 9\mu^2 - 26\mu + 16 = 0$$

This gives $\mu = 2$ or $\frac{8}{9}$. Because all $\mu > 0$, $(\mathbf{X}_0)_1 = (2, 2, 1)$ is a minimum point. For $(\mathbf{X}_0, \boldsymbol{\lambda}_0)_2 = (2, -2, 1, 1)$,

$$|\Delta| = 9\mu^2 - 26\mu + 16 = 0$$

which is the same as in the previous case. Hence $(\mathbf{X}_0)_2 = (2, -2, 1)$ is a minimum point. Finally, for $(\mathbf{X}_0, \boldsymbol{\lambda}_0)_3 = (2.8, 0, 1.4, 1.4)$,

$$|\Delta| = 5\mu^2 - 6\mu - 8 = 0$$

This gives $\mu = 2$ and $-.8$, which means that $(\mathbf{X}_0)_3 = (2.8, 0, 1.4)$ is not an extreme point.

---

## Problem set 20.3c

1. Solve the following linear programming problem by both the Jacobian and the Lagrangean methods:

$$\text{Maximize } f(\mathbf{X}) = 5x_1 + 3x_2$$

subject to

$$g_1(\mathbf{X}) = x_1 + 2x_2 + x_3 - 6 = 0$$

$$g_2(\mathbf{X}) = 3x_1 + x_2 + x_4 - 9 = 0$$

$$x_1, x_2, x_3, x_4 \geq 0$$

2. Find the optimal solution to the problem

$$\text{Minimize } f(\mathbf{X}) = x_1^2 + 2x_2^2 + 10x_3^2$$

subject to

$$g_1(\mathbf{X}) = x_1 + x_2^2 + x_3 - 5 = 0$$

$$g_2(\mathbf{X}) = x_1 + 5x_2 + x_3 - 7 = 0$$

Suppose that $g_1(\mathbf{X}) = .01$ and $g_2(\mathbf{X}) = .02$. Find the corresponding change in the optimal value of $f(\mathbf{X})$.

3. Solve Problem 20.3b-6 by the Lagrangean method and verify that the value of the Lagrange multipliers are the same as the sensitivity coefficients obtained in Problem 20.3b-6.

### 20.3.2 Inequality Constraints

This section shows how the Lagrangean method may be extended to handle inequality constraints. The main contribution of the section is the development of the Kuhn-Tucker conditions, which provide the basic theory for nonlinear programming.

***Extension of the Lagrangean Method.***    Suppose that the problem is given by

$$\text{Maximize } z = f(\mathbf{X})$$

subject to

$$g_i(\mathbf{X}) \leq 0, \quad i = 1, 2, \ldots, m$$

The nonnegativity constraints $\mathbf{X} \geq 0$, if any, are included in the $m$ constraints.

The general idea of extending the Lagrangean procedure is that if the *uncon*strained optimum of $f(\mathbf{X})$ does not satisfy all constraints, the constrained optimum must occur at a boundary point of the solution space. This means that one, or more, of the $m$ constraints must be satisfied in equation form. The procedure thus involves the following steps.

**Step 1.** Solve the unconstrained problem

$$\text{Maximize } z = f(\mathbf{X})$$

If the resulting optimum satisfies all the constraints, stop because all constraints are redundant. Otherwise, set $k = 1$ and go to step 2.

**Step 2.** Activate any $k$ constraints (i.e., convert them into equalities) and optimize $f(\mathbf{X})$ subject to the $k$ active constraints by the Lagrangean

method. If the resulting solution is feasible with respect to the remaining constraints, stop; it is a *local* optimum.[2] Otherwise, activate
another set of $k$ constraints and repeat the step. If *all* sets of active
constraints taken $k$ at a time are considered without encountering a
feasible solution, go to step 3.

**Step 3.** If $k = m$, stop; no feasible solution exists. Otherwise, set $k = k + 1$
and go to step 2.

An important point often neglected in presenting the procedure is that it does *not*
guarantee global optimality even when the problem is well behaved (possesses a *unique*
optimum). Another important point is the implicit misconception that, for $p < q$, the optimum of $f(\mathbf{X})$ subject to $p$ equality constraints is always better than its optimum subject
to $q$ equality constraints. This is true, in general, only if the $q$ constraints form a subset of
the $p$ constraints. The following example is designed to illustrate these points.

---

**Example 20.3-6.**
$$\text{Maximize } z = -(2x_1 - 5)^2 - (2x_2 - 1)^2$$

subject to

$$x_1 + 2x_2 \leq 2$$

$$x_1, x_2 \geq 0$$

The graphical representation in Figure 20-6 should assist in understanding the analytic
procedure. Observe that the problem is well behaved (concave objective function subject to a convex solution space) with the result that a reasonably well-defined algorithm
would guarantee global optimality. Yet, as will be shown, the extended Lagrangean
method produces a local maximum only.

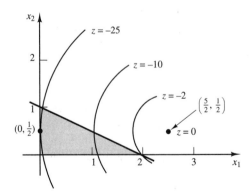

**Figure 20–6**

The unconstrained optimum is obtained by solving

[2] A *local* optimum is defined from among all the optima resulting from optimizing $f(\mathbf{X})$ subject to
*all* combinations of $k$ *equality* constraints, $k = 1, 2, ..., m$.

$$\frac{\partial z}{\partial x_1} = -4(2x_1 - 5) = 0$$

$$\frac{\partial z}{\partial x_2} = -4(2x_2 - 5) = 0$$

This gives $(x_1, x_2) = (\frac{5}{2}, \frac{1}{2})$. Because this solution violates $x_1 + 2x_2 \leq 2$, the constraints are activated one at a time. Consider $x_1 = 0$. The Lagrangean function is

$$L(x_1, x_2, \lambda) = -(2x_1 - 5)^2 - (2x_2 - 1)^2 - \lambda x_1$$

Thus,

$$\frac{\partial L}{\partial x_1} = -4(2x_1 - 5) - \lambda = 0$$

$$\frac{\partial L}{\partial x_2} = -4(2x_2 - 1) \qquad = 0$$

$$\frac{\partial L}{\partial \lambda} = -x_1 \qquad\qquad = 0$$

This gives the solution point $(x_1, x_2) = (0, \frac{1}{2})$, which can be shown by the sufficiency condition to be a maximum. Because this point satisfies all other constraints, the procedure terminates with $(x_1, x_2) = (0, \frac{1}{2})$ as a local optimal solution to the problem. (The remaining constraints $x_2 \geq 0$ and $x_1 = 2x_2 \leq 2$, activated one at a time, yield infeasible solutions.) The objective value is $z = -25$.

In Figure 20-6, the feasible solution $(x_1, x_2) = (2, 0)$, which is the point of intersection of the *two* constraints $x_2 = 0$ and $x_1 + 2x_2 = 2$, yields the objective value $z = -2$. This value is better than the one obtained with one active constraint.

The procedure just described illustrates that the best to be hoped for in using the extended Lagrangean method is a (possibly) good feasible solution. This is particularly so if the objective function is not unimodal. If the functions of the problem are well behaved (e.g., the problem possesses a unique constrained optimum as in Example 20.3-6), the procedure can be rectified to locate the global optimum. Specifically, consider the unconstrained optimum and the constrained optima subject to *all* sets of one active constraint at a time, then two active constraints at a time, and so on, until all $m$ constraints are activated. The best of *all* the *feasible* optima is the global optimum.

If this procedure is followed by Example 20.3-6, it will be necessary to solve seven problems before global optimality is verified. This indicates the limited use of the method in solving problems of any practical size.

***The Kuhn-Tucker Conditions.***    This section develops the Kuhn-Tucker *necessary* conditions for identifying stationary points of a nonlinear constrained problem subject to inequality constraints. The development is based on the Lagrangean method. These conditions are also sufficient under certain rules that will be stated later.

Consider the problem

$$\text{Maximize } z = f(\mathbf{X})$$

subject to

$$\mathbf{g}(\mathbf{X}) \leq \mathbf{0}$$

The inequality constraints may be converted into equations by using *nonnegative* slack variables. Let $\mathbf{S}_i^2(\geq 0)$ be the slack quantity added to the $i$th constraint $g_i(\mathbf{X}) \leq 0$ and

$$\mathbf{S} = (S_1, S_2, \ldots, S_m)^T \quad \text{and} \quad \mathbf{S}^2 = (S_1^2, S_2^2, \ldots, S_m^2)^T$$

where $m$ is the total number of inequality constraints. The Lagrangean function is thus given by

$$L(\mathbf{X}, \mathbf{S}, \boldsymbol{\lambda}) = f(\mathbf{X}) - \boldsymbol{\lambda}[\mathbf{g}(\mathbf{X}) + \mathbf{S}^2]$$

Given the constraints

$$\mathbf{g}(\mathbf{X}) \leq \mathbf{0}$$

a necessary condition for optimality is that $\boldsymbol{\lambda}$ be nonnegative (nonpositive) for maximization (minimization) problems. This is justified as follows. Consider the maximization case. Because $\boldsymbol{\lambda}$ measures the rate of variation of $f$ with respect to $\mathbf{g}$—that is,

$$\boldsymbol{\lambda} = \frac{\partial f}{\partial \mathbf{g}}$$

as the right-hand side of the constraint $\mathbf{g} \leq 0$ increases above zero, the solution space becomes less constrained and hence $f$ cannot decrease. This means that $\boldsymbol{\lambda} \geq 0$. Similarily for minimization, as a resource increases, $f$ cannot increase, which implies that $\boldsymbol{\lambda} \leq \mathbf{0}$. If the constraints are equalities, that is, $\mathbf{g}(\mathbf{X}) = \mathbf{0}$, then $\boldsymbol{\lambda}$ becomes unrestricted in sign (see Problem 20.3d-2).

The restrictions on $\boldsymbol{\lambda}$ must hold as part of the Kuhn-Tucker necessary conditions. The remaining conditions will now be derived.

Taking the partial derivatives of $L$ with respect to $\mathbf{X}, \mathbf{S},$ and $\boldsymbol{\lambda}$, we obtain

$$\frac{\partial L}{\partial \mathbf{X}} = \nabla f(\mathbf{X}) - \boldsymbol{\lambda}\nabla\mathbf{g}(\mathbf{X}) = \mathbf{0}$$

$$\frac{\partial L}{\partial S_i} = -2\lambda_i S_i = 0, \quad i = 1, 2, \ldots, m$$

$$\frac{\partial L}{\partial \boldsymbol{\lambda}} = -(\mathbf{g}(\mathbf{X}) + \mathbf{S}^2) = \mathbf{0}$$

The second set of equations reveals the following results.

**1.** If $\lambda_i$ is not zero, then $S_i^2 = 0$. This means that the corresponding resource is scarce, and consequently it is consumed completely (equality constraint).

**2.** If $S_i^2 > 0$, $\lambda_i = 0$. This means the $i$th resource is not scarce and, consequently, it does not affect the value of $f$ (*i.e.*, $\lambda_i = \frac{\partial f}{\partial g_i} = 0$).

From the second and third sets of equations it follows that

$$\lambda_i g_i(\mathbf{X}) = 0, \quad i = 1, 2, ..., m$$

This new condition essentially repeats the foregoing argument, because if $\lambda_i > 0$, $g_i(\mathbf{X}) = 0$ or $S_i^2 = 0$. Similarly, if $g_i(\mathbf{X}) < 0$, $S_i^2 > 0$, and $\lambda_i = 0$.

The Kuhn-Tucker conditions necessary for $\mathbf{X}$ and $\boldsymbol{\lambda}$ to be a stationary point of the maximization problem can now be summarized as follows:

$$\boldsymbol{\lambda} \geq \mathbf{0},$$

$$\nabla f(\mathbf{X}) - \boldsymbol{\lambda} \nabla \mathbf{g}(\mathbf{X}) = \mathbf{0}$$

$$\lambda_i g_i(\mathbf{X}) = 0, \quad i = 1, 2, ..., m$$

$$\mathbf{g}(\mathbf{X}) \leq \mathbf{0}$$

You can verify that these conditions apply to the minimization case as well, with the exception that $\boldsymbol{\lambda}$ must be nonpositive, as shown previously. In both maximization and minimization, the Lagrange multipliers corresponding to equality constraints must be unrestricted in sign.

*Sufficiency of the Kuhn-Tucker Conditions.* The Kuhn-Tucker necessary conditions are also sufficient if the objective function and the solution space satisfy certain conditions regarding convexity and concavity. These conditions are summarized in Table 20-1.

It is simpler to verify that a function is convex or concave than it is to prove that a solution space is a convex set. For this reason, we provide a list of conditions

**TABLE 20-1**

| Sense of optimization | Required conditions | |
|---|---|---|
| | Objective function | Solution space |
| Maximization | Concave | Convex set |
| Minimization | Convex | Convex set |

that are easier to apply in practice in the sense that the convexity of the solution space can be established by checking directly the convexity or concavity of the

constraint functions. To provide these conditions, we define the generalized nonlinear problems as

$$\text{Maximize or minimize } z = f(\mathbf{X})$$

subject to

$$g_i(\mathbf{X}) \le 0, \quad i = 1, 2, \ldots, r$$

$$g_i(\mathbf{X}) \ge 0, \quad i = r + 1, \ldots, p$$

$$g_i(\mathbf{X}) = 0, \quad i = p + 1, \ldots, m$$

$$L(\mathbf{X}, \mathbf{S}, \boldsymbol{\lambda}) = f(\mathbf{X}) - \sum_{i=1}^{r} \lambda_i[g_i(\mathbf{X}) + S_i^2] - \sum_{i=r+1}^{p} \lambda_i[g_i(\mathbf{X}) - S_i^2] - \sum_{i=p+1}^{m} \lambda_i g_i(\mathbf{X})$$

where $\lambda_i$ is the Lagrangean multiplier associated with constraint $i$. The conditions for establishing the sufficiency of the Kuhn-Tucker conditions are summarized in Table 20-2.

The conditions in Table 20-2 represent only a subset of the conditions in Table
20-1. The reason is that a solution space may be convex without satisfying the conditions in Table 20-2.

**TABLE 20-2**

| Sense of optimization | | Conditions required | | |
|---|---|---|---|---|
| | $f(\mathbf{X})$ | $g_i(\mathbf{X})$ | $\lambda_i$ | |
| Maximization | Concave | Convex | $\ge 0$ | $(1 \le i \le r)$ |
| | | Concave | $\le 0$ | $(r + 1 \le i \le p)$ |
| | | Linear | Unrestricted | $(p + 1 \le i \le m)$ |
| Minimization | Convex | Convex | $\le 0$ | $(1 \le i \le r)$ |
| | | Concave | $\ge 0$ | $(r + 1 \le i \le p)$ |
| | | Linear | Unrestricted | $(p + 1 \le i \le m)$ |

The validity of Table 20-2 rests on the fact that the given conditions yield a
concave Lagrangean function $L(\mathbf{X}, \mathbf{S}, \boldsymbol{\lambda})$ in case of maximization and a convex
$L(\mathbf{X}, \mathbf{S}, \boldsymbol{\lambda})$ in case of minimization. This result is verified by noticing that if $g_i(x)$ is
convex, then $\lambda_i g_i(x)$ is convex if $\lambda_i \ge 0$ and concave if $\lambda_i \le 0$. Similar interpretations can be established for all the remaining conditions. Observe that a linear
function is both convex and concave. Also, if a function $f$ is concave, then $-f$ is convex, and vice versa.

**Example 20.3-7.**

Consider the following minimization problem:

$$\text{Minimize } f(\mathbf{X}) = x_1^2 + x_2^2 + x_3^2$$

subject to

$$g_1(\mathbf{X}) = 2x_1 + x_2 - 5 \leq 0$$
$$g_2(\mathbf{X}) = \phantom{2}x_1 + x_3 - 2 \leq 0$$
$$g_3(\mathbf{X}) = \phantom{2}1 - x_1 \phantom{+ x_3} \leq 0$$
$$g_4(\mathbf{X}) = \phantom{2}2 - x_2 \phantom{+ x_3} \leq 0$$
$$g_5(\mathbf{X}) = \phantom{2}- x_3 \phantom{+ x_3} \leq 0$$

Because this is a minimization problem, it follows that $\boldsymbol{\lambda} \leq \mathbf{0}$. The Kuhn-Tucker conditions are thus given as

$$(\lambda_1, \lambda_2, \lambda_3, \lambda_4, \lambda_5) \leq \mathbf{0}$$

$$(2x_1, 2x_2, 2x_3) - (\lambda_1, \lambda_2, \lambda_3, \lambda_4, \lambda_5) \begin{bmatrix} 2 & 1 & 0 \\ 1 & 0 & 1 \\ -1 & 0 & 0 \\ 0 & -1 & 0 \\ 0 & 0 & -1 \end{bmatrix} = \mathbf{0}$$

$$\lambda_1 g_1 = \lambda_2 g_2 = \cdots = \lambda_5 g_5 = 0$$
$$\mathbf{g}(\mathbf{X}) \leq \mathbf{0}$$

These conditions simplify to the following

$$\lambda_1, \lambda_2, \lambda_3, \lambda_4, \lambda_5 \leq 0$$
$$2x_1 - 2\lambda_1 - \lambda_2 + \lambda_3 = 0$$
$$2x_2 - \lambda_1 + \lambda_4 = 0$$
$$2x_3 - \lambda_2 + \lambda_5 = 0$$
$$\lambda_1(2x_1 + x_2 - 5) = 0$$
$$\lambda_2(\phantom{2}x_1 + x_3 - 2) = 0$$
$$\lambda_3(1 - x_1) = 0$$
$$\lambda_4(2 - x_2) = 0$$
$$\lambda_5 x_3 = 0$$
$$2x_1 + x_2 \leq 5$$
$$x_1 + x_3 \leq 2$$
$$x_1 \geq 1, \quad x_2 \geq 2, \quad x_3 \geq 0$$

The solution is $x_1 = 1, x_2 = 2, x_3 = 0, \lambda_1 = \lambda_2 = \lambda_5 = 0, \lambda_3 = -2, \lambda_4 = -4$. Because both $f(\mathbf{X})$ and the solution space $\mathbf{g}(\mathbf{X}) \leq \mathbf{0}$ are convex, $L(\mathbf{X}, \mathbf{S}, \boldsymbol{\lambda})$ must be convex and the resulting stationary point yields a global constrained minimum. The example demonstrates that it may be difficult to solve the resulting conditions explicitly. Consequently, the procedure is not suitable for numerical computations. The Kuhn-Tucker conditions are central to the development of the nonlinear programming algorithms in Chapter 21.

**Problem set 20.3d**

**1.** Show that the Kuhn-Tucker conditions for the problem:

$$\text{Maximize } f(\mathbf{X})$$

subject to

$$\mathbf{g}(\mathbf{X}) \geq \mathbf{0}$$

are the same as in Section 20.3.2 except that the Lagrange multiplilers $\boldsymbol{\lambda}$ are nonpositive.

2. Consider the following problem:

$$\text{Maximize } f(\mathbf{X})$$

subject to

$$\mathbf{g}(\mathbf{X}) = \mathbf{0}$$

Show that the Kuhn-Tucker conditions are

$$\nabla f(\mathbf{X}) - \boldsymbol{\lambda} \nabla \mathbf{g}(\mathbf{X}) = \mathbf{0}$$

$$\mathbf{g}(\mathbf{X}) = \mathbf{0}$$

$$\boldsymbol{\lambda} \text{ unrestricted in sign}$$

3. Write the Kuhn-Tucker necessary conditions for the following problems.

   (a) Maximize $f(\mathbf{X}) = x_1^3 - x_2^2 + x_1 x_3^2$

   Subject to

   $$x_1 + x_2^2 + x_3 = 5$$

   $$5x_1^2 - x_2^2 - x_3 \geq 0$$

   $$x_1, x_2, x_3 \geq 0$$

   (b) Minimize $f(\mathbf{X}) = x_1^4 + x_2^2 + 5x_1 x_2 x_3$

   Subject to

   $$x_1^2 - x_2^2 + x_3^3 \leq 10$$

   $$x_1^3 + x_2^2 + 4x_3^2 \geq 20$$

4. Consider the problem

$$\text{Maximize } f(\mathbf{X})$$

subject to

$$\mathbf{g}(\mathbf{X}) = \mathbf{0}$$

Given $f(\mathbf{X})$ is concave and $g_i(\mathbf{X})$ $(i = 1, 2, ..., m)$ is a *linear* function, show that the Kuhn-Tucker necessary conditions are also sufficient. Is this result true if $g_i(\mathbf{X})$ is a convex *non*linear function for all $i$? Why?

**5.** Consider the problem

$$\text{Maximize } f(\mathbf{X})$$

subject to

$$g_1(\mathbf{X}) \geq 0, \quad g_2(\mathbf{X}) = 0, \quad g_3(\mathbf{X}) \leq 0$$

Develop the Kuhn-Tucker conditions and give the stipulations under which the conditions are sufficient.

## 20.4 SUMMARY

This chapter provides the classical theory for locating the points of maxima and minima of constrained and unconstrained nonlinear problems. The theory is generally not suitable for computational purposes. Few exceptions exist where the Kuhn-Tucker theory is the basis for the development of efficient computational algorithms. *Quadratic programming,* which we present in the next chapter, is an example of the use of the Kuhn-Tucker necessary conditions.

No sufficiency conditions (similar to those of unconstrained problems and problems with *equality* constraints) can be established for nonlinear programs with inequality constraints. Unless the conditions given in Table 20-1 or 20-2 can be established *in advance,* there is no way of verifying whether a nonlinear programming algorithm converges to a local or a global optimum.

## SELECTED REFERENCES

BAZARRA, M., H. SHRALI, and C. SHETTY, *Nonlinear Programming Theory and Algorithms,* 2nd ed., Wiley, New York, 1993.

BEIGHTLER, C., D. PHILLIPS, and D. WILDE, *Foundations of Optimization,* 2nd ed., Prentice Hall, N.J., 1979.

# Chapter 21

# Nonlinear Programming Algorithms

## 21.1 UNCONSTRAINED ALGORITHMS

This section presents two algorithms for the unconstrained problem: the *direct search* algorithm and the *gradient* algorithm. The first algorithm locates the optimum by direct search over a specified region, and the second uses the gradient of the function to find the optimum.

## 21.1.1 DIRECT SEARCH METHOD

Direct search methods apply primarily to single-variable functions. Although this may appear trivial, it is shown in Section 21.1.2 that optimization of single-variable functions is used to develop multivariable algorithms.

The idea of direct search methods is simple. First, we identify the **interval of uncertainty** that is known to include the optimum is identified. The size of the interval is systematically reduced until the optimum is found. The procedure is such that, the length of the interval including the optimum can be made as small as desired.

This section presents the **dichotomous search** method. We seek to maximize a strictly unimodal function, $f(x)$, over the interval $a \le x \le b$. Define the two points $x_1$ and $x_2$ symmetrically with respect to $a$ and $b$ such that the intervals $a \le x \le x_2$ and $x_1 \le x \le b$ overlap by a finite amount $\Delta$ (see Figure 21–1).

Now evaluate $f(x_1)$ and $f(x_2)$. Three cases will result.

1. If $f(x_1) > f(x_2), x^*$ (optimum $x$) must lie between $a$ and $x_2$.
2. If $f(x_1) < f(x_2), x_1 < x^* < b$.
3. If $f(x_1) = f(x_2), x_1 < x^* < x_2$.

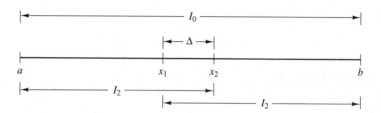

**Figure 21–1**

These results follow directly from the strict unimodality of $f(x)$. In each of these cases, the interval that does not include $x^*$ is discarded in future iterations.

The result of the search is that the maximum of $f(x)$ now lies in a smaller interval. The new interval is further dichotomized into two (overlapping) intervals in the same manner used with the interval $a \leq x \leq b$. Continuing in this manner, we can narrow the interval in which the local maximum lies to any reasonably small $\Delta$.

**Example 21.1-1.**

$$\text{Maximize } f(x) = \begin{cases} 3x, & 0 \leq x \leq 2 \\ -\dfrac{x}{3} + \dfrac{20}{3}, & 2 \leq x \leq 3 \end{cases}$$

We have max $f(x)$ at $x = 2$. Let $x_L$ and $x_R$ define the (left and right) boundaries of the *current* interval. Initially, $x_L = 0$ and $x_R = 3$. Define $x_1$ and $x_2$ as the points dichotomizing an interval so that the associated overlapping intervals are $x_L \leq x \leq x_2$ and $x_1 \leq x \leq x_R$, where $x_1 - x_L = x_R - x_2$ and $\Delta = x_2 - x_1$. This means that

$$x_1 = x_L + \frac{x_R - x_L - \Delta}{2}$$

$$x_2 = x_L + \frac{x_R - x_L + \Delta}{2}$$

Table 21-1 summarizes the computations given $\Delta = .001$.

The last step in Table 21-1 gives $x_L = 1.99737$ and $x_R = 2.00423$. This means that max $f(x)$ occurs at $x^*$, satisfying $1.99737 \leq x^* \leq 2.00423$. If the midpoint is used, this will give $x = 2.0008$, which close to the exact optimum $x^* = 2.0$.

**TABLE 21–1**
COMPUTATIONS FOR DICHOTOMOUS SEARCH METHOD[A]

| $x_L$ | $x_R$ | $x_1$ | $x_2$ | $f(x_1)$ | $f(x_2)$ |
|---|---|---|---|---|---|
| 0 | 3 | 1.4995 [L] | 1.5005 | 4.4985 | 4.5015 [b] |
| 1.4995 | 3 | 2.24925 | 2.25025 [R] | 5.91692 [b] | 5.91658 |
| 1.4995 | 2.25025 | 1.87437 [L] | 1.87537 | 5.62312 | 5.62612 [b] |
| 1.87437 | 2.25025 | 2.06181 | 2.06281 [R] | 5.97939 [b] | 5.97906 |

*Continued*

| $x_L$ | $x_R$ | $x_1$ | $x_2$ | $f(x_1)$ | $f(x_2)$ |
|-------|-------|-------|-------|----------|----------|
| 1.87437 | 2.06281 | 1.96809[L] | 1.96909 | 5.90427 | 5.90727 [b] |
| 1.96809 | 2.06281 | 2.01495 | 2.01595[R] | 5.99502 [b] | 5.99447 |
| 1.96809 | 2.01595 | 1.99152[L] | 1.99252 | 5.97456 | 5.97756 [b] |
| 1.99152 | 2.01595 | 2.00323 | 2.00423[R] | 5.99892 [b] | 5.99859 |
| 1.99152 | 2.00423 | 1.99737[L] | 1.99837 | 5.99213 | 5.99511 [b] |
| 1.99737 | 2.00423 | | | | |

[a]$L(R)$ indicates that $x_L(x_R)$ is set equal to $x_1(x_2)$ in the next step.
[b]$\max\{f(x_1), f(x_2)\}$.

### Problem set 21.1a

1. Solve Example 21.1-1 assuming that $\Delta = .01$. Compare the accuracy of the results with that in Table 21-1.

2. Find the maximum of each of the following functions by dichotomous search. Assume that $\Delta = .05$.

   **(a)** $f(x) = \dfrac{1}{|(x - 3)^3|}$,  $2 \le x \le 4$

   **(b)** $f(x) = x \cos x$,  $0 \le x \le \pi$

   **(c)** $f(x) = x \sin \pi x$,  $1.5 \le x \le 2.5$

   **(d)** $f(x) = -(x - 3)^2$,  $2 \le x \le 4$

   **(e)** $f(x) = \begin{cases} 4x, & 0 \le x \le 2 \\ 4 - x, & 2 \le x \le 4 \end{cases}$

3. Develop an expression for determining the maximum number of iterations needed to terminate the dichotomous search method for a given value of $\Delta$ and an initial interval of uncertainty $I_0 = b - a$.

## 21.1.2 GRADIENT METHOD

This section develops a method for optimizing functions that are twice continuously differentiable. The idea is to generate successive points in the direction of the gradient of the function.

The Newton-Raphson method presented in Section 20.2.2, is a gradient method for solving simultaneous equations. This section presents another technique, called the **steepest ascent** method.

Termination of the gradient method occurs at the point where the gradient vector becomes null. This is only a necessary condition for optimality. Optimality cannot be verified unless it is known a priori that $f(\mathbf{X})$ is concave or convex.

Suppose that $f(\mathbf{X})$ is maximized. Let $\mathbf{X}^0$ be the initial point from which the procedure starts and define $\nabla f(\mathbf{X}^k)$ as the gradient of $f$ at the $k$th point $\mathbf{X}^k$. The idea is to determine a particular path $p$ along which $df/dp$ is maximized at a given point. This result is achieved if successive points $\mathbf{X}^k$ and $\mathbf{X}^{k+1}$ are selected such that

$$\mathbf{X}^{k+1} = \mathbf{X}^k + r^k \nabla f(\mathbf{X}^k)$$

where $r^k$ is a parameter called the optimal **step size.**

The parameter $r^k$ is determined such that $\mathbf{X}^{k+1}$ results in the largest improvement in $f$. In other words, if a function $h(r)$ is defined such that

$$h(r) = f[\mathbf{X}^k + r \nabla f(\mathbf{X}^k)]$$

$r^k$ is the value of $r$ maximizing $h(r)$. Because $h(r)$ is a single-variable function, the search method in Section 21.1.1 may be used to find the optimum provided that $h(r)$ is strictly unimodal.

The proposed procedure terminates when two successive trial points $\mathbf{X}^k$ and $\mathbf{X}^{k+1}$ are approximately equal. This is equivalent to having

$$r^k \nabla f(\mathbf{X}^k) \approx 0$$

Given that $r^k \neq 0$, the necessary condition $\nabla f(\mathbf{X}^k) = 0$ is satisfied at $\mathbf{X}^k$.

---

**Example 21.1-2.**   Consider maximizing the function

$$f(x_1, x_2) = 4x_1 + 6x_2 - 2x_1^2 - 2x_1 x_2 - 2x_2^2$$

$f(x_1, x_2)$ is a quadratic function whose absolute optimum occurs at $(x_1^*, x_2^*) = (\frac{1}{3}, \frac{4}{3})$. It is shown how the problem is solved by the steepest ascent method. Figure 21-2 shows the successive points. The gradients at any two successive points are necessarily orthogonal (perpendicular).

Let the initial point be given by $\mathbf{X}^0 = (1, 1)$. Now

$$\nabla f(\mathbf{X}) = (4 - 4x_1 - 2x_2, 6 - 2x_1 - 4x_2)$$

*First Iteration*

$$\nabla f(\mathbf{X}^0) = (-2, 0)$$

The next point $\mathbf{X}^1$ is obtained by considering

$$\mathbf{X} = (1, 1) + r(-2, 0) = (1 - 2r, 1)$$

Thus,

$$h(r) = f(1 - 2r, 1) = -2(1 - 2r)^2 + 2(1 - 2r) + 4$$

The optimal step size yielding the maximum value of $h(r)$ is $r^1 = \frac{1}{4}$. This gives $\mathbf{X}^1 = (\frac{1}{2}, 1)$.

*Second Iteration*

$$\nabla f(\mathbf{X}^1) = (0, 1)$$

Consider

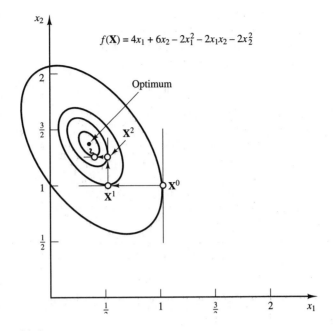

**Figure 21–2**

$$\mathbf{X} = \left(\frac{1}{2}, 1\right) + r(0, 1) = \left(\frac{1}{2}, 1 + r\right)$$

Thus,

$$h(r) = -2(1 + r)^2 + 5(1 + r) + \frac{3}{2}$$

This gives $r^2 = \frac{1}{4}$ or $\mathbf{X}^2 = (\frac{1}{2}, \frac{5}{4})$.
*Third Iteration*

$$\nabla f(\mathbf{X}^2) = \left(-\frac{1}{2}, 0\right)$$

Consider

$$\mathbf{X} = \left(\frac{1}{2}, \frac{5}{4}\right) + r\left(-\frac{1}{2}, 0\right) = \left(\frac{1 - r}{2}, \frac{5}{4}\right)$$

Thus,

$$h(r) = -\left(\frac{1}{2}\right)(1 - r)^2 + \left(\frac{3}{4}\right)(1 - r) + \frac{35}{8}$$

This gives $r^3 = \frac{1}{4}$ or $\mathbf{X}^3 = (\frac{3}{8}, \frac{5}{4})$.
*Fourth Iteration*

$$\nabla f(\mathbf{X}^3) = \left(0, \frac{1}{4}\right)$$

Consider

$$\mathbf{X} = \left(\frac{3}{8}, \frac{5}{4}\right) + r\left(0, \frac{1}{4}\right) = \left(\frac{3}{8}, \frac{5 + r}{4}\right)$$

Thus,

$$h(r) = -\left(\frac{1}{8}\right)(5 + r)^2 + \left(\frac{21}{16}\right)(5 + r) + \frac{39}{32}$$

This gives $r^4 = \frac{1}{4}$, or $\mathbf{X}^4 = (\frac{3}{8}, \frac{21}{16})$.
*Fifth Iteration*

$$\nabla f(\mathbf{X}^4) = \left(-\frac{1}{8}, 0\right)$$

Consider

$$\mathbf{X} = \left(\frac{3}{8}, \frac{21}{16}\right) + r\left(-\frac{1}{8}, 0\right) = \left(\frac{3 - r}{8}, \frac{21}{16}\right)$$

Thus

$$h(r) = -\left(\frac{1}{32}\right)(3 - r)^2 + \left(\frac{11}{64}\right)(3 - r) + \frac{567}{128}$$

This gives $r^5 = \frac{1}{4}$, or $\mathbf{X}^5 = (\frac{11}{32}, \frac{21}{16})$.
*Sixth Iteration*

$$\nabla f(\mathbf{X}^5) = \left(0, \frac{1}{16}\right)$$

Because $\nabla f(\mathbf{X}^5) \approx \mathbf{0}$, the process can be terminated at this point. The *approximate* maximum point is given by $\mathbf{X}^5 = (.3437, 1.3125)$. The exact optimum is $\mathbf{X}^* = (.3333, 1.3333)$.

---

## Problem set 21.1b

1. Show that, in general, the Newton-Raphson method (Section 20.2.2) when applied to a strictly concave quadratic function will converge in exactly one step. Apply the method to the maximization of

$$f(\mathbf{X}) = 4x_1 + 6x_2 - 2x_1^2 - 2x_1x_2 - 2x_2^2$$

2. Carry out at most five iterations for each of the following problems using the method of steepest descent (ascent). Assume that $\mathbf{X}^0 = \mathbf{0}$ in each case.
   (a) min $f(\mathbf{X}) = (x_2 - x_1^2)^2 + (1 - x_1)^2$
   (b) max $f(\mathbf{X}) = \mathbf{c}\mathbf{X} + \mathbf{X}^T\mathbf{A}\mathbf{X}$
      where

$$\mathbf{c} = (1, 3, 5)$$

$$\mathbf{A} = \begin{bmatrix} -5 & -3 & -\dfrac{1}{2} \\ -3 & -2 & 0 \\ -\dfrac{1}{2} & 0 & -\dfrac{1}{2} \end{bmatrix}$$

     **(c)** max $f(x) = 3 - x^2 - x^4$

     **(d)** min $f(\mathbf{X}) = x_1 - x_2 + x_1^2 - x_1 x_2$

## 21.2 CONSTRAINED ALGORITHMS

The general constrained nonlinear programming problem is defined as

$$\text{Maximize (or minimize) } z = f(\mathbf{X})$$

subject to

$$\mathbf{g}(\mathbf{X}) \le \mathbf{0}$$

The nonnegativity conditions $\mathbf{X} \ge \mathbf{0}$ are part of the given constraints. Also, at least one of the functions $f(\mathbf{X})$ and $\mathbf{g}(\mathbf{X})$ is nonlinear and all the functions are continuously differentiable.

     No general algorithm exists for handling nonlinear models, because of the irregular behavior of the nonlinear functions. Perhaps the most general result applicable to the problem is the Kuhn-Tucker conditions. Section 20.3.2 shows that unless $f(\mathbf{X})$ and $\mathbf{g}(\mathbf{X})$ are well-behaved functions (convexity and concavity conditions), the Kuhn-Tucker theory yields only necessary conditions for optimum.

     This section presents a number of algorithms that may be classified generally as *indirect* and *direct* methods. Indirect methods solve the nonlinear problem by dealing with one or more *linear* problems that are based on the original program. Direct methods deal with the nonlinear problem itself.

     The indirect methods presented in this section include separable, quadratic, geometric, and stochastic programming. The direct methods include the method of linear combinations and a brief discussion of the sequential unconstrained maximization technique. Other important nonlinear techniques can be found in the Selected References at the end of the chapter.

### 21.2.1 Separable Programming

A function $f(x_1, x_2, \ldots, x_n)$ is **separable** if it can be expressed as the sum of $n$ single-variable functions $f_1(x_1), f_2(x_2), \ldots, f_n(x_n)$— that is,

$$f(x_1, x_2 \ldots x_n) = f_1(x_1) + f_2(x_2) + \cdots + f_n(x_n)$$

For example, the linear function

$$h(x_1, x_2, \ldots, x_n) = a_1 x_1 + a_2 x_2 + \cdots + a_n x_n$$

(where the $a$'s are constants) is separable. Conversely, the function

$$h(x_1, x_2, x_3) = x_1^2 + x_1 \sin(x_2 + x_3) + x_2 e^{x3}$$

is not separable.

Some nonlinear functions are not directly separable but can be made so by appropriate substitutions. Consider, for example, the case of maximizing $z = x_1x_2$. If we let $y = x_1x_2$, then $\ln y = \ln x_1 + \ln x_2$ and the problem becomes

$$\text{Maximize } z = y$$

subject to

$$\ln y = \ln x_1 + \ln x_2$$

which is separable. The substitution assumes that $x_1$ and $x_2$ are *positive* variables; otherwise, the logarithmic function is undefined.

The case where $x_1$ and $x_2$ assume zero values (i.e., $x_1, x_2 \geq 0$) may be handled as follows. Let $\delta_1$ and $\delta_2$ be positive constants and define

$$w_1 = x_1 + \delta_1$$

$$w_2 = x_2 + \delta_2$$

This means that $w_1$ and $w_2$ are strictly positive. Now

$$x_1x_2 = w_1w_2 - \delta_2w_1 - \delta_1w_2 + \delta_1\delta_2$$

Let $y = w_1w_2$; then the problem is equivalent to

$$\text{Maximize } z = y - \delta_2w_1 - \delta_1w_2 + \delta_1\delta_2$$

subject to

$$\ln y = \ln w_1 + \ln w_2, \ w_1 \geq \delta_1, w_2 \geq \delta_2$$

which is separable.

Other functions that can be made separable (using substitution) are exemplified by $e^{x_1+x_2}$ and $x_1^{x_2}$. A variant of the procedure just presented can be applied to such cases to effect separability.

Separable programming deals with nonlinear problems in which the objective function and the constraints are separable. This section shows how an approximate solution can be obtained for any separable problem by linear approximation and the simplex method of linear programming.

The single-variable function $f(x)$ can be approximated by a piecewise linear function using mixed integer programming (Chapter 9). Suppose that $f(x)$ is to be approximated over the interval $[a, b]$. Define $a_k, k = 1, 2, \ldots, K$, as the $k$th breaking point on the $x$-axis such that $a_1 < a_2 < \cdots < a_k$. The points $a_1$ and $a_k$ coincide with the end points $a$ and $b$ of the interval under study. Thus, $f(x)$ is approximated as follows:

$$f(x) \approx \sum_{k=1}^{K} f(a_k)t_k$$

$$x = \sum_{k=1}^{K} a_k t_k$$

where $t_k$ is a nonnegative weight associated with the $k$th breaking point such that

$$\sum_{k=1}^{K} t_k = 1$$

Mixed integer programming ensures the validity of the approximation. Specifically, the approximation is valid if

1. At most two $t_k$ are positive.
2. If $t_k$ is a positive, then only an adjacent $t_{k+1}$ or $t_{k-1}$ can assume a positive value.

To show how these conditions are satisfied, consider the separable problem

$$\text{Maximize (or minimize) } z = \sum_{i=1}^{n} f_i(x_i)$$

subject to

$$\sum_{i=1}^{n} g_i^j(x_i) \le b_j, \quad j = 1, 2, \ldots, m$$

This problem can be approximated as a mixed integer program as follows. Let the number of breaking points for the $i$th variable $x_i$ equal $K_i$ and let $a_i^k$ be its $k$th breaking value. Let $t_i^k$ be the weight associated with the $k$th breaking point of the $i$th variable. Then the equivalent mixed problem is

$$\text{Maximize (or minimize) } z = \sum_{i=1}^{n} \sum_{k=1}^{K_i} f_i(a_i^k) t_i^k$$

subject to

$$\sum_{i=1}^{n} \sum_{k=1}^{K_i} g_i^j(a_i^k) t_i^k \le b_j, \quad j = 1, 2, \ldots, m$$

$$0 \le t_i^1 \le y_i^1$$

$$0 \le t_i^k \le y_i^{k-1} + y_i^k, \quad k = 2, 3, \ldots, K_i - 1$$

$$0 \le t_i^{K_i} \le y_i^{K_i-1}$$

$$\sum_{k=1}^{K_i-1} y_i^k = 1$$

$$\sum_{k=1}^{K_i} t_i^k = 1$$

$$y_i^k = 0 \text{ or } 1, \quad k = 1, 2, \ldots, K_i; \quad i = 1, 2, \ldots, n$$

The variables for the approximating problem are $t_i^k$ and $y_i^k$.

   This formulation shows how any separable problem can be solved, at least in principle, by mixed integer programming. The difficulty is that the number of constraints increases rather rapidly with the number of breaking points. In particular, the computational feasibility of the procedure is questionable because there are no reliable computer programs for solving large mixed integer programming problems.

Another method for solving the approximate model is the regular simplex method (Chapter 3) using the **restricted basis**. In this case the additional constraints involving $y_i^k$ are disregarded. The restricted basis specifies that *no more* than two *positive* $t_i^k$ can appear in the basis. Moreover, two $t_i^k$ can be positive only if they are adjacent. Thus the strict optimality condition of the simplex method is used to select the entering variable $t_i^k$ *only if* it satisfies the foregoing conditions. Otherwise, the variable $t_i^k$ having the next best optimality indicator $(z_i^k - c_i^k)$ is considered for entering the solution. The process is repeated until the optimality condition is satisfied or until it is impossible to introduce new $t_i^k$ without violating the restricted basis condition, whichever occurs first. The last tableau gives the approximate optimal solution to the problem.

The mixed integer programming method yields a global optimum to the approximate problem, whereas the restricted basis method can only guarantee a local optimum. Also, in the two methods, the approximate solution may not be feasible for the original problem. In fact, the approximate model may give rise to additional extreme points that do not exist in the original problem. This depends on the degree of refinement in the development of the linear approximation.

---

**Example 21.2-1.**    Consider the problem

$$\text{Maximize } z = x_1 + x_2^4$$

subject to

$$3x_1 + 2x_2^2 \leq 9$$

$$x_1, x_2 \geq 0$$

This example illustrates the application of the restricted basis method.

The exact optimum solution to this problem, obtained by inspection, is $x_1 = 0, x_2 = 2.12$ , and $z^* = 20.25$. To show how the approximating method is used, consider the separable functions

$$f_1(x_1) = x_1$$
$$f_2(x_2) = x_2^4$$
$$g_1^1(x_1) = 3x_1$$
$$g_1^2(x_2) = 2x_2^2$$

The functions $f_1(x_1)$ and $g_1^1(x_1)$ are left in their present form, since they are already linear. In this case, $x_1$ is treated as one of the variables. Considering $f_2(x_2)$ and $g_1^2(x_2)$, we assume that there are four breaking points $(K_2 = 4)$. Because the value of $x_2$ cannot exceed 3, it follows that

| $k$ | $a_2^k$ | $f_2(a_2^k)$ | $g_1^2(a_2^k)$ |
|---|---|---|---|
| 1 | 0 | 0 | 0 |
| 2 | 1 | 1 | 2 |
| 3 | 2 | 16 | 8 |
| 4 | 3 | 81 | 18 |

This yields

$$f_2(x_2) \approx t_2^1 f_2(a_2^1) + t_2^2 f_2(a_2^2) + t_2^3 f_2(a_2^3) + t_2^4 f_2(a_2^4)$$
$$\approx 0(t_2^1) + 1(t_2^2) + 16(t_2^3) + 81(t_2^4) = t_2^2 + {}_16t_2^3 + 81t_2^4$$

Similarly,

$$g_1^2(x_2) \approx 2t_2^2 + 8t_2^3 + 18t_2^4$$

The approximation problem thus becomes

$$\text{Maximize } z = x_1 + t_2^2 + 16t_2^3 + 18t_2^4$$

subject to

$$3x_1 + 2t_2^2 + 8t_2^3 + 18t_2^4 \leq 9$$
$$t_2^1 + t_2^2 + t_2^3 + t_2^4 = 1$$
$$t_2^k \geq 0, k = 1, 2, 3, 4$$
$$x_1 \geq 0$$

together with the restricted basis condition.

The initial simplex tableau (with rearranged columns to give a starting solution) is given by

| Basic | $x_1$ | $t_2^2$ | $t_2^3$ | $t_2^4$ | $S_1$ | $t_2^1$ | Solution |
|---|---|---|---|---|---|---|---|
| $z$ | −1 | −1 | −16 | −81 | 0 | 0 | 0 |
| $S_1$ | 3 | 2 | 8 | 18 | 1 | 0 | 9 |
| $t_2^1$ | 0 | 1 | 1 | 1 | 0 | 1 | 1 |

where $S_1$ ($\geq 0$) is a slack variable. (This problem happened to have an obvious starting solution. In general, one may have to use the artificial variables techniques, Section 3.4.)

From the $z$-row coefficients, $t_2^4$ is the entering variable. Since $t_2^1$ is basic, it must leave before $t_2^4$ can enter the solution (restricted basis condition). By the feasibility condition,

$S_1$ must be the leaving variable. This means that $t_2^4$ cannot enter the solution. Next consider $t_2^3$ (next best entering variable). Again $t_2^1$ must leave first. From the feasibility condition, $t_2^1$ is the leaving variable as desired. The new tableau thus becomes

| Basic | $x_1$ | $t_2^2$ | $t_2^3$ | $t_2^4$ | $S_1$ | $t_2^1$ | Solution |
|---|---|---|---|---|---|---|---|
| $z$ | $-1$ | $15$ | $0$ | $-65$ | $0$ | $16$ | $16$ |
| $S_1$ | $3$ | $-6$ | $0$ | $10$ | $1$ | $-8$ | $1$ |
| $t_2^3$ | $0$ | $1$ | $1$ | $1$ | $0$ | $1$ | $1$ |

Clearly, $t_2^4$ is the entering variable. Because $t_2^3$ is in the basis, $t_2^4$ is an admissible entering variable. The simplex method shows that $S_1$ will leave. Thus,

| Basic | $x_1$ | $t_2^2$ | $t_2^3$ | $t_2^4$ | $S_1$ | $t_2^1$ | Solution |
|---|---|---|---|---|---|---|---|
| $z$ | $\dfrac{37}{2}$ | $-24$ | $0$ | $0$ | $\dfrac{13}{2}$ | $-36$ | $22\dfrac{1}{2}$ |
| $t_2^4$ | $\dfrac{3}{10}$ | $-\dfrac{6}{10}$ | $0$ | $1$ | $\dfrac{1}{10}$ | $-\dfrac{8}{10}$ | $\dfrac{1}{10}$ |
| $t_2^3$ | $-\dfrac{3}{10}$ | $\dfrac{16}{10}$ | $1$ | $0$ | $-\dfrac{1}{10}$ | $\dfrac{18}{10}$ | $\dfrac{9}{10}$ |

The tableau shows that $t_2^1$ and $t_2^2$ are candidates for the entering variable. Because $t_2^1$ is not an adjacent point to the basic $t_2^3$ and $t_2^4$, it cannot enter. Also, $t_2^2$ cannot enter because $t_2^4$ cannot leave. The process ends at this point and the solution given is the best feasible solution for the approximate problem.

To find the solution in terms of $x_1$ and $x_2$, we consider

$$t_2^3 = \frac{9}{10} \text{ and } t_2^4 = \frac{1}{10}$$

Thus,

$$x_2 \approx 2t_2^3 + 3t_2^4 = 2\left(\frac{9}{10}\right) + 3\left(\frac{1}{10}\right) = 2.1$$

and $x_1 = 0$ and $z = 22.5$. The approximate optimum value of $x_2$ ($= 2.1$) is close to the true optimum value ($= 2.12$).

*Separable Convex Programming.* A special case of separable programming occurs when the functions $g_i^j(x_i)$ are convex, thus resulting in a convex solution space. In addition, the function $f_i(x_i)$ is convex in case of minimization and concave in case of maximization (see Table 20-2). Under such conditions, the following simplified approximation can be used.

Consider a minimization problem and let $f_i(x_i)$ be as shown in Figure 21-3. The breaking points of the function $f_i(x_i)$ are given by $x_i = a_{ki}, k = 0, 1, ..., K_i$. Let $x_{ki}$ define the increment of the variable $x_i$ in the range $(a_{k-1,i}, a_{ki})$, $k = 1, 2, ..., K_i$, and let $\rho_{ki}$ be the corresponding slope of the line segment in the same range.

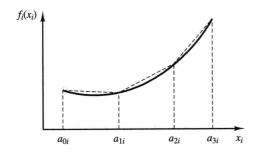

**Figure 21–3**

Then

$$f_i(x_i) \approx \sum_{k=1}^{K_i} (\rho_{ki} x_{ki}) + f_i(a_{oi})$$

$$x_i = \sum_{k=1}^{K_i} x_{ki}$$

provided that

$$0 \le x_{ki} \le a_{ki} - a_{k-1,I}, k = 1, 2, ..., K_i$$

The fact that $f_i(x_i)$ is convex ensures that $\rho_{1i} < \rho_{2i} < \cdots < \rho_{K_i i}$. This means that in the minimization problem, for $p < q$, the variable $x_{pi}$ is more attractive than $x_{qi}$. Consequently, $x_{pi}$ will always enter the solution before $x_{qi}$. The only limitation is that every $x_{ki}$ must be restricted by the upper bound $(a_{ki} - a_{k-1,i})$.

The convex constraint functions $g_i^j(x_i)$ are approximated in essentially the same way. Let $\rho_{ki}^j$ be the slope of the $k$th line segment corresponding to $g_i^j(x_i)$. It follows that the $i$th function is approximated as

$$g_i^j(x_i) \approx \sum_{k=1}^{K_i} \rho_{ki}^j x_{ki} + g_i^j(a_{oi})$$

The complete problem is thus given by

$$\text{Minimize } z = \sum_{i=1}^{n} \left( \sum_{k=1}^{K_i} \rho_{ki} x_{ki} + f_i(a_{oi}) \right)$$

subject to

$$\sum_{i=1}^{n} \left( \sum_{k=1}^{K_i} \rho_{ki}^j x_{ki} + g_i^j(a_{oi}) \right) \le b_j, \quad j = 1, 2, ..., m$$

$$0 \le x_{ki} \le a_{ki} - a_{k-1,i}, \quad k = 1, 2, ..., K_i, \quad i = 1, 2, ..., n$$

where

$$\rho_{ki} = \frac{f_i(a_{ki}) - f_i(a_{k-1,i})}{a_{ki} - a_{k-1,i}}$$

$$\rho_{ki}^j = \frac{g_i^j(a_{ki}) - g_i^j(a_{k-1,i})}{a_{ki} - a_{k-1,i}}$$

The maximization problem is treated essentially the same way. In this case $\rho_{1i} > \rho_{2i} > \cdots > \rho_{K_i i}$, which means that, for $p < q$, the variable $x_{pi}$ will always enter the solution before $x_{qi}$. (See Problem 21.2a-7 for the proof.)

The new problem can be solved by the simplex method with upper bounded variables (Section 7.5.2). The restricted basis concept is not needed because the convexity (concavity) of the functions guarantees the proper selection of variables.

---

**Example 21.2-2.**   Consider the problem

$$\text{Minimize } z = x_1^2 + x_2^2 + 5$$

subject to

$$3x_1^4 + x_2 \le 243$$

$$x_1 + 2x_2^2 \le 32$$

$$x_1, x_2 \ge 0$$

The separable functions of this problem are

$$f_1(x_1) = x_1^2, \quad f_2(x_2) = x_2^2 + 5$$

$$g_1^1(x_1) = 3x_1^4, \quad g_2^1(x_2) = x_2$$

$$g_1^2(x_1) = x_1, \quad g_2^2(x_2) = 2x_2^2$$

These functions satisfy the convexity condition required for the minimization problems.

The range of the variables $x_1$ and $x_2$, calculated from the constraints, are given by $0 \le x_1 \le 3$ and $0 \le x_2 \le 4$. Thus, $x_1$ and $x_2$ are partitioned in these ranges. Let $K_1 = 3$ and $K_2 = 4$ with $a_{01} = a_{02} = 0$. The slopes corresponding to the separable functions are as follows.

*For $i = 1$,*

| $k$ | $a_{k1}$ | $\rho_{k1}$ | $\rho_{k1}^1$ | $\rho_{k1}^2$ | $x_{k1}$ |
|---|---|---|---|---|---|
| 0 | 0 | — | — | — | — |
| 1 | 1 | 1 | 3 | 1 | $x_{11}$ |
| 2 | 2 | 3 | 45 | 1 | $x_{21}$ |
| 3 | 3 | 5 | 195 | 1 | $x_{31}$ |

*For $i = 2$,*

| $k$ | $a_{k2}$ | $\rho_{k2}$ | $\rho_{k2}^1$ | $\rho_{k2}^2$ | $x_{k2}$ |
|-----|----------|-------------|---------------|---------------|----------|
| 0 | 0 | — | — | — | — |
| 1 | 1 | 1 | 1 | 2 | $x_{12}$ |
| 2 | 2 | 3 | 1 | 6 | $x_{22}$ |
| 3 | 3 | 5 | 1 | 10 | $x_{32}$ |
| 4 | 4 | 7 | 1 | 14 | $x_{42}$ |

The complete problem then becomes

$$\text{Minimize } z \approx x_{11} + 3x_{21} + 5x_{31} + x_{12} + 3x_{22} + 5x_{32} + 7x_{42} + 5$$

subject to

$$3x_{11} + 45x_{21} + 195x_{31} + x_{12} + x_{22} + x_{32} + x_{42} \leq 243$$
$$x_{11} + x_{21} + x_{31} + 2x_{12} + 6x_{22} + 10x_{32} + 14x_{42} \leq 32$$
$$0 \leq x_{k1} \leq 1, \quad k = 1, 2, 3$$
$$0 \leq x_{k2} \leq 1, \quad k = 1, 2, 3, 4$$

After solving this problem using upper bounding technique, let $x_{k1}$ and $x_{k2}$ be the corresponding optimal values. Optimal values of $x_1$ and $x_2$ are then given by

$$x_1^* = \sum_{k=1}^{3} x_{k1}^*, \quad x_2^* = \sum_{k=1}^{4} x_{k2}^*$$

## Problem set 21.2a

1. Approximate the following problem as a mixed integer program.

$$\text{Maximize } z = e^{-x_1} + x_1 + (x_2 + 1)^2$$

subject to

$$x_1^2 + x_2 \leq 3$$
$$x_1, x_2 \quad \geq 0$$

2. Repeat Problem 1 using the restricted basis method. Then find the optimal solution.

3. Consider the problem

$$\text{Maximize } z = x_1 x_2 x_3$$

subject to

$$x_1^2 + x_2 + x_3 \leq 4$$

$$x_1, x_2, x_3 \geq 0$$

Approximate the problem as a linear program for use with the restricted basis method.

**4.** Show how the following problem can be made separable.

$$\text{Maximize } z = x_1 x_2 + x_3 + x_1 x_3$$

subject to

$$x_1 x_2 + x_2 + x_1 x_3 \leq 10$$

$$x_1, x_2, x_3 \geq 0$$

**5.** Show how the following problem can be made separable.

$$\text{Minimize } z = e^{2x_1 + x_2^2} + (x_3 - 2)^2$$

subject to

$$x_1 + x_2 + x_3 \leq 6$$

$$x_1, x_2, x_3 \geq 0$$

**6.** Show how the following problem can be made separable.

$$\text{Maximize } z = e^{x_1 x_2} + x_2^2 x_3 + x_4$$

subject to

$$x_1 + x_2 x_3 + x_3 \leq 10$$

$$x_1, x_2, x_3 \leq 0$$

$$x_4 \text{ unrestricted in sign}$$

**7.** Show that in separable convex programming (Section 21.2.1), it is never optimal to have $x_{ki} > 0$ when $x_{k-1,i}$ is not at its upper bound.

**8.** Solve as a separable convex programming problem.

$$\text{Minimize } z = x_1^4 + 2x_2 + x_3^2$$

subject to

$$x_1^2 + x_2 + x_3^2 \leq 4$$

$$|x_1 + x_2| \leq 0$$

$$x_1, x_3 \geq 0$$

$$x_2 \text{ unrestricted in sign}$$

**9.** Solve the following as a separate convex programming problem.

$$\text{Minimize } z = (x_1 - 2)^2 + 4(x_2 - 6)^2$$

subject to

$$6x_1 + 3(x_2 + 1)^2 \leq 12$$

$$x_1, x_2 \geq 0$$

## 21.2.2 Quadratic Programming

A quadratic programming model is defined as follows:

$$\text{Maximize (or minimize) } z = \mathbf{CX} + \mathbf{X}^T\mathbf{DX}$$

subject to

$$\mathbf{AX} \leq \mathbf{b}, \mathbf{X} \geq \mathbf{0}$$

where

$$\mathbf{X} = (x_1, x_2, ..., x_n)^T$$

$$\mathbf{C} = (c_1, c_2, ..., c_n)$$

$$\mathbf{b} = (b_1, b_2, ..., b_m)^T$$

$$\mathbf{A} = \begin{bmatrix} a_{11} & \cdots & a_{1n} \\ \vdots & & \vdots \\ a_{m1} & \cdots & a_{mn} \end{bmatrix}$$

$$\mathbf{D} = \begin{bmatrix} d_{11} & \cdots & d_{1n} \\ \vdots & & \vdots \\ d_{n1} & \cdots & d_{nn} \end{bmatrix}$$

The function $\mathbf{X}^T\mathbf{DX}$ defines a quadratic form (Section A.3) Where $\mathbf{D}$ is symmetric. The matrix $\mathbf{D}$ is negative definite if the problem is maximization, and positive definite if the problem is minimization. This means that $z$ is strictly convex in $\mathbf{X}$ for minimization and strictly concave for maximization. The constraints are assumed linear in this case, which guarantees a convex solution space.

The solution to this problem is based on the Kuhn-Tucker necessary conditions (Section 20.3.2). Because $z$ is strictly convex (or concave) and the solution space is a convex set, these conditions (as proved in Section 20.3.2) are also sufficient for a global optimum.

The quadratic programming problem will be treated for the maximization case. It is trivial to change the formulation to minimization. The problem may be written as

$$\text{Maximize } z = \mathbf{CX} + \mathbf{X}^T\mathbf{DX}$$

subject to

$$\mathbf{G(X)} = \begin{bmatrix} \mathbf{A} \\ -\mathbf{I} \end{bmatrix}\mathbf{X} - \begin{bmatrix} \mathbf{b} \\ \mathbf{0} \end{bmatrix} \leq \mathbf{0}$$

Let

$$\boldsymbol{\lambda} = (\lambda_1, \lambda_2, \ldots, \lambda_m)^T \text{ and } \mathbf{U} = (\mu_1, \mu_2, \ldots, \mu_n)^T$$

be the Lagrange multipliers corresponding to the two sets of constraints $\mathbf{AX} - \mathbf{b} \leq \mathbf{0}$ and $-\mathbf{X} \leq \mathbf{0}$, respectively. Application of the Kuhn-Tucker conditions immediately yields

$$\boldsymbol{\lambda} \geq \mathbf{0}, \mathbf{U} \geq \mathbf{0}$$

$$\nabla z - (\boldsymbol{\lambda}^T, \mathbf{U}^T)\nabla \mathbf{G(X)} = \mathbf{0}$$

$$\lambda_i\left(b_i - \sum_{j=1}^{n} a_{ij}x_j\right) = 0, \quad i = 1, 2, \ldots, m$$

$$\mu_j x_j = 0, \quad j = 1, 2, \ldots, n$$

$$\mathbf{AX} \leq \mathbf{b}, \quad -\mathbf{X} \leq \mathbf{0}$$

Now

$$\nabla z = \mathbf{C} + 2\mathbf{X}^T\mathbf{D}$$

$$\nabla \mathbf{G(X)} = \begin{bmatrix} \mathbf{A} \\ -\mathbf{I} \end{bmatrix}$$

Let $\mathbf{S} = \mathbf{b} - \mathbf{AX} \geq \mathbf{0}$ be the slack variables of the constraints. The conditions reduce to

$$-2\mathbf{X}^T\mathbf{D} + \boldsymbol{\lambda}^T\mathbf{A} - \mathbf{U}^T = \mathbf{C}$$

$$\mathbf{AX} + \mathbf{S} = \mathbf{b}$$

$$\mu_j x_j = 0 = \lambda_i S_i \quad \text{for all } i \text{ and } j$$

$$\boldsymbol{\lambda}, \mathbf{U}, \mathbf{X}, \mathbf{S} \geq \mathbf{0}$$

Because $\mathbf{D}^T = \mathbf{D}$, the transpose of the first set of equations yields

$$-2\mathbf{DX} + \mathbf{A}^T\boldsymbol{\lambda} - \mathbf{U} = \mathbf{C}^T$$

Hence, the necessary conditions may be combined as

$$\begin{bmatrix} -2\mathbf{D} & \mathbf{A}^T & -\mathbf{I} & \mathbf{0} \\ \mathbf{A} & \mathbf{0} & \mathbf{0} & \mathbf{I} \end{bmatrix}\begin{bmatrix} \mathbf{X} \\ \boldsymbol{\lambda} \\ \mathbf{U} \\ \mathbf{S} \end{bmatrix} = \begin{bmatrix} \mathbf{C}^T \\ \mathbf{b} \end{bmatrix}$$

$$\mu_j x_j = 0 = \lambda_i S_i, \qquad \text{for all } i \text{ and } j$$

$$\lambda, \mathbf{U}, \mathbf{X}, \mathbf{S} \geq 0$$

Except for the conditions $\mu_j x_j = 0 = \lambda_i S_i$, the remaining equations are linear functions in $\mathbf{X}, \lambda, \mathbf{U}$, and $\mathbf{S}$. The problem is thus equivalent to solving a set of linear equations, while satisfying the additional conditions $\mu_j x_j = 0 = \lambda_i S_i$. Because $z$ is strictly concave and the solution space is convex, the *feasible* solution satisfying all these conditions must give the unique optimum solution.

The solution of the system is obtained by using phase I of the two-phase method (Section 3.4.2). The only restriction is to satisfy the conditions $\lambda_i S_i = 0 = \mu_j x_j$. This means that if $\lambda_i$ is basic at a *positive level*, $S_i$ cannot become basic at positive level. Similarly, $\mu_j$ and $x_j$ cannot be positive simultaneously. This is the same idea of the *restricted basis* used in Section 21.2.1. Phase I will render all the artificial variables equal to zero only if the problem has a feasible space.

---

**Example 21.2-3.** Consider the problem

$$\text{Maximize } z = 4x_1 + 6x_2 - 2x_1^2 - 2x_1^2 - 2x_1 x_2 - 2x_2^2$$

subject to

$$x_1 + 2x_2 \leq 2$$

$$x_1, x_2 \geq 0$$

This problem can be put in matrix form as follows:

$$\text{Maximize } z = (4, 6)\begin{bmatrix} x_1 \\ x_2 \end{bmatrix} + (x_1, x_2)\begin{bmatrix} -2 & -1 \\ -1 & -2 \end{bmatrix}\begin{bmatrix} x_1 \\ x_2 \end{bmatrix}$$

subject to

$$(1, 2)\begin{bmatrix} x_1 \\ x_2 \end{bmatrix} \leq 2$$

$$x_1, x_2 \geq 0$$

The Kuhn-Tucker conditions are given as

$$\begin{bmatrix} 4 & 2 & 1 & -1 & 0 & 0 \\ 2 & 4 & 2 & 0 & -1 & 0 \\ 1 & 2 & 0 & 0 & 0 & 1 \end{bmatrix}\begin{bmatrix} x_1 \\ x_2 \\ \lambda_1 \\ \mu_1 \\ \mu_2 \\ S_1 \end{bmatrix} = \begin{bmatrix} 4 \\ 6 \\ 2 \end{bmatrix}$$

The initial tableau for phase 1 is obtained by introducing the artificial variables $R_1$ and $R_2$. Thus

| Basic | $x_1$ | $x_2$ | $\lambda_1$ | $\mu_1$ | $\mu_2$ | $R_1$ | $R_2$ | $S_1$ | Solution |
|---|---|---|---|---|---|---|---|---|---|
| $r$ | 6 | 6 | 3 | $-1$ | $-1$ | 0 | 0 | 0 | 10 |
| $R_1$ | 4 | 2 | 1 | $-1$ | 0 | 1 | 0 | 0 | 4 |
| $R_2$ | 2 | 4 | 2 | 0 | $-1$ | 0 | 1 | 0 | 6 |
| $S_1$ | 1 | 2 | 0 | 0 | 0 | 0 | 0 | 1 | 2 |

*First Iteration*

Because $\mu_1 = 0$, the most promising entering variable $x_1$ can be made basic with $R_1$ as the leaving variable. This yields the following tableau:

| Basic | $x_1$ | $x_2$ | $\lambda_1$ | $\mu_1$ | $\mu_2$ | $R_1$ | $R_2$ | $S_1$ | Solution |
|---|---|---|---|---|---|---|---|---|---|
| $r$ | 0 | 3 | $\frac{3}{2}$ | $\frac{1}{2}$ | $-1$ | $-\frac{3}{2}$ | 0 | 0 | 4 |
| $x_1$ | 1 | $\frac{1}{2}$ | $\frac{1}{4}$ | $-\frac{1}{4}$ | 0 | $\frac{1}{4}$ | 0 | 0 | 1 |
| $R_2$ | 0 | 3 | $\frac{3}{2}$ | $\frac{1}{2}$ | $-1$ | $-\frac{1}{2}$ | 1 | 0 | 4 |
| $S_1$ | 0 | $\frac{3}{2}$ | $-\frac{1}{4}$ | $\frac{1}{4}$ | 0 | $-\frac{1}{4}$ | 0 | 1 | 1 |

*Second Iteration*

The most promising variable $x_2$ can be made basic, because $\mu_2 = 0$. This gives

| Basic | $x_1$ | $x_2$ | $\lambda_1$ | $\mu_1$ | $\mu_2$ | $R_1$ | $R_2$ | $S_1$ | Solution |
|---|---|---|---|---|---|---|---|---|---|
| $r$ | 0 | 0 | 2 | 0 | $-1$ | $-1$ | 0 | $-2$ | 2 |
| $x_1$ | 1 | 0 | $\frac{1}{3}$ | $-\frac{1}{3}$ | 0 | $\frac{1}{3}$ | 0 | $-\frac{1}{3}$ | $\frac{2}{3}$ |
| $R_1$ | 0 | 0 | 2 | 0 | $-1$ | 0 | 1 | $-2$ | 2 |
| $x_1$ | 0 | 1 | $-\frac{1}{6}$ | $\frac{1}{6}$ | 0 | $-\frac{1}{6}$ | 0 | $\frac{2}{3}$ | $\frac{2}{3}$ |

*Third Iteration*

Because $S_1 = 0$, $\lambda_1$ can be introduced into the solution. This yields

| Basic | $x_1$ | $x_2$ | $\lambda_1$ | $\mu_1$ | $\mu_2$ | $R_1$ | $R_2$ | $S_1$ | Solution |
|---|---|---|---|---|---|---|---|---|---|
| $r$ | 0 | 0 | 0 | 0 | 0 | $-1$ | $-1$ | 0 | 0 |
| $x_1$ | 1 | 0 | 0 | $-\frac{1}{3}$ | $\frac{1}{6}$ | $\frac{1}{3}$ | $-\frac{1}{6}$ | 0 | $\frac{1}{3}$ |
| $\lambda_1$ | 0 | 0 | 1 | 0 | $-\frac{1}{2}$ | 0 | $\frac{1}{2}$ | $-1$ | 1 |
| $x_2$ | 0 | 1 | 0 | $\frac{1}{6}$ | $-\frac{1}{12}$ | $-\frac{1}{6}$ | $\frac{1}{12}$ | $\frac{1}{2}$ | $\frac{5}{6}$ |

The last tableau gives the optimal solution for phase I. Because $r = 0$, the solution, $x_1^* = \frac{1}{3}$, $x_2^* = \frac{5}{6}$, is feasible. The optimal value of $z$ is computed from the original problem and is equal to 4.16.

### Problem set 21.2b

**1.** Consider the problem

$$\text{Maximize } z = 6x_1 + 3x_2 - 4x_1x_2 - 2x_1^2 - 3x_2^2$$

subject to

$$x_1 + x_2 \le 1$$
$$2x_1 + 3x_2 \le 4$$
$$x_1, x_2 \le 0$$

Show that $z$ is strictly concave and then solve the problem using the quadratic programming algorithm.

**2.** Consider the problem:

$$\text{Minimize } z = 2x_1^2 + 2x_2^2 + 3x_3^2 + 2x_1x_2 + 2x_2x_3 + x_1 - 3x_2 - 5x_3$$

subject to

$$x_1 + x_2 + x_3 \ge 1$$
$$3x_1 + 2x_2 + x_3 \le 6$$
$$x_1, x_2, x_3 \ge 0$$

Show that $z$ is strictly convex and then solve by the quadratic programming algorithm.

### 21.2.3 Geometric Programming

*Geometric* programming solves a special case of nonlinear problems. This technique finds the solution by considering an associated dual problem (to be defined later).

Geometric programming deals with problems in which the objective and the constraint functions are of the following type:

$$z = f(\mathbf{X}) = \sum_{j=1}^{N} U_j$$

where

$$U_j = c_j \prod_{i=1}^{n} x_i^{a_{ij}}, \quad j = 1, 2, ..., N$$

It is assumed that all $c_j > 0$, and that $N$ is finite. The exponents $a_{ij}$ are unrestricted in sign. The function $f(\mathbf{X})$ takes the form of a polynomial except that the exponents $a_{ij}$ may be negative. For this reason, and because all $c_j > 0$, $f(\mathbf{X})$ is called a **posynomial.**

This section will present the unconstrained case of geometric programming. The treatment of the constrained problem is beyond the scope of this chapter. Detailed treatment of the subject is given in Beightler et al. (1979, Chap. 6).

Consider the *minimization* of the posynomial function $f(\mathbf{X})$. This problem will be referred to as the *primal.* The variables $x_i$ are assumed to be *strictly positive* so that the region $x_i \leq 0$ is infeasible. It will be shown later that the requirement $x_i \neq 0$ plays an essential part in the derivation of the results.

The first partial derivative of $z$ must vanish at a minimum point. Thus,

$$\frac{\partial z}{\partial x_k} = \sum_{j=1}^{N} \frac{\partial U_j}{\partial x_k} = \sum_{j=1}^{n} c_j a_{kj}(x_k)^{a_{kj}-1} \prod_{i \neq k} (x_i)^{a_{ij}} = 0, \quad k = 1, 2, ..., n$$

Because each $x_k > 0$ by assumption,

$$\frac{\partial z}{\partial x_k} = 0 = \frac{1}{x_k} \sum_{j=1}^{N} a_{kj} U_j, \quad k = 1, 2, ..., n$$

Let $z^*$ be the minimum value of $z$. It follows that $z^* > 0$, because $z$ is posynomial and each $x_k > 0$. Define

$$y_j = \frac{U_j^*}{z^*}$$

Thus $y_j > 0$ and $\sum_{j=1}^{n} y_j = 1$ The value of $y_j$ represents the relative contribution of the $j$th term $U_j$ to the optimal value of the objective function $z^*$. The *necessary* conditions can now be written as

$$\sum_{j=1}^{N} a_{kj} y_j = 0, \quad k = 1, 2, ..., n$$

$$\sum_{j=1}^{N} y_j = 1, \quad y_j > 0 \text{ for all } j$$

These are known as the **orthogonality** and **normality conditions** and will yield a unique solution for $y_j$ if $(n + 1) = N$ and all the equations are independent. The problem becomes more complex when $N > n + 1$ because the values of $y_j$ are no longer unique. It is shown later that it is possible to determine $y_j$ uniquely for the purpose of minimizing $z$.

Suppose that $y_j^*$ are unique. Then $z^*$ and $x_i^*, i = 1, 2, ..., n$, are determined as follows. Consider

$$z^* = (z^*)^{\sum_{j=1}^{N} y_j^*}$$

Because $z^* = \frac{U_j^*}{y_j^*}$, it follows that

$$z^* = \left(\frac{U_1^*}{y_1^*}\right)^{y_1^*} \left(\frac{U_2^*}{y_2^*}\right)^{y_2^*} \cdots \left(\frac{U_N^*}{y_N^*}\right)^{y_N^*} = \left\{\prod_{j=1}^{N}\left(\frac{c_j}{y_j^*}\right)^{y_j^*}\right\}\left\{\prod_{j=1}^{N}\left(\prod_{i=1}^{N} x_j^{*a_{ij}}\right)^{y_j^*}\right\}$$

$$= \left\{\prod_{j=1}^{N}\left(\frac{c_j}{y_j^*}\right)^{y_j^*}\right\}\left\{\prod_{i=1}^{N}(x_i^*)^{\sum_{i=1}^{n}a_{ij}y_j^*}\right\} = \prod_{j=1}^{N}\left(\frac{c_j}{y_j^*}\right)^{y_j^*}$$

This step is justified because $\sum_{j=1}^{N}a_{ij}y_j = 0$. The value of $z^*$ is thus determined as soon as all $y_j$ are determined. Now, given $y_j^*$ and $z^*$, $U_j^* = y_j^* z^*$ can be determined. The simultaneous solution of the following equations should yield $x_i^*$:

$$U_j^* = c_j \prod_{i=1}^{N}(x_i^*)^{a_{ij}}, \quad j = 1, 2, , n$$

The procedure shows that the solution to the original posynomial $z$ can be transformed into the solution of a set of linear equations in $y_j$. All $y_j^*$ are determined from the necessary conditions for a minimum. It can be shown that these conditions are also sufficient. The proof is given in Beightler et al. (1979, p. 333).

The variables $y_j$ actually define the dual variables associated with the $z$-primal problem. To see this relationship, consider the primal problem in the form

$$z = \sum_{j=1}^{N} y_j\left(\frac{U_j}{y_j}\right)$$

Now define the function

$$w = \prod_{j=1}^{N}\left(\frac{U_j}{y_j}\right)^{y_j} = \prod_{j=1}^{N}\left(\frac{c_j}{y_j}\right)^{y_j}$$

Because $\sum_{j=1}^{N}y_j = 1$ and $y_j > 0$, by Cauchy's inequality,[†] we have

$$w \leq z$$

---

[†] The Cauchy's inequality states that for $z_j > 0$,

$$\sum_{j=1}^{N} w_j z_j \geq \prod_{j=1}^{N}(z_j)^{w_j}, \quad \text{where } w_j > 0 \text{ and } \sum_{j=1}^{N} w_j = 1$$

This is also called the arithmetic–geometric mean inequality.

The function $w$ with its variables $y_1, y_2, \ldots, y_N$ defines the dual problem to the primal. Because $w$ represents the lower bound on $z$ and $z$ is associated with the minimization problem, it follows, by maximizing $w$, that

$$w^* = \max_{y_j} w = \min_{x_i} z = z^*$$

This means that the maximum value of $w\ (= w^*)$ over the values of $y_j$ is equal to the minimum value of $z\ (= z^*)$ over the values of $x_i$.

---

**Example 21.2-4.**

In this example a problem is considered in which $N = n + 1$ so that the solution to the orthogonality and normality conditions is unique. The next example illustrates the other case, where $N > n + 1$.

Consider the problem

$$\text{Minimize } z = 7x_1 x_2^{-1} + 3x_2 x_3^{-2} + 5x_1^{-3} x_2 x_3 + x_1 x_2 x_3$$

This function may be written as

$$z = 7x_1^1 x_2^{-1} x_3^0 + 3x_1^0 x_2^1 x_3^{-2} + 5x_1^{-3} x_2^1 x_3^1 + x_1^1 x_2^1 x_3^1$$

so that

$$(c_1, c_2, c_3, c_4) = (7, 3, 5, 1)$$

$$\begin{bmatrix} a_{11} & a_{12} & a_{13} & a_{14} \\ a_{21} & a_{22} & a_{23} & a_{24} \\ a_{31} & a_{32} & a_{33} & a_{34} \end{bmatrix} = \begin{bmatrix} 1 & 0 & -3 & 1 \\ -1 & 1 & 1 & 1 \\ 0 & -2 & 1 & 1 \end{bmatrix}$$

The orthogonality and normality conditions are thus given by

$$\begin{bmatrix} 1 & 0 & -3 & 1 \\ -1 & 1 & 1 & 1 \\ 0 & -2 & 1 & 1 \\ 1 & 1 & 1 & 1 \end{bmatrix} \begin{bmatrix} y_1 \\ y_2 \\ y_3 \\ y_4 \end{bmatrix} = \begin{bmatrix} 0 \\ 0 \\ 0 \\ 1 \end{bmatrix}$$

This yields the unique solution

$$y_1^* = \frac{12}{24}, \quad y_2^* = \frac{4}{24}, \quad y_3^* = \frac{5}{24}, \quad y_4^* = \frac{3}{24}$$

Thus,

$$z^* = \left(\frac{7}{\left(\frac{12}{24}\right)}\right)^{\frac{12}{24}} \left(\frac{3}{\left(\frac{4}{24}\right)}\right)^{\frac{4}{24}} \left(\frac{5}{\left(\frac{5}{24}\right)}\right)^{\frac{5}{24}} \left(\frac{1}{\left(\frac{3}{24}\right)}\right)^{\frac{3}{24}} = 15.22$$

From the equation $U_j^* = y_j^* z^*$ it follows that

$$7x_1 x_2^{-1} = U_1 = \left(\frac{1}{2}\right)(15.22) = 7.61$$

$$3x_2 x_3^{-2} = U_2 = \left(\frac{1}{6}\right)(15.22) = 2.54$$

$$5x_1^{-3}x_2x_3 = U_3 = \left(\frac{5}{24}\right)(15.22) = 3.17$$

$$x_1x_2x_3 = U_4 = \left(\frac{1}{8}\right)(15.22) = 1.90$$

The solution of these equations is given by

$$x_1^* = 1.315, \; x_2^* = 1.21, \; x_3^* = 1.2$$

which is the optimal solution to the primal.

---

**Example 21.2-5.**   Consider the problem

$$\text{Minimize } z = 5x_1x_2^{-1} + 2x_1^{-1}x_2 + 5x_1 + x_2^{-1}$$

The orthogonality and normality conditions are given by

$$
\begin{bmatrix}
1 & -1 & 1 & 0 \\
-1 & 1 & 0 & -1 \\
1 & 1 & 1 & 1
\end{bmatrix}
\begin{bmatrix}
y_1 \\
y_2 \\
y_3 \\
y_4
\end{bmatrix}
=
\begin{bmatrix}
0 \\
0 \\
1
\end{bmatrix}
$$

Because $N > n + 1$, these equations do not yield $y_j$ directly. Solving for $y_1, y_2,$ and $y_3$ in terms of $y_4$ we get

$$
\begin{bmatrix}
1 & -1 & 1 \\
-1 & 1 & 0 \\
1 & 1 & 1
\end{bmatrix}
\begin{bmatrix}
y_1 \\
y_2 \\
y_3
\end{bmatrix}
=
\begin{bmatrix}
0 \\
y_4 \\
1 - y_4
\end{bmatrix}
$$

or

$$y_1 = \frac{(1 - 3y_4)}{2}$$

$$y_2 = \frac{(1 - y_4)}{2}$$

$$y_3 = y_4$$

The dual problem may now be written as

$$\text{Maximize } w = \left[\frac{5}{.5(1 - 3y_4)}\right]^{.5(1 - 3y_4)}\left[\frac{2}{.5(1 - y_4)}\right]^{.5(1 - y_4)}\left(\frac{5}{y_4}\right)^{y_4}\left(\frac{1}{y_4}\right)^{y_4}$$

Maximization of $w$ is equivalent to maximization of $\ln w$. The latter is easier to manipulate, however. Thus,

$$\ln w = .5(1 - 3y_4)\,\{\ln 10 - \ln(1 - 3y_4)\} + .5(1 - y_4)\{\ln 4 - \ln(1 - y_4)\}$$

$$+ y_4\{\ln 5 - \ln y_4 + (\ln 1 - \ln y_4)\}$$

The value of $y_4$ maximizing $\ln w$ must be unique (because the primal problem has a unique minimum). Hence,

$$\frac{\partial \ln w}{\partial y_4} = \left(\frac{-3}{2}\right)\ln 10 - \left\{\left(\frac{-3}{2}\right) + \left(\frac{-3}{2}\right)\ln(1 - 3y_4)\right\}$$

$$+ \left(\frac{-1}{2}\right)\ln 4 - \left\{\left(\frac{-1}{2}\right) + \left(\frac{-1}{2}\right)\ln(1 - y_4)\right\}$$

$$+ \ln 5 - \{1 + \ln y_4\} + \ln 1 - \{1 + \ln y_4\} = 0$$

This gives, after simplification,

$$-\ln\left(\frac{2 \times 10^{\frac{3}{2}}}{5}\right) + \ln\left[\frac{(1 - 3y_4)^{\frac{3}{2}}(1 - y_4)^{\frac{1}{2}}}{y_4^2}\right] = 0$$

or

$$\frac{\sqrt{(1 - 3y_4)^3(1 - y_4)}}{y_4^2} = 12.6$$

which yields $y_4^* \approx .16$. Hence, $y_3^* = .16$, $y_2^* = .42$, and $y_1^* = .26$. The value of $z^*$ is obtained from

$$z^* = w^* = \left(\frac{5}{.26}\right)^{.26}\left(\frac{2}{.42}\right)^{.42}\left(\frac{5}{.16}\right)^{.16} \approx 9.661$$

Hence,

$$U_3 = .16(9.661) = 1.546 = 5x_1$$
$$U_4 = .16(9.661) = .1546 = x_2^{-1}$$

The equations yield $x_1^* = .309$ and $x_2^* = .647$.

## Problem set 21.2c

1. Solve the following problem by geometric programming.

$$\text{Minimize } z = 2x_1^{-1}x_2^2 + x_1^4x_2^{-2} + 4x_1^2$$

$$x_1, x_2 > 0$$

2. Solve the following problem by geometric programming.

$$\text{Minimize } z = 5x_1x_2^{-1}x_3^2 + x_1^{-2}x_3^{-1} + 10x_2^3 + 2x_1^{-1}x_2x_3^{-3}$$

$$x_1, x_2, x_3 > 0$$

3. Solve the following problem by geometric programming.

$$\text{Minimize } z = 2x_1^2x_2^{-3} + 8x_1^{-3}x_2 + 3x_1x_2$$

4. Solve the following problem by geometric programming.

$$\text{Minimize } z = 2x_1^3x_2^{-3} + 4x_1^{-2}x_2 + x_1x_2 + 8x_1x_2^{-1}$$

$$x_1, x_2 > 0$$

### 21.2.4 Stochastic Programming

Stochastic programming deals with situations where some or all parameters of the problem are described by random variables. Such cases seem typical of real-life problems, where it is difficult to determine the values of the parameters exactly.

The idea of stochastic programming is to convert the probabilistic nature of the problem into an equivalent deterministic situation. This section deals with the technique of **chance-constrained programming,** defined as

$$\text{Maximize } z = \sum_{j=1}^{n} c_j x_j$$

subject to

$$P\left\{ \sum_{j=1}^{n} a_{ij} x_j \le b_i \right\} \ge 1 - \alpha_i, \quad i = 1, 2, , m; \quad x_j \ge 0, \quad \text{for all } j$$

The name "chance-constrained" follows from the fact that each constraint is realized with a minimum probability of $1 - \alpha_i, 0 < \alpha_i < 1$. It is assumed that all $a_{ij}$ and $b_i$ are random variables. Three cases are considered. The first two correspond to the separate considerations of $a_{ij}$ and $b_i$ as random variables. The third case combines the random effects of $a_{ij}$ and $b_i$. In all three cases, it is assumed that the parameters are normally distributed with known means and variances.

***Case* 1.**    Each $a_{ij}$ is normally distributed with mean $E\{a_{ij}\}$ and variance var$\{a_{ij}\}$. Also, the covariance of $a_{ij}$ and $a_{i'j'}$ is given by cov$\{a_{ij}, a_{i'j'}\}$.

Consider the $i$th constraint

$$P\left\{ \sum_{j=1}^{n} a_{ij} x_j \le b_i \right\} \ge 1 - \alpha_i$$

and define

$$h_i = \sum_{j=1}^{n} a_{ij} x_j$$

Then $h_i$ is normally distributed with

$$E\{h_i\} = \sum_{j=1}^{n} E\{a_{ij}\} x_j \quad \text{and} \quad \text{var}\{h_i\} = \mathbf{X}^T \mathbf{D}_i \mathbf{X}$$

where $\mathbf{X} = (x_1, ..., x_n)^T$

$$\mathbf{D}_i = i\text{th covariance matrix} = \begin{bmatrix} \text{var}\{a_{i1}\} & \cdots & \text{cov}\{a_{i1}, a_{in}\} \\ \vdots & & \vdots \\ \text{cov}\{a_{in}, a_{i1}\} & \cdots & \text{var}\{a_{in}\} \end{bmatrix}$$

Now

$$P\{h_i \le b_i\} = P\left\{ \frac{h_i - E\{h_i\}}{\sqrt{\text{var}\{h_i\}}} \le \frac{b_i - E\{h_i\}}{\sqrt{\text{var}\{h_i\}}} \right\} \ge 1 - \alpha_i$$

where $\frac{(h_i - E\{h_i\})}{\sqrt{var\{h_i\}}}$ is standard normal with mean zero and variance one. This means that

$$P\{h_i \le b_i\} = F\left(\frac{b_i - E\{h_i\}}{\sqrt{\mathrm{var}\{h_i\}}}\right)$$

where $\Phi$ represents the CDF of the standard normal distribution. Let $K_{\alpha i}$ be the standard normal value such that

$$F(K_{\alpha i}) = 1 - \alpha_i$$

Then the statement $P\{h_i \le b_i\} \ge 1 - \alpha_i$ is realized if and only if

$$\frac{b_i - E\{h_i\}}{\sqrt{\mathrm{var}\{h_i\}}} \ge K_{\alpha i}$$

This yields the following nonlinear deterministic constraint:

$$\sum_{j=1}^{n} E\{a_{ij}\}x_j + K_{\alpha i}\sqrt{\mathbf{X}^T \mathbf{D}_i \mathbf{X}} \le b_i$$

For the special case where the normal distributions are independent,

$$\mathrm{cov}\{a_{ij}, a_{i'j'}\} = 0$$

and the last constraint reduces to

$$\sum_{j=1}^{n} E\{a_{ij}\}x_j + K_{\alpha i}\sqrt{\sum_{j=1}^{n} \mathrm{var}\{a_{ij}\}x_j^2} \le b_i$$

This constraint can be put in the separable programming form (Section 21.2.1) by using the substitution

$$y_i = \sqrt{\sum_{j=1}^{n} \mathrm{var}\{a_{ij}\}x_j^2}, \text{ for all } i$$

Thus, the original constraint is equivalent to

$$\sum_{j=1}^{n} E\{a_{ij}\}x_j + K_{\alpha i}y_i \le b_i$$

and

$$\sum_{j=1}^{n} \mathrm{var}\{a_{ij}\}x_j^2 - y_i^2 = 0$$

**Case 2.** Only $b_i$ is normal with mean $E\{b_i\}$ and variance $\mathrm{var}\{b_i\}$. The analysis is similar to that of case 1. Consider the stochastic constraint

$$P\left\{b_i \ge \sum_{j=1}^{n} a_{ij}x_j\right\} \ge \alpha_i$$

As in case 1,

$$P\left\{\frac{b_i - E\{b_i\}}{\sqrt{\mathrm{var}\{b_i\}}} \ge \frac{\sum_{j=1}^{n} a_{ij}x_j - E\{b_i\}}{\sqrt{\mathrm{var}\{b_i\}}}\right\} \ge \alpha_i$$

This can hold only if

$$\frac{\sum_{j=1}^{n} a_{ij}x_j - E\{b_i\}}{\sqrt{\text{var}\{b_i\}}} \leq K_{\alpha i}$$

Thus, the stochastic constraint is equivalent to the deterministic linear constraint

$$\sum_{j=1}^{n} a_{ij}x_j \leq E\{b_i\} + K_{\alpha i}\sqrt{\text{var}\{b_i\}}$$

**Case 3.** In this case all $a_{ij}$ and $b_i$ are normal random variables. Consider the constraint

$$\sum_{j=1}^{n} a_{ij}x_j \leq b_i$$

This may be written

$$\sum_{j=1}^{n} a_{ij}x_j - b_i \leq 0$$

Because all $a_{ij}$ and $b_i$ are normal, it follows from the theory of statistics that $\sum_{j=1}^{n} a_{ij}x_j - b_i$ is also normal. This shows that the chance constraint reduces to the same situation given in case 1 and is treated in a similar manner.

---

**Example 21.2-6.**    Consider the chance-constrained problem

$$\text{Maximize } z = 5x_1 + 6x_2 + 3x_3$$

subject to

$$P\{a_{11}x_1 + a_{12}x_2 + a_{13}x_3 \leq 8\} \geq .95$$
$$P\{5x_1 + x_2 + 6x_3 \leq b_2\} \geq .10$$

with all $x_j \geq 0$. Suppose that the $a_{1j}$'s are *independent* normally distributed random variables with the following means and variances:

$$E\{a_{11}\} = 1, E\{a_{12}\} = 3, E\{a_{13}\} = 9$$
$$\text{var}\{a_{11}\} = 25, \text{var}\{a_{12}\} = 16, \text{var}\{a_{13}\} = 4$$

The parameter $b_2$ is normally distributed with mean 7 and variance 9.

From standard normal tables in Appendix D,

$$K_{\alpha 1} = K_{.05} \approx 1.645, \quad K_{\alpha 2} = K_{.10} \approx 1.285$$

For the first constraint, the equivalent deterministic constraint is given by

$$x_1 + 3x_2 + 9x_3 + 1.645\sqrt{25x_1^2 + 16x_2^2 + 4x_3^2} \leq 8$$

and for the second constraint

$$5x_1 + x_2 + 6x_3 \leq 7 + 1.285(3) = 10.855$$

If we let

$$y^2 = 25x_1^2 + 16x_2^2 + 4x_3^2$$

the complete problem then becomes

$$\text{Maximize } z = 5x_1 + 6x_1 + 3x_3$$

subject to

$$x_1 + 3x_2 + 9x_3 + 1.645\, y \le 8$$

$$25x_1^2 + 16x_2^2 + 4x_3^2 - y^2 = 0$$

$$5x_1 + x_2 + 6x_3 \le 10.855$$

$$x_1, x_2, x_3, y \ge 0$$

which can be solved by separable programming.

---

### Problem set 21.2d

**1.** Convert the following stochastic problem into an equivalent deterministic model.

$$\text{Maximixe } z = x_1 + 2x_2 + 5x_3$$

subject to

$$P\{a_1 x_1 + 3x_2 + a_3 x_3 \le 10\} \ge 0.9$$

$$P\{7x_1 + 5x_2 + x_3 \le b_2\} \ge 0.1$$

$$x_1, x_2, x_3 \ge 0$$

Assume that $a_1$ and $a_3$ are independent and normally distributed random variables with means $E\{a_1\} = 2$ and $E\{a_3\} = 5$ and variances $\text{var}\{a_1\} = 9$ and $\text{var}\{a_3\} = 16$. Assume further that $b_2$ is normally distributed with mean 15 and variance 25.

**2.** Consider the following stochastic programming model:

$$\text{Maximize } z = x_1 + x_2^2 + x_3$$

subject to

$$P\{x_1^2 + a_2 x_2^3 + a_3 \sqrt{x_3} \le 10\} \ge 0.9$$

$$x_1, x_2, x_3 \ge 0$$

The parameters $a_2$ and $a_3$ are independent and normally distributed random variables with means 5 and 2, and variance 16 and 25, respectively. Convert the problem into the (deterministic) separable programming form.

### 21.2.5 Linear Combinations Method

This method deals with the following problem in which all constraints are linear:

$$\text{Maximize } z = f(\mathbf{X})$$

subject to

$$\mathbf{AX} \le \mathbf{b}, \quad \mathbf{X} \ge \mathbf{0}$$

The procedure is based on the steepest ascent (gradient) method (Section 21.1.2). However, the direction specified by the gradient vector may not yield a feasible solution for the constrained problem. Also, the gradient vector will not necessarily be null at the optimum (constrained) point. The steepest ascent method must be modified to handle the constrained case.

Let $\mathbf{X}^k$ be the *feasible* trial point at the $k$th iteration. The objective function $f(\mathbf{X})$ can be expanded in the neighborhood of $\mathbf{X}^k$ using Taylor's series. This gives

$$f(\mathbf{X}) \approx f(\mathbf{X}^k) + \nabla f(\mathbf{X}^k)(\mathbf{X} - \mathbf{X}^k) = (f(\mathbf{X}^k) - \nabla f(\mathbf{X}^k)\mathbf{X}^k) + \nabla f(\mathbf{X}^k)\mathbf{X}$$

The procedure calls for determining a feasible point $\mathbf{X} = \mathbf{X}^*$ such that $f(\mathbf{X})$ is maximized subject to the (linear) constraints of the problem. Because $(f(\mathbf{X}^k) - \nabla f(\mathbf{X}^k)\mathbf{X}^k)$ is a constant, the problem for determining $\mathbf{X}^*$ reduce to solving the following linear program:

$$\text{Maximize } w_k(\mathbf{X}) = \nabla f(\mathbf{X}^k)\mathbf{X}$$

subject to

$$\mathbf{AX} \le \mathbf{b}, \mathbf{X} \ge \mathbf{0}$$

Because $w_k$ is constructed from the gradient of $f(\mathbf{X})$ at $\mathbf{X}^k$, an improved solution point can be secured if and only if $w_k(\mathbf{X}^*) > (\mathbf{X}^k)$. From Taylor's expansion, this does not guarantee that $f(\mathbf{X}^*) > f(\mathbf{X}^k)$ unless $\mathbf{X}^*$ is in the neighborhood of $\mathbf{X}^k$. However, given $w_k(\mathbf{X}^*) > w_k(\mathbf{X}^k)$, there must exist a point $\mathbf{X}^{k+1}$ on the line segment $(\mathbf{X}^k, \mathbf{X}^*)$ such that $f(\mathbf{X}^{k+1}) > f(\mathbf{X}^k)$. The objective is to determine $\mathbf{X}^{k+1}$. Define

$$\mathbf{X}^{k+1} = (1 - r)\mathbf{X}^k + r\mathbf{X}^* = \mathbf{X}^k + r(\mathbf{X}^* - \mathbf{X}^k), \quad 0 < r \le 1$$

This means that $\mathbf{X}^{k+1}$ is a **linear combination** of $\mathbf{X}^k$ and $\mathbf{X}^*$. Because $\mathbf{X}^k$ and $\mathbf{X}^*$ are two feasible points in a *convex* solution space, $\mathbf{X}^{k+1}$ is also feasible. By comparison with the steepest ascent method (Section 21.1.2), the parameter $r$ may be regarded as a step size.

The point $\mathbf{X}^{k+1}$ is determined such that $f(\mathbf{X})$ is maximized. Because $\mathbf{X}^{k+1}$ is a function of $r$ only, $\mathbf{X}^{k+1}$ is determined by maximizing

$$h(r) = f[\mathbf{X}^k + r(\mathbf{X}^* = -\mathbf{X}^k)]$$

The procedure is repeated until at the $k$th iteration the condition $w_k(\mathbf{X}^*) \le w_k(\mathbf{X}^k)$ is satisfied. At this point, no further improvements are possible, and the process terminates with $\mathbf{X}^k$ as the best solution point.

The linear programming problems generated at the successive iterations differ only in the coefficients of the objective function. The sensitivity analysis procedures presented in Section 4.7 thus may be used to carry out calculations efficiently.

---

**Example 21.2-7.**   Consider the quadratic programming of Example 21.2-3.

$$\text{Maximize } f(\mathbf{X}) = 4x_1 + 6x_2 - 2x_1^2 - 2x_1x_2 - xx_2^2$$

subject to

$$x_1 + 2x_2 \leq 2$$

$$x_1, x_2 \geq 0$$

Let the initial trial point be $\mathbf{X}^0 = \frac{1}{2}, \frac{1}{2}$, which is feasible. Now

$$\nabla f(\mathbf{X}) = (4 - 4x_1 - 2x_2, 6 - 2x_1 - 4x_2)$$

*First Iteration*

$$\nabla f(\mathbf{X}^0) = (1, 3)$$

The associated linear program maximizes $w_1 = x_1 + 3x_2$ subject to the constraints of the original problem. This gives the optimal solution $\mathbf{X}^* = (0, 1)$. The values of $w_1$ at $\mathbf{X}^0$ and $\mathbf{X}^*$ equal 2 and 3, respectively. Hence a new trial point is determined as

$$\mathbf{X}^1 = \left(\frac{1}{2}, \frac{1}{2}\right) + r\left[(0, 1) - \left(\frac{1}{2}, \frac{1}{2}\right)\right] = \left(\frac{1-r}{2}, \frac{1+r}{2}\right)$$

The maximization of

$$h(r) = f\left(\frac{1-r}{2}, \frac{1+r}{2}\right)$$

yields $r^1 = 1$. Thus $\mathbf{X}^1 = (0, 1)$ with $f(\mathbf{X}^1) = 4$.
*Second Iteration*

$$\nabla f(\mathbf{X}^1) = (2, 2)$$

The objective function of the new linear programming problem is $w_2 = 2x_1 + 2x_2$. The optimum solution to this problem yields $\mathbf{X}^* = (2, 0)$. Because the values of $w_2$ at $\mathbf{X}^1$ and $\mathbf{X}^*$ are 2 and 4 a new trial point must be determined. Thus

$$\mathbf{X}^2 = (0, 1) + r[(2, 0) - (0, 1)] = (2r, 1 - r)$$

The maximization of

$$h(r) = f(2r, 1 - r)$$

yields $r^2 = \frac{1}{6}$. Thus $\mathbf{X}^2 = (\frac{1}{3}, \frac{5}{6})$ with $f(\mathbf{X})^2 \approx 4.16$.

*Third Iteration*

$$\nabla f(\mathbf{X}^2) = (1, 2)$$

The corresponding objective function is $w_3 = x_1 + 2x_2$. The optimum solution of this problem yields the alternative solutions $\mathbf{X}^* = (0, 1)$ and $\mathbf{X}^* = (2, 0)$. The value of $w_3$ for both points equals its value at $\mathbf{X}^2$. Consequently, no further improvements are possible. The *approximate* optimum solution is $\mathbf{X}^2 = (\frac{1}{3}, \frac{5}{6})$ with $f(\mathbf{X}^2) \approx 4.16$. This happens to be the exact optimum.

---

### Problem set 21.2e

**1.** Solve the following problem by the linear combinations method.

$$\text{Minimize } f(\mathbf{X}) = x_1^3 + x_2^3 - 3x_1x_2$$

subject to

$$3x_1 + x_2 \le 3$$
$$5x_1 - 3x_2 \le 5$$
$$x_1, x_2 \ge 0$$

### 21.2.6 SUMT Algorithm

In this section a more general gradient method is presented. It is assumed that the objective function $f(\mathbf{X})$ is concave and each constraint function $g_i(\mathbf{X})$ is convex. Moreover, the solution space must have an interior. This rules out both implicit and explicit use of *equality* constraints.

The SUMT (Sequential Unconstrained Maximization Technique) algorithm is based on transforming the constrained problem into an equivalent *un*constrained problem. The procedure is more or less similar to the use of the Lagrange multipliers method. The transformed problem can then be solved using the steepest ascent method (Section 21.1.2).

To clarify the concept, consider the new function

$$p(\mathbf{X}, t) = f(\mathbf{X}) + t\left(\sum_{i=1}^{m} \frac{1}{g_i(\mathbf{X})} - \sum_{j=1}^{n} \frac{1}{x_j}\right)$$

where $t$ is a nonnegative parameter. The second summation sign is based on the nonnegativity constraints, which must be put in the form $-x_j \le 0$ to conform with the original constraints $g_i(\mathbf{X}) \le 0$. Since $g_i(\mathbf{X})$ is convex, $\frac{1}{g_i(\mathbf{X})}$ is concave. This means that $p(\mathbf{X}, t)$ is concave in $\mathbf{X}$. Consequently, $p(\mathbf{X}, t)$ possesses a unique maximum. The optimization of the original constrained problem is equivalent to optimization of $p(\mathbf{X}, t)$.

The algorithm is initiated by arbitrarily selecting an initial *nonnegative* value for $t$. An initial point $\mathbf{X}^0$ is selected as the first trial solution. This point must be an interior point— that is, it must not lie on the boundaries of the solution space. Given the value of $t$, the steepest ascent method is used to determine the corresponding optimal solution (maximum) of $p(\mathbf{X}, t)$.

The new solution point will always be an interior point because if the solution point is close to the boundaries, at least one of the functions $1/g_i(\mathbf{X})$ or $(-1/x_i)$ will acquire a very large negative value. Because the objective is to maximize $p(\mathbf{X}, t)$, such solution points are automatically excluded. The main result is that successive solution points will always be interior points. Consequently, the problem can always be treated as an unconstrained case.

Once the optimum solution corresponding to a given value of $t$ is obtained, a new value of $t$ is generated and the optimization process (using the steepest ascent method) is repeated. If $t'$ is the current value of $t$, the next value, $t''$, must be selected such that $0 < t'' < t'$.

The SUMT procedure is terminated if, for two successive values of $t$, the corresponding *optimum* values of $\mathbf{X}$ obtained by maximizing $p(\mathbf{X}, t)$ are approximately the same. At this point further trials will produce little improvement.

Actual implementation of SUMT involves more details than have been presented here. Specifically, the selection of an initial value of $t$ is an important factor that can affect the speed of convergence. Further, the determination of an initial interior point may require special techniques. These details can be found in Fiacco and McCormick (1968).

## 21.3 SUMMARY

The solution methods of nonlinear programming can generally be classified as either *direct* or *indirect* procedures. Examples of direct methods are the gradient algorithms, wherein the maximum (minimum) of a problem is sought by following the fastest rate of increase (decrease) of the objective function at a point. In indirect methods, the original problem is replaced by an auxiliary one from which the optimum is determined. Examples of these situations include quadratic programming, separable programming, and stochastic programming.

## SELECTED REFERENCES

BAZARAA, M., H. SHERALL, and C. SHETTY, *Nonlinear Programming, Theory and Algorithms,* 2nd ed., Wiley, New York, 1993.

BEIGHTLER, C., D. PHILLIPS, and D. WILDE, *Foundations of Optimization,* 2nd ed., Prentice Hall, Upper Saddle River, N.J., 1979

FIACCO, A., and G. McCORMICK, *Nonlinear Programming: Sequential Unconstrained Minimization Techniques,* Wiley, New York, 1968.

# Review of Vectors and Matrices

## A.1 VECTORS

### A.1.1 Definition Of A Vector

Let $p_1, p_2, \ldots, p_n$ be any $n$ real numbers and $\mathbf{P}$ an ordered set of these real numbers—that is,

$$\mathbf{P} = (p_1, p_2, \ldots, p_n)$$

Then $\mathbf{P}$ is an $n$-vector (or simply a vector). The $i$th components of $\mathbf{P}$ is given by $p_i$. For example, $\mathbf{P} = (1, 2)$ is a two-dimensional vector.

### A.1.2 Addition (Subtraction) of Vectors

Let

$$\mathbf{P} = (p_1, p_2, \ldots, p_n) \quad \text{and} \quad \mathbf{Q} = (q_1, q_2, \ldots, q_n)$$

be two $n$-vectors. Then the components of the vector $\mathbf{R} = (r_1, r_2, \ldots, r_n)$ such that $\mathbf{R} = \mathbf{P} \pm \mathbf{Q}$ are given by

$$r_i = p_i \pm q_i$$

In general, given the vectors $\mathbf{P}, \mathbf{Q},$ and $\mathbf{S},$

$$\mathbf{P} \pm \mathbf{Q} = \mathbf{Q} \pm \mathbf{P} \qquad \text{(Commutative law)}$$

$$(\mathbf{P} + \mathbf{Q}) + \mathbf{S} = \mathbf{P} + (\mathbf{Q} + \mathbf{S}) \qquad \text{(Associative law)}$$

$$\mathbf{P} + (-\mathbf{P}) = \mathbf{0} \qquad \text{(zero or null vector)}$$

### A.1.3 Multiplication of Vectors by Scalars

Given a vector $\mathbf{P}$ and a scalar (constant) quantity $\theta$, the new vector

$$\mathbf{Q} = \theta\mathbf{P} = (\theta p_1, \theta p_2, ..., \theta p_n)$$

is the scalar product of $\mathbf{P}$ and $\theta$

In general, given the vectors $\mathbf{P}$ and $\mathbf{S}$ and the scalars $\theta$ and $\gamma$,

$$\theta(\mathbf{P} + \mathbf{S}) = \theta\mathbf{P} + \theta\mathbf{S} \qquad \text{(Distributive law)}$$

$$\theta(\gamma\mathbf{P}) = (\theta\gamma)\mathbf{P} \qquad \text{(Associative law)}$$

### A.1.4 Linearly Independent Vectors

The vectors $\mathbf{P}_1, \mathbf{P}_2, ..., \mathbf{P}_n$ are *linearly independent* if and only if, for all real $\theta_j$,

$$\sum_{j=1}^{n} \theta_j \mathbf{P}_j = \mathbf{0}$$

implies that all $\theta_j = 0$. If

$$\sum_{j=1}^{n} \theta_j \mathbf{P}_j = \mathbf{0}$$

for some $\theta \neq 0$, the vectors are said to be *linearly dependent*. For example, the vectors

$$\mathbf{P}_1 = (1, 2) \quad \text{and} \quad \mathbf{P}_2 = (2, 4)$$

are linearly dependent because there exist nonzero $\theta_1 = 2$ and $\theta_2 = -1$ for which

$$\theta_1 \mathbf{P}_1 + \theta_2 \mathbf{P}_2 = \mathbf{0}$$

## A.2 MATRICES

### A.2.1 Definition of a Matrix

A matrix is a rectangular array of elements. The element $a_{ij}$ of the matrix $\mathbf{A}$ occupies the $i$th row and $j$th column of the array. A matrix with $m$ rows and $n$ columns is said to have the order or size $m \times n$. For example,

$$\mathbf{A} = \begin{bmatrix} a_{11} & a_{12} & a_{13} \\ a_{21} & a_{22} & a_{23} \\ a_{31} & a_{32} & a_{33} \\ a_{41} & a_{42} & a_{43} \end{bmatrix} = \|a_{ij}\|_{4 \times 3}$$

is a $(4 \times 3)$-matrix.

### A.2.2 Types of Matrices

**1.** A *square* matrix has $m = n$.

2. An identity matrix is a square matrix in which all the diagonal elements are one and all the off-diagonal elements are zero. For example, a $(3 \times 3)$ identity matrix is given by

$$\mathbf{I}_3 = \begin{bmatrix} 1 & 0 & 0 \\ 0 & 1 & 0 \\ 0 & 0 & 1 \end{bmatrix}$$

3. A *row vector* is a matrix with one row and $n$ columns.

4. A *column vector* is a matrix with $m$ rows and one column.

5. The matrix $\mathbf{A}^T$ is the **transpose** of $\mathbf{A}$ if the element $a_{ij}$ in $\mathbf{A}$ is equal to element $a_{ji}$ in $\mathbf{A}^T$ for all $i$ and $j$. For example, if

$$\mathbf{A} = \begin{bmatrix} 1 & 4 \\ 2 & 5 \\ 3 & 6 \end{bmatrix}$$

then

$$\mathbf{A}^T = \begin{bmatrix} 1 & 2 & 3 \\ 4 & 5 & 6 \end{bmatrix}$$

6. A matrix $\mathbf{B} = \mathbf{0}$ is called a **zero matrix** if every element of $\mathbf{B}$ is zero.

7. Two matrices $\mathbf{A} = \|a_{ij}\|$ and $\mathbf{B} = \|b_{ij}\|$ are equal if and only if they have the same size and $a_{ij} = b_{ij}$ for all $i$ and $j$.

### A.2.3 Matrix Arithmetic Operations

In matrices only addition (subtraction) and multiplication are defined. The division, though not defined, is replaced by inversion (see Section A.2.6).

**Addition (subtraction) of matrices.**    Two matrices $\mathbf{A} = \|a_{ij}\|$ and $\mathbf{B} = \|b_{ij}\|$ can be added together if they are of the same size $(m \times n)$. The sum $\mathbf{D} = \mathbf{A} + \mathbf{B}$ is obtained by adding the corresponding elements. Thus,

$$\|d_{ij}\|_{m \times n} = \|a_{ij} + b_{ij}\|_{m \times n}$$

If the matrices A, B, and C have the same size, then

$$\mathbf{A} \pm \mathbf{B} = \mathbf{B} \pm \mathbf{A} \qquad \text{(Commutative law)}$$

$$\mathbf{A} \pm (\mathbf{B} \pm \mathbf{C}) = (\mathbf{A} \pm \mathbf{B}) \pm \mathbf{C} \qquad \text{(Associative law)}$$

$$(\mathbf{A} \pm \mathbf{B})^T = \mathbf{A}^T \pm \mathbf{B}^T$$

**Product of matrices.**    The product $\mathbf{AB}$ of two matrices $\mathbf{A} = \|a_{ij}\|$ and $\mathbf{B} = \|b_{ij}\|$ is defined if and only if the number of columns of $\mathbf{A}$ equals the number of rows of $\mathbf{B}$. Thus, if $\mathbf{A}$ is of the size $(m \times r)$, then $\mathbf{B}$ is of the size $(r \times n)$, where $m$ an $n$ are arbitrary sizes.

Let $\mathbf{D} = \mathbf{AB}$. Then $\mathbf{D}$ is of the size $(m \times n)$, and its elements $d_{ij}$ are given by

$$d_{ij} = \sum_{k=1}^{r} a_{ik}b_{kj}, \quad \text{for all } i \text{ and } j$$

For example, if

$$\mathbf{A} = \begin{bmatrix} 1 & 3 \\ 2 & 4 \end{bmatrix} \quad \text{and} \quad \mathbf{B} = \begin{bmatrix} 5 & 7 & 9 \\ 6 & 8 & 0 \end{bmatrix}$$

then

$$\mathbf{D} = \begin{bmatrix} 1 & 3 \\ 2 & 4 \end{bmatrix} \begin{bmatrix} 5 & 7 & 9 \\ 6 & 8 & 0 \end{bmatrix} = \begin{bmatrix} (1 \times 5 + 3 \times 6) & (1 \times 7 + 3 \times 8) & (1 \times 9 + 3 \times 0) \\ (2 \times 5 + 4 \times 6) & (2 \times 7 + 4 \times 8) & (2 \times 9 + 4 \times 0) \end{bmatrix}$$

$$= \begin{bmatrix} 23 & 31 & 9 \\ 34 & 46 & 18 \end{bmatrix}$$

In general, $\mathbf{AB} \neq \mathbf{BA}$ even if $\mathbf{BA}$ is defined.

Matrix multiplication follows these general properties:

$$\mathbf{I}_m\mathbf{A} = \mathbf{AI}_n = \mathbf{A}, \quad \text{where } \mathbf{I} \text{ is an identity matrix}$$
$$(\mathbf{AB})\mathbf{C} = \mathbf{A}(\mathbf{BC})$$
$$\mathbf{C}(\mathbf{A} + \mathbf{B}) = \mathbf{CA} + \mathbf{CB}$$
$$(\mathbf{A} + \mathbf{B})\mathbf{C} = \mathbf{AC} + \mathbf{BC}$$
$$\alpha(\mathbf{AB}) = (\alpha\mathbf{A})\mathbf{B} = \mathbf{A}(\alpha\mathbf{B}), \quad \alpha \text{ is a scalar}$$

**Multiplication of partitioned matrices.**    Let $\mathbf{A}$ be an $(m \times r)$-matrix and $\mathbf{B}$ an $(r \times n)$-matrix. If $\mathbf{A}$ and $\mathbf{B}$ are partitioned in to the following submatrices

$$\mathbf{A} = \left[ \begin{array}{c|c|c} \mathbf{A}_{11} & \mathbf{A}_{12} & \mathbf{A}_{13} \\ \hline \mathbf{A}_{21} & \mathbf{A}_{22} & \mathbf{A}_{23} \end{array} \right] \quad \text{and} \quad \mathbf{B} = \left[ \begin{array}{c|c} \mathbf{B}_{11} & \mathbf{B}_{12} \\ \mathbf{B}_{21} & \mathbf{B}_{22} \\ \mathbf{B}_{31} & \mathbf{B}_{32} \end{array} \right]$$

such that the number of columns of $\mathbf{A}_{ij}$ is equal to the number of rows of $\mathbf{B}_{ji}$ for all $i$ and $j$, then

$$\mathbf{A} \times \mathbf{B} = \left[ \begin{array}{c|c} \mathbf{A}_{11}\mathbf{B}_{11} + \mathbf{A}_{12}\mathbf{B}_{21} + \mathbf{A}_{13}\mathbf{B}_{31} & \mathbf{A}_{11}\mathbf{B}_{12} + \mathbf{A}_{12}\mathbf{B}_{22} + \mathbf{A}_{13}\mathbf{B}_{32} \\ \mathbf{A}_{21}\mathbf{B}_{11} + \mathbf{A}_{22}\mathbf{B}_{21} + \mathbf{A}_{23}\mathbf{B}_{31} & \mathbf{A}_{21}\mathbf{B}_{12} + \mathbf{A}_{22}\mathbf{B}_{22} + \mathbf{A}_{23}\mathbf{B}_{32} \end{array} \right]$$

For example,

$$\left[ \begin{array}{c|cc} 1 & 2 & 3 \\ \hline 1 & 0 & 5 \\ 2 & 5 & 6 \end{array} \right] \begin{bmatrix} 4 \\ 1 \\ 8 \end{bmatrix} = \left[ \begin{array}{c} (1)\,(4) + (2 \quad 3)\begin{bmatrix} 1 \\ 8 \end{bmatrix} \\ \hline \begin{bmatrix} 1 \\ 2 \end{bmatrix}(4) + \begin{bmatrix} 0 & 5 \\ 5 & 6 \end{bmatrix}\begin{bmatrix} 1 \\ 8 \end{bmatrix} \end{array} \right] = \left[ \begin{array}{c} 4 + 2 + 24 \\ \hline \begin{bmatrix} 4 \\ 8 \end{bmatrix} + \begin{bmatrix} 40 \\ 53 \end{bmatrix} \end{array} \right] = \begin{bmatrix} 30 \\ 44 \\ 61 \end{bmatrix}$$

### A.2.4 Determinant of a square matrix

Given the n-square matrix

$$\mathbf{A} = \begin{bmatrix} a_{11} & a_{12} & \cdots & a_{1n} \\ a_{21} & a_{22} & \cdots & a_{2n} \\ \vdots & \vdots & & \vdots \\ a_{n1} & a_{n2} & \cdots & a_{nn} \end{bmatrix}$$

consider the product

$$P_{j_1 j_2 \cdots j_n} = a_{1j_1} a_{2j_2} \cdots a_{nj_n}$$

the elements of which are selected such that each column and each row of **A** is represented exactly once among the subscripts of $P_{j_1 j_2 \cdots j_n}$. Next define $\epsilon_{j_1 j_2 \cdots j_n}$ equal to $+1$ if $j_1 j_2 \ldots j_n$ is an even permutation and $-1$ if $j_1 j_2 \ldots j_n$ is an odd permutation. Thus the scalar

$$\sum_\rho \epsilon_{j_1 j_2 \cdots j_n} P_{j_1 j_2 \cdots j_n}$$

is called the determinant of **A,** where $\rho$ represents the summation over all $n!$ permutations. The notation det **A** or $|\mathbf{A}|$ is used to represent the determinant of **A**.

To illustrate, consider

$$\mathbf{A} = \begin{bmatrix} a_{11} & a_{12} & a_{13} \\ a_{21} & a_{22} & a_{23} \\ a_{31} & a_{32} & a_{33} \end{bmatrix}$$

Then

$$|\mathbf{A}| = a_{11}(a_{22}\, a_{33} - a_{23}\, a_{32}) - a_{12}(a_{21}\, a_{33} - a_{31}\, a_{23}) + a_{13}(a_{21}\, a_{32} - a_{22}a_{31})$$

The properties of determinants include the following:

1. If every element of a column or a row is zero, then the value of the determinant is zero.
2. The value of the determinant is not changed if its rows and columns are interchanged.
3. If **B** is obtained from **A** by interchanging any two of its rows (or columns), then $|\mathbf{B}| = -|\mathbf{A}|$.
4. If two rows (or columns) of **A** are identical, then $|\mathbf{A}| = 0$.
5. The value of $|\mathbf{A}|$ remains the same if scalar $\alpha$ times a column (row) vector is added to another column (row) vector.
6. If every element of a column (or a row) of a determinant is multiplied by a scalar $\alpha$, the value of the determinant is multiplied by $\alpha$.
7. If **A** and **B** are two $n$-square matrices, then

$$|\mathbf{AB}| = |\mathbf{A}|\, |\mathbf{B}|$$

*Definition of the Minor of a Determinant.* The minor $M_{ij}$ of the element $a_{ij}$ in the determinant $|\mathbf{A}|$ is obtained from the matrix $\mathbf{A}$ by striking out the $i$th row and $j$th column of $\mathbf{A}$. For example, for

$$\mathbf{A} = \begin{bmatrix} a_{11} & a_{12} & a_{13} \\ a_{21} & a_{22} & a_{23} \\ a_{31} & a_{32} & a_{33} \end{bmatrix}$$

$$M_{11} = \begin{vmatrix} a_{22} & a_{23} \\ a_{32} & a_{33} \end{vmatrix}, \quad M_{22} = \begin{vmatrix} a_{11} & a_{13} \\ a_{31} & a_{33} \end{vmatrix}, \dots$$

*Definition of the Adjoint Matrix.* Let $A_{ij} = (-1)^{i+j} M_{ij}$ be defined as the **cofactor** of the element $a_{ij}$ of the square matrix $\mathbf{A}$. Then, the adjoint matrix of $\mathbf{A}$ is defined as

$$\text{adj } \mathbf{A} = \|A_{ij}\|^T = \begin{bmatrix} A_{11} & A_{21} & \cdots & A_{n1} \\ A_{12} & A_{22} & \cdots & A_{n2} \\ \vdots & \vdots & & \\ A_{1n} & A_{2n} & \cdots & A_{nn} \end{bmatrix}$$

For example, if

$$\mathbf{A} = \begin{bmatrix} 1 & 2 & 3 \\ 2 & 3 & 2 \\ 3 & 3 & 4 \end{bmatrix}$$

then, $A_{11} = (-1)^2(3 \times 4 - 2 \times 3) = 6$, $A_{12} = (-1)^3(2 \times 4 - 2 \times 3) = -2, \dots$, or

$$\text{adj } \mathbf{A} = \begin{bmatrix} 6 & 1 & -5 \\ -2 & -5 & 4 \\ -3 & 3 & -1 \end{bmatrix}$$

## A.2.5 Nonsingular Matrix

A matrix is of a rank $r$ if the largest *square* array in the matrix with nonvanishing determinants is of size $r$. A *square* matrix whose determinant does not vanish is called a **full-rank** or a **nonsingular** matrix. For example,

$$\mathbf{A} = \begin{bmatrix} 1 & 2 & 3 \\ 2 & 3 & 4 \\ 3 & 5 & 7 \end{bmatrix}$$

is a singular matrix because

$$|\mathbf{A}| = 1(21 - 20) - 2(14 - 12) + 3(10 - 9) = 0$$

But A has a rank $r = 2$ because

$$\begin{bmatrix} 1 & 2 \\ 2 & 3 \end{bmatrix} = -1 \neq 0$$

### A.2.6 The Inverse of a Matrix

If **B** and **C** are two $n$-square matrices such that $\mathbf{BC} = \mathbf{CB} = \mathbf{I}$, then **B** is called the inverse of **C** and **C** the inverse of **B**. The common notation for the inverses is $\mathbf{B}^{-1}$ and $\mathbf{C}^{-1}$.

**Theorem**
*If* $\mathbf{BC} = \mathbf{I}$ *and* **B** *is* **nonsingular,** *then* $\mathbf{C} = \mathbf{B}^{-1}$, *which means that the inverse is unique.*

*Proof.*    By assumption,

$$\mathbf{BC} = \mathbf{I}$$

then

$$\mathbf{B}^{-1}\mathbf{BC} = \mathbf{B}^{-1}\mathbf{I}$$

or

$$\mathbf{IC} = \mathbf{B}^{-1}$$

or

$$\mathbf{C} = \mathbf{B}^{-1}$$

Two important results can be proved for nonsingular matrices.

**1.** If **A** and **B** are nonsingular $n$-squre matrices, then $(\mathbf{AB})^{-1} = \mathbf{B}^{-1}\mathbf{A}^{-1}$
**2.** If **A** is nonsingular, then $\mathbf{AB} = \mathbf{AC}$ implies that $\mathbf{B} = \mathbf{C}$.

Matrix inversion is used to solve $n$ linearly independent equations. Consider

$$\begin{bmatrix} a_{11} & a_{12} & \cdots & a_{1n} \\ a_{21} & a_{22} & \cdots & a_{2n} \\ \vdots & \vdots & & \vdots \\ a_{n1} & a_{n2} & \cdots & a_{nn} \end{bmatrix} \begin{bmatrix} x_1 \\ x_2 \\ \vdots \\ x_n \end{bmatrix} = \begin{bmatrix} b_1 \\ b_2 \\ \vdots \\ b_n \end{bmatrix}$$

where $x_i$ represents the unknowns and $a_{ij}$ and $b_i$ are constants. These $n$ equations can be written in matrix form as

$$\mathbf{AX} = \mathbf{b}$$

Because the equations are independent, it follows that **A** is nonsingular. Thus

$$\mathbf{A}^{-1}\mathbf{AX} = \mathbf{A}^{-1}\mathbf{b} \quad \text{or} \quad \mathbf{X} = \mathbf{A}^{-1}\mathbf{b}$$

gives the solution of the $n$ unknowns.

### A.2.7 Methods of Computing the Inverse of a Matrix

**Adjoint matrix method.**     Given $\mathbf{A}$ a nonsingular matrix of size $n$,

$$\mathbf{A}^{-1} = \frac{1}{|\mathbf{A}|} \text{ adj } \mathbf{A} = \frac{1}{|\mathbf{A}|} \begin{bmatrix} A_{11} & A_{21} & \cdots & A_{n1} \\ A_{12} & A_{22} & \cdots & A_{n2} \\ \vdots & \vdots & & \vdots \\ A_{1n} & A_{2n} & \cdots & A_{nn} \end{bmatrix}$$

For example, for

$$\mathbf{A} = \begin{bmatrix} 1 & 2 & 3 \\ 2 & 3 & 2 \\ 3 & 3 & 4 \end{bmatrix}$$

$$\text{adj } \mathbf{A} = \begin{bmatrix} 6 & 1 & -5 \\ -2 & -5 & 4 \\ -3 & 3 & -1 \end{bmatrix} \quad \text{and} \quad |\mathbf{A}| = -7$$

Hence

$$\mathbf{A}^{-1} = \frac{1}{-7} \begin{bmatrix} 6 & 1 & -5 \\ -2 & -5 & 4 \\ -3 & 3 & -1 \end{bmatrix} = \begin{bmatrix} -\dfrac{6}{7} & -\dfrac{1}{7} & \dfrac{5}{7} \\ \dfrac{2}{7} & \dfrac{5}{7} & -\dfrac{4}{7} \\ \dfrac{3}{7} & -\dfrac{3}{7} & \dfrac{1}{7} \end{bmatrix}$$

**Row operations (Gauss-Jordan) method.**     Consider the partitioned matrix $(\mathbf{A} \,|\, \mathbf{I})$, where $\mathbf{A}$ is nonsingular. By premultiplying this matrix by $\mathbf{A}^{-1}$, we obtain

$$(\mathbf{A}^{-1}\mathbf{A} \,|\, \mathbf{A}^{-1}\mathbf{I}) = (\mathbf{I} \,|\, \mathbf{A}^{-1})$$

Thus, by multiplying a sequence of row transformations, the matrix $\mathbf{A}$ is changed to $\mathbf{I}$ and $\mathbf{I}$ is changed to $\mathbf{A}^{-1}$.

For example, consider the system of equations:

$$\begin{bmatrix} 1 & 2 & 3 \\ 2 & 3 & 2 \\ 3 & 3 & 4 \end{bmatrix} \begin{bmatrix} x_1 \\ x_2 \\ x_3 \end{bmatrix} = \begin{bmatrix} 3 \\ 4 \\ 5 \end{bmatrix}$$

The solution of $\mathbf{X}$ and the inverse of basis matrix can be obtained directly by considering

$$\mathbf{A}^{-1}(\mathbf{A} \,|\, \mathbf{I} \,|\, \mathbf{b}) = (\mathbf{I} \,|\, \mathbf{A}^{-1} \,|\, \mathbf{A}^{-1}\mathbf{b})$$

Thus, by a row transformation operation, we get

$$\begin{bmatrix} 1 & 2 & 3 & | & 1 & 0 & 0 & | & 3 \\ 2 & 3 & 2 & | & 0 & 1 & 0 & | & 4 \\ 3 & 3 & 4 & | & 0 & 0 & 1 & | & 5 \end{bmatrix}$$

*Iteration 1*

$$\begin{bmatrix} 1 & 2 & 3 & | & 1 & 0 & 0 & | & 3 \\ 0 & -1 & -4 & | & -2 & 1 & 0 & | & -2 \\ 0 & -3 & -5 & | & -3 & 0 & 1 & | & -4 \end{bmatrix}$$

*Iteration 2*

$$\begin{bmatrix} 1 & 0 & -5 & | & -3 & 2 & 0 & | & -1 \\ 0 & 1 & 4 & | & 2 & -1 & 0 & | & 2 \\ 0 & 0 & 7 & | & 3 & -3 & 1 & | & 2 \end{bmatrix}$$

*Iteration 3*

$$\begin{bmatrix} 1 & 0 & 0 & | & -\dfrac{6}{7} & -\dfrac{1}{7} & \dfrac{5}{7} & | & \dfrac{3}{7} \\[2mm] 0 & 1 & 0 & | & \dfrac{2}{7} & \dfrac{5}{7} & -\dfrac{4}{7} & | & \dfrac{6}{7} \\[2mm] 0 & 0 & 1 & | & \dfrac{3}{7} & -\dfrac{3}{7} & \dfrac{1}{7} & | & \dfrac{2}{7} \end{bmatrix}$$

This gives $x_1 = \frac{3}{7}$, $x_2 = \frac{6}{7}$, and $x_3 = \frac{2}{7}$. The inverse of A is given by the right-hand–side matrix, which is the same as obtained by the method of adjoint matrix.

**Partitioned matrix method.**    Let the two nonsingular matrices **A** and **B** of size $n$ be partitioned as shown subsequently, given that $A_{11}$ is nonsingular.

$$\mathbf{A} = \begin{bmatrix} \mathbf{A}_{11} & \mathbf{A}_{12} \\ (p \times p) & (p \times q) \\ \hline \mathbf{A}_{21} & \mathbf{A}_{22} \\ (q \times p) & (q \times q) \end{bmatrix} \quad \text{and} \quad \mathbf{B} = \begin{bmatrix} \mathbf{B}_{11} & \mathbf{B}_{12} \\ (p \times p) & (p \times q) \\ \hline \mathbf{B}_{21} & \mathbf{B}_{22} \\ (q \times p) & (q \times q) \end{bmatrix}$$

If **B** is the inverse of **A,** then from $\mathbf{AB} = \mathbf{I}_n$, we have

$$\mathbf{A}_{11}\mathbf{B}_{11} + \mathbf{A}_{12}\mathbf{B}_{21} = \mathbf{I}_p$$

$$\mathbf{A}_{11}\mathbf{B}_{12} + \mathbf{B}_{12}\mathbf{A}_{22} = \mathbf{0}$$

Also, from $\mathbf{BA} = \mathbf{I}_n$, we get

$$\mathbf{B}_{21}\mathbf{A}_{11} + \mathbf{B}_{22}\mathbf{A}_{21} = \mathbf{0}$$

$$\mathbf{B}_{21}\mathbf{A}_{12} + \mathbf{B}_{22}\mathbf{A}_{22} = \mathbf{I}_q$$

Because $\mathbf{A}_{11}$ is nonsingular, that is, $|\mathbf{A}_{11}| \neq 0$, solving for $\mathbf{B}_{11}, \mathbf{B}_{12}, \mathbf{B}_{21},$ and $\mathbf{B}_{22}$, we get

$$\mathbf{B}_{11} = \mathbf{A}_{11}^{-1} + (\mathbf{A}_{11}^{-1}\mathbf{A}_{12})\mathbf{D}^{-1}(\mathbf{A}_{21}\mathbf{A}_{11}^{-1})$$

$$\mathbf{B}_{12} = -(\mathbf{A}_{11}^{-1}\mathbf{A}_{12})\mathbf{D}^{-1}$$

$$\mathbf{B}_{21} = -\mathbf{D}^{-1}(\mathbf{A}_{21}\mathbf{A}_{11}^{-1})$$

$$\mathbf{B}_{22} = \mathbf{D}^{-1}$$

where

$$\mathbf{D} = \mathbf{A}_{22} - \mathbf{A}_{21}(\mathbf{A}_{11}^{-1}\mathbf{A}_{12})$$

To illustrate the use of these formulas, partition the matrix

$$\mathbf{A} = \left[\begin{array}{c|cc} 1 & 2 & 3 \\ \hline 2 & 3 & 2 \\ 3 & 3 & 4 \end{array}\right]$$

such that

$$\mathbf{A}_{11} = (1), \quad \mathbf{A}_{12} = (2, 3), \quad \mathbf{A}_{21} = \begin{bmatrix} 2 \\ 3 \end{bmatrix}, \text{ and } \mathbf{A}_{22} = \begin{bmatrix} 3 & 2 \\ 3 & 4 \end{bmatrix}$$

In this case, $\mathbf{A}_{11}^{-1} = 1$ and

$$\mathbf{D} = \begin{bmatrix} 3 & 2 \\ 3 & 4 \end{bmatrix} - \begin{bmatrix} 2 \\ 3 \end{bmatrix} (1) (2, 3) = \begin{bmatrix} -1 & -4 \\ -3 & -5 \end{bmatrix}$$

$$\mathbf{D}^{-1} = -\frac{1}{7}\begin{bmatrix} -5 & 4 \\ 3 & -1 \end{bmatrix} = \begin{bmatrix} \dfrac{5}{7} & -\dfrac{4}{7} \\ -\dfrac{3}{7} & \dfrac{1}{7} \end{bmatrix}$$

Thus,

$$\mathbf{B}_{11} = \left[ -\frac{6}{7} \right] \quad \text{and} \quad \mathbf{B}_{12} = \left[ -\frac{1}{7} \quad \frac{5}{7} \right]$$

$$\mathbf{B}_{21} = \begin{bmatrix} \dfrac{2}{7} \\ \dfrac{3}{7} \end{bmatrix} \quad \text{and} \quad \mathbf{B}_{22} = \begin{bmatrix} \dfrac{5}{7} & -\dfrac{4}{7} \\ -\dfrac{3}{7} & \dfrac{1}{7} \end{bmatrix}$$

which directly give $\mathbf{B} = \mathbf{A}^{-1}$

## A.3 QUADRATIC FORMS

Given

$$\mathbf{X} = (x_1, x_2, \ldots, x_n)^T$$

and

$$\mathbf{A} = \begin{bmatrix} a_{11} & a_{12} & \cdots & a_{1n} \\ a_{21} & a_{22} & \cdots & a_{2n} \\ \vdots & \vdots & & \vdots \\ a_{n1} & a_{n2} & \cdots & a_{nn} \end{bmatrix}$$

the function

$$Q(\mathbf{X}) = \mathbf{X}^T \mathbf{A} \mathbf{X} = \sum_{i=1}^{n} \sum_{j=1}^{n} a_{ij} x_i x_j$$

is called a quadratic form. The matrix $\mathbf{A}$ can always be assumed symmetric because each element of every pair of coefficients $a_{ij}$ and $a_{ji}$ $(i \neq j)$ can be replaced by $\frac{(a_{ij} + a_{ji})}{2}$ without changing the value of $Q(\mathbf{X})$. This assumption has advantages and hence is taken as a requirement.

To illustrate, the quadratic form

$$Q(\mathbf{X}) = (x_1, x_2, x_3) \begin{bmatrix} 1 & 0 & 1 \\ 2 & 7 & 6 \\ 3 & 0 & 2 \end{bmatrix} \begin{bmatrix} x_1 \\ x_2 \\ x_3 \end{bmatrix}$$

is the same as

$$Q(\mathbf{X}) = (x_1, x_2, x_3) \begin{bmatrix} 1 & 1 & 2 \\ 1 & 7 & 3 \\ 2 & 3 & 2 \end{bmatrix} \begin{bmatrix} x_1 \\ x_2 \\ x_3 \end{bmatrix}$$

Note that $\mathbf{A}$ is symmetric in the second case.

The quadratic form is said to be

1. *Positive definite* if $Q(\mathbf{X}) > 0$ for every $\mathbf{X} \neq \mathbf{0}$.
2. *Positive semidefinite* if $Q(\mathbf{X}) \geq 0$ for every $\mathbf{X}$, and there exists $\mathbf{X} \neq \mathbf{0}$ such that $Q(\mathbf{X}) = 0$.
3. *Negative definite* if $-Q(\mathbf{X})$ is positive definite.
4. *Negative semidefinite* if $-Q(\mathbf{X})$ is positive semidefinite.
5. *Indefinite* in all other cases.

It can be proved that the necessary and sufficient conditions for the realization of the preceding cases are

1. $Q(\mathbf{X})$ is positive definite (semidefinite) if the values of the principal minor determinants of $\mathbf{A}$ are positive (nonnegative).[†] In this case, $\mathbf{A}$ is said to be positive definite (semidefinite).

2. $Q(\mathbf{X})$ is negative definite if the value of $k$th principal minor determinants of $\mathbf{A}$ has the sign of $(-1)^k, k = 1, 2, ..., n$. In this case, $\mathbf{A}$ is called negative-definite.

3. $Q(\mathbf{X})$ is a negative-semidefinite if the $k$th principal minor determinant of $\mathbf{A}$ is either zero or has the sign of $(-1)^k, k = 1, 2, ..., n$.

## A.4 CONVEX AND CONCAVE FUNCTIONS

A function $f(X)$ is said to be strictly convex if, for any two distinct points $\mathbf{X}_1$ and $\mathbf{X}_2$,

$$f(\lambda\mathbf{X}_1 + (1 - \lambda)\mathbf{X}_2) < \lambda f(\mathbf{X}_1) + (1 - \lambda)f(\mathbf{X}_2)$$

where $0 < \lambda < 1$. Conversely, a function $f(\mathbf{X})$ is strictly concave if $-f(\mathbf{X})$ is strictly convex.

A special case of the convex (concave) function is the quadratic form (see Section A.3)

$$f(\mathbf{X}) = \mathbf{CX} + \mathbf{X}^T\mathbf{AX}$$

where $\mathbf{C}$ is a constant vector and $\mathbf{A}$ is a symmetric matrix. It can be proved that $f(\mathbf{X})$ is strictly convex if $\mathbf{A}$ is positive definite and $f(\mathbf{X})$ is strictly concave if $\mathbf{A}$ is negative definite.

## SELECTED REFERENCES

HADLEY, G., *Matrix Algebra*, Addison-Wesley, Reading, Mass., 1961.

HOHN, F., *Elementary Matrix Algebra*, 2nd ed., Macmillan, New York, 1964.

## PROBLEMS

■ **A–1**. Show that the following vectors are linearly dependent.

(a) $\begin{bmatrix} 1 \\ -2 \\ 3 \end{bmatrix} \begin{bmatrix} -2 \\ 4 \\ -2 \end{bmatrix} \begin{bmatrix} 1 \\ -2 \\ -1 \end{bmatrix}$

[†]The $k$th *principal minor* determinant of $A_{n\times n}$ is defined by

$$\begin{vmatrix} a_{11} & a_{12} & \cdots & a_{1k} \\ a_{21} & a_{22} & \cdots & a_{2k} \\ \vdots & \vdots & & \vdots \\ a_{k1} & a_{k2} & & a_{kk} \end{vmatrix}, \quad k = 1, 2, ..., n$$

**(b)**
$$\begin{bmatrix} 2 \\ -3 \\ 4 \\ 5 \end{bmatrix} \begin{bmatrix} 4 \\ -6 \\ 8 \\ 10 \end{bmatrix}$$

■ **A–2.** Given

$$\mathbf{A} = \begin{bmatrix} 1 & 4 & 9 \\ 2 & 5 & -8 \\ 3 & 7 & 2 \end{bmatrix} \quad \text{and} \quad \mathbf{B} = \begin{bmatrix} 7 & -1 & 2 \\ 9 & 4 & 8 \\ 3 & 6 & 10 \end{bmatrix}$$

find
(a) $\mathbf{A} + 7\mathbf{B}$
(b) $2\mathbf{A} - 3\mathbf{B}$
(c) $(\mathbf{A} + 7\mathbf{B})^T$

■ **A–3.** In Problem A–2, show that $\mathbf{AB} \neq \mathbf{BA}$

■ **A–4.** Given the partitioned matrices

$$\mathbf{A} = \left[\begin{array}{c|cc} 1 & 5 & 7 \\ 2 & -6 & 9 \\ \hline 3 & 7 & 2 \\ 4 & 9 & 1 \end{array}\right] \quad \text{and} \quad \mathbf{B} = \left[\begin{array}{ccc|c} 2 & 3 & -4 & 5 \\ 1 & 2 & 6 & 7 \\ 3 & 1 & 0 & 9 \end{array}\right]$$

find $\mathbf{AB}$ using partitioning.

■ **A–5.** In Problem A–2, find $\mathbf{A}^{-1}$ and $\mathbf{B}^{-1}$ using the following:
(a) Adjoint matrix method
(b) Row operations method
(c) Partitioned matrix method

■ **A–6.** Verify the formulas given in Section A.2.7 for obtaining the inverse of a partitioned matrix.

■ **A–7.** Find the inverse of

$$\mathbf{A} = \begin{pmatrix} 1 & \mathbf{G} \\ \mathbf{H} & \mathbf{B} \end{pmatrix}$$

where $\mathbf{B}$ is a nonsingular matrix.

■ **A–8.** Show that the quadratic form

$$Q(x_1, x_2) = 6x_1 + 3x_2 - 4x_1x_2 - 2x_1^2 - 3x_2^2 - \frac{27}{4}$$

is negative definite.

■ **A–9.** Show that the quadratic form

$$Q(x_1, x_2, x_3) = 2x_1^2 + 2x_2^2 + 3x_3^2 + 2x_1x_2 + 2x_2x_3$$

is positive definite.

■ **A–10.** Show that the function $f(x) = e^x$ is strictly convex over all real values of $x$.

■ **A–11.** Show that the quadratic function

$$f(x_1, x_2, x_3) = 5x_1^2 + 5x_2^2 + 4x_3^2 + 4x_1x_2 + 2x_2x_3$$

is strictly convex.

■ **A–12.** In Problem A–11, show that $-f(x_1, x_2, x_3)$ is strictly concave.

# Appendix B

# Introduction to Simnet II[†]

## B.1 MODELING FRAMEWORK

The design of SIMNET II views discrete simulation models as queueing systems. The language is based on a **network approach** that uses three suggestive nodes: a **source** from which transactions (customers) arrive, a **queue** where waiting may occur, and a **facility** where service is performed. A fourth node, **auxiliary,** is added to enhance the capabilities of the language.

Nodes in SIMNET II are connected by **branches.** As transactions (also called entities) traverse the branches, they perform important functions that include (1) controlling transaction flow anywhere in the network, (2) collecting pertinent statistics, and (3) performing arithmetic calculations.

During the simulation execution, SIMNET II keeps track of the transactions by placing them in **files.** A file can be thought of as a two-dimensional array in which each row stores information about a single transaction. The columns of the array represent the **attributes** that allow the modeler to keep track of the unique characteristics of each transaction.

SIMNET II uses three types of files.

1. Event calendar
2. Queue
3. Facility

---

[†]This appendix provides the basic features of SIMNET II. Space limitation does not allow the presentation of the intermediate and advanced features of the language. A complete documentation of SIMNET II is given in Hamdy A. Taha, *Simulation with SIMNET II,* second edition, SimTec, Inc., Fayetteville, AR, 1995

The **event calendar (E. FILE)** is the principal file that derives the simulation. It automatically updates and keeps track of the model's events in proper chronological order. The operations of the queues and facilities files are automatically maintained by SIMNET II.

## B.2 STATEMENT REPRESENTATION

The general format of the SIMNET II statement is

```
identifier; field 1; field 2; . . . ; field m:
```

A *node* identifier consists of an arbitrary user-defined name (12 characters maximum) followed by one of the codes *S, *Q, *F, or *A that identifies the name as a source, a queue, a facility, or an auxiliary. A *branch* identifier consists of the code *B only. The fields are separated by semicolons, and the statement must be terminated with a colon. As an illustration, consider

```
ARIV    *S;EX(5);;;;LIM=100:
        *B;QQ;;A(1)=1%:
Q       Q *Q:
```

Source ARIV creates a maximum of 100 transactions with the interarrival time determined from an exponential distribution with a mean of 5 time units. A branch connects source ARIV to queue QQ. A transaction traversing the branch will have its first attribute A(1) set equal to 1 before it enters QQ.

All fields of a statement are *positional* in the sense that their order must be preserved. If a field is not used or is defaulted, its order is preserved by successive semicolons.

Coding in SIMNET II is free formatted as well as uppercase/lowercase insensitive. A statement may be segmented among any number of successive lines by terminating each line with an ampersand (&). For example, the ARIV statement may be coded equivalently as

```
ARIV    *S;EX(5);;;;LI&    !line 1 of ARIV
        M=500:             !line 2 of ARIV
```

A SIMNET II line may include a **comment,** which is prefixed by an exclamation mark (!).

### B.2.1. Source Node

The source node is used to create the arrival of transactions into the network. The definitions of its fields and its graphic symbol are given in Figure B-1.

| SNAME | *S; F1; F2; F3; MULT = F4; LIM = F5; F6; F7; *T: | | |
|---|---|---|---|
| | Field Identifier | | Default |
| F1 | | Interarrival time (expression)[a] | 0 |
| F2 | | Occurrence time of first creation (expression) | 0 |
| F3 | | Mark attribute number with the attribute automatically carrying creation time if F3 > 0 or serial number if F3 < 0 (constant) | None |
| F4 | /m/ | Simultaneous transactions per single creation (constant or variable)[b, c] | 1 |
| F5 | /L/ | Limit on number of creations if F5 > 0 or limit on time of creation if F5 < 0 (constant or variable)[b] | ∞ |
| F6 | /s/ | Output select rule (see Section B.5.1) | None |
| F7 | /r/ | Resources returned by source | None |
| *T | | List of nodes reached from source by direct transfer (see Section B.5.2)[d] | None |

[a]  SIMNET II mathematical expression (see Section B.3)
[b]  For fields F4 through F7, the field number n in the field identifier notation /n/ may be replaced with the descriptive words /Multiple/, /Limit/, /Select/, and /Resources/ or /M/, /L/, /S/, and /R/, respectively.
[c]  Variable may be a nonsubscripted or an array element (see Section B.3).
[d]  The asterisk may be replaced by the descriptive word GOTO-.

**Figure B–1**

### ILLUSTRATIONS

**1.** On arrival at a car registration facility, customers take a number to establish priority for service.

```
CUSTMRS    *S;EX(12);10;-1:
```

Transactions are created from CUSTMRS every EXponential(12) time units, with the *first* transaction arriving at time 10. The third field (;-1:) automatically assigns a distinct *serial number* to attribute A(1) of each transaction. If the third field is changed to (;1:), A(1) will be assigned the *creation time* of the transaction.

**2.** TV units arriving on a conveyor belt every 5 minutes are sent to packaging.

```
TVS    *S;5;goto-PAKAGE:
```

The "goto-" field represents the *T field in Figure B-1. Note that *T is a *floating* field, in the sense that it always occupies the last field of the node regardless of any default fields that may precede it.

**3.** A mill is contracted to receive 100 truckloads of 50 logs each. The mill processes the logs one at a time.

```
TRKS   *S;45;/m/MULT=50;LIM=100;goto-MILL:
```

The LIM field indicates that source TRKS will generate only 100 transactions (trucks). As each transaction leaves TRKS, it will be *replaced* by 50 *identical* transactions representing the logs as shown in the MULT field. The identifier /m/ preceding MULT conveniently suppresses the use of default semicolons.

### B.2.2. Queue Node

Figure B-2 summarizes the queue data.

**ILLUSTRATIONS**

**1.** Rush and regular jobs arrive at a shop randomly with rush jobs taking priority for processing.

```
JOBQ   *Q;;;HI(1):
```

Attribute 1 represents the job type by using $A(1) = 0$ and $A(1) = 1$ to tag regular and rush jobs, respectively. These jobs are ordered in queue JOBQ in ascending order of $A(1)$ by using the queue discipline HI(1). [The opposite of HI(1) is LO(1).] We can suppress the default semicolons by writing the statement equally as

```
JOBQ   *Q;/d/HI(1):
```

**2.** Units of a product are packaged four to a carton. The buffer area can hold a maximum of 75 units. Initially, the buffer is holding 30 units.

```
QUNIT  *Q;75(30);4:
```

Field 1 sets the maximum queue capacity (= 75) and the initial number in the system (= 30). Field 2 indicates that four product units will be converted to a single carton. By default, the attributes of the "carton" transaction will equal those of the LAST of the four transactions forming the carton. The queue discipline is FIFO because field 3 is defaulted.

| | QNAME | *Q; F1(SUBF1); F2(SUBF2); F3; F4; F5; *T: | |
|---|---|---|---|
| | Field<br>Identifier | | Default |
| F1 | | Maximum queue size (constant or<br>variable)[a] | ∞ |
| SUBF1 | | Initial number in queue (constant or<br>variable) | 0 |
| F2 | | Number of waiting transactions<br>required to create *one* leaving<br>transaction (constant or variable) | 1 |
| SUBF2 | | Rule for computing the attributes of<br>the leaving transactions when<br>F2 > 1: SUM, PROD, FIRST, LAST,<br>HI(#), LO(#), where # is an<br>attribute number | LAST |
| F3 | /d/ | Queue discipline: FIFO, LIFO, RAN,<br>HI(#), LO(#), where # is an<br>attribute number | FIFO |
| F4 | /s/ | Output select rule<br>(see Section B.5.1)[b] | None |
| F5 | /r/ | Resources returned by queue | None |
| *T | | List of nodes reached from queue by<br>direct transfer (see Section B.5.2)[c] | None |

[a] Variable may be nonsubscripted or array elements (see Section B.3)
[b] For fields F4 and F5, the field number n in the field identifier notation /n/ may be replaced with
the descriptive words /Discipline/, /Select/, and /Resources/ or /D/, /S/, and /R/, respectively.
[c] The asterisk may be replaced with the descriptive word GOTO-.

**Figure B–2**

## B.2.3.  Facility Node

A facility node consists of one or more (identical) parallel servers. When all the
servers are busy, new transactions cannot enter the facility. When a server completes
a service, the facility *automatically* attempts to pull a new transaction from a predecessor queue, if one exists. Otherwise, the facility goes dormant until a new transaction enters it. Descriptions of the fields of the facility node are given in Figure B-3.

### ILLUSTRATIONS

**1.** A three-server facility starts with two busy servers. The service time is exponential with a mean of 15 minutes. Units completing the service are removed (TERMinated) from the system.

| | Field Identifier | FNAME   *F; F1; F2; F3(SUBF3); F4; F5; *T: | Default |
|---|---|---|---|
| F1 | | Rule for selecting an input *queue* (See Section B.5.1) | None |
| F2 | | Service time (expression)[a] | 0 |
| F3 | | Number of parallel servers (constant or variable)[b] | 1 |
| SUBF3 | | Initial number of busy servers (constant or variable) | 0 |
| F4 | /s/ | Output select rule (see Section B.5.1)[c] | None |
| F5 | /r/ | Resource(s) acquired/released by facility | None |
| *T | | List of nodes reached from facility by direct transfer (see Section B.5.2)[d] | None |

[a] SIMNET II mathematical expression (see Section B.3)
[b] Variable may be a nonsubscripted or an array element (see Section B.3).
[c] For fields F4 and F5, the field number n in the field identifier notation /n/ may be replaced with the descriptive words /Select/ and /Resources/ or /S/ and /R/, respectively.
[d] The asterisk may be replaced with the descriptive word GOTO-.

**Figure B–3**

```
SRVR    *F;;EX(15);3(2);goto-TERM:
```

Field 1 is not needed because it is used only when the facility has multiple input queues. The service time of EX(15) minutes is given in field 2 (any mathematical expression may be used in this field). Field 3 shows that the facility has three parallel servers, with two servers initially busy. The goto-field TERMinates the completed transaction by using the reserved word TERM as a destination.

2. A small shop has one machine and 10 waiting jobs, in addition to the job that is currently being processed. The processing time per job is uniform between 20 and 30 minutes.

```
QJOB    *Q;(10):

FJOB    *F;;UN(20,30);(1);goto-TERM:
```

Because FJOB is initially busy, as indicated by the entry (1) in field 3, the facility will process its resident job in UN(20,30) minutes. After the job leaves FJOB to be TERMinated, the facility will *automatically* "look back" and pull a new job from QJOB. The process is repeated until all 10 jobs are processed.

### B.2.4 Auxiliary Node

The auxiliary is an infinite capacity node that accepts all incoming transactions. The node is mostly suited for representing delays. Also, the auxiliary is the only node that can enter itself, a characteristic that is particularly useful in simulating loops. Figure B-4 describes the fields of the auxiliary node.

| ANAME   *A; F1; F2; F3; T: | | | |
|---|---|---|---|
| | Field Identifier | | Default |
| F1 | | Delay time (expression)[a] | 0 |
| F2 | /s/ | Rule for selecting output node (see Section B.5.1)[b] | None |
| F3 | /r/ | Resource(s) released by auxiliary | None |
| F4 | | List of nodes reached from auxiliary by direct transfer (see Section B.5.2)[c] | None |

[a]  SIMNET II mathematical expression (see Section B.3)
[b]  For fields F2 and F3, the field number n in the field identifier notation /n/ may be replaced with the descriptive words /Select/ and /Resources/ or /S/ and /R/, respectively.
[c]  The asterisk may be replaced with the descriptive word GOTO-.

**Figure B–4**

**ILLUSTRATION**

**1.** Job applicants arrive at an employment office every EX(25) minutes. Each applicant fills out a form and then waits to be interviewed. It takes approximately 15 minutes to complete the form.

```
ARIV    *S;EX(25):

FORM    *A;15:

WAIT    *Q:
```

Filling out the form is represented by the infinite capacity auxiliary FORM because the forms are assumed to be immediately accessible to arriving applicants.

## B.2.5. Basic Rules for the Operation of Nodes

1. A source may not be entered from any node, including another source.
2. A queue may not feed directly into another queue, nor can it feed back into itself.
3. Facilities may follow one another without intervening queues. However, a facility may not feed directly into itself.
4. An auxiliary is the only node that can feed directly into itself.
5. A transaction will skip a queue if the queue is not full to capacity and its successor node accepts the transaction, even if the queue happens to be occupied when the new transaction arrives.
6. If a facility is preceded by a queue, the facility automatically will attempt to draw a waiting transactions immediately when a service is completed. If the queue happens to be empty, the facility will go dormant until it is "revived" by the arrival of a new transaction.
7. Movement of transactions in and out of the queue must be initiated by *other* nodes. The queue itself is not capable of initiating this movement.
8. When facilities follow one another in tandem or when the intervening queues have limited capacities, a transaction completing service in one of the facilities will be **blocked** if its successor node is a full (finite) queue or a busy facility. The **unblocking** will occur automatically in a chain effect when the cause of blocking subsides.

## Problem set B.2a

1. In each of the following cases, what will be the values of attribute $A(1)$ associated with the first three transactions that exit the source node?
   (a) ARIV      *S;5;;1:
   (b) ARIV      *S;5;3;1:
   (c) ARIV      *S;5;3;-1:
2. How many transactions will be generated by each of the following source statements during the first 20 time units of the simulation?
   (a) ARIV      *S;5;/L/LIM=3:
   (b) ARIV      *S;5;/m/MULT=2:
3. The first five transactions arriving at queue QQ have the attributes listed subsequently.

| Transaction | A(1) | A(2) |
|:-----------:|:----:|:----:|
| 1 | 4 | 9 |
| 2 | 7 | −3 |
| 3 | 1 | 10 |

*Continued*

| Transaction | A(1) | A(2) |
|:-----------:|:----:|:----:|
| 4 | 3 | 14 |
| 5 | 2 | 6 |

Show how these transactions will be ordered in QQ in each of the following cases:

**(a)** QQ   *Q:

**(b)** QQ   *Q;/d/LIFO:

**(c)** QQ   *Q;/d/HI(1):

**(d)** QQ   *Q;/d/LO(2):

**4.** For the same data in Problem 3, identify the transactions leaving QQ and their attributes in each of the following cases assuming FIFO queue discipline:

**(a)** QQ   *Q;;2(SUM):

**(b)** QQ   *Q;;4(FIRST):

**(c)** QQ   *Q;;3:

**(d)** QQ   *Q;;2(LO(1)):

**(e)** QQ   *Q;;2(HI(2)):

**5.** Consider the following model segment:

```
QQ   *Q;(3):

FF   *F;;2;(1);goto-TERM:
```

**(a)** How many transactions will be processed by facility FF?

**(b)** Determine the simulation time at which each transaction will leave FF.

**(c)** Repeat (a) and (b), assuming that the model segment is changed as follows:

*Change* **1**

```
QQ   *Q:

FF   *F;;2;(1);goto-TERM:
```

*Change* **2**

```
QQ   *Q;(3):

FF   *F;;2;goto-TERM:
```

*Change* **3**

```
QQ   *Q;(3):

FF   *F;;2;2(1);goto-TERM:
```

**6.** Consider the following source statement:

```
SS   *S;UN(10,15):
```

Suppose that the SIMNET II processor is using the following random numbers stream:

```
.1111, .2342, .6712, .8923, .4687, .3526, . . .
```

Determine the simulation time at which the first three transactions from SS are created.

## B.3 SIMNET II MATHEMATICAL EXPRESSIONS

The rules for constructing and evaluating mathematical expressions in SIMNET II are the same as in FORTRAN. The arithmetic operators include addition (+), subtraction (−), multiplication (*), division (/), and exponentiation (**). An expression may include any legitimate combination of the following elements:

1. User-defined nonsubscripted and array (single- and double-subscripted) variables
2. All familiar algebraic and trigonometric functions (Table B-1)
3. SIMNET II simulation variables that define the status of the simulation during execution (Table B-2)
4. SIMNET II random samples from probabilistic distributions (Table B-3)

Tables B-2 and B-3 provide a partial list of the simulation variables and the random samples. The complete list is in Taha (1995).

**TABLE B-1**
SIMNET II INSTRINSIC FUNCTIONS[+]

| Algebraic | |
|---|---|
| Single argument: | INT, ABS, EXP, SQRT, SIGN, LOG, LOG10 |
| Double arguments: | MOD |
| Multiple arguments: | MAX, MIN |
| Trigonometric (single argument) | |
| Regular: | SIN, COS, TAN |
| Arc: | ASIN, ACOS, ATAN |
| Hyperbolic: | SINH, COSH, TANH |

[+]Arguments may be any SMINET II mathematical expressions.

**TABLE B-2**
PARTIAL LIST OF SIMNET II SIMULATION VARIABLES

| Variable | Definition |
|----------|-----------|
| LEN (auxiliary) | Current number of transactions residing in an auxiliary node |
| LEN/HLEN/LLEN/ALEN (file name) | Current/highest/lowest/average LENgth of a queue, or facility |
| VAL/HVAL/LVAL/AVAL (variable name) | Current/highest/lowest/average VALue of a statistical variable (see Section B.7) |
| COUNT (node or variable name) | Number of transactions that exited a node since the start of the simulation or the cumulative number of updates of a statistical variable |
| RUN.LEN | Length of current run |
| CUR.TIME | Current simulation time |

**TABLE B-3**
PARTIAL LIST OF SIMNET II RANDOM FUNCTIONS

| Function | Definition |
|----------|-----------|
| EX $(p_1, \text{RS})$ | EXponential sample with mean $p_1$ using random stream RS[a] |
| NO $(p_1, p_2, \text{RS})$ | NOrmal sample with mean $p_1$ and standard deviation $p_2$ |
| PO $(p_1, \text{RS})$ | POisson sample with mean $p_1$ |
| RND (RS) | [0, 1] random sample |
| TR $(p_1, p_2, p_3, \text{RS})$ | TRiangular sample in the interval $[p_1, p_3]$ with mode $p_2$ |
| UN $(p_1, p_2,)$ | UNiform sample in the interval $[p_1, p_2]$ |

[a] Arguments $p_1, p_2$, and $p_3$ and random stream RS may be any mathematical expressions. RS must assume a nonzero integer value in the range [-50, +50] corresponding to SIMNET II's 100 random streams. If RS is negative, the **antithetic** [0, 1] random number $(1 - R)$ is used. Default RS = 1.

## B.4 A SIMNET II MODEL EXAMPLE

Customers arrive randomly at a three-clerk post office. The interarrival time is exponential, with a mean of 5 minutes. The service time is also exponential, with a mean of 10 minutes. All arriving customers form one waiting line and are served by free clerks on a FIFO basis.

Figure B-5 provides the network representation of the model and the SIMNET II statements. As you proceed through the explanation of this model, you will find it helpful to refer to the definitions of the nodes summarized in Figures B-1 to B-4.

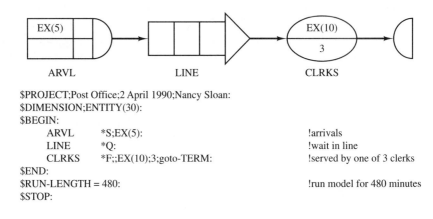

```
$PROJECT;Post Office;2 April 1990;Nancy Sloan:
$DIMENSION;ENTITY(30):
$BEGIN:
      ARVL      *S;EX(5):                              !arrivals
      LINE      *Q:                                    !wait in line
      CLRKS     *F;;EX(10);3;goto-TERM:               !served by one of 3 clerks
$END:
$RUN-LENGTH = 480:                                    !run model for 480 minutes
$STOP:
```

**Figure B–5**

In Figure B-5, the $PROJECT statement provides the model name, date, and analyst name. The $DIMENSION statement uses ENTITY(30) to provide an *estimate* of the memory requirements of the model's files. The statement indicates that no more than 30 transactions are expected in the system at any one time. If the model happens to require more memory during the simulation run, an appropriate message will be posted.

The logic of the model is enclosed between $BEGIN and $END. Transactions automatically are created by source ARVL every EX(5) minutes. The first arrival occurs at time 0 (default of field 2). Arriving transactions will wait in queue LINE if all three clerks are busy. Otherwise, the queue is skipped. When a transaction completes a service, it will be TERMinated. At this point, facility CLRKS will look back at queue LINE and bring in the first-in-line transaction (queue discipline in FIFO by default).

The route of the transaction is defined automatically by the sequence ARVL-LINE-CLRKS because of the physical order of the statements in the model. We will show later that transactions can be routed in any manner in the network by using the goto-field as well as by branching.

The statement between $END and $STOP controls the execution of the simulation. Specifically, $RUN-LENGTH indicates that the simulation will be executed for 480 minutes.

The standard output of the model is given in Figure B-6. Queue LINE has an infinite capacity (designated by asterisks) and an IN : OUT ratio of 1 : 1 signifying that each exiting transaction corresponds to *one* waiting transaction (default for field 2 of LINE). The AVERAGE LENGTH of 1.30 transactions represents the average number of waiting transactions over the entire length of the run. The MIN/MAX/LAST LEN column provides the minimum, maximum, and last length of LINE (= 0, 12, 0 respectively) that occur during the run. The average waiting time of *all* transactions (including those that do not wait) is given by AV. DELAY(ALL) = 6.51 minutes. The next column AV. DELAY(+VE WAIT) shows that the average waiting time for those that *must* wait is 15.63 minutes. Finally, the last column indicates that 58% of the transactions arriving from source ARVL skip LINE, meaning that they do not experience any waiting at all.

```
PROJECT: Post Office        RUN LENGTH =     480.00        NBR RUNS =   1
DATE: 2 April 1990          TRANSIENT PERIOD =      .00    OBS/RUN =    1
ANALYST: Nancy Sloan        TIME BASE/OBS =    480.00

                 *** I N D E P E N D E N T   R U N S   D A T A ***

*** RUN  1:
                        ---------------------
                              Q U E U E S
                        ---------------------
         CAPA-  IN:OUT  AVERAGE  MIN/MAX/  AV. DELAY  AV. DELAY  % ZERO WAIT
         CITY   RATIO   LENGTH   LAST LEN  (ALL)      (+VE WAIT) TRANSACTION
LINE     ****    1: 1    1.31    0/ 12/ 0     6.51       15.63      58.33
                        ---------------------
                            F A C I L I T I E S
                        ---------------------
         NBR    MIN/MAX/  AV. GROSS  AVERAGE   AVERAGE     AVERAGE    AVERAGE
         SRVRS  LAST UTILZ UTILIZ    BLOCKAGE  BLKGE TIME  IDLE TIME  BUSY TIME
CLRKS     3     0/  3/  1   1.9955    .0000      .00        8.44      17.06

*** TRANSACTIONS COUNT AT T =     478.8 OF RUN  1:
NODE       IN     OUT   RESIDING    SKIPPING    UNLINKED/LINKED   TERMINATED
                                    (BLOCKED)   (DESTROYED)
*S:
ARVL              96
*Q:
LINE       40     40       0           56         0/    0            0
*F:
CLRKS      96     95       1    (     0)   (     0)                  95
```

**Figure B–6**

Facility CLRKS has three parallel servers. The second column shows that CLRKS starts empty, reaches a maximum of three busy clerks, and ends the simulation with one busy server. The average gross utilization (third column) indicates that on the average 1.9931 servers (out of 3) were busy throughout the run, thus reflecting a gross percentage utilization of $(\frac{1.9931}{3}) \times 100 = 66.4\%$. The AVERAGE BLOCKAGE records the average *nonproductive* occupancy of the facility (expressed in number of servers) that is the result of being blocked by a succeeding finite queue or facility. This condition does not exist in our example, thus resulting in zero average blockage. In general, the *net* utilization of a facility is the difference between its average gross utilization and its average blockage. The AVERAGE BLKGE TIME represents the average time a facility remains in a blocked state (= 0 in this example). The next to last column represents the average length of time a facility remains idle between busy periods. In this example, when no customers are in the system, each clerk remains idle about 8.48 minutes. The last column provides the average time the facility remains busy before it becomes idle again. Actually, the average busy time can never be less than the average service time per server. In this example, the average busy time is 17.06 minutes. Because the average service time per transaction is 10 minutes, *on the average* each server attends to $\frac{17.06}{10} = 1.706$ customers before becoming idle for 8.479 minutes.

The transactions count given at the end of the report provides a complete history of the flow of transactions during the run. This summary can be helpful in spotting irregularities in the model. For example, a queue build-up may indicate a possible bottleneck. In this example, during the 480-minute run, 96 transactions are created by source ARVL, 40 of which experienced waiting in queue LINE and the remaining 56 skipped the queue. Facility CLRKS received 96 customers and released 95 with 1 transaction remaining unprocessed at the end of the run. The remaining entries in the count are all zeros. In particular, the UNLINKED/LINKED column is used only when the model experiences file manipulations (see Section B.9.3). The (BLOCKED) column will be positive when a facility is blocked. Also, (DESTROYED) will be positive when transactions are destroyed (vanish from the system). Neither case applies to our example.

## B.5  TRANSACTION ROUTING IN SIMNET II

Transactions are routed among the various nodes of the network by using

1. Next-node sequencing
2. Node's select field
3. Node's transfer field *T using GOTO-
4. Branches (*B) emanating from the node

The next-node routing was explained in the preceding sections. This section details the next two types. Routing by branches will be presented in Section B.6.

### B.5.1 Select Routing

Each of SIMNET II's four nodes has a **select field** (see Figures B-1 to B-4) that routes transactions conditionally to one of several destination nodes. In particular, a facility has both input and output select fields because it can pull transactions from one of several input queues as well as send transactions to one of several receiving nodes. Table B-4 gives a partial list of SIMNET II's select rules. The remaining rules are given in Taha (1995).

**TABLE B-4**
PARTIAL LIST OF SELECT RULES

| Rule | Description |
|------|-------------|
| All nodes and TERM [format: rule(node$_1$, node$_2$, ..., node$_m$)]. | |
| POR | Preferred ORder of scanning |
| ROT | ROTational order of scanning |
| Queues and facilities [format: rule(file$_1$, file$_2$, ..., file$_m$)]. | |
| HTE(LTE) | Highest(Lowest) Time file has been Empty |
| Queues and facilities [format: rule(file$_{11}$ ± file$_{12}$ ± ..., ..., file$_{m1}$ ± file$_{m2}$ ± ...)]. | |
| HBC(LBC) | Highest(Lowest) file length |

**ILLUSTRATIONS**

1. SS    *S;UN(10,20);/s/POR(Q1,Q2,A1):

   Transactions leaving source SS will scan the nodes in the preferred order Q1→Q2→A1, and will choose the *first* node that accepts the transaction.

2. QQ  *Q;/s/HTE(F1,F2):

   Transactions leaving queue QQ are sent to either facility F1 or F2, depending on which one has been empty (idle) the longest.

3. AAX    *A;/s/LBC(Q1+F1,Q2-Q1,Q3):

   A transaction leaving auxiliary AAX is sent to *lead node* Q1, Q2, or Q3, depending on which one yields the smallest value of LEN(Q1)+LEN(F1), LEN(Q2)−LEN(Q1), and LEN(Q3), where LEN is the SIMNET II variable that represents the LENgth of the file (see Table B-2).

4. FF     *F;HBC(Q1,Q2,Q3);EX(10);3;LBC(F3,Q4,Q5):

   Facility FF uses both its *input* and *output* select fields. In the input select rule in field 2, when FF "looks back" at queues Q1, Q2, and Q3, it will attempt to draw a transaction from the queue with the highest length (HBC). A transaction leaving FF will select F3, Q4, or Q5 according to the LBC rule—that is, depending on which one has the smallest length.

---

**Example B.5-1   (BANK MODEL).**

Cars arrive at a two-window, drive-in bank according to an exponential interarrival time, with a mean of 5 minutes. A car chooses the right or left lane, depending on which lane is shorter. The service time in either lane is UN(3,4) minutes. The space in each lane, excluding the window, can accommodate at most three cars.

The model network and statements are given in Figure B-7. Transactions are created from source CARS every EX(2) minutes. Field 6 of CARS carries the select rule LBC(QL+WL,QR+WR), indicating that an arriving transaction will enter QL if the number of cars in the left lane (including the window) does not exceed that of the right lane. Otherwise, the right lane is selected. If both QL and QR happen to be full to capacity (i.e., LEN(QL) = 3 and LEN(QR) = 3), transactions arriving from CARS will be destroyed by the system.

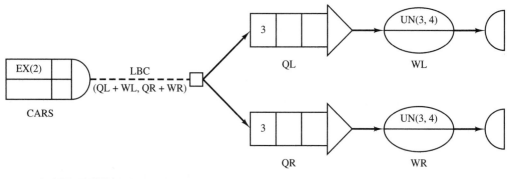

```
$PROJECT;Bank Model;3 April 1990;Nancy Sloan:
$DIMENSION;ENTITY(50):
$BEGIN:
        CARS       *S;EX(2);/s/LBC(QL + WL,QR + WR):        !select shorter lane
        QL         *Q;3:                                    !left lane
        WL         *F;;UN(3,4);goto-TERM:
        QR         *Q;3:                                    !right lane
        WR         *F;;UN(3,4);goto-TERM:
$END:
$RUN-LENGTH = 480:                                          !run model for 480 minutes
$RUNS = 1:                                                  !for one run only
$STOP:
```

**Figure B–7**

---

Notice that the "next-node" ordering of source CARS and queue QL is overridden by the select rule of CARS. Conversely, a transaction leaving QL uses the next-node sequencing to route itself to WL. The same logic applies to QR and WR.

## B.5.2 GOTO Routing (*T-field)

The GOTO field allows additional control over transactions routing in a network by using *either of* the following format:

```
GOTO-node name/transfer type,node name/transfer type,..., repeats
```

The transfer field always occupies the last field of the node statement. Table B-5 summarizes the most common types of transfers. Two other types of transfer, exclusive and dependent, are not presented at this introductory level (see Taha [1995] for details).

**TABLE B-5**
TYPES OF TRANSFER ROUTING

| SIMNET II symbol | Usage |
|---|---|
| A | Always or unconditional transfer (default) |
| Numeric $(0 \leq P \leq 1)$ | Probabilistic transfer, $P$ |
| L | Last choice transfer |

---

**Example B.5-2    (TV INSPECTION).**
Television units arrive for inspection on a conveyor belt from an assembly line at the rate of 5 units per hour. The inspection time is UN(10,15) minutes. Experience shows that 20% of inspected units are adjusted and then sent back for reinspection. The adjustment time is UN(6,8) minutes.

The model network and statements are given in Figure B-8. The routing TVS-QINSP-FINSP is dictated by the next-node sequencing. The probabilistic transfer from FINSP will randomly send 20% of the transactions to QADJ and the remaining 80% to TERM. When adjustment is completed in FADJ, the (default) A-transfer will route the transaction back to QINSP as desired. Notice that the sum of the probabilities in the probabilistic transfers from a node must be 1.

---

**Example B.5-3    (BANK MODEL REVISITED).**
We reconsider the bank model in Example B.5-1. About 90% of the customers who cannot use the drive-in windows will go inside the bank to receive service from one of two tellers. It takes about 3 minutes to park the car and walk inside. The service time is UN(2, 3) minutes.

Figure B-9 gives the new network. The use of the transfer GOTO-AAX/L from node CARS is used to ensure that, as a last choice, a customer who cannot enter one of the drive-in lanes will go to (dummy) auxiliary AAX (with zero delay time) to decide whether to go away or to seek service inside. From AAX, a 0.9-transfer takes the customer inside after parking and a 0.1-transfer TERMinates the transaction.

---

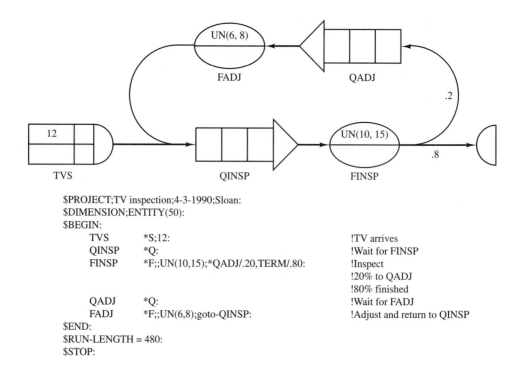

```
$PROJECT;TV inspection;4-3-1990;Sloan:
$DIMENSION;ENTITY(50):
$BEGIN:
        TVS      *S;12:                              !TV arrives
        QINSP    *Q:                                 !Wait for FINSP
        FINSP    *F;;UN(10,15);*QADJ/.20,TERM/.80:   !Inspect
                                                     !20% to QADJ
                                                     !80% finished

        QADJ     *Q:                                 !Wait for FADJ
        FADJ     *F;;UN(6,8);goto-QINSP:             !Adjust and return to QINSP
$END:
$RUN-LENGTH = 480:
$STOP:
```

**Figure B–8**

### Problem set B.5a

**1.** Run the bank model of Example B.5-1 to determine the following:
   **(a)** The average number of cars in each lane.
   **(b)** The percentage of cars in each lane that do not experience any waiting before receiving service.
   **(c)** The percentage of cars that entered the right and left lanes.

**2.** Run the TV model of Example B.5-2 for 480 minutes. Determine the average time a TV unit waits for inspection.

**3. (a)** Run the model of Example B.5-3, and determine the percent utilization of the tellers inside the bank.
   **(b)** Remodel the system, assuming that on entering the bank, the customer will always go to the shorter lane.

**4.** Write a SIMNET II model for the following situation. New customers in a bank arrive every 18 minutes on the average, exponentially distributed. A customer must consult first with a bank officer regarding the opening of the new account. It takes between 15 and 20 minutes, uniformly distributed, to complete this task. Next, the customer goes to one of three tellers to make the initial deposit. This activity takes 5 minutes on the average, exponentially distributed. All customers are served on a FIFO basis. Run the simulation for 480 minutes, and determine the following:

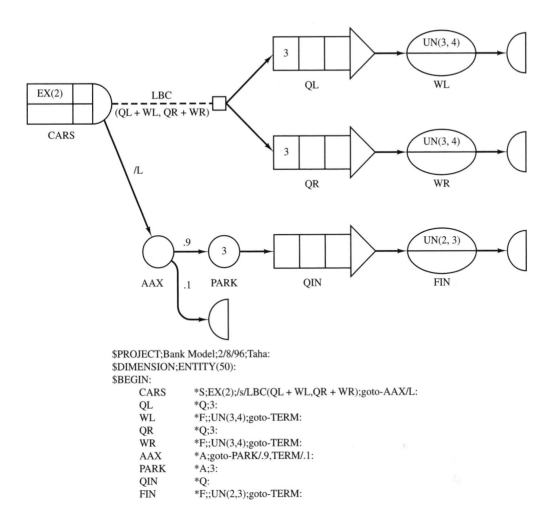

```
$PROJECT;Bank Model;2/8/96;Taha:
$DIMENSION;ENTITY(50):
$BEGIN:
        CARS        *S;EX(2);/s/LBC(QL + WL,QR + WR);goto-AAX/L:
        QL          *Q;3:
        WL          *F;;UN(3,4);goto-TERM:
        QR          *Q;3:
        WR          *F;;UN(3,4);goto-TERM:
        AAX         *A;goto-PARK/.9,TERM/.1:
        PARK        *A;3:
        QIN         *Q:
        FIN         *F;;UN(2,3);goto-TERM:
```

**Figure B–9**

(a) The average length of each queue inside the bank.
(b) The average waiting time in each queue inside the bank.
(c) The percentage of customers in each queue who do not have to wait.
(d) The maximum length of each queue.
(e) The percent utilization of the bank officer and the teller.

## B.6  BRANCHES IN SIMNET II

Branches route transactions among nodes in a manner similar to that of direct transfer (Section B.5.2). We use branches in place of direct transfer when we are interested in performing any of the following functions:

1. Checking logical conditions required before transfer is made to a succeeding node.
2. Executing assignments.
3. Collecting data on (user-defined) statistical variables.
4. Returning resources to base stock.

This information appears in the successive fields of a branch using the format in Figure B-10. Fields F1/SUBF1, F2, F3, and F4 are explained subsequently. The remaining field, F5, dealing with resources, is not covered at this introductory level (see Taha [1995] for details).

| | *B; F1/SUBF1; F2?; F3%; F4%; F5: | | |
| --- | --- | --- | --- |
| | Field Identifier | | Default |
| F1 | | Name of destination node | (Error) |
| SUBF1 | | Branch type (see Table B-6) | A |
| F2 | /c/ | Condition(s) with AND/OR (field must end with ?)[a] | None |
| F3 | /a/ | Assignment(s) (field must end with %) | None |
| F4 | /v/ | List of statistical variables (field must end with %)) (see Section B.7) | None |
| F5 | /r/ | Resources returned by branch | None |

[a] For field F2 through F5, field number n in the notation /n/ of field identifier may be replaced by the descriptive words /Conditions/, /Assignments/, /Variables/, and /Resources/ or /C/, /A/, /V/, and /R/, respectively.

**Figure B–10**

The general format for the conditions field of a branch is as follows:

```
condition 1,AND/OR, . . . ,AND/OR,condition m?
```

The field must terminate with ?. A condition may be arithmetic or logical. Arithmetic conditions have the following general format:

```
left expression(=, >, <, >=, <=, or < >) right expression
```

Logical conditions involve logic switch operations and will be discussed in Section B.7.

As is in all programming languages, AND is evaluated before OR. We can override this default by grouping the conditions using { }. The following examples demonstrate typical arithmetic conditions:

```
1.(A(I)+SAMPLE(J))**2 < SUM, AND, LEN(QQ)=0?

2.{ {V(I) > J,OR,K < M}, AND, XX=LEN(QQ) }?
```

The assignment field F3 of a branch is where all SIMNET II assignments are executed. The field may hold any number of assignments according to the following format:

```
assignment 1,assignment 2,. . . ,assignment m%
```

The field must terminate with %. Assignments in the same field are executed sequentially.

SIMNET II assignments will be executed only by a transaction in motion. If the branch conditions (Field 2) are not satisfied or if the node reached by the branch cannot be entered (e.g., a busy facility), then the branch cannot be taken, or none of its assignments, nor any of its fields, will be activated.

Assignments may be executed unconditionally or conditionally as well as within loops. The syntax of a *conditional assignment* is

```
IF,conditions,THEN,assignments,ELSE,assignments,ENDIF
```

The IF-ENDIF statements may be nested to any depth as the following examples demonstrate:

```
1. IF, {A(1)=1,OR,SUM=0}, AND, K=LEN(QQ),

       THEN,A(1)+A(1)+1,SUM=(K+1)**2,

       ELSE,I=LEN(QQ),J=I+1,

   ENDIF

2. IF,I=1,

       THEN,K=K+1,

       IF,K>2,THEN,J=1,A(K**2)=1,ENDIF,

       ELSE,

       IF,K<=2,THEN,J=0,ENDIF,

   ENDIF
```

The *loop assignment* is similar to FORTRAN. It has the following general format:

```
FOR,index=limit 1,TO,limit 2,STEP,step size,DO,

       assignment 1,

       assignment 2,

             •

             •

             •

       assignment m,

   NEXT
```

The *index* may be any nonsubscripted variable. The parameters *limit 1, limit 2,* and *step size* of the loop may be any SIMNET II mathematical expressions with the *step size* assuming a positive or a negative value. If (STEP, *step size,*) is not specified, a default value of 1 is assumed.

SIMNET II offers the following two *special assignments* (borrowed from C) for use within the FOR-NEXT loop:

1. LOOP=BREAK causes an immediate break away from the loop exactly as if *index* has exceeded *limit 2.*
2. LOOP=CONTINUE causes a skipping of the remaining assignments for the current cycle of the loop.

The following example illustrates the use of FOR-NEXT:

```
IF,I=J,THEN,
    FOR,K=1,TO,J+4,DO,
            IF,K=10,THEN,LOOP=BREAK,ENDIF,
            IF,K=12,THEN A(1)=A(2),ENDIF,
            FOR,L=K+2,TO,1,STEP,-1,DO,
                    nbr_jobs=nbr_jobs+1,
            NEXT,
    NEXT,
ELSE,
    nbr_jobs=nbr_jobs-1,
    FOR,K=1,TO,3,DO,
        A(K)=A(K+1),
    NEXT,
ENDIF
```

The branch types in subfield SUBF1 are given in Table B-6. The A-, P-, and L-types are the same as in direct transfer (Table B-5). The select (S) branches synchronize branch functions of transactions routed via the select field of the node. The conditional (C) branches require that desired conditions be satisfied before a branch is traversed.

Note that conditions cannot be used with the A-branches but are mandatory with the conditional (C) branches. Conditions are optional with all the remaining types.

In SIMNET II, branches of any type in any number may emanate from the same node. These branches may also be ordered sequentially in any manner with two exceptions.

**TABLE B-6**
TYPES OF BRANCHES

| SIMNET II symbol | Usage | Does Branch Accept Conditions? |
|---|---|---|
| S | Select | Yes, optional |
| A | Always (default) | No |
| Numeric (C = 1) | Conditional | Yes, mandatory |
| Numeric (0 < P < 1) | Probabilistic | Yes, optional |
| L | Last choice | Yes, optional |

**1.** The S-branches must always be placed at the top of the list because they must be synchronized with the node's select field, which is acted on before considering any branches.
**2.** The L-branch, if any, must be at the bottom of the list.

**Example B.6-1.**
Transactions arriving from a source SS will select the *shorter* of two queues named Q1 and Q2. During the first 100 time units of the simulation, Q1 and Q2 will not be accessible, and all transactions must go to queue Q3.

Figure B-11 describes the model segment. The select condition LBC(Q1,Q2) routes transactions to the shorter of Q1 and Q2. However, before entering either queue,

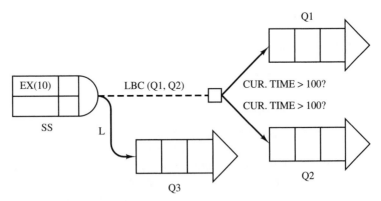

```
SS    *S;EX(10);/S/LBC(Q1, Q2):
      *B;Q1/S;CUR. TIME > 100?:
      *B;Q2/S;CUR. TIME > 100?:
      *B;Q3/L:
```

**Figure B–11**

SIMNET II will check for an S-branch from SS, with a destination node that matches that selected by LBC(Q1,Q2). If Q1 is selected by LBC, the S-branch to Q1 will be checked automatically. Because the branch carries the condition CUR.TIME>100?, Q1 will not be entered until the simulation clock (CUR.TIME) exceeds 100. The same logic applies when Q2 is selected by LBC. The L-branch from source SS is used to route the transactions to Q3 during the first 100 time units.

## Example B.6-2   (BUS LOADING/UNLOADING MODEL).

Buses arrive at a station every EX(30) minutes. The number of passengers on the bus is usually between 20 and 50, uniformly distributed. Between 2 and 6 passengers, uniformly distributed, leave the bus at the station and from 1 to 8 passengers, also uniformly distributed, are usually waiting to board the bus. It takes UN(3,8) seconds per passenger to leave the bus and UN(4,7) seconds to board it. The maximum capacity of the bus is 50 passengers. Simulate the loading/unloading process.

The determination of the number of passengers on the bus and the number to leave and board at the station is achieved by realizing that a uniform *discrete* sample in the interval $(a, b)$ is computed as $INT(UN(a, b + 1))$, where INT is the integer function (see Table B-1).

Figure B-12 gives the model. The A-branch from BUS computes n_on and n_off, the number of passengers on bus (n_on) when it arrives and the number to leave (at the station), respectively. The loop around auxiliary UNLD simulates the unloading of passengers. The first branch is taken conditionally back to UNLD (using the conditional branch code, UNLD/1) if the loop's index I is less than n_off. Each round also increments the index I by 1. After the loop has been satisfied, the L-branch (last choice) takes the transaction to auxiliary LOAD, which simulates the loading process. The number that will board, n_board, equals the smaller of the number of empty seats, n_empty, and the number of passengers waiting at the station, n_wait. Observe that n_board can be determined *equivalently* as

```
n_board=MIN(INT(UN(1,9)),50-n_on+n_off)
```

The procedure we used in the model is intended to demonstrate the use of IF-ENDIF.

## Problem set B.6a

1. Convoys consisting of four empty trucks each leave every EX(3) hours to reach a seaport loading dock in UN(15,20) minutes. At the dock, the trucks are loaded one at a time. The loading time is EX(30) minutes per truck. Loaded trucks move out of the dock again in one convoy. Simulate the system for 100 hours, and determine the amount of time needed until each truck starts loading at the dock. Also, determine the utilization of the loading facility.

2. A bank opens at 8:00 A.M. and closes at 4:30 P.M. Customers arrive every EX(5) minutes. The bank has one inside teller that opens at 8:00 A.M. and one drive-in window that opens an hour later. The service time inside is EX(4) minutes. The drive-in service time is EX(6) minutes. The customer who uses the inside teller will take about 3 minutes to park the car. Simulate the situa-

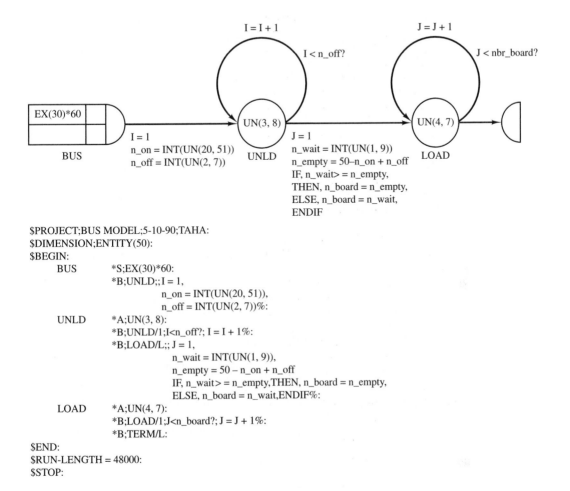

$PROJECT;BUS MODEL;5-10-90;TAHA:
$DIMENSION;ENTITY(50):
$BEGIN:
    BUS        *S;EX(30)*60:
                *B;UNLD;;I = 1,
                            n_on = INT(UN(20, 51)),
                            n_off = INT(UN(2, 7))%:
    UNLD     *A;UN(3, 8):
                *B;UNLD/1;I<n_off?; I = I + 1%:
                *B;LOAD/L;; J = 1,
                            n_wait = INT(UN(1, 9)),
                            n_empty = 50 – n_on + n_off
                            IF, n_wait> = n_empty,THEN, n_board = n_empty,
                            ELSE, n_board = n_wait,ENDIF%:
    LOAD     *A;UN(4, 7):
                *B;LOAD/1;J<n_board?; J = J + 1%:
                *B;TERM/L:
$END:
$RUN-LENGTH = 48000:
$STOP:

**Figure B–12**

tion for 5 days, and determine the average waiting time inside and outside the bank. Also, determine the utilization of the inside teller and the window.

## B.7 STATISTICAL VARIABLES

Field 4 (F4) of a branch is used to compute two types of user-defined statistical variables (a third type, called RUN.END, is not presented here; see Taha [1995]):

1. **Observation-based** (OBS.BASED) variables are those whose average equals the sum of the observation values divided by the number of observations.
2. **Time-based** (TIME.BASED) variables are those whose average equals the area under the curve representing the variable divided by the associated time base.

Before statistical observations can be collected in Field 4 of a branch, the variables themselves must be defined by name, type, observation value, and histogram data using the following statement (which must be placed ahead of $BEGIN):

```
$VARIABLES: Variable name;Type;value;histogram data:
                            •
                            •
                            •

                      repeats
```

The variable name is user defined. The observation value must be defined according to the definitions in Table B-7. The specification for histograms is not covered here, but can be found in Taha (1995).

**TABLE B-7**
STATISTICAL VARIABLES

| Observation Value | Definition |
|---|---|
| **All Types (OBS.BASED and TIME.BASED):** | |
| Expression | Any legitimate SIMNET II mathematical expression |
| **OBS.BASED only** | |
| TRANSIT (#) | Value of the interval CUR.TIME$-$A(#), where # is any SIMNET II expression (> 0), truncated to an integer value, if necessary |
| BET. ARVL | Interval between successive arrivals of transactions. |
| ARVL.TIME | Arrival time of transactions. |
| FIRST | Time of the first arrival. |

In Table B-7, the observation value TRANSIT (#) is particularly useful in computing intervals between two points in the network. This is normally accomplished by assigning the current clock time CUR.TIME to attribute A(#) at a desired start point in the network. When the transaction reaches its desired end point, it will be carrying A(#) with it. TRANSIT (#) then computes the elapsed time by subtracting A(#) from the current clock time CUR.TIME.

The following examples illustrate how statistical variables are defined:

```
$VARIABLES:    SYS TIME;OBS.BASED;TRANSIT(1):

               INV LEVEL;TIME.BASED;I:

               T BET BLKGE;OBS.BASED;BET.ARVL.
```

The gathering of statistics for the OBS.BASED variables requires placing their names in field F4 of the appropriate branch using the following format:

```
variable1 name, variable2 name,...%
```

The field must terminate with %. The TIME.BASED variables are automated; hence, their names need not be placed in field F4 of the branch.

---

**Example B.7-1    (CAR WASH FACILITY).**
Cars arrive at a one-bay car wash facility every EX(10) minutes. Arriving cars enter through a single lane that can accommodate five cars. If the lane is full, arriving cars will go elsewhere. It takes UN(10,15) minutes to wash a car. We want to compute two statistics: the time a car spends in the facility until it is washed, and the interval between successive balks.

Figure B-13 gives the model. It also gives the segment of the output report pertaining to the statistical variables.

When source ARIV creates a transaction, it will automatically set its A(1)=CUR.TIME (because field 3 of ARIV is marked with 1). The first branch from ARIV will attempt to take the transaction to queue LANE. If LANE is full, the transaction will take the L-branch to TERM, signifying balking. The statistical variable BET BALKS has the observation type BET.ARVL and is computed on the branch to TERM. This variable automatically keeps track of the time between balks. Transactions completing WASH will compute SYS TIME as the interval from creation at ARIV until TERMination.

---

## B.8 LOGIC SWITCHES

Queues are buffers where transactions may reside indefinitely. An incoming transaction may skip a queue if the successor node will accept it (e.g., an idle facility). Additionally, a facility completing a service will always attempt to draw a transaction from a predecessor queue. This means that the movements of transactions in and out of a queue are automatically controlled by conditions in *other* nodes in the network, but never by the queue itself.

In some situations, we want to exercise direct control over the operation of the queue. For example, a machine maintenance shutdown can be simulated by "blocking" the path from its predecessor queue, so that no transaction can be drawn by the facility. When maintenance is completed we can "revive" the machine by releasing a waiting transaction from the queue. Logic switches allow the modeler to exercise such control over the queue operation.

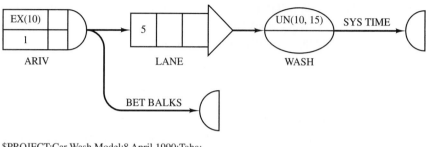

```
$PROJECT;Car Wash Model;8 April 1990;Taha:
$DIMENSION;ENTITY(20),A(1):
$VARIABLES:SYS TIME;obs.based;TRANSIT(1):
            BET BALKS;obs.based;BET.ARVL:
$BEGIN:
    ARIV    *S;EX(10);;1:                !Mark A(1) = CUR.TIME
            *B;LANE:                     !Enter lane if not full
            *B;TERM/L;/v/BET BALKS%:     !Else, balk
    LANE    *Q,5:                        !Lane capacity = 5 cars
    WASH    *F;;UN(10, 15):              !Wash car
            *B;TERM;/v/SYS TIME%:        !Compute SYS TIME
$END:
$RUN-LENGTH = 480:
$STOP:
```

|                | UPDATES | VARIABLES | | | | |
|----------------|---------|-----------|---------|-----------|-----------|-------------|
|                | UPDATES | AV. VALUE | STD DEV | MIN VALUE | MAX VALUE | LAST UPDATE |
| (O)SYS TIME    | 38      | 41.61     | 21.75   | 12.33     | 77.74     | 73.42       |
| (O)BET BALKS   | 9       | 17.15     | 21.40   | .68       | 71.29     | 1.21        |

**Figure B–13**

A logic switch is defined by using the $SWITCHES statement as follows:

```
$SWITCHES:   switch name;initial state;queue 1,queue 2, . . . :
                       •

                       •

                       •

                    repeats
```

The switch name is user defined. The initial state of the switch (before the start of the simulation) may be ON or OFF. The ensuing list of queue names represents those queues controlled by the switch. For example, the statement

```
$SWITCHES: SW;ON;Q1,Q2:
```

indicates that switch SW is initially ON and that it controls the queues names Q1 and Q2.

Modeling of the switch operation is achieved by using **special assignments** of the form:

```
Switch name=ON
Switch name=OFF
```

These assignments are used in two distinct ways.

**1.** As conditions that check the current state of the switch (ON or OFF).

**2.** As assignments that reverse the state of the switch (ON to OFF or OFF to ON).

In the first case, the condition may be integrated (with AND/OR) in the second field of a branch or in the IF-ENDIF statement. In the second case, the assignment is used in the third field of a branch.

A switch *condition* may be regarded as a binary (0-1) test. However, its use as an *assignment* allows us to control the operation of targeted queues. The execution of the assignment (switch name = ON) will *automatically attempt to push the first waiting transaction out of each of the queues listed in the definition of the switch.* If a queue happens to be empty or if the successor node cannot be entered (e.g., unsatisfied branch or busy facility), then no action is taken on that queue.

Remember that pushing transactions out of a controlled queue by a switch can take place only when the assignment (switch name = ON) is executed on a branch. The execution of the assignment (switch name = OFF) alters only the state of the switch but has no effect on its designated queue(s).

---

**Example B.8-1   (MACHINE MAINTENANCE).**

Jobs arrive for processing at a machine every EX(11) minutes. The processing time is EX(12) minutes. Following 8 hours of operation, the machine is shut down for UN(15,20) minutes for maintenance.

Figure B-14 gives the model, which includes two *disjointed* segments. The first segment simulates the maintenance cycle of the machine, and the second segment represents the machine operation. The condition, SW=ON?, on the branch from queue QJOBS to facility MACH controls the output of the queue. Thus, transactions will be permitted to leave QJOBS only if SW is ON.

The state of the switch is controlled by the maintenance segment. Source SS sends *one* transaction to auxiliary DELAY, where it waits for 8 hours, representing the operation time of MACH. When a transaction leaves DELAY, MACH will be due for maintenance. The leaving transaction then executes the assignment, SW = OFF, to halt the flow of transactions from QJOB to MACH. The maintenance transaction then moves into auxiliary MAINT, representing the  period needed to complete the maintenance. When the transaction exits MAINT, it reenters auxiliary DELAY to repeat the cycle. On its way there, it will execute the assignment SW = ON, which will then attempt to push a waiting job out of QJOBS into MACH, as desired. If QJOBS happens to be empty at the time SW = ON is executed, the assignment will simply act to unblock QJOBS so that a newly arriving job can skip the queue and enter MACH.

---

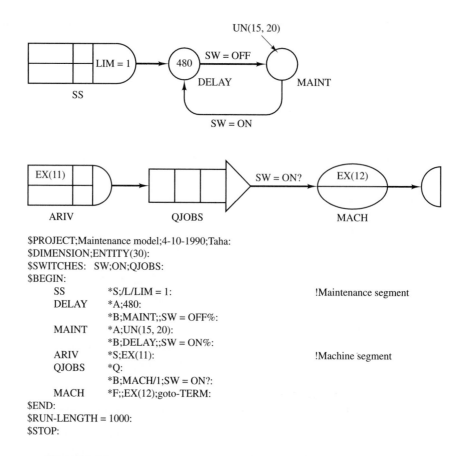

**Figure B–14**

### Problem set B.8a

**1.** In the machine maintenance model of Figure B-14, it is implicitly assumed that repair will start immediately after 480 minutes have elapsed (i.e., when a transaction leaves DELAY). This assumption is correct only if MACHINE happens to be idle at that point. Otherwise, preventive maintenance should not start until MACHINE completes its load. Modify the model to account for this detail.

**2.** Modify the machine maintenance model in Figure B-14 so that preventive maintenance is carried out every 50 completed jobs instead of every 8 hours.

## B.9 SPECIAL ASSIGNMENTS

In Section B.8, we used the special assignment, switch name = ON or OFF, to control the state of a logic switch. Additional SIMNET II special assignments include

1. Source activation/deactivation
2. Statistical variables collection
3. File manipulations applied to queues and facilities
4. Queue parameters control
5. Locating entries in files
6. Attributes control
7. Run length control
8. External files READ/WRITE capability

In this introduction of SIMNET II, we will present only assignments 1 to 3. The remaining assignments are given in Taha (1995).

### B.9.1 Source Activation and Deactivation

In the definition of the source node (Section B.2.1), the fifth field (LIM =) is used to control the number of creations or the length of time the source node is active. These limits, once specified at the start of the simulation, cannot be altered during execution. The source activation/deactivation assignments allow the modeler to *suspend* or *resume* source creations *instantly* at will. The format of these assignments is as follows:

$$\text{SUSPEND} = \text{source name}$$
$$\text{RESUME} = \text{source name}$$

The execution of these assignments *permanently* overrides the time of the first creation and the limit on creations as initially defined in fields F2 and F5 of the source node.

---

**Example B.9-1    (PRODUCTION LINE WITH BREAKDOWNS).**
An automatic production line delivers 1 unit of a product every UN(1,2) minutes for inspection. The inspection time takes 1.5 minutes per unit. The production line is known to break down every EX(120) minutes. It takes UN(5,10) minutes to complete the repair.

In Figure B-15, the source, P_LINE, represents the production line that sends 1 unit into Q_INSPECT every UN(1,2) minutes. The breakdown of the line is simulated by a separate segment. Source S_BREAK sends its first breakdown transaction after 120 minutes from the start of the simulation (thereafter, the breakdown occurs every EX(120) minutes). When the breakdown transaction coming out of S_BREAK executes the SUSPEND assignment, P_LINE stops instantly. After repair occurs, P_LINE is reactivated by executing the RESUME assignment.

---

### B.9.2 Statistical Variables Collection

We have seen in Section B.7 that the statistics of an OBS.BASED variable can be collected by listing the name of the variable in the fourth field of an appropriate branch. The same result can be accomplished using the special assignment

$$\text{COLLECT} = \text{variable name}$$

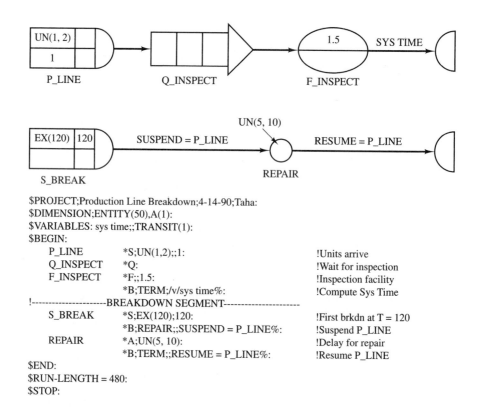

$PROJECT;Production Line Breakdown;4-14-90;Taha:
$DIMENSION;ENTITY(50),A(1):
$VARIABLES: sys time;;TRANSIT(1):
$BEGIN:
```
      P_LINE        *S;UN(1,2);;1:                        !Units arrive
      Q_INSPECT     *Q:                                   !Wait for inspection
      F_INSPECT     *F;;1.5:                              !Inspection facility
                    *B;TERM;/v/sys time%:                 !Compute Sys Time
!---------------------BREAKDOWN SEGMENT--------------------
      S_BREAK       *S;EX(120);120:                       !First brkdn at T = 120
                    *B;REPAIR;;SUSPEND = P_LINE%:         !Suspend P_LINE
      REPAIR        *A;UN(5, 10):                         !Delay for repair
                    *B;TERM;;RESUME = P_LINE%:            !Resume P_LINE
$END:
$RUN-LENGTH = 480:
$STOP:
```

**Figure B–15**

This special assignment is particularly convenient when it is desired to collect statistics about the variable conditionally within an IF-ENDIF statment. Example B.9-3 illustrates this point.

### B.9.3 File Manipulation Assignments

File manipulation assignments allow swapping, deleting, adding, copying, replacing, and locating transactions in queues and facilities. Table B-8 provides a summary of the file manipulation assignments. We refer to the file on the right-hand side of the assignment as the *donor* file. The left-hand side file is called the *recipient* file. For example, in the assignment LAST(QQ) = 1(WW), WW and QQ represent the donor and recipient queues, respectively. The assignment moves the first entry in WW to the tail (LAST) position of QQ. Actually, the quantities *a* and *b* given in Table B-8 can be replaced with any mathematical expression. For example,

$$((J+1)**2+K)(Q1)=(MAX(I+J,K-M))(Q2)$$

is perfectly valid. SIMNET II automatically truncates the expressions to integer values, if necessary.

**TABLE B-8**
FILE MANIPULATION ASSIGNMENTS

| Assignment[a] | Description |
|---|---|
| **Queues only:** | |
| $a$ (Q1) = $b$ (Q2) | Move entry $b$ of Q2 to the $a$th position in Q1 |
| $a$ (Q1) = ALL (Q2) | Move ALL the transactions of Q2 to Q1 starting at the $a$th position of Q1 |
| $a$ (Q1) = TRANS | Place a copy of the TRANSaction currently traversing the branch in the $a$th position of Q1 |
| $a$ (Q1) = DEL | DELete (dispose of) the $a$th entry in Q1 |
| ALL (Q1) = DEL | DELete all the contents of Q1  (Q1 becomes empty) |
| INS (Q1) = $b$ (Q2) | INSert the $b$th entry of Q2 in Q1 per the queue discipline of Q1 |
| INS (Q1) = ALL (Q2) | INSert ALL the transactions of Q2 in Q1 per the queue discipline of Q1 |
| INS (Q1) = TRANS | INSert a copy of the current TRANSaction in Q1 per the queue discipline of Q1 |
| | |
| **Facilities only:** | |
| $a$ (F1) = REL | RELease instantly the $a$th entry in facility F1 |
| ALL(F1) = REL | RELease instantly ALL the contents of facility F1 |
| | |
| **Queues and Facilities:** | |
| $a$ (Q1 or F1) = REP | REPlace the attributes of the $a$th entry in Q1 or F1 with those of the current transaction |
| | |
| COPY = $b$ (Q1 or F1) | Change the attributes of the current transaction traversing the branch to those of the $b$th entry in Q1 or F1 |

[a]a and b may be any SIMNET II mathematical expressions or the symbol LAST. Q1 and Q2 may represent the *same* queue if it is desired to rearrange the order of transactions in a given queue.

Four general rules govern the use of the file manipulation assignments:

**1.** The "queues only" assignments, with the exception of those involving ALL, are *dynamic* in the sense that the recipient queue will automatically attempt to send its received transaction as far as it will go into the network. This action happens momentarily while the assignment is being executed. In the case of the ALL assignments, the modeler is responsible for moving these transactions out of the recipient queue, if necessary, by using a proper switch assignment (Section B.8).

**2.** Automatic movement of transactions will *not* be realized if the execution of the assignment is caused by a file manipulation *nesting*. Nesting occurs when a transaction movement resulting from the execution of a file manipulation assignment causes the execution of *another* file manipulation assignment. For example, if a(Q1) = b(Q2) moves a transaction out of Q1 and the transaction from Q1 executes the assignment a(Q3) = b(Q4), SIMNET II will effect the swap from Q4 to Q3 but will *not* attempt to move the transaction out of Q3. The modeler must use an explicit switch assignment to effect this movement, if desired.

**3.** If the donor file is empty, no action will occur.

**4.** If a recipient *finite-size* queue is full at the time the assignment is executed, an error stop will result unless the donor and recipient queues are one and the same (i.e., reordering transactions in the same queue).

---

**Example B.9-2   (BANK MODEL).**
We revisit Example B.5-1, dealing with the two-lane bank with the additional stipulation that if a lane becomes shorter by at least two cars, the last car in the longer lane jockeys to the last position in the shorter lane.

Figure B-16 gives the model. The only time we need to jockey cars from the longer to the shorter lane is when a car departs from either lane. Facilities WL and WR thus feed into a single auxiliary AX. The branch from AX computes the DIFF, the difference between the number of cars in the right and left lanes. If DIFF $> 1$, we jockey LAST(QR) into LAST(QL). If DIFF $< -1$, the jockeying is reversed.

---

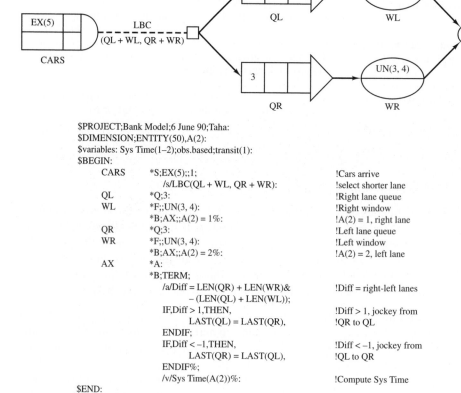

```
$PROJECT;Bank Model;6 June 90;Taha:
$DIMENSION;ENTITY(50),A(2):
$variables: Sys Time(1–2);obs.based;transit(1):
$BEGIN:
        CARS      *S;EX(5);;1;                          !Cars arrive
                  /s/LBC(QL + WL, QR + WR):             !select shorter lane
        QL        *Q;3:                                 !Right lane queue
        WL        *F;;UN(3, 4):                         !Right window
                  *B;AX;;A(2) = 1%:                     !A(2) = 1, right lane
        QR        *Q;3:                                 !Left lane queue
        WR        *F;;UN(3, 4):                         !Left window
                  *B;AX;;A(2) = 2%:                     !A(2) = 2, left lane
        AX        *A:
                  *B;TERM;
                  /a/Diff = LEN(QR) + LEN(WR)&          !Diff = right-left lanes
                     – (LEN(QL) + LEN(WL));
                  IF,Diff > 1,THEN,                     !Diff > 1, jockey from
                     LAST(QL) = LAST(QR),               !QR to QL
                  ENDIF;
                  IF,Diff < –1,THEN,                    !Diff < –1, jockey from
                     LAST(QR) = LAST(QL),               !QL to QR
                  ENDIF%;
                  /v/Sys Time(A(2))%:                   !Compute Sys Time
$END:
$RUN-LENGTH = 480:
$STOP:
```

**Figure B–16**

**Example B.9-3    (TRANSMISSION CHANNEL).**

Messages arrive every UN(7,8) seconds for transmission over a single channel. It takes UN(6,8) seconds to transmit a message. Every UN(600,650) seconds, the channel malfunctions, and any ongoing transmissions must be retransmitted. It takes about 30 seconds to reset the channel.

The model in Figure B-17 consists of two segments representing the transmission channel and the failure-repair cycle. When the channel fails, the transaction leaving auxiliary FAIL turns OFF switch SW to prevent new messages from leaving QMSG. An ongoing transmission in facility CHNL is then RELeased by executing the assignment 1(CHNL) = REL. For identification, the aborted message is tagged with A(2) = −1 *before* it leaves CHNL. The assignment COPY = 1(CHNL) changes the attributes of the transaction leaving FAIL to those of 1(CHNL). Next, we set A(2) = −1 and then execute 1(CHNL) = REP, in effect changing A(2) inside CHNL to −1 while leaving A(1) unchanged. (If CHNL happens to be empty, none of the special assignments will have any effect.)

On leaving CHNL, a transaction having A(2) = −1 (i.e., an aborted message) executes the assignments A(2) = 0 and 1(QMST) = TRANS, which places the aborted message, after resetting its A(2) to zero, at the head of QMSG. Following the repair of the CHNL (exit from RESET), the assignment SW = ON moves the transaction into CHNL for retransmission.

To compute the time a completed transaction spends in the system, we need to compute SYS TIME for only those transactions that have A(2) = 0. We accomplish this result by using COLLECT = SYS TIME with an IF-ENDIF statement that checks the condition A(2) = 0 as the transaction leaves CHNL.

## Problem set B.9a

1. Use the SUSPEND and RESUME assignments to simulate a source that releases transactions on demand only. Specifically, consider the situation where an operator takes EX(10) minutes to complete a job. On completing a job, the operator will then reach for another one. Assume that the source of new jobs is unlimited.

2. A bank opens at 8:00 A.M. and closes at 4:30 P.M. daily. The interarrival time for customers is EX(7) minutes. It takes EX(10) minutes to serve each customer at one of the banks two tellers. At 4:30 P.M., all customers inside the bank must be served. Estimate the maximum, minimum, and average time needed after 4:30 P.M. to serve all the remaining customers.

3. A precast widget is processed by two machines MACH1 and MACH2. The interarrival time of the widgets is EX(.0588) minutes. The processing times at MACH1 and MACH2 are .04 and .0357 minutes, respectively. The floor space available for incoming jobs to MACH1 and MACH2 are 50 and 40 widgets, respectively. The tool at MACH2 fails every EX(8) minutes, at which time it must be removed and discarded. It takes UN(1,3) minutes to repair the tool. Simulate the system for 30 minutes for the purpose of determining the utilization of the machines.

4. Aluminum ingots are melted before being distributed in urns for later use in a manufacturing process. A complete charge of the melting furnace consists

**Figure B–17**

of three ingots. It takes 25 minutes to complete the melting process. The charge is then distributed among three urns. Assume that ingots are available on demand at the furnace. Simulate the model for 480 minutes for the purpose of determining the utilization of the furnace. (Hint: Use an accumulator queue to release the proper charge of the furnace. When the accumulated charge leaves the furnace, "explode" it into three urns using FOR-NEXT to place three copies of the exiting transaction into a new queue representing the urns.)

## B.10  INITIAL DATA

A model in SIMNET II may make use of six types of initial data.

1. Initial file (queues and facilities) entries
2. Discrete probability density functions
3. Table look-up functions
4. Arrays values
5. Constant variables (nonsubscripted) values
6. Functions or mathematical expressions

These data are presented in the model in a *run-specific* format so that several runs, each with different initial data, can be executed in a single simulation session.

### B.10.1  Initial File Entries

Initial entries with specific attribute values are entered using the following format:

```
$INITIAL-ENTRIES: i-j/file 1 name/first entry attributes;
                              .
                              .
                              .
                         last entry attributes:
                              .
                              .
                              .
                    (other files repeats)
              .
              .
              .
        (i-j repeats)
```

where $i$ and $j$ are integer values defining the inclusive range of run numbers for which the given entries apply. The format for each entry is

$$(d)A(1),A(2), \ldots ,A(n)$$

where $d$ is the number of duplicates of the list $A(1), A(2), \ldots, A(n)$ to be inserted in the file (default = 1), and $n$ is the number of attributes as defined by the $DIMEN-SION statement. Each entry terminates with a semicolon with the last entry in a file terminating with colon. Trailing *zero* attributes for any entry may be defaulted by ending the entry with (,;) or (,:).

The following example illustrates the use of $INITIAL-ENTRIES with two queues Q1 and Q2 and one facility F1. The model is assumed to have *two* attributes:

```
$INITIAL-ENTRIES:  1-1/Q1/(2)11,22;12,23;   !first 3 entries of Q1
                          -11,;              !fourth entry (-11,0)
                             ;               !fifth entry (0,0)
                             :               !sixth entry (0,0)
                   F1/-11,-22:               !only entry of F1
                   2-3/Q2/10,20:             !start runs 2 and 3
                   F1/110,220:
```

Although successive entries may be strung on the same line, the given format is more readable.

Example B.10-1 at the end of Section B.10.4 illustrates the use of $INITIAL-ENTRIES.

### B.10.2 Discrete and Discretized Continuous Density Functions

Empirical (discrete) distributions are defined in SIMNET II using the following format:

$$\$DISCRETE\text{-}PDFS: \quad i\text{-}j/N_1/x_{11}, p_{11}; \ldots ; x_{in}, p_{in}:$$

$$\bullet$$
$$\bullet$$
$$\bullet$$

repeats

$$\bullet$$
$$\bullet$$
$$\bullet$$

repeats

where

$N$ = Number of points $(x, p)$ of the discrete function

$x$ = Value of the random variable

$p$ = Discrete probability value associated with $x$

The following example illustrates the definition of discrete functions:

```
$DISCRETE-PDFS:  1-1/3/1,.1;2,.4;3,.5:          !Function #1, run 1

                 2/0,.6;1,.4:                    !Function #2, run 1

              2-3/3/2,.3;3,.5;4,.2:              !Function #1, runs 2, 3
```

SIMNET II samples the discrete function by using the symbol DI($a$,RS), where $a$ represents the function number within its run range, and RS is the random number stream (default = 1). Both $a$ and RS may be any mathematical expressions. If $a$ is positive, sampling is made at the *discrete* points defined by $DISCRETE-PDFS. Otherwise, if $a$ is negative, SIMNET II will convert the discrete points into a *piecewise-linear* probability density function. The DI function may be used directly in a mathematical expression.

### B.10.3 Table Look-Up Functions

Table look-up functions are used to define a dependent variable $y$ as a function of an independent variable $x$. The format of the function is similar to that of $DISCRETE-PDFS.

```
$TABLE-LOOKUPS:  i-j/N₁/x₁₁, y₁₁; x₁₂, y₁₂; . . . . , x₁ₙ₁, y₁ₙ₁:
```
$$\text{\$TABLE-LOOKUPS:}\quad i\text{-}j/N_1/x_{11},\ y_{11};\ x_{12},\ y_{12};\ \dots\dots,\ x_{1n_1},\ y_{1n_1}:$$
$$N_2/x_{21},y_{21};\ x_{22},\ y_{22};\ \dots\dots,\ x_{2n_2},\ y_{2n_2}:$$

```
                     .

                     .

                     .

                 .

                 .

                 .



             repeats
```

The following example illustrates the use of the function:

```
$TABLE-LOOKUPS:  1-1/4/1,2;3,5;6,7;7,9:          !Function #1

                 3/0,0;1,4;2,11:                  !Function #2
```

The symbol TL($n$,$x$) is used to reference table look-up functions, with $n$ representing the number of the function within a given run range and $x$ representing the value of the independent variable. If $n$ is negative, linear interpolation is used to determine the value of $y$. Both $n$ and $x$ could be represented by mathematical expressions. In this case, $n$ will be truncated to an integer value, if necessary, and $x$ must assume a value in the domain in the table look-up function. The function TL may be used directly in a mathematical expression.

In the preceding example, TL(1,3) = 5, whereas TL(1,4) will result in an error because $x = 4$ is undefined for table look-up function number 1. Looking at table number 2, we see that TL($-2$,1.5) = 7.5 as interpolated linearly between $x = 4$ and $x = 11$.

## B.10.4 Initialization of Array Elements

Arrays defined by the $DIMENSION statement may be initialized using the following format:

```
$ARRAYS:
      array 1; i-j/list of values:
                    .

                    .

                    .

                repeats

            .

            .

            .

        repeats
```

There are two formats for the list of values.

**1.** *Explicit* in which each element is explicitly preceded by the subscript(s) defining the element.

**2.** *Implicit* in which subscripts of the listed values are identified by their order in the list. In this case, the entire list must be preceded by the code NS/.

The following example provides an illustration of the use of the two formats given the two arrays BC(2) and YZ(3,2) as defined in the $DIMENSION statement:

```
$ARRAYS:
    BC; 1-1/NS/11,22:        !implicit,BC(1)=11,BC(2)=22
        2-4/2,33:            !explicit,BC(2)=33
    YZ; 1-2/1,2,88;3,1,99:   !explicit,YZ(1,2)=8,YZ(3,1)=99
        3-3/NS/11,22,33:     !implicit,YZ(1,1)=11,YZ(1,2)=22,YZ(2,1)=33
```

When NS is used, the values are taken to represent respective elements of the array (read on a row-by-row basis in the case of the two-dimensional array). The explicit format is useful when it is desired to initialize only selected elements. Note that in the implicit case, any trailing elements that are not assigned values automatically are zero. For example, in run 3, the values of YZ(2,2), YZ(3,1), and YZ(3,2) are all zero by omission.

---

**Example B.10-1   (GRAVEL HAULING OPERATION).**
This example illustrates the use of $INITIAL-ENTRIES and $ARRAYS initialization.
A company uses three 20-ton and two 30-ton trucks for hauling gravel to different customers. The demand for gravel is sufficiently high to keep the operation busy on a con-

tinuous basis. It takes 10 minutes to load a 20-ton truck and 15 minutes to load a 30-ton truck. The round trip to and from customer location is UN(30,60) minutes. The objective of the simulation is to estimate the tonnage hauled by each truck type in a 24-hour period.

Figure B-18 gives the model. The $INITIAL-ENTRIES statement places three 20-ton trucks and two 30-ton trucks in the queue TRKS. Each entry has two attributes: A(1) assigns a serial number representing the truck type, and A(2) specifies the tonnage of the truck. We use the names TYPE and CAPACITY to describe A(1) and A(2)

The loading time at facility LOADS is given by the initial values of the $ARRAY Load_time(1) = 10 and Load_time(2) = 15 for the 20- and 30-ton trucks. Because

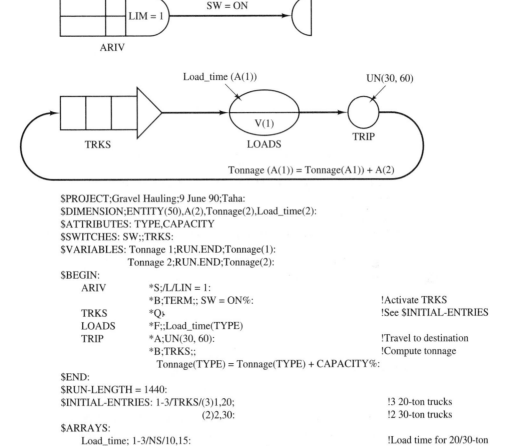

```
$PROJECT;Gravel Hauling;9 June 90;Taha:
$DIMENSION;ENTITY(50),A(2),Tonnage(2),Load_time(2):
$ATTRIBUTES: TYPE,CAPACITY
$SWITCHES: SW;;TRKS:
$VARIABLES: Tonnage 1;RUN.END;Tonnage(1):
            Tonnage 2;RUN.END;Tonnage(2):
$BEGIN:
     ARIV          *S;/L/LIN = 1:
                   *B;TERM;; SW = ON%:                              !Activate TRKS
     TRKS          *Q;                                             !See $INITIAL-ENTRIES
     LOADS         *F;;Load_time(TYPE)
     TRIP          *A;UN(30, 60):                                  !Travel to destination
                   *B;TRKS;;                                       !Compute tonnage
                      Tonnage(TYPE) = Tonnage(TYPE) + CAPACITY%:
$END:
$RUN-LENGTH = 1440:
$INITIAL-ENTRIES: 1-3/TRKS/(3)1,20;                                !3 20-ton trucks
                       (2)2,30:                                    !2 30-ton trucks
$ARRAYS:
     Load_time; 1-3/NS/10,15:                                      !Load time for 20/30-ton
$STOP:
```

**Figure B–18**

A(1) carries the type of the truck (= 1 or 2), the model uses Load_time(A(1)) to define the loading time. After loading is completed, the truck travels to the customer location before returning to TRKS. The tonnage hauled by each truck type is recorded in array

Tonnage (A(1)) to be printed as a RUN.END variable. (A RUN.END variable is computed only once at the very end of the simulation run.)

It is the modeler's responsibility to initiate the movement of the trucks out of TRKS at the start of the simulation. The model employs the dummy source ARIV to release one transaction that executes the assignment SW = ON, thus automatically activating queue TRKS.

### Problem set B.10a

1. Passengers arrive randomly at a bus station. The number of empty seats at the time the bus arrives at the station also varies randomly. It takes about 7 seconds for a passenger to get on the bus. A round trip that brings the bus back to the station takes about 30 minutes. At present, only one bus is in operation. A passenger is willing to wait at the station for no more than 20 minutes.

   The interarrival time for the passengers at the station is determined from histogrammed empirical data as follows:

   | Cell midpoint time (minutes) | 2.0 | 2.5 | 3.0 | 3.5 | 4.0 |
   |---|---|---|---|---|---|
   | Relative frequency | 0.2 | 0.24 | 0.28 | 0.18 | 0.10 |

   The number of empty seats on the bus is 7, 8, or 9, with equal probabilities. Determine the percentage of reneging customers during a simulation run of 480 minutes.

## B.11 SUMMARY

SIMNET II is based on the use of only four nodes, which makes it particularly easy to learn and use. Despite its simple structure, the language is sufficiently powerful to tackle complex situations. The use of *special assignments* within the conditional IF-ENDIF provides powerful modeling capabilities.

The full SIMNET II system is totally interactive both for debugging and obtaining the global statistical results. The full language also includes such important modeling elements as resources, match and assemble, and the important concept of PROCs that allow modeling repetitive actions. The reference listed subsequently provides all the additional information.

## REFERENCE

TAHA, H., *Simulation with SIMNET II*, 2nd ed., SimTec Inc., Fayetteville, AR, 1995.

# TORA and SIMNET II Installation and Execution

Both TORA and SIMNET II run on the IBM PC and true compatible and require MS-DOS 3.2 or later versions. TORA can be executed directly from the floppy disk. SIMNET II must be executed from the hard disk. TORA and SIMNET II each operate within 512K RAM.

## C.1 INSTALLATION AND EXECUTION

The accompanying diskette includes two directories, \Tora and \Simnet. To install either system on the hard drive, simply copy the contents of each system into a separate directory using the DOS copy command.

Instructions for executing TORA and SIMNET II are detailed in the README.DOC (ASCII) files provided in each directory. TORA is totally menu driven, and hence requires no user's manual. An introduction to SIMNET II is given in Appendix B. Both systems operate in totally contained environments that allow creating, editing, and executing TORA and SIMNET II models. The TORA system is custom designed to match the format and notation of the book.

# Appendix D

# *Statistical Tables*

**TABLE D–1**
NORMAL DISTRIBUTION FUNCTION

$$F(z) = \frac{1}{\sqrt{2\pi}} \int_{-\infty}^{z} e^{-(\frac{1}{2})t^2} dt$$

| z | 0.00 | 0.01 | 0.02 | 0.03 | 0.04 | 0.05 | 0.06 | 0.07 | 0.08 | 0.09 |
|-----|--------|--------|--------|--------|--------|--------|--------|--------|--------|--------|
| 0.0 | 0.5000 | 0.5040 | 0.5080 | 0.5120 | 0.5160 | 0.5199 | 0.5239 | 0.5279 | 0.5319 | 0.5359 |
| 0.1 | 0.5398 | 0.5438 | 0.5478 | 0.5517 | 0.5557 | 0.5596 | 0.5636 | 0.5675 | 0.5714 | 0.5753 |
| 0.2 | 0.5793 | 0.5832 | 0.5871 | 0.5910 | 0.5948 | 0.5987 | 0.6026 | 0.6064 | 0.6103 | 0.6141 |
| 0.3 | 0.6179 | 0.6217 | 0.6255 | 0.6293 | 0.6331 | 0.6368 | 0.6406 | 0.6443 | 0.6480 | 0.6517 |
| 0.4 | 0.6554 | 0.6591 | 0.6628 | 0.6664 | 0.6700 | 0.6736 | 0.6772 | 0.6808 | 0.6844 | 0.6879 |
| 0.5 | 0.6915 | 0.6950 | 0.6985 | 0.7019 | 0.7054 | 0.7088 | 0.7123 | 0.7157 | 0.7190 | 0.7224 |
| 0.6 | 0.7257 | 0.7291 | 0.7324 | 0.7357 | 0.7389 | 0.7422 | 0.7454 | 0.7486 | 0.7517 | 0.7549 |
| 0.7 | 0.7580 | 0.7611 | 0.7642 | 0.7673 | 0.7704 | 0.7734 | 0.7764 | 0.7794 | 0.7823 | 0.7852 |
| 0.8 | 0.7881 | 0.7910 | 0.7939 | 0.7967 | 0.7995 | 0.8023 | 0.8051 | 0.8078 | 0.8106 | 0.8133 |
| 0.9 | 0.8159 | 0.8186 | 0.8212 | 0.8238 | 0.8264 | 0.8289 | 0.8315 | 0.8340 | 0.8365 | 0.8389 |
| 1.0 | 0.8413 | 0.8438 | 0.8461 | 0.8485 | 0.8508 | 0.8531 | 0.8554 | 0.8577 | 0.8599 | 0.8621 |
| 1.1 | 0.8643 | 0.8665 | 0.8686 | 0.8708 | 0.8729 | 0.8749 | 0.8770 | 0.8790 | 0.8810 | 0.8830 |
| 1.2 | 0.8849 | 0.8869 | 0.8888 | 0.8907 | 0.8925 | 0.8944 | 0.8962 | 0.8980 | 0.8997 | 0.9015 |
| 1.3 | 0.9032 | 0.9049 | 0.9066 | 0.9082 | 0.9099 | 0.9115 | 0.9131 | 0.9147 | 0.9162 | 0.9177 |
| 1.4 | 0.9192 | 0.9207 | 0.9222 | 0.9236 | 0.9251 | 0.9265 | 0.9279 | 0.9292 | 0.9306 | 0.9319 |
| 1.5 | 0.9332 | 0.9345 | 0.9357 | 0.9370 | 0.9382 | 0.9394 | 0.9406 | 0.9418 | 0.9429 | 0.9441 |
| 1.6 | 0.9452 | 0.9463 | 0.9474 | 0.9484 | 0.9495 | 0.9505 | 0.9515 | 0.9525 | 0.9535 | 0.9545 |
| 1.7 | 0.9554 | 0.9564 | 0.9573 | 0.9582 | 0.9591 | 0.9599 | 0.9608 | 0.9616 | 0.9625 | 0.9633 |
| 1.8 | 0.9641 | 0.9649 | 0.9656 | 0.9664 | 0.9671 | 0.9678 | 0.9686 | 0.9693 | 0.9699 | 0.9706 |
| 1.9 | 0.9713 | 0.9719 | 0.9726 | 0.9732 | 0.9738 | 0.9744 | 0.9750 | 0.9756 | 0.9761 | 0.9767 |

| | | | | | | | | | | |
|---|---|---|---|---|---|---|---|---|---|---|
| 2.0 | 0.9772 | 0.9778 | 0.9783 | 0.9788 | 0.9793 | 0.9798 | 0.9803 | 0.9808 | 0.9812 | 0.9817 |
| 2.1 | 0.9821 | 0.9826 | 0.9830 | 0.9834 | 0.9838 | 0.9842 | 0.9846 | 0.9850 | 0.9854 | 0.9857 |
| 2.2 | 0.9861 | 0.9864 | 0.9868 | 0.9871 | 0.9875 | 0.9878 | 0.9881 | 0.9884 | 0.9887 | 0.9890 |
| 2.3 | 0.9893 | 0.9896 | 0.9898 | 0.9901 | 0.9904 | 0.9906 | 0.9909 | 0.9911 | 0.9913 | 0.9916 |
| 2.4 | 0.9918 | 0.9920 | 0.9922 | 0.9925 | 0.9927 | 0.9929 | 0.9931 | 0.9932 | 0.9934 | 0.9936 |
| 2.5 | 0.9938 | 0.9940 | 0.9941 | 0.9943 | 0.9945 | 0.9946 | 0.9948 | 0.9949 | 0.9951 | 0.9952 |
| 2.6 | 0.9953 | 0.9955 | 0.9956 | 0.9957 | 0.9959 | 0.9960 | 0.9961 | 0.9962 | 0.9963 | 0.9964 |
| 2.7 | 0.9965 | 0.9966 | 0.9967 | 0.9968 | 0.9969 | 0.9970 | 0.9971 | 0.9972 | 0.9973 | 0.9974 |
| 2.8 | 0.9974 | 0.9975 | 0.9976 | 0.9977 | 0.9977 | 0.9978 | 0.9979 | 0.9979 | 0.9980 | 0.9981 |
| 2.9 | 0.9981 | 0.9982 | 0.9982 | 0.9983 | 0.9984 | 0.9984 | 0.9985 | 0.9985 | 0.9986 | 0.9986 |
| 3.0 | 0.9987 | 0.9987 | 0.9987 | 0.9988 | 0.9988 | 0.9989 | 0.9989 | 0.9989 | 0.9990 | 0.9990 |
| 3.1 | 0.9990 | 0.9991 | 0.9991 | 0.9991 | 0.9992 | 0.9992 | 0.9992 | 0.9992 | 0.9993 | 0.9993 |
| 3.2 | 0.9993 | 0.9993 | 0.9994 | 0.9994 | 0.9994 | 0.9994 | 0.9994 | 0.9995 | 0.9995 | 0.9995 |
| 3.3 | 0.9995 | 0.9995 | 0.9995 | 0.9996 | 0.9996 | 0.9996 | 0.9996 | 0.9996 | 0.9996 | 0.9997 |
| 3.4 | 0.9997 | 0.9997 | 0.9997 | 0.9997 | 0.9997 | 0.9997 | 0.9997 | 0.9997 | 0.9997 | 0.9998 |
| 3.5 | 0.9998 | | | | | | | | | |
| 4.0 | 0.99997 | | | | | | | | | |
| 5.0 | 0.9999997 | | | | | | | | | |
| 6.0 | 0.999999999 | | | | | | | | | |

*Source:* MILLER, I., and J. FREUND, *Probability and Statistics for Engineers,* Prentice Hall, Upper Saddle River, N.J., 1985.

**TABLE D–2**
**VALUES OF $t_\alpha^*$**

| $\nu$ | $\alpha = 0.10$ | $\alpha = 0.05$ | $\alpha = 0.025$ | $\alpha = 0.01$ | $\alpha = 0.005$ | $\nu$ |
|---|---|---|---|---|---|---|
| 1 | 3.078 | 6.314 | 12.706 | 31.821 | 63.657 | 1 |
| 2 | 1.886 | 2.920 | 4.303 | 6.965 | 9.925 | 2 |
| 3 | 1.638 | 2.353 | 3.182 | 4.541 | 5.841 | 3 |
| 4 | 1.533 | 2.132 | 2.776 | 3.747 | 4.604 | 4 |
| 5 | 1.476 | 2.015 | 2.571 | 3.365 | 4.032 | 5 |
| 6 | 1.440 | 1.943 | 2.447 | 3.143 | 3.707 | 6 |
| 7 | 1.415 | 1.895 | 2.365 | 2.998 | 3.499 | 7 |
| 8 | 1.397 | 1.860 | 2.306 | 2.896 | 3.355 | 8 |
| 9 | 1.383 | 1.833 | 2.262 | 2.821 | 3.250 | 9 |
| 10 | 1.372 | 1.812 | 2.228 | 2.764 | 3.169 | 10 |
| 11 | 1.363 | 1.796 | 2.201 | 2.718 | 3.106 | 11 |
| 12 | 1.356 | 1.782 | 2.179 | 2.681 | 3.055 | 12 |
| 13 | 1.350 | 1.771 | 2.160 | 2.650 | 3.012 | 13 |
| 14 | 1.345 | 1.761 | 2.145 | 2.624 | 2.977 | 14 |
| 15 | 1.341 | 1.753 | 2.131 | 2.602 | 2.947 | 15 |
| 16 | 1.337 | 1.746 | 2.120 | 2.583 | 2.921 | 16 |
| 17 | 1.333 | 1.740 | 2.110 | 2.567 | 2.898 | 17 |
| 18 | 1.330 | 1.734 | 2.101 | 2.552 | 2.878 | 18 |

| 19 | 1.328 | 1.729 | 2.093 | 2.539 | 2.861 | 19 |
| 20 | 1.325 | 1.725 | 2.086 | 2.528 | 2.845 | 20 |
| | | | | | | |
| 21 | 1.323 | 1.721 | 2.080 | 2.518 | 2.831 | 21 |
| 22 | 1.321 | 1.717 | 2.074 | 2.508 | 2.819 | 22 |
| 23 | 1.319 | 1.714 | 2.069 | 2.500 | 2.807 | 23 |
| 24 | 1.318 | 1.711 | 2.064 | 2.492 | 2.797 | 24 |
| 25 | 1.316 | 1.708 | 2.060 | 2.485 | 2.787 | 25 |
| | | | | | | |
| 26 | 1.315 | 1.706 | 2.056 | 2.479 | 2.779 | 26 |
| 27 | 1.314 | 1.703 | 2.052 | 2.473 | 2.771 | 27 |
| 28 | 1.313 | 1.701 | 2.048 | 2.467 | 2.763 | 28 |
| 29 | 1.311 | 1.699 | 2.045 | 2.462 | 2.756 | 29 |
| inf. | 1.282 | 1.645 | 1.960 | 2.326 | 2.576 | inf. |

*Abridged by permission of Macmillan Publishing Co., Inc., from *Statistical Methods for Research Workers,* 14th ed., by R. A. Fisher. Copyright © 1970 University of Adelaide.

**TABLE D–3**
**VALUES OF $\chi_\alpha^{2*}$**

| $\nu$ | $\alpha = 0.995$ | $\alpha = 0.99$ | $\alpha = 0.975$ | $\alpha = 0.95$ | $\alpha = 0.05$ | $\alpha = 0.025$ | $\alpha = 0.01$ | $\alpha = 0.005$ | $\nu$ |
|---|---|---|---|---|---|---|---|---|---|
| 1 | 0.0000393 | 0.000157 | 0.000982 | 0.00393 | 3.841 | 5.024 | 6.635 | 7.879 | 1 |
| 2 | 0.0100 | 0.0201 | 0.0506 | 0.103 | 5.991 | 7.378 | 9.210 | 10.597 | 2 |
| 3 | 0.0717 | 0.115 | 0.216 | 0.352 | 7.815 | 9.348 | 11.345 | 12.838 | 3 |
| 4 | 0.207 | 0.297 | 0.484 | 0.711 | 9.488 | 11.143 | 13.277 | 14.860 | 4 |
| 5 | 0.412 | 0.554 | 0.831 | 1.145 | 11.070 | 12.832 | 15.056 | 16.750 | 5 |
| | | | | | | | | | |
| 6 | 0.676 | 0.872 | 1.237 | 1.635 | 12.592 | 14.449 | 16.812 | 18.548 | 6 |
| 7 | 0.989 | 1.239 | 1.690 | 2.167 | 14.067 | 16.013 | 18.475 | 20.278 | 7 |
| 8 | 1.344 | 1.646 | 2.180 | 2.733 | 15.507 | 17.535 | 20.090 | 21.955 | 8 |
| 9 | 1.735 | 2.088 | 2.700 | 3.325 | 16.919 | 19.023 | 21.666 | 23.589 | 9 |
| 10 | 2.156 | 2.558 | 3.247 | 3.940 | 18.307 | 20.483 | 23.209 | 25.188 | 10 |
| | | | | | | | | | |
| 11 | 2.603 | 3.053 | 3.816 | 4.575 | 19.675 | 21.920 | 24.725 | 26.757 | 11 |
| 12 | 3.074 | 3.571 | 4.404 | 5.226 | 21.026 | 23.337 | 26.217 | 28.300 | 12 |
| 13 | 3.565 | 4.107 | 5.009 | 5.892 | 22.362 | 24.736 | 27.688 | 29.819 | 13 |
| 14 | 4.075 | 4.660 | 5.629 | 6.571 | 23.685 | 26.119 | 29.141 | 31.319 | 14 |
| 15 | 4.601 | 5.229 | 6.262 | 7.261 | 24.996 | 27.488 | 30.578 | 32.801 | 15 |
| | | | | | | | | | |
| 16 | 5.142 | 5.812 | 6.908 | 7.962 | 26.296 | 28.845 | 32.000 | 34.267 | 16 |
| 17 | 5.697 | 6.408 | 7.564 | 8.672 | 27.587 | 30.191 | 33.409 | 35.718 | 17 |
| 18 | 6.265 | 7.015 | 8.231 | 9.390 | 28.869 | 31.526 | 34.805 | 37.156 | 18 |
| 19 | 6.844 | 7.633 | 8.907 | 10.117 | 30.144 | 32.852 | 36.191 | 38.582 | 19 |
| 20 | 7.434 | 8.260 | 9.591 | 10.851 | 31.410 | 34.170 | 37.566 | 39.997 | 20 |
| | | | | | | | | | |
| 21 | 8.034 | 8.897 | 10.283 | 11.591 | 32.671 | 35.479 | 38.932 | 41.401 | 21 |
| 22 | 8.643 | 9.542 | 10.982 | 12.338 | 33.924 | 36.781 | 40.289 | 42.796 | 22 |
| 23 | 9.260 | 10.196 | 11.689 | 13.091 | 35.172 | 38.076 | 41.638 | 44.181 | 23 |
| 24 | 9.886 | 10.856 | 12.401 | 13.484 | 36.415 | 39.364 | 42.980 | 45.558 | 24 |
| 25 | 10.520 | 11.524 | 13.120 | 14.611 | 37.652 | 40.646 | 44.314 | 46.928 | 25 |

| 26 | 11.160 | 12.198 | 13.844 | 15.379 | 38.885 | 41.923 | 45.642 | 48.290 | 26 |
| 27 | 11.808 | 12.879 | 14.573 | 16.151 | 40.113 | 43.194 | 46.963 | 49.645 | 27 |
| 28 | 12.461 | 13.565 | 15.308 | 16.928 | 41.337 | 44.461 | 48.278 | 50.993 | 28 |
| 29 | 13.121 | 14.256 | 16.047 | 17.708 | 42.557 | 45.772 | 49.588 | 52.336 | 29 |
| 30 | 13.787 | 14.953 | 16.791 | 18.493 | 43.773 | 46.979 | 50.892 | 53.672 | 30 |

[*]This table is based on Table 8 of *Biometrika Tables for Statisticians*, Vol. 1, by permission of the *Biometrika* trustees.

# Answers to Odd-Numbered Problems

## CHAPTER 2

### Set 2.2a

■ **1. (a)** $-x_1 + x_2 \geq 1$.
   **(e)** $.5x_1 - .5x_2 \geq 0$.
■ **3.** $s_1 = 4$ tons, $s_2 = 0$ ton.

### Set 2.3a

■ **3. (a)** $(2.5, 1.75), z = \$19.50$.
   **(b)** $(2, 2), z = \$18$.
   **(c)** $(1, 2), z = \$13$.
   **(d)** $(6, 0), z = \$30$.
   **(e)** Infeasible.
■ **5.** Play 4 hours and work 6 hours, $z = 14$ "pleasurits."

### Set 2.3b

■ **3.** $x_1 = x_2 = z = 0$, which is nonsensical.

### Set 2.3c

■ **1.** $s_1 = 2$ tons, $s_2 = 1$ ton.
■ **3. (a)** Use 40 minutes of machine overtime, $z = \$1517.50$.
   **(b)** No overtime is recommended, $z = \$1513.50$.

## Set 2.4a

■ **1.** (a) $-1 \leq \frac{c_1}{c_2} \leq 1.5$.

  (b) $-1 \leq \frac{c_2}{c_1} \leq \frac{5}{3}$.

  (c) $-1 \leq \frac{c_1}{c_2} < \infty$ if $c_1 = 0$ and $-\frac{1}{3} \leq \frac{c_2}{c_1} < \infty$ if $c_2 = 0$.

■ **3.** (a) 100 $A_1$ cans and 400 $A_2$ cans daily, $z = \$33$.

  (b) $-\infty < \frac{c_1}{c_2} \leq 1$.

■ **5.** (a) \$66,667 personal loans and \$133,333 car loans, $z = \$20,067$. Rate of return $= 10.033\%$.

  (c) Solution remains optimal.

■ **7.** (a) 500 cases of juice and 6000 cases of paste daily, $z = \$6300$.

  (b) $0 \leq \frac{c_1}{c_2} \leq 3$.

## Set 2.4b

■ **1.** (a) 100 type 1 hats and 200 type 2 hats, $z = \$1800$.

  (b) \$4 per unit increase in production of type 2 hats in the range $(200, 500)$.

  (c) \$0 per unit increase in demand limit of type 1 hats in the range $(100, 200)$.

  (d) \$1 per unit increase in demand limit for type 2 hats in the range $(100, 400)$.

■ **3.** (a) $x_1 = 52.94$ units, $x_2 = 14.11$ units, $z = \$148.24$.

  (b) Worth per unit of capacity increase for processes 1, 2, and 3 are \$.1294, \$.1176, and \$0, respectively. Order of priority is process 1 followed by process 2.

■ **5.** (a) 5.128 tons of C1 and 10.256 tons of C2, $z = 153,846$ lb of steam.

  (b) 1 lb relaxation in smoke discharge requirement increases steam output by 7692.2 lb (all per hour).

■ **7.** (a) 480 shirts and 840 blouses per week.

  (b) Workers in cutting, sewing, and packaging must be increased to 92, 134, and 15, respectively.

  (c) Worth per hour of cutting, sewing, and packaging are \$.0247, \$.02867, and 0, respectively.

■ **9.** (a) 50.88 units of HiFi1 and 31.68 units of HiFi2.

  (b) Worth per minute for processes 1, 2, and 3 are 0, 3, and 0, respectively.

## Set 2.5a

■ **1.** (a) Dual price $= \$.5471$ per lb increase in feed mix. A 1-lb increase in feed mix must consist of .588 lb corn and .412 lb soybean meal. Associated increase in cost is $.3 \times .588 + .9 \times .412 = \$.5472$.

  (b) $D_1 = 100$ lb, corn $= 529.41$ lb, soybean meal $= 370.59$ lb, cost $= \$492.36$.

  (c) $d_1 = \$.1, d_2 = \$.15$, solution remains optimal.

  (d) $-.7 \leq \frac{(.3 + d_1)}{(.9 + d_2)} \leq 1$

## Set 2.6a

■ **1.** (a) $x_1 + x_2 + x_3 + (x_4 + x_5) \leq 12$ and $(x_4 + x_5) \geq 4.8$

**(b)** $D_2 = \$7.2$ million. *Method 1:* Dual price $= \$-.0084$ per \$1 loan for $0 \le D_2 \le 7.2$, new $z = \$.936$ million. *Method 2:* Compute new home and commercial loans, given $D_2 = \$7.2$ million from which new $z = \$.936$ million is obtained.

**(c)** $D_1 = \$8$ million and $D_2 = \$4.2$ million results in the feasible solution of \$11 million for home loans and \$9 million for commercial loans to yield \$1.6524 million return on investment.

■ **3. (a) (i)** $D_2 = 4$, minimum number $= 26$ buses. **(ii)** $D_3 = -3$, minimum number $= 23$.

**(b)** $D_1 = 2$, $D_2 = 1$, $D_3 = 2$, $D_4 = 0$, $D_5 = 3$, $D_6 = 2$. New solution $x_1 = 6$, $x_2 = 12$, $x_4 = 9$, and $x_5 = 6$. Total $= 33$ buses.

■ **5. (a)** Let $x_{11} = $ bbls of feedstock regular, $x_{12} = $ bbls of feedstock premium, $x_{21} = $ bbls of cracker regular, and $x_{22} = $ bbls of cracker premium. All units are per day.

Maximize

$$z = 7.7x_{11} + 12.3x_{12} + 5.2x_{21} + 10.4x_{22}$$

subject to

$$5(x_{11} + x_{12} + x_{21} + x_{22}) \le 600,000$$

$$x_{21} + x_{22} \le 40,000$$

$$x_{11} \qquad + x_{21} \qquad \le 80,000$$

$$x_{12} \qquad + x_{22} \le 50,000$$

$$x_{ij} \ge 0, \text{ for all } i \text{ and } j$$

Optimum solution: $x_{11} = 70,000$ bbls/day, $x_{12} = 50,000$ bbls/day, profit $= \$1,154,000$ bbls/day.

**(b)** $D_1 = 50,000$ bbl/day, dual price $= \$1.54$/bbl valid for $-350,000 \le D_1 \le 50,000$. Increase in profit $= \$77,000$/day. Initial cost plus daily cost breaks even with the daily increase in profit in about 57 days. Expansion is recommended.

■ **7. (a)** Let $x_2 = $ executed proportion of project $i$. Solution is $x_1 = x_2 = x_3 = x_4 = 1$, $x_5 = .8413$, $z = \$116,061.10$.

**(b)** Add $x_2 \le x_6$. Solution $x_5 = .0317$; all others $= 1$, $z = \$113,677.80$.

**(c)** Each additional \$1000 contributes \$2888.90, yielding a rate of return of 188.89%.

**(d)** Let $s_i = $ funds left at the end of year $i$. Convert all the constraints to equations using $s_1$ in Equation (1), $s_2 - s_1$ in Equation (2), $s_3 - s_2$ in Equation (3), and $s_4 - s_3$ in Equation (4). Solution calls for selecting all six projects with $z = \$131,300$.

**(e)** Same solution as in (d). Borrowed funds in years 3 and 4 are \$11,100. Rate of return on borrowed money is 137.3%.

■ **9. (a)** Let $x_j = $ amount invested in project $j$ when available, $j = 1, 2, 3, 4$, $y_j = $ amount of bank investment in $j$, $j = 1, 2, ..., 5$.

*Solution*: In year 1, invest \$10,000 in project 2; in year 2, invest \$6000 in project 3; in year 3, invest \$6800 in bank account; and in year 4, invest \$33,642 also in bank account. Accumulated $y_5 = \$53,628.74$ at the start of year 5.

**(b)** Rate of return $= 536.61$.

**(c)** Accumulation at the end of year 5 is reduced by \$3,730.90.

**(d)** $D_1 = 0$, $D_2 = D_3 = D_4 = D_5 = \$1000$. *Solution*: $x_2 = \$10,000$, $x_3 = \$5000$, $y_3 = \$5000$, $y_4 = \$28,825$, and $w = \$46,998.64$.

■ **11. (a)** Produce 28 units of product 1 and 148 units of product 2. Profit is $5280.
  **(b)** Do not pay more than $6 for either machine.
  **(c)** Machining cost must be reduced by at least $20 per unit of product 3.
  **(d)** $10 \leq d_2 \leq 22.50$.
  **(e)** $-13.33 \leq D_2 \leq 445$.

■ **13. (a)** Undertake .7113 of project 1 and none of project 2.
  **(b)** No.
  **(c)** Interest rates: $i_1 = .02, i_2 = .025, i_3 = .171, i_4 = .02$
  **(d)** Net worth per dollar borrowed in period 3 $= 1.1945 - 1.025 \times 1.02 = \$.149$.

■ **15. (a)** Invest $100,000 in plan $A$ in year 1 and $170,000 in plan $B$ in year 2.
  **(b)** One dollar now $= \$5.10$ at end of horizon.

■ **17. (a)** Produce 1800 tons of alloy $A$ and 1000 tons of alloy $B$.
  **(b)** 1000 tons of ore 1 and 3000 tons of ore 3 to $A$, and 2000 tons of ore 2 to $B$.
  **(c)** The specification constraints with negative dual prices may have adverse effect on the profit.
  **(d)** Maximum respective prices are $90, $110, and $30.

## CHAPTER 3

### Set 3.2a

■ **1.** Maximize $z = 2x_1^+ - 2x_1^- + 3x_2 + 5x_3$
  subject to

$$-x_1^+ + x_1^- - x_2 + x_3 \qquad = 5$$
$$-6x_1^+ + 6x_1^- + 7x_2 - 9x_3 - x_4 = 4$$
$$x_1^+ - x_1^- + x_2 + 4x_3 + x_5 = 10$$

all variables are nonnegative.

■ **3.** Minimize $z = y$
  subject to

$$-y + x_1 - x_2 + 3x_3 + s_1 = 0$$
$$-y - x_1 + x_2 - 3x_3 + s_2 = 0$$
$$-y - x_1 + 3x_2 - x_3 + s_3 = 0$$
$$-y + x_1 - 3x_2 + x_3 + s_4 = 0$$

all variables are nonnegative.

### Set 3.2b

■ **1.** $(x_1, x_4) = (0, 4)$ unique and feasible, $(x_1, x_5) = (-6, \frac{14}{3})$ unique and infeasible, $(x_2, x_3) = (0, 2)$ unique and feasible.

■ **3. (a)** Optimum: $x_1 = 8, x_2 = 0, x_3 = 3, x_4 = 0, z = 31$.
   **(b)** Alternative optima: $(x_1, x_2, x_3, x_4) = (4, 0, 0, 0)$ or $(0, 2, 0, 0), z = 4$.

## Set 3.2c

■ **3.** Maximize $z = 2x_1 + 5x_2 + 3x_3 - 15s_1^- - 10s_2^-$ subject to $2x_1 + x_2 + 2x_3 + s_1^+ - s_1^- = 80, x_1 + x_2 + .5x_3 + s_2^+ - s_2^- = 65$, all variables are nonnegative. Optimum: $(x_1, x_2, x_3) = (0, 60, 10), z = \$330$.

## Set 3.3a

■ **3. (a) (i)** $x_8$. **(ii)** $x_3$. **(iii)** $x_1$. **(iv)** None. **(v)** $x_3$.
   **(b) (i)** 20. **(ii)** $-8$. **(iii)** 0. **(iv)** $\infty$ or unbounded. **(v)** 0.
■ **5. (a)** Problem is equivalent to maximize $z = x_1$ subject to $5x_1 \leq 4, 6x_1 \leq 8, 3x_1 \leq 3$. The constraints are dominated by $x_1 \leq \frac{4}{5}$, which is the minimum ratio when $x_1$ is used as the entering variable with $x_2$, $x_3$, and $x_4$ as starting basic solution. Hence, max $z = \frac{4}{5}$.
■ **7. (a)** Optimum at $E = (\frac{5}{2}, 2), z = \frac{39}{2}$.
   **(b)** $A \rightarrow G \rightarrow F \rightarrow E$.
   **(c)** $x_1$ enters: ratios $= (\mathbf{2}, 3, 5), A \rightarrow B, \Delta z = 8$.
   **(d)** $x_2$ enters: ratios $= (\mathbf{1}, 2, 3), A \rightarrow G, \Delta z = 4$.
■ **9.** $A$: basic $(s_1, s_2, s_3, s_4)$, nonbasic $(x_1, x_2, x_3)$.
   $J$: basic $(x_1, s_2, x_2, x_3)$, nonbasic $(s_1, s_3, s_4)$.
■ **11. (a)** Iterations are $A \rightarrow B \rightarrow C \rightarrow D$.
   **(b)** Iterations are $A \rightarrow E \rightarrow D$.
   **(c)** The simplex method requires an extra iteration, showing that it does not always lead to the smallest number of iterations.
   **(d)** The two problems have identical computations except that the objective rows have opposite signs.

## Set 3.4a

■ **3. (a)** $z - (5 - 2M)x_1 - (6 + 3M)x_2 = -3M$.
   **(c)** $z - (3 - 4M)x_1 - (6 - 8M)x_2 - Ms_5 = 5M$.
■ **5.** The starting $z$-equation is $z - x_1 - 12x_2 + 0x_3 + 0x_4 = -8$.
■ **7.** The starting $z$-equation is $z + (2 - 2M)x_1 + (1 + M)x_2 + 0x_3 + 0R = 9 - 4M$.

## Set 3.4b

■ **1. (a)** Artificials are a measure of infeasibility in the problem.
   **(b)** The sum must always be minimized.
■ **3. (a)** Phase I produces $x_1 = \frac{45}{7}$ and $x_2 = \frac{4}{7}$ in four iterations. Phase II produces the same solution in two additional iterations.
■ **5. (a)** Phase I produces $x_2 = 2$ and $R_2 = 0$ in one iteration.
■ **7.** If $x_1, x_3$, or $x_5$ assumes a positive value, then the objective value at the end of Phase I will necessarily increase above zero level (try it!), which shows that the problem will be infeasible if any of these variables is positive.

## Set 3.5a

■ **1. (a)** $A \rightarrow B \rightarrow C \rightarrow D$.
   **(b)** One at $A$, one at $B$, three at $C$, and one at $D$.

## Set 3.5b

■ **1.** Three alternative optima are $(x_1, x_2, x_3) = (0, 0, \frac{10}{3}), (0, 5, 0)$, and $(1, 4, \frac{1}{3})$. $\bar{x}_1 = \alpha_3$, $\bar{x}_2 = 5\alpha_2 + 4\alpha_3, \bar{x}_3 = \frac{10}{3}\alpha_1 + \frac{1}{3}\alpha_3, \alpha_1 + \alpha_2 + \alpha_3 = 1$, and all $\alpha \geq 0$.
■ **3.** At the optimum tableau, the slack associated with the third constraint is basic at zero level (degenerate), and the slack associated with the second constraint is nonbasic and has a zero coefficient in the objective equation (alternative solution).

## Set 3.5d

■ **1.** Request cannot be satisfied. At most 275 tools can be manufactured.

# CHAPTER 4

## Set 4.2a

■ **1.** Maximize $w = 10y_1 + 8y_2$ subject to $y_1 = 2y_2 \leq 5, \ 2y_1 - y_2 \leq 12, \ y_1 + 3y_2 \leq 4$, $y_1 \leq 0, y_2$ unrestricted.
■ **5. (c)** Minimize $w = 5y_1 + 3y_2$ subject to $y_1 - y_2 = 5, \ 2y_1 + 5y_2 + y_3 \geq 6, \ y_1$ unrestricted, $y_2 \leq 0, y_3 \geq 0$.

## Set 4.3a

■ **1.** $2y_1 - y_2 - 12 = 0$ and $y_1 + 3y_2 - 4 = \frac{3}{5}$ yield $y_1 = \frac{29}{5}$ and $y_2 = -\frac{2}{5}$.
■ **3. (a)** Minimize $w = 3y_1 + 4y_2$ subject to $y_1 + 2y_2 \geq 1, \ 2y_1 - y_2 \geq 5, \ y_1 \geq 3, \ y_2$ unrestricted.
   **(b)** $y_1 = 3, y_2 = -1, w = 5$.
■ **5.** $y_1 = 4, y_2 = 0, w = 16$.
■ **9. (a)** Infeasible.
   **(b)** Feasible but not optimal.
   **(c)** Feasible and optimal.

## Set 4.4a

■ **1. (a)** $-\$1500$.
   **(b)** $-\$750$.
   **(c)** $\$0$.
■ **3.** Bago should not pay more than $\$11.88/m^2$ of leather and $\$21.25$ per labor hour.

## Set 4.4b

■ **1.** At least 50%.
■ **3.** Parts PP3 and PP4 are not produced. Rates of deterioration in profit per unit of PP3 and PP4 are $.1429 and $1.1429, respectively.

## Set 4.5a

■ **1. (a)** No, because the dual simplex iterations remain infeasible till the last iteration, when it becomes feasible.
 **(b)** $L \rightarrow I \rightarrow F$.
■ **3. (a)** Optimum is $x_1 = \frac{3}{4}, x_2 = \frac{1}{4}$, and $z = \frac{7}{2}$. Iterations start at $(0,0)$, pass by $(\frac{2}{3}, 0)$, and end at $(\frac{3}{4}, \frac{1}{4})$.
■ **5. (a)** Add the artificial constraint $x_3 \leq M$. Optimum solution is $x_1 = \frac{56}{9}, x_2 = \frac{26}{3}, x_3 = \frac{14}{9}$, and $z = \frac{28}{9}$.

## Set 4.6a

■ **3. (a)** $\mathbf{X}_B = (3, 15)^T, z_1 - c_1 = 0$, and $z_3 - c_3 = 2$. Basis is optimal and feasible.
 **(b)** Optimal but infeasible .
■ **5. (a)** $\mathbf{X}_B = (x_2, x_1)^T = (\frac{18}{5}, \frac{14}{5})^T$ yields $z = 57.2$.
 **(b)** Solution is optimal because $z_3 - c_3 = \frac{3}{5}$ and $z_4 - c_4 = \frac{29}{5}$.
■ **7. (a)** $b_1 = 30, b_2 = 40$.
 **(b)** $y_1 = 5, y_2 = 0$.
 **(c)** $a = 23, b = 5, c = -10$.

## Set 4.7a

■ **1.** New Solution: $(x_1, x_2, x_3) = (0, 95, 240)$, Z = $1390.
■ **3.** $x_1 = \frac{10}{3}, x_2 = 2, z = \frac{74}{4}$.

## Set 4.7b

■ **1. (a)** $-20 \leq D_2 \leq 400, D_3 \geq -20$.
 **(b)** Worth per minute of operation 2 is $2 and of operation 3 is $0.
 **(c)** $x_1 = 0, x_2 = 90$, and $x_3 = 250$. Increase in $z = 40 \times \$2 = \$80$.
 **(d)** $x_1 = 0, x_2 = 100, x_3 = 230$. Change in $z = 30 \times \$0 = \$0$.
 **(e)** $x_1 = 0, x_2 = 90, x_3 = 230, z = 1330$.
■ **3. (a)** Additional profit per hour $= 60 \times \$1 = \$60$, which exceeds the additional overtime cost per hour $(= \$50)$. The result is valid if operation 1 time is in the range $(3.833, 7.333)$ hours. This means that the given conclusion is valid for an additional 10 minutes. Any increase past this limit must be assessed separately.
 **(b)** Additional cost for 2 hours = $110. Additional profit for 2 hours is $120 \times \$2 = \$240$. Hence, additional overtime is justified.
 **(c)** No, because its worth per unit is zero.

(d) New optimum is $x_1 = 0$, $x_2 = 105$, and $x_3 = 230$. Increase in cost is \$6.67, and increase in profit is \$10.

(e) Decrease in profit = \$30, and decrease in cost = \$7.50. Hence, decrease is not recommended.

## Set 4.7C

■ 1. (a) New constraint is redundant.

(b) New solution: $x_1 = 0, x_2 = 88, x_3 = 230, z = \$1{,}326$.

## Set 4.7d

■ 1. (a) Solution remains optimal.

(b) New solution: $x_1 = 10, x_2 = 102.5, x_3 = 215, z = \$860$.

■ 3. (a) $d_1 \leq 4$.

(b) $2 \leq d_2 \leq 8$.

(c) $d_3 \geq -8/3$.

■ 5. (a) $-3 \leq d_1 \leq 1$.

(b) $-2/3 \leq d_2 \leq 6$.

■ 7. (a) $4 - .5d_2 - .25d_2 + 1.5d_3 \geq 0, 1 + .5d_2 \geq 0, 2 - .25d_2 + .5d_3 \geq 0$.

■ 9. (a) Solution does not change.

(b) New solution: $x_1 = 20, x_2 = x_3 = 0, z = \$1{,}400$.

(d) Solution does not change.

■ 11. (a) $\$6 \leq c_1 \leq \$26$.

(b) New solution: $x_1 = 0, x_2 = 165, x_3 = 10, z = \$4{,}105$.

## Set 4.7e

■ 1. 42.86%.

■ 3. (a) Fire engines are not profitable.

(b) Produce 100 fire engines.

# CHAPTER 5

## Set 5.1a

■ 1. (a) F.

(b) T.

(c) T.

■ 3. Denver and Miami will be 150 and 50 cars short of meeting their demands.

- **5.** LA to Denver: 1000 cars; Detroit to Denver: 1100 cars; Detroit to Miami: 200 cars; and New Orleans to Miami: 1200 cars. Denver shortage: 200 cars. Total cost = \$333,200.
- **7. (c)** City 1 will purchase 22.5 million kWh from the network at a cost of \$22,500.
- **9. (b)** Area 1 receives 4 million gallons from refinery 1. Area 2 receives 2 million gallons from refinery 1, 5 million gallons from refinery 2, and 1 million gallons from refinery 3. Area 3 receives 7 million gallons from refinery 3. Total cost = \$243,000.
- **11. (b)** Area 1 receives 4 million gallons from refinery 1. Area 2 receives 2 million gallons from refinery 1 and 5 million gallons from refinery 2, and 1 million gallons from refinery 3. Area 3 receives 4 million gallons from refinery 3. Refinery 3 has 3 million gallons surplus. Total cost = \$207,000.

## Set 5.2a

- **1.** Produce 50 units in period 1 for period 1, produce 180 units in period 2 with 50 units back-ordered for period 2, produce 280 units in period 3 with 70 units back-ordered to period 2 and 30 units carried over to period 4, and produce 270 units in period 4. Total cost = \$31,461.
- **3.** Monday: buy 24; send 12 overnight, and 12 to 2-day. Tuesday: send 6 overnight and 6 to 2-day. Wednesday: buy 8; send 8 overnight and 6 to 2-day. Thursday: send 12 overnight and 8 to 2-day. Friday: send 8 overnight and dispose of 10. Saturday: send 14 overnight. Sunday, dispose of 22. Total cost = \$840.
- **5.** Produce 500 in period 1, with 100 units carried over to period 2; produce 600 units in period 2, with 200 units carried over to period 3 and 180 units carried over to period 4; produce 200 in period 3; and produce 200 in period 4. Total cost = \$190,040.
- **7.** Month 1: buy 200; send 12 to 1-day and 188 to 3-day. Month 2: buy 180, send 148 to 1-day and 32 to 3-day. Month 3: buy 140; send 10 to 1-day and 290 3-day. Month 4: send 198 to 1-day. Month 4: dispose of 230. Month 6: dispose of 290.

## Set 5.3a

- **1. (a)** Northwest: $x_{11} = 5$, $x_{12} = 1$, $x_{22} = 4$, $x_{23} = 3$, $x_{34} = 7$, cost = \$42. Least cost: $x_{11} = 5, x_{13} = 1, x_{22} = 5, x_{23} = 2, x_{33} = 7$, cost = \$37. Vogel: same as least cost.

## Set 5.3b

- **1. (a)** Three iterations: $x_{11} = 1, x_{13} = 5, x_{21} = 4, x_{22} = 5, x_{33} = 5$, cost = \$33.
- **3.** $x_{12} = 10, x_{21} = 20, x_{22} = 10, x_{23} = 50, x_{31} = 5, x_{32} = 10$, with destination 1 40 units short, cost = \$515.
- **5. (a)** \$1475.
    - **(b)** $c_{12} \geq \$3, c_{13} \geq \$8, c_{23} \geq \$13, c_{31} \geq \$7$.

## Set 5.3c

- **1.** $u_1 = 0, u_2 = 5, u_3 = 7, v_1 = -3, v_2 = 2, v_3 = 4, v_4 = 11$, objective value = \$435.

## Set 5.4a

- **1. (a)** 1–5, 2–3, 3–2, 4–4, 5–1, cost = \$21.
- **3.** Worker 5 replaces worker 3.
- **5.** Ticket 1: Leave Dallas on June 3 for return on June 28. Ticket 2: Leave Atlanta on June 7 for return on June 10. Ticket 3: Leave Atlanta on June 12 for return on June 17. Ticket 4: Leave Atlanta on June 21 for return on June 25. Total cost = \$1180. Problem has alternative solutions.

## Set 5.5a

- **1. (b)** $x_{13} = 100, x_{24} = 200, x_{35} = 100, x_{45} = 200, x_{56} = 150$, cost = \$2250. Problem has alternative optima.
- **3. (a)** $x_{15} = 900, x_{24} = 1400, x_{34} = 1000, x_{45} = 1300, x_{46} = 1100, x_{57} = 1000, x_{58} = 1200$, cost = \$8640.
  - **(b)** $x_{15} = 900, x_{24} = 1400, x_{34} = 1000, x_{45} = 1060, x_{46} = 1100, x_{57} = 760, x_{58} = 1200$, cost = \$8016. Dealer 7 is 240 cars short.
- **5.** $x_{12} = 50{,}000, \ x_{37} = 60{,}000, \ x_{75} = 60{,}000, \ x_{54} = 20{,}000, \ x_{56} = 40{,}000, \ x_{62} = 40{,}000$, cost = 2,660,000 gallon miles.

# CHAPTER 6

## Set 6.2a

- **1. (a)** 1−3−4−2.
  - **(b)** 1−5−4−3−1.
  - **(c)** 1−3−4−5−1.
  - **(d)** {1−3, 3−4, 3−5}.
  - **(e)** {1−3, 3−4, 4−2, 2−5}.

## Set 6.3a

- **3.** (SE–LA), (LA–CH), (CH–NY), (NY–DC), (DE–DA), (DA–CH).
- **5.** (1–2), (2–3), (3–4), (4–6), (1–5), (5–7), (5–9), (9–8).

## Set 6.4a

- **1.** Replace at the start of year 1999 and keep till year 2002.
- **3.** Minimum time = 106 seconds.

## Set 6.4b

- **1. (a)** 1−3−6−8, 1−2−3−6−8, 1−3−5−6−8, or 1−2−3−5−6−8, distance = 8.
  - **(c)** 4−5−6−8 or 4−6−8, distance = 8.

- **3.** Replace the car at the start of 1999 and keep it until 2002. Total cost = $9800.
- **5.** Order 100 units in month 1, 140 units in month 2, and 390 units in month 3. Total cost = $7296.

## Set 6.4c

- **1.** **(a)** $5-4-2-1$, distance = 12.
  **(d)** $5-4-4$, distance = 9.
- **3.** 1-2: route $(1-3-2)$, distance = 500 miles.
  1-4: route $(1-3-2-4)$, distance = 700 miles.
  1-5: route $(1-3-5)$, distance = 800 miles.

## Set 6.5a

- **1.** $(1,2),(1,4),(3,4),(3,5)$, capacity = 60.
  $(1,2),(1,3),(4,3),(4,5)$, capacity = 75.

## Set 6.5b

- **1.** **(a)** Surplus capacity: $(2,3) = 40,(2,5) = 10,(4,3) = 5$, all others = 0.
  **(b)** 20, 30, and 20 units.
  **(c)** No because the arcs of node 1 represent the bottleneck.
- **3.** Maximum flow = 25.
- **5.** Maximum flow = 100, pump 4 = 30, pump 5 = 40, pump 6 = 60.
- **7.** Maximum flow = 170.
- **9.** Maximum number of toys = 800.

## Set 6.6b

- **1.** **(a)** Minimize $z = x_{12} + 5x_{13} + 3x_{24} + 4x_{32} + 6x_{34}$
  subject to

$$x_{12} + x_{13} = \phantom{-}50$$

$$-x_{12} + x_{24} - x_{32} = -40$$

$$-x_{13} + x_{32} + x_{34} = \phantom{-}20$$

$$- x_{24} - x_{34} = -30$$

$$30 \le x_{13} \le 40, x_{24} \ge 10, x_{32} \ge 10.$$

  **(b)** Minimize $z = x_{12} + 5x_{13} + 3x_{24} + 4x_{32} + 6x_{34}$
  subject to

$$x_{12} + x_{13} = 20$$

$$-x_{12} + x_{24} - x_{32} = -40$$

$$-x_{13} + x_{32} + x_{34} = 40$$

$$-x_{24} - x_{34} = -20, x_{13} \leq 10.$$

■ **2.** Hire 20 at the start of January and terminate them at the start of March, hire 80 at the start of January and terminate them at the start of May, hire 20 at the start of February and terminate them at the start of March, and hire 90 at the start of April and terminate them at the start of May.

### Set 6.6c

■ **1.** Produce 210 units in period 1 and 220 units in period 3. Total cost = $9,895.
■ **3.** Produce 110 units in period 1, 95 units in period 2, 125 units in period 3, and 100 units in period 4. Carry over 10 units from periods 1 to 2 and 25 units from periods 3 to 4. Back-order 5 units from period 3 to period 2. Total cost = $10,177.50.
■ **5.** School 1 receives 450 students from minority area 2 and 1000 students from nonminority area 1. School 2 receives 500 students from minority area 1, 300 students from minority area 3, and 1000 students from nonminority area 2. Total student–miles = $24,300
■ **7.** $x_{16} = 8, x_{24} = 10, x_{34} = 6, x_{35} = 6, x_{36} = 6$, cost = $146.

### Set 6.7b

■ **1.** 1–3–4–5–6–7; project duration = 19.
■ **3.** $A$–$C$–$D$–$F$–$G$–$H$–$J$–$L$–$N$–$S$–$T$, project duration = 38 days.
■ **5.** Two paths: $A$–$C$–$E$–$F$–$J$–$L$–($M$ or $N$)–$P$–$Q$–$S$–$T$–$U$, project duration = 22.1 days.

### Set 6.7c

■ **1.** $\square_i + D_{ij}$ and $\Delta_j - D_{ij}$.
■ **3. (a)** 10.
  **(b)** 5.
  **(c)** 0.
■ **5. (a)** $B$–$F$; project duration = 45 days.
  **(b)** $A$: $TF = 12, FF = 0$, $C$: $TF = FF = 12$, $D$: $TF = 20, FF = 0$, $E$: $TF = 11, FF = 0$, $G$: $TF = FF = 11$, $H$: $TF = FF = 31$. Activities $A$, $D$, and $E$ are red-flagged.
  **(c)** Delay each of activities $C, D, G$, and $H$ by 5 days. Activity $E$ can start as early as time 20.
  **(d)** Two units.

## CHAPTER 7

### Set 7.2a

■ **1.**

$$\text{Maximize } z = (2, 3, 0, 0, -M)\, (x_1, x_2, \ldots, x_6)^T$$

subject to

$$\begin{bmatrix} 1 & 1 & 0 & | & 1 & 0 & 0 \\ 1 & 2 & 0 & | & 0 & 1 & 0 \\ 5 & -2 & -1 & | & 0 & 0 & 1 \end{bmatrix} \begin{bmatrix} x_1 \\ x_2 \\ \vdots \\ x_6 \end{bmatrix} = \begin{bmatrix} 5 \\ 7 \\ 9 \end{bmatrix}$$

## Set 7.3a

■ **1.** Represent the equations as $\mathbf{P}_1 x_1 + \mathbf{P}_2 x_2 = \mathbf{b}$. Then we have (1) unique solution if $\mathbf{P}_1$ and $\mathbf{P}_2$ are independent, (2) infinity of solutions if $\mathbf{P}_1, \mathbf{P}_2,$ and $\mathbf{b}$ are dependent, and (3) no solution if $\mathbf{P}_1$ and $\mathbf{P}_2$ are dependent and $\mathbf{b}$ is independent.

■ **3. (a)** T.
   **(b)** T.
   **(c)** T.

## Set 7.3b

■ **3.** $(x_1, \ x_2) = \lambda_1(0, \ 0) + \lambda_2(2, \ 0) + \lambda_3(0, \ 2) = (2\lambda_2, \ 2\lambda_3), \ \lambda_1 + \lambda_2 + \lambda_3 = 1, \ \lambda_i \ge 0,$ $i = 1, 2, 3.$

## Set 7.3c

■ **1. (b)** One extreme point in which $x_3 > 0$ and all other variables $= 0$.
   **(c)** No because $x_4$ must be negative.

## Set 7.4a

■ **1.** $\text{Det}(\mathbf{P}_1, \mathbf{P}_2) = -6$, a basis; $\det(\mathbf{P}_2, \mathbf{P}_3) = 0$, not a basis; $\det(\mathbf{P}_3, \mathbf{P}_4) = 1$, a basis.
■ **3.** Because $\det(\mathbf{P}_2, \mathbf{P}_3) = 0, (\mathbf{P}_2, \mathbf{P}_3)$ is not a basis, and hence does not correspond to an extreme point solution.
■ **5.**

| Basic | $x_1$ | $x_2$ | $x_3$ | $x_4$ | $x_5$ | Solution |
|---|---|---|---|---|---|---|
| $z$ | 0 | 0 | $-\dfrac{2}{5}$ | $-\dfrac{1}{5}$ | 0 | $\dfrac{12}{5}$ |
| $x_1$ | 1 | 0 | $-\dfrac{3}{5}$ | $\dfrac{1}{5}$ | 0 | $\dfrac{3}{5}$ |
| $x_2$ | 0 | 1 | $\dfrac{4}{5}$ | $-\dfrac{3}{5}$ | 0 | $\dfrac{6}{5}$ |
| $x_5$ | 0 | 0 | $-1$ | 1 | 1 | 0 |

■ **7. (a)** $\mathbf{P}_1$ leaves.
   **(b)** Yes.
■ **13.** $n - m.$
■ **15.** A tie for the minimum ratio will produce degeneracy. If the constraint coefficient in the entering column corresponding to the zero basic variable is positive, the next iteration will continue to be degenerate. If it is negative or zero, degeneracy will be removed.

■ **17.** **(a)** New $xj = \frac{1}{\beta}$ (old $x_j$).
   **(b)** New $xj = \frac{\alpha}{\beta}$ (old $x_j$).

## Set 7.5a

■ **1.**

$$\begin{bmatrix} 1 & -\frac{3}{4} & -\frac{1}{4} \\ 1 & \frac{1}{2} & -\frac{1}{2} \\ -1 & \frac{1}{2} & \frac{1}{2} \end{bmatrix}$$

■ **3.** If the pivot element used in the formulation of $\xi$ is *not* zero, **B** is a basis.

## Set 7.5b

■ **1. (a)** Iteration 1:

| Basic | $x_1$ | $x_2$ | $x_3$ | $x_4$ | $x_5$ | $x_6$ | Solution |
|-------|-------|-------|-------|-------|-------|-------|----------|
| $z$ | 0 | $-\frac{1}{3}$ | 0 | $\frac{2}{3}$ | 0 | 0 | 8 |
| $x_3$ | | $\frac{4}{3}$ | | | | | 2 |
| $x_1$ | | $\frac{2}{3}$ | | | | | 4 |
| $x_5$ | | $\frac{5}{3}$ | | | | | 5 |
| $x_6$ | | 1 | | | | | 2 |

■ **3.** Optimum: $x_1 = x_2 = x_6 = 0, x_3 = 2, x_4 = 10, x_5 = 8, z = -78$.

## Set 7.5c

■ **3. (a)** Optimum: $x_1 = 0, x_2 = \frac{3}{2}, x_3 = 1, z = 6$.
   **(b)** Optimum: $x_1 = 4, x_2 = \frac{7}{4}, x_3 = 0, z = \frac{83}{4}$.

## Set 7.5d

■ **1. (a)** $(x_1,x_2) = \alpha_1(0,0) + \alpha_2(0,1) + \alpha_3(1,2) + \alpha_4(2,2) + \alpha_5(\frac{10}{3},\frac{4}{3}) + \alpha_6(4,0)$,
   $\alpha_1 + \alpha_2 + \cdots + \alpha_6 = 1$, all $\alpha_i \geq 0$.
   **(b)** No feasible solution space.
   **(c)** $(x_1, x_2) = \alpha_1(0, 0) + \alpha_2(10, 0) + \alpha_3(20, 10) + \alpha_4(20, M) + \alpha_5(0, M)$, $M$ is sufficiently large, $\alpha_1 + \alpha_2 + \cdots + \alpha_5 = 1$, all $\alpha_i \geq 0$.
■ **3.** Substitute $(x_1,x_2) = (\frac{9}{2}\alpha_2 + 4\alpha_3, \alpha_3 + 2\alpha_4), (x_3,x_4) = (4\beta_2 + 9\beta_3, \beta_3 + 10\beta_4)$. The optimum solution is $\alpha_3 = 1$ and $\beta_3 = 1$, which corresponds to $x_1 = 4, x_2 = 1, x_3 = 9, x_4 = 1$,
   $z = 54$.

■ **5.** Optimum: $x_1 = 2, x_2 = 8, x_3 = 0, x_4 = 12, x_5 = 28, x_6 = 0, z = 156$.
■ **7.** Optimum: $y_1 = 0, y_2 = 2, y_3 = 0, y_4 = 5, y_5 = 0, z = 44$.

## Set 7.6b

■ **3. (a)** Minimize $z = 2y_1 + 5y_2$ subject to $2y_1 + y_2 \geq 5, -y_1 + 2y_2 \geq 12, 3y_1 + y_2 \geq 4, y_1$ unrestricted, $y_2 \geq 0$.
   **(b) (i)** Dual is not feasible, hence $(\mathbf{P}_4, \mathbf{P}_3)$ is not optimal. **(ii)** Dual is not feasible, hence $(\mathbf{P}_2, \mathbf{P}_3)$ is not optimal. **(iii)** Dual is feasible, hence $(\mathbf{P}_1, \mathbf{P}_2)$ is optimal. **(iv)** Dual is not feasible, hence $(\mathbf{P}_1, \mathbf{P}_4)$ is not optimal.
■ **5.** $z = 34$.
■ **7.** Minimize $w = \mathbf{Yb}$ subject to $\mathbf{YA} = \mathbf{C}, \mathbf{Y}$ unrestricted.

## Set 7.7a

■ **1.** $-\frac{2}{7} \leq t \leq 1$.
■ **3.** $x_1 = \frac{2}{5}, x_2 = \frac{9}{5}, x_3 = 0, z = \frac{(17 - 29t)}{5}$.
■ **5.** $t_1 = 1$.

## Set 7.7b

■ **1. (a)** $t_1 = 10$, new $\mathbf{B} = (\mathbf{P}_2, \mathbf{P}_3, \mathbf{P}_4)$.
   **(b)** $t_1 = 5$, new $\mathbf{B} = (\mathbf{P}_5, \mathbf{P}_3, \mathbf{P}_6)$.
■ **3.** For $0 \leq t \leq \frac{3}{8}$: $x_1 = \frac{(3 + 7t)}{5}$, $x_2 = \frac{(6 - 11t)}{5}$, $z = \frac{(21 - 11t)}{5}$. For $\frac{3}{8} \leq t \leq \frac{2}{5}$: $x_1 = (-3 + 11t)$, $x_2 = (6 - 15t), z = (6 + 3t)$.

# CHAPTER 8

## Set 8.2a

■ **1.** $G_5$: Minimize $s_5^-, 55x_p + 3.5x_f - .0675x_g + s_5^+ - s_5^- = 0$.
■ **3.** Let $x_1 =$ in-state freshmen, $x_2 =$ out-of-state freshmen, $x_3 =$ international freshmen. $G_1$: minimize $s_1^+$, $G_2$: minimize $s_2^+$, $G_3$: minimize $s_3^+$, $G_4$: minimize $s_4^-$, $G_5$: minimize $s_5^-$ subject to $x_1 + x_2 + x_3 + s_1^+ - s_1^- = 1200, 2x_1 + x_2 - 2x_3 + s_2^+ - s_2^- = 0,$ $-x_1 - x_2 + .9x_3 + s_3^+ - s_3^- = 0, .2x_2 + (\frac{7}{9})x_3 + s_4^+ - s_4^- = 0,$ $.2x_1 - .8x_2 + .2x_3 + s_5^+ - s_5^- = 0$, all variables nonnegative.
■ **5.** Define $x_j =$ number of production runs in shift $j, j = 1, 2, 3$. Minimize $z = s_1^+ + s_1^-$ subject to $-100x_1 + 40x_2 - 80x_3 + s_1^+ - s_1^- = 0, 4 \leq x_1 \leq 5, 10 \leq x_2 \leq 20, 3 \leq x_3 \leq 5$.
■ **7.** Define $x_1$ and $x_2$ as the number of units of products 1 and 2. $G_1$: minimize $s_1^+$, $G_2$: minimize $s_2^+$, $G_3$: minimize $s_3^-$, $G_4$: minimize $s_4^-$, subject to $x_1 + s_1^+ - s_1^- = 80, x_2 + s_2^+ - s_2^- = 60, 5x_1 + 3x_2 + s_3^+ - s_3^- = 480, 6x_1 + 2x_2 + s_4^+ - s_4^- = 480$, all variables are nonnegative.

■ **9.** Let $(x, y)$ define the choice location of the house. $G_1$: minimize $s_1^-$, $G_2$: minimize $s_2^+$, $G_3$: minimize $s_3^-$ subject to $[(x - 1)^2 + (y - 1)^2]^{1/2} + s_1^+ - s_1^- = .25$, $[(x - 20)^2 + (y - 15)^2]^{1/2} + s_2^+ - s_2^- = 10$, $[(x - 4)^2 + (y - 7)^2]^{1/2} + s_3^+ - s_3^- = 1$, all variables are nonnegative.

## Set 8.3a

■ **1.** $x_p = .0201, x_f = .0457, x_s = .0582, x_g = 2$ cents, $s_5^- = 1.45$, all other $s_i = 0$. Gasoline tax falls \$1.45 million short of meeting the desired goal of \$1.6 million.

■ **3.** Solution calls for accepting 840 in state, 240 out of state, and 120 international. ACT goal overachieved by 1.4 points per student. Female-to-male goal underachieved by 141 females.

■ **5.** $x_1 = 4$ runs, $x_2 = 16$ runs, $x_3 = 3$ runs, $s_1^+ = s_1^- = 0$, production of wheels and seats is balanced.

■ **7.** The quota of 80 units of product 1 and 60 units of product 2 can be met with 100 overtime minutes on machine 1 and 120 overtime minutes on machine 2.

■ **9.** $\bar{y} = .8571 + 1.0714x_1 + 2.881x_2 - .9048x_3$.

## Set 8.3b

■ **1.** Optimization of $G_1 = s_1^+$ yields $x_1 = 2.5$ minutes, $x_2 = 3.75$ minutes, $s_1^+ = 5$, and $s_2^- = 0$. $G_1$ is underachieved by 5 million persons, but $G_2$ is automatically satisfied.

■ **3.** **(a)** $x_1 = 5$ concerts, $x_2 = 2.5$ shows, $s_3^+ = 175$, $G_3$ is not met.
    **(b)** $x_1 = 3.6$ concerts, $x_2 = 3.2$ shows, $s_1^+ = 280$, $G_1$ is not met.

# CHAPTER 9

## Set 9.2a

■ **1.** Add the constraints $x_1 \leq x_5$ and $x_3 \leq x_5$. Solution: $x_2 = x_3 = x_5 = 1, z = 90$.

■ **3.** Let $x_{ij}$ = number of bottles of type $i$ given to individual $j$, $i = f(\text{ull}), h(\text{alf})$, and $e(\text{mpty})$, $j = 1, 2, 3$. Feasible solution: $x_{f1} = 3, x_{h1} = 1, x_{e1} = 3, x_{f2} = 3, x_{h2} = 1, x_{e2} = 3, x_{f3} = 1$, $x_{h3} = 5, x_{e3} = 1$. Problem has more than one feasible solution.

■ **5.** Let $x_{ij}$ = number of apples belonging to child $i$ and sold at price $j$. Solution: Jim sells 42 apples for \$$\frac{1}{7}$ each and 8 apples for \$3 each, Bill sells 21 apples for \$$\frac{1}{7}$ each and 9 apples for \$3 each, and John sells his 10 apples for \$3 each. Each child returns with \$30.

■ **7.** Select AFT, TVA, ADV, OSF, and KEN, score = 167.

■ **9.** Side 1: 1–2–4–8, side 2: 3–5–6–7. Minimum capacity = 28 minutes per side.

## Set 9.2b

■ **1.** $x_1 = 600, x_2 = 200, x_3 = 1200, z = \$9800$.

■ **3.** $x_{11} = 1200, x_{13} = 600, x_{22} = 1400, x_{32} = 300, x_{33} = 1000$.

## Set 9.2c

■ **1.** Let $x_{ij} = 1$ if project $i$ precedes project $j$ and zero otherwise. The traffic when project $j$ follows project $i$ is

|   | 1 | 2 | 3 | 4 | 5 | 6 |
|---|---|---|---|---|---|---|
| 1 | — | 4 | 4 | 6 | 6 | 5 |
| 2 | 4 | — | 6 | 4 | 6 | 3 |
| 3 | 4 | 6 | — | 4 | 8 | 7 |
| 4 | 6 | 4 | 4 | — | 6 | 5 |
| 5 | 6 | 6 | 8 | 6 | — | 5 |
| 6 | 5 | 3 | 7 | 5 | 5 | — |

## Set 9.2d

■ **1.** Select routes 5 and 6, distance $= 100$ miles.

■ **3.** Two stations to cover $(1, 3, 5)$ and $(2, 4, 6)$.

## Set 9.2e

■ **1. (a)**

| 5 | 6 | 4 |
|---|---|---|
| 4 | 5 | 6 |
| 6 | 4 | 5 |

   **(b)**

| 6 | 7 | 2 |
|---|---|---|
| 1 | 5 | 9 |
| 8 | 3 | 4 |

■ **3.** Use location 2, $x_1 = 26$, $x_2 = 3$, $x_3 = 0$.

■ **5.** Let $y = 0$ if $x_3 = 0$ and 1 if $x_3 > 5$. Maximize $z = 25x_1 + 30x_2 + 45x_3$ subject to $3x_1 + 4x_2 + 5x_3 \leq 100$, $4x_1 + 3x_2 + 6x_3 \leq 100$, $x_3 - My \leq 0$, $-x_3 + My \leq M - 5$. Solution: $x_1 = 0, x_2 = 11, x_3 = 11, y = 1$.

■ **7.** Replace $b_i$ with $b_i + My_i, y_1 + y_2 + \cdots + y_m = 1, y_i = (0, 1)$.

## Set 9.3a

■ **3. (a)** $x_1 = 2.5, x_2 = 2$ (also, $x_1 = 1, x_2 = 3$), $z = 11$.
**(c)** $x_1 = 4.1667, x_2 = 1, z = 5.1667$.

■ **5. (b)** $x_1 = x_2 = 0, x_3 = 10, z = 50$.

## Set 9.3b

■ **1. (a)** $x_1 = x_2 = x_3 = 1, z = 7$.
**(c)** No feasible solution.

■ **3.** $x_1 = x_2 = x_3 = x_4 = 1, x_5 = 0, z = 95$.

## Set 9.3c

■ **1. (a)** Yes because it passes through a (feasible or infeasible) integer point and does not exclude any feasible integer points.
**(b)** No because it eliminates a feasible integer point.

## Set 9.3d

■ **1.** Cut I: $x_2 \leq 3$. Cut II: $x_1 + x_2 \leq 7$.

■ **3. (b)** Integer solution: $x_1 = 5, x_2 = 2, x_3 = 2, z = 23$. Rounded solution: $x_1 = 5, x_2 = 3$, $x_3 = 3, z = 27$. However, the rounded solution is infeasible because it does not satisfy the second constraint.

## CHAPTER 10

## Set 10.2a

■ **1.** Route: $1 \rightarrow 3 \rightarrow 5 \rightarrow 7$, distance = 21 miles.

## Set 10.3a

■ **1.** Route: $1 \rightarrow 3 \rightarrow 5 \rightarrow 7$, distance = 21 miles.
■ **3.** Route: $1 \rightarrow 2 \rightarrow 3 \rightarrow 5 \rightarrow 7$, distance = 17 miles.

## Set 10.4a

■ **1.** $(m_1, m_2, m_3) = (0, 3, 0)$, revenue = 47.
■ **3.** Food = 1 unit, first aid = 2 units, cloth = 3 units, value = 26 points.

■ **5.** Tomatoes = 2 rows, beans = 1 row, corn = 1 row, score = 30.
■ **7.** Assign funds to precincts 1, 2, and 3, population = 92,000.
■ **9.** $y_1 = y_2 = \cdots = y_n = \frac{c}{n}, z = \left(\frac{c}{n}\right)^n$.

## Set 10.4b

■ **1. (a)** Employments for weeks 1 to 5 are $(6, 5, 3, 6, 8)$.
■ **3.** Cars rented for weeks 1 to 4 are $(7, 4, 8, 8)$, cost = \$6940.

## Set 10.4c

■ **1. (a)** $K \rightarrow R \rightarrow K \rightarrow K$, cost = \$72,800.
■ **3.** $K \rightarrow R \rightarrow K \rightarrow K \rightarrow K$, cost = \$6020.

## Set 10.4d

■ **1.** Year 1: invest \$5000 in First Bank. Year 2: invest \$4090 in Second Bank. Year 3: invest \$3090 in First Bank. Year 4: invest \$2065 in either bank.

## Set 10.5a

■ **1. (a)** $0 \leq x_1 \leq \frac{7}{3}, x_2 = 3 - \frac{2}{7}x_1$.

# CHAPTER 11

## Set 11.3a

■ **1. (a)** $y^* = 346.4$ units, $t_0^* = 11.55$ days, cost/day = \$17.30.
■ **3. (a)** Order 200 units whenever the inventory level drops to 150 units.
　　**(b)** Approximately 91 orders.
■ **5.** Pick up 100 pallets every 20 days.

## Set 11.3b

■ **1.** Take advantage of the discount because the daily cost is \$414 for lots of 1800 towels, and \$356.94 for 2500 towels.
■ **3.** Yes—order 150 units.

## Set 11.3c

■ **1.** $y_1 = 10.85, y_2 = 16.9, y_3 = 22.36$.
■ **3.** $y_1 = 141.42, y_2 = 100, y_3 = 67.1, y_4 = 63.24$.

## Set 11.4a

■ **1. (a)** 500 units in each of periods 1, 4, 7, and 10.
    **(b)** 200 units in each of periods $-1, 2, 5$, and 8, and 300 units in each of periods 1, 4, 7, and 10.

## Set 11.4b

■ **1.** Period 1: 90 units regular time and 50 units overtime. Period 2: 100 units regular time and 60 units overtime. Period 3: 120 units regular time and 80 units overtime. Period 4: 110 units regular time and 50 units overtime.

■ **3.** Period 1: 100 units regular, 50 units overtime, and 23 units subcontracting. Period 2: 40 units regular, 60 units overtime, and 80 units subcontracting. Period 3: 90 units regular, 80 units overtime and 70 units subcontracting. Period 4: 60 units regular and 50 units overtime. Period 5: 70 units regular, 50 units overtime, and 83 units subcontracting.

## Set 11.4c

■ **1. (a)** No.
    **(b) (i)** $1 \leq x_2 \leq 6, 0 \leq x_3 \leq 4, 0 \leq z_1 \leq 5, 1 \leq z_2 \leq 5, 0 \leq z \leq 4$.

## Set 11.4d

■ **1.** Order zero in period 1, 112 in period 2, zero in period 3, and 67 units in period 4, cost = \$632.

■ **3.** Order 50 in period 1 and 260 in period 2, cost = \$3,190.

■ **5.** Order 150 in period 1, 120 in period 2, 110 in period 4, 90 in period 6, 310 in period 7, and 190 units in period 9, cost = \$7090.

## Set 11.4e

■ **1.** Produce 210 in period 1, 255 in period 4, 210 in period 7, and 165 units in period 10.

# CHAPTER 12

## Set 12.2a

■ **1. (a)** .15, .25.
    **(b)** .6.

## Set 12.2b

■ **1.** $E$ and $F$ are mutually exclusive. $P\{E + F\} = \frac{2}{3}$.

## Set 12.2c

- **1.** .4.
- **3.** $\frac{5}{32}$
- **5.** **(a)** .125.
  - **(b)** .6.

## Set 12.3a

- **1.** **(a)** $p(x) = \frac{x}{15}, x = 1, 2, ..., 5$
  - **(b)** .4.
- **3.** $P\{\text{demand} \geq 1100\} = .3$

## Set 12.4a

- **1.** $\frac{2}{3}$ stamp.

## Set 12.4b

- **1.** Mean = 2.67 stamps, var = 1.56.

## Set 12.4c

- **1.** **(a)** For $x_1$ and $x_2$: $p_1 = .4, p_2 = .2, p_3 = .4$.
  - **(b)** No.
  - **(c)** 4.
  - **(d)** 0.
  - **(e)** 48.8.

## Set 12.5a

- **1.** $.5^{10}$.
- **3.** There is a .0547 probability that the correct prediction will be made accidentally.

## Set 12.5b

- **1.** .8646.

## Set 12.5c

- **1.** .3678.

## Set 12.5d

■ **1. (a)** $P\{x \geq 26\} = .0228.$
   **(b)** $P\{x \leq 17\} = .0062.$
■ **3.** $P\{x_1 - x_2 \geq 0\} = .24.$

# CHAPTER 13

## Set 13.2a

■ **1.** $y_{25}^* = 60.33$ units.
■ **3.** Using $n = 3, y_{1990}^* = 1791.3$ car passengers and 938.33 air passengers.
■ **5.** Location 1: Using $n = 5, y_{1995}^* = 238.6$ for term 1, 260.2 for term 2, and 117 for term 3.

## Set 13.3a

■ **1.** $y_{25}^* = 59.63$ units.
■ **3.** $y_{1990}^* = \$26.27$ million.

## Set 13.4a

■ **1.** $y^* = 39.23 + 1.262x, r = .394, y_{25}^* = 70.77$ units.
■ **3.** $y^* = 20.6 + .873x, r = .991, y_{1990}^* = \$30.2$ million.

# CHAPTER 14

## Set 14.2a

■ **1.** $w_A = .44214, w_B = .25184, w_C = .30602.$

## Set 14.2b

■ **1.** $w_S = .331,\quad w_J = .292,\quad w_M = .377.\quad CR_A = .028,\quad CR_{A_I} = .428,\quad CR_{A_E} = .558,$
   $CR_{A_R} = .17,$ consistency of $A$ only is acceptable.
■ **3.** $w_P = .502, w_H = .498. CR_A = .0072 < .1.$
■ **5.** $w_E = .34, w_M = .66.$

## Set 14.3a

■ **1.** $EV(\text{hard}) = \$380, EV(\text{soft}) = -\$50.$

■ **3.** $EV$(utility) $= 7.2\%, EV$(aggressive) $= 13.5\%, EV$(global) $= 11.7\%$.

■ **5.** $EV$(advertise) $= \$625,000, EV$(do not advertise) $= \$360,000$.

■ **7.** $P\{\text{outcome 1}\} = P\{\text{outcome 2}\} = \frac{1}{12}$, $P\{\text{outcome 3}\} = .5, P\{\text{outcome 4}\} = \frac{1}{3}$. All 6 choices yield $EV \leq -\$.53$. Do not play the game.

■ **9.** $EV$(full plant) $= \$3,250,000, EV$(small plant) $= \$900,000$.

■ **11.** $EV$(full plant) $= \$3,300,000, EV$(small plant) $= \$1,667,600$.

## Set 14.3b

■ **1.** Optimal cycle $n = 8$ periods, $EV$(cost per period) $= \$397.50$.

■ **3.** Stock 200 loaves on day 1. On day 2, stock an amount equal to the demand on day 1. $EV$(revenue) $= \$186.84$.

■ **7.** $(\ln L - \frac{L}{200}) \geq 4.089$ and $(\ln L - \frac{L}{100}) \geq 3.505$ are satisfied for $100 \leq L \leq 150$.

## Set 14.3c

■ **1.** $P\{\text{no rain given rain is forecast}\} = .07$.

■ **3.** $EV$(stock) $= \$2491.46, EV$(CD) $= \$800$.

■ **5.** $EV$(planting) $= \$2477.89, EV$(grazing) $= \$7500$.

■ **7.** **(a)** $P\{a_1 \mid s_1\} = .96, \ P\{a_2 \mid s_1\} = .04, \ P\{a_1 \mid s_2\} = .85, \ P\{a_2 \mid s_2\} = .15, \ P\{a_1 \mid s_3\} = .57,$ $P\{a_2 \mid s_3\} = .43$.

  **(b)** If both items are good, ship to $A$; cost $= \$116.44$. If one item is good, ship to $A$; cost $= \$216.86$. If both items are defectives, ship to $A$; cost $= \$471.30$.

## Set 14.3d

■ **1.** **(a)** No advantage, $EV$(return) $= \$5$.

  **(b)** $U(\$10) = 100, U(\$x) = 0, x \neq 10$.

  **(c)** Because $U(\$10) = 100$ and $U(\$5) = 0$, play the game.

■ **3.** **(a)** $p = .667$.

  **(c)** $E\{\text{utility of venture I}\} = 80, E\{\text{utility of venture II}\} = 84$. Select venture II.

## Set 14.4a

■ **1.** **(a)** All criteria select $a_3$.

  **(b)** All criteria tie for $a_2$ and $a_3$.

■ **3.** All criteria select machine 3.

## Set 14.5a

■ **1.** **(a)** Entry $(2, 3)$.

  **(b)** Entry $(1, 3)$.

■ **3.** **(a)** $2 < v < 4$.

  **(b)** $0 < v < 7$.

**(c)** $2 < v < 3$.
**(d)** $-1 < v < 0$.

## Set 14.5b

■ **1.** $(x_1, x_2) = (.5, .5), (y_1, y_2) = (.5, .5), v = 0$.
■ **3.** **(a)** $(x_1, x_2) = (.5, .5), (y_1, y_2, y_3) = (0, \frac{13}{20}, \frac{7}{20}), v = .5$.
    **(b)** $(x_1, x_2, x_3) = (.25, .75, 0), (y_1, y_2) = (.75, .25), v = 5.75$.

## Set 14.5c

■ **3.** **(a)** $UA: (x_1, x_2, x_3, x_4) = (0, .5, 0, .5), DU: (y_1, y_2, y_3, y_4) = (.14, .34, .27, .25), v = .5$.
    **(b)** 30 points, $UA$ favor.
■ **5.** Both players play strategies $(1, 2)$ and $(2, 1)$ with probabilities .571 and .429, respectively.

# CHAPTER 15

## Set 15.2a

■ **1.** Spin 1: continue to spin. Spin 2: continue if spin 1 produces 1 to 6; else, end. Spin 3: continue if spin 2 produces 1 to 6; else, end. Spin 4: continue if spin 3 produces 1 to 5; else, end. Spin 5: continue if spin 4 produces 1 to 4; else, end. Spin 6: end.

## Set 15.3a

■ **1.** Year 1: invest all $10,000. Year 2: invest all accumulated funds. Year 3: invest none. Year 4: invest all accumulated funds.
■ **3.** Period 1: produce two computers. Period 2: production level is determined such that the incoming inventory plus the amount produced equal two computers. Period 3: same as in period 2. Period 4: produce none if incoming inventory is one or zero, and produce one computer if there is a back-order of one computer for period 3.

## Set 15.4a

■ **3.** Game 1: Bet $0 (i.e., do not play). Game 2: bet $1. Game 3: bet $1 if you win in game 2; else, do not play game 3. Maximum probability of making $4 $= .0625$.

# CHAPTER 16

## Set 16.2a

■ **1.** **(a)** Order 1000 units whenever the inventory level drops to 537 units
■ **3.** **(a)** .0023.

(b) Order 300 rolls whenever the inventory drops to 70 rolls.

### Set 16.2b

■ **1. (a)** 3.125 setups.
   **(b)** $312.50/month.
   **(c)** $408.
   **(d)** $2.0397.
   **(e)** .06.
■ **3.** $y^* = 316.85$ units, $R^* = 58.73$ units.

### Set 16.3a

■ **3.** $19 \leq p \leq 35.7$.
■ **5.** 230 copies.
■ **7.** Approximately 39 coats.
■ **9.** $y^* = 5.5$ units.

### Set 16.3b

■ **1.** If $x < 3.52$, order $8 - x$; else, do not order.
■ **3.** If $x < 136$, order $144 - x$; else, do not order.

### Set 16.4a

■ **1.** Period 1: if $x < 9.02$, order $9.02 - x$; else, do not order.
   Period 2: if $x < 7.5$, order $7.5 - x$; else, do not order.

### Set 16.4b

■ **1.** Period 1: if $x < 9.144$, order $9.144 - x$; else, do not order.
   Period 2: if $x < 7.84$, order $7.84 - x$; else, do not order.

## CHAPTER 17

### Set 17.1a

■ **1. (a)** 71%.
   **(b)** Waiting time $\leq 3$ minutes requires at least five cashiers, and efficiency $\geq 90\%$ requires at most two cashiers.

### Set 17.2a

■ **1. (a)** Plane and runway.
   **(b)** Taxi and passenger ride.

■ **5. (a)** None.
  **(g)** Jockey.

## Set 17.3a

■ **1. (a)** Average interarrival time in time units $= \frac{1}{\text{(arrival rate in arrivals per unit time)}}$.

  **(b) (i)** $\lambda = 6$/hour, average interarrival time $= \frac{1}{6}$ hour.
  **(c) (i)** $\mu = 5$/hour, average service time $= .2$ hour.
■ **3. (a)** $f(t) = 20\exp(-20t), t \geq 0$.
  **(b)** .00674.
  **(c)** .632.
  **(d)** 11.67.

## Set 17.3b

■ **1. (a)** F.
  **(b)** T.
■ **3. (a)** .6886
  **(b)** .1738.
  **(c)** .1376.
■ **5.** 75.97 cents.
■ **7. (a)** .4866.
  **(b)** .948 minute.
■ **9. (a)** $f(t) = \left(\frac{1}{10}\right)\exp\left(\frac{-t}{10}\right)$.
  **(b)** $f(t) = \left(\frac{1}{7}\right)\exp\left(\frac{-t}{7}\right)$.

## Set 17.4a

■ **1.** .5595.
■ **3. (a)** 10 arrivals.
  **(b)** .3679.
  **(c)** .6321.
  **(d)** .002479.
■ **5. (a)** 7.5 shelves.
  **(b)** 0.

## Set 17.4b

■ **3. (a)** .4787.
  **(b)** Approximately 25 tickets.
■ **5.** .37116.
■ **7.** .00005.

## Set 17.5a

■ **1. (a)** $(\frac{15}{55}, \frac{24}{55}, \frac{16}{55})$.
   **(b)** 2.02 counters.
   **(c)** .98 counter.
■ **3. (a)** .4445.
   **(b)** .5555.
■ **5. (a)** .00129.
   **(b)** .2273.
   **(c)** 2.9768 tables.
   **(d)** .2796.
■ **7. (a)** $5.5p_1 = 10p_0, 10p_0 + 6P_2 = 14.5P_1, 9P_1 + 6.5p_3 = 14p_2, 8p_2 + 7p_4 = 13.5p_3$.
   **(b)** $p_0 = .08888, p_1 = .1614, p_2 = .2422, p_3 = .2982, p_4 = .2981$.

## Set 17.6a

■ **1. (a)** .1917 car.
   **(b)** .53264 hour.
   **(c)** 1.0104 cars.

## Set 17.6b

■ **1. (a)** 66.67%.
   **(b)** .6667.
   **(c)** .961
   **(d)** $s \geq 11$.
■ **3. (a)** .225 case.
   **(b)** 37.5%.
   **(c)** 2.4 weeks.
■ **5. (a)** .4.
   **(b)** .9.
   **(c)** 2.25.
   **(d)** .0036.

## Set 17.6c

■ **1.** .659.
■ **3.** $\mu \geq 10$.
■ **5.** $37.95.

## Set 17.6d

■ **1. (a)** .3654.
   **(b)** .207 hour.

    **(c)** 3.212 spaces.

    **(d)** .048.

    **(e)** Approximately 10 cars per hour.

■ **3.** At most two seats.

■ **5.** **(a)** .00002.

    **(b)** .00007.

■ **7.** **(a)** .962.

    **(b)** .19 customer per hour.

    **(c)** 1.286 customers.

    **(d)** .1424 hour.

## Set 17.6e

■ **1.** **(a)** .711.

    **(b)** .596.

    **(c)** .4 cab for $c = 2$ and .8 cab for $c = 4$.

    **(d)** Five or more cabs.

■ **3.** **(a)** $c \geq 2$.

    **(b)** $c \geq 4$.

    **(c)** $c \geq 1$.

■ **5.** Ten or more spaces.

■ **7.** **(a)** .65772.

    **(b)** .0662 hour.

    **(c)** 3.29 jobs.

    **(d)** 2.1%.

    **(e)** .667 computer.

## Set 17.6f

■ **1.** **(a)** 1.3 cabs.

    **(b)** .04468.

    **(c)** Three or fewer ($N \leq 7$).

■ **3.** **(a)** .1677 mechanic.

    **(b)** 3.354 jobs.

    **(c)** .9441.

    **(d)** .10559.

    **(e)** 6.7081 jobs.

    **(f)** .9441.

## Set 17.6g

■ **1.** **(a)** 0.

    **(b)** 1.

    **(c)** .63923.

    **(d)** $39,780.

## Set 17.6h

■ **1. (b)** 2.01 repair persons.
     **(c)** .10779.
     **(d)** .34492.
■ **5. (a)** 1.2077 workers.
     **(b)** .22972

## Set 17.7a

■ **1.** 33.3%.
■ **3. (a)** 4.2 homes.
     **(b)** 17 days.
     **(c)** 2.136 days.
■ **5. (a)** .9395 item.
     **(b)** .278.
     **(c)** 74.78 minutes.

## Set 17.9a

■ **1. (b)** Model 3 is the cheapest at $631.20.
■ **3.** Scanner $A$ costs $5.53 per hour, and scanner $B$ costs $4.01 per hour.
■ **5.** 92.65 jobs per week.

## Set 17.9b

■ **1.** Three servers at the cost of $159.77 per hour.
■ **3. (a)** A gain of $5920 per month.
     **(b)** Additional gain of $2880.

## Set 17.9c

■ **1. (a)** Five repair persons.
     **(b)** Six repair persons.

## CHAPTER 18

## Set 18.2a

■ **1. (a)** 90 cm$^2$.
     **(b)** $f(x) = \frac{1}{8}, -7 \leq x \leq 1, f(y) = \frac{1}{8}, -2 \leq y \leq 6, x = -7 + 8R, y = -2 + 9R.$
■ **3. (a)** $0 \leq R \leq .5$, Jim gets $10, $.5 < R \leq 1$, Jan get $10.
     **(b)** $-2.03 \leq \mu \leq 3.63.$
     **(c)** 0.

## Set 18.3a

■ **1. (a)** Discrete.
 **(b)** Continuous.
 **(c)** Discrete.

## Set 18.4a

■ **1.** $A1$: rush job arrival; $A2$: regular job arrival; and $D$: job leaves machine.
■ **3.** $A1$ and $A2$: enter lanes 1 and 2. $A3$: go elsewhere. $D1$ and $D2$: car departs lanes 1 and 2.

## Set 18.4b

■ **1.** 0, .015, .295, .458.
■ **5.** First GOTO uses $0 \le R < .2$ to chose REPAIR and second GOTO uses $.8 \le R \le 1$ to select REPAIR.
■ **7.** $x = a + [R(b - a)(c - a)]^{1/2}, 0 \le R < \frac{(b-a)}{(c-a)}$.

$$x = c - [(c - b)(c - a)(1 - R)]^{1/2}, \frac{(b-a)}{(c-a)} \le R \le 1$$

■ **9.** If $0 \le R \le 1 - 9$, $x = 0$. Otherwise, select $x$ as the largest integer less than or equal to $\frac{ln(1-R)}{ln(q)}$.

## Set 18.4c

■ **1.** .803 hour.
■ **3.** Convolution: $y = 8.1094$, Box-Muller: $y = 7.5365$.
■ **5.** Mean = 25.1, standard deviation = 3.2.
■ **7.** $n = 4$.

## Set 18.4d

■ **1.** $x = .7676$.
■ **3.** $g(x) = .707, 0 \le x \le \frac{\pi}{2}$.
 $h(x) = .637, 0 \le x \le \frac{\pi}{2}$.

## Set 18.5a

■ **1.** $R_4 = .0769, R_5 = .2307, R_6 = .6154, R_7 = .0769, R_8 = .2307$.

## Set 18.6a

■ **1.** Average queue length = 1.11, average waiting time in queue = 11.59, and average facility utilization = .841.

- **3. (a)** Observation.
  - **(b)** Time.
- **5. (a)** One barber.
  - **(b)** 35 minutes.
  - **(c)** 10 minutes.

### Set 18.7a

- **1.** 3.32 time units.
- **3.** $.305 \leq \mu \leq 1.577$.

### Set 18.8a

- **1.** $\bar{z} = 1.81, s_z = .595$.
- **3.** $\bar{z} = -.149, s_z = .67$.

## CHAPTER 19

### Set 19.2a

- **1.** Years 1 and 2: advertise only if product is unsuccessful. Year 3: do not advertise.
- **5.** Order 2 in state 0; otherwise, order none.

### Set 19.3a

- **1.** Advertise whenever in state 1.

## CHAPTER 20

### Set 20.2a

- **1. (a)** None.
  - **(b)** Minimum at $x = 0$.
  - **(e)** Inflection at $x = 0$, minimum at $x = .63$, and maximum at $x = -.63$.
- **3.** Minimum occurs at $(1, 2, 0)$ only.

### Set 20.3a

- **1. (a)** Yes, $\partial c f = -.046$ and $-.04618$.
  - **(b)** $\partial x_1 = -.283 \partial x_2, \partial x_3 = .25 \partial x_2$.
  - **(c)** $\partial x_1 = -.0283$.

**(d)** $\partial cf = -.46$.

## Set 20.3b

■ **1. (a)** No.
■ **3.** $\partial f = 2\partial C^{(2 - n)/n}$.
■ **5.** $\partial f = .472$.

## Set 20.3c

■ **1.** Maximum occurs at $(\frac{12}{5}, \frac{9}{5}, 0, 0)$.

## Set 20.3d

■ **5.** $\lambda_1 \leq 0$, $\lambda_2$ unrestricted, $\lambda_3 \geq 0$. The necessary conditions are sufficient if $f$ is concave, $g_1$ concave, $g_2$ linear, and $g_3$ convex.

# CHAPTER 21

## Set 21.1a

■ **3.** Maximum number of iterations $= 1.44 \ln\{-1 + \frac{(b-a)}{\Delta}\}$.

## Set 21.1b

■ **1.** $(x_1, x_2) = (\frac{1}{3}, \frac{1}{3})$.

## Set 21.2a

■ **3.** Use the substitution $\ln y = \ln x_1 + \ln x_2 + \ln x_3$.

## Set 21.2b

■ **1.** $x_1 = 1, x_2 = 0, z = 4$.

## Set 21.2c

■ **1.** Necessary conditions are not satisfied for $x_j > 0$. The problem has an infimum at $x = 0$.
■ **3.** $(x_1, x_2) = (1.39, 1.13)$.

# Index

# F

# H

# I

# G